해커스 수능 독해
불변의 패턴
유형편이 특별한 이유!

수능 독해 유형을 모두 다 잡으니까!

1

역대 수능/모평/학평 기출
완벽 분석으로
**출제의도를 파고드는
32개의 불변의 패턴**

2

최신 유형별 출제포인트부터
틀리기 쉬운 함정까지
완벽 대비

해커스 수능 독해
불변의 패턴
유형편

해커스 수능 독해
불변의 패턴
실전편

기초부터 실전까지 빈틈없이 대비할 수 있으니까!

3

모든 지문에 제공되는
끊어 읽기와 구문 풀이로
독해력을 기초부터 탄탄히

4

오답률이 높은 고난도 유형까지
빈틈없이 대비할 수 있는
고난도 실전 모의고사

해커스 수능 독해 불변의 패턴 유형편을 검토해주신 선생님들

경기

강상훈	평촌RTS학원
김남균	SDH학원 세교캠퍼스
우재선	리더스 국영수학원
전상호	평촌 이지어학원
최지영	다른영어학원
최희정	SJ클쌤영어

경북

김종완	이엠스토리 영수학원
문재원	포항영신고등학교

대구

김혜란	김혜란 영어학원
박종범	120클럽영어학원
주현아	강고영어학원

서울

김인규	베이스학원
김혜린	아이티씨 고등전문 어학원
양세희	양세희 수능영어학원
이석호	교원더퍼스트캠퍼스학원
최세아	씨앤씨학원

세종

양성욱	조치원 GNB어학원

한나경 | 원힐 영어수학전문학원 |

울산

박순동	JP ENGLISH

전남

나미자	나오미 영어학원
이민정	롱맨어학원

해커스 어학연구소 자문위원단 3기

강원

박정선	잉글리쉬클럽
최현주	최쌤영어

경기

강민정	김진성열정어학원
강상훈	평촌RTS학원
강지인	강지인영어학원
곽은영	나디아잉글리쉬어학원
권계미	A&T+ 영어
김미아	김쌤영어학원
김설화	업라이트잉글리쉬
김성재	스윗스터디학원
김세훈	모두의학원
김수아	더스터디(The STUDY)
김영아	백송고등학교
김유경	벨트어학원
김유경	포시즌스어학원
김유동	이스턴영어학원
김지숙	위디벨럽학원
김지현	이지프레임영어학원
김해빈	해빛영어학원
김현지	지앤비영어학원
박가영	한민고등학교
박영서	스윗스터디학원
박은별	더킹영수학원
박재홍	록키어학원
성승민	SDH어학원 불당캠퍼스
신소연	Ashley English
오귀연	루나영어학원
유신애	에듀포커스학원
윤소정	ILP이화어학원
이동진	이룸학원
이상미	버밍엄영어교습소
이연경	명품M비욘드수학영어학원
이은수	광주세종학원
이지혜	리케이온
이진희	이엠원영수학원
이충기	영어나무
이효명	갈매리드앤톡영어독서학원
임한글	Apsun앞선영어학원
장광명	엠케이영어학원
전상호	평촌이지어학원
전성훈	훈선생영어학원
정선영	코어플러스영어학원
정준	고양외국어고등학교
조연아	카이트학원
채기림	고려대학교EIE영어학원
최지영	다른영어학원
최한나	석사영수전문
최희정	SJ클쌤영어학원
현지환	모두의학원
홍태경	공감국어영어전문학원

경남

강다원	더(the)오르다영어학원
라승희	아이작잉글리쉬
박주언	유니크학원
배송현	두잇영어교습소
안윤서	어썸영어학원
임진희	어썸영어학원

경북

권현미	삼성영어석적우방교실
김으뜸	EIE영어학원 옥계캠퍼스
배세왕	비케이영수전문고등관학원
유영선	아이비티어학원

광주

김유희	김유희영어학원
서희연	SDL영어수학학원
송수일	아이리드영어학원
오진우	SLT어학원수학원
정영철	정영철영어전문학원
최경옥	봉선중학교

대구

권익재	제이슨영어
김병일	독학인학원
김보곤	베스트영어
김연정	달서고등학교
김혜린	김혜린영이학원
문애주	프렌즈입시학원
박정근	공부의힘pnk학원
박희숙	열공열강영어수학학원
신동기	신통외국어학원
위영선	위영선영어학원
윤창원	공터영어학원 상인센터
이승현	학문당입시학원
이주현	이주현영어학원
이현욱	이현욱영어학원
장준현	장쌤독해종결영어학원
주현아	민쌤영어학원
최윤정	최강영어학원

대전

곽선영	위드유학원
김지운	더포스둔산학원
박미현	라시움영어대동학원
박세리	EM101학원

부산

김건희	레지나잉글리쉬 영어학원
김미나	위드중고등영어학원
박수진	정모클영어국어학원
박수진	지니잉글리쉬
박인숙	리더스영어전문학원
옥지윤	더센텀영어학원
윤진희	위니드영어전문교습소
이종ချง	진수학원
정혜린	엠티엔영어학원
조정래	알파카의영어농장
주태양	솔라영어학원

서울

Erica Sull	하버드브레인영어학원
Jung Nick	이은재어학원
강고은	케이앤학원
강신아	교우학원
공현미	이은재어학원
권영진	경동고등학교
김나영	프라임클래스영어학원
김달수	대일외국어고등학교
김대니	채움학원
김문영	창문여자고등학교
김상백	강북세일학원
김연희	이은재어학원
김정은	강북뉴스터디학원
김혜경	대동세무고등학교
남혜원	함영원입시전문학원
노시은	케이앤학원
박선정	강북세일학원
박수진	이은재어학원
박지수	이플러스영수학원
서승희	함영원입시전문학원
신지웅	강북세일학원
양세희	양세희수능영어학원
우정용	제임스영어앤드학원
이박원	이박원어학원
이승혜	스텔라영어
이정욱	이은재어학원
이지연	중계케이트영어학원
임예찬	학습컨설턴트
장지희	고려대학교사범대학부속고등학교
정미라	미라정영어학원
조민규	조민규영어
채가희	대성세그루영수학원
허민	이은재어학원

울산

김기태	그라티아어학원
이민주	로이아카데미
홍영민	더이안영어전문학원

인천

강재민	스터디위드제이쌤
고현순	정상학원
권효진	Genie's English
김솔	전문과외
김정아	밀턴영어학원
서상천	최정서학원
이윤주	트리플원
최예영	영웅아카데미

전남

강희진	강희진영어학원
김두환	해남맨체스터영수학원
송승연	송승연영수학원
윤세광	비상구영어학원

전북

김길자	맨투맨학원
김미영	링크영어학원
김효성	연세입시학원
노빈나	노빈나영어전문학원
라성남	하포드어학원
박재훈	위니드수학지앤비영어학원
박향숙	STA영어전문학원
시종원	시종원영이획원
이상훈	나는학원
장지원	링컨더글라스학원
지근영	한솔영어수학학원
최성령	연세입시학원
최혜영	이든영어수학학원

제주

김랑	KLS어학원
박자은	KLS어학원

충남

김예지	더배움프라임영수학원
김철홍	청경학원
노태겸	최상위학원

충북

라은경	이화윤스영어교습소
신유정	비타민영어클리닉학원

해커스
수능 독해
불패
변의
패턴

유형편

정답이
보이는
패턴만
모았다

🏛 해커스 어학연구소

Contents

CHAPTER 01 목적 파악하기

CHAPTER 02 심경·분위기 파악하기

CHAPTER 03 요지·주장 파악하기

CHAPTER 04 밑줄 의미 추론하기

CHAPTER 05 주제·제목 파악하기

CHAPTER 06 도표 정보 파악하기

CHAPTER 07 세부 정보 파악하기

CHAPTER 08 안내문 정보 파악하기

책의 특징과 구성

1 수능 영어 독해의 모든 유형을 정복하고 내신까지 한 번에 대비!

기출 기반의 빅데이터에서 추출한
불변의 패턴 01~32

유형별로 자주 출제되는 핵심 포인트들을 문제 풀이에 바로 적용할 수 있는 '불변의 패턴'으로 정리하였습니다. 32개의 불변의 패턴들만 익혀두면 쉽고 빠르게 수능 영어 독해의 모든 유형을 정복할 수 있습니다.

문제 풀이 방법을 익히는
패턴맛보기 & 기출문제

패턴에서 학습한 내용을 '패턴맛보기'의 간단한 문제로 점검해보고, '기출문제'에서 패턴을 확인해보며 문제 풀이 방법에 대한 감각을 익힐 수 있습니다.

정답의 단서가 되는 표현들만 모아놓은
실력UP! 기출표현

'실력UP! 기출표현'을 통해 실제 시험에 자주 등장하는 다양한 표현들을 학습할 수 있습니다.

독해의 기본기를 다지고 내신까지 대비하는
실력 UP! 미니 문제

'실력 UP! 미니 문제'를 통해 모든 독해의 기본기인 글의 주제를 찾는 연습뿐만 아니라 서술형 문제까지 풀어 보면서 내신도 함께 대비할 수 있습니다.

2 기본부터 실전까지 체계적으로 반복 학습!

◉ 지문에 대한 이해력을 높여주는
수능 대표 지문 구조 7

수능 영어 독해의 모든 지문을 분석해서 가장 많이 사용되는 대표 지문 구조 7가지를 정리했습니다. '수능 대표 지문 구조 7'을 익혀두면 지문의 흐름을 파악하여 내용을 더 빠르고 정확하게 이해할 수 있고, 정답의 단서도 쉽게 찾을 수 있습니다.

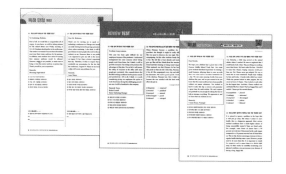

◉ 순서대로 풀기만 하면 복습도 저절로 되는
독해 만점 TEST & REVIEW TEST & 실전 모의고사

각 문제 유형을 '독해 만점 TEST'에서 학습하고, 'REVIEW TEST'에서 복습한 후, 마지막으로 '실전 모의고사'를 통해 점검하며 마무리합니다. 순서대로 풀기만 하면 각 문제 유형에 익숙해지고, 누적 복습 효과를 통해 문제 풀이 실력이 확실하게 향상됩니다.

◉ 고난도 문제까지 철저히 대비하는
고난도 문제 & 고난도 실전 모의고사

'독해 만점 TEST'에서 한 문제씩 제공되는 '고난도 문제'로 난도가 높은 문제에 대한 적응력을 키울 수 있습니다. 또한 오답률이 높은 고난도 유형만 수록한 마지막 '고난도 실전 모의고사'로 3점 배점 문제까지 철저히 대비할 수 있습니다.

◉ 문제에 대한 완벽한 이해로 복습을 돕는
정답 및 해설

상세한 '해설'과 '오답 분석'으로 문제를 완벽하게 이해하고 복습하며 정답률을 높일 수 있습니다. 직독직해 실력을 키우는 끊어 읽기와 '독해가 쉬워지는 구문 풀이'를 담은 '지문 분석'을 통해 전반적인 독해 실력도 향상됩니다.

수능 영어 소개

1. 시험 시간과 문제 수

수능 영어 시험은 70분 동안 진행되고 총 45문제로 구성되어 있다. 시험 시간 70분 중 약 25분은 듣기 평가, 약 45분은 독해 평가에 사용된다. 독해 평가에서 문제 풀이 시간은 평균적으로 한 문제 당 약 1.5분이다. 시험의 난이도에 비해 주어진 시간이 짧기 때문에 평소 시간 안에 문제 푸는 연습을 해두는 것이 매우 중요하다.

평가 영역(시험 시간)	문제 수
듣기 평가(약 25분)	17 문제
독해 평가(약 45분)	28 문제
총 70분	총 45 문제

2. 등급과 점수

수능 영어는 2018학년도부터 받은 점수에 따라 등급이 결정되는 절대 평가로 시행되고 있으며, 100점 만점을 기준으로 0점에서 100점까지 총 9등급으로 나뉜다.

점수	100~90	89~80	79~70	69~60	59~50	49~40	39~30	29~20	19~0
등급	1등급	2등급	3등급	4등급	5등급	6등급	7등급	8등급	9등급

TIP 목표로 하는 대학의 영어 성적 반영 비율과 요구되는 영어 등급 등을 확인하고 수능 영어 학습 목표를 세우는 게 좋다.

3. 수능 영어 독해 유형 소개

수능 영어 독해는 총 28문제로 구성되며, 매해 같은 유형들이 반복해서 출제되고 있다.

문제 번호	문제 유형		배점	문제 수
18	목적 파악하기		2	1 문제
19	심경·분위기 파악하기		2	1 문제
20	주장 파악하기		2	1 문제
21	밑줄 의미 추론하기		2~3	1 문제
22	요지 파악하기		2	1 문제
23	주제 파악하기		2~3	1 문제
24	제목 파악하기		2~3	1 문제
25	도표 정보 파악하기		2	1 문제
26	세부 정보 파악하기		2	1 문제
27	안내문 정보 파악하기		2	2 문제
28				
29	어법상 틀린 것 찾기		2~3	1 문제
30	어휘 적절성 파악하기		2~3	1 문제
31	빈칸 추론하기		2~3	4 문제
32				
33				
34				
35	흐름과 관계 없는 문장 찾기		2	1 문제
36	글의 순서 배열하기		2~3	2 문제
37				
38	주어진 문장의 위치 찾기		2~3	2 문제
39				
40	요약문 완성하기		2	1 문제
41	장문 독해	제목 파악하기	2	2 문제
42		어휘 적절성 파악하기 / 빈칸 추론하기	2	
43		글의 순서 배열하기	2	3 문제
44		지칭하는 대상 추론하기	2	
45		세부 정보 파악하기	2	

수능 대표 지문 구조?

대표 지문 구조 1   주제와 예시

처음 한두 문장에서 지문의 주제가 제시되고, 이를 뒷받침하는 구체적인 예시가 이어지는 지문 구조이다. 수능·모평·학평에서 가장 자주 출제되는 지문 구조이다. 유형을 가리지 않고 자주 출제되는 지문 구조이므로 반드시 알아두어야 한다.

🖹 한눈에 보는 지문 구조

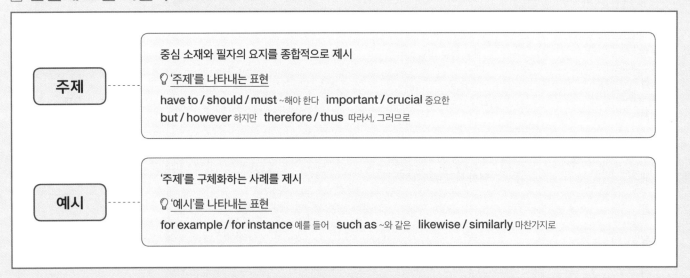

주제 ---- 중심 소재와 필자의 요지를 종합적으로 제시

💡 '주제'를 나타내는 표현

have to / should / must ~해야 한다 important / crucial 중요한
but / however 하지만 therefore / thus 따라서, 그러므로

예시 ---- '주제'를 구체화하는 사례를 제시

💡 '예시'를 나타내는 표현

for example / for instance 예를 들어 such as ~와 같은 likewise / similarly 마찬가지로

🎯 기출로 확인하는 지문 구조

2021년 11월 고2 학평

주제 ----- In order for us to be able to retain valuable pieces of information, our brain 💡has to forget in a manner that is both targeted and controlled.

예시 ----- Can you recall, 💡for example, your very first day of school? You most likely have one or two noteworthy images in your head, 💡such as putting your crayons and pencils into your pencil case. But that's probably the extent of the specifics. Those additional details that are apparently unimportant are actively deleted from your brain the more you go about remembering the situation. The reason for this is that the brain does not consider it valuable to remember all of the details as long as it is able to convey the main message (i.e., your first day of school was great).

우리가 가치 있는 정보들을 기억할 수 있도록, 우리의 뇌는 목표를 삼으면서도 통제된 방식으로 잊어야만 한다. 예를 들어, 당신은 학교에서의 첫날을 기억할 수 있는가? 당신은 아마도 당신의 필통에 크레용과 연필을 넣는 것과 같은 주목할 만한 이미지 한두 개를 머릿속에 가지고 있을 것이다. 그러나 그것이 아마도 (기억할 수 있는) 세부사항의 정도일 것이다. 명백히 중요하지 않은 그러한 추가적인 세부 사항들은 당신이 그 상황을 기억하려고 할수록 당신의 뇌에서 적극적으로 지워진다. 이것의 이유는 뇌가 주요 메시지(즉, 당신의 학교에서의 첫날이 좋았다와 같은)를 전달할 수 있는 한 모든 세부 사항을 기억하는 것이 가치 있다고 여기지 않기 때문이다.

일반적으로 널리 받아들여지는 견해, 즉 통념이 제시되고, 그 통념을 반박하는 필자의 주장이 이어지는 지문 구조이다. 대개 반박 부분이 글의 주제이다.
• 빈출 유형: 요지·주장 파악하기, 주제 파악하기, 빈칸 추론하기, 글의 순서 배열하기, 주어진 문장의 위치 찾기 등

📑 한눈에 보는 지문 구조

통념 ┈┈┈ 중심 소재와 이에 대해 일반적으로 널리 받아들여지는 견해를 요약하여 제시

💡 '통념'을 나타내는 표현

People / We often assume 사람들은 / 우리는 종종 추정한다 **We're often told** 우리는 자주 ~라고 듣는다
It is common ~하는 것이 일반적이다 **Experts say** 전문가들은 ~라고 말한다

반박 ┈┈┈ '통념'과 반대되는 주장을 하는 새로운 발견이나 연구, 조사, 실험의 결과 등을 제시

💡 '반박'을 나타내는 표현

however 하지만 **yet / but** 그러나 **still** 그럼에도 불구하고
nonetheless 그렇더라도 **in contrast** 그에 반해서 **on the other hand** 반면에

🎯 기출로 확인하는 지문 구조

2019년 6월 고1 학평

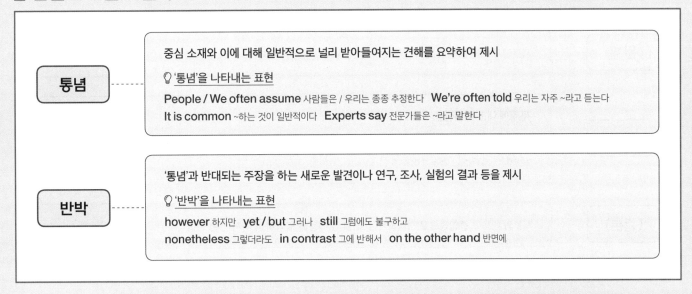

통념 ┈┈┈ 💡People often assume erroneously that if a Hadza adult of Tanzania does not know how to solve an algebraic equation, then he must be less intelligent than we are.

반박 ┈┈┈ 💡Yet there is no evidence to suggest that people from some cultures are fast learners and people from others are slow learners. The study of comparative cultures has taught us that people in different cultures learn different cultural content (attitudes, values, ideas, and behavioral patterns) and that they accomplish this with similar efficiency. The traditional Hadza hunter has not learned algebra because such knowledge would not particularly enhance his adaptation to life in the East African grasslands. However, he would know how to track a wounded bush buck that he has not seen for three days and where to find groundwater.

사람들은 종종 Tanzania Hadza족의 성인이 대수 방정식을 푸는 방법을 모른다면, 그가 우리보다 덜 똑똑함에 틀림없다고 잘못 추정한다. 그러나 어떤 문화권에서 온 사람들은 빠른 학습자이고 다른 문화권에서 온 사람들은 느린 학습자라는 것을 보여주는 증거는 없다. 비교 문화에 대한 연구는 우리에게 다른 문화의 사람들이 다른 문화 콘텐츠(태도, 가치관, 사상, 그리고 행동 양상)를 배운다는 것과 그들이 비슷한 효율로 이것을 성취한다는 것을 가르쳐왔다. 전통적인 Hadza족 사냥꾼은 대수를 배우지 않았는데, 그러한 지식은 그의 동아프리카 초원에서의 적응력을 특별히 향상시켜주지 않기 때문이다. 그러나, 그는 3일 동안 보지 못한 상처 입은 덤불 사슴을 추적하는 방법과 어디에서 지하수를 찾을 수 있는지는 알고 있을 것이다.

대표 지문 구조 3 **문제와 해결**

지문의 도입부에서 어떤 문제 상황이 제시되고, 이어서 이에 대한 해결책이 제시되는 지문 구조이다. 대개 해결 부분이 주제이다.
• 빈출 유형: 요지·주장 파악하기, 밑줄 의미 추론하기, 주제 파악하기, 주어진 문장의 위치 찾기 등

📋 한눈에 보는 지문 구조

문제	지문에서 다룰 중심 소재 및 이와 관련된 질문이나 문제점을 제시
해결	'문제'에 대한 해결책을 제시 💡'해결'을 나타내는 표현 **need to** ~할 필요가 있다 **should / have to / must** ~해야 한다
(결론)	지문의 내용을 종합적으로 정리하거나 '해결'의 내용을 요약하여 다시 한번 언급

🎯 기출로 확인하는 지문 구조

2021년 4월 고3 학평

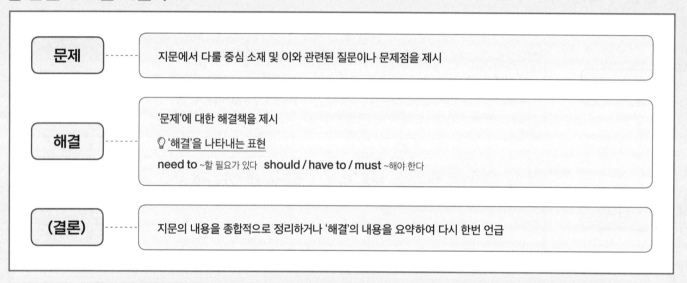

문제

More often than not, modern parents are paralyzed by the fear that they will no longer be liked or even loved by their children if they scold them for any reason. They want their children's friendship above all, and are willing to sacrifice respect to get it. This is not good. A child will have many friends, but only two parents —if that — and parents are more, not less, than friends. Friends have very limited authority to correct.

해결

Every parent therefore 💡needs to learn to tolerate the momentary anger or even hatred directed toward them by their children, after necessary corrective action has been taken, as the capacity of children to perceive or care about long-term consequences is very limited.

결론

Parents are the judges of society. They teach children how to behave so that other people will be able to interact meaningfully and productively with them.

현대의 부모들은 그들이 자녀를 어떤 이유로든 혼내면 더는 자녀의 마음에 들지 않는다거나 심지어 사랑받지 못할 것이라는 두려움에 마비되는 경우가 많다. 그들은 무엇보다도 자녀의 우정을 원하고 그것을 얻기 위해 존경을 기꺼이 희생한다. 이것은 좋지 않다. 아이는 친구는 많이 가질 것이나 부모는 둘 뿐이다. 그렇다면 부모는 친구 이하가 아니라 이상이다. 친구들은 바로잡아 줄 수 있는 권한이 매우 제한적이다. 그러므로, 장기적인 결과를 인지하거나 신경 쓰는 자녀의 능력은 매우 제한적이기 때문에, 모든 부모는 필요한 개선 조치가 취해진 후 자신을 향하는 자녀의 순간적인 분노나 증오까지도 견뎌 내는 것을 배울 필요가 있다. 부모는 사회의 심판관이다. 그들은 다른 사람들이 자녀와 의미 있고 생산적으로 상호 작용할 수 있도록 행동하는 법을 자녀에게 가르친다.

원인과 결과

어떤 현상에 대한 원인을 제시한 후 그로 인해 발생한 결과를 제시하는 지문 구조이다. 대개 결과 부분이 주제이다.
• 빈출 유형: 요지·주장 파악하기, 주제·제목 파악하기, 빈칸 추론하기, 글의 순서 배열하기, 주어진 문장의 위치 찾기, 요약문 완성하기 등

한눈에 보는 지문 구조

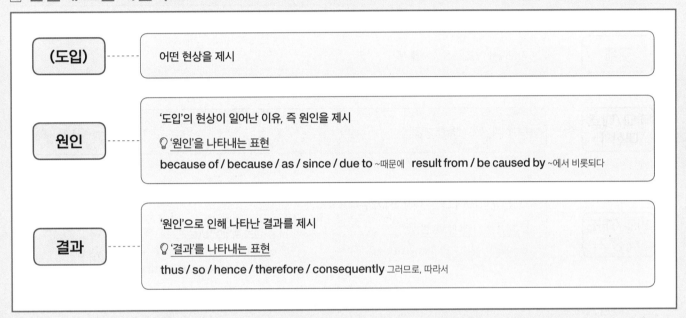

(도입) ······ 어떤 현상을 제시

원인 ······ '도입'의 현상이 일어난 이유, 즉 원인을 제시
💡'원인'을 나타내는 표현
because of / because / as / since / due to ~때문에 result from / be caused by ~에서 비롯되다

결과 ······ '원인'으로 인해 나타난 결과를 제시
💡'결과'를 나타내는 표현
thus / so / hence / therefore / consequently 그러므로, 따라서

기출로 확인하는 지문 구조

2021년 6월 고1 학평

(도입) ······ Research has confirmed that athletes are less likely to participate in unacceptable behavior than are non-athletes.

원인 ······ However, moral reasoning and good sporting behavior seem to decline as athletes progress to higher competitive levels, in part 💡because of the increased emphasis on winning.

결과 ······ 💡Thus winning can be a double-edged sword in teaching character development. Some athletes may want to win so much that they lie, cheat, and break team rules. They may develop undesirable character traits that can enhance their ability to win in the short term. However, when athletes resist the temptation to win in a dishonest way, they can develop positive character traits that last a lifetime. Character is a learned behavior, and a sense of fair play develops only if coaches plan to teach those lessons systematically.

운동 선수는 운동 선수가 아닌 사람들보다 용납할 수 없는 행동을 덜 할 것이라고 연구는 확인했다. 그러나 어느 정도 승리에 대한 강조가 커지기 때문에 운동 선수가 더 높은 경쟁 수준으로 올라감에 따라서 도덕적 분별력과 바람직한 스포츠 행위가 감소하는 것처럼 보인다. 그러므로 승리라는 것은 인성 함양을 가르치는 데 있어서 양날의 검이 될 수 있다. 어떤 선수는 너무나 이기고 싶어서 거짓말하고, 부정행위를 하고 팀 규칙을 위반한다. 그들은 단시간에 이길 수 있는 능력을 강화할 수 있는 바람직하지 못한 인격 특성을 발달시킬지도 모른다. 그러나, 선수가 부정한 방법으로 이기고자 하는 유혹에 저항할 때 그들은 일생동안 지속되는 긍정적인 인격 특성을 계발할 수 있다. 인성은 학습되는 태도이며 그러한 교훈을 코치들이 체계적으로 가르치고자 계획할 때에만 페어 플레이 정신은 발달한다.

대표 지문 구조 5 비교 · 대조

둘 이상의 대상이 가진 공통점이나 차이점을 번갈아 가며 서술하는 지문 구조이다. 비교는 두 대상의 공통점을, 대조는 차이점을 주로 설명한다.
• 빈출 유형: 빈칸 추론하기, 글의 순서 배열하기, 주어진 문장의 위치 찾기, 요약문 완성하기, 장문 독해 등

📑 한눈에 보는 지문 구조

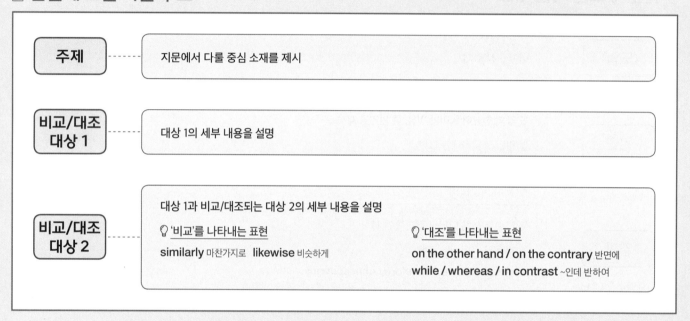

주제	지문에서 다룰 중심 소재를 제시

비교/대조 대상 1	대상 1의 세부 내용을 설명

비교/대조 대상 2

대상 1과 비교/대조되는 대상 2의 세부 내용을 설명

💡 '비교'를 나타내는 표현
similarly 마찬가지로 likewise 비슷하게

💡 '대조'를 나타내는 표현
on the other hand / on the contrary 반면에
while / whereas / in contrast ~인데 반하여

🎯 기출로 확인하는 지문 구조

2020년 3월 고1 학평

주제
Ideas about how much disclosure is appropriate vary among cultures.

대조 대상 1
Those born in the United States tend to be high disclosers, even showing a willingness to disclose information about themselves to strangers. This may explain why Americans seem particularly easy to meet and are good at cocktailparty conversation.

대조 대상 2
💡On the other hand, Japanese tend to do little disclosing about themselves to others except to the few people with whom they are very close. In general, Asians do not reach out to strangers. They do, however, show great care for each other, since they view harmony as essential to relationship improvement. They work hard to prevent those they view as outsiders from getting information they believe to be unfavorable.

얼마나 많은 정보를 공개하는 것이 적절한지에 관한 생각은 문화마다 다르다. 미국에서 태어난 사람들은 정보를 잘 공개하려는 경향이 있고, 심지어 자신에 관한 정보를 낯선 사람에게 기꺼이 공개하려는 의향을 보이기까지 한다. 이것은 미국인들이 특히 만나기 쉬워 보이고 그들이 칵테일 파티에서의 대화에 능숙해보이는 이유를 설명할 수 있다. 반면에, 일본인들은 자신과 매우 친한 소수의 사람들을 제외하고는 타인에게 자신에 관한 정보를 거의 공개하지 않는 경향이 있다. 일반적으로 아시아인들은 낯선 사람에게 관심을 내보이지 않는다. 그러나 그들은 조화를 관계 발전에 필수적이라고 간주하기 때문에 서로를 매우 배려하는 모습을 보인다. 그들은 외부인이라고 간주하는 사람들이 자신이 불리하다고 생각하는 정보를 얻지 못하도록 열심히 애쓴다.

나열 · 열거

인물, 동물, 또는 식물과 같은 중심 소재의 특징을 하나씩 나열하는 지문 구조이다. 나열·열거 구조의 지문은 뚜렷한 주제문이 없는 경우가 많다.
• 빈출 유형: 세부 정보 파악하기, 흐름과 관계 없는 문장 찾기, 글의 순서 배열하기 등

📑 한눈에 보는 지문 구조

설명 1 설명 2 설명 3 ...	중심 소재의 특징이나 요소들을 나열하며 각각의 세부 내용을 설명 💡 '나열 · 열거'를 나타내는 표현 **also** 또한 **in addition to / besides** ~ 외에도 **moreover / furthermore** 게다가

🎯 기출로 확인하는 지문 구조

2020년 3월 고2 학평

설명 1 ┈┈ Dutch mathematician and astronomer Christiaan Huygens was born in The Hague in 1629.

설명 2 ┈┈ He studied law and mathematics at his university, and then devoted some time to his own research, initially in mathematics but then 💡also in optics, working on telescopes and grinding his own lenses.

설명 3 ┈┈ Huygens visited England several times, and met Isaac Newton in 1689. 💡In addition to his work on light, Huygens had studied forces and motion, but he did not accept Newton's law of universal gravitation.

설명 4 ┈┈ Huygens' wideranging achievements included some of the most accurate clocks of his time, the result of his work on pendulums. His astronomical work, carried out using his own telescopes, included the discovery of Titan, the largest of Saturn's moons, and the first correct description of Saturn's rings.

네덜란드의 수학자이자 천문학자인 Christiaan Huygens는 1629년 헤이그에서 태어났다. 그는 대학에서 법과 수학을 공부했고, 그후 처음에는 수학에, 그다음에는 망원경에 대한 작업을 하고 자기 자신의 렌즈를 갈면서 또한 광학에서도 상당 기간을 자신의 연구에 바쳤다. Huygens는 영국을 몇 차례 방문했고, 1689년에 Isaac Newton을 만났다. 빛에 관한 연구 외에도 Huygens는 힘과 운동을 연구했으나, 뉴턴의 만유 인력 법칙을 받아들이지 않았다. Huygens의 광범위한 업적에는 시계추에 대한 그의 연구의 결과물인, 당대의 가장 정확한 시계 중 몇몇이 포함되었다. 자신의 망원경을 사용하여 수행된 그의 천문학 연구에는 토성의 위성 중 가장 큰 타이탄의 발견과 토성의 고리에 대한 최초의 정확한 설명이 포함되었다.

대표 지문 구조 7   시간순 · 과정순

어떤 사건이나 일화를 시간의 흐름이나 사건의 전개 과정에 따라 서술하는 지문 구조이다. 시간순·과정순 구조의 지문은 뚜렷한 주제문이 없는 경우가 많다.
• 빈출 유형: 심경·분위기 파악하기, 세부 정보 파악하기, 글의 순서 배열하기, 장문 독해 등

📑 한눈에 보는 지문 구조

1번째 사건	일련의 사건들을 일어난 시간, 또는 과정 순서로 제시
2번째 사건	
3번째 사건	💡'시간'을 나타내는 표현 💡'과정'을 나타내는 표현
...	

'시간'을 나타내는 표현
in 1990 1990년에   at the age of two 2살 때
today 오늘   yesterday 내일   last week 지난주
next month 다음 달   in the 1980s 1980년대에

'과정'을 나타내는 표현
after ~한 후에   later / afterward 나중에
first 첫째, 첫 번째   next / then 그다음에

🎯 기출로 확인하는 지문 구조

2020년 11월 고1 학평

[1번째 사건] Born 💡in 1867, Sarah Breedlove was an American businesswoman and social activist.

[2번째 사건] Orphaned 💡at the age of seven, her early life was marked by hardship.

[3번째 사건] 💡In 1888, she moved to St. Louis, where she worked as a washerwoman for more than a decade, earning barely more than a dollar a day. During this time, long hours of backbreaking labor and a poor diet caused her hair to fall out. She tried everything that was available but had no success.

[4번째 사건] 💡After working as a maid for a chemist, she invented a successful hair care product and sold it across the country. Not only did she sell, she also recruited and trained lots of women as sales agents for a share of the profits. In the process she became America's first self-made female millionaire and she gave Black women everywhere an opportunity for financial independence.

1867년에 태어난 Sarah Breedlove는 미국인 사업가이자 사회 운동가였다. 7살 때 고아가 된 그녀의 어린 시절은 고난으로 특징지어졌다. 1888년에 그녀는 St. Louis로 이사했고, 그곳에서 10년 넘게 세탁부로 일하며 하루에 겨우 1달러 남짓의 돈을 벌었다. 이 시기 동안, 장시간의 고된 노동과 열악한 식사가 그녀의 머리카락을 빠지게 했다. 그녀는 할 수 있는 모든 것을 시도했지만 성공하지 못했다. 화학자의 가정부로 일한 후 그녀는 성공적인 모발 관리 제품을 발명하여 전국에 판매했다. 그녀는 판매했을 뿐만 아니라, 수익금의 할당을 위해 많은 여성을 판매 대리인으로 모집하여 교육하기도 했다. 그 과정에서 그녀는 미국 최초의 자수성가한 여성 백만장자가 되었고 모든 곳의 흑인 여성들에게 재정적 독립의 기회를 주었다.

CHAPTER 01

목적 파악하기

유형소개 필자가 글을 통해 전달하고자 하는 목적을 파악하는 유형으로, 주로 이메일이나 공지, 광고가 출제됨
문제수 1문제
지시문 다음 글의 목적으로 가장 적절한 것은?

불변의 패턴 01

패턴 빈출도 ★★★★★

글을 쓴 목적은 대부분 글의 중간 이후에 나온다.

지문 듣기

글의 처음에는 인사말, 자기소개, 글을 쓰게 된 배경 설명이 나오고, 글을 쓴 목적은 글의 중간 이후에 나온다.

패턴맛보기

①~③ 중, 글을 쓴 목적이 드러나는 문장을 고르시오.

Dear Residents,

We truly value and appreciate all of our residents, including those with pets. ① We believe that allowing people to live with their pets enriches their lives. While we encourage you to enjoy your pets, we also want to ensure that you do not do so at the expense of your neighbors or your community. ② We have received reports that some residents have been disturbed by noise from dogs barking. Excessive barking by dogs disrupts everyone within hearing. ③ We kindly ask that you keep your dogs' noise levels to a minimum. Thank you for your assistance with this.

해석
주민들께,

우리는 반려동물을 기르는 분들을 포함하여 모든 주민들을 진심으로 소중하게 생각하고 감사하고 있습니다. ① 우리는 사람들이 반려동물과 함께 살도록 하는 것은 그분들의 삶을 풍요롭게 한다고 생각합니다. 우리는 여러분의 반려동물과 즐거운 시간을 보낼 것을 장려하지만, 우리는 또한 여러분의 이웃이나 지역사회에 폐를 끼치면서까지 여러분이 그렇게 하지 않을 것을 확실히 하고자 합니다. ② 우리는 일부 주민들이 반려견이 짖는 소리로 인한 소음으로 방해받고 있다는 신고를 접수했습니다. 개가 과하게 짖는 것은 (그 소리가) 들리는 곳에 있는 모든 분에게 피해를 줍니다. ③ 우리는 여러분이 반려견이 내는 소음을 최소한으로 유지해 주시기를 정중히 요청합니다. 이 일에 협조해주셔서 감사합니다.

해설
글의 중간 이후에 나오는 문장인 ③에서 반려견들이 내는 소음을 최소한으로 유지해줄 것을 요청한다고 했으므로, 이 글의 목적이 드러나는 문장은 ③이다.

정답
③

기출문제 2021년 3월 고2 학평

정답 및 해설 p.2

다음 글의 목적으로 가장 적절한 것은?

My name is Anthony Thompson and I am writing on behalf of the residents' association. Our recycling program has been working well thanks to your participation. However, a problem has recently occurred that needs your attention. Because there is no given day for recycling, residents are putting their recycling out at any time. This makes the recycling area messy, which requires extra labor and cost. To deal with this problem, the residents' association has decided on a day to recycle. I would like to let you know that you can put out your recycling on Wednesdays only. I am sure it will make our apartment complex look much more pleasant. Thank you in advance for your cooperation.

① 재활용품 배출 허용 요일을 알리려고
② 쓰레기 분리배출의 필요성을 설명하려고
③ 쓰레기 분리배출 후 주변 정리를 부탁하려고
④ 입주민 대표 선출 결과를 공지하려고
⑤ 쓰레기장 재정비 비용을 청구하려고

불변의 패턴 02

패턴 빈출도 ★★★★★

글의 목적에 따라 자주 나오는 표현이 있다.

🎧 지문 듣기

요청, 알림, 제안, 불만 등이 자주 나오는 글의 목적인데, **목적별 빈출 표현***을 알아두면 글에서 해당 표현을 찾아 더 빨리 목적을 파악할 수 있다.

패턴맛보기

다음 글에서 글의 목적이 드러나는 문장을 찾아서 밑줄을 그으시오.

Dear Mr. Coleman,

I'm Aaron Brown, the director of TAC company. To celebrate our company's 10th anniversary, we have arranged a small event. It will be an informative afternoon with enlightening discussions on business trends. I recently attended your lecture about recent issues in business and it was really impressive. I am writing this letter to request that you be our guest speaker for the afternoon.

[해석]

Coleman 씨께,

저는 TAC 회사의 이사 Aaron Brown입니다. 저희 회사의 10주년을 기념하고자, 저희는 작은 행사를 마련했습니다. 이것(행사)은 사업 동향에 대해 깨우침을 주는 토론이 마련된 유익한 오후가 될 것입니다. 최근에 저는 사업의 새로운 쟁점에 대한 당신의 강연에 참석하였고 그것은 매우 인상적이었습니다. 저는 오후 행사에 귀하께서 초청 연사가 되어주실 것을 요청하고자 이 편지를 쓰고 있습니다.

[해설]

요청이나 부탁의 상황에 사용되는 표현인 request를 통해 Mr. Coleman에게 오후 행사의 초청 연사가 되어줄 것을 요청하는 글임을 알 수 있다.

[정답]

I am writing this letter to request that you be our guest speaker for the afternoon.

기출문제 2020년 9월 고1 학평

정답 및 해설 p.2

다음 글의 목적으로 가장 적절한 것은?

Dear Wildwood residents,

Wildwood Academy is a local school that seeks to help children with disabilities and learning challenges. We currently have over 200 students enrolled. This year we'd like to add a music class in the hope that each of our students will have the opportunity to develop their musical abilities. To get the class started, we need more instruments than we have now. We are asking you to look around your house and donate any instruments that you may no longer use. Each one donated will be assigned to a student in need. Simply call us and we will be happy to drop by and pick up the instrument.

Sincerely,
Karen Hansen, Principal

① 고장 난 악기의 수리를 의뢰하려고
② 학부모 공개 수업 참석을 권장하려고
③ 음악 수업을 위한 악기 기부를 요청하려고
④ 추가로 개설된 음악 수업 신청을 독려하려고
⑤ 지역 주민을 위한 자선 음악 행사를 홍보하려고

실력UP! 기출표현 목적별 빈출 표현*

| 요청 | request 요청하다 ask 요구하다 urge 간청하다 hope 희망하다 | 제안 | recommend 추천하다 suggest 제안하다 encourage 장려하다 introduce 소개하다 |
| 알림 | announce 공지하다 inform 알리다 remind 상기시키다 notify 알리다 | 불만 | object 반대하다 complain 항의하다 reject 거절하다 |

정답 및 해설 p.3

01 다음 글의 목적으로 가장 적절한 것은?

To Graduating Students,

First of all, we would like to congratulate all of (A)you. As you know, we will be taking pictures for the school album next Friday morning at 10 A.M. Students should gather in the auditorium. This notice is to remind everyone that all students must wear their winter uniforms for the pictures. In addition, some students have asked if wearing their summer uniforms would be allowed. However, (B)this is not possible, so make sure to bring or wear the correct uniform on picture day. Thank you all for your cooperation.

Sincerely,
Blooming High School

① 사진 복장에 관해 알리려고
② 취업하는 학생들을 축하하려고
③ 겨울 교복 구입처를 추천하려고
④ 날짜 및 시간 변동을 공지하려고
⑤ 행사가 열리는 장소를 공지하려고

02 다음 글의 목적으로 가장 적절한 것은?

Dear Mr. Roberson,

Thank you for inviting me to speak at the technology conference in Chicago next month. I am really looking forward to giving a presentation about online marketing. I also think it will be a good chance to meet people who work in the same industry as me. However, there is one problem. I am supposed to give my talk in the morning on August 15, but I have a doctor's appointment that day. Therefore, I'd like to request that you reschedule my presentation for the last day of the conference, August 19. Please let me know if (A)this will create any problems for you.

Sincerely,
Anne Waters

① 발표 참석을 부탁하려고
② 발표 날짜 변경을 요청하려고
③ 온라인 마케팅 강의를 권장하려고
④ 병원 진료 기록 열람이 가능한지 문의하려고
⑤ 마케팅 전문가들을 위한 회의 개최를 건의하려고

실력 UP! 미니 문제 내신 서술형

01. 윗글의 (A), (B)가 지칭하는 바를 영어로 찾아 쓰시오.

(A) _____

(B) _____

실력 UP! 미니 문제 내신 서술형

02. 윗글의 밑줄 친 (A)가 의미하는 것을 우리말로 쓰시오.

(A) _____

03 다음 글의 목적으로 가장 적절한 것은?

Are you tired of staying at expensive hotels that all look the same? Do you want more of a unique travel experience? We have the answer for you. As experienced travelers may know, "couch surfing" is becoming more and more popular, and we highly recommend you try this special way of traveling for your next trip. This option allows you to stay in a local's home and sleep on their couch for free! Not only is it economical but there are also many more advantages. You can discover the culture and traditions of the country and even pick up some of the language. Next time you travel, become a couch surfer and make unforgettable memories with new friends.

① 숙박 시설 폐쇄를 공지하려고
② 최근 여행 트렌드를 문의하려고
③ 새로운 여행 방식을 추천하려고
④ 여행객을 관광지로 초청하려고
⑤ 잘 알려지지 않은 여행지를 홍보하려고

실력 UP! **미니 문제** 내신 서술형

03. 윗글의 요지를 주어진 해석과 일치하도록 <보기>에 있는 단어를 배열하여 문장을 완성하시오.

> 카우치 서핑은 여행자들에게 다양한 혜택을 제공하는 인기 있는 여행 방식이다.
> <보기> is / popular / traveling / travelers / multiple / a / way / provides / with / benefits / couch surfing / of / that

_____

_____ .

04 다음 글의 목적으로 가장 적절한 것은?

To All Marigold Apartment Complex Residents:

Many of (A)us are staying inside more than usual these days. This has led to some friction with regard to noise levels. (B)We hope residents can be a little more mindful of their neighbors. Here are some tips you can follow. When listening to loud music or watching TV, use headphones if possible. Some families have young children who sleep early, so consider doing your laundry or vacuuming during the day instead of at night. Please remember to be considerate of your neighbors and try to follow these tips. We thank you for your cooperation.

Sincerely,
Marigold Management

① 소음을 줄이기 위한 방법을 알려주려고
② 주민들에게 새로운 규정을 알리려고
③ 세입자들을 격려하려고
④ 외부 소음 공해에 관해 경고하려고
⑤ 새로운 입주민들에 관해 알리려고

실력 UP! **미니 문제** 내신 서술형

04. 윗글의 밑줄 친 (A), (B)가 지칭하는 바를 영어로 찾아 쓰시오.

(A) _____

(B) _____

05 다음 글의 목적으로 가장 적절한 것은?

Dear Ms. McEnroe,

As you are aware, this year's engineering contest is coming next week. Also, we have noticed that you have decided to participate again. We were truly amazed at the level of talent your previous works showed last year, so we look forward to enjoying more of your creative works this year. Therefore, we don't want you to forget that the deadline for sending us your final design is fast approaching. The last day to submit your work is next Sunday, December 10th. Works sent after 5 p.m. on this day will not be accepted for the contest. We wish you best of luck.

Sincerely,
Nancy Wang
Engineering Department Manager

① 콘테스트 마감일을 상기시키려고
② 콘테스트 우승자를 발표하려고
③ 콘테스트 심사 기준을 공지하려고
④ 콘테스트 규정의 변동 사항을 알리려고
⑤ 작품 제출 방법을 문의하려고

실력 UP! 미니 문제 내신 서술형

05. 다음 영영 풀이에 적합한 단어를 윗글에서 찾아 쓰시오.

ⓐ natural, inherent ability

→ _____

ⓑ a scheduled time by which a task must be completed

→ _____

06 다음 글의 목적으로 가장 적절한 것은?

Dear Mr. Smith,

Thanks to many of our generous donors, the Browning Public Library has been able to expand the range of services we provide. Regarding this, you recently wrote us to ask about your future donations to our library, and we are pleased to write in response to that question. To donate something, you first have to send a list of your items through our website. We accept used books in good condition, old magazines, and even art pieces as well. Once we have checked your list, we will let you know when and where you can bring your items. If you have any questions about this process, please stop by our Information Desk or contact us through this email address at any time. Thank you for your interest.

Best Regards,
David Wescott
Customer Service Manager

① 건물 확장 공사에 관해 공지하려고
② 도서관에 기부하는 방법을 설명하려고
③ 도서관의 신규 어린이 프로그램을 알리려고
④ 도서관 후원자들에게 변경된 운영 시간을 알리려고
⑤ 건물 확장에 도움을 준 직원들에게 감사를 표하려고

실력 UP! 미니 문제 내신 서술형

06. 다음 질문을 읽고 한 문장의 영어로 답하시오.

Q: What items does the library accept?

A: _____

_____.

07 다음 글의 목적으로 가장 적절한 것은?

Dear Members,

As many of you already know, the Greenwood Recreation Center opened an outdoor ice-skating rink on December 5. Although it has proven to be very popular with our members, there have been a number of injuries. Therefore, we would like to remind everyone to wear the required safety equipment. You should always put on a helmet, elbow and knee pads, and wrist guards before skating. This is particularly important for young or inexperienced skaters. If you have any questions about this policy, please speak to one of our staff members at the reception desk. Thank you for your cooperation, and we hope to see you soon.

Sincerely,
Beth Adams

① 스케이트장 개장일을 공지하려고
② 불량 장비에 대해 환불을 요청하려고
③ 경기 관람 시 지켜야 할 수칙을 전달하려고
④ 지역 주민을 위한 스케이트 강습을 홍보하려고
⑤ 스케이트를 탈 때 안전 장비를 착용할 것을 당부하려고

고난도

08 다음 글의 목적으로 가장 적절한 것은?

Dear Readers,

This month's issue of *Home and Heart* is dedicated to going green. Plastic waste is one of the biggest polluters of the environment. But there are many ways we can help. Instead of using plastic bags for storing food, switch to silicone reusable bags. They are durable and can be cleaned easily. In addition, use a washing bag when doing the laundry. This reduces the amount of small plastic materials that come off of clothes and pollute the water. Using cloth bags for groceries is also an easy way to do your part. Following these practices will do much to help the environment. Remember, even a small change can make a big difference. Thank you for your continued support.

Jane Kendrick
Editor-in-Chief

① 과도한 플라스틱 제품 사용을 비판하려고
② 잡지 기사의 요약본을 제공하려고
③ 신제품에 관한 정보를 제공하려고
④ 플라스틱 사용이 미치는 영향을 밝히려고
⑤ 플라스틱 소비를 줄이는 방안을 소개하려고

실력 UP! 미니 문제 내신 서술형

07. 다음 문장을 우리말로 해석하시오.

Although it has proven to be very popular with our members, there have been a number of injuries.

→ _____

_____ .

실력 UP! 미니 문제 내신 서술형

08. 다음 질문을 읽고 한 문장의 영어로 답하시오.

Q: According to the passage, what are the benefits of using a washing bag when doing laundry?

A: Using a washing bag _____

_____ .

심경·분위기 파악하기

유형 소개 등장인물의 심경이나 글의 분위기를 파악하는 유형으로, 주로 일상 에피소드 나 소설의 한 장면 같은 소재가 출제됨

문제 수 1문제

지시문 다음 글에 드러난 [인물]의 심경 변화로 가장 적절한 것은?
다음 글에 드러난 [인물]의 심경으로 가장 적절한 것은?
다음 글의 상황에 나타난 분위기로 가장 적절한 것은?

불변의 패턴 03

패턴 빈출도 ★★★★★

인물의 심경이나 글의 분위기는 간접적으로 표현된다.

🎧지문 듣기

인물의 심경이나 글의 분위기는 상황이나 배경 설명, 인물의 대사 를 통해 간접적으로 드러나는 경우가 많으며 글의 전반적인 분위 기와 종합하여 정답을 찾는다.

패턴맛보기

밑줄 친 내용에서 유추할 수 있는 분위기로 가장 적절한 것을 고르시오.

It had stopped raining; the earth was refreshed. The frogs were loud in the pond; their throats were <u>swollen with pleasure</u>. Some boys were playing in the little stream that the rain had made by the roadside. It was good to see them and their bright eyes. They were <u>having the time of their lives</u>, and I could see <u>they were very happy</u>.

① sad and gloomy
② merry and lively
③ funny and humorous

[해석]

비가 그쳤고 땅에서는 새로운 기운이 돋아났다. 개구리들은 연못에서 시끄럽게 울 어댔고, 그들의 목은 기쁨으로 부풀어 있었다. 비가 길가에 만들어 놓은 작은 개울 에서 몇 명의 남자아이들이 놀고 있었다. 그들과 그들의 밝은 눈을 볼 수 있어서 좋 았다. 그들은 최고로 즐거운 시간을 보내고 있었고, 나는 그들이 매우 행복하다는 것을 알 수 있었다.

① 슬프고 우울한
② 즐겁고 활기 넘치는
③ 웃기고 유머러스한

[해설]

밑줄 친 부분은 모두 즐겁고 활기찬 분위기를 묘사하는 어구들이므로 글의 분위기 가 ② merry and lively(즐겁고 활기 넘치는)라는 것을 알 수 있다.

[정답]
②

기출문제 2021년 3월 고1 학평

정답 및 해설 p.8

다음 글에 드러난 Shirley의 심경으로 가장 적절한 것은?

On the way home, Shirley noticed a truck parked in front of the house across the street. New neighbors! Shirley was dying to know about them. "Do you know anything about the new neighbors?" she asked Pa at dinner. He said, "Yes, and there's one thing that may be interesting to you." Shirley had a billion more questions. Pa said joyfully, "They have a girl just your age. Maybe she wants to be your playmate." Shirley nearly dropped her fork on the floor. How many times had she prayed for a friend? Finally, her prayers were answered! She and the new girl could go to school together, play together, and become best friends.

① curious and excited
② sorry and upset
③ jealous and annoyed
④ calm and relaxed
⑤ disappointed and unhappy

불변의 패턴04

패턴 빈출도 ★★★★☆

심경 변화의 단서는 처음과 마지막 한두 문장에 있다.

🎧 지문 듣기

처음 한두 문장에서 인물의 처음 심경이 드러나고, 마지막 한두 문장에서 변화된 심경이 드러나기 때문에, 처음과 마지막 한두 문장을 특히 주의 깊게 본다.

TIP 수능 빈출 심경·분위기 어휘*를 미리 학습해두면 좋다.

패턴맛보기

Garnet의 심경을 나타내는 단서를 모두 찾아 밑줄을 그으시오.

> Garnet의 심경: wishful(갈망하는) → excited (신이 난)

Garnet blew out the candles and lay down. It was too hot. She lay there, sweating, and whispered, "I wish the drought would end." Late in the night, slowly, one by one, as if someone were dropping pennies on the roof, came the raindrops. Then, after a few moments, the rain burst strong and loud upon the world. Garnet leaped out of bed and ran to the window. She shouted with joy, "It's raining hard!"

해석

Garnet은 촛불을 불어서 끄고 누웠다. 너무 더웠다. 그녀는 그곳에 누워서 땀을 흘리며 "나는 이 가뭄이 끝났으면 좋겠어."라고 속삭였다. 그날 밤늦게, 누군가가 지붕 위로 동전을 떨어뜨리는 것처럼 천천히, 한 방울씩, 빗방울이 떨어졌다. 그러고 나서, 잠시 후에, 비가 강하고 요란하게 세상으로 쏟아졌다. Garnet은 침대 밖으로 뛰쳐나와 창문으로 달려갔다. 그녀는 "비가 많이 와!"라며 기뻐서 외쳤다.

해설

글의 처음에 Garnet이 "I wish the drought would end(나는 이 가뭄이 끝났으면 좋겠어)"라고 속삭이며 비가 오길 갈망하는 것을 알 수 있다. 그리고, 글의 마지막에서 'She shouted with joy(그녀는 기뻐서 외쳤다)'를 통해 Garnet이 신이 났음을 알 수 있다.

정답

I wish the drought would end
She shouted with joy

기출문제 2019년 9월 고1 학평

정답 및 해설 p.9

다음 글에 드러난 'I'의 심경 변화로 가장 적절한 것은?

I board the plane, take off, and climb out into the night sky. Within minutes, the plane shakes hard, and I freeze, feeling like I'm not in control of anything. The left engine starts losing power and the right engine is nearly dead now. Rain hits the windscreen and I'm getting into heavier weather. I'm having trouble keeping up the airspeed. When I reach for the microphone to call the center to declare an emergency, my shaky hand accidentally bumps the carburetor heat levers, and the left engine suddenly regains power. I push the levers to full. Both engines backfire and come to full power. Feeling that the worst is over, I find my whole body loosening up and at ease.

* carburetor heat lever: 기화기 열 레버

① ashamed → delighted
② terrified → relieved
③ satisfied → regretful
④ indifferent → excited
⑤ hopeful → disappointed

실력UP! 기출표현 수능 빈출 심경·분위기 어휘*

alarmed 불안해하는	embarrassed 쑥스러운	irritated 짜증이 난	scared 무서워하는
annoyed 짜증이 난	envious 부러워하는	nervous 불안해하는	sorrowful 슬퍼하는
bored 지루해하는	excited 신이 난	panicked 겁에 질린	startled 놀란
calm 침착한, 차분한	festive 흥겨운	pleased 기뻐하는	surprised 놀란
confident 확신하고 있는	frightened 겁먹은	proud 자랑스러워하는	thankful 감사하는
confused 혼란스러워하는	grateful 고마워하는	puzzled 당혹스러운	thrilled 흥분한
curious 호기심이 강한	guilty 죄책감이 드는	regretful 후회하는	touched 감동한
delighted 아주 기뻐하는	horrified 겁에 질린	relaxed 느긋한	upset 속상한
depressed 우울한	humorous 재미있는	relieved 안도하는	wishful 갈망하는
disappointed 실망한	indifferent 무관심한	satisfied 만족스러워하는	worried 걱정하는

01 다음 글에 드러난 'I'의 심경으로 가장 적절한 것은?

On my 18th birthday, I received (A)a surprise gift that most would love: a helicopter tour of the Grand Canyon. For me, it was a nightmare because I had always been afraid of flying. But now I had to fly above a huge open canyon. I couldn't say no since it was a thoughtful present from my grandfather. I gathered the small amount of courage that I had and headed toward the helicopter waiting to take me up into the sky. My legs trembled with every step and I was sweating. As we left the ground, I closed my eyes and prayed that it would be over quickly.

① joyful and surprised
② nervous and terrified
③ timid and shy
④ bored and tired
⑤ moody and depressed

실력 UP! 미니 문제 내신 서술형

01. 윗글의 밑줄 친 (A)가 의미하는 것을 우리말로 쓰시오.

(A) _____

02 다음 글에 드러난 Ericka의 심경 변화로 가장 적절한 것은?

Ericka waited restlessly for her daughter, Katie, to come home. It was Katie's first day of school and Ericka was worried. Katie was small for her age. She was also very shy and sometimes had trouble talking to new people. Would she be able to make friends? Suddenly, the door burst open and Katie rushed into the house in her purple shirt, her backpack on her shoulders, and a big smile on her face. "Mom! School was so fun!" she said excitedly. Ericka finally felt the weight of her worries get lifted away. Now, she could rest easy knowing Katie would be fine.

① startled   → exhausted
② fearful   → hurried
③ lonely   → confused
④ frightened → proud
⑤ concerned   → relieved

실력 UP! 미니 문제 내신 서술형

02. 다음 질문을 읽고 영어로 답하시오.

Q: From Ericka's description, what can we know about Katie's characteristics?

A: Katie is _____. Also she is _____ and _____

_____.

03 다음 글에 드러난 Nathan의 심경 변화로 가장 적절한 것은?

Nathan arrived at the hospital at exactly 3 p.m. The rain was pouring and it was a dreary fall day. 'Just like how I feel,' he thought unhappily, looking up at the sky. He walked in with a heavy heart. His cousin Jill had been in a bad car accident. He imagined his aunt and uncle crying, and doctors and nurses whispering in hushed, urgent voices. After hesitating, he slowly opened the door and saw, to his surprise, Jill giggling. "Oh Nathan! I'm so glad you came!" she said with a grin. He walked into the room filled with flowers, balloons, and laughter. He couldn't believe how cheerful it was.

* giggle: 낄낄 웃다, 키득거리다

① afraid → humiliated
② disappointed → suspicious
③ gloomy → amazed
④ enthusiastic → embarrassed
⑤ uninterested → content

04 다음 글에 드러난 Paul의 심경으로 가장 적절한 것은?

Paul had just returned to his campsite after gathering firewood when he noticed that his cat was nowhere to be found. Bella was trained to stay in her cage by the tent, but she currently wasn't there. Paul felt his chest tighten and his breathing speed up. She must have been scared and run away. There was no sign of his playful black cat anywhere. He frantically searched his tent and in the surrounding forest for Bella. But the sun was quickly setting and Paul could feel his anxiety growing. He was in a huge national park and his cat was lost. He didn't have much hope of finding her.

① joyful and happy
② worried and doubtful
③ annoyed and jealous
④ upset and angry
⑤ calm and relaxed

실력 UP! 미니 문제 내신 서술형

03. 다음 영영 풀이에 적합한 단어를 윗글에서 찾아 쓰시오.

ⓐ lacking joy, and evoking a depressing or melancholy mood

→ d_____

ⓑ requiring immediate attention and care in order to prevent a negative outcome

→ u_____

실력 UP! 미니 문제 내신 서술형

04. 다음 문장을 우리말로 해석하시오.

Paul had just returned to his campsite after gathering firewood when he noticed that his cat was nowhere to be found.

→ _____

_____

05 다음 글에 드러난 'I'의 심경 변화로 가장 적절한 것은?

I decided to go to Europe before starting college. My parents were quite nervous since I was going alone. Not me, though. I couldn't wait to explore the world. I wanted to see the amazing architecture and people. I was eager to experience the exotic culture and food. I booked a two-week trip. When I got to Europe, I found the same fast-food restaurants and coffee shops on every street I went. All the young people were wearing the same clothes and speaking the same way. What a letdown! It wasn't what I expected at all. After the two weeks were over, I sadly got on a plane and headed back home.

① anxious   → delighted
② envious   → shocked
③ indifferent → shameful
④ nervous   → confident
⑤ excited   → disappointed

06 다음 글에 드러난 Dylan의 심경 변화로 가장 적절한 것은?

Dylan was about to enter the Castle of Chaos. Halloween was his favourite time of year and he loved haunted houses; he thought they were fun. The Castle of Chaos was famous for being the scariest one. "Are you afraid?" his friends teased. "No way," he said, confidently. Dylan entered the house. He walked through, waiting for the typical monsters to pop out. But all he could hear were odd whispers. Then, it got very cold. This wasn't what he was expecting at all. He was suddenly nervous. Just then, he felt something behind him. He turned around to face a ghost with long black hair staring at him! Dylan shouted in a panic and ran back out the front door as fast as his legs could carry him.

* haunted house: 귀신의 집, 흉가

① hesitant → moved
② bored   → embarrassed
③ lively   → determined
④ fearless → frightened
⑤ jealous → puzzled

실력 UP! 미니 문제 내신 서술형

05. 윗글에서 'I'가 유럽 여행에서 경험하고 싶어 하는 4가지를 찾아 우리말로 쓰시오.

1. _____
2. _____
3. _____
4. _____

실력 UP! 미니 문제 내신 서술형

06. 윗글의 제목을 주어진 해석과 일치하도록 <보기>에 있는 단어를 배열하여 문장을 완성하시오.

Castle of Chaos에서의 뜻밖의 공포
<보기> The / of Chaos / Panic / at the Castle / Unexpected

_____

07 다음 글의 상황에 나타난 분위기로 가장 적절한 것은?

Lily was enjoying every minute of her boat tour that day. The sky was a perfect, cloudless blue and there was a nice salty breeze that kept her cool. She was watching the glassy surface of the sea when she suddenly saw (A)something emerge from its depths. It blew a column of mist into the air before disappearing and then breaking the surface again. The other tourists gasped with excitement and pointed at the display. "It's a whale!" Someone shouted. Lily felt herself smile as she watched not one, but three whales play around the boat. Young children laughed and everyone seemed happy. This would surely be a trip that they all remembered.

① boring
② monotonous
③ weird
④ desperate
⑤ joyful

고난도

08 다음 글에 드러난 Jenna의 심경 변화로 가장 적절한 것은?

Jenna gazed happily at the water as she spread her blanket on the sand. The weather was perfect, and there were only a few other people on the beach. It had been a busy week at work, and she was looking forward to relaxing in the sun. Suddenly, she heard a voice behind her say, "This looks like a good spot!" Turning her head, she saw a group of teenagers setting up a volleyball net. Within a few minutes, one of them shouted, "Game on!" and they started playing loudly. Jenna glared at them as she realized she wouldn't be able to relax with all the noise. Then she sighed with frustration, packed her belongings, and began walking down the beach.

① nervous   → calm
② amused   → jealous
③ confident → envious
④ lazy   → energetic
⑤ satisfied   → irritated

실력 UP! **미니 문제** 내신 서술형

07. 윗글의 밑줄 친 (A)가 의미하는 것을 우리말로 쓰시오.

→

실력 UP! **미니 문제** 내신 서술형

08. 윗글의 제목을 주어진 해석과 일치하도록 <보기>에 있는 단어를 배열하여 문장을 완성하시오.

> 해변가의 시끄러운 방해
> <보기> Interruption / at / the / Noisy / The / Beach

CHAPTER 03

요지·주장 파악하기

불변의 패턴 05

패턴 빈출도 ★★★★★

요지·주장은 처음과 마지막 두세 문장에서 제시된다.

지문 듣기

요지나 주장은 두괄식으로 글의 처음에 제시된 후 마지막에 다시 한번 언급되는 경우가 많다. 글의 처음과 마지막 두세 문장에 집중하면 요지와 주장을 쉽게 찾을 수 있다.

패턴맛보기

(A)와 (B)만을 읽고 글의 요지로 가장 적절한 것을 고르시오.

(A) Studies show that narrative feedback on students' performance is better than grades at both promoting kids' self-motivation to learn and boosting their achievement. When teachers offer information such as "You did a great job of planning your ideas for this paper, and formulating your main argument, but your body paragraphs don't address the question raised by the argument," the student has information that praises the positive elements, addresses failures, and gives useful information for her better performance. (B) In this way, informational feedback works much like praise for efforts, and similarly boosts enthusiasm for the task and later performance.

① 학생은 칭찬을 주고받는 환경에서 더 잘 성장한다.
② 등급보다 서술적 피드백을 제공하는 것이 학생에게 더 유용하다.

해석
(A) 연구들은 학생들의 성과에 대한 서술적 피드백이 아이들의 배우고자 하는 사발적 동기 부여를 촉진하는 것과 그들의 성취를 신장시키는 것 둘 다에 있어서 등급보다 더 낫다는 것을 보여준다. 교사들이 "이 과제물에 있어서 너의 생각을 계획하고 너의 중심 주장을 표현하는 것은 잘했지만 본문 단락들이 그 주장에 의해 제기된 의문점을 다루지 않고 있다."와 같은 정보를 제공할 때, 그 학생은 긍정적인 요소를 칭찬하고 실패한 것들을 언급하며 그녀의 더 나은 성과를 위한 유용한 정보를 주는 정보를 얻는다. (B) 이런 방식으로 정보를 제공하는 피드백은 노력에 대한 칭찬처럼 매우 효과적이며 마찬가지로 그 과업과 이후의 성과에 대한 열정을 신장시킨다.

정답
②

기출문제 2021년 6월 고1 학평

정답 및 해설 p.15

다음 글의 요지로 가장 적절한 것은?

Rather than attempting to punish students with a low grade or mark in the hope it will encourage them to give greater effort in the future, teachers can better motivate students by considering their work as incomplete and then requiring additional effort. Teachers at Beachwood Middle School in Beachwood, Ohio, record students' grades as A, B, C, or I (Incomplete). Students who receive an I grade are required to do additional work in order to bring their performance up to an acceptable level. This policy is based on the belief that students perform at a failure level or submit failing work in large part because teachers accept it. The Beachwood teachers reason that if they no longer accept substandard work, students will not submit it. And with appropriate support, they believe students will continue to work until their performance is satisfactory.

① 학생에게 평가 결과를 공개하는 것은 학습 동기를 떨어뜨린다.
② 학생에게 추가 과제를 부여하는 것은 학업 부담을 가중시킨다.
③ 지속적인 보상은 학업 성취도에 장기적으로 부정적인 영향을 준다.
④ 학생의 자기주도적 학습 능력은 정서적으로 안정된 학습 환경에서 향상된다.
⑤ 학생의 과제가 일정 수준에 도달하도록 개선 기회를 주면 동기부여에 도움이 된다.

불변의 패턴06

패턴 빈출도 ★★★★☆

자주 출제되는 오답의 유형은 정해져 있다.

🎧 지문 듣기

자주 출제되는 오답의 유형을 알아두면 빠르게 소거하면서 정답을 선택할 수 있다.

- **오답의 유형**
- 글과 반대되거나 다른 내용
- 글과 일부만 일치하고 나머지는 다른 내용
- 글에 나오지 않은 소재를 언급한 내용

패턴맛보기

다음 글에서 필자가 주장하는 바로 가장 적절한 것은?

It's not a mistake if it doesn't end up in print. It's the same for email. Nothing bad can happen if you haven't hit the Send key. What you've written can have misspellings, errors of fact, but it doesn't matter. If you haven't sent it, you still have time to fix it. This is easier said than done, of course. Send is your computer's most attractive command. But before you hit the Send key, make sure that you read your document carefully one last time.

① 중요한 이메일은 출력하여 보관해야 한다.
② 이메일을 전송하기 전에 반드시 검토해야 한다.

[해석]
결국 인쇄물로 나오지 않으면 그것은 실수가 아니다. 그것은 이메일에서도 마찬가지다. 전송 버튼을 누르지 않았다면 어떤 나쁜 일도 일어날 수 없다. 여러분이 쓴 글에는 잘못 쓴 철자, 사실의 오류가 있을 수 있지만, 그것은 문제가 되지 않는다. 그것을 전송하지 않았다면, 아직 그것을 고칠 시간이 있다. 물론, 이것은 말은 쉽지만 행동은 어렵다. 전송은 여러분 컴퓨터의 가장 매력적인 명령어이다. 그러나 전송 버튼을 누르기 전에, 반드시 문서를 마지막으로 한 번 주의 깊게 읽어 보라.

[해설]
"전송 버튼을 누르기 전에, 반드시 문서를 마지막으로 한 번 주의 깊게 읽어 보라"고 했으므로 필자가 주장하는 바로 가장 적절한 것은 "이메일을 전송하기 전에 반드시 검토해야 한다."임을 알 수 있다. ①은 글에서 언급된 소재 "이메일(email)"과 "출력(print)"을 통해 글과 일부만 일치하고 나머지는 다른 내용을 말함으로써 혼동을 주는 오답이다.

[정답]
②

기출문제 2019년 3월 고1 학평   정답 및 해설 p.15

다음 글에서 필자가 주장하는 바로 가장 적절한 것은?

It can be tough to settle down to study when there are so many distractions. Most young people like to combine a bit of homework with quite a lot of instant messaging, chatting on the phone, updating profiles on social networking sites, and checking emails. While it may be true that you can multitask and can focus on all these things at once, try to be honest with yourself. It is most likely that you will be able to work best if you concentrate on your studies but allow yourself regular breaks — every 30 minutes or so — to catch up on those other pastimes.

① 공부할 때는 공부에만 집중하라.
② 평소 주변 사람들과 자주 연락하라.
③ 피로감을 느끼지 않게 충분한 휴식을 취하라.
④ 자투리 시간을 이용하여 숙제를 하라.
⑤ 학습에 유익한 기분 전환 활동을 하라.

01 다음 글의 요지로 가장 적절한 것은?

Playing team sports has many benefits for children, but the problem begins when competition starts to overtake the fun part. Of course, a bit of competition is not only a part of sports but it's also good for building character. Overdoing it, though, has negative effects on a young child. Less athletic kids think they're not good enough and feel bad, while more athletic kids can feel pressured to do well all the time. Parents should understand that participation and enjoyment are the most important aspects. When we take the focus off of being competitive, children develop a love for themselves and the sport.

① 신체 건강을 위해 어릴 때부터 다양한 스포츠에 도전해야 한다.
② 경쟁심을 부추기면 운동에 재미를 붙일 수 있다.
③ 스포츠는 훌륭한 인품을 쌓는 데 도움이 된다.
④ 경쟁이 너무 치열한 스포츠는 아이들에게 좋지 않다.
⑤ 부모는 아이들에게 경쟁의 중요성을 인지시켜야 한다.

02 다음 글에서 필자가 주장하는 바로 가장 적절한 것은?

Insecurities can break us down if we are not careful. Just ask a model or athlete. Society designates their bodies as ideal, yet even they might have aspects they don't like about their bodies. Body image is a subjective idea of yourself. (A)This may be quite different from how your body actually appears to others. It's OK not to love every aspect of your body. But it's not OK to think that you are not as good as others or worthless because of (B)it. Accept and love your body for what it can do instead of focusing on perceived imperfections. Just as your personality is unique to you, so is the body that houses it. That makes it beautiful no matter what.

* insecurity: 불안감, 불안정

① 건강한 신체를 유지하기 위해 애써야 한다.
② 사회가 인정하는 미의 기준을 따라가야 한다.
③ 자신의 결점이 무엇인지 아는 것이 중요하다.
④ 내면의 아름다움을 중시하는 문화를 조성해야 한다.
⑤ 우리의 몸을 있는 그대로 받아들이고 사랑해야 한다.

실력 UP! 미니 문제 내신 서술형

01. 다음 문장을 우리말로 해석하시오.

Of course, a bit of competition is not only a part of sports but it's also good for building character.

→ _____

실력 UP! 미니 문제 내신 서술형

02. 윗글의 밑줄 친 (A), (B)가 지칭하는 바를 영어로 찾아 쓰시오.

(A) _____

(B) _____

03 다음 글의 요지로 가장 적절한 것은?

We often go through life on autopilot. Every day, our schedules are filled with school, work, chores, hobbies, and other things that keep us busy. Before we even know it, years have passed us by. But stop for a moment and really think about yourself and the life you are living. Do you feel you are on the correct path mentally, physically, professionally, or spiritually? Being able to reflect on such aspects facilitates a deeper understanding of yourself. When we don't stop to think about our motivations or goals, we fail to develop and end up unhappy and unfulfilled. Take a moment to press pause and meditate. It is a challenging but necessary step for personal growth.

* on autopilot: 자동 조종 모드로, 자동으로

① 스스로에 대한 주관적인 평가는 부정확할 때가 많다.
② 비판적인 자세는 불행한 결과만을 가져온다.
③ 자기 자신에게 엄격한 사람만이 성공할 수 있다.
④ 자아 성찰을 통해 스스로를 이해해야만 발전할 수 있다.
⑤ 바쁜 일상에서도 반드시 충분한 휴식을 취해야 한다.

04 다음 글에서 필자가 주장하는 바로 가장 적절한 것은?

Some people inherently strive for excellence. Others feel they must be perfect in order to be accepted. There is nothing wrong with doing something to the best of your ability. The issue is becoming obsessed with trying to prove you are perfect. If you don't find a good balance, the overwhelming need to excel at everything can sometimes inhibit your progress. You become consumed with tiny imperfections and end up never completing a task. Do not get stuck in (A)this loop or think you are not "good enough." Instead, do the best you can, even if you mess up along the way. The important thing is to keep moving forward.

① 성공한 사람들에게 조언을 구하라.
② 마지막 순간까지 오류가 없는지 점검하라.
③ 인정받고 싶은 욕구를 성장의 동력으로 삼아라.
④ 도전하기 전에 실패의 가능성을 신중히 생각하라.
⑤ 모든 면에서 완벽함을 추구하기보다, 매사에 최선을 다하라.

실력 UP! 미니 문제 내신 서술형

03. 다음 질문을 읽고 한 문장의 영어로 답하시오.

Q: According to the passage, what happens when we fail to press pause and self-reflect?

A: _____ .

실력 UP! 미니 문제 내신 서술형

04. 윗글의 밑줄 친 (A)가 의미하는 것을 우리말로 쓰시오.

(A) _____

05 다음 글의 요지로 가장 적절한 것은?

Over the years, I've met all sorts of managers, and many struggle with one particular aspect of their job. They want the best from their employees but do not know how to convey it. Assessments so often turn into either harsh criticism or timid suggestions. Neither is constructive. Proper feedback is given in a way that points out what needs to be corrected and guides the person to future improvement. As such, managers should focus on observing, not interfering with, the individual's behavior. Ultimately, they should address the things that the employee is capable of changing. When feedback is given correctly, it makes a positive difference for everyone involved.

① 비판은 직원의 자존감에 나쁜 영향을 줄 수 있다.
② 직원들은 서로에게 긍정적인 피드백만을 주어야 한다.
③ 잦은 업무 평가는 오히려 업무가 진행되는 것을 방해한다.
④ 개선될 가능성이 작을지라도 피드백을 주는 것은 중요하다.
⑤ 적절한 피드백은 직원의 성과를 향상시킨다.

06 다음 글에서 필자가 주장하는 바로 가장 적절한 것은?

Sometimes, it feels like everyone wants something from you. A coworker constantly requests help, even though you have too much to do or, maybe friends or neighbors keep asking for favors that intrude on your time. You feel bad saying no, so you end up doing whatever is asked. This leaves you drained and unhappy. That's why personal boundaries are so important. Without some restrictions, your well-being can suffer greatly. A lack of clear boundaries can lower your self-esteem. Resentment builds up and can ultimately ruin relationships. To avoid this, create a limit on how much others can infringe upon you. You don't have to feel guilty or selfish; rather, good boundaries foster healthy and respectful relationships that keep your mind and soul happy.

> * personal boundaries: 개인 바운더리
> (개인이 가상적으로 설정한 타인과의 근접 접촉 범위)

① 개인만의 적절한 바운더리를 가져야 한다.
② 업무상의 바운더리는 사적인 것과 구별해야 한다.
③ 부탁을 너무 단호하게 거절하지 않도록 주의해야 한다.
④ 친밀한 관계를 이루려면 바운더리를 두지 말아야 한다.
⑤ 자존감을 회복하려면 스스로의 내면에 더 솔직해져야 한다.

실력 UP! 미니 문제 내신 서술형

05. 다음 영영 풀이에 적합한 단어를 윗글에서 찾아 쓰시오.

ⓐ a component, portion, or characteristic of something

→ a_____

ⓑ lacking confidence

→ t_____

실력 UP! 미니 문제 내신 서술형

06. 다음 질문을 읽고 한 문장의 영어로 답하시오.

Q: According to the passage, what should we do to avoid the negative circumstances of not having a clear boundary?

A: We should _____

_____.

07 다음 글의 요지로 가장 적절한 것은?

Many of us think small talk is a tedious part of social norms, but this is far from the truth. At its core, small talk is a way to initiate a conversation. Think about the last time you went somewhere you didn't know anyone. Without small talk, there would be nothing to talk about with strangers. Engaging in small talk is a vital skill to master for both social and professional occasions. Good small talk can introduce you to new friends and colleagues and is a great way to network. It doesn't have to be rocket science. A few questions about hobbies or a remark about last night's game can get a conversation going. It can open a whole world of possibilities.

* small talk: 잡담

① 낯선 사람들로부터 예상치 못한 기회를 얻을 수도 있다.
② 말을 잘하는 것은 당신이 성공하도록 도울 수 있다.
③ 잡담은 직업상의 상황에서만 사용되어야 한다.
④ 잡담하는 것에는 많은 이점들이 있다.
⑤ 전문적인 방식으로 말하는 법을 배워라.

08 다음 글에서 필자가 주장하는 바로 가장 적절한 것은?

고난도

Among teachers, a common complaint is that it is difficult to get their students excited about class assignments. This may not be the fault of the students, though. Studies have shown that a young learner's interest in school work has a direct relationship to his or her level of understanding regarding the evaluation criteria. Students who cannot figure out what (A)they must do to receive a high grade often become discouraged and put less effort into a task. In some cases, they may even give up on their work. To provide (B)their students with proper motivation, teachers must make it clear what the students will be evaluated on.

① 학생이 해낼 수 있는 과제를 부여해야 한다.
② 교사는 항상 명확한 평가 기준을 제시해야 한다.
③ 평가의 최종 목표는 학생의 역량을 증진시키는 것이다.
④ 동기 부여를 위해 언제나 적절한 보상을 주어야 한다.
⑤ 과제는 출처가 분명한 자료를 토대로 제공되어야 한다.

실력 UP! 미니 문제 내신 서술형

07. 다음 질문을 읽고 한 문장의 영어로 답하시오.

Q: What does the author say would happen if there were no small talk in situations where you do not know anyone?

A: If there were no small talk, _____

_____ .

실력 UP! 미니 문제 내신 서술형

08. 윗글의 밑줄 친 (A), (B)가 지칭하는 바를 영어로 찾아 쓰시오.

(A) _____

(B) _____

CHAPTER 04
밑줄 의미 추론하기

유형소개 밑줄 친 어구 또는 문장이 함축하고 있는 의미를 추론하는 유형으로, 3점짜리 고난도 문제로 자주 출제됨
문제 수 1문제
지시문 밑줄 친 [어구/문장]이 다음 글에서 의미하는 바로 가장 적절한 것은?

불변의 패턴 07

패턴 빈출도 ★★★★☆

밑줄이 있는 문장은 주제문을 바꿔 말한 것이다.

지문 듣기

밑줄 친 부분이 포함된 문장은 주제문을 다른 표현으로 바꿔 말한 것인 경우가 많다. 따라서 글의 주제를 빠르게 파악하면 밑줄의 의미를 추론하는 데 도움이 된다.

패턴맛보기

다음 글의 주제를 참고해서 밑줄 친 at the "sweet spot"이 의미하는 바로 가장 적절한 것을 고르시오.

> 주제: 좋은 것에도 지나침이 있을 수 있기 때문에 부족과 과잉 모두를 피하는 것이 최선이다.

For almost all things in life, there can be too much of a good thing. Even the best things in life aren't so great in excess. For example, people should be brave, but if someone is too brave they become reckless. People should be trusting, but if someone is too trusting they are considered gullible. For each of these traits, it is best to avoid both deficiency and excess. The best way is to live at the "sweet spot" that maximizes wellbeing.

① 물질적인 부의 영역
② 두 극단의 중간 지점
③ 순간적인 쾌락의 순간

(해석)
인생의 거의 모든 것에 있어서, 좋은 것에도 지나침이 있을 수 있다. 심지어 인생에서 가장 좋은 것들도 지나치면 그렇게 좋지는 않다. 예를 들어, 사람들은 용감해야 하지만, 만약 누군가가 너무 용감하다면 그들은 무모해진다. 사람들은 사람을 믿어야 하지만 만약 누군가가 너무 사람을 믿는다면 그들은 속기 쉬운 사람으로 여겨진다. 각각의 이러한 특성으로 인해, 부족과 과잉 둘 다를 피하는 것이 최선이다. 최선의 방법은 행복을 극대화하는 "가장 적당한 지점"에서 사는 것이다.

(해설)
이 글의 주제는 좋은 것에도 지나침이 있을 수 있기 때문에 부족과 과잉 모두를 피하는 것이 최선이라는 것이므로, 이를 토대로 추론할 수 있는 밑줄 친 sweet spot(가장 적당한 지점)의 의미로 가장 적절한 것은 ② '두 극단의 중간 지점'이다.

(정답)
②

기출문제 2019년 9월 고1 학평

정답 및 해설 p.20

밑줄 친 "There is no there there."가 다음 글에서 의미하는 바로 가장 적절한 것은?

I believe the second decade of this new century is already very different. There are, of course, still millions of people who equate success with money and power — who are determined to never get off that treadmill despite the cost in terms of their wellbeing, relationships, and happiness. There are still millions desperately looking for the next promotion, the next million-dollar payday that they believe will satisfy their longing to feel better about themselves, or silence their dissatisfaction. But both in the West and in emerging economies, there are more people every day who recognize that these are all dead ends — that they are chasing a broken dream. That we cannot find the answer in our current definition of success alone because — as Gertrude Stein once said of Oakland — "There is no there there."

① People are losing confidence in themselves.
② Without dreams, there is no chance for growth.
③ We should not live according to others' expectations.
④ It is hard to realize our potential in difficult situations.
⑤ Money and power do not necessarily lead you to success.

밑줄 친 부분은 비유적이거나 상징적인 표현이다.

🎧지문 듣기

밑줄 친 부분은 글의 내용을 비유적으로 표현하거나 상징적으로 표현하는 경우가 많기 때문에 글자 그대로 해석해서는 의미 파악이 힘들다. 따라서 글의 처음부터 정독해서 읽고 핵심 내용을 파악한 후 밑줄 문장의 숨은 의미를 추론한다.

패턴맛보기

밑줄 친 the omnivore's paradox가 다음 글에서 의미하는 바로 가장 적절한 것은?

Humans are omnivorous. The primary advantage to this is that they can adapt to nearly all earthly environments. The disadvantage is that no single food provides the nutrition necessary for survival. Humans must be flexible enough to eat a variety of items sufficient for physical growth and maintenance, yet cautious enough not to randomly ingest foods that are physiologically harmful and, possibly, fatal. This dilemma, the need to experiment combined with the need for conservatism, is known as the omnivore's paradox.

① 영양이 있는 음식을 원하지만 동시에 이것을 싫어하는 아이러니
② 무엇을 먹을 수 있는지를 판단하는 것의 어려움
③ 음식에 대해 유연하면서 동시에 조심성 있을 필요성

해석
인간은 잡식성이다. 이것의 주요한 이점은 그들이 거의 모든 지구상의 환경에 적응할 수 있다는 것이다. 불리한 점은 단 한 가지의 음식만으로는 생존에 필수적인 영양분을 제공해주지 못한다는 것이다. 인간은 신체적 성장과 유지를 위해 충분한 다양한 것들을 필요한 만큼 먹는 융통성이 있어야 하지만, 생리학적으로 해롭고, 어쩌면 치명적인 음식을 임의로 섭취하지 않을 만큼 충분히 조심스러워야 한다. 이 딜레마, 즉 보수적 경향의 필요성과 동반되는 실험적인 행동의 필요성은 잡식 동물의 역설이라고 알려져 있다.

해설
밑줄 친 '잡식 동물의 역설'은 인간은 다양한 것들을 필요한 만큼 먹는 융통성이 있어야 하지만, 동시에 해롭고 어쩌면 치명적인 음식을 섭취하지 않을 만큼 충분히 조심스러워야 한다는 내용을 비유적으로 표현한 것이다. 따라서, 밑줄 친 the omnivore's paradox(잡식 동물의 역설)가 의미하는 바로 가장 적절한 것은 ③ '음식에 대해 유연하면서 동시에 조심성 있을 필요성'이다.

정답
③

기출문제 2019년 3월 고1 학평

정답 및 해설 p.21

밑줄 친 information blinded가 다음 글에서 의미하는 바로 가장 적절한 것은? [3점]

Technology has doubtful advantages. We must balance too much information versus using only the right information and keeping the decision-making process simple. The Internet has made so much free information available on any issue that we think we have to consider all of it in order to make a decision. So we keep searching for answers on the Internet. This makes us information blinded, like deer in headlights when trying to make personal, business, or other decisions. To be successful in anything today, we have to keep in mind that in the land of the blind, a one-eyed person can accomplish the seemingly impossible. The one-eyed person understands the power of keeping any analysis simple and will be the decision maker when he uses his one eye of intuition.

* intuition: 직관

① unwilling to accept others' ideas
② unable to access free information
③ unable to make decisions due to too much information
④ indifferent to the lack of available information
⑤ willing to take risks in decision-making

01 밑줄 친 <u>feather fanning</u>이 다음 글에서 의미하는 바로 가장 적절한 것은?

Materialism is a way of life in some cultures. In the United States, for instance, there is the sense that the more you own, the happier you'll be, leading some people to develop serious issues like addictions to shopping. For others, spending more money than necessary is less of a problem and more of a way of showing off what they have. This <u>feather fanning</u> is not only for the rich, however. Even members of low-income groups sometimes attempt to use material possessions to influence how others perceive them. For instance, wearing "bling," or jewelry that stands out, is intended to make the statement that the wearer's lifestyle is luxurious, even if that is not at all the case.

* bling: 과도하게 장식한 비싼 보석

① appreciation for beautiful things
② display of luxury and wealth
③ irresponsible spending
④ consequence of instant satisfaction
⑤ relationship between wealth and happiness

실력 UP! 미니 문제 주제 찾기

01. 윗글의 주제로 가장 적절한 것은?
① the psychological benefits of overspending
② how materialism is perceived in different cultures
③ intentions behind displaying material possessions

02 밑줄 친 <u>natural moderator</u>가 다음 글에서 의미하는 바로 가장 적절한 것은?

Recent human activity has contributed greatly to global warming. Nowhere are the effects of global warming more alarming than in the Arctic, where sea ice is vanishing due to temperatures there rising at twice the global average. The function of sea ice goes beyond just supporting wildlife survival in the Arctic; it plays a role that affects the planet as a whole as all the ecosystems on Earth are connected. Light-colored surfaces like sea ice keep the region cool by reflecting the majority of sunlight back into space. Without this <u>natural moderator</u>, it hits the ocean and is absorbed. In turn, more ice melts and sea levels rise, resulting in a cycle that becomes harder to stop the longer it goes on.

* vanish: 사라지다

① a barrier created due to sea ice build-up in the Arctic
② ice that keeps temperatures under control
③ sunlight that restricts rising sea levels
④ limitations forced on wildlife by sea ice
⑤ a temperature that limits the amount of sea ice

실력 UP! 미니 문제 주제 찾기

02. 윗글의 주제로 가장 적절한 것은?
① the effect of greenhouse gases on global warming
② misunderstandings about the nature of Earth's ecosystem
③ the risks triggered by the melting of Arctic sea ice

03 밑줄 친 they get all the breaks가 다음 글에서 의미하는 바로 가장 적절한 것은?

It is tempting to think that highly successful people are lucky and, accordingly, that they get all the breaks. But the truth is that most successful people are no luckier than anyone else. Whether in school, sports, or work—the people who succeed are the ones who put in the hard and necessary work. While most people look forward to taking time off and enjoying (A)their free time, successful people are willing to sacrifice their personal time to achieve their goals. Moreover, they do not easily give up at the first sign of trouble. They know that success does not simply "happen," and that they must work hard to achieve (B)it.

① they take advantage of others
② they have lots of free time
③ they are criticized unfairly
④ they do not have to work hard
⑤ they sometimes make mistakes

04 밑줄 친 trust cannot illuminate the truth가 다음 글에서 의미하는 바로 가장 적절한 것은?

Although many people consider trust to be essential in any good relationship, you shouldn't be too trusting, as this can be an obstacle. This is especially true in negotiations. Studies have found that people who enter into negotiations with feelings of distrust are likely to ask a lot of questions. This is because they aren't sure how trustworthy the other party is. As a result, they gather more information and discuss matters more thoroughly than those who are completely trusting to get a clearer sense of the situation. In effect, when what matters most is the outcome, trust cannot illuminate the truth. In negotiations, people should allow a certain measure of distrust to lead them in their decision making rather than just believing whatever is said.

① questioning nothing guarantees nothing
② trust once lost cannot be regained
③ there has to be a pre-existing relationship
④ we must always have faith in the other party
⑤ it is important to observe the other party's behavior

실력 UP! 미니 문제 내신 서술형

03. 윗글의 밑줄 친 (A), (B)가 지칭하는 바를 영어로 찾아 쓰시오.

(A) _____

(B) _____

실력 UP! 미니 문제 주제 찾기

04. 윗글의 주제로 가장 적절한 것은?

① the benefit of distrust in negotiation
② the necessity of trust in every relationship
③ the need to focus on details during negotiation

05 밑줄 친 removes the guessing game이 다음 글에서 의미하는 바로 가장 적절한 것은?

To meet the nutritional demands of a growing world population, farming will have to get *smarter*. And it's not just a matter of using better seeds or machinery. Just as the world's most successful companies have made progress by using big data, the agricultural world must collect and analyze information to find insights into improving their crop yields. The next generation of smart farms will be data-based, filled with sensors that allow them to measure every variable in each square meter of soil: from luminance and ground temperature, to current moisture levels, to the exact amount of pesticide used. This information, combined with the latest software, removes the guessing game, enabling smart farmers to identify and implement the best possible strategies for their fields.

* luminance: 밝기, 조도

① improves the application of big data in agriculture
② ensures accuracy in the process of farming
③ allows farmers to obtain the best prices
④ inhibits the influence of outside variables
⑤ neglects successful strategies for farming

06 밑줄 친 throwing a stone into the water가 다음 글에서 의미하는 바로 가장 적절한 것은?

Choosing whether or not to eat meat may seem like a personal matter in which factors like health and taste should weigh most heavily. However, there are bigger factors to consider as far as consuming meat is concerned, as it is like throwing a stone into the water. To produce meat, it is first necessary to have land on which to raise cattle and other livestock. As this land is not readily available, forests have to be cleared, often by burning them to the ground. This destroys the habitats of countless animal populations and, over time, can lead to a loss in biodiversity and the extinction of some species. And that's just to start. Greenhouse gas emissions, excessive water use, and numerous other problems that threaten the environment exist, all stemming from our continued demand for meat.

① creating friction between opposing groups
② changing objectives according to demand
③ posing a moral dilemma
④ generating multiple consequences
⑤ raising concerns for numerous people

실력 UP! 미니 문제 내신 서술형

05. 다음 영영 풀이에 적합한 단어를 윗글에서 찾아 쓰시오. (필요한 경우 형태를 변형하시오.)

ⓐ a deep understanding of the inner workings of something

→ i_____

ⓑ a plan or course of action used to accomplish a desired effect

→ s_____

실력 UP! 미니 문제 내신 서술형

06. 다음 문장을 우리말로 해석하시오.

However, there are bigger factors to consider as far as consuming meat is concerned, as it is like throwing a stone into the water.

→ _____

07 밑줄 친 is on the same page가 다음 글에서 의미하는 바로 가장 적절한 것은?

Companies typically have many channels through which they interact with consumers, such as press releases, corporate websites, print and television advertisements, and social media posts. To ensure that these work in harmony, some companies have adopted a strategy called Integrated Marketing Communications (IMC). It involves coordinating all public communications so that customers receive a message that does not contain conflicting information. One barrier to the successful implementation of an IMC strategy is a lack of cooperation among the members of a company. For example, the marketing department might promise a feature the design department is unable to include in a product. To avoid this issue, a team which serves as a control tower must be appointed to make certain that everyone in a company is on the same page.

① deals with similar questions from customers
② provides consistent messages to consumers
③ improves cooperation among companies
④ creates effective product advertisements
⑤ uses familiar marketing methods

실력 UP! 미니 문제 주제 찾기

07. 윗글의 주제로 가장 적절한 것은?
① how the IMC strategy is utilized by companies
② the benefits of using numerous channels for customer communication
③ methods of encouraging collaboration between departments

고난도

08 밑줄 친 rarely hold water가 다음 글에서 의미하는 바로 가장 적절한 것은?

Homeopathy is a popular form of treatment for various diseases that has been heavily criticized by the medical establishment. The reason for the distrust is that there is no evidence that it is effective. Homeopathic "medicines" are created by repeatedly diluting a substance—such as a plant or mineral—in water until almost no chemical trace of it remains. This is done because homeopaths say that the weaker a medicine is, the more powerful its ability to stimulate the body's natural healing power. While doctors agree that such methods are generally not harmful, they urge the public to remember that claims made by homeopaths rarely hold water. The concern is that people with serious illnesses such as cancer might refuse regular medical treatments if they mistakenly put their trust in homeopathy.

* dilute: 희석하다

① are under investigation
② have more supporters
③ are very effective
④ require more money
⑤ are unlikely to be true

실력 UP! 미니 문제 내신 서술형

08. 윗글의 내용을 다음과 같이 요약할 때, 빈칸에 들어갈 알맞은 말을 본문에서 찾아 쓰시오. (필요한 경우, 단어 형태 변경 가능)

Although many people use homeopathy to treat various diseases, it has also been (A) c_____ by the medical establishment because there is no evidence that proves it's (B) e_____.

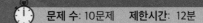

01 다음 글의 목적으로 가장 적절한 것은?

To whom it may concern,

This year has been quite difficult for our employees because of the pandemic. I understand management has some concerns about letting people work from home, but I think it will be good for everyone. I'm writing to let you know the advantages of this plan. First of all, it will ensure the safety of everyone in the office until more people get vaccinated. Also, research shows that flexible working conditions lead to greater morale and productivity. All in all, I think it is worth considering giving our employees the option to work from home during this challenging period. I am sure it will be beneficial to the company.

Sincerely Yours,
Robert Lowell
Senior Marketing Manager

① 재택근무의 장점을 강조하려고
② 연구 조사 결과를 전달하려고
③ 투병 중인 직원들을 격려하려고
④ 직원 건강의 중요성을 알리려고
⑤ 재택근무 이외의 선택지가 있는지 문의하려고

02 다음 글에 드러난 Florence의 심경 변화로 가장 적절한 것은?

When Florence became a candidate for class president, she thought it might be really difficult. She was upset to discover she was right. She tried campaigning, but the other students barely listened to her. She felt like a loser already and wanted to give up. She told her friend about her worries. Her friend said that winning or losing wasn't important. What mattered was that Florence do her best and take pride in what she did. After that, Florence gave it her all. She campaigned every day and talked to her classmates. She made a great speech. On the day of the election, Florence lost. But it didn't matter because she was satisfied with the hard work and effort she put in.

* campaign: 선거 운동을 하다

① desperate   → surprised
② worried   → panicked
③ annoyed   → amused
④ discouraged → proud
⑤ alarmed   → outraged

03 다음 글의 요지로 가장 적절한 것은?

There is an ancient proverb that states "It is better to sweat in practice than to bleed in battle." This idea is just as relevant today, as the ability to excel in any situation relies on preparation. This is particularly true of professionals giving presentations. Giving any kind of presentation, especially a good one, is not an easy task. Nervousness and worry, or even overconfidence, can ruin what could be an excellent performance. The most effective method to combat this is also the most overlooked: practice. It builds confidence and reduces anxiety. The more you practice, the more spontaneous you become as well. Once you can deliver your material in your sleep, you'll know you are ready.

① 훌륭한 발표를 하는 것은 경력의 가장 중요한 부분이다.
② 발표하기를 꺼리는 전문가들은 발전할 수 없을 것이다.
③ 많은 양의 연습을 통해 훌륭한 발표를 할 수 있다.
④ 연습을 열심히 한 사람이 임기응변에도 능하다.
⑤ 자신감을 쌓는 가장 좋은 방법 중 하나는 발표를 하는 것이다.

04 다음 글에서 필자가 주장하는 바로 가장 적절한 것은?

During university, one of the classes I most hated was Classical Literature. I didn't see the need to study something that seemed so outdated in today's society and wondered why it was even being taught at all. After taking the class, I didn't wonder anymore. There were so many ideas and perspectives that opened my imagination. Classical Literature explores themes connected to life such as injustice, revenge, and class. I learned philosophical concepts that I never thought about and caught a glimpse into cultures I never knew. The stories, old as they were, challenged my modern mind. Classical Literature helped me grow not only as a student but more importantly, as a human being.

① 다른 문화를 이해하려면 책을 읽어야 한다.
② 고전 문학은 생각을 넓히는 데 도움이 된다.
③ 철학의 토대를 배우려면 고전 문학을 읽어라.
④ 좋은 작가가 되려면 고전 문학을 배워야 한다.
⑤ 사회학을 전공하려면 고전 문학 수업을 들어야 한다.

05 밑줄 친 have an inner scorecard가 다음 글에서 의미하는 바로 가장 적절한 것은?

Have you ever scrolled through social media only to find a feed full of amazing accomplishments that seem out of reach to you? Like with most people, there will come a time when comparing yourself to others makes you feel as though you're falling short. The truth is that everyone has different talents and opportunities, and it isn't normal for all people to have accomplished the same things at the same points in their lives. Instead of focusing on where you stand in relation to others, it's better to have an inner scorecard when playing the game of life. Doing so will make you feel less compelled to keep up with the other players and more likely to meet whatever objectives that you feel are important. After all, the only person who will care about how you succeeded in the end is you.

① overcome your limitations
② define success for yourself
③ keep your thoughts private
④ get out of your comfort zone
⑤ be humble about your accomplishments

06 다음 글의 목적으로 가장 적절한 것은?

The management of the Arcos Shopping Center has received numerous complaints from visitors. They complain about the lack of available parking. This has been a big problem on weekends. Fortunately, the empty lot behind the shopping center was recently put up for sale. We bought the lot and will be building a new parking garage. The work will begin next month on May 4. It will take around two months to complete. We do not want to cause any interruption to your business. However, please expect some construction noise. We apologize for any inconvenience. If you have questions, please contact my office.

Yours Truly,
Adam Frost

① 상품의 배송 지연에 대해 사과하려고
② 곧 있을 할인 행사를 홍보하려고
③ 주차장 공사 계획을 안내하려고
④ 매장 출구가 혼잡하여 불만을 제기하려고
⑤ 공사로 인해 매장 운영 시간이 변경됨을 안내하려고

07 다음 글에 드러난 Cara의 심경으로 가장 적절한 것은?

Cara reached into her bag and felt her hands begin to tremble. It was empty. Her wallet with all of her money and her passport were gone. She hurriedly stepped out of the line to buy tickets for the museum and walked over to a bench where she emptied her bag. Only a few coins and a map fell out. Cara looked around her with panic. She was in the middle of a city far from her hotel with no money. She also didn't speak the local language and didn't know where to get help. Cara could feel tears filling her eyes as she sat down, and she tried to think of what to do next.

① touched and grateful
② proud and contented
③ desperate and frustrated
④ delighted and excited
⑤ bored and indifferent

08 다음 글의 요지로 가장 적절한 것은?

One of the biggest concerns in modern times is how harmful stress can be to our physical, emotional, and mental health. Certainly, severe and constant stress is not good for anyone. However, stress itself is not always bad. A little bit of stress makes us tougher. It can help us manage difficult situations more easily. When we're stressed, hormones that boost our mental ability and memory are also released. Even when we endure more challenging moments of stress, like going through a breakup or getting a bad grade, it ultimately makes us better. And during these situations, we create strong social bonds by giving each other support. So, don't stress about stress and you will be a healthier you.

① 현대 사회에서 사회적 유대감은 무엇보다 중요하다.
② 당신이 쾌활하다면 스트레스를 이겨낼 수 있다.
③ 스트레스는 몸보다 마음에 더 영향을 미친다.
④ 스트레스는 현대의 가장 큰 문제이다.
⑤ 적당한 스트레스는 도움이 된다.

09 다음 글에서 필자가 주장하는 바로 가장 적절한 것은?

We are taught from a young age that if we work hard enough, we can achieve anything. In addition, self-help books and magazine articles tell us that reaching our goals is up to us. If we have talent after all, we will eventually make it. All of this implies that if we are not "successful," then we are not doing the right things or taking the right steps. However, there are times when hard work and talent are not enough. Sometimes, it is more important to be in the right place at the right time. This is something we must accept. Since we cannot control everything, all we can do is do our best with what we have.

① 재능을 발휘하는 것보다 노력에 의존해라.
② 성공하기 위한 상황과 때를 생각해라.
③ 성공은 노력보다 인내가 더 필요하다.
④ 우리는 언제 성공할 수 있을지 알 수 없다.
⑤ 노력과 능력이 항상 성공을 보장하는 것은 아니다.

10 밑줄 친 "made" and not "born"이 다음 글에서 의미하는 바로 가장 적절한 것은?

History is about more than merely gathering facts, and that's what renowned historian E.H. Carr insists. Instead, history is about interactions between the past and present, and facts and historians. A historian must interpret facts to give them meaning, and they must assign significance to certain facts that they deem significant as they filter through and analyze a large multitude of them. Of course, this implies that history is not neutral, but Carr argues that this is an impossibility anyway, since historians always take sides, which brings such limitations. In his view, history is "made" and not "born." Since cultures evolve, so do evaluations of historical events. In this way, history is an ongoing discussion.

* deem: 여기다

① elements of modern society can be traced to the past
② history is today's interpretation of past facts
③ historical perspectives change little over time
④ historical records consist only of true facts
⑤ a society's structure determines its values

유형 소개 | 글의 핵심 내용인 주제와 이를 함축적으로 표현한 제목을 파악하는 유형
문 제 수 | 각 1문제씩
지 시 문 | 다음 글의 주제로 가장 적절한 것은?
다음 글의 제목으로 가장 적절한 것은?

불변의 패턴 09
패턴 빈출도 ★★★★★
주제문은 처음이나 마지막 두세 문장에 나온다.

지문 듣기

글의 처음과 마지막 두세 문장을 읽으면서 주제문을 찾고, 이 내용을 다른 말로 가장 잘 표현한 정답을 골라야 한다.

패턴맛보기

다음 글의 주제문을 찾아서 밑줄을 그으시오.

If you've ever seen a tree stump, you probably noticed that the top of the stump had a series of rings. These rings can tell us what the weather was like during each year of the tree's life. For example, tree rings usually grow wider in warm, wet years and are thinner in years when it is cold and dry. If the tree has experienced stressful conditions, such as a drought, the tree might hardly grow at all during that time.

[해석]
만약 당신이 나무 그루터기를 본 적이 있다면, 아마도 그루터기의 맨 위에 일련의 나이테가 있는 것을 보았을 것이다. 이 나이테는 우리에게 나무의 일생에서 매해의 날씨가 어땠는지를 알려줄 수 있다. 예를 들어 나이테는 온난하고 습윤했던 해에는 더 커지지만 춥고 건조했던 해에는 얇아진다. 만약 나무들이 가뭄과 같은 혹독한 환경을 겪어왔다면, 그동안은 나무가 아마 거의 자라지 않을지도 모른다.

[해설]
글의 첫 문장은 도입구이고, 두 번째 문장에서 글의 핵심 내용이 언급된다. 이어지는 세 번째 문장부터 마지막 문장까지는 두 번째 문장의 내용에 대한 예시와 부연 설명이다. 따라서 이 글의 주제문은 두 번째 문장인 These rings can tell us ~ of the tree's life.이다.

[정답]
These rings can tell us what the weather was like during each year of the tree's life.

기출문제 2018년 3월 고1 학평
정답 및 해설 p.33

다음 글의 주제로 가장 적절한 것은?

Storyteller Syd Lieberman suggests that it is the story in history that provides the nail to hang facts on. Students remember historical facts when they are tied to a story. According to a report, a high school in Boulder, Colorado, is currently experimenting with a study of presentation of historical material. Storytellers present material in dramatic context to the students, and group discussion follows. Students are encouraged to read further. In contrast, another group of students is involved in traditional research/report techniques. The study indicates that the material presented by the storytellers has much more interest and personal impact than that gained via the traditional method.

① why students should learn history
② essential elements of historical dramas
③ advantages of traditional teaching methods
④ benefits of storytelling in teaching history
⑤ importance of having balanced views on history

불변의 패턴10

패턴 빈출도 ★★★★★

주제문과 함께 자주 나오는 표현이 있다.

🎧지문 듣기

주제문에는 명령문이나 특정 표현들이 자주 함께 쓰인다. **주제문에 자주 등장하는 표현***을 알아두면 글에서 해당 표현을 찾아 정답을 좀 더 빨리 파악할 수 있다.

패턴맛보기

① ~ ③ 중에서 제목의 단서가 명확하게 등장하는 문장을 고르시오.

How Chewing Helps Mammals Survive

① Chewing leads to smaller particles for swallowing, and more exposed surface area for digestive enzymes to act on. ② In other words, it means the extraction of more fuel and raw materials from a mouthful of food. ③ This is especially important for mammals because they heat their bodies from within.

[해석]

씹기가 어떻게 포유류의 생존에 도움이 되었는가

① 씹기는 삼킴을 위한 더 작은 조각들과 소화 효소가 작용하기 위해 더 많이 노출된 표면을 이끌어낸다. ② 다시 말해서, 이것은 한입의 음식으로부터의 더 많은 연료와 원료의 추출을 의미한다. ③ 이것은 그들이 체내에서 그들의 몸을 따뜻하게 해주기 때문에 포유류에게 특히 중요하다.

[정답]

③

기출문제 2021년 3월 고1 학평

정답 및 해설 p.33

다음 글의 제목으로 가장 적절한 것은?

Think, for a moment, about something you bought that you never ended up using. An item of clothing you never ended up wearing? A book you never read? Some piece of electronic equipment that never even made it out of the box? It is estimated that Australians alone spend on average $10.8 billion AUD (approximately $9.99 billion USD) every year on goods they do not use—more than the total government spending on universities and roads. That is an average of $1,250 AUD (approximately $1,156 USD) for each household. All the things we buy that then just sit there gathering dust are waste—a waste of money, a waste of time, and waste in the sense of pure rubbish. As the author Clive Hamilton observes, 'The difference between the stuff we buy and what we use is waste.'

① Spending Enables the Economy
② Money Management: Dos and Don'ts
③ Too Much Shopping: A Sign of Loneliness
④ 3R's of Waste: Reduce, Reuse, and Recycle
⑤ What You Buy Is Waste Unless You Use It

실력UP! 기출표현 | 주제문에 자주 등장하는 표현*

중요성 강조	should/must/have to ~해야 한다 make sure ~을 확실히 해라
	important 중요한 necessary 필요한 try to ~ 하도록 노력해라
대조 / 반전	but/however 그러나 although 비록 in fact 사실은 the truth is 사실은

결론 / 정리	therefore 그러므로 in other words 즉 thus 따라서
법칙 / 통념	in general 일반적으로 believe 믿다
조사 / 연구	according to ~에 따르면

독해 만점 TEST

01 다음 글의 주제로 가장 적절한 것은?

White noise, whether it's the drone of a fan or the regular crash of waves on the shore, is popularly believed to be one of the most effective forms of sleep aid. An entire industry of products has grown up around (A)the concept, with apps and devices that promise to provide soothing sounds that will help you sleep through the night. Some insist that white noise can train you to relax and "switch off" your brain by focusing on a single, gentle stimulus instead of all the thoughts racing around in your head. But despite these claims, research has found little evidence to verify them. Given the active work that our brain has to do when interpreting noise, using one of these may, ironically enough, increase its workload and deny it a chance for needed rest.

* drone: 웅웅거리는 소리   ** stimulus: 자극

① effects of sleeplessness and insomnia

② effective ways to interpret white noise

③ types of white noise that calm our minds

④ products that help you sleep more effectively

⑤ different views regarding white noise's impact on sleep

실력 UP! 미니 문제 내신 서술형

01. 윗글의 밑줄 친 (A)가 의미하는 것을 우리말로 쓰시오.

(A) _____

02 다음 글의 제목으로 가장 적절한 것은?

Thanks to germ theory, we know that maintaining good personal hygiene is important to our health. That is why, from a young age, we are taught to wash ourselves regularly. Soap can lessen our chances of falling ill from contact with harmful bacteria. But more recent research suggests that we may be overdoing (A)this. While it is true that washing with soap can leave our skin clean, the harsh chemicals in it can also remove the natural oils and bacteria that protect our skin. Without these features, the skin becomes dry and can be easily infected. Apparently, when it comes to soap, you can have too much of a good thing.

* germ theory: 세균 이론(질병의 원인은 세균에 의한다는 학설)

① Fight Harmful Germs with Soap

② Can Too Much Soap be Harmful?

③ Soap: Which One is Best for You?

④ The Skin: Our Body's Best Defense

⑤ The Best Reason to Wash Regularly

실력 UP! 미니 문제 내신 서술형

02. 윗글의 밑줄 친 (A)가 의미하는 것을 우리말로 쓰시오.

(A) _____

03 다음 글의 주제로 가장 적절한 것은?

In the digital age, it would seem that there is little reason for our literature to still appear in paper form. After all, physical books, like any number of other obsolete technologies, are no longer strictly necessary with the emergence of E-books and the explosion of content. But some have pushed back against this notion, arguing that E-books have crucial disadvantages compared to their old-fashioned counterparts. Reading on a screen, they point out, requires more energy and induces fatigue faster. It can even disrupt your sleep if done before bed—a time and place books have long been the perfect companion. To make matters worse, on E-books you are also more likely to skim for information rather than lose yourself in the story. This means that the digital reader takes less overall enjoyment from the experience and retains less of what they read.

① the importance of reading fiction
② the efforts to save old literature
③ the causes of sleep difficulties
④ the shortcomings of e-books
⑤ the future of physical books

04 다음 글의 제목으로 가장 적절한 것은?

There is a little-known issue with television, which is that it impairs children's ability to learn language. Data reveals that TV affects language learning in children below the age of two, particularly when it takes the place of human interaction. Children learn language best when they interact with the people around them, because they get to actively engage their brains and respond to what is being said. Most television programming, however, demands only that its young viewers sit passively in front of a screen. When this happens, children's brains do not receive enough stimulation. As a result, it can delay children's ability to learn language.

① Can You Learn a New Language from Watching TV?
② TV: Delaying Language Learning in Children
③ Does Television Harm Children's Health?
④ Passive Language Learning Methods
⑤ The Social Impact of Television

실력 UP! 미니 문제 내신 서술형

03. 다음 영영 풀이에 적합한 단어를 윗글에서 찾아 쓰시오.

ⓐ outdated, having been replaced by newer, superior technology for accomplishing the same task

→ o_____

ⓑ to cause

→ i_____

실력 UP! 미니 문제 내신 서술형

04. 다음 질문을 읽고 한 문장의 영어로 답하시오.

Q: According to the passage, when do children learn language best?

A: _____

_____.

05 다음 글의 주제로 가장 적절한 것은?

Why do you *worry*? You might think doing this helps you to avoid negative outcomes and may even lead you to find solutions. Soon, it becomes the way you approach all problems, real or not. It is a habit. In reality, worry creates only one thing: more worry. It keeps you stuck in the same place, exhausted, much like being on a treadmill. No matter how fast you go, you end up where you began. Whenever you catch yourself worrying too much, you may want to consider trying a different tack. Instead of continuing the cycle, focus on what you want to happen and how you will achieve that result. It will get you off of the treadmill and get you moving forward again.

* treadmill: 쳇바퀴

① ways to move forward despite worrying
② how bad things can lead to solutions
③ how to maintain a cycle of success
④ worrying as a means of focus
⑤ the process of creating habits

06 다음 글의 제목으로 가장 적절한 것은?

Some 5,000 years ago in Mesopotamia—or modern-day Iraq—the debut of money changed the way people lived in numerous ways. For instance, the expanded use of gold and silver currency went hand in hand with the establishment of trade on a wide scale. And with trade, people began to take on specialized professions, including new classes of people like merchants, who profited from being at the center of commercial transactions. Not only that, but money also gave kings more power, since it made it easier to tax people and pay salaries to soldiers and government officials.

① Why Mesopotamia was the Center of the Ancient World
② Gold and Silver: Valuable Metals and Their Many Uses
③ Picturing a World Before the Advent of Money
④ The Downfall of the World's First Kings
⑤ Money: Creator of Human Society

실력 UP! **미니 문제** 내신 서술형

05. 다음 질문을 읽고 한 문장의 영어로 답하시오.

Q: What does the author suggest we do when we find ourselves worrying too much?

A: _____

_____ .

실력 UP! **미니 문제** 내신 서술형

06. 다음 질문을 읽고 한 문장의 영어로 답하시오.

Q: According to the passage, how did money give kings more power?

A: By making it _____

_____ .

07 다음 글의 제목으로 가장 적절한 것은?

In Bram Stoker's 1897 novel *Dracula*, the title character is an ancient vampire with the ability to transform into a bat. While this work of literature strengthened the association between vampires and bats, it was not the origin of (A)it. This can be traced to the 15th century when Europeans first began exploring South America. They discovered a small bat that only feeds on the blood of live animals. It hunts at night and is even known to bite sleeping humans and then consume (B)their blood. Given this, it should come as no surprise that the explorers called it a vampire bat and that people back in Europe were amazed by it. As knowledge of this creature became more widespread, the relationship between bats and the vampires became a part of popular culture.

① Real-Life Vampires found in South America
② Bats and Vampires: Why Are They Linked?
③ Why Stoker Included a Bat in His Novel
④ Dracula: The First European Vampire
⑤ How Do Vampire Bats Drink Blood?

고난도

08 다음 글의 주제로 가장 적절한 것은?

In countries that use the parliamentary system of government, the parliament plays an important role in promoting the will of the people. This is due to the fact that it is a powerful institution that is composed of members who are elected directly by the public. The parliament is the legislative body of the government, meaning that it is able to create and amend laws. Furthermore, it has extensive control over the budget, with the right to approve or reject taxes and spending plans. Finally, the parliament provides oversight of the head of the government and is able to investigate officials who engage in unethical behavior. The fact that so much power is in the hands of the elected members of parliament ensures that the concerns of citizens are the government's most important considerations.

* parliamentary system: 의원 내각제 ** legislative body: 입법 기관

① the origin of today's parliament system
② the process by which a parliament makes a law
③ the public's role in electing government officials
④ the need for a parliament to conduct investigations
⑤ the role of a parliament in promoting public interest

실력 UP! 미니 문제 내신 서술형

07. 윗글의 밑줄 친 (A), (B)가 지칭하는 바를 영어로 찾아 쓰시오.

(A) _____

(B) _____

실력 UP! 미니 문제 내신 서술형

08. 다음 질문을 읽고 한 문장의 영어로 답하시오.

Q: What important role does the parliamentary system of government play?

A: It _____.

CHAPTER 06

도표 정보 파악하기

유형소개 글을 읽고 도표와 일치하지 않는 문장을 고르는 유형으로, 막대/선/원 그래프 또는 표 등 다양한 종류의 도표가 출제됨

문 제 수 1 문제

지 시 문 다음 도표의 내용과 일치하지 않는 것은?

불변의 패턴 11

패턴 빈출도 ★★★★★

도표의 제목과 첫 문장에 무엇에 관한 도표인지 나온다.

지문 듣기

도표의 제목과 첫 문장을 보고 무엇에 관한 도표인지 먼저 파악하면 도표를 더 쉽고 빠르게 이해할 수 있다. 만약 제목만 읽고 파악이 됐다면 첫 문장을 넘기고 바로 선택지부터 읽는다.

패턴맛보기

다음 도표가 무엇에 관한 것인지 우리말로 적으시오.

The Most Spoken Languages Worldwide in 2015

English 1,500 / 375
Chinese 1,100 / 982
Hindi 650 / 460
Spanish 420 / 330
French 370 / 79

■ Total Speakers
□ Native Speakers

0   400   800   1,200   1,600 (million)

* Note: Total Speakers = Native Speakers + Non-native Speakers

The above graph shows the numbers of total speakers and native speakers of the five most spoken languages worldwide in 2015.

→ _____

해석

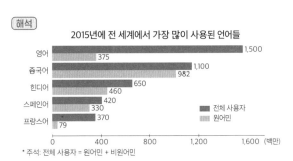

2015년에 전 세계에서 가장 많이 사용된 언어들

영어 1,500 / 375
중국어 1,100 / 982
힌디어 650 / 460
스페인어 420 / 330
프랑스어 370 / 79

■ 전체 사용자
□ 원어민

0   400   800   1,200   1,600 (백만)

* 주석: 전체 사용자 = 원어민 + 비원어민

위 도표는 2015년에 전 세계에서 가장 많이 사용된 다섯 개 언어의 전체 사용자 수와 원어민 수를 보여준다.

정답

2015년에 전 세계에서 가장 많이 사용된 다섯 개 언어의 전체 사용자 수와 원어민 수

기출문제 2018년 9월 고1 학평

정답 및 해설 p.40

다음 도표의 내용과 일치하지 않는 것은?

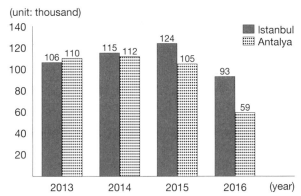

Top Turkish Cities Receiving Tourists

(unit: thousand)

	2013	2014	2015	2016
Istanbul	106	115	124	93
Antalya	110	112	105	59

■ Istanbul
▦ Antalya

(year)

The above graph shows the number of tourists who visited Istanbul and Antalya, the top two most-visited cities in Turkey, from 2013 to 2016. ① The number of tourists to each city was over one hundred thousand every year between 2013 and 2015. ② The city that received the higher number of tourists in 2013 was Antalya, but in the following three years, Istanbul received more tourists than Antalya did. ③ While the number of tourists to Istanbul increased steadily from 2013 to 2015, Antalya received less tourists in 2015 compared to the previous year. ④ Interestingly, in 2016, the number of tourists dropped to less than one hundred thousand for both cities. ⑤ In particular, the number of tourists to Antalya in 2016 was only one-third the number from 2013.

불변의 패턴 12

패턴 빈출도 ★★★★★

정답의 단서는 도표의 수치 변화에 있다.

🎧 지문 듣기

도표의 수치 변화를 나타내는 증가, 감소, 비교, 배수 표현이 정답의 단서가 되는 경우가 많다. 따라서 **수치의 변화를 나타내는 표현***을 알아두고 이를 특히 주의하여 읽는다.

패턴맛보기

도표의 내용과 일치하도록 밑줄 친 부분을 고치시오.

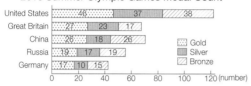

2016 Summer Olympic Games Medal Count

① Of the 5 countries, the United States won the smallest amount of medals in total.

→ _____

② When it comes to gold medals, Great Britain won less than China did.

→ _____

해석

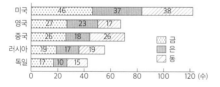

2016년 하계 올림픽 메달 수

① 다섯 국가 중에서, 미국은 가장 적은 수의 메달을 획득했다.
② 금메달의 경우, 영국이 중국보다 더 적게 획득했다.

해설

① 정답의 단서는 최상급 표현 smallest에 있다. 미국이 획득한 메달은 총 120개로 다섯 국가 중에서 가장 많으므로 smallest를 highest 혹은 largest 등으로 고쳐야 한다.
② 정답의 단서는 비교 표현 less에 있다. 영국이 획득한 금메달은 27개로, 26개를 획득한 중국보다 많다. 따라서 less를 more로 고쳐야 한다.

정답

① highest / largest ② more

기출문제 2020년 6월 고1 학평

정답 및 해설 p.40

다음 도표의 내용과 일치하지 <u>않는</u> 것은?

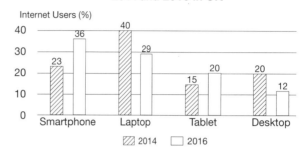

Most Important Device for Internet Access: 2014 and 2016 in UK

The above graph shows what devices British people considered the most important when connecting to the Internet in 2014 and 2016. ① More than a third of UK Internet users considered smartphones to be their most important device for accessing the Internet in 2016. ② In the same year, the smartphone overtook the laptop as the most important device for Internet access. ③ In 2014, UK Internet users were the least likely to select a tablet as their most important device for Internet access. ④ In contrast, they were the least likely to consider a desktop as their most important device for Internet access in 2016. ⑤ The proportion of UK Internet users who selected a desktop as their most important device for Internet access increased by half from 2014 to 2016.

* proportion: 비율

실력UP! 기출표현 수치의 변화를 나타내는 표현*

증가 increase 증가하다 rise 오르다 grow 증가하다 soar 치솟다

감소 decrease 감소하다 decline 감소하다 drop 줄다 reduce 감소하다

비교 more/less than 더 많다/더 적다 higher/lower than 더 크다/더 작다

배수 twice/two times 2배 half 절반 a quarter 4분의 1 one-third 3분의 1

독해 만점 TEST

01 다음 도표의 내용과 일치하지 <u>않는</u> 것은?

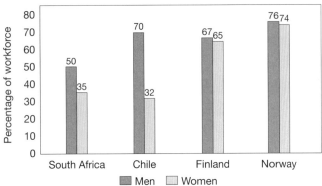

Employment rates of 4 countries (2002)

The above graph shows the male and female employment rates in four different countries in 2002. ① Overall, the percentage of males in the workforce was higher than that of the females in all four countries. ② In South Africa, the percentage of women in the workforce was less than 40 percent. ③ Of the four countries, the largest difference in percentage between men and women in the workforce was in Chile. ④ Both the percentage of men and women in Norway's workforce was higher than the percentage in Chile. ⑤ Compared to the percentage of men in the workforce in South Africa, the percentage of the male workforce in Norway was more than 30 percent higher.

02 다음 도표의 내용과 일치하지 <u>않는</u> 것은?

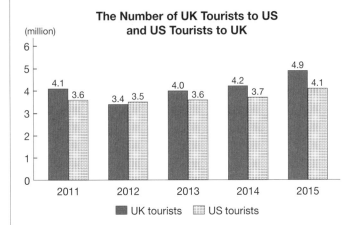

The Number of UK Tourists to US and US Tourists to UK

The above graph shows the number of tourists to and from the UK and US during the period of 2011 to 2015. ① The number of UK tourists to the US in 2011 was more than four million, which was higher compared to that in 2012. ② In 2012, the number of US tourists to the UK was higher than the number of UK tourists to the US. ③ From 2012 to 2015, the number of UK tourists and US tourists to each other's country increased each year. ④ The gap between UK tourists and US tourists was the biggest in 2015. ⑤ The number of US tourists to the UK never went above four million from 2013 to 2015.

실력 UP! 미니 문제 내신 서술형

01. 다음 영영 풀이에 적합한 단어를 윗글에서 찾아 쓰시오.

ⓐ the state of having a job

→ _____

ⓑ the total workers in a society

→ _____

실력 UP! 미니 문제 내신 서술형

02. 다음 문장을 우리말로 해석하시오.

The number of UK tourists to the US in 2011 was more than four million, which was higher compared to that in 2012.

→ _____

03 다음 도표의 내용과 일치하지 <u>않는</u> 것은?

Highest Level of Education Earned by Canadians

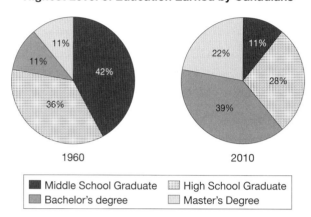

1960

2010

- ■ Middle School Graduate ▦ High School Graduate
- ▨ Bachelor's degree ▢ Master's Degree

The graph above shows the highest level of education earned by Canadians in the years 1960 and 2010. ① In 1960, the percentage of middle school graduates was greater than that of all other completed education groups. ② When it comes to completing middle school only, the percentage was more than 30% higher in 1960 than in 2010. ③ In both 1960 and 2010, the percentage of those whose highest level of education was a high school graduate was more than 30%. ④ The percentage of those who completed a Bachelor's degree and a Master's degree in 1960 was the same. ⑤ Of the levels of education completed, the second lowest percentage in 2010 was Master's degree.

03. 다음 문장을 우리말로 해석하시오.

In 1960, the percentage of middle school graduates was greater than that of all other completed education groups.

→ _____

04 다음 도표의 내용과 일치하지 <u>않는</u> 것은?

The Number of Threatened Fish Species in 5 countries

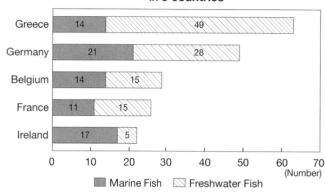

■ Marine Fish ▨ Freshwater Fish

The above graph shows the number of threatened fish species in five countries. ① In Greece, the number of fish species that are threatened in total is more than 60, the greatest total number among the five countries. ② Of the five countries, Germany has the highest number of marine fish species that are threatened. ③ The number of threatened freshwater species in Belgium is the same as France's, but the number of marine fish that are threatened outweighs that of France. ④ There are more freshwater fish species than marine fish species that are threatened in France. ⑤ The number of marine fish species that are threatened in Germany exceeds the total number of fish species that are threatened in Ireland.

04. 다음 영영 풀이에 적합한 단어를 윗글에서 찾아 쓰시오.

ⓐ at risk of becoming an endangered species

→ _____

ⓑ existing in or relating to oceanic ecosystems

→ _____

05 다음 도표의 내용과 일치하지 <u>않는</u> 것은?

The Number of Cars Produced in 2020

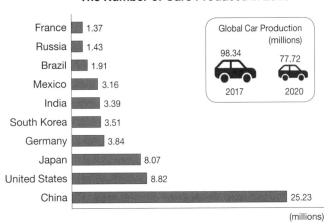

The graph above shows the number of cars produced in millions during 2020 by ten different countries. ① Global car production decreased by over 20 million from 2017 to 2020. ② The combined number of cars produced by France, Russia, and Brazil was fewer than the number of cars produced by the United States. ③ While the number of cars made by South Korea was lower in number than what Germany produced, it was higher than the number of cars produced by India. ④ The gap between the United States and Japan in the number of cars manufactured was less than 1 million. ⑤ It was China that produced the largest number of cars, which was less than three times the number of cars that Japan produced.

06 다음 표의 내용과 일치하지 <u>않는</u> 것은?

Government spending by sector (2009)

	Germany	Italy	UK
Public services	6.6%	8.6%	4.6%
Health	7.1%	7.5%	7.8%
Economic affairs	4.0%	4.5%	4.4%
Education	4.3%	4.6%	6.4%
Environmental protection	0.7%	0.9%	1.0%

The table above shows the percentage of government spending of three different countries in five sectors in 2009. ① Of the three countries, the percentage of government spending for Public services was highest in Italy. ② In Germany, government spending on Health exceeded spending on Economic affairs and environmental protection combined. ③ The second largest percentage of government spending in Italy went to Health. ④ In the UK, government spending on Public services was the third largest among the five sectors, following the government spending used on Economic affairs. ⑤ All three countries used the least amount of government spending on Environmental protection.

실력 UP! 미니 문제 내신 서술형

05. 다음 영영 풀이에 적합한 단어를 윗글에서 찾아 쓰시오.

ⓐ adding together two or more amounts, figures, or quantities

→ _____

ⓑ the separation or difference between two amounts

→ _____

실력 UP! 미니 문제 내신 서술형

06. 다음 영영 풀이에 적합한 단어를 윗글에서 찾아 쓰시오. (필요한 경우 형태를 변형하시오.)

ⓐ to increase beyond another number or amount

→ _____

ⓑ lower than any other corresponding value

→ _____

07 다음 도표의 내용과 일치하지 <u>않는</u> 것은?

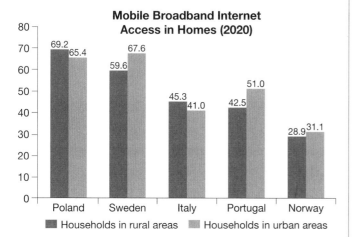

Mobile Broadband Internet Access in Homes (2020)

- Households in rural areas
- Households in urban areas

The above graph shows the percentage of urban and rural households with mobile broadband Internet access for five European countries in 2020. ① The country with the highest percentage of rural households with mobile broadband Internet access was Poland, accounting for 69.2%. ② The percentage of urban households with mobile broadband Internet access in Sweden, Portugal, and Norway exceeded that of rural households. ③ Italy's mobile broadband Internet access in rural areas was less than half, but it was still the third-highest for all countries. ④ Mobile broadband Internet access for urban households in Portugal was less than twice that of rural households in Norway. ⑤ Among the five countries, the gap between the percentage of rural and urban areas with mobile broadband access in Norway was the highest.

고난도

08 다음 도표의 내용과 일치하지 <u>않는</u> 것은?

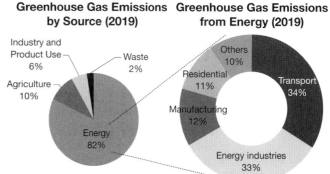

Greenhouse Gas Emissions by Source (2019)

Greenhouse Gas Emissions from Energy (2019)

The two pie charts above show the sources of greenhouse gas emissions in 2019. ① Among the four main categories of sources, more than 80 percent of all greenhouse gas emissions were from energy use. ② In contrast, waste was the smallest source, being responsible for less than five percent of total greenhouse gas emissions. ③ Among the subcategories of energy, transport produced the largest percentage of greenhouse gas emissions at almost 35 percent. ④ Energy industries, which was the second-largest energy subcategory, accounted for less emissions than the manufacturing and residential sectors combined. ⑤ Only 10 percent of emissions resulted from other sources, making this the smallest of the energy subcategories.

실력 UP! 미니 문제 내신 서술형

07. 다음 영영 풀이에 적합한 단어를 윗글에서 찾아 쓰시오.

ⓐ existing in or relating to cities and other populated areas

→ _____

ⓑ the right or ability to use particular things

→ _____

실력 UP! 미니 문제 내신 서술형

08. 다음 문장을 우리말로 해석하시오.

In contrast, waste was the smallest source, being responsible for less than five percent of total greenhouse gas emissions.

→ _____

유형 소개 주어진 글의 세부 정보와 일치하지 않는 선택지를 파악하는 유형으로, 인물/동·식물 등을 소개하는 글이 나옴

문제 수 1문제

지시문 ~에 관한 다음 글의 내용과 일치하지 <u>않는</u> 것은?

불변의 패턴 13

패턴 빈출도 ★★★★★

선택지는 글의 순서대로 나온다.

🎧 지문 듣기

선택지는 글의 흐름 순서대로 제시된다. 선택지를 먼저 보고 글에서 해당하는 부분을 찾아 내용이 일치하는지 확인한다.

(TIP) 대개 ③~⑤ 사이에 정답이 분포하므로 ⑤부터 역순으로 확인하는 습관을 들이면 시간을 단축할 수 있다.

패턴맛보기

다음 글의 내용과 일치하면 T, 일치하지 않으면 F를 고르시오.

George Boole was born in Lincoln, England in 1815. Boole was forced to leave school at the age of sixteen after his father's business collapsed. He taught himself mathematics, natural philosophy and various languages. He began to produce original mathematical research and made important contributions to areas of mathematics. For those contributions, in 1844, he was awarded a gold medal for mathematics by the Royal Society.

① 아버지의 사업 실패 후 학교를 그만두게 되었다. [T / F]
② 수학, 자연 철학, 다양한 언어를 독학했다. [T / F]
③ Royal Society에서 화학으로 금메달을 받았다. [T / F]

해석
George Boole은 1815년에 영국 Lincoln에서 태어났다. Boole은 아버지의 사업이 실패한 후 16세의 나이에 학교를 그만두게 되었다. 그는 수학, 자연 철학, 그리고 다양한 언어를 독학했다. 그는 독창적인 수학적 연구를 만들어내기 시작했고 수학 분야에서 중요한 공헌을 했다. 그러한 공헌으로, 1844년에 그는 Royal Society에서 수학으로 금메달을 받았다.

해설
① 두 번째 문장 Boole was forced to leave school ~ after his father's business collapsed에서 아버지의 사업이 실패한 후 학교를 그만두게 되었다고 했으므로 ①은 글의 내용과 일치한다.
② 세 번째 문장 He taught himself mathematics ~ and various languages에서 그가 수학, 자연 철학, 다양한 언어를 독학했다고 했으므로 ②은 글의 내용과 일치한다.
③ 다섯 번째 문장 he was awarded a gold medal for mathematics by the Royal Society에서 그는 Royal Society에서 수학으로 금메달을 받았다고 했으므로 ③은 글의 내용과 일치하지 않는다.

정답
① T ② T ③ F

기출문제 2020년 9월 고1 학평

정답 및 해설 p.47

Jessie Redmon Fauset에 관한 다음 글의 내용과 일치하지 않는 것은?

Jessie Redmon Fauset was born in Snow Hill, New Jersey, in 1884. She was the first black woman to graduate from Cornell University. In addition to writing novels, poetry, short stories, and essays, Fauset taught French in public schools in Washington, D.C. and worked as a journal editor. While working as an editor, she encouraged many wellknown writers of the Harlem Renaissance. Though she is more famous for being an editor than for being a fiction writer, many critics consider her novel *Plum Bun* Fauset's strongest work. In it, she tells the story of a black girl who could pass for white but ultimately claims her racial identity and pride. Fauset died of heart disease April 30, 1961, in Philadelphia.

* pass for: ~으로 여겨지다

① Cornell University를 졸업한 최초의 흑인 여성이었다.
② Washington, D.C.의 공립학교에서 프랑스어를 가르쳤다.
③ 편집자보다는 소설가로서 더 유명하다.
④ 흑인 소녀의 이야기를 다룬 소설을 썼다.
⑤ Philadelphia에서 심장병으로 사망했다.

불변의 패턴14 | 패턴 빈출도 ★★★★☆
정답은 글에 나온 정보가 일부 변형된 것이다.

지문 듣기

글과 일치하지 않는 선택지가 정답인데, 이 정답은 글에 나온 정보를 살짝 틀리게 말한 것인 경우가 많다. 선택지의 일부만 보고 대조하면 글의 내용과 일치한다고 생각할 수 있으니 주의한다.

패턴맛보기

다음을 읽고 Lithops에 대해 글의 내용과 일치하지 않는 것을 고르시오.

Lithops are plants that are often called 'living stones'. They are plants that are native to the deserts of South Africa but commonly sold in garden centers and nurseries. Lithops are small plants, rarely getting more than an inch above the soil surface and usually with only two leaves.

① 살아있는 돌로 불리는 식물이다.
② 원산지는 남아프리카 사막 지역이다.
③ 토양의 표면 위로 대개 1인치 이상 자란다.

[해석]
리톱스는 종종 '살아있는 돌'로 불리는 식물이다. 그것들은 남아프리카 사막의 토착종이지만, 종묘점과 묘목장에서 흔히 판매된다. 리톱스는 크기가 작은 식물로, 토양의 표면 위로 1인치 이상은 거의 자라지 않으며 보통 단 2개의 잎만을 갖는다.

[해설]
Lithops are small plants, rarely getting more than an inch above the soil surface ~ 에서 리톱스는 토양의 표면 위로 1인치 이상은 거의 자라지 않는다고 했는데, ③은 '토양의 표면 위로 대개 1인치 이상 자란다'고 하여 일부 정보를 잘못 말하였으므로 글의 내용과 일치하지 않는다.

[정답]
③

기출문제 2019년 9월 고1 학평   정답 및 해설 p.47

Mary Cassatt에 관한 다음 글의 내용과 일치하지 않는 것은?

Mary Cassatt was born in Pennsylvania, the fourth of five children born in her well-to-do family. Mary Cassatt and her family traveled throughout Europe in her childhood. Her family did not approve when she decided to become an artist, but her desire was so strong, she bravely took the steps to make art her career. She studied first in Philadelphia and then went to Paris to study painting. She admired the work of Edgar Degas and was able to meet him in Paris, which was a great inspiration. Though she never had children of her own, she loved children and painted portraits of the children of her friends and family. Cassatt lost her sight at the age of seventy, and, sadly, was not able to paint during the later years of her life.

① 유년 시절에 유럽 전역을 여행했다.
② 화가가 되는 것을 가족이 찬성하지 않았다.
③ Edgar Degas를 파리에서 만났다.
④ 자기 자녀의 초상화를 그렸다.
⑤ 70세에 시력을 잃었다.

01 Margaret Murie에 관한 다음 글의 내용과 일치하지 않는 것은?

Margaret Murie was born in Seattle, Washington in 1902. After moving to Alaska with her family, Murie attended college there and became the first woman to graduate from the Alaska Agricultural College and School of Mines. Soon after, she met her husband, and the two moved to Oregon to study elk populations. Murie camped in the wilderness for weeks at a time as she observed the local wildlife. During her studies, Murie increasingly became involved in conservation efforts and became widely recognized for her work. For example, her ideas for preserving entire ecosystems became the foundation for protecting natural parks and large areas of wilderness. Her efforts led her to receiving numerous awards, including the Presidential Medal of Freedom in 1998. She continued to advocate for the environment until she died in 2003 at the age of 101.

① Alaska에서 대학을 다녔다.
② 대학 졸업 이후 연구를 위해 Oregon으로 거처를 옮겼다.
③ 야생 생태계 관찰을 위해 몇 주 내내 야영을 했다.
④ 생태계 보호를 위한 노력으로 널리 알려졌다.
⑤ 공로를 인정받아 사망 이후 대통령 훈장을 받았다.

02 Georgia O'Keeffe에 관한 다음 글의 내용과 일치하지 않는 것은?

Georgia O'Keeffe was born in Wisconsin on November 15, 1887. As the second of seven children, she grew up on a dairy farm and learned art at home. After graduating high school, O'Keeffe studied traditional art in Chicago and New York and taught art in Texas. Her technique changed to more abstract art when she began to study the philosophy of Arthur Wesley Dow, an American painter. She drew many abstract works with charcoal during this time, and her work was first exhibited in 1917. By the 1920s, she had become one of the most influential artists of her time. She was most well-known for her paintings of skyscrapers as well as of natural subjects like deserts, mountains, and especially flowers.

① 일곱 자녀 중 둘째였다.
② Texas에서 미술을 가르친 적이 있다.
③ 다른 예술가에 의해 영감을 받았다.
④ 1917년에 첫 번째 전시회를 열었다.
⑤ 자연에 있는 소재만 그렸다.

실력 UP! 미니 문제 주제 찾기

01. 다음 영영 풀이에 적합한 단어를 윗글에서 찾아 쓰시오.

ⓐ taking part in or devoted to something

→ _____

ⓑ to openly recommend, or argue on behalf of something

→ _____

실력 UP! 미니 문제 주제 찾기

02. 윗글의 주제로 가장 적절한 것은?

① the artistic development of Georgia O'Keeffe
② the effect of nature on the paintings of Georgia O'Keeffe
③ why Georgia O'Keeffe preferred abstract art over traditional art

03 Amelia Earhart에 관한 다음 글의 내용과 일치하지 않는 것은?

Amelia Earhart, an American pilot, was born in Kansas in 1897. Growing up, Earhart went against traditional gender roles. She enjoyed playing basketball, took a class on how to repair cars, and even attended college for a while. During World War I, Earhart volunteered to care for injured soldiers in Toronto, Canada, where she was able to watch the pilots in the Royal Flying Corps train. When she later moved to California, Earhart went on her first flight. She began to take flying lessons afterwards and purchased a plane, nicknamed "the Canary," in 1921. During her career, Earhart set many flying records, including becoming the first woman to fly alone across the Atlantic. She was even given a military award by Congress for her achievements. In 1937, Earhart disappeared while on a flight around the world and was presumed dead.

① 관습적인 성 역할에서 벗어나려고 노력했다.
② 1차 세계대전 당시 부상당한 군인들을 보살폈다.
③ California에서 첫 비행기 조종에 나섰다.
④ 비행 강습을 받았으나 본인 소유의 비행기는 없었다.
⑤ 대서양을 단독 비행한 최초의 여성이었다.

실력 UP! 미니 문제 내신 서술형

03. 윗글의 제목을 주어진 해석과 일치하도록 <보기>에 있는 단어를 배열하여 문장을 완성하시오.

> Amelia Earhart의 생애와 업적
> <보기> Amelia Earhart / The Life / of / Accomplishment / and

04 Rafflesia arnoldii에 관한 다음 글의 내용과 일치하지 않는 것은?

The largest flower in the world is called *Rafflesia arnoldii*, found in the rainforests of Indonesia. It can grow up to three feet wide and weigh up to 15 pounds. This flower is unusual in that it is a parasitic plant with no roots, stems, or leaves. Instead, it attaches to a host plant to obtain water and nutrients. Another odd feature lies in its smell. It does not have the delicate fragrant scent that is usually associated with flowers but rather smells like rotting meat. This stink attracts tiny insects, especially flies, that help this flower to reproduce. Botanists are not sure why this flower evolved to be so big, since its close relatives only produce tiny flowers. In this regard, the flower is somewhat of a mystery.

① 인도네시아에서 발견된다.
② 무게가 15파운드까지 나갈 수 있다.
③ 뿌리를 이용해 다른 식물에 기생한다.
④ 불쾌한 냄새가 난다.
⑤ 작은 곤충들을 끌어들여 번식한다.

실력 UP! 미니 문제 주제 찾기

04. 윗글의 주제로 가장 적절한 것은?
① the odd features of the Rafflesia plant
② methods of survival utilized by parasitic plants
③ reasons for the large size of the Rafflesia flower

05 Juan Ponce de León에 관한 다음 글의 내용과 일치하지 <u>않는</u> 것은?

Spanish explorer Juan Ponce de León was born around 1460. He served as a soldier before beginning his career in exploration. Historians believe that his first voyage to the New World was with Christopher Columbus in 1493. After that, he worked as a captain under a royal governor in that region. Ponce de León was given permission by the Spanish crown to discover new lands and gold while abroad. Eventually, he decided to search for a rumored magical spring called the "fountain of youth." This expedition resulted in his reaching North America. He became the first European to travel to the area, and he named the site Florida for its plants and greenery. He led more voyages to explore the coastline, but was killed by local natives in 1521.

① 탐험가이기 이전에는 군인의 신분이었다.
② 그의 항해에 Columbus가 동행한 적이 있다고 알려졌다.
③ 스페인 국왕은 그가 신대륙과 황금을 찾도록 허가하지 않았다.
④ 소문으로만 듣던 샘을 찾는 과정에서 북아메리카에 도달했다.
⑤ 탐방한 지역을 Florida라고 직접 이름 지었다.

실력 UP! 미니 문제 내신 서술형

05. 윗글의 제목을 주어진 해석과 일치하도록 <보기>에 있는 단어를 배열하여 문장을 완성하시오.

Ponce de León's의 신대륙으로의 탐험
<보기> Explorations / the New World / Ponce de León's / in

06 platypus에 관한 다음 글의 내용과 일치하지 <u>않는</u> 것은?

The platypus is truly one of the most unusual mammals in the world. Native to Australia, it is one of only two mammals to lay eggs. The platypus has often been described as a mix of many different animals. It has the bill and feet of a duck, the body of an otter, and the tail of a beaver. Its appearance is so odd that the first scientists to see a dead one in 1799 thought it was a fake. The platypus is a semi-aquatic animal and hunts for food at the bottom of rivers or streams. They are well-adapted to the water and spend most of their time there. Unlike the females, which are harmless, the males have poison that can cause severe pain to other creatures.

① 알을 낳는 포유류 중 하나이다.
② 신체 부위 중 새와 비슷한 곳이 있다.
③ 1799년에 한 마리가 죽은 채로 발견되었다.
④ 주로 물속에서 생활한다.
⑤ 암컷과 수컷 모두 독을 지닌다.

실력 UP! 미니 문제 주제 찾기

06. 윗글의 주제로 가장 적절한 것은?
① appearance as an adaptation for survival
② the hidden threat posed by the platypus
③ unique characteristics of the platypus

07 Himalayan black bear에 관한 다음 글의 내용과 일치하지 <u>않는</u> 것은?

The Himalayan black bear is a rare type of Asiatic black bear. They have a glossy black coat and a unique white mark shaped like a crescent moon on their chest. Their average length is around 1.5 meters and they can weigh from 90 to 200 kilograms. In the summers, they roam in China, Nepal, Russia, and Tibet, while they descend to more tropical forests in the winter months. These bears mostly feed on plants, but they occasionally eat small mammals and even large animals such as sheep and goats. They have been a protected species since 1977. But like many animals today, they are sadly being threatened due to a loss of habitat and illegal hunting.

① 가슴에 초승달 모양의 하얀 무늬가 있다.
② 몸무게가 최대 200kg까지 나간다.
③ 여름철에는 열대 우림 지역으로 이동한다.
④ 주로 식물을 먹으며, 가끔씩 동물을 잡아 먹기도 한다.
⑤ 1977년부터 보호종으로 지정되었다.

실력 UP! 미니 문제 내신 서술형

07. 다음 질문을 읽고 한 문장의 영어로 답하시오.

Q: According to the passage, what do Himalayan black bears do in the winter months?

A: They _____.

08 Harry Houdini에 관한 다음 글의 내용과 일치하지 <u>않는</u> 것은?

Harry Houdini was born in Budapest, Hungary in 1874. His family immigrated to the United States in 1878. To earn money for his parents, Houdini began working in a circus at the age of nine. In 1894, he launched his career as a magician. Although his early magic tricks were not popular with audiences, he achieved fame as an escape artist. Throughout the early 1900s, Houdini incorporated several dangerous escapes into his act. His most famous trick was called the Chinese Water Torture Cell, which involved being suspended upside down in a locked container of water. In 1926, Houdini started a successful one-man show on Broadway that featured many of his most popular illusions and escapes. Unfortunately, he died that same year after refusing to have surgery because he did not want to cancel a performance.

① 온 가족이 미국으로 이민을 갔다.
② 9살의 나이에 서커스단에서 일하기 시작했다.
③ 초기에 선보인 마술은 엄청난 인기를 끌었다.
④ 1926년에 브로드웨이 쇼에 출연했다.
⑤ 수술받기를 거부하다 사망했다.

실력 UP! 미니 문제 주제 찾기

08. 윗글의 주제로 가장 적절한 것은?

① challenges overcome by Harry Houdini during his life
② the life of famous performer Harry Houdini
③ the most popular trick performed by Harry Houdini

CHAPTER 08

안내문 정보 파악하기

유형 소개 주어진 안내문의 정보와 일치하는, 또는 일치하지 않는 선택지를 파악하는 유형으로, 행사나 경기 등 다양한 소재의 안내문이 출제됨

문제 수 일치 1문제, 불일치 1문제

지시문 ~에 관한 다음 안내문의 내용과 일치하는/일치하지 않는 것은?

불변 패턴 15

패턴 빈출도 ★★★★☆

정답의 단서는 수치가 포함된 부분에 있는 경우가 많다.

지문 듣기

기간, 날짜, 연도, 나이, 가격 등 수치가 포함된 부분에 정답이 있는 경우가 많으므로 이를 중점적으로 보며 정답을 찾는다.

패턴맛보기

다음 글에서 선택지의 내용을 확인할 수 있는 부분에 밑줄을 그으시오.

> **Poetry Workshop**
>
> **When:** Saturday, October 13, 11:00 a.m.–6:00 p.m.
> **Where:** Riverside Public Library
> **Details:**
> • Meet and talk with renowned poets about their poems.
>   Jane Kenny(11:30 a.m.), Michael Weil(12:30 p.m.)
> • Learn how to express your feelings poetically.
> For questions about the workshop, please visit our website.

① 워크숍은 10월 13일 오전 11시부터 시작한다.
② 시인 Jane Kenny는 오전 11시 30분에 만날 수 있다.

해석

> **시 워크숍**
>
> **날짜:** 10월 13일 토요일 오전 11시-오후 6시
> **장소:** Riverside 공립 도서관
> **세부사항:**
> • 저명한 시인들을 만나고 그들이 시에 대해 이야기할 수 있습니다.
>   Jane Kenny(오전 11시 30분), Michael Weil(오후 12시 30분)
> • 당신의 감정을 시적으로 표현하는 방법을 배웁니다.
> 워크숍에 관한 질문은, 저희 웹 사이트를 방문해 주십시오.

정답
① Saturday, October 13, 11:00 a.m.—6:00 p.m.,
② Jane Kenny(11:30 a.m.)

기출문제 2019년 3월 고1 학평

정답 및 해설 p.53

Waverly High School Friendly Chess Tournament에 관한 다음 안내문의 내용과 일치하지 <u>않는</u> 것은?

> ## Waverly High School Friendly Chess Tournament
>
> Saturday, March 23, 10 a.m.
>
> • Where: Waverly High School auditorium
> • Entry Deadline: March 22, 4 p.m.
> • Age Categories: 7-12, 13-15, 16-18
> • Prizes: Gold, Silver, and Bronze for each category
>   - Prize-giving Ceremony: 3 p.m.
>   - Every participant will receive a certificate for entry!
>
> If you are interested, enter online at
> http://www.waverly.org.
>   **For more information, visit our website.**

① Waverly 고등학교 강당에서 열린다.
② 참가 신청 마감은 3월 23일 오전 10시이다.
③ 각 부문별로 금상, 은상, 동상을 수여한다.
④ 시상식은 오후 3시에 있다.
⑤ 참가자 전원에게 참가 증명서를 준다.

불변의 **패턴**16 | 패턴 빈출도 ★★★★☆
예외 조항 및 추가 정보와 관련된 선택지가 정답인 경우가 많다.

🎧지문 듣기

안내문에서는 별표, 괄호, Notice, Note, Additional Information 등으로 예외 조항이나 추가 정보를 제공하는데, 이와 관련하여 정답이 출제되는 경우가 많으니 주의 깊게 살펴본다.

(TIP) 예외 조항과 추가 정보는 보통 지문의 중간 이후에 위치하기 때문에 ⑤부터 역순으로 확인하면 정답을 더 빨리 찾을 수 있다.

패턴맛보기

다음을 읽고 글의 내용과 일치하면 T, 일치하지 않으면 F를 고르시오.

Summer Camp 2022

[Period & Participation]
• July 1-5 (Monday-Friday)
• 8-12 year olds (maximum 20 students per class)

[Programs]
• Cooking
• Outdoor Activities (hiking, rafting, and camping)

※ Notice
• The programs will run regardless of weather conditions.

---

① 참가 연령 제한이 없다. [T / F]
② 야외 프로그램은 운영되지 않는다. [T / F]
③ 기상 조건과 관계없이 프로그램이 진행될 것이다. [T / F]

[해석]

2022년 여름 캠프

[기간 및 참가]
• 7월 1-5일 (월-금요일)
• 8-12세 (한 반당 최대 학생 20명)

[프로그램]
• 요리
• 야외 활동 (하이킹, 래프팅, 그리고 캠핑)

[알림]
• 프로그램은 기상 조건과 관계없이 진행될 것입니다.

[정답]
①F ②F ③T

기출문제 2021년 3월 고1 학평   정답 및 해설 p.54

Great Aquarium에 관한 다음 안내문의 내용과 일치하는 것은?

Great Aquarium

Opening Hours: 10 a.m.-6 p.m., daily
Last entry is at 5 p.m.

Events

Fish Feeding	10 a.m.-11 a.m.
Penguin Feeding	1 p.m.-2 p.m.

Ticket Prices

Age	Price
Kids (12 and under)	$25
Adults (20-59)	$33
Teens (13-19) Seniors (60 and above)	$30

*Ticket holders will receive a free drink coupon.

Booking Tickets
• ALL visitors are required to book online.
• Booking will be accepted up to 1 hour before entry.

---

① 마지막 입장 시간은 오후 6시이다.
② 물고기 먹이 주기는 오후 1시에 시작한다.
③ 60세 이상의 티켓 가격은 33달러이다.
④ 티켓 소지자는 무료 음료 쿠폰을 받는다.
⑤ 예약은 입장 30분 전까지 가능하다.

CH 08

01 Oberman 무선 진공 청소기에 관한 다음 안내문의 내용과 일치하지 <u>않는</u> 것은?

Oberman Cordless Vacuum Cleaner

Instructions:
• Fully charge.
• Remove from charging pod.
• Press POWER button to vacuum.
• Press S button for intense cleaning.
• Press POWER button again to turn off.
• Return to charging pod.

Safety guidelines:
• Always switch off while charging.
• Use only Oberman attachments.
• Do not use on wet surfaces.
• Do not use if power cord is damaged.

WARNING: DO NOT attempt to remove batteries. To change faulty or old batteries, take the appliance to a certified Oberman service center.

---

① S 버튼을 누르면 강력 청소를 할 수 있다.

② POWER 버튼으로 기기를 끌 수 있다.

③ 충전하려면 전원을 꺼야 한다.

④ 바닥이 젖어 있더라도 사용할 수 있다.

⑤ 배터리는 공식 서비스 센터에서 교체되어야 한다.

실력 UP! 미니 문제 내신 서술형

01. 다음 영영 풀이에 적합한 단어를 윗글에서 찾아 쓰시오.

ⓐ using strong energy or effort

→ _____

ⓑ failing, or incapable of operation

→ _____

---

02 Patty's Pastries 로고 대회에 관한 다음 안내문의 내용과 일치하는 것은?

Patty's Pastries Logo Contest

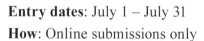

Do you dream of seeing your art on products across the nation? By entering the Patty's Pastries official logo contest, you can turn (A)<u>this fantasy</u> into a reality!

Entry dates: July 1 – July 31
How: Online submissions only
Age and Region: Open to all (professionals and amateurs)

Requirements:
–One entry per person
–No more than three colors
–Include slogan ("Perfection in Pastries")
–Include mascot
–Round shape preferable

To enter, please visit www.pattyspastries/logo.com.
*Once you hit FINAL, your design will be submitted and cannot be changed.

---

① 전문 예술가만을 위한 대회이다.

② 작품은 온라인과 우편을 통해 제출할 수 있다.

③ 서로 다른 네 가지 색깔을 사용해야 한다.

④ 회사는 원형의 로고를 선호한다.

⑤ 최종 제출 후에도 디자인을 수정할 수 있다.

실력 UP! 미니 문제 내신 서술형

02. 윗글의 밑줄 친 (A)가 의미하는 것을 우리말로 쓰시오.

(A) _____

03 Summer Cooking Class에 관한 다음 안내문의 내용과 일치하지 <u>않는</u> 것은?

Summer Cooking Class

Come and join our kid-friendly cooking class to learn all about cooking with fresh ingredients. We welcome all future chefs from ages 9-15.

When: Mon-Fri, August 13-17
Time: 9 a.m. to 4 p.m. (Lunch 12-1)
Price: $200 per child (personal apron included)

What to expect:
-Learn basic cooking techniques.
-Create one main dish and one dessert each day.
-Eat or take home everything you make.
-Receive a cookbook of all recipes for free.

All of our classes are supervised and taught by professional chefs. Parents are welcome to attend and cook with their children on the last day of class.

① 9세에서 15세의 아이들이 참석할 수 있다.
② 주말에는 진행하지 않는다.
③ 조리법이 수록된 요리책은 따로 구매해야 한다.
④ 전문가가 직접 수업을 관리한다.
⑤ 마지막 날에는 학부모와 아이들이 함께 요리할 수 있다.

실력 UP! 미니 문제 내신 서술형

03. 다음 영영 풀이에 적합한 단어를 윗글에서 찾아 쓰시오.

ⓐ a list of ingredients and methods used to cook a specific dish

→ _____

ⓑ to oversee, or manage a group, individual, or especially at a task

→ _____

04 Brentwood College Archery Club에 관한 다음 안내문의 내용과 일치하지 <u>않는</u> 것은?

Brentwood College Archery Club

The Brentwood College Archery Club will be holding a recruitment event to introduce undergraduate students to archery and encourage them to join the club!

Schedule
-From 10:00 a.m. to 4:00 p.m. on Saturday, September 26

Location
-Brentwood College Archery Range
-Located at the south end of the main athletic field, just behind the gym

Activities
-A demonstration of various archery techniques by current club members
-A basic archery lesson for interested students

* free hot dogs will be provided for our attendees from 12:30 to 1:30 p.m.

For more information, please contact the club president at 555-0349.

① 대학교 재학생을 대상으로 모집한다.
② 오후 5시에는 행사에 참여할 수 없다.
③ 체육관 뒤에서 행사를 개최한다.
④ 참가자들에게 무료로 핫도그가 제공된다.
⑤ 문의 사항은 이메일을 통해서 접수된다.

실력 UP! 미니 문제 내신 서술형

04. 다음 질문을 읽고 한 문장의 영어로 답하시오.

Q: According to the passage, what is the purpose of Brentwood College Archery club's recruitment event?

A: It is to _____

_____.

05 Evergreen Youth Adventure Camp에 관한 다음 안내문의 내용과 일치하는 것은?

🎤 Evergreen Youth Adventure Camp 🎤

Our annual youth camp is a great place to get an adventure in nature. Campers can enjoy all sorts of outdoor activities including treasure hunts, making forts, and even rock climbing. We hope your little explorers will join us this year!

When: Tuesday, August 3 - Friday, August 6
Where: Evergreen Campground
Cost: $150 per person (camp t-shirt included)

Details:
- This program is for children ages 9-14.
- All participants should bring sneakers, a jacket, a bathing suit, and personal medicines.
- Registration must be completed online by July 20, and a refund is only available before July 25.
- There will be a bonfire festival that all parents are welcome to on the final day of camp.

Visit www.Evgreencamp.com for more information.

① 실내 암벽 등반 체험이 예정되어 있다.
② 캠프는 화요일부터 5일간 진행된다.
③ 캠프 활동 티셔츠는 참가비에 포함되어 있다.
④ 운동화 및 수영복은 캠프장에서 무료로 제공한다.
⑤ 신청 마감 기한은 7월 25일이다.

실력 UP! 미니 문제 내신 서술형

05. 다음 질문을 읽고 한 문장의 영어로 답하시오.

Q: According to the notice, what materials should the participants bring?

A: All participants are encouraged to _____

_____.

06 Henry Bass Exhibition에 관한 다음 안내문의 내용과 일치하지 <u>않는</u> 것은?

Henry Bass Exhibition

Local renowned artist Henry Bass will put on his 3rd exhibit at the Tate Museum. Come and appreciate this unique artist and his latest works, including five new pieces created especially for our museum.

Hours: 9:00 a.m. to 8:30 p.m. (closed on Mondays)
Exhibit Period: March 1 to May 10

Admission:
- $12 for adults
- Half price for senior citizens(over 65) and students
- No charge for children under 8

* Food or drink is not allowed in the building.

Guided tours are only available with a reservation. No more than 6 people per group. Please call 523-0088 for more information.

① 미술관을 위해 특별히 제작된 5개의 작품이 포함된다.
② 월요일에는 운영하지 않는다.
③ 노인과 학생들의 입장료는 12달러이다.
④ 건물 안에서는 음식물 섭취가 불가능하다.
⑤ 가이드가 동행하는 관람은 최대 6명까지 예약할 수 있다.

실력 UP! 미니 문제 내신 서술형

06. 다음 영영 풀이에 적합한 단어를 윗글에서 찾아 쓰시오.

ⓐ popular or well-known by people, most often because of an accomplishment, skill, or quality

→ _____

ⓑ a sum of money that must be paid for a product or service

→ _____

07 Academic Olympics에 관한 다음 안내문의 내용과 일치하는 것은?

Academic Olympics

The Academic Olympics invites all local middle school teams to compete in a match against wits!

Where: Williamson University
When: May 6-8
Teams:

- Each school is allowed 3 teams with eight members
- There must be at least 2 members from each grade

Events: about 2 hours for each

May 6
• Math: 9 a.m.　　• Science: 2 p.m.
May 7
• History: 10 a.m.　　• Literature: 3 p.m.
May 8
• Sports Day (relay race and capture the flag): 11 a.m.

Academic events will take place in the Science Building and sporting events will take place on the soccer field.

The team with the highest score will be awarded a trophy, and all participants will get a small gift as a souvenir.

---

① 지역 고등학생을 대상으로 개최된다.
② 각 학년별 최소 3명의 인원이 포함되어야 한다.
③ 수학과 과학 경기는 서로 다른 날에 예정되어 있다.
④ 스포츠 경기는 오후 2시에 시작된다.
⑤ 참가자 전원에게 기념품이 지급된다.

실력 UP! 미니 문제 내신 서술형

07. Academic Olympics에서 진행되는 학술 및 스포츠 이벤트는 각각 무엇인지 우리말로 쓰시오.

학술 이벤트: _____

스포츠 이벤트: _____

---

08 Movies in the Park에 관한 다음 안내문의 내용과 일치하지 <u>않는</u> 것은?

Movies in the Park

Aurora County's famous Movies in the Park will soon begin. Join us in this free cinematic outdoor experience that you are sure to love.

Where: Heritage Park
When: Every Friday evening at 8:30 p.m.

You are allowed to bring:
- Chairs, picnic tables, or blankets
- Snacks and drinks
- Pets(must be kept in cage)

Facilities available on site:
- Restrooms and drinking fountains
- Medical tent for emergencies
- Food trucks and vending machines

Park Guidelines:
- Tents can only be set up in reserved areas
- Smoking and drinking are not permitted

For a full schedule of movies, visit www.auroramoviespark.com.

---

① 무료로 관람할 수 있다.
② 야외극장은 매주 금요일마다 열린다.
③ 반려동물은 데려올 수 없다.
④ 화장실과 식수대가 주변에 설치되어 있다.
⑤ 반드시 지정된 구역에만 텐트를 설치해야 한다.

실력 UP! 미니 문제 내신 서술형

08. 다음 문장을 우리말로 해석하시오.

Join us in this free cinematic outdoor experience that you are sure to love.

→ _____

정답 및 해설 p.60

01 April Tree Sale에 관한 다음 안내문의 내용과 일치하는 것은?

April Tree Sale

Come and take advantage of our first tree sale! Don't miss out on some great deals that will make your backyard beautiful.

Sale period:
April 1 – April 20

How to Make a Purchase:
1. Visit our store next to Woodridge Park
2. Select up to three trees (all trees are $20 each)
3. Pay with cash (plant pot not included)
4. Leave your address and contact number for delivery

Delivery Process:
1. Deliveries will be made Tuesdays and Fridays
2. You will receive a message on the day before delivery
3. The delivery takes about 3~4 days on average

*An extra fee will be charged for delivery to islands and mountain areas

Please call 320-9900 for more information.

① 매년 열렸던 행사이다.
② 행사는 한 달 내내 진행된다.
③ 화분을 포함한 가격으로 나무를 판매한다.
④ 화요일 및 금요일마다 배송이 이루어진다.
⑤ 배송 당일에 알림 메시지가 발송된다.

02 다음 글의 주제로 가장 적절한 것은?

Three quarters of consumers now say that they're more likely to make a purchase from a company whose values they agree with, and nearly 60 percent are willing to stop buying from ones they find unethical. To stay competitive, therefore, companies need to project that their company has strong values like compassion or a concern for the environment. Achieving this requires more than preventing wrongdoing; it requires taking positive action. For instance, a company might build a reputation of being "socially responsible" by participating in recycling programs or donating money to causes. This may sound like what a charity does, but these measures lead to building trust with customers. Good actions lead to a good response from consumers and more success as a business.

① problems with creating a responsible image
② popularity of eco-friendly materials
③ surveys as a tool for marketing
④ benefits of living up to customer's values
⑤ charity groups protecting the environment

03 다음 글의 제목으로 가장 적절한 것은?

You may know that shopping while you are hungry can impair your decision making, but did you know being lonely can pose even more problems? According to research from the University of Iowa, a feeling of loneliness can cause you to shop impulsively and make irresponsible financial decisions. This is because a lack of social connections makes us feel empty, and causes us to look for substitutes. Unconsciously, we start to form strong attachments to products instead of people, mistakenly thinking we "need" items we'll probably never use. The lonely shopper thus tends to fill their shopping cart with expensive and mostly useless objects—a tendency which can be both costly and ineffective.

① Strategies You Can Use to Shop More Rationally
② How Being Lonely Affects the Way You Shop
③ The More You Shop, The More You Become Lonely
④ Shopping Addiction and How to Avoid It
⑤ Loneliness: Research into the Surprising Health Risks

04 Maya Lin에 관한 다음 글의 내용과 일치하지 않는 것은?

Maya Lin was born in Athens, Ohio in 1959. She attended Yale University, where she studied architecture and sculpture. During her senior year at Yale, Lin won a competition for her design of an art piece honoring people who had fought in the Vietnam War. Her memorial included a black V-shaped wall covered in the names of 58,000 people who had died or went missing in the war. It was built in Washington D.C. and became one of Lin's most famous accomplishments. In 1988, Lin went on to design another memorial for the civil rights movement. However, after that, she decided to focus on other work, including art inspired by nature. One of her pieces called "wave fields" features grass-covered land that is shaped to look like ocean waves. Much of her modern work tries to highlight climate change.

① Yale University에서 건축을 공부했다.
② 베트남전 참전용사들을 기리는 작품을 디자인했다.
③ Washington D.C.에 세워진 작품은 그녀의 가장 유명한 업적 중 하나로 꼽힌다.
④ 1988년 이전까지는 주로 자연물에서 영감을 받은 작품에 매진했다.
⑤ 파도처럼 보이는 잔디밭을 특징으로 하는 작품을 만들었다.

05 다음 도표의 내용과 일치하지 않는 것은?

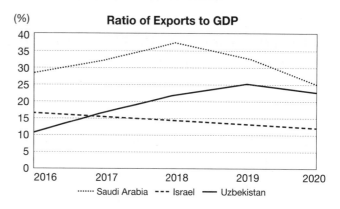

The above graph shows the ratio of exports to GDP in three countries over five years. ① In Israel, the ratio of exports to GDP in 2016 was higher than 10%. ② Of the three countries, Saudi Arabia had the highest ratio of exports to GDP in 2017, followed by Uzbekistan. ③ While Uzbekistan's ratio of exports increased steadily from 2016 to 2019, it was still lower than Israel's in 2019. ④ Saudi Arabia's ratio of exports during the years from 2016 to 2020 never went below 20%. ⑤ In 2020, Uzbekistan had the second highest ratio of exports to GDP while Israel had the lowest.

* GDP: 국내 총생산(Gross Domestic Product)

06 Bliss Mud Festival에 관한 다음 안내문의 내용과 일치하지 <u>않는</u> 것은?

Bliss Mud Festival

The Bliss Mud Festival celebrates our town's unique natural attractions. Since the mid-1990s, the festival has become one of the most anticipated annual events in the region. Come and join thousands of other locals and tourists at this year's festivities!

When: July 21-30
Where: Bliss Creek Campgrounds

Activities:
- Enjoy a mud massage to refresh your skin and help you feel young again
- Relax in a warm mud pool and feel your worries slip away
- Go down a mud slide (not for kids under 5 years old)
- Take part in a one-kilometer obstacle course for the chance to win a prize

What to bring:
- Towels or clothes that can be discarded
- Fresh clothes and shoes (for after the festival)
- Flip-flops or sandals
- Medication and sun protection

*A rock concert will be held nightly on the last two days of the festival.

① 매년 열리는 행사이다.
② 7월 30일까지 행사에 참가할 수 있다.
③ 4살 어린이는 행사 미끄럼틀을 탈 수 없다.
④ 의약품은 참가자들이 직접 가져와야 한다.
⑤ 행사 마지막 3일간은 록 콘서트가 예정되어 있다.

07 다음 글의 제목으로 가장 적절한 것은?

Excess is rarely a good thing. For athletes, this is even true of exercise. Sweating it out and burning calories regularly is healthy, but excessive physical training can take a major toll. Instead of driving individuals to peak levels of performance, pushing too hard can cause them to regress. In extreme cases, too much exercise can even lead to serious injuries. When people experience the effects of overtraining, they can begin having mood swings and suffer from a lack of motivation. Weight loss and an increased resting heart rate are other possible consequences. Any further aggressive training in this state will only make things worse. Therefore, it is important for athletes to moderate the amount of intensive physical activity that they engage in.

① Working Out is Not Enough: The Importance of Diets
② The Best Ways of Achieving your Exercise Goals
③ Effective Training Strategies for Amateurs
④ The Pressure Athletes Feel to Compete Hard
⑤ The Disadvantages of Overtraining for Athletes

08 다음 글의 주제로 가장 적절한 것은?

So-called financial technology—or "fintech" as it's usually known—has completely altered the banking sector in recent years. For instance, fintech brought us rapid and secure digital payment via apps and digital-only banking services that provide the full range of financing options you would have needed to go to a local branch for in the past. Increasingly, anyone with a smartphone can get almost anything a physical bank provides. This greater access to financing and payment options promises a smoother experience for consumers but also a tremendously profitable one for banks, which get more direct access to customers. In general, this technology has revolutionized the industry, increasing overall usability and enhancing the financial experience.

① reasons to be cautious about fintech
② fintech changes creating better banking
③ decision-making strategies of finance banks
④ main qualities of a customer-friendly banker
⑤ fintech usage by banks to help senior customers

09 Robert Capa에 관한 다음 글의 내용과 일치하지 <u>않는</u> 것은?

Famed photojournalist Robert Capa was originally born as Endre Friedmann in Hungary. At the young age of 18, Capa had to leave the country for political reasons. He moved to Germany, where he began photography to pay the bills. Falling in love with this work, he chose his career as a photographer but was forced to leave again because of World War II. This time he settled in Paris. Although Paris was Capa's home, he continued to travel to other countries for work. In fact, it was while he was working in Spain that he took his famous photograph "The Falling Soldier." He was there during the Spanish Civil War. This began his distinguished career as a wartime photojournalist. Unfortunately, Capa's commitment to his job also led to his death. He stepped on a landmine as he photographed soldiers in 1954. He was just 40 years old.

* photojournalist: 보도 사진가

① 정치적인 이유로 본국을 떠났다.
② 생활비를 내기 위해 사진 촬영을 시작했다.
③ 파리에 거처를 둔 채로 활동했다.
④ 스페인 내전과 관련한 작품으로 비난을 받았다.
⑤ 사진 촬영 중 지뢰를 밟아 사망했다.

10 Langston Wedding & Honeymoon Expo에 관한 다음 안내문의 내용과 일치하는 것은?

Langston Wedding & Honeymoon Expo

Langston's largest wedding and honeymoon exhibition will be returning for its fifteenth year at Morris Convention Center. Come and eat delicious food samples, try on the finest dresses, and meet the very best planners to make your dream wedding a reality!

Date:
Saturday, March 2 – Sunday, March 3

Activities:
-Wine and food tastings
-Gifts and prizes
-Bridal fashion show
-Free photo (limited to 1 photo for each)

Cost:
-$20 (for both days)

*Early bird special: 50% discount will be given if you book tickets before February 10

Call 555-6621, or visit our website to book your tickets today!

---

① 올해로 행사 10주년을 맞았다.
② 행사는 3일 동안 진행된다.
③ 사진 촬영은 별도의 금액을 지불해야 한다.
④ 2월 10일 이전에는 입장권을 반값에 구매할 수 있다.
⑤ 웹 사이트를 통해서만 입장권을 예매할 수 있다.

CHAPTER 09
어법상 틀린 것 찾기

유형소개 밑줄 친 단어나 어구 중 어법상 틀린 것을 찾는 유형
문 제 수 1문제
지시문 다음 글의 밑줄 친 부분 중, 어법상 틀린 것은?

불변의 패턴 17

패턴 빈출도 ★★★★★

밑줄은 동사, 분사, 동명사, to부정사에서 많이 나온다.

🎧 지문 듣기

밑줄이 동사, 분사, 동명사, to부정사에 많이 나오므로 이러한 어법 포인트를 집중적으로 학습하여 준비한다.

패턴맛보기

다음 글의 밑줄 친 부분 중, 어법상 틀린 것을 고른 후 올바른 형태로 고쳐 쓰시오.

The most obvious way ① to identify a genuine smile from an insincere one is that a fake smile primarily only affects the lower half of the face, mainly with the mouth alone. The eyes don't really get ② involved. A genuine smile will impact on the muscles and wrinkles around the eyes and less noticeably, the skin between the eyebrow and upper eyelid ③ are lowered slightly with true enjoyment. The genuine smile can impact on the entire face.

→ _____

해석
진짜 미소와 가식적인 것을 식별하는 가장 확실한 방법은 가짜 미소는 얼굴의 아래쪽 절반에만, 즉 대체로 입에만 주로 영향을 준다는 것이다. 눈은 사실상 관여되지 않는다. 진짜 미소는 눈 주위의 근육과 주름에 영향을 미칠 것이고, 덜 눈에 띄게는, 진정한 즐거움을 느끼면 눈썹과 눈 꺼풀 위쪽 사이의 피부가 살짝 내려간다. 진짜 미소는 얼굴 전체에 영향을 줄 수 있다.

해설
③이 포함된 문장의 주어 the skin이 단수명사이므로 복수동사 are를 단수동사 is로 바꿔야 한다.

정답
③, is

기출문제 2020년 6월 고1 학평

정답 및 해설 p.67

다음 글의 밑줄 친 부분 중, 어법상 틀린 것은?

Positively or negatively, our parents and families are powerful influences on us. But even ① stronger, especially when we're young, are our friends. We often choose friends as a way of ② expanding our sense of identity beyond our families. As a result, the pressure to conform to the standards and expectations of friends and other social groups ③ is likely to be intense. Judith Rich Harris, who is a developmental psychologist, ④ arguing that three main forces shape our development: personal temperament, our parents, and our peers. The influence of peers, she argues, is much stronger than that of parents. "The world ⑤ that children share with their peers," she says, "is what shapes their behavior and modifies the characteristics they were born with, and hence determines the sort of people they will be when they grow up."

* temperament: 기질

불변의 패턴18

패턴 빈출도 ★★★★★

밑줄의 품사에 따라 확인해야 하는 것이 정해져 있다.

지문 듣기

- **동사와 준동사**
  밑줄이 동사 자리인지 준동사(분사, 동명사, to부정사) 자리인지 확인한다. 동사일 경우 수 일치 및 태/시제가 맞는지 확인한다. 준동사는 쓰임에 맞는 형태가 쓰였는지 확인한다.

- **대명사, 한정사**
  대명사, 한정사가 그것이 가리키거나 꾸미는 명사와 수 일치하는지 확인한다.

- **형용사, 부사, 비교구문**
  밑줄이 형용사인지 부사인지 확인하고, 각각 올바른 품사를 수식하고 있는지 확인한다. 비교구문은 올바른 형태인지 확인한다.

- **접속사, 관계사**
  밑줄이 접속사인지, 관계사인지를 확인하고, 적절한 접속사 또는 관계사가 사용됐는지 확인한다.

패턴맛보기

다음 네모 안에서 어법상 적절한 것을 고르시오.

ⓐ Artificial light, which typically contains only a few wavelengths of light, do not / does not seem to have the same effect on mood that sunlight has.

ⓑ Some people like the taste of coriander while others find it / them soapy and unpleasant.

ⓒ One would have to filter enormous amounts of water to collect a relative / relatively small amount of plastic.

ⓓ The advantage of non-verbal communication is that / what it offers you the opportunity to express emotions and attitudes properly.

해석

ⓐ 일반적으로 단 몇 개의 빛 파장만을 포함하는 인공 조명은 햇빛이 기분에 미치는 것과 동일한 영향력을 갖고 있지 않는 것 같다.

ⓑ 일부 사람들은 고수의 맛을 좋아하는 반면 다른 사람들은 그것이 비누 같고 불쾌하다고 느낀다.

ⓒ 누군가는 상대적으로 적은 양의 플라스틱을 모으기 위해 상당한 양의 물을 여과해야 할 것이다.

ⓓ 비언어적 의사소통의 이점은 그것이 당신에게 감정과 태도를 적절하게 표현할 기회를 준다는 것이다.

해설

ⓐ 주절에 동사가 없으므로 동사 자리이다. 주어 Artificial light가 단수명사이므로 단수동사 does not이 어법상 적절하다.

ⓑ 대명사가 가리키는 대상은 단수명사 taste of coriander이므로 it이 어법상 적절하다.

ⓒ 형용사 small을 수식하는 것은 부사이므로 부사 relatively가 어법상 적절하다.

ⓓ 주어(it), 동사(offers), 간접목적어(you), 직접목적어(the opportunity)가 모두 있는 완전한 절이 왔으므로 접속사 that이 어법상 적절하다.

정답

ⓐ does not ⓑ it ⓒ relatively ⓓ that

기출문제 2017년 9월 고1 학평

정답 및 해설 p.67

다음 글의 밑줄 친 부분 중, 어법상 틀린 것은?

In perceiving changes, we tend to regard the most recent ① ones as the most revolutionary. This is often inconsistent with the facts. Recent progress in telecommunications technologies is not more revolutionary than ② what happened in the late nineteenth century in relative terms. Moreover, in terms of the consequent economic and social changes, the Internet revolution has not been as ③ important as the washing machine and other household appliances. These things, by vastly reducing the amount of work needed for household chores, ④ allowing women to enter the labor market and virtually got rid of professions like domestic service. We should not put the telescope backward when we look into the past and underestimate the old and overestimate the new. This leads us ⑤ to make all sorts of wrong decisions about national economic policy, corporate policies, and our own careers.

01 다음 글의 밑줄 친 부분 중, 어법상 틀린 것은?

Everyone should try keeping a gratitude journal. It is a good way to reflect on all of the things in life ① what you might feel thankful for. Regularly writing in a gratitude journal can make you more ② appreciative of life and help you maintain a positive outlook. To start a gratitude journal is easy. There are no "rules" and you can write as little or as much as you like. However, I recommend you ③ begin with something simple. For instance, try listing down just a few small examples of things you may have experienced today ④ for which you are grateful. This might include anything from beautiful weather, a task you performed well in school, or even some small kindness ⑤ shown to you by a stranger or friend.

02 다음 글의 밑줄 친 부분 중, 어법상 틀린 것은?

If you are in the market for a new pair of athletic shoes, forget about online shopping. When it comes to ① buying athletic shoes, you will get the best results trying some on in a store. The first thing you should do when trying on shoes is check to see ② whether they fit comfortably on your feet. Walk, jump, or just move around in the shoes to get a good sense of ③ what they might feel like when you wear them. The right shoe should not only fit nicely around the size and shape of your foot but ④ offers good support to prevent the risk of injury. Lastly, try to find out how long the shoes might be expected to last, since having to replace shoes often could become ⑤ costly over time.

실력 UP! 미니 문제 주제 찾기

01. 윗글의 주제로 가장 적절한 것은?
① topics that are common in gratitude journals
② the growing popularity of gratitude journals
③ suggestions for writing a gratitude journal

실력 UP! 미니 문제 내신 서술형

02. 윗글의 요지를 우리말로 쓰시오.

_____

03 다음 글의 밑줄 친 부분 중, 어법상 틀린 것은?

Many students have big dreams for the future but may be disappointed when they realize that dreams take time and effort to achieve. To succeed, it is essential that students not only ① be diligent but also set goals for themselves. When it comes to goals, the smaller, the better. Setting small goals, like reading an extra chapter per night, ② work. That's because small goals are more achievable, and it usually only requires a minimal amount of extra effort to complete ③ them. By contrast, large goals tend to set the bar too ④ high. If students start out with the goal of graduating at the top of their class, for instance, they're likely to feel ⑤ overwhelmed as soon as things go wrong. This can cause the student to lose their motivation and ultimately give up.

03. 윗글의 주제로 가장 적절한 것은?

① problems with only making small goals
② methods to pursuing academic success
③ how to set goals and achieve your dreams

04 다음 글의 밑줄 친 부분 중, 어법상 틀린 것은?

There is perhaps no publication that has ① had as much influence on the modern environmental movement as Rachel Carson's 1962 book *Silent Spring*. In it, she claimed that pesticides like DDT had the power to cause severe harm to animals and ② polluting the world's food supply. She explained ③ that DDT intended to kill pests also poisoned the larger animals that inevitably ate them. Over time, she suggested, all life on Earth could be at risk ④ because of the dangerous effects of chemicals. The book was an unexpected success. It not only helped people understand the connection between nature and human society, but it also affected government policy. By 1975, the United States had banned all the chemicals ⑤ mentioned in Carson's book.

04. 다음 질문을 읽고 한 문장의 영어로 답하시오.

Q: What effect did Carson's book have on government policy in the US?

A: _____

_____ .

05 다음 글의 밑줄 친 부분 중, 어법상 틀린 것은?

Sometimes, traveling by boat, plane, or even car causes us to feel nauseous and even to experience dizziness or headaches. Motion sickness, as these symptoms are ① collectively referred to, is believed to affect many of us. Although debates on what causes (A)this still exist, it's quite clear ② how this happens. In fact, receiving different information from more than one part of the balance-sensing system—the eyes, inner ears, and sensory nerves—③ makes us sick. For example, passengers sitting in the backseat of a car with their view of the front window partially ④ blocked still sense the forward movement of the car through their ears and other senses. Therefore, the brain becomes uncertain about whether or not the body is in fact moving, ⑤ confusing by the different information (B)it is receiving. This miscommunication between the sensory system and the brain triggers motion sickness.

* nauseous: 메스꺼운

06 다음 글의 밑줄 친 부분 중, 어법상 틀린 것은?

The popularity of e-sports, or video game competitions, is on the rise. Today, e-sports is a multi-billion dollar industry backed by celebrities and top brands, with an audience ① rivaling that of traditional sports. However, its beginnings were far humbler. The first game specifically designed for computers, *Spacewar!*, ② was not for commercial use. Despite initially ③ being accessible only to a small group of programmers, it spread once these programmers began to create new versions of the game. By 1972, enough people were aware of it for a leading pop culture magazine to take notice and sponsor ④ that was technically the first-ever e-sports tournament: the "Intergalactic *Spacewar!* Olympics." About two dozen people ⑤ attended the event, and the first prize was a one-year subscription to the magazine.

실력 UP! 미니 문제 내신 서술형

05. 윗글의 밑줄 친 (A), (B)가 지칭하는 바를 영어로 찾아 쓰시오.

(A) _____

(B) _____

실력 UP! 미니 문제 주제 찾기

06. 윗글의 주제로 가장 적절한 것은?

① the economic impact of video games

② the origin of video games and e-sports

③ the advantage of online sports competitions

07 다음 글의 밑줄 친 부분 중, 어법상 틀린 것은?

When preparing for an exam, many students struggle to remember information from the textbook. One easy way to improve their long-term memory is ① to employ active-reading methods. Rather than simply scanning the content, students need to directly interact with it. For example, they can take notes to summarize the main ideas while listening to the lecture, or ② highlighting key terms and concepts to focus on meaningful information. Another active-reading strategy ③ proven to be effective is to make visual representations of important details. According to a recent study, students are more likely to remember data from flow charts, graphs, and diagrams. When facts and figures are presented in these formats, they ④ are retained for a longer period of time. Regardless of the specific techniques used, students who increase their engagement with ⑤ what they read are more likely to remember it.

고난도

08 다음 글의 밑줄 친 부분 중, 어법상 틀린 것은?

Some people stand out in your memory more than most. For me, that person is my grandpa Theodore Lazarus, or Paw Paw. ① Seen at his desk on the phone or in his lounge chair watching TV, Paw Paw was always around. Sometimes, he would go gardening in the backyard or do something practical with his hands. But mostly, I remember Paw Paw liked to spend time ② playing with us. He listened to our stories, read us comics, and used funny expressions like, "No way, Jose!" and "No kiddin'!" ③ which always made us smile. Strangely enough, not once did we ④ heard Paw Paw say that he loved us or that he was proud of us. Yet we always knew that's exactly ⑤ what he felt. We were all extremely sad after Paw Paw passed away. But, I'm glad that I have his memory to keep with me forever.

실력 UP! 미니 문제 내신 서술형

07. 윗글의 내용을 다음과 같이 요약할 때, 빈칸에 들어갈 알맞은 말을 본문에서 찾아 쓰시오.

To improve long-term memory, students can use a _____ methods, or they can increase the e_____ with what they read.

실력 UP! 미니 문제 내신 서술형

08. 다음 영영 풀이에 적합한 단어나 표현을 윗글에서 찾아 쓰시오.

ⓐ serving a purpose that is useful or applicable to daily life

→ _____

ⓑ to an intense extent or tremendous degree

→ _____

어휘 적절성 파악하기

불변의 패턴19

패턴 빈출도 ★★★★★

쓰임이 적절하지 않은 어휘는 문맥과 반대되는 의미로 나온다.

지문 듣기

밑줄 친 단어 중 쓰임이 적절하지 않은 것은 대부분 문맥과 반대되는 의미의 단어로 나온다. 예를 들어, 문맥상 right(옳은)가 나와야 하는 곳에 wrong(그릇된)이 쓰였다면, 이를 정답으로 고르면 되는 것이다. 따라서 정답을 고른 후 그 자리에 밑줄 친 단어의 반의어를 넣어 자연스러운지 확인하면 된다.

패턴맛보기

다음 해석을 참고하여 문맥상 빈칸에 가장 적절한 것을 고르시오.

ⓐ Honesty is a fundamental part of every _____ relationship.

정직함은 모든 굳건한 관계의 근본적인 부분이다.

① strong　　　② weak　　　③ complicated

ⓑ When you develop a reputation for always telling the truth, you will enjoy healthy relationships based on _____ .

당신이 항상 진실만을 말한다는 평판을 쌓으면, 당신은 신뢰를 바탕으로 건강한 관계를 누릴 것이다.

① distrust　　　② cooperation　　　③ trust

ⓒ People who lie get into trouble when someone threatens to _____ their lie.

거짓말을 하는 사람들은 누군가가 그들의 거짓말을 폭로하겠다고 위협하면 곤경에 처하게 된다.

① uncover　　　② conceal　　　③ cover

정답
ⓐ strong　ⓑ trust　ⓒ uncover

기출문제 2020년 3월 고1 학평

정답 및 해설 p.74

다음 글의 밑줄 친 부분 중, 문맥상 낱말의 쓰임이 적절하지 않은 것은?

We often ignore small changes because they don't seem to ① matter very much in the moment. If you save a little money now, you're still not a millionaire. If you study Spanish for an hour tonight, you still haven't learned the language. We make a few changes, but the results never seem to come ② quickly and so we slide back into our previous routines. The slow pace of transformation also makes it ③ easy to break a bad habit. If you eat an unhealthy meal today, the scale doesn't move much. A single decision is easy to ignore. But when we ④ repeat small errors, day after day, by following poor decisions again and again, our small choices add up to bad results. Many missteps eventually lead to a ⑤ problem.

불변의 패턴20 | 패턴 빈출도 ★★★★★
네모 안 어휘들은 보통 서로 반의어 관계이다.

🎧 지문 듣기

각 네모 안의 어휘는 대부분 반의어로 짝지어져 있다. 반의어는 대개 접사가 붙거나(relevant 관련 있는 / irrelevant 관련 없는), 형태가 전혀 다른 어휘들(strength 장점 / weakness 약점)로 구성되어 있다. 보통 전자보다 후자가 더 많이 나오므로 **반의어 관계의 어휘***를 폭넓게 익혀 둔다.

패턴맛보기

다음 해석을 참고하여 괄호 안에서 문맥상 가장 적절한 것을 고르시오.

ⓐ Technological development often forces change, and change is [comfortable / uncomfortable].
과학기술의 발전은 흔히 변화를 강요하는데, 변화는 불편하다.

ⓑ This is one of the main reasons why technology is often [resisted / supported] and why some perceive it as a threat.
이것은 과학기술이 종종 저항을 받고 일부 사람들이 그것을 위협으로 인식하는 주된 이유 중 하나이다.

ⓒ It is important to understand our natural [hate / love] for change when we consider the impact of technology on our lives.
우리는 과학기술이 우리 삶에 끼치는 영향력을 고려할 때 변화에 대한 우리의 본능적인 혐오를 이해하는 것이 중요하다.

[정답]
ⓐ uncomfortable ⓑ resisted ⓒ hate

기출문제 2019년 3월 고1 학평
정답 및 해설 p.74

(A), (B), (C)의 각 네모 안에서 문맥에 맞는 낱말로 가장 적절한 것은?

How does a leader make people feel important? First, by listening to them. Let them know you respect their thinking, and let them (A) silence / voice their opinions. As an added bonus, you might learn something! A friend of mine once told me about the CEO of a large company who told one of his managers, "There's nothing you could possibly tell me that I haven't already thought about before. Don't ever tell me what you think unless I ask you. Is that understood?" Imagine the (B) improvement / loss of self-esteem that manager must have felt. It must have discouraged him and negatively affected his performance. On the other hand, when you make a person feel a great sense of importance, he or she will feel on top of the world — and the level of energy will (C) decrease / increase rapidly.

	(A)	(B)	(C)
①	silence	improvement	decrease
②	silence	loss	increase
③	voice	improvement	decrease
④	voice	loss	decrease
⑤	voice	loss	increase

실력UP! 기출표현 ▶ 반의어 관계의 어휘*

logical 타당한 illogical 모순되는	include 포함시키다 exclude 제외시키다	appear 나타나다 disappear 사라지다	superior 우월한 inferior 열등한
neglect 무시하다 recognize 인정하다	allow 허락하다 forbid 허락하지 않다	physical 육체의 psychological 정신의	polite 공손한 impolite 무례한
narrowly 좁게 widely 넓게	support 지지하다 criticize 비판하다	receptive 수용하는 resistant 저항하는	expand 확대되다 shrink 줄어들다
connectedness 유대감 isolation 고립감	strength 장점 weakness 약점	frequent 빈번한 rare 드문	harmful 해로운 harmless 무해한
intelligent 똑똑한 unintelligent 영리하지 못한	common 흔한 unique 독특한	collective 집단적인 individual 개별적인	assistance 도움 interference 방해

CHAPTER 10 어휘 적절성 파악하기 | 해커스 수능 독해 불변의 패턴 유형편

01 다음 글의 밑줄 친 부분 중, 문맥상 낱말의 쓰임이 적절하지 <u>않은</u> 것은?

Many people fear a future in which robots replace them in the workplace. However, the idea of automation is welcome in the restaurant industry. Human workers can create problems for restaurant owners by needing higher wages with fewer working hours. In contrast, automated systems let owners easily ① <u>operate</u> their business without such conflicts. In addition, human employees are the main ② <u>cause</u> of food contamination. They can easily spread germs that cause outbreaks of disease just by ③ <u>forgetting</u> to wash their hands. Using automated systems to take orders and prepare food ④ <u>raises</u> this risk. Automated systems also make work easier for employees as they can ⑤ <u>complete</u> orders quickly without making mistakes.

02 다음 글의 밑줄 친 부분 중, 문맥상 낱말의 쓰임이 적절하지 <u>않은</u> 것은?

People with low self-esteem often perceive themselves as inferior but do whatever they can to appear ① <u>strong</u>. For those with low self-esteem in leadership positions, the need to look powerful can cause them to try to make their staff ② <u>fear</u> them. For instance, they might threaten to fire employees whenever something goes wrong. Furthermore, they may ③ <u>admit</u> making mistakes, choosing to blame others instead. By behaving this way, they try to make sure that no one will ④ <u>challenge</u> them and that they can hold onto their position. Leaders with poor self-esteem are not aware of their self-value, so they think behaving in this manner is the only way to earn recognition as a leader. Because they do not know their own self-worth, they create a ⑤ <u>toxic</u> environment for the people they manage.

* self-value: 자아 가치

실력 UP! 미니 문제 주제 찾기

01. 윗글의 주제로 가장 적절한 것은?

① how disease outbreaks can be avoided

② the low pay and lack of incentives in restaurants

③ the benefits of automation in the restaurant industry

실력 UP! 미니 문제 주제 찾기

02. 다음 질문을 읽고 한 문장의 영어로 답하시오.

Q: According to the passage, why would leaders with low self-esteem threaten to fire employees or blame others for the mistakes they made?

A: To _____

_____ .

03 다음 글의 밑줄 친 부분 중, 문맥상 낱말의 쓰임이 적절하지 않은 것은?

Invasive plant species pose a very serious threat to biodiversity. This is especially true when a species is introduced to an ecosystem where there are no ① competitors. With nothing challenging it, an invasive plant species can spread very rapidly and easily ② disturb the growth of native plants by consuming whatever light, moisture, and nutrients are available. This can lead to their endangerment or extinction within a few generations. The effects on local birds and wildlife can also be extremely ③ damaging, as many of them rely on these native plants for food. People are ④ unaware of the problems caused by invasive species, and trillions of dollars are spent globally each year to get rid of them. Nonetheless, this often makes the problem ⑤ worse as using pesticides in affected areas can pollute soil and water.

04 다음 글의 밑줄 친 부분 중, 문맥상 낱말의 쓰임이 적절하지 않은 것은?

Active listening is vital to having good interpersonal communication skills. To be an active listener, you must first ① avoid distracting thoughts. This will allow you to pay attention to what the other person is saying. However, just listening is not enough. You must also ② show that you're engaged in what the other person is saying. You can do this by smiling, nodding, and making direct eye contact with the speaker. To be sure that you understand, you can ask the speaker to ③ clarify certain points or summarize what they have said. This involves repeating the main points of the message, which ④ gives the speaker a chance to make a correction if necessary. Finally, before you respond, allow the speaker to finish what they're saying. Interrupting only frustrates the speaker and ⑤ deepens your comprehension.

실력 UP! 미니 문제 주제 찾기

03. 윗글의 주제로 가장 적절한 것은?
① the decline of biodiversity around the world
② how invasive species endanger ecosystems
③ the financial cost of getting rid of invasive species

실력 UP! 미니 문제 주제 찾기

04. 윗글의 주제로 가장 적절한 것은?
① tips for becoming an active listener
② why good interpersonal skills are rare
③ how to make an persuasive argument

05 (A), (B), (C)의 각 네모 안에서 문맥에 맞는 낱말로 가장 적절한 것은?

Imagine being dropped off a thousand miles from home and asked to find your way back. That is what homing pigeons do. Homing pigeons have a natural ability to find their way home over great distances. Ever since the time of the ancient Egyptians, people have (A) utilized / ignored their ability in order to deliver messages between distant locations. But just how are homing pigeons able to navigate? Scientists are uncertain about the exact mechanisms involved, but they believe that a combination of systems can (B) confuse / benefit the pigeons' sense of direction. For instance, they may use the sun to guide their direction or use the iron elements in their beaks to follow Earth's magnetic waves. Another possibility is infrasound, or low-frequency sounds made by natural objects. These sounds are impossible for humans to hear but could enable the homing pigeon to avoid (C) finding / missing its destination.

* homing pigeon: 전서 비둘기, 편지를 보내도록 훈련된 비둘기
** magnetic wave: 자파   *** infrasound: 초저주파 불가청음

 (A)   (B)   (C)
① utilized - confuse - finding
② ignored - confuse - missing
③ utilized - benefit - missing
④ ignored - benefit - finding
⑤ utilized - benefit - finding

실력UP! 미니 문제 내신 서술형

05. 윗글의 내용을 다음과 같이 요약할 때, 빈칸에 들어갈 알맞은 말을 본문에서 찾아 쓰시오. (필요한 경우, 단어 형태 변경 가능)

Homing pigeons can ⓐ n＿＿＿＿＿＿ their way home by combining several different ⓑ s＿＿＿＿＿＿, such as infrasound or detecting magnetic waves.

06 다음 글의 밑줄 친 부분 중, 문맥상 낱말의 쓰임이 적절하지 않은 것은?

In making a decision, using your head simply means relying on your brain to determine which choice would ① bring the superior outcome. This requires an ability to identify relevant facts and use logic to choose the best option. Using your heart, however, means depending on your instincts. This is when people ② reject their feelings and "gut" to determine which choice might be best. This involves remembering previous experiences that might be ③ relevant for the present situation. If current circumstances are like those of the past, a person will likely use prior knowledge while deciding. There are appropriate times to use either the head or the heart. For instance, using your head might not be ④ beneficial in an emergency. When there is no time to stop and think, your heart might be needed to make an ⑤ immediate response.

실력UP! 미니 문제 내신 서술형

06. 윗글의 요지를 주어진 해석과 일치하도록 <보기>에 있는 단어를 배열하여 문장을 완성하시오.

머리를 사용하는 것과 마음을 사용하는 것은 서로 다른 상황에서 이점이 있다.
<보기> using / in / and / your / your / using / beneficial / different / are / head / heart / circumstances

＿＿＿＿＿＿＿＿＿＿＿＿＿＿＿＿＿＿＿＿＿

07 (A), (B), (C)의 각 네모 안에서 문맥에 맞는 낱말로 가장 적절한 것은?

Blame can be loosely defined as a negative reaction toward someone who has shown unsuitable behavior. Although almost everyone has experienced blame, psychologists still struggle to define exactly what it is. One theory is that when we blame people, we are actually (A) judging / accepting them. In effect, the act of blaming someone is the process by which we evaluate others based on personal and social criteria. Another possible explanation of blame is that it is simply a(n) (B) emotional / logical response—we feel anger when we see someone act in a manner that we view as inappropriate. A more recent theory to account for blame argues that it is a (C) change / support of opinion regarding a relationship. This means that when you blame a friend for doing something you find unacceptable, you are actually reconsidering the relationship you have with that person.

(A)	(B)	(C)
① judging	- logical	- change
② accepting	- emotional	- support
③ judging	- emotional	- change
④ accepting	- logical	- change
⑤ judging	- logical	- support

실력 UP! 미니 문제 주제 찾기

07. 윗글의 주제로 가장 적절한 것은?
① different views on the effect of blaming
② theories on the true meaning of blame
③ why blaming is an unhealthy behavior

---

08 다음 글의 밑줄 친 부분 중, 문맥상 낱말의 쓰임이 적절하지 <u>않은</u> 것은?

Gravity is a natural force that most people just take for granted. Unless a person is in outer space, he or she is unlikely to ① ignore this force. But what would happen if gravity suddenly ceased to function here on Earth? The most obvious effects would result from the fact that objects would no longer be ② attracted to each other. This is because Earth would ③ continue spinning, and anything unattached to the surface of the planet would fall away into space. This includes not only solid objects but also the air, and even the water in lakes and oceans. Over time, the planet itself would become ④ smaller since it would continually break apart into tiny pieces. Fortunately, scientists are certain about the impossibility of this scenario occurring. Given that gravity directly corresponds to mass, Earth will ⑤ lose its gravity because of its huge mass.

실력 UP! 미니 문제 내신 서술형

08. 윗글의 내용을 다음과 같이 요약할 때, 빈칸에 들어갈 알맞은 말을 본문에서 찾아 쓰시오. (필요한 경우, 단어 형태 변경 가능)

Although the loss of gravity on Earth would result in several (A) e_____, scientists stress the (B) i_____ of this happening.

CHAPTER 11

빈칸 추론하기

유형 소개 | 빈칸에 들어갈 적절한 단어나 문장을 추론하는 유형으로, 3점짜리 고난도 문제로 자주 출제됨
문 제 수 | 4문제
지 시 문 | 다음 빈칸에 들어갈 말로 가장 적절한 것을 고르시오.

불변의 패턴21 | 패턴 빈출도 ★★★★☆
글의 초반부에 나온 빈칸 문장은 주제문이다.

🎧 지문 듣기

주제문이 초반에 있는 두괄식 글, 또는 주제문이 초반에 나온 후 후반에서 다시 언급되는 양괄식 글이 많이 출제된다. 빈칸이 글의 초반부에 나오면 이어지는 글의 내용을 종합해서 주제문을 완성하는 느낌으로 빈칸에 들어갈 말을 추론해야 한다.

패턴맛보기

다음 글의 내용을 종합해서 글의 주제문을 완성하시오.

> It's hard enough to stick with goals you want to accomplish, but sometimes we make goals we're not even thrilled about in the first place. We set resolutions based on what we're supposed to do, or what others think we're supposed to do, rather than what really matters to us. This makes it nearly impossible to stick to the goal.

You should make goals based on _____.

① a strict deadline
② your own values

해석

> 당신이 달성하고자 하는 목표를 고수하는 것도 충분히 어려운데, 때때로 우리는 애초에 가슴이 설레지도 않는 목표들을 세운다. 우리는 우리에게 정말로 중요한 것보다는, 해야만 하는 것이나 다른 사람들이 생각하기에 우리가 해야만 하는 것에 기반하여 결심을 한다. 이는 그 목표를 고수하는 것을 거의 불가능하게 만든다.

당신은 _____에 기반해서 목표를 세워야 한다.

① 엄격한 마감 기한
② 당신만의 가치관

해설

이 글의 전반적인 내용은 우리에게 정말로 중요한 것보다 우리가 해야한다고 생각하는 일이나 다른 사람들의 생각에 기반하여 목표를 세우는 것은 그 목표를 고수하는 것을 거의 불가능하게 만든다는 것이다. 글의 내용을 종합하면 '당신은 당신만의 가치관에 기반해서 목표를 세워야 한다'는 내용이 되므로 빈칸에 들어갈 말로 가장 적절한 것은 ② your own values(당신만의 가치관)이다.

정답

②

기출문제 2020년 3월 고1 학평
정답 및 해설 p.81

다음 빈칸에 들어갈 말로 가장 적절한 것을 고르시오.

Remember that _____ is always of the essence. If an apology is not accepted, thank the individual for hearing you out and leave the door open for if and when he wishes to reconcile. Be conscious of the fact that just because someone accepts your apology does not mean she has fully forgiven you. It can take time, maybe a long time, before the injured party can completely let go and fully trust you again. There is little you can do to speed this process up. If the person is truly important to you, it is worthwhile to give him or her the time and space needed to heal. Do not expect the person to go right back to acting normally immediately.

* reconcile: 화해하다

① curiosity
② independence
③ patience
④ creativity
⑤ honesty

불변의 패턴22

패턴 빈출도 ★★★★★

후반부의 빈칸 문장은 주제문을 재진술하는 문장이다.

🎧 지문 듣기

글의 후반부에 나오는 빈칸 문장은 앞서 나온 주제문을 다시 한 번 언급하는 문장인 경우가 많다. 따라서 글의 초중반부에서 주제문을 찾아서 확실히 이해한 후, 이를 다른 말로 바꿔 말한 선택지를 찾아야 한다.

패턴맛보기

다음 주제문을 재진술한 문장으로 가장 적절한 것을 고르시오.

주제문: A class requires participation of several people other than a teacher who teaches it, and students who take it.

① A class is in fact the place where students can improve writing skills
② A class is in fact the product of the efforts of hundreds of people
③ A class is in fact most effective when combined with online learning

[해석]
주제문: 수업은 수업을 가르칠 교사와 학생들 외에도 여러 사람의 참여를 필요로 한다.
① 수업은 사실상 학생들이 작문 기술을 향상시킬 수 있는 장소이다
② 수업은 사실상 수많은 사람들의 노력의 결과물이다
③ 수업은 사실상 온라인 학습과 결합될 때 가장 효과적이다

[해설]
주제문은 수업은 수업을 가르칠 교사와 학생들 외에도 여러 사람의 참여를 필요로 한다는 내용이다. 따라서 수업이 여러 사람의 참여를 필요로 한다는 내용을 수업이 수많은 사람의 노력의 결과물이라고 바꿔 말한 ② A class is in fact the product of the efforts of hundreds of people이 주제문을 재진술한 문장으로 가장 적절하다.

[정답]
②

기출문제 2021년 6월 고1 학평

정답 및 해설 p.81

다음 빈칸에 들어갈 말로 가장 적절한 것을 고르시오.

Due to technological innovations, music can now be experienced by more people, for more of the time than ever before. Mass availability has given individuals unheard-of control over their own sound-environment. However, it has also confronted them with the simultaneous availability of countless genres of music, in which they have to orient themselves. People start filtering out and organizing their digital libraries like they used to do with their physical music collections. However, there is the difference that the choice lies in their own hands. Without being restricted to the limited collection of music-distributors, nor being guided by the local radio program as a 'preselector' of the latest hits, the individual actively has to

_____.

The search for the right song is thus associated with considerable effort.

* simultaneous: 동시의

① choose and determine his or her musical preferences
② understand the technical aspects of recording sessions
③ share unique and inspiring playlists on social media
④ interpret lyrics with background knowledge of the songs
⑤ seek the advice of a voice specialist for better performances

01 다음 빈칸에 들어갈 말로 가장 적절한 것을 고르시오.

Many people have a favorite genre that they come back to over and over again. And while reading a familiar type of book can be relaxing, it is unlikely to lead to a broader perspective. For that, people have to read books from a variety of genres, even if it means _____. There is nothing wrong with having a preference for a specific genre, but reading books exclusively from a familiar category means that you will never learn about other topics. In contrast, reading works that take you away from familiar topics almost guarantees that you will encounter new ideas, types of people, and writing styles. This may feel discomforting at first but it will ultimately open you up to new ideas and maybe even cause you to think differently about the world.

① ruining their relationships
② reducing their perspective
③ limiting their memory
④ leaving their comfort zone
⑤ damaging their vocabulary

02 다음 빈칸에 들어갈 말로 가장 적절한 것을 고르시오.

Most websites are now approximately twice as large as they were three years ago. This is due to their more frequent use of videos and images, not to mention the addition of advertising and data-tracking technologies. These are intended to enhance the appearance of websites, help companies meet business objectives, and provide a better user experience. However, all of these factors have increased the density of code that needs to be written, which contributes to a website's complexity and ultimately causes it to load less quickly than before. While having a more attractive appearance helps websites generate more income, the increased bulk and higher level of involvement negatively affect their _____.

* meet: 충족시키다

① growth   ② speed
③ productivity   ④ sound
⑤ image

실력 UP! 미니 문제 내신 서술형

01. 윗글의 요지를 주어진 해석과 일치하도록 <보기>에 있는 단어를 배열하여 문장을 완성하시오.

> 다양한 장르의 책을 읽는 것은 당신의 관점을 확장시킬 수 있다.
> <보기> a variety of / your perspective / Reading books / from / can broaden / genres

_____.

실력 UP! 미니 문제 주제 찾기

02. 윗글의 주제로 가장 적절한 것은?
① changes in advertising and data tracking by computer companies
② trade-offs between the appearance and performance of websites
③ complicated codes needed to maintain modern websites

03 다음 빈칸에 들어갈 말로 가장 적절한 것을 고르시오.

In a 2011 study led by psychology professor Alejandro Lleras, 84 participants were divided into four groups and asked to perform a repetitive task on a computer for 50 minutes. One of the groups was given two short distractions from work. When a four-digit code appeared on their screens, they were asked to stop working briefly. Meanwhile, the other groups worked without interruption for the full duration of the experiment. It was found that the performance of the groups who worked nonstop declined steadily throughout the experiment, whereas the group that stopped momentarily kept their concentration until the end. The findings ultimately suggest that

_____.

① retaining information is possible even with frequent interruptions
② performing multiple tasks at a time can decrease productivity
③ learning lots of information at once is helpful in the short term
④ working on computers can lead to higher performance
⑤ taking breaks improves the ability to focus over time

04 다음 빈칸에 들어갈 말로 가장 적절한 것을 고르시오.

You may as well spend less time scrolling through motivational quotes on social media because _____. These quotes may seem harmless, but they usually use language that overgeneralizes and puts unreasonable pressure on readers. They can also blame people for not creating opportunities for themselves. Consider the following quote by Walt Disney: "All our dreams can come true if we have the courage to pursue them." It sounds pretty inspiring at first but, upon deeper reflection, messages like this reinforce the idea that everyone has the potential to fulfill their aspirations, and if they don't, it's their own fault. Ironically, motivational quotes like this one can increase people's anxiety and depression and make them less driven than before.

* aspiration: 꿈, 열망

① they could be damaging rather than helpful
② it is hard to prove if they are true
③ some are no longer applicable
④ most of them are found in textbooks
⑤ they give you no chance to fulfill your dream

실력 UP! 미니 문제 내신 서술형

03. 윗글의 내용을 다음과 같이 요약할 때, 빈칸에 들어갈 알맞은 말을 본문에서 찾아 쓰시오.

A psychology experiment that had individuals perform
(A) r_____ tasks found that people who were able to
(B) s_____ working momentarily sustained their concentration better easily than people who worked nonstop.

실력 UP! 미니 문제 주제 찾기

04. 윗글의 주제로 가장 적절한 것은?
① the potential side effects of motivational quotes
② the inspiring language of motivational quotes
③ the positive impact of social media on depression

05 다음 빈칸에 들어갈 말로 가장 적절한 것을 고르시오.

As a parent, having an angry outburst in front of your children can be very damaging to them. When you're upset, your first impulse might be to yell or slam a door, but you had better not react to every thing that annoys you. Otherwise, your children will grow up thinking that this sort of behavior is acceptable. Instead of figuring out how to work through their feelings in a calm and healthy way, they will recall how you behaved in similar circumstances and act accordingly. In other words, when put in a situation where they are angry and their ability to control their temper is tested, they will lose control. You must therefore teach them that, although everybody gets upset, it isn't necessary to _____.

① avoid it
② act on it
③ be indifferent
④ keep it hidden
⑤ control the feelings

06 다음 빈칸에 들어갈 말로 가장 적절한 것을 고르시오.

Although there are countless interspecies interactions, the "relationship" between the remora and the shark is an interesting one. In comparison to most sharks, the remora is a tiny creature, typically measuring between one and three feet. The most distinguishing physical characteristic of the remora is its front dorsal fin, which has evolved to take the form of a sucker-like organ over time. It uses this organ to attach itself to a shark as it passes by. In doing so, it obtains not only a fast source of transportation but also protection from predators. Furthermore, when the shark feeds, the remora has access to its leftover food scraps. Since the remora is relatively small and light, the shark hardly notices it and is essentially unaffected by its presence. This is a good example of a relationship between two organisms in which one party _____.

* remora: 빨판상어

① helps the other attract prey
② often puts the other in danger
③ benefits without harming the other
④ exchanges an equal amount of help with the other
⑤ shares its resources with the other for transportation

실력 UP! 미니 문제 주제 찾기

05. 윗글의 주제로 가장 적절한 것은?
① importance of letting children express their emotions
② why parents should control their anger in front of their children
③ circumstances in which the display of anger is necessary

실력 UP! 미니 문제 주제 찾기

06. 윗글의 주제로 가장 적절한 것은?
① comparison of the feeding behavior of two shark species
② the relationship between the remora and the shark
③ physical differences in various marine organisms

07 다음 빈칸에 들어갈 말로 가장 적절한 것을 고르시오.

When it comes to science, many of us fail to consider that _____ . When scientists are presented with a question, (A)they form a hypothesis based on what they already know and then carry out a series of experiments. The outcome may support the hypothesis, but this does not necessarily mean that (B)it is correct. Even if extensive experimentation yielding similar results leads to the widespread acceptance of the hypothesis, it only becomes a theory. Should the theory become a law, there is always the possibility of new evidence arising that can call (C)it into question or refute it entirely. Essentially, as our knowledge of the world grows through scientific investigation, old ideas are replaced by new ones that better align with the most recent findings.

* refute: 반박하다   ** align: 동조하다

① nothing can be proven definitely
② lack of funding presents challenges
③ it is rare to repeat the results of an experiment
④ the public is often misled by complex findings
⑤ methods of collecting evidence vary considerably

실력 UP! 미니 문제 내신 서술형

07. 다음의 (A)~(C)가 지칭하는 바를 영어로 찾아 쓰시오.

(A) _____

(B) _____

(C) _____

08 다음 빈칸에 들어갈 말로 가장 적절한 것을 고르시오.

Behavioral experiments on bees have determined _____ . One of these was an experiment in which researchers put out a blue feeder and a yellow feeder. The only difference between the feeders was that the blue one was empty, while the yellow one was filled with honey. Bees realized that the yellow feeder had honey, so they went there while ignoring the blue one. Even after the honey was removed from the yellow feeder, they continued to associate it with food and come to it. To prove that the bees were truly seeing blue and yellow, multiple blue feeders were put out along with the yellow feeder. The bees continued to go to the yellow feeder first, no matter where it was placed. If the bees were unable to truly see yellow, it is logical to assume that some of them might have explored some of the blue feeders first.

① they can detect sweet scents from great distances
② they have a preference for yellow objects
③ they see light in the ultraviolet spectrum
④ they can distinguish between colors
⑤ they rely on colors to see better

실력 UP! 미니 문제 주제 찾기

08. 윗글의 주제로 가장 적절한 것은?

① the effects of color on the behavior of bees
② the logical behavior exhibited by bees
③ the ability of bees to recognize different colors

09 다음 빈칸에 들어갈 말로 가장 적절한 것을 고르시오.

A study examining prosocial behavior suggests that, as we age, _____ becomes more important. Researchers reached this conclusion by conducting an experiment involving a group of older adults and a group of younger adults. The participants were given devices that measured six levels of grip strength. They were then presented with a set of hypothetical scenarios in which they could either earn money for themselves or another person. For each situation, (A)they were asked whether they were willing to make an effort to earn the money, and if they said yes, they had to squeeze the device hard enough to secure that money. The study found that the older adults were more willing to put in physical effort to gain money for other people than the younger participants. (B)The latter were more concerned with earning money for themselves, showing that aiding other people might become more important as we age.

* grip strength: 악력

① educating younger people
② earning some money
③ redistributing wealth
④ following rules
⑤ helping others

10 다음 빈칸에 들어갈 말로 가장 적절한 것을 고르시오.

It is a common assumption that you'll save time if you drive faster. To a certain extent, this is true. If you need to make a 10-kilometer trip and drive at 20 kilometers an hour, the trip will take you 30 minutes. However, if you accelerate to 30 kilometers an hour, you will arrive at your destination in 20 minutes. That's a 10-minute time saving. Now, imagine speeding up from 30 kilometers an hour to 40 kilometers an hour. You might think you will save another 10 minutes but, if you do the math, you will see that you only save five additional minutes. (A)This downward trend continues the faster you go. Many of us overestimate the time that we can save after we've sped up. This is due to a logical fallacy referred to as the time-saving bias. Essentially, we make (B)an incorrect judgment about _____ because we only focus on the new speed rather than our initial speed.

* fallacy: 오류

① how far away our destination is
② how fast we are able to drive
③ when to increase our speed
④ why time seems to speed up
⑤ how much time we will save

09. 윗글의 밑줄 친 (A), (B)가 지칭하는 바를 영어로 찾아 쓰시오.

(A) _____

(B) _____

10. 윗글의 밑줄 친 (A), (B)가 의미하는 것을 우리말로 쓰시오.

(A) _____

(B) _____

11 다음 빈칸에 들어갈 말로 가장 적절한 것을 고르시오.

Scientists believe that unhatched baby birds _____ from within their eggs by vibrating. To determine this, researchers exposed yellow-legged gull eggs to the sounds of a predator several times a day and found that the eggs vibrated following each experience. Meanwhile, another group of eggs in a control group that was not exposed to the sounds of the predator did not vibrate. The researchers speculate that this response not only demonstrates fear but is typical bird behavior. Birds use a variety of sounds to convey important news all the time, and vibrating from within an egg is no different. It is likely that, despite being confined to their eggs, the young creatures felt threatened as a result of being exposed to the sounds of the predator and wanted to signal their siblings of the danger.

① transmit information to each other
② form a bond with their siblings
③ scare away potential predators
④ accelerate their development
⑤ feel the outside temperature

12 다음 빈칸에 들어갈 말로 가장 적절한 것을 고르시오.

When someone asks, "Could you pass the salt?" the implied meaning is that they would like you to pass them the salt. They do not wish for you to reply with whether you can or cannot complete the task—they simply expect you to do it. Why don't people just say, "Please pass the salt?" The answer has to do with how we approach language. The literal meaning of words is not always important, especially when we speak. What matters more is the situation the speaker is in and their intention. The meaning of a speaker's words may not be immediately obvious to everyone but full of implication, and easily understood by those who are able to put the words into context. The area of linguistics concerned with interpreting meaning is called pragmatics, and it teaches us that _____.

① communication depends on listening
② language has a number of limitations
③ what we say isn't always what we mean
④ unexpected situations are quite common
⑤ correct understanding requires literal meaning

실력 UP! 미니 문제 주제 찾기

11. 윗글의 주제로 가장 적절한 것은?
① how unhatched birds communicate with one another
② the ability of baby birds to recognize threats
③ behavior displayed by mother birds when encountering a predator

실력 UP! 미니 문제 내신 서술형

12. 윗글의 요지를 주어진 해석과 일치하도록 <보기>에 있는 단어를 배열하여 문장을 완성하시오.

> 사람이 말한 것의 의도는 그들이 사용한 단어의 글자 그대로의 의미보다 더 중요하다.
> <보기> of the words / the literal meaning / behind / matters / The intention / what a person says / they use / more than

_____.

CHAPTER 12

흐름과 관계 없는 문장 찾기

불변의 패턴23

패턴 빈출도 ★★★★★

주제만 파악하면 정답이 보인다.

지문 듣기

흐름과 관계 없는 문장을 찾기 위해서는 주제를 명확히 파악해야 한다. 이 유형의 글은 주제문이 초반에 나오는 경우가 많으니 처음 한두 문장에서 주제를 파악하고 이와 관련 없는 문장을 고른다.

패턴맛보기

다음 중 글의 주제와 논리적 연관성이 <u>약한</u> 문장을 고르시오.

주제: 역사를 배우는 것에는 여러 장점이 있다.

① Studying history can make you more knowledgeable or interesting to talk to.
② Studying history helps us ask and answer humanity's Big Questions.
③ Studying history as a profession is a rare career path.

[해석]
① 역사를 공부하는 것은 당신이 대화하기에 더 박식하거나 흥미롭게 만들어 줄 수 있다.
② 역사를 공부하는 것은 우리가 인류의 중대한 문제들을 묻고 답하는 데에 도움이 된다.
③ 직업으로서 역사를 공부하는 것은 흔하지 않은 진로이다.

[해설]
①과 ②은 역사를 배우는 장점에 대한 예시이므로 글의 주제와 강한 논리적 연관성을 갖는다. 반면 ③은 역사를 공부하는 것을 진로로 선택하는 것에 대한 내용으로 글의 주제와 논리적 연관성이 약하므로 정답은 ③ Studying history as a profession is a rare career path.(직업으로서 역사를 공부하는 것은 흔하지 않은 진로이다.)이다.

[정답]
③

기출문제 2019년 6월 고1 학평

정답 및 해설 p.91

다음 글에서 전체 흐름과 관계 <u>없는</u> 문장은?

Words like 'near' and 'far' can mean different things depending on where you are and what you are doing. If you were at a zoo, then you might say you are 'near' an animal if you could reach out and touch it through the bars of its cage. ① Here the word 'near' means an arm's length away. ② If you were telling someone how to get to your local shop, you might call it 'near' if it was a five-minute walk away. ③ It seems that you had better walk to the shop to improve your health. ④ Now the word 'near' means much longer than an arm's length away. ⑤ Words like 'near', 'far', 'small', 'big', 'hot', and 'cold' all mean different things to different people at different times.

불변의 패턴24

핵심 소재만 같고 주제에서 살짝 벗어나는 문장이 정답이다.

🎧 지문 듣기

흐름과 관계 없는 문장은 보통 글의 핵심 소재 또는 관련 소재에 대해 다루지만 주제에서 살짝 벗어나는 내용인 경우가 많다. 언뜻 보기에 자연스럽게 연결되어 보일 수 있으니 주의해야 한다.

패턴맛보기

밑줄 친 문장이 글의 전체 흐름과 관계 없는 이유를 다음과 같이 설명할 때, 빈칸에 들어갈 말로 적절한 것을 각각 찾아 쓰시오.

A snowy owl's ears are not visible from the outside, but it has incredible hearing. ① The feathers on a snowy owl's face guide sounds to its ears, giving it the ability to hear things humans cannot. ② Also, the differing size and location of each ear helps the owl distinguish between sounds. ③ It can hear at the same time the distant hoofbeats of a large deer, the flap of a bird's wings above it, and the digging of a small animal below it. ④ In fact, it has excellent vision both in the dark and at a distance. ⑤ After choosing which sound interests it most, the snowy owl moves its head like a large circular antenna to pick up the best reception.

이 글의 중심 소재는 흰올빼미의 ___(A)___ 이다. ①~③, 그리고 ⑤ 뒤 문장은 모두 흰올빼미의 ___(A)___ 에 관한 것인데, ④은 ___(B)___ 에 관한 것이므로 글의 전체 흐름과 관계 없다.

[해석]

흰올빼미의 귀는 외부에서는 보이지 않지만, 그것은 놀라운 청력을 가지고 있다. ① 흰올빼미의 깃털은 그것의 귀로 소리를 이끌어주는데, 이는 인간이 들을 수 없는 소리를 듣는 능력을 부여해준다. ② 또한 양쪽 귀의 서로 다른 크기와 위치는 올빼미로 하여금 소리들 간의 구분을 가능하게 해준다. ③ 이 올빼미는 멀리서 나는 큰 사슴의 발굽 소리, 자신의 위에 있는 새들의 날개가 펄럭이는 소리, 그리고 자신의 아래에서 작은 동물이 땅을 파는 소리를 동시에 들을 수 있다. ④ 사실, 이 올빼미는 어둠 속에서, 그리고 멀리 떨어진 곳에서도 잘 볼 수 있는 뛰어난 시력을 가졌다. ⑤ 어떤 소리가 가장 이들의 흥미를 돋우는지를 고르면, 흰올빼미는 마치 거대한 원형 안테나가 최상의 수신 상태를 포착하듯 자신의 머리를 돌린다.

[정답]

(A) 청력   (B) 시력

기출문제 2018년 6월 고1 학평

정답 및 해설 p.92

다음 글에서 전체 흐름과 관계 없는 문장은?

Of the many forest plants that can cause poisoning, wild mushrooms may be among the most dangerous. ① This is because people sometimes confuse the poisonous and edible varieties, or they eat mushrooms without making a positive identification of the variety. ② Many people enjoy hunting wild species of mushrooms in the spring season, because they are excellent edible mushrooms and are highly prized. ③ However, some wild mushrooms are dangerous, leading people to lose their lives due to mushroom poisoning. ④ Growing a high-quality product at a reasonable cost is a key aspect to farming edible mushrooms for profit. ⑤ To be safe, a person must be able to identify edible mushrooms before eating any wild one.

* edible: 먹을 수 있는

01 다음 글에서 전체 흐름과 관계 <u>없는</u> 문장은?

Within the animal kingdom, dolphins are believed to have one of the longest social memories. ① A recent study of bottlenose dolphins has revealed that they can remember dolphins they have encountered even after 20 years of separation. ② They are able to do this because dolphins regularly communicate using an array of gestures, clicks, and whistles. ③ Early in life, each dolphin develops a particular whistle that is unique to them. ④ They typically travel within the same family group throughout their lives, which can last anywhere from 10 to 50 years. ⑤ The sound functions similarly to the way that names do among people, providing dolphins an easy way to identify and remember other individuals.

* bottlenose dolphin: 큰돌고래
** click: 클릭, 공기주머니를 튕겨서 내는 딸각 소리

02 다음 글에서 전체 흐름과 관계 <u>없는</u> 문장은?

Thinking good thoughts and performing good deeds are hardly the same thing. People may like to reassure themselves by believing that good thoughts are enough to bring about positive change in the world, but thinking alone is rarely enough. ① If a man is hungry, simply hoping that someone provides him with food is of no real help. ② If everyone who encounters that man shares the same thought but does not do anything about it, he could well end up starving. ③ On the other hand, it would make a world of difference if just one person gave him something to eat. ④ Research has found that people can survive for up to three weeks without food. ⑤ That's why it is important to act on our well-meaning thoughts before it is too late.

실력 UP! **미니 문제** 내신 서술형

01. 윗글의 제목을 주어진 해석과 일치하도록 <보기>에 있는 단어를 배열하여 문장을 완성하시오.

> 돌고래들이 서로를 식별하고 기억하는 방법
>
> <보기> and / How / Each Other / Dolphins / Remember / Identify

실력 UP! **미니 문제** 주제 찾기

02. 윗글의 주제로 가장 적절한 것은?
① why beliefs can modify people's world view
② the influence of good deeds on mental health
③ the need for action over positive thinking

03 다음 글에서 전체 흐름과 관계 <u>없는</u> 문장은?

Vellum is a type of material made from the dry skin of mammals such as calves and sheep. Once (A)it is processed, it can be used as a medium to write or print documents on. Vellum carries a number of benefits for preserving written works, not the least of which is durability. ① The parliaments of Britain and Ireland, for instance, traditionally printed their legislation on vellum for over a thousand years. ② Outside of government, Jewish religious scrolls are still printed on the material to this day. ③ Regular paper is cheap to produce and readily available, so (B)it is more suitable for everyday use. ④ Vellum also has the attraction of being luxurious in appearance. ⑤ Therefore, it is common for some educational institutions to issue traditional diplomas made of vellum.

* vellum: 피지(皮紙)

04 다음 글에서 전체 흐름과 관계 <u>없는</u> 문장은?

Agriculture is one of the fastest-growing sectors in Africa. The need to sustain a vast population means that millions of people across the continent must devote their energy and resources to growing food. ① However, many farmers there rely on outdated tools and methods. ② These tools and methods are not suitable for farming on a large scale, and their continued use could also harm the environment. ③ To unlock the farming sector's full potential without damaging the environment, farmers must turn to emerging technologies, including artificial intelligence, big data, and more. ④ A number of wild African species are currently in danger of extinction. ⑤ Applied in the right circumstances, advanced technologies could help African farmers take full advantage of their continent's abundant natural resources.

실력 UP! 미니 문제 내신 서술형

03. 윗글의 밑줄 친 다음의 (A), (B)가 지칭하는 바를 영어로 찾아 쓰시오.

(A) _____

(B) _____

실력 UP! 미니 문제 주제 찾기

04. 윗글의 주제로 가장 적절한 것은?

① the need for advanced technology in African agriculture

② farming techniques utilized to avoid harming African species

③ the dependence of Africa's population on natural resources

05 다음 글에서 전체 흐름과 관계 <u>없는</u> 문장은?

Nutrition is key to promoting a healthy gut environment, which in turn is essential to maintaining a strong immune system. ① A healthy gut contains the right balance of beneficial microbes to help us digest food, absorb nutrients, and get rid of harmful viruses. ② Without it, we may not get enough nutrition from our food and become vulnerable to serious allergies and diseases. ③ To maintain a healthy gut, it is important to regularly consume foods that contain bioactive compounds as early and as often in life as possible. ④ Babies who consume breast milk tend to show signs of improved immune system later in life. ⑤ In particular, eating lots of fruits, vegetables, and dairy products like yogurt helps us maintain a good microbiome.

* gut: 장(腸) ** microbe: 미생물
*** bioactive compound: 생물 활성 화합물

06 다음 글에서 전체 흐름과 관계 <u>없는</u> 문장은?

When people dream, they typically do not know if the experience is real or not until after they have woken up. ① However, individuals are sometimes able to recognize that they are having a dream and even control their actions while dreaming. ② This phenomenon is known as lucid dreaming, and research indicates it is hard for everyone to experience this. ③ Lucid dreaming has been the subject of many popular science fiction novels and films. ④ In fact, it is believed that only half of all people experience lucid dreams at least once in their lifetime and less than 20 percent have them on a regular basis. ⑤ This is likely because lucid dreaming is related to the ability to monitor one's own thoughts, but most people are not sensitive enough to notice when they are dreaming.

* lucid dreaming: 자각몽

실력 UP! 미니 문제 내신 서술형

05. 윗글의 내용을 다음과 같이 요약할 때, 빈칸에 들어갈 알맞은 말을 본문에서 찾아 쓰시오. (필요한 경우, 단어 형태 변경 가능)

(A) P_____ a healthy gut environment by consuming foods that contain beneficial microbes is (B) e_____ to maintaining a strong immune system.

실력 UP! 미니 문제 주제 찾기

06. 윗글의 주제로 가장 적절한 것은?
① people who enjoy lucid dreaming
② methods for controlling dreams
③ the rare occurrence of lucid dreaming

07 다음 글에서 전체 흐름과 관계 <u>없는</u> 문장은?

The cheetah is a large cat that is native to the grassland areas of Africa. Due to its unique physical characteristics, it is the fastest land animal, capable of accelerating from 0 to 60 mph in only 3 seconds. ① To begin with, it is one of the lightest of the big cats, and its slim build and long legs enable it to run fast. ② In addition, its long muscular tail helps it maneuver and make sharp, quick turns. ③ The respiratory organs of a cheetah also contribute to its ability to move very quickly. ④ The decline of cheetah populations has been a serious problem in Africa, and has brought discussion about reconsidering this animal as endangered. ⑤ For example, its big lungs allow it to take up to 150 breaths per minute when it is running at a high speed.

* respiratory: 호흡의

고난도

08 다음 글에서 전체 흐름과 관계 <u>없는</u> 문장은?

There are many negative aspects surrounding advertisements specifically targeted at young children, and one of these involves a phenomenon called "pester power." ① It describes the tendency of young children to keep asking their parents to buy them products or services that they have previously seen advertised on TV and other media. ② Companies willingly take advantage of children's influence on parents to sell more goods and services to consumers. ③ For parents, children's refusal to obey commands can quickly turn into a problem. ④ This is concerning because young children lack critical thinking and absorb every message from advertisements. ⑤ Not knowing that they are acting just as companies want them to, a lot of children eventually get parents to give in and overspend their money.

* pester power: 부모를 졸라서 바라는 것을 얻어내는 힘

실력 UP! 미니 문제 내신 서술형

07. 윗글의 제목을 주어진 해석과 일치하도록 <보기>에 있는 단어를 배열하여 문장을 완성하시오.

> 속도를 높이는 치타의 신체적 특징
>
> <보기> of the Cheetah / that / Physical Characteristics / Promote Speed / The

실력 UP! 미니 문제 주제 찾기

08. 윗글의 주제로 가장 적절한 것은?

① the negative aspects of advertisements targeted at children
② the tendency of young children to want new products
③ the impact of advertising on children's critical thinking

01 다음 빈칸에 들어갈 말로 가장 적절한 것을 고르시오.

The lifestyle of the Raika tribe in Rajasthan, India, may soon cease to exist. For centuries, the Raikas have herded camels across the Thar Desert, living a semi-nomadic lifestyle and training camels to plough their fields and provide transportation, milk, and wool. However, the last decade has seen many changes that threaten the camels, including a surge in development. The construction of new roads has brought more vehicles to the region, making camels somewhat less useful as "ships of the desert." As a result, their numbers are in sharp decline. Furthermore, the installation of solar and wind farms to support the increase in farmland, made possible by a large-scale irrigation project, has left less space for camels. These advancements have made it more difficult for the Raika to maintain their traditional habits, prompting them to _____.

* plough: 갈다, 경작하다   ** irrigation: 관개(灌漑)

① seek government assistance
② abandon their former ways
③ settle in larger territory
④ struggle for recognition
⑤ pursue bigger dreams

02 다음 빈칸에 들어갈 말로 가장 적절한 것을 고르시오.

The process of urbanization, which was driven by Britain's Industrial Revolution, had major effects, especially with regard to the emergence of _____. Before factories gained attention in Britain, citizens—mostly farmers—had a simpler existence, with little variation in how people lived from village to village. Everyone had similar wealth and lived a similar lifestyle. After the Industrial Revolution, however, people began to flock to cities looking for better opportunities, only to discover that the infrastructure was ill-equipped to provide for them all. While the earliest arrivals were able to claim attractive jobs and housing, the latecomers were stuck with menial labor and poor living conditions. As the industry increased only the wealth of those who were already successful, the gap in status grew larger until a hierarchy became well-established in British society.

* flock: 모이다, 떼 지어 가다

① a more educated population
② revolutionary technologies
③ mass-produced goods
④ distinct social classes
⑤ dangerous diseases

03 다음 글의 밑줄 친 부분 중, 문맥상 낱말의 쓰임이 적절하지 않은 것은?

Being bilingual offers various advantages. For one, it ① increases brain power because it requires a person to switch back and forth between two languages, which involves multitasking skills and creative thinking. Speaking a second language also has an effect on a person's ability to ② concentrate. This is supported by studies showing that bilingual individuals are better at ignoring distractions than their monolingual peers. Furthermore, recent research suggests that these effects aren't ③ lasting. Scientists believe that bilingual people maintain good brain health longer than people who only speak one language. They are able to ④ remember information far more effectively, and dementia and other age-related memory problems do not occur as early or sometimes not at all. Overall, because the brains of bilingual people seem to age at a ⑤ slower rate, they can continue to live fulfilling lives for far longer than others.

* bilingual: 2개 국어를 구사하는 ** dementia: 치매, 정신 이상

04 다음 글에서 전체 흐름과 관계 없는 문장은?

Poor physical fitness among older women is a serious concern. It can impact quality of life and lead to poor mental health. ① At an advanced age, many women need to engage in strength training at least twice a week to maintain adequate physical fitness. ② Unfortunately, many of them lack the proper motivation to engage in regular exercise. ③ To address this issue, experts have found programs aimed at providing social and environmental support helpful. ④ Some exercise routines are more focused on getting the heart rate up, which helps burn fat more quickly. ⑤ These programs, when combined with efforts to increase the affordability and accessibility of fitness programs, help to encourage senior women to find an exercise routine they can adhere to.

05 다음 글의 밑줄 친 부분 중, 어법상 틀린 것은?

As adults, we understand that cooperation can be useful. We know that nobody is capable of doing everything themselves and that everyone needs somebody else's help sometimes. In addition, cooperating on a task often produces better results ① than when the task is performed alone. All of that said, the ability to cooperate does not always come naturally to many people and is something ② that must be taught from a young age. One way to teach children to cooperate is ③ to get them to engage in activities that require teamwork, such as solving a giant puzzle. Another way is for parents and teachers to praise cooperative behavior ④ observing in children as a form of encouragement. Lastly, adults should also act as appropriate models for children and ⑤ demonstrate how best to cooperate with other people, such as by treating others with respect and being open to new ideas.

06 다음 글의 밑줄 친 부분 중, 어법상 틀린 것은?

Russell Baker was an American newspaper columnist known for his humorous observations. He first gained attention in the early 1960s writing satire under a column for The New York Times ① called "The Observer." Baker wrote extensively about many topics ② that concerned society but focused most of his attention on politicians, making fun of Democrats and Republicans alike. In 1974, he moved to the Times' main office in Manhattan and shortly after won his first Pulitzer Prize for commentary. Baker also won recognition for his books, among which ③ were *Growing Up*. Baker won a second Pulitzer for this book, this time for biography. Later, Baker produced *Russell Baker's Book of American Humor*, a comprehensive work ④ whose review of other notable American humorists was well received. In 1998, Baker's Observer column appeared in print for the last time on Christmas Day, around two decades ⑤ before his passing.

* satire: 풍자 작품, 풍자   ** commentary: 평론, 비평

07 다음 글의 밑줄 친 부분 중, 문맥상 낱말의 쓰임이 적절하지 않은 것은?

According to biologists, most animals groom themselves for several reasons. In general, animals groom themselves so that they can maintain their hygiene by ① removing objects like leaves, twigs, or dirt from their bodies. Cats, for example, have ② developed physical features specialized to help in the process. They have extremely rough tongues to lift dirt off their fur. Other animals, like birds, groom themselves to ③ ensure that their bodies are operating normally. They wash, pick at, and straighten ruffled feathers to make sure their bodies function well in flight. Although grooming seems like a necessary daily routine for all animals, there are those animals that seem very ④ interested in this process. For these animals, grooming is secondary to protection. They intentionally ⑤ cover themselves in mud, dead plants, or substances that stink to hide from predators or repel insects.

* groom: (동물의) 털 손질을 하다

08 다음 글에서 전체 흐름과 관계 없는 문장은?

Philosophers and anthropologists have very different approaches, but they both study the same basic topic: the human condition. ① Philosophers study the nature of human existence with the hopes of understanding our position in society through logic. ② Anthropologists, on the other hand, are more concerned with how we actually live in society, examining our diets, actions, and cultural practices. ③ In many cases, there is great overlap between these two fields, which can lead experts from each field to refer to the work of the other. ④ The academic study of anthropology as an independent discipline really began in earnest during the 1800s. ⑤ Philosophers must consider physical aspects that are usually in the domain of anthropologists, and anthropologists must consider the philosophical ethics of civilizations.

09 다음 빈칸에 들어갈 말로 가장 적절한 것을 고르시오.

Advertisers assess the mindset of their customer base and use this information to verbally persuade us into buying goods. Their strategies aren't typically based on logic and objectivity; rather, they tap into our desires and appeal to our emotions by carefully selecting the words they use to describe their products. This is because they know that the _____ we have with a particular word will trigger a corresponding emotional response. We connect words such as "joy," "inspiration," and "happiness" with positive feelings, encouraging us to make a purchase. On the other hand, words like "despair" or "hatred" arouse a very different reaction because we correlate them with negative attitudes. The most effective ads are loaded with words that will compel consumers, consciously and unconsciously, to become interested in and attracted by a product.

* verbally: 말로, 구두로

① associations
② advantages
③ similarities
④ difficulties
⑤ conditions

10 다음 빈칸에 들어갈 말로 가장 적절한 것을 고르시오.

Cosmopolitanism is the idea that people should be citizens of the world and find community at the global level. Arguing against it is difficult from a moral perspective because it emphasizes the idea of all humans being inherently worthy. However, putting it into practice is viewed by many as unrealistic. Those who oppose it say _____.
They believe increased exposure to "otherness" in order to encourage the sense that we are all fundamentally the same requires us to abandon certain traditional values and shared history. It would mean giving equal attention to the needs of people in other parts of the world, which could come at the expense of fellow citizens. This would suggest the need to dismantle patriotism and nationalism, which is unthinkable to many people.

* patriotism: 애국심 ** dismantle: 타도하다, 폐지하다

① individuals will feel forced to share their culture
② some countries would feel culturally superior
③ more border disputes would arise because of it
④ poor countries could be put at even greater risk
⑤ people will feel pressured to give up their culture

CHAPTER 13

글의 순서 배열하기

유형소개 주어진 글 뒤에 이어질 문단들을 논리적 흐름이나 시간 순서에 맞게 배열하는 유형으로, 논설문, 또는 설명문의 글이 많이 출제됨
문제수 2문제
지시문 주어진 글 다음에 이어질 글의 순서로 가장 적절한 것을 고르시오.

불변의 패턴25 | 대명사나 연결어를 찾으면 앞뒤 글의 순서가 보인다.

패턴 빈출도 ★★★★☆

🎧 지문 듣기

각 문단의 첫 문장에 나온 대명사나 연결어를 찾으면 그 앞에 올 내용을 추측할 수 있다. **글의 순서를 알려주는 표현*** 을 참고한다.

- it, that/those, this/these 등의 대명사가 가리키는 내용이 어느 문단에 있는지 찾는다.
- but, however, while 등의 역접 연결어가 있는 문장과 반대되는 내용이 어느 문단에 있는지 찾는다.
- for example, also, so 등의 순접 연결어가 있는 문장과 비슷한 내용이 어느 문단에 있는지 찾는다.

패턴맛보기

주어진 글 다음에 이어지는 각 문장에서 앞 뒤 내용을 추측할 수 있는 대명사 또는 연결어에 밑줄을 그으시오.

> Ideas about how much disclosure is appropriate vary among cultures. Those born in the United States tend to be high disclosers.

(A) This may explain why Americans seem particularly easy to meet.
(B) On the other hand, Japanese tend to do little disclosing about themselves.
(C) Therefore, they might seem less friendly at first.

해석

얼마나 많은 정보를 공개하는 것이 적절한지에 관한 생각은 문화마다 다르다. 미국에서 태어난 사람들은 정보를 잘 공개하려는 경향이 있다.

(A) 이것은 왜 미국인들을 만나는 것이 특히 쉬워 보이는지를 설명해 줄 수 있다.
(B) 반면 일본인은 자신에 대해 거의 공개하지 않는 경향이 있다.
(C) 따라서, 그들은 처음에는 덜 친절해 보일 수 있다.

해설

(A)의 This를 통해 (A)앞에는 This가 가리키는 대상, 또는 내용이 와야함을 알 수 있다.
(B)의 On the other hand를 통해 앞에 (B)와 대조되는 내용이 있는 문장이 와야함을 알 수 있다.
(C)의 Therefore를 통해 (C)는 그 앞에 나오는 내용에 대한 결론, 또는 부연 설명을 다룬 문장이라는 것을 알 수 있다. 또한 they를 통해 (C)앞에 they가 가리키는 대상이 와야함을 알 수 있다.

정답

(A) This (B) On the other hand (C) Therefore, they

기출문제 2019년 6월 고1 학평   정답 및 해설 p.104

주어진 글 다음에 이어질 글의 순서로 가장 적절한 것을 고르시오.

> The next time you're out under a clear, dark sky, look up. If you've picked a good spot for stargazing, you'll see a sky full of stars, shining and twinkling like thousands of brilliant jewels.

(A) It might be easier if you describe patterns of stars. You could say something like, "See that big triangle of bright stars there?" Or, "Do you see those five stars that look like a big letter W?"

(B) But this amazing sight of stars can also be confusing. Try and point out a single star to someone. Chances are, that person will have a hard time knowing exactly which star you're looking at.

(C) When you do that, you're doing exactly what we all do when we look at the stars. We look for patterns, not just so that we can point something out to someone else, but also because that's what we humans have always done.

① (A) – (C) – (B)   ② (B) – (A) – (C)
③ (B) – (C) – (A)   ④ (C) – (A) – (B)
⑤ (C) – (B) – (A)

불변의 패턴26

패턴 빈출도 ★★★★☆

주어진 글을 보고 뒤에 나올 글의 구조를 예측할 수 있다.

🎧 지문 듣기

자주 출제되는 글의 구조를 알아두면, 주어진 글을 통해 글의 구조를 예측하여 글을 더 쉽고 빠르게 이해할 수 있다.

- 주제(주어진 문장) → 예시
- 문제(주어진 문장) → 해결
- 통념(주어진 문장) → 반박 → 결론

패턴맛보기

주어진 글 다음에 이어질 내용으로 알맞은 것을 고르시오.

Making a small request that people will accept will naturally increase the chances of their accepting a bigger request afterwards.

① 주어진 글의 내용을 보충 설명해주는 예시
② 주어진 글에서 언급한 문제에 대한 해결책

[해석]
사람들이 수락할 작은 요구를 하는 것이 나중에 그들이 더 큰 요구를 수락할 가능성을 자연스럽게 증가시킬 것이다.

[해설]
주어진 글은 작은 요구를 하는 것을 통해 나중에 더 큰 요구를 수락할 가능성을 높일 수 있다는 내용이다. 어떻게 작은 요구가 더 큰 요구를 수락할 가능성을 높이는지에 대한 설명이 없고, 이러한 행위에 대한 필자의 견해도 주어지지 않았으므로 다음 문장으로는 주어진 글의 내용을 보충 설명해주는 예시가 이어질 것임을 예상할 수 있다. 따라서 주어진 글 다음에 이어질 내용으로 알맞은 것은 ① '주어진 글의 내용을 보충 설명해주는 예시'이다.

[정답]
①

기출문제 2021년 6월 고1 학평

정답 및 해설 p.104

주어진 글 다음에 이어질 글의 순서로 가장 적절한 것을 고르시오.

People spend much of their time interacting with media, but that does not mean that people have the critical skills to analyze and understand it.

(A) Research from New York University found that people over 65 shared seven times as much misinformation as their younger counterparts. All of this raises a question: What's the solution to the misinformation problem?

(B) One well-known study from Stanford University in 2016 demonstrated that youth are easily fooled by misinformation, especially when it comes through social media channels. This weakness is not found only in youth, however.

(C) Governments and tech platforms certainly have a role to play in blocking misinformation. However, every individual needs to take responsibility for combating this threat by becoming more information literate.

* counterpart: 상대방

① (A) – (C) – (B)　　② (B) – (A) – (C)
③ (B) – (C) – (A)　　④ (C) – (A) – (B)
⑤ (C) – (B) – (A)

실력UP! 기출표현　글의 순서를 알려주는 표현*

순접 연결어	therefore/hence (결과)　for example/for instance (예시)　similarly/likewise (비교)　in addition/moreover (첨가)
역접 연결어	however/but/yet (반전)　while/in contrast/on the other hand (대조)　nevertheless/although/even though (양보)

01 주어진 글 다음에 이어질 글의 순서로 가장 적절한 것을 고르시오.

> Sedimentary rocks can form on land or underwater. In either case, the process follows the same basic steps.

(A) This stage of the process is known as cementation. The crystals act as an adhesive and hold the bits of deposited matter together. Once this stage is complete, the cycle begins all over again.

(B) Rock formation begins when materials such as mud and sand are transported to an area where they can settle, either on the earth's surface or in a body of water. Once the materials have been deposited, they start to build up in layers.

(C) As these accumulate, the weight of each additional layer puts pressure on the ones below it. This compresses the materials, squeezing out any water they may contain. The pressure also causes salt crystals to form.

* cementation: 교결 작용(퇴적물 입자 또는 광물이 퇴적암화 되는 작용)

① (A) – (C) – (B)　　② (B) – (A) – (C)
③ (B) – (C) – (A)　　④ (C) – (A) – (B)
⑤ (C) – (B) – (A)

02 주어진 글 다음에 이어질 글의 순서로 가장 적절한 것을 고르시오.

> All of our thoughts, feelings, and actions are ultimately controlled by the brain.

(A) Quality fuels contain components that enable car engines to operate smoothly and help maintain their longevity. Similarly, highly nutritious foods have vitamins, minerals, and antioxidants that feed the brain and protect it from damage, helping ⓐit stay healthy for longer.

(B) The brain serves an essential function much like the engine in an automobile. It is impossible to operate a car without ⓑone, and the best way to keep it running in peak condition is to supply it with the proper fuel.

(C) In contrast, foods that are low in nutrition, just like non-premium fuels, contain few helpful ingredients and may even be harmful. Processed foods and those with lots of artificial sugars, for example, can cause the brain to produce substances that negatively affect our mood or slow down its normal performance.

* antioxidant: 항산화제

① (A) – (C) – (B)　　② (B) – (A) – (C)
③ (B) – (C) – (A)　　④ (C) – (A) – (B)
⑤ (C) – (B) – (A)

실력 UP! 미니 문제 주제 찾기

01. 윗글의 주제로 가장 적절한 것은?

① the process by which sedimentary rocks form
② the materials that are necessary for rock formation
③ the difference between sedimentary rocks on land and underwater

실력 UP! 미니 문제 내신 서술형

02. 윗글의 ⓐ, ⓑ가 지칭하는 바를 영어로 찾아 쓰시오.

ⓐ _____

ⓑ _____

03 주어진 글 다음에 이어질 글의 순서로 가장 적절한 것을 고르시오.

> While extracting scents and oils from flowers may seem like a difficult DIY project, it's easier than you think.

(A) Next, remove the petals from the flowers and put them in a plastic bag. Crush the petals gently to release the essential oils and then place them in a jar, covering them with olive oil. Gently shake the jar and leave it in a sunny spot for 24 hours.

(B) You don't need complicated equipment to get started; a simple garden containing plants such as roses or lavender is enough. Try to pick flowers that are not yet in full bloom as those that are just beginning to open contain the most fragrant and beneficial oils.

(C) This should be enough time for the petals to release their essence into the olive oil. Remove the old petals, gather new flowers, and repeat the whole process four or five times to get rich, fragrant essential oil.

① (A) – (C) – (B)　　② (B) – (A) – (C)
③ (B) – (C) – (A)　　④ (C) – (A) – (B)
⑤ (C) – (B) – (A)

04 주어진 글 다음에 이어질 글의 순서로 가장 적절한 것을 고르시오.

> There are a few places in which paralegals are allowed to perform the same job as a lawyer. However, most of the time, they are employed by law firms and perform a distinct function from lawyers.

(A) But paralegals also have other fundamental roles. Acting as representatives of a law firm, they are responsible for communicating with clients, and maintaining professional relationships with officials at courts, police departments, and other agencies.

(B) By performing either of ⓐthese basic functions, paralegals enable lawyers to work with maximum efficiency and focus on the needs of their clients. For these reasons, paralegals are considered to be essential personnel at law firms.

(C) Their primary duty is to support practicing lawyers. As such, their activities may include updating and organizing client files, drafting legal documents, or conducting case research, to name a few examples.

* paralegal: 법률 보조원, 패러리걸

① (A) – (C) – (B)　　② (B) – (A) – (C)
③ (B) – (C) – (A)　　④ (C) – (A) – (B)
⑤ (C) – (B) – (A)

실력 UP! 미니 문제 내신 서술형

03. 다음 영영 풀이에 적합한 단어를 윗글에서 찾아 쓰시오. (필요한 경우, 단어 형태 변경 가능)

ⓐ to separate or draw out a substance from something that contains it

→ _____

ⓑ having a positive impact or effect on something else

→ _____

실력 UP! 미니 문제 내신 서술형

04. 윗글의 ⓐ가 지칭하는 바를 영어로 찾아 쓰시오.

① _____

② _____

05 주어진 글 다음에 이어질 글의 순서로 가장 적절한 것을 고르시오.

A basic mechanism of evolution is natural selection, a process whereby particular variations in certain traits become more common over time.

(A) If, however, the butterflies happen to live among birds that eat orange butterflies in particular, the population of orange ones will gradually decrease over time. The white ones, meanwhile, will continue to flourish.

(B) As more time passes, the overall population will start to consist of fewer orange individuals and mostly white ones. The presence of the butterfly-eating birds will have created the natural conditions that favored the selection or survival of white-colored butterflies.

(C) For instance, suppose that the butterfly population in a particular location consists of both orange individuals and white ones. Normally, these butterflies will, in the process of reproduction, pass on each of their unique colors to their offspring.

① (A) – (C) – (B)　　② (B) – (A) – (C)
③ (B) – (C) – (A)　　④ (C) – (A) – (B)
⑤ (C) – (B) – (A)

06 주어진 글 다음에 이어질 글의 순서로 가장 적절한 것을 고르시오.

Independent media refers to any form of media that operates independently of government or corporate interests, so it is considered distinct from mainstream media.

(A) Having an alternative to mainstream media is important because, without it, powerful interests might get away with wrongdoing more easily. Therefore, independent media plays an important role in keeping power in check.

(B) Because they operate independently, members of independent media enjoy more "freedom." That is, they can set their own editorial direction. This creates the impression that they are less biased than mainstream media.

(C) People concerned about bias therefore turn to independent media to gain a different perspective on current events than that portrayed by mainstream media. That is why independent media is sometimes also known as alternative media.

① (A) – (C) – (B)　　② (B) – (A) – (C)
③ (B) – (C) – (A)　　④ (C) – (A) – (B)
⑤ (C) – (B) – (A)

실력 UP! 미니 문제 내신 서술형

05. 윗글의 내용을 다음과 같이 요약할 때, 빈칸에 들어갈 알맞은 말을 본문에서 찾아 쓰시오. (필요한 경우, 단어 형태 변경 가능)

Natural selection results in trait ⓐ v_____ that ultimately become favorable for the ⓑ s_____ of certain individuals in a population.

실력 UP! 미니 문제 주제 찾기

06. 윗글의 주제로 가장 적절한 것은?
① difference between government media and corporate media
② advantages of independent media over mainstream media
③ why independent media is less reliable than other forms of media

07 주어진 글 다음에 이어질 글의 순서로 가장 적절한 것을 고르시오.

If you have ever caught yourself yawning after someone around you does, you may wonder why, especially if you aren't tired or bored.

(A) In fact, being alert was very important millions of years ago, back when humans were prey rather than predators. If danger was near, it is thought that yawning may have been used as a way to increase concentration and, by extension, the likelihood of survival.

(B) Therefore, if someone in a group yawned, the other members of the group would do the same, expressing that they understood the need to be watchful. Over time, contagious yawning has become a way of showing empathy in times of shared boredom or so.

(C) Contagious yawning, as it is known, is believed to have evolved in early humans as a way to help our prehistoric ancestors stay alert. According to some scientists, yawning cools the brain, and people need a cool brain to be alert.

① (A) – (C) – (B)　　② (B) – (A) – (C)
③ (B) – (C) – (A)　　④ (C) – (A) – (B)
⑤ (C) – (B) – (A)

고난도
08 주어진 글 다음에 이어질 글의 순서로 가장 적절한 것을 고르시오.

Too often, people who suffer from insomnia are led to believe that their condition is a result of some personal "failing." Thus, they are told to either stop overthinking, try relaxing, or see a doctor for mental help.

(A) Through their studies of DNA, scientists have discovered that people who suffer from insomnia likely possess genes for sleeplessness in their brain. They have identified seven of these genes in total.

(B) However, researchers have been able to determine that the inability to sleep is not wholly psychological. Rather, sleeplessness is more likely to be biological, meaning it is the result of how people are born.

(C) Any one of the genes can cause people to experience constant bodily movements or an endless stream of thoughts. These conditions can, in turn, contribute to disrupted sleep or cause excessive wakefulness.

* insomnia: 불면증

① (A) – (C) – (B)　　② (B) – (A) – (C)
③ (B) – (C) – (A)　　④ (C) – (A) – (B)
⑤ (C) – (B) – (A)

실력UP! **미니 문제** 내신 서술형

07. 윗글의 내용을 다음과 같이 요약할 때, 빈칸에 들어갈 알맞은 말을 본문에서 찾아 쓰시오. (필요한 경우, 단어 형태 변경 가능)

Millions of years ago, Humans are believed to have

(A) e_____ contagious yawning because it helped them

to remain (B) a_____, increasing their chances of survival.

실력UP! **미니 문제** 주제 찾기

08. 윗글의 주제로 가장 적절한 것은?

① the ways DNA affects people's personalities

② the psychological reasons for sleep disorders

③ how studies have linked insomnia to genetics

CHAPTER 14
주어진 문장의 위치 찾기

유형소개 논리적 흐름상 주어진 문장이 자연스럽게 들어가는 위치를 찾는 유형으로, 3점짜리 고난도 문제로 자주 출제됨

문 제 수 2문제

지 시 문 글의 흐름으로 보아, 주어진 문장이 들어가기에 가장 적절한 곳을 고르시오.

불변의 패턴 27 | 패턴 빈출도 ★★★★☆
주어진 문장에는 앞뒤 문장에 대한 결정적인 단서가 있다.

🎧지문 듣기

주어진 문장에 있는 대명사, 관사, 연결어는 그 문장 앞뒤로 어떤 내용이 오는지 알려주는 중요한 단서이다.

- 대명사와 관사가 있으면 그것이 가리키는 대상이 언급된 문장을 찾는다. 주어진 문장은 그 뒤에 와야 한다.
- 연결어가 있으면, 연결어의 뜻을 바탕으로 논리 관계가 자연스러운 문장을 찾는다.

패턴맛보기

주어진 문장 앞과 뒤에 나올 내용을 ①, ②에서 파악하여 글을 알맞은 순서로 배열하시오.

> By contrast, many present-day stories have a less definitive ending.

① In the classical fairy tale, the conflict is often permanently resolved. Without exception, the hero and heroine live happily ever after.

② Often the conflict in those stories is only partly resolved, or a new conflict appears making the audience think further.

해석

이와 대조적으로, 오늘날의 많은 이야기들은 덜 확정적인 결말을 가진다.

① 고전 동화에서, 갈등은 종종 영구적으로 해결된다. 예외 없이, 남녀 주인공은 영원히 행복하게 산다.

② 흔히 이러한 이야기 속의 갈등은 부분적으로만 해결되거나, 관객들이 더 깊이 생각하게 만드는 새로운 갈등이 나타난다.

해설

주어진 문장의 By contrast(이와 대조적으로)를 통해 주어진 글 앞에는 주어진 글의 내용과 대조되는 내용이 와야함을 알 수 있다. ①은 고전 동화 속 갈등은 남녀 주인공이 영원히 행복하게 사는 내용과 같이 영구적으로 해결된다는 내용을 다루고 있고, ②은 오늘날 이야기 속의 갈등에 대해 이야기하고 있다. ①은 주어진 글의 내용과 대조되는 고전 동화 속 결말에 대한 내용이고, ②은 주어진 글에 대한 부연 설명이므로 글의 알맞은 순서는 ① → 주어진 글 → ②이다.

정답

① → 주어진 글 → ②

기출문제 2019년 3월 고1 학평   정답 및 해설 p.111

글의 흐름으로 보아, 주어진 문장이 들어가기에 가장 적절한 곳을 고르시오.

> This may have worked in the past, but today, with interconnected team processes, we don't want all people who are the same.

Most of us have hired many people based on human resources criteria along with some technical and personal information that the boss thought was important. (①) I have found that most people like to hire people just like themselves. (②) In a team, some need to be leaders, some need to be doers, some need to provide creative strengths, some need to be inspirers, some need to provide imagination, and so on. (③) In other words, we are looking for a diversified team where members complement one another. (④) When putting together a new team or hiring team members, we need to look at each individual and how he or she fits into the whole of our team objective. (⑤) The bigger the team, the more possibilities exist for diversity.

* criteria: 기준

불변의 패턴28

패턴 빈출도 ★★★★☆

뜬금없는 대명사나 지시어, 어색한 연결어가 있는 문장 앞이 정답이다.

🎧 지문 듣기

글의 흐름상 어색한 부분을 찾는 것이 관건이다. 무엇을 가리키는지 명확하지 않은 대명사나 지시어가 나오거나, 연결어가 어색한 경우 그 문장 앞이 정답이다. 정답의 위치에 주어진 문장을 넣어 흐름이 자연스러운지 확인하면 된다.

패턴맛보기

다음 글에서 흐름이 끊기는 부분을 고르시오.

It is important to realize that shopping is really a search for information. (①) You may obtain information from an advertisement, a friend, a salesperson, the Internet, or several other sources. (②) You may also gain information from actual use of the product, such as trying on a dress, or test-driving a car. (③) These costs may include transportation costs and time. (④) Only you can decide whether to take the costs or not.

[해석]

쇼핑은 사실상 정보 탐색이라는 것을 깨닫는 것이 중요하다. 당신은 광고, 친구, 판매원, 인터넷, 또는 여러 기타 출처에서 정보를 얻을 수 있다. 당신은 드레스를 입어보거나 자동차를 시승하는 등, 제품을 실제로 사용해보며 정보를 얻을 수도 있다. 이러한 비용들에는 교통비와 시간이 포함될 수 있다. 그 비용을 지불할지 안 할지는 오직 당신만 결정할 수 있다.

[해설]

③ 앞 문장까지 쇼핑을 위한 정보 탐색의 종류와 방법을 설명한다. 그런데 ③ 뒤 문장에서 These costs(이러한 비용들)를 통해 ③ 앞에서는 언급되지 않았던 "비용"과 관련된 내용이 나오므로 ③ 뒤부터 글의 흐름이 끊긴 것을 알 수 있다.

[정답]
③

기출문제 2020년 3월 고1 학평   정답 및 해설 p.111

글의 흐름으로 보아, 주어진 문장이 들어가기에 가장 적절한 곳을 고르시오.

> In the U.S. we have so many metaphors for time and its passing that we think of time as "a thing," that is "the weekend is almost gone," or "I haven't got the time."

There are some cultures that can be referred to as "people who live outside of time." The Amondawa tribe, living in Brazil, does not have a concept of time that can be measured or counted. (①) Rather they live in a world of serial events, rather than seeing events as being rooted in time. (②) Researchers also found that no one had an age. (③) Instead, they change their names to reflect their stage of life and position within their society, so a little child will give up their name to a newborn sibling and take on a new one. (④) We think such statements are objective, but they aren't. (⑤) We create these metaphors, but the Amondawa don't talk or think in metaphors for time.

* metaphor: 은유 ** sibling: 형제자매

독해 만점 TEST

01 글의 흐름으로 보아, 주어진 문장이 들어가기에 가장 적절한 곳을 고르시오.

> To test (A)their effectiveness, hundreds of patients having minor surgical treatments were divided into five groups.

Those who undergo medical procedures that require them to stay awake often experience anxiety. (①) Thus, a study was performed to see if certain simple methods could be used to keep people's minds occupied during (B)such surgeries. (②) These were listening to music, watching a movie, squeezing a rubber ball, and talking to a nurse. (③) Each was assigned to use one method, while the final group went through the process without any aids. (④) Songs failed to have any effect at all but speaking with a nurse reduced anxiety by 30 percent. (⑤) Watching a film also lowered anxiousness by 25 percent, while the rubber balls reduced such feelings by 18 percent.

02 글의 흐름으로 보아, 주어진 문장이 들어가기에 가장 적절한 곳을 고르시오.

> These cells are connected to our eyes and are thus highly affected by changes in light levels.

Circadian rhythms are internally driven biological processes that follow a 24-hour cycle. (①) They are present in most living things. (②) Circadian rhythms are controlled by nerve cells in our brain, which act as the body's internal clock. (③) This is why we normally start to wake up as the day grows bright and begin to feel restful after it grows dark. (④) This also helps to explain why artificial light can trick our bodies into staying awake. (⑤) And there are other factors besides light that can influence the regulation of our circadian rhythms, including physical movement and body temperature.

* circadian rhythms: 생체리듬

실력 UP! 미니 문제 내신 서술형

01. 윗글의 밑줄 친 (A), (B)가 의미하는 것을 우리말로 쓰시오.

(A) _____

(B) _____

실력 UP! 미니 문제 주제 찾기

02. 윗글의 주제로 가장 적절한 것은?
① how circadian rhythms impact brain cells
② the role circadian rhythms play in our bodies
③ the importance of light in biological processes

03 글의 흐름으로 보아, 주어진 문장이 들어가기에 가장 적절한 곳을 고르시오.

> Its popularity grew among the working classes and extended to people living in Portugal's colonies.

Fado is an important native musical genre from Portugal. It has been performed for nearly 200 years. (①) Its precise origins are unclear, but many scholars believe it began among sailors in the country's capital city, Lisbon. (②) Most early examples deal with the intense longing for home that one feels while living at sea. (③) At the same time, the families left behind also sang these songs to express their yearning to see their loved ones again. (④) Over time, the fado was sung about other similarly mournful topics, such as living a life of poverty. (⑤) In the former Portuguese colonies of Brazil and Indonesia, for example, their traditional songs share characteristics of the fado.

실력 UP! 미니 문제 주제 찾기

03. 윗글의 주제로 가장 적절한 것은?
① the history and characteristics of fado
② the popularity of fado among the working class
③ the spread of fado from Portugal to other countries

04 글의 흐름으로 보아, 주어진 문장이 들어가기에 가장 적절한 곳을 고르시오.

> When you eventually return home, revisit your issue with a clear mind.

Whenever you can't make up your mind about an important life decision, going for a walk is a good idea. It should not be an ordinary walk, however. Take each step slowly and especially pay attention to your breathing in order to relax. (①) It helps to inhale deeply through your nose and exhale slowly through your mouth. (②) The deliberate pace of both will help you consider your thoughts more carefully. (③) You don't need to worry about which streets you should take or where you'll end up. (④) Instead, simply enjoy the passing scenery and let it inspire you to look at things from a different perspective. (⑤) By reconsidering your problem with fresh eyes, the chances of making the right decision greatly increase.

실력 UP! 미니 문제 내신 서술형

04. 윗글의 요지를 우리말로 쓰시오.

_____

05 글의 흐름으로 보아, 주어진 문장이 들어가기에 가장 적절한 곳을 고르시오.

However, this type of thinking can be unreliable and lead to incorrect conclusions.

Associative thinking occurs when we make connections in our brain based on previous experiences. (①) These connections happen subconsciously and almost immediately, causing us to judge situations quickly. (②) When we meet someone for the first time, for instance, we might associate the way a person dresses with a specific personality based on others we have met before who dress the same way. (③) This is one of the reasons we think we can immediately tell a lot about people from the moment we meet them. (④) The error in judgment results from our tendency to build on an initial assumption by finding evidence to support it. (⑤) Such an assumption can cause us to ignore later evidence that, although accurate, contradicts our initial belief.

* subconsciously: 무의식적으로

06 글의 흐름으로 보아, 주어진 문장이 들어가기에 가장 적절한 곳을 고르시오.

Another piece of evidence is that most of its plant and animal species cannot be found anywhere else.

Located in the southern hemisphere, Australia is the smallest continent on the planet, with an area of just over 7,690,000 square kilometers. (①) People commonly refer to Australia as an island, but it has a number of features that clearly indicate that it is a continent. (②) To begin with, while Australia is small by continent standards, it is nearly four times bigger than Greenland, which geographers have identified as the planet's largest island. (③) In addition, the tectonic plate that Australia is located on does not include any other continents. (④) This distinguishes it from Greenland, which is considered to be part of North America because it is on the same plate as this continent. (⑤) The presence of these unique life forms shows that Australia has been physically separated from the other continents for an extremely long period of time.

* tectonic plate: 지각판

실력 UP! 미니 문제 주제 찾기

05. 윗글의 주제로 가장 적절한 것은?
① errors that can be corrected with associative thinking
② the way that subconscious feelings influence our clothing choices
③ how associative thinking can result in false judgment

실력 UP! 미니 문제 내신 서술형

06. 다음 질문을 읽고 한 문장의 영어로 답하시오.
Q: What does the presence of unique life forms show about Australia?
A: _____

_____ .

07 글의 흐름으로 보아, 주어진 문장이 들어가기에 가장 적절한 곳을 고르시오.

> This involves teaching patients to identify harmful behaviors and replace them with positive ones.

Affecting millions of people worldwide, eating disorders are psychological conditions that cause harmful behaviors when it comes to eating food. (①) Although they can take a variety of forms, the two most common affect how much food is eaten. (②) Anorexia is an eating disorder that causes a person to eat too little food, often resulting in extreme weight loss. (③) In contrast, bulimia leads an individual to overeat and then to force himself or herself to vomit immediately afterward. (④) Fortunately, a method called Cognitive Behavioral Therapy (CBT), which is highly effective in helping people overcome eating disorders has been developed. (⑤) For example, patients with bulimia who overeat when they feel stressed may be encouraged to meditate or exercise instead.

고난도

08 글의 흐름으로 보아, 주어진 문장이 들어가기에 가장 적절한 곳을 고르시오.

> On the other hand, if they do prepare and fail, they cannot attribute their failure to outside factors.

Self-sabotage may seem like contradictory behavior for someone who wants to succeed, but a surprising number of people do this. (①) One of the biggest reasons is that most people do not like believing themselves unintelligent. (②) For example, if students intentionally avoid studying for a difficult exam and then get poor scores, they can justify the results by saying they didn't study. (③) Others might point to a lack of sleep or being distracted by personal problems. (④) By blaming something other than their ability, students can feel better about failing because it wasn't really their fault. (⑤) That is, they only failed because even after studying, it turns out that they were not smart enough to pass the test.

* self-sabotage: 자기 훼방

실력 UP! 미니 문제 내신 서술형

07. 윗글의 내용을 다음과 같이 요약할 때, 빈칸에 들어갈 알맞은 말을 본문에서 찾아 쓰시오. (필요한 경우, 단어 형태 변경 가능)

Although eating disorders are widespread and lead to
(A) h＿＿＿＿＿＿＿ behaviors, a treatment called Cognitive Behavioral Therapy has proven successful in helping people
(B) o＿＿＿＿＿＿＿ these conditions.

실력 UP! 미니 문제 내신 서술형

08. 다음 영영 풀이에 적합한 단어를 윗글에서 찾아 쓰시오.

ⓐ causing something to conflict with itself

→ ＿＿＿＿＿＿＿＿＿＿＿＿＿＿＿＿

ⓑ having been enacted willfully and on purpose

→ ＿＿＿＿＿＿＿＿＿＿＿＿＿＿＿＿

CHAPTER 15

요약문 완성하기

유형소개 글의 핵심 내용을 한 문장으로 요약한 요약문의 빈칸에 들어갈 적절한 단어를 찾는 유형으로, 실험, 연구 내용, 개인적 경험 등 다양한 소재의 글이 출제됨

문제수 1문제

지시문 다음 글의 내용을 한 문장으로 요약하고자 한다. 빈칸 (A), (B)에 들어갈 말로 가장 적절한 것은?

불변의 패턴 29

패턴 빈출도 ★★★★★

요약문은 글의 핵심 내용을 간추린 요지이다.

🎧 지문 듣기

요약문은 글의 핵심 내용을 한 문장으로 표현한 요지이다. 문제를 풀 때 먼저 요약문부터 읽고 글의 요지가 무엇인지 파악한 후 글을 읽으면 정답을 더 쉽고 빠르게 찾을 수 있다.

패턴맛보기

다음 요약문을 통해 짐작할 수 있는 글의 내용으로 적절한 것을 고르시오.

According to the experiment, students' interest in a topic (A) _____ when they are encouraged to (B) _____.

① 학생들의 흥미를 불러일으키는 요인에 관한 실험
② 학생들이 실험에 참여하기 싫어하는 이유에 대한 실험
③ 학생들의 참여가 저조한 수업에 관한 실험

[해석]
그 실험에 따르면, 어떤 주제에 대한 학생들의 흥미는 그들이 (B) _____ 하도록 장려될 때 (A) _____ 한다.

[해설]
요약문은 어떠한 실험의 결과에 따르면 어떠한 주제에 대한 학생들의 흥미는 그들이 '무엇'하도록 장려될 때 '무엇'한다는 내용이다. 요약문을 통해 이 글이 어떤 주제에 대해 학생들의 흥미를 불러일으키는 요인에 관한 실험 결과임을 알 수 있으므로, ①이 정답이다.

[정답]
①

기출문제 2021년 3월 고1 학평

정답 및 해설 p.117

다음 글의 내용을 한 문장으로 요약하고자 한다. 빈칸 (A), (B)에 들어갈 말로 가장 적절한 것은?

In one study, researchers asked pairs of strangers to sit down in a room and chat. In half of the rooms, a cell phone was placed on a nearby table; in the other half, no phone was present. After the conversations had ended, the researchers asked the participants what they thought of each other. Here's what they learned: when a cell phone was present in the room, the participants reported the quality of their relationship was worse than those who'd talked in a cell phone-free room. The pairs who talked in the rooms with cell phones thought their partners showed less empathy. Think of all the times you've sat down to have lunch with a friend and set your phone on the table. You might have felt good about yourself because you didn't pick it up to check your messages, but your unchecked messages were still hurting your connection with the person sitting across from you.

* empathy: 공감

↓

The presence of a cell phone _____(A)_____ the connection between people involved in conversations, even when the phone is being _____(B)_____.

	(A)		(B)
①	weakens	⋯	answered
②	weakens	⋯	ignored
③	renews	⋯	answered
④	maintains	⋯	ignored
⑤	maintains	⋯	updated

불변의 패턴30

패턴 빈출도 ★★★★☆

핵심 단어를 다르게 표현한 단어가 정답이다.

🎧지문 듣기

요약문의 빈칸에는 핵심 단어가 들어가는데, 정답의 선택지는 이를 다른 말로 바꾸어 표현한 것이므로 핵심 단어의 유의어로 조합된 선택지를 고른다.

패턴맛보기

다음 글의 밑줄 친 부분을 다르게 표현한 것으로 가장 적절한 말을 찾아서 요약문을 완성하시오.

According to an Australian study, those who are proud of the dishes they make are more likely to enjoy eating vegetarian food and health food. Moreover, this group is more likely than the average person to enjoy eating diverse kinds of food: from salads and seafood to hamburgers and chips.

↓

In general, people who are confident in cooking are more likely to enjoy _____ foods than those who are not.

① various　　　　　② specific
③ healthy

[해석]
호주의 한 연구에 따르면, 자신이 만든 요리를 자랑스러워하는 사람들은 채식과 건강식품을 더 즐겨 먹는 경향이 있다고 한다. 게다가, 이러한 집단은 샐러드와 해산물부터 햄버거와 감자 칩에 이르기까지 다양한 종류의 음식을 먹는 것을 보통 사람들보다 더 즐기는 경향이 있다.

↓

일반적으로 요리에 자신감이 있는 사람들은 그렇지 않은 사람들보다 _____ 한 음식을 즐길 가능성이 더 높다.

① 다양한　　　　　② 특정한
③ 건강한

[해설]
밑줄 친 단어 diverse는 '다양한'을 의미하는 단어이고, 요약문은 요리에 자신감이 있는 사람들은 그렇지 않은 사람들보다 '어떠한' 음식을 즐길 가능성이 더 높다는 내용이다. 선택지 중 diverse를 다르게 표현한 말 중 가장 적절한 것은 various(다양한)이므로 ①이 정답이다.

[정답]
①

기출문제 2018년 6월 고2 학평

정답 및 해설 p.118

다음 글의 내용을 한 문장으로 요약하고자 한다. 빈칸 (A), (B)에 들어갈 말로 가장 적절한 것은?

The wife of American physiologist Hudson Hoagland became sick with a severe flu. Dr. Hoagland was curious enough to notice that whenever he left his wife's room for a short while, she complained that he had been gone for a long time. In the interest of scientific investigation, he asked his wife to count to 60, with each count corresponding to what she felt was one second, while he kept a record of her temperature. His wife reluctantly accepted and he quickly noticed that the hotter she was, the faster she counted. When her temperature was 38 degrees Celsius, for instance, she counted to 60 in 45 seconds. He repeated the experiment a few more times, and found that when her temperature reached 39.5 degrees Celsius, she counted one minute in just 37 seconds. The doctor thought that his wife must have some kind of 'internal clock' inside her brain that ran faster as the fever went up.

↓

The results of Dr. Hoagland's investigation showed that his wife felt _____(A)_____ time had passed than actually had as her body temperature _____(B)_____.

　　(A)　　　　　(B)
① more　⋯　increased
② more　⋯　decreased
③ less　⋯　increased
④ less　⋯　decreased
⑤ less　⋯　changed

01 다음 글의 내용을 한 문장으로 요약하고자 한다. 빈칸 (A), (B)에 들어갈 말로 가장 적절한 것은?

People tend to let their emotions take over and act against their better judgment when they stand to lose a large amount of money. ⓐThis erroneous thinking is called the gambler's fallacy, and the most famous example occurred in 1913 at the Monte Carlo Casino. Because the roulette ball had landed on black 26 times in a row, gamblers concluded that the probability of it landing on black again was next to impossible. They used this, their knowledge of what had already happened, to inform their next move. They bet all their money on red, but the ball landed on black yet again, and they ultimately lost. This is because, according to the laws of probability, there is always an equal chance of the ball landing on black or red in roulette, regardless of any earlier lucky "coincidences." Essentially, each spin produces a random result that is unrelated to any before it.

⇩

In gambling, people mistakenly make decisions based on ____(A)____ outcomes when each event is actually ____(B)____.

	(A)		(B)
①	previous	⋯	intended
②	unknown	⋯	real
③	previous	⋯	independent
④	positive	⋯	likely
⑤	unknown	⋯	unpredictable

실력UP! 미니 문제 내신 서술형

01. 윗글의 밑줄 친 ⓐ가 의미하는 것을 우리말로 쓰시오.

ⓐ _____

_____

02 다음 글의 내용을 한 문장으로 요약하고자 한다. 빈칸 (A), (B)에 들어갈 말로 가장 적절한 것은?

Your sleeping habits could reveal quite a lot about you, such as the type of personality you are likely to have, the composition of your brain, and even how long you may be expected to live. As it happens, morning people tend to display more positive social traits and are less prone to depression, addiction, and other obsessive behavior. Doctors believe these factors contribute to a longer lifespan. Night people, on the other hand, have less white matter in their brains, and as a result have fewer pathways for feel-good hormones such as serotonin. Although night people tend to be more creative and have higher intellectual abilities than morning types, going against the body's natural rhythm over a prolonged period can also shorten their lifespan.

⇩

Morning people are more likely to be ____(A)____ and live longer lives, whereas night people are likely to be more ____(B)____ and creative.

	(A)		(B)
①	cheerful	⋯	confident
②	cheerful	⋯	disciplined
③	optimistic	⋯	intelligent
④	optimistic	⋯	limited
⑤	advantageous	⋯	successful

실력UP! 미니 문제 내신 서술형

02. 윗글에서 아침형 인간과 저녁형 인간 각각의 특징을 찾아 우리말로 쓰시오.

아침형 인간: _____

_____

저녁형 인간: _____

_____

03 다음 글의 내용을 한 문장으로 요약하고자 한다. 빈칸 (A), (B)에 들어갈 말로 가장 적절한 것은?

Experts are divided on the best way to structure primary and secondary education systems. Specialists maintain that youngsters should be encouraged to enter into specific areas of study, such as engineering or the arts, from the earliest age possible. The underlying belief is that education is a social construct that should be used to guide citizens into the roles ⓐthey are best suited for so that they can make significant contributions to society. In contrast, generalists argue that the role of education is to turn students into well-rounded individuals. ⓑThey believe that while learners may choose to focus on one field in college, they should learn about many general subjects when they are young. Such an approach is student-centered and has the goal of creating students who can appreciate a diversity of topics.

* well-rounded: 다재다능한

⇩

Some debate remains over whether children should be guided toward _____(A)_____ careers or given the _____(B)_____ education possible.

	(A)	(B)		(A)	(B)
①	special	⋯ highest	②	social	⋯ longest
③	important	⋯ broadest	④	particular	⋯ broadest
⑤	unique	⋯ highest			

실력 UP! 미니 문제 내신 서술형

03. 윗글의 ⓐ, ⓑ가 지칭하는 바를 영어로 찾아 쓰시오.

ⓐ _____

ⓑ _____

04 다음 글의 내용을 한 문장으로 요약하고자 한다. 빈칸 (A), (B)에 들어갈 말로 가장 적절한 것은?

Although making the f and v sounds while speaking is natural for us now, it might not have always been the case for people. During the Paleolithic period, the majority of ancient humans had teeth that met edge to edge. They needed this jaw structure because of their hunter-gatherer diet, which was made up of tougher foods. Over time, however, people developed agriculture and food therefore became softer. Humans started eating yogurts and stews and this led to alterations in jaw shape. Their upper jaws began to horizontally overlap their lower jaws, giving them the ability to put their lower lip on their upper teeth. Because of this, people could start making the f and v sounds. An adjustment to diet ended up affecting how we communicate, giving us two of the major sounds we use to form speech today.

* Paleolithic: 구석기의

⇩

The addition of softer foods to the human diet _____(A)_____ jaw structure, and this _____(B)_____ people to start using the f and v sounds.

	(A)	(B)		(A)	(B)
①	complicated	⋯ trained	②	changed	⋯ allowed
③	weakened	⋯ trained	④	changed	⋯ attracted
⑤	complicated	⋯ allowed			

실력 UP! 미니 문제 내신 서술형

04. 다음 문장을 우리말로 해석하시오.

Over time, however, people developed agriculture and food therefore became softer.

→ _____

_____

05 다음 글의 내용을 한 문장으로 요약하고자 한다. 빈칸 (A), (B)에 들어갈 말로 가장 적절한 것은?

Some of us see nothing wrong with the relentless pursuit of wealth and social status. But the trouble with human beings is that we are biologically programmed to want more. Throughout our evolutionary history, it was those who sought more resources and an elevated social rank that survived and reproduced. By adopting this mentality in the modern world, however, we are destined to be unhappy. We will never stop striving for bigger and better, whether it is a larger house or a more prominent social circle. We will keep trying to climb the corporate ladder or earn a better spot in the social hierarchy, and when we fail, we will be frustrated. While success may give us momentary pleasure, it will not be long before our desire for more eventually reappears.

⇩

Although people continue to _____(A)_____ more than they have, they never seem to be _____(B)_____ for long.

	(A)		(B)
①	spend	···	disappointed
②	desire	···	satisfied
③	spend	···	satisfied
④	gain	···	disappointed
⑤	desire	···	interested

실력 UP! 미니 문제 내신 서술형

05. 윗글의 요지를 <보기>에 있는 단어만을 활용하여 어법에 맞게 쓰시오.

부와 사회적 지위를 끊임없이 추구하는 것은 만족으로 이어지지 않을 것이다.
<보기> satisfaction / result in / wealth and social status / constantly pursuing / will / not

_____

_____

06 다음 글의 내용을 한 문장으로 요약하고자 한다. 빈칸 (A), (B)에 들어갈 말로 가장 적절한 것은?

Israel Abramov, a behavioral neuroscientist at CUNY's Brooklyn College, studied the difference between how men and women perceive color. To conduct his study, he asked men and women to describe various colors by categorizing them as shades of red, yellow, green, or blue with a percentage. Interestingly, women were able to notice small differences between colors which men described as the same. This may explain previous research showing that women have a much larger and more creative color vocabulary than men. Then, he showed the participants light and dark bars flashing on a screen. This time, men were better than women at noticing variations in brightness, indicating that it was easier for men to spot big differences.

* neuroscientist: 신경 과학자

⇩

Women are able to see _____(A)_____ differences in colors, while men excel at detecting _____(B)_____ changes in the level of light.

	(A)		(B)			(A)		(B)
①	slight	···	minor		②	random	···	simple
③	great	···	similar		④	slight	···	huge
⑤	random	···	excessive					

실력 UP! 미니 문제 내신 서술형

06. 다음 질문을 읽고 한 문장의 영어로 답하시오.

Q: According to the results of the experiment, what were men better than women at?

A: Men were better at _____.

07 다음 글의 내용을 한 문장으로 요약하고자 한다. 빈칸 (A), (B)에 들어갈 말로 가장 적절한 것은?

The secret words and phrases shared exclusively among the members of a household are what linguists call familect. One of the most extensive familect studies was conducted by Cynthia Gordon, a professor of linguistics at Georgetown University. She found that many families continually use a set of terms and expressions, often associated with inside jokes, nicknames, and the words and sounds that young children invent as they learn to talk. As the meaning of these unique expressions is only used within the family group, a special bond that reinforces the family's identity as a team is formed. Even after children have grown up and left the household, using familect is a way to bring the family back together, and to recall their old memories. In a sense, it is a sort of glue holding families together.

⇩

Using familect ____(A)____ a sense of unity and can keep families ____(B)____ .

	(A)		(B)
①	breaks	···	apart
②	distorts	···	happy
③	creates	···	close
④	criticizes	···	close
⑤	develops	···	apart

실력 UP! 미니 문제 내신 서술형

07. 다음 질문을 읽고 한 문장의 영어로 답하시오.

Q: According to the passage, what is the definition of familect?

A: Familect is _____

_____ .

〔고난도〕

08 다음 글의 내용을 한 문장으로 요약하고자 한다. 빈칸 (A), (B)에 들어갈 말로 가장 적절한 것은?

In a 1971 social psychology experiment at Stanford University, student volunteers were assigned to the roles of either prisoner or guard in a simulated prison. Prior to the experiment, none of the students had seemed noticeably more aggressive or passive than anyone else. However, this would soon change. Those assigned to play guards were permitted to maintain order however they wanted. ⓐThey quickly abused their freedom by treating the prisoners unfairly and handing out cruel punishments. Meanwhile, the students playing prisoners were obedient because they were afraid of the consequences of disobeying. Essentially, ⓑthey began exhibiting behaviors that one might expect to see in actual prisoners. It was therefore determined that the behavior of each group of students was a result of the situations they were put in and the roles they were assigned. It was also proposed that the specific conditions of a situation could make people assume roles and adopt personality traits that are not typical for them.

⇩

An experiment studying prison life suggested that ____(A)____ factors cause people to ____(B)____ the roles they are expected to play.

	(A)	(B)		(A)	(B)
①	environmental	··· resist	②	internal	··· adjust
③	biological	··· apply	④	internal	··· reject
⑤	environmental	··· follow			

실력 UP! 미니 문제 내신 서술형

08. 윗글의 ⓐ, ⓑ가 지칭하는 바를 영어로 찾아 쓰시오.

ⓐ _____

ⓑ _____

장문 독해

유형소개 긴 지문을 읽고 문제에 답하는 유형으로, 1지문 2문제(장문 독해①), 1지문 3문제(장문 독해②)가 각각 하나씩 출제됨

지시문 장문 독해①: 윗글의 제목으로 가장 적절한 것은?
　　　　밑줄 친 (a) ~ (e) 중에서 문맥상 낱말의 쓰임이 적절하지 않은 것은?
　　　　or 윗글의 빈칸에 들어갈 말로 가장 적절한 것은?
　　　장문 독해②: 주어진 글 (A)에 이어질 내용을 순서에 맞게 배열한 것으로 가장 적절한 것은?
　　　　밑줄 친 (a) ~ (e) 중에서 가리키는 대상이 나머지 넷과 다른 것은?
　　　　~에 관한 내용으로 적절하지 않은 것은?

불변의 패턴31 · 패턴 빈출도 ★★★★★
장문 독해①은 주로 학술적 내용의 설명문이 나온다.

지문 듣기

의학, 과학, 예술 등 학술적인 분야의 소재를 활용한 설명문이 주로 나오는데, 이 종류의 글은 마지막에 주제문이 나오는 경우가 많다. 주제를 확실히 이해하면 적절한 제목을 파악하거나 문맥에 맞지 않는 어휘를 찾는 것이 훨씬 수월하다.

패턴맛보기

Many high school students study and learn inefficiently because they insist on doing their homework while watching TV or listening to loud music. These teenagers argue that they can study (a) worse with the TV or radio playing. Some professionals actually support their position. They argue that many teenagers can actually study productively under less than ideal conditions because they've been exposed repeatedly to "background noise" since early childhood. This position is certainly not generally shared, however. Many teachers and learning experts are convinced by their own experiences that students who study in a noisy environment often learn (b) inefficiently.

01. 윗글을 읽고 주제문에 밑줄을 그으시오.

02. 밑줄 친 (a)~(b) 중에서 문맥상 낱말의 쓰임이 적절하지 않은 것을 찾아서 바르게 고쳐 쓰시오.

(　　) → ＿＿＿＿＿＿＿＿＿＿＿＿＿＿＿

해석
많은 고등학생들은 TV를 보거나 시끄러운 음악을 들으면서 그들의 숙제를 하는 것을 고집하기 때문에 비효율적으로 공부하고 학습한다. 이런 십대들은 그들이 TV나 라디오를 켜둔 채로 공부를 하면 (a) 더 못하게(→ 더 잘하게) 된다고 주장한다. 실제로 일부 전문가들은 그들의 견해를 지지한다. 그들은 많은 십대들이 어린 시절부터 반복적으로 "배경 소음"에 노출되어 왔기 때문에 실제로 전혀 이상적이지 않은 상황에서 생산적으로 공부할 수 있다고 주장한다. 그러나 이 견해는 분명히 일반적으로 공유되는 것은 아니다. 많은 교사와 학습 전문가들은 시끄러운 환경에서 공부하는 학생들이 흔히 (b) 비효율적으로 학습한다는 것을 그들 자신의 경험으로 확신한다.

해설
01. 글의 내용에 따르면 일부 전문가들은 주의를 산만하게 하는 것과 함께 해야 공부가 더 잘된다는 십대들의 의견에 대해 동의하지만, 이들의 견해는 일반적으로 공유되는 것이 아니며, 많은 교사와 학습 전문가들은 오히려 시끄러운 환경에서 공부하는 학생들이 비효율적이라는 점을 자신들의 경험으로 확신한다고 했다. 따라서 이 글의 주제문은 "많은 교사와 학습 전문가들은 시끄러운 환경에서 공부하는 학생들이 흔히 비효율적으로 학습한다는 것을 그들 자신의 경험으로 확신한다."이다.

02. 일부 전문가들은 많은 십대들이 어린 시절부터 반복적으로 "배경 소음"에 노출되어 왔기 때문에 TV를 보거나 시끄러운 음악이 나오는 환경에서도 생산적으로 공부할 수 있다고 하며 주의를 산만하게 하는 것과 함께 공부하는 십대들의 의견을 지지한다고 했다. 따라서 이런 십대들은 TV나 라디오를 켜둔 채로 공부를 "더 잘하게" 된다고 주장한다는 맥락이 되어야 하므로 (a)의 worse(더 못하게)를 better(더 잘하게)와 같은 어휘로 바꿔야 적절하다.

정답
① Many teachers and learning experts are convinced by their own experiences that students who study in a noisy environment often learn inefficiently.
② (a) → better

[41~42] 다음 글을 읽고, 물음에 답하시오.

A quick look at history shows that humans have not always had the abundance of food that is enjoyed throughout most of the developed world today. In fact, there have been numerous times in history when food has been rather scarce. As a result, people used to eat more when food was available since the availability of the next meal was (a) questionable. Overeating in those times was essential to ensure survival, and humans received satisfaction from eating more than was needed for immediate purposes. On top of that, the highest pleasure was derived from eating the most calorie-dense foods, resulting in a (b) longer lasting energy reserve. Even though there are parts of the world where, unfortunately, food is still scarce, most of the world's population today has plenty of food available to survive and thrive. However, this abundance is new, and your body has not caught up, still naturally (c) rewarding you for eating more than you need and for eating the most calorie-dense foods. These are innate habits and not simple addictions. They are self-preserving mechanisms initiated by your body, ensuring your future survival, but they are (d) irrelevant now. Therefore, it is your responsibility to communicate with your body regarding the new environment of food abundance and the need to (e) strengthen the inborn habit of overeating.

* innate: 타고난

41. 윗글의 제목으로 가장 적절한 것은?

① Which Is Better, Tasty or Healthy Food?
② Simple Steps for a More Balanced Diet
③ Overeating: It's Rooted in Our Genes
④ How Calorie-dense Foods Ruin Our Bodies
⑤ Our Eating Habits Reflect Our Personalities

42. 밑줄 친 (a)~(e) 중에서 문맥상 낱말의 쓰임이 적절하지 않은 것은?

① (a)   ② (b)   ③ (c)   ④ (d)   ⑤ (e)

다양한 일상의 에피소드를 다루는 일화가 나오는데, 주로 배경과 등장 인물들을 소개한 뒤 사건이 전개되며 교훈적 결론을 맺는 구조로 이루어진다. 사건의 논리적 흐름을 이해하여 글의 순서를 먼저 파악하면 지칭 추론과 세부 정보 파악 문제를 더 쉽게 해결할 수 있다.

TIP 지칭 추론 문제는 선택지의 대명사가 가리키는 등장 인물의 이니셜을 표시하면서 푸는 것이 좋다.

패턴맛보기

다음 글을 읽고, 물음에 답하시오.

(A) Deep in the forest, (a) he spotted a beautiful wild deer. It was a large stag.

(B) When (b) he killed the deer with just one shot of his arrow, the king was filled with pride.

(C) Once upon a time, there lived a young king who had a great passion for hunting. Once every year, (c) he would go hunting in the nearby forests.

(D) Like all other years, the hunting season had arrived.

01. 주어진 글의 (A)~(D)를 순서대로 나열하시오.

_____

02. 밑줄 친 (a)~(c)가 공통으로 가리키는 대상을 적으시오.

_____

03. 윗글의 내용과 일치하면 O, 아니면 X를 고르시오.
① 왕은 매년 근처의 숲으로 사냥 여행을 갔다. [O / X]
② 왕은 숲속에서 사슴을 발견하지 못했다. [O / X]
③ 왕은 사냥감을 한발의 화살로 바로 명중시켰다. [O / X]

해석

(C) 먼 옛날에, 사냥에 대한 큰 열정을 가진 젊은 왕이 살았다. 1년에 한 번씩, (c) 그는 근처의 숲으로 사냥을 하러 가곤 했다.

(D) 다른 모든 해처럼, 사냥을 할 계절이 왔다.

(A) 숲속 깊은 곳에서, (a) 그는 아름다운 야생 사슴을 발견했다. 그것은 크기가 큰 수사슴이었다.

(B) (b) 그가 단 한 발의 화살로 그 사슴을 죽였을 때, 왕은 자부심으로 가득 찼다.

해설

01. (C)는 부정관사(a)를 사용하여 사냥에 대한 큰 열정을 가진 한 젊은 왕(a young king)을 처음으로 언급하고 있으므로 주어진 글의 맨 앞에 나와야 한다. (D)의 all other years는 (C)의 Once every year와 연결되므로 (D)는 (C) 다음에 이어지는 것이 적절하다. (A)에서 왕은 아름다운 야생 사슴을 발견했고, (B)에서 그는 단 한발의 화살로 그 사슴을 죽였다고 했으므로 (A) 다음에 (B)가 이어지는 것이 자연스럽다. 따라서 주어진 글의 순서는 (C) - (D) - (A) - (B)이다.

02. 숲에서 수사슴을 발견하고 화살을 쏜 사람은 왕이므로 (a)~(c)가 공통으로 가리키는 대상은 the king / a young king(왕/젊은 왕)이다.

03.
① (C)의 Once every year ~에서 왕은 1년에 한 번씩 근처의 숲으로 사냥을 간다고 했으므로 ①은 글의 내용과 일치한다.
② (A)의 Deep in the forest, he spotted a beautiful wild deer에서 왕은 숲속에서 사슴을 발견했다고 했으므로 ②은 글의 내용과 일치하지 않는다.
③ (B)의 he killed the deer with just one shot of his arrow에서 왕이 한 발의 화살로 사슴을 죽였다고 했으므로 ③은 글의 내용과 일치한다.

정답
01. (C) - (D) - (A) - (B)
02. the king / a young king
03. ① O, ② X, ③ O

[43~45] 다음 글을 읽고, 물음에 답하시오.

(A)

Dorothy was home alone. She was busy with a school project, and suddenly wanted to eat French fries. She peeled two potatoes, sliced them up and put a pot with cooking oil on the stove. Then the telephone rang. It was her best friend Samantha. While chatting away on the phone, Dorothy noticed a strange light shining from the kitchen, and then (a) she remembered about the pot of oil on the stove!

(B)

A while later, after the wound had been treated, the family sat around the kitchen table and talked. "I learned a big lesson today," Dorothy said. Her parents expected (b) her to say something about the fire. But she talked about something different. "I have decided to use kind words more just like you." Her parents were very grateful, because Dorothy had quite a temper.

(C)

Dorothy dropped the phone and rushed to the kitchen. The oil was on fire. "Chill! Take a deep breath," (c) she said to herself. What did they teach us not to do in a situation like this? Don't try to put it out by throwing water on it, because it will cause an explosion, she remembered. She picked up the pot's lid and covered the pot with it to put out the flames. In the process she burned her hands. Dorothy felt dizzy and sat down at the kitchen table.

(D)

A couple of minutes later, her parents came rushing into the house. Samantha had suspected that something might be wrong after Dorothy dropped the phone just like that, and (d) she had phoned Dorothy's parents. Dorothy started to cry. Her mother hugged her tightly and looked at the wound. "Tell me what happened," she said. Dorothy told her, sobbing and sniffing. "Aren't you going to yell at me?" (e) she asked them through the tears. Her father answered with a smile, "I also put my lid on to keep me from exploding." Dorothy looked at him, relieved. "But be careful not to be so irresponsible again."

* sob: 흐느껴 울다   ** sniff: 코를 훌쩍거리다

43. 주어진 글 (A)에 이어질 내용을 순서에 맞게 배열한 것으로 가장 적절한 것은?

① (B) – (D) – (C)   ② (C) – (B) – (D)
③ (C) – (D) – (B)   ④ (D) – (B) – (C)
⑤ (D) – (C) – (B)

44. 밑줄 친 (a)~(e) 중에서 가리키는 대상이 나머지 넷과 다른 것은?

① (a)   ② (b)   ③ (c)   ④ (d)   ⑤ (e)

45. 윗글의 Dorothy에 관한 내용으로 적절하지 않은 것은?

① 감자튀김을 만들려고 감자 두 개를 깎았다.
② 다정한 말을 더 많이 쓰겠다고 다짐했다.
③ 불붙은 기름에 물을 끼얹지 말아야 한다는 것을 기억했다.
④ 뚜껑으로 냄비를 덮어 불을 끄다가 손을 데었다.
⑤ 아버지의 말을 듣고 화를 냈다.

[01~02] 다음 글을 읽고, 물음에 답하시오.

A growing body of evidence suggests that playing video games can positively affect cognitive performance. One of the most notable advantages video gamers have over their non-gamer counterparts is increased _____. Because video games often require rapid responses, with gamers having to make quick decisions and process large amounts of visual information, gamers frequently demonstrate a greater capacity to focus on demanding tasks. Playing video games may also help slow down the mental decline associated with aging. Instead of becoming more forgetful, elderly individuals who play video games experience lasting improvements to their memory. This may be due to the fact that playing video games forces individuals to develop new skills. Learning how to move a character in a game around, for instance, can stimulate the areas of the brain responsible for memory and motor control. Since not learning anything new causes gray matter to shrink over time, it may be possible that people who play games have a better chance of increasing the volume of their gray matter.

* gray matter: 회백질

01 윗글의 제목으로 가장 적절한 것은?

① The Growing Popularity of Video Games Among the Elderly
② The Effect of Video Games on the Brain: Pros and Cons
③ Learning New Skills: The Secret to a Happier Life
④ Why Playing Video Games is Good for the Brain
⑤ Does Gray Matter Volume Impact Memory?

02 윗글의 빈칸에 들어갈 말로 가장 적절한 것은?

① attention
② hunger
③ confusion
④ strength
⑤ outrage

[03~05] 다음 글을 읽고, 물음에 답하시오.

(A)

Emily visited her aunt once a week. She was Emily's favorite relative, and Emily loved talking with her about all sorts of things. One day, as she was visiting, she began to complain to her aunt about some things in her life. Her car wasn't nice enough. Her apartment wasn't big enough. Her clothes weren't fashionable enough. She grumbled about all these things to (a) <u>her</u>.

(B)

She graciously accepted but kept looking at the fancy one her aunt was holding. "Why are you looking at my cup?" (b) <u>she</u> asked. "It's a nice mug," Emily replied. Her aunt smiled. "It's natural to want the best for yourself. There is nothing wrong with wanting nice things." "But if you focus too much on it," (c) <u>she</u> continued "it can cause you to become unhappy."

(C)

Emily nodded. "What you really want is a good cup of coffee," her aunt said. "What you drink it out of does not change how the coffee tastes, does it?" Emily thought about her life. She had a good job and was healthy. She had family and friends who loved her. "You're right," she said. "(d) <u>I</u> have a really good cup of coffee. What more could I want?"

(D)

Her aunt listened to these complaints quietly and then went to the kitchen. (e) <u>She</u> came back with a coffee pot and two mugs. One was very nice and fancy, while the other was plain with a small crack on the handle. She poured coffee into both and handed Emily the plain one.

03 주어진 글 (A)에 이어질 내용을 순서에 맞게 배열한 것으로 가장 적절한 것은?

① (B) – (D) – (C)
② (C) – (B) – (D)
③ (C) – (D) – (B)
④ (D) – (B) – (C)
⑤ (D) – (C) – (B)

04 밑줄 친 (a) ~ (e) 중에서 가리키는 대상이 나머지 넷과 다른 것은?

① (a)
② (b)
③ (c)
④ (d)
⑤ (e)

05 윗글의 Emily에 관한 내용으로 적절하지 <u>않은</u> 것은?

① 매주 이모의 집을 방문했다.
② 이모와 함께 이야기하는 것을 좋아한다.
③ 아파트가 충분히 넓지 않아서 불만을 가졌다.
④ 이모는 그녀가 좋은 것을 갈망하는 것을 이해한다.
⑤ 화려한 머그잔에 든 커피를 마셨다.

[06~07] 다음 글을 읽고, 물음에 답하시오.

It is well established that vitamin D plays an important role in bone health and the prevention and treatment of a wide range of health conditions. However, new research shows that vitamin D may impact us even before birth. Specifically, it can help with fetal brain development, implying that a child's intelligence may be (a) <u>connected</u> to their mother's vitamin D levels while pregnant.

It is common for pregnant women to have insufficient amounts of vitamin D. This is because there are very (b) <u>few</u> foods that contain enough of it naturally. Thus, the sun is actually the best source of vitamin D, since sunlight triggers a chemical reaction in the skin that (c) <u>produces</u> it. However, telling all pregnant women to simply get some sun in order to give their child an advantage is not always practical. Not only can it be dangerous, but women with dark skin do not experience the same results as fairer-skinned women. They are (d) <u>able</u> to produce as much vitamin D through exposure to the sun because their skin has more melanin, which disturbs the Vitamin D production. To give all children an equal chance to develop properly, it is important that health care professionals carefully screen pregnant women to ensure their vitamin D levels (e) <u>stay</u> high.

* trigger: 유발하다

06 윗글의 제목으로 가장 적절한 것은?

① The Role of Melanin in the Human Body
② The Dangers of Too Much Vitamin D
③ The More Sunshine, The Less Vitamin D
④ Vitamin D: Get Enough When You're Pregnant
⑤ Give Your Brain a Boost with Vitamin D Supplements

07 밑줄 친 (a)~(e) 중에서 문맥상 낱말의 쓰임이 적절하지 않은 것은?

① (a)　　② (b)　　③ (c)　　④ (d)　　⑤ (e)

[08~10] 다음 글을 읽고, 물음에 답하시오.

(A)

After his car accident, David had to use a wheelchair to go anywhere. It was difficult for him because he had always loved playing sports and being active, but now he believed it would be impossible. That's why he was surprised when (a) he met Michael at the hospital one day. Michael was also in a wheelchair and asked David, "Do you like to play sports?"

(B)

David failed a lot at that first practice, but he kept going back and getting better. Eventually, (b) he was even invited to play for the team at the national championship tournament. During their final game, David ended up scoring the winning point, helping his team win the tournament. Surrounded by his teammates, David held the trophy high. "I knew you could do it!" Michael exclaimed. David grinned at him, thankful for (c) his encouragement.

(C)

David stared at him with wide eyes. "What do you mean?" (d) he asked. "How would I play sports?" Michael laughed and replied, "You can move around, can't you?" David nodded in response. "Well then, you should be fine! Come to my team's basketball practice next Tuesday. I'll show you how we play."

(D)

(D) On that day, David went to basketball practice and was amazed by how skilled the players were. When it was (e) his turn to play, David told Michael, "I don't think I can do it. I'm just not used to being in a wheelchair." Michael gave him a knowing smile. "David, were you great at any sport the very first time you played it?" David shook his head. "So why would this be any different? You have to practice to get better. I know you can do it." What Michael said made sense to David. He had to at least try.

08 주어진 글 (A)에 이어질 내용을 순서에 맞게 배열한 것으로 가장 적절한 것은?

① (B) – (D) – (C)
② (C) – (B) – (D)
③ (C) – (D) – (B)
④ (D) – (B) – (C)
⑤ (D) – (C) – (B)

09 밑줄 친 (a) ~ (e) 중에서 가리키는 대상이 나머지 넷과 다른 것은?

① (a)
② (b)
③ (c)
④ (d)
⑤ (e)

10 윗글의 David에 관한 내용으로 적절하지 않은 것은?

① 다시는 그가 운동을 할 수 없을 것이라고 생각했다.
② 첫 연습부터 성과가 좋았다.
③ 결승전에서 결승점을 냈다.
④ 화요일 연습에 초대받았다.
⑤ 휠체어에 익숙하지 않아 연습하기를 주저했다.

[11~12] 다음 글을 읽고, 물음에 답하시오.

Streets that have been named after people can be found throughout the world. But how do cities determine who to (a) <u>remember</u> in this way? A study analyzing street names in London, Paris, Vienna, and New York has revealed that street names mostly honor people who made important contributions to their respective societies. Their names are assigned to streets to inspire residents to adopt the (b) <u>values</u> they stood for. To see how street names in the four cities (c) <u>differ</u>, researchers analyzed the people they were named after. In particular, they focused on the ratio of men to women, the historical period they lived in, and the number of foreign figures. It was found that Vienna and London have significantly (d) <u>fewer</u> streets named after women than New York and Paris. This suggests that Vienna and London have taken steps to emphasize the importance of women, while New York and Paris have not. In the three European cities, most streets are named after people from the 19th century, while in New York, the majority of honorees lived in the late 20th century. Finally, Vienna demonstrates the most (e) <u>progressive</u> attitude, with 45 percent of its streets named after foreigners. Despite being global cities, London, Paris, and New York can hardly say the same.

* biased: 편향된, 치중하는

11 윗글의 제목으로 가장 적절한 것은?

① The Importance of Knowing When to Rename Streets
② Do Street Names Affect the Value of Homes?
③ Are Street Names Functional or Political?
④ The Modern Representation in Street Names
⑤ Street Names: A Reflection of Culture and History

12 밑줄 친 (a)~(e) 중에서 문맥상 낱말의 쓰임이 적절하지 <u>않은</u> 것은?

① (a)　　② (b)　　③ (c)　　④ (d)　　⑤ (e)

[13~15] 다음 글을 읽고, 물음에 답하시오.

(A)

As I was attending my first class at university, I saw an unusual sight. A very old lady walked into the class and sat down next to me. "Hi, I'm Daisy," she said as she introduced herself. Daisy was 78 years old and in her third year of college. After class, I was so interested in Daisy that I asked another girl about her. "I'm sorry, I don't know her very well. Maybe you can ask (a) her yourself?" she said.

(B)

I decided to do just that. So one day after class, I walked up to Daisy and asked her how (b) she came to be a student at such a mature age. She replied that she had always wanted to go to college but never had the chance. I wanted to know more about her story, and I asked if we could have lunch together.

(C)

"We don't stop playing because we grow old, we grow old because we stop playing." Daisy taught me that we are never too old to try something new and that we shouldn't ever lose our passion for living. I vowed to follow in (c) her footsteps. She was a true role model and inspiration. She lived her life to the fullest and that is exactly how I wish to live mine.

(D)

We went to a nearby café and (d) she told me all about her life. She had done so many interesting things and lived through so many amazing experiences that I was surprised she still wanted to do so much. A few classmates saw me and came over to join us. They listened to her wonderful stories. One girl said she hoped (e) she would have as much fun as Daisy when she got older. Then, Daisy said something I will never forget.

13 주어진 글 (A)에 이어질 내용을 순서에 맞게 배열한 것으로 가장 적절한 것은?

① (B) – (D) – (C)
② (C) – (B) – (D)
③ (C) – (D) – (B)
④ (D) – (B) – (C)
⑤ (D) – (C) – (B)

14 밑줄 친 (a) ~ (e) 중에서 가리키는 대상이 나머지 넷과 **다른** 것은?

① (a)
② (b)
③ (c)
④ (d)
⑤ (e)

15 윗글에 관한 내용으로 적절하지 **않은** 것은?

① 'I'는 첫 수업에서 흔치 않은 광경을 보았다.
② Daisy는 대학교 3학년이었다.
③ Daisy는 항상 대학교에 가고 싶어 했었다.
④ 'I'는 Daisy처럼 인생을 살기를 희망한다.
⑤ 'I'는 교실에 남아 Daisy의 이야기를 들었다.

고난도

[16~17] 다음 글을 읽고, 물음에 답하시오.

For most people, the opportunity to get free stuff is too good to pass up, and the same goes for food. This cannot be said of most captive animals, however. Extensive research shows that most opt to (a) work for their food. A 1963 study on rats demonstrated this concept quite well and has formed the basis for studies involving other captive animals. Rats were given a choice between having a (b) free meal and accessing food from a container that required them to press a metal bar several times. The rats consistently chose the latter option, even though the food in the container was (c) easier to access. It is believed that the tendency for captive animals to apply effort is related to the (d) lack of stimulation in a cage or artificial setting. Essentially, they perform actions they might normally carry out when hunting or foraging because it is part of their natural instincts to do so. The findings ultimately suggest that providing captive animals with devices like food puzzles could (e) encourage them to act more naturally and prevent them from getting bored, thereby improving their well-being.

* stimulation: 자극   ** forage: 먹이를 찾다

16 윗글의 제목으로 가장 적절한 것은?

① Animals That Work for Humans: Overcoming Challenges
② Who Says There's No Such Thing as a Free Lunch?
③ Why It Is Cruel to Keep Animals in Captivity
④ Worrying Signs of Boredom in Animals
⑤ Why Captive Animals Prefer to Earn Food

17 밑줄 친 (a)~(e) 중에서 문맥상 낱말의 쓰임이 적절하지 않은 것은?

① (a)   ② (b)   ③ (c)   ④ (d)   ⑤ (e)

[18~20] 다음 글을 읽고, 물음에 답하시오.

(A)

Stephen was sitting on a park bench eating a sandwich. He was on a lunch break from work. Stephen did not like his job very much. He thought about how he had always wanted to make a big difference in the world, but he was stuck in a boring job. So, he was not in a very good mood when an old man came up to (a) him.

(B)

However, Stephen felt much worse once he got off work. As (b) he was leaving, he saw the old man again. Stephen saw him asking other people for some food. All he got was just a little bit of bread, but he still seemed so happy to have received it. The image stayed with Stephen as he walked home.

(C)

He apologized for bothering Stephen but asked if he could share a little bit of his food. Stephen needed to eat so he could work the rest of the afternoon, so (c) he said "I'm sorry. I can't." The old man said (d) he understood. Stephen hurriedly ate the rest of his lunch and went back to work, feeling a bit bad.

(D)

He still couldn't get it out of his mind as he lay in bed. Stephen couldn't fall asleep, so he got up and made as many sandwiches as he could. The next day during his lunch break, (e) he found the old man and offered the food. The old man smiled and called out to a friend. When she saw the sandwiches, her face lit up. Stephen smiled. He just made a big difference in the world.

18 주어진 글 (A)에 이어질 내용을 순서에 맞게 배열한 것으로 가장 적절한 것은?

① (B) – (D) – (C)
② (C) – (B) – (D)
③ (C) – (D) – (B)
④ (D) – (B) – (C)
⑤ (D) – (C) – (B)

19 밑줄 친 (a) ~ (e) 중에서 가리키는 대상이 나머지 넷과 다른 것은?

① (a)
② (b)
③ (c)
④ (d)
⑤ (e)

20 윗글에 관한 내용으로 적절하지 <u>않은</u> 것은?

① Stephen은 세상에 큰 변화를 가져오고 싶어했다.
② 나이 든 남자는 빵 조각을 받고 행복해했다.
③ Stephen은 샌드위치를 먹고 기쁜 마음으로 직장에 돌아갔다.
④ Stephen은 나이 든 남자가 마음에 걸려 잠을 설쳤다.
⑤ 나이 든 남자의 친구는 샌드위치를 보고 미소를 지었다.

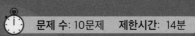

01 글의 흐름으로 보아, 주어진 문장이 들어가기에 가장 적절한 곳을 고르시오.

> This can be similar to the satisfaction people get when they receive a financial reward.

Compliments can truly make us feel good, whether we are giving them or receiving them. (①) Generally speaking, compliments satisfy a deep human need to feel worthy and loved. (②) By giving compliments, we are telling others that we appreciate them. (③) The act of giving compliments also helps us learn to find positive qualities in others. (④) And when we receive compliments, they not only make us feel appreciated but also trigger a pleasing reaction in our brains. (⑤) Overall, when people exchange compliments, it is as if they are rewarding each other with kind words that carry real worth and, over time, help to foster trust, goodwill, and mutual respect.

02 다음 글의 내용을 한 문장으로 요약하고자 한다. 빈칸 (A), (B)에 들어갈 말로 가장 적절한 것은?

During business transactions, one party often has an advantage over the other because they have access to more information. For example, a used car dealer may know that a vehicle doesn't function well and sell it to an unaware customer anyway in order to make a profit. While this behavior is clearly untruthful, an information gap doesn't always have to be negative. Instead of using their specialized knowledge to cheat customers, the used car dealer can use it to repair vehicle problems that the average customer might not notice. This way, buyers are not only happy with reliable vehicles, but they will also recommend the car dealer to other shoppers. This can increase business and allow the dealer to charge higher prices than competitors who let vehicles leave the lot in poor shape.

⇩

> An information gap may result in   (A) , but it can also   (B)   both the buyer and the seller.

     (A)   (B)
① mistrust   ⋯   benefit
② rejection   ⋯   discourage
③ mistrust   ⋯   threaten
④ confusion   ⋯   irritate
⑤ rejection   ⋯   amuse

[03~04] 다음 글을 읽고, 물음에 답하시오.

The attractiveness of food, or how it appears on a plate, influences how we perceive its quality. To determine how diners judge the value of food, researchers working with a chef designed three salads with (a) identical ingredients, dressing, and seasoning. Because there were no differences in the actual taste or quality of the food, and all the ingredients were the same, any opinions about the salads would have to be based on how they looked. The first salad's ingredients were simply tossed and plated, while those of the second were separated from each other and lined up in neat rows. The third salad's ingredients, however, were arranged in an (b) artistic manner. In fact, the design was inspired by an abstract painting by Wassily Kandinsky. Diners not only rated the Kandinsky-inspired salad (c) lower for taste than the other two but they were also willing to pay more than twice as much for it. Although it is difficult to pinpoint exactly why the diners felt this way, it may have something to do with the amount of (d) effort they felt went into the dish. The nice way the food was put onto the plate was (e) pleasing to them and may have suggested that a great amount of care and attention went into their meal.

* abstract painting: 추상화

03 윗글의 제목으로 가장 적절한 것은?

① Improving the Atmosphere in Restaurants With Art
② High-Quality Ingredients: The Key to Your Success
③ Appearance: It Matters When It Comes to Food
④ Can Healthy Options Be Delicious Too?
⑤ Why Food Tastes Better in Restaurants

04 밑줄 친 (a)~(e) 중에서 문맥상 낱말의 쓰임이 적절하지 않은 것은?

① (a) ② (b) ③ (c) ④ (d) ⑤ (e)

05 글의 흐름으로 보아, 주어진 문장이 들어가기에 가장 적절한 곳을 고르시오.

> Instead of looking for changes in sound frequencies, astronomers look for changes in light frequencies.

The Doppler effect describes how frequencies vary in relation to an observer depending on their source's direction of movement. (①) It explains the change in pitch we hear as an ambulance approaches and then moves away from us. (②) In the field of astronomy, it is used in the search for planets outside our solar system. (③) These are observable as colors in the visible spectrum of light from stars. (④) The light appears blue when a star is moving toward us and red in the opposite direction. (⑤) If the colors change over time, then astronomers know that the star's movement is likely being pulled by gravity from a nearby planet.

(A)

As a young girl, Alice lived in her grandmother's house, where she played in a wonderful garden with a wide array of plants. In the spring, the flowers on the plants would bloom, filling the garden with color. When she grew up, Alice bought her own home. That way, she could plant a garden herself. Next door to her lived an old lady named Kathleen, who had no garden of her own.

(B)

Alice was shocked. She walked over to Kathleen's side of the wall and could not believe (a) her eyes. The vines had grown through cracks in the wall and bloomed on the other side, covering it in colorful flowers. Alice was sure that all of her work had been wasted on caring for plants that didn't bloom. (b) She never thought that her work would blossom for somebody else.

(C)

An empty gray wall separated Alice's backyard from Kathleen's home. Alice looked at it and decided to plant her flowers there. (c) She went to a garden store and bought flowering vines to cover the wall. She placed them in good soil, watered them, and protected them from insects. But after six months of caring for the vines, Alice felt disappointed. Although they had grown thick and large and covered the entire wall, they hadn't produced a single flower (d) she could see!

(D)

So, she decided she would replace the vines with another plant. She approached the wall to remove the vines when a voice called out from the other side. It was her neighbor, Kathleen. "I want to thank you," (e) she said with tears in her eyes. "I have been ill for months and unable to leave my house. Seeing your vines bloom with flowers has brought me incredible hope!"

06 주어진 글 (A)에 이어질 내용을 순서에 맞게 배열한 것으로 가장 적절한 것은?

① (B) – (D) – (C)
② (C) – (B) – (D)
③ (C) – (D) – (B)
④ (D) – (B) – (C)
⑤ (D) – (C) – (B)

07 밑줄 친 (a)~(e) 중에서 가리키는 대상이 나머지 넷과 다른 것은?

① (a)   ② (b)   ③ (c)   ④ (d)   ⑤ (e)

08 윗글에 관한 내용으로 적절하지 않은 것은?

① Alice는 자신의 집에 그녀만의 정원을 마련했다.
② Kathleen은 한 송이의 꽃도 볼 수 없었다.
③ Alice와 Kathleen의 집 사이에는 벽이 있었다.
④ Alice는 정원을 6개월 넘게 가꾸었다.
⑤ Kathleen은 몇 달 동안 집 밖에 나가지 못했다.

09 주어진 글 다음에 이어질 글의 순서로 가장 적절한 것을 고르시오.

> Odd pricing refers to the common practice of setting prices in figures that end in "9" or other odd numbers. It is a form of psychological trickery designed to persuade customers to make a purchase.

(A) This variation can also be perceived as a gain. For instance, customers may think they are enjoying significant savings by buying something at $499 instead of $500, even though the actual "gain" is only $1.00.

(B) According to research, one of the reasons odd pricing works is due to specificity. In other words, customers believe that a highly specific price reflects a product's true worth more accurately.

(C) Another reason has to do with perceived loss, in which case customers reading a price from left to right immediately focus on the first digit they see and ignore the rest. Thus, a price of $4.99 is seen as being significantly lower than $5.00, even though the difference between them is only $0.01.

① (A) – (C) – (B)
② (B) – (A) – (C)
③ (B) – (C) – (A)
④ (C) – (A) – (B)
⑤ (C) – (B) – (A)

10 다음 글의 내용을 한 문장으로 요약하고자 한다. 빈칸 (A), (B)에 들어갈 말로 가장 적절한 것은?

> Mathematics and language both rely on elaborate systems of linguistic elements to convey meaning. With language, we communicate ideas through various combinations of characters, morphemes, and grammatical rules. In mathematics, we create systems using numbers, variables, and formulas. The two subjects are similar in that sense. Where they differ is in how they are taught. Language instruction takes a verbal and hands-on approach, while math learning relies on lectures and bookwork. But given that the two subjects have so much in common, math and language instructors should consider adopting one another's methods to deepen the classroom experience. Language courses can be more structured and focused on the actual mechanics of writing. Meanwhile, math teachers can incorporate more group work and discussion of strategies.
>
> * morpheme: 형태소 ** hands-on: 직접 해보는

⇩

> Language and mathematics are ___(A)___ enough that the teaching methods of one can be ___(B)___ to the other for better learning.

	(A)		(B)
①	alike	⋯	replaced
②	clear	⋯	shifted
③	clear	⋯	approached
④	alike	⋯	applied
⑤	elaborate	⋯	described

해커스 수능 독해 불변의 패턴 유형편

실전 모의고사

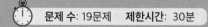

01 다음 글의 목적으로 가장 적절한 것은?

Dear Parents,

We hope your children had a great time at the Pearson Middle School Trade Fair. Our event gives students first-hand experience in running a small business, allowing them to come up with their own ideas and to run these businesses for a day. We saw some amazing booths from your children this year, and we just wanted to let you know that the event would not have been possible without our parent volunteers. You worked so hard to make this day a success and guarantee a great time for each student. We can't express our gratitude to you enough for taking the time to help us manage everything. We appreciate it, and we know that our students do too.

Sincerely,
Connie Evans, Principal

① 행사의 자원봉사자분들께 감사 인사를 전하려고
② 중학생을 위한 프로그램을 광고하려고
③ 부모들께 행사를 공지하려고
④ 학생들에게 자원봉사 활동을 추천하려고
⑤ 무역 박람회를 위한 추가 지원을 요청하려고

02 다음 글에 드러난 'I'의 심경 변화로 가장 적절한 것은?

One Saturday, a little dog arrived at the animal shelter where I worked. He was so neglected that I could barely look at him. The poor thing was nothing more than bones. My heart ached for him. I decided to name him Chance, hoping someone would give him one. But Chance never got adopted. He was so timid that he went unnoticed. People kept walking by him until today. A family with a little boy visited. While the parents looked at other puppies, the boy stood in front of Chance. They looked at each other for the longest time. And then, Chance walked over and licked the boy's hand. The boy hugged him and I smiled. Chance got his second chance.

① sympathetic → pleased
② unhappy → interested
③ surprised → discouraged
④ shocked → jealous
⑤ alarmed → flattered

03 다음 글에서 필자가 주장하는 바로 가장 적절한 것은?

It is natural to ignore a problem in the hope that it will just go away. But when it comes to one's health, this is a dangerous approach. Most serious medical conditions have a much higher chance of being successfully treated if they are found early. For example, some forms of cancer have a 90 percent survival rate if discovered in the early stages compared to a 10 percent survival rate if found later on. This is why doctors encourage everyone to have a regular health checkup once a year. However, people need to do more than this. It is important to watch for symptoms and to report them to a doctor right away. In other words, by carefully monitoring your physical condition, you can increase your chances of having a long, happy life.

① 혼자 해결하기 힘든 문제일수록 신중하게 판단해야 한다.
② 건강에 위협을 줄 만큼 격한 운동은 피해야 한다.
③ 의사들의 조언을 항상 실천하려 노력해야 한다.
④ 자신의 건강 상태를 꾸준히 체크해야 한다.
⑤ 사소한 질병도 무시해서는 안 된다.

04 밑줄 친 attempting to silence them이 다음 글에서 의미하는 바로 가장 적절한 것은?

Art is meant to be an expression of thought through creative means, so the idea that you could put a grade on it is questionable at best. The only way for teachers to really justify grading a piece of art is to assign projects with rules and guidelines to follow. If students are given a clear set of criteria, they will know what objectives to meet in order to achieve the grade they desire. However, all this does for students is build a box around them. It tells them that they have to consider their grades above all else. Students already face enough pressure from being graded in their core subjects, where the material is objective. Since art is a rare subject that allows students to convey their thoughts freely, grading their creations is like attempting to silence them.

① creating unnecessary work
② making them work quietly
③ generating new biases
④ limiting their productivity
⑤ restricting their expression

05 다음 글의 주제로 가장 적절한 것은?

Though copyright laws have been around for centuries, the social media age has brought more people into contact with them than ever. In the past, violating these laws would have required deliberate copying: you would've had to spend time printing knockoff copies of a book or burning bootleg CDs. Nowadays, we're capable of infringing someone's intellectual property with just a few clicks—so fast that we might not even realize it. For those of us whose jobs involve social media, this ease can create financial risk. A lawsuit over something shared online could cost your company up to $150,000 in damages, even if you agree to take it down. For these reasons, legal experts advise caution when posting any material that you did not make or purchase the rights of. Asking permission or finding an alternative may take longer, but doing so will reduce the risk incurred.

* knockoff copy: 불법 복제품 ** bootleg: 불법의, 해적판의

① justifications for borrowing media content from others
② defending the right to intellectual property rights
③ social media's influence on the economy
④ protecting yourself against people who copy content
⑤ the effect of social media on copyright violation

06 다음 도표의 내용과 일치하지 <u>않는</u> 것은?

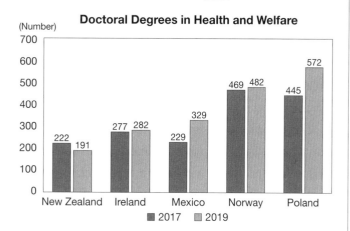

(Number)
Doctoral Degrees in Health and Welfare

■ 2017 ■ 2019

The above graph shows the number of students who earned doctoral degrees in Health and Welfare in five different countries in 2017 and 2019. ① The number of students with doctoral degrees in New Zealand dropped in 2019 compared to 2017. ② In both 2017 and 2019, the number of students with doctoral degrees in Ireland was less than 300. ③ Mexico had fewer students with doctoral degrees than Norway in both 2017 and 2019. ④ Of the five countries, Norway had the highest number of students with doctoral degrees in 2017. ⑤ In 2019, students in Norway with a doctoral degree increased from 2017, while those with a doctoral degree in Poland decreased over that same period.

07 Stephen King에 관한 다음 글의 내용과 일치하지 <u>않는</u> 것은?

Stephen King was born in Portland, Maine, in 1947. After graduating from the University of Maine, he married his wife Tabitha and began working as an English teacher. However, King's true passion was writing. In 1973, he was able to sell his novel *Carrie* to a large publishing company. The subsequent sales from the book allowed him to quit his job and write full-time. Since then, he has published over 60 books and sold more than 300 million copies, mostly in the genres of fantasy, gothic, and especially horror. Many of his horror stories have been made into films that are considered classics today. As such, he is often described as "The King of Horror."

① 영어 교사로 일했다.
② 1973년에 그는 자신의 작품을 한 대형 출판사에 팔았다.
③ 직장을 그만둔 후 *Carrie*를 썼다.
④ 지금까지 60권이 넘는 책을 출간했다.
⑤ 그의 여러 작품들이 영화로 만들어졌다.

08 다음 글의 밑줄 친 부분 중, 어법상 틀린 것은?

Graphic designer Bruno Munari believed that design should serve as "a bridge" between art and life. ① Writing in 1966, he noted that "as long as art stands aside from the problems of life it will only interest a very few people." What he meant was that modern artists appeared more ② concerned with producing work for small groups of people than for society as a whole. He felt artists had lost their connection with society and that the only way to restore it would be through design. For Munari, designing everyday objects like pieces of furniture, signs above storefronts, or ordinary dining utensils ③ presented opportunities to reclaim art's central role. He encouraged designers to place ④ themselves in the thick of life and to create objects that actually made people's lives better. It was the only way Munari believed ⑤ what artists could reestablish their rightful place in society.

* reclaim: 되찾다

09 다음 글의 밑줄 친 부분 중, 문맥상 낱말의 쓰임이 적절하지 않은 것은?

Artificial intelligence, or AI, is almost certainly going to form a large part of people's lives in the future. Even today, AI is used in everything from phones and cars to online shopping and medical research. But as the number of AI applications has ① decreased, so too has the number of associated problems. Some believe that AI itself can figure out the solution, or that it will eventually be able to ② resolve the issues it causes. However, this ③ ignores the role that people play, since significant risks will always be present as long as AI is produced by people. Regarding this, the more ④ powerful AI becomes, the greater the threat that it brings because of its potential impact. It is therefore important that society face the issues surrounding AI while its related problems are still relatively ⑤ minor.

* artificial intelligence: 인공지능

10 다음 빈칸에 들어갈 말로 가장 적절한 것을 고르시오.

Knowing your customers is an essential part of marketing, but this can seem like a daunting task for some, given how diverse large populations can be. Nevertheless, at its core, society is made up of individuals who want to _____, a fact that can be easily exploited to sell products. The vast majority of people, whether they are willing to admit it or not, have a fear of "missing out" and being different from others in their social group. From a marketing perspective, this means that they are more likely to purchase items after seeing their peers do the same. By understanding this herd mentality, marketers can influence consumers' purchasing decisions. Tactics like hiring social media influencers to back products or showing how many times a service has been booked are especially effective. Being able to see how popular something is causes people to view it as valuable and, by extension, makes them want to purchase it for themselves.

* herd mentality: 군중심리

① belong   ② succeed   ③ escape
④ grow   ⑤ compete

11 다음 글에서 전체 흐름과 관계 <u>없는</u> 문장은?

Preserving biodiversity in farming practices is crucial for protecting natural resources. By utilizing techniques that ensure the continuation of as many species as possible, we not only aid in conservation efforts but allow there to be a large enough gene pool to produce a variety of healthy crops. ① There are various farming strategies that can be used to achieve this. ② One such strategy is intercropping, which involves growing crops close together. ③ This allows the plants to use their natural systems with maximum efficiency while also reducing pests with less chemicals. ④ For thousands of years, pests have been one of the major reasons for production loss that farmers have had to deal with. ⑤ Another popular technique is crop rotation, which allows for nutrients in the farming soil to be restored because farmers plant different crops sequentially on the same land.

* intercropping: 간작(間作) ** crop rotation: 윤작(輪作)

12 주어진 글 다음에 이어질 글의 순서로 가장 적절한 것을 고르시오.

> For decades, hydrogen has been promoted as an important form of energy. It is one of the simplest and most abundant elements in the universe and can supply a large amount of energy for electricity, heat, industry, and transportation.

(A) Thanks to recent technological advancements, however, new methods are being developed that allow hydrogen to be produced from purely renewable sources. This means it could still play an important part in achieving a low-carbon future.

(B) What both of these methods have in common is that they are complicated and expensive. They also rely on carbon-heavy fossil fuels that are costly and harmful to the environment.

(C) Unfortunately, hydrogen is typically connected to another compound, so it must be separated. This can be quite complex. For instance, one method to get hydrogen from the air uses very high temperatures. Another method to separate hydrogen from water uses electricity.

① (A) – (C) – (B)
② (B) – (A) – (C)
③ (B) – (C) – (A)
④ (C) – (A) – (B)
⑤ (C) – (B) – (A)

13 글의 흐름으로 보아, 주어진 문장이 들어가기에 가장 적절한 곳을 고르시오.

> Flying directly across the Pacific Ocean would therefore cause a plane to travel across the widest or longest part of the planet.

Most airlines follow a curved flight path over the Pacific Ocean rather than fly directly across it. (①) Part of the reason is that this allows them to stay close to land, which is useful in an emergency. (②) Another has to do with the Earth's spherical shape. (③) Because the Earth is round, it is wider in the middle than it is at the top or the bottom. (④) By flying either above or below the ocean instead, a plane is able to travel a shorter distance. (⑤) This can be verified by taking an artificial globe and measuring the distance between two destinations across the Pacific Ocean, once near the middle and once near the bottom or the top.

* spherical: 구형의

14 다음 글의 내용을 한 문장으로 요약하고자 한다. 빈칸 (A), (B)에 들어갈 말로 가장 적절한 것은?

To test whether DNA can tolerate a space flight and subsequent reentry into Earth's atmosphere, researchers at the University of Zurich placed some on the outside of a rocket that was then launched into space. Upon the rocket's return, researchers were surprised to discover that nearly one-third of the DNA was still "alive," meaning it was still capable of passing on genetic information despite having been exposed to a harsh environment. This finding has led to some intriguing ideas, one of which is that the first DNA on Earth came from outer space. At the same time, they believe humans can then transport DNA from Earth into space and begin life anew on other planets.

⇩

The researchers concluded that DNA can _____(A)_____ harsh environments in space, and they believe it can be used to _____(B)_____ life on other planets.

     (A)   (B)
① withstand ⋯ initiate
② withstand ⋯ study
③ support ⋯ initiate
④ support ⋯ imitate
⑤ alter ⋯ study

[15~16] 다음 글을 읽고, 물음에 답하시오.

With more and more news outlets spreading specific political opinions, journalism is no longer as (a) objective as it used to be. This is problematic for multiple reasons. When journalists include their personal opinions in stories they write, they can influence their audience to think the (b) same way instead of allowing them to form their own opinions. This sort of biased reporting can (c) divide the public as differences in opinion often lead to hostility.

Biased journalism can also result in people turning to the internet, where they can find one-sided news sources that (d) challenge their views. By only exposing themselves to articles and programs containing views they already agree with, they strengthen their belief that their opinion is the only one that matters and can more easily justify their resistance to any other point of view. By contrast, publishing just the facts prevents people from simply (e) accepting someone's opinion as the truth. Instead, it forces them to think for themselves.

15 윗글의 제목으로 가장 적절한 것은?

① The News: Origin of Political Conflict?
② Biased Reporting: The Problems It Causes
③ Do Journalists Influence Political Participation?
④ The Positive Impact of the Internet on News Media
⑤ Journalists' Dilemma: Staying Objective Despite Strong Opinions

16 밑줄 친 (a)~(e) 중에서 문맥상 낱말의 쓰임이 적절하지 않은 것은?

① (a)   ② (b)   ③ (c)   ④ (d)   ⑤ (e)

[17~19] 다음 글을 읽고, 물음에 답하시오.

(A)

Miss Douglas loved being a first-grade teacher, but it wasn't always easy. She was especially worried about little Sarah, who had a hard time making friends. Miss Douglas tried to help her, but sometimes, she wondered if her student even noticed. Still, (a) she loved her job and walked into class every day with a big smile. Today, she was happier than usual because her favorite holiday, Thanksgiving, was coming up.

(B)

The other students were surprised as well. Soon, everyone started guessing whose hand it could be. Some said it must be a farmer's hand who raised turkeys. Others said it was Sarah's hand or her mother's or father's. When Miss Douglas finally asked her, she quietly said "It's (b) yours."

(C)

Miss Douglas was shocked. "(c) Mine? But why..." Then, she remembered all the times she held Sarah's hand. She held her hand to take her to the bathroom or to play outside. She remembered that she held Sarah's little hand over a pencil to show her how to write properly. She remembered how every morning, she would pat Sarah's shoulder and greet (d) her, as she did all the children in her class. Miss Douglas smiled and wiped a tear away.

(D)

In honor of the special day, Miss Douglas had a special assignment for her class. She told them to draw the things they were most thankful for. Students began to work busily. They drew turkeys and big dinners. Some drew their families gathered together, while others drew themselves playing with their friends. But Miss Douglas noticed that little Sarah drew something different. (e) She was quite astonished to see that she had drawn an empty hand.

17. 주어진 글 (A)에 이어질 내용을 순서에 맞게 배열한 것으로 가장 적절한 것은?

① (B) – (D) – (C)
② (C) – (B) – (D)
③ (C) – (D) – (B)
④ (D) – (B) – (C)
⑤ (D) – (C) – (B)

18. 밑줄 친 (a) ~ (e) 중에서 가리키는 대상이 나머지 넷과 다른 것은?

① (a)
② (b)
③ (c)
④ (d)
⑤ (e)

19. 윗글에 관한 내용으로 적절하지 <u>않은</u> 것은?

① Sarah는 친구를 사귀는 것을 어려워했다.
② 추수감사절은 Douglas 선생님이 가장 좋아하는 휴일이었다.
③ Sarah는 자신의 어머니의 손을 그렸다.
④ Douglas 선생님은 Sarah가 올바르게 글씨를 쓰도록 도와주었다.
⑤ Douglas 선생님은 반 학생들에게 그들이 감사한 것을 그리라고 했다.

정답 및 해설 p.153

01 다음 글의 목적으로 가장 적절한 것은?

To Mr. Steve Wilson,

Happy New Year! We here at Prime Gym would like to wish you and your family the very best in the upcoming year. You have been a valued member of our gym for 2 years now. As such, we would like to express our thanks for longtime clients like you. This year, we will be upgrading you to our gold level membership, free of charge. With it, you will be able to receive free PT lessons once a week as well as a total of 10 sports massages per year. Furthermore, you and a guest will have access to our private pool and spa. Thank you again for choosing Prime Gym for all your health and fitness needs.

Sincerely,
Amy State

① 멤버십 가입 조건을 설명하려고
② 헬스클럽에 새로 설치된 장비를 소개하려고
③ 헬스클럽 공사 일정이 변경되었음을 안내하려고
④ 회원의 멤버십 등급이 향상되었음을 알려주려고
⑤ 헬스클럽 이용 시 지켜야 할 안전 수칙을 전달하려고

02 다음 글에 드러난 Warren의 심경 변화로 가장 적절한 것은?

Warren was ready for his solo. He had been practicing every day for months now, and he knew the piano piece by heart. He was positive he would do great. On the day of the performance, he boldly walked up on the stage and stood in front of hundreds of people waiting for his play. He took a deep breath and sat down at the piano. Just as he practiced, he finished the piece without a single mistake. Everyone clapped and cheered. He smiled and began walking off the stage when he stumbled and tripped. He heard a few people laughing. His face turned bright red and he hurried off the stage. He just wanted to crawl under a rock and forget it ever happened.

① helpless   → horrified
② worried   → relieved
③ comfortable → touched
④ panicked   → furious
⑤ confident   → embarrassed

03 다음 글의 요지로 가장 적절한 것은?

If you go to the United States and meet someone, you shake their hand. In Korea, you bow to each other. In France, you kiss the other on the cheek as a greeting. Nonverbal communication like this is a crucial part of social interaction. In fact, one study showed that almost 60 percent of communication was relayed through body language while only 7 percent was conveyed with the actual words a person said. Most nonverbal communication involves five areas: eye contact, touch, gestures, physical distance, and body posture. These areas vary significantly from culture to culture, so learning some common cues is useful. Otherwise, misunderstandings can occur, and you may end up offending someone without meaning to.

① 다양한 비언어적 의사소통을 알아두는 것이 좋다.
② 올바른 대화예절을 아는 것이 중요하다.
③ 우리는 보디랭귀지로 의사소통하는 것에 너무 익숙해져 있다.
④ 다른 나라의 언어를 배우는 것은 문화 교류에 도움이 된다.
⑤ 비언어적 의사소통의 방법은 모든 문화에서 비슷하다.

04 밑줄 친 artistic lineage가 다음 글에서 의미하는 바로 가장 적절한 것은?

How much is your taste in music influenced by the songs you heard in your childhood? The answer might surprise you. According to research, the songs you hear while growing up actually stick with you and become part of your playlists later in life, indicating that we might inherit more than just our genes from our parents. Scientists say that this isn't all that surprising since music tends to help us recall memories; a song can take you back to a family vacation or time spent in your childhood home. This music triggers nostalgia and an emotional response, which is why people tend to listen to songs their parents played as they grew up. This artistic lineage helps define the tastes of future generations, impacting what music they prefer and listen to.

* nostalgia: 향수(鄉愁)

① memories that inspire new music
② skills that are inherited from parents
③ generational differences in musical taste
④ musical styles that occur in different times
⑤ musical preferences that are passed down in families

05 다음 글의 제목으로 가장 적절한 것은?

Most people assume that the longer they work, the more productive they will be. However, recent studies have repeatedly demonstrated that people who work fewer hours a day or fewer days a week often display corresponding improvements in job performance. In contrast, people who work for longer hours are found to be less efficient, less focused, and more likely to experience burnout. The reason for these different outcomes is simple. Work requires energy to perform, and too much of it drains people of the energy they need to continue performing at the same level. People who work less have more time to restore their energy and are therefore more capable of devoting themselves to the work at hand when it is needed.

* burnout: 번아웃, 극도로 피로한 상태

① Matching Worker Pay to Performance
② Don't Assume Hard Work Never Pays Off
③ Inspiration and Innovation: Where to Find It
④ Job Performance from the Factory to the Office
⑤ Less Is More: Fewer Hours Improves Work Performance

06 다음 도표의 내용과 일치하지 <u>않는</u> 것은?

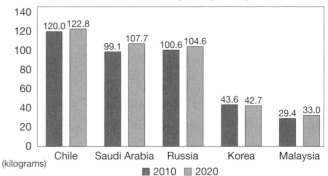

Wheat consumption per capita

The above graph shows the wheat consumption per capita in kilograms of 5 different countries in 2010 and 2020. ① Of the 5 countries, Chile had the highest number of wheat consumption per capita in both 2010 and 2020. ② In 2010, Russia had the second highest wheat consumption per capita, followed by Saudi Arabia with the third highest. ③ For every country except Korea, the wheat consumed per capita was higher in 2020 than in 2010. ④ The difference in wheat consumption per capita between 2010 and 2020 was smaller for Malaysia than it was for Chile. ⑤ Compared to Korea, wheat consumption per capita in Saudi Arabia was more than 50 kilograms higher in 2020.

07 Moorhead Choir Auditions에 관한 다음 안내문의 내용과 일치하는 것은?

Moorhead Choir Auditions

The prestigious Moorhead School of Music is looking for exceptional talents who love to sing. We will be holding auditions for the Concert Choir Group from February 10 to March 28.

Requirements:
- Must be a registered student
- Must have sung in at least one choir before
- Must be able to attend rehearsals (Every Tues. and Thurs., 7-9 p.m.)

The Audition Process
- Sign up for an audition time
- Prepare to perform a singing exercise in one of your vocal range (bass, tenor, alto, or soprano)
- You will also be asked to sight-read a song

For more information, please contact Eric Kim. (ekimchoir@moorheaduni.com)

① 재학생이 아니어도 오디션에 참가할 수 있다.
② 지원자들은 과거에 합창단 경험이 있어야 한다.
③ 리허설은 일주일에 세 번 있다.
④ 지원자들은 아무 때나 오디션을 보러 올 수 있다.
⑤ 지원자들은 서로 다른 네 개의 음역대로 노래를 불러야 한다.

08 다음 글의 밑줄 친 부분 중 어법상 틀린 것은?

Reality television, entertaining though it may be, ① does present problems for society as a whole. To begin with, the term "reality" is misleading. The cameras are supposedly on nonstop, but the only footage that ends up in shows ② to be shocking or dramatic as that's what appeals to viewers. Furthermore, the producers may introduce conflict to encourage arguments between cast members or ③ focus only on the most sensational characters. The manipulation of reality in this way can suggest to viewers that certain extreme behaviors and questionable values are normal. After all, characters on reality shows are ④ meant to be "regular people." The notion that cast members are just like everyone else when most of them are attractive and have what society considers perfect bodies ⑤ leads to low self-esteem in viewers.

09 다음 글의 밑줄 친 부분 중, 문맥상 낱말의 쓰임이 적절하지 않은 것은?

Speaking confidently paves the way for success. If people appear nervous or uncertain when they are talking, the audience may not believe what they are saying. However, if individuals speak with confidence, they are more ① convincing and get their messages across more clearly. In a discussion, people can gain confidence by speaking up at the beginning of a conversation. Anxiety increases over time, so it is ② beneficial to offer an opinion early on. If you fail to do so, discomfort grows, and joining the conversation will only become ③ easier. Practice also makes perfect. Therefore, prepare for an important discussion by thinking about what you want to express ④ before you speak. Lastly, remind yourself to slow down. Speaking too ⑤ quickly gives the impression that you are unsure of what you are saying.

10 다음 빈칸에 들어갈 말로 가장 적절한 것을 고르시오.

Some scientists believe there is a link between brain size and _____. The first members of the genus Homo emerged about three million years ago as *Australopithecus* went extinct. These early human ancestors were responsible for creating the first simple tools associated with a higher level of thought. About a million and a half years later, *Homo erectus*, a species with a bigger brain, appeared. What's interesting is that the appearance of both species occurred at times when weather patterns had begun to vary drastically, ushering in periods of increasingly dry weather or colder temperatures. This made life more unpredictable as food and water were harder to find, so our early ancestors may have evolved bigger brains to come up with solutions. It is speculated that future shifts in environmental conditions may lead to further adaptations to the size of our brains.

* the genus Homo: 인류

① critical thinking
② social interaction
③ physical development
④ longer lifespan
⑤ climate change

11 다음 글에서 전체 흐름과 관계 없는 문장은?

The English lexicon is constantly evolving, with new terms coming from various sources. For instance, technological innovations have often made it necessary to combine existing words in order to more accurately distinguish them. ① Prior to the 1980s, for example, telephones were fixed to one location and could only be used there. ② But when phones that could be used while moving around came along, it became necessary to distinguish them as "mobile phones." ③ Phone companies must license thousands of frequencies to maximize the number of simultaneous mobile phone calls. ④ Similarly, once computers became small and affordable enough for individual consumers to buy, they became known as "personal computers" or PCs. ⑤ More word combinations like these are sure to appear in the future as technology continues to advance and new innovations are discovered.

* lexicon: 어휘 ** simultaneous: 동시의

12 주어진 글 다음에 이어질 글의 순서로 가장 적절한 것을 고르시오.

Uncertainty avoidance describes how well people from different cultural backgrounds tolerate unpredictable events. It provides some insight into how they might respond to new and unfamiliar situations.

(A) To give an example of how the measure works, cultures with "high" uncertainty avoidance usually try to avoid uncertainty. This means that they have a low tolerance for unpredictability and are anxious about the future and anything new. They are therefore more likely to place an emphasis on tradition, order, and stability.

(B) The opposite is true of groups with "low" uncertainty avoidance. Such groups have a high tolerance for unpredictability and feel less fearful about unexpected events. Thus, they are generally more adaptable, innovative, and open to innovative ideas.

(C) The idea of uncertainty avoidance was first proposed by the Dutch sociologist Geert Hofstede during his research into cultural differences between countries. It is one of four measures he used to compare one country with another.

① (A) – (C) – (B)
② (B) – (A) – (C)
③ (B) – (C) – (A)
④ (C) – (A) – (B)
⑤ (C) – (B) – (A)

13 글의 흐름으로 보아, 주어진 문장이 들어가기에 가장 적절한 곳을 고르시오.

For example, individuals started to invent tools, establish a culture and organize into societal groups that began to live together.

Before the dawn of civilization, people were predominantly nomads, living in small groups that acquired food through hunting and gathering. (①) But around 10,000 BC, humans began to establish agricultural hubs and more permanent settlements, which resulted in numerous social changes. (②) Larger groups of people came to live together, and farming practices allowed for excess food production. (③) Due to this abundance of food, not everyone had to focus on providing nourishment, and this enabled people to pursue other "jobs." (④) Eventually, villages and towns became massive cities with dense populations. (⑤) Furthermore, civilizations began to flourish and advancements were made quickly, enabling humans to prosper rather than just survive.

* hub: 중심지

14 다음 글의 내용을 한 문장으로 요약하고자 한다. 빈칸 (A), (B)에 들어갈 말로 가장 적절한 것은?

In 1999, two psychologists, David Dunning and Justin Kruger, conducted a number of tests on a group of students, evaluating their logic, humor, and grammar. What they discovered was that the students who performed the worst also believed they had performed far better than they actually did. They were not only incompetent but also lacked the self-awareness to judge their incompetence accurately. This phenomenon has since become known as the Dunning-Kruger effect. According to Dunning and Kruger, the effect may be caused by something they called the "dual burden." The dual burden describes a condition in which the knowledge that people need to complete a task well is the same knowledge that they need to evaluate themselves correctly. It is as if the incompetent students had two burdens or obstacles to overcome. First, they did not know enough to do well on the tests. Second, their lack of knowledge caused them to be unaware of how badly they did.

⇩

According to the Dunning-Kruger effect, people who perform ____(A)____ also lack the appropriate ____(B)____ to judge themselves accurately.

	(A)		(B)
①	well	···	knowledge
②	well	···	psychology
③	poorly	···	interest
④	poorly	···	awareness
⑤	normally	···	competence

[15~16] 다음 글을 읽고, 물음에 답하시오.

Although using a laptop to take notes is seemingly convenient, taking notes the old-fashioned way may boost your understanding of the material. That's because writing by hand is a slower process than using a laptop. Students who use laptops are able to transcribe the material so quickly that they often just type what is said word for word. Students who put pen to paper, on the other hand, cannot write everything down, so they learn to distinguish important details from irrelevant ones. They can also explain the concepts discussed in a lecture better afterwards because they have to listen very carefully and make sense of the material before they summarize it in their notes.

Furthermore, students who take freehand notes have more _____ when it comes to note-taking than students who use laptops. For example, when you take notes by hand, you have the flexibility to add sketches and diagrams or to circle keywords. Because students may come to associate concepts with them, the end results can be very useful. When you use a computer, on the other hand, all you can do to improve your understanding of a concept is describe it in writing. This is less effective at helping them recall key details when preparing for an exam later.

* freehand: (다른 기구 없이) 손으로만 작성한

15 윗글의 제목으로 가장 적절한 것은?

① Block Online Distractions, and Get Back on Track!
② The Benefits of Freehand Note-Taking over Using Laptops
③ Lecture-Based Classes: Do They Help the Learning Process?
④ How to Determine the Most Efficient Note-Taking Methods
⑤ The Importance of Teaching Handwriting in the Digital Age

16 윗글의 빈칸에 들어갈 말로 가장 적절한 것은?

① freedom ② energy ③ stress
④ ability ⑤ confidence

[17~19] 다음 글을 읽고, 물음에 답하시오.

(A)

Long ago, a rich businessman decided to retire and spend time with his family. His wife had passed away, but he had three sons. His sons always said they were very busy, though, so they only came twice a year. As the man grew older, his sons stopped by less and less to see him. "They don't want to be with (a) me," he thought sadly. "What can I do about this?"

(B)

So, the three sons took turns living with their father, taking care of him and keeping him company. (b) He eventually grew old and died happily after spending so much time with his sons. After the funeral, his sons finally opened the chest and saw all the glass. "What a mean trick!" the eldest complained. But the middle son said "No, we would have neglected him if he hadn't done this." "You're right," said the youngest. "I'm so ashamed. All he wanted was our love."

(C)

He finally came up with a clever plan. The next day, he went to the carpenter and asked him for a large chest. Then, (c) he visited the engineer to make the strongest lock. Finally, he stopped by the glassmaker and asked for broken pieces of glass. The father went home, filled the chest with glass, locked it, and set it under the kitchen table.

* chest: 상자

(D)

The next time (d) his sons visited, they saw it and wondered what was inside. "It's just some things I've been saving," their father replied. Their feet hit the chest as they sat down. They could hear the glass clinking inside. "Listen to those coins! And it's so heavy!" the eldest whispered to (e) his brothers. "It must be all the gold he's saved over the years." The sons decided to take care of their father to inherit the fortune.

17. 주어진 글 (A)에 이어질 내용을 순서에 맞게 배열한 것으로 가장 적절한 것은?

① (B) – (D) – (C)
② (C) – (B) – (D)
③ (C) – (D) – (B)
④ (D) – (B) – (C)
⑤ (D) – (C) – (B)

18. 밑줄 친 (a) ~ (e) 중에서 가리키는 대상이 나머지 넷과 다른 것은?

① (a)
② (b)
③ (c)
④ (d)
⑤ (e)

19. 윗글에 관한 내용으로 적절하지 않은 것은?

① 아들들은 처음에 아버지를 자주 찾아오지 않았다.
② 사업가의 아들들은 교대로 그와 같이 살았다.
③ 막내아들은 아버지의 마음을 몰라준 것을 미안해했다.
④ 아버지는 상자를 깨진 유리로 채웠다.
⑤ 아들들은 아버지의 외로운 모습을 보고 그를 돌보기로 했다.

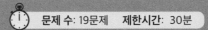

정답 및 해설 p.165

01 다음 글의 목적으로 가장 적절한 것은?

To whom it may concern,

Hello, my name is Kathy Owens. I have been a longtime customer of your airline. I was recently booked on Flight 546 from New York to Hong Kong. I had an important meeting that I could not miss. Unfortunately, when I arrived for my flight, I found out the plane had a serious mechanical problem. The flight was delayed until the next day. I had no choice but to take a different flight, and it still caused me to miss my meeting. As such, I would like to ask for a refund for my original ticket. Thank you for your time.

Regards,
Kathy Owens

① 불친절한 기내 서비스에 대해 불만을 제기하려고
② 구매했던 비행기 티켓의 환불을 요청하려고
③ 항공편이 지연되어 승객들에게 사과하려고
④ 이용 가능한 항공편이 있는지 문의하려고
⑤ 회의 시간이 변경되었음을 공지하려고

02 다음 글에 드러난 Lauren의 심경 변화로 가장 적절한 것은?

Lauren looked at the map. She couldn't understand it. Had she taken a wrong turn somewhere along the hiking trail? She had been searching for the waterfall for hours now and, according to the map, she should be there. She checked the map again and walked in the other direction. She had always been able to get around the mountains, so she didn't know why she was having trouble now. She began to wonder if the map was wrong, when she heard the loud snap of a tree branch. She looked around but saw nothing. Suddenly, she heard a low growl. Her heart started pounding and she could feel herself shaking.

① gloomy → irritated
② furious → eager
③ confused → frightened
④ satisfied → confident
⑤ excited → nervous

03 다음 글의 요지로 가장 적절한 것은?

Millions of people all over the world are becoming more and more concerned about climate change. Unfortunately, among developed countries, only a few are taking the necessary steps against this issue. And only one country has passed a policy that aims to reduce the country's carbon emissions to 70 percent below its 1990 levels by 2030. Thus, it is important for countries and political leaders to take more aggressive action. Experts say that significant action needs to be adopted. Rather than making promises to try, enacting a law is a powerful move that can make a real difference. Hopefully, making more powerful policies will soon become the norm rather than the exception.

① 기후 변화를 막아야 할 책임은 개인에게도 있다.

② 탄소 배출량 감소는 기후 변화를 막는 데 도움이 된다.

③ 기후 변화에 대응하기 위한 조치는 더욱 강력해져야 한다.

④ 이미 시행되고 있는 환경 정책을 보완하는 것이 중요하다.

⑤ 선진국은 개발도상국이 탄소 배출을 줄이는 것을 도와야 한다.

04 밑줄 친 a necessary evil이 다음 글에서 의미하는 바로 가장 적절한 것은?

It's natural for individuals to want to avoid conflict. After all, it can be uncomfortable and awkward. But clashing with other people can benefit rather than harm relationships. If you as an individual disagree with someone you know, it might be better to explain your perspective, on the situation. This is because suppressing your thoughts, feelings, and opinions in order to please someone else can lead to a buildup of angry feelings and an unhealthy relationship over time. Instead, people should practice effective conflict resolution, in which each person is open and willing to hear their counterpart out. This can result in people understanding one another better in the long run. Therefore, accepting that conflict occurs doesn't mean a relationship is doomed to fail; in fact, it is actually a necessary evil.

① a negative event that exposes weaknesses

② a temporary solution that leads to failure

③ a painful way to avoid permanent farewells

④ a guide to start a conversation with strangers

⑤ a pleasant way for people to settle their conflicts

05 다음 글의 제목으로 가장 적절한 것은?

Sports are beneficial in so many ways, from improving fitness to offering individuals a sense of belonging. For adolescents in particular, participating in sports has proven to be especially advantageous for learning about peer cooperation. By working with their peers to overcome challenges and reducing stress while doing so, teenagers who engage in sports see improvements in their mental health and self-confidence, which can ultimately reduce their likelihood of developing anti-social behavior. In this way, sports have even been shown to assist in the fight against crime as they encourage adolescents to spend their time on the field or court instead of engaging in illegal acts. Hence, sports are undoubtedly a useful asset in youth-crime prevention.

① Playing Sports: Good for Some, Not for All

② The Effects of Sports on Self-Confidence

③ Sports as a Method of Physical Recovery

④ Sports: The Key to Stopping Youth Crime

⑤ Team Sports: The Hidden Cause of Illegal Behavior

06 다음 도표의 내용과 일치하지 <u>않는</u> 것은?

Number of Male Deaths **Number of Female Deaths**

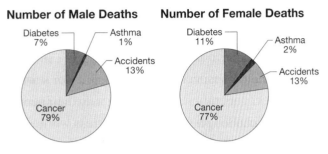

The above charts show the number of male and female deaths caused by cancer, diabetes, asthma, or accidents. ① In both male and female deaths, cancer was the largest cause of death and accounted for more than 75% of deaths each. ② The percentage of deaths caused by accidents exceeded that of deaths caused by diabetes for males. ③ The percentage of death caused by asthma was the lowest for females, though it was still three times higher than asthma deaths in males. ④ Compared to that of females, there were fewer deaths caused by diabetes but more death caused by cancer in males. ⑤ The number of deaths caused by accidents and diabetes combined was still less than the deaths caused by cancer for both males and females.

07 Studio Rock's Beginner Pottery에 관한 다음 안내문의 내용과 일치하는 것은?

Studio Rock's Beginner Pottery

If you're interested in picking up a new hobby, look no further than our weekend pottery workshop for beginners. It's the perfect way to meet new people and unwind after a long week at work!

About classes:
- Classes take place on Saturdays and Sundays.
- Two classes each day: Morning and Afternoon
- $80 per class / $290 for 1 course (4 classes)
 *All materials and tools will be provided.

Learn:
- Pottery wheel (electric and manual)
- Painting
- Decorating
- Hand sculpting

You can register online at our website or call 555-0123 between 8 a.m. and 5 p.m.
*Class sizes are kept to a maximum of five, so sign up early to participate.

① 이 수업은 전문가들만 들을 수 있다.
② 평일에는 두 개의 수업이 진행된다.
③ 전체 한 코스는 4회 수업으로 이루어진다.
④ 학생들은 전기 물레를 사용하는 것만 배운다.
⑤ 수업에는 최소 다섯 명의 학생들이 있다.

08 다음 글의 밑줄 친 부분 중 어법상 틀린 것은?

Although chimpanzees and bonobos are very ① closely related, the fact that they exhibit different behavioral traits suggests that their cognitive skills differ as well. Because chimpanzees have the ability to craft simple tools to assist in ② their foraging, for instance, it stands to reason that they understand cause and effect. In other words, they comprehend that using tools such as sticks ③ make a task easier. Bonobos, on the other hand, ④ are believed to have a theory of mind, which means they can identify different feelings in others and act accordingly. Much of what leads researchers to this conclusion is ⑤ how bonobos interact with one another. They are well-known for providing comfort to others and, unlike chimpanzees, resolving conflicts with affection rather than aggression.

09 다음 글의 밑줄 친 부분 중, 문맥상 낱말의 쓰임이 적절하지 않은 것은?

It's no coincidence that a bad code in a computer is called a virus. Just like viruses infecting people, the electronic variety infects computers. A computer virus needs a file or document where it can "live." It is ① similar to how a human virus requires a host or else it will die. An external element, such as double-clicking a file, can easily ② awake a computer virus. However, until then, the virus remains ③ inactive. Sometimes, a computer virus can be ④ found for months because it doesn't do anything. You have no idea it is in your computer, concealed or buried in a file somewhere. Once it is initiated, however, ⑤ harmful issues start to show up on your system. For instance, a really bad virus can steal your personal information or delete everything on the computer.

10 다음 빈칸에 들어갈 말로 가장 적절한 것을 고르시오.

We all have a constant stream of thoughts going through our head, or a personal narrative we use to give ourselves instructions or make observations about our surroundings. If what we tell ourselves is good, this inner monologue, known as self-talk, can cheer us on and have such a positive effect that _____. For instance, athletes who engage in positive self-talk can put themselves in the right mental state before a game. Any anxiety they feel about failing to live up to the crowd's expectations can lead to a very real inability to perform properly. But engaging in self-talk that calms, motivates, helps them focus, and reminds them of techniques they should use can be incredibly reassuring. This can translate to overcoming any pre-game jitters they might have so they can play to the best of their abilities.

* jitter: 초조, 공포감

① healthier habits are adopted
② we judge our failures less harshly
③ our perception of other people changes
④ decision-making skills are enhanced
⑤ our ability to function improves

11 다음 글에서 전체 흐름과 관계 없는 문장은?

Considering how much social media influences our perceptions, it's not surprising that it has a significant impact on the tourism industry as well. ① Very few people these days rely solely on advertisements or the advice of a travel agent when planning a trip. ② Instead, most turn to sources they trust on social media, like family and friends, who can provide firsthand advice on where to go. ③ By doing so, travelers can minimize their risk of making a bad decision. ④ Some tourist destinations are only popular at certain times of the year. ⑤ The tourism industry has become increasingly aware of this in recent years and is posting visually engaging content and hiring influencers to target potential customers directly.

12 주어진 글 다음에 이어질 글의 순서로 가장 적절한 것을 고르시오.

One of the most important but underestimated inventions is the nail, which is a necessary component in constructing furniture and houses.

(A) Our reliance on this method lessened once we were able to produce objects made of metal. Metal pieces could be hammered on four sides to form sharpened spikes, or nails.

(B) Prior to the creation of the nail, these types of structures were built by interlocking wood in different patterns or joining them with other wooden pieces. They relied mainly on tension to support weight and remain standing.

(C) The nail's sharpened point allowed it to be driven through pieces of wood, joining the pieces together quickly and with far less difficulty than before. So, even though it may appear small and insignificant, the nail has served societies throughout the ages by allowing permanent structures to be built efficiently.

* tension: 장력

① (A) – (C) – (B)
② (B) – (A) – (C)
③ (B) – (C) – (A)
④ (C) – (A) – (B)
⑤ (C) – (B) – (A)

13 글의 흐름으로 보아, 주어진 문장이 들어가기에 가장 적절한 곳을 고르시오.

> To illustrate, they may use three fingers to quickly signal approval without saying any words out loud.

Hand gestures play an important role in communication by allowing us to express ideas for which we may not have the right words at a given time. (①) Indeed, people around the world regularly depend on a variety of hand gestures in everyday interactions. (②) But care should be taken to use appropriate gestures for a particular cultural context. (③) This is because just as words carry different meanings in different cultures, so too can hand gestures invite varied interpretations. (④) For instance, crossing the index and middle fingers has wildly divergent connotations depending on where you do it. (⑤) In America, it is a positive expression of good luck, but in Vietnam, a highly offensive insult!

* connotation: 함의

14 다음 글의 내용을 한 문장으로 요약하고자 한다. 빈칸 (A), (B)에 들어갈 말로 가장 적절한 것은?

> Research into pitch perception, or the ability to detect slight variations in musical sounds, was recently conducted on the Tsimane people, an indigenous tribe living in a remote area of the Bolivian rainforest. The researchers wanted to determine if the Tsimane could recognize the link between different versions of the same note, like middle C and high C. By playing Western music, which is full of such variations, the researchers determined that they could not. The Tsimane had never listened to Western music before, and their own music does not contain such variations. This led the researchers to conclude that pitch perception is not something that we are born with but acquire over time if we are exposed to it.

⇩

> The fact that the Tsimane people could not ____(A)____ different pitches of the same note means that this ability is ____(B)____.

	(A)		(B)
①	know	…	necessary
②	enjoy	…	learned
③	memorize	…	innate
④	fear	…	innate
⑤	identify	…	learned

[15~16] 다음 글을 읽고 물음에 답하시오.

Across the industrialized world, companies are testing autonomous vehicles in large numbers, suggesting that a driverless future could soon be at hand. Apart from helping business run more efficiently and making long commutes bearable, autonomous cars could (a) <u>reduce</u> carbon emissions and the alarming number of deaths that occur each year in accidents. Moreover, most experts (b) <u>doubt</u> development to spread more rapidly in some areas than others. For instance, adoption will likely occur earlier in highly controlled environments such as factory floors, and in places where physical dangers (c) <u>threaten</u> human operators, such as mines. They also predict that driverless robotic vehicles will become more common than passenger cars, since their speeds can easily be (d) <u>limited</u> to run safely alongside pedestrians. Still, challenges remain. For one, autonomous vehicles, which are programmed to follow instructions, have to contend with the (e) <u>unpredictable</u> behavior of human drivers, who do not always follow the rules of the road. In addition, bringing large numbers of driverless cars to our streets safely will require great changes to policy and infrastructure. The public, too, will need to be convinced of their safety. Given these concerns, it's not a good time for champagne yet.

15 윗글의 제목으로 가장 적절한 것은?

① Driverless Cars: Still A Long Way to Go

② The Difficulties in producing Carbon-Free Vehicles

③ What is the Biggest Concern for Automotive Industry Today?

④ Automation: The Future of Technology

⑤ Why We Need Autonomous Vehicles

16 밑줄 친 (a)~(e) 중에서 문맥상 낱말의 쓰임이 적절하지 않은 것은?

① (a)　　② (b)　　③ (c)　　④ (d)　　⑤ (e)

[17~19] 다음 글을 읽고, 물음에 답하시오.

(A)

A man named Vincent became seriously ill one day and had to stay in a hospital room to recover. He was given a shared room with a bed by the door. Across from him, on the opposite side of the room, was another bed by the window. An old man occupied the bed and greeted Vincent as he came in. "It's nice to meet (a) you," he said.

(B)

Weeks went by and Vincent awoke one day to realize that the old man had died. Although this news made Vincent sad, he immediately thought of the bed by the window. Having had nothing but an empty ceiling to stare at for days, (b) he liked the idea of having the view from the window for himself. With the nurse's permission, he moved to the empty bed and looked outside.

(C)

Each day, the old man by the window sat up in bed for an hour. On those occasions, he would look out the window and describe what he saw, such as bright white clouds against a perfectly blue sky or colorfully dressed pedestrians moving around like ants in the street below. Vincent took pleasure in hearing the old man speak. He imagined the scenes as if (c) he were looking at them himself.

(D)

To (d) his amazement, there was nothing outside but a wall. Vincent expressed some surprise to his nurse, who commented that the man was completely blind and was unable to see anything at all. When Vincent wondered aloud why (e) he would take the time to describe so many scenes in detail, the nurse said that he was trying to offer Vincent words of encouragement.

17 주어진 글 (A)에 이어질 내용을 순서에 맞게 배열한 것으로 가장 적절한 것은?

① (B) – (D) – (C)
② (C) – (B) – (D)
③ (C) – (D) – (B)
④ (D) – (B) – (C)
⑤ (D) – (C) – (B)

18 밑줄 친 (a)~(e) 중에서 가리키는 대상이 나머지 넷과 다른 것은?

① (a)
② (b)
③ (c)
④ (d)
⑤ (e)

19 윗글에 관한 내용으로 적절하지 <u>않은</u> 것은?

① Vincent는 다인실을 제공받았다.
② Vincent는 노인의 죽음을 슬퍼했다.
③ 노인은 Vincent에게 매일 창밖 풍경을 묘사했다.
④ Vincent는 노인의 이야기에 싫증이 났다.
⑤ 노인은 Vincent를 격려하고 싶어 했다.

01 다음 글의 주제로 가장 적절한 것은?

Imagine coming across two stories in the news—one about millions of children suffering from severe poverty and another about a single child named Paul who is also in the same situation. If you are like most people, you are more likely to feel greater sympathy for the suffering of Paul than for the millions of other children. The reason for this is something called the "identifiable victim effect," which describes a common bias people have of feeling more empathy for a victim who is specific and identifiable rather than another who is largely faceless or nameless. The bias occurs because our brains lack the capacity to deal with tragedies on a massive scale. And because of the identifiable victim effect, many people ignore problems that affect a great number of victims. Instead, they focus their attention on the smaller number who are identifiable by name.

① why unidentified people can be more sympathetic
② advantages of the identifiable victim effect
③ challenges faced when identifying victims
④ why we lack sympathy for unknown people
⑤ strategies to recognize people in times of crisis

02 다음 글의 제목으로 가장 적절한 것은?

Many animals use camouflage to blend in with their surroundings. But some, like the tiger, have such striking colors and markings that one has to wonder how they succeed. Part of the answer has to do with how animals see color. For instance, whereas human eyes can process a full range of colors, many of the animals in the tiger's environment, such as deer, can only see green and blue. To the deer, therefore, the tiger appears nearly invisible against the green background of the jungle. The tiger's bold stripes also play a part by breaking up the tiger's outline. This helps it remain in camouflage as it creeps among tall grasses and plants while it hunts. So, though a tiger's coat may appear colorful and noticeable to our eyes, it is almost completely undetectable to other animals.

① Deer: A Tiger's Favorite Prey
② Why Animals Need Camouflage
③ Color Perception in the Animal Kingdom
④ The Secrets Behind Tiger Camouflage
⑤ How do Animals Distinguish Shapes?

03 밑줄 친 a closed system이 다음 글에서 의미하는 바로 가장 적절한 것은?

If you walk into a forest, you may see trees filled with fruits, bushes with ripe berries, or plenty of mushrooms and other vegetables sprouting from the ground. Such a harvest has only one farmer: Mother Nature. This is the basis of natural farming, also known as "do-nothing farming." It is an approach to agriculture that encourages the laws of nature and works alongside biodiversity, so that plants can thrive without humanity's touch. Natural farming does not use any of the modern advancements to farming, like machines, pesticides, and fertilizer. Instead, it tries to copy what nature does and allows crops to develop on their own. In this way, it is a closed system, which is more cost-efficient and environmentally-friendly.

① a process needing constant care from farmers
② a plan for more abundant vegetables
③ a practice that can maintain itself
④ a technique that is more agriculturally advanced
⑤ a method that copies ancient farming techniques

04 다음 글의 밑줄 친 부분 중, 어법상 틀린 것은?

Participatory democracy is a political system wherein the power to make political decisions is given to citizens completely. A participatory democracy, while similar to other forms of democracy in that power rests in the hands of the people, ① advocates for more participation and representation than others. That is why it is less likely to be ② corrupted by politicians. However, critics say that this type of democracy is not realistic. In modern day, managing a nation is an ③ extremely complex and integrated endeavor. It calls for time and effort ④ what the average citizen may not have. As such, representatives, ⑤ whose job it is to understand the complexities and consequences of political policies, need to represent the majority.

* participatory democracy: 참여 민주주의

05 다음 글의 밑줄 친 부분 중, 문맥상 낱말의 쓰임이 적절하지 않은 것은?

The principle of double effect argues that "intentional" harm is morally worse than "unintentional" harm. Take driving a car here, for example. Driving is a job requirement for some people, but for others, it has ① become a way for them to have fun. However, driving has been widely ② identified as a leading contributor to global warming. Given that both sets of drivers are polluters, can we say that both should have ③ equal blame? At first, their responsibility might seem similar, since both groups knowingly ④ cause harm. However, while the first group has no choice but to drive, the second group has alternatives. By driving for fun, they are intentionally choosing a ⑤ harmless action even though they can make a different choice. Seen in this light, we can argue that the second group's actions are worse.

06 다음 빈칸에 들어갈 말로 가장 적절한 것을 고르시오.

An ever-expanding awareness of the nutrients in various foods is making some people reconsider their previous views on the vegetarian diet. In the past, their lack of knowledge may have led them to believe that being a vegetarian meant eating only salad, which may fail to satisfy all of a person's nutritional requirements. However, foods such as tofu, beans, and nuts—common staples among most vegetarians—are now commonly known to be excellent sources of protein and other essential nutrients. Meanwhile, hardly can you go online without coming across an article on fruits and vegetables that are considered super foods and a list of all their vitamins, minerals, and benefits. A meat-free diet does not suit everyone's taste, but more and more people are beginning to realize that a vegetarian diet doesn't have to be _____.

* staple: 주식(主食) ** nutrient: 영양소

① inconvenient
② educational
③ balanced
④ expensive
⑤ insufficient

07 주어진 글 다음에 이어질 글의 순서로 가장 적절한 것을 고르시오.

Although often taken for granted today, the common mechanical clock represents one of the most important steps forward in humanity's economic success.

(A) Unfortunately, this method was extremely subjective, and depended not only on being able to see the sun, but also on one's perception of its location. Businesspeople had no real way to plan their activities. However, once accurate mechanical clocks were invented, time could be objectively measured and shared.

(B) Prior to the invention of mechanical clocks, time was measured rather imprecisely, which made business activity difficult to coordinate. People determined when to do things by looking at the location of the sun in the sky and individually deciding the general time of day, such as sunup, midday, and sundown.

(C) Having precise measurements of time allowed businesspeople to set their hours, schedule meetings, coordinate trade activities, and monitor their production schedules. All of these made economic success possible.

① (A) – (C) – (B)
② (B) – (A) – (C)
③ (B) – (C) – (A)
④ (C) – (A) – (B)
⑤ (C) – (B) – (A)

08 글의 흐름으로 보아, 주어진 문장이 들어가기에 가장 적절한 곳을 고르시오.

> "Sympathy," in contrast, is used to mean a person's response to the negative experiences (suffering) of another individual.

The distinction between the words "empathy" and "sympathy" is not very clear, which often leads to confusion. (①) However, one key difference is how we act when we feel each one. (②) "Empathy" is generally used to understand both positive and negative experiences, resulting in pro-social (helping) behavior towards the other. (③) Unlike "empathy," it doesn't necessarily involve doing anything about it (no pro-social behavior). (④) Rather, sympathizing allows a person to acknowledge a situation and just realize the other person is going through a difficult time. (⑤) So while "empathy" may cause a person to directly react to the other, "sympathy" is more of a passive form of simply feeling compassion.

09 밑줄 친 an obstacle to overcome이 다음 글에서 의미하는 바로 가장 적절한 것은?

If there was a drug that could improve memory and make it possible to concentrate for hours on end, one might ask, "Would it be ethical to take it?" With regard to work, it might help people be more productive at the office and finally get that promotion. But as the development of such a drug becomes a reality, it seems that there may be an obstacle to overcome. Some opponents say that companies could start pressuring their employees to use it against their will. In this day and age, most people strive for a healthy work-life balance. However, these drugs would likely only contribute to the creation of a society in which the main focus is work, leaving people with little time to relax and do the things they want to do.

① a strong likelihood that it will never be available
② a small chance that people will not be willing to use it
③ a possibility that it might destroy our work-life balance
④ a minor side effect that can be safely ignored
⑤ a possible problem with the production process

10 다음 글의 밑줄 친 부분 중, 어법상 틀린 것은?

This is the story of two frogs. One frog was fat and the other skinny. One day, while ① searching for food, they inadvertently jumped into a vat of milk. The sides were so slippery ② that it was hard for them to hop out easily. They had nothing to do but swim. After paddling for hours, the skinny frog grew tired, ran out of breath, and ③ crying for help. But the fat frog said, "Keep trying my friend. Something good will happen." Another couple of hours passed. The skinny frog said, "I can't go on any longer," and he decided ④ to stop paddling. Slowly, he drowned in the milk but the fat frog didn't give up. Ten minutes later, the fat frog felt something ⑤ strange under his feet. The milk turned into hard butter at last, and the fat frog finally hopped out of the vat.

* vat: 통   ** paddle: 첨벙거리다

11 다음 글의 밑줄 친 부분 중, 문맥상 낱말의 쓰임이 적절하지 <u>않은</u> 것은?

Philosophy of medicine is a relatively recent field of study that developed in the 21st century. Individuals who study the philosophy of medicine try to ① understand the intellectual aspects of the medical industry better. For example, philosophers of medicine might research moral or ethical issues about health, disease, or treatment. They ask ② conceptual questions: What is the meaning of health? What is the nature of healing? Healthcare professionals ③ lack the time to think about such abstract topics since they have to focus on practical tasks like writing prescriptions and talking to patients. So instead, philosophers of medicine study theories about ④ unimportant decisions that busy doctors and nurses cannot always consider. Philosophers of medicine thus ⑤ have an essential purpose, and contribute to advancements in the medical field.

12 다음 빈칸에 들어갈 말로 가장 적절한 것을 고르시오.

Algorithms on music streaming services utilize users' playlists and listening history to recommend new artists and albums. Recently, research into the accuracy of these recommendations was conducted using two groups of users on a UK music website: those who mostly listen to "mainstream" music and those who mostly listen to non-mainstream music. For the purpose of the study, non-mainstream music was defined as music featuring only acoustic instruments or high-energy music like electronica or hard rock, either with or without vocals. The study found that while the algorithms did well predicting what mainstream music fans might like, they were not as effective at anticipating the same for non-mainstream music listeners. It therefore appears as though _____. This discovery could lead to the creation of more effective algorithms that could result in better and more balanced music recommendations for all users.

* acoustic: 전자 장치를 쓰지 않는 악기로 연주한, 음향의

① users of the UK music website are very influenced by algorithmic tools

② mainstream musicians outnumber non-mainstream musicians

③ recommendation systems are biased toward popular music

④ demand for more alternative music has been largely ignored

⑤ the researchers had difficulty characterizing non-mainstream music

13 주어진 글 다음에 이어질 글의 순서로 가장 적절한 것을 고르시오.

If the weather suddenly changes and your knees start to ache, are the two connected somehow? In fact, they are, and there may actually be a scientific reason behind it.

(A) We feel that tension in places like the hips, knees, hands, or shoulder joints. And that is what produces the pain. So when your grandfather says he knows a storm is coming because his knees hurt, he is telling the truth!

(B) For instance, when barometric pressure drops, such as right before a thunderstorm, there is less pressure on our bodies, allowing the tissue inside to swell. This swollen tissue puts pressure on our joints.

(C) Although we don't often think about it, the air presses down on everything below it, including our bodies. This is called barometric pressure. Our bodies are so sensitive to it that any change has an effect on us.

* barometric pressure: 기압

① (A) – (C) – (B)
② (B) – (A) – (C)
③ (B) – (C) – (A)
④ (C) – (A) – (B)
⑤ (C) – (B) – (A)

14 글의 흐름으로 보아, 주어진 문장이 들어가기에 가장 적절한 곳을 고르시오.

The entertainment industry supports this legislation and argues that users should pay for copyrighted materials in whatever way that they are used.

Over the past two decades, online piracy has become increasingly widespread. (①) Internet users can download or stream all kinds of media, including music, movies, and books with just a few clicks. (②) Not surprisingly, this trend has created friction between entertainment companies and the online community. (③) As a result, a bill has been proposed that would prevent all forms of copyright violations on the Web if passed. (④) Users, on the other hand, believe that any new laws could ultimately block the free flow of information on the Internet. (⑤) Clearly, one side has something to gain and the other has something to lose depending on which group the law favors.

* online piracy: 온라인 저작권 침해

15 다음 빈칸에 들어갈 말로 가장 적절한 것을 고르시오.

The subject of free will has been debated for centuries by philosophers, and none have taken a firmer stance against it than determinists. Determinists do not believe it is possible to have free will or to make independent choices to alter your fate. Rather, they believe that _____. To use a metaphor from science, the earth, year after year, follows a predictable path around the sun. It has no choice but to follow this path because its orbit is influenced or determined by the force of the sun's gravity. Determinists believe something similar occurs with people. People follow a path in life that has been influenced or determined by the force of past actions. Whenever they choose to do something, they are not actually exercising their free will but are behaving exactly as they should, given their particular circumstances.

* determinist: 결정론자

① everything is an outcome of prior events
② one's fate is uncertain at the time of birth
③ pursuing freedom is the goal of philosophy
④ all decisions are based on personal goals
⑤ future outcomes are impossible to predict

16 주어진 글 다음에 이어질 글의 순서로 가장 적절한 것을 고르시오.

Free trade agreements, or FTAs, are essentially contracts drawn to exchange goods and services.

(A) In the ideal scenario, FTAs are mutually beneficial for both. Of course, this isn't always the case with imbalanced conditions, but the major aim is to foster prosperity for all.

(B) Developing economies, on the other hand, benefit from FTAs in other ways. FTAs give access to foreign capital and technical support, both of which can be put to use growing local industries and providing jobs to citizens.

(C) In the case of developed economies, FTAs allow them to open up new markets for their products and outsource the production of goods to countries where costs are low. They are thus able to use their capital for other purposes, such as investing in new lines of business.

① (A) – (C) – (B)
② (B) – (A) – (C)
③ (B) – (C) – (A)
④ (C) – (A) – (B)
⑤ (C) – (B) – (A)

17 다음 글의 내용을 한 문장으로 요약하고자 한다. 빈칸 (A), (B)에 들어갈 말로 가장 적절한 것은?

In 1959, Leon Festinger and James Carlsmith had participants in an experiment spend an hour performing tasks that were designed to be boring and repetitive. When they were done, the participants were paid either $1 or $20 to tell the next participants waiting for their turn that the tasks had been interesting. Then, the participants rated how much they had enjoyed the tasks. Those who were paid $1 were more likely to claim the tasks had been enjoyable than those who were paid $20, even if they did not believe this initially. They did this because they were conflicted about having wasted an hour of their time for only $1. By saying that the tasks had been fun, participants were able to justify having done them and make themselves feel better about the situation. This phenomenon is known as cognitive dissonance, and it tells us that we try to manipulate our beliefs to justify them.

⇩

People _____(A)_____ the way they think when they need a(n) _____(B)_____ reason for a given situation.

	(A)		(B)
①	ignore	…	uncertain
②	express	…	better
③	adjust	…	better
④	adjust	…	worse
⑤	express	…	worse

[18~19] 다음 글을 읽고, 물음에 답하시오.

The movement of Romanticism began in the late 18th century. Departing from the traditional art of the time, it focused heavily on emotions and imagination as well as celebrating the common man. This was in part a response to the Industrial Revolution that (a) shifted society's focus from the natural to innovation and science. Romanticists wanted to instead explore the (b) internal life. Thus, to express this properly, Romantic art had to come from within the mind of the artist. Therefore, it should not be superficial or artificial. Much as its name implies, Romanticism focused on love and joy. However, Romanticists also examined the (c) opposite end of the spectrum and delved deeply into feelings of horror, isolation, and melancholy. A prime example of this is the poem by Edgar Allen Poe titled "The Raven," in which a narrator mourning the loss of his love is visited by a mysterious raven in the middle of the night. The work centered on heightened feelings—in this case, grief and mental instability—that romanticists (d) denied to convey through literature and art. Romanticism eventually peaked in the 1800s and gave way to Realism in the art world. Still, its characteristics (e) remained popular, and its influence can be found everywhere across film, television, literature, music, and art to this day.

* mourn: 애도하다   ** raven: 까마귀

18 윗글의 제목으로 가장 적절한 것은?

① What Romanticism Is, What It Left Us
② Why is Romanticism Popular in Media?
③ The Rise and Fall of Romantic Artists
④ Romanticism: A Missed Opportunity
⑤ The Need for Romantic Art Today

19 밑줄 친 (a) ~ (e) 중에서 문맥상 낱말의 쓰임이 적절하지 **않은** 것은?

① (a) ② (b) ③ (c) ④ (d) ⑤ (e)

MEMO

MEMO

MEMO

해커스 수능독해 불변의 패턴

유형편 | 정답 및 해설

해커스 어학연구소

목적 파악하기

불변의 패턴 01   p.16
글을 쓴 목적은 대부분 글의 중간 이후에 나온다.

기출문제   정답 ①

지문분석

My name is Anthony Thompson / and I am writing on behalf of / the residents' association.
제 이름은 Anthony Thompson입니다 / 그리고 저는 대표하여 (편지를) 쓰고 있습니다 / 입주민 조합

Our recycling program / has been working well / thanks to your participation.
저희의 재활용 프로그램 / 잘 운영되고 있습니다 / 여러분의 참여 덕분에

★ However, / a problem has recently occurred / that needs your attention.
그런데 / 최근 문제가 하나 생겼습니다 / 여러분의 관심이 필요한

Because there is no given day / for recycling, / residents are putting their recycling out / at any time.
정해진 날이 없어서 / 재활용을 위한 / 입주민들은 재활용품을 내놓습니다 / 아무 때나

This makes the recycling area messy, / which requires extra labor and cost.
이것이 재활용 구역을 어지럽힙니다 / 이는 추가 일거리와 비용이 필요하게끔 합니다

To deal with this problem, / the residents' association has decided on / a day to recycle.
이 문제를 해결하기 위해서 / 입주민 조합은 정했습니다 / 재활용하는 날

I would like to let you know / that you can put out your recycling / on Wednesdays only.
저는 여러분께 알려드리고 싶습니다 / 여러분의 재활용품을 내놓을 수 있다는 것 / 오직 수요일에만

I am sure / it will make our apartment complex / look much more pleasant.
저는 확신합니다 / 이것이 저희 아파트 단지를 만들 것이라고 / 훨씬 더 쾌적해 보이게

Thank you in advance for your cooperation.
여러분들의 협조에 미리 감사드립니다

★ 독해가 쉬워지는 구문 풀이

However, a problem has recently **occurred** [that needs your attention].
주어 / 동사구 / 관계절

⇨ [ ]은 주어 a problem을 수식하는 관계절이다.
⇨ occurs는 '~가 생기다, 일어나다'로 해석되지만 목적어를 필요로 하지 않는 자동사이므로 뒤에 나오는 [ ]를 목적어로 착각하지 않도록 주의한다.

어휘 on behalf of ~을 대표하여 residents' association 입주민 조합 recycling 재활용 participation 참여 attention 관심, 주의 given 정해진 messy 어지러운 apartment complex 아파트 단지 in advance 미리 cooperation 협조

해석 제 이름은 Anthony Thompson이고 저는 입주민 조합을 대표하여 (편지를) 쓰고 있습니다. 저희의 재활용 프로그램은 여러분의 참여 덕분에 잘 운영되고 있습니다. 그런데 최근 여러분의 관심이 필요한 문제가 하나 생겼습니다. 재활용을 위해 정해진 날이 없어서 입주민들은 아무 때나 그들의 재활용품을 내놓습니다. 이것은 재활용 구역을 어지럽히고 추가 일거리와 비용이 필요하게끔 합니다. 이 문제를 해결하기 위해서 입주민 조합은 재활용하는 날을 정했습니다. 오직 수요일에만 여러분의 재활용품을 내놓을 수 있다는 것을 여러분께 알려드리고 싶습니다. 이것이 저희 아파

트 단지를 훨씬 더 쾌적해 보이게 만들 것이라고 저는 확신합니다. 여러분의 협조에 미리 감사드립니다.

청소년 축구 토너먼트 시리즈 책임자 Jack D'Adamo 드림

해설 재활용하는 날을 정해서 아파트 입주민들에게 알려주는 글이다. I would like to let you know that you can put out your recycling on Wednesdays only에서 '오직 수요일에만 여러분의 재활용품을 내놓을 수 있다는 것을 여러분께 알려드리고 싶다'고 했으므로 이 글의 목적으로 가장 적절한 것은 ① '재활용품 배출 허용 요일을 알리려고'이다.

오답분석 ②와 ③은 글의 중심 소재인 '쓰레기' 및 '분리배출'을 다루고 있으나, 그것의 필요성을 설명하거나 배출 이후의 정리를 부탁하는 글이 아니므로 오답이다. ④은 글에서 언급된 '입주민 대표'를 활용하여 혼동을 주는 오답이다. ⑤은 글에서 언급된 '쓰레기'를 활용하여 혼동을 주는 오답이다.

불변의 패턴 02   p.17
글의 목적에 따라 자주 나오는 표현이 있다.

기출문제   정답 ③

지문분석

Dear Wildwood residents,
Wildwood 지역 주민들께

Wildwood Academy is a local school / that seeks to help children / with disabilities and learning challenges.
Wildwood Academy는 지역 학교입니다 / 아이들을 돕기 위해 노력하는 / 장애 및 학습상 어려움이 있는

We currently have / over 200 students / enrolled.
저희에게는 지금 있습니다 / 200명 이상 학생들이 / 등록된

This year / we'd like to add a music class / in the hope / that each of our students will have the opportunity / to develop their musical abilities.
올해 / 저희는 음악 수업을 추가하려고 합니다 / 바라며 / 각각의 학생들이 기회를 얻기를 / 그들의 음악적 재능을 키울

To get the class started, / we need more instruments / than we have now.
이 수업이 개설되게 하기 위해 / 저희는 더 많은 악기들이 필요합니다 / 현재 저희가 가지고 있는 것보다

We are asking you / to look around your house / and donate any instruments / that you may no longer use.
저희는 여러분들에게 요청드립니다 / 집을 둘러보기를 / 그리고 어떤 악기든 기부하다 / 더 이상 사용하지 않을

★ Each one donated / will be assigned / to a student / in need.
기부된 각 악기는 / 부여될 것입니다 / 학생에게 / 필요로 하는

Simply call us / and we will be happy to drop by / and pick up the instrument.
저희에게 전화만 해주십시오 / 그러면 저희가 기꺼이 들르겠습니다 / 그리고 악기를 가져가겠습니다

Sincerely,
Karen Hansen, / Principal
Karen Hansen 드림 / 교장

★ 독해가 쉬워지는 구문 풀이

Each one donated will be assigned to a student in need.
수식 받는 명사 과거분사 / 형용사구

⇨ 앞 문장에서 언급된 instrument를 반복 사용하지 않기 위해 부정대명사 one이 쓰였고, 수식 받는 대명사 one이 donate가 나타내는 '기부하는' 행위의 대상이므로 과거분사 donated가 쓰였다.
⇨ in need는 명사 a student를 수식하는 형용사구이다.

어휘 resident 주민, 거주자 seek 노력하다, 추구하다
disability (신체적·정신적) 장애 enroll 등록하다, 입학하다
ability 재능, 역량 look around ~을 둘러보다 assign 부여하다, 배정하다

해석 Wildwood 지역 주민들께,

Wildwood Academy는 장애 및 학습상 어려움이 있는 아이들을 돕기 위해 노력하는 지역 학교입니다. 저희에게는 지금 등록된 학생들이 200명 이상 있습니다. 올해 저희는 각각의 학생들이 그들의 음악적 재능을 키울 기회를 얻기를 바라며 음악 수업을 추가하려고 합니다. 이 수업이 개설되게 하기 위해, 저희는 현재 저희가 가지고 있는 것보다 더 많은 악기들이 필요합니다. 저희는 여러분들이 집을 둘러보고 더 이상 사용하지 않을 어떤 악기든 기부해주시기를 요청드립니다. 기부된 각 악기는 필요로 하는 학생에게 부여될 것입니다. 저희에게 전화만 해주시면 저희가 기꺼이 들러서 악기를 가져가겠습니다.

교장 Karen Hansen 드림

해설 주민들에게 사용하지 않는 악기를 지역 학교에 기부해줄 것을 요청하고 있으므로 요청할 때 자주 사용되는 표현 ask 뒤의 내용을 주목한다. We are asking you to look around your house and donate any instruments that you may no longer use에서 글의 목적이 잘 드러나고 있으므로, 정답은 ③ '음악 수업을 위한 악기 기부를 요청하려고'이다.

오답분석 ①은 음악 수업과 관련된 '악기'를 다루고 있지만 고장 난 악기의 수리를 의뢰하기 위한 글이 아니기 때문에 오답이다. ②과 ⑤은 글과 전혀 관련 없는 내용이다. ④은 음악 수업과 관련된 '음악 수업 신청'을 다루고 있지만 추가로 개설된 음악 수업 신청을 독려하기 위한 글이 아니기 때문에 오답이다.

독해 만점 TEST
p.18

01 ① **02** ② **03** ③ **04** ① **05** ① **06** ② **07** ⑤ **08** ⑤

실력 UP! 미니 문제

01. ⓐ graduating students ⓑ wearing their summer uniforms

02. 발표 일정을 학회 마지막 날로 변경하는 것

03. Couch surfing is a popular way of traveling that provides travelers with multiple benefits

04. (A) Marigold apartment complex residents
    (B) Marigold management

05. ⓐ talent ⓑ deadline

06. The library accepts used books in good condition, old magazines, and even art pieces

07. 비록 이것은 우리 회원들에게 매우 인기가 많은 것으로 드러났지만, 많은 부상이 있어 왔습니다

08. reduces the amount of small plastic materials that come off of clothes and pollute the water

01
정답 ①

지문분석

To Graduating Students,
졸업생 여러분께

First of all, / we would like to congratulate / all of you.
먼저 / 저희는 축하 인사를 전하고 싶습니다 / 여러분 모두에게

As you know, / we will be taking pictures / for the school album / next Friday morning at 10 A.M.
아시다시피 / 우리는 사진 촬영을 할 것입니다 / 학교 앨범에 필요한 / 다음 주 금요일 오전 10시에

Students should gather / in the auditorium.
학생 여러분은 모여야 합니다 / 강당에

★ This notice / is to remind everyone / that all students must wear their winter uniforms / for the pictures.
이 공지는 / 모두에게 상기시켜 주기 위한 것입니다 / 모든 학생들이 동복을 입어야 한다는 점을 / 사진을 위해

In addition, / some students have asked / if wearing their summer uniforms / would be allowed.
이에 덧붙여 / 몇몇 학생들이 문의하였습니다 / 하복을 입는 것이 / 허용되는지를

However, / this is not possible, / so make sure to bring or wear / the correct uniform / on picture day.
그러나 / 이는 가능하지 않습니다 / 그러므로 꼭 가져오거나 입으시기를 바랍니다 / 적합한 복장을 / 촬영 당일에는

Thank you all for your cooperation.
여러분의 협조에 감사드립니다

Sincerely,
Blooming High School
Blooming 고등학교 드림

★ **독해가 쉬워지는 구문 풀이**

This notice is [to remind everyone that all students must wear
　　주어　　동사　　　　　　보어(to부정사구)
their winter uniforms for the pictures].

⇨ [ ]는 to부정사의 명사적 용법으로, 주절의 보어 역할을 한다.
⇨ remind는 <remind + 목적어 + that절> 등으로 표현이 가능하다. 여기서 everyone은 목적어에 해당하고, 이들에게 상기시켜 주는 내용이 that절에 들어간다.

어휘 congratulate 축하 인사를 전하다, 축하하다 gather 모이다 auditorium 강당 remind 상기시키다 allow 허용하다, 허락하다

해석 졸업생 여러분께,

먼저, 저희는 여러분 모두에게 축하 인사를 전하고 싶습니다. 아시다시피, 우리는 다음 주 금요일 오전 10시에 학교 앨범에 필요한 사진 촬영을 할 것입니다. 학생 여러분은 강당에 모여야 합니다. 이 공지는 사진을 위해 모든 학생들이 동복을 입어야 한다는 점을 모두에게 상기시켜 주기 위한 것입니다. 이에 덧붙여, 몇몇 학생들이 하복을 입는 것이 허용되는지를 문의하였습니다. 그러나, 이는 가능하지 않으므로 촬영 당일에는 꼭 적합한 복장을 가져오거나 입으시기를 바랍니다. 여러분의 협조에 감사드립니다.

Blooming 고등학교 드림

해설 졸업반 학생들이 앨범 사진 촬영일에 입어야 할 복장에 관해 알리는 글이다. This notice is to remind everyone that all students must wear their winter uniforms, make sure to bring or wear the correct uniform에서 '이 공지는 모든 학생들이 동복을 입어야 한다는 점을 모두에게 상기시켜 주기 위함이다'와 '꼭 적합한 복장을 가져오거나 입으시기를 바란다'라고 했으므로 이 글의 목적으로 가장 적절한 것은 ① '사진 복장에 관해 알리려고'이다.

오답분석 ②, ③, ④은 글과 관련 없는 내용이다. ⑤은 글의 내용 중 일부만을 말하고 있다.

실력 UP! 미니 문제 01.

정답 (A) graduating students
(B) wearing their summer uniforms

해설 (A) 바로 앞 문장에서 '졸업생 여러분께'라고 한 후, 여러분 모두에게 축하 인사를 전하고 싶다고 했으므로 (A)you는 graduating students를 가리킨다.
(B) 바로 앞 문장에서 몇몇 학생들이 하복을 입는 것이 허용되는지에 대해 문의했다고 한 후, 그러나 이는 가능하지 않다고 했으므로 (B)this는 wearing their summer uniforms를 가리킨다.

02

지문분석

Dear Mr. Roberson,
친애하는 Roberson 씨

Thank you for inviting me / to speak / at the technology conference in Chicago / next month.
저를 초청해 주셔서 감사합니다 / 발표하도록 / 시카고에서 열리는 과학 기술 학회에서 / 다음 달에

★ I am really looking forward to / giving a presentation / about online marketing.
저는 매우 기대하고 있습니다 / 발표를 하는 것을 / 온라인 마케팅에 관한

I also think / it will be a good chance / to meet people / who work in the same industry / as me.
또한 저는 생각합니다 / 이것이 좋은 기회가 될 것이라고 / 사람들을 만나는 / 같은 업계에서 일하는 / 저와

However, / there is one problem.
그러나 / 한 가지 문제가 있습니다

I am supposed to give my talk / in the morning on August 15, / but / I have a doctor's appointment / that day.
저는 강연을 하기로 되어 있습니다 / 8월 15일 오전에 / 그런데 / 저는 병원 예약이 잡혀 있습니다 / 그 날

Therefore, / I'd like to request / that you reschedule my presentation / for the last day of the conference, / August 19.
따라서 / 저는 요청드리고자 합니다 / 당신이 제 발표 일정을 변경해 주시기를 / 학회 마지막 날인 / 8월 19일로

Please let me know / if this will create any problems / for you.
저에게 알려주세요 / 만약 이것이 문제를 일으킨다면 / 당신에게

Sincerely,
Anne Waters
Anne Waters 드림

★ 독해가 쉬워지는 구문 풀이

I am really **looking forward to** giving a presentation about online
　　　　　　　　　　　　　　　　동명사
marketing.

⇨ 'look forward to'는 '~하기를 매우 기대하다'라는 뜻의 표현으로, 이때 to 는 전치사이다. 따라서 명사 역할을 하여 전치사의 목적어 자리에 올 수 있는 동명사 giving이 쓰였다.

어휘 technology (과학) 기술　conference 학회　look forward to ~을 기대하다 presentation 발표　industry 업계　be supposed to do ~ 하기로 되어 있다 talk 강연; 말하다　appointment 예약　request 요청하다 reschedule 일정을 변경하다

해석 친애하는 Roberson 씨,

다음 달에 시카고에서 열리는 과학 기술 학회에서 발표하도록 저를 초청해 주셔서 감사합니다. 저는 온라인 마케팅에 관한 발표를 하는 것을 매우 기대하고 있습니다. 또한, 저는 이것이 저와 같은 업계에서 일하는 사람들을 만나는 좋은 기회가 될 것이라고 생각합니다. 그러나, 한 가지 문제가 있습니다. 저는 8월 15일 오전에 강연을 하기로 되어 있는데, 그날 저는 병원 예약이 잡혀 있습니다. 따라서, 저는 당신이 제 발표 일정을 학회 마지막 날인 8월 19일로 변경해 주시기를 요청드리고자 합니다. 만약 이것이 당신에게 문제를 일으킨다면 저에게 알려주세요.

Anne Waters 드림

해설 발표 일정 변경을 요청하는 글이다. I'd like to request that you reschedule my presentation ~에서 '당신이 제 발표 일정을 변경해 주시기를 요청드리고자 합니다'라고 했으므로 이 글의 목적으로 가장 적절한 것은 ② '발표 날짜 변경을 요청하려고'이다.

오답분석 ①은 '발표 참석'을 다루고 있지만 발표 참석을 부탁하기 위한 글이 아니므로 오답이다. ③, ④, ⑤은 모두 글에서 언급된 일부 소재를 활용하여 혼동을 주는 오답이다.

실력 UP! 미니 문제 02.

정답 발표 일정을 학회 마지막 날로 변경하는 것

해설 바로 앞 문장에서 'I'는 발표 일정을 학회 마지막 날로 변경해 주시기를 요청드린다고 했으므로 (A)this는 '발표 일정을 학회 마지막 날로 변경하는 것'이다.

03

지문분석

Are you tired of / staying at expensive hotels / that all look the same?
~ 에 싫증 나셨나요? / 값비싼 호텔에 머무르는 것 / 모두 똑같아 보이는

Do you want / more of a unique travel experience?
원하시나요 / 조금 더 색다른 여행 경험을

We have the answer / for you.
저희가 해답을 가지고 있습니다 / 여러분을 위한

As experienced travelers may know, / "couch surfing" is becoming more and more popular, / and we highly recommend / you try / this special way of traveling / for your next trip.
경험 많은 여행객들은 아시겠지만 / "카우치 서핑"은 점점 더 인기가 많아지고 있습니다 / 그러므로 저희는 강력하게 추천합니다 / 당신이 시도해보기를 / 이 특별한 방식의 여행을 / 당신의 다음번 여행에

This option allows you to stay / in a local's home / and sleep on their couch / for free!
이 옵션은 당신이 머물게 해줍니다 / 현지인의 집에서 / 그리고 그들의 소파에서 잠을 자게 / 무료로

★ Not only is it economical / but there are also many more advantages.
이것은 경제적일 뿐만 아니라 / 더 많은 장점도 있습니다

You can discover / the culture and traditions of the country / and even pick up / some of the language.
당신은 발견할 수 있습니다 / 그 나라의 문화와 전통을 / 심지어 배울 수도 있습니다 / 약간의 언어를

Next time you travel, / become a couch surfer / and make unforgettable memories / with new friends.
다음에 당신이 여행을 할 때 / 카우치 서퍼가 되어 보세요 / 그리고 잊을 수 없는 추억을 만드세요 / 새로운 친구들과

★ 독해가 쉬워지는 구문 풀이

Not only is it economical but there are also many more
　　　　　 동사 주어　보어
advantages.

⇨ 부정의 의미를 가진 어구 Not only가 절의 앞쪽에 왔으므로, 주어와 동사가 도치되어 '동사 + 주어'의 어순으로 쓰였다.

어휘 be tired of ~에 싫증 나다　couch 소파, 침상 economical 경제적인, 실속 있는　discover 발견하다 pick up 배우다, ~을 알게 되다　unforgettable 잊을 수 없는

해석 모두 똑같아 보이는 값비싼 호텔에 머무르는 것에 싫증 나셨나요? 조금 더 색다른 여행 경험을 원하시나요? 저희가 여러분을 위한 해답을 가지고 있습니다. 경험 많은 여행객들은 아시겠지만, "카우치 서핑"은 점점 더 인기가 많아지고 있으므로, 저희는 당신이 이 특별한 방식의 여행을 당신의 다음번 여행에 시도해보기를 강력하게 추천합니다. 이 옵션은 당신이 현지인의 집에서 머물고, 그들의 소파에서 무료로 잠을 자게 해줍니다! 이것은 경제적일 뿐만 아니라, 더 많은 장점도 있습니다. 당신은 그 나라의 문화와 전통을 발견할 수 있고 심지어 약간의 언어를 배울 수도 있습니다. 다음에 당신이 여행을 할 때 카우치 서퍼가 되어 새로운 친구들과 잊을 수 없는

추억을 만드세요.

[해설] 여행하는 동안 현지인의 집에서 숙박할 수 있는 여행 방식인 카우치 서핑을 추천하는 글이다. As experienced travelers may know, "couch surfing" is becoming more and more popular, and we highly recommend you try this special way of travelling for your next trip에서 '카우치 서핑이 점점 인기가 많아지고 있으니 다음번 여행에서 이것을 시도해보기를 강력하게 추천한다'고 했으므로 이 글의 목적으로 가장 적절한 것은 ③ '새로운 여행 방식을 추천하려고'이다.

[오답분석] ①은 여행과 관련된 소재인 '숙박 시설'을 다루고 있지만 숙박 시설의 폐쇄를 공지하기 위한 글이 아니기 때문에 오답이다. ②은 글의 내용 중 일부만을 말하고 있다. ④은 여행과 관련된 소재인 '관광지'를 다루지만, 여행객을 관광지로 초대하기 위한 글이 아니기 때문에 오답이다. ⑤은 여행과 관련된 소재인 '여행지'를 다루고 있지만 잘 알려지지 않은 여행지를 홍보하기 위한 글이 아니기 때문에 오답이다.

[실력 UP!] 미니 문제 03.

[정답] Couch surfing is a popular way of traveling that provides travelers with multiple benefits

04
정답 ①

[지문분석]

To All Marigold Apartment Complex Residents:
Marigold 아파트 단지 주민 여러분께

Many of us are staying inside / more than usual / these days.
우리 중 많은 분들이 실내에 머무르고 있습니다 / 평소보다 더 많이 / 요즘

This has led to some friction / with regard to noise levels.
이것은 몇몇 마찰로 이어져 오고 있습니다 / 소음 수준에 관한

We hope / residents can be a little more mindful / of their neighbors.
저희는 바랍니다 / 주민들께서 조금 더 신경을 써 줄 수 있길 / 여러분의 이웃에게

Here are some tips / you can follow.
여기에 몇 가지 방법이 있습니다 / 여러분이 따를 수 있는

When listening to loud music / or watching TV, / use headphones / if possible.
시끄러운 음악을 들을 때 / 또는 TV를 볼 때 / 헤드폰을 사용하세요 / 가능하면

Some families have young children / who sleep early, / so / consider doing your laundry or vacuuming / during the day / instead of at night.
몇몇 집에는 어린아이들이 있습니다 / 일찍 잠드는 / 그러므로 / 여러분의 빨래 또는 진공청소기로 청소하는 것을 고려해주세요 / 낮 동안에 / 밤 대신

★ Please remember / to be considerate of your neighbors / and try / to follow these tips.
기억해주세요 / 여러분의 이웃을 배려해야 한다는 것을 / 그리고 노력해주세요 / 이러한 조언들을 지키기 위해

We thank you for your cooperation.
여러분의 협조에 감사드립니다

Sincerely,
Marigold Management
Marigold 관리사무소 드림

★ 독해가 쉬워지는 구문 풀이

Please <u>remember</u> [to be considerate of your neighbors] and <u>try</u>
　　　　동사1　　　　　　　　　　　　　　　　　　　　　　　　　동사2
to follow these tips.

⇨ [ ]는 to부정사의 명사적 용법으로, remember의 목적어 역할을 한다. 동사 remember는 동명사나 to부정사를 모두 목적어로 취할 수 있는 동사인데, '~할 것을 기억하다'라는 미래의 의미를 나타낼 때는 to부정사를 목적어로 취한다.

[어휘] resident 주민 friction 마찰 with regard to ~에 관해
mindful ~에 신경을 쓰는 vacuum 진공청소기로 청소하다
considerate 배려하는

[해석] Marigold 아파트 단지 주민 여러분께:

우리 중 많은 분들이 평소보다 더 많이 실내에 머무르고 있습니다. 이것은 소음 수준에 관한 몇몇 마찰로 이어져 오고 있는데요. 저희는 주민들께서 여러분의 이웃에게 조금 더 신경을 써 줄 수 있길 바랍니다. 여기에 여러분이 따를 수 있는 몇 가지 방법이 있습니다. 시끄러운 음악을 듣거나 TV를 볼 때, 가능하면 헤드폰을 사용하세요. 몇몇 집에는 일찍 잠드는 어린아이들이 있으므로, 밤 대신 낮 동안에 여러분의 빨래 또는 진공청소기로 청소하는 것을 고려해주세요. 여러분의 이웃을 배려해야 한다는 것을 기억해주시고, 이러한 조언들을 지키기 위해 노력해주세요. 여러분의 협조에 감사드립니다.

Marigold 관리사무소 드림

[해설] 아파트 주민들에게 소음을 줄이기 위한 방법을 알려주는 글이다. Here are some tips you can follow에서 '여기에 (소음을 줄이기 위해) 여러분이 따를 수 있는 몇 가지 방법이 있다'고 했으므로 이 글의 목적으로 가장 적절한 것은 ① '소음을 줄이기 위한 방법을 알려주려고'이다.

[오답분석] ②은 주민들이 지켜야 할 '규정'을 다루고 있지만, 구체적으로 '소음'과 관련된 내용이 빠져 있으므로 오답이다. ③, ⑤은 글과 전혀 관련 없는 내용이다. ④은 중심 소재 '소음'을 활용하여 혼동을 주는 오답이다.

[실력 UP!] 미니 문제 04.

[정답] (A) Marigold apartment complex residents
(B) Marigold management

[해설] (A) 이 편지의 수신인은 Marigold 아파트 단지의 주민이고, 바로 앞 문장에서 'Marigold 아파트 단지 주민 여러분께'라고 한 후 우리 중 많은 분들이 재택근무를 하고 있다고 했으므로 (A)us는 Marigold apartment complex residents를 가리킨다.
(B) 이 편지의 발신인은 Marigold 관리사무소이고, (B)가 포함된 문장에서 저희는 주민들께서 여러분의 이웃에게 조금 더 신경을 써 주시길 바란다고 있다고 했으므로 (B)We는 Marigold management를 가리킨다.

05
정답 ①

[지문분석]

Dear Ms. McEnroe,
친애하는 McEnroe씨

As you are aware, / this year's engineering contest / is coming next week.
당신께서도 아시다시피 / 올해의 공학 기술 콘테스트가 / 한 주 앞으로 다가왔습니다

Also, / we have noticed / that you have decided / to participate again.
더불어 / 저희는 알았습니다 / 당신이 ~하기로 결정했음을 / 다시 참가하기로

★ We were truly amazed / at the level of talent / your previous works showed / last year, / so we look forward to / enjoying / more of your creative works / this year.
저희는 진심으로 놀랐습니다 / 재능의 수준에 / 당신의 이전 작품들이 보여줬던 / 작년에 / 그래서 저희는 기대하는 바입니다 / 즐기기를 / 더 많은 당신의 창의적인 작품들 / 올해의

Therefore, / we don't want you to forget / that the deadline for sending us your final design / is fast approaching.
따라서 / 저희는 당신이 잊어버리길 원하지 않습니다 / 저희에게 당신의 최종 작품을 보낼 마감일이 / 빠르게 다가오고 있음을

The last day / to submit your work / is next Sunday, December 10th.
마지막 날은 / 당신의 작품을 제출할 / 다음 주 일요일인 12월 10일입니다

Works sent after 5 p.m. / on this day / will not be accepted for the contest.
오후 5시 이후에 보내진 작품들은 / 이날 / 콘테스트에 받아들여지지 않을 것입니다

We wish you best of luck.
행운을 빕니다

Sincerely,
Nancy Wang
Nancy Wang 드림

Engineering Department Manager
공학부 매니저

★ 독해가 쉬워지는 구문 풀이

We were truly amazed at the level of talent [(that) your previous works showed last year], so we look forward to enjoying more of
<u>목적어(관계절)</u>
your creative works this year.

⇨ [ ]는 선행사 talent를 수식하는 관계절이며, 목적격 관계대명사 which 또는 that이 생략되었다.

[어휘] aware 알고 있는, 의식하는 engineering 공학 기술 notice 알아차리다
participate 참가하다, 참여하다 amazed 놀란 talent 재능, 소질
previous 이전의 look forward to 기대하다, 고대하다 creative 창의적인
deadline 마감일 approach 다가오다, 접근하다 submit 제출하다, 굴복하다
department 학부, 과

[해석] 친애하는 McEnroe씨

당신께서도 아시다시피, 올해의 공학 기술 콘테스트가 한 주 앞으로 다가왔습니다. 더불어, 저희는 당신이 다시 참가하기로 결정했음을 알았습니다. 작년에 당신의 이전 작품들이 보여줬던 재능의 수준에 저희는 진심으로 놀랐고, 그래서 올해 더 많은 당신의 창의적인 작품들을 즐기기를 기대하는 바입니다. 따라서 저희는 당신이 최종 작품을 저희에게 보낼 마감일이 빠르게 다가오고 있음을 잊어버리길 원하지 않습니다. 당신의 작품을 제출할 마지막 날은 다음 주 일요일인 12월 10일입니다. 이날 오후 5시 이후에 보내진 작품들은 콘테스트에 받아들여지지 않을 것입니다. 행운을 빕니다.

공학부 매니저 Nancy Wang 드림

[해설] 공학 기술 콘테스트에 참가 예정인 사람에게 작품 제출 마감일을 알리는 글이다. we don't want you to forget that the deadline for sending us your final design is fast approaching에서 '저희는 당신의 최종 작품을 저희에게 보낼 마감일이 빠르게 다가오고 있음을 당신이 잊어버리길 원하지 않습니다'라고 했으므로 이 글의 목적으로 가장 적절한 것은 ① '콘테스트 마감일을 상기시키려고'이다.

[오답분석] ②, ③, ④은 글의 중심 소재인 '콘테스트'를 활용하여 혼동을 주는 오답이다. ⑤은 글의 중심 소재인 '작품 제출'을 활용하여 혼동을 주는 오답이다.

실력UP! 미니 문제 05.
정답 ⓐ talent ⓑ deadline
해석 ⓐ 타고난, 선천적인 능력
     ⓑ 과업이 완료되어야 하는 예정된 시간

06   정답 ②

지문분석

Dear Mr. Smith,
친애하는 Smith씨

★ Thanks to / many of our generous donors, / the Browning Public Library / has been able / to expand the range of services / we provide.
~ 덕분에 / 우리의 관대하신 수많은 기부자분들 / Browning Public Library / 계속 ~ 해올 수 있었습니다 / 서비스의 폭을 넓히는 것 / 저희가 제공하는

Regarding this, / you recently wrote us to ask / about your future donations / to our library, / and we are pleased / to write in response / to that question.
이와 관련해서 / 최근 당신께서 우리에게 문의 글을 쓰셨습니다 / 향후 기부에 관해 / 저희 도서관을 위한 / 그리고 저희는 기쁩니다 / 답변을 드릴 수 있어서 / 그 문의에 대하여

To donate something, / you first have to send / a list of your items / through our website.
기부를 하시려면 / 당신께서는 먼저 보내 주셔야 합니다 / 물품들의 목록을 / 저희 웹 사이트를 통해

We accept / used books in good condition, / old magazines, / and even art pieces as well.
저희는 받습니다 / 보존 상태가 좋은 중고 도서 / 오래된 잡지 / 그리고 심지어 예술 작품까지도

Once / we have checked your list, / we will let you know / when and where / you can bring your items.
일단 ~하면 / 저희가 당신의 목록을 확인한다 / 저희가 알려 드릴 것입니다 / 언제 그리고 어디로 / 당신의 물건들을 가져와도 되는지

If you have any questions / about this process, / please stop by our Information Desk / or contact us / through this email address / at any time.
문의 사항이 있으시면 / 이 절차에 관해 / 저희 안내데스크에 들르세요 / 또는 연락 주십시오 / 이 이메일 주소를 통해 / 언제든지

Thank you for your interest.
관심을 가져 주셔서 감사드립니다

Best Regards,
David Wescott
David Wescott 드림

Customer Service Manager
고객 서비스 담당자

★ 독해가 쉬워지는 구문 풀이

Thanks to many of our generous donors, <u>the Browning Public Library</u> [has been able to expand] the range of services we provide.
<u>주어</u>   <u>동사</u>

⇨ [ ]는 현재완료시제 표현으로, 과거의 특정 시점으로부터 지금까지 도서관이 서비스의 폭을 지속적으로 넓혀 올 수 있었다는 것을 나타낸다.

[어휘] generous 관대한, 마음이 넓은 donor 기부자 expand 넓히다, 확장하다
range 폭 in response to ~에 대하여, ~에 응하여 condition 상태, 조건
stop by 들르다 interest 관심, 흥미

[해석] 친애하는 Smith씨

우리의 관대하신 수많은 기부자분들 덕분에, Browning Public Library는 제공하는 서비스의 폭을 계속 넓혀 올 수 있었습니다. 이와 관련해서, 최근 당신께서 저희 도서관을 위한 향후 기부에 관해 문의 글을 쓰셨고, 저희는 그 문의에 대한 답변을 드릴 수 있어서 기쁩니다. 기부를 하시려면, 당신께서는 먼저 저희 웹 사이트를 통해 물품들의 목록을 보내 주셔야 합니다. 저희는 보존 상태가 좋은 중고 도서, 오래된 잡지, 그리고 심지어 예술 작품까지도 받습니다. 일단 저희가 당신의 목록을 확인하면, 언제 그리고 어디로 당신의 물건들을 가져와도 되는지 알려 드릴 것입니다. 이 절차에 관해 문의 사항이 있으시면, 저희 안내데스크에 들르시거나, 이 이메일 주소를 통해 언제든지 연락 주십시오. 관심을 가져 주셔서 감사드립니다.

고객 서비스 담당자 David Wescott 드림

[해설] 도서관에 물품을 기부하려는 고객 문의에 응하여 기부 방법을 안내하는

글이다. ask about your future donations에서 '향후 기부에 관해 문의 글을 쓰셨다'고 했고, we are pleased to write in response to that question에서 '그 문의에 대한 답변을 드릴 수 있어서 기쁘다'라고 했으므로, 이 글의 목적으로 가장 적절한 것은 ② '도서관에 기부하는 방법을 설명하려고'이다.

오답분석 ①, ⑤은 글의 내용 중 일부만을 다루고 있다. ③은 글과 전혀 관련 없는 내용이다. ④은 '도서관 기부'와 관련된 '도서관 후원자'를 다루고 있지만, 변경된 운영 시간을 알리기 위한 글이 아니므로 오답이다.

실력UP! 미니 문제 06.

정답 The library accepts used books in good condition, old magazines, and even art pieces

해석 Q: 도서관은 어떤 물품들을 받습니까?
A: 그 도서관은 보존 상태가 좋은 중고 도서, 오래된 잡지, 그리고 심지어 예술 작품까지 받습니다.

해설 We accept used books ~에서 Browning 공립 도서관은 보존상태가 좋은 중고 도서, 오래된 잡지, 그리고 예술 작품 등의 물건을 기부받고 있다는 것을 알 수 있다.

07
정답 ⑤

지문분석

Dear Members,
회원분들께

As many of you already know, / the Greenwood Recreation Center opened / an outdoor ice-skating rink / on December 5.
이미 많은 분들이 아시는 바와 같이 / 그린우드 오락장이 개장했습니다 / 야외 빙상 스케이트장을 / 12월 5일에

★ Although it has proven to be / very popular with our members, / there have been / a number of injuries.
비록 이것(스케이트장)은 드러났지만 / 우리 회원들에게 매우 인기가 많은 것으로 / 있어 왔습니다 / 많은 부상이

Therefore, / we would like to remind everyone / to wear the required safety equipment.
따라서 / 우리는 모든 분들께 다시 한번 알려드리고자 합니다 / 필수 안전 장비를 착용할 것을

You should always put on / a helmet, / elbow and knee pads, / and wrist guards / before skating.
여러분은 항상 착용해야 합니다 / 헬멧을 / 팔꿈치 및 무릎 보호대 / 그리고 손목 보호대를 / 스케이트를 타기 전에

This is particularly important / for young or inexperienced skaters.
이는 특히 중요합니다 / 어리거나 스케이트에 미숙한 사람들에게

If you have any questions / about this policy, / please speak to / one of our staff members / at the reception desk.
만약 문의 사항이 있으시면 / 이 방침에 대해 / 말씀해 주세요 / 우리 직원 중 한 명에게 / 접수처에 있는

Thank you for your cooperation, / and we hope to see you / soon.
협조해 주셔서 감사드립니다 / 그리고 우리는 여러분을 볼 수 있기를 바랍니다 / 곧

Sincerely,
Beth Adams
Beth Adams 드림

★ 독해가 쉬워지는 구문 풀이

Although **it** has proven to be very popular with our members, there have been a number of injuries.
⇨ 대명사 it은 앞 문장의 an outdoor ice-skating rink를 지칭한다.

어휘 recreation 오락 outdoor 야외 ice-skating rink 빙상 스케이트장 prove 드러나다 injury 부상 remind 다시 한번 알려주다 required 필수의 safety equipment 안전 장비 put on 착용하다 pad 보호대 guard 보호대, 경비 particularly 특히 inexperienced 미숙한

policy 방침 reception desk 접수처

해석 회원분들께,
이미 많은 분들이 아시는 바와 같이, 그린우드 오락장이 12월 5일에 야외 빙상 스케이트장을 개장했습니다. 비록 이것(스케이트장)은 우리 회원들에게 매우 인기가 많은 것으로 드러났지만, 많은 부상이 있어 왔습니다. 따라서, 우리는 모든 분들께 필수 안전 장비를 착용할 것을 다시 한번 알려드리고자 합니다. 여러분은 스케이트를 타기 전에 항상 헬멧, 팔꿈치 및 무릎 보호대, 그리고 손목 보호대를 착용해야 합니다. 이는 어리거나 스케이트에 미숙한 사람들에게 특히 중요합니다. 만약 이 방침에 대해 문의 사항이 있으시면, 접수처에 있는 우리 직원 중 한 명에게 말씀해 주세요. 협조해 주셔서 감사드리며, 우리는 여러분을 곧 볼 수 있기를 바랍니다.

Beth Adams 드림

해설 스케이트장 이용객들에게 필수 안전 장비 착용을 당부하는 글이다. we would like to remind everyone to wear the required safety equipment에서 '우리는 모든 분들께 필수 안전 장비를 착용할 것을 다시 한 번 알려드리고자 합니다'라고 했으므로 이 글의 목적으로 가장 적절한 것은 ⑤ '스케이트를 탈 때 안전 장비를 착용할 것을 당부하려고'이다.

오답분석 ①은 중심 소재인 '스케이트장'을 다루고 있지만 개장일을 공지하기 위한 글이 아니므로 오답이다. ②, ③, ④은 글의 내용 중 일부만을 다루고 있다.

실력UP! 미니 문제 07.

정답 비록 이것은 우리 회원들에게 매우 인기가 많은 것으로 드러났지만, 많은 부상이 있어 왔습니다

08
정답 ⑤

지문분석

Dear Readers,
독자분들께

This month's issue of *Home and Heart* / is dedicated to / going green.
Home and Heart 지의 이번 달 호는 / 오직 ~을 위해 할애합니다 / 친환경적으로 되는 것

Plastic waste / is one of the biggest polluters / of the environment.
플라스틱 쓰레기는 / 가장 큰 오염원 중 하나입니다 / 환경의

But / there are many ways / we can help.
그러나 / 많은 방법들이 있습니다 / 우리가 도울 수 있는

Instead of using plastic bags / for storing food, / switch to silicone reusable bags.
비닐봉지를 사용하는 것 대신 / 음식을 보관하기 위해 / 재사용 가능한 실리콘 가방으로 바꾸세요

They are durable / and can be cleaned easily.
그것들은 내구성이 있습니다 / 그리고 쉽게 세척됩니다

In addition, / use a washing bag / when doing the laundry.
이와 함께 / 세탁망을 사용하세요 / 빨래할 때

This reduces / the amount of / small plastic materials / that come off of clothes / and pollute the water.
이것은 줄여줍니다 / 양을 / 작은 플라스틱 입자들을 / 옷에서 떨어져 나오는 / 그리고 물을 오염시키는

★ Using cloth bags / for groceries / is also an easy way / to do your part.
천 가방을 사용하는 것 / 식료품용으로 / 또한 쉬운 방법입니다 / 여러분의 책임을 다하는

Following these practices / will do much / to help the environment.
이러한 습관들을 따르는 것은 / 많은 것을 할 것입니다 / 환경을 돕기 위해

Remember, / even a small change can make / a big difference.
기억하세요 / 작은 변화도 만들 수 있다는 것을 / 큰 차이를

Thank you for your continued support.
지속적인 성원에 감사드립니다

Jane Kendrick
Editor-in-Chief
편집장 드림

★ 독해가 쉬워지는 구문 풀이

[Using cloth bags for groceries] is also an easy way to do your
    주어   동사   보어
part.

⇨ [ ]는 동명사구로, 문장의 주어 자리에 쓰였고 주어로 쓰인 동명사(구)
는 단수 취급한다.
⇨ to do는 to부정사의 형용사적 용법으로, 명사 way를 수식한다.

[어휘] be dedicated to 오직 ~을 위해 할애하다, 전념하다
go green 친환경적으로 되다　polluter 오염원　store 보관하다
reusable 재사용 가능한　durable 내구성이 있는　washing bag 세탁망
material 입자, 물질　grocery 식료품　do one's part ~의 책임을 다하다
practice 습관, 관행　Editor-in-Chief 편집장

[해석] 독자분들께,
　Home and Heart 지의 이번 달 호는 오직 친환경적으로 되는 것을 위해
할애합니다. 플라스틱 쓰레기는 환경의 가장 큰 오염원 중 하나입니다. 그
러나 우리가 도울 수 있는 많은 방법들이 있습니다. 음식을 보관하기 위
해 비닐봉지를 사용하는 것 대신, 재사용 가능한 실리콘 가방으로 바꾸세
요. 그것들은 내구성이 있고 쉽게 세척됩니다. 이와 함께, 빨래할 때 세탁
망을 사용하세요. 이것은 옷에서 떨어져 나와 물을 오염시키는 작은 플라
스틱 입자들의 양을 줄여줍니다. 식료품용으로 천 가방을 사용하는 것 또
한 여러분의 책임을 다하는 쉬운 방법입니다. 이러한 습관들을 따르는 것
은 환경을 돕기 위해 많은 것을 할 것입니다. 작은 변화도 큰 차이를 만들
수 있다는 것을 기억하세요.
지속적인 성원에 감사드립니다.

Jane Kendrick
편집장 드림

[해설] 플라스틱 소비를 줄이는 방안을 독자들에게 전달하는 글이다. Following
these practices will do much to help the environment에서 '이러한
습관들(여러 방안들)을 따르는 것은 환경을 돕기 위해 많은 것을 할 것이
다'라고 했으므로 이 글의 목적으로 가장 적절한 것은 ⑤ '플라스틱 소비
를 줄이는 방안을 소개하려고'이다.

[오답분석] ①과 ④은 중심 소재인 '플라스틱 사용'과 관련된 내용을 다루고 있지만,
이를 비판하거나 그 영향을 밝히기 위한 글이 아니기 때문에 오답이다.
②, ③은 글과 전혀 관련 없는 내용이다.

[실력 UP!] 미니 문제 08.
정답　reduces the amount of small plastic materials that come off of clothes
and pollute the water
해석　Q: 지문에 따르면 세탁할 때 세탁 망을 사용하면 어떤 이점이 있는가?
　　　A: 세탁 망을 사용하는 것은 옷에서 떨어져 나와 물을 오염시키는 작은 플라스틱 입
　　　자들의 양을 줄여준다
해설　This reduces the ~ and pollute the water.에서 세탁 망을 사용하면 물을 오염
시키는 작은 플라스틱 입자의 양을 줄일 수 있다는 것을 알 수 있다.

불변의 패턴 03　　　　　　　　　　　　p.22
인물의 심경이나 글의 분위기는 간접적으로 표현된다.

기출 문제　　　　　　　　　　　　　　　정답 ①

지문분석

On the way home, / Shirley noticed a truck / parked in front of the
house / across the street.
집에 오는 길에 / Shirley는 트럭을 알아차렸다 / 집 앞에 주차되어 있는 / 길 건너편에

New neighbors!
새로운 이웃이다

Shirley was dying to know / about them.
Shirley는 너무 궁금했다 / 그들에 대해

"Do you know anything / about the new neighbors?" / she asked
Pa / at dinner.
아는 게 있어요 / 이사 온 이웃에 대해 / 그녀는 아빠에게 물었다 / 저녁식사 자리에서

He said, / "Yes / and there's one thing / that may be interesting /
to you."
그는 말했다 / 응 / 그리고 한 가지가 있단다 / 아마도 흥미로울 만한 / 너에게

Shirley had a billion more questions.
Shirley는 있었다 / 엄청나게 많은 질문들이

Pa said joyfully, / "They have a girl / just your age.
아빠는 기뻐하며 말했다 / 여자애가 있어 / 딱 네 또래의

Maybe she wants to / be your playmate."
아마 그 아이가 ~하고 싶을 수도 있어 / 너와 같이 노는 친구가 되다

Shirley nearly dropped her fork / on the floor.
Shirley는 포크를 떨어뜨릴 뻔했다 / 바닥에

★ How many times / had she prayed / for a friend?
얼마나 많이 / 그녀가 기도를 했던가 / 친구를 위해

Finally, / her prayers were answered!
마침내 / 그녀의 기도가 응답되었다

She and the new girl / could go to school together, / play together, /
and become best friends.
그녀와 새로운 여자아이는 / 학교도 같이 갈지도 모른다 / 같이 놀고 / 그리고 제일 친한 친
구가 되다

★ 독해가 쉬워지는 구문 풀이
How many times had she prayed for a friend?
　　의문사　　　　 조동사 주어　　본동사

⇨ '의문사 + 조동사 + 주어 + 동사'순의 직접의문문이며, 직접의문문은 간
접의문문과 달리 주어와 동사가 도치되므로, 조동사 had가 주어 she의
앞에 위치한다.

[어휘] neighbor 이웃　joyfully 기뻐하며　playmate 같이 노는 친구

[해석] 집에 오는 길에 Shirley는 길 건너편에 집 앞에 주차되어 있는 트럭을 알
아차렸다. 새로운 이웃이다! Shirley는 그들에 대해 너무 궁금했다. 그녀는
"이사 온 이웃에 대해 아는 게 있어요?라고 저녁식사 자리에서 아빠에게
물었다. 그는 "응, 아마도 너에게 흥미로울 만한 한 가지가 있단다."라고 말
했다. 아빠는 기뻐하며 말했다. "딱 네 또래의 여자애가 있어. 아마 그 아
이가 너와 같이 놀 친구가 되고 싶을 수도 있어." Shirley는 포크를 바닥에
떨어뜨릴 뻔했다. 그녀가 친구를 위해 얼마나 많이 기도를 했던가? 마침내
그녀의 기도가 응답되었다. 그녀와 새로운 여자아이는 학교도 같이 가고,
같이 놀고, 그리고 제일 친한 친구가 될지도 모른다.
① 궁금해하고 들떠 있는

---

② 미안하고 속상한
③ 질투가 나고 짜증 난
④ 차분하고 편안한
⑤ 실망하고 행복하지 않은

[해설] 친구를 원하던 Shirley가 이웃집에 또래 여자아이가 이사 왔다는 소식을 듣고 궁금해하며 들떠 있는 모습을 묘사한 글이다. Shirley was dying to know about them에서 궁금해하는 Shirley의 모습을, Shirley nearly dropped her fork on the floor에서 그녀가 친구를 사귈 수도 있다는 것에 들떠 있는 심경을 느낄 수 있으므로, Shirley의 심경으로 가장 적절한 것은 ① curious and excited(궁금해하고 들떠 있는)이다.

[오답분석] ④ calm and relaxed와 ⑤ disappointed and unhappy는 친구를 사귀고 싶었던 소원이 이루어질지도 몰라 포크를 떨어뜨릴 뻔할 정도로 들뜬 Shirley의 심경과 반대된다. ②의 sorry와 upset, ③ jealous and annoyed는 글 속 상황에서 느낄 심경으로 적절하지 않다.

불변의 패턴 04
p.23
심경 변화의 단서는 처음과 마지막 한두 문장에 있다.

기출 문제
정답 ②

지문분석

I board the plane, / take off, / and climb out / into the night sky.
나는 비행기에 탑승한다 / 그리고 이륙한다 / 그리고 급상승해서 올라간다 / 밤하늘로

Within minutes, / the plane shakes hard, / and I freeze, / feeling like / I'm not in control / of anything.
몇 분 내에 / 비행기가 심하게 흔들린다 / 그리고 나는 몸이 굳는다 / ~라고 느끼며 / 통제할 수 없다 / 아무것도

The left engine starts losing power / and the right engine is nearly dead now.
왼쪽 엔진이 동력을 잃기 시작한다 / 그리고 오른쪽 엔진은 지금 거의 멈췄다

Rain hits the windscreen / and I'm getting into heavier weather.
비가 앞 유리창에 부딪힌다 / 그리고 나는 점점 더 악천후의 날씨 속으로 들어간다

I'm having trouble / keeping up the airspeed.
나는 어렵다 / 대기 속도를 유지하는 것이

When I reach for the microphone / to call the center / to declare an emergency, / my shaky hand accidentally bumps / the carburetor heat levers, / and the left engine suddenly regains power.
내가 마이크에 손을 뻗을 때 / 센터에 연락하려고 / 비상 상황을 알리기 위해 / 나의 떨리는 손이 잘못하여 부딪혔다 / 기화기 열 레버에 / 그리고 왼쪽 엔진이 갑자기 동력을 되찾는다

I push the levers / to full.
나는 레버를 민다 / 끝까지

Both engines backfire / and come to full power.
두 엔진이 모두 역화된다 / 그리고 최대 동력에 이른다

★ Feeling / that the worst is over, / I find my whole body loosening up / and at ease.
생각하며 / 최악의 상황이 끝났다고 / 나는 전신의 긴장이 풀림을 느낀다 / 그리고 마음이 편안해짐을

★ 독해가 쉬워지는 구문 풀이
Feeling that the worst is over, I find my whole body loosening up
　　현재분사구문
and at ease.
⇨ 분사구문의 주어가 따로 없으므로 주절의 주어 I가 분사구문의 의미상 주어이다. I가 feel이 나타내는 '느끼는' 행위의 주체이므로 현재분사 Feeling이 쓰였다.

[어휘] windscreen 앞 유리창 airspeed 대기 속도 accidentally 잘못하여, 우연히
bump 부딪히다 regain 되찾다 backfire 역화하다, 폭발음을 내다

---

loosen up 긴장이 풀리다 at ease 마음이 편안한, 안이하게

[해석] 나는 비행기에 탑승해서, 이륙하고, 밤하늘로 급상승해서 올라간다. 몇 분 내에, 비행기가 심하게 흔들리고 나는 아무것도 통제할 수 없다고 느끼며 몸이 굳는다. 왼쪽 엔진이 동력을 잃기 시작하고 오른쪽 엔진은 지금 거의 멈췄다. 비가 앞 유리창에 부딪히고 나는 점점 더 악천후의 날씨 속으로 들어간다. 나는 대기 속도를 유지하는 것이 어렵다. 내가 비상 상황을 알리기 위해 센터에 연락하려고 마이크에 손을 뻗을 때, 나의 떨리는 손이 잘못하여 기화기 열 레버에 부딪혔고, 왼쪽 엔진이 갑자기 동력을 되찾는다. 나는 레버를 끝까지 민다. 두 엔진이 모두 역화되어 최대 동력에 이른다. 최악의 상황이 끝났다고 생각하며, 나는 전신의 긴장이 풀리고 마음이 편안해짐을 느낀다.

① 부끄러운 → 기쁜
② 두려워하는 → 안도하는
③ 만족하는 → 후회하는
④ 무관심한 → 흥분한
⑤ 기대하는 → 실망한

[해설] 비행기를 조종하는 I가 처음에는 비행기가 심하게 흔들리고 엔진이 동력을 잃어서 두려워하다가 나중에는 엔진의 동력이 되살아나서 안도하는 과정을 묘사하고 있는 글이다. 글의 초반부의 Within minutes, the plane shakes hard, and I freeze, feeling like I'm not in control of anything을 통해 I가 두려워한 것을 알 수 있고, 글의 후반부에서 I find my whole body loosening up and at ease를 통해 안도감을 느꼈다는 것을 알 수 있으므로, I의 심경 변화로 가장 적절한 것은 ② terrified(두려워하는) → relieved(안도하는)이다.

[오답분석] ①의 delighted는 인물의 마지막 심경으로 적절하지만, ashamed는 아니다. ③의 satisfied와 regretful, ④의 indifferent와 excited는 글 속의 상황에서 느낄 심경으로 적절하지 않다. ⑤의 hopeful은 긍정적인 심경으로 I의 첫 심경과 반대되고, disappointed는 부정적인 심경으로 I의 마지막 심경과 반대된다.

독해 만점 TEST
p.24

01 ②　02 ⑤　03 ③　04 ②　05 ⑤　06 ④　07 ⑤　08 ⑤

실력 UP! 미니 문제

01. 그랜드 캐니언 헬리콥터 투어

02. small for her age, very shy, sometimes has trouble talking to new people

03. ⓐ dreary ⓑ urgent

04. Paul은 장작을 줍고 막 캠프장으로 돌아왔을 때 그의 고양이가 어디에도 보이지 않는 것을 알아차렸다

05. 1. 멋진 건축물 2. 사람들 3. 이국적인 문화 4. 음식

06. The Unexpected Panic at the Castle of Chaos

07. 세 마리의 고래

08. The Noisy Interruption at the Beach

01
정답 ②

지문분석

On my 18th birthday, / I received a surprise gift / that most would love: / a helicopter tour of the Grand Canyon.
나의 열여덟 번째 생일에 / 나는 깜짝 선물을 받았다 / 대부분의 사람들이 좋아할 / 그랜드 캐니언 헬리콥터 투어라는

For me, / it was a nightmare / because / I had always been afraid of flying.
나에게 / 그것은 악몽이었다 / 때문에 / 나는 항상 나는 것을 무서워했기

But / now I had to fly / above a huge open canyon.
그러나 / 이제 나는 날아야 했다 / 거대하면서도 탁 트인 협곡 위를

I couldn't say no / since it was a thoughtful present / from my grandfather.
나는 싫다고 말할 수 없었다 / 그것은 사려 깊은 선물이었기 때문이다 / 나의 할아버지께서 주신

★ I gathered / the small amount of courage / that I had / and headed toward the helicopter / waiting to take me / up into the sky.
나는 끌어모았다 / 자그마한 용기를 / 내가 가지고 있던 / 그리고 헬리콥터 쪽으로 향했다 / 나를 데려가기 위해 기다리고 있는 / 하늘 위로

My legs trembled / with every step / and I was sweating.
나의 다리는 덜덜 떨렸다 / 걸음마다 / 그리고 나는 땀을 흘리고 있었다

As we left the ground, / I closed my eyes / and prayed / that it would be over quickly.
우리가 이륙했을 때 / 나는 눈을 감았다 / 그리고 기도했다 / 이것이 빨리 끝나기를

★ 독해가 쉬워지는 구문 풀이

I **gathered** the small amount of courage that I had and **headed**
  주어 동사1   동사2
toward [the **helicopter** waiting] to take me up into the sky.
                    현재분사

⇨ 동사 gathered와 headed는 등위접속사 and로 연결되어 병렬 구조를 이룬다.

⇨ [ ]는 문맥상 '기다리고 있는 헬리콥터'라는 의미로, 수식 받는 명사 helicopter가 wait가 나타내는 '기다리는' 행위의 주체이므로 현재분사 waiting이 쓰였다.

[어휘] open 탁 트인, 펼쳐진 canyon 협곡 thoughtful 사려 깊은 courage 용기 tremble 덜덜 떨리다 [선택지] terrified 무서운, 겁먹은 timid 자신감이 없는, 소심한 moody 시무룩한

[해석] 나의 열여덟 번째 생일에, 나는 대부분의 사람들이 좋아할 그랜드 캐니언 헬리콥터 투어라는 깜짝 선물을 받았다. 나는 항상 나는 것을 무서워했기 때문에 나에게 그것은 악몽이었다. 그러나 이제 나는 거대하면서도 탁 트인 협곡 위를 날아야 했다. 그것은 나의 할아버지께서 주신 사려 깊은 선물이었기 때문에 나는 싫다고 말할 수 없었다. 나는 내가 가지고 있던 자그마한 용기를 끌어모았고 나를 하늘 위로 데려가기 위해 기다리고 있는 헬리콥터 쪽으로 향했다. 나의 다리는 걸음마다 덜덜 떨렸고 나는 땀을 흘리고 있었다. 우리가 이륙했을 때, 나는 눈을 감고 이것이 빨리 끝나기를 기도했다.

① 즐겁고 놀라
② 긴장되고 무서운
③ 자신감이 없고 수줍어하는
④ 지루하고 피곤한
⑤ 시무룩하고 우울한

[해설] 나는 것을 무서워하는 I가 그랜드 캐니언 헬리콥터 투어를 하기 전에 긴장되고 무서워하는 모습을 묘사한 글이다. My legs trembled with every step and I was sweating에서 긴장하는 I의 모습을, I closed my eyes and prayed that it would be over quickly에서 나는 것을 무서워하는 I의 심경을 느낄 수 있으므로, I의 심경으로 가장 적절한 것은 ② nervous and terrified(긴장되고 무서운)이다.

[오답분석] ①의 surprised는 뜻밖의 선물을 받은 I의 심경을 묘사하는 데 적절하지만, joyful은 긍정적인 심경으로 I의 심경과 반대된다. ③의 timid와 shy, ④의 bored와 tired, ⑤의 moody와 depressed는 글 속의 상황에서 느낄 심경으로 적절하지 않다.

실력UP! 미니 문제 01.

정답 그랜드 캐니언 헬리콥터 투어
해설 대부분의 사람들이 좋아할 그랜드 캐니언 헬리콥터 투어라는 깜짝 선물을 받았다고 했으므로 a surprise gift(깜짝 선물)는 '그랜드 캐니언 헬리콥터 투어'이다.

02   정답 ⑤

지문분석

Ericka waited restlessly / for her daughter, Katie, / to come home.
Ericka는 안절부절못하며 기다렸다 / 그녀의 딸 Katie를 / 집으로 돌아오기를

It was Katie's first day of school / and Ericka was worried.
Katie가 학교에 가는 첫날이었다 / 그리고 Ericka는 걱정스러웠다

Katie was small / for her age.
Katie는 작았다 / 그녀의 나이에 비해

She was also very shy / and sometimes had trouble / talking to new people.
그녀는 또한 매우 수줍음이 많았다 / 그리고 때때로 어려움이 있었다 / 새로운 사람들에게 말을 거는 것에

Would she be able to make friends?
그녀가 친구를 만들 수 있을까

Suddenly, / the door burst open / and Katie rushed into the house / in her purple shirt, / her backpack on her shoulders, / and a big smile on her face.
갑자기 / 문이 벌컥 열렸다 / 그리고 Katie가 집 안으로 급히 들어왔다 / 보라색 셔츠를 입은 / 어깨에 가방을 메고 / 얼굴에 함박웃음을 지으면서

"Mom! / School was so fun!" / she said excitedly.
엄마 / 학교가 너무 재미있었어요 / 라며 그녀가 흥분해서 말했다

Ericka finally felt / the weight of her worries / get lifted away.
Ericka는 마침내 느꼈다 / 걱정의 무게가 / 사라지다

★ Now, / she could rest easy / knowing Katie would be fine.
이제 / 그녀는 안심할 수 있었다 / Katie가 괜찮을 것임을 알기에

★ 독해가 쉬워지는 구문 풀이

Now, she could rest easy [knowing Katie would be fine].
                          현재분사구문

⇨ [ ]는 이유를 나타내는 분사구문으로, 'Katie가 괜찮을 것임을 알기에'라고 해석한다.

[어휘] restlessly 안절부절못하며 burst open 벌컥 열리다 rush 급히 하다, 재촉하다 rest easy 안심하다 [선택지] startled 놀란 hurried 조급한, 서두르는 confused 혼란스러운 frightened 겁먹은, 무서워하는 relieved 안도하는

[해석] Ericka는 그녀의 딸 Katie가 집으로 돌아오기를 안절부절못하며 기다렸다. Katie가 학교에 가는 첫날이었고 Ericka는 걱정스러웠다. Katie는 그녀의 나이에 비해 작았다. 그녀는 또한 매우 수줍음이 많았고 때때로 새로운 사람들에게 말을 거는 것에 어려움이 있었다. 그녀가 친구를 만들 수 있을까? 갑자기, 문이 벌컥 열리며 어깨에 보라색 셔츠를 입고 가방을 멘 Katie가 얼굴에 함박웃음을 지으면서 집 안으로 급히 들어왔다. "엄마! 학교가 너무 재미있었어요!"라며 그녀가 흥분해서 말했다. Ericka는 마침내 걱정의 무게가 사라지는 것을 느꼈다. 이제, 그녀는 Katie가 괜찮을 것임을 알기에 안심할 수 있었다.

① 놀란 → 지친
② 두려워하는 → 조급한
③ 외로운 → 혼란스러운
④ 겁먹은 → 자랑스러운
⑤ 걱정하는 → 안도하는

[해설] Ericka가 처음 학교에 간 딸 Katie를 걱정하며 기다리다가, 밝은 모습으로

집에 돌아온 Katie를 보고 안도하는 과정을 묘사하고 있는 글이다. 글의 초반부의 Ericka waited restlessly와 Ericka was worried에서 Ericka가 걱정한 것을 알 수 있고, 글의 후반부에서 Now, she could rest easy knowing Katie would be fine을 통해 안도감을 느꼈다는 것을 알 수 있으므로, Ericka의 심경 변화로 가장 적절한 것은 ⑤ concerned(걱정하는) → relieved(안도하는)이다.

오답분석 ①의 startled와 exhausted, ②의 fearful과 hurried, ③의 lonely와 confused, ④의 frightened는 인물이 느꼈을 심경으로 적절하지 않다.

실력UP! 미니 문제 02.

정답 small for her age, very shy, sometimes has trouble talking to new people

해석 Q: Ericka의 설명으로 Katie의 특징에 대해 알 수 있는 것은?
A: Katie는 그녀의 나이에 비해 작았다. 또한 그녀는 수줍음이 많고 때때로 새로운 사람들에게 말을 거는 것을 어려워한다.

해설 Katie was small for her age.~ had trouble talking to new people.에서 Katie는 나이에 비해 작고, 수줍음이 많고, 때때로 새로운 사람들에게 말을 거는 것에 어려움이 있다는 것을 알 수 있다.

03 정답 ③

지문분석

Nathan arrived at the hospital / at exactly 3 p.m.
Nathan은 병원에 도착했다 / 정확히 오후 3시에

The rain was pouring / and it was a dreary fall day.
비가 퍼붓고 있었다 / 그리고 음울한 가을날이었다

'Just like how I feel,' / he thought unhappily, / looking up at the sky.
딱 내 기분 같네 / 라며 그는 슬프게 생각했다 / 하늘을 올려다보고

He walked in / with a heavy heart.
그는 걸어 들어갔다 / 무거운 마음으로

His cousin Jill / had been in a bad car accident.
그의 사촌 Jill은 / 심한 자동차 사고를 당했었다

He imagined / his aunt and uncle crying, / and doctors and nurses whispering / in hushed, urgent voices.
그는 상상했다 / 그의 숙모와 삼촌이 울고 있는 / 그리고 의사들과 간호사들이 속삭이고 있을 것 / 소리를 낮춘 다급한 목소리로

★ After hesitating, / he slowly opened the door / and saw, / to his surprise, / Jill giggling.
망설인 후에 / 그는 천천히 문을 열었다 / 그리고 보았다 / 놀랍게도 / Jill이 낄낄 웃는 것을

"Oh Nathan! / I'm so glad you came!" / she said with a grin.
아 Nathan / 네가 와줘서 너무 기뻐 / 라며 그녀가 활짝 웃으며 말했다

He walked into the room / filled with flowers, balloons, and laughter.
그는 방 안으로 걸어 들어갔다 / 꽃, 풍선, 그리고 웃음으로 가득 찬

He couldn't believe / how cheerful it was.
그는 믿을 수 없었다 / 그곳이 얼마나 쾌활한지

★ 독해가 쉬워지는 구문 풀이

After hesitating, he slowly opened the door and <u>saw</u>, to his
                    동사
surprise, <u>Jill</u> <u>giggling</u>.
     목적어 목적격보어

⇨ see(saw)는 동사원형을 목적격보어로 취하는 지각동사인데, 목적어가 어떤 행동을 하는 중이라는 의미일 때 지각동사는 현재분사를 목적격보어로 취할 수도 있으므로 giggling이 쓰였다.

어휘 pour 퍼붓다 dreary 음울한, 따분한 whisper 속삭이다
hushed 소리를 낮춘, 조용한 urgent 다급한, 절박한 hesitate 망설이다
to one's surprise 놀랍게도 grin 활짝 웃음 cheerful 쾌활한, 기운찬
선택지 humiliate 창피를 주다, 굴욕감을 주다 suspicious 의심스러워하는
enthusiastic 열정적인, 열광하는 content 만족하는

해석 Nathan은 정확히 오후 3시에 병원에 도착했다. 비가 퍼붓고 있었고 음울한 가을날이었다. '딱 내 기분 같네'라며 그는 하늘을 올려다보고 슬프게 생각했다. 그는 무거운 마음으로 걸어 들어갔다. 그의 사촌 Jill은 심한 자동차 사고를 당했었다. 그는 그의 숙모와 삼촌이 울고 있고 의사들과 간호사들이 소리를 낮춘 다급한 목소리로 속삭이고 있을 것을 상상했다. 망설인 후에, 그는 천천히 문을 열었고 놀랍게도 Jill이 낄낄 웃는 것을 보았다! "아 Nathan! 네가 와줘서 너무 기뻐!"라며 그녀가 활짝 웃으며 말했다. 그는 꽃, 풍선, 그리고 웃음으로 가득 찬 방 안으로 걸어 들어갔다. 그는 그곳이 얼마나 쾌활한지 믿을 수가 없었다.

① 두려운 → 창피한
② 실망한 → 의심스러워하는
③ 우울한 → 놀란
④ 열정적인 → 당황한
⑤ 무관심한 → 만족하는

해설 자동차 사고를 당한 사촌 Jill의 병문안을 간 Nathan이 처음에는 Jill이 걱정돼서 우울해하다가 나중에는 예상과 달리 활짝 웃고 있는 Jill을 보고 놀란 과정을 묘사하고 있는 글이다. 글의 초반부의 it was a dreary fall day와 ~ he thought unhappily를 통해 Nathan이 우울한 것을 알 수 있고, 글의 후반부에서 ~ saw, to his surprise, Jill giggling, He couldn't believe how cheerful it was를 통해 그가 놀랐다는 것을 알 수 있으므로, Nathan의 심경 변화로 가장 적절한 것은 ③ gloomy(우울한) → amazed(놀란)이다.

오답분석 ①의 afraid와 humiliated, ②의 disappointed와 suspicious, ⑤의 uninterested와 content는 글 속의 상황에서 느낄 심경으로 적절하지 않다. ④의 enthusiastic은 긍정적인 심경으로 Nathan의 첫 심경과 반대된다.

실력UP! 미니 문제 03.

정답 ⓐ dreary ⓑ urgent

해석 ⓐ 즐거움이 없으며, 우울하게 하거나 구슬픈 기분을 일깨우는
ⓑ 부정적인 결과를 예방하기 위해 즉각적인 주의와 관리를 필요로 하는

04 정답 ②

지문분석

Paul had just returned / to his campsite / after gathering firewood / when he noticed / that his cat was nowhere to be found.
Paul은 막 돌아왔다 / 그의 캠프장으로 / 장작을 주운 후에 / ~는 것을 알아차렸을 때 / 그의 고양이가 어디에도 보이지 않는다는 것을

Bella was trained / to stay in her cage / by the tent, / but she currently wasn't there.
Bella는 ~하도록 훈련받았다 / 그녀의 우리에 머무르도록 / 텐트 옆에 / 그러나 그녀는 현재 그곳에 없었다

★ Paul felt his chest tighten / and his breathing speed up.
Paul은 그의 가슴이 조이는 것을 느꼈다 / 그리고 그의 호흡이 빨라지는

She must have been scared / and run away.
그녀는 분명 겁을 먹은 것이다 / 그리고 도망치다

There was no sign / of his playful black cat / anywhere.
흔적이 없었다 / 그의 장난기 많은 검은 고양이의 / 어디에도

He frantically searched his tent / and in the surrounding forest / for Bella.
그는 미친 듯이 그의 텐트를 수색했다 / 그리고 주변 숲을 / Bella를 찾아

But / the sun was quickly setting / and Paul could feel / his anxiety growing.
그러나 / 해가 빠르게 지고 있었다 / 그리고 Paul은 ~을 느낄 수 있었다 / 그의 불안감이 커지는

He was in a huge national park / and his cat was lost.
그는 큰 국립공원에 있었다 / 그리고 그의 고양이를 잃어버렸다

He didn't have much hope / of finding her.
그는 가망이 별로 없었다 / 그녀를 찾을

[어휘] campsite 캠프장, 야영지　firewood 장작
nowhere to be found 어디에도 보이지 않다　tighten 조이다, 조여지다
playful 장난기 많은　frantically 미친 듯이, 극도로 흥분하여　anxiety 불안감
[선택지] joyful 즐거운　doubtful 확신이 없는, 의심스러운　jealous 질투 나는

[해석] Paul이 그의 고양이가 어디에도 보이지 않는 것을 알아차렸을 때 그는 장
작을 줍고 막 캠프장으로 돌아왔었다. Bella는 텐트 옆의 우리에 머무르도
록 훈련을 받았지만, 그녀는 현재 그곳에 없었다. Paul은 가슴이 조이고 호
흡이 빨라지는 것을 느꼈다. 그녀는 분명 겁을 먹고 도망친 것이다. 그의 장
난기 많은 검은 고양이의 흔적은 어디에도 없었다. 그는 미친 듯이 그의 텐
트와 주변 숲을 수색하며 Bella를 찾았다. 그러나 해가 빠르게 지고 있었고
Paul은 그의 불안감이 커지는 것을 느낄 수 있었다. 그는 큰 국립공원에 있
었고 그의 고양이를 잃어버렸다. 그는 그녀를 찾을 가망이 별로 없었다.

① 즐겁고 행복한
② 걱정스럽고 확신이 없는
③ 짜증 나고 질투 나는
④ 속상하고 화가 나는
⑤ 침착하고 여유로운

[해설] 캠프장에 온 Paul이 자신의 고양이 Bella를 잃어버려서 불안해하며 찾
아다니는 모습을 묘사한 글이다. He frantically searched his tent and
in the surrounding forest for Bella.과 ~ Paul could feel his anxiety
growing.에서 Paul이 Bella를 찾지 못할까 걱정하는 것을, He didn't
have much hope of finding her.에서 Paul이 Bella를 찾을 수 있다는
확신을 잃어간다는 것을 알 수 있으므로 Paul의 심경으로 가장 적절한 것
은 ② worried and doubtful(걱정스럽고 확신이 없는)이다.

[오답분석] ①의 joyful과 happy, ⑤의 calm과 relaxed는 긍정적인 심경으로 Paul
의 심경과 반대된다. ③의 annoyed와 jealous, ④의 angry는 글 속의 상
황에서 느낄 심경으로 적절하지 않다.

[실력UP!] 미니 문제 04.

[정답] Paul이 그의 고양이가 어디에도 보이지 않는 것을 알아차렸을 때 그는 장작을 줍고
막 캠프장으로 돌아왔었다.

05 　　　　　　　　　　　　　　　　정답 ⑤

지문분석

I decided to go to Europe / before starting college.
나는 유럽에 가기로 결심했다 / 대학에 들어가기 전에

My parents were quite nervous / since I was going alone.
나의 부모님께서는 걱정을 꽤 많이 하셨다 / 내가 혼자 가는 거라서

Not me, / though.
나는 아니었다 / 하지만

I couldn't wait to / explore the world.
나는 어서 빨리 ~하고 싶었다 / 세상을 탐험하다

I wanted to see / the amazing architecture and people.
나는 보고 싶었다 / 멋진 건축물과 사람들을

I was eager to experience / the exotic culture and food.
나는 경험하기를 열망했다 / 이국적인 문화와 음식을

I booked / a two-week trip.
나는 예약했다 / 2주간의 여행을

When I got to Europe, / I found / the same fast-food restaurants
and coffee shops / on every street / I went.
내가 유럽에 도착했을 때 / 나는 발견했다 / 똑같은 패스트푸드 식당과 커피숍을 / 모든 거
리에서 / 내가 갔던

All the young people / were wearing the same clothes / and
speaking the same way.
모든 젊은 사람들이 / 똑같은 옷을 입고 있었다 / 그리고 똑같은 방식으로 말하고 있었다

What a letdown!
정말 실망이었다

★ It wasn't / what I expected / at all.
그것은 ~이 아니었다 / 내가 예상했던 것 / 전혀

After the two weeks were over, / I sadly got on a plane / and
headed back home.
그 2주가 지난 후에 / 나는 슬프게 비행기를 탔다 / 그리고 집으로 돌아갔다

[어휘] architecture 건축물, 건축　eager 열망하는, 갈망하는
exotic 이국적인, 외국의　book 예약하다　letdown 실망, 감소
[선택지] envious 부러워하는, 선망하는　shameful 창피한

[해석] 나는 대학에 들어가기 전에 유럽에 가기로 결심했다. 내가 혼자 가는 거라
서 부모님께서는 걱정을 꽤 많이 하셨다. 하지만 나는 아니었다. 나는 어
서 빨리 세상을 탐험하고 싶었다. 나는 멋진 건축물과 사람들을 보고 싶었
다. 나는 이국적인 문화와 음식을 경험하기를 열망했다. 나는 2주간의 여
행을 예약했다. 유럽에 도착했을 때, 내가 갔던 모든 거리에서 나는 똑같
은 패스트푸드 식당과 커피숍을 발견했다. 모든 젊은 사람들이 똑같은 옷
을 입고, 똑같은 방식으로 말하고 있었다. 정말 실망이었다! 그것은 내가
예상했던 것이 전혀 아니었다. 그 2주가 지난 후에, 나는 슬프게 비행기를
타고 집으로 돌아갔다.

① 불안한　　　　→ 기쁜
② 부러워하는　→ 놀란
③ 무관심한　　→ 창피한
④ 불안해하는 → 자신 있는
⑤ 들뜬　　　　　→ 실망한

[해설] I가 유럽 여행을 떠나기 전에는 새로운 경험을 할 생각에 들떠있었지
만, 나중에는 예상과 다른 유럽의 모습에 실망하는 과정을 묘사하고
있는 글이다. I couldn't wait to explore the world, I was eager to
experience ~를 통해 I가 들떴다는 것을 알 수 있고, 글의 후반부에서
What a letdown을 통해 실망감을 느꼈음을 알 수 있으므로, I의 심경 변
화로 가장 적절한 것은 ⑤ excited(들뜬) → disappointed(실망한)이다.

[오답분석] ①의 anxious는 글 속의 상황에서 느낄 심경으로 적절하지 않으며, ②의
envious, ③의 indifferent와 shameful은 글 속의 상황에서 느낄 심경으
로 적절하지 않다. ④의 nervous는 부정적인 심경으로 I의 첫 심경과 반
대되고, confident는 I의 마지막 심경으로 적절하지 않다.

[실력UP!] 미니 문제 05.

[정답] 1. 멋진 건축물　2. 사람들　3. 이국적인 문화　4. 음식

[해설] I wanted to see ~ and people과 I was eager ~ exotic culture and food에서
I가 유럽에서 the amazing architecture and people(멋진 건축물과 사람들), 그
리고 the exotic culture and food(이국적인 문화와 음식)를 경험하기를 원했다는
것을 알 수 있다.

정답 ④

지문분석

Dylan was about to / enter the Castle of Chaos.
Dylan은 ~하려던 참이었다 / Castle of Chaos에 들어가다

Halloween was his favourite time of year / and he loved haunted houses; / he thought they were fun.
핼러윈은 한 해 중 그가 가장 좋아하는 때였다 / 그리고 그는 귀신의 집을 좋아했다 / 그는 그것들이 재미있다고 생각했다

★ The Castle of Chaos was famous / for being the scariest one.
Castle of Chaos는 유명했다 / 가장 무서운 것으로

"Are you afraid?" / his friends teased.
너 무서워하는 거니 / 라며 그의 친구들이 놀렸다

"No way," he said, confidently.
전혀 / 라고 그가 자신있게 말했다

Dylan entered the house.
Dylan은 그 집에 들어갔다

He walked through, / waiting for the typical monsters / to pop out.
그는 안으로 걸어 들어갔다 / 틀에 박힌 괴물들을 기다리며 / 튀어나올 것을

But / all he could hear / were odd whispers.
하지만 / 그가 들을 수 있던 것은 오직 / 이상한 휘파람뿐이었다

Then, / it got very cold.
그러고는 / 매우 추워졌다

This wasn't / what he was expecting / at all.
이는 ~이 아니었다 / 그가 예상하고 있던 것 / 전혀

He was suddenly nervous.
그는 갑자기 긴장했다

Just then, / he felt something / behind him.
바로 그때 / 그는 무언가를 느꼈다 / 그의 뒤에서

He turned around to face a ghost / with long black hair / staring at him!
그는 뒤돌아서 귀신을 마주 보고 말았다 / 길고 검은 머리카락의 / 그를 쳐다보고 있는

Dylan shouted in a panic / and ran back out the front door / as fast as his legs could carry him.
Dylan은 몹시 당황하여 소리를 질렀다 / 그리고 정문 밖으로 뛰어 돌아갔다 / 전속력으로

★ **독해가 쉬워지는 구문 풀이**

The Castle of Chaos was famous for being the scariest one.
　　　　　　　　　　　　　　전치사　전치사의 목적어(동명사)

⇨ 명사 역할을 하여 전치사의 목적어 자리에 올 수 있는 동명사 being이 쓰였다.

[어휘] be about to ~하려던 참이다, 막 ~하려고 하다　tease 놀리다, 끈질기게 괴롭히다
confidently 자신 있게, 확신을 갖고　typical 틀에 박힌, 일반적인
turn around 뒤돌아보다
as fast as one's legs would carry one 전속력으로
[선택지] hesitant 망설이는　embarrassed 창피한　lively 활기찬, 활발한
determined 단호한, 완강한

[해석] Dylan은 Castle of Chaos에 들어가려던 참이었다. 핼러윈은 한 해 중 그가 가장 좋아하는 때였고 그는 귀신의 집을 좋아했는데, 그는 그것들이 재미있다고 생각했다. Castle of Chaos는 가장 무서운 것으로 유명하다. "너 무서워하는 거니?"라며 그의 친구들이 놀렸다. "전혀"라고 그가 자신 있게 말했다. Dylan은 그 집에 들어갔다. 그는 틀에 박힌 괴물들이 튀어나올 것을 기다리며 안으로 걸어 들어갔다. 하지만, 그가 들을 수 있던 것은 오직 이상한 휘파람뿐이었다. 그러고는, 매우 추워졌다. 이는 그가 예상하고 있던 것이 전혀 아니었다. 그는 갑자기 긴장했다. 바로 그때, 그는 그의 뒤에서 무언가를 느꼈다. 그는 뒤돌아서 그를 쳐다보고 있는 길고 검은 머리카락의 귀신을 마주 보고 말았다! Dylan은 몹시 당황하여 소리를 질렀고 정문 밖으로 전속력으로 뛰어 돌아갔다.

---

① 망설이는 → 감동받은
② 지루한 → 창피한
③ 활기찬 → 단호한
④ 겁 없는 → 무서워하는
⑤ 질투하는 → 어리둥절한

[해설] 귀신의 집을 좋아하는 Dylan이 Castle of Chaos에 들어가며 처음에는 겁 없는 모습을 보이다가 나중에는 그의 예상과 다른 귀신을 보고 무서워하는 과정을 묘사하고 있는 글이다. 글의 중반부의 "Are you afraid?" his friends teased와 "No way," he said를 통해 Dylan이 귀신을 무서워하지 않은 것을 알 수 있다. 그러나 글의 후반부에서 Dylan shouted in a panic and ran back out the front door as fast as his legs could carry him을 통해 결국 무서움을 느꼈다는 것을 알 수 있으므로, Dylan의 심경 변화로 가장 적절한 것은 ④ fearless(겁 없는) → frightened(무서워하는)이다.

[오답분석] ①의 hesitant는 Dylan의 첫 심경과 반대되고, moved는 글 속의 상황에서 느낄 심경으로 적절하지 않다. ②의 bored, ③의 lively와 determined, ⑤의 jealous와 puzzled는 글 속의 상황에서 느낄 심경으로 적절하지 않다.

실력UP! 미니 문제 06.

정답 The Unexpected Panic at the Castle of Chaos

정답 ⑤

지문분석

Lily was enjoying every minute / of her boat tour that day.
Lily는 매 순간을 즐기고 있었다 / 그날 그녀의 보트 투어를

The sky was a perfect, / cloudless blue / and there was a nice salty breeze / that kept her cool.
하늘은 완벽한 것이었다 / 구름 한 점 없는 파란 / 그리고 그곳에 바다 냄새가 나는 좋은 미풍이 불었다 / 그녀를 시원하게 해주는

She was watching / the glassy surface of the sea / when she suddenly saw something / emerge from its depths.
그녀는 보고 있었다 / 바다의 유리와 같은 표면을 / 그녀가 갑자기 무언가를 보았을 때 / 깊은 곳에서 나오는

★ It blew a column of mist / into the air / before / disappearing and then breaking the surface again.
그것은 물기둥을 쏘아 올렸다 / 공기 중으로 / ~에 앞서 / 사라졌다가 다시 수면을 부수기였다

The other tourists gasped with excitement / and pointed at the display.
다른 관광객들은 흥분해서 숨이 턱 막혔다 / 그리고 그 장면을 가리켰다

"It's a whale!"
고래다

Someone shouted.
누군가가 소리쳤다

Lily felt herself smile / as she watched / not one, but three whales / play around the boat.
Lily는 스스로가 미소 짓는 것을 느꼈다 / 그녀가 보며 / 한 마리가 아닌 세 마리의 고래를 / 보트 주변에서 노는

Young children laughed / and everyone seemed happy.
어린아이들은 웃었다 / 그리고 모두가 행복해 보였다

This would surely be a trip / that they all remembered.
이것은 분명 ~한 여행이 될 것이다 / 그들 모두가 기억하는

★ **독해가 쉬워지는 구문 풀이**

It blew a column of mist into the air before [disappearing and then
　　　　　　　　　　　　　　　　　　　　전치사　　　　　등위접속사
breaking the surface again].

⇨ [ ]는 전치사 before의 목적어이며, 동명사 disappearing과 breaking
이 등위접속사 and로 연결되어 병렬 구조를 이룬다.

어휘 cloudless 구름 한 점 없는 salty 바다 냄새가 나는, 바다의
breeze 미풍, 산들바람 glassy 유리와 같은 emerge 나오다, 모습을 드러내다
gasp 숨이 턱 막히다 **선택지** monotonous 단조로운 weird 기이한, 기묘한
desperate 필사적인, 절실한

해석 Lilly는 그날 보트 투어의 매 순간을 즐기고 있었다. 하늘은 구름 한 점 없
는 완벽한 파란색이었고 그녀를 시원하게 해주는 바다 냄새가 나는 좋은
미풍이 불었다. 그녀는 바다의 유리와 같은 표면을 보고 있다가 갑자기 깊
은 곳에서 나오는 무언가를 보았다. 그것은 사라졌다가 다시 수면을 부수
기에 앞서 공기 중으로 물기둥을 쏘아 올렸다. 다른 관광객들은 흥분해서
숨을 헐떡이며 그 장면을 가리켰다. "고래다!" 누군가가 소리쳤다. Lilly는
한 마리가 아니라 세 마리의 고래가 보트 주변에서 노는 것을 보며 스스
로 미소 짓는 것을 느꼈다. 어린아이들은 웃었고 모두가 행복해 보였다. 이
것은 분명 그들 모두가 기억하는 여행이 될 것이다.

① 지루한
② 단조로운
③ 기이한
④ 필사적인
⑤ 즐거운

해설 보트 투어를 하던 중 배 주위에 갑자기 등장한 세 마리의 고래를 보고
기뻐하는 Lily와 승객들의 즐거운 분위기를 묘사한 글이다. The other
tourists gasped with excitement and pointed at the display.와
Young children laughed and everyone seemed happy.에서 즐거운
분위기를 느낄 수 있으므로 글의 분위기로 가장 적절한 것은 ⑤ joyful(즐
거운)이다.

오답 분석 ①의 boring, ③의 weird, ④의 desperate은 부정적인 분위기로 글에서
나타나는 분위기와 반대된다. ②의 monotonous은 글의 분위기로 적절
하지 않다.

실력 UP! 미니 문제 07.

정답 세 마리의 고래

해설 Lily는 바다 깊은 곳에서부터 무언가가 나오는 것을 봤는데, 얼마 후에 다른 승객
이 그것을 가리키며 "고래다!"라고 소리쳤다. 이후 Lily felt herself smile as she
watched not one, but three whales ~라고 나오므로 something(무언가)은 '세
마리의 고래'이다.

08
정답 ⑤

지문분석

Jenna gazed happily / at the water / as she spread her blanket /
on the sand.
Jenna는 행복하게 바라보았다 / 바다를 / 그녀의 담요를 펼치며 / 모래 위에

The weather was perfect, / and there were / only a few other
people / on the beach.
날씨는 완벽했고 / ~이 있었다 / 단 몇 명의 사람들만 / 해변에는

It had been a busy week / at work, / and / she was looking forward
to / relaxing in the sun.
바빴던 한 주였다 / 직장에서 / 그렇기에 / 그녀는 기대하고 있었다 / 태양 아래에서 휴식
을 취하기를

Suddenly, / she heard a voice / behind her / say, / "This looks like
a good spot!"
갑자기 / 그녀는 목소리를 들었다 / 자신의 뒤에서 / 말하는 / 여기가 좋은 자리인 것 같네
라고

★ Turning her head, / she saw a group of teenagers / setting up
a volleyball net.
고개를 돌리자 / 그녀는 한 무리의 청소년들을 보았다 / 배구 네트를 설치하고 있는

Within a few minutes, / one of them shouted, / "Game on" / and
they started playing loudly.
몇 분 이내에 / 그들 중 한 명이 외쳤다 / 경기 시작 / 그리고 그들은 소란스럽게 놀기 시작
했다

Jenna glared at them / as she realized / she wouldn't be able to
relax / with all the noise.
Jenna는 그들을 노려보았다 / 그녀가 깨닫고는 / 그녀가 휴식을 취할 수 없다는 것을 / 온
갖 소음 속에

Then / she sighed with frustration, / packed her belongings, / and
began walking down the beach.
그리고 나서 / 그녀는 좌절감에 한숨을 쉬었다 / 소지품을 챙겼다 / 그리고 해변을 따라 걷
기 시작했다

★ **독해가 쉬워지는 구문 풀이**

[①Turning her head], she saw a group of **teenagers** [②setting up
                                                          현재분사구문
a volleyball net].

⇨ 분사구문 [①]의 앞에는 접속사 및 반복되는 주어가 생략되었다.
⇨ [②]는 명사 teenagers를 수식하는 현재분사구문이다.

어휘 gaze 바라보다 spread 펼치다 blanket 담요 volleyball 배구
glare 노려보다 sigh 한숨을 쉬다 frustration 좌절감, 불만
belongings 소지품 **선택지** irritated 짜증난

해석 Jenna는 그녀의 담요를 모래 위에 펼치며 행복하게 바다를 바라보았다.
날씨는 완벽했고, 해변에는 단 몇 명의 사람들만이 있었다. 직장에서 바빴
던 한 주였기에, 그녀는 태양 아래에서 휴식을 취하기를 기대하고 있었다.
갑자기, 그녀는 자신의 뒤에서 "여기가 좋은 자리인 것 같네!"라고 말하는
목소리를 들었다. 고개를 돌리자, 그녀는 배구 네트를 설치하고 있는 한 무
리의 청소년들을 보았다. 몇 분 이내에, 그들 중 한 명이 "경기 시작!"을 외
쳤고 그들은 소란스럽게 놀기 시작했다. Jenna는 온갖 소음 속에 그녀가
휴식을 취할 수 없다는 것을 깨닫고는 그들을 노려보았다. 그리고 나서 그
녀는 좌절감에 한숨을 쉬고, 소지품을 챙겨서 해변을 따라 걷기 시작했다.

① 불안해 하는 → 침착한
② 즐거워 하는 → 질투하는
③ 자신감 있는 → 부러워 하는
④ 게으른 → 활기에 찬
⑤ 만족스러워 하는 → 짜증난

해설 Jenna가 바닷가에서 만족스러워 하며 휴식을 취하려다가, 근처에 놀
러온 청소년들로 인해 소란스러워지자 짜증이 난 과정을 묘사하고 있
는 글이다. 글의 초반부의 Jenna gazed happily, looking forward to
relaxing~을 통해 만족감을 느낀 것을 알 수 있고, 글의 후반부에서 Then
she sighed with frustration ~을 통해 짜증을 느꼈다는 것을 알 수 있
으므로, Jenna의 심경 변화로 가장 적절한 것은 ⑤ satisfied(만족스러워
하는) → irritated(짜증난)이다.

오답 분석 ①의 nervous는 글 속의 상황에서 느낄 심경으로 적절하지 않고, calm
은 Jenna의 마지막 심경과 반대된다. ②의 jealous, ③의 confident와
envious, ④의 lazy와 energetic은 글 속의 상황에서 느낄 심경으로 적
절하지 않다.

실력 UP! 미니 문제 08.

정답 The Noisy Interruption at the Beach

CHAPTER 03 요지·주장 파악하기

불변의 패턴 05
p.28

요지·주장은 처음과 마지막 두세 문장에서 제시된다.

기출 문제
정답 ⑤

지문분석

★ Rather than attempting / to punish students with a low grade or mark / in the hope / it will encourage them / to give greater effort / in the future, / teachers can better motivate students / by considering their work / as incomplete / and then requiring additional effort.

~하려고 하는 것 대신에 / 낮은 등급이나 점수를 받은 학생들을 벌주다 / 바라면서 / 학생들을 독려할 것 / 더 많은 노력을 하도록 / 앞으로 / 교사들은 학생들에게 더 잘 동기부여를 할 수 있다 / 그들의 과제를 고려함으로써 / 미완성된 것으로 / 그리고 추가적인 노력을 요구한다

Teachers / at Beachwood Middle School / in Beachwood, Ohio, / record students' grades / as A, B, C, or I (Incomplete).

Beachwood 중학교의 교사들은 / Ohio주 Beachwood에 있는 / 학생의 등급을 기록한다 / A, B, C 또는 I(미완성)로

Students / who receive an I grade / are required / to do additional work / in order to bring their performance up / to an acceptable level.

학생들은 / I 등급을 받은 / 요구된다 / 추가 과제를 하도록 / 그들의 성과를 끌어올리기 위해 / 용인되는 수준까지

This policy is based on the belief / that students perform / at a failure level / or submit failing work / in large part / because teachers accept it.

이런 방침은 생각에 근거한다 / 학생들이 수행하는 것이 / 낙제 수준으로 / 또는 낙제 과제를 제출한다 / 대부분 / 교사들이 그것을 받아주기 때문이라는

The Beachwood teachers reason / that if they no longer accept / substandard work, / students will not submit it.

Beachwood의 교사들은 생각한다 / 만약 그들이 더 이상 받아주지 않는다면 / 기준 미달의 과제를 / 학생들이 그것을 제출하지 않을 것이라고

And / with appropriate support, / they believe / students will continue to work / until their performance is satisfactory.

그리고 / 적절한 도움을 통해 / 그들은 생각한다 / 학생들이 계속 노력할 것이라고 / 그들의 성과가 만족스러울 때까지

★ 독해가 쉬워지는 구문 풀이

Rather than attempting to punish students with a low grade or mark in the **hope** (that) it will encourage them to give greater effort in the future, teachers ~ effort.

⇨ '학생들이 앞으로 더 많은 노력을 하도록 독려할 것을 바람'이라는 뜻으로 앞에 있는 명사 hope의 내용을 풀어서 설명하고 있으므로 hope와 명사절(it will encourage ~ in the future) 사이에 동격 that이 생략되었다.

[어휘] attempt ~해보다, 시도하다 punish 벌주다, 처벌하다
encourage 독려하다, 격려하다 acceptable 용인되는, 받아들여지는
reason 생각하다, 추론하다 substandard 기준 미달의, 표준 이하의
performance 성과 satisfactory 만족스러운, 충분한

[해석] [주제문] 학생들이 앞으로 더 많은 노력을 하도록 독려할 것을 바라면서, 교사들은 낮은 등급이나 점수를 받은 학생들을 벌주려고 하는 것 대신에 그들의 과제를 미완성된 것으로 고려하고 추가적인 노력을 요구함으로써 학생들에게 더 잘 동기부여를 할 수 있다. Ohio주 Beachwood에 있는 Beachwood 중학교의 교사들은 학생의 등급을 A, B, C 또는 I(미완성)로 기록한다. I 등급을 받은 학생들은 용인되는 수준까지 그들의 성과를 끌어

올리기 위해 추가 과제를 하도록 요구된다. 이런 방침은 학생들이 낙제 수준으로 수행하거나 낙제 과제를 제출하는 것이 대부분 교사들이 그것을 받아주기 때문이라는 생각에 근거한다. Beachwood의 교사들은 만약 그들이 더 이상 기준 미달의 과제를 받아주지 않는다면, 학생들이 그것을 제출하지 않을 것이라고 생각한다. 그리고 그들은 학생들이 적절한 도움을 통해 그들의 성과가 만족스러울 때까지 계속 노력할 것이라고 생각한다.

[해설] 학생들의 과제를 미완성된 것으로 생각하면서 추가적인 노력을 요구함으로써 교사들은 학생들에게 더 잘 동기부여를 할 수 있다는 내용의 글이므로, 이 글의 요지로 가장 적절한 것은 ⑤ '학생의 과제가 일정 수준에 도달하도록 개선 기회를 주면 동기부여에 도움이 된다.'이다.

[오답분석] ①은 글에서 언급된 소재 '학습 동기'를 활용하여 혼동을 주는 오답이다.
②은 글에서 언급된 소재 '추가 과제'를 활용하여 혼동을 주는 오답이다.
③, ④은 글과 전혀 관련 없는 내용이다.

불변의 패턴 06
p.29

자주 출제되는 오답의 유형은 정해져 있다.

기출 문제
정답 ①

지문분석

It can be tough / to settle down to study / when there are so many distractions.

어려울 수 있다 / 공부하는 것에 전념하는 것이 / 마음을 산만하게 하는 것들이 너무 많이 있을 때

Most young people like / to combine a bit of homework / with quite a lot of instant messaging, / chatting on the phone, / updating profiles on social networking sites, / and checking emails.

대부분의 젊은이들은 좋아한다 / 조금의 과제를 같이 하는 것을 / 꽤 많은 인스턴트 메시지 보내기와 함께 / 전화로 잡담하기 / SNS에 신상 정보 업데이트하기 / 이메일 확인하기

While it may be true / that you can multitask / and can focus / on all these things / at once, / try to be honest / with yourself.

사실일지도 모르지만 / 당신이 동시에 여러 가지 일을 처리할 수 있다 / 그리고 집중할 수 있다 / 이러한 모든 것들에 / 한 번에 / 솔직해져라 / 당신 자신에게

★ It is most likely / that you will be able to work best / if you concentrate on your studies / but allow yourself regular breaks / — every 30 minutes or so — / to catch up on those other pastimes.

아마 ~할 것이다 / 당신은 최고의 결과를 낼 수 있다 / 만약 당신이 공부에 집중한다면 / 그러나 스스로에게 규칙적인 휴식을 허용한다 / 30분 정도마다 / 밀린 그 기분 전환 활동들을 하기 위해

★ 독해가 쉬워지는 구문 풀이

It is most likely [that you will be able **to work** best if you
_{가주어} _{동사}
concentrate on your studies but **allow** yourself regular breaks
진짜 주어
— every 30 minutes or so — to catch up on those other pastimes].

⇨ 주어가 '당신이 공부에 집중하되 밀린 그 기분 전환 활동들을 하기 위해 30분 정도마다 스스로에게 규칙적인 휴식을 허용한다면 최고의 결과를 낼 것이라는 것'이라는 의미로 길기 때문에, 긴 주어를 대신해서 가주어 역할을 할 수 있는 it으로 문장을 시작했다.

⇨ to부정사구 to work best ~ your studies와 (to) allow yourself ~ other pastime은 등위접속사 but으로 연결된 병렬 구조이며, to부정사구 병렬 구조에서 두 번째부터 나오는 to는 생략될 수 있다.

[어휘] settle down 전념하다, 진정하다 distraction 마음을 산만하게 하는 것
break 휴식 catch up on (밀린 일을) 하다, 따라잡다
pastime 기분 전환 활동, 취미, 오락

[해석] [주제문] 마음을 산만하게 하는 것들이 너무 많이 있을 때, 공부하는 것에 전념하는 것이 어려울 수 있다. 대부분의 젊은이들은 조금의 과제와, 꽤 많은

인스턴트 메시지 보내기, 전화로 잡담하기, SNS에 신상 정보 업데이트하기, 이메일 확인하기를 함께 하는 것을 좋아한다. 당신이 동시에 여러 가지 일을 처리할 수 있고 한 번에 이러한 모든 것들에 집중할 수 있다는 것이 사실일지도 모르지만, 당신 자신에게 솔직해져라. 만약 당신이 공부에 집중하되 밀린 그 기분 전환 활동들을 하기 위해 30분 정도마다 스스로에게 규칙적인 휴식을 허용한다면 아마 당신은 최고의 결과를 낼 수 있을 것이다.

[해설] It is most likely that you will be able to work best if you concentrate on your studies ~에서 필자의 주장이 직접적으로 드러난다. 공부와 여러 가지 일을 같이 하기보다는 공부에만 집중하고 다른 기분 전환 활동은 규칙적인 휴식 시간을 정해서 하는 것이 낫다는 내용의 글이므로, 필자의 주장으로 가장 적절한 것은 ① '공부할 때는 공부에만 집중하라.'이다.

[오답분석] ②, ④은 글에서 언급된 내용이 아니다. ③은 글에서 언급된 '휴식'을 활용하여 혼동을 주는 오답이다. ⑤은 글에서 언급된 '기분 전환 활동'을 활용하여 혼동을 주는 오답이다.

독해 만점 TEST
p.30

01 ④　02 ⑤　03 ④　04 ⑤　05 ⑤　06 ①　07 ④　08 ②

[실력 UP!] 미니 문제

01. 물론, 약간의 경쟁은 스포츠의 한 요소일 뿐만 아니라 인격을 함양하기에도 좋다

02. (A) Body image　(B) your body

03. We fail to develop and end up unhappy and unfulfilled

04. 사소한 결점에 사로잡히게 돼서 결국 일을 절대로 완료하지 못하는 것

05. ⓐ aspect　ⓑ timid

06. create a limit on how much others can infringe upon us

07. there would be nothing to talk about with strangers

08. (A) students　(B) teachers

01
정답 ④

[지문분석]

Playing team sports / has many benefits / for children, / but the problem begins / when competition starts to / overtake the fun part.
단체 스포츠를 하는 것은 / 많은 이점이 있다 / 아이들에게 / 하지만 문제는 발생한다 / 경쟁이 ~하기 시작할 때 / 재미의 역할을 넘어서다

★ Of course, / a bit of competition is / not only a part of sports / but it's also good / for building character.
물론 / 약간의 경쟁은 ~이다 / 스포츠의 한 요소일 뿐만 아니라 / 또한 좋다 / 인격을 함양하기에

Overdoing it, / though, / has negative effects / on a young child.
그것을 지나치게 하는 것은 / 하지만 / 부정적인 영향을 끼친다 / 어린아이에게

Less athletic kids think / they're not good enough / and feel bad, / while / more athletic kids can feel pressured / to do well / all the time.
운동에 덜 적극적인 아이들은 생각한다 / 그들이 충분히 훌륭하지 않다고 / 그래서 낙담한다 / 반면에 / 운동에 더 적극적인 아이들은 압박감을 느낄 수 있다 / 잘해야 한다는 / 항상

Parents should understand / that participation and enjoyment are / the most important aspects.
부모는 이해해야 한다 / 참여와 즐거움이 ~임을 / 가장 중요한 측면

When we take the focus off / of being competitive, / children develop a love / for themselves and the sport.
우리가 초점을 두지 않을 때 / 경쟁하는 것에 / 아이들은 애착을 형성한다 / 스스로와 스포츠에 대한

[구문] ★ 독해가 쉬워지는 구문 풀이

Of course, a bit of competition is **not only** a part of sports **but** it's **also** good for building character.
(주어) (동사) (보어)

➡ 상관접속사 not only A but (also) B는 'A뿐만 아니라 B도'라고 해석한다.

[어휘] overtake 넘어서다, 추월하다　part 역할, 요소, 부분　character 인격, 기질　overdo 지나치게 하다, 과장하다　athletic 운동에 적극적인, 건강한　feel pressured 압박감을 느끼다　aspect 측면, 양상　love 애착, 사랑

[해석] 단체 스포츠를 하는 것은 아이들에게 많은 이점이 있지만, 문제는 경쟁이 재미의 역할을 넘어서기 시작할 때 발생한다. 물론, 약간의 경쟁은 스포츠의 한 요소일 뿐만 아니라 인격을 함양하기에도 좋다. 하지만, 그것을 지나치게 하는 것은 어린 아이에게 부정적인 영향을 끼친다. 운동에 덜 적극적인 아이들은 그들이 충분히 훌륭하지 않다고 생각해서 낙담하는 반면, 운동에 더 적극적인 아이들은 항상 잘해야 한다는 압박감을 느낄 수 있다. 부모는 참여와 즐거움이 가장 중요한 측면임을 이해해야 한다. **[주제문]** 우리가 경쟁하는 것에 초점을 두지 않을 때, 아이들은 스스로와 스포츠에 대한 애착을 형성한다.

[해설] 지나친 경쟁은 어린아이에게 부정적인 영향을 끼치고, 경쟁하는 것에 초점을 두지 않을 때 비로소 아이들은 스스로와 스포츠에 대한 애착을 형성한다는 내용의 글이므로, 이 글의 요지로 가장 적절한 것은 ④ '경쟁이 너무 치열한 스포츠는 아이들에게 좋지 않다.'이다.

[오답분석] ①은 글에서 언급된 내용이 아니다. ②과 ⑤은 지나친 경쟁이 좋지 않다는 글의 내용과 반대되는 오답이다. ③은 글의 일부만을 다루고 있는 오답이다.

[실력 UP!] 미니 문제 01.

정답 물론, 약간의 경쟁은 스포츠의 한 요소일 뿐만 아니라 인격을 함양하기에도 좋다

02
정답 ⑤

[지문분석]

Insecurities can break us down / if we are not careful.
불안감은 우리를 무너뜨릴 수 있다 / 만약 우리가 조심하지 않으면

Just ask a model or athlete.
모델이나 운동선수에게 물어보아라

Society designates / their bodies as ideal, / yet / even they might have aspects / they don't like / about their bodies.
사회는 칭한다 / 그들의 체형을 이상적이라고 / 하지만 / 심지어 그들도 ~한 부분이 있을 수도 있다 / 좋아하지 않는 / 자신의 신체에 대해

Body image is / a subjective idea of yourself.
신체상은 ~이다 / 스스로에 대한 주관적인 관념

This may be quite different from / how your body actually appears / to others.
이것은 ~과 상당히 다를지도 모른다 / 당신의 신체가 실제로 보이는 방식 / 다른 사람들에게

It's OK / not to love / every aspect of your body.
괜찮다 / 사랑하지 않아도 / 당신의 신체의 모든 부분을

But / it's not OK to think / that you are not as good as others / or worthless / because of it.
하지만 / 생각하는 것은 괜찮지 않다 / 당신이 다른 사람들만큼 훌륭하지 않다고 / 또는 가치가 없다고 / 그것 때문에

Accept and love your body / for what it can do / instead of focusing on perceived imperfections.
당신의 신체를 인정하고 사랑하라 / 그것(당신의 신체)이 할 수 있는 것에 대해 / 알고 있는 결점에 치중하지 말고

★ Just as your personality is / unique to you, / so is the body / that houses it.

당신의 성격이 ~인 것처럼 / 당신 안의 독특한 것 / 당신의 신체도 그러하다 / 그것을 담고 있는

That makes it beautiful / no matter what.

이는 그것(당신의 신체)을 아름답게 만들어준다 / 무슨 일이 있어도

★ 독해가 쉬워지는 구문 풀이

Just as your personality is unique to you, so is the body that houses it.
　　　　　　　　　　　　　　　　　　　be동사　주어

➡ 「so + do/be/have동사 + 주어」는 '(주어)도 역시 그렇다'라는 의미의 표현으로, do/be/have동사가 주어 앞으로 도치되어 있다.

[어휘] break down 무너뜨리다 athlete 운동선수
designate ~라고 칭하다, 지정하다 subjective 주관적인
worthless 가치 없는 perceived 알고 있는, 인지하고 있는
imperfection 결점, 단점 unique 독특한, 유일한 house 담다, 수용하다
no matter what 무슨 일이 있어도, 반드시

[해석] 만약 우리가 조심하지 않으면 불안감은 우리를 무너뜨릴 수 있다. 모델이나 운동선수에게 물어보아라. 사회는 그들의 체형을 이상적이라고 칭하지만, 심지어 그들도 자신의 신체에 대해 좋아하지 않는 부분이 있을 수도 있다. 신체상은 스스로에 대한 주관적인 관념이다. 이것은 당신의 신체가 실제로 다른 사람들에게 보이는 방식과 상당히 다를지도 모른다. 당신의 신체의 모든 부분을 사랑하지 않아도 괜찮다. 하지만 그것 때문에 당신이 다른 사람들만큼 훌륭하지 않거나 가치가 없다고 생각하는 것은 괜찮지 않다. [주제문] 알고 있는 결점에 치중하지 말고, 당신의 신체가 할 수 있는 것에 대해 그것을 인정하고 사랑하라. 당신의 성격이 당신만의 독특한 것인 것처럼, 그것을 담고 있는 당신의 신체도 그러하다. 이는 무슨 일이 있어도 그것(당신의 신체)을 아름답게 만들어준다.

[해설] 결점에 치중하지 말고 우리의 신체가 할 수 있는 것에 대해 인정하고 사랑하라는 내용의 글이므로, 필자의 주장으로 가장 적절한 것은 ⑤ '우리의 몸을 있는 그대로 받아들이고 사랑해야 한다.'이다.

[오답분석] ①과 ④은 글에서 언급된 내용이 아니다. ②과 ③은 결점에 치중하지 말고 우리의 몸을 있는 그대로 받아들이고 사랑해야 한다는 글의 내용과 반대되는 오답이다.

[실력 UP!] 미니 문제 02.

정답 (A) Body image (B) your body

해설 (A) 바로 앞 문장에서 신체상(Body image)은 스스로에 대한 주관적인 관념이라고 한 후, 이것(This)은 당신의 신체가 실제로 보이는 방식과 상당히 다를 수도 있다고 했으므로 (A)This는 Body image를 가리킨다.
(B) 바로 앞 문장에서 당신의 신체(your body)의 모든 부분을 사랑하지 않아도 된다고 한 후, 그렇지만 그것(it) 때문에 당신을 가치 없다고 생각하는 것은 괜찮지 않다고 했으므로 (B)it은 your body를 가리킨다.

03   정답 ④

지문분석

We often go through life / on autopilot.
우리는 종종 삶을 살아간다 / 자동 조종 모드로

★ Every day, / our schedules are filled with / school, work, chores, hobbies, / and other things / that keep us busy.
매일 / 우리의 스케줄은 ~으로 가득 차 있다 / 학교, 직장, 집안일, 취미 / 그리고 다른 것들 / 우리를 계속해서 바쁘게 하는

Before we even know it, / years have passed us by.
우리가 이를 알아채기도 전에 / 세월은 흘러갔다

But / stop for a moment / and really think about yourself / and the life / you are living.
하지만 / 잠시 멈추어라 / 그리고 스스로에 대해 정말로 생각해 보아라 / 그리고 인생에 대해 / 당신이 살고 있는

Do you feel / you are on the correct path / mentally, physically, professionally, or spiritually?
당신은 느끼는가 / 당신이 올바른 길에 있다고 / 정신적으로, 신체적으로, 직업적으로, 또는 영적으로

Being able to reflect on such aspects / facilitates a deeper understanding / of yourself.
그러한 측면들을 되돌아볼 수 있는 것은 / 더 깊은 이해를 가능하게 한다 / 스스로에 대해

When we don't stop / to think about our motivations or goals, / we fail to develop / and end up unhappy and unfulfilled.
우리가 멈추지 않으면 / 동기 부여나 목표에 대해 생각하기 위해 / 우리는 발전하지 못한다 / 그리고 결국 불행해지고 성취감을 느끼지 못하게 된다

Take a moment / to press pause / and meditate.
시간을 가져라 / 일시 정지 버튼을 누르기 위한 / 그리고 명상해라

It is a challenging but necessary step / for personal growth.
그것은 힘들지만 필수적인 과정이다 / 개인의 성장을 위한

★ 독해가 쉬워지는 구문 풀이

Every day, our schedules are filled with school, work, chores,
　　　　　　주어　　　　　　수동태
hobbies, and other things that keep us busy.
　　　　　　　　　　　　동사 목적어 목적격보어

➡ 주어 our schedules가 동사구 fill with가 나타내는 '채우는' 행위의 대상이므로, 수동태 are filled with가 온 것이 적절하다.
➡ 보어 자리에는 명사나 형용사 역할을 하는 것이 올 수 있으므로 목적어 us 뒤의 목적격보어 자리에 형용사 busy가 쓰였다.

[어휘] chore 집안일, 하기 싫은 일 professionally 직업적으로, 전문적으로
spiritually 영적으로, 정신적으로 reflect on ~을 되돌아보다, 반성하다
facilitate 가능하게 하다, 용이하게 하다 end up 결국 ~하게 되다
unfulfilled 성취감을 못 느끼는, 충족되지 않은 meditate 명상하다, 계획하다

[해석] 우리는 종종 자동 조종 모드로 삶을 살아간다. 매일, 우리의 스케줄은 학교, 직장, 집안일, 취미, 그리고 우리를 계속해서 바쁘게 하는 다른 것들로 가득 차 있다. 우리가 이를 알아채기도 전에, 세월은 흘러갔다. [주제문] 하지만, 잠시 멈추고 스스로와 당신이 살고 있는 인생에 대해 정말로 생각해 보아라. 당신은 정신적으로, 신체적으로, 직업적으로, 또는 영적으로 올바른 길에 있다고 느끼는가? 그러한 측면들을 되돌아볼 수 있는 것은 스스로에 대해 더 깊은 이해를 가능하게 한다. 우리가 동기 부여나 목표에 대해 생각하기 위해 멈추지 않으면, 우리는 발전하지 못하고 결국 불행해지고 성취감을 느끼지 못하게 된다. 일시 정지 버튼을 누르기 위한 시간을 가져라, 그리고 명상해라. 그것은 힘들지만 개인의 성장을 위한 필수적인 과정이다.

[해설] 스스로에 대해 더 깊이 이해하고 성장하기 위해서는 자신과 자신의 인생을 되돌아보는 시간을 가져야 한다는 내용의 글이므로, 이 글의 요지로 가장 적절한 것은 ④ '자아 성찰을 통해 스스로를 이해해야만 발전할 수 있다.'이다.

[오답분석] ①은 글의 핵심 소재 '스스로를 되돌아보는 것'을 활용하여 혼동을 주는 오답이다. ②, ③, ⑤은 글에서 언급된 내용이 아니다.

[실력 UP!] 미니 문제 03.

정답 We fail to develop and end up unhappy and unfulfilled

해석 Q: 지문에 따르면, 우리가 일시정지 버튼을 누르고 자아성찰을 하지 못할 때 어떤 일이 일어나는가?
A: 우리는 발전하지 못하고 결국 불행해지고 성취감을 느끼지 못하게 된다.

해설 When we don't stop to think ~에서 우리가 동기 부여나 목표에 대해 생각하기 위해 멈추지 않으면, 우리는 발전하지 못하고 결국 불행해지고 성취감을 느끼지 못하게 된다는 것을 알 수 있다.

04

정답 ⑤

지문분석

Some people / inherently strive for excellence.
몇몇 사람들은 / 선천적으로 탁월함을 얻으려고 노력한다

Others feel / they must be perfect / in order to be accepted.
다른 사람들은 느낀다 / 그들이 완벽해야 한다고 / 인정받기 위해

There is nothing wrong with / doing something / to the best of your ability.
~에는 아무 문제가 없다 / 무언가를 하는 것 / 당신의 능력을 최대한으로 발휘해서

The issue is / becoming obsessed with trying to prove / you are perfect.
문제는 ~이다 / 증명하기 위해 노력하는 일에 사로잡히게 되는 것 / 당신이 완벽하다는 것을

If you don't find a good balance, / ★ the overwhelming need / to excel at everything / can sometimes inhibit your progress.
만약 당신이 적절한 균형을 찾지 못한다면 / 압도적인 욕구는 / 모든 것에서 뛰어나려는 / 때때로 당신의 발전을 저해할 수도 있다

You become consumed with / tiny imperfections / and end up never completing a task.
당신은 ~에 사로잡히게 된다 / 사소한 결점 / 그리고 결국 일을 절대로 완료하지 못한다

Do not get stuck / in this loop / or think / you are not "good enough."
갇히지 마라 / 이러한 순환에 / 또한 생각하지 마라 / 당신이 "충분히 완벽하지" 않다고도

Instead, / do the best you can, / even if you mess up / along the way.
대신 / 당신이 할 수 있는 최선을 다해라 / 망치더라도 / 도중에

The important thing is / to keep moving forward.
중요한 것은 ~이다 / 계속 앞으로 나아가는 것

★ **독해가 쉬워지는 구문 풀이**

~ the overwhelming **need** [to excel at everything] can sometimes
　　　　　　　　　명사　　to부정사구
inhibit your progress.

⇨ [ ]는 to부정사의 형용사적 용법으로, 명사 need를 수식한다.

[어휘] inherently 선천적으로, 본질적으로　strive for ~을 얻으려고 노력하다
excellence 탁월함, 우수함　obsessed with ~에 사로잡힌
overwhelming 압도적인　excel 뛰어나다　inhibit 저해하다, 억제하다
consumed with ~에 사로잡힌　imperfection 결점, 불완전함
loop 순환, 고리　mess up 망치다　forward 앞으로

[해석] 몇몇 사람들은 선천적으로 탁월함을 얻으려고 노력한다. 다른 사람들은 인정받기 위해 그들이 완벽해야 한다고 느낀다. 당신의 능력을 최대한으로 발휘해서 무언가를 하는 것에는 아무 문제가 없다. 문제는 당신이 완벽하다는 것을 승명하기 위해 노력하는 일에 사로잡히게 되는 것이다. 만약 당신이 적절한 균형을 찾지 못한다면, 모든 것에서 뛰어나려는 압도적인 욕구는 때때로 당신의 발전을 저해할 수도 있다. 당신은 사소한 결점에 사로잡히게 되고, 결국 일을 절대로 완료하지 못한다. 이러한 순환에 갇히지 말고, 당신이 "충분히 완벽하지" 않다고도 생각하지 마라. ▶주제문◀ 대신, 도중에 망치더라도 당신이 할 수 있는 최선을 다해라. 중요한 것은 계속 앞으로 나아가는 것이다.

[해설] 모든 면에서 뛰어나려는 욕구는 오히려 발전을 저해할 수 있기 때문에 도중에 망치더라도 최선을 다하는 것이 중요하다는 내용의 글이므로, 필자의 주장으로 가장 적절한 것은 ⑤ '모든 면에서 완벽함을 추구하기보다, 매사에 최선을 다하라.'이다.

[오답분석] ①, ③, ④은 글에서 언급된 내용이 아니다. ②은 완벽함을 지나치게 추구하지 말라는 글의 내용과 반대되는 오답이다.

▶실력 UP!◀ 미니 문제 04.
정답 사소한 결점에 사로잡히게 돼서 결국 일을 절대로 완료하지 못하는 것

해설 바로 앞 문장에서 모든 것에서 뛰어나려는 압도적인 욕구로 인해 사소한 결점에 사로잡히게 되고, 결국 일을 제대로 완료하지 못하게 된다고 했으므로 (A)this loop(이러한 순환)은 '사소한 결점에 사로잡히게 돼서 결국 일을 절대로 완료하지 못하는 것'이다.

05

정답 ⑤

지문분석

Over the years, / I've met all sorts of managers, / and many struggle with one particular aspect / of their job.
수년 동안 / 나는 모든 유형의 관리자들을 만나왔다 / 그리고 많은 이들은 특정한 한 가지 측면 때문에 어려움을 겪는다 / 그들의 업무에서

They want the best / from their employees / but do not know / how to convey it.
그들은 최고의 성과를 원한다 / 그들의 직원들로부터 / 하지만 알지 못한다 / 이를 전달하는 방법은

Assessments so often turn into / either harsh criticism / or timid suggestions.
평가는 너무나도 자주 ~으로 변한다 / 가혹한 비판이나 / 소심한 제안으로

Neither is constructive.
어느 쪽도 건설적이지 않다

Proper feedback is given / in a way that points out / what needs to be corrected / and guides the person / to future improvement.
적절한 피드백은 주어진다 / 지적하는 방식으로 / 고쳐질 필요가 있는 것을 / 그리고 이들을 나아가게 하는 방식으로 / 훗날의 발전으로

As such, / managers should focus on observing, / not interfering with, / the individual's behavior.
그러한 것에 있어서 / 관리자는 관찰하는 데 중점을 두어야 한다 / 간섭하는 것이 아니라 / 개인의 행동을

Ultimately, / they should address / the things that the employee is capable of changing.
궁극적으로 / 그들은 이야기해야 한다 / 직원이 바꿀 수 있는 것들을

★ When feedback is given correctly, / it makes a positive difference / for everyone involved.
피드백이 올바르게 전달되면 / 그것은 긍정적인 변화를 만든다 / 관련된 모두에게

★ **독해가 쉬워지는 구문 풀이**

When feedback is given correctly, it makes a positive difference
for **everyone** [involved].
　　　　　수식 받는 명사　과거분사

⇨ 수식 받는 명사 everyone이 involve가 나타내는 '관련시키는' 행위의 대상이므로 과거분사 involved가 쓰였다.

[어휘] struggle with 어려움을 겪다　particular 특정한, 특별한
convey 전달하다　assessment 평가, 평가액　turn into ~으로 변하다
harsh 가혹한　criticism 비판　timid 소심한　constructive 건설적인
guide ~을 나아가게 하다, 유도하다
as such 그러한 (자격·지위·기능 등)에 있어서　observe 관찰하다
interfere with ~을 간섭하다, 방해하다　be capable of ~할 수 있다

[해석] 수년 동안, 나는 모든 유형의 관리자들을 만나왔고, 많은 이들은 그들의 업무에서 특정한 한 가지 측면 때문에 어려움을 겪는다. 그들은 직원들로부터 최고의 성과를 원하지만 이를 전달하는 방법은 알지 못한다. 평가는 너무나도 자주 가혹한 비판이나 소심한 제안으로 변한다. 어느 쪽도 건설적이지 않다. ▶주제문◀ 적절한 피드백은 고쳐질 필요가 있는 것을 지적하고 훗날의 발전으로 이들을 나아가게 하는 방식으로 주어진다. 그러한 것에 있어서, 관리자는 개인의 행동을 간섭하는 것이 아니라 관찰하는 데 중점을 두어야 한다. 궁극적으로, 그들은 직원이 바꿀 수 있는 것들을 이야기해야 한다. 피드백이 올바르게 전달되면, 그것은 관련된 모두에게 긍정적인 변화를 만든다.

[해설] 훗날의 발전으로 나아가게 하는 적절한 피드백이 주어졌을 때 업무와 관

련된 모두에게 긍정적인 변화를 만든다는 내용의 글이므로, 이 글의 요지로 가장 적절한 것은 ⑤ '적절한 피드백은 직원의 성과를 향상시킨다.'이다.

①, ③은 글에서 언급된 내용이 아니다. ②은 글의 핵심 소재 '피드백'을 활용하여 헷갈리게 하는 오답이다. ④은 관리자는 피드백으로서 직원이 바꿀 수 있는 것들을 이야기해야 한다는 글의 내용과 반대되는 오답이다

실력 UP! 미니 문제 05.

정답 ⓐ aspect ⓑ timid
해석 ⓐ 어떤 무언가의 요소, 부분, 혹은 특징
　　　ⓑ 자신감이 없는

06　　　　　　　　　　　　　　　　정답 ①

지문분석

Sometimes, / it feels like / everyone wants something / from you.
때때로 / ~하는 것처럼 느껴진다 / 모두가 뭔가를 원한다 / 당신으로부터

A coworker constantly requests help, / even though you have too much to do / or, maybe / friends or neighbors keep asking for favors / that intrude on your time.
동료가 끊임없이 도움을 요청한다 / 당신이 할 일이 매우 많음에도 불구하고 / 또는 어쩌면 / 친구나 이웃이 계속해서 부탁을 한다 / 당신의 시간에 방해가 되는

★ You feel bad / saying no, / so you end up doing / whatever is asked.
당신은 마음이 불편하다 / 거절하는 것이 / 그렇기에 결국 하게 된다 / 요청받는 무엇이든

This leaves you / drained and unhappy.
이것은 당신을 / ~한 상태로 만든다 / 피로하고 불행한

That's why / personal boundaries are so important.
그것이 바로 ~한 이유이다 / 개인 바운더리가 매우 중요하다

Without some restrictions, / your well-being can suffer greatly.
약간의 제한이 없다면 / 당신의 행복은 상당히 반감될 수 있다

A lack of clear boundaries / can lower your self-esteem.
명확한 바운더리가 없다는 것은 / 당신의 자존감을 떨어트릴 수 있다

Resentment builds up / and can ultimately ruin relationships.
분노가 쌓인다 / 그리고 결국 관계를 망쳐버릴 수 있다

To avoid this, / create a limit / on how much others can infringe upon you.
이를 피하기 위해 / 제한을 두어라 / 다른 사람들이 당신을 어느 정도 방해할 수 있을지에

You don't have to / feel guilty or selfish; / rather, / good boundaries foster / healthy and respectful relationships / that keep your mind and soul happy.
당신은 ~할 필요가 없다 / 죄책감이 들거나 이기적이라고 느낄 / 오히려 / 적절한 바운더리는 조성한다 / 건전하면서도 존중하는 관계를 / 당신의 마음과 영혼을 계속 행복하게 해줄

★ 독해가 쉬워지는 구문 풀이

You feel bad saying no, so you end up doing **whatever** is asked.
　　　　　　　　　　　　　　동명사　　　　　　수동태

▷ '결국 ~하게 되다'라는 의미로 「end up + v-ing」를 관용적으로 사용하므로, 동명사 doing이 쓰였다.
▷ 뒤에 수동태 동사(is asked)만 있고 주어가 없는 불완전한 절이 왔으며, 문맥상 '요청받는 무엇이든'이라는 의미가 되는 것이 자연스러우므로 '~하는 무엇이든'이라는 의미로 불완전한 절 앞에 올 수 있는 명사절 접속사 whatever가 쓰였다.

어휘 constantly 끊임없이, 거듭 favor 부탁; 선호하다 intrude 방해하다, 침범하다
drained 피로한, 녹초가 된 restriction 제한, 제약 resentment 분노, 원한
ultimately 결국 infringe upon 방해하다, 침범하다
guilty 죄책감이 드는, 죄책감 foster 조성하다

해석 때때로, 모두가 당신으로부터 뭔가를 원하는 것처럼 느껴진다. 당신이 할 일이 매우 많음에도 불구하고 동료가 끊임없이 도움을 요청하거나, 어쩌

면 친구나 이웃이 계속해서 당신의 시간에 방해가 되는 부탁을 한다. 당신은 거절하는 것이 마음이 불편하기에, 결국 요청받는 무엇이든 하게 된다. 이것은 당신을 피로하고 불행한 상태로 만든다. 그것이 바로 개인 바운더리가 매우 중요한 이유이다. 약간의 제한이 없다면, 당신의 행복은 상당히 반감될 수 있다. 명확한 바운더리가 없다는 것은 당신의 자존감을 떨어트릴 수 있다. 분노가 쌓이고 결국 관계를 망쳐버릴 수 있다. 이를 피하기 위해, 다른 사람들이 당신을 어느 정도까지 방해할 수 있을지에 제한을 두어라. 주제문 당신은 죄책감이 들거나 이기적이라고 느낄 필요가 없으며, 오히려 적절한 바운더리는 당신의 마음과 영혼을 계속 행복하게 해줄 건전하면서도 존중하는 관계를 조성한다.

해설 자신의 행복을 유지하기 위해 개인 바운더리를 갖는 것이 중요하고, 이는 건전하면서도 존중하는 관계를 조성해준다는 내용의 글이므로, 필자의 주장으로 가장 적절한 것은 ① '개인만의 적절한 바운더리를 가져야 한다.'이다.

②, ④은 글의 핵심 어구 '바운더리'를 활용하여 혼동을 주는 오답이다. ③은 거절하는 것에 죄책감이 들거나 이기적이라고 느끼지 말라는 글의 내용과 반대되는 오답이다. ⑤은 글에서 언급된 내용이 아니다.

실력 UP! 미니 문제 06.

정답 create a limit on how much others can infringe upon us
해석 Q: 지문에 따르면, 명확한 바운더리가 없는 부정적인 상황을 피하기 위해 우리는 무엇을 해야 하는가?
　　　A: 우리는 다른 사람들이 우리를 어느 정도까지 방해할 수 있을지에 제한을 두어야 한다.
해설 To avoid this, create ~에서 명확한 바운더리가 없어서 발생하는 문제를 피하기 위해 다른 사람들이 우리를 방해할 수 있는 정도에 제한을 두어야 한다는 것을 알 수 있다.

07　　　　　　　　　　　　　　　　정답 ④

지문분석

Many of us think / small talk is a tedious part of social norms, / but this is far from the truth.
우리들 중 대다수는 생각한다 / 잡담이 사회적 규범의 지루한 부분이라고 / 하지만 이것은 사실과는 거리가 멀다

At its core, / small talk is a way / to initiate a conversation.
본질적으로 / 잡담은 하나의 방법이다 / 대화를 시작하는

Think / about the last time you went / somewhere you didn't know anyone.
생각해 보아라 / 당신이 지난번에 갔던 때를 / 아는 사람이 아무도 없는 곳에

Without small talk, / there would be nothing to talk about / with strangers.
잡담이 없이는 / 이야기를 나눌 것이 하나도 없을 것이다 / 낯선 사람들과

Engaging in small talk / is a vital skill to master / for both social and professional occasions.
잡담을 하는 것은 / 숙달해야 할 중요한 기술이다 / 사회적 그리고 직업상의 상황 모두를 대비해

★ Good small talk can introduce you / to new friends and colleagues / and is a great way to network.
적절한 잡담은 당신을 소개해줄 수 있다 / 새로운 친구들과 동료들에게 / 그리고 정보를 교환하는 훌륭한 방법이다

It doesn't have to / be rocket science.
그것은 ~할 필요가 없다 / 고도의 지능을 요하는 것일

A few questions about hobbies / or a remark about last night's game / can get a conversation going.
취미에 관한 몇 가지 질문 / 또는 어젯밤 경기에 관한 이야기가 / 대화를 이어지게 할 수 있다

It can open / a whole world of possibilities.
그것은 열어줄 수 있다 / 모든 가능성의 세계를

어휘 tedious 지루한, 장황한 norm 규범, 전형적 생활 양식
initiate 시작하다, 창시하다 vital 중요한, 필수적인 occasion 상황, 때
colleague 동료 network 정보를 교환하다, 인맥을 활용하다
rocket science 고도의 지능을 요하는 것 remark 이야기, 견해

해석 우리들 중 대다수는 잡담이 사회적 규범의 지루한 부분이라고 생각하지만, 이것은 사실과는 거리가 멀다. 본질적으로, 잡담은 대화를 시작하는 하나의 방법이다. 아는 사람이 아무도 없는 곳에 당신이 지난번에 갔던 때를 생각해 보아라. 잡담이 없이는, 낯선 사람들과 이야기를 나눌 것이 하나도 없을 것이다. 주제문 잡담을 하는 것은 사회적 그리고 직업상의 상황 모두를 대비해 숙달해야 할 중요한 기술이다. 적절한 잡담은 새로운 친구들과 동료들에게 당신을 소개해줄 수 있고, 정보를 교환하는 훌륭한 방법이다. 그것은 고도의 지능을 요하는 것일 필요가 없다. 취미에 관한 몇 가지 질문이나 어젯밤 경기에 관한 이야기가 대화를 이어지게 할 수 있다. 그것은 모든 가능성의 세계를 열어줄 수 있다.

해설 잡담은 대화를 시작하는 방법이고, 사회적인 상황과 직업상의 상황 모두를 대비해 숙달되어야 하는 중요한 기술이라는 내용의 글이므로, 이 글의 요지로 가장 적절한 것은 ④ '잡담을 하는 것에는 많은 이점들이 있다.'이다.

오답분석 ①, ②, ⑤는 글에서 언급된 내용이 아니다. ③은 글의 요지를 잡담이 오직 직업상의 상황에서만 사용되어야 한다고 잘못 표현한 오답이다.

실력 UP! 미니 문제 07.

정답 there would be nothing to talk about with strangers

해석 Q: 저자가 말하길, 아는 사람이 없는 상황에서 잡담이 없다면 어떤 일이 일어날 것인가?
A: 잡담이 없다면 낯선 사람들과 할 이야기가 없을 것이다.

해설 Without small talk, there would be nothing ~ with strangers에서 잡담이 없다면 낯선 사람들과 이야기를 나눌 것이 하나도 없을 것이라는 것을 알 수 있다.

08
정답 ②

지문분석

> Among teachers, / a common complaint is / that it is difficult / to get their students excited / about class assignments.
> 교사들 사이에서, / 흔한 불평은 / 그것이 어렵다는 것이다 / 그들의 학생들이 흥미를 느끼도록 만드는 것이 / 수입 과제에 대해
>
> This may not be / the fault of the students, / though.
> 이것은 아닐 수도 있다 / 학생들의 잘못 / 그렇지만
>
> Studies have shown / that a young learner's interest / in school work / has a direct relationship / to his or her level of understanding / regarding the evaluation criteria.
> 연구들은 보여주었다 / 어린 학습자의 흥미는 ~임을 / 학업에 대한 / 직접적인 관련이 있다 / 각자의 이해 정도에 / 평가 기준에 관한
>
> ★ Students / who cannot figure out / what they must do / to receive a high grade / often become discouraged / and put less effort / into a task.
> 학생들 / 이해하지 못한 / 그들이 무엇을 해야 하는지 / 높은 점수를 받기 위해서 / 종종 좌절한다 / 그리고 더 적은 노력을 들인다 / 과제에
>
> In some cases, / they may even give up on / their work.
> 경우에 따라서는 / 그들은 심지어 포기할 수도 있다 / 그들의 과제를
>
> To provide their students / with proper motivation, / teachers must make it clear / what the students will be evaluated on.
> 그들의 학생들에게 제공하기 위해서 / 적절한 동기를 / 교사들은 명히 해야 한다 / 학생들이 무엇으로 평가될 것인지

어휘 complaint 불평 assignment 과제 fault 잘못 regarding ~에 관한
evaluation 평가 criteria 기준 figure out 이해하다
discourage 좌절시키다 give up on ~을 포기하다 motivation 동기

해석 교사들 사이에서, 흔한 불평은 그들의 학생들이 수업 과제에 대해 흥미를 느끼도록 만드는 것이 어렵다는 것이다. 그렇지만, 이것은 학생들의 잘못이 아닐 수도 있다. 연구들은 어린 학습자의 학업에 대한 흥미는 평가 기준에 관한 각자의 이해 정도와 직접적인 관련이 있음을 보여주었다. 높은 점수를 받기 위해서 무엇을 해야 하는지 이해하지 못한 학생들은 종종 좌절하고 과제에 더 적은 노력을 들인다. 경우에 따라서는, 그들은 심지어 그들의 과제를 포기할 수도 있다. 그들의 학생들에게 적절한 동기를 제공하기 위해서, 주제문 교사들은 학생들이 무엇으로 평가될 것인지를 명확히 해야 한다.

해설 학생들에게 적절한 동기를 제공하기 위해서 교사들은 학생들이 무엇으로 평가될 것인지를 명확히 해야 한다는 내용의 글이므로, 필자의 주장으로 가장 적절한 것은 ② '교사는 항상 명확한 평가 기준을 제시해야 한다.'이다.

오답분석 ①, ⑤은 글에서 언급된 소재 '과제'를 활용하여 혼동을 주는 오답이다. ③은 글의 핵심 소재 '평가'를 활용하여 혼동을 주는 오답이다. ④은 글에서 언급된 소재 '동기'를 활용하여 혼동을 주는 오답이다.

실력 UP! 미니 문제 08.

정답 (A) students (B) teachers

해설 (A) they가 포함된 문장에서 높은 점수를 받기 위해 무엇을 해야 하는지 이해하지 못한 "학생"들은 종종 좌절하기도 하고, 과제에 더 적은 노력을 들인다고 했으므로 (A)they는 students를 가리킨다.
(B) their가 포함된 문장에서 그들의 학생들에게 적절한 동기를 제공하기 위해 "교사"들은 학생이 무엇으로 평가될 것인지를 명확히 해야 한다고 했으므로, (B)their는 teachers를 가리킨다.

CHAPTER 04 **밑줄 의미 추론하기**

불변의 패턴 07   p.34
밑줄이 있는 문장은 주제문을 바꿔 말한 것이다.

기출 문제   정답 ⑤

지문분석

> I believe / the second decade / of this new century / is already very different.
> 나는 생각한다 / 두 번째 십 년은 / 이 새로운 세기의 / 이미 매우 다르다고

★ There are, / of course, / still millions of people / who equate success / with money and power / — who are determined / to never get off that treadmill / despite the cost / in terms of their wellbeing, relationships, and happiness.

~이 있다 / 물론 / 여전히 수백만 명의 사람들 / 성공을 동일시하는 / 돈 및 권력과 / 그리고 그들은 ~하기로 한 사람들이다 / 그 쳇바퀴에서 절대 내려오지 않는 / 대가를 치렀음에도 불구하고 / 자신의 건강, 관계, 그리고 행복의 관점에서

There are still millions / desperately looking for the next promotion, / the next million-dollar payday / that they believe / will satisfy their longing / to feel better about themselves, / or silence their dissatisfaction.

수백만의 사람들이 여전히 있다 / 다음번 승진을 절실하게 바라는 / 다음번 고액의 월급날과 / 그들이 생각하기에 / 열망을 충족시킬 / 스스로에 대해 더 좋게 느끼고 싶은 / 또는 그들의 불만족을 없앨

But / both / in the West / and in emerging economies, / there are more people every day / who recognize / that these are all dead ends / — that they are chasing a broken dream.

하지만 / 모두 / 서구에서 / 그리고 신흥 경제국들에서 / 매일 더 많은 사람들이 있다 / 깨닫는 / 이러한 것들은 모두 막다른 곳임을 / 즉 그들이 부서진 꿈을 좇고 있음을

That we cannot find the answer / in our current definition of success alone / because — / as Gertrude Stein once said of Oakland / — "There is no there there."

우리는 정답을 찾을 수 없음을 / 성공에 대한 오늘날의 정의 하나만으로는 / ~하기 때문에 / 언젠가 Gertrude Stein이 Oakland에 대해 말했듯이 / "그곳에는 그곳이 없다"

★ 독해가 쉬워지는 구문 풀이

There are, of course, still **millions of people** **who** equate success
　　　　　　　　　　　　　　　　　　주어　　　수식어1(관계절)
with money and power — **who** are determined to never get off
　　　　　　　　　　　　　수식어2(관계절)
that treadmill **despite** the cost in terms of their wellbeing,
　　　　　　　　　전치사　명사
relationships, and happiness.

⇨ 관계대명사 who 뒤에 주어 없이 동사가 바로 왔으므로 who는 주격 관계대명사로 쓰였다.

⇨ 명사 역할을 하는 단어나 구 앞에 올 수 있는 전치사 despite가 명사 앞에 쓰였다.

[어휘] equate 동일시하다, 평균화하다　treadmil 쳇바퀴　promotion 승진, 진급
payday 월급날, 급여(임금) 지급일　satisfy 만족시키다　longing 열망, 갈망
silence ~를 없애다, 가라앉히다　dead end 막다른 곳

[해석] 나는 이 새로운 세기의 두 번째 십 년은 이미 매우 다르다고 생각한다. 물론, 여전히 성공을 돈 및 권력과 동일시하는 수백만 명의 사람들이 있고, 그들은 자신의 건강, 관계, 그리고 행복의 관점에서 대가를 치렀음에도 불구하고 그 쳇바퀴에서 절대 내려오지 않기로 한 사람들이다. 그들이 생각하기에 스스로에 대해 더 좋게 느끼고 싶은 열망을 충족시키거나 그들의 불만족을 없앨 다음번 승진, 다음번 고액의 월급날을 절실하게 바라는 수백만의 사람들이 여전히 있다. [주제문] 하지만 서구와 신흥 경제국들 모두에서 매일 이러한 것들은 모두 막다른 곳임을, 즉 그들이 부서진 꿈을 좇고 있음을 깨닫는 더 많은 사람들이 있다. 언젠가 Gertrude Stein이 Oakland에 대해 말했듯이 "그곳에는 그곳이 없기" 때문에, 우리는 성공에 대한 오늘날의 정의 하나만으로는 정답을 찾을 수 없음을.

① 사람들은 스스로에 대한 자신감을 잃고 있다.
② 꿈 없이는, 성장을 위한 기회가 없다.
③ 우리는 다른 사람들의 기대에 따라 살지 않아야 한다.
④ 어려운 상황에서 우리의 잠재력을 깨닫는 것은 어렵다.
⑤ 돈과 권력이 반드시 당신을 성공으로 이끌어 주지는 않는다.

[해설] 이 글의 주제는 돈과 권력이 곧 성공이라고 생각하지 않는 사람들이 점점 많아지고 있다는 것이므로, 밑줄 친 There is no there there.(그곳에는 그곳이 없다.)가 의미하는 바로 가장 적절한 것은 ⑤ Money and power

do not necessarily lead you to success.(돈과 권력이 반드시 당신을 성공으로 이끌어 주지는 않는다.)이다.

[오답분석] ①, ②, ③, ④은 글에서 언급된 내용이 아니다.

불변의 패턴 08　　　　　　　　p.35
밑줄 친 부분은 비유적이거나 상징적인 표현이다.

기출 문제　　　　　　　　　정답 ③

Technology has doubtful advantages.
기술은 불확실한 이점들이 있다

We must balance / too much information versus / using only the right information / and keeping the decision-making process simple.
우리는 균형을 맞춰야 한다 / 너무 많은 정보 대 / 오로지 정확한 정보만을 사용하는 것 간의 / 그리고 의사 결정 과정을 단순하게 유지하는 것 간의

★ The Internet has made / so much free information / available / on any issue / that we think / we have to consider all of it / in order to make a decision.
인터넷은 해왔다 / 너무나 많은 무료 정보를 / 이용할 수 있게 / 어떤 문제에 대해서든 / 그래서 우리는 생각한다 / 그 모든 것을 고려해야 한다고 / 결정을 내리기 위해

So we keep searching for answers / on the Internet.
그래서 우리는 답을 찾는 것을 계속하고 있다

This makes us information blinded, / like deer in headlights / when trying to make personal, business, or other decisions.
인터넷에서 / 이는 우리를 정보에 눈이 멀게 만든다 / 마치 전조등 앞의 사슴처럼 / 개인적, 사업적, 혹은 그 밖의 결정을 내리려고 노력할 때

To be successful / in anything today, / we have to keep in mind / that in the land of the blind, / a one-eyed person / can accomplish / the seemingly impossible.
성공하기 위해서 / 오늘날 어떤 것에서든 / 우리는 명심해야 한다 / 눈먼 자들의 나라에서는 / 외눈인 사람은 / 성취할 수 있다는 것을 / 겉으로 보기에 불가능한 것을

The one-eyed person / understands the power / of keeping any analysis simple / and will be the decision maker / when he uses / his one eye of intuition.
그 외눈인 사람은 / 힘을 이해한다 / 어떤 분석이라도 단순하게 하는 / 그리고 결정권자가 될 것이다 / 그가 사용할 때 / 직관을 가진 그의 한쪽 눈을

★ 독해가 쉬워지는 구문 풀이

The Internet has made **so much** free information available on any issue **that** we think [(that) we have to consider all of it in order to make a decision].

⇨ 'so + 형용사/부사 + that + 주어 + 동사'구문은 '매우 ~해서 –하다'라는 의미로 해석한다.

⇨ [ ]는 동사 think의 목적어이며, 명사절 접속사 that이 생략되었다.

[어휘] doubtful 불확실한　blind 눈이 먼　headlight 전조등
keep in mind 명심하다　[선택지] indifferent 개의치 않는

[해석] 기술은 불확실한 이점들이 있다. [주제문] 우리는 너무 많은 정보 대 오로지 정확한 정보만을 사용하며 의사결정 과정을 단순하게 유지하는 것 간의 균형을 맞춰야 한다. 인터넷은 어떤 문제에 대해서든 너무나 많은 무료 정보를 이용할 수 있게 해서, 우리는 결정을 내리기 위해 그 모든 것을 고려해야 한다고 생각한다. 그래서 우리는 인터넷에서 답을 찾는 것을 계속하고 있다. 이는 개인적, 사업적 혹은 그 밖의 결정을 내리려고 노력할 때 마치 전조등 앞의 사슴처럼 우리를 정보에 눈이 멀게 만든다. 오늘날 어떤 것에서든 성공하기 위해서, 우리는 눈먼 자들의 나라에서는 외눈인 사람은 겉으로 보기에 불가능한 것을 성취할 수 있다는 것을 명심해야 한다.

그 외눈인 사람은 어떤 분석이라도 단순하게 하는 힘을 이해하며, 그가 직관을 가진 그의 한쪽 눈을 사용할 때 결정권자가 될 것이다.
① 다른 사람들의 생각을 받아들이기 싫어하는
② 무료 정보에 접근할 수 없는
③ 너무 많은 정보로 인해 결정을 내릴 수 없는
④ 이용 가능한 정보의 부족에 개의치 않는
⑤ 의사결정에 있어서 기꺼이 위험을 감수하려고 하는

[해설] 인터넷에 너무 많은 정보가 있는 것이 이점으로 작용하지 않을 수 있으며, 그 정보들을 잘 선별하고 정보를 활용하여 의사결정 과정을 단순하게 유지할 것을 조언하고 있으므로, information blinded(정보에 눈이 먼)가 의미하는 바로 가장 적절한 것은 ③ unable to make decisions due to too much information(너무 많은 정보로 인해 결정을 내릴 수 없는)이다.

[오답분석] ①, ④, ⑤은 글에서 언급된 내용이 아니다. ②은 인터넷이 어떤 문제에 대해서든 너무나 많은 무료 정보를 이용할 수 있게 해왔다는 글의 내용과 반대되는 내용을 다루고 있으므로 오답이다.

독해 만점 TEST
p.36

01 ② **02** ② **03** ④ **04** ① **05** ② **06** ④ **07** ② **08** ⑤

실력 UP! 미니 문제

01. ③
02. ③
03. (A) most people (B) success
04. ①
05. ⓐ insight ⓑ strategy
06. 그러나, 이는 마치 물속으로 돌을 던지는 것과 같기 때문에, 육류 소비에 관한 한 고려해야 할 더 큰 요인들이 있다
07. ①
08. (A) criticized (B) effective

01
정답 ②

지문분석

Materialism is a way of life / in some cultures.
물질만능주의는 하나의 생활 방식이다 / 몇몇 문화에 있는

In the United States, / for instance, / ★there is the sense / that the more you own, / the happier you'll be, / leading some people to develop serious issues / like addictions to shopping.
미국에는 / 예를 들어 / 인식이 있다 / 당신이 더 많이 소유할수록 / 당신이 더 행복할 것이라는 / 이는 일부 사람들에게 심각한 문제들이 생기게 한다 / 쇼핑 중독과 같은

For others, / spending more money than necessary / is less of a problem / and more of a way of showing off / what they have.
다른 어떤 사람들에게는 / 필요한 것보다 더 많은 돈을 쓰는 것은 / 그다지 문제가 아니다 / 그리하며 오히려 과시하는 방법이다 / 그들이 가진 것을

This feather fanning / is not only for the rich, / however.
이러한 깃털 부채질은 / 부유한 사람들만을 위한 것이 아니다 / 그러나

Even members of low-income groups / sometimes / attempt to use material possessions / to influence / how others perceive them.
저소득층 사람들도 / 때때로 / 물질적인 소유물을 이용하려고 한다 / ~에 영향을 주기 위해 / 다른 사람들이 그들을 어떻게 인식하는지

For instance, / wearing "bling," / or jewelry that stands out, / is intended to make the statement / that the wearer's lifestyle is luxurious, / even if that is not at all the case.
예를 들어 / "과도하게 장식한 비싼 보석"을 착용하는 것은 / 즉 눈에 띄는 장신구를 / 말하려는 의도를 지닌다 / 착용한 사람의 삶이 호화롭다고 / 사실은 전혀 그렇지 않음에도

★ **독해가 쉬워지는 구문 풀이**

~ there is the sense that the more you own, the happier you'll be, ~
　　　　　　　　　　동격 that절

⇨ 뒤에 완전한 절(the more you own, the happier you'll be)이 왔고, '당신이 더 많이 소유할수록 당신이 더 행복할 것이라는 인식'이라는 뜻으로 앞에 있는 명사 sense의 내용을 풀어서 설명하고 있으므로 동격 that이 쓰였다.

[어휘] materialism 물질(만능)주의 less of 그다지 ~않다 more of 오히려 ~이다 show off 과시하다, 으스대다 fan 부채질하다, 부추기다 attempt ~하려고 하다 perceive 인식하다, 알아차리다 stand out 눈에 띄다, 두드러지다 statement 말함, 진술 luxurious 호화로운, 고급의 be the case 사실이 그러하다 [선택지] appreciation 감탄, 감상 display 과시, 표시 irresponsible 무책임한 consequence 대가, 영향 satisfaction 만족

[해석] 물질만능주의는 몇몇 문화에 있는 하나의 생활 방식이다. 예를 들어, 미국에는 당신이 더 많이 소유할수록 당신이 더 행복할 것이라는 인식이 있고, 이는 일부 사람들에게 쇼핑 중독과 같은 심각한 문제들이 생기게 한다. [주제문] 다른 어떤 사람들에게는, 필요한 것보다 더 많은 돈을 쓰는 것은 그다지 문제가 아니며 오히려 그들이 가진 것을 과시하는 방법이다. 그러나, 이러한 깃털 부채질은 부유한 사람들만을 위한 것이 아니다. 저소득층 사람들도 다른 사람들이 그들을 어떻게 인식하는지에 영향을 주기 위해 때때로 물질적인 소유물을 이용하려고 한다. 예를 들어, "과도하게 장식한 비싼 보석," 즉, 눈에 띄는 장신구를 착용하는 것은 사실은 전혀 그렇지 않음에도 착용한 사람의 삶이 호화롭다고 말하려는 의도를 지닌다.

① 아름다운 것들에 대한 감탄
② 호사와 부의 과시
③ 무책임한 소비
④ 일시적인 만족의 대가
⑤ 부와 행복 간의 관계

[해설] 물질만능주의는 사람들이 가진 것을 과시하는 방법이며, 저소득층도 그들의 삶이 호화롭다고 말하려는 의도로 물질적인 소유물을 이용한다고 말하고 있으므로, feather fanning(깃털 부채질)이 의미하는 바로 가장 적절한 것은 ② display of luxury and wealth(호사와 부의 과시)이다.

[오답분석] ①, ③은 글의 일부만을 다루고 있는 오답이다. ④, ⑤은 글에서 언급된 내용이 아니다.

실력 UP! 미니 문제 01.

정답 ③

해석 ① 과잉 지출의 심리적 이로움
　　② 서로 다른 문화에서 물질주의가 인식되는 방식
　　③ 물질적 소유물을 보여주려는 행동의 숨은 의도

해설 사람들이 물질적 소유를 과시하는 이유를 다루는 글이므로, 글의 주제로 가장 적절한 것은 ③ intentions behind displaying material possessions(물질적 소유물을 보여주려는 행동의 숨은 의도)이다.

02
정답 ②

지문분석

Recent human activity / has contributed greatly to global warming.
최근 인류의 활동은 / 지구 온난화의 주요한 원인이 되었다

★Nowhere / are the effects of global warming more alarming / than in the Arctic, / where sea ice is vanishing / due to temperatures there / rising at twice the global average.
어디에도 없다 / 지구 온난화의 영향이 더 염려되는 곳은 / 북극보다 / 그곳에서는 해빙이 사라지고 있다 / 그곳의 기온으로 인해 / 지구 평균의 두 배로 높아지고 있는

The function of sea ice / goes beyond just supporting wildlife survival / in the Arctic; / it plays a role / that affects the planet / as a whole / as all the ecosystems on Earth are connected.
해빙의 기능은 / 단순히 야생 동물의 생존을 돕는 것을 넘어선다 / 북극에 있는 / 그리고 그것은 역할을 한다 / 지구에 영향을 미치는 / 전반적으로 / 지구상의 모든 생태계가 연결되어 있기 때문에

Light-colored surfaces / like sea ice / keep the region cool / by reflecting the majority of sunlight / back into space.
밝은색의 표면은 / 해빙같이 / 그 지역을 서늘하게 유지한다 / 햇빛의 대부분을 반사함으로써 / 다시 우주로

Without this underline{natural moderator}, / it hits the ocean / and is absorbed.
이러한 천연 조절 장치가 없다면 / 그것(햇빛)은 바다에 부딪힌다 / 그리고 흡수된다

In turn, / more ice melts / and sea levels rise, / resulting in a cycle / that becomes harder to stop / the longer it goes on.
결국 / 더 많은 얼음이 녹는다 / 그리고 해수면이 상승한다 / 그리고 순환을 야기한다 / 멈추기 더 힘들어지는 / 그것이 더 오래 계속될수록

★ 독해가 쉬워지는 구문 풀이

Nowhere are the effects of global warming more alarming than
　　　　동사　　　　　　주어
in the Arctic, where sea ice is vanishing due to temperatures there rising at twice the global average.

➡ 부정의 의미를 나타내는 어구 Nowhere가 문장의 앞쪽에 와서 동사 are가 주어 the effects of global warming 앞으로 도치되어 있는 문장이다. 따라서 동사는 뒤에 있는 주어에 수 일치되었다.

[어휘] contribute to ~의 원인이 되다 global warming 지구 온난화
alarming 염려되는 the Arctic 북극 sea ice 해빙
go beyond ~을 능가하다, 초과하다 majority 대부분
moderator 조절 장치, 조절기 in turn 결국, 차례차례 sea level 해수면
go on 계속하다 [선택지] build-up 증가 keep under control 통제하다
limitation 제약

[해석] 최근 인류의 활동은 지구 온난화의 주요한 원인이 되었다. 북극보다 지구 온난화의 영향이 더 염려되는 곳은 어디에도 없는데, 그곳에서는 지구 평균의 두 배로 높아지고 있는 그곳의 기온으로 인해 해빙이 사라지고 있다. [주제문] 해빙의 기능은 단순히 북극에 있는 야생 동물의 생존을 돕는 것을 넘어서, 지구상의 모든 생태계가 연결되어 있기 때문에 그것은 지구에 전반적으로 영향을 미치는 역할을 한다. 해빙같이 밝은색의 표면은 햇빛의 대부분을 다시 우주로 반사함으로써 그 지역을 서늘하게 유지한다. 이러한 천연 조절 장치가 없다면, 그것(햇빛)은 바다에 부딪히고 흡수된다. 결국, 더 많은 얼음이 녹고 해수면이 상승하며, 그것이 더 오래 계속될수록 멈추기 더 힘들어지는 순환을 야기한다.

① 북극의 해빙 증가로 인해 생기는 난관
② 기온을 조절하는 얼음
③ 상승하는 해수면을 제한하는 햇빛
④ 해빙에 의해 야생 동물에 가해지는 제약
⑤ 해빙의 양을 제한하는 온도

[해설] 해빙의 역할은 햇빛을 반사함으로써 그 지역을 서늘하게 유지하는 것이라고 했으므로, natural moderator(천연 조절 장치)가 의미하는 바로 가장 적절한 것은 ② ice that keeps temperatures under control(기온을 조절하는 얼음)이다.

[오답분석] ①은 해빙이 사라지면서 나타나는 문제들을 언급한 글의 내용과 반대되므로 오답이다. ③은 글의 핵심 소재 rising sea levels를 활용하여 혼동을 주는 오답이다. ④, ⑤은 글에서 언급된 내용이 아니다.

[실력UP!] 미니 문제 02.
정답 ③

[해석] ① 온실가스가 지구 온난화에 미치는 영향
② 지구 생태계의 본질에 대한 오해
③ 북극 해빙이 녹음으로써 발생한 위험

[해설] 북극 해빙의 역할과 해빙이 사라지면서 생기는 문제에 관한 글이므로, 글의 주제로 가장 적절한 것은 ③ the risks triggered by the melting of Arctic sea ice(북극 해빙이 녹음으로써 발생한 위험)이다.

03　　　　　　　　　　　　　　　　　　정답 ④

지문분석

It is tempting to think / that highly successful people are lucky / and, accordingly, / that they get all the breaks.
생각하고 싶어진다 / 매우 성공한 사람들은 운이 좋다고 / 그래서 그러므로 / 그들은 모든 행운을 얻는다고

But / the truth is / that most successful people are no luckier / than anyone else.
그러나 / 사실은 ~이다 / 대부분의 성공한 사람들이 더 운이 좋은 것은 아니라는 것 / 다른 누구보다

★ Whether in school, sports, or work / —the people who succeed / are the ones / who put in the hard and necessary work.
학교에서나, 스포츠에서나, 직장에서나, / 성공하는 이들은 / 사람들이다 / 어려우면서도 꼭 필요한 일에 몰두하는

While most people look forward to / taking time off and enjoying their free time, / successful people are willing to / sacrifice their personal time / to achieve their goals.
대부분의 사람들이 기대하는 반면 / 잠시 시간을 내서 그들의 자유 시간을 즐기기를 / 성공한 사람들은 기꺼이 ~한다 / 그들의 개인 시간을 희생한다 / 그들의 목표를 이루기 위해

Moreover, / they do not easily give up / at the first sign of trouble.
게다가 / 그들은 쉽게 포기하지 않는다 / 문제의 조짐이 보이자마자

They know / that success does not simply "happen," / and that they must work hard / to achieve it.
그들은 안다 / 성공이 단순히 "일어나지" 않는다는 것을 / 그리고 노력해야 한다는 것을 / 그것을 얻기 위해

★ 독해가 쉬워지는 구문 풀이

Whether in school, sports, or work — the **people** who succeed are
　　　　　　　　　　　　　　　　　　　주어　　　　　　　동사
the **ones** who put in the hard and necessary work.
　　보어

➡ 동일한 명사(people)의 반복을 피하기 위해 부정대명사 ones가 쓰였다. people이 복수명사이므로 복수형 ones를 쓴다.

[어휘] tempt to ~하고 싶은 accordingly 그러므로, 그에 따라
get a break 행운을 얻다, 특혜를 받다 look forward to ~하기를 기대하다
take time off 시간을 내다 give up 포기하다
at the first sign of ~의 조짐이 보이자마자
[선택지] take advantage of ~를 이용하다 criticize 비판하다
unfairly 부당하게

[해석] 매우 성공한 사람들은 운이 좋아서, 그러므로 그들은 모든 행운을 얻는다고 생각하고 싶어진다. [주제문] 그러나 사실은 대부분의 성공한 사람들이 다른 누구보다 더 운이 좋은 것은 아니라는 것이다. 학교에서나, 스포츠에서나, 직장에서나, 성공하는 이들은 어려우면서도 꼭 필요한 일에 몰두하는 사람들이다. 대부분의 사람들이 잠시 시간을 내서 그들의 자유 시간을 즐기기를 기대하는 반면, 성공한 사람들은 그들의 목표를 이루기 위해 기꺼이 개인 시간을 희생한다. 게다가, 그들은 문제의 조짐이 보이자마자 쉽게 포기하지 않는다. 그들은 성공이 단순히 "일어나지" 않으며, 그것을 얻기 위해 노력해야 한다는 것을 안다.

① 그들은 타인을 이용한다
② 그들에게 많은 자유 시간이 있다
③ 그들은 부당하게 비판받는다

④ 그들은 열심히 일하지 않아도 된다
⑤ 그들도 가끔 실수한다

[해설] 성공하는 사람들은 운이 좋아서 모든 행운을 얻는다고 생각하고 싶지만, 그들은 운이 좋은 것이 아니라 어려운 일에 몰두하고 개인 시간을 희생하여 성공을 얻기 위해 노력한다고 했으므로, 밑줄 친 they get all the breaks(모든 행운을 얻는다)가 의미하는 바로 가장 적절한 것은 ④ they do not have to work hard(그들은 열심히 일하지 않아도 된다)이다.

[오답분석] ①, ③, ⑤은 글에서 언급된 내용이 아니다. ②은 글에서 언급된 소재인 free time을 활용하여 혼동을 주는 오답이다.

[실력UP!] 미니 문제 03.

정답 (A) most people (B) success

해설 (A) 바로 앞 부분에서 대부분의 사람들이 그들의 자유 시간을 즐기기를 기대한다고 했으므로, (A)their는 most people(대부분의 사람들)을 가리킨다.
(B) 바로 앞 부분에서 성공한 사람들은 성공이 단순히 일어나지 않는다는 것을 안다고 한 후 그것을 얻기 위해 노력해야 한다는 것을 안다고 했으므로, (B)it는 success(성공)를 가리킨다.

04
정답 ①

[지문분석]

★ Although many people consider trust / to be essential / in any good relationship, / you shouldn't be too trusting, / as this can be an obstacle.
많은 사람들이 신뢰는 ~라고 생각하더라도 / 필수적이라고 / 모든 좋은 관계에서 / 당신은 사람을 너무 믿지 말아야 한다 / 이것이 방해물이 될 수 있기 때문에

This is especially true / in negotiations.
이는 특히 사실이다 / 협상에 있어서

Studies have found / that people who enter into negotiations / with feelings of distrust / are likely to ask a lot of questions.
연구는 ~임을 알아냈다 / 협상에 들어가는 사람들이 / 불신의 감정을 가지고 / 더 많은 질문을 할 것이다

This is because / they aren't sure / how trustworthy the other party is.
이는 ~ 때문이다 / 그들이 확신하지 못한다 / 상대방이 얼마나 믿음직한지

As a result, / they gather more information / and discuss matters more thoroughly / than those who are completely trusting / to get a clearer sense of the situation.
결과적으로 / 그들은 더 많은 정보를 모은다 / 그리고 문제를 더 철저히 논의한다 / (상대를) 전적으로 신뢰하는 이들보다 / 상황에 대한 더 명확한 판단력을 얻기 위해

In effect, / when what matters most is the outcome, / trust cannot illuminate the truth.
사실상 / 가장 중요한 것이 결과인 경우 / 신뢰는 진실을 규명할 수 없다

In negotiations, / people should allow / a certain measure of distrust / to lead them in their decision making / rather than just believing / whatever is said.
협상에서 / 사람들은 허용해야 한다 / 특정한 수준의 불신을 / 그들을 의사결정에 이르게 할 / 그저 믿는 것보다 / 무엇이든 들리는 대로

★ **독해가 쉬워지는 구문 풀이**

Although <u>many people</u> <u>consider</u> <u>trust</u> **to be essential** in any good
　　　　　 주어　　　 동사　 목적어
relationship, ~

⇨ 동사 consider는 목적어(trust)뒤에 '(to be) + 명사·형용사'와 'as + 명사'를 모두 취하는 동사이다.

[어휘] trusting 사람을 믿는 (경향이 있는) obstacle 방해물 distrust 불신
trustworthy 믿음직한 other party 상대방, 당사자
thoroughly 철저하게, 완전히 sense 판단력 in effect 사실상, 요컨대
illuminate 규명하다, 밝게 하다 **[선택지]** guarantee 보장하다 regain 되찾다
pre-existing 이전부터 존재하는 faith 믿음

[해석] 많은 사람들이 모든 좋은 관계에서 신뢰는 필수적이라고 생각하더라도, 이것이 방해물이 될 수 있기 때문에 당신은 사람을 너무 믿는 말아야 한다. 이는 특히 협상에 있어서 사실이다. 연구는 불신의 감정을 가지고 협상에 들어가는 사람들이 더 많은 질문을 할 것임을 알아냈다. 이는 상대방이 얼마나 믿음직한지 그들이 확신하지 못하기 때문이다. 결과적으로, 그들은 상황에 대한 더 명확한 판단력을 얻기 위해 전적으로 (상대를) 신뢰하는 이들보다 더 많은 정보를 모으고 문제를 더 철저히 논의한다. 사실상, 가장 중요한 것이 결과인 경우, 신뢰는 진실을 규명할 수 없다. **[주제문]** 협상에서, 사람들은 무엇이든 들리는 대로 그저 믿는 것보다 그들을 의사결정에 이르게 할 특정한 수준의 불신을 허용해야 한다.

① 아무것도 묻지 않는 것은 아무것도 보장할 수 없다
② 한번 잃은 신뢰는 다시 되찾을 수 없다
③ 이전부터 존재하는 관계가 있어야 한다
④ 우리는 언제나 상대방에게 믿음을 가져야 한다
⑤ 상대방의 행동을 관찰하는 것이 중요하다

[해설] 모든 좋은 관계에 신뢰가 필수적이지만, 협상에서 상대방에게 불신의 감정을 가진다면 더 많은 질문을 하게 되고 결과적으로 더 많은 정보를 모아 더 명확한 판단력을 얻을 수 있다고 말하고 있으므로, trust cannot illuminate the truth(신뢰는 진실을 규명할 수 없다)가 의미하는 바로 가장 적절한 것은 ① questioning nothing guarantees nothing(아무것도 묻지 않는 것은 아무것도 보장할 수 없다)이다.

[오답분석] ②, ③은 글에서 언급된 내용이 아니다. ④은 협상에서 특정한 수준의 불신을 허용해야 한다는 글의 내용과 반대되는 내용을 다루고 있으므로 오답이다. ⑤은 글에서 언급된 소재인 other party를 활용하여 혼동을 주는 오답이다.

[실력UP!] 미니 문제 04.

정답 ①

해석 ① 협상 시 불신의 이점
② 모든 관계에서 신뢰의 필요성
③ 협상 과정에서 세부사항에 집중할 필요성

해설 협상에서 상대방에 대한 특정한 수준의 불신을 갖는 것이 주는 이점에 대한 글이므로, 이 글의 주제로 가장 적절한 것은 ① the benefit of distrust in negotiation(협상 시 불신의 이점)이다.

05
정답 ②

[지문분석]

To meet the nutritional demands / of a growing world population, / farming will have to get *smarter*.
영양에 관한 수요를 충족시키려면 / 증가하는 세계 인구의 / 농업은 *더 스마트해*져야 할 것이다

And / it's not just a matter / of using better seeds or machinery.
그리고 / 그것은 문제만은 아니다 / 더 좋은 종자나 기계를 사용하는 것의

Just as the world's most successful companies / have made progress / by using big data, / the agricultural world / must collect and analyze information / to find insights / into improving their crop yields.
세계에서 가장 성공한 회사들이 ~한 것과 마찬가지로 / 성과를 내왔다 / 빅데이터를 이용하여 / 농업 분야도 / 정보를 수집하고 분석해야 한다 / 통찰력을 찾기 위해 / 그들의 농작물 수확량 개선에 대한

The next generation of smart farms / will be data-based, / filled with sensors / that allow them to measure every variable / in each square meter of soil: / from luminance and ground temperature, / to current moisture levels, / to the exact amount of pesticide used.
스마트 농업의 다음 세대는 / 데이터를 기반으로 할 것이다 / 센서로 가득 채워지며 / 그들이 모든 변수를 측정하게 해주는 / 토양의 각 제곱미터 내 / 밝기와 지면 온도에서부터 / 현재 수분 수준까지 / 사용된 농약의 정확한 양까지

★ This information, / combined with the latest software, / removes the guessing game, / enabling smart farmers / to identify and implement the best possible strategies / for their fields.
이러한 정보는 / 최신 소프트웨어와 결합된 / 추리 게임을 끝낸다 / 영리한 농부들이 ~할 수 있게 하여 / 가능한 최선의 전략을 찾고 실행하게 / 그들의 토지를 위해

★ 독해가 쉬워지는 구문 풀이

This information, combined with the latest software, removes the
　　주어　　　　　　　　　　삽입구　　　　　　　　　동사
guessing game, **enabling** smart farmers to identify and implement
　목적어　　　　　　　　　　　현재분사구문
the best ~

⇨ This information은 enable이 나타내는 '할 수 있게 하는' 행위의 주체이므로 현재분사 enabling이 쓰였다.

⇨ 동사 enable은 목적격보어로 to부정사를 취하는 동사이다.

[어휘] nutritional 영양에 관한　demand 수요　farming 농업, 농사
machinery 기계　insight 통찰력　crop yield 농작물 수확량
variable 변수　square meter 평방미터　ground temperature 지면 온도
moisture 수분　pesticide 농약, 살충제　implement 실행하다, 시행하다
strategy 전략　[선택지] inhibit 억제하다, 금지하다　neglect 등한시하다

[해석] 증가하는 세계 인구의 영양에 관한 수요를 충족시키려면, 농업은 *더 스마트*해져야 할 것이다. 그리고 그것은 더 좋은 종자나 기계를 사용하는 것의 문제만은 아니다. [주제문] 세계에서 가장 성공한 회사들이 빅데이터를 이용하여 성과를 내온 것과 마찬가지로, 농업 분야도 그들의 농작물 수확량 개선에 대한 통찰력을 찾기 위해 정보를 수집하고 분석해야 한다. 스마트 농업의 다음 세대는 밝기와 지면 온도에서부터 현재 수분 수준 및 사용된 농약의 정확한 양까지, 토양의 각 제곱미터 내 모든 변수를 측정하게 해주는 센서로 가득 채워지며 데이터를 기반으로 할 것이다. 최신 소프트웨어와 결합된 이러한 정보는, 영리한 농부들이 그들의 토지를 위해 가능한 최선의 전략을 찾고 실행할 수 있게 하여 추리 게임을 끝낸다.

① 농업에 사용되는 빅데이터의 활용 방법을 개선한다
② 농사짓는 과정에서 정확성을 보장한다
③ 농부들이 가장 좋은 값을 받도록 해준다
④ 외부 변수의 영향을 억제한다
⑤ 농업을 위한 성공적인 전략을 등한시한다

[해설] 스마트 농업은 정보를 모으고 분석하여 그 데이터를 기반으로 농부들이 토지를 위한 최선의 전략을 찾고 실행하게 해준다고 말하고 있으므로, 밑줄 친 removes the guessing game(추리 게임을 끝낸다)이 의미하는 바로 가장 적절한 것은 ② ensures accuracy in the process of farming(농사짓는 과정에서 정확성을 보장한다)이다.

[오답분석] ①은 글의 일부만을 다루고 있는 오답이다. ③은 글에서 언급된 내용이 아니다. ④는 글에서 언급된 소재인 'variable'을 활용하여 혼동을 주는 오답이다. 변수를 측정하는 것만 언급되었고, 억제하는 것은 글에서 언급되지 않은 내용이다. ⑤는 스마트 농업이 데이터를 기반으로 토지를 위한 최선의 전략을 찾고 실행하게 해준다고 한 글의 내용과 반대되는 내용을 다루고 있으므로 오답이다.

[실력 UP!] 미니 문제 05.

정답 ⓐ insight　ⓑ strategy
해석 ⓐ 어떤 것의 내적 작용들에 대한 심도 있는 이해
　　　 ⓑ 원하는 효과를 성취하기 위해 사용된 계획이나 방책

06 　　　　　　　　　　　　　　　　　정답 ④

지문분석

Choosing / whether or not to eat meat / may seem like a personal matter / in which factors like health and taste / should weigh most heavily.
결정하는 것은 / 고기를 먹을지 말지를 / 개인적인 문제처럼 보일 수 있다 / 건강 및 맛과 같은 요인들이 / 가장 많이 중요시되어야 하는

However, / there are bigger factors to consider / as far as consuming meat is concerned, / as it is like throwing a stone / into the water.
그러나 / 고려해야 할 더 큰 요인들이 있다 / 육류 소비에 관한 한 / 이는 마치 돌을 던지는 것과 같기 때문에 / 물속으로

To produce meat, / it is first necessary / to have land / on which to raise / cattle and other livestock.
고기를 생산하기 위해서는 / 우선 필수적이다 / 땅을 소유하는 것이 / 키울 / 소와 다른 가축을

As this land is not readily available, / forests have to be cleared, / often by burning them to the ground.
이러한 땅은 쉽게 구할 수 없기 때문에 / 숲이 개간되어야 한다 / 종종 그것을 완전히 태움으로써

This destroys / the habitats of countless animal populations / and, over time, / can lead to / a loss in biodiversity and the extinction of some species.
이는 파괴한다 / 수많은 동물 개체군의 서식지를 / 그리고 시간이 지날수록 / ~으로 이어질 수 있다 / 종 다양성의 상실과 일부 종의 멸종

And / that's just to start.
그리고 / 그것은 단지 시작에 불과하다

★ Greenhouse gas emissions, / excessive water use, / and numerous other problems / that threaten the environment / exist, / all stemming from our continued demand / for meat.
온실가스 배출 / 과도한 물 사용 / 그리고 수많은 다른 문제들이 / 환경을 위협하는 / 있다 / 그런데 모든 것은 우리의 지속적인 수요에서 생겨난다 / 육류에 대한

★ 독해가 쉬워지는 구문 풀이

Greenhouse gas emissions, excessive water use, and numerous
　　　　　　　　　　　　　　주절의 주어
other problems that threaten the environment exist, **all** stemming
　　　　　　　　　　　　　　　　　　　　　동사　분사구문의 주어
from our continued demand for meat.
　　현재분사구문

⇨ 주절의 주어(Greenhouse ~ the environment)와 분사구문의 주어(all)가 일치하지 않으면 분사구문의 주어를 생략할 수 없으므로 현재분사 stemming 앞에 주어(all)가 쓰였다.

[어휘] weigh 중요시되다　heavily 많이　consume 소비하다　cattle 소
livestock 가축　readily 쉽게　clear 개간하다, 개척하다
to the ground 완전히　habitat 서식지　population 개체군
biodiversity 종 다양성　extinction 멸종　greenhouse gas 온실가스
emission 배출　excessive 과도한　numerous 수많은
stem from ~에서 생겨나다, 기인하다　continued 지속적인
[선택지] friction 마찰　pose 제기하다

[해석] 고기를 먹을지 말지를 결정하는 것은 건강 및 맛과 같은 요인들이 가장 많이 중요시되어야 하는 개인적인 문제처럼 보일 수 있다. 그러나, 이는 마치 물속으로 돌을 던지는 것과 같기 때문에, [주제문] 육류 소비에 관한 한 고려해야 할 더 큰 요인들이 있다. 고기를 생산하기 위해서는, 우선 소와 다른 가축을 키울 땅을 소유하는 것이 필수적이다. 이러한 땅은 쉽게 구할 수 없기 때문에, 종종 숲을 완전히 태움으로써 개간되어야 한다. 이는 수많은 동물 개체군의 서식지를 파괴하며, 시간이 지날수록, 종 다양성의 상실과 일부 종의 멸종으로 이어질 수 있다. 그리고 그것은 단지 시작에 불과하다. 온실가스 배출, 과도한 물 사용, 그리고 환경을 위협하는 수많은 다른 문제들이 있는데, 모든 것은 육류에 대한 우리의 지속적인 수요에서 생겨난다.

① 적대 관계의 단체들 간에 마찰을 조성하는 것
② 수요에 따라 목표를 변화시키는 것
③ 도덕적 딜레마를 제기하는 것
④ 복합적인 결과를 발생시키는 것
⑤ 수많은 사람들의 우려를 일으키는 것

[해설] 육류 소비는 개인적인 문제로 보일 수 있지만 고려해야 할 더 큰 요인들이 있고, 이것은 숲의 개간, 동물 서식지 파괴, 환경 문제로 이어질 수 있다고 말하고 있으므로, 밑줄 친 throwing a stone into the water(물속으로 돌을 던지는 것)가 의미하는 바로 가장 적절한 것은 ④ generating multiple consequences(복합적인 결과를 발생시키는 것)이다.

[오답분석] ①, ③은 글에서 언급된 내용이 아니다. ②, ⑤은 글의 일부만을 다루고 있는 오답이다.

[실력 UP!] 미니 문제 06.

[정답] 그러나, 이는 마치 물속으로 돌을 던지는 것과 같기 때문에, 육류 소비에 관한 한 고려해야 할 더 큰 요인들이 있다

07　　　　　　　　　　정답 ②

[지문분석]

Companies typically have many channels / through which they interact with consumers, / such as press releases, corporate websites, print and television advertisements, / and social media posts.
기업들은 일반적으로 많은 수단을 가지고 있다 / ~를 통해 고객들과 소통한다 / 보도 자료, 기업 홈페이지, 인쇄 및 TV 광고와 같은 / 그리고 소셜 미디어 게시글(과 같은)

To ensure / that these work in harmony, / some companies have adopted / a strategy called Integrated Marketing Communications (IMC).
반드시 ~하게 하기 위해서 / 이들이 호흡이 맞도록 / 몇몇 기업들은 채택했다 / 통합적 마케팅 커뮤니케이션(IMC)이라고 불리는 전략

It involves / coordinating all public communications / so that customers receive a message / that does not contain conflicting information.
그것은 포함한다 / 모든 홍보 활동을 조정하는 것 / 고객들이 메시지를 받도록 / 상충하는 정보를 포함하지 않는

One barrier to the successful implementation / of an IMC strategy / is a lack of cooperation / among the members of a company.
성공적인 실행에 있어 하나의 장애물 / IMC 전략의 / 협력의 부재이다 / 기업 구성원 간

★ For example, / the marketing department might promise a feature / the design department is unable / to include in a product.
예를 들어 / 마케팅 부서는 기능을 보증할지도 모른다 / 디자인 부서가 할 수 없는 / 상품에 추가하는

To avoid this issue, / a team which serves as a control tower / must be appointed / to make certain / that everyone in a company / is on the same page.
이 문제를 피하기 위해서 / 관제탑 역할을 하는 팀 / 지정되어야 한다 / 확실하게 하기 위해서 / 기업에 있는 모두가 / 같은 페이지에 있다

★ 독해가 쉬워지는 구문 풀이

For example, the marketing department might promise **a feature**
[the design department is unable to include in a product].
　　　　　　　　수식어(관계절)

⇨ [ ]는 선행사 feature를 수식하는 관계절이며, feature 뒤에 목적격 관계대명사 that이 생략되었다.

[어휘] typically 일반적으로　channel 수단　interact 소통하다
press release 보도 자료　corporate 기업의　advertisement 광고
ensure 반드시 ~하게 하다　work in harmony 호흡이 맞다　adopt 채택하다
strategy 전략　integrate 통합하다　coordinate 조정하다, 관장하다

public communication 홍보 활동　barrier 장애물　implementation 실행
cooperation 협력　department 부서　feature 기능　control tower 관제탑
appoint 지정하다　[선택지] consistent 일관된　improve 증진시키다
familiar 익숙한

[해설] 기업들은 일반적으로 보도 자료, 기업 홈페이지, 인쇄 및 TV 광고, 그리고 소셜 미디어 게시글과 같은, 고객들과 소통하는 많은 수단을 가지고 있다. 이들이 반드시 호흡이 맞게 하기 위해서, 몇몇 기업들은 통합적 마케팅 커뮤니케이션(IMC)이라고 불리는 전략을 채택했다. [주제문] 그것은 고객들이 상충하는 정보를 포함하지 않는 메시지를 받도록 모든 홍보 활동을 조정하는 것을 포함한다. IMC 전략의 성공적인 실행에 있어 하나의 장애물은 기업 구성원 간 협력의 부재이다. 예를 들어, 마케팅 부서는 디자인 부서가 상품에 추가할 수 없는 기능을 보증할지도 모른다. 이 문제를 피하기 위해서, 기업에 있는 모두가 같은 페이지에 있다는 것을 확실하게 하기 위한 관제탑 역할을 하는 팀이 지정되어야 한다.

① 고객들의 비슷한 문의를 다룬다
② 고객들에게 일관된 메시지를 제공한다
③ 기업들 간 협력을 증진시킨다
④ 효과적인 상품 광고를 제작한다
⑤ 익숙한 마케팅 방법을 사용한다

[해설] IMC 전략은 고객들이 상충하는 정보를 포함하지 않는 메시지를 받도록 모든 홍보 활동을 조정한다고 말하고 있으므로, is on the same page (같은 페이지에 있다)가 의미하는 바로 가장 적절한 것은 ② provides consistent messages to consumers(고객들에게 일관된 메시지를 제공한다)이다.

[오답분석] ①, ③, ④, ⑤은 모두 글에서 언급된 일부 소재만을 다루고 있는 오답이다.

[실력 UP!] 미니 문제 07.

[정답] ①

[해석] ① IMC 전략이 기업에서 활용되는 방법
② 고객과의 소통을 위해 다양한 수단을 사용하는 것의 이점
③ 부서 간 협동을 장려하는 방법

[해설] 어떻게 기업이 IMC 전략을 통해 소비자와 상호작용하는 많은 수단들이 반드시 호흡이 맞게 하는지에 대해 설명하고 있으므로, 글의 주제로 가장 적절한 것은 ① how the IMC strategy is utilized by companies(IMC 전략이 기업에서 활용되는 방법)이다.

08　　　　　　　　　　정답 ⑤

[지문분석]

Homeopathy is a popular form of treatment / for various diseases / that has been heavily criticized / by the medical establishment.
동종 요법은 대중적인 형태의 치료법이다 / 다양한 질병을 위한 / 상당히 비판받아온 / 의료계에 의해

★ The reason for the distrust is / that there is no evidence / that it is effective.
불신의 이유는 ~이다 / 증거가 없다는 것 / 그것이 효과적이라는

Homeopathic "medicines" are created / by repeatedly diluting a substance / —such as a plant or mineral— / in water / until almost no chemical trace of it remains.
동종 요법의 "약"은 만들어진다 / 물질을 반복적으로 희석함으로써 / 식물이나 광물과 같은 / 물에 / 그것의 화학적 흔적이 거의 남아있지 않을 때까지

This is done / because homeopaths say / that the weaker a medicine is, / the more powerful its ability / to stimulate / the body's natural healing power.
이것은 행해진다 / 동종 요법 지지자들이 주장하기 때문에 / 약이 묽을수록 / 그것의 능력이 강력하다 / 촉진시키는 / 신체의 자연 치유력

While doctors agree / that such methods are generally not harmful, / they urge the public / to remember / that claims made by homeopaths / rarely hold water.
비록 의사들은 동의하지만 / 그러한 방법이 대체로 위험하지 않다고 / 그들은 대중에게 권고한다 / 기억하도록 / 동종 요법 지지자들에 의한 주장이 ~라고 / 좀처럼 이치에 맞지 않음을

The concern is / that people with serious illnesses / such as cancer / might refuse regular medical treatments / if they mistakenly put their trust / in homeopathy.
우려되는 것은 / 심각한 질환을 앓는 사람들 / 암과 같은 / 일반적인 의학적 치료를 거부할 수도 있다 / 만약 그들이 잘못 믿는다면 / 동종 요법을

★ 독해가 쉬워지는 구문 풀이

The reason for the distrust is [①that there is no evidence that it is effective].
동격의 that절

⇨ 명사절 [①]는 위 문장의 보어이다.

⇨ '그것이 효과적이라는 증거'라는 뜻으로 앞에 있는 명사 evidence의 내용을 풀어서 설명하고 있으므로 동격 that이 쓰였다.

어휘 homeopathy 동종 요법 treatment 치료법 criticize 비판하다
medical establishment 의료계 distrust 불신 evidence 증거
substance 물질 mineral 광물 chemical 화학적인 trace 흔적
remain 남아 있다 homeopath 동종 요법 지지자
stimulate 촉진시키다, 자극하다 rarely 좀처럼 ~않다 hold water 이치에 맞다
urge (강력히) 권고하다 public 대중 concern 우려
선택지 investigation 연구

해석 동종 요법은 의료계에 의해 상당히 비판받아온 다양한 질병을 위한 대중적인 형태의 치료법이다. 불신의 이유는 그것이 효과적이라는 증거가 없다는 것이다. 동종 요법의 "약"은 식물이나 광물과 같은 물질을 그것의 화학적 흔적이 거의 남아있지 않을 때까지 물에 반복적으로 희석함으로써 만들어진다. 이것은 동종 요법 지지자들이 약이 묽을수록 신체의 자연 치유력을 촉진시키는 능력이 강력하다고 주장하기 때문에 행해진다. 비록 의사들은 그러한 방법이 대체로 위험하지 않다고 동의하지만, [주제문] 그들은 동종 요법 지지자들에 의한 주장이 좀처럼 이치에 맞지 않음을 기억하도록 대중에게 권고한다. 우려되는 것은 암과 같은 심각한 질환을 앓는 사람들이 만약 동종 요법을 잘못 믿는다면 일반적인 의학적 치료를 거부할 수도 있다는 것이다.

① 연구 중이다
② 더 많은 지지자를 보유하다
③ 매우 효과적이다
④ 비용이 더 든다
⑤ 사실일 가능성이 거의 없다

해설 의료계에서 동종 요법을 불신하는 이유는 그것이 효과적이라는 증거가 없기 때문이라고 했으므로, rarely hold water(좀처럼 이치에 맞지 않다)가 의미하는 바로 가장 적절한 것은 ⑤ are unlikely to be true(사실일 가능성이 거의 없다)이다.

오답분석 ①, ②, ④은 글에서 언급된 내용이 아니다. ③은 글에서 언급된 소재 effective를 활용하여 혼동을 주는 오답이다.

실력UP! 미니 문제 08.

정답 (A) criticized (B) effective
해석 비록 많은 사람들이 다양한 질병을 치료하기 위해 동종 요법을 사용하지만, 그것이 (B) 효과적이라는 것을 증명하는 증거가 없기 때문에 또한 의료계로부터 상당히 (A) 비판을 받아왔다.
해설 동종 요법은 다양한 질병을 위한 대중적인 형태의 치료법인데, 그것은 의료계에서 상당히 "비판을 받아왔으며," 불신의 이유는 그것이 "효과적"이라는 증거가 없기 때문이라고 했으므로, 요약문의 빈칸에 들어갈 말로 가장 적절한 것은 (A) criticized(비판받는), (B) effective(효과적인)이다.

01 ① 02 ④ 03 ③ 04 ② 05 ② 06 ③ 07 ③ 08 ⑤
09 ⑤ 10 ②

01
정답 ①

지문분석

To whom it may concern,
관계자분께

This year has been quite difficult / for our employees / because of the pandemic.
올해는 꽤 힘들었습니다 / 우리 직원들이 / 전 세계적인 전염병으로 인해

I understand / management has some concerns / about letting people work from home, / but I think / it will be good for everyone.
저는 이해합니다 / 경영진이 우려를 갖고 있다는 것을 / 직원들이 재택근무를 하도록 허용하는 것과 관련하여 / 하지만 저는 생각합니다 / 이것이 모두에게 이로울 것이라고

I'm writing / to let you know / the advantages of this plan.
저는 이 편지를 씁니다 / 당신에게 알리기 위해 / 이 계획의 장점들을

First of all, / it will ensure the safety of everyone / in the office / until more people get vaccinated.
첫째로 / 이것은 모두의 안전을 보장해 줄 것입니다 / 사무실에 있는 / 더 많은 사람들이 백신 접종을 받을 때까지

Also, / research shows / that flexible working conditions lead / to greater morale and productivity.
또한 / 연구 결과는 보여줍니다 / 유연한 근무 환경이 이어진다는 것을 / 더 증진된 사기와 생산성으로

★ All in all, / I think / it is worth considering / giving our employees the option / to work from home / during this challenging period.
무엇보다도 / 저는 생각합니다 / 고려할 만한 가치가 있다고 / 우리 직원들에게 선택권을 주는 것은 / 재택근무를 할 / 이렇게 힘든 시기에

I am sure / it will be beneficial / to the company.
저는 확신합니다 / 이것이 도움이 될 것이라고 / 회사에

Sincerely Yours,
Robert Lowell
Senior Marketing Manager
선임 마케팅 관리자 드림

★ 독해가 쉬워지는 구문 풀이

All in all, I think it **is worth considering** [giving our employees the option to work from home during this challenging period].
동명사의 목적어

⇨ be worth -ing는 '~할 가치가 있다'라고 해석한다.
⇨ [ ]는 동명사 considering의 목적어 역할을 하는 동명사구이다.

어휘 pandemic 전 세계적인 전염병 management 경영진, 경영
work from home 재택근무를 하다 ensure 보장하다
vaccinate 백신 접종을 하다 flexible 유연한
working condition 근무 환경 morale 사기, 의욕 productivity 생산성
option 선택권 challenging 힘든, 도전적인

해석 관계자분께,

올해는 전 세계적인 전염병으로 인해 우리 직원들이 꽤 힘들었습니다. 저는 직원들이 재택근무를 하도록 허용하는 것과 관련하여 경영진이 우려를 갖고 있다는 것을 이해하지만, 저는 이것이 모두에게 이로울 것이라고 생각합니다. 저는 당신에게 이 계획의 장점들을 알리기 위해 이 편지를 씁니다. 첫째로, 이것은 더 많은 사람들이 백신 접종을 받을 때까지, 사무실에 있는 모두의 안전을 보장해 줄 것입니다. 또한, 연구 결과는 유연한 근

무 환경이 더 증진된 사기와 생산성으로 이어진다는 것을 보여줍니다. 무엇보다도, 저는 이렇게 힘든 시기에 우리 직원들에게 재택근무를 할 선택권을 주는 것은 고려할 만한 가치가 있다고 생각합니다. 저는 이것이 회사에 도움이 될 것이라고 확신합니다.

Robert Lowell
선임 마케팅 관리자 드림

[해설] 재택근무가 가진 장점을 회사 경영진에게 전달하는 글이다. I'm writing to let you know the advantages of this plan에서 '이 계획(재택근무)의 장점들을 알리기 위해 편지를 쓴다'고 했으므로 이 글의 목적으로 가장 적절한 것은 ① '재택근무의 장점을 강조하려고'이다.

[오답분석] ②과 ④은 글의 내용 중 일부만을 다루고 있다. ③은 글과 전혀 관련 없는 내용이다. ⑤은 중심 소재인 '재택근무'를 다루고 있지만, 재택근무 이외의 선택지가 있는지 문의하기 위한 글이 아니기 때문에 오답이다.

02
정답 ④

지문분석

When Florence became a candidate / for class president, / she thought / it might be really difficult.
Florence가 후보가 되었을 때 / 반장의 / 그녀는 생각했다 / 그것이 정말 어려울 것이라고

She was upset / to discover / she was right.
그녀는 속상했다 / 알게 되어 / 그녀가 옳았다는 것을

She tried campaigning, / but the other students / barely listened to her.
그녀는 선거 운동을 해보았다 / 하지만 다른 학생들은 / 그녀의 말을 거의 듣지 않았다

She felt like a loser already / and wanted to give up.
그녀는 이미 패자인 것 같이 느꼈다 / 그리고 포기하고 싶었다

She told her friend / about her worries.
그녀는 친구에게 이야기했다 / 그녀의 마음고생에 대해

Her friend said / that winning or losing wasn't important.
그녀의 친구는 말했다 / 이기거나 지는 것은 중요하지 않다고

★ What mattered was / that Florence do her best / and take pride / in what she did.
중요했던 것은 ~이었다 / Florence가 최선을 다하는 것 / 그리고 자부심을 갖는 것이다 / 그녀가 했던 것에 대해

After that, / Florence gave it her all.
그 후에 / Florence는 그것에 그녀의 모든 것을 쏟아부었다

She campaigned every day / and talked to her classmates.
그녀는 매일 선거운동을 했다 / 그리고 반 친구들에게 말을 걸었다

She made a great speech.
그녀는 훌륭한 연설을 했다

On the day of the election, / Florence lost.
선거 당일에 / Florence는 패했다

But / it didn't matter / because she was satisfied / with the hard work and effort / she put in.
하지만 / 그것은 중요하지 않았다 / 그녀는 만족했기 때문에 / 수고와 노력에 / 자신이 들인

★ 독해가 쉬워지는 구문 풀이

What mattered was that Florence do her best and take pride in
　주어　　　　　동사　　　　　　　　　보어
what she did.

⇨ 뒤에 동사(mattered)만 있고 주어가 없는 불완전한 절이 왔으므로 관계대명사 What이 주어 역할을 하는 명사절을 이끌고 있다.
⇨ that이 이끄는 절은 be동사(was)의 보어 역할을 하는 명사절이다.

[어휘] worry 마음고생, 걱정　matter 중요하다; 문제　hard work 수고, 노력
[선택지] desperate 자포자기한, 절박한　panic 당황하게 하다
outraged 격분한, 분개한

[해석] Florence가 반장 후보가 되었을 때, 그녀는 그것이 정말 어려울 것이라고 생각했다. 그녀가 옳았다는 것을 알게 되어 그녀는 속상했다. 그녀는 선거 운동을 해보았지만, 다른 학생들은 그녀의 말을 거의 듣지 않았다. 그녀는 이미 패자인 것 같이 느꼈고, 포기하고 싶었다. 그녀는 친구에게 그녀의 마음고생에 대해 이야기했다. 그녀의 친구는 이기거나 지는 것은 중요하지 않다고 말했다. 중요했던 것은 Florence가 최선을 다하고 그녀가 했던 것에 대해 자부심을 갖는 것이었다. 그 후에, Florence는 그것에 그녀의 모든 것을 쏟아부었다. 그녀는 매일 선거운동을 하고 반 친구들에게 말을 걸었다. 그녀는 훌륭한 연설을 했다. 선거 당일에, Florence는 패했다. 하지만, 그녀는 자신이 들인 수고와 노력에 만족했기 때문에 그것은 중요하지 않았다.

① 자포자기한 → 놀란
② 걱정하는 → 당황한
③ 짜증 난 → 즐거워하는
④ 낙담한 → 자랑스러운
⑤ 불안해하는 → 격분한

[해설] Florence가 반장 후보로서 선거 운동을 하면서 낙담했지만 친구의 조언대로 최선을 다했고, 결국 떨어졌음에도 자신의 노력에 자랑스러워하는 과정을 묘사하고 있는 글이다. 글의 중반부의 She felt like a loser already and wanted to give up을 통해 Florence가 낙담한 것을 알 수 있고, 글의 후반부에서 she was satisfied with the hard work and effort she put in을 통해 만족하고 자랑스러워했음을 알 수 있으므로, Florence의 심경 변화로 가장 적절한 것은 ④ discouraged(낙담한) → proud(자랑스러운)이다.

[오답분석] ①의 desperate는 Florence의 처음 심경으로 적절하지만, 마지막 심경으로 surprised는 적절하지 않다. ②의 panicked와 ⑤의 outraged는 모두 부정적인 심경으로, Florence의 마지막 심경과 반대된다. ③의 annoyed와 amused는 Florence가 느꼈을 심경으로 적절하지 않다.

03
정답 ③

지문분석

There is an ancient proverb / that states / "It is better / to sweat in practice / than to bleed in battle."
옛 격언이 있다 / ~라고 말하는 / 더 낫다 / 연습에서 땀을 흘리는 것이 / 전투에서 피를 흘리는 것보다

This idea / is just as relevant today, / as the ability to excel / in any situation / relies on preparation.
이 관념은 / 오늘날에도 마찬가지로 유의미하다 / 타인을 뛰어넘는 능력은 ~기 때문에 / 어떠한 상황에서도 / 준비에 달려있다

This is particularly true of professionals / giving presentations.
이것은 전문가들에게는 더욱 그러하다 / 발표를 하는

Giving any kind of presentation, / especially a good one, / is not an easy task.
어떤 종류의 발표를 하는 것이든 / 특히 훌륭한 발표는 / 쉬운 일이 아니다

Nervousness and worry, / or even overconfidence, / can ruin / what could be an excellent performance.
긴장과 걱정 / 혹은 심지어 자만심도 / 엉망으로 만들 수 있다 / 최고의 발표가 될 수도 있던 것을

The most effective method / to combat this / is also the most overlooked: / practice.
가장 효과적인 방법은 / 이를 방지하는 / 또한 가장 간과되는 것이기도 하다 / 연습이다

It builds confidence / and reduces anxiety.
그것(연습)은 자신감을 키운다 / 그리고 불안을 줄여준다

★ The more you practice, / the more spontaneous you become / as well.
당신이 더 연습할수록 / 당신은 더 자연스러워진다 / 또한

Once you can deliver your material / in your sleep, / you'll know / you are ready.
당신이 당신의 발표물에 대해 말할 수 있게 된다면 / 잠결에도 / 당신은 깨닫게 될 것이다 / 당신이 준비되었음을

★ 독해가 쉬워지는 구문 풀이

The <u>more</u> you practice, the <u>more spontaneous</u> you become as
　　　비교급　　　　　　　　　　비교급
well.

⇨ '더 ~할수록, 더 …하다'라는 의미로 <the + 비교급 ~, the + 비교급 …>
이 쓰였다.

어휘 proverb 격언, 속담　sweat 땀을 흘리다; 땀　bleed 피를 흘리다
relevant 유의미한, 관련 있는　excel (타인을) 뛰어넘다, 능가하다
rely on ~에 달려있다, 의존하다　overconfidence 자만심
ruin 엉망으로 만들다, 망치다　combat 방지하다
overlook 간과하다, 눈감아주다　anxiety 불안, 염려
spontaneous 자연스러운, 자발적인

해석 "전투에서 피를 흘리는 것보다 연습에서 땀을 흘리는 것이 더 낫다"라고 말하는 옛 격언이 있다. 이 관념은 오늘날에도 마찬가지로 유의미하고, 주제문 어떠한 상황에서도 타인을 뛰어넘는 능력은 준비에 달려있기 때문에 이것은 발표를 하는 전문가들에게는 더욱 그러하다. 어떤 종류의 발표를 하는 것이든, 특히 훌륭한 발표는 쉬운 일이 아니다. 긴장과 걱정, 혹은 심지어 자만심도 최고의 발표가 될 수도 있던 것을 엉망으로 만들 수 있다. 이를 방지하는 가장 효과적인 방법은 또한 가장 간과되는 방법이기도 한데, 그것은 연습이다. 그것(연습)은 자신감을 키우고 불안을 줄여준다. 당신이 더 연습할수록, 당신은 또한 더 자연스러워진다. 당신이 잠결에도 발표물에 대해 말할 수 있게 된다면, 당신은 당신이 준비되었음을 깨닫게 될 것이다.

해설 글의 핵심 소재는 '발표'와 '연습'이며, 훌륭한 발표를 하기 위한 가장 효과적인 방법은 잠결에도 발표를 할 수 있을 정도로 연습을 하는 것이라는 내용의 글이므로, 이 글의 요지로 가장 적절한 것은 ③ '많은 양의 연습을 통해 훌륭한 발표를 할 수 있다.'이다.

오답분석 ①, ②은 글의 핵심 소재인 '발표'를 다루고 있으나, 또 다른 핵심 소재인 '연습'에 관한 언급이 없으므로 오답이다. ④은 글의 핵심 소재인 '연습'을 다루고 있으나, 나머지 핵심 소재인 '발표'에 관한 언급이 없으므로 오답이다. ⑤은 글의 핵심 소재인 '발표'와 글에서 언급된 '자신감'을 연결 지어 혼동을 주는 오답이다.

04
정답 ②

지문분석

During university, / one of the classes / I most hated / was Classical Literature.
대학시절에 / 수업 중 하나는 / 내가 가장 싫어하던 / 고전 문학이었다

I didn't see the need / to study something / that seemed so outdated / in today's society / and ★ wondered / why it was even being taught / at all.
나는 필요성을 이해하지 못했다 / 무언가를 공부해야 할 / 매우 구식처럼 보이는 / 현대 사회에서 / 그리고 의문이 들었다 / 왜 그것을 배우고 있는지도 / 도대체

After taking the class, / I didn't wonder anymore.
수업을 들은 후 / 나는 더 이상 의문을 갖지 않게 되었다

There were so many ideas and perspectives / that opened my imagination.
아주 많은 사상과 관점들이 있었다 / 나의 상상력을 열어준

Classical Literature explores themes / connected to life / such as injustice, revenge, and class.
고전 문학은 주제를 탐구한다 / 삶에 관련된 / 불평등, 원한, 그리고 계급과 같은

I learned philosophical concepts / that I never thought about / and caught a glimpse into cultures / I never knew.
나는 철학적 개념을 배웠다 / 내가 한 번도 생각해 보지 않았던 / 그리고 문화도 잠깐 들여다봤다 / 전혀 알지 못했던

The stories, / old as they were, / challenged my modern mind.
그 이야기들은 / 이미 오래된 / 나의 현대적 사고에 이의를 제기했다

Classical Literature helped me grow / not only as a student / but more importantly, / as a human being.
고전 문학은 나를 성장시키도록 도와주었다 / 학생으로서뿐만 아니라 / 더 중요하게는 / 한 명의 인간으로서도

★ 독해가 쉬워지는 구문 풀이

~ wondered <u>why</u> <u>it</u> was even <u>being taught</u> at all.
　　　　　　의문사　주어　　　　　동사

⇨ why it was even being taught는 동사 wondered의 목적어로 쓰인 <의문사 + 주어 + 동사> 순의 간접 의문문(명사절)이다.

어휘 classical literature 고전 문학　perspective 관점, 견해
explore 탐구하다, 개척하다　theme 주제　injustice 불평등, 부당함
revenge 원한, 복수　philosophical 철학적인
a glimpse into ~을 잠깐 들여다봄　challenge 이의를 제기하다, 도전하다
human being 인간, 사람

해석 대학시절에, 내가 가장 싫어하던 수업 중 하나는 고전 문학이었다. 나는 현대 사회에서 매우 구식처럼 보이는 무언가를 공부해야 할 필요성을 이해하지 못했고, 도대체 왜 그것을 배우고 있는지도 의문이 들었다. 수업을 들은 후, 나는 더 이상 의문을 갖지 않게 되었다. 나의 상상력을 열어준 아주 많은 사상과 관점들이 있었다. 고전 문학은 불평등, 원한, 그리고 계급과 같은 삶에 관련된 주제를 탐구한다. 나는 내가 한 번도 생각해 보지 않았던 철학적 개념을 배웠고, 전혀 알지 못했던 문화도 잠깐 들여다봤다. 이미 오래된 그 이야기들은 나의 현대적 사고에 이의를 제기했다. 고전 문학은 나를 학생으로서뿐만 아니라, 더 중요하게는 한 명의 인간으로서도 성장시키도록 도와주었다.

해설 글의 핵심 소재는 '고전 문학'과 '성장'이며, 고전 문학을 통해 이전에 접해 보지 않았던 철학적 개념과 문화를 알게 되고 기존의 사고를 더 넓힐 수 있었다는 내용의 글이므로, 필자의 주장으로 가장 적절한 것은 ② '고전 문학은 사고를 넓히는 데 도움이 된다.'이다.

오답분석 ①은 글의 핵심 소재인 '고전 문학'과 '성장'이 모두 언급되지 않은 오답이다. ③, ④, ⑤은 글의 핵심 소재인 '고전 문학'을 다루고 있으나 나머지 핵심 소재 '성장'에 대한 언급이 없고, 글에 언급된 다른 소재들을 활용하여 혼동을 주는 오답이다.

05
정답 ②

지문분석

Have you ever scrolled through social media / only to find a feed / full of amazing accomplishments / that seem out of reach to you?
소셜 미디어를 넘겨본 적이 있는가 / 게시물을 결국 보게 되다 / 놀라운 성과들로 가득한 / 당신은 해내지 못할 것처럼 보이는

Like with most people, / there will come a time / when comparing yourself to others / makes you feel / as though you're falling short.
대부분의 사람들과 마찬가지로 / 때가 올 것이다 / 스스로를 타인과 비교하는 것이 ~할 때 / 당신을 느끼게 만드는 / 마치 당신이 모자란 것처럼

The truth is / that everyone has / different talents and opportunities, / and it isn't normal / for all people / to have accomplished the same things / at the same points / in their lives.
사실은 ~이다 / 모든 사람이 가진다 / 서로 다른 재능과 기회를 / 그리고 흔하지 않다 / 모든 사람이 / 똑같은 것을 이뤄내는 것은 / 똑같은 시기에 / 그들의 삶에서

Instead of focusing on / where you stand / in relation to others, / it's better / to have an inner scorecard / when playing the game of life.
~에 중점을 두기보다 / 당신이 어디에 서 있는지 / 타인과 비교해서 / 더 좋다 / 내면의 득점표를 가지는 것이 / 삶이라는 게임을 할 때는

Doing so / will make you feel less compelled / to keep up with the other players / ★ and more likely to meet / whatever objectives / that you feel are important.
그렇게 하는 것은 / 당신이 ~해야 한다는 생각을 덜 느끼게 만들어 줄 것이다 / 다른 참가자들을 따라잡는 / 그리고 더 이룰 수 있도록 / 어느 목표라도 / 당신이 중요하다고 느끼는

After all, / the only person / who will care about / how you succeeded in the end / is you.
어쨌든 / 유일한 사람은 / ~에 관심을 가질 / 마지막에 당신이 어떻게 성공해냈는지 / 바로 당신이다

★ 독해가 쉬워지는 구문 풀이

~ and more likely to meet whatever objectives that you feel are
　　　　　　　　　　　　　　복합관계형용사　　명사
important.

⇨ whatever는 뒤에 오는 명사(objectives)를 수식하는 복합관계형용사로 쓰였다.

[어휘] scroll through 넘겨보다, 스크롤 하다 accomplishment 성과
out of reach 해내지 못하는, 힘이 미치지 않는 fall short 모자라다
in relation to ~와 비교해서 inner 내면의 scorecard 득점표
compel ~하게 만들다 keep up with ~를 따라잡다 objective 목표
[선택지] limitation 한계 define 정의하다 private 비밀의
comfort zone 안전지대 humble 겸손한 accomplishment 성취

[해석] 소셜 미디어를 넘겨보다 당신은 해내지 못할 것처럼 보이는 놀라운 성과들로 가득한 게시물을 결국 보게 된 적이 있는가? 대부분의 사람들과 마찬가지로, 스스로를 타인과 비교하는 것이 마치 당신이 모자란 것처럼 느끼게 만드는 때가 올 것이다. 사실은 모든 사람이 서로 다른 재능과 기회를 가지며, 모든 사람이 그들의 삶에서 똑같은 시기에 똑같은 것을 이뤄내는 것이 흔하지는 않다. [주제문] 타인과 비교해서 당신이 어디에 서 있는지에 중점을 두기보다, 삶이라는 게임을 할 때는 내면의 득점표를 가지는 것이 더 좋다. 그렇게 하는 것은 당신이 다른 참가자들을 따라잡아야 한다는 생각을 덜 느끼게 만들어 줄 것이며, 당신이 중요하다고 느끼는 어느 목표라도 더 이룰 수 있도록 만들어 줄 것이다. 어쨌든, 마지막에 당신이 어떻게 성공해냈는지에 관심을 가질 유일한 사람은 바로 당신이다.

① 당신의 한계를 극복하는
② 당신 스스로 성공을 정의하는
③ 당신의 생각을 비밀로 하는
④ 당신의 안전지대에서 벗어나는
⑤ 당신의 성취에 대해 겸손한

[해설] 마지막에 당신이 어떻게 성공해냈는지에 관심을 가질 유일한 사람은 바로 당신이기 때문에 타인과 비교하는 것보다는 자신만의 기준을 가지는 것이 중요하다는 내용의 글이므로, 밑줄 친 have an inner scorecard(내면의 득점표를 가지는)가 의미하는 바로 가장 적절한 것은 ② define success for yourself(당신 스스로 성공을 정의하는)이다.

[오답분석] ①과 ④은 내면의 득점표를 가지라는 것과 관련 없는 오답이다. ③, ⑤은 글의 일부를 다루는 소재 private와 accomplishments를 활용하여 혼동을 주는 오답이다.

[지문분석]

The management / of the Arcos Shopping Center / has received numerous complaints / from visitors.
경영진은 / Arcos 쇼핑 센터의 / 수많은 불만을 들어왔습니다 / 방문객들로부터

They complain / about the lack / of available parking.
그들은 불평합니다 / 부족에 대해 / 이용 가능한 주차 장소의

This has been a big problem / on weekends.
이는 큰 문제였습니다 / 주말에

Fortunately, / the empty lot / behind the shopping center / was recently put up for sale.
다행히도 / 빈 부지가 / 쇼핑 센터 뒤의 / 최근 경매에 나왔습니다

We bought the lot / and will be building a new parking garage.
저희는 그 부지를 매입했습니다 / 그리고 새로운 주차장을 지을 것입니다

The work will begin / next month / on May 4.
이 작업은 시작될 것입니다 / 다음 달인 / 5월 4일에

★ It will take / around two months / to complete.
이것은 걸릴 것입니다 / 약 두 달이 / 완공하는 데

We do not want / to cause any interruption / to your business.
저희는 원하지 않습니다 / 어떠한 방해 요인도 야기하기를 / 여러분의 장사에

However, / please expect / some construction noise.
하지만 / 예상해주시기 바랍니다 / 어느 정도의 공사 소음은

We apologize / for any inconvenience.
저희는 사과 드립니다 / 모든 불편에 대해

If you have questions, / please contact my office.
문의 사항이 있으시면 / 제 사무실로 연락 주십시오

Yours Truly,
Adam Frost
Adam Frost 올림

★ 독해가 쉬워지는 구문 풀이

It will take around two months to complete.
　　　　　　　　　　시간　　　　to부정사

⇨ It takes ~ to는 '-하는 데 ~이 걸리다'라는 의미의 to부정사 관용 표현이다.

[어휘] lot 부지, 구획 put up for sale 경매에 나오다, 팔려고 내놓다
interruption 방해 요인, 중단

[해석] Arcos 쇼핑 센터의 경영진은 방문객들로부터 수많은 불만을 들어왔습니다. 그들은 이용 가능한 주차 장소의 부족에 대해 불평합니다. 이는 주말에 큰 문제였습니다. 다행히도, 쇼핑 센터 뒤의 빈 부지가 경매에 나왔습니다. 저희는 그 부지를 매입했고 새로운 주차장을 지을 것입니다. 이 작업은 다음 달인 5월 4일에 시작될 것입니다. 이것은 완공하는 데 약 두 달이 걸릴 것입니다. 저희는 여러분의 장사에 어떠한 방해 요인도 야기하기를 원하지 않습니다. 하지만, 어느 정도의 공사 소음은 예상해주시기 바랍니다. 저희는 모든 불편에 대해 사과 드립니다. 문의 사항이 있으시면, 제 사무실로 연락 주십시오.

Adam Frost 올림

[해설] 쇼핑 센터의 새로운 주차장 건설 계획에 대해 알리고, 발생할 수도 있는 불편에 대해 양해를 구하고 있다. We bought the lot and will be building a new parking garage에서 '부지를 매입했고 새로운 주차장을 지을 것이다'라고 했으므로 이 글의 목적으로 가장 적절한 것은 ③ '주차장 공사 계획을 안내하려고'이다.

[오답분석] ①, ②은 글과 관련 없는 내용이다. ④은 혼잡한 시설에 대한 불만을 다루고 있지만 불만을 제기하기 위한 글이 아니므로 오답이다. ⑤은 주차장 공사 일정을 다루고 있지만 매장 운영 시간이 변경된 것은 아니므로 오답이다.

정답 ③

Cara reached into her bag / and felt her hands begin to tremble.
Cara는 자신의 가방 안으로 손을 뻗었다 / 그리고 그녀의 손이 떨리는 것을 느꼈다

It was empty.
그것은 비어있었다

Her wallet with all of her money / and her passport were gone.
그녀의 모든 돈이 있는 지갑 / 그리고 그녀의 여권이 사라졌다

She hurriedly stepped out of the line / to buy tickets for the museum / and walked over to a bench / where she emptied her bag.
그녀는 서둘러 줄에서 나왔다 / 박물관 입장권을 사기 위한 / 그리고 벤치로 걸어갔다 / 그녀의 가방을 비운

Only a few coins and a map fell out.
동전 몇 개와 지도 한 장만 떨어졌다

Cara looked around her / with panic.
Cara는 그녀 주위를 둘러보았다 / 공포에 질려

She was in the middle of a city / far from her hotel / with no money.
그녀는 도시 한복판에 있었다 / 그녀의 호텔에서 멀리 떨어진 / 돈이 없는 상태로

★ She also didn't speak / the local language / and didn't know / where to get help.
그녀는 또한 말하지 못했다 / 그 나라의 언어를 / 그리고 알지 못했다 / 어디서 도움을 받아야 할지

Cara could feel tears filling her eyes / as she sat down, / and she tried to think / of what to do next.
Cara는 눈물이 차오르는 것을 느꼈다 / 그녀가 자리에 앉으면서 / 그리고 그녀는 생각하려고 애썼다 / 다음에 무엇을 해야 할지

★ 독해가 쉬워지는 구문 풀이

She also didn't speak the local language and didn't know [where to
　　　　　　　　　　　　　　　　　　　　동사　　　목적어
get help].

⇨ 명사구 [ ]는 동사 know의 목적어이다.
⇨ where to get은 '의문사 + to부정사'로 쓰인 to부정사의 명사적 용법으로, '어디서 도움을 받아야 할지'로 해석된다.

어휘 tremble 떨다, 떨리다　wallet 지갑　**선택지** touched 감동한　grateful 감사하는　contented 만족해하는　lively 활기 넘치는, 활발한　monotonous 단조로운

해석 Cara는 가방 안으로 손을 뻗으며 그녀의 손이 떨리는 것을 느꼈다. 그것은 비어있었다. 그녀의 모든 돈과 여권이 들어있던 지갑이 사라졌다. 그녀는 박물관 입장권을 사기 위한 줄에서 서둘러 나와 벤치로 걸어가 가방을 비웠다. 동전 몇 개와 지도 한 장만 떨어졌다. Cara는 공포에 질려 그녀의 주위를 둘러보았다. 그녀는 돈이 없는 상태로 호텔에서 멀리 떨어진 도시 한복판에 있었다. 그녀는 그 나라의 언어를 할 줄 몰랐고 어디서 도움을 받아야 할지 몰랐다. Cara는 자리에 앉으면서 눈물이 차오르는 것을 느꼈고, 다음에 무엇을 해야 할지 생각하려고 애썼다.

① 감동하고 감사한
② 뿌듯하고 만족해하는
③ 절망적이고 좌절한
④ 활기차고 축제적인
⑤ 단조롭고 지루한

해설 가방 속에 있던 자신의 돈과 여권이 사라진 것을 발견한 Cara가 언어가 안 통하는 낯선 곳에서 앞으로 어떻게 해야 할지 고민하며 좌절하는 모습을 묘사한 글이다. with panic, Cara could feel tears filling her eyes as she sat down~에서 Cara가 좌절한 것을 알 수 있으므로 Cara의 심경으로 가장 적절한 것은 ③ desperate and frustrated(절망적이고 좌절한)이다.

오답분석 ④ delighted와 excited는 긍정적인 심경으로 Cara의 심경과 반대된다. ①의 touched와 grateful, ② proud와 contented, ⑤의 bored와 indifferent는 글 속의 상황에서 느낄 심경으로 적절하지 않다.

정답 ⑤

One of the biggest concerns / in modern times / is how harmful stress can be / to our physical, emotional, and mental health.
가장 큰 관심사 중 하나는 / 현대에서 / 스트레스가 얼마나 해로울 수 있는가이다 / 우리의 신체적, 정서적, 그리고 정신적 건강에 있어서

Certainly, / severe and constant stress is not good / for anyone.
분명히 / 심각하고 지속적인 스트레스는 좋지 않다 / 누구에게나

However, / stress itself is not always bad.
하지만 / 스트레스 자체가 항상 나쁜 것은 아니다

A little bit of stress / makes us tougher.
어느 정도의 스트레스는 / 우리를 더 강하게 만든다

It can help us / manage difficult situations / more easily.
그것은 우리에게 도움이 될 수 있다 / 어려운 상황을 헤쳐나가는 데 / 좀 더 쉽게

When we're stressed, / hormones / that boost our mental ability and memory / are also released.
우리가 스트레스를 받을 때 / 호르몬이 / 우리의 정신력과 기억력을 향상시키는 / 또한 분비된다

★ Even when we endure / more challenging moments / of stress, / like going through a breakup / or getting a bad grade, / it ultimately makes us better.
우리가 견딜 때에도 / 더 힘든 순간들을 / 스트레스의 / 이별을 겪는 것처럼 / 또는 낮은 성적을 받는 것 / 그것은 궁극적으로 우리를 더 성장시킨다

And / during these situations, / we create strong social bonds / by giving each other support.
그리고 / 이러한 상황 속에서 / 우리는 강한 사회적 유대를 형성한다 / 서로에게 지지를 해줌으로써

So, / don't stress / about stress / and you will be / a healthier you.
따라서 / 스트레스를 받지 말아라 / 스트레스에 대해서 / 그러면 당신은 ~이 될 것이다 / 더 건강한 자신이

★ 독해가 쉬워지는 구문 풀이

[Even when we endure more challenging moments of stress,
{like going through a breakup or getting a bad grade}], it
　　　　　동명사　　　　　　　등위접속사　동명사
ultimately makes us better.

⇨ [ ]는 주절(it ~ better)을 수식하는 부사절이다.
⇨ { }는 부사절을 수식하기 위해 삽입된 전치사구이다. 동명사 going과 getting은 등위접속사 or로 연결된 병렬 구조이며, 각각 전치사 like의 목적어이다.

어휘 severe 심각한, 엄격한　constant 지속적인　boost 향상시키다, 북돋우다　release 분비하다, 놓아주다　endure 견디다　challenging 힘든　breakup 이별, 분해　ultimately 궁극적으로　bond 유대, 끈

해설 현대에서 가장 큰 관심사 중 하나는 스트레스가 우리의 신체적, 정서적, 그리고 정신적 건강에 있어서 얼마나 해로울 수 있는가이다. 분명히, 심각하고 지속적인 스트레스는 누구에게나 좋지 않다. **주제문** 하지만, 스트레스 자체가 항상 나쁜 것은 아니다. 어느 정도의 스트레스는 우리를 더 강하게 만든다. 그것은 어려운 상황을 좀 더 쉽게 헤쳐나가는 데 우리에게 도움이 될 수 있다. 우리가 스트레스를 받을 때, 우리의 정신력과 기억력을 향상시키는 호르몬이 또한 분비된다. 이별을 겪거나 낮은 성적을 받는 것처럼 우리가 더 힘든 스트레스의 순간들을 견딜 때에도, 그것은 궁극적으로 우리를 더 성장시킨다. 그리고 이러한 상황 속에서, 우리는 서로에게 지지를 해줌으로써 강한 사회적 유대를 형성한다. 따라서, 스트레스에 대해서 스트레스를 받지 말아라, 그러면 당신은 더 건강한 자신이 될 것이다.

09   정답 ⑤

지문분석

We are taught / from a young age / that if we work hard enough, / we can achieve anything.
우리는 배웠다 / 어릴 때부터 / 만약 우리가 충분히 열심히 노력하면 / 우리는 어떤 것이든 이룰 수 있다고

In addition, / self-help books and magazine articles / tell us / that reaching our goals / is up to us.
더욱이 / 자기계발서 및 잡지 기사는 / 우리에게 말한다 / 목표에 도달하는 것이 / 우리에게 달려 있다고

If we have talent / after all, / we will eventually make it.
만약 우리가 재능이 있다면 / 어쨌든 / 우리는 결국 성공할 것이다

All of this implies / that if we are not "successful," / then we are not doing the right things / or taking the right steps.
이 모든 것은 의미한다 / 만약 우리가 "성공하지" 못한다면 / 그렇다면 우리는 적절한 일을 하지 않고 있다 / 또는 적절한 조치를 취한다

★ However, / there are times / when hard work and talent / are not enough.
하지만 / 때가 있다 / 노력과 재능으로는 / 충분하지 않은

Sometimes, / it is more important / to be in the right place / at the right time.
때때로 / 더욱 중요하다 / 적절한 상황에 있는 것이 / 적절한 때에

This is something / we must accept.
이것은 어떤 것이다 / 우리가 받아들여야 하는

Since we cannot control everything, / all we can do is / do our best / with what we have.
우리가 모든 것을 통제할 수는 없기 때문에 / 우리가 할 수 있는 전부는 / 최선을 다하는 것이다 / 우리가 가진 것으로

★ **독해가 쉬워지는 구문 풀이**

However, there are times <u>when</u> <u>hard work and talent</u> <u>are</u> <u>not</u>
            관계부사   주어   동사
<u>enough</u>.
보어

⇨ 뒤에 주어(hard work and talent), 동사(are), 보어(not enough)가 모두 있는 완전한 절이 왔고, 시간을 나타내는 선행사 time을 수식할 수 있는 관계부사 when이 쓰였다.

[어휘] self-help book 자기계발서   be up to ~에게 달려 있다   after all 어쨌든 make it 성공하다   imply 의미하다, 함축하다   place 상황, 기회 accept 받아들이다

[해석] 우리는 만약 우리가 충분히 열심히 노력하면 어떤 것이든 이룰 수 있다고 어릴 때부터 배웠다. 더욱이, 자기계발서 및 잡지 기사는 목표에 도달하는 것이 우리에게 달려 있다고 말한다. 만약 우리가 어쨌든 재능이 있다면, 우리는 결국 성공할 것이다. 이 모든 것은 만약 우리가 "성공하지" 못한다면 우리는 적절한 일을 하지 않고 있거나 적절한 조치를 취하지 않고 있다는 것을 의미한다. 하지만, 노력과 재능으로는 충분하지 않을 때가 있다. 때때로, 적절한 때에 적절한 상황에 있는 것이 더욱 중요하다. 이것은 우리가

받아들여야 하는 것이다. [주제문] 우리가 모든 것을 통제할 수는 없기 때문에, 우리가 할 수 있는 전부는 우리가 가진 것으로 최선을 다하는 것이다.

[해설] 성공에 있어서 노력과 재능만으로 충분하지 않을 때가 있고, 우리가 할 수 있는 것은 우리가 가진 것으로 최선을 다하는 것이라는 내용의 글이므로, 필자가 주장하는 바로 가장 적절한 것은 ⑤ '노력과 능력이 항상 성공을 보장하는 것은 아니다.'이다.

[오답분석] ①은 글에서 언급된 '재능'과 '노력'을 활용하여 혼동을 주는 오답이다. ②, ③, ④은 글에서 언급된 내용이 아니다.

10   정답 ②

지문분석

History is / about more than / merely gathering facts, / and that's / what renowned historian E.H. Carr insists.
역사란 ~이다 / 그 이상의 / 단순히 사실을 수집하는 것 / 그리고 그것이 ~이다 / 명성 있는 역사가 E.H. Carr가 주장하는 바

Instead, / history is about interactions / between the past and present, / and facts and historians.
대신에 / 역사는 상호 작용에 관한 것이다 / 과거와 현재 간의 / 그리고 사실 및 사학자들 간의

A historian must interpret facts / to give them meaning, / and they must assign significance / to certain facts / that they deem significant / as they filter through and analyze / a large multitude of them.
사학자는 사실을 해석해야만 한다 / 그것들에 의미를 부여하기 위해서 / 그리고 그들은 중요성을 부여해야 한다 / 어떤 사실에 / 그들이 중요하다고 여기는 / 그들이 걸러내고 분석하면서 / 광범위한 다수의 사실을

Of course, / this implies / that history is not neutral, / but Carr argues / that this is an impossibility / anyway, / since historians always take sides, / which brings such limitations.
물론 / 이것은 의미한다 / 역사가 중립적이지 않다는 것을 / 하지만 Carr는 주장한다 / 이것 (역사적 중립을 지키는 것)이 불가능한 일이라고 / 어차피 / 사학자들은 언제나 자신의 편을 정하기 때문에 / 이는 앞선 제약을 동반한다

In his view, / history is "made" / and not "born."
그의 관점에서 / 역사는 "만들어지는" 것이다 / 그리고 "탄생하는" 것이 아니다

★ Since cultures evolve, / so do / evaluations of historical events.
문화가 발달하면서 / ~도 그러하다 / 역사적 사건에 대한 평가

In this way, / history is an ongoing discussion.
이런 면에서 / 역사는 계속 진행 중인 토론이다

★ **독해가 쉬워지는 구문 풀이**

Since cultures evolve, so <u>do</u> <u>evaluations of historical events</u>.
                   동사   주어

⇨ 「so + do/be/have동사 + 주어」는 '(주어)도 역시 그렇다'라는 의미의 표현으로, do/be/have동사가 주어 앞으로 도치되어 있다. 반복되는 동사가 일반동사의 현재형 evolve이므로 do동사의 현재형 do가 쓰였다.

[어휘] gather 수집하다   renowned 명성 있는   historian 사학자, 역사가 interaction 상호 작용   interpret 해석하다   assign 부여하다, 지정하다 significance 중요성   multitude 다수   neutral 중립적인 impossibility 불가능한 일   evolve 발달하다, 진화하다   evaluation 평가 ongoing 계속 진행 중인   [선택지] be traced to ~에서 기원을 찾다 perspective 관점   consist 이루어지다   determine 결정하다

[해석] 역사란 단순히 사실을 수집하는 것 그 이상이고 그것이 명성 있는 역사가 E.H. Carr가 주장하는 바이다. [주제문] 대신에, 역사는 과거와 현재, 그리고 사실 및 사학자들 간의 상호 작용에 관한 것이다. 사학자는 사실에 의미를 부여하기 위해서 그것을 해석해야만 하고, 그리고 그들은 광범위한 다수의 사실을 걸러내고 분석하면서 그들이 중요하다고 여기는 어떤 사실에 중요성을 부여해야 한다. 물론, 이것은 역사가 중립적이지 않다는 것을

의미하지만, Carr는 이것(역사적 중립을 지키는 것)이 어차피 불가능한 일이라고 주장하는데, 사학자들은 언제나 자신의 편을 정하고, 이는 앞선 제약들을 동반하기 때문이다. 그의 관점에서, 역사는 "만들어지는" 것이지 "탄생하는" 것이 아니다. 문화가 발달하면서, 역사적 사건에 대한 평가도 그러하다. 이런 면에서, 역사는 계속 진행 중인 토론이다.

① 현대 사회의 요소들은 과거에서 기원을 찾을 수 있다
② 역사는 과거 사실들에 대한 현재의 해석이다
③ 역사적인 관점은 시간이 지나면서 거의 변하지 않는다
④ 역사적인 기록은 진실된 사실만으로 이루어져 있다
⑤ 한 사회의 구조는 그것의 가치 기준을 결정한다

[해설] 역사란 사실의 수집 그 이상의 것으로, 사학자들은 사실을 해석하고 걸러내고 분석하면서 중요하다고 여기는 어떤 사실에 중요성을 부여한다고 했으므로, 밑줄 친 "made" and not "born"("만들어지는" 것이지 "탄생하는" 것이 아니다)이 의미하는 바로 가장 적절한 것은 ② history is today's interpretation of past facts(역사는 과거 사실들에 대한 현재의 해석이다)이다.

[오답분석] ①, ⑤은 글에서 언급된 내용이 아니다. ③, ④은 글의 중심 소재인 '역사'를 활용하여 혼동을 주는 오답이다.

CHAPTER 05 주제·제목 파악하기

불변의 패턴 09   p.44
주제문은 처음이나 마지막 두세 문장에 나온다.

기출 문제   정답 ④

지문분석

Storyteller Syd Lieberman suggests / that it is the story in history / that provides the nail / to hang facts on.
스토리텔러 Syd Lieberman은 시사한다 / 바로 역사 속의 이야기라고 / 못을 제공하는 것은 / 사실을 걸기 위한

Students remember historical facts / when they are tied / to a story.
학생들은 역사적 사실을 기억한다 / 그것들이 연결될 때 / 이야기와

According to a report, / a high school / in Boulder, Colorado, / is currently experimenting / with a study of presentation of historical material.
한 보고서에 따르면 / 한 고등학교에서 / Colorado주 볼더에 있는 / 현재 실험을 하고 있다 / 역사적 자료 제시의 연구에 관한

Storytellers present material / in dramatic context / to the students, / and group discussion follows.
스토리텔러들이 자료를 제시한다 / 생동적인 맥락에서 / 학생들에게 / 그리고 그룹 토론이 이어진다

Students are encouraged / to read further.
학생들은 장려된다 / 더 많이 읽도록

In contrast, / another group of students is involved / in traditional research / report techniques.
이와 달리 / 또 다른 그룹의 학생들은 참여한다 / 전통적인 조사 / 보고 방식에

★ The study indicates / that the material presented by the storytellers / has much more interest and personal impact / than that gained / via the traditional method.
이 연구는 보여준다 / 스토리텔러들에 의해서 제시된 자료가 / 훨씬 더 많은 흥밋거리와 개인적인 영향력을 지닌다는 것을 / 얻게 된 자료보다 / 전통적인 방법을 통해서

★ 독해가 쉬워지는 구문 풀이

The study indicates [that the material presented by the
　　　　　　　　　　명사절 접속사　　　주어
storytellers has much more interest and personal impact than
　　　　　　동사
that gained via the traditional method].
지시대명사

⇨ 명사절 [ ]는 동사 indicates의 목적어이다.
⇨ 지시대명사 that은 앞의 the material을 가리키며, 같은 명사의 반복을 피하고자 사용되었다.
⇨ 문맥상 '얻게 된 자료'라는 의미로, 수식 받는 대명사 that이 '얻은' 행위의 대상이므로 과거분사 gained가 쓰였다.

[어휘] dramatic 생동적인, 급격한 context 맥락, 문맥, 환경
involve 참여시키다, 수반하다 indicate 보여주다
[선택지] essential 필수적인, 극히 중요한 balanced 균형 잡힌, 안정된

[해석] 스토리텔러 Syd Lieberman은 사실을 걸기 위한 못을 제공하는 것은 바로 역사 속의 이야기라고 시사한다. 학생들은 역사적 사실이 이야기와 연결될 때 그것들을 기억한다. 한 보고서에 따르면, Colorado주 볼더에 있는 한 고등학교에서 현재 역사적 자료 제시의 연구에 대한 실험을 하고 있다. 스토리텔러들이 학생들에게 자료를 생동적인 맥락에서 제시하고, 그룹 토론이 이어진다. 학생들은 더 많이 읽도록 장려된다. 이와 달리, 또 다른 그룹의 학생들은 전통적인 조사/보고 방식에 참여한다. [주제문] 이 연구는 스토리텔러들에 의해서 제시된 자료가 전통적인 방법을 통해서 얻게 된 자료보다 훨씬 더 많은 흥밋거리와 개인적인 영향력을 지닌다는 것을 보여준다.

① 학생들이 역사를 배워야 하는 이유
② 역사 드라마의 필수 요소들
③ 전통적인 교수 방법의 장점들
④ 역사를 가르치는 것에 있어서 스토리텔링의 이점들
⑤ 역사에 대한 균형 잡힌 시각을 갖는 것의 중요성

[해설] 글의 초반부에서 학생들은 역사적 사실이 이야기와 연결될 때 그것들을 기억한다고 하고, 후반부에서 연구는 스토리텔러들에 의해서 제시된 자료가 전통적인 방법을 통해서 얻게 된 자료보다 훨씬 더 많은 흥밋거리와 개인적인 영향력을 지닌다는 것을 보여준다고 했으므로, 이 글의 주제로 가장 적절한 것은 ④ benefits of storytelling in teaching history(역사를 가르치는 것에 있어서 스토리텔링의 이점들)이다.

[오답분석] ①은 글의 핵심 소재 중 일부분인 '역사'만 다루고 있으며, 글과 관련 없는 learn을 활용하여 혼동을 주는 오답이다. ②은 글의 핵심 소재 중 일부분인 '역사'만 다루고 있으며, 글에서 언급된 dramatic context를 활용하여 혼동을 주는 오답이다. ③은 글의 핵심 소재 중 일부분인 '긍정적 요인'만 다루고 있으며, 글에서 언급된 'traditional method'를 활용하여 혼동을 주는 오답이다. ⑤은 글의 내용과 관련 없는 balanced view를 활용하여 혼동을 주는 오답이다.

불변의 패턴 10   p.45
주제문과 함께 자주 나오는 표현이 있다.

기출 문제   정답 ⑤

지문분석

Think, / for a moment, / about something / you bought / that you never ended up using.
생각해보아라 / 잠시 / ~것에 대해 / 당신이 산 / 결국 한 번도 사용하지 않은

An item of clothing / you never ended up wearing?
옷 한 벌 / 결국 한 번도 입지 않은

A book / you never read?
책 / 한 번도 읽지 않은

Some piece of electronic equipment / that never even made it / out of the box?
어떤 전자 기기 / 심지어 꺼내지지도 않은 / 상자 밖으로

It is estimated / that Australians alone spend on / average $10.8 billion AUD / (approximately $9.99 billion USD) / every year / on goods they do not use—/ more than the total government spending / on universities and roads.
추산된다 / 호주인들만 해도 쓰는 것으로 / 평균 108억 호주 달러를 / (약 99억 9천 미국 달러) / 매년 / 사용하지 않는 물건들에 / 이는 정부 지출 총액을 넘는다 / 대학과 도로에 사용하는

That is an average of $1,250 AUD / (approximately $1,156 USD) / for each household.
그것은 평균 1,250 호주 달러이다 / (약 1,156 미국 달러) / 각 가구당

★ All the things / we buy / that then just sit there gathering dust / are waste—/ a waste of money, a waste of time, / and waste in the sense of pure rubbish.
모든 물건들은 / 우리가 사는 / 그 뒤에 그저 그 자리에서 먼지만 쌓고 있는 / 낭비이다 / 돈 낭비 / 시간 낭비 / 순전한 쓰레기라는 의미에서 낭비

As the author Clive Hamilton observes, / 'The difference / between the stuff we buy / and what we use / is waste.'
작가인 Clive Hamilton이 말하는 것처럼 / 차이는 / 우리가 사는 물건 간에 / 그리고 우리가 사용하는 것 / 낭비이다

★ 독해가 쉬워지는 구문 풀이

[All the **things** {①we buy} {②that then just sit there gathering
주어
dust}] are waste—a waste of money, a waste of time, and waste
동사 보어
in the sense of pure rubbish.

⇨ 명사구 [ ]는 문장 전체의 주어이며, 동사는 are, 보어는 waste인 2형식 문장이다. a waste of money ~ pure rubbish는 보어 waste를 부연 설명한다.

⇨ {①}과 {②}는 각각 선행사 things를 수식하는 관계절이다. {①}의 앞에는 목적격 관계대명사 which 또는 that이 생략되었다.

[어휘] end up ~ing 결국 ~하다 household 가구, 세대
in the sense of ~이라는 의미에서 pure 순전한, 순수한
rubbish 쓰레기 (같은 것); 하찮은 observe (관찰에 의하여) 말하다, 관찰하다
[선택지] enable 가능하게 하다 economy 경제 (활동), 절약
management 관리, 경영

[해석] 당신이 사놓고 결국 한 번도 사용하지 않은 것에 대해 잠시 생각해보아라. 결국 한 번도 입지 않은 옷 한 벌? 한 번도 읽지 않은 책? 심지어 상자 밖으로 꺼내지지도 않은 어떤 전자 기기? 호주인들만 해도 매년 평균 108억 호주 달러(약 99억 9천 미국 달러)를 사용하지 않는 물건들에 쓰는 것으로 추산되는데, 이는 대학과 도로에 사용하는 정부 지출 총액을 넘는다. 그것은 각 가구당 평균 1,250 호주 달러(약 1,156 미국 달러)이다. **[주제문]** 우리가 사고 난 뒤에 그저 그 자리에서 먼지만 쌓고 있는 모든 물건들은 낭비인데, 돈 낭비, 시간 낭비이자 순전한 쓰레기라는 의미에서 낭비이다. 작가인 Clive Hamilton이 말하는 것처럼 '우리가 사는 물건과 우리가 사용하는 것 간의 차이는 낭비이다'.

① 소비가 경제 활동을 가능하게 한다
② 돈 관리: 해야 할 것과 하지 않아야 할 것
③ 지나친 쇼핑: 외로움의 신호
④ 낭비의 3R: 줄이고, 다시 사용하고, 재활용하기
⑤ 당신이 사는 것은 그것을 사용하지 않는 한 낭비이다

[해설] 이 글의 중심 내용은 우리가 구매한 뒤에 사용하지 않는 모든 물건들이 낭

비라는 것이므로, 이 글의 제목으로 가장 적절한 것은 ⑤ What You Buy Is Waste Unless You Use It(당신이 사는 것은 그것을 사용하지 않는 한 낭비이다)이다.

[오답분석] ①은 글의 핵심 소재에 대한 언급이 없으며, 글에서 언급된 spending을 활용하여 혼동을 주는 오답이다. ②은 글의 핵심 소재에 대한 언급이 없으며, 글의 일부를 다루는 지엽적인 소재 money를 활용하여 혼동을 주는 오답이다. ③은 글의 내용과 관련 없는 내용이다. ④은 글의 핵심 소재 중 일부분인 '낭비'만 다루고 있으며, 글의 내용과 관련 없는 reduce, reuse, recycle을 활용하여 혼동을 주는 오답이다.

독해 만점 TEST
p 46

01 ⑤ **02** ② **03** ④ **04** ② **05** ① **06** ⑤ **07** ② **08** ⑤

실력 UP! 미니 문제

01. 백색소음이 수면에 도움을 주는 가장 효과적인 방법 중 하나라는 것

02. 비누로 씻는 것

03. ⓐ obsolete ⓑ induce

04. Children learn language best when they interact with the people around them

05. Focus on what you want to happen and how you will achieve that result

06. easier to tax people and pay salaries to soldiers and government officials

07. (A) the association between vampires and bats
    (B) sleeping humans

08. plays an important role in promoting the will of the people

01
정답 ⑤

지문분석

★ White noise, / whether it's the drone of a fan / or the regular crash of waves / on the shore, / is popularly believed / to be one of the most effective forms / of sleep aid.
백색소음은 / 그것이 선풍기의 웅웅거리는 소리든지 / 아니면 파도가 부서지는 규칙적인 소리든지 / 해안의 / 일반적으로 여겨진다 / 가장 효과적인 방법 중 하나라고 / 수면에 도움을 주는

An entire industry of products / has grown up / around the concept, / with apps and devices / that promise to provide soothing sounds / that will help you sleep / through the night.
모든 산업의 제품들은 / 성장해왔다 / 그 기본적 개념을 활용하며 / 앱과 장치와 함께 / 안정적인 소리를 제공할 것을 약속하는 / 당신이 숙면하는 것을 도와줄 / 밤새

Some insist / that white noise can train you / to relax and "switch off" your brain / by focusing on a single, gentle stimulus / instead of all the thoughts / racing around in your head.
일부 사람들은 주장한다 / 백색소음은 당신을 훈련시켜 줄 수 있다고 / 긴장을 풀고 뇌의 "스위치를 끄도록" / 한 가지의 부드러운 자극에 집중함으로써 / 온갖 생각 대신에 / 당신 머릿속에서 여기저기를 질주하는

But / despite these claims, / research has found little evidence / to verify them.
하지만 / 이러한 주장에도 불구하고 / 연구는 근거를 거의 찾지 못했다 / 그것을 증명할

Given the active work / that our brain has to do / when interpreting noise, / using one of these / may, ironically enough, / increase its workload / and deny it a chance / for needed rest.
활동적인 작업을 고려해보면 / 우리의 뇌가 해야 하는 / 소음을 해석할 때 / 이것들 중 하나를 이용하는 것은 / 충분히 아이러니하게도 / 그것의(뇌의) 작업량을 늘릴 수도 있다 / 그래서 기회를 주지 않는다 / 필요한 휴식을 취할

어휘 white noise 백색소음　form 방법, 수법　around ~이 활용되어
concept (상품·판매의) 기본적 개념, 테마　soothing 안정적인
verify 증명하다, 확인하다　interpret 해석하다, 이해하다
deny A B A에게 B를 주지 않다　**선택지** sleeplessness 불면
insomnia 불면증

해석 선풍기의 웅웅거리는 소리든지 아니면 해안의 파도가 부서지는 규칙적인
소리든지, 일반적으로 백색소음은 수면에 도움을 주는 가장 효과적인 방
법 중 하나라고 여겨진다. 밤새 당신이 숙면하는 것을 도와줄 안정적인 소
리를 제공할 것을 약속하는 앱 및 장치와 함께, 모든 산업의 제품들은 그
기본적 개념을 활용하며 성장해왔다. 일부 사람들은 당신 머릿속에서 여
기저기를 질주하는 온갖 생각 대신에 한 가지의 부드러운 자극에 집중함
으로써 백색소음은 당신이 긴장을 풀고 뇌의 "스위치를 끄도록" 훈련시켜
줄 수 있다고 주장한다. **주제문** 하지만 이러한 주장에도 불구하고, 연구는
그것을 증명할 근거를 거의 찾지 못했다. 소음을 해석할 때 우리의 뇌가
해야 하는 활동적인 작업을 고려해보면, 충분히 아이러니하게도, 이것(앱
및 장치)들 중 하나를 이용하는 것은 그것의(뇌의) 작업량을 늘릴 수 있어
서 필요한 휴식을 취할 기회를 주지 않는다.

① 불면과 불면증의 영향
② 백색소음을 이해하는 효과적인 방법
③ 우리의 마음을 진정시키는 백색소음의 유형
④ 더 효과적으로 수면을 취하도록 도와주는 제품들
⑤ 백색소음이 수면에 끼치는 영향에 대한 상이한 관점

해설 일부 사람들은 백색소음이 수면 중 뇌의 스위치를 끄도록 훈련시켜줄 수
있다고 하였으나, 글의 후반부에서 이를 증명할 수 있는 근거를 거의 찾지
못했고, 오히려 백색 소음은 뇌가 휴식을 취할 기회를 주지 않는다고 했으
므로, 이 글의 주제로 가장 적절한 것은 ⑤ different views regarding
white noise's impact on sleep(백색소음이 수면에 끼치는 영향에 대한
상이한 관점)이다.

오답분석 ①은 글의 핵심 소재인 '백색 소음'에 대한 언급이 없으며, 글의 핵심 소재
sleep과 관련된 소재를 활용하여 혼동을 주는 오답이다. ②, ③은 글의 핵
심 소재 중 일부인 '백색 소음'을 활용하여 혼동을 주는 오답이다. ④은
글에서 언급된 소재인 product를 활용하여 혼동을 주는 오답이다.

실력 UP! 미니 문제 01.

정답 백색소음이 수면에 도움을 주는 가장 효과적인 방법 중 하나라는 것

해설 바로 앞 문장에서 백색소음은 수면에 도움을 주는 방법 중 하나라고 여겨진다고 한
후 모든 산업의 제품들은 그 기본적 개념을 활용하며 성장해왔다고 했으므로 (A)the
concept(그 기본적 개념)은 '백색소음이 수면에 도움을 주는 가장 효과적인 방법
중 하나라는 것'을 의미한다.

02　　　　　　　　　　　　　　　　　　　정답 ②

지문분석

Thanks to germ theory, / we know / that maintaining good
personal hygiene / is important to our health.
세균 이론 덕분에 / 우리는 알고 있다 / 바람직한 개인 위생 상태를 유지하는 것이 ~라는 것
을 / 우리 건강에 중요하다

That is why, / from a young age, / we are taught / to wash
ourselves regularly.
그것이 바로 이유이다 / 어릴 때부터 / 우리가 교육받은 / 스스로 규칙적으로 씻도록

Soap can lessen our chances / of falling ill / from contact with
harmful bacteria.
비누는 가능성을 줄여 줄 수 있다 / 병에 걸릴 / 해로운 박테리아와의 접촉으로 인해

But / more recent research suggests / that we may be overdoing
this.
하지만 / 더 최근의 연구는 시사한다 / 우리가 이것을 너무 지나치게 하고 있을지도 모른
다고

★ While it is true / that washing with soap / can leave our skin
clean, / the harsh chemicals in it / can also remove the natural
oils and bacteria / that protect our skin.
사실이지만 / 비누로 씻는 것이 ~라는 것은 / 우리의 피부를 깨끗하게 해줄 수 있다 / 그 안
에 있는 너무 강한 화학물질은 / 자연적인 유분과 박테리아도 없앨 수 있다 / 우리의 피부
를 보호하는

Without these features, / the skin becomes dry / and can be
easily infected.
이 요소들이 없으면 / 피부는 건조해진다 / 그리고 쉽게 감염될 수 있다

Apparently, / when it comes to soap, / you can have too much of
a good thing.
확실히 / 비누에 관한 한 / 너무 지나치면 좋지 않을 수 있다

어휘 maintain 유지하다　hygiene 위생 상태, 청결　fall ill 병에 걸리다
harmful 해로운　overdo ~을 지나치게 하다　harsh 너무 강한, 지독한
chemical 화학물질; 화학의　infect 감염시키다　apparently 확실히
when it comes to ~에 관한 한, ~에 관해서는　**선택지** defense 방어술, 방어

해석 세균 이론 덕분에, 우리는 바람직한 개인 위생 상태를 유지하는 것이 우리
건강에 중요하다는 것을 알고 있다. 그것이 바로 우리가 어릴 때부터 스스
로 규칙적으로 씻도록 교육받은 이유이다. 비누는 해로운 박테리아와의
접촉으로 인해 병에 걸릴 가능성을 줄여 줄 수 있다. 하지만 더 최근의 연
구는 우리가 이것을 너무 지나치게 하고 있을지도 모른다고 시사한다. 비
누로 씻는 것이 우리의 피부를 깨끗하게 해줄 수 있다는 것은 사실이지만,
그 안에 있는 너무 강한 화학물질은 우리의 피부를 보호하는 자연적인 유
분과 박테리아도 없앨 수 있다. 이 요소들이 없으면, 피부는 건조해지고
쉽게 감염될 수 있다. **주제문** 확실히, 비누에 관한 한, 너무 지나치면 좋지
않을 수 있다.

① 비누로 해로운 세균에 맞서라
② 너무 과도한 비누칠은 해로울 수 있을까?
③ 비누: 어떤 것이 당신에게 가장 잘 맞을까?
④ 피부: 신체 최고의 방어술
⑤ 규칙적으로 씻어야 하는 가장 타당한 이유

해설 글의 후반부에서 비누에 관한 한, 너무 지나치면 좋지 않을 수 있다고 했으
므로, 이 글의 제목으로 가장 적절한 것은 ② Can Too Much Soap be
Harmful?(너무 과도한 비누칠은 해로울 수 있을까?)이다.

오답분석 ①과 ③은 글의 핵심 소재 '비누'를 다루고 있으나, ①은 글의 일부를 다루
는 지엽적인 소재 germs를 다루고 있고, ③은 글과 관련 없는 내용을 다
루고 있으므로 오답이다. ④은 글의 일부를 다루는 지엽적인 소재 skin을
활용하여 혼동을 주는 오답이다. ⑤은 글에서 언급된 wash regularly를
활용하여 혼동을 주는 오답이다.

실력 UP! 미니 문제 02.

정답 비누로 씻는 것

해설 최근의 연구는 우리가 '이것'을 지나치게 하고 있을지도 모른다고 시사한다고 한 후, 비누로 씻는 것(washing with soap)이 피부를 보호하는 자연적인 유분과 박테리아도 없앨 수 있다고 했으므로, (A)this(이것)는 '비누로 씻는 것'을 의미한다.

03
정답 ④

지문분석

In the digital age, / it would seem / that there is little reason / for our literature / to still appear / in paper form.
디지털 시대에서 / ~처럼 보일 것이다 / 이유는 거의 없다 / 문학 작품이 / 여전히 나타날 / 종이 형태로

★ After all, / physical books, / like any number of other obsolete technologies, / are no longer strictly necessary / with the emergence of E-books / and the explosion of content.
어찌 되었건 / 물리적 형태의 책은 / 다른 많은 구식 기술처럼 / 더 이상 전적으로 필요하지는 않다 / 전자책의 등장으로 인해 / 그리고 콘텐츠의 폭발적인 증가

But / some have pushed back / against this notion, / arguing / that E-books have crucial disadvantages / compared to their old-fashioned counterparts.
하지만 / 일부는 반발한다 / 이러한 견해에 대해 / 주장하면서 / 전자책이 결정적인 단점을 가지고 있다고 / 오래된 그들의 상대에 비해

Reading on a screen, / they point out, / requires more energy / and induces fatigue faster.
화면을 통해 독서를 하는 것은 / 그들이 지적하기를 / 더 많은 에너지를 필요로 한다 / 그리고 더 빨리 피로를 유발한다

It can even disrupt your sleep / if done before bed / — a time and place / books have long been the perfect companion.
그것은 당신의 수면을 방해할 수도 있다 / 만약 잠자리에 들기 전에 이것이 행해진다면 / 때와 장소인 / 오랫동안 책이 완벽히 짝을 이루었던

To make matters worse, / on E-books / you are also more likely to / skim for information / rather than lose yourself / in the story.
설상가상으로 / 전자책에서는 / 당신은 또한 ~할 가능성이 더 크다 / 정보를 위해 대충 읽을 / 몰두하기보다 / 이야기에

This means / that the digital reader takes less overall enjoyment / from the experience / and retains less / of what they read.
이는 의미한다 / 디지털 독서가들이 전반적인 즐거움을 덜 느낀다는 것을 / 그 경험에서 오는 / 그리고 더 적게 간직한다 / 그들이 읽는 것을

> ★ **독해가 쉬워지는 구문 풀이**
>
> After all, **physical books**, [like any number of other obsolete technologies], are no longer strictly necessary with the emergence of E-books and the explosion of content.
> (주어) (수식어구(전치사 + 명사구)) (동사)
>
> ⇨ [ ]은 physical books를 부연 설명하는 전치사구이다.

어휘 appear 나타나다, 나오다 obsolete 구식의 strictly 전적으로, 엄격히 emergence 등장, 출현 explosion 폭발적인 증가, 폭발 notion 견해, 관념 crucial 결정적인, 중대한 counterpart 상대, (대응 관계에 있는) 것 induce 유발하다, 유도하다 fatigue 피로 companion 짝을 이루는 to make matters worse 설상가상으로 skim 대충 읽다, 걷어 내다 lose oneself in ~에 몰두하다, 열중하다 overall 전반적인 retain 간직하다, 유지하다 [선택지] shortcoming 단점, 결점

해석 디지털 시대에서, 문학 작품이 여전히 종이 형태로 나타날 이유는 거의 없는 것처럼 보일 것이다. 어찌 되었건, 다른 많은 구식 기술처럼 물리적 형태의 책은 전자책의 등장과 콘텐츠의 폭발적인 증가로 인해 더 이상 전적으로 필요하지는 않다. [주제문] 하지만 일부는 전자책이 오래된 그들의 상대에 비해 결정적인 단점을 가지고 있다고 주장하면서 이러한 견해에 대해 반발한다. 그들이 지적하기를, 화면을 통해 독서를 하는 것은 더 많은 에너지를 필요로 하고 더 빨리 피로를 유발한다. 만약 오랫동안 책이 완벽

히 짝을 이루었던 때와 장소인 잠자리에 들기 전에 이것이 행해진다면 그것은 당신의 수면을 방해할 수도 있다. 설상가상으로, 전자책에서는, 또한 이야기에 몰두하기보다 정보를 위해 대충 읽을 가능성이 더 크다. 이는 디지털 독서가들이 그 경험에서 오는 전반적인 즐거움을 덜 느끼고 그들이 읽는 것을 더 적게 간직한다는 것을 의미한다.

① 소설 읽기의 중요성
② 고대 문학을 지키려는 노력들
③ 수면 장애의 원인
④ 전자책의 단점
⑤ 물리적 형태를 가진 책의 미래

해설 글의 중후반부에서 전자책이 결정적인 단점을 가지고 있다고 주장하며 화면을 통해 독서를 하는 것은 더 많은 에너지를 필요로 하고, 더 빨리 피로를 유발하며, 잠들기 전의 독서는 수면을 방해할 수도 있다고 했다. 또한, 전자책에서는 이야기에 몰두하기보다 정보를 위해 대충 읽을 가능성이 더 크다고 했으므로, 이 글의 주제로 가장 적절한 것은 ④ the shortcomings of e-books(전자책의 단점)이다.

오답분석 ①은 글의 핵심 소재 '전자책'에 대한 언급이 없으며, 글과 관련 없는 소재를 다루고 있다. ②는 글의 일부를 다루는 지엽적 소재인 literature를, ③은 sleep을, ⑤는 physical books를 활용하여 혼동을 주는 오답이다.

실력 UP! 미니 문제 03.

정답 ⓐ obsolete ⓑ induce

해석 ⓐ 같은 과업을 달성함에 있어 더 새롭고, 더 우수한 기술에 의해 대체되어 구식이 된
ⓑ 유발하다

04
정답 ②

지문분석

There is a little-known issue / with television, / which is that it impairs children's ability / to learn language.
잘 알려지지 않은 쟁점이 있다 / 텔레비전에 관해서 / 이는 그것이 아동의 능력을 해친다는 것이다 / 언어를 배우는

Data reveals / that TV affects language learning / in children below the age of two, / particularly when it takes the place / of human interaction.
자료는 보여준다 / 텔레비전이 언어 습득에 영향을 미친다는 것을 / 2살 미만 아동의 / 특히 그것이 대신할 때 / 대인 상호 작용을

Children learn language best / when they interact with the people / around them, / because they get to actively engage their brains / and respond / to what is being said.
아동은 언어를 가장 잘 배운다 / 사람들과 상호 작용할 때 / 그들 주변의 / 적극적으로 그들의 뇌를 관여시키게 되기 때문에 / 그리고 반응한다 / 들리는 것에

★ Most television programming, / however, / demands only / that its young viewers sit passively / in front of a screen.
대부분의 텔레비전 프로그램 편성은 / 하지만 / 오로지 요구한다 / 그들의 어린 시청자들이 수동적으로 앉아 있기만을 / 화면 앞에

When this happens, / children's brains do not receive enough stimulation.
이러한 일이 일어날 때 / 아동의 뇌는 충분한 자극을 받지 못한다

As a result, / it can delay children's ability / to learn language.
그 결과 / 이는 아동의 능력을 지연시킬 수 있다 / 언어를 습득하는

> ★ **독해가 쉬워지는 구문 풀이**
>
> Most television programming, however, **demands** only that its
> (동사)
> young viewers (should) **sit** passively in front of a screen.
> (동사원형)
>
> ⇨ 요구의 의미를 가진 동사 demand(demands)의 목적어로 쓰인 that 절이 문맥상 '앉아 있어야 한다'라는 의미로 당위성을 띠고 있으므로, should가 생략된 동사원형 sit이 쓰였다.

[어휘] little-known 잘 알려지지 않은 particularly 특히
take the place of ~을 대신하다 interaction 상호 작용
engage 관여시키다 passively 수동적으로 stimulation 자극, 흥분

[해석] 텔레비전에 관해서 잘 알려지지 않은 쟁점이 있는데, 이는 그것이 언어를 배우는 아동의 능력을 해친다는 것이다. **[주제문]** 자료는 특히 텔레비전이 대인 상호 작용을 대신할 때 2살 미만 아동의 언어 습득에 영향을 미친다는 것을 보여준다. 아동은 들리는 것에 적극적으로 그들의 뇌를 관여시키고 반응하게 되기 때문에 그들 주변의 사람들과 상호 작용할 때 언어를 가장 잘 배운다. 하지만, 대부분의 텔레비전 프로그램 편성은 그들의 어린 시청자들이 화면 앞에 오로지 수동적으로 앉아 있기만을 요구한다. 이러한 일이 일어날 때, 아동의 뇌는 충분한 자극을 받지 못한다. 그 결과, 이는 언어를 습득하는 아동의 능력을 지연시킬 수 있다.

① TV를 보면서 새로운 언어를 배울 수 있을까?
② TV: 아동의 언어 습득을 지연시키는 것
③ 텔레비전이 아동의 건강을 해칠까?
④ 수동적인 언어 습득 방식
⑤ 텔레비전의 사회적 영향

[해설] 이 글의 중심 내용은 텔레비전을 보며 화면 앞에 수동적으로 앉아 있기만 하는 것은 아동의 뇌에 충분한 자극을 주지 못해 2살 미만 아동의 언어 습득을 지연시킨다는 내용의 글이므로, 이 글의 제목으로 가장 적절한 것은 ② TV: Delaying Language Learning in Children(TV: 아동의 언어 습득을 지연시키는 것)이다.

[오답분석] ①은 글의 일부를 다루는 소재 '텔레비전', '언어 습득 능력'만이 언급된 오답이다. ③은 글과 관련 없는 health를 활용하여 혼동을 주는 오답이다. ④은 글과 관련 없는 passive를 활용하여 혼동을 주는 오답이다. ⑤은 글의 일부를 다루는 지엽적인 소재 '텔레비전'을 활용하여 혼동을 주는 오답이다.

[실력 UP!] 미니 문제 04.
정답 Children learn language best when they interact with the people around them
해석 Q: 지문에 따르면, 아이들이 언제 언어를 가장 잘 배운다고 하는가?
A: 아이들은 그들 주변의 사람들과 상호 작용할 때 언어를 가장 잘 배운다.
해설 Children learn language best when they interact with the people around them에서 아이들은 주변의 사람들과 상호 작용할 때 언어를 가장 잘 배운다고 했다.

05

정답 ①

[지문분석]

Why do you *worry*?
당신은 왜 *걱정하는가*

★ You might think / doing this helps you / to avoid negative outcomes / and may even lead you / to find solutions.
당신은 생각할 수도 있다 / 그것이 당신이 도와줄 것이라 / 나쁜 결과를 피하도록 / 그리고 심지어 당신을 이끌지도 모른다 / 해결책을 찾도록

Soon, / it becomes the way / you approach all problems, / real or not.
곧 / 이것이 방식이 된다 / 당신이 모든 문제에 접근하는 / 진짜든 아니든

It is a habit.
이것은 습관이다

In reality, / worry creates only one thing: / more worry.
현실에서 / 걱정은 오직 한 가지만을 만들어낼 뿐이다 / 더 많은 걱정

It keeps you / stuck in the same place, / exhausted, / much like being on a treadmill.
그것은 당신을 계속 ~하게 하다 / 같은 곳에 빠져 있게 / 그리고 지쳐 있게 / 마치 꼭 쳇바퀴 위에 있는 것처럼

No matter how fast you go, / you end up / where you began.
당신이 아무리 빠르게 가더라도 / 당신은 결국 ~하게 된다 / 당신이 출발한 곳에 있게

Whenever you catch yourself / worrying too much, / you may want to consider / trying a different tack.
당신이 스스로를 발견할 때마다 / 너무 걱정하는 / 당신은 고려해 보는 것이 좋을 것이다 / 다른 방향을 시도해 보는 것을

Instead of continuing the cycle, / focus on / what you want to happen / and how you will achieve that result.
그 순환을 반복하는 것 대신에 / ~에 집중하라 / 당신이 일어나길 바라는 일 / 그리고 당신이 그 결과를 어떻게 얻을 것인지

It will get you off / of the treadmill / and get you moving / forward again.
이는 당신을 꺼낼 것이다 / 쳇바퀴에서 / 그리고 나아가게 해줄 것이다 / 다시 앞으로

★ 독해가 쉬워지는 구문 풀이

You might think [doing this **helps** you to avoid negative outcomes].
　　　　　　　　　　　　　　　목적어　목적격보어

⇨ 명사절 [ ]는 동사 think의 목적어이며, 명사절 접속사 that은 생략되었다.
⇨ 동사 help는 목적격보어로 동사원형 또는 to부정사를 취하는 준 사역 동사이다.

[어휘] approach 접근하다 stuck 빠져 있는, 갇힌
exhaust 지치게 하다, 소모시키다 end up 결국~되다 tack 방향
forward 앞으로 **[선택지]** despite ~에도 불구하고 maintain 유지하다
means 수단

[해석] 당신은 왜 *걱정하는가*? 당신은 그것이 당신이 나쁜 결과를 피하도록 도와주고, 심지어 해결책을 찾도록 당신을 이끌지도 모른다고 생각할 수도 있다. 곧, 이것이 진짜든 아니든 당신이 모든 문제에 접근하는 방식이 된다. 이것은 습관이다. 현실에서, 걱정은 더 많은 걱정이라는 오직 한 가지만을 만들어낼 뿐이다. 그것은 당신을 계속 같은 곳에 빠져 있게 하며, 마치 꼭 쳇바퀴 위에 있는 것처럼 지쳐 있게 한다. 당신이 아무리 빠르게 가더라도, 당신은 결국 출발한 곳에 있게 된다. 당신이 너무 걱정하는 스스로를 발견할 때마다, 다른 방향을 시도해보는 것을 고려해 보는 것이 좋을 것이다. **[주제문]** 그 순환을 반복하는 것 대신에, 당신이 일어나길 바라는 일과 당신이 그 결과를 어떻게 얻을 것인지에 집중하라. 이는 당신을 쳇바퀴에서 꺼내서 다시 앞으로 나아가게 해줄 것이다.

① 걱정이 있음에도 불구하고 앞으로 나아가는 방법
② 나쁜 일이 해결책으로 이어질 수 있는 방법
③ 성공 주기를 유지하는 방법
④ 집중하는 수단으로서의 걱정
⑤ 습관을 만드는 과정

[해설] 이 글의 중심 내용은 걱정을 하는 것은 더 많은 걱정을 만들어낼 뿐이므로, 그 대신 일어나길 바라는 일과 그 결과를 어떻게 얻을 것인지에 집중하면 다시 앞으로 나아갈 수 있을 것이라는 내용의 글이다. 그러므로, 이 글의 주제로 가장 적절한 것은 ① ways to move forward despite worrying(걱정이 있음에도 불구하고 앞으로 나아가는 방법)이다.

[오답분석] ②과 ③은 글의 핵심 소재 '걱정'에 대한 언급이 없는 오답이다. ④은 글의 핵심 소재 '걱정'을 다루고 있으나, 글의 일부를 다루는 지엽적인 소재 focus를 활용하여 혼동을 주는 오답이다. ⑤은 글의 일부를 다루는 지엽적인 소재 habit을 활용하여 혼동을 주는 오답이다.

[실력 UP!] 미니 문제 05.
정답 Focus on what you want to happen and how you will achieve that result
해석 Q: 너무 많이 걱정을 하는 스스로를 발견했을 때, 필자는 우리가 어떻게 해야 할 것을 제안하는가?
A: 당신이 일어나길 바라는 일과 당신이 그 결과를 어떻게 얻을 것인지에 집중하라.
해설 Instead of continuing the cycle, ~에서 그 순환을 반복하는 것 대신에, 당신이 일어나길 바라는 일과 그 결과를 어떻게 얻을 것인지에 집중하라고 했다.

지문분석

Some 5,000 years ago in Mesopotamia / — or modern-day Iraq — / the debut of money / changed the way people lived / in numerous ways.
약 5천 년 전 메소포타미아에서 / 오늘날의 이라크인 / 돈의 등장은 / 사람들이 사는 방식을 바꾸었다 / 여러 방면에서

For instance, / the expanded use of gold and silver currency / went hand in hand with / the establishment of trade / on a wide scale.
예를 들어 / 금화와 은화의 확대된 사용은 / ~과 관련되어 있다 / 무역 체제 확립 / 대규모의

And with trade, / people began / to take on specialized professions, / including new classes of people / like merchants, / who profited from / being at the center / of commercial transactions.
그리고 무역과 함께 / 사람들은 시작했다 / 전문적인 일들을 맡기 / 새로운 계층의 사람들을 포함하여 / 상인과 같은 / 그리고 그들은 이윤을 얻었다 / 중심에 있으면서 / 상거래의

Not only that, but / money also gave kings more power, / ★since it made it easier / to tax people and pay salaries / to soldiers and government officials.
그뿐만 아니라 / 돈은 왕들에게 더 큰 권력을 주기도 했다 / 이는 돈이 더 용이하게 해주었기 때문이다 / 사람들에게 세금을 부과하는 것과 임금을 지불하는 것을 / 군인 및 정부 관료들에게

★ 독해가 쉬워지는 구문 풀이

~ since it made it easier [to tax people and pay salaries to soldiers
　　　　동사 가목적어 목적격보어　　　　　진짜 목적어
and government officials].

⇨ 동사 make는 5형식 동사로 쓰일 때 'make + 목적어 + 목적격보어' 형태를 취하며, '~이 ~하게 만들다'라는 의미를 나타낸다. 이때, to부정사구 목적어(to tax ~ officials)가 목적격보어(easier)와 함께 오면 진짜 목적어를 목적격보어 뒤로 보내고, 목적어가 있던 자리에 가목적어 it을 쓴다.

어휘 modern-day 오늘날의, 현재의　debut 등장, 출시, 데뷔　currency 통화
go hand in hand with ~과 관련되다　establishment 확립
scale 규모, 저울　take on (일 등을) 맡다, (책임을) 지다　merchant 상인
commercial 상업의　transaction 거래　tax 세금을 부과하다
official 관료　**선택지** advent 출현　downfall 몰락

해석 약 5천 년 전, 오늘날의 이라크인 메소포타미아에서 **주제문** 돈의 등장은 여러 방면에서 사람들이 사는 방식을 바꾸었다. 예를 들어, 금화와 은화의 확대된 사용은 대규모의 무역 체제 확립과 관련되어 있다. 그리고 무역과 함께, 사람들은 상인과 같은 새로운 계층의 사람들을 포함하여, 전문적인 일들을 맡기 시작했고, 상인들은 상거래의 중심에 있으면서 이윤을 얻었다. 그뿐만 아니라, 돈은 왕들에게 더 큰 권력을 주기도 했는데, 이는 돈이 사람들에게 세금을 부과하고 군인 및 정부 관료들에게 임금을 지불하는 것을 더 용이하게 해주었기 때문이다.

① 메소포타미아는 왜 고대 사회의 중심이었는가
② 금과 은: 가치 있는 금속, 그리고 그것들의 많은 쓰임새
③ 돈이 출현하기 이전의 세상을 상상하기
④ 세계 초대 왕들의 몰락
⑤ 돈: 인간 사회의 창조자

해설 이 글의 중심 내용은 돈의 등장이 무역 체계의 확립, 새로운 계층의 등장, 확대된 왕의 권력과 같이 여러 방면에서 사람들이 사는 방식을 바꾸어 놓았다는 내용의 글이므로, 이 글의 제목으로 적절한 것은 ⑤ Money: Creator of Human Society(돈: 인간 사회의 창조자)이다.

오답분석 ①은 글의 핵심 소재 '돈'에 대한 언급이 없으며, 글의 일부를 다루는 지엽적 소재인 메소포타미아를 활용하여 혼동을 주는 오답이다. ②은 금과 은이라는 글의 일부를 다루는 지엽적 소재를 활용하여 혼동을 주는 오답이다. ③은 '돈'을 다루고 있으나, 글과 관련 없는 내용으로 혼동을 주는 오답이다. ④은 글의 일부를 다루는 지엽적 소재인 kings를 활용하여 혼동을 주는 오답이다.

실력 UP! 미니 문제 06.

정답 easier to tax people and pay salaries to soldiers and government officials

해석 Q: 지문에 따르면, 돈이 어떻게 왕에게 더 많은 권력을 주었는가?
A: 사람들에게 세금을 부과하고 군인 및 정부 관료들에게 임금을 지불하는 것을 더 용이하게 해줌으로써.

해설 Not only that, but money ~ and government officials에서 돈은 왕이 사람들에게 세금을 부과하고 군인과 정부 관료들의 임금 지불하는 것을 더 용이하게 해줬다는 것을 알 수 있다.

지문분석

★In Bram Stoker's 1897 novel *Dracula*, / the title character is an ancient vampire / with the ability / to transform into a bat.
Bram Stoker의 1897년 소설 *드라큘라*에서 / 주인공은 고대 흡혈귀이다 / 능력을 가진 / 박쥐로 변하는

While / this work of literature / strengthened the association / between vampires and bats, / it was not the origin of it.
~인 반면에 / 이 문학 작품이 / 연관성을 굳혔다 / 흡혈귀와 박쥐 간의 / 그것(문학 작품)이 그 연관성의 시초는 아니었다

This can be traced / to the 15th century / when Europeans first began / exploring South America.
이는 거슬러 올라갈 수 있다 / 15세기로 / 유럽인들이 처음 시작했던 / 남아메리카를 탐험하기

They discovered / a small bat / that only feeds on / the blood of live animals.
그들은 발견했다 / 작은 박쥐를 / 오로지 ~만 먹고 사는 / 살아 있는 동물들의 피

It hunts at night / and is even known / to bite sleeping humans / and then consume their blood.
그것은 밤에 사냥을 한다 / 그리고 심지어 알려져 있다 / 잠든 사람들을 깨문다고 / 그리고 나서 그들의 피를 먹는다고

Given this, / it should come as no surprise / that the explorers called it / a vampire bat / and that people back in Europe / were amazed by it.
이를 고려해볼 때 / 전혀 놀랄 만한 일이 아니었다 / 탐험가들이 그것을 ~라 이름 붙인 것 / 흡혈박쥐라고 / 그리고 유럽에 남아 있는 사람들이 ~한 것 / 그로 인해 놀랐다

As knowledge of this creature / became more widespread, / the relationship between bats and the vampires / became a part of popular culture.
이 생물체에 대한 인식이 ~하면서 / 점차 널리 퍼졌다 / 박쥐와 흡혈귀 간의 상관관계는 / 대중문화의 하나가 되었다

★ 독해가 쉬워지는 구문 풀이

In Bram Stoker's 1897 novel *Dracula*, the title character is an
　　　　　　　　　　　　　　　주어　　　　동사
ancient vampire with the ability **to transform** into a bat.
　보어

⇨ to transform은 to부정사의 형용사적 용법으로, 명사 ability를 수식한다.

어휘 novel 소설; 새로운　ancient 고대의　vampire 흡혈귀
transform 변하다, 바꾸다　literature 문학　strengthen ~을 굳히다, 강화하다
association 연관(성), 협회　trace (기원 등을) 거슬러 올라가다, 추적하다
explore 탐험하다　feed on ~를 먹고 살다　bite 깨물다
consume 먹다, 소비하다　given ~을 고려해 볼 때　call 이름 붙이다, 부르다
creature 생물체

해석 Bram Stoker의 1897년 소설 *드라큘라*에서, 주인공은 박쥐로 변하는 능력을 가진 고대 흡혈귀이다. 이 문학 작품이 흡혈귀와 박쥐 간의 연관성을 굳혔지만, 그것(문학 작품)이 그 연관성의 시초는 아니었다. 이는 유럽인

들이 남아메리카를 처음 탐험하기 시작했던 15세기로 거슬러 올라갈 수 있다. 그들은 오로지 살아 있는 동물들의 피만 먹고 사는 작은 박쥐를 발견했다. 그것은 밤에 사냥을 하고, 심지어 잠든 사람들을 깨우고 나서 그들의 피를 먹는다고 알려져 있다. 이를 고려해볼 때, 탐험가들이 그것을 흡혈박쥐라고 이름 붙이고, 유럽에 남아 있는 사람들이 그로 인해 놀랐던 것은 전혀 놀랄 만한 일이 아니었다. (주제문) 이 생물체에 대한 인식이 점차 널리 퍼지면서, 박쥐와 흡혈귀 간의 상관관계는 대중문화의 하나가 되었다.

① 남아메리카에서 발견된 실존하는 흡혈귀
② 박쥐와 흡혈귀: 그들은 왜 짝이 지어졌는가?
③ 스토커는 그의 소설에 왜 박쥐를 포함시켰는가
④ 드라큘라: 최초의 유럽 흡혈귀
⑤ 흡혈 박쥐는 어떻게 피를 마실까?

(해설) 이 글의 중심 내용은 남아메리카에서 흡혈박쥐를 처음 발견한 유럽 탐험가들로 인해 박쥐와 흡혈귀 간의 연관성이 시작되었으며, 흡혈박쥐에 대한 인식이 널리 퍼지면서 이들의 상관관계가 대중문화의 하나가 되었다는 내용의 글이므로, 이 글의 제목으로 적절한 것은 ② Bats and Vampires: Why Are They Linked?(박쥐와 흡혈귀: 그들은 왜 짝이 지어졌는가?)이다.

(오답 분석) ①, ⑤은 각각 글의 지엽적 소재 'South America', 'Blood'를 활용하여 혼동을 주는 오답이다. ③은 글의 핵심 소재 중 하나인 '흡혈귀'에 대한 언급이 없고, 글의 지엽적 소재와 연결 지어 혼동을 주는 오답이다. ④은 글의 핵심 소재 중 하나인 '박쥐'에 대한 언급이 없고 글의 지엽적 소재와 연결 지어 혼동을 주는 오답이다.

(실력 UP!) 미니 문제 07.

정답 (A) the association between vampires and bats
(B) sleeping humans

해설 (A) 이 문학 작품이 흡혈귀와 박쥐 간의 연관성을 굳혔으나, 그것이 그 연관성의 시초는 아니었다고 했으므로, (A)it는 the association between vampires and bats(흡혈귀와 박쥐 간의 연관성)를 가리킨다.
(B) 유럽인들이 발견한 그 박쥐는 밤에 사냥을 하며 잠든 사람들을 깨우고 나서 그들의 피를 먹는다고 알려져 있다고 했으므로, (B)their는 sleeping humans(잠든 사람들)를 가리킨다.

08   정답 ⑤

지문분석

In countries / that use the parliamentary system of government, / the parliament plays an important role / in promoting the will of the people.
국가에서 / 의원 내각제를 사용하는 / 의회는 중요한 역할을 한다 / 국민의 의사를 증진시키는

★ This is due to the fact that / it is a powerful institution / that is composed of members / who are elected directly / by the public.
이는 ~라는 사실 때문이다 / 그것은 강력한 기관이다 / 의원들로 구성된 / 직접적으로 선출된 / 국민에 의해

The parliament / is the legislative body of the government, / meaning / that it is able to create and amend laws.
의회는 / 정부의 입법 기관이다 / 이는 의미한다 / 그것이 법을 만들고 개정할 수 있다는 것을

Furthermore, / it has extensive control / over the budget, / with the right / to approve or reject / taxes and spending plans.
뿐만 아니라 / 그것은 광범위한 지배권을 가진다 / 예산에 대한 / 권한으로 / 승인하거나 거부하는 / 세금 및 지출 계획을

Finally, / the parliament provides oversight / of the head of the government / and / is able to investigate / officials who engage in unethical behavior.
마지막으로 / 의회는 감사를 실시한다 / 행정부에 대한 / 그리고 / 수사할 수 있다 / 비윤리적 행동에 관여하는 공무원을

The fact / that so much power is in the hands of / the elected members of parliament / ensures / that the concerns of citizens / are the government's most important considerations.
사실은 / 많은 권한이 ~의 손에 있다는 / 선출된 의회 구성원 / 반드시 ~하도록 한다 / 시민들의 관심사가 / 정부의 가장 중요한 고려 사항임을

★ **독해가 쉬워지는 구문 풀이**

This is due to the fact that it is a powerful institution **that** is
                                            동격의 that절
composed of members **who** are elected directly by the public.

⇨ '국민에 의해 직접적으로 선출된 의원들로 구성된 강력한 기관이라는 사실'이라는 뜻으로 앞에 있는 명사 fact의 내용을 풀어서 설명하고 있으므로 동격 that이 쓰였다.

⇨ 관계대명사 that과 who는 각각 선행사 powerful institution, members를 수식하는 주격 관계대명사이다.

(어휘) parliament 의회 play a role in ~에서 역할을 하다 promote 증진시키다 will 의사 due to the fact ~라는 사실로 인하여 institution 기관 compose 구성하다 elect 선출하다 public 국민 amend 개정하다 extensive 광범위한 budget 예산 right 권한; 옳은 approve 승인하다 reject 거부하다 tax 세금 spending 지출 oversight 감사, 감독 investigate 수사하다 official 공무원; 공식적인 engage in ~에 관여하다 unethical 비윤리적인 in the hands of ~의 손에 있는 concern 관심사, 걱정 citizen 시민 consideration 고려 사항 (선택지) conduct 진행하다

(해설) 의원 내각제를 사용하는 국가에서, 의회는 국민의 의사를 증진시키는 중요한 역할을 한다. 이는 그것이 국민에 의해 직접적으로 선출된 의원들로 구성된 강력한 기관이라는 사실 때문이다. 의회는 정부의 입법 기관인데, 이는 그것이 법을 만들고 개정할 수 있다는 것을 의미한다. 뿐만 아니라, 그것은 세금 및 지출 계획을 승인하거나 거부하는 권한으로 예산에 대한 광범위한 지배권을 가진다. 마지막으로, 의회는 정부 수반에 대한 감사를 실시하고 비윤리적 행동에 관여하는 공무원을 수사할 수 있다. (주제문) 많은 권한이 선출된 의회 구성원의 손에 있다는 사실은 반드시 시민들의 관심사가 정부의 가장 중요한 고려 사항이 되도록 한다.

① 오늘날 의회 체계의 기원
② 의회가 법을 만드는 과정
③ 공무원을 선출하는 것에 있어서 국민의 역할
④ 의회가 수사를 진행해야 할 필요성
⑤ 공익 증진을 위한 의회의 역할

(해설) 이 글의 중심 내용은 의회는 국민의 의사를 증진시키는 중요한 역할을 하며, 많은 권한이 의회 구성원의 손에 있다는 사실은 반드시 시민들의 관심사가 정부의 가장 중요한 고려 사항이 되도록 한다는 내용의 글이므로, 이 글의 주제로 가장 적절한 것은 ⑤ the role of a parliament in promoting public interest(공익 증진을 위한 의회의 역할)이다.

(오답 분석) ①, ②, ④은 모두 글의 핵심 소재인 '의회'를 다루고 있으나, ①은 글과 관련 없는 내용을, ②과 ④은 글의 일부를 다루는 지엽적 소재를 활용하여 혼동을 주는 오답이다. ③은 글의 핵심 소재에 대한 언급이 없으므로 오답이다.

(실력 UP!) 미니 문제 08.

정답 plays an important role in promoting the will of the people

해석 Q: 의원 내각제가 맡은 중요한 역할은 무엇인가?
A: 그것은 국민의 의사를 증진시키는 중요한 역할을 맡는다.

해설 the parliament plays an important role in promoting the will of the people에서 의회는 국민의 의사를 증진시키는 중요한 역할을 맡는다는 것을 알 수 있다.

도표 정보 파악하기

불변의 패턴 11 · p.50

도표의 제목과 첫 문장에 무엇에 관한 도표인지 나온다.

기출 문제 · 정답 ⑤

지문분석

The above graph shows / the number of tourists / who visited Istanbul and Antalya, / the top two most-visited cities / in Turkey, / from 2013 to 2016.
위 도표는 보여준다 / 관광객의 수를 / 이스탄불과 안탈리아에 방문한 / 사람들이 가장 많이 방문하는 두 도시인 / 터키에서 / 2013년부터 2016년까지

① The number of tourists / to each city / was over one hundred thousand every year / between 2013 and 2015.
관광객 수는 / 각 도시의 / 매년 10만 명 이상이었다 / 2013년과 2015년 사이에

② ★ The city / that received the higher number of tourists / in 2013 / was Antalya, / but in the following three years, / Istanbul received more tourists / than Antalya did.
도시는 / 더 많은 수의 관광객을 받은 / 2013년에 / 안탈리아였다 / 하지만 이후 3년 동안은 / 이스탄불이 더 많은 관광객을 받았다 / 안탈리아보다

③ While the number of tourists / to Istanbul / increased steadily / from 2013 to 2015, / Antalya received less tourists / in 2015 / compared to the previous year.
관광객 수는 ~한 반면 / 이스탄불의 / 지속적으로 증가했다 / 2013년부터 2015년까지 / 안탈리아는 더 적은 관광객을 받았다 / 2015년에 / 전년도에 비해

④ Interestingly, / in 2016, / the number of tourists dropped / to less than one hundred thousand / for both cities.
흥미롭게도 / 2016년에 / 관광객의 수가 감소했다 / 10만 명 미만으로 / 두 도시 모두

⑤ In particular, / the number of tourists / to Antalya in 2016 / was only(→ more than) one-third the number / from 2013.
특히 / 관광객 수는 / 2016년 안탈리아의 / 수치의 1/3에 불과했다(→ 을 넘어섰다) / 2013년도

> **★ 독해가 쉬워지는 구문 풀이**
>
> [The city that received the higher number of tourists in 2013] was
>   수식어(관계절)   동사
> Antalya, ~
> ⇨ [ ]는 문장의 주어이며, that ~ tourists in 2013은 선행사 The city를 수식하는 주격 관계대명사절이다.

어휘 steadily 지속적으로, 점차 in particular 특히

해석 관광객을 가장 많이 받는 터키 도시들

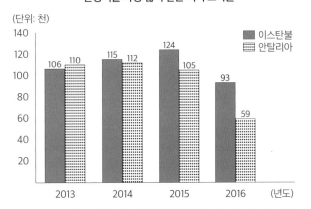

(단위: 천)
이스탄불 / 안탈리아
2013: 106 / 110
2014: 115 / 112
2015: 124 / 105
2016: 93 / 59

위 도표는 터키에서 사람들이 가장 많이 방문하는 두 도시인 이스탄불

과 안탈리아에 2013년부터 2016년까지 방문한 관광객의 수를 보여준다. ① 2013년과 2015년 사이에 각 도시의 관광객 수는 매년 10만 명 이상이었다. ② 2013년에 더 많은 수의 관광객을 받은 도시는 안탈리아였지만, 이후 3년 동안은 이스탄불이 안탈리아보다 더 많은 관광객을 받았다. ③ 이스탄불의 관광객 수는 2013년부터 2015년까지 지속적으로 증가한 반면, 안탈리아는 전년도에 비해 2015년에 더 적은 관광객을 받았다. ④ 흥미롭게도, 2016년에 두 도시 모두 관광객의 수가 10만 명 미만으로 감소했다. ⑤ 특히, 2016년 안탈리아의 관광객 수는 2013년도 수치의 1/3에 불과했다(→ 을 넘어섰다).

[해설] 도표의 제목과 글의 도입부를 통해 위 도표가 터키에서 사람들이 가장 많이 방문하는 두 도시인 이스탄불과 안탈리아에 2013년부터 2016년까지 방문한 관광객 수에 관한 것임을 알 수 있다. 2013년에 안탈리아의 관광객 수는 11만 명이고, 2016년은 5만 9천 명으로, 2016년도의 관광객 수가 2013년의 1/3 이상이므로, 도표의 내용과 일치하지 않는 것은 ⑤이다.

[오답분석] ①은 2013년과 2015년 사이에 이스탄불과 안탈리아 관광객 수가 모두 10만 명 이상이었으므로 도표의 내용과 일치한다. ②은 2013년에 안탈리아의 관광객 수는 11만 명으로 이스탄불보다 더 많았고, 2014, 2015, 2016년에는 이스탄불의 관광객 수가 11만 5천 명, 12만 4천 명, 9만 3천 명으로 같은 년도 안탈리아보다 더 많았으므로 도표의 내용과 일치한다. ③은 2013년에서 2015년까지 이스탄불 관광객 수는 10만 6천 명, 11만 5천 명, 12만 4천 명으로 계속 증가했고, 안탈리아 관광객 수는 2014년에 11만 2천 명에서 2015년에 10만 5천 명으로 감소했으므로 도표의 내용과 일치한다. ④은 2016년에 이스탄불의 관광객 수는 9만 3천 명, 안탈리아 관광객 수는 5만 9천 명이므로 도표의 내용과 일치한다.

불변의 패턴 12 · p.51

정답의 단서는 도표의 수치 변화에 있다.

기출 문제 · 정답 ⑤

지문분석

The above graph shows / what devices British people considered / the most important / when connecting to the Internet / in 2014 and 2016.
위 도표는 보여준다 / 영국인들이 어떤 기기를 생각했는지를 / 가장 중요하다고 / 인터넷에 접속할 때 / 2014년과 2016년에

★ ① More than a third of UK Internet users / considered smartphones / to be their most important device / for accessing the Internet / in 2016.
영국 인터넷 사용자들의 3분의 1 이상이 / 스마트폰을 ~라고 생각했다 / 가장 중요한 기기라고 / 인터넷에 접속하는 데 / 2016년도에

② In the same year, / the smartphone overtook the laptop / as the most important device / for Internet access.
같은 해에 / 스마트폰이 노트북을 앞질렀다 / 가장 중요한 기기로서 / 인터넷 접속을 위한

③ In 2014, / UK Internet users / were the least likely to select a tablet / as their most important device / for Internet access.
2014년에 / 영국 인터넷 사용자들은 / 태블릿을 가장 적게 선택했을 것이다 / 가장 중요한 기기로 / 인터넷 접속을 위한

④ In contrast, / they were the least likely to consider a desktop / as their most important device / for Internet access / in 2016.
이와 달리 / 그들은 데스크톱을 가장 적게 고려했을 것이다 / 가장 중요한 기기로 / 인터넷 접속을 위한 / 2016년에는

⑤ The proportion / of UK Internet users / who selected a desktop / as their most important device / for Internet access / increased (→ decreased) by half / from 2014 to 2016.
비율은 / 영국 인터넷 사용자들의 / 데스크톱을 선택한 / 가장 중요한 기기로 / 인터넷 접속을 위한 / 절반 가량 증가했다(→ 감소했다) / 2014년에서 2016년 사이에

★ 독해가 쉬워지는 구문 풀이

<u>More than a third of UK Internet users</u> <u>considered</u> <u>smartphones</u>
　　　　　주어　　　　　　　　　　　　동사　　　　　목적어
<u>to be their most important device</u> for accessing the Internet in
　　목적격보어
2016.

⇨ 동사 consider는 목적어(smartphones) 뒤에 목적격보어로 '(to be) + 명사·형용사'와 'as + 명사'를 모두 취할 수 있다.

[어휘] access 접속, 접근　consider 생각하다, 고려하다
overtake 앞지르다, 추월하다

[해석]

인터넷 접속을 위해 가장 중요한 기기:
2014년 및 2016년 영국

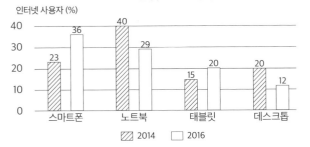

인터넷 사용자 (%)

위 도표는 2014년과 2016년에 영국인들이 인터넷에 접속할 때 어떤 기기를 가장 중요하다고 생각했는지를 보여준다. ① 2016년도에 영국 인터넷 사용자들의 3분의 1 이상이 스마트폰을 인터넷에 접속하기 위해 가장 중요한 기기라고 생각했다. ② 같은 해에, 스마트폰이 인터넷 접속을 위한 가장 중요한 기기로서 노트북을 앞질렀다. ③ 2014년에, 영국 인터넷 사용자들은 인터넷 접속을 위한 가장 중요한 기기로 태블릿을 가장 적게 선택했을 것이다. ④ 이와 달리, 그들은 2016년에는 인터넷 접속을 위한 가장 중요한 기기로 데스크톱을 가장 적게 고려했을 것이다. ⑤ 인터넷 접속을 위한 가장 중요한 기기로 데스크톱을 선택한 영국 인터넷 사용자들의 비율은 2014년에서 2016년 사이에 절반 가량 증가했다(→ 감소했다).

[해설] 이 글에서는 ①의 More than a third, ②의 overtook, ③과 ④의 the least, ⑤의 increased by half가 도표 내의 수치를 올바르게 설명하고 있는지 확인해야 한다. 2014년에 인터넷 접속을 위한 가장 중요한 기기로 데스크톱을 선택한 영국 인터넷 사용자의 비율은 20%이고 2016년도에는 12%로, 절반만큼 증가한 것이 아니라 반대로 감소하였으므로 도표의 내용과 일치하지 않는 것은 ⑤이다.

[오답분석] ①은 2016년에 인터넷 접속을 위한 가장 중요한 기기로 스마트폰을 생각한 사용자의 비율은 36%로, 이는 전체 사용자의 3분의 1 이상이므로 도표의 내용과 일치한다. ②은 2016년에 인터넷 접속을 위한 가장 중요한 기기로 스마트폰을 선택한 사용자의 비율은 36%로, 노트북을 선택한 비율인 29%를 앞질렀으므로 도표의 내용과 일치한다. ③은 2014년에 인터넷 접속을 위한 가장 중요한 기기로 태블릿을 선택한 사용자의 비율은 15%로, 이는 네 가지 기기 중에서 가장 적으므로 도표의 내용과 일치한다. ④은 2016년에 인터넷 접속을 위한 가장 중요한 기기로 데스크톱을 선택한 사용자의 비율은 12%로, 이는 네 가지 기기 중에서 가장 적으므로 도표의 내용과 일치한다.

독해 만점 TEST

p.52

01 ⑤　02 ⑤　03 ③　04 ⑤　05 ⑤　06 ④　07 ⑤　08 ④

[실력 UP!] 미니 문제

01. ⓐ employment　ⓑ workforce
02. 2011년에 미국으로 간 영국인 관광객 수는 400만 명 이상이었고, 이는 2012년의 그것과 비교했을 때 더 많았다

03. 1960년에는, 중학교 졸업자의 비율이 모든 다른 최종 학력 집단의 비율보다 높았다
04. ⓐ threatened　ⓑ marine
05. ⓐ combined　ⓑ gap
06. ⓐ exceed　ⓑ least
07. ⓐ urban　ⓑ access
08. 그에 반해서, 폐기물은 전체 온실가스 배출의 5% 미만을 담당하는 가장 작은 원천이었다

01

정답 ⑤

The above graph shows / the male and female employment rates / in four different countries / in 2002.
위 도표는 보여준다 / 남성과 여성의 취업률을 / 서로 다른 4개국의 / 2002년에

① Overall, / the percentage of males / in the workforce / was higher than that of the females / in all four countries.
전반적으로 / 남성의 비율은 / 노동 인구 중 / 여성의 그것(비율)보다 더 높았다 / 네 개의 모든 국가에서

② In South Africa, / the percentage of women / in the workforce / was less than 40 percent.
남아프리카 공화국에서는 / 여성의 비율이 / 노동 인구 중 / 40%보다 더 적었다

③ Of the four countries, / the largest difference in percentage / between men and women / in the workforce / was in Chile.
네 국가에서 / 비율 차이가 가장 큰 곳은 / 남성과 여성의 / 노동 인구 중 / 칠레였다

④ Both the percentage of men and women / in Norway's workforce / was higher / than the percentage in Chile.
남성과 여성의 비율 모두는 / 노르웨이 노동 인구 중 / 더 높았다 / 칠레의 비율보다

★ ⑤ Compared to the percentage of men / in the workforce in South Africa, / the percentage of the male workforce / in Norway / was more(→ less) than 30 percent higher.
남성의 비율과 비교했을 때 / 남아프리카 공화국의 노동 인구 중 / 남성 노동 인구 비율은 / 노르웨이의 / 30%보다 더 높았다(→ 덜 높았다)

★ 독해가 쉬워지는 구문 풀이

[Compared to the percentage of men in the workforce in South
　분사구문의 분사
Africa], the percentage of the male workforce in Norway was more
　　　　　　　　　　　　　주어　　　　　　　　　　　　동사
than 30 percent higher.

⇨ [ ]의 앞에는 접속사 및 반복되는 주어, 그리고 Being이 생략되었다. 분사구문으로 바꾼 후 분사구문 맨 앞의 Being은 주로 생략한다.

[어휘] employment rate 취업률　percentage 비율
workforce 노동 인구, 노동력

[해석]

4개국의 취업률 (2002)

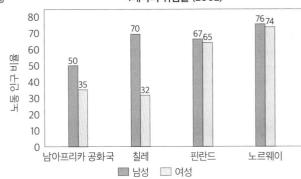

위 도표는 2002년에 서로 다른 4개국의 남성과 여성의 취업률을 보여준다. ① 전반적으로, 네 개의 모든 국가에서 노동 인구 중 남성의 비율은 여

성의 비율보다 더 높았다. ② 남아프리카 공화국에서는, 노동 인구 중 여성의 비율이 40%보다 더 적었다. ③ 네 국가에서, 노동 인구 중 남성과 여성의 비율 차이가 가장 큰 곳은 칠레였다. ④ 노르웨이 노동 인구 중 남성과 여성의 비율 모두는 칠레의 비율보다 더 높았다. ⑤ 남아프리카 공화국의 노동 인구 중 남성의 비율과 비교했을 때, 노르웨이의 남성 노동 인구 비율은 30%보다 더 높았다(→ 덜 높았다).

[해설] 도표의 제목과 글의 도입부를 통해 이 도표가 2002년의 4개국의 남성과 여성 취업률에 관한 것임을 알 수 있다. 이 글에서는 ①과 ④의 higher, ②의 less than 40 percent, ③의 the largest, ⑤의 more than 30 percent higher가 도표 내의 수치를 올바르게 설명하고 있는지 확인해야 한다. 남아프리카 공화국의 남성 노동 인구 비율은 50%, 노르웨이의 남성 노동 인구 비율은 76%로, 두 비율의 차이는 26%이므로 도표의 내용과 일치하지 않는 것은 ⑤이다.

[오답 분석] ①은 모든 국가에서 노동 인구 중 남성의 비율이 여성보다 높으므로 도표의 내용과 일치한다. ②은 남아프리카 공화국 노동 인구 중 여성의 비율이 35%로 40%에 미치지 못하므로 도표의 내용과 일치한다. ③은 네 국가 중 남성과 여성 노동 인구 수의 차이가 가장 큰 곳은 38%의 차이를 보이는 칠레이므로 도표의 내용과 일치한다. ④은 노르웨이의 노동 인구 중 남성의 비율은 76%, 여성의 비율은 74%로 칠레의 남성, 여성 노동 인구 비율보다 더 높으므로 도표의 내용과 일치한다.

[실력 UP!] 미니 문제 01.

정답 ⓐ employment ⓑ workforce
해석 ⓐ 직장을 가진 상태
　　　 ⓑ 사회 내의 전체 노동자

02
정답 ⑤

[지문분석]

The above graph shows / the number of tourists to and from the UK and US / during the period / of 2011 to 2015.
위 도표는 보여준다 / 영국과 미국을 오고 간 관광객 수를 / 기간 동안 / 2011년부터 2015년까지의

★ ① The number of UK tourists / to the US / in 2011 / was more than four million, / which was higher / compared to that / in 2012.
영국인 관광객 수는 / 미국으로 간 / 2011년에 / 400만 명 이상이었다 / 그리고 이는 더 많았다 / 그것과 비교했을 때 / 2012년의

② In 2012, / the number of US tourists / to the UK / was higher / than the number of UK tourists / to the US.
2012년에는 / 미국인 관광객 수가 / 영국으로 간 / 더 많았다 / 영국인 관광객 수보다 / 미국으로 간

③ From 2012 to 2015, / the number of UK tourists and US tourists / to each other's country / increased each year.
2012년부터 2015년까지 / 영국인 관광객과 미국인 관광객 수는 / 서로의 나라에 간 / 해마다 증가했다

④ The gap / between UK tourists and US tourists / was the biggest / in 2015.
차이는 / 영국인 관광객과 미국인 관광객 사이의 / 가장 컸다 / 2015년에

⑤ The number of US tourists / to the UK / never went above four million / from 2013 to 2015(→ went above four million in 2015).
미국인 관광객 수는 / 영국으로 간 / 400만 명을 넘은 적이 없다 / 2013년부터 2015년까지(→ 2015년에 400만 명을 넘었다)

★ **독해가 쉬워지는 구문 풀이**

[The number of UK tourists to the US in 2011] was more than four
million, **which** was higher compared to that in 2012.
　　　　　　관계대명사 동사

⇨ 계속적 용법으로 쓰인 관계대명사 which는 [ ]를 수식한다.

[어휘] period 기간 gap 차이 overall 전반적으로

[해설] (백만)

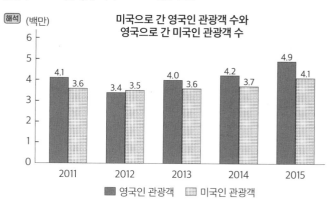

미국으로 간 영국인 관광객 수와
영국으로 간 미국인 관광객 수

■ 영국인 관광객　▤ 미국인 관광객

위 도표는 2011년부터 2015년까지의 기간 동안 영국과 미국을 오고 간 관광객 수를 보여준다. ① 2011년에 미국으로 간 영국인 관광객 수는 400만 명 이상이었고, 이는 2012년의 그것과 비교했을 때 더 많았다. ② 2012년에는, 영국으로 간 미국인 관광객 수가 미국으로 간 영국인 관광객 수보다 더 많았다. ③ 2012년부터 2015년까지, 서로의 나라에 간 영국인 관광객과 미국인 관광객 수는 해마다 증가했다. ④ 영국인 관광객과 미국인 관광객 사이의 차이는 2015년에 가장 컸다. ⑤ 영국으로 간 미국인 관광객 수는 2013년부터 2015년까지 400만 명을 넘은 적이 없다(→ 2015년에 400만 명을 넘었다).

[해설] 도표의 제목과 글의 도입부를 통해 이 도표가 2011년부터 2015년 사이에 미국으로 간 영국인 관광객 수와 영국으로 간 미국인 관광객 수에 관한 것임을 알 수 있다. 이 글에서는 ①의 more than과 higher, ②의 higher, ③의 increased, ④의 the biggest, ⑤의 never went above가 도표 내의 수치를 올바르게 설명하고 있는지 확인해야 한다. 2013년부터 2015년까지의 기간 중, 2015년에 영국으로 간 미국인 관광객의 수가 410만 명을 기록하였으므로 도표의 내용과 일치하지 않는 것은 ⑤이다.

[오답 분석] ①은 2011년에 미국으로 간 영국인 관광객이 410만 명으로 400만 명 이상이었고, 그다음 해인 2012년의 340만 명보다 더 많으므로 도표의 내용과 일치한다. ②은 2012년에 영국으로 간 미국인 관광객이 미국으로 간 영국인 관광객보다 10만 명 더 많으므로 도표의 내용과 일치한다. ③은 2012년부터 2015년까지 미국인과 영국인의 관광객 수는 모두 해마다 증가했으므로 도표의 내용과 일치한다. ④은 영국인과 미국인 관광객 수의 차이가 가장 컸던 해는 약 80만명의 차이를 기록한 2015년이었으므로 도표의 내용과 일치한다.

[실력 UP!] 미니 문제 02.

정답 2011년에 미국으로 간 영국인 관광객 수는 400만 명 이상이었고, 이는 2012년의 그것과 비교했을 때 더 많았다

03
정답 ③

[지문분석]

The graph above shows / the highest level of education / earned by Canadians / in the years 1960 and 2010.
위 도표는 보여준다 / 최종 학력을 / 캐나다인이 취득한 / 1960년과 2010년에

① In 1960, / the percentage of middle school graduates / was greater / than that of all other completed education groups.
1960년에는 / 중학교 졸업자의 비율이 / 더 높았다 / 모든 다른 최종 학력 집단의 그것(비율)보다

② When it comes to / completing middle school only, / the percentage / was more than 30% higher / in 1960 / than in 2010.
~에 관해서는 / 중학교까지만 수료하는 것 / 그 비율이 / 30% 이상 높았다 / 1960년에 / 2010년보다

③ In both 1960 and 2010(→ In 1960), / the percentage of those / whose highest level of education / was a high school graduate / was more than 30%.
1960년과 2010년 모두(→ 1960년에) / 사람들의 비율은 / 최종 학력이 / 고등학교 졸업이다 / 30% 이상이다

★ ④ The percentage of those / who completed a Bachelor's degree and a Master's degree / in 1960 / was the same.
사람들의 비율은 / 학사 학위와 석사 학위를 수료한 / 1960년에 / 동일했다

⑤ Of the levels of education completed, / the second lowest percentage / in 2010 / was Master's degree.
수료한 학력 중에서 / 두 번째로 낮은 비율은 / 2010년에 / 석사 학위였다

★ 독해가 쉬워지는 구문 풀이

The percentage of **those** [who completed a Bachelor's degree and
　　　　　　　　주어
a Master's degree in 1960] was the same.
　　　　　　　　　　　　　　　동사

⇨ 관계절[who ~ in 1960]의 수식을 받으면서 '~한 사람들'이라는 뜻의 대명사인 those가 쓰였다.

[어휘] level of education 학력 earn 취득하다, 얻다 graduate 졸업자; 졸업하다 Bachelor's degree 학사 학위 Master's degree 석사 학위

[해석]

캐나다인이 취득한 최종 학력

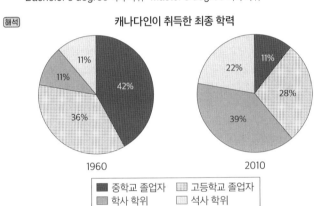

1960　　　　　　2010

■ 중학교 졸업자　　▨ 고등학교 졸업자
■ 학사 학위　　　　□ 석사 학위

위 도표는 1960년과 2010년에 캐나다인이 취득한 최종 학력을 보여준다. ① 1960년에는, 중학교 졸업자의 비율이 모든 다른 최종 학력 집단의 비율보다 더 높았다. ② 중학교까지만 수료하는 것에 관해서는, 2010년보다 1960년에 그 비율이 30% 이상 높았다. ③ 1960년과 2010년 모두 (→ 1960년에), 최종 학력이 고등학교 졸업자였던 사람들의 비율은 30% 이상이었다. ④ 1960년에 학사 학위와 석사 학위를 수료한 사람들의 비율은 동일했다. ⑤ 수료한 학력 중에서, 2010년에 두 번째로 낮은 비율은 석사 학위였다.

[해설] 도표의 제목과 글의 도입부를 통해 이 도표가 1960년과 2010년에 캐나다인이 취득한 최종 학력의 비율에 관한 것임을 알 수 있다. 이 글에서는 ①의 greater, ②의 more than 30% higher, ③의 both와 more than 30%, ④의 the same, ⑤의 the second lowest가 도표 내의 수치를 올바르게 설명하고 있는지 확인해야 한다. 고등학교 졸업이 최종 학력인 사람들의 비율은 1960년에는 36%였지만 2010년에는 28%로 두해 모두 30% 이상인 것은 아니므로, 도표의 내용과 일치하지 않는 것은 ③이다.

[오답분석] ①은 1960년에 중학교 졸업자의 비율은 42%로, 그 외 모든 다른 최종 학력 비율보다 더 높으므로 도표의 내용과 일치한다. ②은 중학교 졸업자 비율만 봤을 때 1960년의 비율이 42%로, 2010년의 11%보다 30% 이상 높으므로 도표의 내용과 일치한다. ④은 1960년에 학사 학위와 석사 학위를 수료한 사람들의 비율은 각각 11%로 동일하므로 도표의 내용과 일치한다. ⑤은 2010년에 석사 학위 수료 비율은 22%로, 11%에 이어 두번째로 낮으므로 도표의 내용과 일치한다.

[실력UP!] 미니 문제 03.

[정답] 1960년에는, 중학교 졸업자의 비율이 모든 다른 최종 학력 집단의 비율보다 높았다

04　　　　　　　　　　　　　　　　　　정답 ⑤

[지문분석]

The above graph shows / the number of threatened fish species / in five countries.
위 도표는 나타낸다 / 멸종 위기에 처한 어종의 수를 / 다섯 개 국가에서

① In Greece, / the number of fish species / that are threatened / in total / is more than 60, / the greatest total number / among the five countries.
그리스에서 / 어종의 수는 / 멸종 위기에 처한 / 총 / 60개 이상이다 / 가장 높은 총계 / 다섯 국가 중에서

② Of the five countries, / Germany has the highest number of marine fish species / that are threatened.
다섯 국가 중 / 독일이 가장 많은 수의 바닷물고기 종을 가지고 있다 / 멸종 위기에 처한

③ The number of threatened freshwater species / in Belgium / is the same as France's, / ★but the number of marine fish / that are threatened / outweighs that of France.
멸종 위기에 처한 민물고기 종의 수는 / 벨기에서 / 프랑스의 그것과 같다 / 하지만 바닷물고기의 수는 / 멸종 위기에 처한 / 프랑스의 그것보다 더 많다

④ There are more freshwater fish species / than marine fish species / that are threatened / in France.
민물고기 종이 더 많다 / 바닷물고기 종보다 / 멸종 위기에 처한 / 프랑스에는

⑤ The number of marine fish species / that are threatened / in Germany / exceeds(→ is lower than) / the total number of fish species / that are threatened / in Ireland.
바닷물고기 종의 수 / 멸종 위기에 처한 / 독일에서 / 초과한다(→ ~보다 적다) / 전체 어종의 수를 / 멸종 위기에 처한 / 아일랜드에서

★ 독해가 쉬워지는 구문 풀이

but **the number** of marine fish [that are threatened] outweighs
　　　　　　　　　　　　선행사
that of France.
지시대명사

⇨ [ ]는 선행사 fish를 수식하는 관계절이다.
⇨ 지시대명사 that은 앞 문장의 the number를 지칭하며, 같은 명사의 반복을 피하고자 사용되었다.

[어휘] threatened 멸종 위기에 처한 in total 총, 합쳐서 marine 바다의, 해양의 freshwater 민물의, 담수의 outweigh ~보다 더 많다 exceed 초과하다

[해석]

5개국의 멸종 위기에 처한 어종의 수

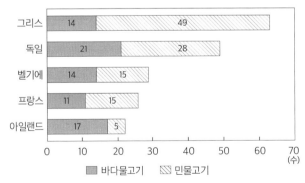

■ 바다물고기　　▨ 민물고기

위 도표는 다섯 개 국가에서 멸종 위기에 처한 어종의 수를 나타낸다. ① 그리스에서, 멸종 위기에 처한 총 어종의 수는 다섯 국가 중에서 가장 높은 총계인 60종 이상이다. ② 다섯 국가 중, 독일이 멸종 위기에 처한 바닷물고기 종의 수를 가장 많이 가지고 있다. ③ 벨기에서 멸종 위기에 처한 민물고기 종의 수는 프랑스의 그것과 같지만, 멸종 위기에 처한 바닷물고기의 수는 프랑스의 그것보다 더 많다. ④ 프랑스에는 멸종 위기에 처

한 바닷물고기 종보다 민물고기 종이 더 많다. ⑤ 독일에서 멸종 위기에 처한 바닷물고기 종의 수는 아일랜드에서 멸종 위기에 처한 전체 어종의 수를 초과한다(→ 수보다 적다).

[해설] 도표의 제목과 글의 도입부를 통해 이 도표가 다섯 개 국가에서 멸종 위기에 처한 어종의 수에 관한 것임을 알 수 있다. 이 글에서는 ①의 more than 60와 the greatest, ②의 the highest, ③의 the same과 outweigh, ④의 more, ⑤의 exceed가 도표 내의 수치를 올바르게 설명하고 있는지 확인해야 한다. 독일에서 멸종 위기에 처한 바닷물고기 종은 21종으로, 아일랜드에서 멸종 위기에 처한 전체 어종의 수인 22종보다 적으므로, 도표의 내용과 일치하지 않는 것은 ⑤이다.

[오답분석] ①은 그리스에서 멸종 위기에 처한 어종은 총 63종이고 다섯 개 국가 중 가장 많은 숫자이므로 도표의 내용과 일치한다. ②은 독일이 21종으로, 다섯 개 국가 중 멸종 위기에 처한 가장 많은 바닷물고기 종을 가진 나라이므로 도표의 내용과 일치한다. ③은 벨기에와 프랑스에서 멸종 위기인 민물고기 종의 수는 15종으로 같고, 바닷물고기 종의 수는 11종으로 14종인 벨기에가 더 많으므로 도표의 내용과 일치한다. ④은 프랑스에는 멸종 위기에 처한 민물고기 종이 15종으로, 이는 11종인 바닷물고기 종의 수보다 더 많으므로 도표의 내용과 일치한다.

[실력 UP!] 미니 문제 04.

정답 ⓐ threatened   ⓑ marine
해석 ⓐ 멸종위기종이 될 위험에 처한
   ⓑ 해양 생태계에 살거나 관련된

05

정답 ⑤

[지문분석]

The graph above shows / the number of cars / produced / in millions / during 2020 / by ten different countries.
위 도표는 보여준다 / 자동차의 수를 / 생산된 / 백만 단위로 / 2020년 한 해 동안 / 서로 다른 10개의 국가에서

① Global car production decreased / by over 20 million / from 2017 to 2020.
전 세계 자동차 생산량은 감소했다 / 2천만 대 이상 가량 / 2017년에서 2020년까지

② The combined number of cars / produced by France, Russia, and Brazil / was fewer / than the number of cars / produced by the United States.
자동차의 합친 수량은 / 프랑스, 러시아, 그리고 브라질에 의해 생산된 / 더 적었다 / 자동차의 수보다 / 미국에 의해 생산된

★ ③ While / the number of cars / made by South Korea / was lower in number / than what Germany produced, / it was higher / than the number of cars / produced by India.
~인 반면 / 지동치의 수는 / 대한민국에 의해 만들어진 / 수적으로 더 적었다 / 독일이 생산한 것보다 / 더 많았다 / 자동차의 수보다는 / 인도에 의해 생산된

④ The gap / between the United States and Japan / in the number of cars / manufactured / was less than 1 million.
격차는 / 미국과 일본 간의 / 자동차 수에 있어서 / 생산된 / 100만보다 더 적었다

⑤ It was China / that produced the largest number of cars, / which was less(→ more) / than three times the number of cars / that Japan produced.
중국이었다 / 가장 많은 수의 자동차를 생산한 것은 / 그리고 그 수는 더 적었다(→ 더 많았다) / 자동차 수의 3배보다 / 일본이 생산한

★ 독해가 쉬워지는 구문 풀이

While the number of cars made by South Korea was lower in
      단수주어   수식어(분사구)   단수동사
number than [what Germany produced], ~
              관계   주어 동사
              대명사

⊃ 'the number of + 복수명사(cars)'는 단수취급하므로 단수동사 was가 쓰였다.
⊃ [ ]는 전치사 than의 목적어 역할을 하는 명사절이고, 주어(Germany)와 타동사(produced)만 있고 목적어가 없는 불완전한 절이 왔으므로, '~하는 것'이라는 의미로 불완전한 절 앞에 오는 관계대명사 what이 쓰였다.

[어휘] different 서로 다른, 여러 가지의 in number 수적으로, 숫자상으로 manufacture 생산하다

[해석]

2020년에 생산된 자동차의 수

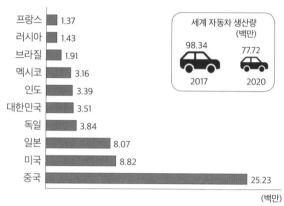

국가	생산량 (백만)
프랑스	1.37
러시아	1.43
브라질	1.91
멕시코	3.16
인도	3.39
대한민국	3.51
독일	3.84
일본	8.07
미국	8.82
중국	25.23

세계 자동차 생산량 (백만)
98.34 (2017)   77.72 (2020)

위 도표는 2020년 한 해 동안 서로 다른 10개의 국가에서 생산된 자동차의 수를 백만 단위로 보여준다. ① 전 세계 자동차 생산량은 2017년부터 2020년까지 2천만 대 이상 가량 감소했다. ② 프랑스, 러시아, 그리고 브라질에 의해 생산된 자동차의 합친 수량은 미국에 의해 생산된 자동차의 수보다 더 적었다. ③ 대한민국에 의해 만들어진 자동차의 수는 독일이 생산한 것보다 수적으로 더 적은 반면, 인도에 의해 생산된 자동차의 수보다는 더 많았다. ④ 생산된 자동차 수에 있어서 미국과 일본 간의 격차는 100만보다 더 적었다. ⑤ 가장 많은 수의 자동차를 생산한 것은 중국이었고, 그 수는 일본이 생산한 자동차 수의 3배보다 더 적었다(→ 더 많았다).

[해설] 도표의 제목과 글의 도입부를 통해 이 도표가 2020년에 10개의 국가에서 생산된 자동차의 수에 관한 것임을 알 수 있다. 이 글에서는 ①의 decreased, ②의 fewer than, ③의 lower와 higher, ④의 less than, ⑤의 the largest와 less than three times가 도표 내의 수치를 올바르게 설명하고 있는지 확인해야 한다. 중국이 생산한 자동차 수는 2,523만이고, 이는 일본이 생산한 자동차 수인 807만의 3배인 2,421만보다 많으므로, 도표의 내용과 일치하지 않는 것은 ⑤이다.

[오답분석] ①은 2017년의 전 세계 자동차 생산량은 9,834만이고 2020년은 7,772만으로, 2020년에는 2017년보다 2,062만이 감소했으므로 도표의 내용과 일치한다. ②은 프랑스, 러시아, 브라질에서 생산된 자동차 수는 각각 137만, 143만, 191만이며, 세 국가의 합인 471만은 미국의 882만보다 더 적으므로 도표의 내용과 일치한다. ③은 대한민국에서 생산된 자동차 수는 351만으로, 독일의 384만보다 더 적고 인도의 339만보다 더 크므로 도표의 내용과 일치한다. ④은 미국과 일본에서 생산된 자동차 수는 각각 882만과 807만으로, 그 격차인 75만은 100만보다 더 적으므로 도표의 내용과 일치한다.

[실력 UP!] 미니 문제 05.

정답 ⓐ combined   ⓑ gap
해석 ⓐ 둘 또는 이상의 수치나 수량을 함께 더한
   ⓑ 두 수량 간의 구분 또는 차이

06

지문분석

The table above shows / the percentage of government spending / of three different countries / in five sectors / in 2009.
위 표는 보여준다 / 정부 지출 비율을 / 서로 다른 세 국가의 / 다섯 개 분야에서의 / 2009년에

① Of the three countries, / the percentage of government spending / for Public services / was highest / in Italy.
세 국가 중 / 정부 지출의 비율은 / 공공 서비스를 위한 / 가장 높았다 / 이탈리아에서

★ ② In Germany, / government spending on Health / exceeded spending / on Economic affairs and Environmental protection combined.
독일에서는 / 보건 분야에 대한 정부 지출이 / 지출을 넘어섰다 / 경제 문제와 환경 보호 분야를 합친

③ The second largest percentage / of government spending in Italy / went to Health.
두 번째로 큰 비율은 / 이탈리아에서 정부 지출의 / 보건 분야에 주어졌다

④ In the UK, / government spending on Public services / was the third largest among the five sectors, / following(→ preceding) the government spending / used on Economic affairs.
영국에서 / 공공 서비스 분야의 정부 지출은 / 다섯 개 분야 중 세 번째로 많았다 / 정부 지출에 뒤이어(→ 앞서) / 경제 문제에 사용된

⑤ All three countries / used the least amount / of government spending / on Environmental protection.
세 국가 모두 / 가장 적은 양을 사용했다 / 정부 지출의 / 환경 보호에

> ★ **독해가 쉬워지는 구문 풀이**
>
> In Germany, government spending on Health exceeded [spending
> 　　　　　　 　주어　　　　　　　　　　 동사
> on Economic affairs and Environmental Protection] combined.
> 　　　　　　　　　　목적어
>
> ⇨ 과거분사 combined는 [ ] 전체를 수식한다.

어휘 government spending 정부 지출 sector 분야
public services 공공 서비스 affair 문제, 일
environmental protection 환경 보호 go to ~에 주어지다

해석
분야별 정부 지출(2009)

	독일	이탈리아	영국
공공 서비스	6.6%	8.6%	4.6%
보건	7.1%	7.5%	7.8%
경제 문제	4.0%	4.5%	4.4%
교육	4.3%	4.6%	6.4%
환경 보호	0.7%	0.9%	1.0%

위 표는 2009년에 서로 다른 세 국가의 다섯 개 분야에서의 정부 지출 비율을 보여준다. ① 세 국가 중, 공공 서비스를 위한 정부 지출의 비율은 이탈리아에서 가장 높았다. ② 독일에서는, 보건 분야에 대한 정부 지출이 경제 문제와 환경 보호 분야를 합친 지출을 넘어섰다. ③ 이탈리아에서 정부 지출의 두 번째로 큰 비율은 보건 분야에 주어졌다. ④ 영국에서 공공 서비스 분야의 정부 지출은 경제 문제에 사용된 정부 지출에 뒤이어(→ 앞서) 다섯 개 분야 중 세 번째로 많았다. ⑤ 세 국가 모두 정부 지출의 가장 적은 양을 환경 보호에 사용했다.

해설 표의 제목과 글의 도입부를 통해 이 표가 2009년에 세 국가가 다섯 개의 분야에 사용한 정부 지출의 비율에 관한 것임을 알 수 있다. 이 글에서는 ①의 highest, ②의 exceeded, ③의 the second largest, ④의 the third largest와 following, ⑤의 the least가 표에서 언급하는 수치를 올

바르게 설명하고 있는지 확인해야 한다. 영국이 공공 서비스 분야에 사용한 정부 지출 비율은 4.6%로, 보건 분야에 사용된 7.8%와 교육 분야에 사용된 6.4%에 이어 세 번째로 많이 사용되었고, 이는 4.4%의 비율로 그 뒤를 잇는 경제 문제보다 앞선 순위이므로, 표의 내용과 일치하지 않는 것은 ④이다.

오답분석 ①은 이탈리아의 공공 서비스 정부 지출 비율은 8.6%로, 세 국가 중 가장 높으므로 표의 내용과 일치한다. ②는 독일에서 보건 분야 정부 지출 비율은 7.1%로, 경제 문제와 환경 보호에 사용된 것을 합친 비율인 4.7%를 넘어섰으므로 표의 내용과 일치한다. ③은 이탈리아에서 보건 분야 정부 지출 비율은 7.5%로, 가장 높은 비율인 8.6%의 공공 서비스 다음이므로 표의 내용과 일치한다. ⑤는 세 국가 모두 환경 보호 분야에 가장 적은 비율의 정부 지출을 사용하였으므로 표의 내용과 일치한다.

실력 UP! 미니 문제 06.

정답 ⓐ exceed ⓑ least
해석 ⓐ 별도의 숫자 또는 수량을 넘어 증가하는
ⓑ 상응하는 어떤 값보다도 작은

07

지문분석

The above graph shows / the percentage of urban and rural households / with mobile broadband Internet access / for five European countries / in 2020.
위 도표는 보여준다 / 도시와 시골 가정의 비율을 / 이동 광대역 인터넷 접속이 가능한 / 유럽 5개국의 / 2020년도

① The country / with the highest percentage of rural households / with mobile broadband Internet access / was Poland, / accounting for 69.2%.
국가는 / 시골 가정의 비율이 가장 높은 / 이동 광대역 인터넷 접속이 가능한 / 폴란드였다 / 69.2%를 차지한

★ ② The percentage of urban households / with mobile broadband Internet access / in Sweden, Portugal, and Norway / exceeded / that of rural households.
도시 가정의 비율 / 이동 광대역 인터넷 접속이 가능한 / 스웨덴, 포르투갈, 그리고 노르웨이에서 / 넘어섰다 / 시골 가정의 비율을

③ Italy's mobile broadband Internet access / in rural areas / was less than half, / but / it was still the third-highest / for all countries.
이탈리아의 이동 광대역 인터넷 접속은 / 시골 가정의 / 절반 이하였다 / 하지만 / 그래도 여전히 세 번째로 높았다 / 전체 국가 중에서

④ Mobile broadband Internet access / for urban households in Portugal / was less than twice / that of rural households in Norway.
이동 광대역 인터넷 접속은 / 포르투갈 도시 가정의 / 두 배보다 적었다 / 노르웨이 시골 가정의 그것(이동 광대역 인터넷 접속)의

⑤ Among the five countries, / the gap / between the percentage of rural and urban areas / with mobile broadband access / in Norway / was the highest(→ lowest).
다섯 국가 중에서 / 차이 / 시골 및 도시 가정 비율 간 / 이동 광대역 접속의 / 노르웨이의 / 가장 높았다(→ 가장 낮았다)

> ★ **독해가 쉬워지는 구문 풀이**
>
> **The percentage** of urban households with mobile broadband Internet access in Sweden, Portugal, and Norway exceeded **that** of rural households.
>
> ⇨ 대명사 that은 앞의 The percentage를 지칭하며, 반복을 피하기 위해 사용되었다.

어휘 urban 도시의 rural 시골의 household 가정 broadband 광대역
exceed 넘어서다

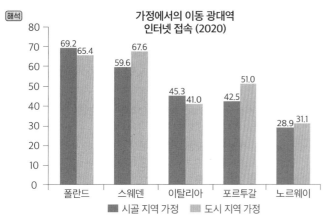

가정에서의 이동 광대역 인터넷 접속 (2020)

폴란드 69.2 / 65.4
스웨덴 59.6 / 67.6
이탈리아 45.3 / 41.0
포르투갈 42.5 / 51.0
노르웨이 28.9 / 31.1

■ 시골 지역 가정　■ 도시 지역 가정

위 도표는 2020년도 유럽 5개국의 이동 광대역 인터넷 접속이 가능한 도시와 시골 가정의 비율을 보여준다. ① 이동 광대역 인터넷 접속이 가능한 시골 가정의 비율이 가장 높은 국가는 69.2%를 차지한 폴란드였다. ② 스웨덴, 포르투갈 및 노르웨이에서 이동 광대역 인터넷 접속이 가능한 도시 가정의 비율은 시골 가정의 비율을 넘어섰다. ③ 이탈리아 시골 가정의 이동 광대역 인터넷 접속은 절반 이하였으나, 그래도 여전히 전체 국가 중에서 세 번째로 높았다. ④ 포르투갈 도시 가정의 이동 광대역 인터넷 접속은 노르웨이 시골 가정의 그것(이동 광대역 인터넷 접속)의 두 배보다 적었다. ⑤ 다섯 국가 중에서, 노르웨이의 시골 및 도시 가정의 이동 광대역 접속 비율 간 차이가 가장 높았다(→ 가장 낮았다).

해설 도표의 제목과 글의 도입부를 통해 위 도표가 2020년도 유럽 5개국의 이동 광대역 인터넷 접속이 가능한 도시와 시골 가정의 비율에 관한 것임을 알 수 있다. 이 글에서는 ①의 the highest percentage of rural과 69.2%, ②의 exceeded, ③의 less than half, still the third-highest, ④의 less than twice, ⑤의 the highest가 도표의 내용을 올바르게 설명하고 있는지 확인해야 한다. 노르웨이의 시골 및 도시 가정의 이동 광대역 인터넷 접속 비율 간 차이는 2.2%로, 이는 다섯 국가 중 가장 낮으므로 도표의 내용과 일치하지 않는 것은 ⑤이다.

오답분석 ①은 폴란드의 이동 광대역 인터넷 접속이 가능한 시골 가정의 비율이 69.2%로 가장 높으므로 도표의 내용과 일치한다. ②는 스웨덴, 포르투갈 및 노르웨이에서 이동 광대역 인터넷 접속이 가능한 도시 가정의 비율은 각각 67.6%, 51.0%, 31.1%이며, 이는 세 국가 각각의 시골 가정의 비율인 59.6%, 42.5%, 28.9%를 넘어섰으므로 도표의 내용과 일치한다. ③은 이탈리아 시골 가정의 이동 광대역 인터넷 접속 비율이 45.3%로, 이는 절반 이하이며 전체 국가 중에서 세 번째로 높은 수치이므로 도표의 내용과 일치한다. ④는 포르투갈 도시 가정의 이동 광대역 인터넷 접속은 51.0%이며, 이는 노르웨이 시골 가정의 인터넷 접속 비율인 28.9%의 두 배보다 더 적었으므로 도표의 내용과 일치한다.

실력 UP! 미니 문제 07.

정답 ⓐ urban ⓑ access

해석 ⓐ 도시 및 다른 인구 밀집 지역에 있거나 관련된
ⓑ 특정한 것을 사용할 수 있는 권리나 능력

08
정답 ④

지문분석

The two pie charts above / show the sources of greenhouse gas emissions / in 2019.
위의 두 가지 원 도표는 / 온실가스 배출의 원천을 보여준다 / 2019년

① Among the four main categories of sources, / more than 80 percent of all greenhouse gas emissions / were from energy use.
네 개의 주요 원천 중에서 / 전체 온실가스 배출의 80% 이상은 / 에너지 사용으로부터 나왔다

② In contrast, / waste was the smallest source, / being responsible for less than five percent / of total greenhouse gas emissions.
그에 반해서 / 폐기물은 가장 작은 원천이었다 / 5% 미만을 담당하는 / 전체 온실가스 배출의

③ Among the subcategories of energy, / transport produced the largest percentage / of greenhouse gas emissions / at almost 35 percent.
에너지의 하위 범주들 중에서 / 수송이 가장 큰 비율을 초래했다 / 온실가스 배출의 / 거의 35%에 달하는

④ Energy industries, / which was the second-largest energy subcategory, / accounted for less(→ more) emissions / than the manufacturing and residential sectors combined.
에너지 산업 / 두 번째로 큰 에너지 하위 범주였던 / 더 적은(→ 더 많은) 비율을 차지했다 / 제조 및 주거 분야 배출이 합쳐진 것보다

★⑤ Only 10 percent of emissions / resulted from other sources, / making this / the smallest of the energy subcategories.
배출량의 10%만이 / 기타 원천으로부터 기인했다 / 이는 이것을 ~로 만들었다 / 에너지 하위 범주에서 가장 적은 것으로

> ★ 독해가 쉬워지는 구문 풀이
>
> Only 10 percent of emissions resulted from other sources, [making this the smallest of the energy subcategories].
> 목적어　　　　　　　　목적격보어
>
> ⇨ [ ]는 분사구문의 부사절이며, 접속사 및 반복되는 주어(10 percent of emissions)가 생략되었다.

어휘 greenhouse gas 온실가스　emission 배출　waste 폐기물
subcategory 하위 범주　transport 수송　manufacture 제조
residential 주거의　sector 분야

해석

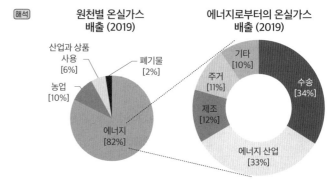

원천별 온실가스 배출 (2019)

산업과 상품 사용 [6%]
농업 [10%]
폐기물 [2%]
에너지 [82%]

에너지로부터의 온실가스 배출 (2019)

기타 [10%]
주거 [11%]
제조 [12%]
에너지 산업 [33%]
수송 [34%]

주제문 위의 두 가지 원 도표는 2019년 온실가스 배출의 원천을 보여준다. ① 네 개의 주요 원천 중에서, 전체 온실가스 배출의 80% 이상은 에너지 사용으로부터 나왔다. ② 그에 반해서, 폐기물은 전체 온실가스 배출의 5% 미만을 담당하는 가장 작은 원천이었다. ③ 에너지의 하위 범주들 중에서, 수송이 온실가스 배출의 거의 35%에 날하는 가장 큰 비율을 초래했다. ④ 두 번째로 큰 에너지 하위 범주였던 에너지 산업은 제조 및 주거 분야 배출이 합쳐진 것보다 더 적은(→ 더 많은) 비율을 차지했다. ⑤ 배출량의 10%만이 기타 원천으로부터 기인했는데, 이는 이것을 에너지 하위 범주에서 가장 작은 것으로 만들었다.

해설 도표의 제목과 글의 도입부를 통해 두 도표가 2019년 온실가스 배출의 원천에 관한 것임을 알 수 있다. 이 글에서는 ①의 more than 80 percent, ②의 the smallest와 less than five percent of total, ③의 the largest, ④의 second-largest와 combined, ⑤의 10 percent와 the smallest가 도표 내의 수치를 올바르게 설명하고 있는지 확인해야 한다. 에너지 산업의 배출 비율은 33%이고, 제조와 주거 분야로부터의 배출 비율은 각각 12%, 11%로 이 둘을 합치면 23%이다. 따라서 에너지 산업의 배출 비율(33%)은 제조 및 주거 분야 배출 비율의 합(23%)보다 더 많으므로, 도표의 내용과 일치하지 않는 것은 ④이다.

오답
분석 ①은 에너지 사용으로부터 배출된 온실가스가 82%이므로 도표의 내용과 일치한다. ②은 폐기물로부터 배출된 온실가스가 2%로, 가장 적은 비율을 차지하므로 도표의 내용과 일치한다. ③은 수송으로부터 배출된 온실가스가 34%로, 가장 큰 비율을 차지하므로 도표의 내용과 일치한다. ⑤은 기타 근원으로부터 배출된 온실가스가 10%로, 가장 적은 비율을 차지하므로 도표의 내용과 일치한다.

실력 UP! 미니 문제 08.

해석 그에 반해서, 폐기물은 전체 온실가스 배출의 5% 미만을 담당하는 가장 작은 원천이었다

CHAPTER 07 세부 정보 파악하기

불변의 패턴 13   p.56
선택지는 글의 순서대로 나온다.

기출 문제   정답 ③

지문분석

Jessie Redmon Fauset was born / in Snow Hill, New Jersey, / in 1884.
Jessie Redmon Fauset은 태어났다 / New Jersey주의 Snow Hill에서 / 1884년에

She was the first black woman / to graduate from Cornell University.
그녀는 최초의 흑인 여성이었다 / Cornell University를 졸업한

In addition to writing / novels, poetry, short stories, and essays, / Fauset taught French / in public schools in Washington, D.C. / and worked / as a journal editor.
쓰는 것뿐만 아니라 / 소설, 시, 단편 소설, 수필을 / Fauset은 프랑스어를 가르쳤다 / Washington, D.C.의 공립학교에서 / 그리고 일했다 / 학술지 편집자로서

While working / as an editor, / she encouraged many wellknown writers / of the Harlem Renaissance.
일하는 동안 / 편집자로 / 그녀는 많은 유명한 작가들을 고무시켰다 / 흑인 예술 문화 부흥 운동의

★ Though she is more famous / for being an editor / than for being a fiction writer, / many critics consider her novel *Plum Bun* / Fauset's strongest work.
비록 그녀가 더 유명하더라도 / 편집자로서 / 소설가보다는 / 많은 비평가들은 그녀의 소설 *Plum Bun*을 여긴다 / Fauset의 가장 훌륭한 작품으로

In it, / she tells the story / of a black girl / who could pass for white / but ultimately claims / her racial identity and pride.
그 속에서 / 그녀는 이야기를 한다 / 한 흑인 소녀의 / 백인으로 여겨질 수 있었다 / 하지만 결국에는 주장한다 / 자신의 인종 정체성과 자부심을

Fauset died of heart disease April 30, 1961, / in Philadelphia.
Fauset은 1961년 4월 30일에 심장병으로 사망했다 / Philadelphia에서

★ 독해가 쉬워지는 구문 풀이

Though she **is** more **famous** [①**for** being an editor] than [②**for** being a fiction writer], many critics consider her novel *Plum Bun*
　　　　　　　　　　　　　주어　　　　동사　　　목적어
Fauset's strongest work.

➡ 'be동사 + famous + for + 명사(구)' 구문은 '~로 유명하다'로 해석된다.
➡ 전치사구 [①]과 [②]는 전치사 than으로 연결되어 병렬 구조를 이룬다.

어휘 Harlem Renaissance 흑인 예술 문화 부흥 운동, 할렘 르네상스
ultimately 결국에는 racial identity 인종 정체성 pride 자부심, 긍지

해석 Jessie Redmon Fauset은 1884년에 New Jersey의 Snow Hill에서 태어났다. 그녀는 Cornell University를 졸업한 최초의 흑인 여성이었다. 소설, 시, 단편 소설, 수필을 쓰는 것뿐만 아니라, Fauset은 Washington, D.C.의 공립학교에서 프랑스어를 가르쳤고, 학술지 편집자로서 일했다. 편집자로 일하는 동안, 그녀는 흑인 예술 문화 부흥 운동의 많은 유명한 작가들을 고무시켰다. 비록 그녀가 소설가보다는 편집자로서 더 유명하더라도, 많은 비평가들은 그녀의 소설 *Plum Bun*을 Fauset의 가장 훌륭한 작품으로 여긴다. 그 속에서, 그녀는 백인으로 여겨질 수 있었지만 결국에는 자신의 인종 정체성과 자부심을 주장하는 한 흑인 소녀의 이야기를 한다. Fauset은 1961년 4월 30일에 Philadelphia에서 심장병으로 사망했다.

해설 she is more famous for being an editor than for being a fiction writer를 통해 Jessie Redmon Fauset이 소설가보다는 편집자로 더 유명하다는 것을 알 수 있으므로, 글의 내용과 일치하지 않는 것은 ③ '편집자보다는 소설가로서 더 유명하다.'이다.

오답
분석 ①은 She was the first black woman to graduate from Cornell University라고 했으므로 글의 내용과 일치한다. ②은 Fauset taught French in public schools in Washington, D.C라고 했으므로 글의 내용과 일치한다. ④은 In it, she tells the story of a black girl이라고 했으므로 글의 내용과 일치한다. ⑤은 Fauset died of heart disease ~ in Philadelphia라고 했으므로 글의 내용과 일치한다.

불변의 패턴 14   p.57
정답은 글에 나온 정보가 일부 변형된 것이다.

기출 문제   정답 ④

지문분석

Mary Cassatt was born / in Pennsylvania, / the fourth of five children / born in her well-to-do family.
Mary Cassatt는 태어났다 / Pennsylvania에서 / 다섯 자녀 중 넷째로 / 부유한 가정에서 태어난

Mary Cassatt and her family traveled / throughout Europe / in her childhood.
Mary Cassatt와 그녀의 가족은 여행했다 / 유럽 전역을 / 어린 시절에

Her family did not approve / when she decided to become an artist, / ★ but her desire was so strong, / she bravely took the steps / to make art her career.
그녀의 가족은 찬성하지 않았다 / 그녀가 화가가 되기로 결심했을 때 / 하지만 그녀의 열망은 너무 강해서 / 그녀는 용감하게 발을 내디뎠다 / 미술을 그녀의 진로로 만들기 위해

She studied first / in Philadelphia / and / then went to Paris / to study painting.
그녀는 먼저 공부했다 / Philadelphia에서 / 그리고 / 그러고 나서 파리로 갔다 / 그림을 공부하기 위해

She admired / the work of Edgar Degas / and was able to meet him / in Paris, / which was a great inspiration.
그녀는 ~에 감탄했다 / Edgar Degas의 작품 / 그리고 그를 만날 수 있었다 / 파리에서 / 그런데 그것은 큰 영감이 되었다

Though she never had / children of her own, / she loved children / and painted portraits / of the children of her friends and family.
비록 그녀는 둔 적은 없었지만 / 자기의 자녀를 / 그녀는 아이들을 사랑했다 / 그리고 초상화를 그렸다 / 그녀의 친구들과 가족의 아이들의

Cassatt lost her sight / at the age of seventy, / and, sadly, / was not able to paint / during the later years of her life.
Cassatt는 시력을 잃었다 / 70세의 나이에 / 그리고 슬프게도 / 그림을 그릴 수 없었다 / 그녀의 노년 동안

어휘 well-to-do 부유한　admire 감탄하다　inspiration 영감　portrait 초상화

해석 Mary Cassatt는 부유한 가정에서 태어난 다섯 자녀 중 넷째로, Pennsylvania에서 태어났다. Mary Cassatt와 그녀의 가족은 어린 시절에 유럽 전역을 여행했다. 그녀의 가족은 그녀가 화가가 되기로 결심했을 때 찬성하지 않았지만, 그녀의 열망은 너무 강해서, 그녀는 미술을 그녀의 진로로 만들기 위해 용감하게 발을 내디뎠다. 그녀는 먼저 Philadelphia에서 공부했고 그러고 나서 그림을 공부하기 위해 파리로 갔다. 그녀는 Edgar Degas의 작품에 감탄했고 그를 파리에서 만날 수 있었는데, 그것은 큰 영감이 되었다. 비록 그녀는 자기의 자녀를 둔 적은 없었지만, 그녀는 아이들을 사랑했고 그녀의 친구들과 가족의 아이들의 초상화를 그렸다. Cassatt는 70세의 나이에 시력을 잃었으며, 슬프게도 그녀의 노년 동안 그림을 그릴 수 없었다.

해설 Though she never had children of her own ~을 통해 그녀는 자기의 자녀를 둔 적이 없었다고 했으므로, 글의 내용과 일치하지 않는 것은 ④ '자기 자녀의 초상화를 그렸다.'이다.

오답분석 ①은 Mary Cassatt and her family traveled throughout Europe in her childhood라고 했으므로 글의 내용과 일치한다. ②은 Her family did not approve when she decided to become an artist라고 했으므로 글의 내용과 일치한다. ③은 She admired the work of Edgar Degas and was able to meet him in Paris라고 했으므로 글의 내용과 일치한다. ⑤은 Cassatt lost her sight at the age of seventy라고 했으므로 글의 내용과 일치한다.

독해 만점 TEST　　　　　　　　　　　　p.58

01 ⑤　02 ⑤　03 ④　04 ③　05 ③　06 ⑤　07 ③　08 ③

실력UP! 미니 문제

01. ⓐ involved　ⓑ advocate
02. ①
03. The Life and Accomplishment of Amelia Earhart
04. ①
05. Ponce de León's Explorations in the New World
06. ③
07. descend to more tropical forests
08. ②

01　　　　　　　　　　　　　　　　정답 ⑤

지문분석

Margaret Murie was born / in Seattle, Washington / in 1902.
Margaret Murie는 태어났다 / Washington주 Seattle에서 / 1902년에

After moving to Alaska / with her family, / Murie attended college there / and became the first woman / to graduate from the Alaska Agricultural College and School of Mines.
알래스카로 이사간 후 / 그녀의 가족과 함께 / Murie는 그곳에서 대학을 다녔다 / 그리고 첫 번째 여성이 되었다 / 알래스카 농업 광산 대학을 졸업한

Soon after, / she met her husband, / and the two moved to Oregon / to study elk populations.
곧 / 그녀는 그녀의 남편을 만났다 / 그리고 그 둘은 Oregon주로 이동했다 / 엘크 개체군을 연구하기 위해

Murie camped in the wilderness / for weeks / at a time / as she observed the local wildlife.
Murie는 황무지에서 야영을 했다 / 몇 주 동안 / 한 번에 / 그녀가 지역의 야생 동물을 관찰했을 때

★ During her studies, / Murie increasingly became involved / in conservation efforts / and became widely recognized / for her work.
연구를 하는 과정에서 / Murie는 점차 몰두하기 시작했다 / 자연보호 활동에 / 그리고 널리 인정받게 되었다 / 그녀의 노력으로

For example, / her ideas for preserving entire ecosystems / became the foundation / for protecting natural parks and large areas of wilderness.
예를 들어 / 전체 생태계를 보존하려는 그녀의 방법들 / 기반이 되었다 / 자연 공원 및 광활한 황무지 보호의

Her efforts led her / to receiving numerous awards, / including the Presidential Medal of Freedom in 1998.
그녀의 노력들은 그녀를 이끌었다 / 수많은 상을 받도록 / 1998년 대통령 훈장을 포함하여

She continued to advocate / for the environment / until she died in 2003 / at the age of 101.
그녀는 꾸준히 대변했다 / 환경을 / 2003년 그녀가 사망할 때까지 / 101세의 나이로

어휘 elk 엘크, 뿔이 큰 사슴의 일종　population 개체군, 개체 수　camp in 야영하다　wilderness 황무지, 황야, 자연　increasingly 점차, 점점　involved 몰두한, 열중한　conservation effort 자연보호 활동　recognized 인정받은, 공인의　preserve 보존하다, 보호하다　ecosystem 생태계　foundation 기반, 기초　advocate 변호하다, 옹호하다

해석 Margaret Murie는 1902년에 Washington주 Seattle에서 태어났다. 그녀의 가족과 함께 알래스카로 이사간 후, Murie는 그곳에서 대학을 다녔고, 알래스카 농업 광산 대학을 졸업한 첫 번째 여성이 되었다. 곧, 그녀는 그녀의 남편을 만났고, 그 둘은 엘크 개체군을 연구하기 위해 Oregon주로 이동했다. Murie가 지역의 야생 동물을 관찰했을 때 그녀는 한 번에 몇 주 동안 황무지에서 야영을 했다. 연구를 하는 과정에서, Murie는 자연보호 활동에 점차 몰두하기 시작했고 그녀의 노력들로 널리 인정받게 되었다. 예를 들어, 전체 생태계를 보존하려는 그녀의 방법들은 자연 공원 및 광활한 황무지 보호의 기반이 되었다. 그녀의 노력들은 1998년 대통령 훈장을 포함하여 수많은 상을 받도록 그녀를 이끌었다. 그녀는 2003년 101세의 나이로 사망할 때까지 꾸준히 환경을 대변했다.

해설 ~ including the Presidential Medal of Freedom in 1998. She continued to advocate for the environment until she died in 2003 at the age of 101를 통해 그녀가 사망한 것은 2003년이지만, 대통령 훈장을 받은 것은 1998년임을 알 수 있으므로, 글의 내용과 일치하지 않는 것은 ⑤ '공로를 인정받아 사망 이후 대통령 훈장을 받았다.'이다.

오답분석 ①은 After moving to Alaska with her family, Murie attended college there라고 했으므로 글의 내용과 일치한다. ②은 Soon after, ~ and the two moved to Oregon이라고 했으므로 글의 내용과 일치한다. ③은 Murie camped in the wilderness for weeks ~ as she observed the local wildlife라고 했으므로 글의 내용과 일치한다. ④은 Murie increasingly became involved in conservation efforts and became widely recognized for her work라고 했으므로 글의 내용과 일치한다.

정답 ⓐ involved ⓑ advocate

해석 ⓐ 어떤 일에 참여하거나 깊이 헌신한 상태
ⓑ 공개적으로 추천하거나 어떤 것을 대신해 주장을 펼침

02   정답 ⑤

지문분석

Georgia O'Keeffe was born / in Wisconsin / on November 15, 1887.
Georgia O'Keeffe는 태어났다 / Wisconsin주에서 / 1887년 11월 15일에

As the second of seven children, / she grew up / on a dairy farm / and learned art / at home.
일곱 자녀 중 둘째로 / 그녀는 자랐다 / 낙농장에서 / 그리고 미술을 배웠다 / 집에서

After graduating high school, / O'Keeffe studied traditional art / in Chicago and New York / and taught art / in Texas.
고등학교를 졸업한 후 / O'Keeffe는 전통 미술을 공부했다 / 시카고와 뉴욕에서 / 그리고 미술을 가르쳤다 / Texas에서

Her technique changed / to more abstract art / when she began to study / the philosophy of Arthur Wesley Dow, / an American painter.
그녀의 기법은 변해 갔다 / 더 추상적인 예술로 / 그녀가 공부하기 시작하면서 / Arthur Wesley Dow의 철학을 / 미국 화가인

She drew many abstract works / with charcoal / during this time, / and her work was first exhibited / in 1917.
그녀는 많은 추상화 작품들을 그렸다 / 목탄으로 / 이 시기 동안 / 그리고 그녀의 작품은 처음으로 전시되었다 / 1917년에

By the 1920s, / she had become / one of the most influential artists / of her time.
1920년대 즈음 / 그녀는 되었다 / 가장 영향력 있는 예술가 중 한 명이 / 그녀의 시대에서

★ She was most well-known / for her paintings of skyscrapers / as well as of natural subjects / like deserts, mountains, and especially flowers.
그녀는 가장 잘 알려져 있었다 / 고층 건물의 그림으로도 / 자연물뿐만 아니라 / 사막, 산, 그리고 특히 꽃과 같은

> ★ 독해가 쉬워지는 구문 풀이
>
> She **was** most **well-known for** her paintings [①of skyscrapers] as well as [②of natural subjects like deserts, mountains, and especially flowers].
>   상관접속사
>
> ⇨ 'be동사 + known + for + 명사(구)' 구문은 '~로 잘 알려진'이라고 해석한다.
> ⇨ 전치사구[①]과 [②]는 상관접속사 as well as로 연결되어 병렬 구조를 이룬다.

어휘 dairy 낙농(업)의 abstract 추상적인, 추상파의 philosophy 철학
charcoal 목탄 exhibit 전시하다 influential 영향력 있는
skyscraper 고층 건물

해석 Georgia O'Keeffe는 1887년 11월 15일에 Wisconsin주에서 태어났다. 일곱 자녀 중 둘째로, 그녀는 낙농장에서 자랐고, 집에서 미술을 배웠다. 고등학교를 졸업한 후, O'Keeffe는 시카고와 뉴욕에서 전통 미술을 공부했고 Texas에서 미술을 가르쳤다. 그녀의 기법은 그녀가 미국 화가인 Arthur Wesley Dow의 철학을 공부하기 시작하면서 더 추상적인 예술로 변해 갔다. 그녀는 이 시기 동안 목탄으로 많은 추상화 작품들을 그렸고, 그녀의 작품은 1917년에 처음으로 전시되었다. 1920년대 즈음, 그녀는 그녀의 시대에서 가장 영향력 있는 예술가 중 한 명이 되었다. 그녀는 사막, 산, 그리고 특히 꽃과 같은 자연물뿐만 아니라 고층 건물의 그림으로도 가장 잘 알려져 있었다.

해설 이 글의 마지막 문장 She was most well-known for her paintings of skyscrapers as well as of natural subjects를 통해 자연물뿐만 아니라 고층 건물의 그림도 그렸다는 것을 알 수 있으므로, 글의 내용과 일치하지 않는 것은 ⑤ '자연에 있는 소재만 그렸다.'이다.

오답분석 ①은 As the second of seven children이라고 했으므로 글의 내용과 일치한다. ②은 taught art in Texas라고 했으므로 글의 내용과 일치한다. ③은 Her technique changed to more abstract art when she began to study the philosophy of Arthur Wesley Dow, an American painter라고 했으므로 글의 내용과 일치한다. ④은 her work was first exhibited in 1917이라고 했으므로 글의 내용과 일치한다.

정답 ①

해석 ① Georgia O'Keeffe의 예술적 발전
② 자연이 Georgia O'Keeffe의 그림에 미치는 영향
③ Georgia O'Keeffe가 전통 미술보다 추상 미술을 선호한 이유

해설 Georgia O'Keeffe의 학력 사항과 화풍 등, 예술가로서 그녀의 생애에 관한 글이므로, 글의 주제로 가장 적절한 것은 ① the artistic development of Georgia O'Keeffe이다.

03   정답 ④

지문분석

Amelia Earhart, an American pilot, / was born in Kansas in 1897.
미국 비행사 Amelia Earhart는 / 1897년 Kansas에서 태어났다

Growing up, / Earhart went against / traditional gender roles.
자라면서 / Earhart는 반대했다 / 관습적인 성 역할에

She enjoyed playing basketball, / took a class on how to repair cars, / and even attended college / for a while.
그녀는 농구 하는 것을 즐겼다 / 자동차 수리 방법에 대한 수업을 들었다 / 그리고 심지어 대학에 다니기도 했다 / 한동안

During World War I, / Earhart volunteered / to care for injured soldiers / in Toronto, Canada, / ★ where she was able to watch / the pilots in the Royal Flying Corps / train.
1차 세계대전 동안 / Earhart는 자원했다 / 부상당한 군인들을 간호하기 위해 / 캐나다 Toronto에서 / 그곳에서 그녀는 볼 수 있었다 / 항공대 소속의 조종사들이 / 훈련하는 것을

When she later moved to California, / Earhart went on her first flight.
그녀가 나중에 California로 이동했을 때 / Earhart는 그녀의 첫 비행에 나섰다

She began to take flying lessons / afterwards / and purchased a plane, / nicknamed "the Canary," / in 1921.
그녀는 비행 강습을 받기 시작했다 / 이후 / 그리고 비행기 한 대를 구입했다 / "the Canary"(카나리아)라는 애칭을 붙인 / 1921년에

During her career, / Earhart set many flying records, / including becoming the first woman / to fly alone across the Atlantic.
그녀의 경력에서 / Earhart는 많은 비행 기록을 남겼다 / 최초의 여성이 되었다는 점을 포함하여 / 대서양을 단독 비행한

She was even given / a military award / by Congress / for her achievements.
그녀는 심지어 받았다 / 군 훈장을 / 미 의회로부터 / 그녀의 업적으로

In 1937, / Earhart disappeared / while on a flight around the world / and was presumed dead.
1937년 / Earhart는 실종되었다 / 세계를 누비는 비행을 하던 도중 / 그리고 사망한 것으로 추정된다

> ★ 독해가 쉬워지는 구문 풀이
>
> ~ where she was able to <u>watch</u> the <u>pilots in the Royal Flying Corps</u>
>   동사   목적어
> <u>train</u>.
> 목적격보어
>
> ⇨ watch는 목적격보어로 동사원형을 취할 수 있는 지각동사이므로 동사원형 train이 쓰였다.

어휘 go against ~에 반대하다, 거스르다 traditional 관습적인, 전통적인
volunteer 자원하다, 봉사하다 injured 부상당한, 다친
Royal Flying Corps (당시 영국군) 항공대 go on 나서다, 나가다
the Atlantic 대서양 military award 군 훈장 Congress 의회
achievement 업적, 성과 presume 추정하다

해석 미국 비행사 Amelia Earhart는 1897년 Kansas에서 태어났다. 자라면서, Earhart는 관습적인 성 역할에 반대했다. 그녀는 농구 하는 것을 즐겼고, 자동차 수리 방법에 대한 수업을 들었으며, 심지어 한동안 대학에 다니기도 했다. 1차 세계대전 동안, Earhart는 캐나다 Toronto에서 부상당한 군인들을 간호하기 위해 자원했는데, 그곳에서 그녀는 항공대 소속의 조종사들이 훈련하는 것을 볼 수 있었다. 그녀가 나중에 California로 이동했을 때, Earhart는 그녀의 첫 비행에 나섰다. 이후 그녀는 비행 강습을 받기 시작했고, 1921년에 "the Canary"(카나리아)라는 애칭을 붙인 비행기 한 대를 구입했다. 그녀의 경력에서, Earhart는 대서양을 단독 비행한 최초의 여성이 되었다는 점을 포함하여, 많은 비행 기록을 남겼다. 그녀는 심지어 그녀의 업적으로 미 의회로부터 군 훈장을 받았다. 1937년, Earhart는 세계를 누비는 비행을 하던 도중 실종되었고, 사망한 것으로 추정된다.

해설 She began to take flying lessons afterwards and purchased a plane, nicknamed "the Canary," in 1921을 통해 비행 강습을 받기 시작하면서 비행기 한 대를 구매했다고 했으므로, 글의 내용과 일치하지 않는 것은 ④ '비행 강습을 받았으나 본인 소유의 비행기는 없었다.'이다.

오답분석 ①은 Growing up, Earhart went against traditional gender roles라고 했으므로 글의 내용과 일치한다. ②은 During World War I, Earhart volunteered to care for injured soldiers in Toronto, Canada라고 했으므로 글의 내용과 일치한다. ③은 When she later moved to California, Earhart went on her first flight라고 했으므로 글의 내용과 일치한다. ⑤은 Earhart set many flying records, including becoming the first woman to fly alone across the Atlantic이라고 했으므로 글의 내용과 일치한다.

실력 UP! 미니 문제 03.

정답 The Life and Accomplishment of Amelia Earhart

04 정답 ③

지문분석

The largest flower / in the world / is called *Rafflesia arnoldii*, / found in the rainforests / of Indonesia.
가장 큰 꽃은 / 세계에서 / *라플레시아 아르놀디*로 불린다 / 우림에서 발견된다 / 인도네시아의

It can grow / up to three feet wide / and weigh / up to 15 pounds.
그것은 자랄 수 있다 / 폭이 3피트까지 / 그리고 무게가 나간다 / 15파운드까지

This flower is unusual / in that it is a parasitic plant / with no roots, stems, or leaves.
이 꽃은 특이하다 / 기생 식물이라는 점에서 / 뿌리도, 줄기도, 잎도 없는

★ Instead, / it attaches to a host plant / to obtain water and nutrients.
대신, / 그것은 숙주 식물에 달라붙는다 / 물과 영양분을 얻기 위해

Another odd feature / lies in its smell.
또 다른 이상한 특징은 / 그것의 냄새에 있다

It does not have the delicate fragrant scent / that is usually associated with flowers / but rather / smells like rotting meat.
그것은 섬세하면서도 달콤한 향기를 가지고 있지 않다 / 보통의 꽃에서 연상되는 / ~이 아니고 오히려 / 썩어가는 고기와 같은 냄새가 난다

This stink attracts tiny insects, / especially flies, / that help this flower / to reproduce.
이 악취는 작은 곤충들을 끌어들인다 / 특히 파리 / 이 꽃을 돕는 / 번식하도록

Botanists are not sure / why this flower evolved to be so big, / since its close relatives / only produce tiny flowers.
식물학자는 확실히 알지 못한다 / 이 꽃이 너무나 커지도록 진화한 이유를 / 이것과 가까운 계통의 식물들은 ~하기 때문에 / 작은 꽃들만 피운다

In this regard, / the flower is / somewhat of a mystery.
그러한 면에서 / 이 꽃은 ~이다 / 다소 불가사의한

★ 독해가 쉬워지는 구문 풀이

Instead, it attaches to a host plant **to obtain** water and nutrients.
                                              to부정사(~하기 위해서)

⇨ to obtain은 to부정사의 부사적 용법으로, 목적을 나타낸다.

어휘 rainforest 우림 wide 폭이 ~인 weigh 무게가 나가다
parasitic 기생의, 기생하는 stem 줄기 host 숙주 obtain 얻다
nutrient 영양분 odd 이상한, 색다른 delicate 섬세한
fragrant 달콤한, 향기로운 scent 향기 associate 연상하다
rot 썩다, 부패하다 stink 악취 reproduce 번식하다 somewhat 다소

해석 세계에서 가장 큰 꽃은 *라플레시아 아르놀디*로 불리고, 인도네시아의 우림에서 발견된다. 그것은 폭이 3피트까지 자라고 15파운드까지 무게가 나갈 수 있다. 이 꽃은 뿌리도, 줄기도, 잎도 없는 기생 식물이라는 점에서 특이하다. 대신, 그것은 물과 영양분을 얻기 위해 숙주 식물에 달라붙는다. 또 다른 이상한 특징은 그것의 냄새에 있다. 그것은 보통의 꽃에서 연상되는 섬세하면서도 달콤한 향기를 가지고 있지 않고, 오히려 썩어가는 고기와 같은 냄새가 난다. 이 악취는 이 꽃을 번식하도록 돕는 작은 곤충들, 특히 파리를 끌어들인다. 이것과 가까운 계통의 식물들은 작은 꽃들만 피우기 때문에, 식물학자는 이 꽃이 너무나 커지도록 진화한 이유를 확실히 알지 못한다. 그러한 면에서, 이 꽃은 다소 불가사의하다.

해설 이 글의 세 번째 문장 This flower is unusual in that it is a parasitic plant with no roots, stems, or leaves를 통해 이 꽃은 뿌리도, 줄기도, 잎도 없는 기생 식물이라는 것을 알 수 있으므로, 글의 내용과 일치하지 않는 것은 ③ '뿌리를 이용해 다른 식물에 기생한다.'이다.

오답분석 ①은 found in the rainforests of Indonesia라고 했으므로 글의 내용과 일치한다. ②은 weigh up to 15 pounds라고 했으므로 글의 내용과 일치한다. ④은 but rather smells like rotting meat라고 했으므로 글의 내용과 일치한다. ⑤은 This stink attracts tiny insects, especially flies, that help this flower to reproduce라고 했으므로 글의 내용과 일치한다.

실력 UP! 미니 문제 04.

정답 ①

해석 ① 라플레시아 식물의 색다른 특징들
② 기생 식물에 의해 활용되는 생존 방법들
③ 라플레시아 꽃의 크기가 큰 이유

해설 서식지, 생존 전략, 냄새 등, 라플레시아 꽃의 색다른 특징에 관한 내용의 글이므로, 글의 주제로 가장 적절한 것은 ① the odd features of the Rafflesia plant이다.

05 정답 ③

지문분석

Spanish explorer Juan Ponce de León / was born around 1460.
스페인 탐험가 Juan Ponce de León은 / 1460년경에 태어났다

He served as a soldier / before beginning his career / in exploration.
그는 군인으로 복무했다 / 경력을 시작하기에 앞서 / 탐험 분야에서

Historians believe / that his first voyage to the New World / was with Christopher Columbus / in 1493.
역사학자들은 생각한다 / 신대륙을 향한 그의 첫 번째 항해는 ~한 것으로 / Christopher Columbus와 함께 했다 / 1493년에

After that, / he worked as a captain / under a royal governor in that region.
이후에 / 그는 대위로 임명되어 일했다 / 그 지역 왕실 소속 총독 휘하의

Ponce de León was given permission / by the Spanish crown / to discover new lands and gold / while abroad.
Ponce de León은 허가를 받았다 / 스페인 국왕으로부터 / 신대륙과 황금을 찾도록 / 타지에 있는 동안

Eventually, / he decided / to search for a rumored magical spring / called the "fountain of youth."
마침내 / 그는 결심했다 / 소문으로만 듣던 신비로운 샘을 찾기로 / "젊음의 샘"이라 불리는

★ This expedition / resulted in / his reaching North America.
이 탐험은 / 결과를 불러왔다 / 그가 북아메리카에 도달하는

He became the first European / to travel to the area, / and he named the site Florida / for its plants and greenery.
그는 최초의 유럽인이 되었다 / 그 지역을 탐방한 / 그리고 그 지역을 Florida라고 이름 지었다 / 그 땅의 목초와 나무들을 보고는

He led more voyages / to explore the coastline, / but was killed by local natives / in 1521.
그는 더 많은 항해를 이끌었다 / 해안 지대를 탐사하고자 / 그러나 원주민들에 의해 죽임을 당했다 / 1521년에

★ 독해가 쉬워지는 구문 풀이

This expedition resulted in [**his reaching** North America].
　　　　　　　　　　　동명사의 의미상 주어

⇨ [ ]는 전치사 in의 목적어 역할을 하는 동명사구이다.
⇨ 동명사의 의미상 주어는 소유격 대명사(his)의 형태로 쓰이는 것이 일반적이나, 전치사 in의 목적어 자리이기도 하므로 목적격 him을 써도 된다. 두 경우 의미상 큰 차이는 없다.

[어휘] exploration 탐험 voyage 항해, 여행 captain (육군) 대위, 선장
royal 왕실의 governor 총독, 주지사 permission 허가, 허락
crown 국왕 rumor 소문이 돌다; 소문 spring 샘; 도약하다 fountain 샘, 분수
expedition 탐험 site 지역, 현장 greenery 나무, 푸른 잎
coastline 해안 지대 native 원주민의, 토착의

[해석] 스페인 탐험가 Juan Ponce de León은 1460년경에 태어났다. 그는 탐험 분야에서 경력을 시작하기에 앞서 군인으로 복무했다. 역사학자들은 1493년에 신대륙을 향한 그의 첫 번째 항해는 Christopher Columbus와 함께 했던 것으로 생각한다. 이후에, 그는 그 지역 왕실 소속 총독 휘하의 대위로 임명되어 일했다. Ponce de León은 타지에 있는 동안 신대륙과 황금을 찾도록 스페인 국왕으로부터 허가를 받았다. 마침내 그는 "젊음의 샘"이라 불리는 소문으로만 듣던 신비로운 샘을 찾기로 결심했다. 이 탐험은 그가 북아메리카에 도달하는 결과를 불러왔다. 그는 그 지역을 탐방한 최초의 유럽인이 되었으며, 그 땅의 목초와 나무들을 보고는 그 지역을 Florida라고 이름 지었다. 그는 해안 지대를 탐사하고자 더 많은 항해를 이끌었으나 1521년에 원주민들에 의해 죽임을 당했다.

[해설] Ponce de León was given permission by the Spanish crown to discover new lands and gold while abroad를 통해 타지에 있는 동안 신대륙과 황금을 찾도록 스페인 국왕으로부터 허가를 받았다고 했으므로, 글의 내용과 일치하지 않는 것은 ③ '스페인 국왕은 그가 신대륙과 황금을 찾도록 허가하지 않았다.'이다.

[오답분석] ①은 He served as a soldier before beginning his career in exploration이라고 했으므로 글의 내용과 일치한다. ②은 Historians believe that his first voyage to the New World was with Christopher Columbus in 1493라고 했으므로 글의 내용과 일치한다. ④은 he decided to search for a rumored magical spring called the "fountain of youth." This expedition resulted in his reaching North America라고 했으므로 글의 내용과 일치한다. ⑤은 He became the first European to travel to the area, and he named the site

Florida라고 했으므로 글의 내용과 일치한다.

실력 UP! 미니 문제 05.

정답 Ponce de León's Explorations in the New World

06
정답 ⑤

[지문분석]

The platypus is truly / one of the most unusual mammals / in the world.
오리너구리는 정말로 ~이다 / 가장 독특한 포유류 중 하나 / 세상에서

Native to Australia, / it is one of only two mammals / to lay eggs.
호주 태생인 / 이것은 단 두 종류의 포유류 중 하나이다 / 알을 낳는

The platypus has often been described / as a mix of / many different animals.
오리너구리는 종종 묘사되어왔다 / 혼합체로 / 많은 다양한 동물들의

It has / the bill and feet of a duck, / the body of an otter, / and the tail of a beaver.
그것은 가지고 있다 / 오리의 부리와 발 / 수달의 몸통 / 그리고 비버의 꼬리

Its appearance is so odd that / the first scientists / to see a dead one / in 1799 / thought it was a fake.
그것의 생김새는 너무 이상한 나머지 / 최초의 과학자들은 / 죽어 있는 한 마리의 오리너구리를 봤다 / 1799년에 / 그것이 가짜라고 생각했다

The platypus is a semi-aquatic animal / and hunts for food / at the bottom of rivers or streams.
오리너구리는 반수생동물이다 / 그리고 먹이를 사냥한다 / 강과 개울의 바닥에서

They are well-adapted to the water / and spend most of their time there.
그들은 물에 잘 적응한다 / 그리고 그들 시간의 대부분을 그곳에서 보낸다

★ Unlike the females, / which are harmless, / the males have poison / that can cause severe pain / to other creatures.
암컷들과 달리 / 위험하지 않은 / 수컷들은 독을 지니고 있다 / 극심한 고통을 유발할 수 있는 / 다른 생물들에게

★ 독해가 쉬워지는 구문 풀이

Unlike the females, [①**which are harmless**], the males have
　　　　　　　　선행사　　　　관계절
poison [②**that can cause severe pain to other creatures**].
선행사　　　　　　　　　　관계절

⇨ [①]은 선행사 the females를 수식하는 관계절이다.
⇨ [②]는 선행사 poison을 수식하는 관계절이다.

[어휘] mammal 포유류 native to ~태생의 bill 부리 otter 수달
appearance 생김새 fake 가짜의, 거짓의 aquatic 수생의 stream 개울
well-adapted 잘 적응한 harmless 위험하지 않은, 무해한 severe 극심한
creature 생물, 생명체

[해석] 오리너구리는 정말로 세상에서 가장 독특한 포유류 중 하나이다. 호주 태생인 이것은 알을 낳는 단 두 종류의 포유류 중 하나이다. 오리너구리는 종종 많은 다양한 동물들의 혼합체로 묘사되어왔다. 그것은 오리의 부리와 발, 수달의 몸통, 그리고 비버의 꼬리를 가지고 있다. 그것의 생김새는 너무 이상한 나머지 1799년에 죽어 있는 한 마리의 오리너구리를 봤던 최초의 과학자들은 그것이 가짜라고 생각했다. 오리너구리는 반수생동물이며 강과 개울의 바닥에서 먹이를 사냥한다. 그들은 물에 잘 적응하고 그들 시간의 대부분을 그곳에서 보낸다. 위험하지 않은 암컷들과 달리, 수컷들은 다른 생물들에게 극심한 고통을 유발할 수 있는 독을 지니고 있다.

[해설] 이 글의 마지막 문장 Unlike the females, which are harmless, the males have poison을 통해 위험하지 않은 암컷들과 달리 수컷들은 독을 지닌다고 했으므로 글의 내용과 일치하지 않는 것은 ⑤ '암컷과 수컷 모두 독을 지닌다.'이다.

실력UP! 미니 문제 06.

정답 ③

해석 ① 생존을 위한 적응 수단으로서의 생김새
② 오리너구리에 의한 숨겨진 위협
③ 오리너구리의 독특한 특징

해설 오리너구리의 생태와 독특한 특징에 관한 글이므로, 글의 주제로 가장 적절한 것은 ③ unique characteristics of the platypus이다.

07
정답 ③

지문분석

The Himalayan black bear / is a rare type / of Asiatic black bear.
히말라야곰은 / 희귀종이다 / 반달가슴곰의

They have a glossy black coat / and a unique white mark / shaped like a crescent moon / on their chest.
그들에게는 윤이 나는 검정 가죽이 있다 / 그리고 특유의 하얀 무늬(가 있다) / 초승달처럼 생긴 / 그들의 가슴에는

Their average length / is around 1.5 meters / and they can weigh / from 90 to 200 kilograms.
그들의 평균 몸길이는 / 대략 1.5미터이다 / 그리고 몸무게는 나갈 수 있다 / 90에서 200 킬로그램까지

In the summers, / they roam in China, Nepal, Russia, and Tibet, / while they descend to more tropical forests / in the winter months.
여름철에 / 그들은 중국, 네팔, 러시아 그리고 티베트를 떠돈다 / 반면 더욱 열대 우림 쪽으로 내려간다 / 겨울철에는

These bears mostly feed on plants, / but they occasionally eat small mammals / and even large animals / such as sheep and goats.
이 곰들은 주로 식물을 먹고 산다 / 하지만 그들은 때때로 작은 포유류를 먹기도 한다 / 비롯해 심지어 큰 동물들 / 양이나 염소와 같은

★ They have been a protected species / since 1977.
그들은 보호종으로 지정되었다 / 1977년 이래로

But like many animals today, / they are sadly being threatened / due to a loss of habitat and illegal hunting.
하지만 오늘날의 많은 동물들처럼 / 안타깝게도 그들은 위협받고 있다 / 서식지 감소와 불법 사냥(밀렵)으로 인해

★ 독해가 쉬워지는 구문 풀이

They **have been** a protected species **since** 1977.

⇨ 현재완료 표현인 have been은 과거 특정 시점으로부터 현재까지 이어지는 상황을 묘사하는데 주로 쓰이며, 특정 시점을 언급할 때는 전치사 since와 함께 쓴다.

어휘 rare 희귀한 glossy 윤이 나는 crescent moon 초승달
roam 떠돌다, 배회하다 descend 내려가다 feed on ~을 먹고살다
occasionally 때때로 mammal 포유류 threaten 위협하다 loss 감소, 소실
habitat 서식지 illegal hunting 불법 사냥, 밀렵

해석 히말라야곰은 반달가슴곰의 희귀종이다. 그들에게는 윤이 나는 검정 가죽이 있으며, 그들의 가슴에는 초승달처럼 생긴 특유의 하얀 무늬가 있다. 그들의 평균 몸길이는 대략 1.5미터이고 몸무게는 90에서 200킬로그램까지 나갈 수 있다. 여름철에 그들은 중국, 네팔, 러시아 그리고 티베트를 떠도는 반면 겨울철에는 더욱 열대 우림 쪽으로 내려간다. 이 곰들은 주로 식물을 먹고 살지만, 그들은 때때로 작은 포유류를 비롯해 심지어 양이나

염소와 같은 큰 동물들을 먹기도 한다. 그들은 1977년 이래로 보호종으로 지정되었다. 하지만 오늘날의 많은 동물처럼, 안타깝게도 그들은 서식지 감소와 불법 사냥(밀렵)으로 인해 위협받고 있다.

해설 In the summers, they roam in China, Nepal, Russia, and Tibet, while they descend to more tropical forests in the winter months를 통해 이 곰들은 여름과 달리 겨울철에는 더욱 열대 우림 쪽으로 내려간다고 했으므로, 글의 내용과 일치하지 않는 것은 ③ '여름철에는 열대 우림 지역으로 이동한다.'이다.

실력UP! 미니 문제 07.

정답 descend to more tropical forests

해석 Q: 지문에 따르면 히말라야곰은 겨울철에 무엇을 하는가?
A: 그들은 열대 우림으로 내려간다.

해설 ~ while they descend to more tropical forests in the winter months.에서 히말라야곰들이 여름에는 중국, 네팔, 러시아, 티베트를 떠돌다가 겨울철에는 열대 우림으로 내려간다는 것을 알 수 있다.

08
정답 ③

지문분석

Harry Houdini was born / in Budapest, Hungary / in 1874.
Harry Houdini는 태어났다 / 헝가리 Budapest에서 / 1874년에

His family immigrated to the United States / in 1878.
그의 가족은 미국으로 이민을 갔다 / 1878년에

To earn money for his parents, / Houdini began working in a circus / at the age of nine.
부모님을 위해 돈을 벌고자 / Houdini는 서커스단에서 일하기 시작했다 / 9살이라는 나이에

In 1894, / he launched his career / as a magician.
1894년에 / 그는 그의 경력을 시작했다 / 마술사로서

Although / his early magic tricks / were not popular with audiences, / he achieved fame / as an escape artist.
비록 / 그의 초창기 마술은 / 관객들에게 인기가 없었지만 / 그는 명성을 얻었다 / 탈출 곡예사로서

Throughout the early 1900s, / Houdini incorporated / several dangerous escapes / into his act.
1900년대 초반 동안 / Houdini는 포함시켰다 / 몇 가지의 위험한 탈출 묘기를 / 그의 연출에

His most famous trick / was called the Chinese Water Torture Cell, / which involved / being suspended upside down / in a locked container of water.
그의 가장 유명한 묘기는 / 중국 물고문 틀로 불렸으며 / 그것은 동반되었다 / 거꾸로 매달리는 상황이 / 잠긴 물통 안에서

In 1926, / Houdini started / a successful one-man show on Broadway / that featured / many of his most popular illusions and escapes.
1926년에 / Houdini는 시작했다 / 브로드웨이에서 성공적인 1인 공연을 / 특색으로 삼는 / 그의 가장 인기 있는 속임수와 탈출 묘기 다수를

★ Unfortunately, / he died that same year / after refusing to have surgery / because he did not want to cancel / a performance.
불행하게도 / 같은 해에 그는 사망했다 / 수술 받기를 거부한 이후 / 취소하고 싶지 않아서 / 공연을

★ 독해가 쉬워지는 구문 풀이

Unfortunately, he died that same year after refusing to have
 접속사 현재분사구문
surgery because he did not want to cancel a performance.

➡ 문맥상 '그가 수술 받기를 거부하다'라는 의미로, he가 refuse가 나타내는 '거절하는' 행위의 주체이므로 현재분사 refusing이 쓰였다. 분사구문 앞에 있는 접속사(after)는 의미를 명확하게 하기 위해 남았다.

[어휘] launch 시작하다 magician 마술사 audience 관객 achieve 얻다
fame 명성 escape 탈출 torture 고문 suspend 매달다
upside-down 거꾸로 container 통 one-man 1인의, 혼자 하는
feature 특색으로 삼다 illusion 속임수, 환상

[해석] Harry Houdini는 1874년에 헝가리 Budapest에서 태어났다. 그의 가족은 1878년에 미국으로 이민을 갔다. Houdini는 부모님을 위해 돈을 벌고자, 9살이라는 나이에 서커스단에서 일하기 시작했다. 1894년에 그는 마술사로서 그의 경력을 시작했다. 비록 그의 초창기 마술은 관객들에게 인기가 없었지만, 그는 탈출 곡예사로서 명성을 얻었다. 1900년대 초반 동안, Houdini는 그의 연출에 몇 가지의 위험한 탈출 묘기를 포함시켰다. 그의 가장 유명한 묘기는 중국 물고문 틀로 불렸으며, 그것은 잠긴 물통 안에서 거꾸로 매달리는 상황이 동반되었다. 1926년, Houdini는 그의 가장 인기 있는 속임수와 탈출 묘기 다수를 특색으로 삼는 성공적인 1인 공연을 브로드웨이에서 시작했다. 불행하게도, 같은 해에 그는 공연을 취소하고 싶지 않아서 수술 받기를 거부한 이후 사망했다.

[해설] Although his early magic tricks were not popular with audiences를 통해 그의 초창기 마술은 관객들에게 인기가 없다고 했으므로, 글의 내용과 일치하지 않는 것은 ③ '초기에 선보인 마술은 엄청난 인기를 끌었다.'이다.

[오답분석] ①은 His family immigrated to the United States in 1878이라고 했으므로 글의 내용과 일치한다. ②은 Houdini began working in a circus at the age of nine이라고 했으므로 글의 내용과 일치한다. ④은 In 1926, Houdini started a successful one-man show on Broadway라고 했으므로 글의 내용과 일치한다. ⑤은 he died that same year after refusing to have surgery라고 했으므로 글의 내용과 일치한다.

[실력 UP!] 미니 문제 08.

정답 ②

해석 ① Harry Houdini가 그의 일생 동안 극복했던 어려움
② 유명한 공연가 Harry Houdini의 생애
③ Harry Houdini에 의해 공연된 가장 유명한 마술

해설 이 글은 Harry Houdini의 출생, 공연가로서의 활동, 죽음 등 그의 생애에 대한 내용이므로, 글의 주제로 가장 적절한 것은 ① the life of famous performer Harry Houdini(유명한 공연가 Harry Houdini의 생애)이다.

CHAPTER 08 안내문 정보 파악하기

불변의 패턴 15
p.62
정답의 단서는 수치가 포함된 부분에 있는 경우가 많다.

기출 문제
정답 ②

지문분석

Waverly High School
Friendly Chess Tournament
Waverly 고등학교 친선 체스 토너먼트

Saturday, March 23, 10 a.m.
3월 23일 토요일 오전 10시

• Where: / Waverly High School auditorium
장소 / Waverly 고등학교 강당

• Entry Deadline: / March 22, 4 p.m.
참가 신청 마감 / 3월 22일 오후 4시

• Age Categories: / 7-12, 13-15, 16-18
연령 부문 / 7~12세, 13~15세, 16~18세

• Prizes: / Gold, Silver, and Bronze / for each category
상 / 금상, 은상, 동상 / 각 부문별

-Prize-giving Ceremony: / 3 p.m.
시상식 / 오후 3시

-Every participant will receive / a certificate for entry!
모든 참가자는 받을 것입니다 / 참가 증명서를

If you are interested, / enter online / at http://www.waverly.org.
관심이 있다면 / 온라인으로 참가를 신청하세요 / http://www.waverly.org에서

★ For more information, / visit our website.
더 많은 정보를 원하시면 / 저희 웹 사이트를 방문하세요

★ 독해가 쉬워지는 구문 풀이

For more information, **visit** our website.
 명령문의 동사원형

➡ 명령문은 주로 주어를 생략하고 동사원형으로 시작한다.

[어휘] friendly 친선의 entry 참가 category 부문 certificate 증명서

[해석]
Waverly 고등학교 친선 체스 토너먼트
3월 23일 토요일 오전 10시

• 장소: Waverly 고등학교 강당
• 참가 신청 마감: 3월 22일 오후 4시
• 연령 부문: 7~12세, 13~15세, 16~18세
• 상: 각 부문별 금상, 은상, 동상
  - 시상식: 오후 3시
  - 모든 참가자는 참가 증명서를 받을 것입니다!
관심이 있다면, http://www.waverly.org에서 온라인으로 참가를 신청하세요.
더 많은 정보를 원하시면, 저희 웹 사이트를 방문하세요.

[해설] Entry Deadline: March 22, 4 p.m.을 통해 참가 신청 마감은 3월 22일 오후 4시라는 것을 알 수 있으므로, 글의 내용과 일치하지 않는 것은 ② '참가 신청 마감은 3월 23일 오전 10시이다.'이다.

[오답분석] ①은 Where: Waverly High School auditorium이라고 했으므로 글의 내용과 일치한다. ③은 Prizes: Gold, Silver, and Bronze for each category라고 했으므로 글의 내용과 일치한다. ④은 Prize-giving Ceremony: 3 p.m.이라고 했으므로 글의 내용과 일치한다. ⑤은 Every participant will receive a certificate for entry라고 했으므로 글의 내용과 일치한다.

불변의 패턴 16

p.63

예외 조항 및 추가 정보와 관련된 선택지가 정답인 경우가 많다.

기출 문제

정답 ④

지문분석

Great Aquarium
Great 수족관

Opening Hours: / 10 a.m.-6 p.m., daily
개장 시간: / 매일 오전 10시-오후 6시

Last entry is at 5 p.m.
마지막 입장은 오후 5시입니다

Events 행사

Fish Feeding 물고기 먹이 주기	10 a.m.-11 a.m. 오전 10시-오전 11시
Penguin Feeding 펭귄 먹이 주기	1 p.m.-2 p.m. 오후 1시-오후 2시

Ticket Prices 티켓 가격

Age 나이	Price 가격
Kids (12 and under) 어린이 (12세 이하)	$25 25달러
Adults (20-59) 성인 (20-59세)	$33 33달러
Teens (13-19) 10대(13-19세) Seniors (60 and above) 노인 (60세 이상)	$30 30달러

*Ticket holders / will receive a free drink coupon.
티켓 소지자는 / 무료 음료 쿠폰을 받을 것입니다

Booking Tickets 티켓 예약

• ★ ALL visitors are required / to book online.
모든 방문객들은 요구됩니다 / 온라인으로 예약할 것이

• Booking will be accepted / up to 1 hour before entry.
예약은 받아질 것입니다 / 입장 1시간 전까지

★ 독해가 쉬워지는 구문 풀이

ALL visitors are required to book online.
　주어　　　　　동사

⇨ 주어 ALL visitors가 동사 require가 나타내는 '요구하는' 행위의 대상이므로 수동태 are required가 쓰였다. require는 to부정사를 목적격 보어로 취하는 5형식 동사이므로, 뒤에 있는 to book은 목적격보어이다.

어휘 holder 소지자, 보유자 book 예약하다 entry 입장, 출입

해석

Great 수족관

개장 시간: 매일 오전 10시-오후 6시
마지막 입장은 오후 5시입니다.

행사

물고기 먹이 주기	오전 10시-오전 11시
펭귄 먹이 주기	오후 1시-오후 2시

티켓 가격

나이	가격
어린이 (12세 이하)	25달러
성인 (20-59세)	33달러
10대(13-19세) 노인 (60세 이상)	30달러

* 티켓 소지자는 무료 음료 쿠폰을 받을 것입니다.

티켓 예약
• 모든 방문객들은 온라인으로 예약할 것이 요구됩니다.
• 예약은 입장 1시간 전까지 받아질 것입니다.

해설 티켓 가격에 대해 부연 설명하고 있는 부분의 *Ticket holders will receive a free drink coupon을 통해 티켓 소지자가 무료 음료 쿠폰을 받을 것임을 알 수 있으므로, 글의 내용과 일치하는 것은 ④ '티켓 소지자는 무료 음료 쿠폰을 받는다.'이다.

오답분석 ①은 Last entry is at 5 p.m.이라고 했으므로 글의 내용과 일치하지 않는다. ②은 Fish Feeding 10 a.m.-11 a.m.이라고 했으므로 글의 내용과 일치하지 않는다. ③은 Seniors (60 and above) $30라고 했으므로 글의 내용과 일치하지 않는다. ⑤은 Booking will be accepted up to 1 hour before entry라고 했으므로 글의 내용과 일치하지 않는다.

독해 만점 TEST

p.64

01 ④ 02 ④ 03 ③ 04 ⑤ 05 ③ 06 ③ 07 ⑤ 08 ③

실력 UP! 미니 문제

01. ⓐ intense ⓑ faulty
02. 전국 각지의 제품에서 자신의 그림을 보는 것
03. ⓐ recipe ⓑ supervise
04. introduce students to archery and encourage them to join the club
05. bring sneakers, a jacket, a bathing suit, and personal medicines
06. ⓐ renowned ⓑ charge
07. 학술 이벤트: 수학, 과학, 역사, 문학
    스포츠 이벤트: 계주, 깃발 잡기
08. 당신이 반드시 사랑하게 될 이 무료 야외 영화 감상 체험에 함께하세요

01

정답 ④

지문분석

Oberman Cordless Vacuum Cleaner
Oberman 무선 진공 청소기

Instructions:
사용법

• Fully charge.
완전히 충전하세요

• Remove / from charging pod.
분리하세요 / 충전용 거치대에서

• Press POWER button / to vacuum.
POWER 버튼을 누르세요 / 진공 청소하려면

• Press S button / for intense cleaning.
S 버튼을 누르세요 / 강력 청소를 하려면

• Press POWER button again / to turn off.
POWER 버튼을 다시 누르세요 / 전원을 끄려면

• Return / to charging pod.
가져다 놓으세요 / 충전용 거치대로

Safety guidelines:
안전 지침

• Always switch off / while charging.
항상 전원을 끄세요 / 충전 중에는

- Use / only Oberman attachments.
사용하세요 / Oberman사의 부속품만

- Do not use / on wet surfaces.
사용하지 마세요 / 젖어 있는 표면에

- ★ Do not use / if power cord is damaged.
사용하지 마세요 / 전원 코드가 망가졌다면

WARNING: / DO NOT attempt / to remove batteries.
경고 / ~하려고 하지 마세요 / 배터리를 분리하다

To change / faulty or old batteries, / take the appliance / to a certified Oberman service center.
교체하려면 / 불량이거나 오래된 배터리를 / 기기를 가져가세요 / Oberman 공인 서비스 센터로

★ 독해가 쉬워지는 구문 풀이

Do not use if power cord is damaged.
　　　　　부사절 접속사　　　　　현재시제

⇨ if가 이끄는 절이 조건의 의미를 나타내는 부사절이므로, 전원 코드가 망가진 것이 미래에 일어날 일이더라도 현재시제 is damaged로 쓴다.

[어휘] cordless 무선의 vacuum 진공 청소기; 진공 청소하다 instruction 사용법
charge 충전하다 remove 분리하다 pod 거치대 intense 강력한
guideline 지침 attachment 부속품 faulty 불량인 appliance 기기
certified 공인된

[해석]

Oberman 무선 진공 청소기

사용법:
- 완전히 충전하세요.
- 충전용 거치대에서 분리하세요.
- 진공 청소하려면 POWER 버튼을 누르세요.
- 강력 청소를 하려면 S 버튼을 누르세요.
- 전원을 끄려면 POWER 버튼을 다시 누르세요.
- 충전용 거치대로 가져다 놓으세요.

안전 지침:
- 충전 중에는 항상 전원을 끄세요.
- Oberman사의 부속품만 사용하세요.
- 젖어 있는 표면에 사용하지 마세요.
- 전원 코드가 망가졌다면 사용하지 마세요.
경고: 배터리를 분리하려고 하지 마세요. 불량이거나 오래된 배터리를 교체하려면, Oberman 공인 서비스 센터로 기기를 가져가세요.

[해설] Do not use on wet surfaces를 통해 젖어 있는 표면에는 사용하면 안 된다는 것을 알 수 있으므로, 글의 내용과 일치하지 않는 것은 ④ '바닥이 젖어 있더라도 사용할 수 있다.'이다.

[오답 분석] ①은 Press S button for intense cleaning이라고 했으므로 글의 내용과 일치한다. ②은 Press POWER button again to turn off라고 했으므로 글의 내용과 일치한다. ③은 Always switch off while charging 이라고 했으므로 글의 내용과 일치한다. ⑤은 To change faulty or old batteries, take the appliance to a certified Oberman service center라고 했으므로 글의 내용과 일치한다.

[실력 UP!] 미니 문제 01.

정답 ⓐ intense ⓑ faulty
해석 ⓐ 강한 에너지나 노력을 활용하는
　　 ⓑ 작동에 실패한, 또는 작동할 수 없는

지문분석

Patty's Pastries Logo Contest
Patty's Pastries 로고 대회

Do you dream of seeing your art / on products / across the nation?
당신의 그림을 보기를 꿈꾸시나요 / 제품에서 / 전국 각지의

★ By entering / the Patty's Pastries official logo contest, / you can turn this fantasy / into a reality!
참가함으로써 / Patty's Pastries의 공식 로고 대회에 / 당신은 이 꿈을 바꿀 수 있습니다 / 현실로

Entry dates: / July 1 – July 31
응모일: / 7월 1일 - 7월 31일

How: / Online submissions only
응모 방법: / 온라인 제출만 가능

Age and Region: / Open to all / (professionals and amateurs)
나이와 지역: / 누구나 참여 가능 / (전문가와 비전문가)

Requirements:
요건:

-One entry / per person
1개의 응모작 / 1인당

-No more than three colors
색상은 3개가 넘지 않도록

-Include slogan / ("Perfection in Pastries")
표어 포함하기 / ("페이스트리의 완벽함")

-Include mascot
마스코트 포함하기

-Round shape preferable
둥근 형태를 선호함

To enter, / please visit www.pattyspastries/logo.com.
참가하시려면 / www.pattyspastries/logo.com을 방문하세요

*Once you hit FINAL, / your design will be submitted / and cannot be changed.
일단 FINAL 버튼을 누르면 / 당신의 디자인이 제출될 것입니다 / 그리고 수정은 할 수 없습니다

★ 독해가 쉬워지는 구문 풀이

By **entering** the Patty's Pastries official logo contest, you can turn
전치사 전치사의 목적어
　　　　　(동명사)
this fantasy into a reality!

⇨ 명사 역할을 하여 전치사의 목적어 자리에 올 수 있는 동명사 entering 이 쓰였다.

[어휘] pastry 페이스트리 official 공식의 turn into ~을 ~로 바꾸다
entry 응모, 응모작 submission 제출 requirement 요건
slogan 표어 mascot 마스코트 preferable 선호하는 submit 제출하다

[해석]

Patty's Pastries 로고 대회

전국 각지의 제품에서 당신의 그림을 보기를 꿈꾸시나요? Patty's Pastries의 공식 로고 대회에 참가함으로써, 당신은 이 꿈을 현실로 바꿀 수 있습니다!
응모일: 7월 1일 - 7월 31일
응모 방법: 온라인 제출만 가능
나이와 지역: 누구나 참여 가능(전문가와 비전문가)
요건:
- 1인당 1개의 응모작

- 색상은 3개가 넘지 않도록
- 표어 포함하기("페이스트리의 완벽함")
- 마스코트 포함하기
- 둥근 형태를 선호함

참가하시려면, www.pattyspastries/logo.com을 방문하세요.
* 일단 FINAL 버튼을 누르면, 당신의 디자인이 제출될 것이며 수정은 할 수 없습니다.

[해설] Round shape preferable을 통해 둥근 형태를 선호한다는 것을 알 수 있으므로, 글의 내용과 일치하는 것은 ④ '회사는 원형의 로고를 선호한다.'이다.

[오답분석] ①은 Open to all(professionals and amateurs)이라고 했으므로 글의 내용과 일치하지 않는다. ②은 How: Online submissions only라고 했으므로 글의 내용과 일치하지 않는다. ③은 No more than three colors 라고 했으므로 글의 내용과 일치하지 않는다. ⑤은 Once you hit FINAL, your design will be submitted and cannot be changed라고 했으므로 글의 내용과 일치하지 않는다.

[실력 UP!] 미니 문제 02.

정답 전국 각지의 제품에서 자신의 그림을 보는 것
해설 전국 각지의 제품에서 당신의 그림을 보기를 꿈꾸는지 물어본 후 로고 대회에 참가함으로써 이 꿈을 현실로 바꿀 수 있다고 했으므로, (A)this fantasy(이 꿈)는 '전국 각지의 제품에서 자신의 그림을 보는 것'을 의미한다.

03 정답 ③

[지문분석]

Summer Cooking Class
여름 요리 교실

Come and join / our kid-friendly cooking class / to learn all about cooking / with fresh ingredients.
오셔서 참가하세요 / 저희의 어린이 전용 요리 교실에 / 요리에 관한 모든 것을 배우시려면 / 신선한 재료로 하는

We welcome / all future chefs / from ages 9-15.
저희는 환영합니다 / 모든 주방장 꿈나무들을 / 9세에서 15세까지의

When: / Mon-Fri, / August 13-17
언제 / 월-금 / 8월 13일-17일

Time: / 9 a.m. to 4 p.m. / (Lunch 12-1)
시간 / 오전 9시에서 오후 4시 / (점심시간 12시-1시)

Price: / $200 / per child / (personal apron included)
참가비 / 200달러 / 아동 한 명당 / (개인용 앞치마 포함됨)

What to expect:
기대하실 수 있는 것

-Learn / basic cooking techniques.
배우게 됩니다 / 기초적인 요리 기법들을

-Create / one main dish and one dessert / each day.
만들게 됩니다 / 주 요리 하나와 후식 하나를 / 매일

-Eat or take home / everything you make.
먹거나 집에 가져갈 수 있습니다 / 여러분이 만든 모든 것은

-Receive / a cookbook of all recipes / for free.
받게 됩니다 / 모든 조리법이 수록된 요리책을 / 무료로

★ All of our classes / are supervised and taught / by professional chefs.
저희의 모든 수업은 / 관리되고 교육됩니다 / 전문 주방장들에 의해

Parents are welcome / to attend and cook / with their children / on the last day of class.
부모님이 얼마든지 ~할 수 있습니다 / 참석해서 요리할 / 자녀들과 함께 / 수업 마지막 날은

★ **독해가 쉬워지는 구문 풀이**

All of our classes are supervised and taught by professional chefs.
　주어　　　　　복수동사　수동태
(All of + 복수명사)

⇨ 주어 All of our classes에서 All of는 동사가 of 뒤의 명사에 수 일치해야 하는 부분/수량표현이므로 복수명사 classes에 수 일치하는 복수동사 are가 쓰였다.
⇨ 주어 All of our classes가 동사 supervise가 나타내는 '관리하는' 행위의 대상이므로, 수동태 are supervised가 쓰였다.

[어휘] ingredient 재료　apron 앞치마　dessert 후식
supervise 관리하다, 지도하다　attend 참석하다

[해석]

여름 요리 교실
신선한 재료로 하는 요리에 관한 모든 것을 배우시려면 저희의 어린이 전용 요리 교실에 오셔서 참가하세요. 저희는 9세에서 15세까지의 모든 주방장 꿈나무들을 환영합니다.

언제: 월-금, 8월 13일-17일
시간: 오전 9시에서 오후 4시 (점심시간 12시-1시)
참가비: 아동 한 명당 200달러 (개인용 앞치마 포함됨)

기대하실 수 있는 것:
- 기초적인 요리 기법들을 배우게 됩니다.
- 매일 주 요리 하나와 후식 하나를 만들게 됩니다.
- 여러분이 만든 모든 것은 먹거나 집에 가져갈 수 있습니다.
- 모든 조리법이 수록된 요리책을 무료로 받게 됩니다.

저희의 모든 수업은 전문 주방장들에 의해 관리되고 교육됩니다. 수업 마지막 날은 부모님이 얼마든지 참석해서 자녀들과 함께 요리할 수 있습니다.

[해설] Receive a cookbook of all recipes for free를 통해 모든 조리법이 수록된 요리책을 무료로 받게 된다는 것을 알 수 있으므로, 글의 내용과 일치하지 않는 것은 ③ '조리법이 수록된 요리책은 따로 구매해야 한다.'이다.

[오답분석] ①은 We welcome all future chefs from ages 9-15이라고 했으므로 글의 내용과 일치한다. ②은 When: Mon-Fri라고 했으므로 글의 내용과 일치한다. ④은 All of our classes are supervised and taught by professional chefs라고 했으므로 글의 내용과 일치한다. ⑤은 Parents are welcome to attend and cook with their children on the last day of class라고 했으므로 글의 내용과 일치한다.

[실력 UP!] 미니 문제 03.

정답 ⓐ recipe　ⓑ supervise
해석 ⓐ 특정한 음식을 요리하는 데 사용되는 재료 및 조리법을 수록한 것
　　　ⓑ 집단이나 개인, 특히 특정한 과업에 대한 감독 또는 관리

04 정답 ⑤

[지문분석]

Brentwood College Archery Club
Brentwood 대학교 양궁 동아리

★ The Brentwood College Archery Club / will be holding a recruitment event / to introduce undergraduate students to archery / and / encourage them to join the club!
Brentwood 대학교 양궁 동아리는 / 신규 모집 행사를 개최할 것입니다 / 재학생들에게 양궁을 소개하기 위해 / 그리고 / 그들에게 동아리 가입을 권장하기 위해

Schedule
일정

-From 10:00 a.m. to 4:00 p.m. / on Saturday, September 26
오전 10시부터 오후 4시까지 / 9월 26일 토요일

Location
장소

-Brentwood College Archery Range
Brentwood 대학교 양궁 연습장

-Located at the south end / of the main athletic field, / just behind the gym
남쪽 끝에 위치해 있음 / 주 운동장의 / 체육관 바로 뒤

Activities
행사

-A demonstration of various archery techniques / by current club members
다양한 양궁 기술 시범 / 동아리 기존 회원들의

-A basic archery lesson / for interested students
기초 양궁 수업 / 관심 있는 학생들을 위한

* free hot dogs will be provided / for our attendees / from 12:30 to 1:30 p.m.
무료 핫도그가 제공될 것입니다 / 참석자들을 위한 / 12시 30분부터 오후 1시 30분까지

For more information, / please contact the club president / at 555-0349.
더 많은 정보를 위해서는 / 동아리 회장에게 연락해 주세요 / 555-0349로

★ 독해가 쉬워지는 구문 풀이

The Brentwood College Archery Club will be holding a recruitment event **to introduce** undergraduate students to archery **and (to) encourage** them to join the club!

➡ to부정사의 부사적 용법으로 사용된 to introduce와 to encourage는 등위접속사 and로 연결되어 병렬 구조를 이루며, to부정사구 병렬 구조에서 두 번째부터 나열된 to부정사는 to를 생략할 수 있다.

어휘 archery 양궁 hold 개최하다, 잡다 recruitment 모집
encourage 권장하다 undergraduate 재학생 range 연습장, 범위
athletic field 운동장 demonstration 시범 various 다양한
attendee 참석자

해석
Brentwood 대학교 양궁 동아리

Brentwood 대학교 양궁 동아리는 재학생들에게 양궁을 소개하고 동아리 가입을 권장하기 위해 신규 모집 행사를 개최할 것입니다!

일정
- 9월 26일 토요일 오전 10시부터 오후 4시까지

장소
- Brentwood 대학교 양궁 연습장
- 주 운동장의 남쪽 끝, 체육관 바로 뒤

행사
- 동아리 기존 회원들의 다양한 양궁 기술 시범
- 관심 있는 학생들을 위한 기초 양궁 수업

* 12시 30분부터 오후 1시 30분까지 참석자들을 위한 무료 핫도그가 제공될 것입니다.

더 많은 정보를 위해서는, 동아리 회장에게 555-0349로 연락해 주세요.

해설 For more information, please contact the club president at 555-0349를 통해 문의사항은 전화를 통해서 접수됨을 알 수 있으므로, 글의 내용과 일치하지 않는 것은 ⑤ '문의사항은 이메일을 통해서 접수된다.'이다.

실력 UP! 미니 문제 04.

정답 introduce students to archery and encourage them to join the club

해석 Q: 지문에 따르면 Brentwood College 양궁 동아리 모집 행사의 목적은 무엇인가?
A: 재학생들에게 양궁을 소개하고 그들에게 동아리 가입을 권장하기 위함이다.

해설 The Brentwood College Archery Club will be ~ to join the club에서 Brentwood College 양궁 동아리는 목적은 재학생들에게 양궁을 소개하고 그들에게 동아리 가입을 권장하기 위해 모집 행사를 열었다는 것을 알 수 있다.

05 정답 ③

지문분석

Evergreen Youth Adventure Camp
Evergreen 청소년 모험 캠프

Our annual youth camp / is a great place / to get an adventure in nature.
저희 청소년 연례 캠프는 / 최적의 장소입니다 / 자연 속에서 모험을 할

Campers can enjoy / all sorts of outdoor activities / including treasure hunts, making forts, and even rock climbing.
캠핑 참가자들은 즐길 수 있습니다 / 모든 종류의 야외 활동을 / 보물 찾기, 요새 만들기, 심지어 암벽 등반을 포함한

We hope / your little explorers will join us / this year!
저희는 기대합니다 / 여러분의 꼬마 탐험가들이 저희와 함께 하기를 / 올해에

When: / Tuesday, August 3 - Friday, August 6
시간 / 8월 3일 화요일 - 8월 6일 금요일

Where: / Evergreen Campground
장소 / Evergreen 캠핑장

Cost: / $150 per person / (camp t-shirt included)
참가비 / 1인당 150달러 / (캠프 티셔츠 포함)

Details:
세부사항

-This program is for children / ages 9-14
이 프로그램은 아동을 위한 것입니다 / 9-14세의

-All participants should bring / sneakers, a jacket, a bathing suit, and personal medicines.
모든 참가자들은 가져와야 합니다 / 운동화, 재킷, 수영복, 그리고 개인 상비약을

-Registration must be completed online / by July 20, / and a refund is only available / before July 25.
접수는 반드시 온라인에서 작성되어야 합니다 / 7월 20일까지 / 그리고 환불은 ~만 가능합니다 / 7월 25일 전에

-★ There will be a bonfire festival / that all parents are welcome to / on the final day of camp.
모닥불 축제가 있을 것입니다 / 모든 부모님들께서 얼마든지 함께하실 수 있는 / 캠프 마지막 날에

Visit www.Evgreencamp.com / for more information.
www.Evgreencamp.com에 방문하세요 / 더 많은 정보를 위해서는

★ 독해가 쉬워지는 구문 풀이

There will be a bonfire festival **that all parents are welcome to** on
　　　　　　　　　　　　　　　　　　 관계절
the final day of camp.

➡ 목적격 관계대명사 that은 선행사 a bonfire festival을 수식하는 관계절을 이끈다.

해석

Evergreen 청소년 모험 캠프

저희 청소년 연례 캠프는 자연 속에서 모험을 할 최적의 장소입니다. 캠핑 참가자들은 보물 찾기, 요새 만들기, 심지어 암벽 등반을 포함한 모든 종류의 야외 활동을 즐길 수 있습니다. 저희는 올해에 여러분의 꼬마 탐험가들이 저희와 함께 하기를 기대합니다.

시간: 8월 3일 화요일 - 8월 6일 금요일

장소: Evergreen 캠핑장

참가비: 1인당 150달러 (캠프 티셔츠 포함)

세부사항:

- 이 프로그램은 9-14세의 아동을 위한 것입니다.
- 모든 참가자들은 운동화, 재킷, 수영복, 그리고 개인 상비약을 가져와야 합니다.
- 접수는 반드시 7월 20일까지 온라인에서 작성되어야 하고, 환불은 7월 25일 전에만 가능합니다.
- 모든 부모님들께서 얼마든지 함께하실 수 있는 모닥불 축제가 캠프 마지막 날에 있을 것입니다.

더 많은 정보를 위해서는 www.Evgreencamp.com에 방문하세요.

해설 Cost: $150 per person (camp t-shirt included)을 통해 참가비에 캠프 티셔츠가 포함되어 있다는 것을 알 수 있으므로, 글의 내용과 일치하는 것은 ③ '캠프 활동 티셔츠는 참가비에 포함되어 있다.'이다.

오답분석 ①은 Campers can enjoy all sorts of outdoor activities ~ and even rock climbing이라고 했으므로 글의 내용과 일치하지 않는다. ②은 When: Tuesday, August 3 - Friday, August 6라고 했으므로 글의 내용과 일치하지 않는다. ④은 All participants should bring sneakers, a jacket, a bathing suit ~ 라고 했으므로 글의 내용과 일치하지 않는다. ⑤은 Registration must be completed online by July 20라고 했으므로 글의 내용과 일치하지 않는다.

실력UP! 미니 문제 05.

정답 bring sneakers, a jacket, a bathing suit, and personal medicines

해석 Q: 안내문에 따르면 참가자들은 어떤 물건들을 가져가야 하는가?
A: 모든 참가자들은 운동화, 재킷, 수영복, 그리고 개인 상비약을 가져오도록 권장된다.

해설 All participants should bring~에서 모든 참가자들은 운동화, 재킷, 수영복, 그리고 개인 상비약을 가져와야 한다는 것을 알 수 있다.

06 정답 ③

지문분석

Henry Bass Exhibition
Henry Bass Exhibition 전시회

Local renowned artist Henry Bass / will put on his 3rd exhibit / at the Tate Museum.
지역의 저명한 예술가인 Henry Bass는 / 그의 세 번째 전시회를 개최할 것입니다 / Tate 미술관에서

★Come / and appreciate / this unique artist and his latest works, / including five new pieces / created especially for our museum.
오세요 / 그리고 감상하세요 / 이 독특한 예술가와 그의 최신 작품들을 / 5점의 새로운 작품을 포함한 / 우리 미술관을 위해 특별히 제작된

Hours: / 9:00 a.m. to 8:30 p.m. / (closed on Mondays)
시간 / 오전 9시부터 저녁 8시 30분까지 / (월요일 휴관)

Exhibit Period: / March 1 to May 10
전시 기간 / 3월 1일부터 5월 10일까지

Admission:
입장료

-$12 / for adults
12달러 / 성인은

-Half price / for senior citizens(over 65) and students
절반 가격 / 노인(65세 이상) 및 학생들은

-No charge / for children under 8
무료 / 8세 미만 아동은

* Food or drink is not allowed / in the building.
음식 또는 음료는 허용되지 않습니다 / 건물 내에서

Guided tours / are only available with a reservation.
가이드 투어는 / 예약으로만 이용 가능합니다

No more than 6 people / per group.
6명 이내여야 합니다 / 그룹 당

Please call 523-0088 / for more information.
523-0088로 전화 주십시오 / 더 많은 정보를 위해서는

★ 독해가 쉬워지는 구문 풀이

Come and appreciate this unique artist and his latest works, [including five new pieces created especially for our museum].
                                        과거분사

⇨ [ ]는 주절 (Come ~ works)를 수식하는 분사구문의 부사절이다.
⇨ 수식 받는 명사구(five new pieces)가 '제작하는' 행위의 대상이므로 과거분사 created가 쓰였다.

해석

Henry Bass Exhibition 전시회

지역의 저명한 예술가인 Henry Bass는 Tate 미술관에서 그의 세 번째 전시회를 개최할 것입니다. 오셔서, 이 독특한 예술가와, 우리 미술관을 위해 특별히 제작된 5점의 새로운 작품을 포함한 그의 최신 작품들을 감상하세요.

시간: 오전 9시부터 저녁 8시 30분까지 (월요일 휴관)

전시 기간: 3월 1일부터 5월 10일까지

입장료:

- 성인은 12달러
- 노인(65세 이상)과 학생들은 절반 가격
- 8세 미만 아동은 무료

* 음식 또는 음료는 건물 내에서 허용되지 않습니다.

가이드 투어는 예약으로만 이용 가능합니다. 그룹 당 6명 이내여야 합니다. 더 많은 정보를 위해서는 523-0088로 전화 주십시오.

해설 Admission: Half price for senior citizens(over 65) and students를 통해 노인과 학생들의 입장료는 성인 입장료의 절반 가격인 6달러라는 것을 알 수 있으므로, 글의 내용과 일치하지 않는 것은 ③ '노인과 학생들의 입장료는 12달러이다.'이다.

오답분석 ①은 appreciate ~ including five new pieces created especially for our museum이라고 했으므로 글의 내용과 일치한다. ②은 Hours: 9:00 a.m. to 8:30 p.m. (closed on Mondays)라고 했으므로 글의 내용과 일치한다. ④은 Food or drink is not allowed in the building이라고 했으므로 글의 내용과 일치한다. ⑤은 Guided tours ~, No more than 6 people per group이라고 했으므로 글의 내용과 일치한다.

정답 ⓐ renowned ⓑ charge

해석 ⓐ 대체로 성과, 기술 또는 품질 때문에 사람들에게 인기 있거나 잘 알려진
　　 ⓑ 제품이나 서비스에 대해 지불해야 하는 금액

07
정답 ⑤

지문분석

Academic Olympics
Academic Olympics

★The Academic Olympics invites / all local middle school teams /
to compete in a match / against wits!
The Academic Olympics는 초대합니다 / 모든 인근 중학교 팀을 / 대회에 참가할 / 지성을 겨루는

Where: / Williamson University
장소 / Williamson 대학교

When: / May 6-8
시간 / 5월 6-8일

Teams:
팀

-Each school is allowed / 3 teams with eight members
각 학교는 인정됩니다 / 8명의 구성원으로 된 세 팀이

-There must be at least 2 members / from each grade
최소 2명의 구성원이 있어야 합니다 / 각 학년별로

Events: / about 2 hours / for each
행사 / 대략 두 시간씩 / 각각

May 6
5월 6일

•Math: / 9 a.m.　　•Science: / 2 p.m.
수학 / 오전 9시　　과학 / 오후 2시

May 7
5월 7일

•History: / 10 a.m.　　•Literature: / 3 p.m.
역사 / 오전 10시　　문학 / 오후 3시

May 8
5월 8일

•Sports Day / (relay race and capture the flag): / 11 a.m.
운동회 날 / (계주 및 깃발 잡기) / 오전 11시

Academic events will take place / in the Science Building / and
sporting events will take place / on the soccer field.
학술 이벤트는 열릴 것입니다 / 과학관에서 / 그리고 운동회는 열릴 것입니다 / 축구장에서

The team with the highest score / will be awarded a trophy, / and
all participants will get a small gift / as a souvenir.
가장 높은 점수를 받은 팀이 / 트로피를 받게 될 것입니다 / 그리고 모든 참가자들은 작은 선물을 받을 것입니다 / 기념품으로

★ 독해가 쉬워지는 구문 풀이

The Academic Olympics invites all local middle school teams [to
　　　　　　　　　　　　　　　　　　　　　　　　명사구
compete] in a match against wits!
to부정사

⇨ [ ]는 명사구 all local middle school teams를 수식하는 형용사 역할
을 하는 to부정사이다.

어휘 wit 지성, 지혜 literature 문학 take place 열리다, 일어나다

해석

Academic Olympics

The Academic Olympics는 지성을 겨루는 대회에 참가할 모든 인근 중학교 팀을 초대합니다!

장소: Williamson 대학교

시간: 5월 6-8일

팀:

- 각 학교는 8명의 구성원으로 된 세 팀이 인정됩니다
- 각 학년별로 최소 2명의 구성원이 있어야 합니다

행사: 각각 대략 두 시간씩

5월 6일
　•수학: 오전 9시　　•과학: 오후 2시
5월 7일
　•역사: 오전 10시　　•문학: 오후 3시
5월 8일
　•운동회 날 (계주 및 깃발 잡기): 오전 11시

학술 이벤트는 과학관에서 열릴 것이며 운동회는 축구장에서 열릴 것입니다.

가장 높은 점수를 받은 팀이 트로피를 받게 될 것이고, 모든 참가자들은 기념품으로 작은 선물을 받을 것입니다.

해설 all participants will get a small gift as a souvenir를 통해 모든 참가자들은 기념품으로 작은 선물을 받을 것이라는 것을 알 수 있으므로, 글의 내용과 일치하는 것은 ⑤ '참가자 전원에게 기념품이 지급된다.'이다.

오답분석 ①은 The Academic Olympics invites all local middle school teams ~ 라고 했으므로 글의 내용과 일치하지 않는다. ②은 There must be at least 2 members from each grade라고 했으므로 글의 내용과 일치하지 않는다. ③은 May 6 - Math: 9 a.m., Science: 2 p.m.라고 했으므로 글의 내용과 일치하지 않는다 ④은 Sports Day (relay race and capture the flag): 11 a.m.라고 했으므로 글의 내용과 일치하지 않는다.

정답 학술 이벤트: 수학, 과학, 역사, 문학
　　 스포츠 이벤트: 계주, 깃발 잡기

해설 학술 이벤트: Events의 Math: 9 a.m.~ Literature: 3 p.m.를 통해 Academic Olympics에서 진행하는 학술 이벤트로는 수학, 과학, 역사, 문학이 있다는 것을 알 수 있다.
　　 스포츠 이벤트: Events의 Sports Day (relay race and capture the flag): 11 a.m.를 통해 스포츠 이벤트로는 relay race(계주)와 capture the flag(깃발 잡기)가 있다는 것을 알 수 있다.

08
정답 ③

지문분석

Movies in the Park
공원 속 영화 감상

Aurora County's famous Movies in the Park / will soon begin.
Aurora 주의 유명한 공원 속 영화 감상 / 곧 개최될 것입니다

Join us / in this free cinematic outdoor experience / that you are
sure to love.
함께 하세요 / 이 무료 야외 영화 감상 체험에 / 당신이 반드시 사랑하게 될

Where: / Heritage Park
장소 / Heritage 공원

When: / Every Friday evening at 8:30 p.m.
시간 / 매주 금요일 밤 8시 30분

You are allowed to bring:
여러분은 가져오실 수 있습니다

-Chairs, picnic tables, or blankets
의자, 피크닉 테이블 또는 담요

-Snacks and drinks
간식과 음료

-Pets(must be kept in cage)
반려동물(반드시 이동장에 넣어 두어야 함)

Facilities / available on site:
시설물들 / 현장에서 사용 가능한

-Restrooms and drinking fountains
화장실 및 식수대

-Medical tent / for emergencies
구호 천막 / 응급 상황을 대비한

-Food trucks and vending machines
푸드 트럭과 자판기

Park Guidelines:
공원 지침

-★ Tents can only be set up / in reserved areas
텐트는 ~만 설치될 수 있습니다 / 지정된 장소에

-Smoking and drinking are not permitted
흡연과 음주는 허용되지 않습니다

For a full schedule of movies, / visit www.auroramoviespark.com.
전체 영화 상영 표를 보려면 / www.auroramoviespark.com에 방문하세요

★ 독해가 쉬워지는 구문 풀이

Tents can only be set up in reserved areas
허가의 의미

⇨ 조동사 can은 문맥에 따라 능력, 요청, 허가 등 다양한 의미를 내포할 수 있으며, 여기서는 텐트 설치에 대한 '허가'의 의미로 사용되었다.

[어휘] cinematic 영화의 cage 이동장, 우리, 새장 emergency 응급 상황
reserved 지정된 permit 허용하다, 허락하다

[해석]

공원 속 영화 감상

Aurora 주의 유명한 공원 속 영화 감상이 곧 개최될 것입니다. 당신이 반드시 사랑하게 될 이 무료 야외 영화 감상 체험에 함께하세요.
장소: Heritage 공원
시간: 매주 금요일 밤 8시 30분

여러분은 가져오실 수 있습니다:
- 의자, 피크닉 테이블 또는 담요
- 간식과 음료
- 반려 동물(반드시 이동장에 넣어 두어야 함)

현장에서 사용 가능한 시설물들:
- 화장실 및 식수대
- 응급 상황을 대비한 구호 천막
- 푸드 트럭과 자판기

공원 지침:
- 텐트는 지정된 장소에만 설치될 수 있습니다
- 흡연과 음주는 허용되지 않습니다

전체 영화 상영 표를 보려면, www.auroramoviespark.com에 방문하세요.

[해설] You are allowed to bring: Pets(must be kept in cage)를 통해 반려 동물을 이동장에 넣어 둔 채로 데려올 수 있다는 것을 알 수 있으므로, 글의 내용과 일치하지 않는 것은 ③ '반려동물은 데려올 수 없다.'이다.

[오답분석] ①은 Join us in this free cinematic outdoor experience ~ 라고 했으므로 글의 내용과 일치한다. ②은 When: Every Friday evening at 8:30 p.m이라고 했으므로 글의 내용과 일치한다. ④은 Facilities available on site: Restrooms and drinking fountains라고 했으므로 글의 내용과 일치한다. ⑤은 Tents can only be set up in reserved areas라고 했으므로 글의 내용과 일치한다.

[실력 UP!] 미니 문제 08.

[정답] 당신이 반드시 사랑하게 될 이 무료 야외 영화 감상 체험에 함께하세요

 **REVIEW TEST** CHAPTER 05-08   p.68

01 ④	02 ④	03 ②	04 ④	05 ③	06 ⑤	07 ⑤	08 ②
09 ④	10 ④						

---

01   정답 ④

[지문분석]

April Tree Sale
4월의 나무 할인

Come / and take advantage of / our first tree sale!
오세요 / 그래서 즐기세요 / 우리의 첫 번째 나무 할인 행사를

Don't miss out on / some great deals / that will make your backyard beautiful.
놓치지 마세요 / 몇몇의 좋은 거래들을 / 당신의 뒷마당을 아름답게 만들

Sale period:
할인 기간

April 1 – April 20
4월 1일 - 4월 20일

How to Make a Purchase:
구매하는 법

1. Visit / our store next to Woodridge Park
방문하세요 / Woodridge 공원 옆에 있는 우리 가게에

2. Select / up to three trees / (all trees are $20 each)
고르세요 / 나무를 세 그루까지 / 모든 나무는 각각 20달러입니다

3. Pay with cash / (plant pot not included)
현금으로 결제하세요 / (화분은 포함되지 않음)

4. Leave your address and contact number / for delivery
당신의 주소와 연락처를 남기세요 / 배송을 위해

Delivery Process:
배송 절차

1. ★ Deliveries will be made / Tuesdays and Fridays
배송은 될 것입니다 / 화요일과 금요일마다

2. You will receive a message / on the day before delivery
당신은 메시지를 받을 것입니다 / 배송 전날에

3. The delivery takes about 3~4 days / on average
배송은 3~4일이 걸립니다 / 평균적으로

* An extra fee will be charged / for delivery / to islands and mountain areas
추가 금액이 부과될 것입니다 / 배송에는 / 도서 및 산간 지역

Please call 320-9900 / for more information.
320-9900로 전화주세요 / 더 많은 정보를 위해서는

Deliveries will be made Tuesdays and Fridays
　　　　　　　　수동태

⇨ 주어 Deliveries가 동사 made가 나타내는 '하는' 행위의 대상이므로, 수동태 be made가 온 것이 적절하다.

[어휘] sale 할인, 판매　take advantage of 즐기다, 이용하다, 활용하다
deal 거래, 물건　backyard 뒷마당　up to ~까지　plant pot 화분
on average 평균적으로

[해석]

4월의 나무 할인

오셔서 우리의 첫 번째 나무 할인 행사를 즐기세요! 당신의 뒷마당을 아름답게 만들 몇몇 좋은 거래들을 놓치지 마세요.

할인 기간:
4월 1일 - 4월 20일

구매하는 법:
1. Woodridge 공원 옆에 있는 우리 가게에 방문하세요
2. 나무를 세 그루까지 고르세요 (모든 나무는 각각 20달러입니다)
3. 현금으로 결제하세요 (화분은 포함되지 않음)
4. 배송을 위해 당신의 주소와 연락처를 남기세요

배송 절차:
1. 배송은 화요일과 금요일마다 될 것입니다
2. 당신은 배송 전날에 메시지를 받을 것입니다
3. 배송은 평균적으로 3~4일이 걸립니다

* 도서 및 산간 지역 배송에는 추가 금액이 부과될 것입니다

더 많은 정보를 위해서는 320-9900로 전화주세요.

[해설] Deliveries will be made Tuesdays and Fridays를 통해 배송은 화요일과 금요일마다 된다는 것을 알 수 있으므로, 글의 내용과 일치하는 것은 ④ '화요일 및 금요일마다 배송이 이루어진다.'이다.

[오답분석] ①은 Come and take advantage of our first tree sale이라고 했으므로 글의 내용과 일치하지 않는다. ②은 Sale period: April 1 - April 20이라고 했으므로 글의 내용과 일치하지 않는다. ③은 Pay with cash (plant pot not included)라고 했으므로 글의 내용과 일치하지 않는다. ⑤은 You will receive a message on the day before delivery라고 했으므로 글의 내용과 일치하지 않는다.

02　　　　　　　　　　　　　　　　정답 ④

지문분석

★ Three quarters of consumers / now say / that they're more likely to make a purchase / from a company / whose values they agree with, / and nearly 60 percent / are willing to stop buying / from ones / they find unethical.
소비자의 4분의 3은 / 이제는 말한다 / 그들은 더욱 구매를 할 것 같다고 / 기업으로부터 / 그들이 동의하는 가치관을 가진 / 그리고 약 60퍼센트는 / 구매하는 것을 그만둘 의향이 있다 / 기업에서 / 그들이 비윤리적이라고 생각하는

To stay competitive, / therefore, / companies need to project / that their company has strong values / like compassion / or a concern for the environment.
계속해서 경쟁력을 가지려면 / 따라서 / 기업들은 표명해야 한다 / 그들 기업이 견실한 가치들을 지니고 있다는 것을 / 연민과 같은 / 또는 환경에 대한 관심

Achieving this requires / more than preventing wrongdoing; / it requires / taking positive action.
이것을 이루어내는 것은 필요로 한다 / 잘못된 행위를 예방하는 것 이상을 / 그런데 그것은 필요로 한다 / 긍정적인 조치를 취하는 것을

For instance, / a company might build a reputation / of being "socially responsible" / by participating in recycling programs / or donating money to causes.
예를 들어 / 한 기업은 명성을 쌓을 수 있다 / "사회적으로 책임을 다한다"는 / 재활용 프로그램에 참여함으로써 / 또는 대의명분에 돈을 기부한다

This may sound like / what a charity does, / but these measures / lead to building trust / with customers.
이는 마치 ~처럼 들릴 수도 있다 / 자선 단체가 하는 일 / 하지만 이러한 조치들은 / 신뢰를 형성하는 것으로 이어진다 / 고객들과의

Good actions lead to a good response / from consumers / and more success / as a business.
좋은 행동들은 좋은 반응으로 이어진다 / 소비자들로부터의 / 그리고 더 많은 성공 / 기업으로서의

Three quarters of consumers now say that they're more likely to make a purchase from a company whose values they agree with, ~
　　　　　　　　　　　　　　　　소유격 관계대명사　　주어　동사

⇨ 문맥상 명사 values와 함께 '기업의 가치'라는 뜻을 나타내며, 뒤에 주어(they), 동사(agree with)만 있고 목적어는 없는 불완전한 절이 왔으므로, 「whose + 명사」를 만드는 소유격 관계대명사 whose가 쓰였다.

[어휘] unethical 비윤리적인　competitive 경쟁력을 가진, 경쟁의
compassion 연민, 동정　wrongdoing 잘못된 행위　reputation 명성, 평판
responsible 책임을 다할 수 있는　cause 대의명분, 원인　measure 조치, 대책
[선택지] popularity 인기

[해석] 소비자의 4분의 3은 이제는 그들이 동의하는 가치관을 가진 기업으로부터 더욱 구매를 할 것 같고, 약 60퍼센트는 그들이 비윤리적이라고 생각하는 기업에서 구매하는 것을 그만둘 의향이 있다고 말한다. [주제문] 따라서, 계속해서 경쟁력을 가지려면, 기업들은 그들 기업이 환경에 대한 연민이나 관심과 같은 견실한 가치들을 지니고 있다는 것을 표명해야 한다. 이것을 이루어내는 것은 잘못된 행위를 예방하는 것 이상을 필요로 하는데, 그것은 긍정적인 조치를 취하는 것을 필요로 한다. 예를 들어, 한 기업은 재활용 프로그램에 참여하거나 대의명분에 돈을 기부함으로써 "사회적으로 책임을 다한다"는 명성을 쌓을 수 있다. 이는 마치 자선 단체가 하는 일처럼 들릴 수도 있지만, 이러한 조치들은 고객들과의 신뢰를 형성하는 것으로 이어진다. 좋은 행동들은 소비자들로부터의 좋은 반응과 기업으로서의 더 많은 성공으로 이어진다.

① 책임감 있는 이미지를 만드는 것의 문제점
② 친환경적인 소재의 인기
③ 마케팅 도구로서의 설문조사
④ 고객이 가진 가치관에 부응하는 것의 이점
⑤ 환경을 보호하는 자선 단체들

[해설] 오늘날의 많은 고객들은 그들이 동의하는 가치관을 가진 기업으로부터 물건을 구매하기 때문에 기업들이 경쟁력을 가지려면 그들이 견실한 가치들을 지니고 있다는 것을 표명해야 하며, "사회적으로 책임을 다한다"는 명성을 쌓는 등의 조치를 취함으로써 고객들과의 신뢰를 형성해야 한다는 내용의 글이므로, 이 글의 주제로 가장 적절한 것은 ④ benefits of living up to customer's values(고객이 가진 가치관에 부응하는 것의 이점)이다.

[오답분석] ①의 '책임감 있는 이미지를 만드는 것의 문제점'은 긍정적인 조치를 취하는 것이 고객과의 신뢰 형성 및 기업의 더 많은 성공 등으로 이어진다는 글의 내용과 반대되는 내용이기 때문에 오답이다. ②, ⑤은 글의 일부를 포함하는 지엽적인 소재를 다루고 있는 오답이다. ③은 글과 관계없는 내용이므로 오답이다.

03

지문분석

You may know / that shopping while you are hungry can impair / your decision making, / but did you know / being lonely can pose / even more problems?

당신은 알 수도 있다 / 배고플 동안 쇼핑하는 것이 해칠 수 있다는 것을 / 당신의 의사결정을 / 하지만 알았는가 / 외로움이 야기할 수 있다는 것을 / 훨씬 더 많은 문제를

According to research / from the University of Iowa, / a feeling of loneliness can cause you / to shop impulsively / and make irresponsible financial decisions.

연구에 따르면 / 아이오와 대학교의 / 외로움은 당신이 ~하게 할 수 있다 / 충동적으로 물건을 사게 / 그리고 무책임한 금전적 결정을 내리게

This is because / a lack of social connections / makes us feel empty, / and causes us to look for substitutes.

이것은 ~하기 때문이다 / 사회적 관계의 결핍이 / 우리를 공허하게 느끼게 한다 / 그리하여 우리가 대체물을 찾게 만든다

★ Unconsciously, / we start to form / strong attachments to products / instead of people, / mistakenly thinking / we "need" items / we'll probably never use.

무의식적으로 / 우리는 형성하기 시작한다 / 물건에 강한 애착 / 사람 대신 / 잘못 생각하면서 / 우리는 물건이 "필요하다"고 / 우리가 아마 절대 사용하지 않을

The lonely shopper thus / tends to fill their shopping cart / with expensive and mostly useless objects / —a tendency / which can be both costly and ineffective.

따라서 외로운 쇼핑객은 / 그들의 쇼핑 카트를 채우는 경향이 있다 / 비싸면서도 주로 불필요한 물건들로 / 이는 경향이다 / 비용이 많이 들면서도 비효율적인

★ 독해가 쉬워지는 구문 풀이

Unconsciously, we start to form strong attachments to products instead of people, mistakenly thinking we "need" items we'll probably never use.
현재분사구문

⇨ 분사구문의 주어가 따로 없으므로 주절의 주어 we가 분사구문의 의미상 주어이다. we는 think가 나타내는 '생각하는' 행위의 주체이므로 현재분사 thinking이 쓰였다.

[어휘] impair 해치다, 약화시키다 pose 야기하다, 제기하다 loneliness 외로움 impulsively 충동적으로 irresponsible 무책임한 substitute 대체물 unconsciously 무의식적으로 attachment 애착 mistakenly 잘못하여 costly 비용이 많이 드는 ineffective 비효율적인 [선택지] strategy 전략 rationally 합리적으로 addiction 중독

[해석] 당신은 배고플 동안 쇼핑하는 것이 당신의 의사결정을 해칠 수 있다는 것을 알 수도 있지만, 외로움이 훨씬 더 많은 문제를 야기할 수 있다는 것을 알았는가? 아이오와 대학교의 연구에 따르면, 외로움은 당신이 충동적으로 물건을 사고 무책임한 금전적 결정을 내리게 할 수 있다. 이것은 사회적 관계의 결핍이 우리를 공허하게 느끼게 하여 우리가 대체물을 찾게 만들기 때문이다. 무의식적으로, 우리는 아마 절대 사용하지 않을 물건이 "필요하다"고 잘못 생각하면서, 사람 대신 물건에 강한 애착을 형성하기 시작한다. 따라서 외로운 쇼핑객은 비싸면서도 주로 불필요한 물건들로 그들의 쇼핑 카트를 채우는 경향이 있는데, 이는 비용이 많이 들면서도 비효율적인 경향이다.

① 더 합리적으로 물건을 사기 위해 당신이 이용할 수 있는 전략들
② 외로움은 당신이 쇼핑하는 방식에 어떻게 영향을 끼치는가
③ 당신이 물건을 더 많이 살수록, 더 외로워진다
④ 쇼핑 중독과 그것을 피하는 방법
⑤ 외로움: 건강상의 놀랄만한 위험에 관한 연구

[해설] 글의 핵심 소재는 '쇼핑'과 '외로움'이다. 외로움은 충동적으로 물건을 사고 무책임한 금전적 결정을 내리게 할 수 있다는 내용의 글이므로, 제목으로 가장 적절한 것은 ② How Being Lonely Affects the Way You Shop (외로움은 당신이 쇼핑하는 방식에 어떻게 영향을 끼치는가)이다.

[오답분석] ①, ④, ⑤은 글의 핵심 소재 중 하나만을 활용하여 혼동을 주는 오답이다. ③은 글의 핵심 소재인 '쇼핑'과 '외로움'을 모두 언급하였으나, 두 소재의 인과관계를 반대로 기술한 오답이다.

04

지문분석

Maya Lin was born / in Athens, Ohio / in 1959.
Maya Lin은 태어났다 / Ohio주 Athens에서 / 1959년에

She attended Yale University, / where she studied architecture and sculpture.
그녀는 Yale 대학을 다녔다 / 그곳에서 그녀는 건축과 조각을 공부했다

During her senior year at Yale, / Lin won a competition / for her design of an art piece / honoring people / who had fought in the Vietnam War.
Yale 대학 4학년을 보내던 중 / Lin은 대회에서 우승했다 / 예술 작품을 디자인한 것으로 / 사람들을 기리는 / 베트남 전쟁에 참가했던

Her memorial / included a black V-shaped wall / covered in the names of 58,000 people / who had died or went missing in the war.
그녀가 만든 기념비는 / V 모양의 검정색 벽을 포함했다 / 58,000명의 사람들의 이름으로 덮인 / 전쟁에서 죽거나 실종된

It was built / in Washington D.C. / and became / one of Lin's most famous accomplishments.
그것은 세워져 있다 / Washington D.C.에 / 그리고 되었다 / Lin의 가장 유명한 업적 중 하나가

In 1988, / Lin went on / to design another memorial / for the civil rights movement.
1988년에 / 이어서 Lin은 ~에 착수했다 / 또 다른 기념비를 디자인하는 것 / 미국 인권 운동에 관한

However, / after that, / she decided to focus on / other work, / including art / inspired by nature.
그러나 / 그 이후에는 / 그녀는 ~에 몰두하기로 결심했다 / 다른 작품들 / 예술 작품들을 포함하여 / 자연에서 영감을 받은

★ One of her pieces / called "wave fields" / features grass-covered land / that is shaped / to look like ocean waves.
그녀의 작품들 중 하나 / "wave fields"라 불리는 / 잔디로 덮인 땅을 특징으로 한다 / 조형된 / 마치 바다의 파도처럼 보이도록

Much of her modern work / tries to highlight / climate change.
그녀의 현대 작품들 중 대다수 / 주목하려고 한다 / 기후 변화

★ 독해가 쉬워지는 구문 풀이

One of her pieces **called** "wave fields" features grass-covered land
주어   동사
that is shaped **to look** like ocean waves.

⇨ 수식 받는 명사(One of her pieces)는 call이 나타내는 "부르는" 행위의 대상이므로 과거분사 called가 쓰였다.
⇨ to look은 to부정사의 부사적 용법으로, 목적의 의미를 나타낸다.

[어휘] attend 다니다, 참석하다 architecture 건축, 설계 sculpture 조각 senior 4학년의, 노령의, 선임의 competition 대회, 경쟁 honor ~을 기리다, 경의를 표하다 memorial 기념비 accomplishment 업적 inspire 영감을 주다, 격려하다 feature ~을 특징으로 하다, 특색이 되다 highlight 주목하다, 강조하다

[해석] Maya Lin은 1959년에 Ohio주 Athens에서 태어났다. 그녀는 Yale 대학을 다녔고, 그곳에서 그녀는 건축과 조각을 공부했다. Yale 대학 4학년을 보내던 중, Lin은 베트남 전쟁에 참가했던 사람들을 기리는 예술 작품을 디자인한 것으로 대회에서 우승했다. 그녀가 만든 기념비는 전쟁에서 죽거

나 실종된 58,000명의 사람들의 이름으로 덮인 V 모양의 검정색 벽을 포함했다. 그것은 Washington D.C.에 세워져 있으며, Lin의 가장 유명한 업적 중 하나가 되었다. 이어서 1988년에 Lin은 미국 인권 운동에 관한 또 다른 기념비를 디자인하는 것에 착수했다. 그러나, 그 이후에는 자연에서 영감을 받은 예술 작품들을 포함하여 다른 작품들에 몰두하기로 결심했다. 그녀의 작품들 중 "wave fields"라 불리는 하나는 마치 바다의 파도처럼 보이도록 조형된 잔디로 덮인 땅을 특징으로 한다. 그녀의 현대 작품들 중 대다수는 기후 변화에 주목하려고 한다.

해설 However, after that, she decided to focus on other work, including art inspired by nature를 통해 1988년 이후에는 자연에서 영감을 받은 예술 작품들을 포함하여 다른 작품들에 몰두했다고 했으므로, 글의 내용과 일치하지 않는 것은 ④ '1988년 이전까지는 주로 자연물에서 영감을 받은 작품에 매진했다.'이다.

오답분석 ①은 She attended Yale University, where she studied architecture and sculpture라고 했으므로 글의 내용과 일치한다. ②은 Lin won a competition for her design of an art piece honoring people who had fought in the Vietnam War라고 했으므로 글의 내용과 일치한다. ③은 It was built in Washington D.C. and became one of Lin's most famous accomplishments라고 했으므로 글의 내용과 일치한다. ⑤은 One of her pieces called "wave fields" features grass-covered land that is shaped to look like ocean waves라고 했으므로 글의 내용과 일치한다.

05 정답 ③

지문분석

The above graph shows / the ratio of exports to GDP / in three countries / over five years.
위 그래프는 나타낸다 / GDP 대비 수출 비율을 / 세 나라의 / 5년간

① In Israel, / the ratio of exports to GDP in 2016 / was higher than 10%.
이스라엘의 / 2016년 GDP 대비 수출 비율은 / 10퍼센트보다 더 높았다

② ★ Of the three countries, / Saudi Arabia had the highest ratio of exports to GDP / in 2017, / followed by Uzbekistan.
세 국가 중에서, / 사우디아라비아가 GDP 대비 수출 비율이 가장 높았다 / 2017년에 / 그리고 우즈베키스탄이 그 뒤를 이었다

③ While / Uzbekistan's ratio of exports / increased steadily / from 2016 to 2019, / it was still lower(→ higher) / than Israel's / in 2019.
~에도 불구하고 / 우즈베키스탄의 수출 비율은 / 지속적으로 증가했다 / 2016년부터 2019년까지 / 그것은 여전히 낮았다(→ 높았다) / 이스라엘의 수출 비율보다 / 2019년에는

④ Saudi Arabia's ratio of exports / during the years from 2016 to 2020 / never went below 20%.
사우디아라비아의 수출 비율은 / 2016년부터 2020년 동안 / 20퍼센트 아래로 내려간 적이 한 번도 없었다

⑤ In 2020, / Uzbekistan had the second highest / ratio of exports to GDP, / while Israel / had the lowest.
2020년에 / 우즈베키스탄은 두 번째로 높았다 / GDP 대비 수출 비율이 / 반면에 이스라엘은 / 가장 낮았다

★ 독해가 쉬워지는 구문 풀이

Of the three countries, Saudi Arabia had the highest ratio of exports to GDP in 2017, followed by Uzbekistan.
                                                          과거분사구문

⇨ 분사구문에 주어가 따로 없으므로 주절의 주어 Saudi Arabia가 분사구문의 의미상 주어이다. 문맥상 '우즈베키스탄이 그 뒤를 이었다'라는 의미로, Saudi Arabia가 follow가 나타내는 '뒤를 잇는' 행위의 대상이므로 과거분사 followed가 쓰였다.

어휘 ratio 비율   export 수출

해설 (%)

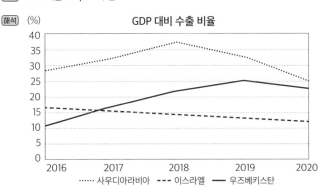

GDP 대비 수출 비율

······ 사우디아라비아   --- 이스라엘   — 우즈베키스탄

위 그래프는 세 국가의 5년간 GDP 대비 수출 비율을 나타낸다. ① 2016년 이스라엘의 GDP 대비 수출 비율은 10퍼센트보다 더 높았다. ② 세 국가 중에서, 사우디아라비아가 2017년에 GDP 대비 수출 비율이 가장 높았고, 우즈베키스탄이 그 뒤를 이었다. ③ 우즈베키스탄의 수출 비율은 2016년부터 2019년까지 지속적으로 증가했음에도 불구하고, 2019년에는 이스라엘의 수출 비율보다 여전히 낮았다(→ 높았다). ④ 2016년부터 2020년 동안 사우디아라비아의 수출 비율은 20퍼센트 아래로 내려간 적이 한 번도 없었다. ⑤ 2020년에 우즈베키스탄은 GDP 대비 수출 비율이 두 번째로 높았던 반면 이스라엘은 가장 낮았다.

해설 도표의 제목과 글의 도입부를 통해 이 도표가 세 국가의 5년간 GDP 대비 수출 비율에 관한 것임을 알 수 있다. 2016년부터 2019년까지 우즈베키스탄의 수출 비율은 지속적으로 증가하였고, 2019년에 우즈베키스탄의 수출 비율은 약 25%로, 이는 같은 해 15% 미만의 수출 비율을 기록한 이스라엘보다 큰 수치이므로, 도표의 내용과 일치하지 않는 것은 ③이다.

오답분석 ①은 이스라엘의 2016년 수출 비율이 15퍼센트 이상이었으므로 도표의 내용과 일치한다. ②은 2017년에 수출 비율은 사우디아라비아, 우즈베키스탄, 그리고 이스라엘 순으로 높았으므로 도표의 내용과 일치한다. ④은 2016년부터 2020년까지 사우디아라비아의 수출 비율은 20퍼센트 아래로 내려간 적이 없으므로 도표의 내용과 일치한다. ⑤ 2020년에 우즈베키스탄의 GDP 대비 수출 비율은 두 번째로 높고, 이스라엘은 가장 낮았으므로 도표의 내용과 일치한다.

06 정답 ⑤

지문분석

Bliss Mud Festival
Bliss 머드 축제

The Bliss Mud Festival celebrates / our town's unique natural attractions.
Bliss 머드 축제는 알립니다 / 우리 도시의 독특한 자연 명소를

Since the mid-1990s, / the festival has become / one of the most anticipated annual events / in the region.
1990년대 중반부터 / 이 축제는 되었습니다 / 가장 기대되는 연례 행사 중 하나가 / 지역에서

Come and join / thousands of other locals and tourists / at this year's festivities!
오셔서 함께하세요 / 수천 명의 다른 주민들 및 관광객들과 / 올해의 축제 행사에

When: / July 21-30
언제 / 7월 21-30일

Where: / Bliss Creek Campgrounds
어디에서 / Bliss Creek 캠핑장

Activities:
활동

★ -Enjoy a mud massage / to refresh your skin / and help you feel young again
머드 마사지를 즐기세요 / 피부의 생기를 되찾게 하는 / 그리고 다시 젊음을 느끼게 도와주는

-Relax in a warm mud pool / and feel your worries slip away
따뜻한 머드 풀장에서 휴식을 취하세요 / 그리고 걱정거리들이 사라지는 것을 느껴보세요

-Go down a mud slide / (not for kids under 5 years old)
머드 미끄럼틀을 타고 내려가보세요 / (5세 미만의 아이는 안 됨)

-Take part in a one-kilometer obstacle course / for the chance / to win a prize
1킬로미터의 장애물 경기에 참가하세요 / 기회를 (얻기) 위해 / 상품을 탈 수 있는

What to bring:
준비물

-Towels or clothes / that can be discarded
수건이나 옷 / 버려도 되는

-Fresh clothes and shoes / (for after the festival)
새 옷과 신발 / (축제 후의 용도로)

-Flip-flops or sandals
슬리퍼나 샌들

-Medication and sun protection
의약품 및 햇빛 차단용품

*A rock concert will be held nightly / on the last two days / of the festival.
록 콘서트가 밤마다 열릴 것입니다 / 마지막 이틀 동안 / 축제의

★ 독해가 쉬워지는 구문 풀이

Enjoy a mud massage [to refresh your skin and help you feel
　　　　　　　　　　　　to부정사　　　　　　　to를 생략한 동사원형
young again]

⇨ [ ]는 목적을 나타내는 to부정사의 부사적 용법이다.
⇨ to refresh와 to help는 등위접속사 and로 연결된 병렬 구조이며, 병렬 구조에서 두 번째부터 나열된 to부정사는 to를 생략할 수 있다.

[어휘] celebrate (세상에) 알리다, 선전하다　anticipated 기대되는, 대망의
festivity 축제 행사　refresh 생기를 되찾게 하다, 상쾌하게 하다
slip away 사라지다　take part in 참가하다　obstacle 장애물
flip-flop 슬리퍼, 끈을 끼워서 신는 샌들　nightly 밤마다

[해석]
Bliss 머드 축제
Bliss 머드 축제는 우리 도시의 독특한 자연 명소를 알립니다. 1990년대 중반부터, 이 축제는 지역에서 가장 기대되는 연례 행사 중 하나가 되었습니다. 오셔서 수천 명의 다른 주민들 및 관광객들과 올해의 축제 행사에 함께하세요!

언제: 7월 21-30일
어디에서: Bliss Creek 캠핑장
활동:
- 피부의 생기를 되찾게 하고 다시 젊음을 느끼게 도와주는 머드 마사지를 즐기세요
- 따뜻한 머드 풀장에서 휴식을 취하고 걱정거리들이 사라지는 것을 느껴보세요
- 머드 미끄럼틀을 타고 내려가보세요 (5세 미만의 아이는 안 됨)
- 상품을 탈 수 있는 기회를 (얻기) 위해 1킬로미터의 장애물 경기에 참가하세요
준비물:
- 버려도 되는 수건이나 옷
- 새 옷과 신발 (축제 후의 용도로)
- 슬리퍼나 샌들

- 의약품 및 햇빛 차단용품
*록 콘서트가 축제의 마지막 이틀 동안 밤마다 열릴 것입니다.

[해설] 부연 설명을 하는 부분인 *A rock concert will be held nightly on the last two days of the festival을 통해 록 콘서트가 축제의 마지막 이틀 동안 밤마다 열린다는 것을 알 수 있으므로, 글의 내용과 일치하지 않는 것은 ⑤ '행사 마지막 3일간은 록 콘서트가 예정되어 있다.'이다.

[오답분석] ①은 the festival has become one of the most anticipated annual events in the region이라고 했으므로 글의 내용과 일치한다. ②은 When: July 21-30라고 했으므로 글의 내용과 일치한다. ③은 Go down a mud slide (not for kids under 5 years old)라고 했으므로 글의 내용과 일치한다. ④은 What to bring과 Medication and sun protection이라고 했으므로 글의 내용과 일치한다.

07　　　　　　정답 ⑤

지문분석

Excess is rarely a good thing.
지나침이 좋은 것인 경우는 드물다

For athletes, / this is even true of exercise.
운동 선수들에게 있어 / 이것은 심지어 운동도 마찬가지이다

★ Sweating it out / and burning calories regularly / is healthy, / but excessive physical training / can take a major toll.
땀을 내는 것 / 그리고 규칙적으로 칼로리를 태우는 것은 / 건강에 좋다 / 하지만 과도한 체력 훈련은 / 큰 피해를 가져올 수 있다

Instead of driving individuals / to peak levels of performance, / pushing too hard / can cause them to regress.
개인을 이끄는 대신 / 최고 수준의 성과로 / 너무 강하게 밀어붙이는 것은 / 그들이 퇴보하도록 만들 수 있다

In extreme cases, / too much exercise / can even lead to serious injuries.
극단적인 경우 / 지나친 운동 / 심각한 부상으로 이어질 수도 있다

When people experience / the effects of overtraining, / they can begin having mood swings / and suffer from a lack of motivation.
사람들이 경험할 때 / 과도한 훈련의 영향을 / 그들은 감정 기복이 생기기 시작할 수 있다 / 그리고 동기 결핍을 겪는다

Weight loss / and an increased resting heart rate / are other possible consequences.
체중 감소 / 및 안정 시 심박수의 증가는 / 발생할 수 있는 또 다른 결과이다

Any further aggressive training / in this state / will only make things worse.
더 이상의 적극적인 훈련은 / 이 상태에서 / 상황을 악화시키기만 할 것이다

Therefore, / it is important for athletes / to moderate the amount of intensive physical activity / that they engage in.
그러므로 / 운동선수들에게 중요하다 / 격렬한 신체활동의 양을 조절하는 것은 / 그들이 하는

★ 독해가 쉬워지는 구문 풀이

Sweating it out and burning calories regularly is healthy, ~
　　　　　　주어　　　　　　　　　　　　　　단수동사

⇨ 땀을 내고 칼로리를 태우는 것은 의미상 하나의 덩어리로 해석되므로 단수 동사 is가 쓰였다.

[어휘] athlete 운동선수　be true of ~은 마찬가지이다, ~에 적용되다
take a toll 피해를 가져오다, 타격을 주다　peak 최고의　regress 퇴보하다
overtrain 과도하게 훈련하다　mood swing 감정 기복　motivation 동기
resting heart rate 안정 시 심박수　consequence 결과
aggressive 적극적인, 공격적인　[선택지] work out 운동하다
amateur 초보자, 비전문가　disadvantage 불이익, 단점

[해석] 지나침이 좋은 것인 경우는 드물다. 운동 선수들에게 있어, 이것은 심지어 운동도 마찬가지이다. [주제문] 규칙적으로 땀을 내고 칼로리를 태우는 것은 건강에 좋지만, 과도한 체력 훈련은 큰 피해를 가져올 수 있다. 개인을 최고 수준의 성과로 이끄는 대신, 너무 강하게 밀어붙이는 것은 그들이 퇴보하도록 만들 수 있다. 극단적인 경우 지나친 운동은 심각한 부상으로 이어질 수도 있다. 사람들이 과도한 훈련의 영향을 경험할 때, 그들은 감정기복이 생기기 시작하고 동기 결핍을 겪을 수 있다. 체중 감소 및 안정 시 심박수의 증가는 발생할 수 있는 또 다른 결과이다. 이 상태에서 더 이상의 적극적인 훈련은 상황을 악화시키기만 할 것이다. 그러므로 그들이 하는 격렬한 신체활동의 양을 조절하는 것은 운동선수들에게 중요하다.

① 운동하는 것으로는 충분하지 않다: 식이요법의 중요성
② 당신의 운동 목표를 달성하는 최고의 방법
③ 초보자를 위한 효과적인 훈련 전략
④ 운동선수들이 힘들게 경쟁하며 느끼는 압박
⑤ 운동선수들에게 있어 과도한 훈련의 불이익

[해설] 글의 핵심 소재는 '과도한 운동'과 '과도한 운동이 가져올 수 있는 피해'이다. 과도한 운동은 운동 선수들에게도 큰 피해를 가져올 수 있으며, 이것이 어떤 결과를 초래할 수 있는지에 대한 내용의 글이므로 글의 제목으로 가장 적절한 것은 ⑤ The Disadvantages of Overtraining for Athletes (운동선수들에게 있어 과도한 훈련의 불이익)이다.

[오답분석] ①, ②, ③, ④은 모두 글의 핵심 소재가 아닌 다른 소재들을 언급하여 혼동을 주는 오답이다. ①, ②은 글에서 자주 언급된 '운동'을 활용하여 혼동을 주는 오답이다. ③, ④은 글에서 언급된 소재인 '훈련', '운동선수'를 활용하여 혼동을 주는 오답이다.

08 　　　　　　　　　　정답 ②

지문분석

So-called financial technology / —or "fintech" / as it's usually known / —has completely altered the banking sector / in recent years.
이른바 금융 기술 / 혹은 "핀테크"는 / 일반적으로 알려진 대로 / 은행업 분야를 완전히 바꿔놓았다 / 최근 몇 년간

★ For instance, / fintech brought us / rapid and secure digital payment / via apps and digital-only banking services / that provide the full range of financing options / you would have needed to go / to a local branch for / in the past.
예를 들어 / 핀테크는 우리에게 가져다주었다 / 빠르면서도 안전한 디지털 결제 방식을 / 앱과 디지털 전용 뱅킹 서비스를 통해 / 폭넓은 금융 옵션을 제공하는 / 당신은 가야 했다 / 인근 지점에 / 과거였다면

Increasingly, / anyone with a smartphone / can get almost anything / a physical bank provides.
점점 / 스마트폰을 가진 누구든지 / 거의 모든 것을 얻을 수 있다 / 물리적 형태의 은행이 제공하는

This greater access / to financing and payment options / promises a smoother experience / for consumers / but also a tremendously profitable one / for banks, / which get more direct access / to customers.
이러한 더 많은 이용 기회는 / 금융 및 결제 옵션에 대한 / 더 원활한 경험을 제공한다 / 고객들에게 / 뿐만 아니라 엄청나게 이익이 되는 것(경험)을 / 은행에도 / 즉, 그것은(은행은) 더 직접적으로 접근할 수 있는 기회를 얻는다 / 고객들에게

In general, / this technology has revolutionized the industry, / increasing overall usability / and enhancing the financial experience.
전반적으로 / 이러한 기술은 업계에 혁명을 일으켰다 / 그리고 종합적인 편리함을 높이면서 / 그리고 금융 관련 경험을 향상시키면서

★ 독해가 쉬워지는 구문 풀이

For instance, fintech brought us ~ via apps and digital-only banking services [that provide the full range of financing options
　　　　　　　선행사1　　　　　　수식어1(관계절)　　　　　　선행사2
{you would have needed to go to a local branch for in the past}].
　　　　　수식어2(관계절)
⇨ [ ]는 선행사 services를 수식하는 관계절이다.
⇨ { }는 선행사 options를 수식하는 관계절이며, 전치사 for의 목적어를 대신하는 목적격 관계대명사 that 또는 which가 생략되었다.

[어휘] so-called 이른바, 소위　full range of 폭넓은　financing 금융, 재정　tremendously 엄청나게, 무시무시하게　revolutionize ~에 혁명을 일으키다, 혁명화하다　usability 편리함, 유용성　enhance 향상시키다, 높이다　[선택지] decision-making 의사결정　-friendly ~에 친화적인, ~에 적합한

[해석] 이른바 금융 기술, 혹은 일반적으로 알려진 대로 "핀테크"는 최근 몇 년간 은행업 분야를 완전히 바꿔놓았다. 예를 들어, 핀테크는 폭넓은 금융 옵션을 제공하는 앱과 디지털 전용 뱅킹 서비스를 통해 우리에게 빠르면서도 안전한 결제 방식을 가져다주었는데, 과거였다면 인근 지점에 가야 했었다. 점점, 스마트폰을 가진 누구든지 물리적 형태의 은행이 제공하는 거의 모든 것을 얻을 수 있다. 금융 및 결제 옵션에 대한 이러한 더 많은 이용 기회는 고객들에게 더 원활한 경험뿐만 아니라 은행에도 엄청나게 이익이 되는 경험을 제공하는데, 즉, 은행은 고객들에게 더 직접적으로 접근할 수 있는 기회를 얻는다. [주제문] 전반적으로, 이러한 기술은 종합적인 편리함을 높이고 금융 관련 경험을 향상시키면서 업계에 혁명을 일으켰다.

① 핀테크에 주의해야 하는 이유
② 더 나은 뱅킹을 만들어내는 핀테크 변화
③ 금융 은행의 의사결정 전략
④ 고객 친화적인 은행원의 주요한 자질
⑤ 고령층 고객들을 돕기 위한 은행의 핀테크 활용

[해설] 글의 핵심 소재는 '핀테크'와 그것의 '긍정적 요인'이다. 금융 기술인 핀테크가 종합적인 편리함을 높이고 금융 관련 경험을 향상시킴으로써 은행업 분야를 완전히 바꿔놓았다는 내용의 글이므로, 이 글의 주제로 가장 적절한 것은 ② fintech changes creating better banking(더 나은 뱅킹을 만들어내는 핀테크 변화)이다.

[오답분석] ①, ⑤은 글의 핵심 소재 'fintech'를 활용하여 혼동을 주는 오답이다. ③은 글에서 언급된 소재 'banks'를 활용하여 혼동을 주는 오답이다. ④은 글에서 언급되고 있지 않다.

09 　　　　　　　　　　정답 ④

지문분석

Famed photojournalist Robert Capa / was originally born / as Endre Friedmann / in Hungary.
유명한 보도 사진가인 Robert Capa는 / 원래 태어났다 / Endre Friedmann이라는 이름으로 / 헝가리에서

At the young age of 18, / Capa had to leave the country / for political reasons.
18세의 어린 나이에 / Capa는 그 나라를 떠나야 했다 / 정치적인 이유로

He moved to Germany, / where he began photography / to pay the bills.
그는 독일로 옮겨갔다 / 그곳에서 그는 사진 촬영을 시작했다 / 고지서의 돈을 내기 위해

Falling in love with this work, / he chose his career / as a photographer / but was forced to leave again / because of World War II.
이 일에 매력을 느끼면서 / 그는 그의 진로를 선택했다 / 사진가로서 / 하지만 그 나라를 떠나야만 했다 / 제2차 세계 대전으로 인해

This time / he settled in Paris.
이번에 / 그는 파리에 정착했다

Although Paris was Capa's home, / he continued to travel / to other countries / for work.
파리가 Capa의 거처였지만 / 그는 계속해서 옮겨 다녔다 / 다른 나라들로 / 일 때문에

★ In fact, / it was while he was working / in Spain / that he took / his famous photograph "The Falling Soldier."
실제로 / 그것은 바로 그가 일하던 때였다 / 스페인에서 / 찍은 것은 / 그의 유명한 사진인 / "쓰러지는 병사"를

He was there / during the Spanish Civil War.
그는 그곳에 있었다 / 스페인 내전 중에

This began his distinguished career / as a wartime photojournalist.
이것(이 사진)으로부터 그의 유명한 경력이 시작되었다 / 전시 보도 사진가로서의

Unfortunately, / Capa's commitment / to his job / also led to his death.
안타깝게도 / Capa의 헌신은 / 일에 대한 / 또한 그의 죽음으로 이어졌다

He stepped on a landmine / as he photographed soldiers / in 1954.
그는 지뢰를 밟았다 / 군인들의 사진을 찍다가 / 1954년에

He was just 40 years old.
그는 겨우 40세였다

★ 독해가 쉬워지는 구문 풀이

In fact, **it** was [while he was working in Spain] **that** he took his
　　　　　　　　　　　　강조 대상
famous photograph "The Falling Soldier."

⇨ 'it + be동사 + (강조의 대상) + that ~' 형태의 강조 구문이다. 강조 대상
에 명사, 부사, to부정사 등이 올 수 있으며, [ ]처럼 부사절 전체를 강조
할 수도 있다.

어휘 work one's way up 점점 출세하다, (회사에서 윗자리로) 차근차근 밟아 올라가다
Spanish Civil War 스페인 내전　distinguished 유명한, 차별화된
wartime 전시의; 전시　commitment 헌신

해석 유명한 보도 사진가인 Robert Capa는 원래 Endre Friedmann이라는 이름으로 헝가리에서 태어났다. 18세의 어린 나이에, Capa는 정치적인 이유로 그 나라를 떠나야 했다. 그는 독일로 옮겨갔고, 그곳에서 고지서의 돈을 내기 위해 사진 촬영을 시작했다. 이 일에 매력을 느끼면서 그는 사진가로서 그의 진로를 선택했지만 제2차 세계 대전으로 인해 다시 떠나야만 했다. 이번에 그는 파리에 정착했다. 파리가 Capa의 거처였지만, 그는 일 때문에 계속해서 다른 나라들로 옮겨 다녔다. 실제로, 그의 유명한 사진인 "쓰러지는 병사"를 찍은 것은 바로 그가 스페인에서 일하던 때였다. 그는 스페인 내전 중에 그곳에 있었다. 이것(이 사진)으로부터 전시 보도 사진가로서의 그의 유명한 경력이 시작되었다. 안타깝게도, 일에 대한 Capa의 헌신은 또한 그의 죽음으로 이어졌다. 그는 1954년에 군인들의 사진을 찍다가 지뢰를 밟았다. 그는 겨우 40세였다.

해설 it was while he was working in Spain that he took his famous photograph "The Falling Soldier." He was there during the Spanish Civil War를 통해 Robert Capa가 스페인에서 일하면서 스페인 내전 중에 찍은 사진 "쓰러지는 병사"로부터 전시 보도 사진가로서의 유명한 경력이 시작되었다고 했으므로, 글의 내용과 일치하지 않는 것은 ④ '스페인 내전과 관련한 작품으로 비난을 받았다'이다.

오답분석 ①은 Capa had to leave the country for political reasons라고 했으므로 글의 내용과 일치한다. ②는 he began photography to pay the bills라고 했으므로 글의 내용과 일치한다. ③은 Although Paris was Capa's home, he continued to travel to other countries for work라고 했으므로 글의 내용과 일치한다. ⑤는 Capa's commitment to his job also led to his death. He stepped on a landmine as he photographed soldiers ~ 라고 했으므로 글의 내용과 일치한다.

지문분석

Langston Wedding & Honeymoon Expo
Langston 결혼 및 신혼여행 박람회

Langston's largest wedding and honeymoon exhibition / will be returning / for its fifteenth year / at Morris Convention Center.
Langston 최대 규모의 결혼 및 신혼여행 박람회 / 돌아올 것입니다 / 15주년을 맞이하여 / Morris 컨벤션 센터에

★ Come and eat delicious food samples, / try on the finest dresses, / and meet the very best planners / to make your dream wedding a reality!
오셔서 맛있는 시식용 음식을 드세요 / 가장 멋진 드레스를 입어 보세요 / 그리고 최고의 플래너들을 만나보세요 / 당신이 꿈꾸는 결혼식을 현실로 만들어줄

Date:
날짜

Saturday, March 2 – Sunday, March 3
3월 2일 토요일 - 3월 3일 일요일

Activities:
행사들

-Wine and food tastings
와인 및 음식 시식회

-Gifts and prizes
선물 및 경품

-Bridal fashion show
결혼식 패션쇼

-Free photo / (limited to 1 photo / for each)
무료 사진 촬영 / (사진 1장으로 제한됨 / 한 사람당)

Cost:
금액

-$20 / (for both days)
20달러 / (양일간)

*Early bird special: / 50% discount will be given / if you book tickets / before February 10
얼리버드 스페셜 / 50% 할인을 제공받을 것입니다 / 입장권을 예매하신다면 / 2월 10일 전에

Call 555-6621, / or visit our website / to book your tickets today!
555-6621에 전화하세요 / 또는 우리 웹 사이트에 방문하세요 / 오늘 당신의 입장권을 예매하려면

★ 독해가 쉬워지는 구문 풀이

Come and **eat** delicious food samples, **try** on the finest dresses, and **meet** the very best planners to make your dream wedding a reality!

⇨ 동사 come, eat, try, meet는 등위접속사 and로 연결되어 병렬 구조를 이룬다.

어휘 expo 박람회, 전람회　exhibition 박람회, 전시회　reality 현실
tasting 시식회, 시음회　prize 경품, 상품
early bird special 얼리버드 스페셜, 선착 서비스　book 예매하다, 예약하다

해석
Langston 결혼 및 신혼여행 박람회
Langston 최대 규모의 결혼 및 신혼여행 박람회가 15주년을 맞이하여 Morris 컨벤션 센터에 돌아올 것입니다. 오셔서 맛있는 시식용 음식도 드시고, 가장 멋진 드레스도 입어 보시고, 당신이 꿈꾸는 결혼식을 현실로 만들어줄 최고의 플래너들도 만나보세요!

날짜:
3월 2일 토요일 - 3월 3일 일요일

행사들:
- 와인 및 음식 시식회
- 선물 및 경품
- 결혼식 패션쇼
- 무료 사진 촬영 (한 사람당 사진 1장으로 제한됨)

금액:
- 20달러 (양일간)

*얼리버드 스페셜: 2월 10일 전에 입장권을 예매하신다면 50% 할인을 제공받으실 것입니다

오늘 당신의 입장권을 예매하려면 555-6621에 전화하거나, 우리 웹사이트에 방문하세요!

[해설] Early bird special: 50% discount will be given ~ before February 10을 통해 2월 10일 전에 입장권을 예매하면 50% 할인을 제공받는다는 것을 알 수 있으므로, 글의 내용과 일치하는 것은 ④ '2월 10일 이전에는 입장권을 반값에 구매할 수 있다.'이다.

[오답분석] ①은 Langston's largest wedding and honeymoon exhibition will be returning for its fifteenth year ~라고 했으므로 글의 내용과 일치하지 않는다. ②은 Date: Saturday, March 2 - Sunday, March 3라고 했으므로 글의 내용과 일치하지 않는다. ③은 Activities: Free photo라고 했으므로 글의 내용과 일치하지 않는다. ⑤은 Call 555-6621, or visit our website to book ~ 라고 했으므로 글의 내용과 일치하지 않는다.

CHAPTER 09 어법상 틀린 것 찾기

불변의 패턴 17   p.72
밑줄은 동사, 분사, 동명사, to부정사에서 많이 나온다.

기출 문제   정답 ④

지문분석

Positively or negatively, / our parents and families / are powerful influences / on us.
긍정적이든 부정적이든 / 우리의 부모님 및 가족들은 / 강력한 영향을 주는 사람들이다 / 우리에게

★ But / even ① stronger, / especially when we're young, / are our friends.
하지만 / 훨씬 더 강력한 영향을 준다 / 특히 우리가 어렸을 때에는 / 우리의 친구들이

We often choose friends / as a way / of ② expanding our sense of identity / beyond our families.
우리는 종종 친구를 선택한다 / 방법으로 / 우리의 정체성을 확장시키는 / 가족의 범위를 넘어서

As a result, / the pressure to conform / to the standards and expectations / of friends and other social groups / ③ is likely to be intense.
그 결과 / 충족시켜야 한다는 압박감이 / 기준과 기대를 / 친구 및 다른 사회적 집단의 / 심해질 수도 있다

Judith Rich Harris, / who is a developmental psychologist, / ④ arguing(→ argues) / that three main forces shape our development: / personal temperament, our parents, and our peers.
Judith Rich Harris는 / 발달 심리학자인 / 주장한다 / 세 가지의 주요한 영향력이 우리의 발달을 형성한다고 / 개인의 기질, 부모, 또래

The influence of peers, / she argues, / is much stronger / than that of parents.
또래의 영향은 / 그녀가 주장하기를 / 훨씬 더 강력하다 / 부모의 영향보다

"The world / ⑤ that children share / with their peers," / she says, / "is what shapes their behavior / and modifies the characteristics / they were born with, / and hence determines the sort of people / they will be / when they grow up."
세상은 / 아이들이 공유하는 / 그들의 또래와 / 라고 그녀는 말한다 / 그들의 행동을 형성하는 것이다 / 그리고 특성을 바꾼다 / 그들이 가지고 태어난 / 그렇기 때문에 사람의 유형을 결정한다 / 그들이 될 / 그들이 자랐을 때

★ 독해가 쉬워지는 구문 풀이

But **even stronger**, especially when we're young, **are our friends**.
주격보어   삽입절   동사   주어

⇨ 형용사 주격보어 even stronger를 강조하기 위해 도치된 문장이며, 주어는 our friends, 동사는 are이다.

[어휘] influence 영향을 주는 사람·것, 영향   conform 충족시키다, 일치하다
social group 사회적 집단   force 영향력, 힘   peer 또래
modify 바꾸다, 수정하다

[해석] 긍정적이든 부정적이든, 우리의 부모님 및 가족들은 우리에게 강력한 영향을 주는 사람들이다. 하지만 특히 우리가 어렸을 때에는, 우리의 친구들이 훨씬 더 강력한 영향을 준다. 우리는 종종 가족의 범위를 넘어서 우리의 정체성을 확장시키는 방법으로 친구를 선택한다. 그 결과, 친구 및 다른 사회적 집단의 기준과 기대를 충족시켜야 한다는 압박감이 심해질 수도 있다. 발달 심리학자인 Judith Rich Harris는 세 가지의 주요한 영향력인 개인의 기질, 부모, 또래가 우리의 발달을 형성한다고 주장한다. 그녀가 주장하기를, 또래의 영향은 부모의 영향보다 훨씬 더 강력하다. "아이들이 그들의 또래와 공유하는 세상은 그들의 행동을 형성하며 그들이 가지고 태어난 특성을 바꾸고, 그렇기 때문에 그들이 자랐을 때 그들이 될 사람의 유형을 결정한다."라고 그녀는 말한다.

[해설] 절에는 반드시 주어와 동사가 있어야 하는데, 현재분사는 동사의 역할을 할 수 없고 동사 자리에는 '동사'나 '조동사 + 동사원형'이 와야 하므로, ④의 arguing을 argues로 고쳐야 한다.

[오답분석] ①은 주격보어 even stronger가 문장 앞쪽에 와서 동사 are가 주어 our friends 앞으로 도치되었으므로 형용사 stronger를 사용한 것은 어법상 적절하다. ②은 명사 역할을 하여 전치사 of의 목적어 자리에 올 수 있는 동명사 expanding을 사용한 것은 어법상 적절하다. ③은 주어가 단수 명사 the pressure이므로 단수동사 is를 사용한 것은 어법상 적절하다. ⑤은 뒤에 주어(children), 동사(share)만 있고 목적어가 없는 불완전한 절이 왔으며, 문맥상 '아이들이 그들의 또래와 공유하는 세상'이라는 의미이므로 선행사 The world를 수식하는 관계대명사 that을 사용한 것은 어법상 적절하다.

불변의 패턴 18   p.73
밑줄의 품사에 따라 확인해야 하는 것이 정해져 있다.

지문분석

In perceiving changes, / we tend to regard / the most recent
① ones / as the most revolutionary.
변화를 인식하는 데에 있어서 / 우리는 여기는 경향이 있다 / 가장 최근의 변화를 / 가장 혁
신적인 것으로

This is often inconsistent / with the facts.
이는 종종 일치하지 않는다 / 사실과

Recent progress / in telecommunications technologies / is
not more revolutionary / than ② what happened / in the late
nineteenth century / in relative terms.
최근의 발전은 / 통신 기술에서의 / 더 혁신적이지는 않다 / 일어났던 것보다 / 19세기 말
에 / 상대적으로

Moreover, / in terms of the consequent economic and social
changes, / ★the Internet revolution has not been as ③ important /
as the washing machine and other household appliances.
게다가 / 그 결과로 일어나는 경제적 및 사회적 변화의 측면에서 / 인터넷 혁명은 중요하지
는 않았다 / 세탁기와 다른 가전용 기기들만큼

These things, / by vastly reducing the amount / of work / needed
for household chores, / ④ allowing(→ allowed) women / to
enter the labor market / and virtually got rid of professions / like
domestic service.
이러한 것들은 / 양을 크게 줄임으로써 / 노동의 / 가사에 필요한 / 여성들이 ~할 수 있게 했
다 / 노동 시장에 진입하다 / 사실상 직종을 없애 버렸다 / 가사 서비스와 같은

We should not put the telescope backward / when we look into
the past / and underestimate the old / and overestimate the new.
우리는 망원경을 거꾸로 놓지 않아야 한다 / 과거를 들여다볼 때 / 그리고 예전 것을 과소
평가한다 / 그리고 새로운 것을 과대평가한다

This leads us / ⑤ to make all sorts of wrong decisions / about
national economic policy, / corporate policies, / and our own
careers.
이것은 우리를 이끈다 / 모든 잘못된 결정을 내리도록 / 국가의 경제 정책에 관해 / 기업의
정책 / 그리고 우리 자신의 진로

★ 독해가 쉬워지는 구문 풀이

~ the Internet revolution has not been as ③ important as the
washing machine and other household appliances.

⇨ 문맥상 '세탁기와 다른 가전용 기기들만큼 중요하지는 않은'이라는 뜻이
되는 것이 적절하고 앞뒤에 as ~ as가 있으므로, 원급 비교구문을 만들
수 있는 형용사의 원급 important가 쓰였다.

어휘 perceive 인식하다, 인지하다　revolutionary 혁신적인, 혁명적인
inconsistent 일치하지 않는, 모순된　telecommunications 통신
relative 상대적인　term 조건, 기간　appliance (가정용) 기기
chore 일, 하기 싫은 일　labor market 노동 시장　virtually 사실상, 가상으로
profession 직종, 직업　domestic 가사의, 국내의
underestimate 과소평가하다　overestimate 과대평가하다

해석 변화를 인식하는 데에 있어서, 우리는 가장 최근의 변화를 가장 혁신적인
것으로 여기는 경향이 있다. 이는 종종 사실과 일치하지 않는다. 통신 기
술에서의 최근의 발전은 상대적으로 19세기 말에 일어났던 것보다 더 혁
신적이지는 않다. 게다가, 그 결과로 일어나는 경제적 및 사회적 변화의 측
면에서, 인터넷 혁명은 세탁기와 다른 가전용 기기들만큼 중요하지는 않
았다. 이러한 것들은 가사에 필요한 노동의 양을 크게 줄임으로써 여성들
이 노동시장에 진입할 수 있게 했고, 사실상 가사 서비스와 같은 직종을
없애 버렸다. 우리는 과거를 들여다볼 때 망원경을 거꾸로 놓고 예전 것을
과소평가하고 새로운 것을 과대평가하지 않아야 한다. 이것은 우리가 국
가의 경제 정책, 기업의 정책, 그리고 우리 자신의 진로에 관해 모든 잘못
된 결정을 내리도록 이끈다.

해설 절에는 반드시 주어와 동사가 있어야 하는데, 현재분사는 동사의 역할을

할 수 없고 동사 자리에는 '동사'나 '조동사 + 동사원형'이 와야 하므로,
④의 allowing을 allowed로 고쳐야 한다.

오답분석 ①은 복수명사 changes를 가리키므로 복수대명사 ones를 사용한 것은
어법상 적절하다. ②은 주어가 없는 불완전한 절(happened ~ century)
을 이끌며 전치사 than의 목적어 자리에 올 수 있는 명사절 접속사 what
을 사용한 것은 어법상 적절하다. ③은 문맥상 '세탁기와 다른 가전용 기
기들만큼 중요하지는 않은'이라는 의미로, as ~ as 사이에 형용사의 원급
important를 사용한 것은 어법상 적절하다. ⑤은 동사 lead가 to부정사
를 목적격보어로 취하는 동사이므로 to make를 사용한 것은 어법상 적
절하다.

독해 만점 TEST　　　　　　　　　　　　　　p.74

01 ①　**02** ④　**03** ②　**04** ②　**05** ⑤　**06** ④　**07** ②　**08** ④

실력 UP! 미니 문제

01. ③
02. 운동용 신발을 살 때는 매장에서 직접 신어보는 것이 좋다.
03. ③
04. By 1975, the United States had banned all the chemicals
    mentioned in Carson's book
05. (A) motion sickness　(B) the brain
06. ②
07. (A) active-reading　(B) engagement
08. ⓐ practical　ⓑ extremely

01　　　　　　　　　　　　　　　　　정답 ①

지문분석

Everyone should try / keeping a gratitude journal.
모든 사람은 ~해 봐야 한다 / 감사 일기를 쓰는 것을

It is a good way / to reflect on / all of the things in life / ① what
(→ that) you might feel thankful for.
그것은 좋은 방법이다 / 되돌아보는 / 삶의 모든 것을 / 당신이 감사하다고 느낄 수 있는

Regularly writing in a gratitude journal / can make you more
② appreciative / of life / and help you maintain / a positive outlook.
감사 일기에다 주기적으로 글을 쓰는 것은 / 당신이 더 감사하게 만들 수 있다 / 삶에 대해 /
그리고 당신이 유지하도록 도와줄 수 있다 / 긍정적인 태도를

To start a gratitude journal / is easy.
감사 일기를 시작하는 것은 / 쉽다

There are no "rules" / and ★ you can write / as little or as much
as / you like.
"규칙"은 없다 / 그러니 당신은 쓸 수 있다 / ~만큼 적게 또는 많이 / 당신이 원하는

However, / I recommend / you ③ begin with something simple.
하지만 / 나는 추천한다 / 당신이 사소한 것으로 시작하기를

For instance, / try listing down / just a few small examples / of
things you may have experienced today / ④ for which you are
grateful.
예를 들어 / 적도록 해 봐라 / 몇 가지 작은 예시 정도를 / 당신이 오늘 경험했을 수도 있는
것의 / 당신에게 감사한

This might include anything / from beautiful weather, / a task
you performed well in school, / or even some small kindness /
⑤ shown to you / by a stranger or friend.
이것은 어떤 것이라도 포함할 수 있다 / 좋은 날씨부터 / 학교에서 잘한 일 / 또는 심지어 작
은 친절까지 / 당신에게 보여진 / 모르는 사람이나 친구로부터

○

~ you can write **as little or as much as** you like.
　주어　　동사　　└ 부사의 원급 ┘

⇨ 두 대상의 동등함을 나타내는 원급 표현은 'as/so + 형용사/부사의 원급 + as(~만큼 -한)'의 형태로 나타낼 수 있다.

[어휘] keep (일기·기록 등을) 쓰다　gratitude 감사, 고마움　journal 일기, 신문
reflect on ~을 되돌아보다, 반성하다　appreciative 감사하는
outlook 태도, 관점　grateful 감사하는　kindness 친절　stranger 모르는 사람

[해석] 〔주제문〕 모든 사람은 감사 일기를 써 봐야 한다. 그것은 당신이 감사하다고 느낄 수 있는 삶의 모든 것을 되돌아보는 좋은 방법이다. 감사 일기에다 주기적으로 글을 쓰는 것은 당신이 삶에 대해 더 감사하게 만들고 당신이 긍정적인 태도를 유지하도록 도와줄 수 있다. 감사 일기를 시작하는 것은 쉽다. "규칙"은 없으니 당신은 원하는 만큼 적게 또는 많이 쓸 수 있다. 하지만, 나는 당신이 사소한 것으로 시작하기를 추천한다. 예를 들어, 당신이 오늘 경험했을 수도 있는 당신에게 감사한 것의 몇 가지 작은 예시 정도를 적도록 해 봐라. 이것은 좋은 날씨부터, 학교에서 잘한 일, 또는 심지어 모르는 사람이나 친구로부터 당신에게 보여진 작은 친절까지 어떤 것이라도 포함할 수 있다.

[해설] ①은 앞과 뒤에 절이 하나씩 위치했으므로 접속사 혹은 관계대명사가 필요한 자리이다. 뒤에 나오는 절이 주어(you)와 동사구(might feel thankful for)만 있고 전치사 for의 목적어가 없으므로 불완전한 절을 이끌며, 선행사 things를 수식할 수 있는 관계대명사 that이 와야한다. 따라서 ①의 what을 that으로 고쳐야 한다.

[오답분석] ②은 동사 make의 목적어 you의 상태를 설명하는 목적격보어 자리이고, 보어 자리에는 명사나 형용사 역할을 하는 것이 올 수 있으므로 형용사 appreciative를 사용한 것은 어법상 적절하다. ③은 제안의 의미를 가진 동사 recommend의 목적어로 쓰인 that절이 문맥상 '시작하기를 추천한다'라는 의미로 어떤 일을 해야 한다는 당위성을 띠는 내용이므로 should를 생략한 동사원형 begin을 사용한 것은 어법상 적절하다. ④은 '전치사 + 관계대명사'에서 전치사는 선행사 또는 관계절의 동사(구)에 따라 결정되는데, 문맥상 '당신이 감사한 것'이라는 의미가 되어야 자연스럽고 선행사 things와 함께 쓰여 'you are grateful for things'라는 표현을 완성하는 전치사 for가 와야 하므로, for which를 사용한 것은 어법상 적절하다. ⑤은 수식 받는 명사 kindness가 shown이 나타내는 '보여주는' 행위의 대상이므로 과거분사 shown을 사용한 것은 어법상 적절하다.

[실력UP!] 미니 문제 01.

정답 ③

해석 ① 감사 일기에서 흔히 볼 수 있는 주제들
② 감사 일기의 높아지는 인기
③ 감사 일기를 쓰는 것에 대한 제안

해설 감사 일기를 쓸 때의 장점 및 쓰는 법을 알려주며 감사 일기를 쓸 것을 제안하는 글이므로, 이 글의 주제로 가장 적절한 것은 ③ suggestions for writing a gratitude journal이다.

02

정답 ④

[지문분석]

If you are in the market for / a new pair of athletic shoes, / forget about online shopping.
만약 당신이 ~을 사고 싶다면 / 새로운 운동용 신발 한 켤레를 / 온라인 쇼핑은 잊어라

When it comes to / ① buying athletic shoes, / you will get the best results / trying some on / in a store.
~에 관한 한 / 운동용 신발을 사는 것 / 최선의 결과를 얻을 것이다 / 몇 가지를 신어봐야 / 매장에서

★ The first thing you should do / when trying on shoes / is check to see / ② whether they fit comfortably / on your feet.
당신이 해야 할 첫 번째는 / 신발을 신어볼 때 / 보고 확인하는 것이다 / 그것이 편안하게 맞는지 / 당신의 발 둘레에

Walk, jump, or just move around / in the shoes / to get a good sense of / ③ what they might feel like / when you wear them.
걷고, 뛰고, 아니면 그냥 움직여봐라 / 신발을 신고 / ~에 대해 충분한 판단을 하기 위해 / 그것이 어떤 느낌이 들지 / 당신이 신발을 신었을 때

The right shoe should not only fit nicely / around the size and shape of your foot / but ④ offers(→ offer) good support / to prevent the risk of injury.
가장 적당한 신발은 잘 맞을 뿐만 아니라 ~일 것이다 / 당신의 발 크기와 모양에 / 제대로 지탱하게 해준다 / 부상의 위험을 막도록

Lastly, / try to find out / how long / the shoes might be expected to last, / since having to replace shoes often / could become ⑤ costly / over time.
마지막으로 / 알아내 보아라 / 얼마나 오랫동안 / 그 신발이 유지될 것으로 예상되는지 / 신발을 자주 바꿔야 하는 것은 ~할 수 있으므로 / 많은 돈이 든다 / 시간이 지남에 따라

The first thing {you should do} when trying on shoes is (to) check
　　　　　　　　　주어　　　　　　　　　　to부정사 보어
to see [whether they fit comfortably around your feet].

⇨ { }는 주어 thing을 수식하는 관계절로 목적격 관계대명사 that 또는 which가 생략되어 있다.
⇨ [ ]는 동사 see의 목적어 역할을 하는 명사절이다.

[어휘] athletic 운동 경기의, 체육의　when it comes to ~에 관한 한
comfortably 편안하게　sense 판단, 느낌　injury 부상
find out 알아내다, 발견하다　costly 많은 돈이 드는, 대가가 큰

[해석] 만약 당신이 새로운 운동용 신발 한 켤레를 사고 싶다면, 온라인 쇼핑은 잊어라. 〔주제문〕 운동용 신발을 사는 것에 관한 한, 매장에서 몇 가지를 신어봐야 최선의 결과를 얻을 것이다. 신발을 신어볼 때 당신이 해야 할 첫 번째는 그것이 당신의 발 둘레에 편안하게 맞는지 보고 확인하는 것이다. 당신이 신발을 신었을 때 어떤 느낌이 들지에 대해 충분한 판단을 하기 위해 신발을 신고 걷고, 뛰고, 아니면 그냥 움직여봐라. 가장 적당한 신발은 당신의 발 크기와 모양에 잘 맞을 뿐만 아니라, 부상의 위험을 막도록 제대로 지탱하게 해줄 것이다. 마지막으로, 신발을 자주 바꿔야 하는 것은 시간이 지남에 따라 많은 돈이 들 수 있으므로 그 신발이 얼마나 오랫동안 유지될 것으로 예상되는지 알아내 보아라.

[해설] not only A but (also) B 구문으로, B는 not only 다음에 나온 동사 fit와 병렬 구조를 이루어야 한다. 주어(The right shoe)가 단수주어이지만 not only 앞에 should가 왔으므로 동사원형 fit가 쓰였고, B자리에도 동사원형이 와야 한다. 따라서 ④의 offers를 offer로 고쳐야 한다.

[오답분석] ①은 When it comes to의 to는 전치사이므로 동명사 buying이 온 것은 어법상 적절하다. ②은 동사의 목적어 자리에는 명사 역할을 하는 것이 와야 하고, 문맥상 '그것이 편안하게 맞는지'라는 의미를 나타내는 명사절 접속사 whether를 사용한 것은 어법상 적절하다. ③은 목적어가 없는 불완전한 절(they might feel like)을 이끌며 전치사의 목적어 자리에 올 수 있는 명사절 접속사 what을 사용한 것은 어법상 적절하다. ⑤은 become은 주격보어를 취하는 동사이므로 형용사 costly를 사용한 것은 어법상 적절하다.

[실력UP!] 미니 문제 02.

정답 운동용 신발을 살 때는 매장에서 직접 신어보는 것이 좋다.

해설 운동용 신발을 살 때는 매장에서 직접 신어보면서 발 둘레에 잘 맞는지 등의 여러 사항들을 확인해보는 것이 좋다는 내용의 글이므로, 글의 요지는 '운동용 신발을 살 때는 매장에서 직접 신어보는 것이 좋다'이다.

정답 ②

지문분석

Many students have big dreams / for the future / but may be disappointed / when they realize / that dreams take time and effort / to achieve.
많은 학생들이 큰 꿈을 가지고 있다 / 미래에 대한 / 하지만 어쩌면 실망할 수 있다 / 그들이 알면 / 꿈은 시간과 노력이 든다는 것을 / 이루는 데

To succeed, / it is essential / that students not only ① be diligent / but also set goals for themselves.
성공하기 위해서 / ~이 필수적이다 / 학생들이 부단히 노력해야 할 뿐만 아니라 / 스스로 목표를 세워야 하는 것도

When it comes to goals, / the smaller, the better.
목표에 관한 한 / 작을수록 더 좋다

Setting small goals, / like reading an extra chapter / per night, / ② work(→ works).
작은 목표를 세우는 것은 / 추가로 한 단원을 읽는 것과 같은 / 밤마다 / 효과가 있다

That's because / small goals are more achievable, / and it usually only requires / a minimal amount of extra effort / to complete ③ them.
이는 ~하기 때문이다 / 작은 목표는 달성하기 더 쉽다 / 그리고 대개 ~만 요구한다 / 최소한의 추가적인 노력을 / 그것을 이루는 데

By contrast, / large goals tend to set the bar / too ④ high.
그에 반해서 / 큰 목표는 장애물을 세우는 경향이 있다 / 너무 높이

If students start out / with the goal of graduating / at the top of their class, / for instance, / they're likely to feel ⑤ overwhelmed / as soon as things go wrong.
만약 학생들이 시작한다면 / 졸업하는 목표를 가지고 / 반 1등으로 / 예를 들어 / 그들은 당황하게 될 것이다 / 일이 잘못되자마자

★ This can cause the student / to lose their motivation / and ultimately give up.
이것은 그 학생이 ~하게 만들 수 있다 / 동기를 잃게 / 그리고 결국 포기하게

★ 독해가 쉬워지는 구문 풀이

This can **cause** the student to lose their motivation **and** ultimately
　　　　　동사　　　목적어　　　목적격보어　　　　　등위접속사
　　　　　　　　　　　　　　　　(to부정사)

give up.
to를 생략한 동사원형

⇨ 동사 cause는 to부정사를 목적격보어로 취하는 5형식 동사이다.

⇨ to부정사구 to lose their motivation과 (to) ultimately give up은 등위접속사 and로 연결된 병렬 구조이며, to부정사구 병렬 구조에서 두 번째부터 나열된 to부정사는 to를 생략할 수 있다.

어휘 achieve 이루다, 성취하다　diligent 부단히 노력하는, 부지런한
for oneself 스스로, 자기를 위하여　bar 장애물, 막대기
overwhelm 당황하게 하다　go wrong 잘못되다　motivation 동기
ultimately 결국, 마침내

해석 많은 학생들이 미래에 대한 큰 꿈을 가지고 있지만, 꿈을 이루는 데 시간과 노력이 든다는 것을 알면 그들은 어쩌면 실망할 수 있다. 성공하기 위해서, 학생들이 부단히 노력해야 할 뿐만 아니라 스스로 목표를 세워야 하는 것도 필수적이다. (주제문)목표에 관한 한, 작을수록 더 좋다. 밤마다 추가로 한 단원을 읽는 것과 같은 작은 목표를 세우는 것은 효과가 있다. 이는 작은 목표는 달성하기 더 쉽고, 대개 그것을 이루는 데 최소한의 추가적인 노력만을 요구하기 때문이다. 그에 반해서, 큰 목표는 장애물을 너무 높이 세우는 경향이 있다. 예를 들어, 만약 학생들이 반 1등으로 졸업하는 목표를 가지고 시작한다면, 일이 잘못되자마자 그들은 당황하게 될 것이다. 이것은 그 학생이 동기를 잃고 결국 포기하게 만들 수 있다.

해설 ②의 주어 Setting small goals는 단수 취급하는 동명사구 주어이므로 ②의 work를 단수동사 works로 고쳐야 한다.

오답분석 ①은 주절에 요구의 의미를 가진 형용사 essential이 쓰인 문장의 that 절이 문맥상 '학생들이 ~해야 하는 것이 필수적이다'라는 의미로 어떤 일을 해야 한다는 당위성을 띠는 내용이므로 should를 생략한 동사원형 be를 사용한 것은 어법상 적절하다. ③은 대명사가 가리키는 대상이 복수명사 small goals이므로 복수대명사 them을 사용한 것은 어법상 적절하다. ④은 동사 set을 수식하고 있으므로 부사 high를 사용한 것은 어법상 적절하다. ⑤은 감각동사 feel의 주격보어 자리이며, 주어 they가 overwhelm이 나타내는 '당황하게 하는' 행위의 대상이므로 과거분사 overwhelmed를 사용한 것은 어법상 적절하다.

실력 UP! 미니 문제 03.

정답 ③

해석 ① 작은 목표만을 세우는 것의 문제점
② 학문적 성공을 추구하기 위한 방법들
③ 목표를 설정하고 꿈을 이루는 방법

해설 목표를 세우는 것은 중요하고, 큰 꿈보단 작은 목표를 세우는 것이 효과적이라는 내용의 글이므로, 글의 주제로 가장 적절한 것은 ③ how to set goals and achieve your dreams이다.

정답 ②

지문분석

There is perhaps no publication / that has ① had as much influence / on the modern environmental movement / as Rachel Carson's 1962 book / *Silent Spring*.
출판물은 아마도 없을 것이다 / 큰 영향을 끼쳤던 / 현대 환경 운동에 / Rachel Carson의 1962년 책만큼 / *침묵의 봄*

In it, / she claimed / that pesticides like DDT / had the power / to cause severe harm to animals / and ② polluting(→ pollute) the world's food supply.
그 책에서 / 그녀는 주장했다 / DDT 같은 살충제가 / 영향력이 있다고 / 동물에게 심각한 해를 야기할 / 그리고 세계의 식량 공급원을 오염시킬

★ She explained / ③ that DDT intended to kill pests / also poisoned the larger animals / that inevitably ate them.
그녀는 설명했다 / 해충을 죽이는 데 쓰이는 DDT가 / 더 큰 동물도 독살시켰다고 / 불가피하게 그것을 먹은

Over time, / she suggested, / all life on Earth / could be at risk / ④ because of the dangerous effects / of chemicals.
시간이 지남에 따라 / 그녀는 시사했다 / 지구상의 모든 생명이 / 위험에 처할 수도 있다고 / 위험한 영향으로 인해 / 화학 물질의

The book was an unexpected success.
그 책은 뜻밖의 성공이었다

It not only / helped people understand the connection / between nature and human society, / but it also affected government policy.
그것은 ~했을 뿐만 아니라 / 사람들이 관계를 이해하는 데 도움이 되었다 / 자연과 인간 사회 간의 / 정부 정책에도 영향을 미쳤다

By 1975, / the United States had banned all the chemicals / ⑤ mentioned in Carson's book.
1975년까지 / 미국은 모든 화학 물질을 금지했다 / Carson의 책에 언급된

★ 독해가 쉬워지는 구문 풀이

She explained that DDT **intended** to kill pests also **poisoned** the
　　　　　　　　　주어　　과거분사　　　　　　　　　　　동사
larger animals that inevitably ate them.

⇨ 문맥상 '해충을 죽이는 데 쓰이는'이라는 의미로, 주어 DDT가 intend가 나타내는 '~하는 데 쓰고자 하는' 행위의 대상이므로 과거분사 intended가 쓰였다.

어휘 perhaps 아마도, 어쩌면　publication 출판물, 발행
claim 주장하다, 요구하다　power 영향력, 힘　severe 심각한

---

pollute 오염시키다   intend (어떤 목적)에 쓰고자 하다, 의도하다
pest 해충, 유해 동물 inevitably 불가피하게, 필연적으로
unexpected 뜻밖의, 예상치 않은   ban 금지하다, 금하다
mention 언급하다, 말하다

[해석] Rachel Carson의 1962년 책 *침묵의 봄*만큼 현대 환경 운동에 큰 영향을 끼쳤던 출판물은 아마도 없을 것이다. 그 책에서, 그녀는 DDT 같은 살충제가 동물에게 심각한 해를 야기하고 세계의 식량 공급원을 오염시킬 영향력이 있다고 주장했다. 그녀는 해충을 죽이는 데 쓰이는 DDT가 불가피하게 그것을 먹은 더 큰 동물도 독살시켰다고 설명했다. 그녀는 화학 물질의 위험한 영향으로 인해 시간이 지남에 따라 지구상의 모든 생명이 위험에 처할 수도 있다고 시사했다. 그 책은 뜻밖의 성공이었다. [주제문] 그것은 사람들이 자연과 인간 사회 간의 관계를 이해하는 데 도움이 되었을 뿐만 아니라, 정부 정책에도 영향을 미쳤다. 1975년까지, 미국은 Carson의 책에 언급된 모든 화학 물질을 금지했다.

[해설] 문맥상 '살충제가 심각한 해를 야기하고 오염시킬 영향력'이라는 의미로 명사 the power를 수식하는 to부정사 2개가 나열되는 것이 자연스러우므로 to cause와 대등한 to부정사 to pollute가 와야 하지만, 뒤에 나열된 to부정사는 to를 생략할 수 있으므로 ②의 polluting을 동사원형 pollute로 고쳐야 한다.

[오답분석] ①은 문맥상 '지금까지 큰 영향을 끼쳤다'는 의미이므로 현재완료 have[has] + p.p.를 만드는 과거분사 had를 사용한 것은 어법상 적절하다. ③은 주어(DDT), 동사(poisoned), 목적어(the larger animals)를 갖춘 완전한 절(DDT ~ poisoned the larger animals ~)을 이끌며 문장의 목적어 자리에 쓰여 명사절을 이끄는 접속사 that을 사용한 것은 어법상 적절하다. ④는 뒤에 명사구(the dangerous effects)가 왔으므로 전치사 because of를 사용한 것은 어법상 적절하다. ⑤는 수식 받는 명사 chemicals가 mentioned가 나타내는 '언급하는' 행위의 대상이므로 과거분사 mentioned를 사용한 것은 어법상 적절하다.

[실력UP! 미니 문제 04.]

정답 By 1975, the United States had banned all the chemicals mentioned in Carson's book

해석 Q: Carson의 책이 미국의 정부 정책에 어떤 영향을 미쳤는가?
A: 1975년까지, 미국은 Carson의 책에 언급된 모든 화학 물질을 금지했다.

해설 Carson의 책은 사람들이 자연과 인간 사회 간의 관계를 이해하는 데 도움이 되었을 뿐만 아니라 정부 정책에도 영향을 미쳤다고 한 후, 1975년까지, 미국은 그녀의 책에 언급된 모든 화학 물질을 금지했다고 했다.

05
정답 ⑤

[지문분석]

Sometimes, / traveling by boat, plane, or even car / causes us / to feel nauseous / and even to experience dizziness or headaches.
가끔 / 배, 비행기, 또는 심지어 차를 타고 여행하는 것은 / 우리로 하여금 ~하게 하다 / 메스껍게 하는 / 그리고 심지어 현기증이나 두통을 경험하게

Motion sickness, / as these symptoms are ① collectively referred to, / is believed / to affect many of us.
멀미 / 일괄적으로 이 증상들은 불리며 / 여겨진다 / 많은 사람들에게 영향을 끼친다고

Although / debates on / what causes this / still exist, / it's quite clear / ② how this happens.
~지만 / ~에 관한 논의 / 무엇이 이것을 야기하는지 / 아직 존재한다 / 꽤나 명확하다 / 이것이 어떻게 일어나는지

In fact, / receiving different information / from more than one part of the balance-sensing system /—the eyes, inner ears, and sensory nerves—/ ③ makes us sick.
사실 / 다른 정보를 받아들이는 것 / 균형 감각계의 하나 이상의 부분으로부터 / 눈, 내이, 그리고 감각 신경 / 우리를 메스껍게 만든다

★ For example, / passengers / sitting in the backseat of a car / with their view / of the front window / partially ④ blocked / still sense the forward movement of the car / through their ears and other senses.
예를 들어 / 승객들 / 차의 뒷자리에 앉아있는 / 시야가 ~한 상태 / 앞 유리창의 / 일부 차단된 / 여전히 차가 앞으로 가는 움직임을 느낀다 / 그들의 귀와 다른 감각들을 통해

Therefore, / the brain becomes uncertain / about whether or not the body is in fact moving, / ⑤ confusing(→ confused) by the different information / it is receiving.
그러므로 / 뇌는 불확실해진다 / 신체가 실제로 움직이고 있는지 아닌지에 대해 / 서로 다른 정보들에 의해 혼란스러워지며 / 그것이 전달받고 있는

This miscommunication / between the sensory system and the brain / triggers motion sickness.
이러한 의사소통 오류가 / 감각 기관과 뇌의 / 멀미를 유발한다

★ 독해가 쉬워지는 구문 풀이

For example, passengers sitting in the backseat of a car with their
                                              주어
view of the front window partially blocked still sense the forward
      수식 받는 명사구   과거분사   동사
movement of the car through their ears and other senses.

⇨ 수식 받는 명사구가 block이 나타내는 '막는' 행위의 대상이므로 과거분사 blocked가 쓰였다.

[어휘] dizziness 현기증 motion sickness 멀미 symptom 증상
collectively 일괄하여, 전체적으로 exist 존재하다 inner ear 내이
sensory 감각의 nerve 신경 sick 메스꺼운 passenger 승객 block 막다
forward 앞으로 가는 uncertain 불확실한 confuse 혼란스럽게 만들다
miscommunication 의사소통 오류 trigger 유발하다

[해석] 가끔, 배, 비행기, 또는 심지어 차를 타고 여행하는 것은 우리로 하여금 메스껍게 하고, 심지어 현기증이나 두통을 경험하게 한다. 일괄적으로 이 증상들은 멀미라고 불리며, 많은 사람들에게 영향을 끼친다고 여겨진다. 무엇이 이것을 야기하는지에 관한 논의는 아직 존재하지만, 이것이 어떻게 일어나는지는 꽤나 명확하다. 사실, [주제문] 눈, 내이, 그리고 감각 신경과 같은 균형 감각계의 하나 이상의 부분으로부터 다른 정보를 받아들이는 것은 우리를 메스껍게 만든다. 예를 들어, 차의 뒷자리에 앉아있는 승객들은 앞 유리창의 시야가 일부 차단된 상태에서 그들의 귀와 다른 감각들을 통해 여전히 차가 앞으로 가는 움직임을 느낀다. 그러므로, 뇌는 그것이 전달받고 있는 서로 다른 정보들에 의해 혼란스러워지며 신체가 실제로 움직이고 있는지 아닌지에 대해 불확실해진다. 이러한 감각 기관과 뇌의 의사소통 오류가 멀미를 유발한다.

[해설] 수식 받는 명사 the brain과 분사는 '혼란스러워진'이라는 의미의 수동 관계이다. 수동 관계를 나타내는 분사는 과거분사이므로, ⑤의 confusing을 confused로 고쳐야 한다.

[오답분석] ①은 부사는 동사, 형용사, 다른 부사, 문장 전체를 수식하는데, 부사가 동사구 are referred to를 수식하고 있으므로 부사 collectively를 사용한 것은 어법상 적절하다. ②는 '의문사 + 주어 + 동사'의 어순으로 쓰인 간접의문문이므로 의문사 자리에 올 수 있는 how를 사용한 것은 어법상 적절하다. ③은 주어가 동명사구 receiving different information이므로 단수동사 makes를 사용한 것은 어법상 적절하다. ④는 수식 받는 명사 their view와 분사가 '시야가 막힌'이라는 의미의 수동 관계이므로 과거분사 blocked를 사용한 것은 어법상 적절하다.

[실력UP! 미니 문제 05.]

정답 (A) motion sickness
(B) the brain

해설 (A) 멀미는 많은 사람들에게 영향을 끼친다고 여겨진다고 한 후, 무엇이 이것을 야기하는지에 관한 논의가 아직 존재하지만 이것이 어떻게 일어나는지는 꽤나 명백하다고 했으므로, (A)this는 motion sickness(멀미)를 가리킨다.

(B) 뇌는 실제로 몸이 움직이고 있는지 불확실해진다고 한 후, 그것이 전달받고 있는 서로 다른 정보들에 의해 혼란스러워진다고 했으므로, (B)it는 the brain(뇌)을 가리킨다.

06
정답 ④

지문분석

The popularity of e-sports, / or video game competitions, / is on the rise.
e스포츠의 인기가 / 즉 비디오 게임 경기 / 상승하고 있다

Today, / e-sports is a multi-billion dollar industry / backed by celebrities and top brands, / with an audience / ① rivaling that of traditional sports.
오늘날 / e스포츠는 수십억 달러의 산업이다 / 유명인 및 일류 브랜드의 후원을 받는 / 관중과 더불어 / 전통 스포츠의 그것(관중)에 필적하는

However, / its beginnings were far humbler.
하지만 / 그 시초는 훨씬 더 보잘것없었다

The first game / specifically designed for computers, / *Spacewar!*, / ② was not for commercial use.
첫 번째 게임인 / 컴퓨터용으로 특별히 제작된 / *Spacewar!* 는 / 상업용이 아니었다

Despite initially ③ being accessible / only to a small group of programmers, / it spread / once these programmers began / to create new versions of the game.
처음에 이용 가능했음에도 불구하고 / 오로지 소수의 프로그래머들 집단에게만 / 그것은 퍼져 나갔다 / 이 프로그래머들이 시작하자 / 그 게임의 새로운 버전을 만들어내기

★ By 1972, / enough people were aware of it / for a leading pop culture magazine / to take notice and sponsor / ④ that(→ what) was technically the first-ever e-sports tournament: / the "Intergalactic *Spacewar!* Olympics."
1972년쯤에 / 충분히 많은 사람들이 그것에 대해 알게 되었다 / 선두적인 대중문화 잡지가 / 주목하고 후원하게 되다 / 엄밀히 말하면 사상 최초의 e스포츠 토너먼트였던 것 / Intergalactic *Spacewar!* Olympics에

About two dozen people ⑤ attended the event, / and the first prize was a one-year subscription / to the magazine.
약 24명이 그 행사에 참여했다 / 그리고 1등 상은 1년 구독권이었다 / 그 잡지의

★ **독해가 쉬워지는 구문 풀이**

By 1972, enough people were aware of it [for a leading pop culture magazine **to take notice** and **(to) sponsor**] ~
　　　　　　　　　　　　　　　　전치사구

⇨ [ ]는 enough를 수식하는 전치사구로, '~하기에 충분한'이라고 해석한다.

⇨ to take notice와 (to) sponsor는 등위접속사 and로 연결된 병렬 구조이다. 뒤에 나열된 to부정사는 to를 생략할 수 있다.

어휘 on the rise 상승 중인, 오름세에　celebrity 유명인, 연예인
rival ~에 필적하다, ~과 겨루다　humble 보잘것없는, 초라한
pop culture 대중문화　take notice 주목하다, 주의하다
technically 엄밀히 말하면, 기술적으로　first-ever 사상 최초의, 생애 처음의
dozen 12의, 다수의　subscription 구독권

해석 e스포츠, 즉 비디오 게임 경기의 인기가 상승하고 있다. 오늘날, e스포츠는 전통 스포츠의 관중에 필적하는 관중과 더불어, 유명인 및 일류 브랜드의 후원을 받는 수십억 달러의 산업이다. 하지만, 그 시초는 훨씬 더 보잘것없었다. 컴퓨터용으로 특별히 제작된 첫 번째 게임인 *Spacewar!* 는 상업용이 아니었다. 처음에 오로지 소수의 프로그래머들 집단에게만 이용 가능했음에도 불구하고, 이 프로그래머들이 그 게임의 새로운 버전을 만들어내기 시작하자 그것은 퍼져 나갔다. 1972년쯤에, 충분히 많은 사람들이 그것에 대해 알게 되자, 선두적인 대중문화 잡지가 Intergalactic *Spacewar!* Olympics라는, 엄밀히 말하면 사상 최초의 e스포츠 토너먼트였던 것에 주목하고 후원하게 되었다. 약 24명이 그 행사에 참여했고, 1등 상은 그 잡지의 1년 구독권이었다.

해설 뒤에 동사(was)와 주격보어(the first-ever e-sports tournament)만 있고 주어가 없는 불완전한 절이 왔으며, notice and sponsor의 목적어, 즉 선행사가 없으므로 선행사를 포함하면서 불완전한 절을 이끄는 관계대명사 what이 쓰여야 하므로 ④의 that을 what으로 고쳐야 한다.

오답분석 ①은 수식 받는 명사 audience가 rival이 나타내는 '필적하는' 행위의 주체이므로 현재분사 rivaling을 사용한 것은 어법상 적절하다. ②은 주어 The first game은 단수명사이므로 단수동사 was를 사용한 것은 어법상 적절하다. ③은 명사 역할을 하여 전치사(Despite)의 목적어 자리에 올 수 있는 동명사 being을 사용한 것은 어법상 적절하다. ⑤은 사람들이 행사에 참여한 것은 과거에 있었던 일이므로 과거시제 attended를 사용한 것은 어법상 적절하다.

실력 UP! 미니 문제 06.

정답 ②

해석 ① 비디오 게임의 경제적 효과
② 비디오 게임과 e스포츠의 기원
③ 온라인 스포츠 경기의 장점

해설 최초의 게임인 *Spacewar!*와 최초의 e스포츠 토너먼트인 Intergalactic *Spacewar!* Olympics에 관한 글이므로, 글의 주제로 가장 적절한 것은 ② the origin of video games and e-sports이다.

07
정답 ②

지문분석

When preparing for an exam, / many students struggle / to remember information / from the textbook.
시험을 준비할 때, / 많은 학생들은 애쓴다 / 자료를 기억하려고 / 교과서의

One easy way / to improve their long-term memory / is ① to employ active-reading methods.
한 가지 쉬운 방법 / 그들의 장기 기억을 향상시키는 / 능동적 읽기 방법을 이용하는 것이다

★ Rather than simply scanning the content, / students need to / directly interact with it.
내용을 단순히 훑어보기보다는 / 학생들은 ~할 필요가 있다 / 그것과 직접적으로 상호작용할

For example, / they can take notes / to summarize the main ideas / while listening to the lecture, / or / ② highlighting(→ highlight) key terms and concepts / to focus on meaningful information.
예를 들어 / 그들은 필기를 할 수 있다 / 주요 개념들을 요약하기 위해 / 강의를 들으면서 / 혹은 / 중요한 단어나 개념에 강조 표시를 할 수 있다 / 의미 있는 정보에 주목하기 위해

Another active-reading strategy / ③ proven to be effective / is to make visual representations / of important details.
또 하나의 능동적 읽기 전략은 / 효과적으로 증명된 / 시각적 표현을 만드는 것이다 / 중요한 세부 사항들의

According to a recent study, / students are more likely to remember / data from flow charts, graphs, and diagrams.
최근의 연구에 따르면 / 학생들은 더 기억하기 쉽다 / 순서도, 그래프, 그리고 도표의 자료를

When facts and figures are presented / in these formats, / they ④ are retained for a longer period of time.
사실과 수치가 제시되면 / 이러한 형식들로 / 그들은 더 오랜 기간 동안 유지된다

Regardless of / the specific techniques used, / students / who increase their engagement / with ⑤ what they read / are more likely to remember it.
~에 상관없이 / 사용된 구체적인 기법 / 학생들은 / 더 몰두하는 / 그들이 읽는 것에 / 기억할 가능성이 더 높다

★ **독해가 쉬워지는 구문 풀이**

Rather than simply scanning the content, students need to directly
　　　　　　전치사　　　명사
interact with it.

⇨ 명사 역할을 하여 전치사의 목적어 자리에 올 수 있는 동명사 scanning이 쓰였다.

어휘 struggle 애쓰다 long-term 장기간의 employ 이용하다
active-reading 능동적 읽기 scan 훑어보다 interact with 상호작용하다
take notes 필기하다 summarize 요약하다 highlight 강조하다
strategy 전략 representation 표현 flow chart 순서도 diagram 도표
figure 수치 format 형식 retain 유지하다 regardless of ~와 관계없이
specific 구체적인 engagement 몰두, 참여

해석 시험을 준비할 때, 많은 학생들은 교과서의 자료를 기억하려고 애쓴다. 그들의 **주제문** 장기 기억을 향상시키는 한 가지 쉬운 방법은 능동적 읽기 방법을 이용하는 것이다. 내용을 단순히 훑어보기보다는, 학생들은 그것과 직접적으로 상호작용할 필요가 있다. 예를 들어, 그들은 주요 개념들을 요약하기 위해 강의를 들으면서 필기를 할 수 있고, 혹은 의미 있는 정보에 주목하기 위해 중요한 단어나 개념에 강조 표시를 할 수 있다. 효과적으로 증명된 또 하나의 능동적 읽기 전략은 중요한 세부 사항들의 시각적 표현을 만드는 것이다. 최근의 연구에 따르면, 학생들은 순서도, 그래프, 그리고 도표의 자료를 더 기억하기 쉽다. 이러한 형식들로 사실과 수치가 제시되면, 그들은 더 오랜 기간 동안 유지된다. 사용된 구체적인 기법에 상관없이, 그들이 읽는 것에 더 몰두하는 학생들은 그것을 기억할 가능성이 더 높다.

해설 ②는 등위접속사 or로 이어지는 동사이므로, 앞에 나온 동사 take와 병렬 구조를 이루어야 한다. 주어 they 뒤에 can이 왔으므로 동사원형 take가 쓰였고, 병렬 구조를 이루는 or 뒤에도 can이 생략된 동사원형이 와야 한다. 따라서 ②의 highlighting을 highlight로 고쳐야 한다.

오답분석 ①은 be동사(is)의 보어 자리인데, to부정사는 명사 역할을 하며 보어 자리에 올 수 있으므로 to부정사 to employ를 사용한 것은 어법상 적절하다. ③은 수식 받는 명사 strategy가 proven이 나타내는 '증명된' 행위의 대상이므로 과거분사 proven을 사용한 것은 어법상 적절하다. ④는 they가 '그들은 ~ 유지된다'라는 의미의 수동 관계에서의 주어이므로 수동태 are retained를 사용한 것은 어법상 적절하다. ⑤는 뒤에 주어(they)와 동사(read)만 있고 목적어가 없는 불완전한 절이 왔으며, 문맥상 '그들이 읽는 것'이라는 의미이므로 선행사 the thing을 포함하는 목적격 관계대명사 what을 사용한 것은 어법상 적절하다.

실력 UP! 미니 문제 07.
정답 (A) active-reading   (B) engagement
해석 장기 기억을 향상시키기 위해, 학생들은 (A) 능동적 읽기 방법을 이용하거나, 그들이 읽는 것에 더 (B) 몰두할 수 있다.
해설 글 초반에서 학생들의 장기 기억을 향상시키는 한 가지 쉬운 방법은 능동적 읽기 방법을 이용하는 것이라고 했고, 글 후반에서는 구체적인 기법에 상관없이, 학생들은 그들이 읽는 것에 더 몰두함으로써 읽은 것들을 기억할 가능성이 더 높다고 했다. 따라서 요약문의 빈칸에 들어갈 말로 가장 적절한 것은 (A) active-reading(능동적 읽기), (B) engagement(몰두)이다.

08
정답 ④

지문분석

Some people stand out / in your memory / more than most.
일부 사람들은 두드러진다 / 당신의 기억에서 / 대부분의 사람들보다 더

For me, / that person is my grandpa / Theodore Lazarus, or Paw Paw.
나에게 / 그 사람은 나의 할아버지이다 / Theodore Lazarus, 즉 Paw Paw

① Seen at his desk on the phone / or in his lounge chair watching TV, / Paw Paw was always around.
그의 책상에서 통화하고 있는 모습을 보이며 / 또는 그의 안락의자에서 텔레비전을 시청하고 있는 / Paw Paw는 항상 주변에 있었다

Sometimes, / he would go gardening / in the backyard / or do something practical / with his hands.
때때로, / 그는 정원을 가꾸러 가곤 했다 / 뒷마당으로 / 또는 실용적인 무언가를 하곤 했다 / 그의 손으로

But mostly, / I remember / Paw Paw liked to spend time / ② playing with us.
하지만 주로 / 나는 기억한다 / Paw Paw가 시간 보내기를 좋아했던 것을 / 우리와 함께 노는 데

He listened to our stories, / read us comics, / and used funny expressions / like, "No way, Jose!" and "No kiddin'!" / ③ which always made us smile.
그는 우리의 이야기를 들어주었다 / 우리에게 만화책을 읽어주었다 / 그리고 재미있는 표현들을 썼다 / "절대 아니야!"와 "그럴 리가"와 같은 / 이것은 항상 우리를 웃게 만들었다

Strangely enough, / not once did we ④ heard(→ hear) / Paw Paw say / that he loved us / or that he was proud of us.
참 이상하게도 / 우리는 한 번도 듣지 못했다 / Paw Paw가 말하는 것을 / 그가 우리를 사랑한다고 / 또는 우리가 자랑스럽다고

Yet / we always knew / that's exactly ⑤ what he felt.
하지만 / 우리는 항상 알고 있었다 / 그것이 바로 정확히 그가 느꼈던 것임을

We were all extremely sad / after Paw Paw passed away.
우리는 모두 매우 슬펐다 / Paw Paw가 돌아가신 후에

★ But, / I'm glad / that I have his memory / to keep with me forever.
하지만 / 나는 기쁘다 / 그의 기억을 갖게 되어 / 나와 영원히 함께 할

> ★ 독해가 쉬워지는 구문 풀이
>
> But, I'm glad that I have his memory to keep with me forever.
>   명사절 주어 동사   목적어
>   접속사
>
> ⇨ 뒤에 주어(I), 동사(have), 목적어(his memory)가 모두 있는 완전한 절이 왔고, 문맥상 '나는 그의 기억을 갖게 되어 기뻤다'라는 의미로 문장에 생각/감정 형용사 glad가 있으므로 <생각/감정 형용사 + that + 완전한 절> 구문을 만드는 접속사 that이 쓰였다.

어휘 stand out 두드러지다, 눈에 띄다 lounge chair 안락의자
garden 정원을 가꾸다 backyard 뒷마당 practical 실용적인, 현실적인
comic 만화책; 재미있는 strangely enough 이상하게도 extremely 매우
pass away 돌아가시다, 떠나가다

해석 **주제문** 일부 사람들은 대부분의 사람들보다 더 당신의 기억에서 두드러진다. 나에게, 그 사람은 나의 할아버지인 Theodore Lazarus, 즉 Paw Paw이다. Paw Paw는 책상에서 통화하고 있거나 안락의자에서 텔레비전을 시청하고 있는 모습을 보이며, 항상 주변에 있었다. 때때로, 그는 정원을 가꾸러 뒷마당으로 가거나 그의 손으로 실용적인 무언가를 하곤 했다. 하지만, 주로 나는 Paw Paw가 우리와 함께 노는 데 시간 보내기를 좋아했던 것을 기억한다. 그는 우리의 이야기를 들어주고 우리에게 만화책을 읽어주며 "절대 아니야!"와 "그럴 리가!"와 같은 재미있는 표현들을 썼는데, 이것은 항상 우리를 웃게 만들었다. 참 이상하게도, 우리는 Paw Paw가 우리를 사랑한다거나 우리가 자랑스럽다고 말하는 것을 한 번도 듣지 못했다. 하지만, 우리는 그것이 바로 정확히 그가 느꼈던 것임을 항상 알고 있었다. Paw Paw가 돌아가신 후에 우리는 모두 매우 슬펐다. 하지만 나는 나와 영원히 함께 할 그의 기억을 갖게 되어 기쁘다.

해설 부정의 의미를 가진 어구 not once가 앞으로 나오면서 어순이 도치된 문장이다. 일반동사(heard)가 쓰였으므로 일반동사 대신 조동사가 도치된 'not once + do/does/did + 주어 + 동사원형' 형태가 되어야 한다. 따라서 ④의 heard를 동사원형 hear로 고쳐야 한다.

오답분석 ①은 주어 Paw Paw가 '보여지는' 행위의 대상이므로 과거분사 Seen을 사용한 것은 어법상 적절하다. ②은 '~하는 데 시간을 보내다'는 'spend + 시간/돈 + -ing'를 사용하여 나타낼 수 있으므로 동명사 playing을 사용한 것은 어법상 적절하다. ③은 관계절이 앞에 나온 절에 대한 부연 설명을 하고 관계절 내에서 주어 역할을 하고 있으므로, 계속적 용법으로 쓰일 수 있는 주격 관계대명사 which를 사용한 것은 어법상 적절하다. ⑤은 뒤에 주어(he)와 동사(felt)만 있고 보어가 없는 불완전한 절이 왔으므로, '~하는 것'이라는 의미로 불완전한 절 앞에 올 수 있는 명사절 접속사 what을 사용한 것은 어법상 적절하다.

정답 ⓐ practical ⓑ extremely

해석 ⓐ 일상생활에 유용하거나 적용할 수 있도록 도움이 되는
　　　ⓑ 극도의 정도 또는 엄청난 정도로

CHAPTER 10 어휘 적절성 파악하기

불변의 패턴 19　　　　　　　　　p.78
쓰임이 적절하지 않은 어휘는 문맥과 반대되는 의미로 나온다.

기출 문제　　　　　　　　　정답 ③

지문분석

We often ignore small changes / because they don't seem to / ① matter very much / in the moment.
우리는 종종 작은 변화들을 무시한다 / 그것들이 ~하지 않아 보이기 때문에 / 크게 중요하다 / 당장은

If you save a little money now, / you're still not a millionaire.
만약 당신이 지금 약간의 돈을 모으더라도 / 당신은 여전히 백만장자가 아니다

If you study Spanish / for an hour tonight, / you still haven't learned the language.
만약 당신이 스페인어를 공부하더라도 / 오늘 밤 한 시간 동안 / 당신은 여전히 그 언어를 익힌 것이 아니다

We make a few changes, / but the results never seem to come ② quickly / and so we slide back into / our previous routines.
우리는 약간의 변화를 만든다 / 하지만 그 결과는 결코 빨리 나타나지 않는 것 같다 / 그래서 우리는 ~으로 복귀한다 / 이전의 일상

★ The slow pace of transformation / also makes it ③ easy (→ difficult) / to break a bad habit.
변화의 느린 속도는 / 또한 그것을 쉽게(→ 어렵게) 만든다 / 나쁜 습관을 버리기

If you eat an unhealthy meal today, / the scale doesn't move much.
만약 당신이 오늘 건강에 좋지 않은 음식을 먹어도 / 저울 눈금은 크게 움직이지 않는다

A single decision is easy / to ignore.
한 번의 결정은 쉽다 / 무시하기가

But / when we ④ repeat small errors, / day after day, / by following poor decisions / again and again, / our small choices add up to bad results.
하지만 / 우리가 작은 잘못들을 반복한다면 / 매일 / 잘못된 결정을 따름으로써 / 반복적으로 / 우리의 작은 선택들은 결국 좋지 않은 결과가 된다

Many missteps eventually / lead to a ⑤ problem.
많은 실수는 결국 / 문제를 일으킨다

★ 독해가 쉬워지는 구문 풀이

The slow pace of transformation also makes it easy
　　　　　　　　　　　　　　　　　가짜 목적어
　　　　　　　　　　　　　　　　　목적어 보어
to break a bad habit.
진짜 목적어(to부정사구)

⇨ 동사 make는 5형식 동사로 쓰일 때 'make + 목적어 + 목적격보어' 형태를 취하며, '~이 -하게 만들다'라는 의미를 나타낸다. 이때, to부정사구 목적어(to break a bad habit)가 목적격보어(easy)와 함께 오면 진짜 목적어를 목적격보어 뒤로 보내고, 목적어가 있던 자리에 가짜 목적어 it을 써야 한다.

어휘 in the moment 당장은　slide into 복귀하다　routine 일상, 판에 박힌 일
pace 속도　transformation 변화, 변신　add up to 결국 ~가 되다
misstep 실수, 잘못된 조치

해석 작은 변화들은 당장은 크게 ① 중요하지 않아 보이기 때문에 우리는 종종 그것들을 무시한다. 만약 당신이 지금 약간의 돈을 모으더라도, 당신은 여전히 백만장자가 아니다. 만약 당신이 오늘 밤 한 시간 동안 스페인어를 공부하더라도, 당신은 여전히 그 언어를 익힌 것이 아니다. 우리는 약간의 변화를 만들지만, 그 결과는 결코 ② 빨리 나타나지 않는 것 같아서 우리는 이전의 일상으로 복귀한다. 변화의 느린 속도는 또한 나쁜 습관을 버리기 ③ 쉽게(→ 어렵게) 만든다. 만약 당신이 오늘 건강에 좋지 않은 음식을 먹어도, 저울 눈금은 크게 움직이지 않는다. 한 번의 결정은 무시하기가 쉽다. 하지만 우리가 잘못된 결정을 반복적으로 따름으로써 작은 잘못들을 매일 ④ 반복한다면, 우리의 작은 선택들은 결국 좋지 않은 결과가 된다. 많은 실수들은 결국 ⑤ 문제를 일으킨다.

해설 약간의 변화는 그 결과가 빨리 나타나지 않기 때문에, 변화의 느린 속도는 나쁜 습관을 버리기 어렵게 만든다는 맥락이 되어야 하므로, ③의 easy를 difficult와 같은 어휘로 바꾸어야 문맥상 적절하다.

오답분석 ①은 우리는 작은 변화들이 당장은 크게 "중요하지" 않아 보여서 종종 그것들을 무시한다는 문맥이 되어야 하므로 matter가 오는 것이 적절하다. ②은 우리는 약간의 변화를 만들지만 그 결과는 결코 "빨리" 나타나지 않는 것 같다는 문맥이 되어야 하므로 quickly가 오는 것이 적절하다. ④은 우리가 작은 잘못들을 매일 "반복한다"면 결국 좋지 않은 결과가 된다는 문맥이 되어야 하므로 repeat가 오는 것이 적절하다. ⑤은 많은 실수들이 결국 "문제"를 일으킨다는 문맥이 되어야 하므로 problem이 오는 것이 적절하다.

불변의 패턴 20　　　　　　　　　p.79
네모 안 어휘들은 보통 서로 반의어 관계이다.

기출 문제　　　　　　　　　정답 ⑤

지문분석

How does a leader make / people feel important?
리더는 어떻게 만드는가 / 사람들을 중요하다고 느끼게

First, / by listening to them.
첫째 / 그들에게 귀를 기울임으로써이다

Let them know / you respect their thinking, / and let them (A) silence / voice / their opinions.
그들에게 알려주라 / 당신이 그들의 생각을 존중한다는 것을 / 그리고 그들이 말로 표현할 수 있도록 하라 / 그들의 의견을

As an added bonus, / you might learn something!
덤으로 / 당신은 무언가를 배울 수도 있다

A friend of mine / once told me / about the CEO of a large company / who told one of his managers, / "There's nothing you could possibly tell me / that I haven't already thought about before.
내 친구가 / 한 번은 나에게 말했다 / 한 대기업의 최고 경영자에 대해 / 자신의 관리자 중 한 명에게 말을 한 / 당신이 나에게 말해줄 수 있는 것은 아무것도 없어 / 내가 전에 이미 생각해보지 않았던 것은

★ Don't ever tell me / what you think / unless I ask you.
나에게 절대 말하지 마 / 당신이 생각하는 것을 / 내가 당신에게 물어보지 않으면

Is that understood?"
이해했나

Imagine / the (B) improvement / loss of self-esteem / that manager must have felt.
상상해 보아라 / 자존감의 상실을 / 관리자가 틀림없이 느꼈을

It must have discouraged him / and negatively affected / his performance.
그것은 그를 낙담시켰을 것이다 / 그리고 부정적인 영향을 미쳤다 / 그의 성과에

On the other hand, / when you make a person feel / a great sense of importance, / he or she will feel / on top of the world — / and the level of energy / will (C) decrease / increase rapidly.
반면에 / 당신이 한 사람에게 느끼게 할 때 / 대단히 중요하다는 인식을 / 그 사람은 느낄 것이다 / 천하를 얻은 기분을 / 그리고 활력의 수준은 / 급격히 증가할 것이다

★ 독해가 쉬워지는 구문 풀이

Don't ever tell me [①**what** you think] [②unless I ask you].

⇨ 명사절 [①]은 뒤에 주어(you)와 동사 (think)만 있고 목적어가 없는 불완전한 절이며, 앞에 선행사가 없으므로 관계대명사 what이 사용되었다.

⇨ [②]은 앞 문장 전체(Don't ~ think)를 수식하는 부사절이다

[어휘] respect 존중하다 thinking 생각 silence 침묵시키다 voice 말로 표현하다 opinion 의견 CEO 최고 경영자 improvement 향상 loss 상실 self-esteem 자존감 discourage 낙담시키다 negatively 부정적으로 affect 영향을 미치다 performance 성과 on top of the world 천하를 얻은 기분인 rapidly 급속히

[해석] (주제문) 리더는 어떻게 사람들을 중요하다고 느끼게 만드는가? 첫째, 그들에게 귀를 기울임으로써이다. 당신이 그들의 생각을 존중한다는 것을 그들에게 알려주고, 그들이 그들의 의견을 (A) 말로 표현할 수 있도록 하라. 덤으로, 당신은 무언가를 배울 수도 있다! 한 번은 내 친구가 나에게, 자신의 관리자 중 한 명에게 '당신이 말할 수 있는 것에서 내가 전에 이미 생각해보지 않았던 것은 아무것도 없어. 내가 당신에게 묻지 않는 한 절대 당신이 생각하는 것을 나에게 말하지 마. 이해했니?'라고 말한 한 대기업의 최고 경영자에 대해 이야기한 적이 있다. 관리자가 틀림없이 느꼈을 자존감의 (B) 상실을 상상해 보아라. 그것은 그를 낙담시키고 그의 성과에 부정적인 영향을 미쳤을 것이다. 반면에, 당신이 한 사람에게 대단히 중요하다는 인식을 느끼게 할 때, 그 사람은 천하를 얻은 기분을 느낄 것이고, 활력의 수준은 급격히 (C) 증가할 것이다.

　　　　(A)　　　　(B)　　　(C)
① 침묵시키다　 - 향상 - 감소하다
② 침묵시키다　 - 상실 - 증가하다
③ 말로 표현하다 - 향상 - 감소하다
④ 말로 표현하다 - 상실 - 감소하다
⑤ 말로 표현하다 - 상실 - 증가하다

[해설] (A) 리더는 사람들에게 귀를 기울임으로써 그들의 생각을 존중한다는 것을 그들에게 알려 주고, 그들이 그들의 의견을 "말로 표현할" 수 있도록 해야 한다는 의미가 되어야 하므로 voice가 문맥상 적절하다.
(B) 관리자가 들은 이야기가 그를 낙담시키고 성과에 부정적인 영향을 미쳤을 것이라고 했으므로 그가 느꼈을 자존감의 "상실"을 상상해 보라는 의미가 되어야 한다. 따라서 loss가 문맥상 적절하다.
(C) 한 사람에게 자신이 대단히 중요하다는 인식을 느끼게 할 때, 그 사람은 천하를 얻은 기분을 느낄 것이고 활력 수준이 급격히 "증가할" 것이라는 의미가 되어야 하므로 increase가 문맥상 적절하다. 따라서 정답으로 가장 적절한 것은 ⑤ voice - loss - increase이다.

독해 만점 TEST
p.80

01 ④　02 ③　03 ④　04 ⑤　05 ③　06 ②　07 ③　08 ⑤

실력 UP! 미니 문제
01. ③

---

02. make sure that no one will dare to challenge them and that they can hold onto their position
03. ②
04. ①
05. ⓐ navigate　ⓑ system
06. Using your head and using your heart are beneficial in different circumstances
07. ②
08. (A) effects　(B) impossibility

01
정답 ④

지문분석

Many people fear a future / in which robots replace them / in the workplace.
많은 사람들은 미래를 두려워한다 / 로봇이 그들을 대체하는 / 직장에서

However, / the idea of automation / is welcome / in the restaurant industry.
하지만 / 자동화라는 개념은 / 환영받는다 / 요식업계에서

Human workers can create problems for restaurant owners / by needing higher wages / with fewer working hours.
사람 직원들은 레스토랑 사장들에게 문제를 일으킬 수 있다 / 더 높은 임금을 요구함으로써 / 적은 노동시간과 함께

In contrast, / automated systems let owners / easily ① operate their business / without such conflicts.
이와는 대조적으로 / 자동화 시스템은 사장들로 하여금 ~하게 해준다 / 쉽게 사업을 운영하도록 / 그러한 갈등 없이

In addition, / human employees are the main ② cause / of food contamination.
게다가 / 사람 직원은 주요한 원인이다 / 식품 오염의

★ They can easily spread germs / that cause outbreaks of disease / just by ③ forgetting to wash their hands.
그들은 세균을 쉽게 퍼트릴 수 있다 / 질병의 발생을 야기하는 / 단지 그들의 손을 씻을 것을 잊어버림으로써

Using automated systems / to take orders and prepare food / ④ raises(→ reduces) this risk.
자동화된 장치를 이용하는 것은 / 주문을 받고 음식을 준비하기 위해 / 이러한 위험을 증가(→ 감소)시킨다

Automated systems / also make work easier / for employees / as they can ⑤ complete orders quickly / without making mistakes.
자동화된 장치는 / 또한 작업을 더 쉽게 만든다 / 직원들의 / 주문을 빠르게 처리할 수 있기 때문에 / 오류를 발생시키지 않고

★ 독해가 쉬워지는 구문 풀이

They can easily spread germs that cause outbreaks of disease
　　　　　　　　　　　　　　　　　수식어(관계절)
just by **forgetting to wash** their hands.
　　　　동사(forget) 목적어(to부정사)

⇨ 동사 forget은 동명사나 to부정사를 모두 목적어로 취할 수 있는 동사인데, '(미래에) ~할 것을 잊어버리다'라는 의미를 나타낼 때는 to부정사를 목적어로 취한다.

[어휘] workplace 직장, 일터 automation 자동화 welcome 환영받는 contamination 오염, 더러움 germ 세균, 병균 outbreak 발생, 발발

[해석] 많은 사람들은 직장에서 로봇이 그들을 대체하는 미래를 두려워한다. (주제문) 하지만, 자동화라는 개념은 요식업계에서 환영받는다. 사람 직원들은 적은 노동시간과 함께 더 높은 임금을 요구함으로써 레스토랑 사장들에게 문제를 일으킬 수 있다. 이와는 대조적으로, 자동화 시스템은 사장들로 하여금 그러한 갈등 없이 쉽게 사업을 ① 운영하도록 해준다. 게다가, 사람 직원은 식품 오염의 주요한 ② 원인이다. 그들은 단지 손을 씻을 것을 ③ 잊

어버림으로써 질병의 발생을 야기하는 세균을 쉽게 퍼트릴 수 있다. 주문을 받고 음식을 준비하기 위해 자동화된 장치를 이용하는 것은 이러한 위험을 ④ 증가(→ 감소)시킨다. 또한 자동화된 장치는 오류를 발생시키지 않고 주문을 빠르게 ⑤ 처리할 수 있기 때문에 직원들의 작업을 더 쉽게 만든다.

[해설] 이 글은 요식업계에서 자동화가 가진 이점들에 관한 글이다. 따라서 사람 직원은 세균을 쉽게 퍼트려 질병의 발생을 야기할 수 있으나 자동화된 장치를 사용해 음식을 준비하면 이러한 위험을 "감소시킬" 수 있다는 맥락이 되어야 하므로, ④의 raises는 reduces와 같은 어휘로 바꾸어야 문맥상 적절하다.

[오답분석] ①은 사장에게 문제 상황을 자주 만들어내는 사람 직원과 달리 자동화 시스템은 그러한 갈등 없이 사업을 "운영하도록" 해준다는 문맥이 되어야 하므로 operate가 오는 것이 적절하다. ②은 사람 직원이 식품 오염의 주요한 "원인"이며, 이들이 세균을 쉽게 퍼트릴 수 있다는 문맥이 되어야 하므로 cause가 오는 것이 적절하다. ③은 손 씻기를 "잊어버림"으로써 질병의 발생을 야기하고, 이로 인해 세균을 쉽게 퍼트릴 수 있다는 문맥으로 이어져야 하므로 forgetting이 오는 것이 적절하다. ⑤은 오류를 발생시키지 않으면서 주문을 빠르게 "처리하여" 작업을 더 쉽게 만든다는 문맥이 되어야 하므로 complete가 오는 것이 적절하다.

[실력 UP!] 미니 문제 01.

정답 ③

해석 ① 질병 발생을 막을 수 있는 방법
② 식당에서의 낮은 임금과 장려금 부족
③ 요식업계에서 자동화의 이점

해설 요식업계에서 자동화가 환영받는 이유에 관한 글이므로, 글의 주제로 가장 적절한 것은 ③ the benefits of automation in the restaurant industry이다.

02 　　　　　　　　　　정답 ③

[지문분석]

People with low self-esteem / often perceive themselves / as inferior / but do whatever they can / to appear ① strong.
자존감이 낮은 사람들은 / 종종 자신을 여긴다 / 열등하다고 / 하지만 그들이 할 수 있는 무엇이든 한다 / 강단 있게 보이기 위해

For those with low self-esteem / in leadership positions, / the need to look powerful / can cause them to try / to make their staff ② fear them.
자존감이 낮은 사람들에게 있어 / 리더의 위치에 있는 / 영향력 있게 보이고자 하는 욕구는 / 그들이 애쓰게 할 수 있다 / 그들의 직원이 그들을 무서워하게 만들도록

For instance, / they might threaten / to fire employees / whenever something goes wrong.
예를 들어 / 그들은 협박할지도 모른다 / 직원들을 해고하겠다고 / 무언가 일이 잘못될 때마다

Furthermore, / they may ③ admit(→ deny) making mistakes, / choosing to blame others instead.
더 나아가 / 그들은 실수하는 것을 인정할(→ 부인할) 수 있다 / 대신 다른 사람을 탓하기로 결정하며

★ By behaving this way, / they try to make sure / that no one will ④ challenge them / and that they can hold onto their position.
이런 방식으로 행동함으로써 / 그들은 반드시 ~할 수 있도록 노력한다 / 그 어떤 사람도 그들에게 이의를 제기하지 못한다 / 또 그들의 지위를 유지할 수 있다

Leaders with poor self-esteem / are not aware of their self-value, / so they think / behaving in this manner / is the only way / to earn recognition / as a leader.
열등한 자존감을 가진 리더는 / 그들의 자아 가치를 인지하지 못한다 / 그래서 그들은 생각한다 / 이런 방식으로 행동하는 것이 / 유일한 방법이라고 / 인정을 받는 / 지도자로서

Because they do not know / their own self-worth, / they create a ⑤ toxic environment / for the people they manage.
그들이 ~을 모르기 때문에 / 자신의 자아 가치를 / 그들은 해가 되는 환경을 만들어낸다 / 그들이 관리하는 사람들에게

★ 독해가 쉬워지는 구문 풀이

By behaving this way, they try to make sure [①**that** no one will challenge them] and [②**that** they can hold onto their position].
　　　　　　　명사절 접속사　　　　　　　　명사절 접속사

⇨ [①]과 [②]는 각각 make sure의 목적어이며, 등위접속사 and로 연결되어 병렬 구조를 이룬다. 2개의 that 모두 명사절 접속사 that이 쓰였다.

[어휘] perceive ~로 여기다 　inferior 열등한 　staff 직원 　threaten 협박하다
fire 해고하다 　go wrong (일 등이) 잘못되다 　dare 감히 ~하다
challenge 이의를 제기하다 　recognition 인정
inability ~할 수 없는 것, 불가능 　worth 가치 　toxic 해가 되는, 치명적인; 독

[해석] [주제문] 자존감이 낮은 사람들은 종종 자신을 열등하다고 여기지만 ① 강단있게 보이기 위해 그들이 할 수 있는 무엇이든 한다. 리더의 위치에 있는 자존감이 낮은 사람들에게 있어, 영향력 있게 보이고자 하는 욕구는 그들의 직원이 그들을 ② 무서워하게 만들도록 애쓰게 할 수 있다. 예를 들어, 그들은 무언가 일이 잘못될 때마다 직원들을 해고하겠다고 협박할지도 모른다. 더 나아가, 그들은 대신 다른 사람을 탓하기로 결정하며 실수하는 것을 ③ 인정할(→ 부인할) 수 있다. 이런 방식으로 행동함으로써, 그들은 그 어떤 사람도 감히 그들에게 ④ 이의를 제기하지 못하게 하고, 또 그들의 지위를 반드시 유지할 수 있도록 노력한다. 열등한 자존감을 가진 리더는 그들의 자아 가치를 인지하지 못해서 이런 방식으로 행동하는 것이 지도자로서 인정을 받는 유일한 방법이라고 생각한다. 그들이 자신의 자아 가치를 모르기 때문에, 그들은 그들이 관리하는 사람에게 ⑤ 해가 되는 환경을 만들어낸다.

[해설] 자존감이 낮은 사람들은 다른 사람을 탓하기로 결정하며 실수하는 것을 "부인할" 수 있다는 맥락이 되어야 하므로, ③의 admit은 deny와 같은 어휘로 바꾸어야 문맥상 적절하다.

[오답분석] ①은 그들은 "강단 있게" 보이기 위해 할 수 있는 무엇이든 한다는 문맥이 되어야 하므로 strong이 오는 것이 적절하다. ②은 자존감이 낮은 리더가 영향력 있게 보이고자 하는 욕구는 직원이 그를 "무서워하게" 만들도록 애쓰게 할 수 있다는 문맥이 되어야 하므로 fear가 오는 것이 적절하다. ④은 직원을 협박하거나, 다른 사람을 탓함으로써 그 어떤 사람도 감히 그들에게 "이의를 제기하지" 못한다는 문맥이 되어야 하므로 challenge가 오는 것이 적절하다. ⑤은 그들 자신의 가치를 인지하지 못하기 때문에 그들이 관리하는 사람들에게 "해가 되는" 환경을 만들어 낸다는 문맥이 되어야 하므로 toxic이 오는 것이 적절하다.

[실력 UP!] 미니 문제 02.

정답 make sure that no one will dare to challenge them and that they can hold onto their position

해석 Q. 지문에 따르면, 왜 자존감이 낮은 지도자들은 직원들을 해고한다고 협박하거나 그들이 저지른 실수에 대해 다른 사람들을 탓하는가?
A: 그 어떤 사람도 감히 그들에게 이의를 제기하지 못하게 하고, 또 그들의 지위를 반드시 유지할 수 있도록 하기 위함이다.

해설 By behaving this way ~ hold onto their position에서 자존감이 낮은 지도자는 사람들이 자신에게 이의를 제기하지 못하게 하고, 그들의 지위를 반드시 유지할 수 있도록 직원들을 해고한다고 협박하거나 그들이 저지른 실수에 대해 다른 사람들을 탓한다는 것을 알 수 있다.

03 　　　　　　　　　　정답 ④

[지문분석]

Invasive plant species pose / a very serious threat / to biodiversity.
침입성 식물종은 가한다 / 매우 심각한 위험을 / 생물의 다양성에

This is especially true / when a species is introduced / to an ecosystem / where there are no ① competitors.
이는 특히 더 그렇다 / 어떤 생물 종이 도입될 때 / 생태계에 / 경쟁자가 없는

★ With nothing challenging it, / an invasive plant species can spread very rapidly / and easily ② disturb the growth / of native plants / by consuming / whatever light, moisture, and nutrients / are available.

그것에 대항하는 어떠한 것도 없기에 / 침입성 식물종은 아주 빠르게 퍼져나갈 수 있다 / 그리고 성장을 쉽게 방해한다 / 토착 식물의 / 섭취하면서 / 그 어떤 빛, 수분, 영양분이든 지 / 얻을 수 있는

This can lead / to their endangerment or extinction / within a few generations.

이는 초래할 수 있다 / 그들의 멸종 위기나 절멸을 / 몇 세대 내에

The effects on local birds and wildlife / can also be extremely ③ damaging, / as many of them rely on these native plants / for food.

토착 조류와 야생동물에게 미치는 영향은 / 마찬가지로 몹시 해로울 수 있는데 / 이는 이들 중 다수가 이 토착 식물을 의존하기 때문이다 / 먹이로써

People are ④ unaware(→ aware) of the problems / caused by invasive species, / and trillions of dollars are spent / globally each year / to get rid of them.

사람들은 문제들을 모르고(→ 인지하고) 있다 / 침입종에 의해 야기되는 / 그리고 수조 달러 가 사용된다 / 매년 세계적으로 / 그것을 없애기 위해

Nonetheless, / this often makes the problem ⑤ worse / as using pesticides / in affected areas / can pollute soil and water.

그럼에도 불구하고 / 이는 종종 문제를 더 안 좋게 만든다 / 살충제를 사용하는 것은 ~하기 때문에 / 피해를 본 지역에 / 토양과 물을 오염시킬 수 있다

★ 독해가 쉬워지는 구문 풀이

[With nothing challenging it], an invasive plant species can spread
　　　　대명사　현재분사　　　　　　　주어　　　　　　　　동사1
very rapidly and easily disturb the growth of native plants ~
　　　　　　　　　　　　　동사2

⇨ [ ]는 <with + 목적어 + 형용사/분사> 구문이며, '~한채'로 해석한다.
⇨ 수식 받는 대명사 nothing이 challenge가 나타내는 '대항하는' 행위의 주체이므로 현재분사 challenging이 쓰였다.

어휘 invasive plant 침입성 식물 pose 가하다 introduce 도입하다, 들여오다 ecosystem 생태계 native 토착의, 태생의 consume 섭취하다, 사용하다 endangerment 멸종 위기의 상태, 위험에 빠진 상태 extinction 절멸, 멸종 damaging 해로운, 악영향을 주는 trillion 1조, 엄청난 양 affected 피해를 본, 영향을 받은

해석 **주제문** 침입성 식물종은 생물의 다양성에 매우 심각한 위협을 가한다. 이는 어떤 생물 종이 ① 경쟁자가 없는 생태계에 도입될 때 특히 더 그렇다. 그것에 대항하는 어떠한 것도 없기에, 침입성 식물종은 아주 빠르게 퍼져나가며, 얻을 수 있는 그 어떤 빛, 수분, 영양분이든지 섭취하면서 토착 식물의 성장을 쉽게 ② 방해할 수 있다. 이는 몇 세대 내에 그들의 멸종 위기나 절멸을 초래할 수 있다. 토착 조류와 야생동물에게 미치는 영향도 마찬가지로 ③ 해로울 수 있는데, 이는 이들 중 다수가 이 토착 식물을 먹이로써 의존하기 때문이다. 사람들은 침입종에 의해 야기되는 문제들을 ④ 모르고(→ 인지하고) 있고, 그것을 없애기 위해 매년 세계적으로 수조 달러가 사용된다. 그럼에도 불구하고, 피해를 본 지역에 살충제를 사용하는 것은 토양과 물을 오염시킬 수 있기 때문에 이는 종종 문제를 더 ⑤ 안 좋게 만든다.

해설 사람들이 침입종에 의해 야기되는 문제들을 인지하고 있고 그 문제를 없애기 위해 매년 수조 달러가 사용된다는 맥락이 되어야 하므로, ④의 unaware를 aware와 같은 어휘로 바꾸어야 문맥상 적절하다.

오답분석 ①은 생물 종이 그것에 대항하는 어떠한 "경쟁자"도 없는 생태계에 도입될 때 특히 더 위협을 가한다는 문맥이 되어야 하므로 competitors가 오는 것이 적절하다. ②은 침입성 식물종이 얻을 수 있는 그 어떤 빛, 수분, 영양분이든지 섭취하면서 토착 식물의 성장을 쉽게 "방해할" 수 있다는 문맥이 되어야 하므로 disturb가 오는 것이 적절하다. ③은 토착 조류 및 야생동물이 토착 식물을 먹이로써 의존하고 있기 때문에 침입성 식물종에 의

한 토착 식물의 멸종 및 절멸이 이들에 끼치는 영향도 "해로울" 수 있다는 문맥이 되어야 하므로 damaging이 오는 것이 적절하다. ⑤은 살충제를 사용하는 것은 토양과 물을 오염시켜 종종 문제를 "더 안 좋게" 만든다는 문맥이 되어야 하므로 worse가 오는 것이 적절하다.

실력UP! 미니 문제 03.

정답 ②

해석 ① 전 세계에서 생물 다양성의 감소
② 침입종들이 생태계를 위험에 빠뜨리는 방법
③ 침입종 제거에 드는 재정적 비용

해설 침입성 식물종이 침입한 생태계와 그들이 토착종에 야기하는 문제에 관한 글이므로, 글의 주제로 가장 적절한 것은 ② how invasive species endanger ecosystems 이다.

04　　　　　　　　　　　　　　　　　　정답 ⑤

지문분석

Active listening is vital / to having good interpersonal communication skills.

적극적인 경청은 필수적이다 / 좋은 대인 의사소통 기술을 갖는 데

To be an active listener, / you must first ① avoid / distracting thoughts.

적극적으로 듣는 사람이 되려면 / 당신은 먼저 피해야 한다 / 정신을 산만하게 하는 생각들을

★ This will allow you / to pay attention / to what the other person is saying.

이는 당신이 ~할 수 있게 해줄 것이다 / 주목하게 / 다른 사람이 말하고 있는 것에

However, / just listening is not enough.

하지만 / 그저 듣는 것만으로는 충분하지 않다

You must also ② show / that you're engaged / in what the other person is saying.

당신은 또한 보여주어야 한다 / 당신이 몰두해 있음을 / 다른 사람이 말하고 있는 것에

You can do this / by smiling, nodding, and making direct eye contact / with the speaker.

당신은 이것을 할 수 있다 / 미소를 짓고, 고개를 끄덕이고, 직접적인 눈 맞춤을 함으로써 / 화자와

To be sure / that you understand, / you can ask the speaker / to ③ clarify certain points / or summarize what they have said.

확실히 하고자 한다면 / 당신이 이해하는 것을 / 당신은 화자에게 요청할 수 있다 / 특정 부 분을 명확히 해달라고 / 또는 그들이 말한 것을 요약해달라고

This involves repeating the main points / of the message, / which ④ gives the speaker a chance / to make a correction / if necessary.

이것은 요점을 되풀이해서 말하는 것을 포함한다 / 메시지의 / 그런데 이는 화자에게 기회 를 준다 / 잘못을 바로잡을 / 필요할 경우

Finally, / before you respond, / allow the speaker to finish / what they're saying.

마지막으로 / 당신이 대답하기 전에 / 화자가 마무리 지을 수 있도록 해 주어라 / 그가 말하 고 있는 것을

Interrupting only frustrates the speaker / and ⑤ deepens(→ limits) your comprehension.

이야기를 중단시키는 것은 화자를 실망하게 할 뿐이다 / 그리고 당신의 이해를 깊어지게 할(→ 제한할)

★ 독해가 쉬워지는 구문 풀이

This will **allow** you to pay attention to **what** the other person is
　　　　　동사　목적어 목적격보어　　　　　전치사
saying.

⇨ allow는 to부정사를 목적격보어로 취하는 동사이다.
⇨ 전치사 to의 목적어, 즉, 선행사를 포함하고, 불완전한 절 앞에 올 수 있는 관계대명사 what이 쓰였다.

어휘 active 적극적인, 활발한

interpersonal communication skill 대인 의사소통 기술
distract (정신을) 산만하게 하다, (주의를) 딴 데로 돌리다
pay attention to ~에 주목하다 engaged 몰두해 있는
nod (고개를) 끄덕이다, 까딱하다 interrupt (이야기를) 중단시키다
frustrate 실망하게 하다

해석 **주제문** *적극적인* 경청은 좋은 대인 의사소통 기술을 갖는 데 필수적이다. 적극적으로 듣는 사람이 되려면, 당신은 먼저 정신을 산만하게 하는 생각들을 ① 피해야 한다. 이는 당신이 다른 사람이 말하고 있는 것에 주목할 수 있게 해줄 것이다. 하지만, 그저 듣는 것만으로는 충분하지 않다. 당신은 또한 다른 사람이 말하고 있는 것에 당신이 몰두해 있음을 ② 보여주어야 한다. 당신은 미소를 짓고, 고개를 끄덕이고, 화자와 직접적인 눈 맞춤을 함으로써 이것을 할 수 있다. 당신이 이해하는 것을 확실히 하고자 한다면, 당신은 특정 부분을 ③ 명확히 하거나 그들이 말한 것을 요약해달라고 화자에게 요청할 수 있다. 이것은 메시지의 요점을 되풀이해서 말하는 것을 포함하는데, 이는 필요할 경우 화자에게 잘못을 바로잡을 기회를 ④ 준다. 마지막으로, 당신이 대답하기 전에 화자가 그가 말하고 있는 것을 마무리 지을 수 있도록 해 주어라. 이야기를 중단시키는 것은 화자를 실망하게 하고 당신의 이해를 ⑤ 깊어지게 할(→ 제한할) 뿐이다.

해설 좋은 대인 의사소통 기술 중의 하나는 화자가 말하고 있는 것을 마무리 짓게 하는 것이며, 이야기를 중단시키는 것은 당신의 이해를 "제한한다"는 맥락이 되어야 하므로, ⑤의 deepens를 limits와 같은 어휘로 바꾸어야 문맥상 적절하다.

오답 분석 ①은 적극적으로 들으려면 먼저 정신을 산만하게 하는 생각들을 "피해야" 한다는 문맥이 되어야 하므로 avoid가 오는 것이 적절하다. ②은 듣는 것만으로는 충분하지 않으며, 다른 사람이 말하고 있는 것에 당신이 몰두해 있음을 "보여주어야" 한다는 문맥이 되어야 하므로 show가 오는 것이 적절하다. ③은 이해하는 것을 확실히 하고자 한다면 특정 부분을 "명확히 해달라"고 화자에게 요청할 수 있다는 문맥이 되어야 하므로 clarify가 오는 것이 적절하다. ④은 그들이 말한 것을 요약하거나 요점을 되풀이하는 것이 화자에게 잘못을 바로잡을 기회를 "준다"는 문맥이 되어야 하므로 gives가 오는 것이 적절하다.

실력 UP! 미니 문제 04.

정답 ①

해석 ① 적극적으로 듣는 사람이 되기 위한 팁
② 좋은 대인 의사소통 기술이 드문 이유
③ 설득력 있는 주장을 하는 방법

해설 좋은 대인 의사소통 기술을 갖는 데 필수적인 적극적인 경청을 하는 방법에 관한 글이므로, 글의 주제로 가장 적절한 것은 ① tips for becoming an active listener이다.

05
정답 ③

지문분석

★ Imagine / being dropped off a thousand miles / from home / and asked / to find your way back.
상상해보아라 / 1,000마일 떨어진 곳에 내려졌다고 / 집에서 / 그리고 요구를 받았다 / 되돌아오라는

That is / what homing pigeons do.
그것이 바로 ~이다 / 전서 비둘기가 하는 일

Homing pigeons have a natural ability / to find their way home / over great distances.
전서 비둘기는 타고난 능력이 있다 / 집으로 되돌아오는 / 먼 거리를 거쳐

Ever since the time of the ancient Egyptians, / people have (A) utilized / ignored / their ability / in order to deliver messages / between distant locations.
고대 이집트 시대 이후로 / 인류는 이용해왔다 / 그들의 능력을 / 메시지를 전하기 위해 / 멀리 떨어진 장소 간의

But / just how / are homing pigeons able to navigate?
하지만 / 도대체 어떻게 / 전서 비둘기는 길을 찾을 수 있는가

Scientists are uncertain / about the exact mechanisms involved, / but they believe / that a combination of systems can (B) confuse / benefit / the pigeons' sense of direction.
과학자들은 알지 못한다 / 관련된 정확한 방법에 대해 / 하지만 그들은 생각한다 / 여러 체계의 조합이 도움을 줄 수 있다고 / 비둘기의 방향 감각에

For instance, / they may use the sun / to guide their direction / or use the iron elements / in their beaks / to follow Earth's magnetic waves.
예를 들어 / 그들은 태양을 이용할 수도 있다 / 그래서 그들의 방향을 이끌다 / 또는 철 성분을 이용한다 / 그들 부리에 있는 / 그래서 지구의 자파를 따라간다

Another possibility is infrasound, / or low-frequency sounds / made by natural objects.
다른 가능성은 초저주파이다 / 즉 낮은 주파수의 소리 / 자연 물체에 의해 만들어지는

These sounds are impossible / for humans to hear / but could enable the homing pigeon / to avoid (C) finding / missing / its destination.
이러한 소리들은 불가능하다 / 인간이 듣기에 / 하지만 전서 비둘기가 ~하게 할 수 있다 / 놓치는 것을 방지하도록 / 그들의 목적지를

> ★ 독해가 쉬워지는 구문 풀이
>
> **Imagine** being dropped off a thousand miles from home and
> 명령문의 동사원형
> asked to find your way back.
>
> ⇨ 명령문은 주로 주어를 생략하고 동사원형으로 시작한다.

어휘 find one's way back 되돌아오다 navigate 길을 찾다, 항해하다
mechanism 방법, 체계 frequency 주파수

해석 집에서 1,000마일 떨어진 곳에 내려져서 되돌아오라는 요구를 받았다고 상상해보아라. 그것이 바로 전서 비둘기가 하는 일이다. **주제문** 전서 비둘기는 먼 거리를 거쳐 집으로 되돌아오는 타고난 능력이 있다. 고대 이집트 시대 이후로, 인류는 멀리 떨어진 장소 간의 메시지를 전하기 위해 그들의 능력을 (A) 이용해왔다. 하지만 전서 비둘기는 도대체 어떻게 길을 찾을 수 있는가? 과학자들은 관련된 정확한 방법에 대해 알지 못하지만, 그들은 여러 체계의 조합이 비둘기의 방향 감각에 (B) 도움을 줄 수 있다고 생각한다. 예를 들어, 그들은 태양을 이용해서 그들의 방향을 이끌거나 그들 부리에 있는 철 성분을 이용해서 지구의 자파를 따라갈 수도 있다. 다른 가능성은 초저주파, 즉 자연 물체에 의해 만들어지는 낮은 주파수의 소리이다. 이러한 소리들은 인간이 듣기에 불가능하지만 전서 비둘기가 그들의 목적지를 (C) 놓치는 것을 방지하게 할 수 있다.

(A)　　　　(B)　　　　(C)
① 이용하는 – 혼란시키다 – 찾는
② 무시하는 – 혼란시키다 – 놓치는
③ 이용하는 – 도움을 주다 – 놓치는
④ 무시하는 – 도움을 주다 – 찾는
⑤ 이용하는 – 도움을 주다 – 찾는

해설 (A) 멀리 떨어진 장소 간의 메시지를 전하기 위해 그들의 능력을 "이용해 왔다"는 의미가 되어야 하므로 utilized가 문맥상 적절하다.
(B) 과학자들은 여러 체계의 조합이 비둘기의 방향 감각에 "도움을 줄 수 있다"고 생각한다는 의미가 되어야 하므로 benefit가 문맥상 적절하다.
(C) 초저주파는 전서 비둘기가 그들의 목적지를 "놓치는 것"을 방지해준다는 의미가 되어야 하므로 missing이 문맥상 적절하다.
따라서 정답으로 가장 적절한 것은 ③ utilized- benefit – missing이다.

실력 UP! 미니 문제 05.

정답 ⓐ navigate ⓑ system

해석 전서 비둘기는 초저주파 같은 여러 다른 ⓑ 체계를 조합하거나 자파를 감지하여 집으로 가는 ⓐ 길을 찾을 수 있다.

전서 비둘기는 태양과 초저주파를 이용하거나, 지구의 자파를 따라가는 등의 여러 체계를 조합해서 위치를 알아낸다고 했으므로, 요약문의 빈칸에 들어갈 말로 가장 적절한 것은 @ navigate(길을 찾다), ⓑ system(체계)이다.

06 정답 ②

지문분석

In making a decision, / using your head simply means / relying on your brain / to determine / which choice would ① bring the superior outcome.
결정을 내릴 때 / 당신의 머리를 사용한다는 것은 단순히 의미한다 / 당신의 뇌에 의존한다는 것을 / 알아내기 위해 / 어떤 선택이 최선의 결과를 가져올지를

This requires an ability / to identify relevant facts / and use logic / to choose the best option.
이것은 능력을 요구한다 / 관련 사실들을 확인하는 / 그리고 논리를 이용하는 / 최고의 선택지를 고르기 위해

★ Using your heart, / however, / means / depending on your instincts.
당신의 마음을 사용하는 것은 / 반면에 / 의미한다 / 당신의 본능에 의지하는 것을

This is when / people ② reject(→ trust) their feelings and "gut" / to determine / which choice might be best.
이것은 ~하는 경우이다 / 사람들이 그들의 느낌과 "직감"을 거부하는(→ 믿는) / 알아내기 위해 / 어떤 결정이 최선일지

This involves / remembering previous experiences / that might be ③ relevant / for the present situation.
이것은 포함한다 / 이전의 경험을 생각해 내는 것을 / 관련 있을지 모르는 / 현재 상황과

If current circumstances are / like those of the past, / a person will likely use prior knowledge / while deciding.
만약 현재 상황이 ~이라면 / 과거의 그것(상황)과 유사하다 / 아마도 어떤 사람은 기존의 지식을 사용할 가능성이 있을 것이다 / 결정을 내릴 때

There are appropriate times / to use / either the head or the heart.
적절한 때가 있다 / 사용할 / 머리나 마음 어느 쪽 하나를

For instance, / using your head might not be ④ beneficial / in an emergency.
예를 들어 / 머리를 사용하는 것이 도움이 되지 않을 수 있다 / 응급 상황에서는

When there is no time / to stop and think, / your heart might be needed / to make an ⑤ immediate response.
시간이 없을 때는 / 멈춰서 생각할 / 당신의 마음이 ~할 필요가 있을지도 모른다 / 즉각적인 반응을 할

> ★ 독해가 쉬워지는 구문 풀이
>
> [①Using your heart], however, means [②depending on your instincts].
> 단수주어(동명사구)   동사   목적어(동명사구)
>
> ⇨ 동명사구 [①]은 문장의 주어, 동명사구 [②]는 동사 means의 목적어이며, 동명사(구) 주어는 단수 취급한다.

어휘 rely 의존하다　determine 알아내다, 결정하다　superior 최선의, 상급의
relevant 관련 있는　logic 논리　instinct 본능　gut 직감, 내장
circumstance 상황　appropriate 적절한　beneficial 도움이 되는
emergency 응급 상황　immediate 즉각적인　response 반응, 대응

해석 결정을 내릴 때, 당신의 머리를 사용한다는 것은 단순히 어떤 선택이 최선의 결과를 ① 가져올지를 알아내기 위해 당신의 뇌에 의존하는 것을 의미한다. 이것은 관련 사실들을 확인하고 최고의 선택지를 고르기 위해 논리를 이용하는 능력을 요구한다. 반면에 당신의 마음을 사용하는 것은 당신의 본능에 의지하는 것을 의미한다. 이것은 사람들이 어떤 결정이 최선일지 알아내기 위해 그들의 느낌과 "직감"을 ② 거부하는(→ 믿는) 경우이다. 이것은 현재 상황과 ③ 관련 있을지 모르는 이전의 경험을 생각해 내는 것을 포함한다. 만약 현재 상황이 과거의 그것(상황)과 유사하다면, 아마도 어떤 사람은 결정을 내릴 때 기존의 지식을 사용할 가능성이 있을 것이다.

머리나 마음 어느 쪽 하나를 사용할 적절한 때가 있다. 예를 들어, 응급 상황에서는 머리를 사용하는 것이 ④ 도움이 되지 않을 수 있다. 멈춰서 생각할 시간이 없을 때는, 당신의 마음이 ⑤ 즉각적인 반응을 할 필요가 있을지도 모른다.

해설 머리를 사용하는 상황과 달리 사람들은 어떤 결정이 최선일지 알아내기 위해 그들의 느낌과 직감을 "믿는" 경우가 있다는 맥락이 되어야 하므로, ②의 reject를 trust와 같은 단어로 바꾸어야 문맥상 적절하다.

오답분석 ①은 어떤 선택이 최선의 결과를 "가져올지" 알아내기 위해 관련 사실들을 확인하고 논리를 이용해서 최고의 선택지를 고른다는 문맥으로 이어져야 하므로 ①은 bring이 오는 것이 적절하다. 마음을 사용하여 결정을 내리는 것은 현재 상황과 "관련 있을"지 모르는 이전의 경험을 생각해 내는 것을 포함한다는 문맥으로 이어져야 하므로 ③은 relevant가 오는 것이 적절하다. 머리를 사용하는 것이 응급 상황에서는 도움이 되지 않을 수 있다는 문맥으로 이어져야 자연스러우므로 ④은 beneficial이 오는 것이 적절하다. 이와 더불어 멈춰서 생각할 시간이 없을 때는 "즉각적인" 반응을 할 필요가 있을지도 모른다는 문맥으로 이어져야 하므로 ⑤은 immediate가 오는 것이 적절하다.

실력UP! 미니 문제 06.

정답 Using your head and using your heart are beneficial in different circumstances

07 정답 ③

지문분석

Blame can be loosely defined / as a negative reaction / toward someone / who has shown unsuitable behavior.
비난은 막연히 정의될 수 있다 / 부정적인 반응으로 / 누군가를 향한 / 적합하지 않은 행동을 보인

Although / almost everyone has experienced blame, / psychologists still struggle / to define exactly / what it is.
~임에도 불구하고 / 거의 모두가 비난을 경험해봤다 / 심리학자들은 여전히 애쓰다 / 정확히 정의하기 위해서 / 그것(비난)이 무엇인지

One theory is / that when we blame people, / we are actually (A) judging / accepting them.
한 학설은 ~이다 / 우리가 사람들을 비난할 때라는 것 / 우리는 사실 그들을 판단하고 있다

In effect, / the act of blaming someone / is the process / by which we evaluate others / based on personal and social criteria.
사실상 / 누군가를 비난하는 행위는 / 과정이다 / 우리가 타인을 평가하는 / 개인적인 그리고 사회적인 기준에 근거하여

Another possible explanation of blame is / that it is simply a(n) (B) emotional / logical response / —we feel anger / when we see someone act / in a manner / that we view as inappropriate.
비난에 대한 또 하나의 그럴싸한 설명은 ~이다 / 그것이 단순히 감정적인 반응이라는 것 / 우리는 분노를 느낀다 / 누군가가 행동하는 것을 볼 때 / ~한 태도로 / 우리가 부적절하다고 보는

A more recent theory / to account for blame / argues / that it is a (C) change / support of opinion / regarding a relationship.
더 최근의 학설 / 비난을 설명하기 위한 / 주장한다 / 그것이 견해의 변화라는 것 / 관계에 관한

★ This means / that when you blame a friend / for doing something / you find unacceptable, / you are actually reconsidering the relationship / you have with that person.
이것은 의미한다 / 당신이 친구를 비난할 때 / 무언가를 하는 것으로 / 당신이 받아들일 수 없다고 여기는 / 사실 당신은 관계를 재고하는 중이다 / 당신과 그 사람 사이의

This means that when you blame a friend for doing something [①(that) you find **unacceptable**], you are actually reconsidering the relationship [②(that) you have with that person].

⇨ [①]은 선행사 something을 수식하는 관계절이다. unacceptable은 동사 find가 쓰인 5형식 문장의 목적격보어로서, 생략된 목적격 관계대명사 that을 수식한다.

⇨ [②]는 선행사 relationship을 수식하는 관계절이며, 목적격 관계대명사 that 또는 which가 생략되었다.

어휘 loosely 막연히 define 정의하다 unsuitable 적합하지 않은 psychologist 심리학자 struggle 애쓰다 judge 판단하다 in effect 사실상 evaluate 평가하다 criteria 기준 logical 이성적인, 논리적인 inappropriate 부적절한 recent 최근의 account for 설명하다 regarding ~에 관한 unacceptable 받아들일 수 없는 reconsider 재고하다

해석 비난은 적합하지 않은 행동을 보인 누군가를 향한 부정적인 반응으로 막연히 정의될 수 있다. 거의 모두가 비난을 경험해 봤음에도 불구하고, 심리학자들은 그것(비난)이 무엇인지 정확히 정의하기 위해서 여전히 애쓴다. 한 학설은 우리가 사람들을 비난할 때, 우리는 사실 그들을 (A) 판단하고 있다는 것이다. 사실상, 누군가를 비난하는 행위는 우리가 개인적인 그리고 사회적인 기준에 근거하여 타인을 평가하는 과정이다. 비난에 대한 또 하나의 그럴싸한 설명은 그것이 우리가 누군가가 우리가 부적절하다고 보는 태도로 행동하는 것을 볼 때 분노를 느끼는 것처럼 단순히 (B) 감정적인 반응이라는 것이다. 비난을 설명하기 위한 더 최근의 학설은 그것이 관계에 관한 견해의 (C) 변화라는 것을 주장한다. 이것은 당신이 받아들일 수 없다고 여기는 무언가를 하는 것으로 친구를 비난할 때, 사실 당신은 당신과 그 사람 사이의 관계를 재고하는 중이라는 것을 의미한다.

	(A)	(B)	(C)
①	판단하는	이성적인	변화
②	받아들이는	감정적인	지지
③	판단하는	감정적인	변화
④	받아들이는	이성적인	변화
⑤	판단하는	이성적인	지지

해설 (A) 개인적이거나 사회적인 기준에 근거하여 타인을 평가한다는 내용으로 보아 우리가 사람들을 비난할 때, 우리는 사실 그들을 "판단하고" 있다는 의미가 되어야 하므로 judging이 문맥상 적절하다.
(B) 부적절한 행동을 보고 분노를 느낀다는 내용으로 보아 비난이 단순히 "감정적인" 반응일 수도 있다는 의미가 되어야 하므로 emotional이 문맥상 적절하다.
(C) 관계를 재고하는 중이라는 내용으로 보아 비난은 관계에 관한 견해의 "변화"라는 의미가 되어야 하므로 change가 문맥상 적절하다
따라서 정답으로 가장 적절한 것은 ③ judging- emotional - change이다.

실력 UP! 미니 문제 07.

정답 ②
해석 ① 비난의 효과에 대한 서로 다른 견해
② 비난의 진정한 의미에 대한 학설들
③ 비난이 도덕상 좋지 않은 행동인 이유
해설 심리학자들은 비난이 정확히 무엇인지를 정의하기 위해 여전히 애쓴다고 하며, 그들이 제시하고 있는 여러 학설에 대해 설명하고 있으므로, 글의 주제로 가장 적절한 것은 ① theories on the true meaning of blame(비난의 진정한 의미에 대한 학설들)이다.

지문분석

Gravity is a natural force / that most people just take for granted.
중력은 자연력이다 / 대부분의 사람들이 그저 당연하게 여기는

★ Unless a person is in outer space, / he or she is unlikely / to ① ignore this force.
사람이 우주 공간에 있지 않는 한 / 그 사람은 생각지도 못한다 / 이 힘을 무시하는 것

But what would happen / if gravity suddenly ceased / to function here on Earth?
그러나 무슨 일이 일어날 것인가? / 만약 중력이 갑자기 중단한다면 / 이곳 지구에서 기능하기를

The most obvious effects / would result from the fact / that objects would no longer be ② attracted / to each other.
가장 분명한 영향들은 / 사실에서 비롯될 것이다 / 물체들이 더 이상 끌어당겨지지 않을 것이다 / 서로에게

This is because / Earth would ③ continue spinning, / and anything / unattached to the surface / of the planet / would fall away / into space.
이것은 ~ 때문이다 / 지구가 계속해서 회전할 것이다 / 그리고 무엇이든 / 지면에 붙어있지 않은 / 행성의 / 떨어져 나갈 것이다 / 우주로

This includes / not only solid objects / but also the air, / and even the water in lakes and oceans.
이것은 포함한다 / 고체 물질뿐만 아니라 / 공기 / 그리고 심지어 호수나 바다의 물까지도

Over time, / the planet itself would become ④ smaller / since it would continually break apart / into tiny pieces.
시간이 지나면서 / 지구 자체는 더 작아질 것이다 / 계속해서 분해될 것이기 때문에 / 작은 조각들로

Fortunately, / scientists are certain / about the impossibility / of this scenario occurring.
다행스럽게도 / 과학자들은 확신한다 / 불가능에 / 이 시나리오가 발생하는 것의

Given that / gravity directly corresponds to mass, / Earth will ⑤ lose(→ keep) its gravity / because of its huge mass.
~을 고려하면 / 중력이 질량에 정비례하여 부합한다 / 지구는 그것의 중력을 잃을(→ 유지할) 것이다 / 그것의 거대한 질량 덕분에

Unless a person is in outer space, he or she is unlikely to ignore this force.

⇨ 문맥상 '사람이 우주 공간에 있지 않는 한'이라는 의미로 절(a person is in outer space)과 절(he or she is ~ this force)을 연결하는 '~하지 않는 한'이라는 뜻의 부사절 접속사 unless가 쓰였다.

어휘 gravity 중력 take for granted 당연한 일로 여기다 cease 중단하다 function 기능하다 attract 끌어당기다 unattached 붙어있지 않은 solid 고체의 impossibility 불가능 occur 발생하다 directly 정비례하여 correspond 부합하다 mass 질량

해석 중력은 대부분의 사람들이 그저 당연하게 여기는 자연력이다. 사람이 우주 공간에 있지 않는 한, 이 힘을 ① 무시하는 것은 생각지도 못할 일이다. 그러나 만약 중력이 이곳 지구에서 기능하기를 갑자기 중단한다면 무슨 일이 일어날 것인가? 가장 분명한 영향들은 물체들이 서로에게 더 이상 ② 끌어당겨지지 않을 것이라는 사실에서 비롯될 것이다. 이것은 지구가 ③ 계속해서 회전할 것이고, 행성의 지면에 붙어있지 않은 무엇이든 우주로 떨어져 나갈 것이기 때문이다. 이것은 고체 물질뿐만 아니라 공기 그리고 심지어 호수나 바다의 물까지도 포함한다. 시간이 지나면서, 작은 조각들로 계속해서 분해될 것이기 때문에 지구 자체는 ④ 더 작아질 것이다. 다행스럽게도, 과학자들은 이 시나리오가 발생하는 것의 불가능에 확신한다. 중력이 질량에 정비례하여 부합한다는 것을 고려하면, 지구는 그것의 거대한 질량 덕분에 중력을 ⑤ 잃을(→ 유지할) 것이다.

[해설] 이 글은 중력이 지구에서 기능하기를 중단한다면 어떤 일이 벌어지는지에 관한 글이다. 중력은 질량에 정비례하여 부합하므로, 지구는 거대한 질량 덕분에 중력을 "유지할" 것이라는 맥락이 되어야 하므로, ⑤의 lose를 keep과 같은 어휘로 바꾸어야 문맥상 적절하다.

[오답분석] ①은 사람들이 우주 공간에 있지 않는 한, 중력을 "무시하는" 것은 생각지도 못할 일이라는 문맥이 되어야 하므로 ignore가 오는 것이 적절하다. ②은 중력이 없다면 물체들이 서로에게 더 이상 "끌어당겨지지" 않을 것이라는 문맥이 되어야 하므로 attracted가 오는 것이 적절하다. ③은 지구가 "계속해서" 회전하여, 행성의 지면에 붙어있지 않은 무엇이든 우주로 떨어져 나갈 것이라는 문맥으로 이어져야 하므로 continue가 오는 것이 적절하다. ④은 시간이 지나면서, 작은 조각들로 계속해서 분해될 것이기 때문에 지구 자체는 "더 작아질" 것이라는 문맥이 되어야 하므로 smaller가 오는 것이 적절하다.

[실력 UP!] 미니 문제 08.

정답 (A) effects   (B) impossibility

해석 비록 지구 중력의 손실이 여러 가지 (A) 영향들을 초래할지라도, 과학자들은 이러한 사건의 (B) 불가능성을 강조한다.

해설 중력이 지구에서 기능하기를 갑자기 중단한다면 발생할 수 있는 영향들에 대해 설명하고 있고, 다행스럽게도 과학자들은 이 시나리오가 발생하는 것의 불가능에 확신한다고 했으므로, 요약문의 빈칸에 들어갈 말로 가장 적절한 것은 (A) effects(영향들), (B) impossibility(불가능성)이다.

CHAPTER 11 빈칸 추론하기

불변의 패턴 21   p.84
글의 초반부에 나온 빈칸 문장은 주제문이다.

기출 문제   정답 ③

[지문분석]

Remember / that **patience** is always of the essence.
기억해라 / **인내**가 항상 가장 중요하다는 것을

If an apology is not accepted, / thank the individual / for hearing you out / and leave the door open / for if and when / he wishes to reconcile.
만약 사과가 받아들여지지 않는다면, / 그 사람에게 감사해라 / 당신의 말을 끝까지 들어준 것에 / 그리고 문을 열어두어라 / 경우와 때를 위해 / 그 사람이 화해하고 싶을

★ Be conscious of the fact / that just because someone accepts your apology / does not mean / she has fully forgiven you.
사실을 자각해라 / 누군가가 당신의 사과를 받아들인다고 해서 / 의미하지 않는다 / 그녀가 당신을 완전히 용서했다는 것

It can take time, / maybe a long time, / before the injured party / can completely let go / and fully trust you again.
시간이 걸릴 수 있다 / 어쩌면 오랜 시간 / 상처받은 당사자가 / 완전히 떨쳐 버릴 수 있기 전까지 / 그리고 당신을 다시 완전히 믿는

There is little / you can do / to speed this process up.
거의 없다 / 당신이 할 수 있는 것은 / 이 과정의 속도를 높이기 위해서

If the person is truly important / to you, / it is worthwhile / to give him or her / the time and space needed / to heal.
만약 그 사람이 정말로 중요하다면 / 당신에게 / 가치가 있다 / 그 사람에게 줄 / 필요한 시간과 공간을 / 치유하기 위해

Do not expect / the person to go right back / to acting normally immediately.
기대하지 말아라 / 그 사람이 곧장 돌아갈 것이라고 / 바로 평소처럼 행동하는 것으로

★ 독해가 쉬워지는 구문 풀이

Be conscious of the fact that just because someone accepts
　　　　　　　　　　　　　　　동격의 that절
your apology does not mean she has fully forgiven you.

▷ '누군가가 당신의 사과를 받아들인다고 해서 그녀가 당신을 완전히 용서했다는 것을 의미하지 않는다는 사실'이라는 뜻으로 앞에 있는 명사 the fact의 내용을 풀어서 설명하고 있으므로 동격 that이 쓰였다.

[어휘] of the essence 가장 중요한   hear out ~의 말을 끝까지 들어주다   conscious 자각하는   let go (걱정·근심 등을) 떨쳐 버리다   worthwhile 가치 있는   immediately 바로, 곧   (선택지) curiosity 호기심   patience 인내(력), 참을성

[해석] **[주제문]** 인내가 항상 가장 중요하다는 것을 기억하라. 만약 사과가 받아들여지지 않는다면, 그 사람이 당신의 말을 끝까지 들어준 것에 감사하고, 그 사람이 화해하고 싶을 경우와 때를 위해 문을 열어두어라. 누군가가 당신의 사과를 받아들인다고 해서 그녀가 당신을 완전히 용서했다는 것을 의미하지 않는다는 사실을 자각해라. 상처받은 당사자가 완전히 떨쳐 버리고 당신을 다시 완전히 믿을 수 있기 전까지 시간이 걸릴 수 있고, 어쩌면 오랜 시간이 걸릴 수도 있다. 이 과정의 속도를 높이기 위해서 당신이 할 수 있는 것은 거의 없다. 만약 그 사람이 당신에게 정말로 중요하다면, 치유하기 위해 필요한 시간과 공간을 그 사람에게 줄 가치가 있다. 그 사람이 바로 평소처럼 행동하는 것으로 곧장 돌아갈 것이라고 기대하지 말아라.

① 호기심
② 자립
③ 인내
④ 창의성
⑤ 정직

[해설] 빈칸 문장은 이 글의 주제문이므로, 이를 다시 언급한 문장이나 부연 설명하는 문장을 파악해야 한다. 빈칸 문장에서 '무엇'이 항상 가장 중요하다고 하고, 글의 후반에서 상처받은 당사자가 완전히 떨쳐 버리고 당신을 다시 완전히 믿을 수 있기 전까지 시간이 걸릴 수 있다고 했다. 따라서 빈칸 문장은 "인내"가 항상 가장 중요하다는 것을 기억하라는 의미가 되는 것이 자연스러우므로 ③ patience(인내)가 정답이다.

[오답분석] ①, ②, ④, ⑤은 글의 내용과 관련이 없으므로 오답이다.

불변의 패턴 22   p.85
후반부의 빈칸 문장은 주제문을 재진술하는 문장이다.

기출 문제   정답 ①

[지문분석]

Due to technological innovations, / music can now be experienced / by more people, / for more of the time / than ever before.
기술 혁신으로 인해 / 음악은 이제 경험될 수 있다 / 더 많은 사람에 의해 / 더 오랜 시간 동안 / 이전보다

Mass availability / has given individuals unheard-of control / over their own sound-environment.
대규모의 이용 가능성은 / 개인에게 전례 없는 통제권을 주었다 / 그들 자신의 음향 환경에 대한

However, / it has also confronted them / with the simultaneous availability / of countless genres of music, / in which they have to orient themselves.
하지만 / 그것은 그들이 맞닥뜨리게 했고 / 동시에 이용 가능한 상황에 / 수많은 장르의 음악을 / 그들은 그 상황에 스스로를 맞춰야 한다

People start filtering out / and organizing their digital libraries / like they used to do / with their physical music collections.
사람들은 필터링하기 시작한다 / 그리고 그들의 디지털 라이브러리를 구성하는 것 / 그들이 했던 것처럼 / 물리적 형태의 음악 수집

However, / there is the difference / that the choice lies in their own hands.
하지만 / 차이가 있다 / 선택이 그들 마음대로라는

★ Without being restricted / to the limited collection / of music-distributors, / nor being guided / by the local radio program / as a 'preselector' / of the latest hits, / the individual actively has to **choose and determine / his or her musical preferences**.
국한되지 않은 상황에서 / 제한된 수집물에 / 음악 배급업자들의 / 또는 유도되지도 않으며 / 지역 라디오 프로그램에 의해 / '사전 선택자'로서의 / 최신 히트곡의 / 개인은 적극적으로 **선택하고 결정해야 한다** / **자신의 음악적 선호도를**

The search / for the right song / is thus associated with considerable effort.
검색은 / 적절한 노래의 / 따라서 상당한 노력과 연관된다

★ 독해가 쉬워지는 구문 풀이

[**Without** {①being restricted to the limited collection of music-distributors}, **nor** {②being guided by the local radio program as a 'preselector' of the latest hits}], the individual actively has to choose and determine his or her musical preferences.

⇨ 동명사구 {①}과 {②}는 각각 전치사 Without의 목적어이며, 등위접속사 nor로 연결된 병렬 구조이다.

⇨ [ ]는 주절 [the individual ~ musical preferences]을 수식하는 전치사구이다.

[어휘] mass 대규모의, 대중의 unheard-of 전례 없는, 금시초문의
confront 맞닥뜨리다, 닥치다 orient 맞추다, 지향하게 하다
in hand 자기 마음대로, 지배하여 associate 연관되다, 결부 짓다
considerable 상당한 [선택지] preference 선호(도) inspire 영감을 주다
interpret (의미를) 해석하다

[해석] 기술 혁신으로 인해, 음악은 이제 이전보다 더 많은 사람에 의해 더 오랜 시간 동안 경험될 수 있다. 대규모의 이용 가능성은 개인에게 그들 자신의 음향 환경에 대한 전례 없는 통제권을 주었다. 하지만, 그것은 그들이 동시에 수많은 장르의 음악을 이용 가능한 상황에 맞닥뜨리게 했고 그들은 그 상황에 스스로를 맞춰야 한다. 사람들은 물리적 형태의 음악 수집을 했던 것처럼 그들의 디지털 라이브러리를 필터링하고 구성하기 시작한다. 하지만, 선택이 그들 마음대로라는 차이가 있다. 음악 배급업자들의 제한된 수집물에 국한되지도, 최신 히트곡의 '사전 선택자'로서의 지역 라디오 프로그램에 의해 유도되지도 않은 상황에서, [주제문] 개인은 적극적으로 **자신의 음악적 선호도를 선택하고 결정**해야 한다. 따라서 적절한 노래의 검색은 상당한 노력과 연관된다.

① 자신의 음악적 선호도를 선택하고 결정한다
② 녹음 과정의 기술적 측면들을 이해한다
③ 독특하고 영감을 주는 플레이리스트를 소셜 미디어에서 공유한다
④ 노래의 배경지식을 바탕으로 가사를 해석한다
⑤ 더 나은 공연을 위해 발성 전문가의 조언을 구한다

[해설] 빈칸 문장은 이 글의 주제문이므로, 이를 다시 언급한 문장이나 부연 설명하는 문장을 파악해야 한다. 빈칸 문장에서 개인은 적극적으로 '무엇을 해야' 한다고 하고, 글의 중반에서 대규모의 음악 이용 가능성은 개인에게 전례 없는 통제권을 주었으나 동시에 수많은 장르의 음악을 이용 가능한 상황에 맞닥뜨리게 했다고 했다. 따라서 빈칸 문장은 음악 배급자들의 제한된 수집에 국한되지도, 지역 라디오 프로그램에 의해 유도되지도 않고 개인이 적극적으로 "자신의 음악적 선호도를 선택하고 결정해야" 한다는 의미가 되는 것이 자연스러우므로 ① choose and determine his or her musical preferences(자신의 음악적 선호도를 선택하고 결정한다)

가 정답이다.

[오답분석] ②의 녹음 과정의 기술적 측면들을 이해한다는 내용은 글의 내용과 관련이 없다. ③의 플레이리스트를 소셜 미디어에서 공유한다는 내용은 글에서 언급되고 있지 않다. ④은 글의 핵심 단어인 songs를 활용하여 혼동을 주는 오답이다. 더 나은 공연을 위해 발성 전문가의 조언을 구한다는 ⑤은 글의 주제와 관련이 없다.

독해 만점 TEST p.86

01 ④ 02 ② 03 ⑤ 04 ① 05 ② 06 ③ 07 ① 08 ④
09 ⑤ 10 ⑤ 11 ① 12 ③

실력 UP! 미니 문제

01. Reading books from a variety of genres can broaden your perspective
02. ②
03. (A) repetitive   (B) stop
04. ①
05. ②
06. ②
07. (A) scientists   (B) hypothesis   (C) law
08. ③
09. (A) participants   (B) the younger participants
10. (A) 속도가 높아짐에 따라 절약되는 시간이 적어지는 것
    (B) 속도를 높인 후 절약할 수 있는 시간을 과대평가하는 것
11. ①
12. The intention behind what a person says matters more than the literal meaning of the words they use

---

01 정답 ④

지문분석

★ Many people / have a favorite genre / that they come back to / over and over again.
많은 사람들은 / 선호하는 장르가 있다 / 그들이 찾는 / 몇 번이고 반복해서

And while / reading a familiar type of book / can be relaxing, / it is unlikely / to lead to a broader perspective.
그리고 ~하지만 / 익숙한 유형의 책을 읽는 것 / 안정감을 줄 수 있다 / 가능성은 거의 없다 / 넓은 관점으로 이끌

For that, / people have to read books / from a variety of genres, / even if it means / **leaving their comfort zone**.
이 때문에 / 사람들은 책을 읽어야 한다 / 다양한 장르의 / 비록 그것이 뜻할지라도 / **그들의 안전지대에서 벗어남을**

There is nothing wrong / with having a preference for a specific genre, / but reading books / exclusively from a familiar category / means / that you will never learn / about other topics.
잘못된 것은 아니다 / 특정 장르를 선호하는 것이 / 하지만 책만 읽는 것은 / 오로지 친숙한 범주의 / 의미한다 / 당신이 결코 배우지 못할 것을 / 다른 주제에 대해

In contrast, / reading works / that take you away from familiar topics / almost guarantees / that you will encounter / new ideas, types of people, and writing styles.
이와 달리 / 작품들을 읽는 것 / 익숙한 주제에서 당신을 벗어나게 해 줄 / 거의 보장한다 / 당신이 마주하게 될 것을 / 새로운 사고, 사람들의 유형, 그리고 문체를

This may feel discomforting / at first / but it will ultimately open you / up to new ideas / and maybe even cause you / to think differently / about the world.
이것은 불편하게 느껴질 수도 있다 / 처음에는 / 그러나 결국 당신이 마음을 열게 할 것이다 / 새로운 생각을 향해 / 그리고 심지어 당신을 ~하게 만들 것이다 / 다르게 생각하도록 / 세상에 대해

어휘 unlikely 아마도 ~하지 않는 perspective 관점 a variety of 다양한
genre 장르 preference 선호 exclusively 오로지 guarantee 보장하다
discomforting 불편하게 하는 **선택지** ruin 약화시키다
comfort zone (심리적) 안전지대

해석 많은 사람들은 그들이 몇 번이고 반복해서 찾는 선호하는 장르가 있다. 그리고 익숙한 유형의 책을 읽는 것이 안정감을 줄 수 있지만, 넓은 관점으로 이끌 가능성은 거의 없다. **주제문** 이 때문에, 비록 그것이 **그들의 안전지대에서 벗어남**을 뜻할지라도, 사람들은 다양한 장르의 책을 읽어야 한다. 특정 장르를 선호하는 것이 잘못된 것은 아니지만, 오로지 친숙한 범주의 책만 읽는 것은 당신이 결코 다른 주제에 대해 배우지 못할 것을 의미한다. 이와 달리, 익숙한 주제에서 당신을 벗어나게 해 줄 작품들을 읽는 것은 당신이 새로운 사고, 사람들의 유형, 그리고 문제를 마주하게 될 것을 거의 보장한다. 이것은 처음에는 불편하게 느껴질 수도 있으나 결국 새로운 생각을 향해 당신이 마음을 열게 할 것이며 심지어 당신이 세상에 대해 다르게 생각하도록 만들 것이다.

① 그들의 인간 관계를 약화시킴
② 그들의 관점을 축소시킴
③ 그들의 기억력을 제한함
④ 그들의 안전지대에서 벗어남
⑤ 그들의 어휘력을 감퇴시킴

해설 빈칸 문장은 이 글의 주제문이므로, 이를 다시 언급한 문장이나 부연 설명하는 문장을 파악해야 한다. 빈칸 문장에서 다양한 장르의 책을 읽는 것이 '무엇'을 뜻할지라도, 사람들은 그것을 해야 한다고 하고, 글의 후반에서 더 다양한 독서 목록을 가지는 것이 처음에는 "겁이 날 수도 있으나" 결국 새로운 생각을 향해 마음을 열게 할 것이라고 했다. 따라서 빈칸에는 ④ leaving their comfort zone(그들의 안전지대에서 벗어남)이 와서 다양한 장르의 책을 읽는 것이 그들의 안전지대에서 벗어남을 뜻할지라도 그것을 해야 한다는 의미가 되어야 한다.

오답분석 ①의 '인간 관계'는 글에서 언급된 소재인 '사람'을 활용하여 혼동을 주는 오답이다. ②의 '관점을 축소시킨다는 것'은 글의 주제를 반대로 진술한 오답이다. ③의 '기억력'은 글과 상관없는 오답이다. ⑤의 '어휘력'은 글의 핵심 소재 '책'에서 연상되는 내용을 활용하여 혼동을 주는 오답이다.

실력 UP! 미니 문제 01.

정답 Reading books from a variety of genres can broaden your perspective

02
정답 ②

지문분석

★ Most websites are now / approximately twice as large / as they
were three years ago.
현재 대부분의 웹사이트는 ~이다 / 대략 두 배만큼 더 크다 / 3년 전의 그것들보다

This is due to their more frequent use / of videos and images, /
not to mention the addition / of advertising and data-tracking
technologies.
이것은 그들의 더욱 빈번한 사용으로 인한 것이다 / 영상과 사진의 / 합세는 말할 것도 없고 /
광고와 자료 추적 기술의

These are intended / to enhance the appearance of websites, /
help companies meet business objectives, / and provide a better
user experience.
이들은 계획된다 / 웹사이트의 외관을 강화하도록 / 회사가 사업 목표를 충족시키는 것을
돕도록 / 그리고 더 나은 사용자 경험을 제공하도록

However, / all of these factors / have increased the density of
code / that needs to be written, / which contributes to a website's
complexity / and ultimately causes it to load less quickly / than
before.
그러나 / 이러한 요소들 모두는 / 코드의 밀도를 증가시켰다 / 쓰여야 하는 / 그런데 이는
웹사이트의 복잡함의 원인이다 / 그리고 결국 그것이 덜 빠르게 로딩되도록 만든다 / 이
전보다

While / having a more attractive appearance / helps websites
generate more income, / the increased bulk and higher level of
involvement / negatively affect their **speed**.
반면에 / 더 매력적인 외관을 가지는 것은 / 웹사이트가 더 많은 수입을 창출하도록 돕는다 /
커진 규모와 더 높은 관여도는 / 그것의 **속도**에 부정적으로 영향을 미친다

어휘 approximately 대략 frequent 빈번한
not to mention ~은 말할 것도 없이 tracking 추적
intend 계획하다, 의도하다 enhance 강화하다 density 밀도
contribute to ~의 원인이다 complexity 복잡함 load 로딩되다
generate 창출하다 income 수입 bulk 규모
level of involvement 관여도(재화나 서비스를 구매할 때 소비자가 정보 탐색에 시간과 노력을 기울이는 정도) negatively 부정적으로

해석 현재 대부분의 웹사이트는 3년 전의 그것들보다 대략 두 배만큼 더 크다. 이것은 광고와 자료 추적 기술의 합세는 말할 것도 없고, 영상과 사진의 더욱 빈번한 사용으로 인한 것이다. 이들은 웹사이트의 외관을 강화하고, 회사가 사업 목표를 충족시키는 것을 도우며, 더 나은 사용자 경험을 제공하도록 계획된다. 그러나, 이러한 요소들 모두는 쓰여야 하는 코드의 밀도를 증가시켰는데, 이는 웹사이트의 복잡함의 원인이며 결국 그것이 이전보다 덜 빠르게 로딩되도록 만든다. **주제문** 더 매력적인 외관을 가지는 것은 웹사이트가 더 많은 수입을 창출하도록 돕는 반면, 커진 규모와 더 높은 관여도는 그것의 **속도**에 부정적으로 영향을 미친다.

① 성장
② 속도
③ 생산성
④ 소리
⑤ 이미지

해설 빈칸 문장은 이 글의 주제문이므로, 이를 다시 언급한 문장이나 부연 설명하는 문장을 파악해야 한다. 빈칸 문장에서 웹사이트의 커진 규모와 더 높은 관여도는 웹사이트의 '무엇'에 부정적으로 영향을 미친다고 하고, 앞 문장에서 웹사이트의 복잡함이 원인이 되어 결국 웹사이트가 이전보다 덜 빠르게 로딩되도록 만든다고 했다. 따라서 빈칸에는 커진 규모와 더 높은 관여도가 웹사이트의 "속도"에 부정적으로 영향을 미친다는 의미가 되는 것이 자연스러우므로 ② speed(속도)가 정답이다.

오답분석 ①의 '성장'은 글의 내용과 관련이 없다. ③의 '생산성'에 대한 내용은 글에서 언급되고 있지 않다. ④과 ⑤은 글에서 언급된 소재 videos and images를 활용하여 혼동을 주는 오답이다.

실력 UP! 미니 문제 02.

정답 ②
해석 ① 컴퓨터 회사에 의한 광고 및 데이터 추적의 변화

② 웹사이트의 외관과 성능 간의 상호 절충
③ 현대의 웹사이트를 관리하기 위해 필요한 복잡한 코드들

해설 더 매력적인 외관은 웹사이트가 더 많은 수입을 창출하도록 돕지만, 웹사이트의 속도에는 부정적인 영향을 미친다는 내용의 글이므로, 글의 주제로 가장 적절한 것은 ② trade-offs between the appearance and performance of websites이다.

03
정답 ⑤

지문분석

In a 2011 study / led by psychology professor Alejandro Lleras, / 84 participants were divided into four groups / and asked to perform a repetitive task / on a computer / for 50 minutes.
2011년 연구에서 / 심리학 교수 Alejandro Lleras에 의해 진행된 / 84명의 참가자들이 네 개의 그룹으로 나누어졌다 / 그리고 반복적인 작업을 수행하도록 요구되었다 / 컴퓨터로 / 50분 동안

One of the groups was given / two short distractions / from work.
그 그룹 중 하나에게는 주어졌다 / 두 번의 짧은 기분 전환이 / 작업으로부터

When a four-digit code appeared / on their screens, / they were asked / to stop working briefly.
네 자리 숫자 코드가 나타났을 때 / 그들의 화면에 / 그들은 지시받았다 / 잠시 일하는 것을 중단하도록

Meanwhile, / the other groups worked / without interruption / for the full duration of the experiment.
한편 / 다른 그룹은 작업했다 / 중단 없이 / 실험의 전체 기간 동안

★ It was found / that the performance of the groups / who worked nonstop / declined steadily / throughout the experiment, / whereas the group that stopped momentarily / kept their concentration / until the end.
드러났다 / 그룹의 성과는 ~인 것으로 / 쉬지 않고 작업한 / 지속적으로 떨어졌다 / 실험 내내 / 반면에 잠깐씩 중단했던 그룹은 / 집중력을 유지했다 / 끝까지

The findings ultimately suggest / that **taking breaks improves the ability** / **to focus** / **over time**.
그 연구 결과는 궁극적으로 시사한다 / **휴식을 취하는 것은 능력을 향상시킨다는 것을** / 집중하는 / 오랜 시간 동안

★ **독해가 쉬워지는 구문 풀이**

It was found that the performance of the groups who worked
가주어   동사   진짜 주어
nonstop declined steadily throughout the experiment, whereas ~.

⇨ 주어가 '쉬지 않고 작업한 그룹의 성과는 ~ 끝까지 집중력을 유지했다는 것'이라는 의미로 길기 때문에, 긴 주어를 대신해서 가주어 역할을 할 수 있는 It으로 문장을 시작했다.

어휘 psychology 심리학 repetitive 반복적인 task 작업, 일 distraction 기분 전환 digit 자리, 숫자, 번호 briefly 잠시, 간략히 interruption 중단, 방해 performance 성과, 실행 steadily 지속적으로 momentarily 잠깐씩, 곧 finding (연구 등의) 결과, 발견 [선택지] retain 기억하다, 보유하다 at a time 동시에, 한 번에

해석 심리학 교수인 Alejandro Lleras에 의해 진행된 2011년 연구에서, 84명의 참가자들이 네 개의 그룹으로 나누어져 50분 동안 컴퓨터로 반복적인 작업을 수행하도록 요구되었다. 그 그룹 중 하나에게는 작업으로부터 두 번의 짧은 기분 전환이 주어졌다. 그들의 화면에 네 자리 숫자 코드가 나타났을 때, 그들은 잠시 일하는 것을 중단하도록 지시받았다. 한편, 다른 그룹은 실험의 전체 기간 동안 중단 없이 작업했다. 쉬지 않고 작업한 그룹의 성과는 실험 내내 지속적으로 떨어졌고, 반면에 잠깐씩 중단했던 그룹은 끝까지 집중력을 유지했다는 것이 드러났다. [주제문] 그 연구 결과는 **휴식을 취하는 것은 오랜 시간 동안 집중하는 능력을 향상시킨다는 것을** 궁극적으로 시사한다.

① 정보를 기억하는 것은 잦은 중단이 있더라도 가능하다
② 여러 작업을 동시에 하는 것은 생산성을 떨어뜨릴 수 있다

③ 많은 정보를 한 번에 습득하는 것은 단기적으로 도움이 된다
④ 컴퓨터로 작업하는 것은 더 향상된 성과를 이끌어 낼 수 있다
⑤ 휴식을 취하는 것은 오랜 시간 동안 집중하는 능력을 향상시킨다

해설 빈칸 문장은 이 글의 주제문이므로, 이를 다시 언급한 문장이나 부연 설명하는 문장을 파악해야 한다. 빈칸 문장에서 연구 결과는 '무엇'을 궁극적으로 시사한다고 하고, 글의 중반에서 쉬지 않고 작업한 그룹의 성과는 지속해서 떨어진 반면에 잠깐씩 중단했던 그룹은 끝까지 집중했다고 했다. 따라서 빈칸에는 그 연구 결과는 "휴식을 취하는 것은 오랜 시간 동안 집중하는 능력을 향상시킨다"는 것을 궁극적으로 시사한다는 의미가 되는 것이 자연스러우므로 ⑤ taking breaks improves the ability to focus over time(휴식을 취하는 것은 오랜 시간 동안 집중하는 능력을 향상시킨다)이 정답이다.

오답분석 ①은 글의 핵심 소재 '중단'을 활용하여 혼동을 주는 오답이다. ②은 글의 핵심 소재 '생산성'을 활용하여 혼동을 주는 오답이다. ③의 '많은 정보를 한 번에 습득하는 것'은 글의 내용과 상관없는 오답이다. ④은 글의 핵심 소재 '성과'를 활용하여 혼동을 주는 오답이다.

실력 UP! 미니 문제 03.

정답 (A) repetitive (B) stop

해석 개인이 (A) 반복적인 업무를 수행하도록 한 심리 실험은 일을 잠깐씩 (B) 멈출 수 있었던 사람들이 쉬지 않고 일했던 사람들보다 더 수월하게 그들의 집중력을 유지했다고 밝혔다.

해설 50분 동안 반복적인 작업을 수행하는 실험을 통해 쉬지 않고 작업한 그룹의 성과는 실험 내내 지속적으로 떨어졌고, 반면에 잠깐씩 일을 중단했던 그룹은 끝까지 집중력을 유지했다는 것이 밝혀졌다고 했으므로, 요약문의 빈칸에 들어갈 말로 가장 적절한 것은 (A) repetitive(반복적인), (B) stop(멈추다)이다.

04
정답 ①

지문분석

You may as well / spend less time / scrolling through motivational quotes / on social media / because **they could be damaging** / **rather than helpful**.
당신은 ~하는 편이 낫다 / 시간을 덜 쓰는 / 동기를 주는 인용구를 넘겨보는 것에 / 소셜 미디어에서 / **그것이 해로울 수 있기 때문에** / **생산적이기보다**

These quotes may seem harmless, / but they usually use language / that overgeneralizes / and puts unreasonable pressure on readers.
이러한 문구들은 악의가 없는 것처럼 보일 수 있다 / 하지만 그것들은 표현을 사용하는 경향이 있다 / 일반화가 지나치는 / 그리고 읽는 사람에게 무리한 부담을 준다

They can also blame people / for not creating opportunities / for themselves.
그것들은 또한 사람들을 비난할 수도 있다 / 기회를 만들지 않는 것에 대해서 / 스스로

Consider the following quote / by Walt Disney: / "All our dreams can come true / if we have the courage / to pursue them."
다음 인용구를 생각해 보아라 / 월트 디즈니의 / 우리의 모든 꿈들은 실현될 수 있다 / 우리가 용기가 있다면 / 그것을 추구할

It sounds pretty inspiring / at first / but, upon deeper reflection, / ★ messages like this / reinforce the idea / that everyone has the potential / to fulfill their aspirations, / and if they don't, / it's their own fault.
그것은 매우 영감을 주는 것처럼 보인다 / 처음에는 / 하지만, 더 깊이 생각해보면 / 이와 같은 메시지는 / 견해를 뒷받침한다 / 모든 사람이 가능성을 지닌다는 / 그들의 꿈을 이룰 / 그런데 만약 그들이 꿈을 이루지 못한다면 / 그것은 그들의 책임이다

Ironically, / motivational quotes / like this one / can increase people's anxiety and depression / and make them less driven / than before.
역설적으로 / 동기를 주는 인용구는 / 이것과 같이 / 사람들의 불안과 우울함을 증대시킬 수 있다 / 그리고 그들을 덜 의욕 넘치게 만든다 / 이전보다

[어휘] may as well ~하는 편이 낫다　motivational 동기를 주는
quote 인용구, 인용문　harmless 악의가 없는, 무해한　language 표현, 말
overgeneralize 지나치게 일반화하다　unreasonable 무리한, 부당한
consider 생각해 보다, 고려하다　reflection 생각, 숙고
reinforce 뒷받침하다, 강화하다　ironically 역설적으로　driven 의욕이 넘치는
[선택지] applicable 적용할 수 있는　fulfill 이루다

[해석] [주제문] 그것(인용구를 넘겨보는 것)이 생산적이기보다 해로울 수 있기 때문에 당신은 소셜 미디어에서 동기를 주는 인용구를 넘겨보는 것에 시간을 덜 쓰는 편이 낫다. 이러한 문구들은 악의가 없는 것처럼 보일 수 있지만, 그것들은 일반화가 지나치고 읽는 사람에게 무리한 부담을 주는 표현을 사용하는 경향이 있다. 그것들은 또한 스스로 기회를 만들지 않는 것에 대해서 사람들을 비난할 수도 있다. 월트 디즈니의 다음 인용구를 생각해 보아라: "우리의 모든 꿈들은 우리가 그것을 추구할 용기가 있다면 실현될 수 있다." 그것은 처음에는 매우 영감을 주는 것처럼 보이지만, 더 깊이 생각해보면, 이와 같은 메시지는 모든 사람이 그들의 꿈을 이룰 가능성을 지니는데, 만약 그들이 꿈을 이루지 못한다면 그것은 그들의 책임이라는 견해를 뒷받침한다. 역설적으로, 이것과 같이 동기를 주는 인용구는 사람들의 불안과 우울함을 증대시키고 그들을 이전보다 덜 의욕 넘치게 만들 수 있다.

① 그것이 생산적이기보다 해로울 수 있다
② 그것들이 사실인지 증명하기가 쉽지 않다
③ 몇몇은 더 이상 적용할 수 없는 것들이다
④ 그것들 중 대부분은 교과서에서 발견된다
⑤ 그것들은 당신이 꿈을 이룰 여지를 주지 않는다

[해설] 글의 초반부에 위치한 빈칸을 포함한 문장은 주제문이므로, 이를 다시 언급한 문장이나 부연 설명하는 문장을 파악해야 한다. 빈칸 문장에서 '어떠한 이유로' 동기를 주는 인용구를 넘겨보는 것에 시간을 덜 쓰는 편이 낫다고 했고, 글의 후반에서 동기를 주는 인용구는 역설적으로 사람들의 불안과 우울함을 증대시키고 덜 의욕 넘치게 만들 수 있다고 했다. 따라서 빈칸에는 "그것(인용구를 넘겨보는 것)이 생산적이기보다 해로울 수 있기" 때문에 당신은 동기를 주는 인용구를 넘겨보는 것에 시간을 덜 쓰는 편이 낫다는 의미가 되는 것이 자연스러우므로 ① damaging rather than productive(그것이 생산적이기보다 해로울 수 있다)가 정답이다.

[오답분석] ②의 '사실인지 증명하기', ③의 '더 이상 적용할 수 없는 것들', ④의 '교과서에서 발견된다'는 글의 내용과 상관없는 오답이다. ⑤는 글에서 언급된 소재 '꿈'을 활용하여 혼동을 주는 오답이다.

[실력 UP!] 미니 문제 04.

정답 ①
해석 ① 동기를 주는 인용구의 잠재적인 부작용
② 동기를 주는 인용구의 고무적인 언어
③ 우울증에 대한 소셜 미디어의 긍정적인 영향
해설 동기를 주는 인용구들을 넘겨보는 것이 역효과를 낼 수 있다는 것에 대한 글이므로, 글의 주제로 가장 적절한 것은 ① the potential side effects of motivational quotes이다.

05　　　　　　　　　　　　　　　　　　　　　　정답 ②

[지문분석]

As a parent, / having an angry outburst / in front of your children / can be very damaging / to them.
부모로서 / 분노를 폭발시키는 것은 / 당신의 자녀들 앞에서 / 매우 악영향을 줄 수 있다 / 그들에게

When you're upset, / your first impulse might be / to yell or slam a door, / but you had better not / react to every thing that annoys you.
당신이 화났을 때 / 당신의 첫 번째 충동은 ~일 수 있다 / 소리를 지르거나 문을 쾅 닫는 것 / 그러나 당신은 ~하지 않는 것이 낫다 / 당신을 짜증 나게 하는 모든 것에 반응하는

Otherwise, / your children will grow up / thinking / that this sort of behavior is acceptable.
그렇지 않으면 / 당신의 자녀들은 자랄 것이다 / 생각하며 / 이러한 종류의 행동이 용인되는 것이라고

★ Instead of figuring out / how to work through their feelings / in a calm and healthy way, / they will recall / how you behaved / in similar circumstances / and act accordingly.
생각해내는 대신 / 그들의 감정을 해결하는 방법을 / 침착하고 건강한 방식으로 / 그들은 기억해 낼 것이다 / 당신이 어떻게 행동했는지를 / 비슷한 상황에서 / 그리고 그에 따라 행동하다

In other words, / when put in a situation / where they are angry / and their ability to control their temper / is tested, / they will lose control.
다시 말해서 / 상황에 놓였을 때 / 그들이 화가 난 / 그리고 그들의 인내심을 조절하는 그들의 능력이 / 시험받는다 / 그들은 통제력을 잃게 될 것이다

You must therefore teach them / that, although everybody gets upset, / it isn't necessary / to **act on it**.
따라서 당신은 그들에게 가르쳐야 한다 / 비록 모두가 화가 나더라도 / 당연하지는 않다 / **그에 따라 행동하는** 것이

[어휘] outburst 폭발　damaging 악영향을 주는　impulse 충동　yell 소리 지르다
slam (문 등을) 쾅 닫다　acceptable 용인되는　figure out 생각해 내다
recall 기억해 내다　circumstance 상황　accordingly 그에 따라
temper 인내심　lose control 통제력을 잃다　upset 화난, 속상한
necessary 당연한　[선택지] indifferent 무관심한

[해석] 부모로서, 당신의 자녀들 앞에서 분노를 폭발시키는 것은 그들에게 매우 악영향을 줄 수 있다. 당신이 화났을 때, 당신의 첫 번째 충동은 소리를 지르거나 문을 쾅 닫는 것일 수 있는데, 당신은 당신을 짜증 나게 하는 모든 것에 반응하지 않는 것이 낫다. 그렇지 않으면, 당신의 자녀들은 이러한 종류의 행동이 용인되는 것이라고 생각하며 자랄 것이다. 침착하고 건강한 방식으로 그들의 감정을 해결하는 방법을 생각해내는 대신, 그들은 당신이 비슷한 상황에서 어떻게 행동했는지를 기억해 내고 그에 따라 행동할 것이다. 다시 말해서, 그들이 화가 나고 그들의 인내심을 조절하는 능력을 시험받는 상황에 놓였을 때, 그들은 통제력을 잃게 될 것이다. [주제문] 따라서 당신은, 비록 모두가 화가 나더라도 **그에 따라 행동하는** 것이 당연하지는 않다는 것을 그들에게 가르쳐야 한다.

① 그것을 회피하는
② 그에 따라 행동하는

③ 무관심한
④ 그것을 계속 숨기는
⑤ 감정을 통제하는

[해설] 빈칸 문장은 이 글의 주제문이므로, 이를 다시 언급한 문장이나 부연 설명하는 문장을 파악해야 한다. 빈칸 문장에서 모두가 화가 나더라도 '무엇' 하는 것이 당연하지는 않다고 아이에게 가르쳐야 한다고 했고, 글의 초반에서 모든 짜증에 반응하지 않는 것이 낫다고 했다. 따라서 빈칸에는 모두가 화가 나더라도, "그에 따라 행동하는" 것이 당연하지는 않다는 것을 가르쳐야 한다는 의미가 되는 것이 자연스러우므로 ② act on it(그에 따라 행동하는)이 정답이다.

[오답분석] ①의 '회피하는 것', ③의 '무관심한 것', ④의 '그것을 숨기는 것'은 글의 내용과 상관없는 오답이다. ⑤은 화난 감정에 매번 반응하지 않는 것이 좋다는 글의 주제와 반대되는 내용이므로 오답이다.

[실력UP!] 미니 문제 05.

정답 ②

해석 ① 아이들이 자신의 감정을 표현하도록 하는 것의 중요성
② 부모가 자녀들 앞에서 화를 조절해야 하는 이유
③ 분노의 표출이 꼭 필요한 상황들

해설 자녀들 앞에서 분노를 표출하는 것이 그들에게 악영향을 미칠 수 있으므로 모든 짜증에 반응하지 않도록 자신을 통제하는 것이 좋다는 내용의 글이므로, 글의 주제로 가장 적절한 것은 ② why parents should control their anger in front of their children이다.

06   정답 ③

[지문분석]

Although there are countless interspecies interactions, / the "relationship" / between the remora and the shark / is an interesting one.
비록 수많은 종(種) 간 상호작용이 있지만 / "관계"는 / 빨판상어와 상어 간의 / 흥미로운 것이다

In comparison to most sharks, / the remora is a tiny creature, / typically measuring between one and three feet.
대부분의 상어와 비교했을 때 / 빨판상어는 작은 생물이다 / 일반적으로 1에서 3피트 사이로 측정되는

The most distinguishing physical characteristic / of the remora / is its front dorsal fin, / which has evolved / to take the form of a sucker-like organ over time.
가장 특색 있는 신체적 특성은 / 빨판상어의 / 그것의 앞 등지느러미이다 / 이것은 진화했다 / 시간이 지나며 빨판 같은 기관의 형태를 가지도록

It uses this organ / to attach itself to a shark / as it passes by.
이것(빨판상어)은 이 기관을 사용한다 / 상어에 자신을 부착시키기 위해 / 그것(상어)이 지나갈 때

In doing so, / it obtains not only / a fast source of transportation / but also protection from predators.
그렇게 하면서 / 그것은 획득할 뿐만 아니라 / 더 빠른 이동 수단 / 천적들로부터의 보호도

Furthermore, / when the shark feeds, / the remora has access / to its leftover food scraps.
게다가 / 상어가 먹이를 먹을 때 / 빨판상어는 얻을 수 있다 / 그것이 먹다 남은 먹이 찌꺼기도

Since / the remora is relatively small and light, / the shark hardly notices it / and is essentially unaffected / by its presence.
~이기 때문에 / 빨판상어는 비교적 작고 가볍다 / 상어는 좀처럼 그것을 알아차리지 못한다 / 그리고 본래 영향을 받지 않는다 / 그것(빨판상어)의 존재에

★ This is a good example / of a relationship between two organisms / in which one party **benefits** / **without harming the other**.
이것은 좋은 예이다 / 두 유기체 간 관계의 / 한쪽이 득을 보는 / 다른 쪽을 해치지 않으면서

[어휘] interspecies 종(種) 간의 typically 일반적으로, 보통 distinguishing 특색 있는, 특징적인 dorsal fin 등지느러미 sucker 빨판 attach 부착하다, 붙다 transportation 이동 수단 predator 천적, 포식자 have access to (~를) 얻다, 이용하다, 활용하다 leftover 먹다 남은 scrap 찌꺼기, 조각 unaffected 영향을 받지 않은 presence 존재
[선택지] exchange 주고받다

[해설] 비록 수많은 종(種) 간 상호작용이 있지만, 빨판상어와 상어 간의 "관계"는 흥미로운 것이다. 대부분의 상어와 비교했을 때, 빨판상어는 일반적으로 1에서 3피트 사이로 측정되는 작은 생물이다. 빨판상어의 가장 특색 있는 신체적 특성은 그것의 앞 등지느러미인데, 이것은 시간이 지나며 빨판 같은 기관의 형태를 가지도록 진화했다. 이것(빨판상어)은 상어가 지나갈 때 그것(상어)에 자신을 부착시키기 위해 이 기관을 사용한다. 그렇게 하면서, 그것은 더 빠른 이동 수단뿐만 아니라 천적들로부터의 보호도 획득한다. 게다가, 상어가 먹이를 먹을 때, 빨판상어는 그것이 먹다 남은 먹이 찌꺼기도 얻을 수 있다. 빨판상어는 비교적 작고 가볍기 때문에, 상어는 좀처럼 그것을 알아차리지 못하며, 본래 그것(빨판상어)의 존재에 영향을 받지 않는다. [주제문] 이것은 한쪽이 **다른 쪽을 해치지 않으면서 득을 보는** 두 유기체 간 관계의 좋은 예이다.

① 다른 쪽이 먹이를 유인하는 것을 돕다
② 다른 쪽을 종종 위험에 빠트리다
③ 다른 쪽을 해치지 않으면서 득을 보다
④ 다른 쪽과 같은 양의 도움을 주고받다
⑤ 이동 수단을 위해 다른 쪽과 그것의 자원을 공유하다

[해설] 빈칸 문장은 이 글의 주제문이므로, 이를 다시 언급한 문장이나 부연 설명하는 문장을 파악해야 한다. 빈칸 문장에서 빨판상어와 상어의 관계는 한쪽이 '무엇을 하는' 두 유기체 간 관계의 좋은 예라고 했다. 글의 중반에서, 빨판상어는 상어에 자신을 부착하여 이동 수단으로 활용하거나, 천적들로부터 보호를 받고, 먹이도 얻을 수 있다고 했다. 그리고 빈칸 앞 문장에서 상어는 빨판상어를 알아차리지 못하고, 본래 빨판상어의 존재에 영향을 받지 않는다고 했다. 따라서 빈칸에는 빨판상어와 상어의 관계는 한 쪽이 "다른 쪽을 해치지 않으면서 득을 보는" 두 유기체 간 관계의 좋은 예라는 의미가 되는 것이 자연스러우므로 ③ benefits without harming the other(다른 쪽을 해치지 않으면서 득을 보다)가 정답이다.

[오답분석] ①, ④은 글의 핵심 소재인 '득을 보는' 상황을 서술하고 있으나, 글에서 상어는 본래 빨판상어의 존재에 영향을 받지 않는다고 했으므로 오답이다. ②은 글의 내용과 상관없는 오답이다. ⑤은 글에서 언급된 소재 '이동 수단'을 활용하여 혼동을 주는 오답이다.

[실력UP!] 미니 문제 06.

정답 ②

해석 ① 두 상어 종의 섭식 행동 비교
② 빨판상어와 상어의 관계
③ 다양한 해양 유기체의 신체적 차이

해설 빨판상어와 상어 간 관계는 한 쪽이 다른 쪽을 해치지 않으면서 득을 보는 관계임을 설명하고 있는 글이므로, 글의 주제로 가장 적절한 것은 ② the relationship between the remora and the shark이다.

07
정답 ①

지문분석

When it comes to science, / many of us fail to consider / that **nothing can be proven definitely**.
과학에 관한 한 / 우리 중 다수는 생각하지 못한다 / **그 어느 것도 뚜렷하게 증명될 수 없다**는 것을

When scientists are presented with a question, / they form a hypothesis / based on what they already know / and then / carry out a series of experiments.
과학자들은 의문이 생길 때 / 가설을 만든다 / 그들이 이미 알고 있는 것에 근거해서 / 그리고 그 후에 / 일련의 실험을 수행한다

The outcome may support the hypothesis, / but this does not necessarily mean / that it is correct.
그 결과는 가설을 뒷받침할 수도 있다 / 하지만 이는 반드시 의미하지는 않는다 / 그것이 옳다는 것을

Even if extensive experimentation / yielding similar results / leads to the widespread acceptance / of the hypothesis, / it only becomes a theory.
아주 많은 실험이 ~하더라도 / 비슷한 결과를 산출해내는 / 일반적인 수용으로 이어지더라도 / 그 가설의 / 그것은 단지 이론이 될 뿐이다

★Should the theory become a law, / there is always the possibility / of new evidence arising / that can call it into question / or refute it entirely.
만일 그 이론이 법칙이 된다면 / 가능성은 항상 있다 / 새로운 증거가 발생할 / 그것에 의문을 제기할 수 있거나 / 또는 전적으로 반박하는

Essentially, / as our knowledge of the world / grows through scientific investigation, / old ideas are replaced / by new ones / that better align with / the most recent findings.
기본적으로 / 세상에 대한 우리의 지식은 ~하므로 / 과학 연구를 통해 확장된다 / 이전의 신념은 대체된다 / 새로운 것들로 / 더욱 동조하는 / 가장 최신의 발견에

★ **독해가 쉬워지는 구문 풀이**

[Should the theory become a law], there is always the possibility
      주어   동사원형
of new evidence arising that can call it into question or refute it entirely.

⇨ [ ]는 가정법 문장에서 If가 생략되어 주어와 should가 도치되면서 'Should + 주어 + 동사원형'의 어순으로 쓰였다. 미래에 일어날 가능성이 거의 없거나, 불가능한 일이 일어날 것이라고 가정해서 말할 때는 가정법 미래 문장을 쓴다.

어휘 hypothesis 가설, 가정 carry out 수행하다, 이행하다
necessarily 반드시, 꼭 experimentation 실험 (활동·과정)
yield (결과 등을) 산출하다, 내다 acceptance 수용
call ~ into question ~에 의문을 제기하다, ~을 의심하다
〔선택지〕definitely 뚜렷하게, 분명히 present 야기하다, (곤란 등이) 생기게 하다
mislead 현혹시키다 considerably 상당히, 많이

해석 〔주제문〕과학에 관한 한, 우리 중 다수는 **그 어느 것도 뚜렷하게 증명될 수 없다**는 것을 생각하지 못한다. 과학자들은 의문이 생길 때, 그들이 이미 알고 있는 것에 근거해서 가설을 만들고 그 후에 일련의 실험을 수행한다. 그 결과는 가설을 뒷받침할 수도 있지만, 이는 반드시 그것이 옳다는 것을 의미하지는 않는다. 비슷한 결과를 산출해내는 아주 많은 실험이 그 가설의 일반적인 수용으로 이어지더라도, 그것은 단지 이론이 될 뿐이다. 만일 그 이론이 법칙이 된다면, 그것에 의문을 제기하거나 전적으로 반박할 수 있는 새로운 증거가 발생할 가능성은 항상 있다. 기본적으로, 세상에 대한 우리의 지식은 과학 연구를 통해 확장되므로, 이전의 신념은 가장 최신의 발견에 더욱 동조하는 새로운 것들로 대체된다.

① 그 어느 것도 뚜렷하게 증명될 수 없다
② 자금 부족은 문제를 야기한다
③ 실험의 결과가 되풀이되는 것은 드물다
④ 대중은 종종 복잡한 결과에 현혹된다
⑤ 증거를 모으는 방법은 상당히 다르다

해설 빈칸 문장은 이 글의 주제문이므로, 이를 다시 언급한 문장이나 부연 설명하는 문장을 파악해야 한다. 빈칸 문장에서 과학에 관한 한 우리 중 다수는 '무엇하다'는 것을 생각하지 못한다고 하고, 이어서 실험의 결과는 가설을 뒷받침할 수도 있지만, 그것이 가설이 옳다는 것을 의미하지는 않으며, 이론이 법칙이 되어도 그에 반하는 새로운 증거가 발생할 가능성이 항상 있다고 했다. 따라서 빈칸에는 과학에 관한 한 우리 중 다수는 "그 어느 것도 뚜렷하게 증명될 수 없다"는 것을 생각하지 못한다는 의미가 되는 것이 자연스러우므로 ① nothing can be proven definitely(그 어느 것도 뚜렷하게 증명될 수 없다)가 정답이다.

오답분석 ②의 '자금 부족'은 글과 상관없는 오답이다. ③은 글의 핵심 소재 '실험 결과'를 활용하여 혼동을 주는 오답이다. ④은 글에서 언급된 소재 '결과'를 활용하여 혼동을 주는 오답이다. ⑤은 글의 핵심 소재 '실험'과 연관되는 소재인 '증거'를 활용하여 혼동을 주는 오답이다.

실력 UP! 미니 문제 07.

정답 (A) scientists (B) hypothesis (C) law

해설 (A) '과학자들은 의문이 생길 때'라고 말한 후 그들은 이미 알고 있는 것에 근거해서 가설을 만든다고 했으므로, (A)they가 가리키는 것은 scientists(과학자들)이다.
(B) 실험의 결과가 가설을 뒷받침할 수도 있다고 한 후 이는 그것이 옳다는 것을 의미하지는 않는다고 했으므로, (B)it이 가리키는 것은 hypothesis(가설)이다.
(C) 이론이 법칙이 되는 경우를 가정한 후, 그것에 의문을 제기하거나 그것을 반박할 수 있는 새로운 증거가 발생할 가능성이 항상 있다고 했으므로, (C)it이 가리키는 것은 law(법칙)이다.

08 정답 ④

지문분석

Behavioral experiments / on bees / have determined / **they can distinguish** / **between colors**.
행동 실험은 / 벌을 대상으로 한 / 밝혀냈다 / **그들이 구별할 수 있음을** / **색깔을**

One of these was an experiment / in which researchers put out / a blue feeder and a yellow feeder.
이것(행동 실험)들 중 하나는 실험이었다 / 연구원들이 놓아둔 / 파란색 먹이통과 노란색 먹이통을

The only difference / between the feeders / was that the blue one was empty, / while the yellow one / was filled with honey.
유일한 차이점은 / 먹이통 사이의 / 파란색 통은 비어 있다는 점이었다 / 반면 노란색 통은 / 꿀로 가득 차 있었다

★Bees realized / that the yellow feeder had honey, / so they went there / while ignoring the blue one.
벌들은 알아차렸다 / 노란색 먹이통에 꿀이 있다는 것을 / 그래서 그곳으로 갔다 / 파란색 통을 무시한 채

Even after the honey was removed / from the yellow feeder, / they continued to associate it / with food / and come to it.
꿀이 없어진 후에도 / 노란색 먹이통에서 / 그들은 계속해서 그것을 연관 지어 생각했다 / 먹이와 / 그리고 그곳에 왔다

To prove / that the bees were truly seeing blue and yellow, / multiple blue feeders were put out / along with the yellow feeder.
증명하기 위해 / 벌들이 정말로 파란색과 노란색을 볼 수 있는지 / 여러 개의 파란색 먹이통들이 놓였다 / 노란색 먹이통 사이에

The bees continued to go / to the yellow feeder first, / no matter where it was placed.
벌들은 계속해서 갔다 / 먼저 노란색 먹이통으로 / 그것이 어디에 놓였든지

If the bees / were unable to truly see yellow, / it is logical to assume / that some of them might have explored / some of the blue feeders / first.
만약 벌들이 ~했다면 / 정말로 노란색을 볼 수 없었다 / ~라고 생각하는 것이 타당하다 / 그들 중 일부는 살펴봤을지도 모른다 / 몇몇 파란색 먹이통을 / 먼저

CHAPTER 11 빈칸 추론하기 **87**

★ 독해가 쉬워지는 구문 풀이

Bees realized that the yellow feeder had honey, so they went there while ignoring the blue one.
접속사 현재분사구문

⇨ 분사구문에 주어가 따로 없으므로 주절의 주어 Bees가 분사구문의 의미상 주어이다. 문맥상 '벌들이 파란색 통을 무시하다'라는 의미로, Bees가 ignore가 나타내는 '무시하는' 행위의 주체이므로 현재분사 ignoring이 쓰였다. 분사구문 앞에 있는 접속사(while)는 의미를 명확하게 하기 위해 남았다.

어휘 behavioral 행동의, 행동에 관한 feeder 먹이통, 공급 장치
ignore 무시하다 associate 연관 지어 생각하다, 관련시키다
logical 타당한, 논리적인 assume 생각하다 explore 살펴보다
선택지 detect 감지하다, 발견하다 scent 냄새, 향기
ultraviolet 자외선; 자외선의 distinguish 구별하다, 구분하다

해석 주제문 벌을 대상으로 한 행동 실험은 **그들이 색깔을 구별할 수 있음**을 밝혀냈다. 이것(행동 실험)들 중 하나는 연구원들이 파란색 먹이통과 노란색 먹이통을 놓아둔 실험이었다. 먹이통 사이의 유일한 차이점은 파란색 통은 비어 있는 반면, 노란색 통은 꿀로 가득 차 있었다는 점이었다. 벌들은 노란색 먹이통에 꿀이 있다는 것을 알아차렸고, 그래서 파란색 통을 무시한 채 그곳으로 갔다. 꿀이 노란색 먹이통에서 없어진 후에도, 그들은 계속해서 그것을 먹이와 연관 지어 생각하고 그곳에 왔다. 벌들이 정말로 파란색과 노란색을 볼 수 있는지 증명하기 위해, 여러 개의 파란색 먹이통들이 노란색 먹이통 사이에 놓였다. 벌들은 그것이 어디에 놓였든지 계속해서 먼저 노란색 먹이통으로 갔다. 만약 벌들이 정말로 노란색을 볼 수 없었다면, 그들 중 일부는 몇몇 파란색 먹이통을 먼저 살펴봤었을지도 모른다고 생각하는 것이 타당하다.

① 그들이 먼 거리에서도 달콤한 냄새를 감지할 수 있다
② 그들이 노란색 물체를 선호한다
③ 그들이 자외선 스펙트럼에 있는 빛을 본다
④ 그들이 색깔을 구별할 수 있다
⑤ 그들이 더 잘 보기 위해 색깔에 의존한다

해설 빈칸 문장은 이 글의 주제문이므로, 이를 다시 언급한 문장이나 부연 설명하는 문장을 파악해야 한다. 빈칸 문장에서 벌을 대상으로 한 행동 실험은 '무엇'을 밝혀냈다고 하고, 이어서 실험에서 노란색 통에 꿀이 있음을 알아차린 벌들은 이후에도 꿀의 유무나 위치에 상관없이 노란색 통에 갔다고 했다. 따라서 빈칸에는 벌을 대상으로 한 행동 실험은 "그들이 색깔을 구별할 수 있음"을 밝혀냈다는 의미가 되는 것이 자연스러우므로 ④ they can distinguish between colors(그들이 색깔을 구별할 수 있다)가 정답이다.

오답 분석 ①은 글의 내용과 상관없는 오답이다. ②은 글에서 언급된 '노란색'을 활용하여 혼동을 주는 오답이다. ③은 글의 내용과 상관없는 오답이다. ⑤은 글의 핵심 소재 '색깔'을 활용하여 혼동을 주는 오답이다.

실력 UP! 미니 문제 08.

정답 ③

해석 ① 색이 벌의 행동에 미치는 영향
② 벌들에게서 보여지는 논리적인 행동
③ 서로 다른 색깔을 인식하는 벌들의 능력

해설 벌을 대상으로 한 행동 실험을 통해 그들이 색깔을 구별할 수 있다는 것을 밝혔다는 내용의 글이므로, 글의 주제로 가장 적절한 것은 ③ the ability of bees to recognize different colors이다.

09

정답 ⑤

지문분석

A study / examining prosocial behavior / suggests that, / as we age, / **helping others** becomes more important.
한 연구는 / 친사회적 행동을 조사한 / ~ 한다는 것을 시사한다 / 우리가 나이를 먹을수록 / **다른 사람들을 돕는 것**이 더 중요해진다

Researchers reached this conclusion / by conducting an experiment / involving a group of older adults / and a group of younger adults.
연구원들은 이러한 결론에 도달하였다 / 한 실험을 시행하면서 / 노인 집단을 포함하는 / 청년 집단과

★The participants were given devices / that measured six levels / of grip strength.
참가자들에게 도구가 주어졌다 / 여섯 단계로 측정하는 / 악력을

They were then presented / with a set of hypothetical scenarios / in which they could either earn money / for themselves or another person.
그다음 그들에게 제시되었다 / 일련의 가상의 상황들이 / 그들이 돈을 벌 수 있는 / 스스로 혹은 타인을 위해서

For each situation, / they were asked / whether they were willing to make an effort / to earn the money, / and if they said yes, / they had to squeeze the device / hard enough / to secure that money.
각 상황마다 / 그들은 질문을 받았다 / 그들이 기꺼이 노력할 것인지 / 돈을 벌기 위해 / 그리고 만약 그들이 동의했을 경우 / 그들은 도구를 쥐어야 했다 / 충분히 강하게 / 그 돈을 확보하기 위해

The study found that / the older adults were more willing to put in / physical effort / to gain money for other people / than the younger participants.
이 연구는 밝혀냈다 / 노인들이 더 기꺼이 행사한다는 것을 / 물리적 노력을 / 다른 사람을 위한 돈을 벌기 위해 / 청년 참가자들보다

The latter were more concerned with / earning money for themselves, / showing / that aiding other people / might become more important / as we age.
후자(청년들)는 더 관심을 가졌다 / 자신을 위해 돈을 버는 데 / 그런데 이것은 보여준다 / 타인을 돕는 것이 ~라는 것을 / 더 중요하게 된다 / 우리가 늙어갈수록

★ 독해가 쉬워지는 구문 풀이

The participants were given devices **that** measured six levels of grip strength.
주어 4형식 수동태 직접 목적어

⇨ 주어 The participants가 동사 give가 나타내는 '주는' 행위의 대상이므로, 수동태 were given이 쓰였다. 동사 give는 목적어 2개가 올 수 있는 4형식 동사이므로, 수동태 동사 뒤에 남은 직접 목적어 devices를 보고 능동태 동사가 와야 한다고 착각하지 않도록 주의한다.

어휘 examine 조사하다, 관찰하다 prosocial 친사회적인 conduct 시행하다
device 도구, 장치 hypothetical 가상의 squeeze 꽉 쥐다
secure 확보하다; 안전한 be willing to 기꺼이 ~ 하다 physical 물리적인
latter 후자(後者) priority 우선순위 선택지 redistribute 재분배하다
wealth 부, 재산

해석 주제문 친사회적 행동을 조사한 한 연구는 우리가 나이를 먹을수록 **다른 사람들을 돕는 것**이 더 중요해진다는 것을 시사한다. 연구원들은 노인 집단과 청년 집단을 포함하는 한 실험을 시행하면서 이러한 결론에 도달하였다. 참가자들에게 여섯 단계로 악력을 측정하는 도구가 주어졌다. 그다음 그들에게 스스로 혹은 타인을 위해서 돈을 벌 수 있는 일련의 가상의 상황들이 제시되었다. 각 상황마다, 그들은 돈을 벌기 위해 기꺼이 노력할 것인지 질문을 받았고, 만약 그들이 동의했을 경우, 그들은 그 돈을 확보하기 위해 도구를 충분히 강하게 쥐어야 했다. 이 연구는 노인들이 청년 참가자들보다 다른 사람을 위한 돈을 벌기 위해 더 기꺼이 물리적 노력을 행사한다는 것을 밝혀냈다. 후자(청년들)는 자신을 위해 돈을 버는 데 더

관심을 가졌는데, 이것은 우리가 늙어갈수록 타인을 돕는 것이 더 중요하게 된다는 것을 보여준다.

① 청년들을 교육하는 것
② 어느 정도 돈을 버는 것
③ 부를 재분배하는 것
④ 규칙을 따르는 것
⑤ 다른 사람들을 돕는 것

해설 글의 초반부에 위치한 빈칸을 포함한 문장은 주제문이므로, 이를 다시 언급한 문장이나 부연 설명하는 문장을 파악해야 한다. 빈칸 문장에서 한 연구는 우리가 나이를 먹을수록 '무엇'이 더 중요해진다고 했고, 글의 후반에서 노인들이 젊은이들보다 다른 사람을 위한 돈을 벌기 위해 더 기꺼이 물리적 노력을 행사했으며, 이는 우리가 늙어갈수록 타인을 돕는 것이 더 우선순위가 된다는 것을 보여준다고 했다. 따라서 빈칸에는 한 연구는 우리가 나이를 먹을수록 "다른 사람들을 돕는 것"이 더 중요해진다는 것을 시사한다는 의미가 되는 것이 자연스러우므로 ⑤ helping others(다른 사람들을 돕는 것)가 정답이다.

오답분석 ①은 글의 핵심 소재인 '청년'을 활용하여 혼동을 주는 오답이다. ②는 글에서 언급된 소재 '돈'을 활용하여 혼동을 주는 오답이다. ③은 글에서 언급된 소재 '돈'과 연상되는 '부'를 활용하여 혼동을 주는 오답이다. ④는 글의 내용과 상관없는 오답이다.

실력 UP! 미니 문제 09.

정답 (A) participants　(B) the younger participants

해설 (A) 참가자들에게 스스로 혹은 타인을 위해서 돈을 벌 수 있는 가상의 상황이 제시되었다고 한 후 각 상황마다 그들은 돈을 벌기 위해 기꺼이 노력할 것인지 질문을 받았다고 했으므로, (A)they가 가리키는 것은 participants(참가자들)이다.

(B) 노인들이 청년 참가자들보다 다른 사람을 위한 돈을 벌기 위해 더 기꺼이 물리적 노력을 행사한다는 것을 밝혀냈다고 한 후 후자는 자신을 위해 돈을 버는 데 더 관심을 가졌다고 했으므로, (B)The latter가 가리키는 것은 the younger participants(청년 참가자들)이다.

10　　　　　　　　　　　정답 ⑤

지문분석

It is a common assumption / that you'll save time / if you drive faster.
이것은 당연한 가정이다 / 당신이 시간을 절약할 것이라는 것은 / 만약 당신이 더 빨리 운전하면

To a certain extent, / this is true.
어느 정도까지 / 이것은 사실이다

If you need to make a 10-kilometer trip / and drive at 20 kilometers an hour, / the trip will take you 30 minutes.
만약 당신이 10킬로미터의 이동을 해야 한다면 / 그리고 시속 20킬로미터로 운전한다면 / 당신은 이동하는 데 30분이 걸릴 것이다

However, / if you accelerate / to 30 kilometers an hour, / you will arrive at your destination / in 20 minutes.
하지만 / 만약 당신이 속도를 높인다면 / 시속 30킬로미터로 / 당신은 목적지에 도착할 것이다 / 20분 이내에

That's a 10-minute time saving.
그것은 10분의 시간 절약이다

Now, / imagine speeding up / from 30 kilometers an hour / to 40 kilometers an hour.
이제 / 속도를 높인다고 상상해보자 / 시속 30킬로미터에서 / 시속 40킬로미터로

You might think / you will save / another 10 minutes / but, / if you do the math, / you will see / that you only save / five additional minutes.
당신은 생각할지도 모른다 / 당신이 절약할 것이라고 / 10분을 더 / 하지만 / 만약 당신이 계산해본다면 / 당신은 알게 될 것이다 / 겨우 절약한다는 것을 / 5분만 추가로

This downward trend continues / the faster you go.
이 하락세는 계속된다 / 당신이 더 빨리 가면 갈수록

★ Many of us overestimate the time / that we can save / after we've sped up.
우리 중 대부분이 시간을 과대평가하는 / 우리가 절약할 수 있는 / 우리가 속도를 높인 후

This is due to a logical fallacy / referred to as / the time-saving bias.
이는 논리적 오류 때문이다 / ~이라고 불리는 / 시간 절약 편중

Essentially, / we make an incorrect judgment / about **how much time we will save** / because we only focus on the new speed / rather than our initial speed.
본래 / 우리는 잘못된 판단을 내린다 / **우리가 얼마나 많은 시간을 절약할 것인지**에 대해 / 새로운 속도에만 집중하기 때문에 / 우리의 처음 속도보다는

★ 독해가 쉬워지는 구문 풀이

Many of us overestimate the time [①that we can save] [②after we've sped up].

⇨ [①]은 선행사 the time을 수식하는 관계절이며, 목적격 관계대명사 that은 생략할 수 있다.
⇨ [②]은 주절(Many ~ save) 전체를 수식하는 부사절이다.

어휘 assumption 가정, 가설　accelerate 속도를 높이다, 가속화하다
downward 하락하는　overestimate 지나치게 어림하다, 과대평가하다
refer to as ~라고 부르다　bias 편중, 치우침　judgment 판단, 추정
initial 처음의, 시작의　선택지 destination 목적지

해석 만약 당신이 더 빨리 운전하면 시간을 절약할 것이라는 것은 당연한 가정이다. 어느 정도까지, 이것은 사실이다. 만약 당신이 10킬로미터의 이동을 해야 하고 시속 20킬로미터로 운전한다면, 당신은 이동하는 데 30분이 걸릴 것이다. 하지만, 만약 당신이 시속 30킬로미터로 속도를 높인다면, 당신은 20분 이내에 목적지에 도착할 것이다. 그것은 10분의 시간 절약이다. 이제, 시속 30킬로미터에서 시속 40킬로미터로 속도를 높인다고 상상해보자. 당신은 10분을 더 절약할 것이라고 생각할지도 모르지만, 만약 당신이 계산해본다면, 겨우 5분만 추가로 절약한다는 것을 알게 될 것이다. 이 하락세는 당신이 더 빨리 가면 갈수록 계속된다. 우리 중 대부분이 우리가 속도를 높인 후 절약할 수 있는 시간을 과대평가하는 이유는 시간 절약 편중이라고 불리는 논리적 오류 때문이다. 주제문 본래, 우리는 처음 속도보다는 새로운 속도에만 집중하기 때문에 **우리가 얼마나 많은 시간을 절약할 것인지**에 대해 잘못된 판단을 내린다.

① 우리의 목적지가 얼마나 멀리 떨어져 있는지
② 우리가 얼마나 빠르게 운전할 수 있는지
③ 언제 우리의 속도를 높일지
④ 시간이 왜 더 빨리 가는 것처럼 보이는지
⑤ 우리가 얼마나 많은 시간을 절약할 것인지

해설 빈칸 문장은 이 글의 주제문이므로, 이를 다시 언급한 문장이나 부연 설명하는 문장을 파악해야 한다. 빈칸 문장에서 '무엇'에 대해 우리가 잘못된 판단을 내린다고 하고, 글의 후반에서 우리가 속도를 높인 후 절약할 수 있는 시간을 과대평가하는 이유는 시간 절약 편중이라고 불리는 논리적 오류 때문이라고 했다. 따라서 빈칸에는 본래 우리는 처음 속도보다는 새로운 속도에만 집중하기 때문에 "우리가 얼마나 많은 시간을 절약할 것인지"에 대해 잘못된 판단을 내린다는 의미가 되는 것이 자연스러우므로 ⑤ how much time we will save(우리가 얼마나 많은 시간을 절약할 것인지)가 정답이다.

오답분석 ①은 글에서 언급된 소재 '목적지'를 활용하여 혼동을 주는 오답이다. ②은 글에서 언급된 소재 '빠르게' 및 '운전'을 활용하여 혼동을 주는 오답이다. ③은 글의 핵심 소재 '속도를 높인다'를 활용하여 혼동을 주는 오답이다. ④은 글의 핵심 소재 '시간'을 활용하여 혼동을 주는 오답이다.

정답 (A) 속도가 높아짐에 따라 절약되는 시간이 적어지는 것
(B) 속도를 높인 후 절약할 수 있는 시간을 과대평가하는 것

해설 (A) 시속 20킬로미터에서 30킬로미터로 속도를 높이면 10분을 절약할 수 있는데, 시속 30킬로미터에서 40킬로미터로 속도를 높인다면 5분만 절약한다는 것을 알게 된다고 했으므로, (A)This downward trend(이 하락세)는 '속도가 높아짐에 따라 절약되는 시간이 적어지는 것'을 의미한다.
(B) 우리는 처음 속도보다는 새로운 속도에만 집중하기 때문에 더 빨리 운전한다면 시간을 더 절약할 것이라는 잘못된 판단을 하게 된다고 했으므로, (B)an incorrect judgment는 '속도를 높인 후 절약할 수 있는 시간을 과대평가하는 것'이다.

11 정답 ①

지문분석

Scientists believe / that unhatched baby birds / **transmit information to each other** / from within their eggs / by vibrating.
과학자들은 믿는다 / 부화하지 않은 새끼 새들이 ~한다는 것을 / **서로에게 정보를 전달한다** / 그들의 알 내부에서부터 / 진동함으로써

To determine this, / researchers exposed yellow-legged gull eggs / to the sounds of a predator / several times a day / and found that the eggs vibrated / following each experience.
이것을 밝히기 위해 / 연구원들은 노랑발 갈매기 알들을 노출시켰다 / 포식자의 소리에 / 하루에 여러 번 / 그리고 알들이 진동한다는 것을 알아냈다 / 각각의 경험에 따라

Meanwhile, / another group of eggs in a control group / that was not exposed to the sounds of the predator / did not vibrate.
한편 / 대조군에 있는 다른 알들의 집단 / 포식자의 소리에 노출되지 않았던 / 진동하지 않았다

The researchers speculate / that this response not only demonstrates fear / but is typical bird behavior.
연구원들은 추측한다 / 이 반응이 두려움을 보여주는 것뿐만 아니라 / 그러나 일반적인 새의 행동이다

Birds use a variety of sounds / to convey important news all the time, / and vibrating from within an egg / is no different.
새들은 다양한 소리를 사용한다 / 매번 중요한 정보를 전달하기 위해 / 그리고 알 내부에서 진동하는 것 / 이와 다를 바 없다

★ It is likely that, / despite being confined to their eggs, / the young creatures felt threatened / as a result of being exposed / to the sounds of the predator / and wanted to signal their siblings of the danger.
~할 가능성이 크다 / 그들의 알에 갇혀 있음에도 불구하고 / 어린 생명체들은 위협을 느꼈다 / 노출된 결과로 / 포식자의 소리에 / 그래서 그들의 형제들에게 위험 신호를 보내기를 원했다

★ 독해가 쉬워지는 구문 풀이

It is likely **that**, [despite being confined to their eggs], the young
　　　　　　　　　　　전치사구　　　　　　　　　　주어
creatures **felt** threatened as a result of being exposed to the
　　　　　　　동사1
sounds of the predator and **wanted** to signal their siblings of the
　　　　　　　　　　　　　　　　　　동사2
danger.
⇨ 주절의 동사 felt와 wanted는 등위접속사 and로 연결되어 병렬 구조를 이룬다.

어휘 unhatched 부화하지 않은　within 내부에서　vibrate 진동하다
determine 밝히다　expose 노출시키다　yellow-legged gull 노랑발 갈매기
predator 포식자　meanwhile 한편　control group 대조군
speculate 추측하다　demonstrate 보여주다　convey 전달하다
confine 가두다　signal 신호를 보내다　[선택지] transmit 전달하다
bond 유대감　potential 잠재적인　accelerate 가속하다

해석 [주제문] 과학자들은 부화하지 않은 새끼 새들이 그들의 알 내부에서부터 진동함으로써 **서로에게 정보를 전달한다**고 믿는다. 이것을 밝히기 위해,

---

연구원들은 노랑발 갈매기 알들을 하루에 여러 번 포식자의 소리에 노출시켰고, 각각의 경험에 따라 알들이 진동한다는 것을 알아냈다. 한편, 포식자의 소리에 노출되지 않았던 대조군에 있는 다른 알들의 집단은 진동하지 않았다. 연구원들은 이 반응이 두려움을 보여주는 것뿐만 아니라 일반적인 새의 행동이라고 추측한다. 새들은 매번 중요한 정보를 전달하기 위해 다양한 소리를 사용하고, 알 내부에서 진동하는 것도 이와 다를 바 없다. 그들의 알에 갇혀 있음에도 불구하고, 포식자의 소리에 노출된 결과로 어린 생명체들은 위협을 느껴서 그들의 형제들에게 위험 신호를 보내기를 원했을 가능성이 크다.

① 서로에게 정보를 전달한다
② 그들의 형제와 유대감을 형성한다
③ 잠재적 포식자를 겁주어 쫓아버린다
④ 그들의 성장을 가속한다
⑤ 외부 온도를 느낀다

해설 빈칸 문장은 이 글의 주제문이므로, 이를 다시 언급한 문장이나 부연 설명하는 문장을 파악해야 한다. 빈칸 문장에서 부화하지 않은 새끼 새들이 그들의 알 내부에서부터 진동함으로써 '무엇을 한다'고 하고, 글의 후반에서 새들은 매번 중요한 정보를 전달하기 위해 다양한 소리를 사용하며, 알 내부에서 진동하는 것도 이와 다를 바 없다고 했다. 따라서 빈칸 문장은 새끼 새들이 알 내부에서 진동함으로써 "서로에게 정보를 전달한다"는 의미가 되는 것이 자연스러우므로 ① transmit information to each other(서로에게 정보를 전달한다)가 정답이다.

오답분석 ②과 ③은 글에서 각각 언급된 소재 '형제' 및 '포식자'를 활용하여 혼동을 주는 오답이다. ④과 ⑤은 글의 내용과 상관없는 오답이다.

정답 ①

해석 ① 알에서 부화되지 않은 새들이 서로 의사소통하는 방법
② 아기 새의 위협을 인지하는 능력
③ 포식자를 마주칠 때 어미 새가 보이는 행동

해설 새들은 중요한 소식을 알리기 위해 다양한 소리를 사용한다고 하며, 알 내부로부터의 진동도 다를 바가 없다고 했으므로, 글의 주제로 가장 적절한 것은 ① how unhatched birds communicate with one another(알에서 부화되지 않은 새들이 서로 의사소통하는 방법)이다.

12 정답 ③

지문분석

When someone asks, / "Could you pass the salt?" / the implied meaning is / that they would like you / to pass them the salt.
누군가가 물을 경우 / 소금 좀 건네줄 수 있어요? / 함축된 의미는 ~이다 / 그들은 당신이 ~ 하기를 원한다 / 그들에게 소금을 건네주기를

★ They do not wish for you / to reply with / whether you can or cannot complete the task / —they simply expect you to do it.
그들은 당신에게 바라지 않는다 / 대답하기를 / 당신이 그 일을 해낼 수 있는지 또는 없는지 / 그들은 단지 당신이 그것을 하기를 바란다

Why don't people just say, / "Please pass the salt?"
그들은 왜 그저 말하지 않는가? / 소금 좀 건네주세요

The answer has to do with / how we approach language.
그 답은 ~와 관련이 있다 / 우리가 어떻게 언어에 접근하는지

The literal meaning of words / is not always important, / especially when we speak.
단어들의 글자 그대로의 뜻이 / 항상 중요한 것은 아니다 / 특히 우리가 말할 때

What matters more / is the situation the speaker is in / and their intention.
더 중요한 것은 / 화자가 처해 있는 상황이다 / 그리고 그들의 의도

The meaning of a speaker's words / may not be immediately obvious to everyone / but full of implication, / and easily understood by those / who are able to / put the words into context.
화자가 쓰는 단어의 의미 / 모두에게 즉각 분명하지 않을 수 있다 / 그러나 함축으로 가득 차 있는 / 그리고 그들에게 쉽게 이해된다 / ~를 할 수 있는 사람들 / 단어를 맥락에 적용하다

The area of linguistics / concerned with interpreting meaning / is called pragmatics, / and it teaches us / that **what we say isn't always what we mean**.
언어학의 분야 / 뜻을 해석하는 것과 관련 있는 / 화용론이라고 불리다 / 그리고 그것은 우리에게 가르쳐준다 / 우리가 말하는 것이 언제나 우리가 의미하는 것은 아니라는 것을

★ 독해가 쉬워지는 구문 풀이

They do not wish for you to reply with [**whether** you can or cannot complete the task]—they simply expect you to do it.

⇨ [ ]는 전치사 with의 목적어이다.
⇨ [ ]와 같이 의문사가 없는 간접의문문은 <if/whether + 주어 + 동사>의 어순을 갖는다.

어휘 imply 함축하다 whether ~인지 아닌지 have to do with ~와 관련이 있다 approach 접근하다 literal 글자 그대로의 especially 특히 matter 중요하다 intention 의도 immediately 즉각 obvious 분명한 implication 함축 context 맥락 linguistics 언어학 concerned with ~와 관련된 interpret 해석하다 pragmatics 화용론
선택지 depend on ~에 의존하다 limitation 한계

해석 누군가가 "소금 좀 건네줄 수 있어요?"라고 물을 경우, 함축된 의미는 그들은 당신이 그들에게 소금을 건네주기를 원한다는 것이다. 그들은 당신이 그 일을 해낼 수 있는지 또는 없는지 대답하기를 바라지 않으며, 그들은 단지 당신이 그것을 하기를 바란다. 그들은 왜 그저 "소금 좀 건네주세요"라고 말하지 않는가? 그 답은 우리가 어떻게 언어에 접근하는지와 관련이 있다. 특히 우리가 말할 때, 단어들의 글자 그대로의 뜻이 항상 중요한 것은 아니다. 더 중요한 것은 화자가 처해 있는 상황과 그들의 의도이다. 화자가 쓰는 단어의 의미는 모두에게 즉각 분명하지 않으나 함축으로 가득 차 있을 수 있고, 단어를 맥락에 적용할 수 있는 사람들에게 쉽게 이해된다. 뜻을 해석하는 것과 관련 있는 언어학의 분야는 화용론이라고 불리고, 주제문 그것은 **우리가 말하는 것이 언제나 우리가 의미하는 것은 아니라는 것**을 가르쳐준다.

① 의사소통은 듣기에 의존한다
② 언어는 많은 한계를 가지고 있다
③ 우리가 말하는 것이 언제나 우리가 의미하는 것은 아니다
④ 예상치 못한 상황은 꽤 흔하다
⑤ 정확한 이해는 글자 그대로의 의미를 필요로 한다

해설 빈칸 문장은 이 글의 주제문이므로, 이를 다시 언급한 문장이나 부연 설명하는 문장을 파악해야 한다. 빈칸 문장에서 화용론은 '무엇'을 가르쳐준다고 하고, 글의 중반에서 우리가 말할 때 단어의 글자 그대로의 뜻보다 화자가 처해 있는 상황과 그들의 의도가 중요하다고 했다. 따라서 빈칸에는 화용론은 "우리가 말하는 것이 언제나 우리가 의미하는 것은 아니라는 것"을 가르쳐준다는 의미가 되는 것이 자연스러우므로 ③ what we say isn't always what we mean(우리가 말하는 것이 언제나 우리가 의미하는 것은 아니다)이 정답이다.

오답분석 ①의 '의사소통은 듣기에 의존한다', ②의 '언어는 많은 한계를 가지고 있다'는 글의 내용과 상관없는 오답이다. ④은 글의 핵심 소재 '상황'을 활용하여 혼동을 주는 오답이다. ⑤은 정확한 이해는 글자 그대로의 의미를 필요로 한다는 내용은 글의 주제를 반대로 진술한 오답이다.

실력UP! 미니 문제 12.

정답 The intention behind what a person says matters more than the literal meaning of the words they use

---

CHAPTER 12 흐름과 관계 없는 문장 찾기

불변의 패턴 23   p.92
주제만 파악하면 정답이 보인다.

기출 문제   정답 ③

지문분석

Words like 'near' and 'far' / can mean different things / depending on / where you are / and what you are doing.
'near'와 'far'와 같은 단어들은 / 여러 가지 것들을 의미할 수 있다 / ~에 따라 / 당신이 어디에 있는지에 / 그리고 무엇을 하고 있는지

★ If you were at a zoo, / then you might say / you are 'near' an animal / if you could reach out / and touch it / through the bars / of its cage.
만약 당신이 동물원에 있다면 / 당신은 말할지도 모른다 / 동물 '가까이'에 있다고 / 손을 뻗을 수 있는 경우에 / 그리고 동물을 만진다 / 창살 사이로 / 동물 우리의

① Here / the word 'near' / means an arm's length away.
여기서 / 'near'라는 단어는 / 팔 길이만큼의 거리를 의미한다

② If you were telling someone / how to get to your local shop, / you might call it 'near' / if it was a five-minute walk away.
만약 당신이 누군가에게 말해주고 있다면 / 동네 가게에 가는 방법을 / 그것을 '가까이'라고 일컬을지도 모른다 / 걸어서 5분 거리인 경우에

(③ It seems / that you had better walk / to the shop / to improve your health.)
~인 것 같다 / 당신은 걸어가는 것이 더 낫다 / 가게에 / 건강을 증진시키기 위해

④ Now / the word 'near' / means much longer / than an arm's length away.
이제 / 'near'라는 단어는 / 훨씬 더 긴 것을 의미한다 / 팔 길이만큼의 거리보다

⑤ Words / like 'near', 'far', 'small', 'big', 'hot', and 'cold' / all mean different things / to different people / at different times.
단어들은 / 'near', 'far', 'small', 'big', 'hot', 'cold'와 같은 / 모두 다른 것을 의미한다 / 다른 사람들에게 / 다른 때에

★ 독해가 쉬워지는 구문 풀이

[①If you were at a zoo], [②then you might say you are 'near' an animal {if you could reach out and touch it through the bars of its cage}].

⇨ [②]는 문장 전체의 주절이며, [①]는 주절[②]를 수식하는 부사절이다.
⇨ { }는 주절[②] 안에 있는 절(then ~ animal)을 수식하는 부사절이다.

어휘 reach out (손을) 뻗다 improve 증진시키다, 향상하다

해석 'near'와 'far'와 같은 단어들은 당신이 어디에 있는지와 무엇을 하고 있는지에 따라 여러 가지 것들을 의미할 수 있다. 만약 당신이 동물원에 있다면, 동물 우리의 창살 사이로 손을 뻗어서 동물을 만질 수 있는 경우에 당신은 동물 '가까이'에 있다고 말할지도 모른다. ① 여기서 'near'라는 단어는 팔 길이만큼의 거리를 의미한다. ② 만약 당신이 누군가에게 동네 가게에 가는 방법을 말해주고 있다면, 걸어서 5분 거리인 경우에 그것을 '가까이'라고 일컬을지도 모른다. (③ 당신은 건강을 증진시키기 위해 가게에 걸어가는 것이 더 나을 것 같다) ④ 이제 'near'라는 단어는 팔 길이만큼의 거리보다 훨씬 더 긴 것을 의미한다. ⑤ 주제문 'near', 'far', 'small', 'big', 'hot', 'cold'와 같은 단어들은 모두 다른 때에 다른 사람들에게 다른 것을 의미한다.

해설 이 글의 주제는 'near', 'far'와 같은 단어들은 당신이 어디에 있는지와 무엇을 하고 있는지에 따라 여러 가지 것들을 의미할 수 있다는 것이다. 대

부분의 문장이 여러 상황과 위치에서 단어가 갖는 의미에 대해 예를 드는 내용으로 주제와 관련 있는데, 건강 증진을 위해 걸어가는 것이 훨씬 더 낫다는 ③은 글의 흐름과 관계없는 문장이다.

오답분석 ①은 바로 앞 문장의 동물원 예시에서 단어가 어떤 의미를 갖는지 설명하는 문장이고 ②과 ④은 동네 가게로 가는 방법을 들어 설명한 두 번째 예시로 글의 주제와 연관되어 있다. ⑤은 첫 번째 문장을 다른 말로 바꾸어 설명한 문장이라 흐름에 자연스럽다.

불변의 패턴 24
p.93

핵심 소재만 같고 주제에서 살짝 벗어나는 문장이 정답이다.

기출 문제
정답 ④

지문분석

Of the many forest plants / that can cause poisoning, / wild mushrooms may be / among the most dangerous.
많은 산림 식물 중에서 / 중독을 일으킬 수 있는 / 야생 버섯이 ~일 수 있다 / 가장 위험한 것들 중 하나

① This is because / people sometimes confuse / the poisonous and edible varieties, / or they eat mushrooms / without making a positive identification / of the variety.
이는 ~하기 때문이다 / 사람들이 때때로 혼동한다 / 독성이 있는 종류와 먹을 수 있는 종류를 / 또는 그들이 버섯을 먹는다 / 확실한 확인을 하지 않고 / 종류에 대한

② Many people enjoy / hunting wild species of mushrooms / in the spring season, / because they are excellent edible mushrooms / and are highly prized.
많은 사람들이 즐긴다 / 야생 버섯 종을 찾아다니는 것을 / 봄철에 / 그것들이 훌륭한 식용 버섯이기 때문에 / 그리고 매우 귀하게 여겨진다

③ ★ However, / some wild mushrooms are dangerous, / leading people to lose their lives / due to mushroom poisoning.
그러나 / 몇몇 야생 버섯들은 위험하다 / 사람들이 목숨을 잃게 하므로 / 버섯의 독성으로 인해

(④ Growing a high-quality product / at a reasonable cost / is a key aspect / to farming edible mushrooms / for profit.)
높은 품질의 상품을 기르는 것이 / 합리적인 비용으로 / 핵심적인 측면이다 / 식용 버섯 양식의 / 이윤을 위한

⑤ To be safe, / a person must be able to identify edible mushrooms / before eating any wild one.
안전하려면 / 개인은 먹을 수 있는 버섯을 식별할 수 있어야 한다 / 어떠한 야생 버섯을 먹기 전에

★ 독해가 쉬워지는 구문 풀이

However, some wild mushrooms are dangerous, [leading people to lose their lives due to mushroom poisoning].

⇨ [ ]는 주절(some ~ dangerous)을 수식하는 분사구문의 부사절이며, 결과를 의미한다. 접속사 및 반복되는 주어(some wild mushrooms)는 생략되었다.

어휘 among ~ 중의 하나로 identification 확인, 식별 prized 귀한, 가치 있는 reasonable 합리적인

해석 중독을 일으킬 수 있는 많은 산림 식물 중에서, 야생 버섯이 가장 위험한 것들 중 하나일 수 있다. ① 이는 사람들이 때때로 독성이 있는 종류와 먹을 수 있는 종류를 혼동하거나, 그들이 종류에 대한 확실한 확인을 하지 않고 버섯을 먹기 때문이다. ② 야생 버섯 종들이 훌륭한 식용 버섯이고 매우 귀하게 여겨지기 때문에 많은 사람들이 봄철에 야생 버섯 종을 찾아다니는 것을 즐긴다. ③ 그러나, 몇몇 야생 버섯들은 버섯의 독성으로 인해 사람들이 목숨을 잃게 하므로 위험하다. (④ 합리적인 비용으로 높은 품질의 상품을 기르는 것이 이윤을 위한 식용 버섯 양식의 핵심적인 측면

이다.) ⑤ 안전하려면, 개인은 어떠한 야생 버섯을 먹기 전에 먹을 수 있는 버섯을 식별할 수 있어야 한다.

해설 이 글의 주제는 야생 버섯의 독성은 위험하기 때문에 먹을 수 있는 버섯을 식별해서 먹어야 한다는 것이다. 대부분이 야생 버섯의 위험성에 대한 내용으로 주제와 관련 있는데, 식용 버섯 재배 및 그 이윤에 대해 언급한 ④은 글의 흐름과 관계없는 문장이다.

오답분석 ①은 야생 버섯이 위험하다는 첫 번째 문장의 이유를 설명하는 내용이다. ②과 ③은 사람들이 야생 버섯을 찾는 이유와 몇몇 야생 버섯이 목숨까지 잃게 할 정도로 위험하다는 내용으로 주제와 연관되어 있다. ⑤은 안전하게 야생 버섯을 먹기 위한 당부의 말이므로 글의 흐름에 자연스럽다.

독해 만점 TEST
p.94

01 ④ **02** ④ **03** ③ **04** ④ **05** ④ **06** ③ **07** ④ **08** ③

실력 UP! 미니 문제

01. How Dolphins Identify and Remember Each Other
02. ③
03. (A) Vellum   (B) Regular paper
04. ①
05. (A) Promoting   (B) essential
06. ③
07. The Physical Characteristics of the Cheetah that Promote Speed
08. ①

01
정답 ④

지문분석

Within the animal kingdom, / dolphins are believed to have / one of the longest social memories.
동물계에서 / 돌고래는 갖는다고 여겨진다 / 가장 긴 사회적 기억력 중 하나를

① ★ A recent study / of bottlenose dolphins / has revealed / that they can remember dolphins / they have encountered / even after 20 years of separation.
최근의 한 연구는 / 큰돌고래에 대한 / 밝혀냈다 / 그들이 돌고래들을 기억할 수 있다는 것을 / 그들이 만났던 / 헤어진 지 20년이 지난 후에도

② They are able to do this / because dolphins regularly communicate / using an array of gestures, clicks, and whistles.
그들은 이렇게 할 수 있다 / 돌고래들이 주기적으로 의사소통하기 때문에 / 일련의 몸짓, 클릭, 휘파람을 이용하여

③ Early in life, / each dolphin develops a particular whistle / that is unique to them.
어릴 때 / 각각의 돌고래는 특별한 휘파람을 만들어낸다 / 그들만의 독자적인

(④ They typically travel / within the same family group / throughout their lives, / which can last anywhere / from 10 to 50 years.)
그들은 보통 이동한다 / 같은 무리의 집단을 벗어나지 않고 / 사는 내내 / 그런데 이는 대략 지속된다 / 10년에서 50년까지

⑤ The sound functions / similarly to the way / that names do / among people, / providing dolphins an easy way / to identify and remember other individuals.
그 소리는 기능한다 / 방식과 비슷하게 / 이름이 행하는 / 사람들 사이에서 / 그리고 돌고래에게 쉬운 방법을 제공한다 / 다른 개체를 식별하고 기억하는

★ 독해가 쉬워지는 구문 풀이

A recent study of bottlenose dolphins has revealed [that
　　　　　　　　　　　　　　　　　　　　　동사　　명사절
　　　　　　　　　　　　　　　　　　　　　　　　접속사
they can remember dolphins they have encountered even after
주어　　　　동사　　　목적어
20 years of separation].

⇨ 명사절 [ ]는 동사 revealed의 목적어이며, 명사절 접속사 that은 생략
될 수 있다.

[어휘] animal kingdom 동물계　memory 기억력　encounter 만나다
separation 헤어짐, 분리　an array of 일련의　typically 보통, 일반적으로
function 기능하다, 작용하다　identify 식별하다

[해석] 동물계에서, 돌고래는 가장 긴 사회적 기억력 중 하나를 갖는다고 여겨진
다. ① 큰돌고래에 대한 최근의 한 연구는 그들이 만났던 돌고래들을 헤어
진 지 20년이 지난 후에도 기억할 수 있다는 것을 밝혀냈다. ② 돌고래들
이 일련의 몸짓, 클릭, 휘파람을 이용하여 주기적으로 의사소통하기 때문
에 그들은 이렇게 할 수 있다. ③ 어릴 때, 각각의 돌고래는 그들만의 독자
적인 특별한 휘파람을 만들어낸다. (④ 그들은 보통 사는 내내 같은 무리
의 집단을 벗어나지 않고 이동하는데, 이는 대략 10년에서 50년까지 지속
된다.) ⑤ 그 소리는 사람들 사이에서 이름이 행하는 방식과 비슷하게 기
능하면서, 돌고래에게 다른 개체를 식별하고 기억하는 쉬운 방법을 제공
한다.

[해설] 이 글의 주제는 돌고래의 긴 사회적 기억력이다. 대부분이 돌고래의 기억
력과 기억하는 방법에 대한 내용으로 주제와 관련 있는데, 돌고래가 같은
무리의 집단을 벗어나지 않고 10~50년 동안 함께 이동한다는 ④은 글의
흐름과 관계없는 문장이다.

[오답 분석] ①, ②은 돌고래가 20년 전의 일도 기억하는데, 독특한 의사소통 방법 때
문에 그렇다는 내용으로 주제와 연관되어 있다. ③과 ④은 돌고래가 기억
하는 방법으로 사용되는 독특한 의사소통에 대한 부연 설명으로 글의 흐
름에 자연스럽다.

[실력 UP!] 미니 문제 01.

정답　How Dolphins Identify and Remember Each Other

02　　　　　　　　　　　　　　　　　　　정답 ④

[지문분석]

Thinking good thoughts / and performing good deeds / are hardly
the same thing.
좋은 생각을 하는 것 / 그리고 좋은 행동을 하는 것은 / 전혀 같은 것이 아니다

People may like to reassure themselves / by believing / that good
thoughts are enough / to bring about positive change / in the
world, / but thinking alone is rarely enough.
사람들은 자신들을 안심시키고 싶어 할 수도 있다 / 믿음으로써 / 좋은 생각만으로 충분
하다고 / 긍정적인 변화를 가져오기 위해 / 세상에 / 하지만 생각하는 것만으로는 별로 충
분하지 않다

① If a man is hungry, / simply hoping / that someone provides
him with food / is of no real help.
만약 한 사람이 굶주리고 있다면 / 바라는 것만으로는 / 누군가가 그에게 음식을 주기를 /
진정한 도움이 되지 않는다

② If everyone / who encounters that man / shares the same
thought / but does not do anything / about it, / he could well end
up starving.
만약 모든 사람들이 ~한다면 / 그 사람과 마주치는 / 똑같은 생각을 하다 / 하지만 아무것
도 하지 않는다 / 그것에 대해 / 아마 그는 굶어 죽을 것이다

③ ★ On the other hand, / it would make a world of difference / if
just one person gave him / something to eat.
반면에 / 그것은 큰 차이를 만들 것이다 / 만약 단 한 명이라도 그에게 준다면 / 먹을 것을

(④ Research has found / that people can survive / for up to three
weeks / without food.)
연구는 알아냈다 / 사람들이 생존할 수 있음을 / 3주까지 / 음식 없이도

⑤ That's why / it is important / to act on our well-meaning
thoughts / before it is too late.
그것이 바로 ~한 이유이다 / ~이 중요하다 / 선의의 생각에 따라 행동하는 것 / 너무 늦기
전에

★ 독해가 쉬워지는 구문 풀이

On the other hand, it would make a world of difference if just one
person gave him something [to eat].
　　　　　　　　　　　　　　명사　　to부정사

⇨ [ ]는 명사 something을 수식하는 형용사 역할을 하는 to부정사이다.

[어휘] deed 행동, 행위　reassure 안심시키다, 확신시키다
bring about 가져오다, 생기게 하다　be of help 도움이 되다　well 아마, 잘
starve 굶어 죽다, 굶주리다　world of difference 큰 차이
act on ~에 따라 행동하다, ~에 영향을 주다
well-meaning 선의의, 악의가 없는

[해석] 좋은 생각을 하는 것과 좋은 행동을 하는 것은 전혀 같은 것이 아니다. 사
람들은 세상에 긍정적인 변화를 가져오기 위해 좋은 생각만으로 충분하
다고 믿음으로써 자신을 안심시키고 싶어 할 수도 있지만, 생각하는 것만
으로는 별로 충분하지 않다. ① 만약 한 사람이 굶주리고 있다면, 누군가
가 그에게 음식을 주기를 바라는 것만으로는 진정한 도움이 되지 않는다.
② 만약 그 사람과 마주치는 모든 사람들이 똑같은 생각을 하지만 그것에
대해 아무것도 하지 않는다면, 아마 그는 결국 굶어 죽을 것이다. ③ 반면
에, 만약 단 한 명이라도 그에게 먹을 것을 준다면, 그것은 큰 차이를 만들
것이다. (④ 연구는 사람들이 음식 없이도 3주까지 생존할 수 있음을 알아
냈다.) ⑤ [주제문] 그것이 바로 너무 늦기 전에 선의의 생각에 따라 행동하
는 것이 중요한 이유이다.

[해설] 이 글의 주제는 선의의 생각에 따라 행동하는 것이 중요하다는 것이다. 대
부분 좋은 생각이 좋은 행동으로 이어지는 것과 관련된 내용으로 주제와
관련 있는데, 사람의 생존 조건에 대해 언급한 ④은 글의 흐름과 관계없는
문장이다.

[오답 분석] ①, ②, ③은 좋은 생각이 좋은 행동으로 이어져야 한다는 주장을 설명하
는 예시로 주제와 연관되어 있다. ⑤은 선의의 생각에 따라 행동하는 것이
중요하다는 주제문을 다시 언급한 문장으로 글의 흐름에 자연스럽다.

[실력 UP!] 미니 문제 02.

정답　③
해석　① 믿음이 사람들의 세계관을 바꿀 수 있는 이유
　　　② 선행이 정신건강에 미치는 영향
　　　③ 긍정적인 생각보다 행동하는 것의 필요성
해설　선의의 생각은 행동하지 않고 갖고 있는 것만으로는 의미가 없다는 것에 대한 글이므
로, 글의 주제로 가장 적절한 것은 ③ the need for action over positive thinking
이다.

03　　　　　　　　　　　　　　　　　　　정답 ③

[지문분석]

Vellum is a type of material / made from the dry skin / of mammals /
such as calves and sheep.
피지는 소재의 한 종류이다 / 건조된 가죽으로 만들어지는 / 포유동물의 / 송아지나 양
과 같은

Once it is processed, / it can be used / as a medium / to write or
print documents on.
그것이 가공되고 나면 / 사용될 수 있다 / 도구로써 / 그 위에 글을 쓰거나 문서를 인쇄하는

Vellum carries a number of benefits / for preserving written works, / not the least of which / is durability.
피지는 많은 장점을 지닌다 / 쓰인 글을 보존하는 데 / 그중 적잖은 부분은 / 내구성이다

① The parliaments of Britain and Ireland, / for instance, / traditionally printed their legislation / on vellum / for over a thousand years.
영국과 아일랜드 의회는 / 예를 들어 / 전통적으로 법률을 기록했다 / 피지에 / 천 년 넘게

② Outside of government, / Jewish religious scrolls are still printed / on the material / to this day.
정부 문서를 제외하고는 / 유대교의 책들이 아직도 인쇄된다 / 그 소재에 / 오늘날까지

(③ Regular paper is cheap to produce / and readily available, / so it is more suitable / for everyday use.)
일반 종이는 생산하기에 저렴하다 / 그리고 손쉽게 구할 수 있는 / 그래서 더 적합하다 / 일상적 용도로

④ Vellum also has the attraction / of being luxurious / in appearance.
피지는 또한 매력도 있다 / 고급스럽다는 / 보기에

⑤ ★ Therefore, / it is common / for some educational institutions / to issue traditional diplomas / made of vellum.
그래서 / ~은 흔한 일이다 / 일부 교육 기관이 / 전통 졸업 증서를 발행하는 것 / 피지로 만들어진

★ 독해가 쉬워지는 구문 풀이

Therefore, it is common for some educational institutions to issue
가주어   to부정사 의미상 주어
traditional diplomas made of vellum.
진짜 주어

⇨ 주어가 '피지로 만들어진 전통 졸업 증서를 발행하는 것'이라는 의미로 길기 때문에, 긴 주어를 대신해서 가주어 역할을 할 수 있는 it으로 문장을 시작했다. to issue가 나타내는 '발행하는' 행위를 하는 some educational institutions는 to부정사의 의미상 주어이므로 for some educational institutions의 형태로 쓰였다.

[어휘] material 소재, 옷감, 원자재 mammal 포유동물 calf 송아지, 종아리 medium 도구, 수단, 매체 print 새기다, 인쇄하다, 글씨를 (인쇄체로) 쓰다 preserve 보존하다 durability 내구성, 내구력 parliament 의회, 국회 Jewish 유대교의, 유대인의 scroll 책, 두루마리 readily 손쉽게, 순조롭게 in appearance 보기에는 diploma 졸업 증서, 학위

[해석] 피지는 송아지나 양과 같은 포유동물의 건조된 가죽으로 만들어지는 소재의 한 종류이다. 그것이 가공되고 나면, 그 위에 글을 쓰거나 문서를 인쇄하는 도구로써 사용될 수 있다. 피지는 쓰인 글을 보존하는 데 많은 장점을 지니는데, 그중 적잖은 부분은 내구성이다. ① 예를 들어, 영국과 아일랜드 의회는 전통적으로 천 년 넘게 피지에 법률을 기록했다. ② 정부 문서를 제외하고는, 유대교의 책들이 오늘날까지 아직도 그 소재에 인쇄된다. (③ 일반 종이는 생산하기에 저렴하고 손쉽게 구할 수 있어서 일상적 용도로 더 적합하다.) ④ 피지는 또한 보기에 고급스럽다는 매력도 있다. ⑤ 그래서, 일부 교육 기관이 피지로 만들어진 전통 졸업 증서를 발행하는 것은 흔한 일이다.

[해설] 이 글의 주제는 피지의 다양한 장점과 용도이다. 대부분 피지의 장점과 그것의 용도에 대한 내용으로 주제와 관련 있는데, 일반 종이의 장점과 용도를 언급한 ③은 글의 흐름과 관계없는 문장이다.

[오답분석] ①, ②은 피지의 내구성이 좋다는 점 때문에 오랫동안 피지를 사용해온 경우를 언급하고 있고 ④, ⑤은 피지의 또 다른 장점과 용도를 설명하고 있으므로 글의 흐름에 자연스럽다.

실력 UP! 미니 문제 03.

정답 (A) Vellum (B) Regular paper

해설 (A) 피지는 포유동물의 건조된 가죽으로 만들어진 소재의 한 종류라고 한 후 그것이 가공되고 나면 그 위에 글을 쓰거나 문서를 인쇄하는 도구로써 사용될 수 있다고 했으므로, (A)it이 가리키는 것은 Vellum(피지)이다.

(B) 일반 종이는 생산하기에 저렴하고 손쉽게 구할 수 있다고 한 후 그래서 그것이 일상적 용도로 더 적합하다고 했으므로, (B)it이 가리키는 것은 Regular paper(일반 종이)이다.

04   정답 ④

지문분석

Agriculture is / one of the fastest-growing sectors / in Africa.
농업은 ~이다 / 가장 빠르게 성장하는 분야 중 하나 / 아프리카에서

The need / to sustain a vast population / means / that millions of people / across the continent / must devote their energy and resources / to growing food.
필요성은 / 막대한 인구를 부양해야 할 / 의미한다 / 수백만 명의 사람들이 / 그 대륙 전체의 / 그들의 에너지와 자원을 쏟아야 한다는 것을 / 식량을 생산하는 일에

① However, / many farmers there rely on / outdated tools and methods.
하지만 / 그곳의 많은 농부들은 ~에 의존하고 있다 / 구식 도구와 방법에

② These tools and methods are not suitable / for farming / on a large scale, / and their continued use / could also harm the environment.
이러한 도구와 방법은 적합하지 않다 / 농사를 짓기에 / 대규모로 / 그리고 그것들의 지속적인 사용은 / 환경에 피해를 줄 수도 있다

③ To unlock the farming sector's full potential / without damaging the environment, / farmers must turn to emerging technologies, / including artificial intelligence, big data, and more.
농경지의 최대 잠재력을 드러내기 위해서 / 환경에 해를 끼치지 않으면서 / 농부들은 최신 기술에 의존해야 한다 / 인공지능, 빅데이터, 그리고 그 이상의 것을 비롯한

(④ A number of wild African species / are currently in danger / of extinction.)
많은 야생 아프리카 종들이 / 현재 위기에 있다 / 멸종의

⑤ ★ Applied in the right circumstances, / advanced technologies could help African farmers / take full advantage of their continent's abundant natural resources.
적절한 상황에 적용된다면 / 선진 기술은 아프리카 농부들을 도울 수 있다 / 그들 대륙의 풍부한 천연자원을 온전히 활용하도록

★ 독해가 쉬워지는 구문 풀이

Applied in the right circumstances, advanced technologies
과거분사구문   주어
could help African farmers take full advantage of their continent's
동사   목적어   목적격보어
abundant natural resources.

⇨ 분사구문에 주어가 따로 없으므로 주절의 주어 advanced technologies가 분사구문의 의미상 주어이다. 문맥상 '선진 기술이 적용된다'라는 의미로, advanced technologies가 apply가 나타내는 '적용하는' 행위의 대상이므로 과거분사 Applied가 쓰였다.

[어휘] agriculture 농업 sustain 부양하다, 견디다 devote 쏟다, 전념하다 outdated 구식의, 시대에 뒤진 on a large scale 대규모로 potential 잠재력 turn to ~에 의존하다, ~로 되다 emerging 최신의, 떠오르는 artificial intelligence 인공 지능 advanced 선진의, 고급의 natural resource 천연자원

[해석] 농업은 아프리카에서 가장 빠르게 성장하는 분야 중 하나이다. 막대한 인구를 부양해야 할 필요성은 그 대륙 전체의 수백만 명의 사람들이 식량을 생산하는 일에 그들의 에너지와 자원을 쏟아야 한다는 것을 의미한다. ① 하지만, 그곳의 많은 농부들은 구식 도구와 방법에 의존하고 있다. ② 이러한 도구와 방법은 대규모로 농사를 짓기에 적합하지 않고, 그것들의 지속적인 사용은 환경에 피해를 줄 수도 있다. ③ 환경에 해를 끼치지 않으면서 농경지의 최대 잠재력을 드러내기 위해서, 농부들은 인공지능, 빅데이터, 그리고 그 이상의 것을 비롯한 최신 기술에 의존해야 한다. (④ 많은 야생 아프리카 종들이 현재 멸종 위기에 있다.) ⑤ [주제문] 적절한 상

황에 적용된다면, 선진 기술은 아프리카 농부들이 그들 대륙의 풍부한 천연자원을 온전히 활용하도록 도울 수 있다.

해설 이 글의 주제는 현재 아프리카 농업의 문제점과 이를 해결하기 위한 선진 기술 도입이 필요하다는 것이다. 대부분이 아프리카 농업의 문제점과 선진 기술 도입에 대한 내용으로 주제와 관련이 있는데, 야생동물들이 멸종 위기에 있다는 ④은 글의 흐름과 관계없는 문장이다.

오답분석 ①, ②은 아프리카 농업의 문제점, ③, ⑤은 이에 따른 선진 기술 도입의 필요성에 대한 내용으로 글의 흐름에 자연스럽다.

실력 UP! 미니 문제 04.

정답 ①

해석 ① 아프리카 농업에서 첨단기술의 필요성
② 아프리카 생물종의 피해를 막기 위해 활용되는 농업 기술
③ 천연자원에 대한 아프리카 인구의 의존도

해설 구식 도구에 의존하고 있는 아프리카 농업의 문제와 최신 기술을 도입할 필요성에 관한 글이므로, 글의 주제로 가장 적절한 것은 ① the need for advanced technology in African agriculture이다.

05
정답 ④

지문분석

Nutrition is key / to promoting a healthy gut environment, / which in turn is essential / to maintaining a strong immune system.
영양 섭취는 중요하다 / 건강한 장 환경을 활성화하는 데 / 그리고 이는 결과적으로 필수적이다 / 강한 면역 체계를 유지하는 데

① A healthy gut contains the right balance / of beneficial microbes / to help us digest food, / absorb nutrients, / and get rid of harmful viruses.
건강한 장은 적절한 균형이 잡혀있다 / 유익한 미생물들의 / 우리가 음식을 소화하는 것을 돕는 / 그리고 영양분을 흡수한다 / 그리고 해로운 바이러스를 제거한다

② Without it, / we may not get enough nutrition / from our food / and become vulnerable / to serious allergies and diseases.
그것 없이는 / 우리는 충분한 영양분을 얻지 못할 수 있다 / 음식에서 / 그리고 취약해진다 / 심각한 알레르기나 질병에

③ To maintain a healthy gut, / it is important / to regularly consume foods / that contain bioactive compounds / as early and as often / in life / as possible.
건강한 장을 유지하기 위해서 / ~이 중요하다 / 음식을 주기적으로 섭취하는 것 / 생물 활성 화합물을 함유한 / 이른 시기에 그리고 자주 / 삶 속에서 / 가능한 한

(④ Babies / who consume breast milk / tend to show signs / of improved immune system / later in life.)
아기들은 / 모유를 먹는 / 징후를 보이는 경향이 있다 / 증진된 면역 체계의 / 나중에 살면서

⑤ ★ In particular, / eating lots of fruits, vegetables, and dairy products / like yogurt / helps us / maintain a good microbiome.
특히 / 많은 과일, 채소, 유제품을 먹는 것은 / 요구르트와 같은 / 우리가 ~하도록 도와준다 / 좋은 체내 미생물 생태계를 유지한다

★ 독해가 쉬워지는 구문 풀이

In particular, underline{eating lots of fruits, vegetables, and dairy products}
　　　　　　　　　　단수주어(동명사구)
like yogurt underline{helps} underline{us} underline{maintain} a good microbiome.
　　　　　　동사　목적어　목적격보어(동사원형)

⇨ 주어 eating lots of fruits, ~ dairy products like yogurt는 단수 취급하는 동명사구 주어이므로 단수동사 helps가 쓰였다.

⇨ helps는 to부정사를 목적격보어로 취하지만 to를 생략하고 동사원형을 취할 수도 있다.

어휘 nutrition 영양 섭취, 영양물　promote 활성화하다, 촉진하다
in turn 결과적으로, 차례차례　immune 면역의, 면제된　absorb 흡수하다
vulnerable 취약한, 연약한　consume 섭취하다　breast milk 모유
sign 징후, 표시　dairy product 유제품　microbiome 체내 미생물 생태계

해설 **주제문** 영양 섭취는 건강한 장 환경을 활성화하는 데 중요하고, 이는 결과적으로 강한 면역 체계를 유지하는 데 필수적이다. ① 건강한 장은 우리가 음식을 소화하고 영양분을 흡수하며 해로운 바이러스를 제거하는 것을 돕는 유익한 미생물들의 적절한 균형이 잡혀있다. ② 그것 없이는, 우리는 음식에서 충분한 영양분을 얻지 못하고 심각한 알레르기나 질병에 취약해질 수 있다. ③ 건강한 장을 유지하기 위해서, 생물 활성 화합물을 함유한 음식을 삶 속에서 가능한 한 이른 시기에, 그리고 자주 주기적으로 섭취하는 것이 중요하다. (④ 모유를 먹는 아기들은 나중에 살면서 증진된 면역 체계의 징후를 보이는 경향이 있다.) ⑤ 특히, 많은 과일, 채소, 요구르트와 같은 유제품을 먹는 것은 우리가 좋은 체내 미생물 생태계를 유지하도록 도와준다.

해설 이 글의 주제는 영양 섭취가 건강한 장 환경을 활성화하는 데 필수적이라는 것이다. 대부분이 장 건강을 유지하기 위한 방법에 대한 내용으로 주제와 관련이 있는데, 모유를 먹는 아기의 면역 체계에 대해 언급한 ④은 글의 흐름과 관계없는 문장이다.

오답분석 ①, ②은 건강한 장의 조건들을 언급하였고, ③, ⑤은 이를 유지하기 위해 필요한 방법에 대한 내용으로 글의 흐름에 자연스럽다.

실력 UP! 미니 문제 05.

정답 (A) Promoting　(B) essential

해석 이로운 미생물을 함유한 음식을 섭취함으로써 건강한 장 환경을 (A) 활성화하는 것은 강한 면역 체계를 유지하는 데 (B) 필수적이다.

해설 글에서 건강한 장을 유지하기 위해, 생물 활성 화합물을 함유한 음식을 가능한 한 빨리, 주기적으로 섭취하는 것은 결과적으로 강한 면역 체계를 유지하는 데 필수적이라고 했으므로, 요약문의 빈칸에 들어갈 말로 가장 적절한 것은 (A) Promoting(활성화하는 것), (B) essential(필수적인)이다.

06
정답 ③

지문분석

When people dream, / they typically do not know / if the experience is real or not / until after they have woken up.
사람들이 꿈을 꿀 때 / 그들은 일반적으로 알지 못한다 / 그 경험이 진짜인지 아닌지 / 그들이 잠에서 깰 때까지

① However, / individuals / are sometimes able to recognize / that they are having a dream / and / even control their actions / while dreaming.
그러나 / 사람들은 / 가끔 인식할 수 있다 / 그들이 꿈을 꾸고 있다는 것을 / 그리고 / 그들의 행동을 조종할 수도 있다 / 꿈을 꾸는 동안

② This phenomenon / is known as lucid dreaming, / and research indicates / it is hard for everyone to experience this.
이 현상은 / 자각몽으로 알려져 있다 / 그리고 연구 조사는 보여준다 / 모든 사람이 이것을 경험하기는 힘들다는 것을

(③ Lucid dreaming / has been the subject / of many popular science fiction novels and films.)
자각몽은 / 소재가 되어왔다 / 많은 유명 공상 과학 소설 및 영화의

④ In fact, / it is believed that / only half of all people / experience lucid dreams / at least once in their lifetime / and / less than 20 percent / have them on a regular basis.
사실 / 여겨진다 / 모든 사람의 절반만이 / 자각몽을 경험한다 / 일생에서 적어도 한 번은 / 그리고 / 20% 미만이 / 그것을 정기적으로 꾼다고

⑤ This is likely because / lucid dreaming is related to / the ability to monitor / one's own thoughts, / ★ but / most people are not sensitive enough / to notice when they are dreaming.
이것은 아마 ~ 때문일 것이다 / 자각몽이 관련이 있다 / 조정하는 능력과 / 사람의 생각을 / 그러나 / 대부분의 사람들은 충분히 민감하지 않다 / 그들이 꿈을 꿀 때 알아차릴 만큼

어휘 typically 일반적으로 experience 경험 individual 사람, 개인
recognize 인식하다 phenomenon 현상 research 연구 (조사)
indicate 보여주다 science fiction 공상과학의 lifetime 일생
on a regular basis 정기적으로 likely ~할 것 같은 ability 능력
monitor 조정하다, 관찰하다 sensitive 민감한

해석 사람들이 꿈을 꿀 때, 그들은 일반적으로 그들이 잠에서 깰 때까지 그 경험이 진짜인지 아닌지 알지 못한다. ① 그러나, 사람들은 가끔 그들이 꿈을 꾸고 있다는 것을 인식할 수 있고, 꿈을 꾸는 동안 그들의 행동을 조종할 수도 있다. 주제문 ② 이 현상은 자각몽으로 알려져 있으며, 연구 조사는 모든 사람이 이것을 경험하기는 힘들다는 것을 보여준다. (③ 자각몽은 많은 유명 공상 과학 소설 및 영화의 소재가 되어왔다.) ④ 사실 모든 사람의 절반만이 일생에서 적어도 한 번은 자각몽을 경험하고, 20% 미만이 그것을 정기적으로 꾼다고 여겨진다. ⑤ 이것은 아마 자각몽이 사람의 생각을 조정하는 능력과 관련이 있으나, 대부분의 사람들은 그들이 꿈을 꿀 때 알아차릴 만큼 충분히 민감하지 않기 때문일 것이다.

해설 이 글의 주제는 모든 사람이 자각몽이라는 현상을 경험하기는 어렵다는 것이다. 대부분이 많은 사람들은 자각몽을 경험하기 어렵다는 내용으로 주제와 관련이 있는데, 자각몽이 소설 및 영화 소재로 사용된다고 언급한 ③은 글의 흐름과 관계 없는 문장이다.

실력 UP! **미니 문제 06.**

정답 ③

해석 ① 자각몽을 즐기는 사람들
② 꿈을 통제하는 방법
③ 드물게 발생하는 자각몽

해설 자각몽으로 알려진 현상은 모든 사람이 경험하기는 어렵다고 하며 인간의 절반만 그들의 일생에서 이것을 경험하는 것으로 여겨진다고 했으므로, 글의 주제로 가장 적절한 것은 ③ the rare occurrence of lucid dreaming(드물게 발생하는 자각몽)이다.

07
정답 ④

지문분석

The cheetah is a large cat / that is native to / the grassland areas of Africa.
치타는 큰 고양이과 동물이나 / 태생의 / 아프리카 초원

★ Due to / its unique physical characteristics, / it is the fastest land animal, / capable of accelerating / from 0 to 60 mph / in only 3 seconds.
~으로 인해 / 그것의 독특한 신체적 특성 / 그것은 가장 빠른 육상 동물이다 / 가속할 수 있는 / 0에서 시속 60마일로 / 3초 만에

① To begin with, / it is one of the lightest / of the big cats, / and / its slim build and long legs / enable it to run fast.
우선 / 그것은 가장 가벼운 것 중의 하나이다 / 큰 고양이과 동물들 중 / 그리고 / 그것의 날씬한 체구와 긴 다리는 / 그것이 빠르게 달리는 것을 가능하게 해준다

② In addition, / its long muscular tail helps / it maneuver / and / make sharp, quick turns.
또한 / 그것의 길고 근육이 발달한 꼬리는 도와준다 / 그것이 조종하는 것을 / 그리고 / 급격하고 빠르게 방향을 바꾸는 것을

③ The respiratory organs of a cheetah / also contribute to its ability / to move very quickly.
치타의 호흡 기관 / 역시 그것의 능력에 기여한다 / 매우 빠르게 움직이는

(④ The decline of cheetah populations / has been a serious problem in Africa, / and has brought discussion about / reconsidering this animal as endangered.)
치타 개체수의 감소는 / 아프리카에서 심각한 문제였으며 / ~에 대한 논의를 불러일으켰다 / 이 동물을 멸종 위기에 처한 것으로 재고하는 것

⑤ For example, / its big lungs allow it / to take up to 150 breaths / per minute / when it is running at a high speed.
예를 들어 / 치타의 큰 폐는 그것이 할 수 있도록 해준다 / 150회의 호흡을 하도록 / 분당 / 치타가 빠른 속도로 달릴 때

어휘 native 태생의 grassland 초원 unique 독특한 physical 신체적인
characteristic 특성 capable of ~할 수 있는 accelerate 가속하다
mph 시속 ~마일 light 가벼운; 빛 slim 날씬한 build 체구; 짓다
enable ~을 할 수 있게 하다 muscular 근육이 발달한 maneuver 조종하다
sharp 급격한 organ 장기 (기관) contribute 기여하다 ability 능력
decline 감소 population 개체수, 인구 discussion 논의
reconsider 재고하다 endangered 멸종 위기에 처한 per ~당

해석 치타는 아프리카 초원 태생의 큰 고양이과 동물이다. 주제문 그것의 독특한 신체적 특성으로 인해 그것은 가장 빠른 육상 동물이며, 3초 만에 0에서 시속 60마일로 가속할 수 있다. ① 우선, 그것은 큰 고양이과 동물들 중 가장 가벼운 것 중 하나이며, 그것의 날씬한 체구와 긴 다리는 그것이 빠르게 달리는 것을 가능하게 해준다. ② 또한, 그것의 길고 근육이 발달한 꼬리는 그것이 급격하고 빠르게 방향을 조종하고 바꾸는 것을 도와준다. ③ 치타의 호흡 기관 역시 그것이 매우 빠르게 움직이는 능력에 기여한다. (④ 치타 개체수의 감소는 아프리카에서 심각한 문제였으며, 이 동물을 멸종 위기에 처한 것으로 재고하는 것에 대한 논의를 불러일으켰다.) ⑤ 예를 들어, 치타의 큰 폐는 치타가 빠른 속도로 달릴 때 분당 150회의 호흡을 하도록 해준다.

해설 이 글의 주제는 가장 빠른 육상 동물인 치타의 독특한 신체적 특성에 대한 것이다. 대부분이 어떠한 신체적 특성으로 인해 치타가 빠르게 달릴 수 있는지를 설명하는 내용으로 주제와 관련이 있는데, 치타의 멸종 위기 상황에 대해 언급한 ④은 글의 흐름과 관계 없는 문장이다.

실력 UP! **미니 문제 07.**

정답 The Physical Characteristics of the Cheetah that Promote Speed

08
정답 ③

지문분석

There are many negative aspects / surrounding advertisements / specifically targeted / at young children, / and one of these involves a phenomenon / called "pester power."
많은 부정적인 측면이 있다 / 광고와 관련된 / 특히 대상으로 하는 / 어린아이들을 / 그런데 이것들 중 하나는 현상을 포함한다 / "부모를 졸라서 바라는 것을 얻어내는 힘"이라고 불리는

① It describes the tendency / of young children / to keep asking their parents / to buy them products or services / that they have previously seen / advertised on TV and other media.
그것은 경향을 말한다 / 어린아이들의 / 그들의 부모에게 계속 요구하는 / 제품이나 서비스를 사달라고 / 이전에 봤던 / TV나 다른 매체에서 광고되는 것을

② Companies willingly take advantage of children's influence / on parents / to sell more goods and services / to consumers.

기업은 아이들의 영향력을 기꺼이 이용한다 / 부모에 대한 / 더 많은 제품과 서비스를 판매하기 위해 / 소비자에게

(③ For parents, / children's refusal / to obey commands / can quickly turn into a problem.)

부모들에게 있어 / 아이들의 거부는 / 지시를 따르는 것에 대한 / 곧 문제가 될 수 있다

④ This is concerning / because young children lack critical thinking / and absorb every message / from advertisements.

이것은 염려스럽다 / 어린아이들은 비판적인 사고가 부족하기 때문에 / 그리고 모든 메시지를 받아들인다 / 광고의

⑤ ★ Not knowing / that they are acting / just as companies want them to, / a lot of children eventually get parents to give in / and overspend their money.

알지 못한 채 / 그들이 행동하고 있다는 것을 / 기업이 그들로 하여금 하기 원하는 대로 / 많은 아이들은 결국 부모가 항복하게 만든다 / 그리고 그들의 돈을 많이 쓰게

★ 독해가 쉬워지는 구문 풀이

[**Not** knowing that they are acting just as companies want them
　　　분사
to], a lot of children eventually get parents to give in and overspend
　　　　　　주어　　　　　　　　동사　　목적어　　　└ 목적격보어 ┘
their money.

▷ [ ]는 '~을 알지 못한 채'라는 뜻으로 분사 knowing을 부정하는 부정어 Not이 knowing 앞에 쓰였다.

어휘 surrounding 관련된　phenomenon 현상, 사건　willingly 기꺼이, 자진해서　take advantage of ~을 이용하다, ~을 기회로 활용하다　obey 따르다, 순종하다　command 지시　critical 비판적인, 중요한　give in 항복하다, 제출하다　overspend 돈을 많이 쓰다

해석 (주제문) 특히 어린아이들을 대상으로 하는 광고와 관련된 많은 부정적인 측면이 있는데, 이것들 중 하나는 "부모를 졸라서 바라는 것을 얻어내는 힘"이라고 불리는 현상을 포함한다. ① 그것은 어린아이들이 이전에 TV나 다른 매체에서 광고되는 것을 봤던 제품이나 서비스를 사달라고 그들의 부모에게 계속 요구하는 경향을 말한다. ② 기업은 더 많은 제품과 서비스를 소비자에게 판매하기 위해 부모에 대한 아이들의 영향력을 기꺼이 이용한다. (③ 부모들에게 있어, 지시를 따르는 것에 대한 아이들의 거부는 곧 문제가 될 수 있다.) ④ 어린아이들은 비판적인 사고가 부족하고 광고의 모든 메시지를 받아들이기 때문에 이것은 염려스럽다. ⑤ 기업이 그들로 하여금 하기 원하는 대로 그들이 행동하고 있다는 것을 알지 못한 채, 많은 아이들은 결국 부모가 항복하고 그들의 돈을 많이 쓰게 만든다.

해설 이 글의 주제는 어린이를 대상으로 하는 광고가 부모와 자녀에게 미치는 영향에 대한 것이다. 대부분이 어린이를 대상으로 하는 광고의 부정적 측면을 언급하고 있는데, 아이들이 부모의 지시를 거부하여 문제가 된다는 ③은 글의 흐름과 관계 없는 문장이다.

실력 UP! 미니 문제 08.

정답 ①

해석 ① 어린이를 대상으로 하는 광고의 부정적인 측면
② 새로운 물건을 원하는 아이들의 경향
③ 광고가 아이들의 비판적 사고에 미치는 영향

해설 아이들을 대상으로 하는 광고가 아이들의 사고와 부모의 소비 계획에 미치는 부정적인 영향에 관한 글이므로, 글의 주제로 가장 적절한 것은 ① the negative aspects of advertisements targeted at children이다.

01　　정답 ②

지문분석

The lifestyle of the Raika tribe / in Rajasthan, India, / may soon cease to exist.

Raika족의 생활 방식은 / 인도 라자스탄의 / 곧 소멸할 수도 있다

For centuries, / the Raikas have herded camels / across the Thar Desert, / living a semi-nomadic lifestyle / and training camels / to plough their fields / and provide transportation, milk, and wool.

수 세기 동안 / Raika족은 낙타를 몰아왔다 / 타르 사막 전역에 걸쳐 / 반유목 생활을 하면서 / 그리고 낙타를 훈련시키면서 / 그들의 밭을 갈며 / 이동 수단, 우유, 그리고 털을 제공하도록

However, / the last decade has seen many changes / that threaten the camels, / including a surge in development.

그러나 / 지난 10년 동안 많은 변화들이 있었다 / 낙타를 위협하는 / 개발의 급증을 포함한

The construction of new roads / has brought more vehicles to the region, / making camels somewhat less useful / as "ships of the desert."

새로운 도로의 건설은 / 그 지역으로 더 많은 차량을 불러들였다 / 동시에 낙타를 다소 쓸모가 없게 만들었다 / "사막의 배"로서의

As a result, / their numbers are in sharp decline.

그 결과 / 그들의 수는 가파른 감소세에 있다

★ Furthermore, / the installation of solar and wind farms / to support the increase in farmland, / made possible by a large-scale irrigation project, / has left less space for camels.

게다가 / 태양광 및 풍력 발전소의 건설은 / 농경지의 확장을 지원하기 위한 / 대규모 관개 프로젝트 덕분에 가능했던 / 낙타의 입지를 더 좁혔다

These advancements / have made it more difficult / for the Raika / to maintain their traditional habits, / prompting them / to **abandon their former ways**.

이러한 발전은 / 더 힘들게 만들었다 / Raika족을 / 그들의 전통적 관습을 유지하기 / 그들이 ~하도록 했다 / **그들의 기존 방식을 포기하도록**

★ 독해가 쉬워지는 구문 풀이

Furthermore, [the installation of solar and wind farms to support
　　　　　　　　　　　　　　　　　　주어
the increase in farmland, {made possible by a large-scale irrigation
　　　　선행사
project}], has left less space for camels.
　　　　　　동사

▷ [ ]는 문장의 주어이다.
▷ { }는 선행사 increase를 수식하는 관계절로, 앞에 관계대명사와 be동사가 생략되었다.

어휘 cease to exist 소멸하다　herd 몰다　nomadic 유목 생활을 하는　transportation 이동 수단, 수송　notable 눈에 띄는　surge 급증　installation 설치　farm 발전소　prompt ~하게 하다, 촉진하다
(선택지) assistance 지원　settle 정착하다　recognition 인정

해석 인도 라자스탄의 Raika족의 생활 방식은 곧 소멸할 수도 있다. 수 세기 동안, Raika족은 반유목 생활을 하고 낙타가 그들의 밭을 갈며 이동 수단, 우유, 그리고 털을 제공하도록 훈련시키면서, 타르 사막 전역에 걸쳐 낙타를 몰아왔다. 그러나, 지난 10년 동안 낙타를 위협하는 개발의 급증을 포함한 많은 변화들이 있었다. 새로운 도로의 건설은 그 지역으로 더 많은 차량을 불러들였고, 동시에 "사막의 배"로서의 낙타를 다소 쓸모가 없게 만들다. 그 결과, 그들의 수는 가파른 감소세에 있다. 게다가, 대규모 관개 프

로젝트 덕분에 가능했던 농경지의 확장을 지원하기 위한 태양광 및 풍력 발전소의 건설은, 낙타의 입지를 더 좁혔다. (주제문) 이러한 발전은 Raika족이 그들의 전통적 관습을 유지하기 더 힘들게 만들었고 **그들의 기존 방식을 포기하도록** 했다.

① 정부 지원을 모색하도록
② 그들의 기존 방식을 포기하도록
③ 더 넓은 영토에 정착하도록
④ 인정받기 위해 노력하도록
⑤ 더 큰 꿈을 추구하도록

(해설) 빈칸 문장은 이 글의 주제문이므로, 이를 다시 언급한 문장이나 부연 설명하는 문장을 파악해야 한다. 글의 초반부(The lifestyle ~ cease to exist)에서 Raika족의 생활 방식은 곧 소멸할 수도 있다고 하며, 글 중후반을 통틀어 새로운 도로, 태양광 및 풍력 발전소의 건설로 인해 낙타들의 수가 가파른 감소세에 있어 입지가 좁아졌다고 했다. 따라서 빈칸에는 ② abandon their former ways(그들의 기존 방식을 포기하도록)가 와서 발전은 Raika족이 낙타와 함께했던 그들의 기존 생활 방식을 포기하도록 했다는 의미가 되어야 한다.

(오답분석) ①의 정부 지원을 모색하게 하는 것과 ③의 더 넓은 영토에 정착하도록 하는 것에 대한 내용은 글에서 언급되고 있지 않다. ④의 인정받기 위해 노력하게 하는 것과 ⑤의 더 큰 꿈을 추구하는 것은 글의 내용과 관련이 없다.

02
정답 ④

지문분석

The process of urbanization, / which was driven by Britain's Industrial Revolution, / had major effects, / especially with regard to the emergence / of **distinct social classes**.
도시화 과정은 / 영국의 산업 혁명에 의해 주도된 / 주요한 영향을 미쳤다 / 특히 출현에 있어서 / **뚜렷한 사회 계층의**

Before factories gained attention in Britain, / citizens—mostly farmers— / had a simpler existence, / with little variation in / how people lived / from village to village.
영국에 공장들이 주목을 받기 전에 / 대부분 농민이었던 시민들은 / 단순한 삶을 살았다 / 거의 차이가 없는 / 사람들이 사는 방식에 / 마을마다

Everyone had similar wealth / and lived a similar lifestyle.
모두가 비슷한 부를 지녔고 / 비슷한 생활방식으로 살았다

★ After the Industrial Revolution, / however, / people began to flock to cities / looking for better opportunities, / only to discover that / the infrastructure was ill-equipped / to provide for them all.
산업 혁명 이후 / 그러나 / 사람들은 도시로 모여들기 시작했다 / 더 좋은 기회를 찾아 / 결국 깨달았을 뿐이었다 / 사회 기반 시설이 열악했다는 것을 / 그들 모두에게 (기회를) 주기에는

While the earliest arrivals / were able to claim attractive jobs and housing, / the latecomers were stuck with / menial labor and poor living conditions.
초기 정착민은 ~한 반면 / 매력적인 일자리와 거주지를 얻을 수 있었다 / 후발주자들은 강요당했다 / 하찮은 일과 열악한 거주 환경을

As the industry increased only the wealth / of those who were already successful, / the gap in status grew larger / until a hierarchy became well-established / in British society.
산업이 재산만을 불리면서 / 이미 성공한 사람들의 / 신분 간의 격차가 더 커졌다 / 계급 제도가 정착될 때까지 / 영국 사회에

★ **독해가 쉬워지는 구문 풀이**

After the Industrial Revolution, however, people <u>began</u> to flock to
　　　　　　　　　　　　　　　　　　　　주어　　동사
cities <u>looking for better opportunities</u>, [only to discover that the
　　　　　현재분사구문
infrastructure was ill-equipped to provide for them all].

⇨ [　]는 <only + to + discover/find + ~> 구문으로, '결국 ~하게 되다'로 해석한다.

(어휘) urbanization 도시화 Industrial Revolution 산업 혁명 emergence 출현 existence 삶, 존재 variation 차이 only to 결국 ~하다 infrastructure 사회 기반 시설 ill-equipped 열악한, 준비가 안 된 claim 얻다, 요구하다 latecomer 후발주자 be stuck with (주로 싫은 일 등을) 강요당하다 menial 하찮은 status 신분, 지위 hierarchy 계급 제도 well-established 정착된, 자리 잡은 (선택지) revolutionary 혁신적인 mass-produced 대량으로 생산된 distinct 뚜렷한

(해설) (주제문) 영국의 산업 혁명에 의해 주도된 도시화 과정은 특히 **뚜렷한 사회 계층의** 출현에 있어서 주요한 영향을 미쳤다. 영국에 공장들이 주목을 받기 전에, 대부분 농민이었던 시민들은 마을마다 사람들이 사는 방식에 거의 차이가 없는 단순한 삶을 살았다. 모두가 비슷한 부를 지녔고, 비슷한 생활방식으로 살았다. 그러나 산업 혁명 이후, 사람들은 더 좋은 기회를 찾아 도시로 모여들기 시작했는데, 그들은 모두에게 (기회를) 주기에는 사회 기반 시설이 열악했다는 것을 결국 깨달았을 뿐이었다. 초기 정착민은 매력적인 일자리와 거주지를 얻을 수 있었던 반면, 후발주자들은 하찮은 일과 열악한 거주 환경을 강요당했다. 산업이 이미 성공한 사람들의 재산만을 불리면서 영국 사회에 계급 제도가 정착될 때까지 신분 간의 격차가 더 커졌다.

① 교육을 더 많이 받은 집단
② 혁신적인 기술
③ 대량 생산 제품
④ 뚜렷한 사회 계층
⑤ 위험한 질병

(해설) 빈칸 문장은 이 글의 주제문이므로 이를 다시 언급한 문장이나 부연 설명하는 문장을 파악해야 한다. 빈칸 문장에서 영국의 산업 혁명에 의해 주도된 도시화 과정은 특히 '무엇'의 출현에 주요한 영향을 미쳤다고 하고, 글의 후반에서 산업의 발전은 이미 성공한 사람들의 재산만을 불리면서, 계급 제도가 정착될 때까지 신분 격차가 더 커졌다고 했다. 따라서 빈칸에는 ④ distinct social classes(뚜렷한 사회 계층)가 와서 영국의 도시화 과정은 특히 "뚜렷한 사회 계층"의 출현에 있어 주요한 영향을 미쳤다는 의미가 되어야 한다.

(오답분석) ①의 교육을 더 많이 받은 집단, ③의 대량 생산 제품, ⑤ 위험한 질병에 대한 내용은 글에서 언급되고 있지 않다. ②은 글에서 언급된 소재 revolution을 활용하여 헷갈리게 하는 오답이다.

03
정답 ③

지문분석

Being bilingual / offers various advantages.
2개 국어를 구사하는 것은 / 다양한 이점들을 제공한다

For one, / it ① increases brain power / because it requires a person / to switch back and forth between two languages, / which involves / multitasking skills and creative thinking.
우선 / 그것은 뇌의 능력을 향상시킨다 / 개인에게 필요로 하기 때문에 / 두 언어를 왔다 갔다 전환할 것을 / 그리고 이는 동반한다 / 다중 작업 처리 능력과 창의적 사고를

Speaking a second language / also has an effect / on a person's ability / to ② concentrate.
제2 언어를 말하는 것은 / 또한 영향을 미친다 / 개인의 능력에 / 집중하는

★ This is supported / by studies / showing / that bilingual individuals are better / at ignoring distractions / than their monolingual peers.
이것은 뒷받침된다 / 연구에 의해 / 보여주는 / 2개 국어 구사자들이 더 탁월하다는 것을 / 방해 요인을 무시하는 일에 / 1개 국어를 구사하는 그들의 동년배보다

Furthermore, / recent research suggests / that these effects aren't ③ lasting(→ temporary).
게다가 / 최근 연구는 보여준다 / 이러한 영향이 지속되지(→ 일시적이지) 않음을

Scientists believe / that bilingual people / maintain good brain health longer / than people who only speak one language.
과학자들은 생각한다 / 2개 국어 구사자들이 ~라고 / 좋은 뇌 건강을 더 오래 유지하다 / 하나의 언어만 구사하는 사람들보다

They are able to ④ remember information / far more effectively, / and dementia and other age-related memory problems / do not occur / as early / or sometimes not at all.
그들은 정보를 기억할 수 있다 / 훨씬 더 효과적으로 / 그리고 치매나 나이와 관련된 다른 기억력 문제들이 / 발생하지 않는다 / 이른 시기에는 / 혹은 때로는 전혀

Overall, / because the brains of bilingual people / seem to age / at a ⑤ slower rate, / they can continue to live / fulfilling lives / for far longer / than others.
전반적으로 / 2개 국어 구사자들의 뇌가 ~하기 때문에 / 노화하는 것으로 보인다 / 더 느린 속도로 / 그들은 지속하며 살 수 있다 / 만족스러운 삶을 / 훨씬 더 오랫동안 / 다른 사람들보다

★ 독해가 쉬워지는 구문 풀이

This is supported by studies [showing that bilingual individuals {are better at ignoring} distractions than their monolingual peers].
　　　　　　　　　　　수식어(관계절)

⇨ [ ]는 studies를 수식하는 관계절이다.
⇨ { }는 <be + good/better + at + (동)명사>구문으로, '~에 탁월하다'로 해석된다.

어휘 switch back and forth 왔다 갔다 전환하다　multitasking 다중 작업 (처리)
second language 제2 언어　distraction 방해 요인, 주의를 산만하게 하는 것
monolingual 1개 국어를 구사하는　peer 동년배
fulfilling 만족스러운, 성취감을 주는

해석 주제문 2개 국어를 구사하는 것은 다양한 이점들을 제공한다. 우선, 그것은 개인이 두 언어를 왔다 갔다 전환할 것을 필요로 하고, 이는 다중 작업 처리 능력과 창의적 사고를 동반하기 때문에 뇌의 능력을 ①향상시킨다. 제2 언어를 말하는 것은 개인의 ②집중하는 능력에도 영향을 미친다. 이 것은 2개 국어 구사자들이 1개 국어를 구사하는 그들의 동년배보다 방해 요인을 무시하는 일에 더 탁월하다는 것을 보여주는 연구에 의해 뒷받침된다. 게다가, 최근 연구는 이러한 영향이 ③지속되지(→ 일시적이지) 않음을 보여준다. 과학자들은 2개 국어 구사자들이 하나의 언어만 구사하는 사람들보다 좋은 뇌 건강을 더 오래 유지한다고 생각한다. 그들은 정보를 훨씬 더 효과적으로 ④기억할 수 있고 치매나 나이와 관련된 다른 기억력 문제들이 이른 시기에 혹은 때로는 전혀 발생하지 않는다. 전반적으로, 2개 국어 구사자들의 뇌가 ⑤더 느린 속도로 노화하는 것으로 보이기 때문에, 그들은 다른 사람들보다 훨씬 더 오랫동안 만족스러운 삶을 지속하며 살 수 있다.

해설 2개 국어를 구사하는 것의 영향은 "지속되지" 않는 것이 아니고 노년에 들면서도 정신적으로 더 예리한 상태를 유지하게 해준다는 맥락이 되어야 하므로, ③의 lasting을 temporary와 같은 어휘로 바꾸어야 문맥상 적절하다.

오답분석 ①은 2개 국어를 구사하는 것은 다양한 이점들을 제공하며, 다중 작업 처리 능력과 창의적 사고를 동반하기 때문에 뇌의 능력을 "향상시킨다"는 문맥이 되어야 하므로 increases가 오는 것이 적절하다. ②은 2개 국어 구사자들이 방해 요인을 무시하는 일에 더 탁월하기 때문에 제2언어를 말하는 것은 "집중하는" 능력에 영향을 미친다는 문맥이 되어야 하므로 concentrate가 오는 것이 적절하다. ④은 정보를 훨씬 더 효과적으로 "기억할" 수 있고 노년에 나이와 관련된 기억력 문제가 일찍 발생하지 않는다는 문맥이 되어야 하므로 remember가 오는 것이 적절하다. ⑤은 2개 국어 구사자들의 뇌가 "더 느린" 속도로 노화하기 때문에 더 오랫동

안 만족스러운 삶을 지속하며 살 수 있다는 문맥이 되어야 하므로 slower가 오는 것이 적절하다.

04

지문분석

Poor physical fitness / among older women / is a serious concern.
약한 체력은 / 나이 든 여성의 / 심각한 문제이다

It can impact quality of life / and lead to poor mental health.
그것은 삶의 질에 영향을 미칠 수 있다 / 그리고 쇠약한 정신 건강으로 이어질 수 있다

① At an advanced age, / many women need to engage in / strength training / at least twice a week / to maintain adequate physical fitness.
노년에 / 많은 여성들은 해야 한다 / 체력 훈련을 / 최소 일주일 중 이틀은 / 적당한 체력을 유지하기 위해

② Unfortunately, / many of them / lack the proper motivation / to engage in regular exercise.
안타깝게도 / 그들 중 다수가 / 적절한 동기가 없다 / 규칙적인 운동을 할

③ To address this issue, / experts have found / programs aimed at providing / social and environmental support helpful.
이 문제를 해결하기 위해 / 전문가들은 발견했다 / 제공을 목표로 한 프로그램들이 / 사회적 및 환경적 지원이 도움이 된다는 것을

(④ Some exercise routines are more focused / on getting the heart rate up, / which helps / burn fat more quickly.)
몇몇 운동 루틴은 더 집중되어 있다 / 심박수를 높이는 것에 / 그리고 이는 도와준다 / 지방을 더 빠르게 태우도록

⑤ ★ These programs, / when combined with efforts / to increase the affordability and accessibility / of fitness programs, / help to encourage senior women / to find an exercise routine / they can adhere to.
이러한 프로그램들은 / 노력이 겸비된다면 / 구입 능력과 접근 가능성을 증대시키기 위한 / 체력 단련 프로그램에 대한 / 고령 여성들을 장려하는 데 도움이 된다 / 운동 과정을 찾도록 / 그들이 충실할 수 있는

★ 독해가 쉬워지는 구문 풀이

These programs, **when** combined with efforts to increase the
　　주어　　　　　　　　　　　　삽입구
affordability and accessibility of fitness programs, ~

⇨ 분사구문의 뜻을 분명하게 해주기 위해 분사구문의 부사절 접속사 (when)가 분사구문 앞에 생략되지 않고 남아있을 수 있다.

어휘 physical fitness 체력　at an advanced age 노년에
engage in (무언가를) 하다, ~에 관여하다　strength 체력, 힘
adequate 적당한, 충분한　address 해결하다, 연설하다　aim 목표로 하다
routine 루틴, 정해진 과정, 일과　heart rate 심박수　affordability 구입 능력
accessibility 접근 가능성, 접근하기 쉬움　adhere to ~에 충실하다

해석 나이 든 여성의 약한 체력은 심각한 문제이다. 그것은 삶의 질에 영향을 미치고 쇠약한 정신 건강으로 이어질 수 있다. ① 노년에, 많은 여성들은 적당한 체력을 유지하기 위해 일주일 중 최소 이틀은 체력 훈련을 해야 한다. ② 안타깝게도, 그들 중 다수가 규칙적인 운동을 할 적절한 동기가 없다. ③ 이 문제를 해결하기 위해, 전문가들은 사회적 및 환경적 지원 제공을 목표로 한 프로그램들이 도움이 된다는 것을 발견했다. (④ 몇몇 운동 루틴은 심박수를 높이는 것에 더 집중되어 있는데, 이는 지방을 더 빠르게 태우도록 도와준다.) ⑤ 체력 단련 프로그램에 대한 구입 능력과 접근 가능성을 증대시키기 위한 노력이 겸비된다면, 이러한 프로그램들은 고령 여성들이 충실할 수 있는 운동 과정을 찾도록 장려하는 데 도움이 된다.

해설 이 글의 주제는 나이 든 여성들이 규칙적인 운동을 할 적절한 동기가 없다는 문제점과 이를 해결하기 위한 방안이다. 대부분이 노년 여성에게 필요한 체력 훈련의 양과 동기 부여 및 이를 도울 수 있는 방안에 대한 내용으

로 주제와 연결되어 있다. 하지만 심박수를 높이는 데 집중된 운동 루틴들이 지방을 더 빠르게 태운다는 ④은 글의 흐름과 관계없는 문장이다.

[오답분석] ①, ②은 노년 여성들에게 필요한 체력 훈련의 양과 이를 실천하기 어려운 이유에 대한 내용으로 주제와 연관되어 있다. ③, ⑤은 노년 여성들의 체력 훈련을 돕기 위한 프로그램에 대한 소개로 글의 흐름에 자연스럽다.

05 정답 ④

[지문분석]

As adults, / we understand / that cooperation can be useful.
성인으로서 / 우리는 안다 / 협력이 유익할 수 있음을

★ We know / that nobody is capable of / doing everything themselves / and that everyone needs / somebody else's help sometimes.
우리는 안다 / 그 누구도 ~할 수 없다는 것을 / 모든 것을 혼자서 함 / 그리고 모두가 필요로 한다는 것을 / 때때로 다른 누군가의 도움을

In addition, / cooperating on a task / often produces better results / ① than when the task is performed alone.
또한 / 업무상 협력하는 것은 / 종종 더 나은 결과를 만들어낸다 / 그 업무가 단독으로 수행되었을 때보다

All of that said, / the ability to cooperate / does not always come naturally / to many people / and is something ② that must be taught / from a young age.
모두 그렇게 말하지만 / 협력하는 능력은 / 언제나 당연하게 생기지 않는다 / 많은 사람들에게 / 그리고 가르쳐져야 하는 것이다 / 어릴 때부터

One way / to teach children to cooperate / is ③ to get them to engage in activities / that require teamwork, / such as solving a giant puzzle.
한 가지 방법 / 아이들에게 협력하는 것을 가르치는 / 활동에 그들이 참여하도록 만드는 것이다 / 팀워크를 필요로 하는 / 거대한 퍼즐을 푸는 것 같이

Another way is / for parents and teachers / to praise cooperative behavior / ④ observing(→ observed) in children / as a form of encouragement.
다른 방법은 ~이다 / 부모와 교사가 / 협동적인 행동을 칭찬하는 것 / 아이들에게서 관찰되는 / 격려의 형태로

Lastly, / adults should also act / as appropriate models for children / and ⑤ demonstrate / how best to cooperate with other people, / such as by treating others with respect / and being open to new ideas.
마지막으로 / 어른들은 또한 행동해야 한다 / 아이들을 위한 적절한 본보기로서 / 그리고 보여주다 / 다른 사람과 협력하는 최선의 방법을 / 존경심을 가지고 다른 사람들을 대하거나 / 그리고 새로운 생각을 받아들이는 것

★ 독해가 쉬워지는 구문 풀이

We know that nobody is capable of doing everything themselves
　　　　　　　 단수대명사　 단수동사
and that everyone needs somebody else's help sometimes.
　　　　　 단수대명사　 단수동사

⇨ nobody와 everyone은 단수 취급하는 대명사이므로, 단수동사 is와 needs가 쓰였다.

[어휘] cooperation 협력, 협동　naturally 당연하게, 자연스럽게
cooperative 협동적인　engage in ~에 참여하다, 종사하다
observe 관찰하다　demonstrate 보여주다, 입증하다　treat 대하다, 여기다
be open to ~을 받아들이다

[해석] 성인으로서, 우리는 협력이 유익할 수 있음을 안다. 우리는 그 누구도 모든 것을 혼자서 할 수 없고 모두가 때때로 다른 누군가의 도움을 필요로 한다는 것을 안다. 또한, 업무상 협력하는 것은 그 업무가 단독으로 수행되었을 때보다 종종 더 나은 결과를 만들어낸다. **[주제문]** 모두 그렇게 말하지만, 협력하는 능력은 많은 사람들에게 언제나 당연하게 생기지 않고, 어릴 때

부터 가르쳐져야 하는 것이다. 아이들에게 협력하는 것을 가르치는 한 가지 방법은 거대한 퍼즐을 푸는 것 같이 팀워크를 필요로 하는 활동에 그들이 참여하도록 만드는 것이다. 다른 방법은 부모와 교사가 아이들에게서 관찰되는 협동적인 행동을 격려의 형태로 칭찬하는 것이다. 마지막으로, 어른들은 또한 존경심을 가지고 다른 사람들을 대하거나 새로운 생각을 받아들이는 등 아이들을 위한 적절한 본보기로서 행동하고 다른 사람과 협력하는 최선의 방법을 보여주어야 한다.

[해설] 수식 받는 명사 behavior와 분사가 아이들에게서 '관찰된 행동'이라는 의미의 수동 관계이므로, ④의 observing을 observed로 고쳐야 한다.

[오답분석] ①은 '형용사/부사의 비교급(better) + than'의 형태로 비교급 표현을 나타내면서, 절을 이끌 수 있는 접속사 than을 사용한 것은 어법상 적절하다. ②은 뒤에 동사(must be taught)만 있고 주어가 없는 불완전한 절이 왔으며, 문맥상 '가르쳐져야 하는 것'이라는 의미이므로 선행사 something을 수식하는 주격 관계대명사 that을 사용한 것은 어법상 적절하다. ③은 be동사(is)의 보어 자리이며, to부정사는 명사 역할을 하며 보어 자리에 올 수 있으므로 to부정사 to get을 사용한 것은 어법상 적절하다. ⑤은 같은 문장 성분을 대등하게 연결하는 등위접속사 and 앞에 조동사 should의 영향을 받은 동사원형 act가 있으므로 병렬 구조를 이루는 동사원형 demonstrate를 사용한 것은 어법상 적절하다.

06 정답 ③

[지문분석]

Russell Baker was an American newspaper columnist / known for his humorous observations.
Russell Baker는 미국의 신문 칼럼니스트였다 / 그의 해학적인 비평으로 유명한

He first gained attention / in the early 1960s / writing satire under a column / for The New York Times / ① called "The Observer."
그는 처음 주목을 받았다 / 1960년대 초반에 / 칼럼 내에서 풍자 글을 쓰면서 / The New York Times의 / "The Observer"라 불리는

★ Baker wrote extensively / about many topics / ② that concerned society / but focused most of his attention / on politicians, / making fun of Democrats and Republicans alike.
Baker는 광범위하게 글을 썼다 / 많은 주제에 대해 / 사회와 관련 있는 / 하지만 그의 관심의 대부분을 두었다 / 정치인들에게 / 그리고 민주당원과 공화당원 모두를 조롱했다

In 1974, / he moved to the Times' main office / in Manhattan / and shortly after / won his first Pulitzer Prize / for commentary.
1974년에 / 그는 Times의 본사로 옮겼다 / 맨해튼에 있는 / 그리고 직후에 / 그의 첫 번째 퓰리처상을 받았다 / 평론 부문에서

Baker also won recognition / for his books, / among which ③ were(→ was) *Growing Up*.
Baker는 또한 인정을 받았다 / 그의 저서들에 대해 / 그중에는 *Growing Up*이 있었다

Baker won a second Pulitzer / for this book, / this time for biography.
Baker는 두 번째 퓰리처상을 받았다 / 이 책으로 / 이번에는 전기 부문에서

Later, / Baker produced *Russell Baker's Book of American Humor*, / a comprehensive work / ④ whose review of other notable American humorists / was well received.
이후에 / Baker는 *Russell Baker's Book of American Humor*를 썼다 / 모음집인 / 다른 유명한 미국 유머 작가들에 대한 그 책의 비평은 / 호평을 받았다

In 1998, / Baker's Observer column appeared in print / for the last time / on Christmas Day, / around two decades / ⑤ before his passing.
1998년에 / Baker의 Observer 칼럼은 출판되어 나왔다 / 마지막으로 / 성탄절에 / 20년 쯤인 / 그가 죽기 전

어휘 columnist 칼럼니스트, 정기 기고가 humorous 해학적인, 재미있는
observation 비평, 관찰 concern 관련 있다, 관여하다
make fun of ~을 조롱하다 Democrat 민주당원 Republican 공화당원
recognition 인정, 인식 comprehensive 포괄적인, 종합적인
notable 유명한, 중요한 humorist 유머 작가 be well received 호평을 받다
appear in print 출판되어 나오다 passing 죽음, 경과

해석 Russell Baker는 그의 해학적인 비평으로 유명한 미국의 신문 칼럼니스트
였다. 그는 The New York Times의 "The Observer"라 불리는 칼럼 내에
서 풍자 글을 쓰면서 1960년대 초반에 처음 주목을 받았다. Baker는 사회
와 관련 있는 많은 주제에 대해 광범위하게 글을 썼지만 그의 관심의 대부
분을 정치인들에게 두면서 민주당원과 공화당원 모두를 조롱했다. 1974
년에, 그는 맨해튼에 있는 Times의 본사로 옮겼고 직후에 평론 부문에서
그의 첫 번째 퓰리처상을 받았다. Baker는 또한 그의 저서들에 대해 인정
을 받았고, 그중에는 *Growing Up*이 있었다. Baker는 이 책으로 이번에
는 전기 부문에서 두 번째 퓰리처상을 받았다. 이후에 Baker는 모음집인
*Russell Baker's Book of American Humor*를 썼는데, 다른 유명한 미국
유머 작가들에 대한 그 책의 비평은 호평을 받았다. 1998년에, Baker의
Observer 칼럼은 그가 죽기 20년 전쯤인 성탄절에 마지막으로 출판되어
나왔다.

해설 전치사 among이 '~ 중에'라는 의미로 쓰여 문장 앞에 와서 주어와 동
사가 도치된 문장이다. among which were *Growing Up*에서 주어는
*Growing Up*으로 단수이므로, ③의 were를 was로 고쳐야 한다.

오답분석 ①은 수식 받는 명사 a column과 분사가 '~라 불리는 칼럼'이라는 의미
의 수동 관계이므로 과거분사 called를 사용한 것은 어법상 적절하다.
②은 뒤에 동사(concerned)와 목적어(society)만 있고 주어가 없는 불
완전한 절이 왔으며, 문맥상 '사회와 관련 있는 많은 주제'라는 의미이므
로 선행사 many topics를 수식하는 주격 관계대명사 that을 사용한 것
은 어법상 적절하다. ④은 선행사(a comprehensive work)가 사물이고
관계절 내에서 review는 a comprehensive work에 속하는 비평이므로
사물을 가리키는 소유격 관계대명사 whose를 사용한 것은 어법상 적절
하다. ⑤은 전치사는 명사 역할을 하는 것 앞에 와야 하므로 '동명사의 의
미상 주어 + 동명사(his passing)' 앞에 전치사 before를 사용한 것은 어
법상 적절하다.

07
정답 ④

지문분석

★ According to biologists, / most animals groom themselves / for
several reasons.
생물학자들에 따르면 / 대부분의 동물은 스스로를 털 손질을 한다 / 몇 가지 이유로

In general, / animals groom themselves / so that they can
maintain their hygiene / by ① removing objects like leaves, twigs,
or dirt / from their bodies.
일반적으로 / 동물들은 스스로를 털 손질을 한다 / 그들이 청결을 유지할 수 있도록 / 나뭇
잎, 가지, 또는 흙과 같은 것들을 제거함으로써 / 그들의 몸에서

Cats, / for example, / have ② developed physical features /
specialized to help / in the process.
고양이는 / 예를 들어 / 신체적 특징을 발달시켜왔다 / 도움이 되도록 특화된 / 이 과정에서

They have extremely rough tongues / to lift dirt / off their fur.
이들은 굉장히 거친 혀를 가지고 있다 / 흙을 털어 내기 위한 / 이들의 털에서

Other animals, / like birds, / groom themselves to ③ ensure / that
their bodies are operating normally.
다른 동물들은 / 새와 같은 / 확실하게 하고자 스스로를 털 손질을 한다 / 그들의 몸이 정
상적으로 기능하는지

They wash, pick at, and straighten / ruffled feathers / to make
sure their bodies function well / in flight.
그들은 씻고, 뽑고, 그리고 곧게 펴낸다 / 헝클어진 깃털을 / 반드시 몸이 잘 기능하도록 /
비행 중에

Although grooming seems like / a necessary daily routine
for all animals, / there are those animals / that seem very
④ interested(→ uninterested) / in this process.
털 손질이 ~처럼 보임에도 불구하고 / 모든 동물의 필수적인 하루 일과 / 동물들이 있다 /
매우 관심이 있어(→ 관심이 없어) 보이는 / 이 과정에

For these animals, / grooming is secondary / to protection.
이들에게 / 털 손질은 부차적인 것이다 / 안전에 비하면

They intentionally ⑤ cover themselves / in mud, dead plants, or
substances / that stink / to hide from predators / or repel insects.
이들은 그들의 몸을 일부러 뒤덮는다 / 진흙, 죽은 식물, 혹은 물질로 / 냄새나는 / 포식자로
부터 숨거나 / 벌레를 쫓아내기 위해

어휘 biologist 생물학자 hygiene 청결, 위생 twig 가지 specialized 특화된
extremely 굉장히, 극도로 ensure 확실하게 하다 make sure 반드시 ~하다
flight 비행 secondary 부차적인 predator 포식자 repel 쫓아내다

해석 **주제문** 생물학자들에 따르면, 대부분의 동물은 몇 가지 이유로 스스로를
털 손질을 한다. 일반적으로, 동물들은 나뭇잎, 가지, 또는 흙과 같은 것들
을 그들의 몸에서 ①제거함으로써 청결을 유지할 수 있도록 스스로를 털
손질을 한다. 예를 들어, 고양이는 이 과정에서 도움이 되도록 특화된 신
체적 특징을 ②발달시켜왔다. 이들은 털에서 흙을 털어 내기 위한 굉장히
거친 혀를 가지고 있다. 새와 같은 다른 동물들은 그들의 몸이 정상적으로
기능하는지 ③확실하게 하고자 스스로를 털 손질을 한다. 그들은 비행 중
에 반드시 몸이 잘 기능하도록 헝클어진 깃털을 씻고, 뽑고, 그리고 곧게
펴낸다. 털 손질이 모든 동물의 필수적인 하루 일과처럼 보임에도 불구하
고, 이 과정에 매우 ④관심이 있어(→ 관심이 없어) 보이는 동물들이 있다.
이들에게, 털 손질은 안전에 비하면 부차적인 것이다. 이들은 포식자로부
터 숨거나 벌레를 쫓아내기 위해 진흙, 죽은 식물, 혹은 냄새 나는 물질로
그들의 몸을 일부러 ⑤뒤덮는다.

해설 털 손질이 모든 동물의 필수적인 하루 일과처럼 보임에도 불구하고 털 손
질에 매우 "관심이 없어" 보이는 동물들이 있고, 그들에게 털 손질은 안전
에 비하면 부차적인 것이라는 맥락이 되어야 하므로, ④의 interested를
uninterested와 같은 어휘로 바꾸어야 문맥상 적절하다.

오답분석 ①은 털 손질을 함으로써 나뭇잎, 가지, 또는 흙을 "제거한다"는 문맥이 되
어야 하므로 removing이 오는 것이 적절하다. ②은 고양이와 같은 동물
은 털 손질에 도움이 되도록 특화된 신체적인 특징을 "발달시켜왔다"는
문맥이 되어야 하므로 developed가 오는 것이 적절하다. ③은 새와 같
은 동물이 비행 중에 몸이 정상적으로 기능하는지 "확실하게 하고자" 스

스로를 털 손질한다는 문맥이 되어야 하므로 ensure가 오는 것이 적절하다. ⑤은 포식자로부터 숨거나 벌레를 쫓아내기 위해 진흙, 죽은 식물, 혹은 냄새나는 물질로 스스로를 "뒤덮는다"는 문맥이 되어야 하므로 cover가 오는 것이 적절하다.

08
정답 ④

지문분석

> Philosophers and anthropologists / have very different approaches, / but they both study the same basic topic: / the human condition.
> 철학자와 인류학자는 / 매우 다른 접근법을 취한다 / 하지만 그들 모두 동일한 기본 주제를 연구한다 / 인간의 생활이라는
>
> ① Philosophers study the nature / of human existence / with the hopes of understanding / our position in society / through logic.
> 철학자는 본질을 연구한다 / 인간 존재의 / 이해하기를 바라며 / 인간의 사회적 위치를 / 논리를 통해
>
> ② ★ Anthropologists, / on the other hand, / are more concerned with / how we actually live / in society, / examining our diets, actions, and cultural practices.
> 인류학자는 / 반면에 / ~에 더 관심을 둔다 / 우리가 실제로 어떻게 살고 있는지 / 사회에서 / 그리고 우리의 식습관, 행동 및 문화적 관례를 조사하며
>
> ③ In many cases, / there is great overlap / between these two fields, / which can lead experts from each field / to refer to the work / of the other.
> 많은 경우에 / 상당한 공통점이 있다 / 이 두 가지 분야 간에 / 그리고 이것은 각 분야의 전문가들을 이끌 수 있다 / 연구를 참고하도록 / 상대 분야의
>
> (④ The academic study of anthropology / as an independent discipline / really began / in earnest / during the 1800s.)
> 인류학에 관한 학술적 연구는 / 독립된 학문으로서 / 사실상 시작되었다 / 본격적으로 / 1800년대 중반에
>
> ⑤ Philosophers must consider physical aspects / that are usually in the domain of anthropologists, / and anthropologists must consider the philosophical ethics / of civilizations.
> 철학자는 물리적 측면들을 고려해야 한다 / 일반적으로 인류학자의 영역에 있는 / 그리고 인류학자는 철학적 윤리를 고려해야 한다 / 문명의

> **★ 독해가 쉬워지는 구문 풀이**
>
> Anthropologists, on the other hand, are more concerned with [how we actually live] in society, ~
> 의문사 주어　　　　　동사
>
> ⇨ [ ]는 전치사 with의 목적어로 쓰인 「의문사 + 주어 + 동사」 순의 간접 의문문(명사절)이다.

어휘 anthropologist 인류학자　condition 생활, 조건　nature 본질, 자연
practice 관례　overlap 공통점, 중복　refer to ~을 참고하다, 언급하다
discipline 학문, 규율　in earnest 본격적으로, 진지하게　ethic 윤리
civilization 문명

해석 철학자와 인류학자는 매우 다른 접근법을 취하지만, 그들 모두 인간의 생활이라는 동일한 기본 주제를 연구한다. ① 철학자는 논리를 통해 인간의 사회적 위치를 이해하기를 바라며, 인간 존재의 본질을 연구한다. ② 반면에, 인류학자는 우리의 식습관, 행동 및 문화적 관례를 조사하며 우리가 실제로 사회에서 어떻게 살고 있는지에 더 관심을 둔다. (주제문) ③ 많은 경우에, 이 두 가지 분야 간에 상당한 공통점이 있고, 이것은 각 분야의 전문가들이 상대 분야의 연구를 참고하도록 이끌 수 있다. (④ 독립된 학문으로서 인류학에 관한 학술적 연구는 사실상 1800년대 중반에 본격적으로 시작되었다) ⑤ 철학자는 일반적으로 인류학자의 영역에 있는 물리적 측면들을 고려해야 하고, 인류학자는 문명의 철학적 윤리를 고려해야 한다.

해설 이 글의 주제는 철학자와 인류학자는 동일한 주제를 연구하기 때문에 두

전문가는 상대 분야의 연구를 참고할 수 있다는 것이다. 대부분이 철학자와 인류학자의 연관성에 대한 내용으로 주제와 관련 있는데, 독립된 학문으로서 인류학의 학술적 연구가 시작된 시기에 대해 언급한 ④은 글의 흐름과 관계없는 문장이다.

오답분석 ①과 ②은 철학자와 인류학자가 연구하는 대상에 대해 언급하고 있으므로 주제와 연관되어 있다. ③과 ⑤은 두 학문은 공통점이 있으므로 교류를 통해 서로의 연구를 참고해야 한다는 내용이므로 글의 흐름에 자연스럽다.

09
정답 ①

지문분석

> Advertisers assess the mindset / of their customer base / and use this information / to verbally persuade us / into buying goods.
> 광고주는 사고방식을 가늠한다 / 그들의 고객층의 / 그리고 이 정보를 사용한다 / 우리를 말로 설득하기 위해 / 물건을 사도록
>
> Their strategies aren't typically / based on logic and objectivity; / rather, / they tap into our desires / and appeal to our emotions / by carefully selecting the words / they use / to describe their products.
> 그들의 전략은 일반적으로 ~하지 않는다 / 논리와 객관성에 기반한 / 그보다 / 그들은 우리의 욕망을 이용한다 / 그리고 우리의 감정에 호소한다 / 신중하게 단어를 고름으로써 / 그들이 사용하는 / 그들의 제품을 설명하기 위해
>
> This is because / they know / that the **associations** / we have with a particular word / will trigger a corresponding emotional response.
> 이것은 ~하기 때문이다 / 그들은 안다 / **연상들**이 / 우리가 특정한 단어에 가지는 / 그에 상응하는 감정적 반응을 촉발할 것임을
>
> We connect words / such as "joy," "inspiration," and "happiness" / with positive feelings, / encouraging us / to make a purchase.
> 우리는 단어를 연결 짓는다 / "즐거움," "영감," "행복"과 같은 / 긍정적인 감정과 / 우리를 부추긴다 / 구매하도록
>
> On the other hand, / words like "despair" or "hatred" / arouse a very different reaction / because we correlate them / with negative attitudes.
> 반면에 / "절망"이나 "혐오"와 같은 단어는 / 매우 다른 반응을 불러일으킨다 / 우리가 그것들을 연관시키기 때문에 / 부정적인 태도와
>
> ★ The most effective ads are loaded / with words / that will compel consumers, / consciously and unconsciously, / to become interested in and attracted by a product.
> 가장 효과적인 광고는 가득 차 있다 / 단어들로 / 고객들을 ~하게 만드는 / 의식적으로 또 무의식적으로 / 흥미를 느끼거나 제품에 끌린다고 느끼는

> **★ 독해가 쉬워지는 구문 풀이**
>
> The most effective ads are loaded with words that will [compel
> 　　　　　　　　　　　　　　　　　　　선행사　주격
> 　　　　　　　　　　　　　　　　　　　　　관계대명사
> consumers, consciously and unconsciously, **to become**
> interested in and attracted by a product].
>
> ⇨ that은 선행사 words를 수식하는 주격 관계대명사이다.
> ⇨ 'compel + A + to부정사 + B'는 'A가 B 하도록 만들다'라고 해석한다.

어휘 advertiser 광고주　assess 가늠하다, 평가하다　mindset 사고방식
logic 논리　objectivity 객관성　tap into ~을 이용하다　trigger 촉발하다
inspiration 영감　despair 절망　hatred 혐오　arouse 불러일으키다
correlate 서로 연관시키다　be loaded with ~로 가득 차 있다
compel ~하게 만들다　consciously 의식적으로　(선택지) association 연상

해석 광고주는 고객층의 사고방식을 가늠하고 우리가 물건을 사도록 말로 설득하기 위해 이 정보를 사용한다. 그들의 전략은 일반적으로 논리와 객관성에 기반하지 않고, 그보다, 그들은 그들의 제품을 설명하기 위해 그들이 사용하는 단어를 신중하게 고름으로써 우리의 욕망을 이용하고 우리

의 감정에 호소한다. [주제문] 이것은 우리가 특정한 단어에 가지는 **연상들**이 그에 상응하는 감정적 반응을 촉발할 것임을 알기 때문이다. 우리는 "즐거움," "영감," "행복"과 같은 단어를 긍정적인 감정과 연결 지어서 구매하도록 부추긴다. 반면에, "절망"이나 "혐오"와 같은 단어는 우리가 그것들을 부정적인 태도와 연관시키기 때문에 매우 다른 반응을 불러일으킨다. 가장 효과적인 광고는 고객들이, 의식적으로 또 무의식적으로, 제품에 흥미를 느끼거나 끌린다고 느끼게 만드는 단어들로 가득 차 있다.

① 연상들
② 이점들
③ 유사성들
④ 어려움들
⑤ 조건들

[해설] 빈칸 문장은 이 글의 주제문이므로, 이를 다시 언급한 문장이나 부연 설명하는 문장을 파악해야 한다. 빈칸 문장에서, 광고주는 우리가 특정한 단어에 가지는 '무엇'이 그에 상응하는 감정적 반응을 촉발할 것임을 안다고 했다. 빈칸 문장 뒤에서 빈칸 문장을 뒷받침하는 세부 문장들에 따르면, 우리는 "즐거움"과 같은 단어를 통해 긍정적인 감정을 연결 짓고(connect), "절망"과 같은 단어를 통해 부정적인 태도를 연관 짓는다고(correlate) 했으므로, 빈칸 문장의 빈칸에는 connect나 correlate와 유사한 단어가 들어가야 한다. 따라서 빈칸에는 ① associations(연상들)가 와서 광고주는 우리가 특정한 단어에 가지는 "연상들"이 그에 상응하는 감정적 반응을 촉발할 것임을 알고 있다는 의미가 되어야 한다.

[오답분석] ②의 이점들과 ④의 어려움들은 글의 내용과 관련이 없다. ③의 유사성들과 ⑤의 조건들에 관한 내용은 글에서 언급되고 있지 않다.

10 정답 ⑤

[지문분석]

Cosmopolitanism is the idea / that people should be citizens / of the world / and find community / at the global level.
세계주의는 사상이다 / 사람들이 시민이어야 한다는 / 세계의 / 그리고 공동체를 찾아야 한다 / 전 지구적 차원에서

Arguing against it / is difficult / from a moral perspective / because it emphasizes the idea / of all humans being inherently worthy.
그것에 대해 반대 주장을 하는 것은 / 어렵다 / 도덕적 관점에서 / 그것은 관념을 강조하기 때문에 / 모든 사람들이 본질적으로 가치 있다는

However, / putting it into practice is viewed / by many / as unrealistic.
그러나 / 그것을 실천하는 것은 여겨진다 / 많은 사람들에게서 / 비현실적인 것으로

Those who oppose it / say / **people will feel pressured / to give up their culture.**
그것에 반대하는 사람들은 / 말한다 / **사람들이 압박감을 느낄 것이라고 / 그들의 문화를 포기해야 한다는**

★ They believe / increased exposure to "otherness" / in order to encourage the sense / that we are all fundamentally the same / requires us to abandon / certain traditional values and shared history.
그들은 생각한다 / "다름"에 더 많이 노출되는 것은 / 인식을 조장하고자 / 우리가 모두 근본적으로 동일하다는 / 우리가 포기하도록 요구한다 / 특정한 전통 가치와 공유된 역사를

It would mean / giving equal attention / to the needs of people / in other parts of the world, / which could come at the expense of / fellow citizens.
그것은 의미할 것이다 / 동일한 관심을 기울이는 것을 / 사람들의 요구에 / 세계 다른 지역 / 그런데 이것은 희생시킬 수도 있다 / 동료 시민들을

This would suggest the need / to dismantle patriotism and nationalism, / which is unthinkable / to many people.
이는 필요성을 제안할 수도 있다 / 애국심과 민족주의를 타도할 / 하지만 그것은 감히 생각도 할 수 없는 일이다 / 많은 사람들에게는

They believe [increased **exposure** to "otherness" in order to encourage the sense {that we are all fundamentally the same}
　　　　　　　　동격의 that 주어 동사
requires us to abandon certain traditional values and shared
명사절의 동사
history].

⇨ 명사절 [ ]는 동사 believe의 목적어이며, 앞에 명사절 접속사 that이 생략되었다.
⇨ 명사절의 주어는 increased ~ the same이고 동사는 requires이다.
⇨ { }는 '우리가 모두 근본적으로 동일하다는 인식'이라는 뜻으로 앞에 있는 명사 the sense의 내용을 풀어서 설명하고 있으므로 동격의 that이 쓰였다.

[어휘] moral 도덕적인, 도의적인 perspective 관점, 시각 emphasize 강조하다 inherently 본질적으로, 선천적으로 put ~ into practice ~을 실천하다 otherness 다름, 타성 encourage 조장하다 fundamentally 근본적으로, 완전히 abandon 포기하다, 버리다 at the expense of ~의 희생으로 fellow 동료인, 동류인 nationalism 민족주의, 국가주의 unthinkable 감히 생각도 할 수 없는, 상상도 할 수 없는 [선택지] superior 우월한, 우수한 border 국경, 경계 dispute 분쟁; 논쟁하다

[해석] 세계주의는 사람들이 세계의 시민이어야 하고 전 지구적 차원에서 공동체를 찾아야 한다는 사상이다. 그것은 모든 사람들이 본질적으로 가치 있다는 관념을 강조하기 때문에 도덕적 관점에서 그것에 대해 반대 주장을 하는 것은 어렵지만, 그것을 실천하는 것은 많은 사람들에게 비현실적인 것으로 여겨진다. [주제문] 그것에 반대하는 사람들은 **사람들이 그들의 문화를 포기해야 한다는 압박감을 느낄 것이라고** 말한다. 그들은 우리가 모두 근본적으로 동일하다는 인식을 조장하고자 "다름"에 더 많이 노출되는 것은 우리가 특정한 전통 가치와 공유된 역사를 포기하도록 요구한다고 생각한다. 그것은 세계 다른 지역 사람들의 요구에 동일한 관심을 기울이는 것을 의미하는데, 이것은 동료 시민들을 희생시킬 수도 있다. 이것은 애국심과 민족주의를 타도할 필요성을 제안할 수도 있지만, 그것은 많은 사람들에게는 감히 생각도 할 수 없는 일이다.

① 개인은 그들의 문화를 공유하도록 강요받는다고 느낄 것이다
② 일부 국가는 문화적으로 우월하다고 느낄 것이다
③ 그것으로 인해 더 많은 국경 분쟁이 발생할 것이다
④ 빈곤 국가들은 심지어 더 큰 위기에 처할 수도 있다
⑤ 사람들이 그들의 문화를 포기해야 한다는 압박감을 느낄 것이다

[해설] 빈칸 문장은 이 글의 주제문이므로, 이를 다시 언급한 문장이나 부연 설명하는 문장을 파악해야 한다. 먼저 빈칸 문장에서 그것(세계주의)에 반대하는 사람들은 '무엇이라고' 말한다고 했는데, 빈칸의 앞 문장(putting it ~ as unrealistic)에서 세계주의를 실행하는 것은 많은 사람들에게 비현실적인 것으로 여겨진다고 했고, 빈칸 뒤 문장(They believe ~ shared history)에서 이것이 우리가 특정한 전통 가치와 공유된 역사를 포기하도록 요구한다고 했다. 또한, 뒤에 이어지는 문장에서 세계주의를 위해 동료 시민들을 희생시키거나, 애국심 및 민족주의를 타도하는 것은 많은 이들에게는 감히 생각도 할 수 없는 일이라고 했다. 따라서 빈칸에는 ⑤ people will feel pressured to give up their culture(사람들이 그들의 문화를 포기해야 한다는 압박감을 느낄 것이다)가 오는 것이 자연스럽다.

[오답분석] ①은 글의 핵심 소재 중 하나인 '개인'과 '문화'를 다루고 있으나, 글의 내용과 반대로 문화를 공유하도록 강요받는다고 했으므로 오답이다. ②는 글의 핵심 소재인 '문화'에 관한 내용이지만, 특정 문화의 우월성을 우려하는 내용이 아니므로 오답이다. ③의 더 많은 국경 분쟁이 발생한다는 것과 ④의 빈곤 국가들이 더 큰 위기에 처한다는 것은 글의 핵심 소재인 '세계주의'에서 연상될 수 있는 내용을 활용하여 혼동을 주는 오답이다.

불변의 패턴 25　　　　　　　　　　　　p.102

대명사나 연결어를 찾으면 앞뒤 글의 순서가 보인다.

기출 문제　　　　　　　　　　　　　　정답 ②

지문분석

> The next time / you're out / under a clear, dark sky, / look up.
> 다음에 / 당신이 나가 있을 때 / 맑고 어두운 하늘 아래에 / 위를 올려다보아라
>
> If you've picked a good spot / for stargazing, / you'll see a sky / full of stars, / shining and twinkling / like thousands of brilliant jewels.
> 만약 당신이 좋은 장소를 골랐다면 / 별을 관측하기에 / 하늘을 보게 될 것이다 / 별로 가득한 / 빛나고 반짝거리는 / 수천 개의 화려한 보석들처럼

(A) It might be easier / if you describe patterns / of stars.
그것은 더 쉬울 것이다 / 만약 당신이 모양을 묘사한다면 / 별들의

You could say something like, / "See that big triangle of bright stars / there?"
당신은 ~과 같이 말할 수 있을 것이다 / 저 큰 삼각형의 밝은 별들이 보이나요 / 저기에

Or, / "Do you see those five stars / that look like a big letter W?"
또는 / 저 다섯 개의 별이 보이나요 / 대문자 W처럼 보이는

(B) But / this amazing sight / of stars / can also be confusing.
하지만 / 이 놀라운 광경은 / 별들의 / 또한 혼란스러울 수도 있다

Try and point out a single star / to someone.
별 하나를 가리켜서 보여줘 봐라 / 누군가에게

★ Chances are, / that person will have a hard time / knowing exactly / which star you're looking at.
아마 ~일 것이다 / 그 사람은 어려울 것이다 / 정확하게 알기 / 당신이 어떤 별을 보고 있는지를

(C) When you do that, / you're doing exactly / what we all do / when we look at the stars.
그렇게 할 때 / 당신은 정확하게 하고 있는 것이다 / 우리 모두가 하는 것을 / 우리가 별을 볼 때

We look for patterns, / not just so / that we can point something out / to someone else, / but also because that's / what we humans have always done.
우리는 규칙들을 찾는데 / 이는 ~만이 아니라 / 우리가 무엇을 가리켜서 보여줄 수 있기 위해서 / 다른 누군가에게 / 그게 바로 ~이기도 때문이다 / 우리 인간들이 항상 해온 것

> **★ 독해가 쉬워지는 구문 풀이**
>
> **Chances are, that** person will have a hard time knowing exactly
> 　　　　　　　주어　　　　　조동사+동사
>
> [which star you're looking at].
>
> ⇨ chances are는 '~일 것이다'로 해석되는 숙어 표현이다.
> ⇨ that은 지시형용사로 쓰였으며, person을 수식한다.
> ⇨ which는 star를 수식하는 의문형용사이며, [ ]는 의문형용사가 사용된 간접 의문문으로, <의문형용사 + 명사 + 주어 + 동사>의 어순을 갖는다

[어휘] stargaze 별을 관측하다　brilliant 화려한, 훌륭한　jewel 보석
pattern 모양, 형태　chances are 아마 ~일 것이다

[해석] 다음에 당신이 맑고 어두운 하늘 아래에 나가 있을 때, 위를 올려다보아라. 만약 당신이 별을 관측하기에 좋은 장소를 골랐다면, 수천 개의 화려한 보석들처럼 빛나고 반짝거리는 별로 가득한 하늘을 보게 될 것이다.

(B) 하지만 이 놀라운 별들의 광경은 또한 혼란스러울 수도 있다. 누군가에게 별 하나를 가리켜서 보여줘 봐라. 아마 그 사람은 당신이 어떤 별을 보고 있는지를 정확하게 알기 어려울 것이다.

(A) 만약 당신이 별들의 모양을 묘사한다면 그것은 더 쉬울 것이다. 당신은 "저기에 저 큰 삼각형의 밝은 별들이 보이나요?"와 같이 말할 수 있을 것이다. 또는, "대문자 W처럼 보이는 저 다섯 개의 별이 보이나요?"

(C) 그렇게 할 때, 당신은 우리가 별을 볼 때 우리 모두가 하는 것을 정확하게 하고 있는 것이다. 우리는 규칙들을 찾는데, 이는 다른 누군가에게 무엇을 가리켜서 보여줄 수 있기 위해서만이 아니라, 그게 바로 우리 인간들이 항상 해온 것이기도 때문이다.

[해설] 주어진 글은 별을 관측하기에 좋은 장소에서 당신은 보석들처럼 빛나고 반짝거리는 별로 가득한 하늘을 보게 될 것이라는 내용이다. (B) 첫 문장의 '이 놀라운 광경'(this amazing sight)이 주어진 글의 '보석들처럼 빛나고 반짝거리는 별로 가득한 하늘'을 나타내므로, (B)가 주어진 글 다음에 이어지는 것이 자연스럽다. (A) It might be easier의 It은 (B)의 knowing exactly which star you're looking at을 나타내므로 (B) 다음에 이어지는 것이 자연스럽다. (C) 첫 문장의 that은 (A)의 describe patterns of stars를 나타내므로 (A) 다음에 이어지는 것이 자연스럽다. 따라서 글의 순서로 가장 적절한 것은 ② (B)-(A)-(C)이다.

불변의 패턴 26　　　　　　　　　　　　p.103

주어진 글을 보고 뒤에 나올 글의 구조를 예측할 수 있다.

기출 문제　　　　　　　　　　　　　　정답 ②

지문분석

> People spend much of their time / interacting with media, / but that does not mean / that people have the critical skills / to analyze and understand it.
> 사람들은 많은 시간을 보낸다 / 미디어와 상호작용하면서 / 하지만 그게 의미하지는 않는다 / 사람들이 중요한 기술을 가지고 있다는 것을 / 그것을 분석하고 이해하는

(A) Research / from New York University / found / that people over 65 / shared seven times as much misinformation / as their younger counterparts.
조사는 / New York 대학교의 / 알아냈다 / 65세 이상의 사람들이 / 7배 더 많은 잘못된 정보를 공유한다는 것을 / 더 젊은 사람들보다

All of this raises a question: / What's the solution / to the misinformation problem?
이 모든 것은 의문을 제기한다 / 해결책은 무엇인가 / 잘못된 정보 문제에 대한

(B) ★ One well-known study / from Stanford University / in 2016 / demonstrated / that youth are easily fooled / by misinformation, / especially when it comes through social media channels.
유명한 한 연구는 / Stanford 대학교의 / 2016년 / 보여주었다 / 젊은이들이 쉽게 속는다는 것을 / 잘못된 정보에 의해 / 특히 소셜 미디어 채널을 통해서라면

This weakness is not found / only in youth, / however.
이러한 취약함은 발견되는 것은 아니다 / 젊은이에게서만 / 그러나

(C) Governments and tech platforms certainly have a role / to play / in blocking misinformation.
정부와 기술 플랫폼은 분명 역할을 가지고 있다 / 해야 할 / 잘못된 정보를 차단하는 데에 있어서

However, / every individual needs to take responsibility / for combating this threat / by becoming more information literate.
그러나 / 모든 개인은 책임을 져야 한다 / 이러한 위협에 맞서 싸우는 / 좀 더 정보를 잘 다루게 됨으로써

★ 독해가 쉬워지는 구문 풀이

One well known study from Stanford University in 2016
　　　　　　　　　　　　　　　　　　　주어
demonstrated [that youth are easily fooled by misinformation,
　동사　　　명사절 접속사
especially {when **it** comes through social media channels}].

⇨ [ ]는 동사 demonstrated의 목적어 역할을 하는 명사절이다.

⇨ { }는 명사절 [ ]을 수식하는 부사절이며, 대명사 it은 misinformation
을 가리킨다.

[어휘] critical 중요한, 결정적인　misinformation 잘못된 정보, 오보
fool 속이다, 기만하다　weakness 취약함　combat 맞서 싸우다
literate ~을 다룰 줄 아는, 글을 쓰고 읽을 수 있는

[해석] 사람들은 미디어와 상호작용하면서 많은 시간을 보내지만, 그게 사람들
이 그것을 분석하고 이해하는 중요한 기술을 가지고 있다는 것을 의미하
지는 않는다.
(B) 2016년 Stanford 대학교의 유명한 한 연구는 특히 소셜 미디어 채널
을 통해서라면 젊은이들이 잘못된 정보에 의해 쉽게 속는다는 것을 보여
주었다. 그러나, 이러한 취약함은 젊은이에게서만 발견되는 것은 아니다.
(A) New York 대학교의 조사는 65세 이상의 사람들이 더 젊은 사람들보
다 7배 더 많은 잘못된 정보를 공유한다는 것을 알아냈다. 이 모든 것은 의
문을 제기한다: 잘못된 정보 문제에 대한 해결책은 무엇인가?
(C) 정부와 기술 플랫폼은 분명 잘못된 정보를 차단하는 데에 있어서 해
야 할 역할을 가지고 있다. [주제문] 그러나, 모든 개인은 좀 더 정보를 잘 다
루게 됨으로써 이러한 위협에 맞서 싸우는 책임을 져야 한다.

[해설] 주어진 문장에서 사람들이 미디어에 많은 시간을 보내는 것이 그것을 분
석하고 이해하는 중요한 기술을 가진다는 것을 의미하지는 않는다는 점
을 문제로서 제기한다. 이에 대한 예시로 (B)에서 연구를 통해 젊은이들이
소셜 미디어를 통해서 잘못된 정보에 쉽게 속을 수 있다는 결과와 추가로
다른 결과도 도출하였음을 언급한다. (A)에서는 65세 이상의 사람들이 젊
은 사람들보다 7배 더 많은 잘못된 정보를 공유한다고 하며, (B)의 마지막
문장에서 언급한 또 다른 조사 결과를 설명하고 있으므로 (A) 다음에 이
어지는 것이 자연스럽다. 마지막으로 (C)에서는 (B) 마지막 문장에서 제기
된 의문점에 대한 해결 방안으로서, 개인이 정보를 잘 다루게 됨으로써 잘
못된 정보의 위협에 맞서 싸우는 책임을 져야 한다는 것을 제시한다. 따라
서 글의 순서로 가장 적절한 것은 ② (B)-(A)-(C)이다.

독해 만점 TEST
p.104

01 ③　02 ②　03 ②　04 ④　05 ④　06 ③　07 ④　08 ②

[실력 UP!] 미니 문제

01. ①
02. ⓐ the brain　ⓑ the engine
03. ⓐ extract　ⓑ beneficial
04. ① to support practicing lawyers
　　② acting as representatives of a law firm
05. ⓐ variations　ⓑ survival
06. ②
07. (A) evolved　(B) alert
08. ③

01
정답 ③

[지문분석]

Sedimentary rocks can form / on land or underwater.
퇴적암은 형성될 수 있다 / 육지 또는 물속에서

In either case, / the process follows / the same basic steps.
어느 쪽이든 / 그 과정은 따른다 / 동일한 기본적인 단계를

(A) This stage of the process / is known as cementation.
이러한 과정의 단계는 / 교결 작용으로 알려져 있다

The crystals act as an adhesive / and hold the bits of deposited matter together.
그 결정체는 접착제의 역할을 한다 / 그리고 침전된 물질의 조각들을 한데 모은다

Once this stage is complete, / the cycle begins / all over again.
이 단계가 끝나면 / 이 주기는 시작된다 / 처음부터 다시

(B) Rock formation begins / when materials such as mud and sand are transported / to an area / where they can settle, / either on the earth's surface or in a body of water.
바위층의 형성이 시작된다 / 진흙 및 모래와 같은 물질이 옮겨지면 / 영역으로 / 그것들이 가라앉을 수 있는 / 지표면 위나 수역 속 중 한 곳에서

Once the materials have been deposited, / they start to build up / in layers.
물질들이 침전되면 / 그것은 쌓이기 시작한다 / 층층이

(C) As these accumulate, / the weight of each additional layer / puts pressure on the ones / below it.
이들이 축적되면서 / 추가된 각 층의 무게는 / 층에 압력을 가한다 / 그것의 아래에 있는

This compresses the materials, / squeezing out any water / they may contain.
이는 그 물질들을 압축시켜서 / 어떠한 수분이든 짜낸다 / 그것이 포함하고 있을 수도 있는

★ The pressure also causes / salt crystals to form.
그 압력은 또한 ~하게 한다 / 소금 결정이 만들어지도록

★ 독해가 쉬워지는 구문 풀이

The pressure also causes salt crystals to form.
　　　　　　　동사　　　목적어　　목적격보어

⇨ 동사 cause는 to부정사를 목적격보어로 취할 수 있다.

[어휘] sedimentary rock 퇴적암　underwater 물속에서　crystal 결정체
adhesive 접착제　deposit 침전시키다　transport 옮기다
settle 가라앉다, 정착하다　build up 쌓이다　layer 층
accumulate 축적되다　compress 압축시키다　squeeze out 짜내다

[해석] [주제문] 퇴적암은 육지 또는 물속에서 형성될 수 있다. 어느 쪽이든, 그 과
정은 동일한 기본적인 단계를 따른다.
(B) 진흙 및 모래와 같은 물질이 지표면 위나 수역 속 중 한 곳에서 그것들
이 가라앉을 수 있는 영역으로 옮겨지면 바위층의 형성이 시작된다. 물질
들이 침전되면, 그것은 층층이 쌓이기 시작한다.
(C) 이들이 축적되면서, 추가된 각 층의 무게는 그것의 아래에 있는 층에
압력을 가한다. 이는 그 물질들을 압축시켜서, 그것이 포함하고 있을 수
도 있는 어떠한 수분이든 짜낸다. 그 압력은 또한 소금 결정이 만들어지
게 한다.
(A) 이러한 과정의 단계는 교결 작용으로 알려져 있다. 그 결정체는 접착
제의 역할을 하고 침전된 물질의 조각들을 한데 모은다. 이 단계가 끝나
면, 이 주기는 처음부터 다시 시작된다.

[해설] 주어진 글은 퇴적암이 육지 또는 물속에서 형성되는 과정에서 동일한 기
본적인 단계를 따른다는 내용이다. (B) 첫 문장의 '바위층의 형성이 시
작된다'(Rock formation begins)는 주어진 글에서 언급한 퇴적암 형성
과정의 시작을 나타내고 있으므로 그 바로 다음에 이어지는 것이 자연

스럽다. (C) 첫 문장의 As these accumulate에서 these는 (B) 마지막 문장에서 층층이 쌓이기 시작하는 물질들(the materials)을 나타내므로 (B) 다음에 이어지는 것이 자연스럽다. (A) 두 번째 문장의 The crystals 는 (C) 마지막 문장에서 언급된 salt crystals를 가리키는 것으로 (C) 바로 다음에 (A)가 오는 것이 적절하다. 따라서 글의 순서로 가장 적절한 것은 ③ (B)-(C)-(A)이다.

[실력UP!] 미니 문제 01.

정답 ①

해석 ① 퇴적암이 형성되는 과정
② 암석 형성에 필요한 물질들
③ 육지와 수중 퇴적암의 차이

해설 퇴적암이 형성되는 과정을 각 단계별로 설명하고 있는 글이므로, 글의 주제로 가장 적절한 것은 ① the process by which sedimentary rocks form이다.

02 　　　　　　　　　　　　　　　　　정답 ②

지문분석

> All of our thoughts, feelings, and actions are / ultimately controlled / by the brain.
> 우리의 모든 생각, 감정, 그리고 행동은 / 결국 통제된다 / 뇌에 의해

(A) Quality fuels contain components / that enable car engines to operate smoothly / and help maintain their longevity.
고급 연료는 성분을 함유하고 있다 / 자동차 엔진이 매끄럽게 작동하게 해주는 / 그리고 엔진의 수명이 오래 유지되도록 도와주는

Similarly, / highly nutritious foods / have vitamins, minerals, and antioxidants / that feed the brain / and protect it from damage, / helping it stay healthy / for longer.
마찬가지로 / 영양가가 매우 높은 음식은 / 비타민, 미네랄, 항산화제를 가지고 있다 / 뇌에 영양분을 공급하고 그것(뇌)을 손상으로부터 보호하는 / 그런데 그것들은 뇌가 건강한 상태를 유지하도록 도와준다 / 더 오래

(B) The brain serves / an essential function / much like the engine in an automobile.
뇌는 수행한다 / 필수적인 기능을 / 마치 자동차의 엔진과 매우 같은

It is impossible / to operate a car without one, / ★ and the best way / to keep it running in peak condition / is to supply it with the proper fuel.
~은 불가능하다 / 그것(엔진) 없이 자동차를 운행하는 것은 / 그리고 최선의 방법은 / 최상의 상태로 그것(엔진)이 계속 작동하도록 하는 / 그것(엔진)에 알맞은 연료를 공급하는 것이다

(C) In contrast, / foods that are low in nutrition, / just like non-premium fuels, / contain few helpful ingredients / and may even be harmful.
반대로 / 영양가가 낮은 음식은 / 저급한 연료와 같은 / 유익한 성분을 거의 함유하고 있지 않다 / 그리고 심지어는 해로울 수도 있다

Processed foods / and those with lots of artificial sugars, / for example, / can cause the brain / to produce substances / that negatively affect our mood / or slow down its normal performance.
가공식품 / 및 인공 합성 당분이 함유된 음식은 / 예를 들어 / 뇌가 ~하도록 할 수 있다 / 물질을 만들어 내도록 / 우리의 기분에 부정적으로 영향을 미치는 / 또는 뇌의 정상적인 기능을 둔화시키는

★ **독해가 쉬워지는 구문 풀이**

~ and the best way [①to keep it running in peak condition] is [②to supply it with the proper fuel].
　　　　　주어　　　　　　　　　　　　　　　　동사　　보어

⇨ [①]은 to부정사의 형용사적 용법으로, way를 수식한다.
⇨ [②]는 to부정사의 명사적 용법으로, 문장의 보어 역할을 한다.

[어휘] ultimately 결국　quality 고급의　component 성분　operate 작동하다　smoothly 매끄럽게　longevity 수명, 장수　similarly 마찬가지로　nutritious 영양가가 높은　essential 필수적인　function 기능　peak 최상의　supply 공급하다　proper 알맞은　premium 고급의　ingredient 성분　processed 가공한　artificial sugar 인공 합성 당분　substance 물질　negatively 부정적으로　slow down 둔화시키다

[해석] [주제문] 우리의 모든 생각, 감정, 그리고 행동은 결국 뇌에 의해 통제된다.
(B) 뇌는 마치 자동차의 엔진과 매우 같은 필수적인 기능을 수행한다. 그것(엔진) 없이 자동차를 운행하는 것은 불가능하며, 최상의 상태로 그것(엔진)이 계속 작동하도록 하는 최선의 방법은 엔진에 알맞은 연료를 공급하는 것이다.
(A) 고급 연료는 자동차 엔진이 매끄럽게 작동하게 해주고, 엔진의 수명이 오래 유지되도록 도와주는 성분을 함유하고 있다. 마찬가지로, 영양가가 매우 높은 음식은 뇌에 영양분을 공급하고 그것(뇌)을 손상으로부터 보호하는 비타민, 미네랄, 항산화제를 가지고 있는데, 그것들은 뇌가 건강한 상태를 더 오래 유지하도록 도와준다.
(C) 반대로, 저급한 연료와 같은 영양가가 낮은 음식은 유익한 성분을 거의 함유하고 있지 않고 심지어는 해로울 수도 있다. 예를 들어, 가공식품 및 인공 합성 당분이 함유된 음식은 뇌가 우리의 기분에 부정적으로 영향을 미치는 물질을 만들어내거나, 뇌의 정상적인 기능을 둔화시킬 수 있다.

[해설] 주어진 글은 뇌가 우리의 모든 것을 통제한다는 내용이므로, 그 뒤에 뇌(Brain)에 대해 언급하며 이를 자동차의 엔진에 비유한 (B)가 오는 것이 자연스럽다. (B)의 마지막 문장에서 최상의 상태로 엔진을 유지하기 위해 필요한 proper fuel(알맞은 연료)과 (A)의 첫 번째 문장 Quality fuels(고급 연료)가 연관되는 내용이므로 (A)가 와야 한다. 그 뒤에 (C)의 In contrast(반대로)를 보면 (B)의 '고급 연료'의 설명과 대조되는 내용인 non-premium fuels(저급한 연료)의 특징이 언급되므로 마지막으로 (C)가 오는 것이 자연스럽다. 따라서 글의 순서로 가장 적절한 것은 ② (B)-(A)-(C)이다.

[실력UP!] 미니 문제 02.

정답 ⓐ the brain　ⓑ the engine

해설 ⓐ 영양가가 매우 높은 음식은 뇌에 영양분을 공급하고 뇌를 손상으로부터 보호하는 비타민, 미네랄, 항산화제를 가지고 있다고 한 후 그것들은 뇌가 건강한 상태를 더 오래 유지하도록 도와준다고 했으므로, ⓐit이 가리키는 것은 the brain(뇌)이다.
ⓑ 뇌는 마치 자동차의 엔진과 매우 같은 필수적인 기능을 수행한다고 한 후 그것 없이 자동차를 운행하는 것은 불가능하다고 했으므로, ⓑone이 가리키는 것은 the engine(엔진)이다.

03 　　　　　　　　　　　　　　　　　정답 ②

지문분석

> While / extracting scents and oils from flowers / may seem like a difficult DIY project, / it's easier than you think.
> ~이긴 하지만 / 꽃들로부터 향기와 오일을 추출해내는 것은 / 어려운 DIY 프로젝트처럼 보일 수 있다 / 그것은 당신이 생각하는 것보다 쉽다

(A) Next, / remove the petals from the flowers / and put them in a plastic bag.
다음으로 / 꽃에서 꽃잎들을 제거해라 / 그리고 그것들을 비닐봉지에 넣어라

Crush the petals gently / to release the essential oils / and then place them in a jar, / covering them with olive oil.
꽃잎들을 부드럽게 으깨라 / 방향유를 배출시키기 위해 / 그리고 그것들을 병 안에 넣어라 / 그것들을 올리브유로 뒤덮어

Gently shake the jar / and leave it in a sunny spot for 24 hours.
병을 부드럽게 흔들어라 / 그리고 양지에 24시간 동안 놔두어라

(B) You don't need complicated equipment / to get started; / a simple garden / containing plants such as roses or lavender / is enough.
당신은 복잡한 장비가 필요하지 않다 / 시작하는 데 / 단순한 정원 하나 / 장미와 라벤더 같은 식물이 있는 / 충분하다

★ Try to pick flowers / that are not yet in full bloom / as / those that are just beginning to open / contain the most fragrant and beneficial oils.
꽃을 따도록 해라 / 아직 만개하지 않은 / ~ 때문에 / 막 피기 시작하는 그것(꽃)들은 / 가장 향기롭고 유익한 오일을 함유하다

(C) This should be enough time / for the petals to release their essence / into the olive oil.
이것은 충분한 시간일 것이다 / 꽃잎들이 그들의 진액을 방출시키기에 / 올리브유에

Remove the old petals, / gather new flowers, / and repeat the whole process four or five times / to get rich, fragrant essential oil.
이전의 꽃잎들을 제거해라 / 새로운 꽃들을 모아라 / 그리고 전체 과정을 네 번이나 다섯 번 반복해라 / 풍부하고, 향기로운 방향유를 얻기 위해서

★ 독해가 쉬워지는 구문 풀이

Try to pick flowers that are not yet in full bloom as **those** that are just
　　　　　　　　　　　　　　　　　　　　　　　　　　　지시대명사
beginning to open contain the most fragrant and beneficial oils.

⇨ 지시대명사 those는 앞의 flowers를 지칭하며, 같은 명사의 반복을 피하고자 사용되었다.

[어휘] extract 추출하다 scent 향기 remove 제거하다 petal 꽃잎 crush 으깨다 essential oils 방향유 gently 부드럽게 complicated 복잡한 equipment 장비 full bloom 만개 beneficial 유익한 release 방출하다 essence 진액 fragrant 향기로운

[해석] [주제문] 꽃들로부터 향기와 오일을 추출해내는 것은 어려운 DIY 프로젝트처럼 보일 수 있긴 하지만, 그것은 당신이 생각하는 것보다 쉽다.
(B) 당신은 시작하는 데 복잡한 장비가 필요하지 않다. 장미와 라벤더 같은 식물이 있는 단순한 정원 하나면 충분하다. 막 피기 시작하는 꽃들은 가장 향기롭고 유익한 오일을 함유하고 있기 때문에 아직 만개하지 않은 꽃을 따도록 해라.
(A) 다음으로, 꽃에서 꽃잎들을 제거하고, 그것들을 비닐봉지에 넣어라. 방향유를 배출시키기 위해 꽃잎들을 부드럽게 으깨고, 그것들을 올리브유로 뒤덮어 병 안에 넣어라. 병을 부드럽게 흔들고, 양지에 24시간 동안 놔두어라.
(C) 이것은 꽃잎들이 올리브유에 그들의 진액을 방출시키기에 충분한 시간일 것이다. 풍부하고, 향기로운 방향유를 얻기 위해서 이전의 꽃잎들을 제거하고, 새로운 꽃들을 모아서 전체 과정을 네 번이나 다섯 번 반복해라.

[해설] 주어진 글은 꽃들로부터 향기와 오일을 추출해내는 것은 생각보다 쉽다는 내용이다. (B) 첫 문장의 '시작하는 데'(to get started)가 주어진 글에서 언급한 꽃들로부터 향기와 오일을 추출해내는 과정의 시작을 나타내고 있으므로 주어진 글 다음에 이어지는 것이 자연스럽다. (A) 첫 문장의 Next는 (B) 다음 과정을 나타내므로 (B) 다음에 이어지는 것이 자연스럽다. (C) 첫 문장의 This should be enough time에서 This는 (A) 마지막 문장의 24 hours를 나타내므로 (A) 다음에 이어지는 것이 자연스럽다. 따라서 글의 순서로 가장 적절한 것은 ② (B)-(A)-(C)이다.

[실력UP!] 미니 문제 03.

정답 ⓐ extract ⓑ beneficial
해석 ⓐ 어떠한 물질을 그것을 포함하고 있는 것으로부터 분리하거나 끌어내는
　　ⓑ 다른 것에 긍정적인 영향이나 효과를 주는

지문분석

There are a few places / in which paralegals are allowed / to perform the same job / as a lawyer.
몇몇 장소가 있다 / 법률 보조원이 허락되는 / 똑같은 일을 수행하도록 / 변호사와

However, / most of the time, / they are employed by law firms / and perform a distinct function / from lawyers.
하지만 / 대부분의 경우 / 그들은 법률 사무소에 고용된다 / 그래서 다른 역할을 수행한다 / 변호사들과는

(A) But / paralegals also have / other fundamental roles.
그러나 / 법률 보조원은 또한 가지고 있다 / 다른 근본적인 역할을

Acting as representatives of a law firm, / they are responsible for / communicating with clients, / and maintaining professional relationships / with officials at courts, police departments, and other agencies.
법률 사무소의 대변인으로서 활동하며 / 그들은 담당한다 / 고객과의 소통 / 그리고 직업상의 관계 유지 / 법원, 경찰서 및 다른 기관의 공무원과

(B) By performing / either of these basic functions, / paralegals enable lawyers / to work with maximum efficiency / and focus on the needs of their clients.
수행함으로써 / 이러한 기본적인 역할들 중 어느 하나를 / 법률 보조원은 변호사가 ~할 수 있도록 해준다 / 최대한 효율적으로 근무하도록 / 그리고 그들 고객의 요구사항에 집중하도록

★ For these reasons, / paralegals are considered / to be essential personnel / at law firms.
이러한 이유로 / 법률 보조원은 여겨진다 / 필수적인 인원으로 / 법률 사무소에

(C) Their primary duty is / to support practicing lawyers.
그들의 주된 임무는 ~이다 / 활동 중인 변호사를 보조하는 것

As such, / their activities may include / updating and organizing client files, / drafting legal documents, / or conducting case research, / to name a few examples.
따라서 / 그들의 활동은 포함할 수 있다 / 고객 파일 갱신 및 정리 / 법률 문서 초고 작성 / 또는 사건 조사 / 몇 가지 예시를 들어보자면

★ 독해가 쉬워지는 구문 풀이

For these reasons, <u>paralegals</u> <u>are considered</u> <u>to be essential</u>
　　　　　　　　　　　주어　　　　　　수동태　　　　to be + 형용사
personnel at law firms.

⇨ 동사 consider는 목적어 뒤에 '(to be) + 명사·형용사'와 'as + 명사'를 모두 취할 수 있으며, 해당 문장은 수동태 문장이므로 목적어 없이 수동태 동사 뒤에 to be essential이 쓰였다.

[어휘] function 역할 fundamental 근본적인 representative 대변인, 대표자 responsible 담당의 official 공무원 court 법원 agency 기관 efficiency 효율성 essential 필수적인 personnel 인원 primary 주된 as such 따라서 update 갱신하다 organize 정리하다 draft 초고를 작성하다

[해석] 법률 보조원이 변호사와 똑같은 일을 수행하도록 허락되는 몇몇 장소가 있다. 하지만, 대부분의 경우, 그들은 법률 사무소에 고용되어서 변호사들과는 다른 역할을 수행한다.
(C) 그들의 주된 임무는 활동 중인 변호사를 보조하는 것이다. 따라서, 몇 가지 예시를 들어보자면, 그들의 활동은 고객 파일 갱신 및 정리, 법률 문서 초고 작성, 또는 사건 조사를 포함할 수 있다.
(A) 그러나 법률 보조원은 다른 근본적인 역할을 또한 가지고 있다. 법률 사무소의 대변인으로서 활동하며, 그들은 고객과의 소통, 그리고 법원, 경찰서 및 다른 기관의 공무원과 직업상의 관계 유지를 담당한다.
(B) 이러한 기본적인 역할들 중 어느 하나를 수행함으로써, 법률 보조원은 변호사가 최대 효율적으로 근무하고, 그들 고객의 요구사항에 집중

할 수 있도록 해준다. 이러한 이유들로, 법률 보조원은 법률 사무소에 필수적인 인원으로 여겨진다.

[해설] 주어진 글은 법률 보조원은 대부분 법률 사무소에 의해 고용되어 변호사들과는 다른 역할을 수행한다는 내용이다. (C)의 Their primary duty(그들의 주된 임무)는 주어진 글의 '법률 보조원의 주된 임무'를 가리키므로 주어진 글 바로 다음에 오는 것이 적절하다. (A) other fundamental roles(다른 근본적인 역할)는 (C)에서 언급한 primary duty와 이어지는 또 다른 역할을 의미하며, (C)에서 언급되지 않은 법률 보조원의 임무에 대한 추가 설명을 하고 있으므로 (A)는 (C) 뒤에 오는 것이 적절하다. (B)의 these basic functions(이러한 기본적인 역할)는 (C)에서 설명한 primary duty와 (A)에서 설명한 other fundamental roles를 통틀어 가리키므로 (A) 바로 다음에 오는 것이 적절하다. 따라서 글의 순서로 가장 적절한 것은 ④ (C)-(A)-(B)이다.

실력UP! 미니 문제 04.

정답 ① to support practicing lawyers
② acting as representatives of a law firm

해설 these basic functions는 (C)에서 언급된 주된 임무(primary duty)와 (A)에서 언급된 다른 근본적인 역할(other fundamental roles)을 가리킨다. 따라서 하나는 to support practicing lawyers(변호사를 보조하는 것)과 다른 하나는 acting as representatives of a law firm(법률 사무소의 대변인으로 활동하는 것)이다.

05 정답 ④

지문분석

A basic mechanism of evolution / is natural selection, / a process / whereby particular variations in certain traits / become more common / over time.
진화의 기본적인 기제는 / 자연 선택이다 / 하나의 과정 / 어떤 형질 중에서 특정한 변이가 / 더 흔해지다 / 시간이 지나면서

(A) If, / however, / the butterflies happen to live / among birds / that eat orange butterflies in particular, / the population of orange ones / will gradually decrease / over time.
만약 / 하지만 / 그 나비들이 우연히 살게 된다면 / 새들 사이에서 / 특히 주황색 나비를 잡아먹는 / 주황색 개체의 개체 수는 / 점점 감소할 것이다 / 시간이 지날수록

The white ones, / meanwhile, / will continue to flourish.
흰색 개체는 / 반면 / 계속해서 잘 자랄 것이다

(B) As more time passes, / the overall population will start to consist of / fewer orange individuals and mostly white ones.
더 오랜 시간이 지나면서 / 전체 개체군은 구성되기 시작할 것이다 / 주황색 개체는 더 적고 거의 모두 흰색 개체로

★ The presence of the butterfly-eating birds / will have created the natural conditions / that favored the selection or survival / of white-colored butterflies.
나비를 잡아먹는 새의 출현은 / 자연조건을 만들어낼 것이다 / 선택 또는 생존에 도움이 되는 / 흰 나비의

(C) For instance, / suppose / that the butterfly population in a particular location / consists of / both orange individuals and white ones.
예를 들어 / 가정하자 / 특정 지역의 나비 개체군이 ~라고 / 이루어져 있다 / 주황색 개체와 흰색 개체로

Normally, / these butterflies will, / in the process of reproduction, / pass on / each of their unique colors / to their offspring.
일반적으로 / 이 나비들은 ~할 것이다 / 번식의 과정에서 / 물려줄 것이다 / 그들 각자의 고유한 색깔을 / 그들의 자손에게

★ 독해가 쉬워지는 구문 풀이

The presence of the butterfly-eating birds will have created the
　　　　　　주어　　　　　　　　　　　　　　　will have + p.p
natural conditions that [favored the selection or survival of white-
　　　　　　　　　　　　주격　　동사
　　　　　　　　　　관계대명사
colored butterflies].

⇨ will have created는 미래완료시제로, 현재나 과거부터 시작된 특정한 사건으로 인해 미래의 어느 시점에 완료되는 결과를 의미한다.
⇨ 관계대명사 that 뒤에 주어 없이 동사가 바로 왔으므로 that은 주격 관계대명사이다.

[어휘] mechanism 기제　evolution 진화　natural selection 자연 선택
variation 변이, 변형　trait 형질, 특성　population 개체 수, 개체군
gradually 점점　flourish 잘 자라다　presence 출현　favor 돕다, 조력하다
reproduction 번식　offspring 자손

[해석] **[주제문]** 진화의 기본적인 기제는 자연 선택인데, 이것은 어떤 형질 중에서 특정한 변이가 시간이 지나면서 더 흔해지는 하나의 과정이다.
(C) 예를 들어, 특정 지역의 나비 개체군이 주황색 개체와 흰색 개체로 이루어져 있다고 가정하자. 일반적으로, 이 나비들은 번식의 과정에서 그들 각자의 고유한 색깔을 자손에게 물려줄 것이다.
(A) 하지만, 만약 그 나비들이 특히 주황색 나비를 잡아먹는 새들 사이에서 우연히 살게 된다면, 주황색 개체의 개체 수는 시간이 지날수록 점점 감소할 것이다. 반면, 흰색 개체는 계속해서 잘 자랄 것이다.
(B) 더 오랜 시간이 지나면서, 전체 개체군은 주황색 개체는 더 적어지고, 거의 모두 흰색 개체로 구성되기 시작할 것이다. 나비를 잡아먹는 새의 출현은 흰 나비의 선택 또는 생존에 도움이 되는 자연조건을 만들어 낼 것이다.

[해설] 주어진 글은 진화의 기본적인 기제인 자연 선택은 시간이 지나면서 어떤 형질 중에서 특정한 변이가 더 흔해지는 과정이라는 내용이다. (C) 첫 문장의 For instance를 통해 주어진 글에서 언급한 '자연 선택'의 예시를 들고 있으므로 주어진 글 뒤에 오는 것이 적절하다. (A) 첫 문장의 the butterflies는 (C) 마지막 문장의 these butterflies를 가리키므로 (A)는 (B) 뒤에 오는 것이 자연스럽다. (A)의 마지막 문장에 흰색 개체가 계속해서 잘 자랄 것이라고 했고, (B) 첫 문장에서 시간이 지나면서 거의 모두 흰색 개체로 구성되기 시작할 것이라고 했으므로 (B)는 (A) 뒤에 오는 것이 적절하다. 따라서 글의 순서로 가장 적절한 것은 ④ (C)-(A)-(B)이다.

실력UP! 미니 문제 05.

정답 ⓐ variations　ⓑ survival

해석 자연 선택은 궁극적으로 개체군 내 특정 개체의 ⓑ 생존에 유리한 형질의 ⓐ 변이를 초래한다.

해설 자연 선택을 통해 한 개체가 지닌 특정한 형질들의 변이가 그 개체의 생존에 유리하게 작용하면서 점점 개체군 전체에 그 변이가 더 흔해지는 과정을 설명한 글이므로, 요약문의 빈칸에 들어갈 말로 가장 적절한 것은 ⓐ variations(변이), ⓑ survival(생존)이다.

06 정답 ③

지문분석

Independent media refers to / any form of media / that operates independently / of government or corporate interests, so it is considered / distinct from mainstream media.
독립 매체는 가리킨다 / 모든 형태의 매체를 / 독립적으로 운영되는 / 정부나 기업의 이해관계로부터 / 그러므로 이것은 간주된다 / 대중 매체와는 다른 것으로

(A) Having an alternative to mainstream media / is important / because, without it, / powerful interests might get away with wrongdoing / more easily.
대중 매체의 대체재가 있다는 것은 / 중요하다 / 그것이 없다면 ~이기 때문이다 / 권력을 가진 이해 관계자들이 범죄에서 벗어날 수 있다 / 더 쉽게

Therefore, / independent media plays an important role / in keeping power in check.
따라서 / 독립 매체는 중요한 역할을 한다 / 권력을 견제하는 데 있어

(B) Because they operate independently, / members of independent media / enjoy more "freedom."
그들은 독립적으로 운영되기 때문에 / 독립 매체의 구성원들은 / 더 많은 "자유"를 누린다

That is, / they can set / their own editorial direction.
즉 / 그들은 설정할 수 있다 / 그들만의 편집 방향을

This creates the impression / that they are less biased / than mainstream media.
이는 인상을 준다 / 그들이 덜 편향되어 있다는 / 대중 매체보다

(C) ★ People concerned about bias / therefore / turn to independent media / to gain a different perspective / on current events / than that portrayed / by mainstream media.
편향을 우려하는 사람들은 / 따라서 / 독립 매체에 의존한다 / 다른 시각을 얻기 위해 / 최근의 사건에 관하여 / 묘사된 것과는 / 대중 매체에 의해

That is why / independent media is / sometimes also known / as alternative media.
이것이 ~한 이유이다 / 독립 매체가 ~이다 / 종종 ~로도 알려진 / 대안 매체로

> ★ 독해가 쉬워지는 구문 풀이
>
> People ~ turn to independent media to gain a different perspective
> 주어   동사   단수명사
> on current events than that portrayed by mainstream media.
>   단수대명사
>
> ⇨ 대명사가 가리키는 대상은 단수명사 perspective이므로, 단수대명사 that이 쓰였다.

[어휘] independent 독립의 operate 운영되다 corporate 기업의
interest 이해관계 distinct 다른 alternative 대체재, 대안
mainstream 대중의, 주류의
get away with (범죄 등의 책임을) 벗어나다, 피하다 wrongdoing 범죄
keep in check 견제하다, 억제하다 editorial 편집의 bias 편향
perspective 시각, 관점 portray 묘사하다

[해석] [주제문] 독립 매체는 정부나 기업의 이해관계로부터 독립적으로 운영되는 모든 형태의 매체를 가리키므로, 이것은 대중 매체와는 다른 것으로 간주된다.
(B) 그들은 독립적으로 운영되기 때문에, 독립 매체의 구성원들은 더 많은 "자유"를 누린다. 즉, 그들은 그들만의 편집 방향을 설정할 수 있다. 이는 그들이 대중 매체보다 덜 편향되어 있다는 인상을 준다.
(C) 따라서 편향을 우려하는 사람들은 최근의 사건에 관하여 대중 매체에 의해 묘사된 것과는 다른 시각을 얻기 위해 독립 매체에 의존한다. 이것이 독립 매체가 종종 대안 매체로도 알려진 이유다.
(A) 대중 매체의 대체재가 있다는 것은 중요한데, 그것이 없다면 권력을 가진 이해 관계자들이 범죄에서 더 쉽게 벗어날 수 있기 때문이다. 따라서, 독립 매체는 권력을 견제하는 데 있어 중요한 역할을 한다.

[해설] 주어진 글은 독립 매체의 정의를 설명하는 내용이다. (B) 첫 문장의 they operate independently는 주어진 글의 operate independently를 반복하여 독립 매체의 특성을 설명하고 있으므로 주어진 글 다음에 오는 것이 적절하다. (C)에서 편향을 우려하는 사람들이 독립 매체에 의존한다고 했으므로 독립 매체는 대중매체보다 덜 편향되어 있다는 인상을 준다는 (B) 다음에 와야 한다. (C) 마지막 문장의 alternative media가 (A) 첫 문장의 Having an alternative to mainstream media와 연결되므로 글의 순서로 가장 적절한 것은 ③ (B)-(C)-(A)이다.

실력UP! 미니 문제 06.

[정답] ②

[해석] ① 정부 매체와 기업 매체 간의 차이점
② 대중 매체에 비해 독립 매체가 갖는 장점
③ 독립 매체가 다른 형태의 매체보다 신뢰성이 떨어지는 이유

[해설] 독립 매체가 대중 매체에 비해 덜 편향적이라서 권력을 견제하는 데 있어 중요한 역할을 한다는 등 독립 매체의 장점에 관한 글이므로, 글의 주제로 가장 적절한 것은 ② advantages of independent media over mainstream media이다.

07
정답 ④

지문분석

> If you have ever caught yourself yawning / after someone around you does, / you may wonder why, / especially if you aren't tired or bored.
> 만약 당신이 하품하는 자신을 발견한 적이 있다면 / 당신 주위의 누군가가 그런(하품한) 이후 / 당신은 왜일까 궁금해 할 것이다 / 특히 낭신이 피곤하거나 지루하지 않다면

(A) In fact, / being alert / was very important / millions of years ago, / back when humans were prey / rather than predators.
사실 / 경계하는 것 / 굉장히 중요했다 / 수백만 년 전 / 과거에 인류가 사냥감이었을 때 / 포식자보다는

If danger was near, / it is thought / that yawning may have been used / as a way to increase concentration / and, by extension, the likelihood of survival.
만약 위험이 가까이 있다면, / 생각된다 / 하품이 쓰였을 것으로 / 집중력을 높이는 방법으로서 / 그리고, 더 나아가, 생존의 가능성을

(B) Therefore, / if someone in a group yawned, / the other members of the group / would do the same, / expressing / that they understood / the need to be watchful.
그러므로 / 한 집단의 누군가가 하품을 했다면 / 그 집단의 다른 구성원들 / 똑같이 할 것이다 / 표현하며 / 그들이 이해했음을 / 조심할 필요

Over time, / contagious yawning / has become a way / of showing empathy / in times / of shared boredom or so.
시간이 지나면서 / 전염성 하품은 / 하나의 방법이 되었다 / 공감을 표현하는 / ~ 때에 / 모두에게 (공유된) 지루한 일 등의

(C) ★ Contagious yawning, as it is known, / is believed to have evolved / in early humans / as a way to help / our prehistoric ancestors / stay alert.
전염성 하품이라 알려진 이것은 / 진화해왔다고 믿어진다 / 초기 인류 사이에서 / 도울 방법으로서 / 우리의 선사 시대 조상들 / 계속 경계를 하도록

According to some scientists, / yawning cools the brain, / and people need a cool brain / to be alert.
일부 과학자들에 따르면 / 하품은 두뇌를 식히다 / 그리고 사람들은 냉철한 두뇌가 필요하다 / 방심하지 않기 위해서

> ★ 독해가 쉬워지는 구문 풀이
>
> Contagious yawning, as it is known, is believed to have evolved in
> early human **as** a way [to **help** our prehistoric ancestors stay alert].
>   목적어   목적격보어
>
> ⇨ 전치사 as는 동사 evolve와 함께 '~로 진화하다'라는 의미를 나타낸다.
> ⇨ [ ]는 명사 a way를 수식하여 형용사적 용법으로 쓰인 to부정사구이며, 동사 help는 목적격보어로 동사원형 또는 to부정사를 취하는 준 사역동사이다.

[어휘] yawn 하품하다 wonder 궁금해하다 alert 경계하는, 방심하지 않는
prey 사냥감, 먹이 predator 포식자 concentration 집중력
by extension 더 나아가 likelihood 가능성 survival 생존
express 표현하다 watchful 조심하는 contagious 전염성의
empathy 공감 boredom 지루한 일 evolve 진화하다
prehistoric 선사 시대의 ancestor 조상

만약 당신 주위의 누군가가 하품한 이후 하품하는 자신을 발견한 적이 있다면, 특히 당신이 피곤하거나 지루하지 않다면, 당신은 왜일까 궁금해 할 것이다.

(C) [주제문] 전염성 하품이라 알려진 이것은 초기 인류 사이에서 우리의 선사 시대 조상들이 계속 경계를 하도록 도울 방법으로서 진화해왔다고 믿어진다. 일부 과학자들에 따르면 하품은 두뇌를 식히고, 사람들은 방심하지 않기 위해서 냉철한 두뇌가 필요하다.

(A) 사실, 수백만 년 전, 과거에 인류가 포식자보다는 사냥감이었을 때, 경계하는 것은 굉장히 중요했다. 만약 위험이 가까이 있다면, 하품이 집중력, 그리고 더 나아가, 생존의 가능성을 높이는 방법으로서 쓰였을 것으로 생각된다.

(B) 그러므로, 한 집단의 누군가가 하품을 했다면, 그 집단의 다른 구성원들도 그들이 조심할 필요를 이해했음을 표현하며 똑같이 할 것이다. 시간이 지나면서, 전염성 하품은 모두에게(공유된) 지루한 일 등의 때에 공감을 표현하는 하나의 방법이 되었다.

해설 주어진 글은 우리가 피곤하거나 지루하지 않은 상황에서도 주위에서 하품한 누군가를 따라 자신 역시 하품하는 이유에 대한 의문을 제기하는 글이다. 이에 대한 답으로 (C)에서 전염성 하품이 조상들이 계속 경계를 하도록 도울 방법으로서 진화해왔다고 믿어진다는 것을 언급하므로 (C)는 주어진 글 다음에 오는 것이 적절하다. (A)에서는 과거 인류가 포식자보다는 사냥감이었을 때 경계하는 것이 중요했다고 하므로 이러한 경계 태세에 관해 먼저 언급한 (C) 다음에 오는 것이 적절하다. (B)에서는 과거에 한 집단의 누군가가 하품을 했다면, 다른 구성원들도 조심할 필요를 이해했음을 표현하기 위해 똑같이 하품을 했을 것이라는 구체적인 내용을 설명하고 있으므로 마지막에 오는 것이 적절하다. 따라서 글의 순서로 가장 적절한 것은 ④ (C) - (A) - (B)이다.

[실력 UP!] 미니 문제 07.

정답 (A) evolved   (B) alert

해석 수백만 년 전, 인간들은 이것(전염성 하품)이 생존의 가능성을 높이면서 그들이 계속 (B) 경계하도록 도와주기 때문에 전염성 하품을 (A) 진화시켜왔다고 여겨진다.

해설 전염성 하품은 초기 인류 사이에서 우리의 조상이 계속 경계를 하도록 도울 방법으로 진화해왔다고 믿어진다고 했으므로, 요약문의 빈칸에 들어갈 말로 가장 적절한 것은 (A) evolved(진화한), (B) alert(경계하는)이다.

08

정답 ②

[지문분석]

> Too often, / people who suffer from insomnia / are led to believe / that their condition is / a result of some personal "failing."
> 너무 자주 / 불면증에 시달리는 사람들은 / 믿게 된다 / 그들의 상태가 ~라고 / 개인적인 "실패"의 결과
>
> ★ Thus, / they are told / to either stop overthinking, / try relaxing, / or see a doctor / for mental help.
> 따라서 / 그들은 말을 듣는다 / 너무 많이 생각하는 것을 멈추거나 / 긴장을 풀거나 / 또는 진료를 받으라는 / 정신적 도움을 위해

(A) Through their studies of DNA, / scientists have discovered / that people who suffer from insomnia / likely possess genes for sleeplessness / in their brain.
DNA 연구를 통해 / 과학자들은 발견했다 / 불면증에 시달리는 사람들이 ~라는 것을 / 불면 유전자를 지닐 가능성이 있다 / 그들의 뇌에

They have identified / seven of these genes in total.
그들은 발견했다 / 총 일곱 개의 이러한 유전자를

(B) However, / researchers have been able to determine / that the inability to sleep / is not wholly psychological.
그러나 / 연구자들은 밝혀낼 수 있었다 / 수면 불능이 / 전적으로 심리적인 것은 아님을

Rather, / sleeplessness is more likely to be biological, / meaning it is the result of / how people are born.
도리어 / 불면은 생물학적인 것일 가능성이 더 있는데 / 즉 불면은 ~의 결과라는 것이다 / 사람들이 태어난 방식의

(C) Any one of the genes / can cause people to experience / constant bodily movements / or an endless stream of thoughts.
이 유전자들 중 어느 것이든 / 사람들로 하여금 겪도록 만들 수 있다 / 지속적인 신체 움직임을 / 또는 끊임없는 생각의 흐름을

These conditions can, / in turn, / contribute to disrupted sleep / or cause excessive wakefulness.
이러한 상태는 / 결국 / 수면 방해의 원인이 된다 / 또는 지나친 각성 상태를 일으킬 수 있다

> ★ 독해가 쉬워지는 구문 풀이
>
> Thus, they are told to either stop overthinking, try relaxing, or see
>   상관접속사 동사1   동사2   동사3
>   (either ~or)
> a doctor for mental help.
> ⇨ 상관접속사 either 뒤의 첫 번째 동사 stop과 병렬 구조를 이루는 동사 원형 try와 see가 쓰였다.

어휘 failing 실패, 결점 overthink 너무 많이 생각하다 possess 지니다 sleeplessness 불면 determine 밝혀내다 inability 불능 wholly 전적으로 psychological 심리적인, 정신적인 biological 생물학적인 constant 지속적인 endless 끊임없는 in turn 결국 contribute to ~의 원인이 되다 disrupt 방해하다 excessive 지나친 wakefulness 각성 상태

해석 너무 자주, 불면증에 시달리는 사람들은 그들의 상태가 개인적인 "실패"의 결과라고 믿게 된다. 따라서, 그들은 너무 많이 생각하는 것을 멈추거나, 긴장을 풀거나, 또는 정신적 도움을 위해 진료를 받으라는 말을 듣는다.

(B) 그러나, 연구자들은 수면 불능이 전적으로 심리적인 것은 아님을 밝혀낼 수 있었다. [주제문] 도리어, 불면은 생물학적인 것일 가능성이 더 있는데, 즉 불면은 사람들이 태어난 방식의 결과라는 것이다.

(A) DNA 연구를 통해, 과학자들은 불면증에 시달리는 사람들이 그들의 뇌에 불면 유전자를 지닐 가능성이 있다는 것을 발견했다. 그들은 총 일곱 개의 이러한 유전자를 발견했다.

(C) 이 유전자들 중 어느 것이든 사람들로 하여금 지속적인 신체 움직임 또는 끊임없는 생각의 흐름을 겪도록 만들 수 있다. 결국 이러한 상태는 수면 방해의 원인이 되거나 지나친 각성 상태를 일으킬 수 있다.

해설 주어진 글은 불면증에 시달리는 사람이 개인적 실패의 결과라고 믿게 되어 정신적 도움을 위해 진료를 받으라는 말을 듣는다는 내용이다. (B)는 However를 통해 주어진 내용과 반대되는 내용인 불면이 전적으로 심리적인 것은 아니고 생물학적인 가능성이 있다고 했으므로 주어진 글 다음에 오는 것이 자연스럽다. (A)의 첫 문장에서 불면 유전자를 발견했다고 했으므로 생물학적 가능성에 대해 먼저 언급한 (B) 다음에 오고, (C) 첫 문장의 the genes(이 유전자들)는 (A)의 seven of these genes(일곱 개의 이러한 유전자)를 가리키므로 (C)는 (A) 다음에 오는 것이 적절하다. 따라서 글의 순서로 가장 적절한 것은 ② (B) - (A) - (C)이다.

[실력 UP!] 미니 문제 08.

정답 ③

해석 ① DNA가 사람들의 성격에 영향을 미치는 방법
② 수면 장애의 심리적 이유
③ 연구들이 불면증을 유전학과 어떻게 연관시켰는지

해설 불면이 유전학적 요인으로 인한 것일지도 모른다는 연구 결과에 관한 글이므로, 글의 주제로 가장 적절한 것은 ③ how studies have linked insomnia to genetics 이다.

CHAPTER 14 주어진 문장의 위치 찾기

불변의 패턴 27　　　　　　　　　　　　　p.108
주어진 문장에는 앞뒤 문장에 대한 결정적인 단서가 있다.

기출 문제　　　　　　　　　　　　　　　정답 ②

지문분석

Most of us have hired many people / based on human resources criteria / along with some technical and personal information / that the boss thought / was important.
우리의 대부분은 많은 사람들을 고용해왔다 / 인적 자원 기준에 근거하여 / 전문적이면서도 개인적인 정보에 따른 / 사장이 생각하기에 / 중요한

(①) I have found / that most people like to hire people / just like themselves.
나는 알게 되었다 / 대부분의 사람들이 사람을 고용하고 싶어 한다는 것을 / 그들 자신과 비슷한

(②) (This may have worked / in the past, / but today, / with interconnected team processes, / we don't want / all people who are the same.)
이는 유효했을 수도 있다 / 과거에는 / 하지만 오늘날에는 / 상호 연결된 팀의 업무 과정으로 인해 / 우리는 원하지 않는다 / 모두가 똑같은 사람이기를

In a team, / some need to be leaders, / some need to be doers, / some need to provide creative strengths, / some need to be inspirers, / some need to provide imagination, / and so on.
팀 내에서 / 일부는 리더여야 한다 / 그리고 일부는 실행가여야 한다 / 그리고 일부는 창의력을 제공해야 한다 / 그리고 일부는 격려를 해주는 사람이어야 한다 / 그리고 일부는 상상력을 제공해야 한다 / 등

(③) In other words, / we are looking for a diversified team / where members complement one another.
다시 말해 / 우리는 다양화된 팀을 원하고 있다 / 구성원들이 서로를 보완하는

(④) ★ When putting together a new team / or hiring team members, / we need to look at each individual / and how he or she fits into / the whole of our team objective.
새로운 팀을 만들 때 / 혹은 팀원을 고용하는 / 우리는 각 개인을 살펴보아야 한다 / 그리고 그 사람이 어떻게 적합한지를 / 우리의 팀 목적의 전반에

(⑤) The bigger the team, / the more possibilities exist / for diversity.
팀이 크면 클수록 / 가능성이 더 많이 존재한다 / 다양성에 대한

★ 독해가 쉬워지는 구문 풀이

[When **putting** together a new team or **hiring** team members],
　접속사　　　　　　　　　　　　　현재분사구문
we need to look at each individual and how he or she fits into the whole of our team objective.

⇨ [ ]는 주절(we ~ objective)을 수식하는 분사구문의 부사절이다. 주절과 반복되는 주어(we)는 생략되었으나, 분사구문 앞에 있는 부사절 접속사 When은 의미를 명확히 하고자 생략되지 않았다.
⇨ 현재분사 putting과 hiring은 등위접속사 or로 연결된 병렬 구조이다.

어휘 hire 고용하다　technical 전문적인　interconnected 상호 연결된
doer 실행가, 행위자　look for 원하다　diversified 다양화된
complement 보완하다, 보충하다　put together 만들다, 준비하다
fit into ~에 적합하다, 어울리다　objective 목적

해석 우리의 대부분은 사장이 생각하기에 중요한, 전문적이면서도 개인적인 정보에 따른 인적 자원 기준에 근거하여 많은 사람들을 고용해왔다. 나는 대부분의 사람들이 그들 자신과 비슷한 사람을 고용하고 싶어 한다는 것을 알게 되었다. (이는 과거에는 유효했을 수도 있지만, 오늘날에는 상호 연결된 팀의 업무 과정으로 인해 우리는 모두가 똑같은 사람이기를 원하

지 않는다.) 팀 내에서, 일부는 리더여야 하고, 일부는 실행가여야 하며, 일부는 창의력을 제공해야 하고, 일부는 격려를 해주는 사람이어야 하며, 일부는 상상력 등을 제공해야 한다. 다시 말해, 우리는 구성원들이 서로를 보완하는 다양화된 팀을 원하고 있다. 새로운 팀을 만들거나 팀원을 고용할 때, 우리는 각 개인과, 그 사람이 어떻게 우리의 팀 목적 전반에 적합한지를 살펴보아야 한다. 팀이 크면 클수록, 다양성에 대한 가능성이 더 많이 존재한다.

해설 주어진 문장의 This may have worked in the past를 통해 주어진 글 앞에 This가 지칭하는 것이 과거에는 유효했다는 내용이 언급됨을 알 수 있다. 또한, but today ~ we don't want all people who are the same을 통해 This가 지칭하는 것이 오늘날에는 유효하지 않으며, 오늘날에는 '우리는 모두가 똑같은 사람이기를 원하지 않는다'는 것을 알 수 있다. ① 뒤 문장에서 글쓴이는 '대부분의 사람들은 그들 자신과 비슷한 사람을 고용하고 싶어 한다는 것'을 알게 되었다고 했으나, ② 뒤 문장에서는 팀 내에서 각자에게 다양한 역할이 요구된다고 설명한다. 따라서 주어진 문장이 들어가기에 가장 적절한 곳은 ②이다.

오답분석 ① 뒤 문장은 첫 번째 문장에 이어서 인력 고용에 있어서 사람들이 원하는 기준에 대해 언급하고 있으므로, 앞 문장과 연결된다. ③ 뒤 문장들은 팀의 다양성에 관련된 내용이므로 ③ 앞 문장과 연결되며 문장들 간의 흐름이 자연스럽다.

불변의 패턴 28　　　　　　　　　　　　　p.109
뜬금없는 대명사나 지시어, 어색한 연결어가 있는 문장 앞이 정답이다.

기출 문제　　　　　　　　　　　　　　　정답 ④

지문분석

There are some cultures / that can be referred to / as "people who live outside of time."
몇몇 문화권이 있다 / 일컬어질 수 있는 / "시간 밖에서 사는 사람들"이라고

The Amondawa tribe, / living in Brazil, / does not have a concept / of time / that can be measured or counted.
Amondawa 부족에게는 / 브라질에 사는 / 개념이 없다 / 시간의 / 측정되거나 세어질 수 있는

(①) Rather / they live in a world / of serial events, / rather than / seeing events / as being rooted / in time.
도리어 / 그들은 세상에서 산다 / 연속되는 사건들의 / ~보다는 / 사건들을 보기 / 바탕을 두면서 / 시간에

(②) Researchers also found / that no one had an age.
연구자들은 또한 알아냈다 / 누구에게도 나이가 없음을

(③) Instead, / they change their names / to reflect their stage of life / and position within their society, / so a little child / will give up their name / to a newborn sibling / and take on a new one.
대신에 / 그들은 이름을 바꾼다 / 자신들의 생애 단계를 반영하기 위해 / 그리고 사회 내의 위치 / 그래서 어린아이는 / 자신의 이름을 넘겨준다 / 새로 태어난 형제자매에게 / 그리고 새로운 이름을 얻는다

(④) (★ In the U.S. / we have so many metaphors / for time and its passing / that we think of time / as "a thing," / that is / "the weekend is almost gone," / or "I haven't got the time.")
미국에서 / 우리는 매우 많은 은유가 있다 / 시간과 그 흐름에 관한 / 그래서 시간을 생각한다 / "물건"으로 / 즉 / "주말이 거의 다 지나갔다" / 또는 "나는 시간이 없다"

We think / such statements are objective, / but they aren't.
우리는 생각한다 / 그러한 말들이 객관적이라고 / 하지만 그렇지 않다

(⑤) We create these metaphors, / but the Amondawa don't talk or think / in metaphors for time.
우리는 이런 은유를 만들어낸다 / 하지만 Amondawa 사람들은 말하거나 생각하지 않는다 / 시간에 대한 은유로

[어휘] serial 연속되는　root 바탕을 두다, 뿌리를 두다
give up A to B A를 B에게 넘겨주다　take on 얻다, 지다　passing 흐름
that is 즉, 다시 말해서　statement 말, 진술　objective 객관적인

[해석] "시간 밖에서 사는 사람들"이라고 일컬어질 수 있는 몇몇 문화권이 있다.
브라질에 사는 Amondawa 부족에게는 측정되거나 세어질 수 있는 시간
의 개념이 없다. 도리어, 그들은 시간에 바탕을 두면서 사건들을 보기보다
는 연속되는 사건들의 세상에서 산다. 연구자들은 또한 누구에게도 나이
가 없음을 알아냈다. 대신에, 그들은 자신들의 생애 단계와 사회 내의 위
치를 반영하기 위해 이름을 바꾸어서, 어린아이는 자신의 이름을 새로 태
어난 형제자매에게 넘겨주고 새로운 이름을 얻는다. (미국에서, 우리는 시
간과 그 흐름에 관한 매우 많은 은유가 있어서 시간을 "물건"으로 생각하
는데, 즉 "주말이 거의 다 지나갔다"나 "나는 시간이 없다."와 같은 것이
다.) 우리는 그러한 말들이 객관적이라고 생각하지만, 그렇지 않다. 우리는
이런 은유를 만들어내지만, Amondawa 사람들은 시간에 대한 은유로 말
하거나 생각하지 않는다.

[해설] ④ 앞 문장까지 브라질의 Amondawa 부족을 소개하며, 측정되거나 세
어질 수 있는 시간의 개념이 없는 그들의 문화를 설명한다. 그런데 ④ 뒤
문장에 such statements(그러한 말)가 나오는데 ④의 앞에는 "말"에 관
한 언급이 없으므로 ④의 앞과 뒤에서 글의 흐름이 끊기는 것을 알 수 있
다. 따라서 주어진 문장이 들어가기에 가장 적절한 곳은 ④이다.

[오답분석] ① 뒤 문장은 앞 문장에 이어서 Amondawa 부족에게 있어서의 시간의
개념을 설명하고, ②과 ③ 뒤 문장은 그들이 나이의 개념을 사용하는 대
신 이름을 바꿈으로써 자신의 생애 단계와 사회 내의 위치를 나타낸다
는 내용이므로 문장의 흐름이 자연스럽다. 또한 ⑤의 앞, 뒤 문장은 시간
을 은유적으로 표현한 말에 관한 내용이므로 자연스럽게 이어진다.

독해 만점 TEST

p.110

01. ③　02. ③　03. ⑤　04. ⑤　05. ④　06. ⑤　07. ⑤　08. ⑤

실력 UP! 미니 문제

01. (A) 음악 듣기, 영화 보기, 고무 공 꽉 쥐기, 간호사에게 말 걸기
　　(B) 그들이 깨어있도록 요구하는 의료 수술

02. ②

03. ①

04. 삶의 중요한 결정에 대해 마음을 정할 수 없을 때는 산책을 하며 생각을 정리
　　하라.

05. ③

06. It has been physically separated from the other continents for
　　an extremely long period of time

07. (A) harmful　(B) overcome

08. ⓐ contradictory　ⓑ intentionally

지문분석

★ Those / who undergo medical procedures / that require them to
stay awake / often experience anxiety.
사람들은 / 의료 수술을 받는 / 그들이 깨어있도록 요구하는 / 종종 불안을 겪는다

(①) Thus, / a study was performed / to see / if certain simple
methods could be used / to keep people's minds occupied /
during such surgeries.
따라서 / 한 실험이 진행되었다 / 확인하기 위해 / 어떤 간단한 방법이 사용될 수 있을지를 /
사람들의 정신을 몰두하게 하는 데 / 그러한 수술 중에

(②) These were listening to music, / watching a movie, / squeezing
a rubber ball, / and talking to a nurse.
이것은 음악 듣기였다 / 영화 보기 / 고무 공 꽉 쥐기 / 그리고 간호사에게 말 걸기

(③) (To test their effectiveness, / hundreds of patients / having
minor surgical treatments / were divided / into five groups.)
그것들의 효과를 시험하기 위해 / 수백 명의 환자들이 / 간단한 수술 치료를 받는 / 나뉘었
다 / 다섯 개의 집단으로

Each was assigned / to use one method, / while the final group
went through the process / without any aids.
각 집단은 지정되었다 / 한 가지 방법을 사용하도록 / 하지만 마지막 집단은 / 수술을 마쳤
다 / 어떠한 도움 없이

(④) Songs failed to have any effect / at all / but speaking with a
nurse / reduced anxiety / by 30 percent.
노래는 어떠한 효과도 가져오지 못했다 / 전혀 / 하지만 간호사와 이야기하는 것은 / 불안
감을 줄였다 / 30%만큼

(⑤) Watching a film also / lowered anxiousness / by 25 percent, /
while the rubber balls reduced such feelings / by 18 percent.
영화를 보는 것도 / 불안을 줄였다 / 25%만큼 / 반면 고무공은 그러한 감정을 줄였다 /
18%만큼

[어휘] undergo ~을 받다, 경험하다　procedure 수술, 시술, 절차
perform 진행하다, 수행하다　occupy 몰두하다, 마음을 끌다　squeeze 꽉 쥐다
effectiveness 효과　surgical 수술의　assign 지정하다
anxiousness 불안

[해석] 그들이 깨어있도록 요구하는 의료 수술을 받는 사람들은 종종 불안을 겪
는다. 따라서, 그러한 수술 중에 어떤 간단한 방법이 사람들의 정신을 몰
두하게 하는 데 사용될 수 있을지를 확인하기 위해 한 실험이 진행되었다.
이것은 음악 듣기, 영화 보기, 고무 공 꽉 쥐기, 그리고 간호사에게 말 걸기
였다. (그것들의 효과를 시험하기 위해, 간단한 수술 치료를 받는 수백 명
의 환자들이 다섯 개의 집단으로 나뉘었다.) 각 집단은 한 가지 방법을 사
용하도록 지정되었지만, 마지막 집단은 어떠한 도움 없이 수술을 마쳤다.
노래는 어떠한 효과도 전혀 가져오지 못했지만, 간호사와 이야기하는 것
은 불안감을 30%만큼 줄였다. 영화를 보는 것도 25%만큼 불안을 줄인
반면, 고무공은 그러한 감정을 18%만큼 줄였다.

[해설] 주어진 문장의 To test their effectiveness, divided into five groups
를 통해 주어진 문장 앞에는 효과가 검증되어야 할 대상이 언급되어야 함
을 알 수 있고, 주어진 문장 뒤에는 다섯 개로 나뉜 집단에 관한 내용이 이
어져야 함을 알 수 있다. ③의 앞에서 언급된 네 가지 방법은 주어진 문장
의 their가 지칭하는 대상이며, ③ 뒤의 Each와 the final group은 주어
진 문장에서 언급된 집단을 지칭함을 알 수 있다. 따라서 주어진 문장이
들어가기에 가장 적절한 곳은 ③이다.

오답분석 ③ 앞 문장까지는 수술 중에 사람들의 정신을 몰두하게 하는 방법의 효과를 시험하기 위한 실험이 진행되었으며, 시험의 대상이 된 방법들이 무엇인지 언급하고 있으므로 문장의 흐름이 자연스럽다. ⑤ 뒤 문장들은 실험 집단을 나눈 방식 및 실험 결과를 설명하고 있으므로 자연스럽게 이어진다.

실력 UP! 미니 문제 01.

정답 (A) 음악 듣기, 영화 보기, 고무 공 꽉 쥐기, 간호사에게 말 걸기
(B) 그들이 깨어있도록 요구하는 의료 수술

해설 (A) 사람들의 정신을 몰두하게 하는 데 사용될 수 있는 방법으로 음악 듣기, 영화 보기, 고무 공 꽉 쥐기, 간호사에게 말 걸기가 제시되었고, 그것들의 효과를 시험하기 위해 환자들을 집단으로 나눴다고 했으므로 (A)their는 '음악 듣기, 영화 보기, 고무 공 꽉 쥐기, 간호사에게 말 걸기'를 의미한다.
(B) 그들이 깨어있도록 요구하는 의료 수술에서 사람들의 정신을 몰두하게 하고 불안감을 줄이는 방법을 찾기 위한 실험이므로, (B)such surgeries(그러한 수술)은 '그들이 깨어있도록 요구하는 의료 수술'을 의미한다.

02   정답 ③

지문분석

Circadian rhythms are / internally driven biological processes / that follow a 24-hour cycle.
생체리듬은 ~이다 / 체내에서 이루어지는 생물학적 과정 / 24시간의 주기를 따르는

(①) They are present / in most living things.
그것은 존재한다 / 대부분의 생물체 내에

(②) Circadian rhythms are controlled / by nerve cells / in our brain, / which act / as the body's internal clock.
생체리듬은 통제된다 / 신경 세포에 의해 / 우리 뇌 속의 / 이들은 역할 한다 / 신체 내부의 시계로서

(③) (These cells are connected / to our eyes / and are thus highly affected / by changes in light levels.)
이 세포들은 연결되어 있다 / 우리의 눈에 / 그리고 따라서 크게 영향을 받는다 / 조도의 변화에

★ This is why / we normally start to wake up / as the day grows bright / and begin to feel restful / after it grows dark.
이것이 이유이다 / 우리가 일반적으로 잠에서 깨기 시작하는 / 날이 점점 밝아지면서 / 그리고 편안함을 느끼기 시작한다 / 날이 어두워진 후에

(④) This also helps to explain / why artificial light can trick our bodies / into staying awake.
이것은 또한 설명하는 것을 도와준다 / 인공조명이 우리의 신체를 속일 수 있는 이유를 / 깨어있도록

(⑤) And / there are other factors / besides light / that can influence the regulation / of our circadian rhythms, / including physical movement and body temperature.
그리고 / 다른 요인들이 있다 / 빛 외에도 / 조절에 영향을 줄 수 있는 / 우리의 생체리듬 / 신체의 움직임과 체온을 포함하여

★ 독해가 쉬워지는 구문 풀이

This is [why we normally start to wake up as the day grows
        의문사 주어   동사1
bright and begin to feel restful after it grows dark].
       동사2

⇨ [ ]는 동사 is의 보어로 쓰인 <의문사 + 주어 + 동사> 순의 간접 의문문(명사절)이다.
⇨ start와 begin은 등위접속사 and로 연결되어 병렬 구조를 이룬다.

어휘 biological 생물학적인 present 존재하는, 참석하는 cell 세포
internally 체내에서 restful 편안한, 차분한 artificial 인공의
trick into ~하도록 속이다 factor 요인 regulation 조절

해석 생체리듬은 24시간의 주기를 따르는, 체내에서 이루어지는 생물학적 과정이다. 그것은 대부분의 생물체 내에 존재한다. **[주제문]** 생체리듬은 우리 뇌 속의 신경 세포에 의해 통제되는데, 이들은 신체 내부의 시계로서 역할

한다. (이 세포들은 우리의 눈에 연결되어 있어서 조도의 변화에 크게 영향을 받는다.) 이것이 우리가 일반적으로 날이 점점 밝아지면서 잠에서 깨기 시작하고 날이 어두워진 후에 편안함을 느끼기 시작하는 이유이다. 이것은 또한 인공조명이 우리의 신체가 깨어있도록 속일 수 있는 이유를 설명하는 것을 도와준다. 그리고 신체의 움직임과 체온을 포함하여, 빛 외에도 우리의 생체리듬 조절에 영향을 줄 수 있는 다른 요인들이 있다.

해설 주어진 문장의 These cells(이 세포들)를 보아 주어진 문장 앞에는 세포와 관련된 내용이 언급되어야 하며, 이는 ③ 앞 문장의 nerve cells in our brain을 지칭한다. 또한, 주어진 문장의 affected by changes in light levels(조도의 변화에 영향을 받는)로 보아, 주어진 문장의 뒤에는 조도의 변화로 인한 영향과 관련된 내용이 나와야 한다는 것을 알 수 있다. ③ 뒤 문장에서 '이것이 우리가 날이 밝아지면서 잠에서 깨기 시작하고 날이 어두워진 후에 편안함을 느끼기 시작하는 이유'라고 했으므로 주어진 문장이 들어가기에 가장 적절한 곳은 ③이다.

오답분석 ③ 앞 문장까지는 대부분의 생물체 내에 존재하는 생체리듬이 통제되는 방식과 그것의 역할에 대해 설명하고 있으므로 문장의 흐름이 자연스럽다. ③, ④, ⑤ 뒤 문장들은 생체리듬과 조도는 연관성이 있기 때문에 인공조명이 우리의 신체에 영향을 미칠 수 있다고 하며, 빛 외에도 생체리듬 조절에 영향을 줄 수 있는 요인들이 있다고 설명하고 있으므로 문장이 자연스럽게 이어진다.

실력 UP! 미니 문제 02.

정답 ②

해석 ① 생체리듬이 뇌세포에 미치는 영향
② 생체리듬이 우리 몸에서 하는 역할
③ 생물학적 과정에서 빛의 중요성

해설 생체리듬의 정의와 역할, 그리고 특징에 관한 글이므로, 글의 주제로 가장 적절한 것은 ② the role circadian rhythms play in our bodies이다.

03   정답 ⑤

지문분석

Fado is / an important native musical genre / from Portugal.
파두는 ~이다 / 중요한 고유 음악 장르 / 포르투갈의

It has been performed / for nearly 200 years.
그것은 연주되어왔다 / 200년 가까이

(①) Its precise origins are unclear, / but many scholars believe / it began among sailors / in the country's capital city, Lisbon.
그것의 정확한 기원은 분명하지 않다 / 하지만 많은 학자들은 믿는다 / 그것이 선원들 사이에서 시작되었다고 / 그 나라의 수도인 리스본의

(②) Most early examples / deal with the intense longing / for home / that one feels / while living at sea.
초창기 대부분의 전형은 / 강렬한 갈망을 다룬다 / 고향에 대한 / 누군가 느끼는 / 바다에 살면서

(③) ★ At the same time, / the families left behind / also sang these songs / to express their yearning / to see their loved ones again.
동시에 / 남겨진 가족들 / 또한 이 노래를 불렀다 / 갈망을 표현하기 위해 / 그들의 사랑하는 사람들을 다시 보고 싶다는

(④) Over time, / the fado was sung / about other similarly mournful topics, / such as living a life of poverty.
시간이 흐르면서 / 파두는 노래되었다 / 다른 비슷한 구슬픈 주제에 관해 / 빈곤한 삶을 사는 것 같은

(⑤) (Its popularity grew / among the working classes / and extended to people / living in Portugal's colonies.)
그것의 인기는 커졌다 / 노동자 계급에서 / 그리고 사람들에게로 퍼졌다 / 포르투갈의 식민지에 사는

                                 ↻

In the former Portuguese colonies / of Brazil and Indonesia, / for example, / their traditional songs share / characteristics of the fado.
포르투갈의 과거 식민지였던 / 브라질과 인도네시아 / 예를 들어 / 그들의 전통 가요는 같은 ~을 갖는다 / 파두의 특징을

> ★ 독해가 쉬워지는 구문 풀이
>
> At the same time, the families left behind also sang these songs [①to express their yearning] [②to see their loved ones again].
> to부정사(~하기 위해서)　명사　to부정사
>
> ⇨ [①]는 to부정사의 부사적 용법으로, 목적을 의미한다.
> ⇨ [②]는 to부정사의 형용사적 용법으로, 명사 yearning을 수식한다.

[어휘] fado 파두(포르투갈의 민요·춤) precise 정확한 origin 기원
deal with 다루다 intense 강렬한 longing 갈망, 열망 yearning 갈망
mournful 구슬픈 poverty 빈곤 popularity 인기
working class 노동자 계급 extend 퍼지다 colony 식민지

[해석] 파두는 포르투갈의 중요한 고유 음악 장르이다. 그것은 200년 가까이 연주되어왔다. 그것의 정확한 기원은 분명하지 않지만, 많은 학자들은 그것이 그 나라의 수도인 리스본의 선원들 사이에서 시작되었다고 믿는다. 초창기 대부분의 전형은 누군가 바다에 살면서 느끼는 고향에 대한 강렬한 갈망을 다룬다. 동시에, 남겨진 가족들 또한 그들의 사랑하는 사람들을 다시 보고 싶다는 갈망을 표현하기 위해 이 노래를 불렀다. 시간이 흐르면서, 파두는 빈곤한 삶을 사는 것 같은 다른 비슷한 구슬픈 주제에 관해 노래되었다. (노동자 계급에서 그것의 인기는 커졌고 포르투갈의 식민지에 사는 사람들에게로 퍼졌다.) 예를 들어, 포르투갈의 과거 식민지였던 브라질과 인도네시아에서, 그들의 전통 가요는 파두와 같은 특징을 갖는다.

[해설] 주어진 문장의 Portugal's colonies를 통해 주어진 문장 뒤에는 포르투갈의 식민지에 관한 내용이 나와야 한다는 것을 알 수 있다. 주어진 문장의 Portugal's colonies는 ⑤ 뒤 문장의 the former Portuguese colonies of Brazil and Indonesia로 이어지고 있다. 따라서 주어진 문장이 들어가기에 가장 적절한 곳은 ⑤이다.

[오답분석] ⑤ 앞 문장까지는 포르투갈의 중요한 고유 음악 장르인 파두의 기원 및 주제에 대해 설명하는 내용이므로 문장의 흐름이 자연스럽다.

[실력 UP!] 미니 문제 03.
정답 ①
해석 ① 파두의 역사와 특징
② 노동 계급에서 파두의 인기
③ 포르투갈에서 다른 나라로의 파두의 확산
해설 파두의 기원과 노래의 주제 등 그것의 특징에 관한 글이므로, 글의 주제로 가장 적절한 것은 ① the history and characteristics of fado이다. ②과 ③은 지엽적인 내용만 다루고 있어서 정답이 될 수 없다.

04
정답 ⑤

[지문분석]

★ Whenever you can't / make up your mind / about an important life decision, / going for a walk / is a good idea.
당신이 ~할 수 없을 때는 언제나 / 마음을 정하다 / 인생의 중요한 결정에 대해 / 산책을 하러 가는 것은 / 좋은 생각이다

It should not be / an ordinary walk, / however.
그것은 ~이어서는 안 된다 / 평범한 산책 / 그러나

Take each step slowly / and especially pay attention / to your breathing / in order to relax.
각 발걸음을 천천히 내디더라 / 그리고 특히 집중하라 / 당신의 호흡에 / 긴장을 풀기 위해

(①) It helps to inhale deeply / through your nose / and exhale slowly / through your mouth.
그것은 숨을 깊이 들이마시도록 돕는다 / 당신의 코를 통해 / 그리고 천천히 숨을 내쉬도록 / 당신의 입을 통해

(②) The deliberate pace of both / will help you consider your thoughts / more carefully.
두 호흡의 느긋한 속도는 / 당신의 생각을 고찰하도록 도울 것이다 / 더 신중하게

(③) You don't need to worry about / which streets you should take / or where you'll end up.
당신은 ~에 대해 걱정할 필요가 없다 / 어떤 길을 가야 할지 / 또는 마지막에는 어디로 갈지

(④) Instead, / simply enjoy the passing scenery / and let it inspire you / to look at things / from a different perspective.
대신 / 지나가는 풍경을 그저 즐겨라 / 그리고 그것이 당신에게 영감을 주게 해라 / 사물을 보도록 / 다른 시각으로

(⑤) (When you eventually return home, / revisit your issue / with a clear mind.)
당신이 마침내 집에 돌아오면 / 당신의 문제를 다시 돌아보아라 / 명료한 마음을 가지고

By reconsidering your problem / with fresh eyes, / the chances / of making the right decision / greatly increase.
당신의 문제를 재고함으로써 / 새로운 시각으로 / 가능성은 / 옳은 선택을 할 / 대단히 증가한다

> ★ 독해가 쉬워지는 구문 풀이
>
> Whenever you can't make up your mind about an important life
> 복합관계부사
> decision, ~
>
> ⇨ 문맥상 '당신이 마음을 정할 수 없을 때는 언제나'라는 의미가 되어야 자연스러우므로 복합관계부사 Whenever(~할 때는 언제나)가 쓰였다.

[어휘] inhale 숨을 들이마시다 exhale 숨을 내쉬다 deliberate 느긋한
end up 마지막에 ~ 되다 scenery 풍경 inspire 영감을 주다
perspective 시각 revisit 다시 돌아보다 reconsider 재고하다

[해석] [주제문] 당신이 인생의 중요한 결정에 대해 마음을 정할 수 없을 때는 언제나, 산책을 하러 가는 것은 좋은 생각이다. 그러나, 그것은 평범한 산책이어서는 안 된다. 각 발걸음을 천천히 내딛고 긴장을 풀기 위해 당신의 호흡에 특히 집중하라. 그것은 당신의 코를 통해 숨을 깊이 들이마시고 당신의 입을 통해 천천히 숨을 내쉬도록 돕는다. 두 호흡의 느긋한 속도는 당신의 생각을 더 신중하게 고찰하도록 도울 것이다. 당신은 어떤 길을 가야 할지 또는 마지막에는 어디로 갈지에 대해 걱정할 필요 없다. 대신, 지나가는 풍경을 그저 즐기고 그것이 당신에게 사물을 다른 시각으로 보도록 영감을 주게 해라. (당신이 마침내 집에 돌아오면, 명료한 마음을 가지고 당신의 문제를 다시 돌아보아라) 당신의 문제를 새로운 시각으로 재고함으로써, 옳은 선택을 할 가능성은 대단히 증가한다.

[해설] 주어진 문장의 eventually return home을 통해 주어진 문장 앞에는 이미 집을 떠났으나 아직 돌아오지 않은 상황이 묘사되어야 한다. ① 앞에 이미 산책의 시작을 의미하는 going for a walk가 있고, ④ 뒤 문장까지 산책하는 방법에 대해 설명하고 있다. 또한 ⑤ 뒤 문장의 reconsidering your problem with fresh eyes는 주어진 문장의 revisit your issue with a clear mind와 자연스럽게 연결된다. 따라서 주어진 문장이 들어가기에 가장 적절한 곳은 ⑤이다.

[오답분석] ①~④ 문장들은 모두 산책하는 방법에 대한 내용이므로 산책이 끝나고 집에 돌아온 뒤의 내용인 주어진 문장이 들어가기에 적절하지 않다.

[실력 UP!] 미니 문제 04.
정답 삶의 중요한 결정에 대해 마음을 정할 수 없을 때는 산책을 하며 생각을 정리하라.
해설 중요한 결정에 대해 마음을 정할 수 없을 때 호흡과 주변 환경에 집중하고 천천히 산책을 하며 생각을 정리하는 방법에 대한 글이므로, 글의 요지는 '삶의 중요한 결정에 대해 마음을 정할 수 없을 때는 산책을 하며 생각을 정리하라.'이다.

05

정답 ④

지문분석

Associative thinking occurs / when we make connections / in our brain / based on previous experiences.
연상적 사고는 발생한다 / 우리가 연결 지어 생각할 때 / 뇌 속에서 / 이전 경험에 기반해

(①) These connections happen / subconsciously and almost immediately, / causing us / to judge situations quickly.
이러한 연상은 발생한다 / 무의식적이면서도 거의 즉각적으로 / 그리고 이는 우리가 ~하게 한다 / 상황을 빠르게 판단하게

(②) When we meet someone / for the first time, / for instance, / we might associate / the way a person dresses / with a specific personality / based on others / we have met before / who dress the same way.
우리가 누군가를 만날 때 / 처음으로 / 예를 들어 / 우리는 연결 지어 생각할 수 있다 / 개인이 옷을 입는 방식을 / 특정한 성격과 / 다른 사람들에 근거하여 / 우리가 이전에 만났던 / 같은 방식으로 옷을 입는

(③) ★ This is one of the reasons / we think / we can immediately tell a lot / about people / from the moment / we meet them.
이는 이유 중 하나이다 / 우리가 생각하는 / 우리는 많은 것을 바로 알 수 있다고 / 사람들에 대해 / 순간부터 / 우리가 그들을 만난

(④) (However, / this type of thinking / can be unreliable / and lead to incorrect conclusions.)
그러나 / 이런 종류의 사고는 / 신뢰할 수 없다 / 그리고 잘못된 결론으로 이어질 수 있다

The error in judgment / results from our tendency / to build on an initial assumption / by finding evidence / to support it.
이 판단의 오류는 / 우리의 경향에서 비롯된다 / 최초 가정에 의지하는 / 증거를 찾음으로써 / 그것(가정)을 뒷받침할

(⑤) Such an assumption / can cause us to ignore later evidence / that, / although accurate, / contradicts our initial belief.
그러한 가정은 / 우리가 이후의 증거를 무시하도록 만들 수 있다 / ~하는 / 비록 정확하더라도 / 우리의 처음 신념에 반대되는

★ **독해가 쉬워지는 구문 풀이**

This is one of the reasons ①we think ②we can immediately tell a
　　　　　　　　　주어 동사 　　　　　　　　보어
lot about people from the moment ③we meet them.

⇨ ①에는 관계대명사 that이 생략되었다.
⇨ ②에는 명사절 접속사 that이 생략되었다.
⇨ ③에는 관계부사 when이 생략되었다.

어휘 associative thinking 연상적 사고 associate 연결 지어 생각하다
unreliable 신뢰할 수 없는 tendency 경향 build on 의지하다
initial 최초의, 처음의 assumption 가정 accurate 정확한
contradict 반대되다

해석 연상적 사고는 우리가 뇌 속에서 이전 경험에 기반해 연결 지어 생각할 때 발생한다. 이러한 연상은 무의식적이면서도 거의 즉각적으로 발생하는데, 이는 우리가 상황을 빠르게 판단하게 한다. 예를 들어, 우리는 누군가를 처음으로 만날 때 우리가 이전에 만났던, 같은 방식으로 옷을 입는 다른 사람들에 근거하여 개인이 옷을 입는 방식을 특정한 성격과 연결 지어 생각할 수 있다. 이는 우리가 사람들을 만난 순간부터 그들에 대해 많은 것을 바로 알 수 있다고 생각하는 이유 중 하나이다. (주제문) (그러나, 이런 종류의 사고는 신뢰할 수 없으며 잘못된 결론으로 이어질 수 있다) 이 판단의 오류는 최초 가정을 뒷받침할 증거를 찾음으로써 그것(최초 가정)에 의지하는 우리의 경향에서 비롯된다. 그러한 가정은 비록 정확하더라도, 우리의 처음 신념과 반대되는 이후의 증거를 무시하도록 만들 수 있다.

해설 이 글의 ④ 앞 문장까지는 우리는 옷을 입는 방식과 개인의 성격을 연결 지어 생각하는 등 연상적 사고를 통해 상황을 빠르게 판단할 수 있다고 하다가, ④ 뒤 문장부터는 갑자기 판단의 오류에 의지하는 우리의 경향에 대해 언급하므로 ④의 앞과 뒤에서 글의 흐름이 끊기는 것을 알 수 있다. 따

라서 주어진 문장이 들어가기에 가장 적절한 곳은 ④이다.

오답분석 ④ 앞 문장까지는 연상적 사고를 통해 우리는 상황을 빠르게 판단할 수 있다고 하고, 그러한 연상적 사고의 예시를 설명하므로 문장의 흐름이 자연스럽다. ④ 뒤 문장들은 연상적 사고에 따른 판단의 오류가 발생하는 이유를 제시하고, 우리가 의지하는 최초 가정이 어떠한 결과를 가져올 수 있는지 설명하고 있으므로 문장이 자연스럽게 이어진다.

실력 UP! 미니 문제 05.

정답 ③

해석 ① 연상적 사고로 고칠 수 있는 오류들
② 잠재된 감정이 우리의 옷 선택에 영향을 미치는 방식
③ 연상적 사고가 어떻게 잘못된 판단을 초래할 수 있는지

해설 연상적 사고는 우리가 빠른 판단을 할 수 있도록 도움을 주지만, 이러한 판단은 잘못된 결론으로 이어질 수 있다는 것에 관한 글이므로, 글의 주제로 가장 적절한 것은 ③ how associative thinking can result in false judgment이다.

06

정답 ⑤

지문분석

Located in the southern hemisphere, / Australia is the smallest continent / on the planet, / with an area of just over 7,690,000 square kilometers.
남반구에 위치한 / 호주는 가장 작은 대륙이다 / 지구상에서 / 7,690,000 제곱킬로미터가 조금 넘는 면적을 가진

(①) People commonly refer to Australia / as an island, / but it has a number of features / that clearly indicate / that it is a continent.
사람들은 흔히 호주를 지칭하다 / 섬으로 / 그러나 그것은 많은 특성들을 가지고 있다 / 확실하게 나타내는 / 그곳이 대륙이라는 것

(②) To begin with, / while Australia is small by continent standards, / it is nearly four times bigger than Greenland, / which geographers have identified / as the planet's largest island.
우선 / 호주가 대륙의 기준에서는 작지만 / 그것은 그린란드보다 거의 네 배나 크다 / 그것은 지리학자들이 확인했다 / 지구상에서 가장 큰 섬으로

(③) In addition, / the tectonic plate / that Australia is located on / does not include any other continents.
게다가 / 지각판 / 호주가 위치해 있는 / 다른 어떤 대륙들도 포함하지 않는다

(④) This distinguishes it from Greenland, / which is considered to be part of North America / because it is on the same plate / as this continent.
이는 그린란드와 그것을 구별되도록 한다 / 북아메리카의 일부로 여겨지는 / 그것(그린란드)이 같은 판 위에 있기 때문이다 / 이 대륙과

(⑤) (★ Another piece of evidence is / that most of its plant and animal species / cannot be found anywhere else.)
또 다른 증거는 ~이다 / 그곳(호주)의 대부분의 식물과 동물 종 / 다른 곳 어디에서도 찾아볼 수 없다는 것

The presence of these unique life forms / shows / that Australia has been physically separated / from the other continents / for an extremely long period of time.
이러한 독특한 생명체의 존재 / 보여준다 / 호주가 물리적으로 분리되어 있었다는 것 / 다른 대륙들로부터 / 매우 긴 시간 동안

★ **독해가 쉬워지는 구문 풀이**

Another piece of evidence is that most of its plant and animal
　　　주어　　　　　　동사　　　　　　　　보어(명사절)
species cannot be found anywhere else.

⇨ that이 이끄는 절은 be동사(was)의 보어 역할을 하는 명사절이다.

어휘 southern hemisphere 남반구 continent 대륙 refer to 지칭하다
feature 특성 indicate 보여주다 geographer 지리학자 identify 확인하다
distinguish 구별하다 presence 존재 unique 독특한 separate 분리하다

해석 (주제문) 남반구에 위치한 호주는 7,690,000 제곱킬로미터가 조금 넘는 면

적을 가진 지구상에서 가장 작은 대륙이다. 사람들은 흔히 호주를 섬으로 지칭하지만, 호주는 그곳이 대륙이라는 것을 확실하게 나타내는 많은 특성들을 가지고 있다. 우선, 호주가 대륙의 기준에서는 작지만, 그것은 지리학자들이 지구상에서 가장 큰 섬으로 확인한 그린란드보다 거의 네 배나 크다. 게다가, 호주가 위치해 있는 지각판은 다른 어떤 대륙들도 포함하지 않는다. 이는 북아메리카 대륙과 그것(그린란드)이 같은 판 위에 있기 때문에 북아메리카의 일부로 여겨지는 그린란드와 그것을 구별되도록 한다. (또 다른 증거는 그곳(호주)의 대부분의 식물과 동물 종을 다른 곳 어디에서도 찾아볼 수 없다는 것이다.) 이러한 독특한 생명체의 존재는 호주가 매우 긴 시간 동안 다른 대륙들로부터 물리적으로 분리되어 있었다는 것을 보여준다.

[해설] 주어진 문장의 Another piece of evidence(또 다른 증거)를 보아, 주어진 문장 앞에는 증거에 관한 내용이 하나 이상 언급되어야 하며, 이는 ②에서 ④ 뒤 문장까지 이어지는 면적 및 지각판과 관련된 내용들이다. 또한, 주어진 문장의 most of its plant and animal species(대부분의 식물과 동물 종)로 보아, 주어진 문장의 뒤에는 두 번째 증거로서 동식물과 관련한 내용이 나와야 한다는 것을 알 수 있으며, 이는 ⑤ 뒤의 The presence of these unique life forms(이러한 독특한 생명체의 존재)로 이어진다. 따라서 주어진 문장이 들어가기에 가장 적절한 곳은 ⑤이다.

[오답분석] ⑤ 앞 문장까지는 호주가 대륙인 첫 번째 이유와 관련된 면적 및 지각판에 대해 설명하는 내용이므로 문장의 흐름이 자연스럽다.

[실력 UP!] 미니 문제 06.

[정답] It has been physically separated from the other continents for an extremely long period of time

[해석] Q: 독특한 생명체의 존재는 호주에 대해 무엇을 나타내는가?
A: 그것은 매우 긴 시간 동안 다른 대륙들로부터 물리적으로 분리되어 있었다.

[해설] The presence of these unique life forms shows that ~에서 독특한 생명체의 존재는 호주가 매우 긴 시간 동안 다른 대륙들로부터 물리적으로 분리되어 있었음을 보여준다는 것을 알 수 있다.

07
정답 ⑤

[지문분석]

Affecting millions of people worldwide, / eating disorders are psychological conditions / that cause harmful behaviors / when it comes to / eating food.
세계적으로 수백만 명의 사람들에게 영향을 미치는 / 섭식 장애는 정신적인 상태이다 / 위험한 행동을 유발하는 / ~에 관한 / 음식 섭취

(①) Although they can take a variety of forms, / the two most common / affect / how much food is eaten.
그것들은 다양한 유형을 취할 수 있지만, / 가장 흔한 두 가지(유형)은 / 영향을 미치다 / 얼마나 많은 음식이 섭취되는지

(②) Anorexia is an eating disorder / that causes a person to eat too little food, / often resulting in extreme weight loss.
거식증은 섭식 장애이다 / 사람이 너무 적은 양의 음식을 먹게 만드는 / 종종 과도한 체중 감소를 야기하는

(③) In contrast, / bulimia leads an individual / to overeat / and then to force himself or herself / to vomit immediately afterward.
그에 반해서 / 폭식증은 개인을 이끈다 / 과식하도록 / 그리고 그다음 본인에게 강요하도록 / 그 이후 바로 구토하기를

(④) ★ Fortunately, / a method called Cognitive Behavioral Therapy (CBT), / which is highly effective / in helping people overcome eating disorders / has been developed.
다행히도 / 인지 행동 치료라 불리는 방법이 / 굉장히 효과적인 / 사람들이 섭식 장애를 극복하도록 돕는 데 / 개발되었다

(⑤) (This involves teaching patients / to identify harmful behaviors / and replace them with positive ones.)
이것은 환자들을 가르치는 것을 포함한다 / 위험한 행동을 식별하는 것 / 그리고 그것들을 긍정적인 것들로 대체하는 것

For example, / patients with bulimia / who overeat when they feel stressed / may be encouraged / to meditate or exercise instead.
예를 들어 / 폭식증 환자들은 / 스트레스를 받을 때 과식하는 / 장려될 것이다 / 대신에 명상이나 운동을 하도록

★ 독해가 쉬워지는 구문 풀이
Fortunately, a method [①called Cognitive Behavioral Therapy (CBT)], [②**which is highly effective in helping people overcome** eating disorders] has been developed.
과거분사구문
수식어(관계절)
⇨ [①]은 수식 받는 명사 a method가 call이 나타내는 '부르는' 행위의 대상이므로 과거분사 called가 쓰였다.
⇨ [②]은 선행사 a method를 수식하는 주격 관계대명사절이다.

[어휘] disorder 장애 psychological 정신적인 condition 질환, 상태
anorexia 거식증 bulimia 폭식증, 과식 overeat 과식하다 vomit 구토하다
Cognitive Behavioral Therapy(CBT) 인지 행동 치료
overcome 극복하다 identify 식별하다 encourage 장려하다
meditate 명상하다

[해석] 세계적으로 수백만 명의 사람들에게 영향을 미치는, 섭식 장애는 음식 섭취에 관한 위험한 행동을 유발하는 정신적인 질환이다. 그것들은 다양한 유형을 취할 수 있지만, 가장 흔한 두 가지 유형은 얼마나 많은 음식이 섭취되는지에 영향을 미친다. 거식증은 사람이 너무 적은 양의 음식을 먹게 만들어 종종 과도한 체중 감소를 야기하는 섭식 장애이다. 그에 반해서, 폭식증은 개인이 과식을 한 다음 그 이후 본인에게 바로 구토하기를 강요하도록 이끈다. 다행히도, 사람들이 섭식 장애를 극복하도록 돕는 데 굉장히 효율적인 인지 행동 치료라 불리는 방법이 개발되었다. (이것은 환자들이 위험한 행동을 식별하고 그것들을 긍정적인 것들로 대체하는 것을 가르치는 것을 포함한다.) 예를 들어, 스트레스를 받을 때 과식하는 폭식증 환자들은 대신에 명상이나 운동을 하도록 장려될 것이다.

[해설] 주어진 문장의 This involves teaching patients(이것은 환자들을 가르치는 것을 포함한다)를 보아 주어진 문장 앞에는 환자를 가르치는 것과 관련된 내용이 언급되어야 하며, 이는 ⑤ 앞 문장의 Cognitive Behavioral Therapy (CBT)를 지칭한다. 또한, 주어진 문장의 replace them with positive ones(긍정적인 것들로 대체하다)로 보아, 주어진 문장의 뒤에는 위험한 행동이 긍정적인 것들로 대체된 것과 관련된 내용이 나와야 한다는 것을 알 수 있다. ⑤ 뒤 문장에서 '폭식증 환자들은 대신에 명상이나 운동을 하도록 장려될 것이다'라고 했으므로 주어진 문장이 들어가기에 가장 적절한 곳은 ⑤이다.

[오답분석] ⑤ 앞 문장까지는 섭식 장애의 정의와 그것의 가장 흔한 두 가지 유형에 대해 설명하는 내용이므로 문장의 흐름이 자연스럽다.

[실력 UP!] 미니 문제 07.

[정답] (A) harmful (B) overcome

[해석] 섭식 장애가 널리 퍼졌고 (A) 위험한 행동들을 이끌지라도, 인지 행동 치료라고 불리는 치료법은 사람들이 이러한 질환을 (B) 극복하도록 돕는 데 성공적인 것으로 드러났다.

[해설] 세계적으로 수백만 명의 사람들에게 영향을 미치는 섭식 장애는 음식 섭취에 관한 위험한 행동을 유발하는 정신적인 질환이라고 했고, 이것을 극복하도록 돕는 데 굉장히 효율적인 인지 행동 치료라 불리는 방법이 개발되었다고 했으므로, 요약문의 빈칸에 들어갈 말로 가장 적절한 것은 (A) harmful(위험한), (B) overcome(극복하다)이다.

08

지문분석

Self-sabotage may seem / like contradictory behavior / for someone who wants to succeed, / but a surprising number of people / do this.
자기 훼방은 보일 수도 있다 / 모순된 행동처럼 / 성공하고 싶은 사람에게 / 하지만 놀랄 정도로 많은 사람들이 / 이 행동을 한다

(①) One of the biggest reasons is / that most people do not like / believing themselves unintelligent.
가장 큰 이유 중 하나는 ~이다 / 대부분의 사람은 좋아하지 않는다는 것 / 그들 자신이 어리석다고 생각하는 것을

(②) For example, / if students intentionally avoid studying / for a difficult exam / and then get poor scores, / they can justify the results / by saying / they didn't study.
예를 들어 / 만약 학생들이 공부를 일부러 하지 않는다면 / 어려운 시험의 / 그러고 나서 부진한 점수를 받는다 / 그들은 결과를 정당화할 수 있다 / 말함으로써 / 그들은 공부를 하지 않았다고

(③) Others might point to / a lack of sleep / or being distracted / by personal problems.
다른 학생들은 언급할 수도 있다 / 수면 부족이라고 / 또는 방해 받았다고 / 개인적인 일들로 인해

(④) By blaming something / other than their ability, / students can feel better / about failing / because it wasn't really their fault.
다른 것을 탓함으로써 / 그들의 능력 대신 / 학생들은 기분이 나아질 수 있다 / 실패한 것에 대해 / 이는 그것이 실제로 그들의 잘못이 아니었기 때문이다

(⑤) (On the other hand, / if they do prepare and fail, / they cannot attribute their failure / to outside factors.)
반면에 / 만약 그들이 정말로 준비하고도 실패한다면 / 그들은 실패를 돌릴 수 없다 / 외부 요인의 탓으로

★ That is, / they only failed because / even after studying, / it turns out / that they were not smart enough / to pass the test.
즉 / 그들은 ~ 때문에 그냥 망친 것이다 / 공부를 했음에도 불구하고 / 알고 보니 ~이다 / 그들이 충분히 똑똑하지 않았다 / 시험을 통과할 만큼

★ 독해가 쉬워지는 구문 풀이

That is, they only failed because even after studying, it turns out that they were not smart enough to pass the test.
　　　　　　　　　　　　　　　　　　　　　　　형용사

▷ '충분히 똑똑한'이라는 의미로 enough가 형용사 smart를 수식하고 있으므로, smart 뒤에 쓰였다.

▷ 문장 구조를 재배열하면 다음과 같다. That is, it turns out that they only failed because they were not smart enough to pass the test, even after studying.

어휘 contradictory 모순된　unintelligent 어리석은　justify 정당화하다
point 언급하다, 가리키다　distract 방해하다　blame ~를 탓하다
attribute ~탓으로 돌리다

해설 **주제문** 성공하고 싶은 사람에게 자기 훼방은 모순된 행동처럼 보일 수도 있지만, 놀랄 정도로 많은 사람들이 이 행동을 한다. 가장 큰 이유 중 하나는 대부분의 사람은 그들 자신이 어리석다고 생각하는 것을 좋아하지 않는다는 것이다. 예를 들어, 만약 학생들이 어려운 시험의 공부를 일부러 하지 않고 나서, 부진한 점수를 받는다면, 그들은 공부하지 않았다고 말함으로써 결과를 정당화할 수 있다. 다른 학생들은 수면 부족이라거나 개인적인 일들로 인해 방해 받았다고 언급할 수도 있다. 그들의 능력 대신 다른 것을 탓함으로써, 학생들은 실패한 것에 대해 기분이 나아질 수 있는데 이는 그것이 실제로 그들의 잘못이 아니었기 때문이다. (반면에, 만약 그들이 정말로 준비하고도 실패한다면, 그들은 실패를 외부 요인의 탓으로 돌릴 수 없다.) 즉, 그들은 그냥 망친 것인데, 공부를 했음에도 불구하고 알고 보니 그들이 시험을 통과할 만큼 충분히 똑똑하지 않았기 때문이다.

해설 주어진 문장의 if they do prepare and fail~(그들이 정말로 준비하고도 실패한다면)을 통해 주어진 문장 뒤에는 준비를 제대로 하고도 실패한 내용이 이어져야 함을 알 수 있다. 또한, they cannot attribute their failure to outside factors를 통해 주어진 문장의 뒤에는 실패를 외부 요인의 탓으로 돌릴 수 없다는 내용이 이어져야 함을 알 수 있다. 주어진 문장의 On the other hand를 통해 주어진 문장의 앞과 뒤 내용이 서로 반대되어야 함을 알 수 있고, 주어진 문장의 내용을 통해 학생들이 제대로 준비하고 실패하면 외부 요인을 탓할 수 없다는 것과 관련된 내용이 뒤이어 나와야 함을 알 수 있다. ⑤ 앞 문장까지 학생들이 준비하지 않고 외부 요인을 탓하는 내용이 왔고, ⑤ 뒤 문장에서 공부를 했음에도 학생들이 충분히 똑똑하지 않아서 시험을 망쳤다는 내용이 나왔으므로 주어진 문장이 들어가기에 가장 적절한 곳은 ⑤이다.

오답분석 ⑤ 앞 문장까지는 많은 사람들이 자기 훼방이라는 행동을 하는 이유를 설명하고, 그것의 예시로서 학생들이 어려운 시험의 공부를 일부러 하지 않는 경우에 대한 내용만을 언급하므로 문장의 흐름이 자연스럽다.

실력 UP! 미니 문제 08.

정답 ⓐ contradictory　ⓑ intentionally

해석 ⓐ 어떤 것이 그 자체와 모순되게 하는 것
　　　ⓑ 의도적으로 그리고 고의로 행해진

CHAPTER 15 요약문 완성하기

불변의 패턴 29　　　　　　　　　　p.114
요약문은 글의 핵심 내용을 간추린 요지이다.

기출 문제

지문분석

In one study, / researchers asked pairs of strangers / to sit down / in a room / and chat.
한 연구에서 / 연구원들은 짝을 이룬 모르는 사람들이 ~하게 했다 / 앉도록 / 한 방에 / 그리고 이야기하도록

In half of the rooms, / a cell phone was placed / on a nearby table; / in the other half, / no phone was present.
그 방의 절반에는 / 휴대전화가 놓여 있었다 / 근처의 탁자 위에 / 그리고 다른 절반에는 / 휴대전화가 없었다

After the conversations had ended, / the researchers asked the participants / what they thought / of each other.
대화가 끝난 후 / 연구원들은 참가자들에게 물었다 / 어떻게 생각했는지를 / 서로에 대해

Here's / what they learned: / when a cell phone was present / in the room, / the participants reported / the quality / of their relationship / was worse / than those who'd talked / in a cell phone-free room.
여기 있다 / 그들이 알게 된 것 / 휴대전화가 있었을 때 / 방에 / 참가자들은 전했다 / 질이 / 그들의 관계의 / 더 나빴다고 / 이야기했던 사람들보다 / 휴대전화가 없는 방에서

The pairs / who talked in the rooms / with cell phones / thought / their partners showed less empathy.
짝들은 / 방에서 이야기했던 / 휴대폰이 있는 / 생각했다 / 그들의 파트너가 더 적은 공감을 보여주었다고

★ Think / of all the times / you've sat down / to have lunch / with a friend / and set your phone / on the table.
떠올려보아라 / 모든 때를 / 당신이 앉았던 / 점심을 먹기 위해 / 친구와 / 그리고 당신의 휴대전화를 놓았다 / 탁자 위에

You might have felt good / about yourself / because you didn't pick it up / to check your messages, / but your unchecked messages / were still hurting your connection / with the person / sitting across from you.
당신이 좋게 느꼈을 수도 있다 / 당신 스스로에 대해 / 휴대전화를 집지 않았기 때문에 / 메시지를 확인하기 위해 / 하지만 당신의 확인되지 않은 메시지는 / 여전히 관계를 망치고 있었다 / 사람과의 / 당신 맞은편에 앉아 있는

⇩

The presence of a cell phone / (A) weakens the connection / between people / involved in conversations, / even when the phone is being (B) ignored.
휴대전화의 존재는 / 관계를 약화한다 / 사람들 간의 / 대화에 참여하는 / 심지어 휴대전화가 무시되고 있을 때도

★ 독해가 쉬워지는 구문 풀이

Think of all the times [you've **sat** down to have lunch with a friend
명령문의
동사원형
and (have) **set** your phone on the table].

⇨ 명령문은 주로 주어를 생략한 채 동사원형(Think)을 사용한다.
⇨ 과거분사 sat과 set은 등위접속사 and로 연결되어 병렬 구조를 이루며, 반복되는 have는 생략되었다.

[어휘] report 전하다, 알리다 involve 참여하다, 관여하다 [선택지] renew 갱신하다

[해석] 한 연구에서, 연구원들은 짝을 이룬 모르는 사람들이 한 방에 앉아서 이야기하도록 했다. 그 방의 절반에는 근처의 탁자 위에 휴대전화가 놓여 있었고, 다른 절반에는 휴대전화가 없었다. 대화가 끝난 후, 연구원들은 참가자들에게 서로에 대해 어떻게 생각했는지를 물었다. 여기 그들이 알게 된 것이 있다: 방에 휴대전화가 있었을 때, 참가자들은 휴대전화가 없는 방에서 이야기했던 사람들보다 그들의 관계의 질이 더 나빴다고 전했다. 휴대폰이 있는 방에서 이야기했던 짝들은 그들의 파트너가 더 적은 공감을 보여주었다고 생각했다. 당신이 친구와 점심을 먹기 위해 앉아서 탁자 위에 당신의 휴대전화를 놓았던 모든 때를 떠올려보라. 당신이 메시지를 확인하기 위해 휴대전화를 집지 않았기 때문에 당신 스스로에 대해 좋게 느꼈을 수도 있지만, 당신의 확인되지 않은 메시지는 여전히 당신 맞은편에 앉아 있는 사람과의 관계를 망치고 있었다.

⇩

휴대전화의 존재는 심지어 휴대전화가 (B) 무시되고 있을 때도 대화에 참여하는 사람들 간의 관계를 (A) 약화한다.

　　(A)　　　　(B)
① 약화하다 … 응답되다
② 약화하다 … 무시되다
③ 갱신하다 … 응답되다
④ 유지하다 … 무시되다
⑤ 유지하다 … 업데이트되다

[해설] 요약문은 휴대전화의 존재는 심지어 휴대전화가 '(B)되고' 있을 때도 대화에 참여하는 사람들 간의 관계를 '(A)한다'는 내용이다. 글에서 탁자에 놓인 휴대전화는 메시지를 확인하지 않더라도 맞은편에 앉아서 대화하고 있는 사람과의 관계를 망친다고 했다. 요약문의 (A)에는 글에서 언급된 'showed less empathy', 'hurting your connection'과 관련된 'weakens'가, (B)에는 글에서 언급된 'didn't pick it up', 'unchecked'와 관련된 'ignored'가 적절하므로 ② weakens(약화하다) - ignored(무시되다)가 정답이다.

[오답분석] 탁자에 놓인 휴대전화가 맞은편에 앉아서 대화에 참여하는 사람과의 관계를 망친다고 했으므로 ③의 renews, ④와 ⑤의 maintains는 (A)에 들

어갈 단어로 적절하지 않다. 휴대폰을 집어 메시지를 확인하지 않더라도 탁자에 놓인 휴대전화가 다른 사람과의 관계에 영향을 미친다고 했으므로 ①과 ③의 answered, ⑤의 updated는 (B)에 들어갈 단어로 적절하지 않다.

불변의 패턴 30　　　　　　　　　　　p.115
핵심 단어를 다르게 표현한 단어가 정답이다.

기출 문제　　　　　　　　　　　정답 ①

[지문분석]

The wife / of American physiologist Hudson Hoagland / became sick / with a severe flu.
아내 / 미국의 생리학자인 Hudson Hoagland의 / 아프게 되었다 / 심한 독감으로

Dr. Hoagland was curious / enough to notice / that whenever he left his wife's room / for a short while, / she complained / that he had been gone / for a long time.
Hoagland 박사는 호기심이 많았다 / 주목할 만큼 충분히 / 그가 아내의 방을 떠날 때마다 / 잠시 동안 / 그녀가 불평하는 것을 / 그가 없었다고 / 오랫동안

★ In the interest of / scientific investigation, / he asked his wife / to count to 60, / with each count / corresponding / to what she felt was one second, / while he kept a record / of her temperature.
~를 위해 / 과학적 연구 / 그는 아내에게 요청했다 / 60까지 세어달라고 / 각각의 횟수로 / 해당하는 / 그녀가 1초라고 느낀 것에 / 그가 기록하는 동안 / 그녀의 체온을

His wife reluctantly accepted / and he quickly noticed / that the hotter she was, / the faster she counted.
그의 아내는 마지못해 받아들였다 / 그리고 그는 금세 알아차렸다 / 그녀가 열이 나면 날수록 / 더 빨리 숫자를 센다는 것을

When her temperature was 38 degrees Celsius, / for instance, / she counted / to 60 / in 45 seconds.
그녀의 체온이 섭씨 38도였을 때 / 예를 들어 / 그녀는 세었다 / 60까지 / 45초 만에

He repeated the experiment / a few more times, / and found / that when her temperature / reached 39.5 degrees Celsius, / she counted one minute / in just 37 seconds.
그는 실험을 반복했다 / 몇 번 더 / 그리고 발견했다 / 그녀의 체온이 / 섭씨 39.5도에 이르렀을 때 / 그녀가 1분을 세었다는 것을 / 단 37초 만에

The doctor thought / that his wife / must have some kind of 'internal clock' / inside her brain / that ran faster / as the fever went up.
그 박사는 생각했다 / 그의 아내가 / 일종의 '체내 시계'를 가지고 있음이 틀림없다고 / 머릿속에 / 더 빨리 가는 / 열이 높아질수록

⇩

The results of Dr. Hoagland's investigation / showed / that his wife felt (A) more time had passed / than actually had / as her body temperature (B) increased.
Hoagland 박사의 연구 결과는 / 보여주었다 / 그의 아내가 더 많은 시간이 흘렀던 것처럼 느꼈음을 / 실제보다 / 그녀의 체온이 높아짐에 따라

★ 독해가 쉬워지는 구문 풀이

In the interest of scientific investigation, he asked his wife to count to 60, with each count corresponding to [{①what she felt}
　　　　　　　　　　　　　　　　　전치사　　　목적어(명사절)
was {②one second}], while he kept a record of her temperature.

⇨ 명사절 [ ]는 전치사 to의 목적어이다.
⇨ {①}은 명사절의 주어, {②}는 보어이다.

[어휘] in the interest of ~을 위해 investigation 연구, 조사 corresponding (~에) 해당하는, 상응하는 reluctantly 마지못해, 억지로 internal 체내의, 내부의

해석 미국의 생리학자인 Hudson Hoagland의 아내가 심한 독감으로 아프게
해석 미국의 생리학자인 Hudson Hoagland의 아내가 심한 독감으로 아프게 되었다. Hoagland 박사는 그가 잠시 동안 아내의 방을 떠날 때마다, 그가 오랫동안 없었다고 그녀가 불평하는 것을 주목할 만큼 충분히 호기심이 많았다. 과학적 연구를 위해, 그가 그녀의 체온을 기록하는 동안, 그는 아내에게 1초라고 느낀 것에 해당하는 각각의 횟수로 60까지 세어달라고 요청했다. 그의 아내는 마지못해 받아들였고, 그는 그녀가 열이 나면 날수록 더 빨리 숫자를 센다는 것을 금세 알아차렸다. 예를 들어, 그녀의 체온이 섭씨 38도였을 때, 그녀는 45초 만에 60까지 세었다. 그는 몇 번 더 실험을 반복했고, 그녀의 체온이 섭씨 39.5도에 이르렀을 때, 그녀가 단 37초 만에 1분을 세었다는 것을 발견했다. 그 박사는 그의 아내가 열이 높아질수록 더 빨리 가는 일종의 '체내 시계'를 머릿속에 가지고 있음이 틀림없다고 생각했다.

⇩

> Hoagland 박사의 연구 결과는 그의 아내가 체온이 (B) 높아짐에 따라, 실제보다 (A) 더 많은 시간이 흘렀던 것처럼 느꼈음을 보여 주었다.

    (A)   (B)
① 더 많은 … 높아졌다
② 더 많은 … 낮아졌다
③ 더 적은 … 높아졌다
④ 더 적은 … 낮아졌다
⑤ 더 적은 … 변했다

해설 Hoagland 박사의 아내가 체온이 '(B)함'에 따라, 실제보다 '(A)한' 시간이 흘렀던 것처럼 느꼈다는 내용이다. 글에서 Hoagland의 아내가 열이 나면 날수록 더 빨리 숫자를 셌다고 했다. 요약문의 (A)에는 글에서 언급된 'the faster she counted'와 관련된 'more'가, (B)에는 글에서 언급된 'the hotter she was', 'the fever went up'과 관련된 'increased'가 적절하므로 ① more(더 많은) - increased(높아졌다)가 정답이다.

오답분석 열이 나면 날수록 더 빨리 숫자를 셌다고 했으므로 ③, ④, ⑤의 less는 (A)에 들어갈 단어로 적절하지 않다. 아내가 열이 높아질수록 '체내 시계'가 더 빨리 가는 것 같다고 했으므로 ②과 ④의 decreased, 그리고 ⑤의 changed은 (B)에 들어갈 단어로 적절하지 않다.

독해 만점 TEST
p.116

01 ③ 02 ③ 03 ④ 04 ② 05 ② 06 ④ 07 ③ 08 ⑤

실력 UP! 미니 문제

01. (많은 양의 돈을 잃을 것 같을 때) 감정이 장악하여 더 나은 판단과는 반대로 행동하는 경향

02. 아침형 인간: 더 긍정적이고 우울증, 중독 그리고 다른 강박적인 행동을 보일 가능성이 더 적다, 저녁형 인간보다 오래 사는 경향이 있다
저녁형 인간: 뇌에 백질이 더 적고, 창의적이고, 더 높은 지적 능력을 가지고 있다, 아침형 인간보다 수명이 짧다

03. ⓐ citizens ⓑ generalists

04. 그러나, 시간이 지남에 따라 인류는 농업을 발전시켰고, 그에 따라 음식이 더 부드러워졌다.

05. Constantly pursuing wealth and social status will not result in satisfaction

06. noticing variations in brightness

07. the secret words and phrases shared exclusively among the members of a household

08. ⓐ Those assigned to play guards
ⓑ the students playing prisoners

지문분석

People tend to / let their emotions take over / and act / against their better judgment / when they stand to lose / a large amount of money.
사람들은 ~하는 경향이 있다 / 그들의 감정이 장악하게 하는 / 그리고 행동한다 / 더 나은 판단과는 반대로 / 그들이 잃을 것 같을 때 / 많은 양의 돈을

This erroneous thinking / is called the gambler's fallacy, / and the most famous example / occurred in 1913 / at the Monte Carlo Casino.
이러한 잘못된 사고는 / 도박꾼의 오류라고 불린다 / 그리고 가장 유명한 예시는 / 1913년에 발생했다 / Monte Carlo 카지노에서

Because the roulette ball had landed on black / 26 times in a row, / gamblers concluded / that the probability of it landing on black again / was next to impossible.
룰렛 공이 검은색 위에 멈춰 섰기 때문에 / 스물여섯 번 연속으로 / 도박꾼들은 단정했다 / 그것이 다시 검은색에 멈춰 설 확률은 / 거의 있을 수 없다고

★ They used this, / their knowledge of what had already happened, / to inform their next move.
그들은 이것을 이용했다 / 즉 그들이 이미 일어난 일에 대한 정보를 / 다음 수를 알아내기 위해서

They bet all their money / on red, / but the ball landed / on black yet again, / and they ultimately lost.
그들은 돈 전부를 걸었다 / 빨간색에 / 하지만 공은 멈춰 섰다 / 또다시 검은색에 / 그리고 그들은 결국 졌다

This is because, / according to the laws of probability, / there is always an equal chance / of the ball landing on black or red / in roulette, / regardless of any earlier lucky "coincidences."
왜냐하면 이것은 ~하기 때문이다 / 확률의 법칙에 따르면 / 확률은 항상 같다 / 공이 검은색이나 빨간색에 멈춰 설 / 룰렛에서 / 행운이 깃든 어떠한 앞선 "우연"과도 상관없이

Essentially, / each spin produces a random result / that is unrelated to any / before it.
본래 / 각각의 스핀은 무작위의 결과를 도출한다 / 어떠한 것(스핀)과도 관련 없는 / 그것 이전의

⇩

> In gambling, / people mistakenly make decisions / based on (A) previous outcomes / when each event is actually (B) independent.
> 도박에서 / 사람들은 잘못된 결정을 내린다 / 이전의 결과에 기반한 / 각 사건이 실제로 서로 관련이 없을 때에도

★ 독해가 쉬워지는 구문 풀이

They used this, [①their knowledge of what had already happened], [②to inform their next move].
           삽입구

⇨ [①]은 this를 부연 설명하기 위해 삽입된 명사구이다.
⇨ [②]는 to부정사의 부사적 용법으로, 목적의 의미를 나타낸다.

어휘 take over 장악하다, 차지하다 judgment 판단 stand to ~할 것 같다 erroneous 잘못된 fallacy 오류 probability 확률 impossible 있을 수 없는 coincidence 우연 essentially 본래, 기본적으로 mistakenly 잘못하여
선택지 independent 서로 관련이 없는 unpredictable 예측 불가능한

해석 **주제문** 사람들은 그들이 많은 양의 돈을 잃을 것 같을 때 그들의 감정이 장악하게 하고, 더 나은 판단과는 반대로 행동하는 경향이 있다. 이러한 잘못된 사고는 도박꾼의 오류라고 불리며, 가장 유명한 예시는 1913년 Monte Carlo 카지노에서 발생했다. 룰렛 공이 스물여섯 번 연속으로 검은색 위에 멈춰 섰기 때문에, 도박꾼들은 그것이 다시 검은색에 멈춰 설 확률은 거의 있을 수 없다고 단정했다. 그들은 다음 수를 알아내기 위해서 이것, 즉 이미 일어난 일에 대한 정보를 이용했다. 그들은 돈 전부를 빨간

색에 걸었지만, 공은 또다시 검은색에 멈춰 섰고, 그들은 결국 졌다. 왜냐하면 이것은 확률의 법칙에 따르면, 공이 룰렛에서 검은색이나 빨간색에 멈춰 설 확률은 행운이 깃든 어떠한 앞선 "우연들"과도 상관없이 항상 같기 때문이다. 본래, 각각의 스핀은 그것 이전의 어떠한 것(스핀)과도 관련 없는 무작위의 결과를 도출한다.

⇩

> 도박에서, 각 사건이 실제로 (B) 서로 관련이 없을 때에도 사람들은 (A) 이전의 결과에 기반한 잘못된 결정을 내린다.

	(A)		(B)
①	이전의	…	의도된
②	알려지지 않은	…	실제적인
③	이전의	…	서로 관련이 없는
④	긍정적인	…	가능성 있는
⑤	알려지지 않은	…	예측 불가능한

[해설] 요약문은 도박에서 각 사건이 실제로는 '(B)'일 때에도 사람들은 '(A)'의 결과에 기반하여 잘못된 결정을 내린다는 내용이다. 글에서 Monte Carlo 카지노에서 도박꾼들은 다음 수를 알아내기 위해서 이미 일어난 일에 대한 정보를 이용했는데, 공이 룰렛의 검은색이나 빨간색에 멈춰 설 확률은 어떠한 앞선 우연들과도 상관없이 항상 같기 때문에 그들은 졌다고 설명했다. 따라서 요약문의 (A)에는 글에서 언급된 'earlier', 'before'와 관련된 'previous'가, (B)에는 글에서 언급된 'regardless of', 'random', 'unrelated to'와 관련된 'independent'가 적절하므로 ③ previous(이전의) - independent(서로 관련이 없는)가 정답이다.

[오답분석] 1913년 Monte Carlo 카지노의 예시는 이미 일어난 일을 근거로 잘못된 선택을 내리는 것을 보여주므로 ②과 ⑤의 unknown, ④의 positive는 (A)에 들어갈 단어로 적절하지 않다. 도박의 각 사건은 확률적으로 무작위의 결과를 도출한다고 했으므로 ①의 intended, ②의 real, ④ likely는 (B)에 들어갈 단어로 적절하지 않다.

[실력 UP!] 미니 문제 01.

정답 (많은 양의 돈을 잃을 것 같을 때) 감정이 장악하여 더 나은 판단과는 반대로 행동하는 경향

해설 바로 앞 문장에서 "사람들은 많은 돈을 잃을 것 같을 때 감정이 장악하여 더 나은 판단과는 반대로 행동하는 경향이 있다"고 한 후, 이러한 잘못된 사고(This erroneous thinking)는 도박꾼의 오류라 불린다고 하였으므로, ⓐThis erroneous thinking은 "(많은 양의 돈을 잃을 것 같을 때) 감정이 장악하여 더 나은 판단과는 반대로 행동하는 경향"을 의미한다.

02
정답 ③

[지문분석]

Your sleeping habits / could reveal quite a lot / about you, / such as the type of personality / you are likely to have, / the composition of your brain, / and even how long / you may be expected to live.
당신의 수면 습관은 / 꽤 많은 걸 알려줄 수 있다 / 당신에 대해 / 예를 들어 성격의 유형 등 / 당신이 가지고 있을 법한 / 당신의 뇌 구조 / 그리고 심지어 얼마나 오래 / 당신이 살 것으로 예상되는지

As it happens, / morning people tend to display / more positive social traits / and are less prone to / depression, addiction, and other obsessive behavior.
공교롭게도 / 아침형 인간은 보이는 경향이 있다 / 더 긍정적인 사회적 특성을 / 그리고 ~할 가능성이 더 적다 / 우울증, 중독 그리고 다른 강박적인 행동

Doctors believe / these factors contribute to / a longer lifespan.
의사들은 생각한다 / 이러한 요소가 ~에 도움이 된다고 / 더욱 긴 수명

Night people, / on the other hand, / have less white matter in their brains, / and as a result / have fewer pathways / for feel-good hormones / such as serotonin.
저녁형 인간은 / 반면 / 뇌에 백질이 더 적다 / 그래서 결과적으로 / 경로를 더 적게 가지고 있다 / 기분을 좋게 해주는 호르몬이 다니는 / 세로토닌과 같은

★ Although / night people / tend to be more creative / and have higher intellectual abilities / than morning types, / going against the body's natural rhythm / over a prolonged period / can also shorten their lifespan.
비록 ~이긴 하지만 / 저녁형 인간이 / 더 창의적인 경향이 있다 / 그리고 더 높은 지적 능력을 가지고 있다 / 아침형 인간보다 / 신체의 자연스러운 리듬을 거스르는 것은 / 장기간에 걸쳐 / 그들의 수명을 또한 단축할 수도 있다

⇩

> Morning people are more likely / to be (A) optimistic / and live longer lives, / whereas night people are likely / to be more (B) intelligent and creative.
> 아침형 인간은 더 ~하는 경향이 있다 / 긍정적인 / 그리고 오래 사는 / 반면 저녁형 인간은 ~하는 경향이 있다 / 더 지적이고 창의적인

★ 독해가 쉬워지는 구문 풀이

[①Although night people tend to be more creative and have
부사절 접속사
higher intellectual abilities than morning types], [②going against
the body's natural rhythm over a prolonged period] can also
동명사구(주어)
shorten their lifespan.

⇨ [①]은 '비록 ~이지만'이라는 양보의 의미를 나타내는 부사절이다.
⇨ [②]는 동명사구로, 주절의 주어 자리에 쓰였다.

[어휘] sleeping habit 수면 습관 reveal 알려주다, 밝히다 composition 구조, 구성
as it happens 공교롭게도, 마침 display (감정·성질 등을) 보이다, 나타내다
trait 특성 prone to ~할 가능성이 있다 depression 우울증
obsessive 강박적인 contribute to ~에 도움이 되다, 기여하다
white matter (뇌·척수의) 백질 pathway 경로 intellectual 지적의
prolonged 장기의, 오래 계속되는 [선택지] disciplined 훈련 받은
optimistic 긍정적인, 낙관적인 advantageous 유리한

[해석] [주제문] 당신의 수면 습관은 예를 들어 당신이 가지고 있을 법한 성격의 유형, 당신의 뇌 구조, 그리고 심지어 당신이 얼마나 오래 살 것으로 예상되는지 등 당신에 대해 꽤 많은 걸 알려줄 수 있다. 공교롭게도, 아침형 인간은 더 긍정적인 사회적 특성을 보이는 경향이 있고 우울증, 중독 그리고 다른 강박적인 행동을 할 가능성이 더 적다. 의사들은 이러한 요소가 더욱 긴 수명에 도움이 된다고 생각한다. 반면 저녁형 인간은 뇌에 백질이 더 적어서, 결과적으로 세로토닌과 같은 기분을 좋게 해주는 호르몬이 다니는 경로를 더 적게 가지고 있다. 비록 저녁형 인간이 아침형 인간보다 더 창의적이고 더 높은 지적 능력을 가지고 있는 경향이 있긴 하지만, 장기간에 걸쳐 신체의 자연스러운 리듬을 거스르는 것은 그들의 수명을 또한 단축할 수도 있다.

⇩

> 아침형 인간은 더 (A) 긍정적이고 오래 사는 경향이 있는 반면, 저녁형 인간은 더 (B) 지적이고 창의적인 경향이 있다.

	(A)	(B)
①	쾌활한	자신감 있는
②	쾌활한	훈련 받은
③	긍정적인	지적인
④	긍정적인	제한된
⑤	유리한	성공한

[해설] 요약문은 아침형 인간이 저녁형 인간보다 더 '(A)하고' 오래 사는 경향이

있는 반면, 저녁형 인간은 아침형 인간보다 더 '(B)하고' 창의적인 경향이 있다는 내용이다. 글에서 아침형 인간은 더 긍정적인 사회적 특성을 보이면서 우울증, 중독, 다른 강박적인 행동을 덜 겪어 긴 수명에 도움이 된다고 했고, 저녁형 인간은 더 창의적이고 지적 능력이 높은 경향이 있지만, 장기간 신체의 정상적인 리듬을 거스름에 따라 그들의 수명을 단축할 수 있다고 했다. 따라서 요약문의 (A)에는 글에서 언급된 'positive'와 관련된 'optimistic'이, (B)에는 글에서 언급된 'higher intellectual abilities'와 관련된 'intelligent'가 적절하므로 ③ optimistic(긍정적인) - intelligent(지적인)가 정답이다.

오답분석 아침형 인간이 더 긍정적인 사회적 특성을 보이는 경향이 있다고 했으므로 ①과 ②의 cheerful, ④의 optimistic 모두 답이 될 수 있지만, 그와 짝을 이루는 ① confident, ② disciplined, ④ limited는 저녁형 인간의 특성으로 언급되지 않았으므로 오답이다. ⑤의 advantageous와 successful 역시 글의 내용과 관련 없으므로 오답이다.

실력 UP! 미니 문제 02.

정답 아침형 인간: 더 긍정적이고 우울증, 중독 그리고 다른 강박적인 행동을 보일 가능성이 더 적다, 저녁형 인간보다 오래 사는 경향이 있다
저녁형 인간: 뇌에 백질이 더 적고, 창의적이고, 더 높은 지적 능력을 가지고 있다, 아침형 인간보다 수명이 짧다

해설 아침형 인간: morning people tend to ~ longer life span에서 아침형 인간은 더 긍정적인 사회적 특성을 보이는 경향이 있고 우울증, 중독 그리고 다른 강박적인 행동을 보일 가능성이 더 적으며 더 긴 수명에 도움이 되는 특징을 가진다는 내용이 나온다.
저녁형 인간: Night people, on the other hand ~ their lifespan에서 저녁형 인간은 뇌에 백질이 더 적고, 더 창의적이고 더 높은 지적 능력을 가지고 있는 경향이 있으나, 장기간에 걸쳐 신체의 자연스러운 리듬을 거스르는 것이 그들의 수명을 단축할 수도 있다는 내용이 나온다.

03

정답 ④

지문분석

Experts are divided / on the best way / to structure primary and secondary education systems.
전문가들은 의견이 나뉘어 있다 / 최선의 방법을 놓고 / 초등 및 중등 교육 제도를 구성하는

Specialists maintain / that youngsters should be encouraged / to enter into specific areas of study, / such as engineering or the arts, / from the earliest age possible.
특성화 교육을 지지하는 사람들은 주장한다 / 청소년들이 권장되어야 한다고 / 특정 학문 분야에 진입하도록 / 공학이나 인문학처럼 / 가능한 한 어린 나이에

★ The underlying belief is / that education is a social construct / that should be used / to guide citizens into the roles / they are best suited for / so that they can make significant contributions / to society.
기본적인 신념은 ~이다 / 교육이란 사회적 구성물이라는 것 / 활용되어야 하는 / 시민들을 역할로 인도하기 위해 / 그들에게 가장 잘 맞는 / 그들이 중대한 기여를 할 수 있도록 / 사회에

In contrast, / generalists argue / that the role of education is / to turn students into / well-rounded individuals.
반면 / 보편적 교육을 지지하는 사람들은 주장한다 / 교육의 역할이 ~이라고 / 학생들을 ~으로 만들기 위함이다 / 다재다능한 개인

They believe / that while learners may choose / to focus on one field / in college, / they should learn / about many general subjects / when they are young.
그들은 생각한다 / 학습자가 선택할 수도 있지만 / 한 분야에 집중하는 쪽으로 / 대학에서는 / 그들은 배워야 한다고 / 다양한 교양 과목을 / 그들이 어릴 때는

Such an approach / is student-centered / and has the goal / of creating students / who can appreciate a diversity of topics.
그러한 접근법은 / 학생 중심적이다 / 그리고 목표로 한다 / 학생들을 양성하는 것을 / 다양한 주제를 올바르게 이해할 수 있는

⇩

Some debate remains over / whether children should be guided / toward (A) particular careers / or given the (B) broadest education / possible.
~에 대한 논쟁은 여전히 있다 / 아이들이 지도되어야 하는지 / 특정한 진로로 / 아니면 가장 광범위한 교육을 받아야 하는지 / 가능한 한

★ 독해가 쉬워지는 구문 풀이

The underlying belief is [that education is a social construct
명사절 접속사
{that should be used to guide citizens into the roles <they are
주격 관계대명사
best suited for> so that they can make significant contributions
관계절
to society}].

⇨ [ ]는 주어 belief의 보어 역할을 하는 명사절이다.
⇨ { }는 선행사 construct를 수식하는 관계절이다.
⇨ < >는 선행사 roles를 수식하는 관계절이며, 목적격 관계대명사는 생략되었다.

어휘 structure 구성하다, 구조화하다 engineering 공학 arts 인문학 underlying 기본적인 construct 구성물, 구조물 significant 중대한, 커다란 contribution 기여, 이바지 general subject 교양 과목 appreciate 올바르게 이해하다, 진가를 알다 debate 논쟁, 논의
선택지 broad 광범위한

해설 **주제문** 전문가들은 초등 및 중등 교육 제도를 구성하는 최선의 방법을 놓고 의견이 나뉘어 있다. 특성화 교육을 지지하는 사람은 청소년들이 가능한 한 어린 나이에 공학이나 인문학처럼 특정 학문 분야에 진입하도록 권장되어야 한다고 주장한다. 기본적인 신념은 교육이란 시민들이 사회에 중대한 기여를 할 수 있도록 그들에게 가장 잘 맞는 역할로 인도하기 위해 활용되어야 하는 사회적 구성물이라는 것이다. 반면, 보편적 교육을 지지하는 사람들은 교육의 역할이 학생들을 다재다능한 개인으로 만들기 위함이라고 주장한다. 그들은 학습자가 대학에서는 한 분야에 집중하는 쪽으로 선택할 수도 있지만, 그들이 어릴 때는 다양한 교양 과목을 배워야 한다고 생각한다. 그러한 접근법은 학생 중심적이며 다양한 주제를 올바르게 이해할 수 있는 학생들을 양성하는 것을 목표로 한다.

⇩

아이들이 (A) 특정한 진로로 지도되어야 하는지 아니면 가능한 한 (B) 가장 광범위한 교육을 받아야 하는지에 대한 논쟁은 여전히 있다.

	(A)	(B)
①	특별한	가장 고등의
②	사회적인	가장 긴
③	중요한	가장 광범위한
④	특정한	가장 광범위한
⑤	독특한	가장 고등의

해설 요약문은 아이들이 '(A)한' 진로로 지도되어야 하는지, 아니면 가능한 한 '(B)한' 교육을 받아야 하는지에 대한 논쟁이 여전히 있다는 내용이다. 글에서 초등 및 중등 교육 제도 구성에 대한 최선의 방법을 놓고, 가능한 한 어린 나이에 특정 학문 분야에 진입하도록 해야 할지, 아니면 다양한 교양 과목을 배워서 다재다능한 개인으로 만들어야 할지 전문가들의 의견이 갈린다고 했다. 따라서 요약문의 (A)에는 글에서 언급된 'specific'과 관련된 'particular'가, (B)에는 글에서 언급된 'well-rounded', 'general subject', 'diversity of topics'와 관련된 'broadest'가 적절하므로 ④ particular(특정한) - broadest(가장 광범위한)가 정답이다.

오답분석 특성화 교육을 지지하는 사람은 가능한 한 어린 나이에 특정 학문에 진입할 수 있도록 권장되어야 한다고 했으므로 ②의 social과 ③의 important

는 (A)에 들어갈 단어로 적절하지 않다. 보편적 교육을 지지하는 사람들은 학습자들이 대학에서 특정한 분야에 집중하는 것을 선택할지라도 어릴 때는 다양한 교양 과목을 배워야 한다고 했으므로 ①, ⑤의 highest와 ②의 longest는 (B)에 들어갈 단어로 적절하지 않다.

실력 UP! 미니 문제 03.

정답 ⓐ citizens ⓑ generalists

해설 ⓐ 교육이란 시민들을 그들(they)에게 가장 잘 맞는 역할로 인도하기 위해 활용되어야 하는 사회적 구성물이라고 했으므로, ⓐthey가 가리키는 것은 citizens(시민들)이다.

ⓑ 보편적 교육을 지지하는 사람들은 교육의 역할이 학생들을 다재다능한 개인으로 만드는 것이라고 주장한다고 한 후 그들(They)은 어릴 때는 다양한 교양 과목을 배워야 한다고 생각한다고 했으므로, ⓑthey가 가리키는 것은 generalists(보편적 교육을 지지하는 사람들)이다.

04
정답 ②

지문분석

Although making the f and v sounds / while speaking / is natural / for us now, / it might not have always been the case / for people.
f와 v 소리를 내는 것이 ~하더라도 / 말하면서 / 자연스럽다 / 지금 우리에게는 / 항상 그렇지는 않았을 수도 있다 / 인류에게 있어

During the Paleolithic period, / the majority of ancient humans / had teeth / that met edge to edge.
구석기 시대에 / 대부분의 고대 인류는 / 치아를 가지고 있었다 / 끝과 끝이 닿는

They needed this jaw structure / because of their hunter-gatherer diet, / which was made up of / tougher foods.
그들은 이러한 턱 구조가 필요했다 / 수렵 채집 식생활로 인해 / 그런데 이 식생활은 ~으로 이루어져 있었다 / 더 질긴 음식

Over time, / however, / people developed agriculture / and food therefore became softer.
시간이 지남에 따라 / 그러나 / 인류는 농업을 발전시켰다 / 그리고 그에 따라 음식이 더 부드러워졌다

★ Humans started eating yogurts and stews / and this led to alterations / in jaw shape.
인간은 요구르트와 스튜를 먹기 시작했다 / 그리고 이는 변형으로 이어졌다 / 턱 모양의

Their upper jaws / began to horizontally overlap / their lower jaws, / giving them the ability / to put their lower lip / on their upper teeth.
그들의 위턱은 / 가로로 덮기 시작했다 / 그들의 아랫턱을 / 이것은 그들이 ~할 수 있게 했다 / 아랫입술을 대는 / 윗니에

Because of this, / people could start / making the f and v sounds.
이로 인해 / 인류는 시작할 수 있었다 / f와 v 소리를 내기

An adjustment to diet / ended up affecting / how we communicate, / giving us two of the major sounds / we use / to form speech today.
식생활의 변화는 / 결국 영향을 주었다 / 우리가 의사소통하는 방식에 / 두 가지의 주요 소리를 선사하며 / 우리가 사용하는 / 오늘날 발화하기 위해 /

⇩

The addition of softer foods / to the human diet (A) changed jaw structure, / and this (B) allowed people to start / using the f and v sounds.
더 부드러운 음식이 추가된 것은 / 인류의 식생활에 / 턱 구조를 변화시켰다 / 그리고 이는 인류가 ~하게 해 주었다 / f와 v 소리를 내는 것을

★ 독해가 쉬워지는 구문 풀이

Humans started eating yogurts and stews and this led to alterations
　　　　　　　　 동사　 목적어(동명사)
in jaw shape.

⇨ start는 목적어로 동명사와 to부정사 모두 취할 수 있고, 이때 의미 차이는 크게 없다.

어휘 majority 대부분 jaw 턱, 턱뼈 hunter-gatherer 수렵 채집(민) alteration 변형, 변경 adjustment 변화, 조정 speech 발화, 말하는 것

해석 지금 우리에게는 말하면서 f와 v 소리를 내는 것이 자연스럽더라도, 인류에게 있어 항상 그렇지는 않았을 수도 있다. 구석기 시대에, 대부분의 고대 인류는 끝과 끝이 닿는 치아를 가지고 있었다. 그들은 수렵 채집 식생활로 인해 이러한 턱 구조가 필요했는데, 이 식생활은 더 질긴 음식으로 이루어져 있었다. 그러나, 시간이 지남에 따라 인류는 농업을 발전시켰고, 그에 따라 음식이 더 부드러워졌다. 인간은 요구르트와 스튜를 먹기 시작했고, 이는 턱 모양의 변형으로 이어졌다. 그들의 위턱은 아랫턱을 가로로 덮기 시작했고, 이것이 그들이 아랫입술을 윗니에 댈 수 있게 했다. 이로 인해, 인류는 f와 v 소리를 내기 시작할 수 있었다. [주제문] 식생활의 변화는 오늘날 우리가 발화하기 위해 사용하는 두 가지의 주요 소리를 선사하며, 결국 우리가 의사소통하는 방식에 영향을 주었다.

⇩

인류의 식생활에 더 부드러운 음식이 추가된 것은 턱 구조를 (A) 변화시켰고, 이는 인류가 f와 v 소리를 내게 (B) 해 주었다.

　　　　(A)　　　　　　(B)
① 복잡하게 했다 ⋯ 훈련시켰다
② 변화시켰다 ⋯ ~하게 해 주었다
③ 약화시켰다 ⋯ 훈련시켰다
④ 변화시켰다 ⋯ 끌어들였다
⑤ 복잡하게 했다 ⋯ ~하게 해 주었다

해설 요약문은 인류의 식생활에 더 부드러운 음식이 추가된 것은 턱 구조를 '(A)했고', 이는 인류가 f와 v 소리를 내게 '(B)했다'는 내용이다. 글에서 인간이 요구르트와 스튜처럼 더 부드러운 음식을 먹기 시작한 것이 턱 모양의 변형으로 이어졌고, 이러한 식생활의 변화가 오늘날 우리가 사용하는 두 가지의 주요 소리인 f와 v를 내게 했다고 했다. 따라서 요약문의 (A)에는 글에서 언급된 'alterations'와 관련된 'changed'가, (B)에는 글에서 언급된 'giving them the ability', 'could start making ~' 등과 관련된 'allowed'가 적절하므로 ② changed(변화시켰다) - allowed(~하게 해 주었다)가 정답이다.

오답분석 더 부드러운 음식을 먹기 시작하면서 끝과 끝이 닿는 치아 구조가 위턱이 아랫턱을 가로로 덮도록 바뀌었다고 했으므로 ①, ⑤의 complicated와 ③의 weakened는 (A)에 들어갈 단어로 적절하지 않다. 턱 구조의 변화는 인류가 f와 v 소리를 내게 했다고 했으므로 ①, ③의 trained와 ④의 attracted는 (B)에 들어갈 단어로 적절하지 않다.

실력 UP! 미니 문제 04.

정답 그러나, 시간이 지남에 따라 인류는 농업을 발전시켰고, 그에 따라 음식이 더 부드러워졌다.

05
정답 ②

지문분석

Some of us see nothing wrong / with the relentless pursuit / of wealth and social status.
우리 중 일부는 아무런 문제가 없다고 여긴다 / 끊임없이 추구하는 것에 / 부와 사회적 지위를

But / the trouble with human beings / is that we are biologically programmed / to want more.
그러나 / 인간이 가지고 있는 문제는 / 우리가 생물학적으로 프로그램화되어 있다는 것이다 / 더 많이 원하도록

★Throughout our evolutionary history, / it was those / who sought more resources / and an elevated social rank / that survived and reproduced.
진화의 역사에 걸쳐 / 바로 사람들이었다 / 더 많은 자원을 추구한 / 그리고 높은 사회적 계급 / 살아남고 번식했던 것은

By adopting this mentality / in the modern world, / however, / we are destined to be unhappy.
이러한 사고방식을 취함으로써 / 현대 사회에서 / 그러나 / 우리는 불행해질 수밖에 없는 운명이다

We will never stop / striving for bigger and better, / whether it is a larger house / or a more prominent social circle.
우리는 멈추지 않을 것이다 / 더 크고 더 좋은 것을 얻으려고 노력하는 것을 / 그것이 더 큰 집이든 / 혹은 더 저명한 사회적 집단이든

We will keep trying / to climb the corporate ladder / or earn a better spot / in the social hierarchy, / and when we fail, / we will be frustrated.
우리는 끊임없이 노력할 것이다 / 회사의 서열 사다리를 오르려고 / 또는 더 나은 자리를 얻으려고 / 사회적 계층에서 / 그리고 실패하면 / 우리는 좌절감에 빠질 것이다

While success may give us / momentary pleasure, / it will not be long before / our desire for more / eventually reappears.
성공은 우리에게 주지만 / 순간적인 만족을 / 머지않아 ~할 것이다 / 더 많은 걸 원하는 우리의 욕망이 / 결국 다시 나타나다

⇩

Although people continue to (A) desire / more than they have, / they never seem / to be (B) satisfied for long.
비록 사람들은 꾸준히 원함에도 불구하고 / 그들이 가진 것 이상을 / 그들은 결코 ~하지 못하는 듯하다 / 만족스러운 상태를 오래 유지하는

★ 독해가 쉬워지는 구문 풀이

Throughout our evolutionary history, it was **those** who sought more resources and an elevated social rank **that** survived and reproduced.
　　　　　　　　　　　　강조 대상

⇨ it-that 강조 구문은 '~한 것은 바로 -이다'라는 의미로, 주어 이외에도 목적어/보어/수식어 등이 it과 that 사이에 와서 강조될 수 있다.
⇨ 관계절 who ~ social rank의 수식을 받으면서 '~한 사람들'이라는 뜻의 대명사인 those가 쓰였다.

[어휘] relentless 끊임없는, 끈질긴 pursuit 추구 social status 사회적 지위 biologically 생물학적으로 evolutionary 진화의, 점진적인 elevated (지위가) 높은 reproduce 번식하다 mentality 사고방식 destined ~할 운명인 strive for ~을 얻으려고 노력하다 social circle 사회적 집단, 사교계 corporate 회사의 hierarchy 계층 frustrated 좌절감에 빠진 momentary 순간적인

[해석] 우리 중 일부는 부와 사회적 지위를 끊임없이 추구하는 것에 아무런 문제가 없다고 여긴다. 그러나 인간이 가지고 있는 문제는 우리가 더 많이 원하도록 생물학적으로 프로그램화되어 있다는 것이다. 진화의 역사에 걸쳐, 살아남고 번식했던 것은 바로 더 많은 자원과 높은 사회적 계급을 추구한 사람들이었다. 그러나 현대 사회에서 이러한 사고방식을 취함으로써, 우리는 불행해질 수밖에 없는 운명이다. 더 큰 집이든 혹은 더 저명한 사회적 집단이든, 우리는 더 크고 더 좋은 것을 얻으려고 노력하는 것을 멈추지 않을 것이다. 우리는 회사의 서열 사다리를 오르거나 사회적 계층에서 더 나은 자리를 얻으려고 끊임없이 노력할 것이고, 실패하면 우리는 좌절감에 빠질 것이다. [주제문] 성공은 우리에게 순간적인 만족을 주지만, 머지않아 더 많은 걸 원하는 우리의 욕망이 결국 다시 나타날 것이다.

⇩

비록 사람들은 그들이 가진 것 이상을 꾸준히 (A) 원함에도 불구하고, 그들은 (B) 만족스러운 상태를 결코 오래 유지하지는 못하는 듯하다.

	(A)	(B)
①	쓰다	실망한
②	원하다	만족스러운
③	쓰다	만족스러운
④	얻다	실망한
⑤	원하다	관심 있는

[해설] 요약문은 비록 사람들이 그들이 가진 것 이상을 꾸준히 '(A)'에도 불구하고 그들은 '(B)한' 상태를 결코 오래 유지하지는 못하는 듯하다는 내용이다. 글에서 인간은 더 많이 원하도록 프로그램화되어 있고, 더 크고 좋은 것을 얻기 위해 노력하여 성공한다면 순간적인 만족을 얻을 수는 있지만, 그것보다 더 많은 것을 원하는 우리의 욕망이 머지않아 다시 나타날 것이라고 했다. 따라서 요약문의 (A)에는 글에서 언급된 'pursuit', 'want', 'striving for'와 관련된 'desire'가, (B)에는 글에서 언급된 'momentary pleasure'와 관련된 'satisfied'가 적절하므로 ② desire(원하다) - satisfied(만족스러운)가 정답이다.

[오답분석] 우리는 더 많이 원하도록 프로그램화되어 있고 더 크고 좋은 것을 얻으려고 노력하는 것을 멈추지 않을 것이라고 했으므로 ①과 ③의 spend는 (A)에 들어갈 단어로 적절하지 않다. 성공은 우리에게 순간적인 만족을 주지만, 머지않아 더 많은 것을 원하는 우리의 욕망이 다시 나타날 것이라고 했으므로 ①, ④의 disappointed와 ⑤의 interested는 (B)에 들어갈 단어로 적절하지 않다.

[실력 UP!] 미니 문제 05.

정답 Constantly pursuing wealth and social status will not result in satisfaction

06　　　　　　　　　　　　　　　　　정답 ④

[지문분석]

Israel Abramov, / a behavioral neuroscientist / at CUNY's Brooklyn College, / studied the difference between / how men and women perceive color.
Israel Abramov는 / 행동 신경과학자 / 뉴욕 시립대학 산하 브루클린 대학의 / 차이를 연구했다 / 남성과 여성이 색상을 인지하는 방법의

To conduct his study, / he asked men and women / to describe various colors / by categorizing them / as shades of red, yellow, green, or blue / with a percentage.
그의 연구를 수행하기 위해 / 그는 남성과 여성에게 요청했다 / 다양한 색상들을 묘사해 달라고 / 분류하면서 / 빨강, 노랑, 초록 혹은 파란 색조로 / 비율과 함께

Interestingly, / women were able to notice / small differences between colors / which men described as the same.
흥미롭게도 / 여성은 알아차릴 수 있었다 / 색상들 간의 미묘한 차이를 / 남성이 동일한 것으로 묘사했던

★This may explain previous research / showing / that women have / a much larger / and more creative color vocabulary / than men.
이것은 이전의 연구를 설명해 줄지도 모른다 / 보여주며 / 여성이 가지고 있음을 / 훨씬 더 광범위하고 / 더 창의적인 색상 어휘를 / 남성보다

Then, / he showed the participants / light and dark bars / flashing on a screen.
그다음 / 그는 참가자들에게 보여주었다 / 밝은 막대와 어두운 막대를 / 화면에 번쩍이는

This time, / men were better than women / at noticing variations in brightness, / indicating / that it was easier for men / to spot big differences.
이번에는 / 남성이 여성보다 더 뛰어났다 / 밝기의 변화를 알아차리는 것에 / 이는 보여준다 / 남성에게 더 쉬웠다는 것을 / 큰 차이를 발견하는 것이

⇩

> Women are able to see / (A) <u>slight</u> differences in colors, / while / men excel at detecting / (B) <u>huge</u> changes in the level of light.
> 여성은 알아챌 수 있다 / 색상의 근소한 차이를 / 반면 / 남성은 감지하는 데 뛰어나다 / 빛의 수준의 큰 변화를

★ 독해가 쉬워지는 구문 풀이

This may explain previous research [**showing** that women have a much larger and more creative color vocabulary than men].

⇨ 현재분사 showing이 이끄는 [ ]는 주절(This ~ research)를 수식하는 분사구문이다.

어휘 behavioral 행동에 관한 perceive 인지하다 conduct 수행하다 describe 묘사하다 various 다양한 categorize 분류하다 shade 색조 percentage 비율 notice 알아차리다 previous 이전의 vocabulary 어휘 participant 참가자 bar 막대 flash 번쩍이다 variation 변화 brightness 밝음 indicate 나타내다 spot 발견하다 [선택지] slight 근소한 minor 작은 random 무작위의 similar 유사한 excessive 지나친

해석 뉴욕 시립대학 산하 브루클린 대학의 행동 신경과학자 Israel Abramov는 남성과 여성이 색상을 인지하는 방법의 차이를 연구했다. 그의 연구를 수행하기 위해, 그는 남성과 여성에게 다양한 색상들을 빨강, 노랑, 초록 혹은 파란 색조로 분류하면서 비율과 함께 묘사해 달라고 요청했다. 흥미롭게도, 남성이 동일한 것으로 묘사했던 색상들 간의 미묘한 차이를 여성이 알아차릴 수 있었다. 이것은 여성이 남성보다 훨씬 더 광범위하고 창의적인 색상 어휘를 가지고 있음을 보여주며 이전의 연구를 설명해 줄지도 모른다. 그다음, 그는 참가자들에게 화면에 번쩍이는 밝은 막대와 어두운 막대를 보여주었다. 이번에는, 남성이 여성보다 밝기의 변화를 알아차리는 것에 더 뛰어났는데, 이는 큰 차이를 발견하는 것이 남성에게 더 쉬웠다는 것을 보여준다.

⇩

> 여성은 색상의 (A) 근소한 차이를 알아챌 수 있는 반면, 남성은 빛의 수준의 (B) 큰 변화를 감지하는 데 뛰어나다.

    (A)   (B)
① 근소한   … 작은
② 무작위의 … 간단한
③ 엄청난   … 유사한
④ 근소한   … 큰
⑤ 무작위의 … 지나친

해설 요약문은 여성은 색상의 '(A)한' 차이를 알아챌 수 있는 반면, 남성은 빛의 수준의 '(B)한' 변화를 감지하는 데 뛰어나다는 내용이다. 글에서 여성은 색상들 간의 미묘한 차이를 알아차릴 수 있다고 하고, 남성은 밝기의 큰 차이를 더 잘 발견했다고 했다. 따라서 요약문의 (A)에는 글에서 언급된 'women were able to notice small differences'와 관련된 'slight'가, (B)에는 글에서 언급된 'it was easier for men to spot big differences'와 관련된 'huge'가 적절하므로 요약문의 빈칸에 들어갈 말로 가장 적절한 것은 ④ slight(근소한) - huge(큰)이다.

오답분석 여성은 미묘한 차이를 인식할 수 있다고 했으므로 ②, ⑤의 random과 ③의 great는 (A)에 들어갈 단어로 적절하지 않다. 남성은 큰 차이를 발견할 수 있다고 했으므로 ①의 minor, ②의 simple, ③의 similar, ⑤의 excessive는 (B)에 들어갈 단어로 적절하지 않다.

실력UP! 미니 문제 06.

정답 noticing variations in brightness

해석 Q: 실험의 결과에 따르면, 남자는 여자보다 어떤 것을 더 잘하는가?

A: 남자는 밝기의 변화를 알아차리는 것을 더 잘했다.

해설 This time, men were better than women at noticing variations in brightness ~에서 남자가 여자보다 밝기의 변화를 더 잘 알아차린다는 것을 알 수 있다.

07   정답 ③

지문분석

> The secret words and phrases / shared exclusively / among the members of a household / are what linguists call familect.
> 비밀 단어와 문구들 / 독점적으로 공유되는 / 가족 구성원들 사이에서 / 언어학자들이 familect라고 부르는 것이다
>
> One of the most extensive familect studies / was conducted by Cynthia Gordon, / a professor of linguistics / at Georgetown University.
> 가장 대규모의 familect 연구 중 하나는 / Cynthia Gordon에 의해 수행되었다 / 언어학 교수인 / Georgetown 대학교의
>
> She found that / many families continually use / a set of terms and expressions, / often associated with / inside jokes, nicknames, / and the words and sounds / that young children invent / as they learn to talk.
> 그녀는 발견했다 / 많은 가족들이 계속해서 사용한다는 것을 / 용어와 표현들을 / 보통 ~과 관련된 / 자기들끼리만 아는 농담, 별명 / 그리고 단어 및 소리 / 어린 아이들이 만들어내는 / 말하는 법을 배울 때
>
> ★ As / the meaning of these unique expressions / is only used within the family group, / a special bond / that reinforces the family's identity / as a team / is formed.
> ~때문에 / 이러한 독특한 표현들의 의미는 / 가족 집단 내에서만 사용된다 / 특별한 유대감이 / 가족의 정체성을 강화하는 / 하나의 팀으로서 / 형성된다
>
> Even after / children have grown up / and left the household, / using familect / is a way / to bring the family back together, / and to recall their old memories.
> 후에도 / 아이들이 성장하여 / 집을 떠난 / familect를 사용하는 것은 / 방법이다 / 가족을 다시 결합시키고 / 그들의 옛 추억을 회상하는
>
> In a sense, / it is a sort of glue / holding families together.
> 어떤 의미에서 / 그것은 일종의 접착제이다 / 가족들을 뭉치게 하는

⇩

> Using familect / (A) <u>creates</u> a sense of unity / and can keep families (B) <u>close</u>.
> Familect를 사용하는 것은 / 통일감을 형성하고 / 가족들을 가깝게 유지시킬 수 있다

★ 독해가 쉬워지는 구문 풀이

[①**As** the meaning of these unique expressions is only used within the family group], <u>a special bond</u> that reinforces the family's identity [②**as** a team] <u>is created</u>.
        주어   동사

⇨ 부사절 접속사 As가 이끄는 [①]은 주절(a special ~ created)을 수식하는 부사절이다.

⇨ [②]의 as는 전치사로 쓰여, 명사 family's identity를 수식하는 전치사구를 이끈다.

어휘 phrase 문구 share 공유하다 exclusively 독점적으로 household 가족, 가정 linguist 언어학자 extensive 대규모의 conduct 수행하다 professor 교수 linguistics 언어학 continually 계속해서 term 용어 associate 관련시키다 inside joke 자기들끼리만 아는 농담 nickname 별명 invent 만들어내다, 발명하다 bond 유대감 reinforce 강화하다 identity 정체성 a sort of 일종의 [선택지] apart 따로 distort 왜곡하다 criticize 비판하다

해석 가족 구성원들 사이에서 독점적으로 공유되는 비밀 단어와 문구들은 언

어학자들이 familect라고 부르는 것이다. 가장 대규모의 familect 연구 중 하나는 Georgetown 대학교의 언어학 교수인 Cynthia Gordon에 의해 수행되었다. 그녀는 많은 가족들이 보통 자기들끼리만 아는 농담, 별명, 그리고 어린 아이들이 말하는 법을 배울 때 만들어내는 단어 및 소리와 관련된 용어와 표현들을 계속해서 사용한다는 것을 발견했다. 주제문 이러한 독특한 표현들의 의미는 가족 집단 내에서만 사용되기 때문에, 하나의 팀으로서 가족의 정체성을 강화하는 특별한 유대감이 형성된다. 아이들이 성장하여 집을 떠난 후에도, familect를 사용하는 것은 가족을 다시 결합시키고, 그들의 옛 추억을 회상하는 방법이다. 어떤 의미에서, 그것은 가족들을 뭉치게 하는 일종의 접착제이다.

⇩

Familect를 사용하는 것은 통일감을 (A) 형성하고 가족들을 (B) 가깝게 유지시킬 수 있다.

(A)		(B)
① 약화시키다	…	따로
② 왜곡하다	…	행복하게
③ 형성하다	…	가깝게
④ 비판하다	…	가깝게
⑤ 만들다	…	따로

해설 요약문은 familect를 사용하는 것은 통일감을 '(A)하고' 가족들을 '(B)하게' 유지시킬 수 있다는 내용이다. 글에서 familect의 사용은 하나의 팀으로서 가족의 정체성을 강화시키고, 아이들이 집을 떠난 후에도 다시 결합시킨다고 했다. 따라서 요약문의 (A)에는 글에서 언급된 'a special bond ~ is formed'와 관련된 'creates'가, (B)에는 글에서 언급된 'bring the family back together'와 관련된 'close'가 적절하므로 요약문의 빈칸에 들어갈 말로 가장 적절한 것은 ③ creates(형성하다) - close(가깝게) 이다.

오답분석 하나의 팀으로서 가족의 정체성을 강화시킨다고 했으므로 ①의 breaks와 ②의 distorts, ④의 criticizes는 (A)에 들어갈 단어로 적절하지 않다. 또한, 가족을 다시 결합시킨다고 했으므로 ①, ⑤의 apart는 (B)에 들어갈 단어로 적절하지 않다.

실력UP! 미니 문제 07.

정답 the secret words and phrases shared exclusively among the members of a household

해설 Q: 지문에 따르면 familect의 정의는 무엇인가?
A: Familect는 가족 구성원들 사이에서 독점적으로 공유되는 비밀 단어와 문구들이다.

해설 The secret words ~ are what linguists call familect에서 언어학자들은 familect를 가족 구성원들 사이에서 독점적으로 공유되는 비밀 단어와 문구라고 부른다는 것을 알 수 있다.

08
정답 ⑤

지문분석

In a 1971 social psychology experiment / at Stanford University, / student volunteers were assigned / to the roles of either prisoner or guard / in a simulated prison.
1971년 사회 심리학 실험에서 / 스탠포드 대학교의 / 학생 지원자에게 지정됐다 / 죄수 또는 간수 둘 중 하나의 역할이 / 모의 감옥의

Prior to the experiment, / none of the students / had seemed noticeably more aggressive or passive / than anyone else.
실험 이전에는 / 학생들 중 누구도 ~ 않았다 / 눈에 띄게 더 공격적이거나 수동적으로 보였다 / 다른 사람들보다

However, / this would soon change.
하지만 / 이는 곧 바뀌게 된다

Those / assigned to play guards / were permitted to maintain order / however they wanted.
사람들은 / 간수 역할을 하도록 지정된 / 질서를 유지하도록 허락되었다 / 그들이 어떤 방식을 사용하든

They quickly abused their freedom / by treating the prisoners unfairly / and handing out cruel punishments.
그들은 그들의 자유를 곧 남용했다 / 죄수들을 부당하게 대우함으로써 / 그리고 잔인한 벌을 주는 것

Meanwhile, / the students playing prisoners / were obedient / because they were afraid of / the consequences of disobeying.
반면에 / 죄수 역할을 하는 학생들은 / 복종했다 / ~가 두려웠기 때문에 / 불복종의 결과

Essentially, / they began exhibiting behaviors / that one might expect to see / in actual prisoners.
본질적으로 / 그들은 행동을 보이기 시작했다 / 사람들이 볼 수 있을 법한 / 실제 죄수들로부터

★ It was therefore determined / that the behavior of each group of students / was a result of the situations / they were put in / and the roles / they were assigned.
그 결과 밝혀졌다 / 각 학생 집단의 행동은 / 상황의 결과임이 / 그들이 처한 / 그리고 역할 / 그들에게 부여된

It was also proposed / that the specific conditions of a situation / could make people assume roles / and adopt personality traits / that are not typical for them.
또한 제시되었다 / 어떤 상황의 특정 조건이 ~라고 / 사람들이 역할을 맡게 만들 수 있다 / 그리고 성격적 특성을 취한다 / 그들에게 평소와 다른

⇩

An experiment studying prison life suggested / that (A) environmental factors cause people / to (B) follow the roles / they are expected to play.
감옥 생활을 연구한 한 실험은 주장했다 / 환경적인 요인이 사람들이 ~하게 한다고 / 역할에 따르게 / 그들이 하도록 기대되는

★ 독해가 쉬워지는 구문 풀이

It was therefore determined that the behavior of each group of
가주어 동사
students was a result of the situations they were put in and the
진짜 주어(명사절)
roles they were assigned.

⇨ 주어가 '각 학생 집단의 행동은 그들이 처한 상황과 그들에게 부여된 역할의 결과임'이라는 의미로 길기 때문에, 긴 주어를 대신해서 가주어 역할을 할 수 있는 It으로 문장을 시작했다.

어휘 assign 지정하다, 맡기다 simulated 모의의 noticeably 눈에 띄게 aggressive 공격적인 passive 수동적인 permit 허락하다 abuse 남용하다 hand out 주다 obedient 복종하는 consequence 결과 disobey 불복종하다 exhibit 보이다 specific 특정한, 구체적인 assume 맡다, 추측하다 trait 특성, 특징 typical 평소의, 일반적인
선택지 internal 내부의 adjust 적응하다 reject 거절하다

해석 1971년 스탠포드 대학교의 사회 심리학 실험에서, 학생 지원자에게 모의 감옥의 죄수 또는 간수 둘 중 하나의 역할이 지정됐다. 실험 이전에는, 학생들 중 누구도 다른 사람들보다 눈에 띄게 더 공격적이거나 수동적으로 보이지 않았다. 하지만, 이는 곧 바뀌게 된다. 간수 역할을 하도록 지정된 사람들은 그들이 어떤 방식을 사용하든 질서를 유지하도록 허락되었다. 그들은 죄수들을 부당하게 대우하고 잔인한 벌을 줌으로써 그들의 자유를 곧 남용했다. 반면에, 죄수 역할을 하는 학생들은 불복종의 결과가 두려웠기 때문에 복종했다. 본질적으로, 그들은 사람들이 실제 죄수들로부터 볼 수 있을 법한 행동을 보이기 시작했다. 주제문 그 결과 각 학생 집단의 행동은 그들이 처한 상황과 그들에게 부여된 역할의 결과임이 밝혀졌다. 또한 어떤 상황의 특정 조건이 사람들이 평소와 다른 역할을 맡고 성격적 특성을 취하게 만들 수 있다고 제시되었다.

⇩

감옥 생활을 연구한 한 실험은 (A) 환경적인 요인이 사람들이 그들이 하도록 기대되는 역할에 (B) 따르게 한다고 주장했다.

         (A)   (B)
① 환경적인   … 반대하다
② 내부의   … 적응하다
③ 생물학적인 … 적용하다
④ 내부의   … 거절하다
⑤ 환경적인   … 따르다

[해설] 요약문은 감옥 생활을 연구한 실험은 '(A)' 요인이 사람들이 그들이 하도록 기대되는 역할에 '(B)'하게 한다고 주장했다는 내용이다. 글에서 학생들이 실험에서 보인 행동은 그들이 처한 상황과 그들에게 부여된 역할의 결과이고, 상황의 특정 조건은 그들이 평소와 다른 역할을 맡고 성격적 특성을 취하게 만들 수 있다는 결과를 제시했다. 따라서 요약문의 (A)에는 글에서 언급된 'situations they were put in', 'specific conditions of a situation'과 관련된 'environmental'이, (B)에는 글에서 언급된 'assume', 'adopt' 등과 관련된 'follow'가 적절하므로 ⑤ environmental(환경적인) - follow (따르다)이다.

[오답분석] 학생들이 처한 상황과 그들에게 부여된 역할이 그들이 특정 행동을 보이는 원인이라 했으므로 ②, ④의 internal과 ③의 biological은 (A)에 들어갈 단어로 적절하지 않다. 특정 상황의 조건이 학생들이 기대되는 역할에 따르게 한다고 했으므로 ①의 resist와 ④의 reject는 (B)에 들어갈 단어로 적절하지 않다.

실력 UP! 미니 문제 08.

정답 ⓐ Those assigned to play guards ⓑ the students playing prisoners

해설 ⓐ 간수 역할을 하도록 지정된 사람들은 그들이 어떤 방식을 사용하든 질서를 유지하도록 허락되었다고 한 후 그들은 죄수들을 부당하게 대우하고 잔인한 벌을 주었다고 했으므로, ⓐ는 Those assigned to play guards(간수 역할을 하도록 지정된 사람들)를 가리킨다.
ⓑ 죄수 역할을 하는 학생들은 불복종의 결과가 두려웠기 때문에 복종했다고 한 후 본질적으로 그들을 사람들이 실제 죄수들로부터 볼 수 있을 법한 행동을 보이기 시작했다고 했으므로, ⓑ는 the students playing prisoners(죄수 역할을 하는 학생들)이다.

CHAPTER 16 장문 독해

불변의 패턴 31
p.120

장문 독해①은 주로 학술적 내용의 설명문이 나온다.

기출 문제 41 ~ 42

지문분석

A quick look / at history / shows / that humans have not always had / the abundance of food / that is enjoyed / throughout most of the developed world / today.
잠깐 살펴보는 것은 / 역사를 / 보여준다 / 인간이 항상 경험했던 것은 아님을 / 음식의 풍부함을 / 누려지는 / 대부분의 발전한 세상에서 / 오늘날

In fact, / there have been numerous times / in history / when food has been rather scarce.
사실 / 수많은 시기가 있었다 / 역사상 / 음식이 상당히 부족했던

As a result, / people used to eat more / when food was available / since the availability of the next meal / was (a) questionable.
그 결과 / 사람들은 더 많이 먹곤 했다 / 음식이 있을 때 / 다음 식사의 가능성이 ~하기 때문에 / 불확실했다

Overeating in those times / was essential / to ensure survival, / and humans received satisfaction / from eating / more than was needed / for immediate purposes.
그러한 시기의 과식은 / 필수적이었다 / 생존을 보장하기 위해 / 그리고 인간은 만족을 얻었다 / 먹는 것에서 / 필요한 것보다 더 많이 / 당장의 목표치에

On top of that, / the highest pleasure / was derived from / eating the most calorie-dense foods, / resulting in a (b) longer lasting energy reserve.
뿐만 아니라 / 가장 큰 기쁨은 / ~에서 왔다 / 칼로리가 가장 높은 음식을 먹는 것 / 그리고 이는 더 오래 지속되는 에너지 비축으로 이어졌다

Even though there are parts / of the world / where, unfortunately, food is still scarce, / most of the world's population today / has plenty of food / available to survive and thrive.
비록 일부 지역이 있다 / 세계의 / 안타깝게도 음식이 여전히 부족한 / 오늘날 세계 인구의 대부분은 / 많은 음식을 가지고 있다 / 생존하고 번영하기 위해 이용 가능한

★ However, / this abundance is new, / and your body has not caught up, / still naturally (c) rewarding you / for eating / more than you need / and for eating the most calorie-dense foods.
그러나 / 이러한 풍요는 새로 나타난 것이다 / 그러므로 당신의 몸이 따라가지 못했다 / 그래서 당신에게 여전히 당연하게 보상한다 / 먹는 것에 대해 / 당신이 필요한 것보다 더 많이 / 그리고 칼로리가 가장 높은 음식을 먹는 것에 대해

These are innate habits / and not simple addictions.
이것들은 타고난 습관이다 / 단순한 중독이 아닌

They are self-preserving mechanisms / initiated by your body, / ensuring your future survival, / but they are (d) irrelevant now.
그것들은 자기 보호 체계이다 / 당신의 몸에 의해 일어난 / 그리고 당신의 미래 생존을 보장한다 / 하지만 그것들은 이제 부적절하다

Therefore, / it is your responsibility / to communicate with your body / regarding the new environment / of food abundance / and the need / to (e) strengthen(→ change) the inborn habit of overeating.
따라서 / 당신의 책임이다 / 당신의 몸과 소통하는 것은 / 새로운 환경에 대해 / 음식의 풍요가 있는 / 그리고 필요 / 타고난 과식 습관을 강화시킬(→ 변화시킬)

★ 독해가 쉬워지는 구문 풀이

However, this abundance is new, and your body has not caught up, [still naturally rewarding you {**for eating** more than you need and **for eating** the most calorie-dense foods}].

⇨ [ ]는 앞의 주절을 수식하는 분사구문의 부사절이며, 접속사 및 주어 (your body)가 생략되었다.
⇨ 전치사구 for eating은 등위접속사 and로 연결된 병렬 구조이다.

[어휘] abundance 풍부 numerous 수많은 scarce 부족한, 드문
ensure 보장하다 immediate 당장의, 즉시의 pleasure 기쁨, 즐거움
derive from ~에서 왔다, 파생하다 dense ~가 높은, 많은 고밀도의
rewarding 보상하는, 보람 있는 irrelevant 부적절한, 상관없는 inborn 타고난

[해석] 역사를 잠깐 살펴보는 것은 인간이 오늘날 대부분의 발전한 세상에서 누려지는 음식의 풍부함을 항상 경험했던 것은 아님을 보여준다. 사실, 역사상 음식이 상당히 부족했던 수많은 시기가 있었다. 그 결과, 사람들은 다음 식사의 가능성이 (a) 불확실했기 때문에 음식이 있을 때 더 많이 먹곤 했다. 그러한 시기의 과식은 생존을 보장하기 위해 필수적이었고, 인간은 당장의 목표치에 필요한 것보다 더 많이 먹는 것에서 만족을 얻었다. 뿐만 아니라, 가장 큰 기쁨은 칼로리가 가장 높은 음식을 먹는 것에서 왔고, 이는 (b) 더 오래 지속되는 에너지 비축으로 이어졌다. 안타깝게도, 비록 음식이 여전히 부족한 세계의 일부 지역들이 있더라도, 오늘날 세계 인구의 대부분은 생존하고 번영하기 위해 이용 가능한 많은 음식을 가지고 있다. 그러나, 이러한 풍요는 새로 나타난 것이므로 당신의 몸이 따라가지 못해

서 당신이 필요한 것보다 더 많이 먹고 칼로리가 가장 높은 음식을 먹는 것에 대해 당신에게 여전히 당연하게 (c) 보상한다. 이것들은 타고난 습관이지 단순한 중독이 아니다. 그것들은 당신의 몸에 의해 일어난 자기 보호 체계이고 당신의 미래 생존을 보장하지만, 그것들은 이제 (d) 부적절하다. [주제문] 따라서, 음식의 풍요가 있는 새로운 환경과 타고난 과식 습관을 (e) 강화시킬(→ 변화시킬) 필요에 대해 당신의 몸과 소통하는 것은 당신의 책임이다.

41   정답 ③

[해석] ① 맛있는 음식과 건강에 좋은 음식 중 어느 것이 더 나은가?
② 더 균형 잡힌 식습관을 위한 간단한 방법들
③ 과식: 그것은 우리의 유전자에 자리잡혀 있다
④ 고칼로리 음식이 우리의 몸을 망가뜨리는 방법
⑤ 우리의 식습관은 우리의 성격을 반영한다

[해설] 음식이 부족했던 시기에는 음식이 있으면 더 많이 먹던 것이 우리의 생존을 보장하기 위해 필수적이었기에 과식이 우리의 타고난 습관이 되었다는 내용의 글이므로, 글의 제목으로 가장 적절한 것은 ③ Overeating: It's Rooted in Our Genes(과식: 그것은 우리의 유전자에 자리잡혀 있다)이다.

[오답분석] ①은 글의 핵심 소재 food를 활용하여 혼동을 주는 오답이다. ②은 글의 핵심 소재 overeating 및 food에서 연상되는 Diet를 활용하여 혼동을 주는 오답이다. ④은 글에서 언급된 Calorie-dense Foods를 활용하여 혼동을 주는 오답이다. ⑤은 글의 핵심 소재 Eating Habits를 활용하여 혼동을 주는 오답이다.

42   정답 ⑤

[해설] 과거에는 음식이 부족했기 때문에 음식이 있을 때 더 많이 먹어 두어서 생존을 보장해야 했던 것과 달리, 현재는 음식이 풍요로운 시기이므로 우리는 몸과 소통하여 타고난 과식 습관을 변화시켜야 한다는 맥락이 되어야 하므로, ⑤의 strengthen을 change와 같은 어휘로 바꾸어야 문맥상 적절하다.

[오답분석] ①은 다음 식사의 가능성이 "불확실"했기 때문에 음식이 있을 때 더 많이 먹곤 했다는 문맥이 되어야 하므로 questionable이 오는 것이 적절하다. ②은 칼로리가 가장 높은 음식을 먹는 것이 "더 오래" 지속되는 에너지 비축으로 이어졌다는 문맥이 되어야 하므로 longer가 오는 것이 적절하다. ③은 몸이 오늘날의 음식의 풍요를 따라가지 못해서 필요한 것보다 더 많이 먹고 칼로리가 가장 높은 음식을 먹는 것에 대해 여전히 당연하게 "보상"한다는 문맥이 되어야 하므로 rewarding이 오는 것이 적절하다. ④은 타고난 과식 습관은 자기 보호 체계이고 미래 생존을 보장하지만 음식이 풍요로운 현재에서는 "부적절"하다는 문맥이 되어야 하므로 irrelevant가 오는 것이 적절하다.

불변의 패턴 32   p.122
장문 독해②는 일상의 에피소드를 다루는 일화가 나온다.

기출 문제 43 ~ 45

[지문분석]

(A) Dorothy was home / alone.
Dorothy는 집에 있었다 / 혼자

She was busy / with a school project, / and suddenly wanted to eat French fries.
그녀는 바빴다 / 학교 과제로 / 그리고 갑자기 감자튀김이 먹고 싶어졌다

She peeled two potatoes, / sliced them up / and put a pot with cooking oil / on the stove.
그녀는 감자 2개의 껍질을 벗기고 / 얇게 썰었다 / 그리고 식용유를 두른 냄비를 올려 놓았다 / 가스레인지 위에

Then / the telephone rang.
그때 / 전화기가 울렸다

It was her best friend Samantha.
그것은 그녀의 가장 친한 친구 Samatha였다

While chatting away on the phone, / Dorothy noticed / a strange light shining / from the kitchen, / and then (a) she remembered / about the pot of oil / on the stove!
전화로 수다를 떨던 도중 / Dorothy는 알아챘다 / 이상한 빛이 나는 것을 / 부엌에서 / 그리고 그때 그녀는 떠올랐다 / 기름을 두른 냄비가 / 가스레인지 위에 있는

(B) A while later, / after the wound had been treated, / the family sat around the kitchen table / and talked.
잠시 후 / 상처가 치료된 후 / 가족은 부엌 식탁에 둘러 앉아 / 이야기를 나눴다

"I learned a big lesson today," / Dorothy said.
저는 오늘 큰 교훈을 배웠어요 / Dorothy는 말했다

Her parents expected / (b) her to say / something about the fire.
그녀의 부모는 예상했다 / 그녀가 말할 것을 / 화재에 관한 무언가를

But / she talked / about something different.
그러나 / 그녀는 이야기했다 / 다른 것에 대해

"I have decided / to use kind words more / just like you."
저는 결심했어요 / 다정한 말을 더 많이 하기로 / 엄마 아빠처럼

★ Her parents were very grateful, / because Dorothy had quite a temper.
그녀의 부모는 매우 고맙게 여겼다 / 왜냐하면 Dorothy는 꽤나 다혈질이었기 때문이다

(C) Dorothy dropped the phone / and rushed to the kitchen.
Dorothy는 전화기를 떨어뜨렸다 / 그리고 부엌으로 서둘러 갔다

The oil was on fire.
기름에는 불이 붙어 있었다

"Chill! / Take a deep breath," / (c) she said to herself.
진정해 / 심호흡을 해 / 그녀는 자신에게 말했다

What did they teach us / not to do / in a situation like this?
그들이 우리에게 가르친 것은 뭐지 / 하지 말라고 / 이런 상황에서

Don't try to put it out / by throwing water on it, / because it will cause an explosion, / she remembered.
그것을 끄려고 하지마 / 그것에 물을 뿌려서 / 그것은 폭발을 일으킬 것이므로 / 그녀는 기억했다

She picked up / the pot's lid / and covered the pot with it / to put out the flames.
그녀는 들었다 / 냄비의 뚜껑을 / 그리고 그것으로 냄비를 덮었다 / 불을 끄기 위해

In the process / she burned her hands.
그 과정에서 / 그녀는 손에 화상을 입었다

Dorothy felt dizzy / and / sat down at the kitchen table.
Dorothy는 현기증을 느꼈으며 / 그리고 부엌 식탁에 앉았다

(D) A couple of minutes later, / her parents came rushing / into the house.
몇 분 후 / 그녀의 부모님은 급하게 달려왔다 / 집으로

Samantha had suspected / that something might be wrong / after Dorothy dropped the phone / just like that, / and / (d) she had phoned Dorothy's parents.
Samatha는 의심했었다 / 무언가 잘못되었을 거라고 / Dorothy가 전화기를 떨어뜨린 후 / 그렇게 / 그리고 그녀가 Dorothy의 부모님에게 전화를 한 것이다

Dorothy started to cry.
Dorothy는 울기 시작했다

Her mother hugged her tightly / and looked at the wound.
그녀의 엄마는 그녀를 꼭 껴안았고 / 상처를 보았다

"Tell me what happened," / she said.
무슨 일이 있었는지 말해주렴 / 그녀는 말했다

Dorothy told her, / sobbing and sniffing.
Dorothy는 그녀에게 말했다 / 흐느껴 울고 훌쩍거리며

"Aren't you going to yell / at me?" / (e) she asked them / through the tears.
소리 지르지 않을 거예요? / 저에게 / 그녀는 그들에게 물었다 / 눈물을 흘리며

Her father answered / with a smile, / "I also put my lid on / to keep me / from exploding."
그녀의 아버지는 대답했다 / 미소를 지으며 / 나도 내 뚜껑을 덮는단다 / 나를 막으려고 / (감정이) 폭발하는 것을

Dorothy looked at him, / relieved.
Dorothy는 그를 쳐다보았다 / 안심하며

"But be careful / not to be so irresponsible / again."
하지만 조심하렴 / 그렇게 무책임하지 않도록 / 다시는

★ 독해가 쉬워지는 구문 풀이

Her parents were very grateful, because Dorothy had **quite a temper**.

⇨ '꽤나 ~한'이라는 표현을 사용할 때 주로 활용되는 <quite/what/such + (관사 a/an) + (형용사) + 명사>구문이다.

[어휘] peel 껍질을 벗기다 slice (얇게) 썰다 pot 냄비 cooking oil 식용유 stove 가스레인지, 화로 ring 울리다 chat 수다를 떨다 wound 상처 have a temper 다혈질이다 rush 서둘러서 가다 chill 진정하다; 냉기 explosion 폭발 lid 뚜껑 flame 불, 불길 dizzy 현기증이 나는 suspect 의심하다 irresponsible 무책임한

[해석] (A) Dorothy는 집에 혼자 있었다. 그녀는 학교 과제로 바빴고, 갑자기 감자튀김이 먹고 싶어졌다. 그녀는 감자 2개의 껍질을 벗고 얇게 썰고, 식용유를 두른 냄비를 가스레인지 위에 올려 놓았다. 그때 전화기가 울렸다. 그것은 그녀의 가장 친한 친구 Samantha였다. 전화로 수다를 떨던 도중 Dorothy는 부엌에서 이상한 빛이 나는 것을 알아챘고, 그때 (a) 그녀는 가스레인지 위에 있는 기름을 두른 냄비가 떠올랐다.

(C) Dorothy는 전화기를 떨어뜨리고 부엌으로 서둘러 갔다. 기름에는 불이 붙어 있었다. "진정해! 심호흡을 해," (c) 그녀는 자신에게 말했다. 그들이 우리에게 이런 상황에서 하지 말라고 가르친 게 뭐지? 폭발을 일으킬 것이므로 그것에 물을 뿌려서 끄려고 하지 말라는 것을 그녀는 기억했다. 그녀는 냄비의 뚜껑을 들고 불을 끄기 위해 그것으로 냄비를 덮었다. 그 과정에서 그녀는 손에 화상을 입었다. Dorothy는 현기증을 느끼고 부엌 식탁에 앉았다.

(D) 몇 분 후, 그녀의 부모님은 집으로 급하게 달려왔다. Samantha는 Dorothy가 전화기를 그렇게 떨어뜨린 후 무언가 잘못되었을 거라고 의심했었고, (d) 그녀가 Dorothy의 부모님에게 전화를 한 것이다. Dorothy는 울기 시작했다. 그녀의 엄마는 그녀를 꼭 껴안고 상처를 보았다. "무슨 일이 있었는지 말해주렴," 그녀는 말했다. Dorothy는 흐느껴 울고 훌쩍거리며 그녀에게 말했다. "저에게 소리 지르지 않을 거예요? (e) 그녀는 눈물을 흘리며 그들에게 물었다. 그녀의 아버지는 미소를 지으며 대답했다, "나도 (감정이) 폭발하는 것을 막으려고 내 뚜껑을 덮는단다." Dorothy는 안심하며 그를 쳐다보았다. "하지만 다시는 그렇게 무책임하지 않도록 조심하렴."

(B) 잠시 후, 상처가 치료된 후, 가족은 부엌 식탁에 둘러 앉아 이야기를 나눴다. "저는 오늘 큰 교훈을 배웠어요," Dorothy는 말했다. 그녀의 부모는 (b) 그녀가 화재에 관한 무언가를 말할 것을 예상했다. 그러나 그녀는 다른 것에 대해 이야기했다. "저는 엄마 아빠처럼 다정한 말을 더 많이 하기로 결심했어요." 그녀의 부모는 매우 고맙게 여겼는데, Dorothy는 꽤나 다혈질이었기 때문이다.

43
정답 ③

[해설] (A)는 Dorothy가 감자튀김이 먹고 싶어 냄비를 가스레인지 위에 올렸

다가, 전화를 하느라 깜빡해서 불이 났다는 내용이다. (C)의 Dorothy dropped the phone은 (A)에서 친구와 전화를 하다 가스레인지에 올려 놓은 냄비를 떠올려서 놀란 것을 나타내므로 (A) 다음에 오는 것이 적절하다. (D)의 Her mother ~ looked at the wound는 (C)의 In the process she burned her hands의 상처를 의미하므로 (C) 다음에 오는 것이 적절하다. (B)의 after the wound had been treated는 (D)에서 상처를 본 부모님이 치료해주신 것을 나타내므로, (D) 다음에 오는 것이 적절하다. 따라서 글의 순서로 가장 적절한 것은 ③ (C)-(D)-(B)이다.

44
정답 ④

[해설] (a), (b), (c), (e)는 모두 Dorothy를 가리키지만 (d)는 Samantha를 가리키므로 ④이 정답이다.

45
정답 ⑤

[해설] Dorothy looked at him, relieved를 통해 아버지의 말을 들은 Dorothy가 안심했다는 것을 알 수 있으므로, Dorothy에 관한 내용과 일치하지 않는 것은 ⑤ '아버지의 말을 듣고 화를 냈다'이다.

[오답분석] ①은 ~ suddenly wanted to eat French fries와 She peeled two potatoes라고 했으므로 글의 내용과 일치한다. ②은 I have decided to use kind words more ~라고 했으므로 글의 내용과 일치한다. ③은 Don't try to put it out ~ she remembered라고 했으므로 글의 내용과 일치한다. ④은 She picked up the pot's lid and covered the pot과 In the process she burned her hands라고 했으므로 글의 내용과 일치한다.

독해 만점 TEST
p.124

01 ④	02 ①	03 ④	04 ④	05 ⑤	06 ④	07 ④	08 ③
09 ③	10 ②	11 ⑤	12 ④	13 ①	14 ⑤	15 ⑤	16 ⑤
17 ③	18 ②	19 ④	20 ③				

01 ~ 02

[지문분석]

A growing body of evidence suggests / that playing video games can positively affect / cognitive performance.
늘어나는 근거는 시사한다(시사하는 근거가 늘어나고 있다) / 비디오 게임을 하는 것이 긍정적으로 영향을 미칠 수 있음을 / 인지 능력에

★ One of the most notable advantages / video gamers have / over their non-gamer counterparts / is increased **attention**.
가장 주목할 만한 이점 중 하나는 / 비디오 게임을 하는 사람들이 갖는 / 게임을 하지 않는 쪽보다 / 향상된 **주의력**이다

Because video games / often require rapid responses, / with gamers / having to make quick decisions / and process large amounts of visual information, / gamers / frequently demonstrate a greater capacity / to focus on demanding tasks.
비디오 게임은 ~이기 때문에 / 신속한 반응을 종종 요구한다 / 게임을 하는 사람들이 / 신속한 결정을 내리도록 / 그리고 대량의 시각 정보를 처리하도록 / 게임을 하는 사람들은 / 더 뛰어난 능력을 자주 보여준다 / 힘든 작업에 집중하는

Playing video games / may also help / slow down the mental decline / associated with aging.
비디오 게임을 하는 것은 / 또한 도움이 될 수도 있다 / 정신 쇠퇴를 늦추는 데 / 노화와 관련된

Instead of becoming more forgetful, / elderly individuals / who play video games / experience lasting improvements / to their memory.

더 잘 잊어버리게 되기는커녕 / 노령의 사람들은 / 비디오 게임을 하는 / 지속적인 향상을 경험한다 / 그들의 기억력의

This may be / due to the fact / that playing video games / forces individuals / to develop new skills.

이는 ~일 수도 있다 / 사실 때문에 / 비디오 게임을 하는 것 ~라는 / 사람들로 하여금 ~하게 한다 / 새로운 능력을 발달시키다

Learning / how to move a character in a game around, / for instance, / can stimulate the areas of the brain / responsible for memory and motor control.

배우는 것은 / 게임 속 캐릭터를 돌아다니게 하는 방법을 / 예를 들어 / 뇌의 부분을 자극할 수 있다 / 기억력과 운동 제어를 담당하는

Since not learning anything new / causes gray matter to shrink / over time, / it may be possible / that people who play games / have a better chance / of increasing the volume / of their gray matter.

어떠한 새로운 것도 배우지 않는 것은 ~하므로 / 회백질을 오그라들게 한다 / 시간이 지나면서 / ~이 가능할 수도 있다 / 게임을 하는 사람들이 / 더 좋은 기회를 얻는다 / 양을 늘릴 / 그들의 회백질의

★ 독해가 쉬워지는 구문 풀이

One of the most notable advantages video gamers have over their
주어(one of + 명사)   수식어(관계절)
non-gamer counterparts is increased attention.
                        단수동사

▷ 주어 one of the most notable advantages에서 one of는 단수 취급하는 표현이므로 단수동사 is가 쓰였다. video gamers have ~ counterparts는 수 일치에 영향을 미치지 않는 수식어(관계절)이다.

어휘 suggest 시사하다, 제안하다 cognitive 인지의, 인식의
notable 주목할 만한, 중요한 counterpart 반대 쪽, 상대
demonstrate 보여주다, 입증하다 capacity 능력, 용량 decline 쇠퇴, 감소
forgetful 잘 잊어버리는, 잊기 쉬운 elderly 노령의
motor control 운동 제어 shrink 오그라들다, 줄어들다

해석 주제문 비디오 게임을 하는 것이 인지 능력에 긍정적 영향을 미칠 수 있음을 시사하는 근거가 늘어나고 있다. 게임을 하지 않는 쪽보다 비디오 게임을 하는 사람들이 갖는 가장 주목할 만한 이점 중 하나는 향상된 **주의력**이다. 비디오 게임은 게임을 하는 사람들이 신속한 결정을 내리거나 대량의 시각 정보를 처리하도록 하며, 신속한 반응을 종종 요구하기 때문에 게임을 하는 사람들은 힘든 작업에 집중하는 더 뛰어난 능력을 자주 보여준다. 비디오 게임을 하는 것은 또한 노화와 관련된 정신 쇠퇴를 늦추는 데 도움이 될 수도 있다. 더 잘 잊어버리게 되기는커녕, 비디오 게임을 하는 노령의 사람들은 그들의 기억력의 지속적인 향상을 경험한다. 이는 비디오 게임을 하는 것이 사람들로 하여금 새로운 능력을 발달시키게 한다는 사실 때문일 수도 있다. 예를 들어, 게임 속 캐릭터를 돌아다니게 하는 방법을 배우는 것은 기억력과 운동 제어를 담당하는 뇌의 부분을 자극할 수 있다. 어떠한 새로운 것도 배우지 않는 것은 시간이 지나면서 회백질을 오그라들게 하므로, 게임을 하는 사람들이 그들의 회백질의 양을 늘릴 더 좋은 기회를 얻는 것이 가능할 수도 있다.

01
정답 ④

해석 ① 노령층 사이에서 늘어나는 비디오 게임의 인기
② 비디오 게임이 뇌에 미치는 영향: 장단점
③ 새로운 기술을 배우는 것: 더 행복한 삶의 비결
④ 비디오 게임을 하는 것이 뇌에 좋은 이유
⑤ 회백질의 양이 기억력에 영향을 미치는가?

어휘 pros and cons 장단점, 찬반양론

해설 비디오 게임을 하는 것이 인지 능력에 긍정적인 영향을 미칠 수 있다는 근거가 늘어나고 있다고 한 후 몇몇 근거들을 설명하는 내용의 글이므로, 글의 제목으로 가장 적절한 것은 ④ Why Playing Video Games is Good for the Brain(비디오 게임을 하는 것이 뇌에 좋은 이유)이다.

오답 분석 ①은 글의 핵심 소재 Video Games, Elderly를 활용하여 혼동을 주는 오답이다. ③은 글에서 언급되고 있지 않다. ④은 글의 핵심 소재 Video Games, Brain을 활용하여 혼동을 주는 오답이다. ⑤는 글에서 언급된 소재 Gray Matter를 활용하여 혼동을 주는 오답이다.

02
정답 ①

해석 ① 주의력   ② 허기   ③ 혼동
④ 강인함   ⑤ 분노

해설 이 글의 주제문인 '비디오 게임을 하는 것이 인지 능력에 긍정적으로 영향을 미칠 수 있음을 시사하는 근거가 늘어나고 있다'를 다시 언급한 문장이나 부연 설명하는 문장을 파악해야 한다. 비디오 게임은 게임을 하는 사람들에게 신속한 반응을 종종 요구하며, 그들은 힘든 작업에 집중하는 더 뛰어난 능력을 자주 보여준다고 했다. 따라서 비디오 게임을 하는 사람들이 갖는 가장 주목할 만한 이점 중 하나는 향상된 "주의력"이라는 의미가 되는 것이 자연스러우므로 ① attention(주의력)이 정답이다.

오답 분석 ②, ④, ⑤은 글의 내용과 상관없는 오답이다. ③은 "힘든 작업에 집중하는 더 뛰어난 능력을 보인다"는 지문의 내용과 반대되는 오답이다.

03 ~ 05

지문분석

(A) Emily visited her aunt / once a week.
Emily는 그녀의 이모를 방문했다 / 일주일에 한 번

She was Emily's favorite relative, / and Emily loved talking with her / about all sorts of things.
그녀는 Emily가 가장 좋아하는 친척이었다 / 그리고 Emily는 그녀와 이야기하는 것을 좋아했다 / 많은 것에 대해

One day, / as she was visiting, / she began to complain / to her aunt / about some things / in her life.
하루는 / 그녀가 방문하고 있을 때 / 그녀는 불평하기 시작했다 / 그녀의 이모에게 / 몇몇 것에 대해 / 자기 삶의

Her car / wasn't nice enough.
그녀의 차는 / 충분히 멋지지 않았다

Her apartment / wasn't big enough.
그녀의 아파트는 / 충분히 넓지 않았다

Her clothes / weren't fashionable enough.
그녀의 옷은 / 충분히 최신 유행의 것이 아니었다

She grumbled / about all these things to (a) her.
그녀는 투덜거렸다 / 이러한 모든 것에 대해 / 그녀에게

(B) ★ She graciously accepted / but kept looking at the fancy one / her aunt was holding.
그녀는 고맙게 받았다 / 하지만 화려한 것을 계속 보았다 / 그녀의 이모가 들고 있던

"Why are you looking at my cup?" / (b) she asked.
왜 내 컵을 보고 있니 / 라며 그녀가 물었다

"It's a nice mug," / Emily replied.
멋진 머그잔이네요 / 라고 Emily가 답했다

Her aunt smiled.
그녀의 이모가 미소 지었다

"It's natural / to want the best / for yourself.
당연한 거야 / 가장 좋은 것을 원하는 건 / 스스로를 위해

There is nothing wrong / with wanting nice things."
아무런 문제가 없어 / 좋은 것을 원하는 것엔

"But / if you focus too much / on it," / (c) <u>she</u> continued / "it can cause you to become unhappy."

하지만 / 만약 네가 너무 많이 초점을 둔다면 / 그것에 / 그녀가 이어서 말했다 / 그것은 네가 불행해지게 만들 수 있어

(C) Emily nodded.

Emily가 고개를 끄덕였다

"What you really want / is a good cup of coffee," / her aunt said.

네가 정말로 원하는 것은 / 맛있는 커피 한 잔이야 / 라고 그녀의 이모가 말했다

"What you drink it out of / does not change / how the coffee tastes, / does it?"

네가 그것을 무엇으로 마시는지는 / 바꾸지 않아 / 커피가 어떤 맛이 나는지를 / 그렇지

Emily thought / about her life.

Emily가 생각했다 / 그녀의 삶에 대해

She had a good job / and was healthy.

그녀는 좋은 직장이 있었다 / 그리고 건강했다

She had family and friends / who loved her.

그녀는 가족과 친구들이 있었다 / 그녀를 사랑하는

"You're right," / she said.

이모가 맞아요 / 라며 그녀가 말했다

"(d) I have / a really good cup of coffee.

저는 마시고 있어요 / 정말로 맛있는 커피 한 잔을

What more could I want?"

제가 무엇을 더 원하겠어요

(D) Her aunt listened / to these complaints / quietly / and then went to the kitchen.

그녀의 이모는 들었다 / 이러한 불평을 / 조용히 / 그리고 나서 주방으로 갔다

(e) <u>She</u> came back / with a coffee pot and two mugs.

그녀는 돌아왔다 / 커피 주전자와 머그잔 두 개를 가지고

One was very nice and fancy, / while the other was plain / with a small crack / on the handle.

하나는 매우 멋지고 화려했다 / 반면 다른 것은 평범했다 / 그리고 작게 금이 가 있었다 / 손잡이에

She poured coffee into both / and handed Emily the plain one.

그녀는 두 잔 모두에 커피를 부었다 / 그리고 Emily에게 평범한 잔을 주었다

★ 독해가 쉬워지는 구문 풀이

She graciously <u>accepted</u> but <u>kept looking</u> at the fancy one [her
주어   동사1   동사2
aunt was holding].
수식어(관계절)

⇨ 동사 keep은 동명사(looking)를 목적어로 취한다.

⇨ [ ]는 선행사로 one을 취하는 관계절이다.

[어휘] all sorts of 많은 fashionable 최신 유행의
grumble 투덜거리다, 넜두리하다 graciously 고맙게도, 우아하게
nod (고개를) 끄덕이다, 까딱하다 out of ~으로, ~에서 fancy 화려한, 비싼
plain 평범한, 분명한 crack 금, 틈새

[해석] (A) Emily는 일주일에 한 번 그녀의 이모를 방문했다. 그녀는 Emily가 가장 좋아하는 친척이었고, Emily는 많은 것에 대해 그녀와 이야기하는 것을 좋아했다. 하루는, 그녀가 방문하고 있을 때 Emily는 자기 삶의 몇몇 것에 대해 그녀의 이모에게 불평하기 시작했다. 그녀의 차는 충분히 멋지지 않았다. 그녀의 아파트는 충분히 넓지 않았다. 그녀의 옷은 충분히 최신 유행의 것이 아니었다. 그녀는 이러한 모든 것에 대해 (a) <u>그녀</u>에게 투덜거렸다.
(D) 그녀의 이모는 이러한 불평을 조용히 듣고 나서 주방으로 갔다. (e) <u>그녀</u>는 커피 주전자와 머그잔 두 개를 가지고 돌아왔다. 하나는 매우 멋지고 화려한 반면, 다른 것은 평범하고 손잡이에 작게 금이 가 있었다. 그녀는 두 잔 모두에 커피를 부었고 Emily에게 평범한 잔을 주었다.
(B) 그녀는 고맙게 받았지만, 그녀의 이모가 들고 있던 화려한 것을 계속 보았다. "왜 내 컵을 보고 있니?"라며 (b) <u>그녀</u>가 물었다. "멋진 머그잔이네

요."라고 Emily가 답했다. 그녀의 이모가 미소 지었다. "스스로를 위해 가장 좋은 것을 원하는 건 당연한 거야. 좋은 것을 원하는 것엔 아무런 문제가 없어." "하지만 만약 네가 그것에 너무 많이 초점을 둔다면" (c) <u>그녀</u>가 이어서 말했다. "그것은 네가 불행해지게 만들 수 있어."
(C) Emily가 고개를 끄덕였다. "네가 정말로 원하는 것은 맛있는 커피 한 잔이야"라고 그녀의 이모가 말했다. "네가 그것을 무엇으로 마시는지는 커피가 어떤 맛이 나는지를 바꾸지 않아, 그렇지?" Emily가 그녀의 삶에 대해 생각했다. 그녀는 좋은 직장이 있었고 건강했다. 그녀는 그녀를 사랑하는 가족과 친구들이 있었다. "이모가 맞아요"라며 그녀가 말했다. "(d) <u>저</u>는 정말로 맛있는 커피 한 잔을 마시고 있어요. 제가 무엇을 더 원하겠어요?"

03 　　　　　　　　　　　　　　정답 ④

[해설] (A)는 Emily가 일주일에 한 번 그녀의 이모를 방문했는데, 하루는 이모에게 자신의 삶에서 몇몇 것에 대해 불평했다는 내용이다. (D)의 these complaints는 (A)의 grumbled about all these things의 all these things를 가리키므로 (A) 다음에 오는 것이 적절하다. (B)의 the fancy one은 (D)의 One was very nice and fancy, while the other was plain에서의 One을 가리키므로 (D) 다음에 오는 것이 적절하다. (C)의 Emily nodded는 (B)에서 좋은 것을 원하는 것에 너무 많은 초점을 둔다면 불행해지게 된다는 그녀의 이모의 조언을 받아들이는 것을 나타내므로 (B) 다음에 오는 것이 적절하다. 따라서 ④ (D)-(B)-(C)가 정답이다.

04 　　　　　　　　　　　　　　정답 ④

[해설] (a), (b), (c), (e)는 모두 Emily의 이모를 가리키지만 (d)는 Emily를 가리키므로 ④이 정답이다.

05 　　　　　　　　　　　　　　정답 ⑤

[해설] She poured coffee into both and handed Emily the plain one을 통해 Emily에게는 화려한 컵이 아닌 평범한 컵을 건네주었다는 것을 알 수 있으므로, Emily에 관한 내용과 일치하지 않는 것은 ⑤ '화려한 머그잔에 든 커피를 마셨다.'이다.

[오답분석] ①은 Emily visited her aunt once a week라고 했으므로 글의 내용과 일치한다. ②은 Emily loved talking with her about all sorts of things라고 했으므로 글의 내용과 일치한다. ③은 Her apartment wasn't big enough라고 했으므로 글의 내용과 일치한다. ④은 It's natural to want the best for yourself라고 했으므로 글의 내용과 일치한다.

06 ~ 07

[지문분석]

It is well established / that vitamin D plays an important role / in bone health / and the prevention and treatment / of a wide range of health conditions.

충분히 입증되었다 / 비타민 D가 중요한 역할을 한다는 것은 / 뼈 건강에 / 그리고 예방과 치료에 / 다양한 건강상 질병의

However, / new research shows / that vitamin D may impact us / even before birth.

그러나 / 새로운 연구는 보여준다 / 비타민 D가 우리에게 영향을 줄 수도 있음을 / 출생 전에도

Specifically, / it can help / with fetal brain development, / implying / that a child's intelligence may be (a) <u>connected</u> / to their mother's vitamin D levels / while pregnant.

구체적으로 / 그것은 도움이 될 수 있다 / 태아의 뇌 발달에 / 그런데 이것은 암시한다 / 아이의 지능이 연관될 수도 있음을 / 엄마의 비타민 D 수치와 / 임신 기간 동안

It is common / for pregnant women / to have insufficient amounts / of vitamin D.
~은 일반적이다 / 임신한 여성에게 / 불충분한 양이 있다는 것 / 비타민 D의

This is because / there are very (b) few foods / that contain enough of it / naturally.
이는 ~하기 때문이다 / 음식이 거의 없다 / 충분한 양의 그것(비타민 D)이 함유된 / 자연 상태에서

Thus, / the sun is actually the best source / of vitamin D, / since sunlight triggers a chemical reaction / in the skin / that (c) produces it.
따라서 / 사실상 하는 최고의 원천이다 / 비타민 D의 / 햇빛이 화학 반응을 유발시키기 때문에 / 피부에서 / 그것(비타민 D)을 생성하는

However, / telling all pregnant women / to simply get some sun / in order to give their child an advantage / is not always practical.
그러나 / 모든 임신부에게 말하는 것은 / 어느 정도 햇빛을 쬐라고 / 아이에게 도움이 되고자 / 항상 현실적이지는 않다

★ Not only can it be dangerous, / but women with dark skin / do not experience the same results / as fairer-skinned women.
그것은 위험할 수 있을 뿐만 아니라 / 어두운 피부를 가진 여성들은 / 같은 효과를 경험하지 못한다 / 더 흰 피부를 가진 여성들만큼

They are (d) able (→ unable) / to produce as much Vitamin D / through exposure to the sun / because / their skin has more melanin, / which disturbs the Vitamin D production.
그들은 ~할 수 있다(→ 할 수 없다) / 비타민 D를 그만큼 생성시키는 것 / 햇빛에 대한 노출만으로는 / 왜냐하면 / 그들의 피부에 멜라닌이 더 많이 있다 / 그것은 비타민 D 생성을 방해한다

To give all children an equal chance / to develop properly, / it is important / that health care professionals carefully screen / pregnant women / to ensure / their vitamin D levels (e) stay high.
모든 아이들에게 동일한 기회를 주려면 / 제대로 성장할 / ~이 중요하다 / 의료 전문가들이 주의 깊게 검진하는 것 / 임산부를 / 확실히 하기 위해 / 그들의 비타민 D 수치가 높은 편을 유지하도록

★ 독해가 쉬워지는 구문 풀이

Not only can it be dangerous, but women with dark skin do not
부정   조동사 주어
의미의 어구
experience the same results as fairer-skinned women.

⇨ 부정의 의미를 가진 어구 Not only가 절의 앞쪽에 왔으므로 조동사인 can이 주어 앞으로 도치되었다.

어휘 establish 입증하다, 설립하다   condition 병, 조건
specifically 구체적으로, 특히   fetal 태아의   pregnant 임신한, 풍요한
insufficient 불충분한   practical 현실적인, 실제적인   fair-skinned 피부가 흰
disturb 방해하다   health care professional 의료 전문가

해석 비타민 D가 뼈 건강과 다양한 건강상 질병의 예방과 치료에 중요한 역할을 한다는 것은 충분히 입증되었다. 그러나, 새로운 연구는 비타민 D가 출생 전에도 우리에게 영향을 줄 수도 있음을 보여준다. [주제문] 구체적으로, 그것은 태아의 뇌 발달에 도움이 될 수 있는데, 이것은 아이의 지능이 임신 기간 동안 엄마의 비타민 D 수치와 (a) 연관될 수도 있음을 암시한다. 임신한 여성에게 불충분한 양의 비타민 D가 있다는 것은 일반적이다. 이는 자연 상태에서 충분한 양의 그것(비타민 D)이 함유된 음식이 (b) 거의 없기 때문이다. 따라서, 사실상 하는 비타민 D의 최고의 원천인데, 햇빛은 피부에서 그것(비타민 D)을 (c) 생성하는 화학 반응을 유발시키기 때문이다. 그러나, 아이에게 도움이 되고자 모든 임산부에게 어느 정도 햇빛을 쬐라고 말하는 것은 항상 현실적이지는 않다. 그것은 위험할 수 있을 뿐만 아니라, 어두운 피부를 가진 여성들은 더 흰 피부를 가진 여성들만큼 같은 효과를 경험하지 못한다. 그들의 피부에는 비타민 D 생성을 방해하는 멜라닌이 더 많이 있기 때문에 햇빛에 대한 노출만으로는 비타민 D를 그만큼 생성 (d) 시킬 수 있다(→ 시킬 수 없다). 모든 아이들에게 제대로 성장할 동일한 기회를 주려면, 의료 전문가들이 임산부들의 비타민 D

수치가 확실히 높은 편을 (e) 유지하도록 하기 위해 그들을 주의 깊게 검진하는 것이 중요하다.

06
정답 ④

해석 ① 인체 내에서 멜라닌의 역할
② 과도한 비타민 D의 위험
③ 빛을 많이 쬘수록 비타민 D는 덜 얻는다
④ 비타민 D: 당신이 임신 중일 때 충분히 얻어라
⑤ 비타민 D 보충으로 당신의 뇌에 활력을 불어넣어라

어휘 boost (활력) 등을 불어넣다

해설 임산부가 충분한 비타민 D를 섭취하는 것이 태아의 뇌 발달과 지능에 영향을 미칠 수 있기 때문에 비타민 D 수치가 확실히 높은 편을 유지하도록 주의 깊게 검진하는 것이 중요하다라는 내용의 글이므로, 글의 제목으로 가장 적절한 것은 ④ Vitamin D: Get Enough When You're Pregnant (비타민 D: 당신이 임신 중일 때 충분히 얻어라)이다.

오답 분석 ①은 글에서 언급된 소재 Melanin을 활용하여 혼동을 주는 오답이다. ②은 글의 핵심 소재 Vitamin D를, ③은 Sunshine과 Vitamin D를 활용하여 혼동을 주는 오답이다. ⑤은 글의 핵심 소재 Vitamin D와, 글에서 언급된 소재 Brain을 활용하여 혼동을 주는 오답이다.

07
정답 ④

해설 어두운 피부를 가진 여성들은 비타민 D 생성을 방해하는 멜라닌이 피부에 더 많으므로, 더 흰 피부를 가진 여성들과 똑같은 효과를 경험하지 못하며, 따라서 햇빛에 노출되더라도 비타민 D를 최대한으로 생성"시킬 수 없다"는 맥락이 되어야 하므로 ④의 able(~할 수 있다)을 unable(~할 수 없다)과 같은 어휘로 바꾸어야 문맥상 적절하다.

오답 분석 ①은 출생 전에도 우리가 비타민 D의 영향을 받을 수 있기 때문에 아이의 지능이 임신 기간 동안 산모의 비타민 D 수치와 "연관된다"는 맥락이 되어야 하므로 connected가 오는 것이 적절하다. ②은 임신한 여성에게 비타민 D가 불충분한 일이 일반적이고, 이는 충분한 양의 비타민 D를 함유한 음식이 "거의 없기" 때문이라는 문맥이 되어야 하므로 few가 오는 것이 적절하다. ③은 햇빛이 비타민 D를 생성하는 최고의 원천인데, 그것은 햇빛이 피부에서 비타민 D를 "생성하는" 화학 반응을 유발시키기 때문이라는 맥락이 되어야 하므로 produces가 오는 것이 적절하다. ⑤은 모든 아이들에게 그들이 제대로 성장할 동일한 기회를 주려면, 의료 전문가들이 임산부들을 주의 깊게 검진해서 그들의 비타민 D 수치가 확실하게 높은 편을 "유지하도록" 해야 한다는 맥락이 되어야 하므로 stay가 오는 것이 적절하다.

08 ~ 10

지문분석

(A) After his car accident, / David had to use a wheelchair / to go anywhere.
자동차 사고 이후에 / David는 휠체어를 사용해야 했다 / 어디든 가려면

It was difficult / for him / because he had always loved / playing sports and being active, / but now / he believed / it would be impossible.
이것은 힘들었다 / 그에게 / 그는 항상 좋아했기 때문에 / 운동하는 것과 활동적인 것을 / 그리고 이제 / 그는 생각했다 / 그것이 불가능할 것이라고

That's why / he was surprised / when (a) he met Michael at the hospital / one day.
그것이 ~한 이유이다 / 그가 놀랐던 / 그가 Michael을 병원에서 만났을 때 / 어느 날

Michael was also in a wheelchair / and asked David, / "Do you like to play sports?"
Michael 또한 휠체어를 타고 있었다 / 그리고 David에게 물었다 / 당신은 운동하는 것을 좋아하나요

(B) David failed a lot / at that first practice, / but he kept going back / and getting better.
David는 많이 실패했다 / 그 첫 연습에서 / 하지만 그는 계속 다시 시도했다 / 그리고 계속 실력이 더 나아졌다

Eventually, / (b) he was even invited / to play for the team / at the national championship tournament.
결국 / 그는 심지어 초대되었다 / 그 팀을 위해 경기하도록 / 전국 선수권 대회에서

During their final game, / David ended up scoring the winning point, / helping his team win the tournament.
결승전에서 / David는 결국 결승점을 득점했다 / 그리고 그의 팀이 대회에서 우승하도록 도왔다

Surrounded by his teammates, / David held the trophy high.
그의 팀원들에 둘러싸여서 / David는 트로피를 높이 들었다

"I knew / you could do it!" / Michael exclaimed.
저는 알았어요 / 당신이 할 수 있을 줄 / Michael이 소리쳤다

David grinned at him, / thankful for (c) his encouragement.
David는 그를 향해 활짝 웃었다 / 그의 격려에 고마워하며

(C) David stared at him / with wide eyes.
David는 그를 처다보았다 / 눈을 동그랗게 뜨고

"What do you mean?" / (d) he asked.
무슨 말씀이신가요 / 라며 그가 물었다

"How would I play sports?"
제가 어떻게 운동을 하겠어요

Michael laughed and replied, / "You can move around, / can't you?"
Michael은 웃으며 대답했다 / 당신은 움직일 수 있잖아요 / 그렇지 않나요

David nodded / in response.
David는 고개를 끄덕였다 / 대답으로

"Well then, / you should be fine!
그렇다면 / 당신은 지장이 없을 거예요

Come to my team's basketball practice / next Tuesday.
저희 팀의 농구 연습에 오세요 / 다음 주 화요일에

I'll show you / how we play."
제가 보여드릴게요 / 저희가 어떻게 경기하는지

(D) On that day, / David went to basketball practice / and was amazed / by how skilled the players were.
그날 / David는 농구 연습에 갔다 / 그리고 놀랐다 / 선수들의 실력이 얼마나 좋은지에

When it was (e) his turn / to play, / David told Michael, / ★ "I don't think I can do it.
그가 할 차례가 되었을 때 / David는 Michael에게 말했다 / 저는 못할 것 같아요

I'm just not used to / being in a wheelchair."
저는 아직 ~에 익숙하지 않아요 / 휠체어를 타는 것

Michael gave him a knowing smile.
Michael은 그에게 다 안다는 듯한 미소를 지었다

"David, / were you great / at any sport / the very first time you played it?"
David / 당신은 잘했나요 / 그 어떤 스포츠든 / 처음 했을 때

David shook his head.
David는 고개를 저었다

"So / why would this be any different?
그럼 / 이것이라고 뭐가 다를까요

You have to practice / to get better.
당신은 연습해야 해요 / 더 잘하기 위해

I know / you can do it."
제가 알아요 / 당신이 할 수 있다는 것을

What Michael said / made sense / to David.
Michael이 했던 말은 / 이해가 되었다 / David에게

He had to at least try.
그는 적어도 시도를 해야 했다

★ 독해가 쉬워지는 구문 풀이

"I don't think [I can do it]. I'm just not used to being in a wheelchair."
동명사

⇨ 명사절 [ ]는 동사 think의 목적어이며, 명사절 접속사 that이 생략되었다.
⇨ be used to 뒤에 동명사가 올 때는 '~하는 데 익숙하다'라는 의미이다.

어휘 national championship tournament 전국 선수권 대회
winning point 결승점 exclaim 소리치다 grin 활짝 웃다
encouragement 격려 nod 고개를 끄덕이다 make sense 이해가 되다

해석 (A) 자동차 사고 이후에, David는 어디든 가려면 휠체어를 사용해야 했다. 그는 운동하는 것과 활동적인 것을 항상 좋아했기 때문에 이것은 그에게 힘들었고, 이제 그는 그것이 불가능할 것이라고 믿었다. 그것이 어느 날 (a) 그가 Michael을 병원에서 만났을 때 놀랐던 이유이다. Michael 또한 휠체어를 타고 있었고 David에게 물었다, "당신은 운동하는 것을 좋아하나요?"
(C) David는 눈을 동그랗게 뜨고 그를 처다보았다. "무슨 말씀이신가요?"라며 (d) 그가 물었다. "제가 어떻게 운동을 하겠어요?" Michael은 웃으며 대답했다, "당신은 움직일 수 있잖아요, 그렇지 않나요?" David는 대답으로 고개를 끄덕였다. "그렇다면, 당신은 지장이 없을 거예요! 다음 주 화요일 저희 팀의 농구 연습에 오세요. 저희가 어떻게 경기하는지 제가 보여드릴게요."
(D) 그날, David는 농구 연습에 갔고 선수들의 실력이 얼마나 좋은지에 놀랐다. (e) 그가 할 차례가 되었을 때, David는 Michael에게 말했다, "저는 못할 것 같아요. 저는 아직 휠체어를 타는 것에 익숙하지 않아요." Michael은 그에게 다 안다는 듯한 미소를 지었다. "David, 당신은 그 어떤 스포츠든 처음 했을 때 잘했나요?" David는 고개를 저었다. "그럼 이것이라고 뭐가 다를까요? 당신은 더 잘하기 위해 연습해야 해요. 당신이 할 수 있다는 것을 제가 알아요." Michael이 했던 말은 David에게 이해가 되었다. 그는 적어도 시도를 해야 했다.
(B) David는 그 첫 연습에서 많이 실패했지만, 그는 계속 다시 시도했고, 실력이 계속 더 나아졌다. 결국, (b) 그는 심지어 전국 선수권 대회에서 그 팀을 위해 경기하도록 초대되었다. 결승전에서, David는 결국 결승점을 득점했고, 그의 팀이 대회에서 우승하도록 도왔다. 그의 팀원들에 둘러싸여서, David는 트로피를 높이 들었다. "저는 당신이 할 수 있을 줄 알았어요!" Michael이 소리쳤다. David는 (c) 그의 격려에 고마워하며, 그를 향해 활짝 웃었다.

08
정답 ③

해설 (A)는 David가 자동차 사고 이후에 휠체어를 타야 했고 그는 운동하고 활동적인 것을 항상 좋아했지만 이제는 불가능할 것이라고 믿던 중 Michael을 만났다는 내용이다. (C)의 David stared at him의 him은 (A)에서 David에게 운동하는 것을 좋아하냐고 물으며 다가온 Michael을 가리키므로 (A) 다음에 오는 것이 적절하다. (D)의 On that day에서 that day는 (C)의 basketball practice next Tuesday를 가리키므로 (C) 다음에 오는 것이 적절하다. (B)는 David가 첫 연습에서는 많이 실패했지만 계속 연습하면서 실력이 나아지고 심지어 전국 선수권 대회에서 팀이 우승하도록 도왔다는 내용이므로 Michael이 휠체어를 타면서 운동하는 것도 잘하려면 연습해야 한다고 한 (D) 뒤에 오는 것이 적절하다. 따라서 ③ (C) - (D) - (B)가 정답이다.

09
정답 ③

해설 (a), (b), (d), (e)는 모두 David를 가리키지만 (c)는 Michael을 가리키므로 ③이 정답이다.

10
정답 ②

해설 David failed a lot at that first practice를 통해 David는 첫 연습에서는 많이 실패했다는 것을 알 수 있으므로, David에 관한 내용과 일치하지 않는 것은 ② '첫 연습부터 성과가 좋았다'이다.

오답 분석 ①은 he believed it(playing sports and being active) would be impossible라고 했으므로 글의 내용과 일치한다. ③은 David ended up scoring the winning point라고 했으므로 글의 내용과 일치한다. ④은 Come to my(Michael) team's basketball practice next Tuesday라고 했으므로 글의 내용과 일치한다. ⑤은 I(David) don't think I can do it. I'm just not used to being in a wheelchair라고 했으므로 글의 내용과 일치한다.

11 ~ 12

지문분석

Streets / that have been named after people / can be found / throughout the world.
도로들은 / 사람들의 이름을 따서 명명된 / 발견된다 / 전 세계에서

But / how do cities determine / who to (a) remember / in this way?
하지만 / 도시는 어떻게 정하는가 / 기억할 누군가를 / 이러한 방식으로

A study / analyzing street names / in London, Paris, Vienna, and New York / has revealed / that street names mostly honor people / who made important contributions / to their respective societies.
한 조사는 / 도로명을 분석한 / 런던, 파리, 빈(비엔나), 뉴욕의 / 보여주었다 / 도로명이 대부분 사람들을 기린다는 것을 / 중대한 기여를 한 / 그들 각각의 사회에

Their names are assigned to streets / to inspire residents / to adopt the (b) values / they stood for.
그들의 이름이 도로에 부여된다 / 주민들을 고취시키기 위해 / 가치를 받아들이도록 / 그들이 상징하는

To see / how street names in the four cities (c) differ, / researchers analyzed / the people they were named after.
알아보기 위해 / 네 도시의 도로명이 어떻게 다른지 / 조사원들은 분석했다 / 이름이 붙여진 사람들을

In particular, / they focused on / the ratio of men to women, / the historical period they lived in, / and the number of foreign figures.
특히 / 그들은 주목했다 / 여성 대비 남성의 비율 / 그들이 살았던 역사적 시기 / 그리고 외국인들의 수

It was found / that Vienna and London have significantly (d) fewer(→ more) streets / named after women / than New York and Paris.
~이 드러났다 / 빈과 런던에는 도로가 현저히 더 적다(→ 더 많다)는 것이 / 여성의 이름을 따서 명명된 / 뉴욕 및 파리보다

This suggests / that Vienna and London have taken steps / to emphasize the importance of women, / while New York and Paris have not.
이는 시사한다 / 빈과 런던이 조치를 취했다 / 여성의 가치를 강조하려는 / 반면 뉴욕과 파리는 그렇지 않음을

In the three European cities, / most streets are named after people / from the 19th century, / while / in New York, / the majority of honorees / lived in the late 20th century.
유럽의 세 도시에서 / 대부분의 도로는 사람들의 이름을 따서 명명된다 / 19세기의 / 반면 뉴욕에서 / 그 영예를 받은 대부분의 사람이 / 20세기 후반에 살았다

Finally, / Vienna demonstrates / the most (e) progressive attitude, / with 45 percent of its streets / named after foreigners.
마지막으로 / 빈은 보여준다 / 가장 진보적인 사고방식을 / 도로의 45퍼센트가 / 외국인들의 이름을 따서 명명되었으므로

★ Despite being global cities, / London, Paris, and New York / can hardly say the same.
세계적인 도시임에도 불구하고 / 런던, 파리, 뉴욕은 / 똑같다고 보기는 힘들다

★ 독해가 쉬워지는 구문 풀이

Despite being global cities, London, Paris, and New York can
　　전치사　　동명사구
hardly say the same.

⇨ 명사 역할을 하는 단어나 구 앞에 올 수 있는 전치사 Despite가 동명사구 being global cities 앞에 쓰였다.

어휘 name after ~의 이름을 따서 명명하다 reveal 보여주다, 밝히다 honor 기리다, 예우하다 assign 부여하다, 배정하다 inspire 고취시키다 adopt 받아들이다, 취하다 stand for ~을 상징하다, 나타내다 metric (측정) 기준; 미터법의 take steps 조치를 취하다 emphasize 강조하다 importance 가치, 중요성 majority 대부분, 대다수 honoree 영예를 받는 사람, 수상자 progressive 진보적인, 점진적인 attitude 사고방식, 태도

해석 사람들의 이름을 따서 명명된 도로들은 전 세계에서 발견된다. 하지만, 도시는 이러한 방식으로 (a) 기억할 누군가를 어떻게 정하는가? 런던, 파리, 빈(비엔나), 뉴욕의 도로명을 분석한 한 조사는 도로명이 대부분 그들 각각의 사회에 중대한 기여를 한 사람들을 기린다는 것을 보여주었다. 그들이 상징하는 (b) 가치를 주민들이 받아들이도록 고취시키기 위해 그들의 이름이 도로에 부여된다. 네 도시의 도로명이 어떻게 (c) 다른지 알아보기 위해, 조사원들은 (도로에 자신들의) 이름이 붙여진 사람들을 분석했다. 특히, 그들은 여성 대비 남성의 비율, 그들이 살았던 역사적 시기, 그리고 외국인들의 수에 주목했다. 빈과 런던에는 뉴욕 및 파리보다 여성의 이름을 따서 명명된 도로가 현저히 (d) 더 적다(→ 더 많다)는 것이 드러났다. 이는 빈과 런던이 여성의 가치를 강조하려는 조치를 취한 반면, 뉴욕과 파리는 그렇지 않음을 시사한다. 유럽의 세 도시에서, 대부분의 도로는 19세기 사람들의 이름을 따서 명명된 반면, 뉴욕에서 그 영예를 받은 대부분의 사람들은 20세기 후반에 살았다. 마지막으로, 빈은 도로의 45퍼센트가 외국인들의 이름을 따서 명명되었으므로, 가장 (e) 진보적인 사고방식을 보여준다. 런던, 파리, 뉴욕은 세계적인 도시임에도 불구하고 똑같다고 보기는 힘들다.

11
정답 ⑤

해석 ① 도로명을 바꿀 시점을 아는 것의 중요성
② 도로명이 주택의 가치에 영향을 미치는가?
③ 도로명은 실용적인가 또는 정치적인가?
④ 도로명 속 현대적 표현
⑤ 도로명: 문화와 역사의 반영

어휘 representation 표현, 대표 reflection 반영, 반사

해설 사람들의 이름을 따서 명명된 도로명은 각 도시에 중대한 기여를 한 사람들을 기리기 위한 것이며, 네 도시의 도로명은 성별 비율의 차이, 인물이 살았던 시기, 명명된 외국인의 수를 기준으로 다르다는 내용의 글이므로, 글의 제목으로 가장 적절한 것은 ⑤ Street Names: A Reflection of Culture and History(도로명: 문화와 역사의 반영)이다.

오답 분석 ①, ③, ④은 글의 핵심 소재인 street와 name을, ②은 글의 핵심 소재인 street names와 value를 활용하여 혼동을 주는 오답이다.

12
정답 ④

해설 빈과 런던은 여성의 가치를 강조하려는 조치를 취했기 때문에 그곳에는 여성의 이름을 따서 명명된 도로가 "더 많다"는 맥락이 되어야 하므로,

④의 fewer(더 적은)를 more(더 많은)와 같은 어휘로 바꾸어야 문맥상 적절하다.

 오답분석 ①은 각 사회에 중대한 기여를 한 사람들의 이름을 따서 도로명을 짓고 그들을 "기억"한다는 문맥이 되어야 하므로 remember가 오는 것이 적절하다. ②은 도로명이 사회에 중대한 기여를 한 사람들을 기린다는 것을 보여주었다는 앞 문장에 이어서, 그것은 그들이 상징하는 "가치"를 주민들이 받아들이도록 고취시키기 위함이라는 문맥이 되어야 하므로 values가 오는 것이 적절하다. ③은 네 도시의 도로명이 어떻게 "다른지"를 알아보기 위해 조사원들이 사람들을 분석했다는 문맥이 되어야 하므로 differ가 오는 것이 적절하다. ⑤은 사람의 이름을 딴 비엔나의 도로명 중 45%가 외국인의 이름을 따서 명명되었기 때문에 가장 "진보적인" 사고방식을 보여준다는 문맥이 되어야 하므로 progressive가 오는 것이 적절하다.

13 ~ 15

지문분석

(A) As I was attending my first class / at university, / I saw an unusual sight.
내가 첫 수업에 참석했을 때 / 대학교에서 / 나는 드문 광경을 보았다

A very old lady walked / into the class / and sat down / next to me.
나이가 아주 많은 한 여성이 걸어 들어왔다 / 교실로 / 그리고 앉았다 / 내 옆에

"Hi, / I'm Daisy," / she said / as she introduced herself.
안녕 / 나는 Daisy야 / 라며 그녀는 말했다 / 스스로를 소개하면서

Daisy was 78 years old / and in her third year / of college.
Daisy는 78세였다 / 그리고 3학년이었다 / 대학의

After class, / I was so interested in Daisy / that I asked another girl / about her.
수업 후에 / 나는 Daisy에게 매우 호기심이 생겼다 / 그래서 다른 여학생에게 물어보았다 / 그녀에 대해

"I'm sorry, / I don't know her very well. / Maybe you can ask (a) her / yourself?" / she said.
미안 / 나는 그녀를 잘 몰라 / 아마 네가 그녀에게 물어봐도 될 걸 / 직접 / 이라고 그녀가 말했다

(B) I decided / to do just that.
나는 결심했다 / 바로 그렇게 하기로

So / one day after class, / I walked up to Daisy / and asked her / how (b) she came to be a student / at such a mature age.
그래서 / 어느 날 수업 후 / 나는 Daisy에게 걸어갔다 / 그리고 그녀에게 물어보았다 / 어떻게 그녀가 학생이 되었는지 / 그렇게 장년의 나이에

She replied / that she had always wanted / to go to college / but never had the chance.
그녀는 답했다 / 항상 ~하고 싶었다고 / 대학에 들어가고 / 하지만 전혀 기회가 없었다

I wanted to know more / about her story, / and I asked / if we could have lunch together.
나는 더 알고 싶었다 / 그녀의 이야기에 대해 / 그리고 물어보았다 / 우리가 함께 점심을 먹을 수 있을지

(C) "We don't stop playing / because we grow old, / we grow old / because we stop playing."
우리는 즐기는 것을 멈추지 않아 / 나이 들었다고 / 우리가 나이가 드는 거야 / 즐기는 것을 멈추기 때문에라며

Daisy taught me / that we are never too old / to try something new / and that we shouldn't ever lose / our passion for living.
Daisy는 내게 가르쳐주었다 / 우리가 결코 나이가 많지 않다고 / 새로운 것을 시도하기에 / 그리고 우리의 절대 잃어서는 안 된다 / 삶에 대한 열정을

I vowed / to follow in (c) her footsteps.
나는 다짐했다 / 그녀의 선례를 좇아가기로

She was a true role model / and inspiration.
그녀는 진정한 롤 모델이었다 / 그리고 영감을 주는 사람

She lived her life / to the fullest / and that is exactly / how I wish to live mine.
그녀는 그녀의 인생을 살았다 / 최대한으로 / 그리고 그건 정확히 ~이다 / 내가 내 인생을 살아가고 싶은 방식

(D) We went to a nearby café / and (d) she told me all / about her life.
우리는 근처 카페에 갔다 / 그리고 그녀는 모든 것을 내게 말해주었다 / 그녀의 인생에 대한

★ She had done / so many interesting things / and lived through / so many amazing experiences / that I was surprised / she still wanted to do so much.
그녀는 했었다 / 아주 많은 흥미로운 일을 / 그리고 겪었다 / 아주 많은 놀라운 경험들을 / 그래서 나는 놀랐다 / 그녀가 아직도 그렇게 많은 것을 하고 싶어 한다는 것에

A few classmates saw me / and came over / to join us.
몇몇 반 친구들이 나를 보았다 / 그리고 다가왔다 / 우리와 함께하려고

They listened to her wonderful stories.
그들은 그녀의 놀라운 이야기를 들었다

One girl said / she hoped / (e) she would have as much fun / as Daisy / when she got older.
한 여학생은 말했다 / 그녀가 바란다고 / 그녀가 즐겁게 지내기를 / Daisy만큼 / 나이가 들었을 때

Then, / Daisy said something / I will never forget.
그때 / 무언가를 Daisy가 말했다 / 내가 절대 잊지 못할

★ 똑해가 쉬워지는 구문 풀이

She [had done **so** many interesting things and (had) lived through
주어   동사1   등위접속사   동사2
so many amazing experiences] **that** I was surprised she still
wanted to do so much.

⇨ [ ]는 등위접속사 and로 연결된 병렬 구조이며, lived 앞에 반복되는 had는 생략되었다.

⇨ '매우 ~해서 …하다'라는 의미로 <so/such ~ that …> 구조를 사용한다.

어휘 mature 나이든, 성숙한 vow 다짐하다; 맹세
follow in someone's footsteps ~의 선례를 좇아가다, ~의 발자취를 따라가다
inspiration 영감을 주는 사람, 영감 to the fullest 최대한으로, 완전하게
live through ~을 겪다 have fun 즐겁게 지내다 grow old 나이 들다, 늙다

해석 (A) 내가 대학교에서 첫 수업에 참석했을 때, 나는 드문 광경을 보았다. 나이가 아주 많은 한 여성이 교실로 걸어 들어와서 내 옆에 앉았다. 그녀는 "안녕, 나는 Daisy야"라고 말하며 스스로를 소개했다. Daisy는 78세였고 대학 3학년이었다. 수업 후에, 나는 Daisy에게 매우 호기심이 생겨서 다른 여학생에게 그녀에 대해 물어보았다. "미안, 나는 그녀를 잘 몰라. 아마 네가 직접 (a) 그녀에게 물어봐도 될 걸?"이라고 그녀가 말했다.
(B) 나는 바로 그렇게 하기로 결심했다. 그래서 어느 날 수업 후, 나는 Daisy에게 걸어가서 어떻게 (b) 그녀가 그렇게 장년의 나이에 학생이 되었는지 그녀에게 물어보았다. 그녀는 항상 대학에 들어가고 싶었지만 전혀 기회가 없었다고 답했다. 나는 그녀의 이야기에 대해 더 알고 싶었고, 우리가 함께 점심을 먹을 수 있을지 물어보았다.
(D) 우리는 근처 카페에 갔고 (d) 그녀는 그녀의 인생에 대한 모든 것을 내게 말해주었다. 그녀는 아주 많은 흥미로운 일을 했었고 아주 많은 놀라운 경험들을 겪어서 나는 그녀가 아직도 그렇게 많은 것을 하고 싶어 한다는 것에 놀랐다. 몇몇 반 친구들이 나를 보았고 우리와 함께하려고 다가왔다. 그들은 그녀의 놀라운 이야기를 들었다. 한 여학생은 (e) 그녀가 나이가 들었을 때 Daisy만큼 즐겁게 지내기를 바란다고 말했다. 그때, 내가 절대 잊지 못할 무언가를 Daisy가 말했다.
(C) "우리는 나이 들었다고 즐기는 것을 멈추지 않아, 우리가 즐기는 것을 멈추기 때문에 나이가 드는 거야."라며 Daisy는 우리가 새로운 것을 시도하기에 결코 나이가 많지 않고 삶에 대한 우리의 열정을 절대 잃어서는 안 된다고 내게 가르쳐주었다. 나는 (c) 그녀의 선례를 좇아가기로 다짐

했다. 그녀는 진정한 롤 모델이자 영감을 주는 사람이었다. 그녀는 그녀의 인생을 최대한으로 살았고, 그건 정확히 내가 내 인생을 살아가고 싶은 방식이다.

13
정답 ①

[해설] (A)는 대학교 첫 수업에서 78세의 Daisy를 만나 그녀에 대해 더 알고 싶었다는 내용이다. (B)의 I decided to do just that의 that은 (A)의 you(I) can ask her(Daisy) yourself를 가리키므로 (A) 다음에 오는 것이 적절하다. (D)는 근처 카페에 가서 Daisy의 인생에 대한 많은 이야기를 들었다는 내용이므로 나는 그녀의 이야기에 대해 더 알고 싶었고, 우리가 함께 점심을 먹을 수 있을지 물어보았다고 한 (B) 뒤에 와야 한다. (C)는 우리가 나이 들었다고 즐기는 것을 멈추는 것이 아니라 즐기는 것을 멈추기 때문에 나이가 드는 것이라고 Daisy가 말했다는 내용이므로 내가 절대 잊지 못할 무언가를 Daisy가 말했다고 한 (D) 뒤에 와야 한다. 따라서 ① (B)-(D)-(C)가 정답이다.

14
정답 ⑤

[해설] (a), (b), (c), (d)는 모두 Daisy를 가리키지만 (e)는 한 여학생을 가리키므로 ⑤가 정답이다.

15
정답 ⑤

[해설] We went to a nearby café and she told me all about her life를 통해 교실에 남아 들은 것이 아니라 근처 카페에서 Daisy의 이야기를 들었다는 것을 알 수 있으므로, 글의 내용과 일치하지 않는 것은 ⑤ 'I'는 교실에 남아 Daisy의 이야기를 들었다'이다.

[오답 분석] ①은 As I was attending my first class at university, I saw an unusual sight라고 했으므로 글의 내용과 일치한다. ②은 Daisy was 78 years old and in her third year of college라고 했으므로 글의 내용과 일치한다. ③은 she had always wanted to go to college but never had the chance라고 했으므로 글의 내용과 일치한다. ④은 I vowed to follow in her footsteps라고 했으므로 글의 내용과 일치한다.

16 ~ 17

[지문분석]

For most people, / the opportunity to get free stuff / is too good to pass up, / and the same goes for food.
대부분의 사람들에게 / 공짜 물건을 받을 기회는 / 놓치기엔 너무 아깝다 / 그리고 음식도 마찬가지이다

This cannot be said / of most captive animals, / however.
이렇게 말할 수 없다 / 대부분의 포획된 동물에 대해서는 / 그러나

Extensive research shows / that most opt to (a) <u>work</u> / for their food.
광범위한 연구는 보여준다 / 대부분이 노력하기를 선택한다는 것을 / 먹이를 얻기 위해

A 1963 study / on rats / demonstrated this concept quite well / and has formed / the basis for studies / involving other captive animals.
1963년의 연구는 / 쥐에 대한 / 이 개념을 아주 잘 입증했다 / 그리고 만들었다 / 연구의 기반을 / 다른 포획된 동물을 포함하는

★ Rats were given a choice / between having a (b) <u>free</u> meal and accessing food / from a container / that required them / to press a metal bar several times.
쥐들은 선택권을 받았다 / 공짜 음식을 얻는 것과 음식을 얻는 것 사이에서 / 용기에 든 / 그들에게 요구하는 / 쇠막대를 여러 번 누르도록

The rats consistently chose the latter option, / even though the food in the container / was (c) <s>easier</s>(→ harder) to access.
쥐들은 꾸준히 후자의 옵션을 골랐다 / 용기에 든 음식이 ~임에도 불구하고 / 얻기에 더 쉬웠다(→ 더 어려웠다)

It is believed / that the tendency / for captive animals to apply effort / is related to the (d) <u>lack</u> of stimulation / in a cage or artificial setting.
~라고 여겨진다 / 경향은 / 포획된 동물이 노력을 쏟는 / 자극 부족과 관련된다 / 우리 안이나 인공적인 환경에서의

Essentially, / they perform actions / they might normally carry out / when hunting or foraging / because it is part of their natural instincts / to do so.
본래 / 그들은 행동들을 한다 / 그들이 보통 하는 / 사냥하거나 먹이를 찾을 때 / 그들의 타고난 본능의 일부이기 때문에 / 그렇게 하는 것이

The findings ultimately suggest / that providing captive animals with devices / like food puzzles / could (e) <u>encourage</u> them / to act more naturally / and prevent them from getting bored, / thereby improving their well-being.
결국 연구 결과는 시사한다 / 포획된 동물에게 상치를 제공하는 것이 / 먹잇감 놀이와 같은 / 그들을 자극할 수 있다 / 더 자연스럽게 행동하도록 / 그리고 지루해질 수 없게 한다 / 그리고 그렇게 함으로써 그들의 행복을 증진한다

★ 독해가 쉬워지는 구문 풀이

<u>Rats</u> <u>were given</u> <u>a choice</u> between having a free meal and
주어　　수동태　　직접목적어
accessing food from a container that required them to press a metal bar several times.

▷ 주어 Rats가 동사 give가 나타내는 '주는' 행위의 대상이므로, 수동태 were given이 쓰였다. 동사 give는 목적어 2개가 올 수 있는 4형식 동사이므로, 수동태 동사 뒤에 직접목적어 a choice가 남아 있다.

[어휘] stuff 물건　pass up (기회를) 놓치다, 거절하다
the same goes for ~도 마찬가지이다　captive 포획된　opt 선택하다
access 얻다　consistently 꾸준히, 끊임없이　latter 후자의; 후자
apply 쏟다, 기울이다　essentially 본래, 기본적으로
thereby 그렇게 함으로써, 그것 때문에　well-being 행복, 안녕

[해석] 대부분의 사람들에게, 공짜 물건을 받을 기회는 놓치기엔 너무 아까우며, 음식도 마찬가지이다. 그러나, 대부분의 포획된 동물에 대해서는 이렇게 말할 수 없다. [주제문] 광범위한 연구는 대부분이 먹이를 얻기 위해 (a) 노력하기를 선택한다는 것을 보여준다. 쥐에 대한 1963년의 연구는 이 개념을 아주 잘 입증했고 다른 포획된 동물을 포함하는 연구의 기반을 만들었다. 쥐들은 (b) 공짜 음식을 얻는 것과 그들에게 쇠막대를 여러 번 누르도록 요구하는 용기에 든 음식을 얻는 것 사이에서 선택권을 받았다. 쥐들은 용기에 든 음식이 얻기에 (c) <s>더 쉬웠음</s>(→ 더 어려웠음)에도 불구하고 꾸준히 후자의 옵션을 골랐다. 포획된 동물이 노력을 쏟는 경향은 우리 안이나 인공적인 환경에서의 자극 (d) 부족과 관련된다고 여겨진다. 본래, 그들은 사냥하거나 먹이를 찾을 때 그들이 보통 하는 행동들을 하는데, 이것은 그렇게 하는 것이 그들의 타고난 본능의 일부이기 때문이다. 결국 연구 결과는 포획된 동물에게 먹잇감 놀이와 같은 장치를 제공하는 것이 그들이 더 자연스럽게 행동하도록 (e) 자극하고 지루해질 수 없게 하며, 그렇게 함으로써 그들의 행복을 증진할 수 있음을 시사한다.

16
정답 ⑤

[해석] ① 인간을 위해 일하는 동물: 난관 극복하기
② 공짜 점심 같은 것은 없다고 누가 말하는가?
③ 동물을 가둬 놓는 것이 왜 잔인한가?
④ 동물의 권태에 대해 우려되는 징후들
⑤ 왜 포획된 동물은 노력해서 먹이를 얻기를 선호하는가

어휘 overcome 극복하다 cruel 잔인한 boredom 권태

해설 대부분의 포획 동물은 먹이를 얻기 위해 공짜로 제공되는 음식을 받는 것보다 타고난 본능에 따라 사냥을 하거나 먹이를 찾는 것과 같이 노력하는 경향을 보인다는 내용의 글이므로, 글의 제목으로 가장 적절한 것은 ⑤ Why Captive Animals Prefer to Earn Food(왜 포획된 동물은 노력해서 먹이를 얻기를 선호하는가)이다.

오답분석 ①은 글에서 언급된 소재 Animals를, ②은 글에서 언급된 소재 free를 활용하여 혼동을 주는 오답이다. ③은 글의 핵심 소재인 Animals in Captivity를 활용하여 혼동을 주는 오답이다. ④은 글에서 언급된 소재 Animals를 활용하여 혼동을 주는 오답이다.

17
정답 ③

해설 쥐들은 용기에 든 음식이 얻기에 "더 어려움"에도 불구하고 공짜 음식이 아닌 용기에 든 음식을 얻고자 선택했다는 맥락이 되어야 하므로, ③의 easier(더 쉬운)를 harder(더 어려운)와 같은 어휘로 바꾸어야 문맥상 적절하다.

오답분석 ①은 공짜 음식을 선호하는 사람들과 달리 포획된 동물들 중 대부분은 먹이를 얻기 위해 "노력한다"는 문맥이 되어야 하므로 work가 오는 것이 적절하다. ②는 쥐들이 "공짜" 먹이 대신 쇠막대를 여러 번 누르도록 요구하는 용기에 든 음식을 꾸준히 골랐다는 문맥이 되어야 하므로 free가 오는 것이 적절하다. ④는 본래 동물들이 자극에 대한 욕구를 충족시키려는 그들의 본능의 일부로 어떤 행동을 하지만, 포획된 동물들은 이러한 자극이 "부족하다"는 맥락이 되어야 하므로 lack이 오는 것이 적절하다. ⑤는 포획된 동물에게 먹잇감 놀이와 같은 장치를 제공하는 것이 그들이 더 자연스럽게 행동하도록 "자극한다"는 문맥이 되어야 하므로 encourage가 오는 것이 적절하다.

18 ~ 20

지문분석

(A) Stephen was sitting / on a park bench / eating a sandwich.
Stephen은 앉아 있었다 / 공원 벤치에 / 샌드위치를 먹으며

He was on a lunch break / from work.
그는 점심시간이었다 / 직장에서

Stephen did not like his job / very much.
Stephen은 그의 일을 좋아하지는 않았다 / 아주 많이

★ He thought / about how he had always wanted / to make a big difference / in the world, / but he was stuck / in a boring job.
그는 떠올렸다 / 그가 항상 얼마나 원했는지 / 큰 변화를 가져오기를 / 세상에 / 하지만 그는 갇혀 있었다 / 지루한 일에

So, / he was not in a very good mood / when an old man came up to (a) him.
그래서 / 그는 기분이 그다지 좋지는 않았다 / 나이 든 한 남자가 그에게 다가왔을 때

(B) However, / Stephen felt much worse / once he got off work.
하지만 / Stephen은 기분이 더 나빠졌다 / 퇴근하자마자

As (b) he was leaving, / he saw the old man again.
그가 가고 있을 때 / 그는 그 나이 든 남자를 또 봤다

Stephen saw him asking other people / for some food.
Stephen은 그가 다른 사람들에게 구걸하는 것을 봤다 / 음식을

All he got / was just a little bit of bread, / but he still seemed so happy / to have received it.
그 남자가 받은 것 전부는 / 고작 작은 빵 조각에 불과했다 / 하지만 그는 그래도 행복해 보였다 / 그것을 받아서

The image / stayed with Stephen / as he walked home
그 모습은 / 계속 Stephen에게 남아 있었다 / 그가 집에 걸어갈 때

(C) He apologized / for bothering Stephen / but asked / if he could share a little bit / of his food.
그는 사과했다 / Stephen을 귀찮게 한 것에 대해 / 그렇지만 물었다 / 그가 약간 나눠줄 수 있을지 / 그의 음식을

Stephen needed to eat / so he could work / the rest of the afternoon, / so (c) he said / "I'm sorry / I can't."
Stephen은 식사를 해야 했다 / 일을 할 수 있도록 / 남은 오후에 / 그래서 그는 말했다 / 미안합니다 / 저는 그렇게 할 수 없어요

The old man said / (d) he understood.
나이 든 남자는 말했다 / 그가 이해한다고

Stephen hurriedly ate / the rest of his lunch / and went back to work, / feeling a bit bad.
Stephen은 서둘러서 먹었다 / 남은 점심을 / 그리고 직장에 돌아갔다 / 약간 기분이 좋지 않은 채

(D) He still couldn't get it / out of his mind / as he lay in bed.
그는 여전히 그것을 떨쳐낼 수 없었다 / 그의 머릿속으로부터 / 그가 잠자리에 들었을 때

Stephen couldn't fall asleep, / so he got up / and made as many sandwiches / as he could.
Stephen은 잠들 수 없었다 / 그래서 그는 일어났다 / 그리고 많은 샌드위치를 만들었다 / 그가 할 수 있는 한

The next day / during his lunch break, / (e) he found the old man / and offered the food.
다음 날 / 점심시간 중에 / 그는 그 나이 든 남자를 발견했다 / 그리고 음식을 주었다

The old man smiled / and called out to a friend.
나이 든 남자는 미소를 지었다 / 그리고 친구 한 명을 불러왔다

When she saw the sandwiches, / her face lit up.
그녀가 샌드위치를 봤을 때 / 그녀의 얼굴이 밝아졌다

Stephen smiled.
Stephen은 미소를 지었다

He just made a big difference / in the world.
그는 방금 막 커다란 변화를 만들었다 / 세상에

★ 독해가 쉬워지는 구문 풀이

He thought about how <u>he</u> <u>had always wanted</u> to make a big
　　　　　　　　　의문사 주어　　　　동사
difference in the world, ~

⇨ how he had always wanted ~ in the world는 전치사 about의 목적어로 쓰인 <의문사 + 주어 + 동사> 순의 간접 의문문(명사절)이다.

어휘 lunch break 점심시간 stuck 갇힌 get off work 퇴근하다
bother 귀찮게 하다, 방해하다 call out ~를 부르다
face light up 얼굴이 밝아지다

해석 (A) Stephen은 샌드위치를 먹으며 공원 벤치에 앉아 있었다. 그는 직장에서 점심시간이었다. Stephen은 그의 일을 아주 많이 좋아하지는 않았다. 그는 세상에 큰 변화를 가져오기를 그가 항상 얼마나 원했는지 떠올렸지만, 그는 지루한 일에 갇혀 있었다. 그래서, 나이 든 한 남자가 (a) 그에게 다가왔을 때 그는 기분이 그다지 좋지는 않았다.
(C) 그는 Stephen을 귀찮게 한 것에 대해 사과하긴 했지만, 그가 그의 음식을 약간 나눠줄 수 있을지 물었다. Stephen은 남은 오후에 일을 할 수 있도록 식사를 해야 해서 (c) 그는 "미안합니다. 저는 그렇게 할 수 없어요."라고 말했다. 나이 든 남자는 (d) 그가 이해한다고 말했다. Stephen은 서둘러서 남은 점심을 먹고 약간 기분이 좋지 않은 채 직장에 돌아갔다.
(B) 하지만, Stephen은 퇴근하자마자 기분이 더 나빠졌다. (b) 그가 가고 있을 때 그는 그 나이 든 남자를 또 봤다. Stephen은 그가 다른 사람들에게 음식을 구걸하는 것을 봤다. 그 남자가 받은 것 전부는 고작 작은 빵 조각에 불과했지만, 그는 그래도 그것을 받아서 행복해 보였다. 그 모습은 그가 집에 걸어갈 때 계속 Stephen에게 남아 있었다.
(D) 그가 잠자리에 들었을 때 그는 여전히 그의 머릿속으로부터 그것을 떨쳐낼 수 없었다. Stephen은 잠들 수 없어서, 그는 일어나서 그가 할 수 있

는 한 많은 샌드위치를 만들었다. 다음 날 점심시간 중에, (e) 그는 그 나이든 남자를 발견했고 음식을 주었다. 나이든 남자는 미소를 지었고 친구한 명을 불러왔다. 그녀가 샌드위치를 봤을 때, 그녀의 얼굴이 밝아졌다. Stephen은 미소를 지었다. 그는 방금 막 세상에 커다란 변화를 만들었다.

18 정답 ②

[해설] (A)는 Stephen이 점심 식사로 샌드위치를 먹으며 공원 벤치에 앉아있을 때 나이든 한 남자가 다가왔다는 내용이다. (C)는 그 남자가 와서 Stephen의 음식을 조금 나누어 줄 수 있을지 물어봤지만 그는 거절한 후 서둘러 남은 점심을 먹고 직장으로 다시 돌아갔다는 내용이므로 나이든 한 남자가 다가왔다고 한 (A) 뒤에 와야 한다. (B)는 퇴근할 때 그 남자가 음식을 구걸하다가 작은 빵 한 조각을 받고 행복해하는 모습을 봤다는 내용이므로 점심시간에 공원에서 그 남자를 만났다고 한 (C) 뒤에 와야 한다. (D)는 잠자리에 들었을 때도 그 남자 때문에 잠을 이루지 못하고 결국 일어나서 그가 만들 수 있는 한 많은 샌드위치를 만들었다는 내용이므로 퇴근하고 집에 가는 길에도 그 남자의 모습이 남아있었다고 한 (B) 뒤에 와야 한다. 따라서 ② (C)-(B)-(D)가 정답이다.

19 정답 ④

[해설] (a), (b), (c), (e)는 모두 Stephen을 가리키지만 (d)는 나이든 남자를 가리키므로 ④이 정답이다.

20 정답 ③

[해설] (C)의 Stephen hurriedly ate the rest of his lunch and went back to work, feeling a bit bad를 통해 샌드위치를 먹고 직장에 돌아갔으나 약간 기분이 좋지 않음을 알 수 있으므로, 글의 내용과 일치하지 않는 것은 ③ 'Stephen은 샌드위치를 먹고 기쁜 마음으로 직장에 돌아갔다'이다.

[오답분석] ①은 He thought about how he always wanted to make a big difference in the world라고 했으므로 글의 내용과 일치한다. ②은 All he got was just a little bit of bread, but he still seemed so happy to have received it이라고 했으므로 글의 내용과 일치한다. ④은 He still couldn't get it out of his mind as he lay in bed, Stephen couldn't fall asleep~ 이라고 했으므로 글의 내용과 일치한다. ⑤은 When she saw the sandwiches, her face lit up이라고 했으므로 글의 내용과 일치한다.

REVIEW TEST CHAPTER 13-16 p.132

01 ⑤   02 ①   03 ③   04 ③   05 ③   06 ③   07 ⑤   08 ②
09 ③   10 ④

01 정답 ⑤

[지문분석]

Compliments can truly / make us feel good, / whether we are giving them / or receiving them.
칭찬은 진정으로 ~할 수 있다 / 우리를 기분 좋게 만들다 / 우리가 그것을 해주든지 / 그것을 받든지 간에

(①) ★ Generally speaking, / compliments satisfy a deep human need / to feel worthy and loved.
일반적으로 말하면 / 칭찬은 인간의 깊은 욕구를 만족시킨다 / 가치 있고 사랑받는다고 느끼려는

(②) By giving compliments, / we are telling others / that we appreciate them.
칭찬을 해줌으로써 / 우리는 타인에게 이야기하는 것이다 / 우리가 그들의 진가를 알아본다고

(③) The act of giving compliments / also helps us / learn to find positive qualities / in others.
칭찬하는 행위는 / 또한 우리를 도와준다 / 긍정적인 특징을 찾는 것을 배우도록 / 타인으로부터

(④) And / when we receive compliments, / they not only make us feel appreciated / but also trigger a pleasing reaction / in our brains.
그리고 / 우리가 칭찬을 받을 때 / 그것은 우리가 인정받는다고 느끼게 해줄 뿐만 아니라 / 기분 좋은 반응을 촉발시킨다 / 우리 뇌 속의

(⑤) (This can be similar / to the satisfaction / people get / when they receive a financial reward.)
이것은 비슷할 수 있다 / 만족감과 / 사람들이 얻는 / 금전적인 보상을 받을 때

Overall, / when people exchange compliments, / it is as if they are rewarding each other / with kind words / that carry real worth / and, over time, / help to foster / trust, goodwill, and mutual respect.
대체로 / 사람들이 칭찬을 주고받을 때 / 이는 마치 그들이 서로에게 보상을 해주는 것 같다 / 상냥한 말로 / 진정한 가치를 지니는 / 그리하며 시간이 흐름에 따라 / 촉진하도록 돕는다 / 신뢰, 호의, 그리고 상호 존중을

> ★ 독해가 쉬워지는 구문 풀이
>
> [Generally speaking], compliments satisfy a deep human need to
>   주어   동사   목적어
> feel worthy and loved.
>
> ⇨ [ ]는 비인칭 독립분사구문 중 하나로, '일반적으로 말하면'이라고 해석한다. 비인칭 독립분사구문은 주어가 people, you, we 등 일반인일 때 쓰인다.

[어휘] compliment 칭찬 worthy 가치 있는 appreciate 진가를 알아보다, 인정하다 trigger 촉발시키다 satisfaction 만족감 financial 금전적인 foster 촉진하다 goodwill 호의 mutual 상호의

[해석] **[주제문]** 칭찬은 우리가 그것을 해주든지 그것을 받든지 간에, 우리를 진정으로 기분 좋게 만들 수 있다. 일반적으로 말하면, 칭찬은 가치 있고 사랑받는다고 느끼려는 인간의 깊은 욕구를 만족시킨다. 칭찬을 해줌으로써, 우리는 타인에게 우리가 그들의 진가를 알아본다고 이야기하는 것이다. 칭찬하는 행위는 또한 우리가 타인으로부터 긍정적인 특징을 찾는 것을 배우도록 도와준다. 그리고 우리가 칭찬을 받을 때, 그것은 우리가 인정받는다고 느끼게 해줄 뿐만 아니라 우리 뇌 속의 기분 좋은 반응을 촉발시킨다. (이것은 사람들이 금전적인 보상을 받을 때 얻는 만족감과 비슷할 수 있다.) 대체로, 사람들이 칭찬을 주고받을 때, 이는 마치 그들이 진정한 가치를 지니며 시간이 흐름에 따라 신뢰, 호의, 그리고 상호 존중을 촉진하도록 돕는 상냥한 말로 서로에게 보상을 해주는 것 같다.

[해설] 주어진 문장을 통해 주어진 문장의 주변에 사람들이 금전적인 보상을 받을 때 얻는 만족감과 This 사이에 유사성이 있다는 내용이 나와야 함을 알 수 있다. 칭찬을 받는 것이 뇌 속의 기분 좋은 반응을 촉발시킨다고 한 ⑤ 앞 내용은 주어진 문장의 This가 지칭하는 것이며, ⑤ 앞의 a pleasing reaction은 주어진 문장의 satisfaction으로 이어진다. 또한 ⑤ 뒤에서 실질적인 가치를 지닌 말로 서로에게 보상을 해주는 것 같다는 내용은 주어진 문장의 financial reward와 연결된다. 따라서 주어진 문장이 들어가기에 가장 적절한 곳은 ⑤이다.

[오답분석] ⑤ 앞 문장까지는 칭찬의 기능 및 역할에 대해 언급하고, 이어서 우리가 칭찬을 받을 때 느끼는 감정에 대해 설명하고 있으므로 문장들이 자연스럽게 이어진다. 또한 ⑤ 앞 문장까지는 모두 정답의 단서인 satisfaction과 financial reward와 관련된 내용이 언급되지 않으므로 주어진 문장이 들어가기에 적절하지 않다.

지문분석

During business transactions, / one party often has an advantage / over the other / because they have access / to more information.
상거래에서, / 보통 한 쪽이 유리한 위치에 있다 / 다른 한 쪽보다 / 이는 그들이 이용할 수 있기 때문이다 / 더 많은 정보를

For example, / a used car dealer may know / that a vehicle doesn't function well / and sell it / to an unaware customer anyway / in order to make a profit.
예를 들어, / 중고차 딜러는 알 수도 있다 / 어떤 자동차가 잘 작동하지 않는다는 것을 / 그런데도 그것을 판매한다 / 어차피 알아채지 못하는 고객에게 / 이윤을 내기 위해

While this behavior is clearly untruthful, / an information gap doesn't always have to be negative.
이러한 행동은 분명히 거짓말을 하는 것이지만 / 정보 격차가 항상 부정적일 필요는 없다

★ Instead of using their specialized knowledge / to cheat customers, / the used car dealer can use it / to repair vehicle problems / that the average customer might not notice.
그들의 전문 지식을 사용하는 것 대신 / 고객을 속이기 위해 / 그 중고차 딜러는 그것(지식)을 활용할 수 있다 / 차량의 결함을 수리하기 위해 / 평범한 손님은 알아차리지 못할

This way, / buyers are not only happy / with reliable vehicles, / but they will also recommend the car dealer / to other shoppers.
이렇게 하면 / 구매자는 만족할 뿐만 아니라 / 믿을 수 있는 자동차에 / 또한 그 자동차 딜러를 추천할 것이다 / 다른 구매자들에게

This can increase business / and allow the dealer to charge higher prices / than competitors / who let vehicles leave the lot / in poor shape.
이것은 거래를 늘려줄 수 있다 / 그리고 그 딜러가 더 높은 가격을 청구하게 해준다 / 경쟁자들보다 / 자동차가 차고지를 나가게 두는 / 형편없는 상태로

⇩

An information gap / may result in (A) mistrust, / but it can also (B) benefit / both the buyer and the seller.
정보 격차는 / 불신을 야기할 수도 있다 / 하지만 이것은 또한 이익을 줄 수 있다 / 구매자와 판매자 모두에게

★ 독해가 쉬워지는 구문 풀이

Instead of [①using their specialized knowledge to cheat
　　　　　　동명사
customers], the used car dealer can use it to repair vehicle
problems [②that the average customer might not notice].
목적격 관계대명사

⇨ [①]는 전치사 instead of의 목적어이다.
⇨ [②]는 선행사 problems를 수식하는 관계대명사절이며, 목적격 관계대명사 that은 생략할 수 있다.

어휘 business transaction 상거래　untruthful 거짓말을 하는
specialized 전문의, 특수한　cheat 속이다　reliable 믿을 수 있는
competitor 경쟁자　lot 차고지, 부지　[선택지]mistrust 불신
rejection 거절　discourage 낙담시키다　irritate 짜증 나게 하다

해석 상거래에서, 보통 한 쪽이 다른 한 쪽보다 유리한 위치에 있는데 이는 그들이 더 많은 정보를 이용할 수 있기 때문이다. 예를 들어, 중고차 딜러는 어떤 자동차가 잘 작동하지 않는다는 것을 알 수도 있지만 이윤을 내기 위해 어차피 알아채지 못하는 고객에게 그것을 판매한다. [주제문] 이러한 행동은 분명히 거짓말을 하는 것이지만, 정보 격차가 항상 부정적일 필요는 없다. 고객을 속이기 위해 그들의 전문 지식을 사용하는 것 대신, 그 중고차 딜러는 평범한 손님은 알아차리지 못할 차량의 결함을 수리하기 위해 그것(지식)을 활용할 수 있다. 이렇게 하면, 구매자는 믿을 수 있는 자동차에 만족할 뿐만 아니라, 또한 그 자동차 딜러를 다른 구매자들에게 추천할 것이다. 이것은 거래를 늘려주고, 자동차가 형편없는 상태로 차고지를

나가게 두는 경쟁자들보다 그 딜러가 더 높은 가격을 청구하게 해줄 수 있다.

⇩

정보 격차는 (A) 불신을 야기할 수도 있지만, 이것은 또한 구매자와 판매자 모두에게 (B) 이익을 줄 수 있다.

　　(A)　　　(B)
① 불신 … 이익을 주다
② 거절 … 낙담시키다
③ 불신 … 위협하다
④ 혼란 … 짜증 나게 하다
⑤ 거절 … 즐겁게 하다

해설 요약문은 정보 격차가 '(A)'를 야기할 수도 있지만 구매자와 판매자 모두에게 '(B)'할 수 있다는 내용이다. 글에서 정보 격차를 이용한 행동은 분명히 거짓말을 하는 것이지만, 정보 격차가 항상 부정적인 필요는 없으며 이것을 활용하면 구매자는 믿을 수 있는 자동차에 만족하게 되고, 딜러 역시 더 높은 가격을 청구하게 해줄 수 있다고 했다. 따라서 요약문의 (A)에는 글에서 언급된 'untruthful'과 관련된 'mistrust'가, (B)에는 글에서 언급된 'happy', 'allow ~ to charge higher prices'와 관련된 'benefit'가 적절하므로 ① mistrust(불신) - benefit(이익을 주다)가 정답이다.

오답분석 구매자와 판매자 사이의 정보 격차가 야기할 수 있는 결과로 지문에서 언급된 내용은 거짓말과 불신이므로 ②과 ⑤의 rejection과 ④의 confusion은 (A)에 들어갈 단어로 적절하지 않다. 또한, 글의 후반에서 이러한 정보 격차를 활용하면 구매자와 판매자 모두가 만족할 수 있다고 했으므로, ②의 discourage, ③의 threaten, ④의 irritate, ⑤의 amuse는 (B)에 들어갈 단어로 적절하지 않다.

---

03 ~ 04

지문분석

The attractiveness of food, / or how it appears on a plate, / influences / how we perceive its quality.
음식의 매력 / 즉 그것이 접시 위에서 어떻게 보이는지는 / 영향을 준다 / 우리가 어떻게 그것의 품질을 인지하는지에

To determine / how diners judge the value of food, / researchers working with a chef / designed three salads / with (a) identical ingredients, dressing, and seasoning.
알아내기 위해 / 식사를 하는 손님들이 어떻게 음식의 가치를 판단하는지를 / 요리사와 함께 일하는 연구원들이 / 세 가지의 샐러드를 만들었다 / 동일한 재료, 드레싱, 양념으로

Because there were no differences / in the actual taste or quality of the food, / and all the ingredients were the same, / any opinions about the salads / would have to be based / on how they looked.
차이가 없었기 때문에 / 실제 맛이나 음식의 질에는 / 그리고 모든 재료가 같았다 / 샐러드에 대한 모든 판단은 / 근거해야 할 것이다 / 그것들이 어떻게 보이는지에

The first salad's ingredients / were simply tossed and plated, / while those of the second were separated / from each other / and lined up / in neat rows.
첫 번째 샐러드의 재료들은 / 단순히 버무려서 그릇에 놓았다 / 반면 두 번째 것들은 떼어 놓았다 / 서로에게서 / 그리고 나열됐다 / 정돈된 줄로

The third salad's ingredients, / however, / were arranged / in an (b) artistic manner.
세 번째 샐러드의 재료들은 / 그러나 / 배열되었다 / 예술적인 방식으로

In fact, / the design was inspired / by an abstract painting / by Wassily Kandinsky.
실제로 / 그 디자인은 영감을 받았다 / 추상화에서 / Wassily Kandinsky의

Diners / not only rated / the Kandinsky-inspired salad / (c) lower (→ higher) / for taste / than the other two / but they were also willing to pay / more than twice as much / for it.
식사를 하는 손님들은 / 평가했을 뿐만 아니라 / Kandinsky에게서 영감을 받은 샐러드를 / 더 낮게(→ 더 높게) / 맛에 있어서 / 다른 두 개보다 / 그들은 또한 지불할 의향이 있었다 / 두 배 이상 더 / 그것에

Although it is difficult / to pinpoint exactly / why the diners felt this way, / it may have something to do with / the amount of (d) effort / they felt / went into the dish.
비록 어렵더라도 / 정확히 설명하는 것은 / 식사를 하는 손님들이 왜 이렇게 느꼈는지 / 그 것은 ~과 관련이 있을 수도 있다 / 노력의 양 / 그들이 느낀 / 음식에 들어간

★ The nice way / the food was put onto the plate / was (e) pleasing / to them / and may have suggested / that a great amount of care and attention / went into their meal.
세련된 방식은 / 음식이 접시에 놓인 / 만족스러웠다 / 그들에게 / 그리고 암시했을 수도 있다 / 상당한 주의와 관심이 / 그들의 음식에 기울여졌음을

★ 독해가 쉬워지는 구문 풀이

The nice way [the food was put onto the plate] was pleasing to
　　　　선행사　　　　관계부사절
them ~

⇨ [ ]는 선행사 way를 수식하는 관계부사절이다.

어휘 attractiveness 매력, 매력적인 것 perceive 인지하다
determine 알아내다, 결정하다 diner 식사를 하는 손님, 작은 식당
seasoning 양념 toss (샐러드를) 버무리다, 던지다
pinpoint 정확히 설명하다, 정확히 찾아내다
have something to do with ~과 관련이 있다 attention 주의

해석 주제문 음식의 매력, 즉 그것이 접시 위에서 어떻게 보이는지는 우리가 어떻게 그것의 품질을 인지하는지에 영향을 준다. 식사를 하는 손님들이 어떻게 음식의 가치를 판단하는지를 알아내기 위해, 요리사와 함께 일하는 연구원들이 (a) 동일한 재료와 드레싱, 양념으로 세 가지의 샐러드를 만들었다. 실제 맛이나 음식의 질에는 차이가 없었고 모든 재료가 같았기 때문에, 샐러드에 대한 모든 판단은 그것들이 어떻게 보이는지에 근거해야 할 것이다. 첫 번째 샐러드의 재료들은 단순히 버무려서 그릇에 놓인 반면, 두 번째 것들은 서로에게서 떼어 놓고 정돈된 줄로 나열됐다. 그러나, 세 번째 샐러드의 재료들은 (b) 예술적인 방식으로 배열되었다. 실제로, 그 디자인은 Wassily Kandinsky의 추상화에서 영감을 받았다. 식사를 하는 손님들은 Kandinsky에게서 영감을 받은 샐러드를 다른 두 개보다 맛에 있어서 (c) 더 낮게(→ 더 높게) 평가했을 뿐만 아니라, 그들은 또한 그것에 두 배 이상 더 지불할 의향이 있었다. 비록 식사를 하는 손님들이 왜 이렇게 느꼈는지를 정확히 설명하는 것은 어렵더라도, 그것은 그들이 느낀 음식에 들어간 (d) 노력의 양과 관련이 있을 수도 있다. 음식이 접시에 놓인 세련된 방식은 그들에게 (e) 만족스러웠고, 그들의 음식에 상당한 주의와 관심이 기울여졌음을 암시했을 수도 있다.

03   정답 ③

해석 ① 예술 작품으로 식당의 분위기 개선하기
② 고급 재료들: 당신의 성공의 핵심
③ 외관: 그것은 음식에 관해서라면 중요하다
④ 건강에 좋은 선택이 맛있을 수도 있을까?
⑤ 음식이 식당에서 더 맛있는 이유

어휘 atmosphere 분위기, 대기

해설 음식이 접시 위에서 어떻게 보이는지는 그 음식의 품질을 인지하는 데 영향을 미친다는 내용의 글이므로, 글의 제목으로 가장 적절한 것은 ③ Appearance: It Matters When It Comes to Food(외관: 그것은 음식에 관해서라면 중요하다)이다.

오답분석 ①은 글의 핵심 소재인 Art를 활용하여 혼동을 주는 오답이다. ②은 글의 핵심 소재인 Quality를 글에서 언급된 소재 Ingredients와 연결 지어 혼동을 주는 오답이다. ④과 ⑤은 글에 등장한 taste와 관련된 내용을 활용하여 혼동을 주는 오답이다.

04   정답 ③

해설 손님들은 Kandinsky의 추상화에서 영감을 받아 예술적인 방식으로 재료를 배열한 샐러드의 맛을 더 높게 평가했을 뿐만 아니라, 가격 또한 두 배 이상 더 지불할 의향이 있었다는 맥락이 되어야 하므로, ③의 lower(더 낮게)를 higher(더 높게)와 같은 어휘로 바꾸어야 문맥상 적절하다.

오답분석 ①은 연구원들이 "동일한" 재료, 드레싱, 양념을 사용하여 실제로 맛이나 음식의 질에는 차이가 없도록 하고, 재료의 배열만 바꾼 세 가지의 샐러드를 만들었다는 문맥이 되어야 하므로 identical이 오는 것이 적절하다. ②은 세 번째 샐러드의 재료들이 Wassily Kandinsky의 추상화에서 영감을 받아 "예술적인" 방식으로 배열되었다는 문맥이 되어야 하므로 artistic이 오는 것이 적절하다. ④은 글의 후반에서 그들이 먹은 음식에 상당한 주의와 관심이 기울여졌음을 암시했을 수도 있다고 했으므로, 손님들이 음식을 어떻게 느끼는지는 음식에 들어간 "노력"의 양과 관련이 있다는 문맥이 되어야 한다. 따라서 effort가 오는 것이 적절하다. ⑤은 예술적 작품에 영감을 받아 재료를 배열한 샐러드가 손님들에게 "만족스러웠고" 그 음식에 상당한 주의와 관심이 기울여졌음을 암시했을 수 있다는 문맥이 되어야 하므로 pleasing이 오는 것이 적절하다.

05   정답 ③

지문분석

★ The Doppler effect describes / how frequencies vary / in relation to an observer / depending on their source's direction of movement.
도플러 효과는 설명한다 / 주파수가 어떻게 달라지는지를 / 관측자와 관련하여 / 근원의 이동 방향에 따라

(①) It explains the change in pitch / we hear / as an ambulance approaches / and then moves away / from us.
그것은 음높이의 변화를 설명해준다 / 우리가 듣는 / 구급차가 가까워질 때 / 그리고 멀어질 때 / 우리에게서

(②) In the field of astronomy, / it is used / in the search for planets / outside our solar system.
천문학 분야에서 / 그것은 사용된다 / 행성 탐색에 / 우리 태양계 바깥의

(③) (Instead of looking for changes / in sound frequencies, / astronomers look for changes / in light frequencies.)
변화를 찾는 대신 / 음성 주파수의 / 천문학자들은 변화를 찾는다 / 빛의 주파수의

These are observable / as colors / in the visible spectrum of light / from stars.
이것은 식별이 가능하다 / 색깔처럼 / 빛의 가시 스펙트럼 / 별에서 나오는

(④) The light appears blue / when a star is moving / toward us / and red / in the opposite direction.
빛은 파란색으로 보인다 / 별이 이동할 때 / 우리 쪽으로 / 그리고 빨간색으로 / 반대 방향에서는

(⑤) If the colors change / over time, / then astronomers know / that the star's movement is likely being pulled / by gravity / from a nearby planet.
만약 그 색깔이 바뀐다면 / 시간이 지나면서 / 천문학자들은 인지한다 / 그 별의 움직임이 아마도 당겨지고 있는 중이라는 것을 / 중력에 의해 / 인근 행성의

★ 독해가 쉬워지는 구문 풀이

The Doppler effect describes [how frequencies vary] in relation to
　　　　　　　　　　　　　　의문사　　주어　　동사
an observer depending on their source's direction of movement.

어휘 frequency 주파수 source 근원, 근원지, 원천 pitch 음높이
astronomer 천문학자 observable 식별 가능한 visible 가시적인
spectrum 스펙트럼 gravity 중력 nearby 인근의, 주변의 planet 행성

해석 도플러 효과는 관측자와 관련하여 근원의 이동 방향에 따라 주파수가 어떻게 달라지는지를 설명한다. 그것은 구급차가 우리에게서 가까워졌다가 멀어질 때 우리가 듣는 음높이의 변화를 설명해준다. 천문학 분야에서, 그것은 우리 태양계 바깥의 행성 탐색에 사용된다. (음성 주파수의 변화를 찾는 대신, 천문학자들은 빛의 주파수의 변화를 찾는다) 이것은 별에서 나오는 빛의 가시 스펙트럼 색깔처럼 식별이 가능하다. 빛은 별이 우리 쪽으로 이동할 때 파란색으로 보이고, 반대 방향에서는 빨간색으로 보인다. 만약 시간이 지나면서 그 색깔이 바뀐다면, 천문학자들은 그 별의 움직임이 아마도 인근 행성의 중력에 의해 당겨지고 있는 중이라는 것을 인지한다.

해설 주어진 문장의 Instead of, changes in sound frequencies를 통해 주어진 문장의 앞에는 음성 주파수의 변화에 관한 내용이 나와야 하고, 주어진 문장 뒤에는 changes in light frequencies, 즉, 빛의 주파수의 변화에 관한 내용이 등장해야 함을 알 수 있다. 또한, astronomer를 통해 주어진 글 앞에 천문학과 관련된 내용이 언급되어야 함을 알 수 있다. 이 글은 음성 주파수의 변화와 관련된 도플러 효과에 관한 내용으로 시작하여, 그것이 천문학 분야의 연구에도 사용된다는 내용으로 이어진다. ③ 앞 문장에, 도플러 효과가 천문학 분야에서도 사용된다고 했으며, ③ 뒤의 These, observable as colors와 visible은 주어진 글의 changes in light frequencies를 부연 설명하는 내용이므로 주어진 문장이 들어가기에 가장 적절한 곳은 ③이다.

오답분석 ③ 앞 문장까지는 도플러 효과의 정의와 예시, 천문학 분야에서 그것이 어떻게 사용되는지에 대해 언급하고 있으므로 문장이 자연스럽게 이어진다. 또한 ③ 뒤 문장부터는 빛의 가시 스펙트럼 색깔이 빛의 이동 방향에 따라 어떤 색으로 보이는지, 그 색깔의 변화를 통해 천문학자들이 인지할 수 있는 것에 대해 설명하고 있으므로 문장의 흐름이 자연스럽다.

06 ~ 08

지문분석

(A) As a young girl, / Alice lived / in her grandmother's house, / where she played / in a wonderful garden / with a wide array of plants.
어린 소녀일 때 / Alice는 살았다 / 그녀의 할머니의 집에서 / 그리고 그곳에서 그녀는 놀았다 / 멋진 정원에서 / 다양한 식물늘이 있는

In the spring, / the flowers on the plants / would bloom, / filling the garden / with color.
봄이 되면 / 식물의 꽃이 / 피어났다 / 그리고 정원을 채웠다 / 색색깔로

When she grew up, / Alice bought her own home.
그녀가 어른이 되었을 때 / Alice는 그녀 자신의 집을 샀다

That way, / she could plant a garden herself.
그렇게 해서 / 그녀는 직접 정원을 가꿀 수 있었다

Next door to her / lived an old lady / named Kathleen, / who had no garden / of her own.
그녀의 옆집에는 / 나이 든 부인이 살았다 / Kathleen이라는 이름의 / 그리고 그 부인은 정원을 가지고 있지 않았다 / 자신의

(B) Alice was shocked.
Alice는 충격을 받았다

She walked over / to Kathleen's side of the wall / and could not believe (a) her eyes.
그녀는 걸어갔다 / Kathleen 쪽 너머의 벽으로 / 그리고 그녀의 눈을 의심했다

The vines had grown / through cracks / in the wall / and bloomed / on the other side, / covering it / in colorful flowers.
덩굴 식물이 자랐다 / 틈 사이로 / 벽의 / 그리고 꽃을 피웠다 / 반대쪽에서 / 그리고 벽을 덮고 있었다 / 화려한 꽃들로

Alice was sure / that all of her work had been wasted / on caring for plants / that didn't bloom.
Alice는 확신했었다 / 그녀의 모든 노력이 낭비되었다고 / 식물을 돌보는 것에 / 꽃이 피지 않는

(b) She never thought / that her work would blossom / for somebody else.
그녀는 전혀 생각하지 못했다 / 그녀의 노력이 꽃피웠을 것이라 / 다른 누군가를 위해

(C) An empty gray wall / separated Alice's backyard / from Kathleen's home.
아무것도 없는 회색 벽이 / Alice의 뒤뜰을 나눴다 / Kathleen의 집과

Alice looked at it / and decided to plant her flowers there.
Alice는 그것을 보았다 / 그리고는 그곳에 꽃들을 심기로 했다

(c) She went to a garden store / and bought flowering vines / to cover the wall.
그녀는 정원용품점에 갔다 / 그리고 꽃을 피우는 덩굴 식물을 샀다 / 벽을 덮을

She placed them / in good soil, / watered them, / and protected them / from insects
그녀는 그것들을 넣었다 / 좋은 흙 속에 / 그리고 물을 주었다 / 그리고 보호했다 / 벌레들로부터

But / after six months / of caring for the vines, / Alice felt disappointed.
하지만 / 6개월이 지나고 / 덩굴 식물들을 보살핀 지 / Alice는 실망했다

Although they had grown thick and large / and covered the entire wall, / they hadn't produced a single flower / (d) she could see!
그것들이 두껍고 크게 자랐지만 / 그리고 벽 전체를 덮었다 / 그것들은 단 한 송이의 꽃도 피우지 않았다 / 그녀가 볼 수 있는

(D) So, / she decided / she would replace the vines / with another plant.
그래서 / 그녀는 ~하기로 했다 / 그 덩굴 식물을 바꿀 것이다 / 다른 식물로

She approached the wall / to remove the vines / when a voice called out / from the other side.
그녀가 벽에 다가갔다 / 덩굴 식물을 없애려고 / 그때 한 목소리가 들렸다 / 반대쪽에서

It was her neighbor, / Kathleen.
그것은 그녀의 이웃이었다 / Kathleen

"I want to thank you," / (e) she said / with tears in her eyes.
당신에게 감사하고 싶어요 / 라고 그녀가 말했다 / 눈에 눈물이 맺힌 채

"I have been ill / for months / and unable to leave my house.
저는 몇 달 동안 아팠어요 / 그리고 집에서 나갈 수 없었어요

★ Seeing your vines bloom / with flowers / has brought me incredible hope!"
당신의 덩굴 식물이 피우는 것을 보는 게 / 꽃을 / 제게 엄청난 희망을 주었어요

★ 독해가 쉬워지는 구문 풀이

Seeing your vines bloom with flowers has brought me incredible hope!"
　　주어(동명사구)　　　　　　단수동사

⇨ 주어 Seeing your vines bloom with flowers는 단수 취급하는 동명사구 주어이므로 단수동사 has가 쓰였다.

어휘 a wide array of 다양한, 다수의 grow up 어른이 되다, 자라다
vine 덩굴 식물, 포도나무 crack 틈, 금 bloom 꽃이 피다; 꽃
blossom 꽃을 피우다 soil 흙, 토양 entire 전체
approach 다가가다, 접근하다 remove 없애다, 제거하다 ill 아픈, 병 든
incredible 엄청난, 믿을 수 없는

해석 (A) 어린 소녀일 때 Alice는 그녀의 할머니의 집에서 살았고, 그곳에서 그녀는 다양한 식물들이 있는 멋진 정원에서 놀았다. 봄이 되면, 식물의 꽃이 피어났고 정원을 색색깔로 채웠다. 그녀가 어른이 되었을 때, Alice는

그녀 자신의 집을 샀다. 그렇게 해서, 그녀는 직접 정원을 가꿀 수 있었다. 그녀의 옆집에는 Kathleen이라는 이름의 나이 든 부인이 살았고, 그 부인은 자신의 정원을 가지고 있지 않았다.

(C) 아무것도 없는 회색 벽이 Kathleen의 집과 Alice의 뒤뜰을 나눴다. Alice는 그것을 보고 그곳에 꽃들을 심기로 했다. (c)그녀는 정원용품점에 가서 벽을 덮을 꽃을 피우는 덩굴 식물을 샀다. 그녀는 그것들을 좋은 흙 속에 넣고 물을 주고 벌레들로부터 보호했다. 하지만, 덩굴 식물들을 보살핀 지 6개월이 지나고 Alice는 실망했다. 그것들이 두껍고 크게 자라서 벽 전체를 덮었지만, (d)그녀가 볼 수 있는 단 한 송이의 꽃도 피우지 않았다!

(D) 그래서 그녀는 그 덩굴 식물을 다른 식물로 바꾸기로 했다. 그녀가 덩굴 식물을 없애려고 벽에 다가갔던 그때 반대쪽에서 한 목소리가 들렸다. 그것은 그녀의 이웃인 Kathleen이었다. "당신에게 감사하고 싶어요"라고 (e)그녀가 눈에 눈물이 맺힌 채 말했다. "저는 몇 달 동안 아팠고 집에서 나갈 수 없었어요. 당신의 덩굴 식물이 꽃을 피우는 것을 보는 게 제게 엄청난 희망을 주었어요!"

(B) Alice는 충격을 받았다. 그녀는 Kathleen 쪽 너머의 벽으로 걸어갔고 (a)그녀의 눈을 의심했다. 덩굴 식물이 벽의 틈 사이로 자라서 반대쪽에서 꽃을 피웠고, 화려한 꽃들로 벽을 덮고 있었다. Alice는 그녀의 모든 노력이 꽃이 피지 않는 식물을 돌보는 것에 낭비되었다고 확신했었다. (b)그녀는 그녀의 노력이 다른 누군가를 위해 꽃피웠을 것이라 전혀 생각하지 못했다.

06 정답 ③

해설 (A)는 Alice가 어른이 되고 나서 꽃이 가득한 자신만의 정원을 만들었고 옆집에는 Kathleen이라는 이웃이 살았다는 내용이다. (C)는 이웃과의 경계를 나누는 회색 벽을 보고 꽃을 심기로 결정했다는 내용이므로, 자신의 집을 사서 직접 정원을 가꿀 수 있게 되었다는 (A) 뒤에 와야 한다. (D)는 Alice가 덩굴 식물을 다른 식물로 바꾸기로 했다는 내용이므로, 6개월간 덩굴 식물을 보살폈으나 단 한 송이의 꽃도 피우지 않았다고 한 (C) 뒤에 와야 한다. (B)는 Alice의 집 쪽에는 보이지 않던 꽃이 Kathleen의 집 쪽의 벽에 화려하게 핀 것을 보고 눈을 의심했다는 내용이므로, Kathleen이 덩굴 식물이 꽃을 피우는 것을 보며 희망을 갖게 되고, 그에 따른 감사를 표현하고 있는 (D) 뒤에 와야 한다. 따라서 ③ (C) - (D) - (B)가 정답이다.

07 정답 ⑤

해설 (a), (b), (c), (d)는 Alice를 가리키지만 (e)는 Kathleen을 가리키므로 ⑤이 정답이다.

08 정답 ②

해설 Seeing your vines bloom with flowers has brought me incredible hope!를 통해 Kathleen이 Alice의 덩굴 식물이 꽃을 피우는 것을 보았음을 알 수 있으므로, 글의 내용과 일치하지 않는 것은 ② 'Kathleen은 한 송이의 꽃도 볼 수 없었다'이다.

오답분석 ①은 Alice bought her own home. That way, she could plant a garden herself라고 했으므로 글의 내용과 일치한다. ③은 An empty gray wall separated Alice's backyard from Kathleen's home이라고 했으므로 글의 내용과 일치한다. ④은 after six months of caring for the vines, Alice felt disappointed라고 했으므로 글의 내용과 일치한다. ⑤은 I have been ill for months and unable to leave my house라고 했으므로 글의 내용과 일치한다.

09 정답 ③

지문분석

Odd pricing refers to / the common practice of setting prices / in figures / that end in "9" or other odd numbers.
단수 가격 책정은 가리킨다 / 가격을 정하는 일반적인 관행을 / 숫자로 / "9" 또는 다른 홀수로 끝나는

It is a form of psychological trickery / designed to persuade customers / to make a purchase.
그것은 심리적 속임수의 한 형태이다 / 고객들을 설득하기 위해 고안된 / 구매하도록

(A) This variation can also be perceived / as a gain.
이러한 차이는 또한 인식될 수 있다 / 이득으로

For instance, / customers may think / they are enjoying significant savings / by buying something at $499 instead of $500, / even though the actual "gain" is only $1.00.
예를 들어 / 고객들은 생각할지도 모른다 / 큰 절약을 누리고 있다고 / 무언가를 500달러 대신 499달러에 구매함으로써 / 비록 실제 "이득"은 고작 1달러지만

(B) According to research, / one of the reasons odd pricing works / is due to specificity.
연구에 따르면 / 단수 가격 정책이 효과 있는 이유 중 하나는 / 구체성 때문이다

In other words, / customers believe / that a highly specific price / reflects a product's true worth / more accurately.
다시 말해서 / 고객들은 믿는다 / 매우 구체적인 가격이 ~라고 / 제품의 진정한 가치를 반영한다 / 더 정확히

★ (C) Another reason has to do with / perceived loss, / in which case / customers / reading a price from left to right / immediately focus on the first digit / they see / and ignore the rest.
또 다른 이유는 ~과 관련이 있는데 / 지각된 손실 / 이 경우에 / 고객들은 / 가격을 왼쪽에서 오른쪽으로 읽는 / 즉시 첫 번째 숫자에 바로 집중한다 / 그들이 보는 / 그리고 나머지는 무시한다

Thus, / a price of $4.99 is seen / as being significantly lower than $5.00, / even though the difference between them is only $0.01.
따라서 / 4.99달러라는 가격은 보인다 / 5.00달러보다 상당히 더 낮은 것처럼 / 비록 가격의 차이가 고작 0.01달러일지라도

★ 독해가 쉬워지는 구문 풀이

Another reason has to do with perceived loss, [①in which case] customers [②reading a price from left to right] immediately focus
수식 받는 명사 ── 현재분사
on the first digit they see and ignore the rest.

⇨ [①]는 "이 경우에"라는 의미의 숙어 표현으로, in that case와 바꿔 쓸 수 있다.

⇨ [②]에서 수식 받는 명사 customer가 read가 나타내는 '읽는' 행위의 주체이므로 현재분사 reading이 쓰였다.

어휘 odd pricing 단수 가격 책정 practice 관행 set 정하다 figure 숫자
odd 홀수의 trickery 속임수 design 고안하다 variation 차이, 변형
gain 이득 specificity 구체성, 특수성 accurately 정확히
reflect 반영하다 perceive 지각하다 loss 손실
in which case 이 경우에, 그런 경우에는 digit 숫자

해석 단수 가격 책정은 "9" 또는 다른 홀수로 끝나는 숫자로 가격을 정하는 일반적인 관행을 가리킨다. 그것은 고객들을 구매하도록 설득하기 위해 고안된 심리적 속임수의 한 형태이다.
(B) 연구에 따르면, 단수 가격 정책이 효과 있는 이유 중 하나는 구체성 때문이다. 다시 말해서, 고객들은 매우 구체적인 가격이 제품의 진정한 가치를 더 정확히 반영한다고 믿는다.
(C) 또 다른 이유는 지각된 손실과 관련이 있는데, 이 경우에 가격을 왼쪽에서 오른쪽으로 읽는 고객들은 그들이 보는 첫 번째 숫자에 바로 집중하고 나머지는 무시한다. 따라서, 비록 가격의 차이가 고작 0.01달러일지라

도, 4.99달러라는 가격은 5.00달러보다 상당히 더 낮은 것처럼 보인다. (A) 이러한 차이는 또한 이득으로 인식될 수 있다. 예를 들어, 고객들은 비록 실제 "이득"은 고작 1달러지만, 무언가를 500달러 대신 499달러에 구매함으로써 큰 절약을 누리고 있다고 생각할지도 모른다.

(해설) 주어진 글은 고객들을 구매하도록 설득하기 위해 고안된 심리적 속임수의 한 형태인 단수 가격 책정에 대한 내용이다. (B)의 one of the reasons odd pricing works(단수 가격 정책이 효과 있는 이유 중 하나)를 언급하며 구매를 유도하기 위한 심리적 속임수에 대해 설명하기 시작하므로 (B)는 주어진 글 바로 다음에 오는 것이 적절하다. (C)의 Another reason은 (B)의 내용에 대한 부연 설명을 하고 있으므로 단수 가격 책정이 효과 있는 이유 중 하나가 구체성 때문이라고 한 (B) 뒤에 오는 것이 적절하다. (A)의 This variation(이러한 차이)은 (C)의 4.99달러가 0.01달러 차이인 5.00달러보다 더 낮아 보이는 것을 가리키므로 가격을 왼쪽에서 오른쪽으로 읽는 고객들은 첫 번째 숫자에 집중하고 나머지는 무시한다고 한 (C) 바로 다음에 오는 것이 적절하다. 따라서 글의 순서로 가장 적절한 것은 ③ (B)-(C)-(A)이다.

10
정답 ④

지문분석

Mathematics and language both rely on / elaborate systems / of linguistic elements / to convey meaning.
수학과 언어는 모두 ~에 의존한다 / 정교한 체계 / 언어적 요소로 이루어진 / 의미를 전달하기 위해

With language, / we communicate ideas through various combinations / of characters, morphemes, and grammatical rules.
언어와 관련해서 / 우리는 다양한 조합을 통해 의사를 전달한다 / 문자, 형태소 그리고 문법 규칙의

In mathematics, / we create systems / using numbers, variables, and formulas.
수학에서 / 우리는 체계를 구성한다 / 숫자, 변수 그리고 공식을 이용해

The two subjects are similar / in that sense.
두 과목은 비슷하다 / 그런 의미에서

★ Where they differ / is in how they are taught.
그들이 다른 부분은 / 가르치는 방법에 있다

Language instruction takes / a verbal and hands-on approach, / while math learning relies on / lectures and bookwork.
언어 교육은 취한다 / 구두적이고 직접 해보는 접근 방식을 / 반면 수학 학습은 ~에 의존한다 / 강의와 교재를 통한 학습

But given that / the two subjects have so much in common, / math and language instructors should consider / adopting one another's methods / to deepen the classroom experience.
하지만 ~을 고려한다면 / 두 과목이 굉장히 많은 공통점을 가진다는 점 / 수학과 언어 교사들은 잘 생각해 보아야 한다 / 서로의 방식을 차용하는 것을 / 교실에서의 경험에 깊이를 더하기 위해

Language courses can be more structured / and focused on / the actual mechanics of writing.
언어 수업은 더 구조화될 수 있다 / 그리고 ~에 초점을 맞춘다 / 글쓰기의 실제적 방법에

Meanwhile, / math teachers can incorporate / more group work and discussion / of strategies.
한편 / 수학 교사들은 도입할 수 있다 / 더 많은 조별 활동과 토론을 / (수업) 전략에

⇩

Language and mathematics are (A) alike enough / that the teaching methods of one can be (B) applied / to the other / for better learning.
언어와 수학은 충분히 유사하다 / 그러므로 하나의 교수법이 적용될 수 있다 / 다른 과목에 / 더 나은 학습을 위해

★ 독해가 쉬워지는 구문 풀이
[①Where they differ] is in [②how they are taught].
　　주어　　　　　　　　동사

⇨ [①]은 의문사 where가 이끄는 명사절이며 문장의 주어로 쓰였고, [②]는 의문사 how가 이끄는 명사절이며 전치사 in의 목적어로 쓰였다.

(어휘) elaborate 정교한　linguistic 언어적, 어학상의　convey 전달하다
variable 변수　formula 공식　approach 접근　bookwork 교재를 통한 학습
deepen 깊이를 더하다, 깊어지다　mechanic 방법
incorporate 도입하다, 결합하다　(선택지) shift 변경하다, 변화하다

(해석) 수학과 언어는 모두 의미를 전달하기 위해 언어적 요소로 이루어진 정교한 체계에 의존한다. 언어와 관련해서, 우리는 문자, 형태소 그리고 문법 규칙의 다양한 조합을 통해 의사를 전달한다. 수학에서 우리는 숫자, 변수 그리고 공식을 이용해 체계를 구성한다. 그런 의미에서 두 과목은 비슷하다. 그들이 다른 부분은 가르치는 방법에 있다. 언어 교육은 구두적이고 직접 해보는 접근 방식을 취하는 반면, 수학 학습은 강의와 교재를 통한 학습에 의존한다. (주제문) 하지만 두 과목이 굉장히 많은 공통점을 가진다는 점을 고려한다면, 수학과 언어 교사들은 교실에서의 경험에 깊이를 더하기 위해 서로의 방식을 차용하는 것을 잘 생각해 보아야 한다. 언어 수업은 더 구조화될 수 있고 글쓰기의 실제적 방법에 초점을 맞출 수 있다. 한편, 수학 교사들은 더 많은 조별 활동과 토론을 (수업) 전략에 도입할 수 있다.

⇩

언어와 수학은 충분히 (A) 유사하므로 더 나은 학습을 위해 하나의 교수법이 다른 과목에 (B) 적용될 수 있다.

(A)	(B)
① 유사한	대체된
② 분명한	변경된
③ 분명한	접목된
④ 유사한	적용된
⑤ 정교한	설명된

(해설) 요약문은 언어와 수학이 충분히 '(A)하므로' 더 나은 학습을 위해 한 교수법이 다른 과목에 '(B)될' 수 있다는 내용이다. 글에서 언어와 수학이 서로 비슷하여 많은 공통점을 공유하므로 각 과목의 교사들이 서로의 교수법을 차용하는 것을 잘 생각해 보아야 한다고 했다. 따라서 요약문의 (A)에는 글에서 언급된 'similar', 'have so much in common'과 관련된 'alike'가, (B)에는 글에서 언급된 'adopting', 'incorporate'와 관련된 'applied'가 적절하므로 ④ alike(유사한) - applied(적용된)가 정답이다.

(오답분석) 글에서 두 과목이 서로의 방법을 차용하는 것을 서술하고 있으므로, 서로를 대체한다고 표현한 ①의 replaced는 적절하지 않다. ②과 ③의 clear는 '분명한' 또는 '명확한'이라는 의미로, 두 과목이 서로 '비슷하다'는 의미를 나타낼 수 없으므로 적절하지 않다. 본 글에서 두 과목이 정교한(elaborate) 체계에 의존한다고 했으나, 두 과목이 서로의 방법을 차용할 수 있는 이유는 '정교함'이 아닌 '유사하기' 때문이므로 ⑤의 elaborate는 적절하지 않다. 또한 ⑤의 described는 '설명된'이라는 의미로 서로의 방법을 차용한다는 의미를 나타낼 수 없다.

01 ①	02 ①	03 ④	04 ⑤	05 ⑤	06 ⑤	07 ③	08 ⑤
09 ①	10 ①	11 ④	12 ⑤	13 ④	14 ①	15 ②	16 ④
17 ④	18 ④	19 ③					

01
정답 ①

지문분석

Dear Parents,
학부모님들께

We hope / your children had a great time / at the Pearson Middle School Trade Fair.
저희는 바랍니다 / 여러분의 자녀들이 좋은 시간을 보냈기를 / Pearson 중학교 무역 박람회에서

★ Our event gives students first-hand experience / in running a small business, / allowing them to come up with / their own ideas / and to run these businesses / for a day.
저희의 행사는 학생들에게 직접적인 경험을 제공합니다 / 소기업을 운영하는 / 그들이 ~을 생각해내게 하면서 / 그들만의 아이디어를 / 그리고 그 사업체를 운영할 수 있게 하면서 / 하루 동안

We saw some amazing booths / from your children / this year, / and we just wanted to let you know / that the event would not have been possible / without our parent volunteers.
저희는 몇몇 멋진 부스들을 보았습니다 / 여러분의 자녀들에게서 / 올해 / 그리고 여러분께 꼭 알려드리고 싶었습니다 / 그 행사가 가능하지 않았을 것임을 / 학부모 자원봉사자분들 없이는

You worked so hard / to make this day a success / and guarantee a great time / for each student.
여러분들께서는 매우 열심히 힘써주셨습니다 / 이날을 성공적으로 만들기 위해 / 그리고 좋은 시간을 보장하기 위해 / 각각의 학생들에게

We can't express our gratitude to you enough / for taking the time / to help us manage everything.
저희는 여러분께 아무리 감사를 표현해도 부족합니다 / 시간을 내어 / 저희를 도와 모든 것을 관리하는

We appreciate it, / and we know / that our students do too.
감사드립니다 / 그리고 저희는 생각합니다 / 학생들도 또한 그러하다고(감사드린다고)

Sincerely,
Connie Evans, Principal
교장 Connie Evans 드림

★ **독해가 쉬워지는 구문 풀이**

Our event gives students first-hand experience in running a small
　주어　　동사　간접 목적어　　직접 목적어
business, [**allowing** them to come up with their own ideas and
　　　　　　　　　　　　현재분사구문
to run these businesses for a day].

⇨ [ ]는 분사구문이며, 접속사와 주어가 생략되었다.

어휘 trade fair 무역 박람회 first-hand 직접적인, 직접 경험한
come up with ~을 생각해내다, 제안하다 run a business 사업체를 운영하다
booth 부스, 점포, 전시장 volunteer 자원봉사자; 자원하다
guarantee 보장하다, 보증하다 gratitude 감사 appreciate 감사하다

해석 학부모님들께,

저희는 여러분의 자녀들이 Pearson 중학교 무역 박람회에서 좋은 시간을 보냈기를 바랍니다. 저희의 행사는 학생들이 그들만의 아이디어를 생각해내고, 하루 동안 그 사업체를 운영할 수 있게 하면서, 학생들에게 소

기업을 운영하는 직접적인 경험을 제공합니다. 올해 저희는 여러분의 자녀들에게서 몇몇 멋진 부스들을 보았고, 그 행사가 학부모 자원봉사자분들 없이는 가능하지 않았을 것임을 여러분께 꼭 알려드리고 싶었습니다. 여러분들께서는 이날을 성공적으로 만들고 각각의 학생들에게 좋은 시간을 보장하기 위해 매우 열심히 힘써주셨습니다. 시간을 내어 저희를 도와 모든 것을 관리해 주신 것에 대해서 저희는 여러분께 아무리 감사를 표현해도 부족합니다. 감사드리며, 학생들도 또한 그러하다고(감사드린다고) 생각합니다.

교장 Connie Evans 드림

해설 무역 박람회 행사를 여는 것을 도와준 학부모 자원봉사자들께 감사 인사를 전달하는 글이다. ~ the event would not have been possible without our parent volunteers ~ We can't express our gratitude to you enough for taking the time to help us manage everything. 에서 '이 행사를 성공적으로 만들기 위해 매우 열심히 힘써주신 학부모 자원봉사자들께 아무리 감사를 표현해도 부족하다'고 했으므로, 이 글의 목적으로 가장 적절한 것은 ① '행사의 자원봉사자분들께 감사 인사를 전하려고'이다.

오답분석 ②, ③, ⑤은 글과 전혀 관련 없는 내용이다. ④은 학교 행사와 관련된 소재인 자원봉사 활동을 다루고 있지만, 학생들에게 자원봉사 활동을 추천하기 위한 글이 아니기 때문에 오답이다.

02
정답 ①

지문분석

One Saturday, / a little dog arrived at the animal shelter / where I worked.
어느 토요일에 / 작은 개 한 마리가 동물 보호소에 왔다 / 내가 일하는

He was so neglected / that I could barely look at him.
그는 너무 심하게 방치되었다 / 그래서 나는 그를 거의 쳐다볼 수 없었다

The poor thing was nothing more than bones.
그 불쌍한 녀석은 뼈밖에 없었다

My heart ached for him.
그로 인해 나의 마음이 아팠다

★ I decided to name him Chance, / hoping / someone would give him one.
나는 그에게 Chance라고 이름을 붙이기로 했다 / 바라면서 / 누군가가 그에게 그것(기회)을 주기를

But / Chance never got adopted.
하지만 / Chance는 결코 입양되지 않았다

He was so timid / that he went unnoticed.
그는 매우 소심했다 / 그래서 눈에 띄지 않았다

People kept walking by him / until today.
사람들은 그를 지나쳐 걸어갔다 / 오늘까지

A family with a little boy visited.
어린 소년이 있는 가족이 방문했다

While the parents looked at other puppies, / the boy stood / in front of Chance.
그 부모가 다른 강아지들을 보는 동안 / 그 소년은 섰다 / Chance 앞에

They looked at each other / for the longest time.
그들은 서로 바라보았다 / 아주 오랫동안

And then, / Chance walked over / and licked the boy's hand.
그러고는 / Chance가 걸어갔다 / 그리고 그 소년의 손을 핥았다

The boy hugged him / and I smiled.
그 소년은 그를 안아주었다 / 그리고 나는 미소를 지었다

Chance got his second chance.
Chance는 그의 두 번째 기회를 얻었다

★ 독해가 쉬워지는 구문 풀이

I decided to name him Chance, [hoping someone would give him
　　　　　5형식 동사 목적어 목적격보어
one.]

⇨ 동사 name은 'name + 목적어 + 목적격보어'의 형태로 쓰여, '(목적어)를 (목적격보어)라고 이름을 붙이다'라고 해석한다.

⇨ one은 Chance(기회)를 가리키는 부정대명사이다.

어휘 shelter 보호소, 피난처 neglected 방치된, 도외시된 barely 거의 ~않다
nothing more than ~밖에 없는, ~에 불과한 ache 아프다
name 이름을 붙이다 unnoticed 눈에 띄지 않는, 간과되는 lick 핥다
선택지 sympathetic 동정하는, 동조하는 discouraged 낙담한
jealous 질투하는 alarmed 불안해하는 flattered 우쭐해 하는

해석 어느 토요일에, 작은 개 한 마리가 내가 일하는 동물 보호소에 왔다. 그는 너무 심하게 방치되어서 나는 그를 거의 쳐다볼 수 없었다. 그 불쌍한 녀석은 뼈밖에 없었다. 그로 인해 나의 마음이 아팠다. 나는 누군가가 그에게 그것(기회)을 주기를 바라면서 그에게 Chance라고 이름을 붙이기로 했다. 하지만, Chance는 결코 입양되지 않았다. 그는 매우 소심해서 눈에 띄지 않았다. 오늘까지 사람들은 그를 지나쳐 걸어갔다. 어린 소년이 있는 가족이 방문했다. 그 부모가 다른 강아지들을 보는 동안, 그 소년은 Chance 앞에 섰다. 그들은 서로를 아주 오랫동안 바라보았다. 그러고는 Chance가 걸어가서 그 소년의 손을 핥았다. 그 소년은 그를 안아주었고 나는 미소를 지었다. Chance는 그의 두 번째 기회를 얻었다.

① 동정하는 　→ 기쁜
② 불행한 　　→ 관심 있는
③ 놀란 　　　→ 낙담한
④ 충격을 받은 → 질투하는
⑤ 불안해하는 → 우쭐해 하는

해설 동물 보호소에서 일하는 I가 입양되지 못하는 개 Chance를 보고 불쌍해하다가 Chance가 새로운 주인을 만나게 되는 것을 보고 기뻐하는 과정을 묘사하고 있는 글이다. 글의 초반부의 My heart ached for him에서 I가 Chance를 동정하고 있다는 것을 알 수 있고, 글의 후반부에서 I smiled를 통해 Chance가 입양될 것 같자 기뻐하는 것을 알 수 있으므로, I의 심경 변화로 가장 적절한 것은 ① sympathetic(동정하는) → pleased(기쁜)이다.

오답분석 ②의 interested, ④의 shocked와 jealous, ⑤의 alarmed와 flattered는 글 속의 상황에서 느낄 심경으로 적절하지 않다. ③의 discouraged는 부정적인 감정으로 인물의 마지막 심경과 반대된다.

03　　　　　　　　　　　　　　　　　정답 ④

지문분석

It is natural / to ignore a problem / in the hope / that it will just go away.
그것은 자연스럽다 / 문제를 무시하는 / 바라면서 / 그것이 그냥 사라지기를

But / when it comes to / one's health, / this is a dangerous approach.
그러나 / ~에 관한 한 / 사람의 건강 / 이는 위험한 접근이다

Most serious medical conditions / have a much higher chance / of being successfully treated / if they are found early.
대부분의 심각한 질병들 / 훨씬 높은 가능성을 가지고 있다 / 성공적으로 치료될 / 그것들이 조기에 발견된다면

★ For example, / some forms of cancer / have a 90 percent survival rate / if discovered / in the early stages / compared to / a 10 percent survival rate / if found / later on.
예를 들어 / 몇몇 종류의 암 / 생존율이 90퍼센트이다 / 발견된다면 / 초기 단계에 / ~에 비해 / 10퍼센트의 생존율 / 만약 발견된다면 / 나중에

This is why / doctors encourage everyone / to have a regular health checkup / once a year.
이것이 ~하는 이유이다 / 의사들이 모두에게 권장하는 / 정기적인 건강 검진을 받으라고 / 1년에 한 번

However, / people need to / do more than this.
그러나 / 사람들은 ~할 필요가 있다 / 이보다 더 (자주)

It is important / to watch for symptoms / and to report them / to a doctor / right away.
그것은 중요하다 / 증상을 살펴보는 것 / 그리고 그것들을 알리는 것 / 의사에게 / 즉시

In other words, / by carefully monitoring / your physical condition, / you can increase / your chances of / having a long, happy life.
다시 말해서 / 주의하여 관찰함으로써 / 당신의 신체 상태를 / 당신은 증가시킬 수 있다 / 당신의 ~할 가능성 / 길고, 행복한 인생을 살

★ 독해가 쉬워지는 구문 풀이

For example, some forms of cancer have a 90 percent survival rate [if (they are) **discovered** in the early stages], compared to a 10 percent survival rate [if (they are) **found** later on].

⇨ '만약 ~라면'이라는 뜻을 분명하게 하기 위해 분사구문(discovered in the early stages, found later on) 앞에 접속사(If)가 왔다.

어휘 ignore 무시하다 approach 접근 medical condition 질병
successfully 성공적으로 treat 치료하다 cancer 암 survival rate 생존율
discover 발견하다 encourage 권장하다 checkup 건강 검진
symptom 증상 report 알리다 monitor 관찰하다 physical 신체의

해석 문제가 그냥 사라지기를 바라면서 그것을 무시하는 것은 자연스럽다. 그러나 사람의 건강에 관한 한, 이는 위험한 접근이다. 대부분의 심각한 질병들은 그것들이 조기에 발견된다면 성공적으로 치료될 훨씬 높은 가능성을 가지고 있다. 예를 들어, 몇몇 종류의 암은 나중에 발견된다면 생존율이 10퍼센트인 것에 비해, 초기 단계에 발견된다면 생존율이 90퍼센트이다. 이것이 의사들이 모두에게 1년에 한 번 정기적인 건강 검진을 받으라고 권장하는 이유이다. 그러나, 사람들은 이보다 더 (자주) 할 필요가 있다. 증상을 살펴보고 그것들을 즉시 의사에게 알리는 것은 중요하다. 【주제문】 다시 말해서, 당신의 신체 상태를 주의하여 관찰함으로써 당신은 당신의 길고, 행복한 인생을 살 가능성을 증가시킬 수 있다.

해설 자신의 신체 상태를 주의하여 관찰함으로써 길고, 행복한 인생을 살 가능성을 증가시킬 수 있다는 내용의 글이므로, 필자의 주장으로 가장 적절한 것은 ④ '자신의 건강 상태를 꾸준히 체크해야 한다'이다.

오답분석 ①은 글과 전혀 관련 없는 내용이다. ②은 글에서 언급된 소재 '건강'을 활용하여 혼동을 주는 오답이다. ③은 글에서 언급된 소재 '의사'를 활용하여 혼동을 주는 오답이다. ⑤은 글에서 언급된 소재 '질병'을 활용하여 혼동을 주는 오답이다.

04　　　　　　　　　　　　　　　　　정답 ⑤

지문분석

Art is meant to be an expression of thought / through creative means, / so the idea / that you could put a grade on it / is questionable at best.
예술은 생각의 표현이라고 여겨진다 / 창의적인 수단들에 의한 / 그 때문에 ~한 생각은 / 당신이 그것에 성적을 매길 수 있다는 / 기껏해야 의문의 여지가 있을 뿐이다

The only way / for teachers / to really justify grading a piece of art / is to assign projects / with rules and guidelines to follow.
유일한 방법은 / 선생님들이 / 예술 작품에 점수를 매기는 것을 실제로 정당화할 / 과제를 내는 것이다 / 따라야 할 규칙과 지침이 있는

If students are given / a clear set of criteria, / they will know / what objectives to meet / in order to achieve the grade / they desire.
만약 학생들에게 부여된다면 / 분명한 기준들이 / 그들은 알게 될 것이다 / 달성해야 하는 목표가 무엇인지 / 점수를 얻기 위해 / 그들이 원하는

★ However, / all this does for students / is build a box around them.
하지만 / 이것이 학생들을 위해 해주는 것이라고는 / 그들 주변에 틀을 만드는 것뿐이다

It tells them / that they have to consider their grades / above all else.
그것은 그들에게 알려준다 / 그들이 자신의 점수를 생각해야 한다고 / 다른 무엇보다도

Students already face enough pressure / from being graded / in their core subjects, / where the material is objective.
학생들은 이미 충분한 부담에 직면한다 / 점수가 매겨지는 것으로부터 / 그들의 주요 과목에서 / (학습) 자료가 객관적인

Since art is a rare subject / that allows students / to convey their thoughts freely, / grading their creations / is like attempting / to silence them.
미술은 보기 드문 과목이므로 / 학생들이 ~하게 하는 / 그들의 생각을 자유롭게 전달하도록 / 그들의 창작물에 점수를 매기는 것은 / ~한 시도처럼 보일 수 있다 / 그들을 침묵시키려는

★ 독해가 쉬워지는 구문 풀이

However, [①all this does for students] is [②(to) build a box around them].
　　　　　　　　 주어　　　　　　　　 동사　　　　　 보어

⇨ [①]은 문장의 주어, [②]은 보어이다.
⇨ [②]의 build 앞에는 to가 생략되었다.

어휘 be meant to be ~인 것으로 여겨지다
questionable 의문의 여지가 있는, 의심스러운　at best 기껏해야, 고작
criteria 기준들　objective 목표; 객관적인　box 틀　face 직면하다, 마주하다
convey 전달하다　선택지 generate 만들어내다, 발생시키다　restrict 제한하다

해석 주제문 예술은 창의적인 수단들에 의한 생각의 표현이라고 여겨지기 때문에, 당신이 그것에 성적을 매길 수 있다는 생각은 기껏해야 의문의 여지가 있을 뿐이다. 선생님들이 예술 작품에 점수를 매기는 것을 실제로 정당화할 유일한 방법은 따라야 할 규칙과 지침이 있는 과제를 내는 것이다. 만약 학생들에게 분명한 기준들이 부여된다면 그들은 그들이 원하는 점수를 얻기 위해 달성해야 하는 목표가 무엇인지 알게 될 것이다. 하지만, 이것이 학생들을 위해 해주는 것이라고는 그들 주변에 틀을 만드는 것 뿐이다. 그것은 그들에게 그들이 다른 무엇보다도 자신의 점수를 생각해야 한다고 알려준다. 학생들은 (학습) 자료가 객관적인 주요 과목에서 점수가 매겨지는 것으로부터 이미 충분한 부담에 직면한다. 미술은 학생들이 그들의 생각을 자유롭게 전달하도록 하는 보기 드문 과목이므로, 그들의 창작물에 점수를 매기는 것은 그들을 침묵시키려는 시도처럼 보일 수 있다.

① 불필요한 일을 만드는 것
② 그들이 조용히 작업하게 하는 것
③ 새로운 편견을 만들어내는 것
④ 그들의 생산성을 제한하는 것
⑤ 그들의 표현을 제한하는 것

해설 미술은 학생들이 생각을 자유롭게 전달하도록 하는 보기 드문 과목이므로 그들의 창작물에 점수를 매기는 것은 학생 주변에 틀을 만들고, 그들에게 다른 무엇보다도 자신의 점수를 생각해야 한다고 알려주는 것이라고 했으므로, attempting to silence them(그들을 침묵시키려는 시도)이 의미하는 바로 가장 적절한 것은 ⑤ restricting their expression(그들의 표현을 제한하는 것)이다.

오답 분석 ①, ③은 글에서 언급된 내용이 아니다. ②은 밑줄 친 부분의 silence에서 연상되는 quietly를 활용하여 혼동을 주는 오답이다. ④은 글의 핵심 어휘인 restricting의 유의어 limiting을 활용하여 혼동을 주는 오답이다.

지문분석

Though copyright laws have been around / for centuries, / the social media age / has brought more people into contact / with them / than ever.
비록 저작권법이 존재해왔지만 / 수 세기 동안 / 소셜 미디어 시대는 / 더 많은 사람들이 접하게 해 주었다 / 그것들을 / 그 어느 때보다도 더

In the past, / violating these laws / would have required deliberate copying: / you would've had to spend time / printing knockoff copies of a book / or burning bootleg CDs.
과거에 / 이 법을 위반한다는 것은 / 의도적인 복제를 하는 것을 필요로 했을 것이다 / 당신은 시간을 써야 했을 것이다 / 책의 불법 복제품을 인쇄하는 데에 / 또는 불법 CD를 굽는 것

Nowadays, / we're capable of infringing / someone's intellectual property / with just a few clicks / —so fast / that we might not even realize it.
오늘날 / 우리는 침해할 수 있다 / 누군가의 지적 재산을 / 단 몇 번의 클릭만으로 / 너무나도 빨라서 / 우리는 심지어 그것을 알아차리지 못할 수도 있다

★ For those of us / whose jobs involve social media, / this ease / can create financial risk.
우리 중 ~한 사람들에게 / 업무가 소셜 미디어를 수반하는 / 이러한 용이함은 / 재정적 위험을 야기할 수 있다

A lawsuit / over something shared online / could cost your company / up to $150,000 / in damages, / even if you agree to take it down.
소송은 / 온라인에서 공유된 무언가에 대한 / 당신 회사가 내게 할 수 있다 / 15만 달러까지 / 피해 보상금으로 / 설령 당신이 그것을 내리기로 합의하더라도

For these reasons, / legal experts advise caution / when posting any material / that you did not make / or purchase the rights of.
이러한 이유로 / 법률 전문가는 조심할 것을 충고한다 / 어떠한 자료를 게시할 때 / 당신이 만들지 않은 / 또는 권리를 취득하지 않은

Asking permission or finding an alternative / may take longer, / but doing so will reduce / the risk incurred.
허가를 요청하거나 대안을 찾는 것이 / 더 오래 걸릴 수도 있다 / 하지만 그렇게 하는 것은 줄일 것이다 / 발생되는 위험을

★ 독해가 쉬워지는 구문 풀이

For those of us [whose jobs involve social media], this ease can create financial risk.

⇨ 선행사 those가 '~한 사람들'이라는 뜻으로 쓰였고, 관계절 내에서 jobs가 '우리'의 업무를 나타내므로 소유격 관계대명사 whose가 쓰였다.

어휘 copyright 저작권, 판권　around 존재하여, 주위에
bring into contact with ~을 접하게 해 주다　violate 위반하다, 침해하다
deliberate 의도적인, 고의의　infringe (법적 권리를) 침해하다, 제한하다
damages 피해 보상금　take down 내리다, 치우다　alternative 대안
incur 발생시키다, 초래하다　선택지 justification 정당화, 변명　violation 침해

해석 주제문 비록 저작권법이 수 세기 동안 존재해왔지만, 소셜 미디어 시대는 더 많은 사람들이 그 어느 때보다도 더 그것들을 접하게 해 주었다. 과거에, 이 법을 위반한다는 것은 의도적인 복제를 하는 것을 필요로 했을 것이고, 당신은 책의 불법 복제품을 인쇄하거나 불법 CD를 굽는 데에 시간을 써야 했을 것이다. 오늘날, 우리는 단 몇 번의 클릭만으로 누군가의 지적 재산을 침해할 수 있는데, 이것은 너무나도 빨라서 우리는 심지어 그것을 알아차리지 못할 수도 있다. 우리 중 업무가 소셜 미디어를 수반하는 사람들에게, 이러한 용이함은 재정적 위험을 야기할 수 있다. 온라인에서 공유된 무언가에 대한 소송은 설령 당신이 그것을 내리기로 합의하더라도 당신 회사가 피해 보상금으로 15만 달러까지 내게 할 수 있다. 이러한 이유들로, 법률 전문가는 당신이 만들지 않거나 권리를 취득하지 않은 어떠한 자료를 게시할 때 조심할 것을 충고한다. 허가를 요청하거나 대안을

찾는 것이 더 오래 걸릴 수도 있지만, 그렇게 하는 것은 발생되는 위험을 줄일 것이다.

① 타인에게서 미디어 콘텐츠를 차용하는 것에 대한 정당화
② 지적 재산권에 대한 권리를 옹호하는 것
③ 소셜 미디어가 경제에 미치는 영향
④ 콘텐츠를 복제하는 사람들에게 맞서 스스로를 보호하는 것
⑤ 소셜 미디어가 저작권 침해에 미치는 영향

[해설] 소셜 미디어 시대에서는 단 몇 번의 클릭만으로, 쉽게 다른 사람의 지적 재산을 침해할 수 있기 때문에 주의해야 한다고 했으므로, 이 글의 주제로 가장 적절한 것은 ⑤ the effect of social media on copyright violation(소셜 미디어가 저작권 침해에 미치는 영향)이다.

[오답분석] ①, ④은 글에서 언급되고 있지 않다. ②은 글의 핵심 소재 intellectual property를 활용하여 혼동을 주는 오답이다. ③은 글의 핵심 어구 social media를 활용하여 혼동을 주는 오답이다.

06 정답 ⑤

[지문분석]

The above graph shows the number of students / who earned doctoral degrees in Health and Welfare / in five different countries / in 2017 and 2019.
위 그래프는 학생 수를 나타낸다 / 보건복지 박사 학위를 취득한 / 서로 다른 5개국에서 / 2017년과 2019년에

★ ① The number of students with doctoral degrees / in New Zealand / dropped in 2019 / compared to 2017.
박사 학위가 있는 학생 수는 / 뉴질랜드에서 / 2019년에 하락했다 / 2017년과 비교했을 때

② In both 2017 and 2019, / the number of students with doctoral degrees / in Ireland / was less than 300.
2017년과 2019년 모두 / 박사 학위가 있는 학생 수는 / 아일랜드에서 / 300명보다 더 적었다

③ Mexico had fewer students / with doctoral degrees / than Norway / in both 2017 and 2019.
멕시코는 학생들이 더 적었다 / 박사 학위가 있는 / 노르웨이보다 / 2017년과 2019년 모두

④ Of the five countries, / Norway had the highest number of students / with doctoral degrees / in 2017.
다섯 국가 중에서 / 노르웨이는 학생 수가 가장 많았다 / 박사 학위가 있는 / 2017년에

⑤ In 2019, / students in Norway / with a doctoral degree / increased from 2017, / while those with a doctoral degree in Poland / decreased(→ increased) / over that same period.
2019년에 / 노르웨이의 학생은 / 박사 학위가 있는 / 2017년보다 증가했다 / 반면에 폴란드에서 박사 학위가 있는 학생들은 / 감소했다(→ 증가했다) / 같은 기간 동안

★ 독해가 쉬워지는 구문 풀이

The number of students with doctoral degrees in New Zealand
　　　　　　　　　　　주어
dropped in 2019 **compared to** 2017.
　동사

⇨ 분사구문 compared to ~는 '~와 비교하면'이라고 해석한다.

[어휘] earn 취득하다, 얻다　doctoral degree 박사 학위
health and welfare 보건복지

[해석]

보건복지 박사 학위

위 그래프는 서로 다른 5개국에서 2017년과 2019년에 보건복지 박사 학위를 취득한 학생 수를 나타낸다. ① 2019년에 뉴질랜드에서 박사 학위가 있는 학생 수는 2017년과 비교했을 때 하락했다. ② 아일랜드에서 박사 학위가 있는 학생 수는 2017년과 2019년 모두, 300명보다 더 적었다. ③ 멕시코는 박사 학위가 있는 학생들이 2017년과 2019년 모두 노르웨이보다 더 적었다. ④ 다섯 국가 중에서, 2017년에 노르웨이는 박사 학위가 있는 학생 수가 가장 많았다. ⑤ 2019년에, 박사 학위가 있는 노르웨이의 학생은 2017년보다 증가한 반면, 폴란드에서 박사 학위가 있는 학생들은 같은 기간 동안 감소했다(→ 증가했다).

[해설] 도표의 제목과 글의 도입부를 통해 위 도표가 서로 다른 5개국의 2017과 2019년에 보건복지 박사 학위를 얻은 학생 수에 관한 것임을 알 수 있다. 이 글에서는 ①의 dropped, ②의 less than, ③의 fewer, ④의 the highest, ⑤의 increased와 decreased가 도표 내의 수치를 올바르게 설명하고 있는지 확인해야 한다. 2017년에 비해 2019년에 노르웨이뿐만 아니라 폴란드에서도 박사 학위가 있는 학생 수는 증가하였으므로, 도표의 내용과 일치하지 않는 것은 ⑤이다.

[오답분석] ①은 2019년에 뉴질랜드에서 박사 학위가 있는 학생 수는 191명으로 222명이었던 2017년에 비해 감소했으므로 도표의 내용과 일치한다. ②은 아일랜드에서 박사 학위가 있는 학생 수는 2017년에 277명, 2019년에 282명으로, 모두 300명보다 더 적으므로 도표의 내용과 일치한다. ③은 멕시코에 박사 학위가 있는 학생 수가 2017년에 229명, 2019년에 329명이며, 노르웨이는 2017년에 469명, 2019년에 482명으로, 두 해 모두 멕시코가 노르웨이보다 더 적으므로 도표의 내용과 일치한다. ④은 2017년에 박사 학위가 있는 학생 수가 노르웨이가 469명으로 다섯 국가 중 가장 많으므로 도표의 내용과 일치한다.

07 정답 ③

[지문분석]

Stephen King was born / in Portland, / Maine, / in 1947.
Stephen King은 태어났다 / Portland에서 / Maine 주 / 1947년에

After graduating from the University of Maine, / he married his wife Tabitha / and began working / as an English teacher.
Maine 대학교를 졸업한 후 / 그는 그의 아내 Tabitha와 결혼했다 / 그리고 일하기 시작했다 / 영어 교사로

However, / King's true passion was writing.
그러나 / King의 진정한 열정은 글쓰기였다

In 1973, / he was able to sell his novel *Carrie* / to a large publishing company.
1973년에 / 그는 그의 소설 *Carrie*를 팔 수 있었다 / 한 대형 출판사에

The subsequent sales / from the book / allowed him to quit his job / and write full-time.
뒤이은 판매액은 / 그 책의 / 그가 일을 그만두게 해주었다 / 그리고 전업으로 글을 쓰게

Since then, / he has published over 60 books / and sold more than 300 million copies, / mostly in the genres of fantasy, gothic, and especially horror.
그 이후로 / 그는 60권 이상의 책을 냈다 / 그리고 3억 부 이상을 팔았다 / 주로 판타지, 고딕, 그리고 특히 공포 장르에서

★ Many of his horror stories / have been made into films / that are considered classics / today.
그의 공포 소설 중 많은 것은 / 영화로 만들어졌다 / 고전으로 여겨지는 / 오늘날에

As such, / he is often described / as "The King of Horror."
그것으로써 / 그는 종종 평가된다 / "공포소설의 King(왕)"으로

★ 독해가 쉬워지는 구문 풀이

Many of his horror stories **have been made into** films that are
　　　주어　　　　　　　　　　현재완료 수동태
considered classics today.

⇨ 주어 Many of his horror stories와 동사 make가 '그의 공포 소설 중 많은 것은 만들어졌다'라는 의미의 수동 관계이므로 현재완료 수동태가 쓰였다.

어휘 passion 열정　subsequent 뒤이은, 그 이후의　sales 판매액, 매출(량)
full-time 전업의　publish (책을) 내다, 출판하다　genre 장르, 유형
gothic 고딕파의(중세적 분위기)　describe ~라고 평가하다, 묘사하다

해석 Stephen King은 1947년에 Maine 주의 Portland에서 태어났다. Maine 대학교를 졸업한 후, 그는 그의 아내 Tabitha와 결혼했고 영어 교사로 일하기 시작했다. 그러나, King의 진정한 열정은 글쓰기였다. 1973년에, 그는 한 대형 출판사에 그의 소설 *Carrie*를 팔 수 있었다. 그 책의 뒤이은 판매액은 그가 일을 그만두고 전업으로 글을 쓰게 해주었다. 그 이후로, 그는 60권 이상의 책을 냈고 주로 판타지, 고딕, 그리고 특히 공포 장르에서 3억 부 이상을 팔았다. 그의 공포 소설 중 많은 것은 오늘날에 고전으로 여겨지는 영화로 만들어져 왔다. 그것으로써, 그는 종종 "공포소설의 King(왕)"으로 평가된다.

해설 이 글의 중반부 The subsequent sales from the book allowed him to quit his job and write full-time을 통해 *Carrie*를 쓰기 전이 아닌 쓰고 난 이후에 일을 그만두고 전업으로 글을 쓰기 시작했다고 했으므로, 글의 내용과 일치하지 않는 것은 ③ '직장을 그만둔 후 *Carrie*를 썼다.'이다.

오답분석 ①은 began working as an English teacher라고 했으므로 글의 내용과 일치한다. ②은 In 1973, he was able to sell his novel *Carrie* to a large publishing company라고 했으므로 글의 내용과 일치한다. ④은 he has published over 60 books라고 했으므로 글의 내용과 일치한다. ⑤는 Many of his horror stories have been made into films라고 했으므로 글의 내용과 일치한다.

08　　　　　　　　　　　　　　　　정답 ⑤

지문분석

Graphic designer Bruno Munari believed / that design should serve as "a bridge" / between art and life.
그래픽 디자이너인 Bruno Munari는 생각했다 / 디자인이 "다리" 역할을 해야 한다고 / 예술과 인생 사이의

① Writing in 1966, / he noted / that "as long as art stands / aside from the problems of life / it will only interest / a very few people."
1966년에 집필하면서 / 그는 언급했다 / 예술이 하는 한 / 삶의 문제들에서 동떨어져 있는 / 그것은 ~의 관심만 끌 것이다 / 아주 극소수 사람들

★ What he meant was / that modern artists appeared / more ② concerned with producing work / for small groups of people / than for society as a whole.
그가 의미한 바는 ~이었다 / 현대 예술가들이 ~처럼 보인다는 것 / 작품을 만드는 것에 더 관심이 있는 / 소수 집단의 사람들을 위한 / 사회 전체를 위해서보다는

He felt / artists had lost their connection with society / and that the only way to restore it / would be through design.
그는 느꼈다 / 예술가들이 사회와의 연결성을 잃어버렸다고 / 그리고 그것을 회복하는 유일한 방법은 ~라고 / 디자인을 통해서라고

For Munari, / designing everyday objects / like / pieces of furniture, / signs above storefronts, / or ordinary dining utensils / ③ presented opportunities / to reclaim art's central role.
Munari에게, / 일상적인 물건을 디자인하는 것은 / ~과 같은 / 가구 / 가게 앞의 간판 / 또는 일반적인 식기구 / 기회를 제공하는 것이었다 / 예술의 가장 중요한 역할을 되찾을

He encouraged designers / to place ④ themselves in the thick of life / and to create objects / that actually made people's lives better.
그는 디자이너들을 격려했다 / 삶의 현장 속에 스스로를 두도록 / 그리고 물건을 만들도록 / 사람들의 삶을 실제로 더 낫게 만드는

It was the only way / Munari believed / ⑤ what(→ that) artists could reestablish their rightful place / in society.
그것은 유일한 방법이었다 / Munari가 생각하는 / 예술가들이 그들의 적절한 본분을 회복할 수 있는 / 사회에서

★ 독해가 쉬워지는 구문 풀이

[①**What he meant**] **was** [②that modern artists appeared more
　　　주어　　　　　 동사
concerned with producing work for small groups of people than for society as a whole].

⇨ 명사절 [①]은 문장의 주어, 명사절 [②]는 보어이다.
⇨ 관계대명사 what은 선행사를 포함하며, the thing which로 바꿔 쓸 수 있다.

어휘 serve as ~의 역할을 하다　note 언급하다, 적다　as a whole 전체로서
storefront 가게 앞　ordinary 일반적인, 일상적인　utensil 기구, 도구
central 가장 중요한, 중심의　in the thick of ~의 현장 속에
reestablish 회복하다, 복구하다　rightful 적절한, 걸맞은　place 본분, 입장

해석 주제문 그래픽 디자이너인 Bruno Munari는 디자인이 예술과 인생 사이의 "다리" 역할을 해야 한다고 생각했다. 1966년에 집필하면서, 그는 "예술이 삶의 문제들에서 동떨어져 있는 한, 그것은 아주 극소수 사람들의 관심만 끌 것이다."라고 언급했다. 그가 의미한 바는 현대 예술가들이 사회 전체를 위해서보다는 소수 집단의 사람들을 위한 작품을 만드는 것에 더 관심이 있는 것처럼 보인다는 것이었다. 그는 예술가들이 사회와의 연결성을 잃어버렸고 그것을 회복하는 유일한 방법은 디자인을 통해서라고 느꼈다. Munari에게, 가구, 가게 앞의 간판, 또는 일반적인 식기구와 같은 일상적인 물건을 디자인하는 것은 예술의 가장 중요한 역할을 되찾을 기회를 제공하는 것이었다. 그는 디자이너들이 삶의 현장 속에 스스로를 두고 사람들의 삶을 실제로 더 낫게 만드는 물건을 만들도록 격려했다. 그것은 Munari가 생각하는 예술가들이 사회에서 그들의 적절한 본분을 회복할 수 있는 유일한 방법이었다.

해설 완전한 절(artists ~ in society)을 이끌며 동사 believed의 목적어 자리에 쓰였으므로 ⑤의 what을 접속사 that으로 고쳐야 한다.

오답분석 ①은 분사구문의 주어가 따로 없으므로 주절의 주어 he가 분사구문의 의미상 주어이며, he는 write가 나타내는 '쓰는' 행위의 주체이므로 현재분사 Writing을 사용한 것은 어법상 적절하다. ②은 동사 appear(appeared)는 주격보어를 취하는 동사인데, 보어 자리에는 명사나 형용사 역할을 하는 것이 올 수 있으므로 형용사 역할을 하는 과거분사 concerned를 사용한 것은 어법상 적절하다. ③은 절에는 반드시 주어와 동사가 있어야 하는데, 동사 자리에는 '동사'나 '조동사 + 동사원형'이 와야 하므로 동사 presented를 사용한 것은 어법상 적절하다. ④은 동사 place의 목적어 themselves가 지칭하는 대상이 encouraged의 목적어 designers와 동일하므로, 재귀대명사 themselves를 사용한 것은 어법상 적절하다.

지문분석

Artificial intelligence, / or AI, / is almost certainly going to form / a large part of people's lives / in the future.
인공지능, / 즉 AI는, / 거의 확실히 구성할 것이다 / 사람들의 삶의 많은 부분을 / 미래에

Even today, / AI is used in everything / from phones and cars / to online shopping and medical research.
오늘날조차도, / AI는 모든 것에 사용되고 있다 / 전화기와 자동차부터 / 온라인 쇼핑과 의학 연구에 이르기까지

But / as the number of AI applications has ① decreased(→ increased), / so too has / the number of associated problems.
하지만 / AI의 활용 횟수가 감소하면서(→ 증가하면서) / ~도 그러해졌다 / 관련된 문제의 수

★ Some believe / that AI itself can figure out the solution, / or that it will eventually / be able to ② resolve the issues / it causes.
어떤 이들은 믿는다 / AI가 스스로 해결책을 생각해 낼 수 있을 것이라고 / 또는 그것이 결국에는 / 문제를 해결할 수 있다 / 자신이 야기하는

However, / this ③ ignores / the role that people play, / since significant risks will always be present / as long as AI is produced / by people.
그러나 / 이는 무시한다 / 사람이 하는 역할을 / 중대한 위험 요소가 항상 존재할 것이기 때문이다 / AI가 만들어진 이상 / 사람에 의해

Regarding this, / the more ④ powerful AI becomes, / the greater the threat / that it brings / because of its potential impact.
이 점을 고려할 때 / AI가 더 영향력이 커질수록 / 위협도 커진다 / 그것이 가져올 / 그것의 잠재적 영향력으로 인해

It is therefore important / that society face the issues / surrounding AI / while its related problems are still relatively ⑤ minor.
따라서 ~은 중요하다 / 사회가 문제를 인정하고 대처해야 하는 것은 / AI에 대한 / 그것과 관련된 문제들이 아직 상대적으로 작을 때

★ 독해가 쉬워지는 구문 풀이

Some believe [①that AI **itself** can figure out the solution], or [②that it will eventually be able to resolve the issues it causes].

⇨ 강조 용법으로 사용된 재귀대명사 itself는 '스스로'를 의미하며 생략이 가능하다.

⇨ [①]과 [②]는 각각 believe의 목적어 역할을 하는 명사절이다.

어휘 certainly 확실히, 분명히 application 활용, 이용 associated 관련된 figure out 생각해내다, 찾아내다 solution 해결책 eventually 결국에 resolve 해결하다 significant 중대한, 중요한 potential 잠재적인 face the issue 문제를 인정하고 대처하다 surrounding ~과 관련된, ~에 대한

해석 (주제문) 인공지능, 즉 AI는 거의 확실히 미래에 사람들의 삶의 많은 부분을 구성할 것이다. 오늘날조차도, AI는 전화기와 자동차부터 온라인 쇼핑과 의학 연구에 이르기까지 모든 것에 사용되고 있다. 하지만 AI의 활용 횟수가 ① 감소하면서(→ 증가하면서), 관련된 문제의 수도 그러해졌다. 어떤 이들은 AI가 스스로 해결책을 생각해 내고, 또는 자신이 야기하는 문제도 결국에는 ② 해결할 수 있을 것이라고 믿는다. 그러나, 이는 사람이 하는 역할을 ③ 무시하는 것인데, AI가 사람에 의해 만들어진 이상 중대한 위험 요소가 항상 존재할 것이기 때문이다. 이 점을 고려할 때, AI가 더 ④ 영향력이 커질수록, 그것의 잠재적 영향력으로 인해 그것이 가져올 위협도 커진다. 따라서 그것과 관련된 문제들이 아직 상대적으로 ⑤ 작을 때 사회가 AI에 대한 문제를 인정하고 대처해야 하는 것은 중요하다.

해설 오늘날 AI는 전화기와 자동차부터 온라인 쇼핑과 의학 연구에 이르기까지 모든 것에 사용되고 있으며, 미래에도 사람들의 삶의 많은 부분을 구성할 것이 거의 확실하다고 했으므로, AI의 활용 횟수가 "증가하면서" 관련된 문제의 수도 함께 증가했다는 맥락이 되어야 한다. 따라서 ①의 decreased를 increased와 같은 어로 바꾸어야 문맥상 적절하다.

오답분석 ②은 AI가 스스로 해결책을 생각해 내고 그것이 야기하는 문제도 스스로 "해결할" 수 있을 것이라는 문맥이 되어야 하므로 resolve가 오는 것이 적절하다. ③은 AI가 스스로 해결책을 생각해 내고 문제를 해결할 수 있을 것이라고 믿는 것은 사람이 하는 역할을 "무시하는" 것이라는 문맥이 되어야 하므로 ignores가 오는 것이 적절하다. ④은 AI의 잠재적 영향으로 인해 이것이 가져올 위험도 커지기 때문에 "영향력이 커질수록" 위협도 커진다는 문맥이 되어야 하므로 powerful이 오는 것이 적절하다. ⑤은 AI에 대한 문제들이 아직 상대적으로 "작을" 때 사회는 그 문제를 인정하고 대처해야 한다는 문맥이 되어야 하므로 minor가 오는 것이 적절하다.

지문분석

Knowing your customers / is an essential part of marketing, / but this can seem like / a daunting task / for some, / given how diverse large populations can be.
당신의 고객을 아는 것은 / 마케팅의 필수적인 부분이다 / 그런데 이것은 ~처럼 보일 수 있다 / 벅찬 업무 / 일부에게는 / 많은 사람들이 얼마나 가지각색일 수 있는지를 고려했을 때

Nevertheless, / at its core, / society is made up of individuals / who want to **belong**, / a fact / that can be easily exploited / to sell products.
그럼에도 불구하고 / 본질적으로 / 사회는 ~한 개인들로 이루어져 있다 / **속하기**를 원하는 / 사실이다 / 쉽게 이용될 수 있는 / 제품을 팔기 위해

The vast majority of people, / whether they are willing to admit it or not, / have a fear of "missing out" / and being different from others / in their social group.
대부분의 사람들은 / 그들이 그것을 기꺼이 인정하든 하지 않든 / "소외되는 것"에 대해 두려움을 가지고 있다 / 그리고 다른 사람들과 다르다는 것에 / 그들의 사회 무리 안의

From a marketing perspective, / this means / that they are more likely to purchase items / after seeing their peers do the same.
마케팅 관점에서 / 이는 의미한다 / 그들이 물건을 살 가능성이 더 높다는 것을 / 그들의 또래가 같은 것을 하는(물건을 사는) 것을 본 후

By understanding this herd mentality, / marketers can influence / consumers' purchasing decisions.
이러한 군중심리를 이해함으로써 / 마케팅 담당자는 영향을 미칠 수 있다 / 소비자의 구매 결정에

Tactics / like hiring social media influencers / to back products / or showing / how many times a service has been booked / are especially effective.
전략들 / 소셜 미디어 인플루언서를 고용하는 것과 같은 / 제품을 보증해줄 / 또는 보여주는 것 / 서비스가 얼마나 많이 예약되었는지를 / 특히 효과적이다

★ Being able to see / how popular something is / causes people to view it / as valuable / and, / by extension, / makes them want to purchase it / for themselves.
볼 수 있는 것은 / 어떤 것이 얼마나 인기 있는지를 / 사람들이 그것을 여기게 한다 / 가치 있다고 / 그리고 / 더 나아가 / 그들이 그것을 사고 싶어지도록 만든다 / 자신을 위해

★ 독해가 쉬워지는 구문 풀이

[**Being** able to see how popular something is] **causes** people
　　단수주어(동명사구)　　　　　　　　　단수동사1
to view it as valuable and, by extension, **makes** them want to
　　　　　　　　　　　　　　　　　　　단수동사2
purchase it for themselves.

⇨ [ ]는 동명사구로, 문장의 주어 자리에 쓰였고, 주어로 쓰인 동명사(구)는 단수 취급한다.

어휘 essential 필수적인 daunting 벅찬 diverse 가지각색인, 다양한 at its core 본질적으로 exploit 이용하다 vast majority 대부분의 miss out 소외되다, 누락시키다 perspective 관점 tactic 전략 back 보증하다, 지지하다 by extension 더 나아가 (선택지)compete 경쟁하다

해석 당신의 고객을 아는 것은 마케팅의 필수적인 부분인데, 많은 사람들이 얼

마나 가지각색일 수 있는지를 고려했을 때, 이것이 일부에게는 벅찬 업무처럼 보일 수 있다. (주제문) 그럼에도 불구하고, 본질적으로, 사회는 **속하기**를 원하는 개인들로 이루어져 있으며, 이는 제품을 팔기 위해 쉽게 이용될 수 있는 사실이다. 대부분의 사람들은, 그들이 그것을 기꺼이 인정하든 하지 않든, "소외되는 것"과 그들의 사회 무리 안의 다른 사람들과 다르다는 것에 대해 두려움을 가지고 있다. 마케팅 관점에서, 이는 그들이 그들의 또래가 같은 것을 하는(물건을 사는) 것을 본 후 물건을 살 가능성이 더 높다는 것을 의미한다. 이러한 군중심리를 이해함으로써, 마케팅 담당자는 소비자의 구매 결정에 영향을 미칠 수 있다. 제품을 보증해줄 소셜 미디어 인플루언서를 고용하거나 서비스가 얼마나 많이 예약되었는지를 보여주는 것과 같은 전략들이 특히 효과적이다. 어떤 것이 얼마나 인기 있는지를 볼 수 있는 것은 사람들이 그것을 가치 있다고 여기게 하며, 더 나아가, 그들이 자신을 위해 그것을 사고 싶어지도록 만든다.

① 속하다   ② 성공하다   ③ 탈출하다
④ 성장하다   ⑤ 경쟁하다

[해설] 빈칸 문장은 이 글의 주제문이므로, 이를 다시 언급한 문장이나 부연 설명하는 문장을 파악해야 한다. 빈칸 문장에서 본질적으로 사회는 '무엇하기를' 원하는 개인들로 이루어져 있다고 하고, 빈칸 바로 뒤의 문장에서 대부분의 사람들이 소외되는 것과 자신이 속한 사회 무리의 다른 사람들과 다르다는 것에 대해 두려움을 가지고 있다고 했다. 따라서 빈칸에는 사회는 "속하기"를 원하는 개인들로 이루어져 있다는 의미가 되는 것이 자연스러우므로 ① belong(속하다)이 정답이다.

[오답분석] ②의 '성공하다', ④의 '성장하다'와 ⑤의 '경쟁하다'는 글의 내용과 관련이 없다. ③은 사람들이 사회 무리 안에 속하기를 원한다는 글의 내용과 반대되는 내용이므로 오답이다.

11
정답 ④

지문분석

Preserving biodiversity / in farming practices / is crucial / for protecting natural resources.
생물의 다양성을 지키는 것은 / 농업 방식에서 / 필수적이다 / 천연자원을 보호하기 위해

By utilizing techniques / that ensure the continuation / of as many species as possible, / ★ we not only aid / in conservation efforts / but allow there to be a large enough gene pool / to produce a variety of healthy crops.
기술을 활용함으로써 / 존속을 보장하는 / 가능한 한 많은 종들의 / 우리는 촉진시킬 뿐만 아니라 / 보존 활동을 / 충분히 큰 유전자 풀이 생기게 하여 / 다양한 건강한 작물을 생산하기 위한

① There are various farming strategies / that can be used / to achieve this.
다양한 농업 전략이 있다 / 사용될 수 있는 / 이를 달성하기 위해

② One such strategy is intercropping, / which involves growing crops / close together.
이러한 전략 중 하나는 간작이다 / 이것은 작물을 기르는 것을 필요로 한다 / 가까이에서 같이

③ This allows the plants / to use their natural systems / with maximum efficiency / while also reducing pests / with less chemicals.
이는 식물이 ~하게 해준다 / 그들의 자생 체계를 이용하게 / 최대한의 효율로 / 동시에 또한 해충을 줄여준다 / 더 적은 화학 물질로

(④ For thousands of years, / pests have been one of the major reasons / for production loss / that farmers have had to deal with.)
수천 년 동안 / 해충은 주요 원인 중 하나였다 / 생산량 손실의 / 농부들이 대처해야 했던

⑤ Another popular technique is crop rotation, / which allows for nutrients / in the farming soil / to be restored / because farmers plant different crops sequentially / on the same land.
또 다른 대중적인 기법은 윤작이다 / 이는 영양분이 ~하게 한다 / 농사를 짓는 토양 내의 / 회복되게 / 농부들이 연속해서 다른 작물을 심기 때문에 / 같은 땅에

[어휘] biodiversity 생물의 다양성 crucial 필수적인 natural resource 천연자원 utilize 활용하다 continuation 존속, 지속 aid 촉진시키다, 돕다 conservation 보존 effort 활동, 노력 gene pool 유전자 풀, 유전자 공급원 natural 자생의, 타고난 deal with ~에 대처하다, 대항하다 sequentially 연속하여, 결과로서

[해석] (주제문) 농업 방식에서 생물의 다양성을 지키는 것은 천연자원을 보호하기 위해 필수적이다. 가능한 한 많은 종들의 존속을 보장하는 기술을 활용함으로써, 우리는 보존 활동을 촉진시킬 뿐만 아니라, 다양한 건강한 작물을 생산하기 위한 충분히 큰 유전자 풀이 생기게 한다. ① 이를 달성하기 위해 사용될 수 있는 다양한 농업 전략이 있다. ② 이러한 전략 중 하나는 간작으로, 이것은 작물들을 가까이에서 같이 기르는 것을 필요로 한다. ③ 이는 식물이 그들의 자생 체계를 최대한의 효율로 이용하게 해주고, 동시에 또한 더 적은 화학 물질로 해충을 줄여준다. (④ 수천 년 동안 해충은 농부들이 대처해야 했던 생산량 손실의 주요 원인 중 하나였다.) ⑤ 또 다른 대중적인 기법은 윤작으로, 이는 농부들이 같은 땅에 연속해서 다른 작물을 심기 때문에 농사를 짓는 토양 내의 영양분이 회복되게 한다.

[해설] 이 글의 주제는 생물의 다양성을 지키기 위한 농업 기술과 전략을 이용함으로써 보존 활동을 촉진시키고 다양한 건강한 작물을 생산하기 위한 충분히 큰 유전자 풀이 생기게 한다는 것이다. ①, ②, ③, ⑤이 생물의 다양성을 지키는 농업 방식인 간작과 윤작에 대해 설명하는 내용으로 주제와 관련이 있는 반면, 해충이 생산량 손실의 주요한 원인 중 하나였음을 언급한 ④은 글의 흐름과 관계없는 문장이다.

[오답분석] ①, ②, ③, ⑤은 글의 주제와 관련하여 생물의 다양성을 지키는 농업 방식에 대한 예시를 설명하고 있으므로 글의 흐름에 자연스럽다.

12
정답 ⑤

지문분석

For decades, / hydrogen has been promoted / as an important form of energy.
수십 년간 / 수소는 홍보되어 왔다 / 중요한 형태의 에너지로서

It is one of the simplest / and most abundant elements / in the universe / and can supply a large amount of energy / for electricity, heat, industry, and transportation.
이것은 가장 단순한 것 중 하나이다 / 그리고 가장 풍부한 원소 / 우주에서 / 그리고 많은 양의 에너지를 공급할 수 있다 / 전기, 난방, 산업, 그리고 이동 수단에

(A) Thanks to / recent technological advancements, / however, / new methods are being developed / that allow hydrogen to be produced / from purely renewable sources.
~ 덕분에 / 최근의 기술 발전 / 하지만 / 새로운 방법들이 개발되고 있다 / 수소가 생산될 수 있도록 하는 / 전적으로 재생 가능한 자원으로부터

This means / it could still play an important part / in achieving a low-carbon future.
이는 의미한다 / 그것(수소)이 여전히 중요한 역할을 할 수 있다는 것을 / 저탄소 미래를 달성하는 데 있어

★ (B) What both of these methods have in common is / that they are complicated and expensive.
이 두 가지 방법이 공통적으로 가지고 있는 점은 / 그것들이 복잡하고 비용이 많이 든다는 것이다

They also rely on / carbon-heavy fossil fuels / that are costly and harmful / to the environment.
그것들은 또한 ~에 의존한다 / 고탄소 화석 연료 / 비경제적이면서 해로운 / 환경에

(C) Unfortunately, / hydrogen is typically connected to / another compound, / so / it must be separated.
안타깝게도 / 수소는 일반적으로 ~에 결합되어 있다 / 다른 화합물 / 그래서 / 그것은 분리되어야만 한다

This can be quite complex.
이것은 꽤 복잡할 수 있다

For instance, / one method / to get hydrogen from the air / uses very high temperatures.
예를 들어 / 하나의 방법은 / 공기에서 수소를 얻는 / 매우 높은 온도를 이용한다

Another method / to separate hydrogen from water / uses electricity.
또 다른 방법은 / 물에서 수소를 추출하는 / 전기를 사용한다

★ 독해가 쉬워지는 구문 풀이

[**What** both of these methods have in common] is that they are
　　단수주어(명사절)　　　　　　　　　　　단수동사
complicated and expensive.

⇨ [ ]는 what이 이끄는 명사절로, 문장의 주어 역할을 한다. 이 경우, 주어는 단수 취급한다.

어휘 hydrogen 수소 promote 홍보하다 transportation 이동 수단 thanks to ~덕분에 purely 전적으로 renewable 재생 가능한 carbon 탄소 fossil fuel 화석 연료 costly 비경제적인, 대가가 큰 compound 화합물

해석 수십 년간, 수소는 중요한 형태의 에너지로서 홍보되어 왔다. 이것은 우주에서 가장 단순하면서도 가장 풍부한 원소 중 하나이며 전기, 난방, 산업, 그리고 이동 수단에 많은 양의 에너지를 공급할 수 있다.
(C) 안타깝게도, 수소는 일반적으로 다른 화합물에 결합되어 있어서 분리되어야만 한다. 이것은 꽤 복잡할 수 있다. 예를 들어, 공기에서 수소를 얻는 하나의 방법은 매우 높은 온도를 이용한다. 물에서 수소를 추출하는 또 다른 방법은 전기를 사용한다.
(B) 이 두 가지 방법이 공통적으로 가지고 있는 점은 그것들이 복잡하고 비용이 많이 든다는 것이다. 그것들은 또한 비경제적이면서, 환경에 해로운 고탄소 화석 연료에 의존한다.
(A) 하지만, 최근의 기술 발전 덕분에, 전적으로 재생 가능한 자원으로부터 수소가 생산될 수 있도록 하는 새로운 방법들이 개발되고 있다. 이는 저탄소 미래를 달성하는 데 있어 그것(수소)이 여전히 중요한 역할을 할 수 있다는 것을 의미한다.

해설 주어진 글은 수소가 우주에서 가장 단순하고 풍부한 원소 중 하나이며 전기, 난방, 산업, 이동 수단에 많은 양의 에너지를 공급할 수 있다는 내용이다. (C)는 Unfortunately를 통해 주어진 글에서 언급된 장점에 대한 반전 설명을 하고 있으므로 주어진 글 뒤에 오는 것이 자연스럽다. (B)의 both of these methods(이 두 가지 방법)는 (C)의 '공기에서 수소를 얻는 방법'과 '물에서 수소를 추출하는 방법'을 가리키므로 (C) 뒤에 와야 한다. (A)는 however를 통해 (B)의 내용에 대한 반전 설명을 하면서 재생 가능한 자원으로부터 수소를 생산하는 새로운 방법이 개발되고 있다는 내용이므로 수소를 얻는 기존의 두 가지 방법이 비경제적이면서 환경에 해로운 고탄소 화석 연료에 의지한다고 한 (B) 뒤에 오는 것이 자연스럽다. 따라서 글의 순서로 가장 적절한 것은 ⑤ (C)-(B)-(A)이다.

지문분석

Most airlines follow / a curved flight path / over the Pacific Ocean / rather than fly directly / across it.
대부분의 항공사는 따른다 / 휘어진 비행경로를 / 태평양 위로 / 곧장 비행하기보다는 / 그것(태평양)을 가로질러

(①) Part of the reason is / that this allows them / to stay close to land, / which is useful / in an emergency.
그 이유 중 일부는 ~이기 때문이다 / 이것이 그들로 하여금 ~ 할 수 있게 한다 / 육지에 더 가까이 있게 / 이것은 유용하다 / 비상시에

(②) Another has to do with / the Earth's spherical shape.
또 다른 이유는 ~와 관련이 있다 / 지구의 구 형태

(③) ★ Because the Earth is round, / it is wider / in the middle / than it is at the top or the bottom.
지구는 둥글기 때문에 / 더 넓다 / 가운데 부분이 / 위나 아래보다

(④) (Flying directly / across the Pacific Ocean / would therefore cause a plane to travel / across the widest or longest part / of the planet.)
곧장 비행하는 것은 / 태평양을 가로질러 / 따라서 비행기가 이동하게 할 것이다 / 가장 넓거나 가장 긴 부분을 거쳐서 / 지구의

By flying / either above or below the ocean / instead, / a plane is able to travel / a shorter distance.
비행함으로써 / 바다(태평양) 위쪽이나 아래쪽 둘 중 한 곳으로 / 대신 / 비행기는 이동할 수 있다 / 더 짧은 거리를

(⑤) This can be verified / by taking an artificial globe / and measuring the distance / between two destinations / across the Pacific Ocean, / once near the middle / and once near the bottom or the top.
이것은 증명될 수 있다 / 인공 지구본을 가져옴으로써 / 그리고 거리를 측정하는 것 / 두 목적지 사이의 / 태평양을 가로지르는 / 한 번은 중앙 근처로 / 그리고 한 번은 아래나 위 근처로

★ 독해가 쉬워지는 구문 풀이

Because the Earth is round, it is wider in the middle **than** it is (wider)
　　　　　　　　　　　　　　　　　　　　　　　接속사
at the top or the bottom.

⇨ 접속사(than)로 연결된 병렬 구조에서 반복되는 wider는 생략할 수 있다.

어휘 airline 항공사 curved 휘어진 the Pacific Ocean 태평양 emergency 비상 (사태) distance 거리 verify 증명하다 artificial 인공의 globe 지구본 destination 목적지

해석 대부분의 항공사는 그것(태평양)을 곧장 가로질러 비행하기보다는 태평양 위로 휘어진 비행경로를 따른다. 그 이유 중 일부는 이것이 그들로 하여금 육지에 더 가까이 있게 해주기 때문인데, 이것은 비상시에 유용하다. 또 다른 이유는 지구의 구 형태와 관련이 있다. 지구는 둥글기 때문에, 위나 아래보다 가운데 부분이 더 넓다. (따라서 태평양을 가로질러 곧장 비행하는 것은 비행기가 지구의 가장 넓거나, 가장 긴 부분을 거쳐서 이동하게 할 것이다.) 대신 바다(태평양) 위쪽이나 아래쪽 둘 중 한 곳으로 비행함으로써, 비행기는 더 짧은 거리를 이동할 수 있다. 이것은 인공 지구본을 가져와서 태평양을 가로지르는 두 목적지 사이의 거리를, 한 번은 중앙 근처로 그리고 한 번은 아래나 위 근처로 측정함으로써 증명될 수 있다.

해설 주어진 문장의 therefore ~ planet을 통해 주어진 문장 앞에는 태평양을 가로질러 비행하지 않는 이유가 나와야 한다는 것을 알 수 있다. ①~③ 뒤 문장까지 대부분의 항공사가 태평양을 곧장 가로질러 비행하지 않는 두 가지 이유를 설명하고 있고, ④ 뒤 문장에서 By flying either above or below the ocean instead를 통해 태평양을 가로질러 비행하지 않는 대신 사용되는 방법에 대해 설명하고 있으므로 주어진 문장이 들어가기에 가장 적절한 곳은 ④이다.

①, ② 뒤 문장은 첫 번째 문장에 이어서 대부분의 항공사가 태평양을 곧장 가로질러 비행하지 않는 이유에 대해 언급하고 있고, ③ 뒤 문장은 앞 문장에 대한 보충 설명이므로 문장의 흐름이 자연스럽다. ⑤ 뒤 문장의 This는 ④ 뒤 문장의 a plane is able to travel a shorter distance(비행기는 더 짧은 거리를 이동할 수 있다)를 가리키므로 문장의 흐름이 자연스럽다.

14   정답 ①

지문분석

★ To test / whether DNA can tolerate a space flight / and subsequent reentry into Earth's atmosphere, / researchers at the University of Zurich / placed some / on the outside of a rocket / that was then launched into space.
실험하기 위해 / DNA가 우주 비행을 견딜 수 있을지 / 그리고 지구의 대기로의 추후 재진입을 / Zurich 대학의 연구원들은 / 몇몇(DNA)을 배치했다 / 로켓의 외부에 / 그 이후에 (그것들은) 우주로 발사됐다

Upon the rocket's return, / researchers were surprised to discover / that nearly one-third of the DNA was still "alive", / meaning / it was still capable of passing on / genetic information / despite having been exposed to a harsh environment.
로켓이 귀환하자마자 / 연구원들은 발견하고는 놀랐다 / DNA의 거의 삼 분의 일이 아직 "살아있는" 것을 / 이는 의미한다 / 그것(DNA)이 여전히 전달할 수 있는 것을 / 유전 정보를 / 혹독한 환경에 노출되었음에도 불구하고

This finding has led to some intriguing ideas, / one of which is / that the first DNA on Earth / came from outer space.
이 발견은 몇몇 흥미로운 발상으로 이어졌다 / 그중 하나는 ~이다 / 지구상 첫 번째 DNA가 ~라는 것 / 우주로부터 왔다

At the same time, / they believe / humans can then transport DNA / from Earth into space / and begin life anew / on other planets.
동시에 / 그들은 믿는다 / 그렇다면 인간이 DNA를 이동시킬 수 있다고 / 지구에서 우주로 / 그리고 삶을 새로이 시작한다 / 다른 행성에서

⇩

The researchers concluded / that DNA can (A) withstand harsh environments in space, / and they believe / it can be used to (B) initiate life / on other planets.
연구원들은 결론지었다 / DNA가 우주의 혹독한 환경을 견딜 수 있다고 / 그리고 그들은 믿는다 / 그것이 삶을 시작하는 데 사용될 수 있다고 / 다른 행성에서

★ 독해가 쉬워지는 구문 풀이

[To test whether DNA can tolerate a space flight and subsequent reentry into Earth's atmosphere], researchers at the University of
주어
Zurich placed **some** on the outside of a rocket [that was then
동사   목적어   수식어(관계절)
launched into space].
⇨ some은 앞의 DNA를 가리키는 대명사로 쓰였으며, 복수명사 혹은 셀 수 없는 명사를 대신할 때 사용할 수 있다.
⇨ [ ]는 선행사 rocket을 수식하는 관계절이다.

어휘 tolerate 견디다   subsequent 추후의   reentry 재진입   atmosphere 대기   launch 발사하다   pass on ~을 전달하다   genetic 유전의   harsh 혹독한   intriguing 흥미로운   transport 이동시키다   anew 새로이, 다시 한번
선택지 withstand 견디다   initiate 시작하다   imitate 모방하다   alter 바꾸다

해석 DNA가 우주 비행과 추후 지구 대기로의 재진입을 견딜 수 있을지 실험하기 위해, Zurich 대학의 연구원들은 몇몇(DNA)을 로켓의 외부에 배치했고 그 이후에 (그것들은) 우주로 발사됐다. 로켓이 귀환하자마자, 연구원들은 DNA의 거의 삼 분의 일이 아직 "살아있는" 것을 발견하고는 놀랐는데, 주제문 이는 그것(DNA)이 혹독한 환경에 노출되었음에도 불구하고 여

전히 유전 정보를 전달할 수 있다는 것을 의미한다. 이 발견은 몇몇 흥미로운 발상으로 이어졌는데, 그중 하나는 지구상 첫 번째 DNA가 우주로부터 왔다는 것이다. 동시에, 그들은 그렇다면 인간이 DNA를 지구에서 우주로 이동시켜 다른 행성에서 삶을 새로이 시작할 수 있다고 믿는다.

⇩

연구원들은 DNA가 우주의 혹독한 환경을 (A) 견딜 수 있다고 결론지었고, 그것이 다른 행성에서 삶을 (B) 시작하는 데 사용될 수 있다고 믿는다.

     (A)   (B)
① 견디다   …   시작하다
② 견디다   …   연구하다
③ 지지하다   …   시작하다
④ 지지하다   …   모방하다
⑤ 바꾸다   …   연구하다

해설 요약문은 연구원들이 DNA가 우주의 혹독한 환경을 '(A)'할 수 있음을 결론지었고, 그것이 다른 행성에서 삶을 '(B)하는' 데 사용될 수 있다고 믿는다는 내용이다. 글에서 몇몇 DNA가 배치된 로켓이 우주로 발사됐고, 그것들 중 거의 삼 분의 일이 여전히 살아있는 채로 귀환했으며, 이것은 DNA가 우주의 혹독한 환경을 견딜 수 있음을 의미할 뿐만 아니라 DNA를 우주로 이동시켜 다른 행성에서 삶을 새로이 시작할 수 있음을 믿게 되었다고 했다. 따라서 요약문의 (A)에는 글에서 언급된 'still alive', 'despite having been exposed to a harsh environment'와 관련된 'withstand'가, (B)에는 글에서 언급된 'begin life anew'와 관련된 'initiate'가 적절하므로 ① withstand(견디다) - initiate(시작하다)가 정답이다.

오답분석 우주 비행 후 귀환한 로켓에 배치한 DNA가 여전히 살아있었다고 했으므로 ③과 ④의 support와 ⑤의 alter는 (A)에 들어갈 단어로 적절하지 않다. DNA를 지구에서 우주로 이동시켜 다른 행성에서 새로운 삶을 시작할 수 있다는 것을 믿게 되었다고 했으므로 ②과 ⑤의 study, 그리고 ④의 imitate는 (B)에 들어갈 단어로 적절하지 않다.

15 ~ 16

지문분석

With more and more news outlets / spreading specific political opinions, / journalism is no longer as (a) objective / as it used to be.
점점 더 많은 언론 매체가 / 특정 정치적 견해를 확산시키면서 / 저널리즘은 더 이상 객관적이지 않다 / 이전에 그랬던 것만큼

This is problematic / for multiple reasons.
이것은 문제가 된다 / 여러 가지 이유로

When journalists include their personal opinions / in stories / they write, / they can influence their audience / to think the (b) same way / instead of allowing them / to form their own opinions.
기자들이 자신의 개인적인 견해를 포함할 때 / 기사에 / 그들이 작성하는 / 그들은 독자에게 영향을 미칠 수 있다 / 똑같은 방식으로 생각하도록 / ~ 하도록 하는 대신 / 자신만의 견해를 형성하도록

This sort of biased reporting / can (c) divide the public / as differences in opinion / often lead to hostility.
이런 유형의 편향된 보도는 / 대중을 분열시킬 수 있다 / 의견의 차이는 ~ 하기 때문에 / 종종 적대감으로 이어지다

Biased journalism / can also result in / people turning to the internet, / where they can find / one-sided news sources / that (d) challenge(→ support) their views.
편향된 저널리즘은 / 또한 결국 ~하게 만든다 / 사람들이 인터넷에 의지하게 / 거기서 그들은 찾을 수 있다 / 편파적인 뉴스자료를 / 그들의 견해를 문제 삼는(→ 뒷받침하는)

★ By only exposing themselves to articles and programs / containing views / they already agree with, / they strengthen their belief / that their opinion is the only one that matters / and can more easily justify their resistance / to any other point of view.
자신을 기사와 프로그램에만 노출시킴으로써 / 관점을 담고 있는 / 그들이 이미 동의하는 / 그들은 믿음을 견고하게 한다 / 그들의 의견만이 중요한 것이라는 / 그리고 저항도 더 쉽게 정당화할 수 있다 / 다른 어떤 관점에 대한

By contrast, / publishing just the facts / prevents people from simply (e) accepting someone's opinion / as the truth.
반면에 / 단지 사실만을 알리는 것은 / 사람들이 단순히 누군가의 의견을 받아들이는 것을 방지한다 / 입증된 사실로

Instead, / it forces them to think / for themselves.
대신에 / 그것은 그들이 생각하게 만든다 / 스스로

★ 독해가 쉬워지는 구문 풀이

By only exposing themselves ~ they already agree with, they strengthen their **belief** [that their opinion is the only one that matters and can more easily justify their resistance to any other point of view].
동격 that절
⇨ 명사절 [ ]는 명사 belief와 동격을 이룬다.

[어휘] news outlet 언론 매체, 언론 기관 multiple 여러 가지, 다양한
journalist 기자, 언론인, 저널리스트 story 기사, 이야기
biased 편향된, 선입견이 있는 divide 분열하다, 가르다 hostility 적대감, 반감
turn to ~에 의지하다, ~이 되다 one-sided 편파적인, 한쪽으로 치우친
matter 중요하다; 문제 resistance 저항 point of view 관점, 견해
force ~하게 만들다, 강요하다

[해석] (주제문) 점점 더 많은 언론 매체가 특정 정치적 견해를 확산시키면서, 저널리즘은 더 이상 이전에 그랬던 것만큼 (a) 객관적이지 않다. 이것은 여러 가지 이유로 문제가 된다. 기자들이 그들이 작성하는 기사에 자신의 개인적인 견해를 포함할 때, 그들은 독자가 자신만의 견해를 형성하도록 하는 대신 (b) 똑같은 방식으로 생각하도록 영향을 미칠 수 있다. 의견의 차이는 종종 적대감으로 이어지기 때문에 이런 유형의 편향된 보도는 대중을 (c) 분열시킬 수 있다.
편향된 저널리즘은 결국 사람들을 인터넷에 의지하게 만드는데, 거기서 그들은 그들의 견해를 (d) 문제 삼는(→ 뒷받침하는) 편파적인 뉴스 자료를 찾을 수 있다. 그들이 이미 동의하는 관점을 담고 있는 기사와 프로그램에만 자신을 노출시킴으로써, 그들은 그들의 의견만이 중요한 것이라는 믿음을 견고하게 하고 다른 어떤 관점에 대한 저항도 더 쉽게 정당화할 수 있다. 반면에, 단지 사실만을 알리는 것은 사람들이 단순히 누군가의 의견을 입증된 사실로 (e) 받아들이는 것을 방지한다. 대신에, 그것은 그들이 스스로 생각하게 만든다.

15
정답 ②

[해석] ① 뉴스: 정치적 갈등의 근원인가?
② 편향된 보도: 그것이 야기하는 문제들
③ 언론인이 정치 참여에 영향을 미치는가?
④ 인터넷이 언론 매체에 미치는 긍정적인 영향
⑤ 언론인의 딜레마: 강경한 견해에도 불구하고 객관성을 유지하는 것

[해설] 기자의 개인적인 견해를 포함하는 편향된 기사는 독자가 그들만의 견해를 형성하는 것을 방해하고 그들이 더욱 더 편향된 기사만을 찾게 한다는 내용의 글이므로, 글의 제목으로 가장 적절한 것은 ② Biased Reporting: The Problems It Causes(편향된 보도: 그것이 야기하는 문제들)이다.

[오답분석] ①과 ③은 글의 일부만을 다루고 있는 오답이다. ④은 사람들은 인터넷에서 그들의 견해를 뒷받침하는 편파적인 뉴스 자료를 찾는다고 했으므로

글의 내용과 반대된다. ⑤은 글에서 언급되고 있지 않다.

[어휘] participation 참여

16
정답 ④

[해설] 편향된 저널리즘은 사람들을 인터넷에 의지하게 만들고, 결국 인터넷에서 자신의 견해를 "뒷받침하는" 편파적인 뉴스만을 찾도록 이어질 수 있다는 맥락이 되어야 하므로, ④의 challenge(문제 삼다)를 support(뒷받침하다)와 같은 어휘로 바꾸어야 문맥상 적절하다.

[오답분석] ①은 더 많은 언론 매체가 특정 정치적 견해를 확산시키면서 저널리즘은 이제 이전만큼 "객관적이지" 않다는 문맥이 되어야 하므로 objective가 오는 것이 적절하다. ②은 기자들이 기사에 개인적인 견해를 포함할 때 그들은 독자들도 그들과 "똑같은" 방식으로 생각하게 만들 수 있다는 문맥이 되어야 하므로 same이 오는 것이 적절하다. ③은 의견의 차이는 적대감으로 이어질 수 있기에 편향된 보도가 대중을 "분열시킬" 수 있다는 문맥이 되어야 하므로 divide가 오는 것이 적절하다. ⑤은 사실만을 알리는 것은 사람들이 단순히 사실을 "받아들이는" 것을 방지하고 스스로 생각하게 만든다는 문맥이 되어야 하므로 accepting이 오는 것이 적절하다.

---

17 ~ 19

[지문분석]

(A) Miss Douglas loved / being a first-grade teacher, / but it wasn't always easy.
Douglas 선생님은 좋아했다 / 1학년 선생님인 것을 / 하지만 그것이 언제나 쉽지만은 않았다

She was especially worried / about little Sarah, / who had a hard time making friends.
그녀는 특히 걱정했다 / 어린 Sarah에 대해 / 친구를 사귀기 어려워하는

Miss Douglas tried to help her, / but sometimes, / she wondered / if her student even noticed.
Douglas 선생님은 그녀를 도와주려고 노력했다 / 하지만 때때로 / 그녀는 궁금했다 / 그녀의 학생(Sarah)이 이를 알아주기라도 할지

Still, / (a) she loved her job / and walked into class every day / with a big smile.
그럼에도 / 그녀는 그녀의 직업을 좋아했다 / 그리고 매일 교실로 들어갔다 / 함박웃음을 지으며

Today, / she was happier than usual / because her favorite holiday, / Thanksgiving, / was coming up.
오늘 / 그녀는 평소보다 더 기뻤다 / 왜냐하면 그녀가 가장 좋아하는 휴일이 ~이기 때문이다 / 추수감사절이 / 다가오고 있었다

(B) The other students were surprised / as well.
다른 학생들은 놀랐다 / 또한

Soon, / everyone started guessing / whose hand it could be.
곧 / 모두가 추측하기 시작했다 / 그것이 누구의 손일지

Some said / it must be a farmer's hand / who raised turkeys.
몇몇은 말했다 / 농부의 손임이 틀림없다고 / 칠면조를 길러낸

Others said / it was Sarah's hand / or her mother's / or father's.
다른 아이들은 말했다 / Sarah의 손이라고 / 또는 그녀의 어머니의 것 / 또는 아버지의 것

When Miss Douglas finally asked her, / she quietly said / "It's (b) yours."
Douglas 선생님이 마침내 그녀에게 물어봤을 때 / 그녀는 조용히 말했다 / 이것은 당신의 손이에요

(C) Miss Douglas was shocked.
Douglas 선생님은 충격을 받았다

"(c) Mine? / But why..."
나의 손 / 하지만 왜

Then, / she remembered all the times / she held Sarah's hand.
그리고 나서 / 그녀는 모든 순간을 떠올렸다 / 그녀가 Sarah의 손을 잡았던

She held her hand / to take her to the bathroom / or to play outside.
그녀는 그녀의 손을 잡았다 / 그녀를 화장실에 데려가기 위해 / 또는 밖에서 놀기 위해

She remembered / that she held Sarah's little hand / over a pencil / to show her / how to write properly.
그녀는 떠올렸다 / 그녀가 Sarah의 작은 손을 잡았던 것을 / 연필 위로 / 그녀에게 보여주기 위해 / 올바르게 글씨를 쓰는 법을

She remembered / how every morning, / she would pat Sarah's shoulder / and greet (d) her, / as she did all the children / in her class.
그녀는 떠올렸다 / 매일 아침 ~하곤 했던 것을 / Sarah의 어깨를 쓰다듬었다 / 그리고 그녀에게 인사했다 / 다른 아이들에게도 했던 것처럼 / 그녀 반의

Miss Douglas smiled / and wiped a tear away.
Douglas 선생님은 미소지었다 / 그리고 눈물을 닦아냈다

(D) In honor of the special day, / Miss Douglas had a special assignment / for her class.
이 특별한 날을 기념하여 / Douglas 선생님은 특별한 과제를 내주었다 / 그녀의 학생들을 위한

★ She told them to draw / the things they were most thankful for.
그녀는 그들에게 그리라고 했다 / 가장 감사했던 것을

Students began to work busily.
학생들은 바쁘게 움직이기 시작했다

They drew / turkeys and big dinners.
그들은 그렸다 / 칠면조와 푸짐한 식사를

Some drew their families / gathered together, / while others drew themselves / playing with their friends.
일부는 그들의 가족을 그렸다 / 함께 모여 있는 / 반면 다른 아이들은 스스로를 그렸다 / 그들의 친구들과 함께 놀고 있는

But / Miss Douglas noticed / that little Sarah drew something / different.
그러나 / Douglas 선생님은 알아챘다 / 어린 Sarah가 무언가를 그렸다는 것을 / 다른

(e) She was quite astonished / to see / that she had drawn an empty hand.
그녀는 꽤 깜짝 놀랐다 / ~을 보고 / 그녀가 빈손을 그린 것을

★ 독해가 쉬워지는 구문 풀이

She told them to draw the things [they were most thankful for].
　　　　　　　　　　　　　　　　　수식어(관계절)

⇨ [ ]는 선행사 things 뒤에 목적격 관계대명사 that 또는 which가 생략된 관계대명사절이다.
⇨ 전치사 for는 관계대명사가 생략되지 않았을 경우 관계대명사와 함께 [ ]의 앞에 올 수 있다.

어휘 turkey 칠면조 properly 올바르게 in the honor of ~을 기념하여 assignment 과제 gather 모이다 astonished 깜짝 놀란

해석 (A) Douglas 선생님은 1학년 선생님인 것을 좋아했지만, 그것이 언제나 쉽지만은 않았다. 그녀는 친구를 사귀기 어려워하는 어린 Sarah에 대해 특히 걱정했다. Douglas 선생님은 그녀를 도와주려고 노력했지만, 때때로는 그녀의 학생(Sarah)이 이를 알아주기라도 할지 궁금했다. 그럼에도, (a) 그녀는 그녀의 직업을 좋아했고 매일 함박웃음을 지으며 교실로 들어갔다. 오늘, 그녀는 평소보다 더 기뻤는데 왜냐하면 그녀가 가장 좋아하는 휴일인 추수감사절이 다가오고 있었기 때문이다.
(D) 이 특별한 날을 기념하여, Douglas 선생님은 그녀의 학생들을 위한 특별한 과제를 내주었다. 그녀는 그들에게 가장 감사했던 것을 그리라고 했다. 학생들은 바쁘게 움직이기 시작했다. 그들은 칠면조와 푸짐한 식사를 그렸다. 일부는 그들의 가족이 함께 모여 있는 것을 그린 반면, 다른 아이들은 그들의 친구들과 함께 놀고 있는 스스로를 그렸다. 그러나 Douglas 선생님은 어린 Sarah가 다른 무언가를 그렸다는 것을 알아챘다. (e) 그녀는 그녀가 빈손을 그린 것을 보고 꽤 깜짝 놀랐다.

(B) 다른 학생들 또한 놀랐다. 곧, 모두가 그것이 누구의 손일지 추측하기 시작했다. 몇몇은 칠면조를 길러낸 농부의 손임이 틀림없다고 말했다. 다른 아이들은 Sarah의 손이거나 그녀의 어머니나 아버지의 것이라고 말했다. Douglas선생님이 마침내 그녀에게 물어봤을 때, 그녀는 조용히 "이것은 (b) 당신의 손이에요."라고 말했다.
(C) Douglas 선생님은 충격을 받았다. "(c) 나의 손? 하지만 왜…" 그러고 나서, 그녀는 Sarah의 손을 잡았던 모든 순간을 떠올렸다. 그녀는 그녀를 화장실에 데려가거나 밖에서 놀기 위해 그녀의 손을 잡았다. 그녀에게 올바르게 글씨를 쓰는 법을 보여주기 위해 연필 위로 그녀가 Sarah의 작은 손을 잡았던 것을 떠올렸다. 그녀는 매일 아침, 그녀 반의 다른 아이들에게도 했던 것처럼, Sarah의 어깨를 쓰다듬으며 (d) 그녀에게 인사하곤 했던 것을 떠올렸다. Douglas 선생님은 미소지으면서 눈물을 닦아냈다.

17 　　　　　　　　　　　　　정답 ④

해설 (A)는 Douglas 선생님이 학생들 중 Sarah에 대해 평소 걱정하는 마음이 있었다는 것과, 오늘은 추수감사절이 다가오고 있어 평소보다 더 기뻤다는 내용이다. (D)는 추수감사절을 맞이해서 감사한 것을 그리는 과제를 냈다는 내용이고, (D)의 the special day는 (A)의 Thanksgiving을 가리키므로 (A) 다음에 오는 것이 적절하다. (B)는 다른 학생들 또한 놀라면서 모두 Sarah가 그린 손이 누구의 손일지 추측하기 시작했다는 내용이므로 Sarah가 그린 빈손을 보고 Douglas 선생님이 깜짝 놀랐다고 한 (D) 뒤에 와야 한다. (C)는 Sarah가 그린 손이 Douglas 선생님의 것이라는 이야기를 듣고 그녀가 Sarah의 손을 잡아주었던 많은 순간들을 떠올리며 눈물을 흘렸다는 내용이므로 Sarah가 그린 빈손이 Douglas 선생님의 것이라고 한 (B) 뒤에 와야 한다. 따라서 글의 순서로 가장 적절한 것은 ④ (D) - (B) - (C)이다.

18 　　　　　　　　　　　　　정답 ④

해설 (a), (b), (c), (e)는 Douglas 선생님을 가리키지만 (d)는 Sarah를 가리키므로 ④이 정답이다.

19 　　　　　　　　　　　　　정답 ③

해설 When Miss Douglas finally asked her, she quietly said "It's yours"를 통해 Sarah가 그린 빈손의 주인이 Douglas 선생님이었다는 것을 알 수 있으므로, 글의 내용과 일치하지 않는 것은 ③ 'Sarah는 자신의 어머니의 손을 그렸다.'이다.

오답 분석 ①은 She was especially worried about little Sarah, who had a hard time making friends라고 했으므로 글의 내용과 일치한다. ②은 her favorite holiday, Thanksgiving, was coming up이라고 했으므로 글의 내용과 일치한다. ④은 she held Sarah's little hand over a pencil to show her how to write properly라고 했으므로 글의 내용과 일치한다. ⑤은 She told them to draw the things they were most thankful for라고 했으므로 글의 내용과 일치한다.

제2회 실전 모의고사 　　　　　　　　p.146

01 ④	02 ⑤	03 ①	04 ⑤	05 ⑤	06 ④	07 ②	08 ②
09 ③	10 ⑤	11 ③	12 ④	13 ④	14 ④	15 ②	16 ①
17 ③	18 ⑤	19 ⑤					

지문분석

To Mr. Steve Wilson,
Steve Wilson님께

Happy New Year!
새해 복 많이 받으세요

We here at Prime Gym / would like to wish / you and your family / the very best / in the upcoming year.
저희 Prime 체육관에서는 / ~하길 바랍니다 / 귀하와 귀하의 가족분들께 / 행운이 있으시길 / 다가오는 해에

★ You have been a valued member / of our gym / for 2 years now.
귀하께서는 소중한 고객이십니다 / 저희 체육관의 / 현재 2년째

As such, / we would like to / express our thanks / for longtime clients / like you.
이로써 / 저희는 ~하고 싶습니다 / 감사를 표하다 / 오랜 고객분들께 / 귀하와 같은

This year, / we will be upgrading you / to our gold level membership, / free of charge.
올해 / 저희는 귀하를 올려드릴 것입니다 / 저희 골드 레벨 멤버십으로 / 무료로

With it, / you will be able to receive / free PT lessons / once a week / as well as a total of 10 sports massages / per year.
그것으로 / 귀하께서는 받을 수 있게 될 것입니다 / 무료 PT 수업 / 일주일에 한 번씩 / 총 10번의 스포츠 마사지 뿐만 아니라 / 매년

Furthermore, / you and a guest / will have access to / our private pool and spa.
게다가 / 귀하와 귀하의 손님 한 분은 / 이용하실 수 있을 것입니다 / 저희의 개인 수영장과 온천을

Thank you again / for choosing Prime Gym / for all your health and fitness needs.
다시 한번 감사드립니다 / Prime 헬스클럽을 선택해주신 것에 대해 / 귀하의 건강과 신체 단련의 필요를 위해

Sincerely,
Amy State
Amy State 드림

★ **독해가 쉬워지는 구문 풀이**

You **have been** a valued member of our gym **for 2 years** now.
　　　현재완료

⇨ have + p.p로 표현되는 현재완료시제는 과거와 현재를 모두 포함하는 시간 표현 <for + 시간>과 주로 함께 쓰인다.

어휘 valued 소중한, 귀중한　longtime 오랜　free of charge 무료로
private 개인의　fitness 신체 단련, 건강

해석 Steve Wilson님께,
　새해 복 많이 받으세요! 저희 Prime 체육관에서는 다가오는 해에 귀하와 귀하의 가족분들께 행운이 있으시길 바랍니다. 귀하께서는 현재 2년째 저희 체육관의 소중한 고객이십니다. 이로써, 저희는 귀하와 같은 오랜 고객분들께 감사를 표하고 싶습니다. 올해, 저희는 귀하를 무료로 저희 골드 레벨 멤버십으로 올려드릴 것입니다. 그것으로, 귀하께서는 매년 총 10번의 스포츠 마사지 뿐만 아니라 무료 PT 수업도 일주일에 한 번씩 받을 수 있게 될 것입니다. 게다가, 귀하와 귀하의 손님 한 분은 저희의 개인 수영장과 온천을 이용하실 수 있을 것입니다. 귀하의 건강과 신체 단련의 필요를 위해 Prime 헬스클럽을 선택해주신 것에 대해 다시 한번 감사드립니다.
　Amy State 드림

해설 헬스클럽의 오랜 회원에게 멤버십 등급이 향상되었음을 알려주고 이에 따른 혜택을 안내하는 내용의 글이다. we will be upgrading you to our gold level membership에서 '귀하를 저희 골드 레벨 멤버십으로 올려드릴 것입니다'라고 했으므로, 정답은 ④ '회원의 멤버십 등급이 향상되었

음을 알려주려고'이다.

오답분석 ①은 '멤버십'을 다루고 있지만 가입 조건을 설명하는 글이 아니므로 오답이다. ②, ③, ⑤은 글과 관련 없는 내용이다.

지문분석

Warren was ready / for his solo.
Warren은 준비가 되어 있었다 / 그의 독주를 위한

He had been practicing every day / for months now, / and he knew the piano piece by heart.
그는 매일 연습해왔다 / 지금까지 몇 달째 / 그리고 그는 그 피아노곡을 외우고 있었다

He was positive / he would do great.
그는 자신이 있었다 / 그가 잘 해낼 것이라는

★ On the day of the performance, / he boldly walked up on the stage / and stood in front of hundreds of people / waiting for his play.
공연 날에 / 그는 대담하게 무대 위로 걸어 올라갔다 / 그리고 수백 명의 사람들 앞에 섰다 / 그의 연주를 기다리는

He took a deep breath / and sat down at the piano.
그는 심호흡했다 / 그리고 피아노에 앉았다

Just as he practiced, / he finished the piece / without a single mistake.
그가 연습했던 바로 그대로 / 그는 그 곡을 끝냈다 / 단 한 번의 실수 없이

Everyone clapped and cheered.
모든 사람들이 박수를 치고 환호했다

He smiled / and began walking off the stage / when he stumbled and tripped.
그는 미소를 지었다 / 그리고 무대에서 내려오기 시작했다 / 바로 그때 그는 발을 헛디뎌 걸려 넘어졌다

He heard a few people laughing.
그는 몇몇 사람들이 웃는 것을 들었다

His face turned bright red / and he hurried off the stage.
그의 얼굴은 새빨갛게 변했다 / 그리고 그는 급히 무대를 떠났다

He just wanted / to crawl under a rock / and forget it ever happened.
그는 그저 ~하고 싶었다 / 쥐구멍으로 들어가다 / 그리고 그 일이 일어났다는 것조차 잊다

★ **독해가 쉬워지는 구문 풀이**

On the day of the performance, he boldly **walked** up on the stage
　　　　　　　　　　　　　　　　　　　　　동사1
and **stood** in front of hundreds of people [waiting for his play].
　　동사2

⇨ walked와 stood는 등위접속사 and로 연결되어 병렬 구조를 이룬다.
⇨ [ ]에서 수식 받는 명사 people이 wait이 나타내는 '기다리는' 행위의 주체이므로, 현재분사 waiting이 쓰였다.

어휘 solo 독주　know by heart 외우다　piece 곡　positive 자신 있는, 긍정적인
boldly 대담하게　take a deep breath 심호흡하다　cheer 환호하다
stumble 발을 헛디디다　trip 걸려 넘어지다　hurry off 급히 떠나다
crawl under a rock 쥐구멍으로 들어가다　[선택지] helpless 무력한
horrified 겁에 질린　relieved 안도하는　comfortable 편안한
touched 감동한　panicked 당황한　furious 몹시 화가 난

해석 Warren은 그의 독주를 위한 준비가 되어 있었다. 그는 지금까지 몇 달째 매일 연습해왔고, 그는 그 피아노곡을 외우고 있었다. 그는 그가 잘 해낼 것이라는 자신이 있었다. 공연 날에, 그는 대담하게 무대 위로 걸어 올라갔고 그의 연주를 기다리는 수백 명의 사람들 앞에 섰다. 그는 심호흡했고 피아노에 앉았다. 그가 연습했던 바로 그대로, 그는 단 한 번의 실수 없이 그 곡을 끝냈다. 모든 사람들이 박수를 치고 환호했다. 그는 미소를 지으며 무대에서 내려오기 시작했는데 바로 그때 발을 헛디뎌 걸려 넘어졌다.

그는 몇몇 사람들이 웃는 것을 들었다. 그의 얼굴은 새빨갛게 변했고 그는 급히 무대를 떠났다. 그는 그저 쥐구멍으로 들어가 그 일이 일어났다는 것조차 잊고 싶었다.

① 무력한 → 겁에 질린
② 걱정하는 → 안도하는
③ 편안한 → 감동한
④ 당황한 → 몹시 화가 난
⑤ 자신 있는 → 창피해하는

[해설] Warren이 피아노 독주를 하기 전에는 자신 있어 했지만, 독주가 끝난 후 무대에서 내려오면서 발을 헛디뎌 걸려 넘어져서 창피해하는 과정을 묘사하고 있는 글이다. 글의 초반부에서 He was positive he would do great, he boldly walked up ~을 통해 Warren이 자신 있어 하는 것을 알 수 있고, 글의 후반부에서 He just wanted to crawl under a rock and forget it ever happened를 통해 그가 넘어진 것을 창피해한다는 것을 알 수 있으므로, Warren의 심경 변화로 가장 적절한 것은 ⑤ confident(자신 있는) → embarrassed(창피해하는)이다.

[오답분석] ①의 helpless와 horrified는 글 속의 상황에서 느낄 심경으로 적절하지 않다. ②의 worried는 부정적인 심경으로 인물의 첫 심경과 반대되고, relieved는 긍정적인 심경으로 인물의 마지막 심경과 반대된다. ③의 comfortable은 인물의 첫 심경으로 적절하지만, 마지막 심경으로 touched는 적절하지 않다. ④의 panicked는 부정적인 심경으로 인물의 첫 심경과 반대되고, furious는 글 속의 상황에서 느낄 심경으로 적절하지 않다.

03 정답 ①

지문분석

If you go to the United States / and meet someone, / you shake their hand.
만약 당신이 미국에 간다면 / 그리고 누군가를 만나면 / 당신은 그들과 악수를 한다

In Korea, / you bow to each other.
한국에서 / 당신은 서로에게 고개를 숙인다

In France, / you kiss the other on the cheek / as a greeting.
프랑스에서 / 당신은 다른 사람의 뺨에 입맞춤을 한다 / 인사로

★ Nonverbal communication like this / is a crucial part / of social interaction.
이와 같은 비언어적 의사소통은 / 중요한 부분이다 / 사회적 상호 작용의

In fact, / one study showed / that almost 60 percent of communication was relayed / through body language / while only 7 percent was conveyed / with the actual words / a person said.
실제로 / 한 연구는 보여주었다 / 의사소통의 거의 60퍼센트는 전달된다는 것을 / 보디랭귀지를 통해 / 의사소통의 7퍼센트만이 전달되는 반면 / 실제 단어로 / 사람이 말하는

Most nonverbal communication / involves five areas: / eye contact, touch, gestures, physical distance, and body posture.
대부분의 비언어적 의사소통은 / 5가지 영역을 포함한다 / 눈 맞춤, 접촉, 몸짓, 물리적 거리, 그리고 자세

These areas vary significantly / from culture to culture, / so learning some common cues / is useful.
이 영역들은 크게 다르다 / 문화마다 / 그러므로 공통적인 몇몇 신호를 알아두는 것이 / 도움이 된다

Otherwise, / misunderstandings can occur, / and you may end up offending someone / without meaning to.
그렇지 않으면 / 오해가 발생할 수 있다 / 그리고 당신은 누군가를 불쾌하게 할지도 모른다 / 의도치 않게

Nonverbal communication [like this] is a crucial part of social
　　　　　　　　　　　　수식어(전치사구)
interaction.

⇨ [ ]는 전치사구로 명사 communication을 수식한다.
⇨ this는 지시대명사로, 앞 문장에서 언급된 미국, 한국, 프랑스에서의 비언어적 의사소통을 가리킨다.

[어휘] bow 고개를 숙이다, 절하다   greeting 인사
nonverbal 비언어적인, 말로 할 수 없는   crucial 중요한   interaction 상호 작용
relay 전달하다, 교대시키다   physical 물리적인, 신체의
significantly 크게, 현저히   cue 신호, 단서   otherwise 그렇지 않으면
misunderstanding 오해, 착오   end up ~하게 되다
offend 불쾌하게 하다, 위반하다   mean to 의도하다, ~할 셈이다

[해석] 만약 당신이 미국에 가서 누군가를 만나면, 당신은 그들과 악수를 한다. 한국에서, 당신은 서로에게 고개를 숙인다. 프랑스에서, 당신은 인사로 다른 사람의 뺨에 입맞춤을 한다. 이와 같은 비언어적 의사소통은 사회적 상호 작용의 중요한 부분이다. 실제로, 한 연구는 의사소통의 7퍼센트만이 사람이 말하는 실제 단어로 전달되는 반면, 의사소통의 거의 60퍼센트는 보디랭귀지를 통해 전달된다는 것을 보여주었다. 대부분의 비언어적 의사소통은 눈 맞춤, 접촉, 몸짓, 물리적 거리, 그리고 자세라는 5가지 영역을 포함한다. [주제문] 이 영역들은 문화마다 크게 다르므로, 공통적인 몇몇 신호를 알아두는 것이 도움이 된다. 그렇지 않으면, 오해가 발생할 수 있고, 당신은 의도치 않게 누군가를 불쾌하게 할지도 모른다.

[해설] 비언어적 의사소통은 문화마다 크게 다르므로 오해가 발생하는 것을 방지하기 위해서는 공통적인 몇몇 신호를 알아두는 것이 도움이 된다는 내용의 글이므로, 이 글의 요지로 가장 적절한 것은 ① '다양한 비언어적 의사소통을 알아두는 것이 좋다.'이다.

[오답분석] ②, ③, ④는 글에서 언급된 내용이 아니다. ⑤은 비언어적 의사소통 방법은 문화마다 차이가 있다고 한 글의 내용과 반대된다.

04 정답 ⑤

지문분석

How much / is your taste in music influenced / by the songs / you heard / in your childhood?
얼마나 많이 / 당신의 음악 취향은 영향을 받는가 / 노래에 의해 / 당신이 들었던 / 어린 시절에

The answer might surprise you.
답변은 당신을 놀라게 할 수 있다

★ According to research, / the songs you hear / while growing up / actually stick with you / and become part of your playlists / later in life, / indicating / that we might inherit / more than just our genes / from our parents.
연구에 따르면 / 당신이 듣는 노래들은 / 자라면서 / 실제로 당신의 곁에 머문다 / 그리고 당신의 재생 목록의 일부가 된다 / 이후에 / 이것은 ~을 나타낸다 / 우리가 물려받을 수도 있다는 것을 / 우리의 유전자 그 이상을 / 우리의 부모님으로부터

Scientists say / that this isn't all that surprising / since music tends to help us / recall memories; / a song can take you back / to a family vacation / or time / spent in your childhood home.
과학자들은 말한다 / 이것이 그렇게 놀랄만한 일은 아니라고 / 음악은 도움을 주는 경향이 있기 때문에 / 기억을 떠올리는 데 / 노래는 당신에게 상기시켜 줄 수 있다 / 가족 여행을 / 또는 ~한 시간을 / 당신의 어린 시절의 집에서 보낸

This music triggers / nostalgia and an emotional response, / which is why / people tend to listen to songs / their parents played / as they grew up.
이 음악은 유발한다 / 향수와 감정적인 반응을 / 이것은 ~하는 이유이다 / 사람들이 노래를 듣는 경향이 있는 / 그들의 부모님이 들려주었던 / 그들이 자라면서

This artistic lineage helps define / the tastes of future generations, / impacting / what music they prefer and listen to.
이러한 예술적인 혈통은 설명하는 데 도움을 준다 / 미래 세대의 취향을 / 영향을 미치며 / 그들이 어떤 음악을 선호하고 듣는지에

★ 독해가 쉬워지는 구문 풀이

According to research, the **songs** [①you hear while growing up]
　　　　　　　　　　　주어
actually **stick** with you and **become** part of your playlists later in
　　　동사1　　　　　　　　　　동사2
life, [②indicating {that we might inherit more than just our genes
　　　　　　명사절 접속사
from our parents}].

⇨ [①]은 선행사 songs 뒤에 목적격 관계대명사 that 또는 which가 생략된 관계절이 온 형태이다.

⇨ 동사 stick과 become은 등위접속사 and로 연결된 병렬 구조이다.

⇨ [②]는 분사구문이며, { }는 동사 indicate의 목적어 역할을 하는 명사절이다.

[어휘] stick with ~의 곁에 머물다　inherit 물려받다　recall 떠올리다
take ~ back to ~에게 -을 상기시키다　trigger 유발하다　emotional 감정적인
lineage 혈통　impact 영향을 미치다　(선택지) inspire 영감을 주다
preference 취향

[해석] 당신이 어린 시절에 들었던 노래에 의해 당신의 음악 취향은 얼마나 많이 영향을 받는가? 답변은 당신을 놀라게 할 수 있다. (주제문) 연구에 따르면, 당신이 자라면서 듣는 노래들은 실제로 당신의 곁에 머물러 이후에 당신의 재생 목록의 일부가 되며, 이것은 우리가 우리의 부모님으로부터 유전자 그 이상을 물려받을 수도 있다는 것을 나타낸다. 과학자들은 이것이 그렇게 놀랄만한 일은 아니라고 말하는데, 음악은 우리가 기억을 떠올리는 데 도움을 주는 경향이 있기 때문이다. 노래는 당신에게 가족 여행이나 당신의 어린 시절의 집에서 보낸 시간을 상기시켜 줄 수 있다. 이 음악은 향수와 감정적인 반응을 유발하는데, 이것이 사람들이 그들이 자라면서 그들의 부모님이 들려주었던 노래를 듣는 경향이 있는 이유이다. 이러한 예술적인 혈통은 그들이 어떤 음악을 선호하고 듣는지에 영향을 미치며 미래 세대의 취향을 설명하는 데 도움을 준다.

① 새로운 음악에 영감을 주는 기억
② 부모님으로부터 물려받은 기술
③ 음악적 취향에서의 세대 차이
④ 서로 다른 시대에서 나타나는 음악적 스타일
⑤ 집안 내에서 전승되는 음악적 취향

[해설] 우리가 자라면서 부모님이 들려줬던 노래들은 오랫동안 우리 곁에 머물러 이후에 우리의 재생 목록의 일부가 된다고 말하고 있으므로, 밑줄 친 artistic lineage(예술적인 혈통)가 의미하는 바로 가장 적절한 것은 ⑤ musical preferences that are passed down in families(집안 내에서 전승되는 음악적 취향)이다.

[오답분석] ①, ②, ④은 글에서 언급된 내용이 아니다. ③은 부모님으로부터 세대를 거쳐 음악적 취향을 물려받게 된다고 한 글의 내용과 반대되는 내용을 다루고 있으므로 오답이다.

05

정답 ⑤

지문분석

Most people assume / that the longer they work, / the more productive they will be.
대부분의 사람들은 생각한다 / 그들이 더 많이 일할수록 / 그들이 더 생산적일 것이라고

★ However, / recent studies have repeatedly demonstrated / that people who work / fewer hours a day / or fewer days a week / often display corresponding improvements / in job performance.
하지만 / 최근 연구는 여러 차례 증명했다 / 일하는 사람들이 / 하루에 더 적은 시간을 / 또는 한 주에 더 적은 날을 / 그에 상응하는 개선점을 종종 보여준다는 것을 / 업무 성과에 있어서

In contrast, / people who work / for longer hours / are found / to be less efficient, / less focused, / and more likely to experience burnout.
이와 반대로 / 일하는 사람들은 / 더 오랜 시간 동안 / 밝혀졌다 / 덜 효율적이다 / 집중력이 떨어지다 / 그리고 번아웃을 겪을 가능성이 더 높은 것으로

The reason / for these different outcomes / is simple.
이유는 / 이러한 서로 다른 결과의 / 간단하다

Work requires energy / to perform, / and too much of it / drains people of the energy / they need / to continue performing / at the same level.
일은 에너지를 필요로 한다 / 그것을 해낼 / 그리고 너무 많은 일은 / 사람들로 하여금 에너지를 소모시킨다 / 그들이 필요로 하는 / 계속해서 일을 해내는 데 / 동일한 수준으로

People / who work less / have more time / to restore their energy / and are therefore / more capable of devoting themselves / to the work at hand / when it is needed.
사람들은 / 더 적게 일하는 / 시간이 더 많다 / 그들의 에너지를 회복할 / 그리고 그 결과 / 더 전념할 수 있다 / 주어진 일에 / 필요할 때

★ 독해가 쉬워지는 구문 풀이

However, recent studies have repeatedly demonstrated [that people who work fewer hours a day or fewer days a week often display corresponding improvements in job performance].

⇨ [ ]는 명사절로 demonstrated의 목적어 역할을 하며, 명사절을 이끄는 접속사 that은 생략할 수 있다.

[어휘] assume 생각하다, 추측하다　demonstrate 증명하다
corresponding 상응하는　improvement 개선점　performance 성과, 수행
drain 소모시키다　restore 회복하다　devote oneself to ~에 전념하다, 몰두하다
(선택지) inspiration 영감　innovation 혁신

[해석] 대부분의 사람들은 그들이 더 많이 일할수록, 더 생산적일 것이라고 생각한다. (주제문) 하지만, 최근 연구는 하루에 더 적은 시간을, 또는 한 주에 더 적은 날을 일하는 사람들이 종종 업무 성과에 있어서 그에 상응하는 개선점을 보여준다는 것을 여러 차례 증명했다. 이와 반대로, 더 오랜 시간 동안 일하는 사람들은 덜 효율적이고, 집중력이 떨어지며, 번아웃을 겪을 가능성이 더 높은 것으로 밝혀졌다. 이러한 서로 다른 결과의 이유는 간단하다. 일은 그것을 해낼 에너지를 필요로 하며, 너무 많은 일은 사람들로 하여금 동일한 수준으로 계속해서 일을 해내는 데 그들이 필요로 하는 에너지를 소모시킨다. 더 적게 일하는 사람들은 그들의 에너지를 회복할 시간이 더 많고, 그 결과 필요할 때 주어진 일에 더 전념할 수 있다.

① 근로자의 급여를 성과에 맞추는 것
② 근면은 결코 보상받을 수 없다고 생각하지 마라
③ 영감과 혁신: 어디서 찾아야 할까
④ 공장에서부터 사무실에 이르는 업무 성과
⑤ 더 적을수록 더 낫다: 짧은 근무 시간이 업무 성과를 높인다

[해설] 이 글의 중심 내용은 더 적은 시간 동안 일하는 것이 에너지를 회복하는 데 더 많은 시간을 보낼 수 있게 하여 높은 업무 성과를 내는 것을 가능하게 한다는 것이므로, 이 글의 제목으로 가장 적절한 것은 ⑤ Less Is More: Fewer Hours Improves Work Performance(더 적을수록 더 낫다: 짧은 근무 시간이 업무 성과를 높인다)이다.

[오답분석] ①, ④은 글의 핵심 어구인 Performance를 활용하여 혼동을 주는 오답이다. ②은 덜 일하는 것이 더 높은 성과를 내는 데 도움이 된다는 글의 주제와 반대되는 내용이므로 오답이다. ③은 글에서 언급되고 있지 않다.

06

지문분석

The above graph shows / the wheat consumption per capita / in kilograms / of 5 different countries / in 2010 and 2020.
위 도표는 보여준다 / 1인당 밀 소비량을 / 킬로그램 단위로 / 서로 다른 5개국의 / 2010년과 2020년에

① Of the 5 countries, / Chile had / the highest number of wheat consumption / per capita / in both 2010 and 2020.
5개국 중에서, / 칠레가 보였다 / 가장 많은 밀 소비량을 / 1인당 / 2010년과 2020년 모두

② ★ In 2010, / Russia had the second highest wheat consumption per capita, / followed by Saudi Arabia with the third highest.
2010년에 / 러시아는 1인당 밀 소비량이 두 번째로 많았다 / 세 번째로 많았던 사우디아라비아가 그 뒤를 이었다

③ For every country except Korea, / the wheat consumed per capita was higher / in 2020 than in 2010.
한국을 제외한 모든 나라들에서는 / 1인당 소비된 밀이 더 많았다 / 2010년보다 2020년에

④ The difference in wheat consumption per capita / between 2010 and 2020 / was smaller(→ larger) for Malaysia than it was for Chile.
1인당 밀 소비량의 차이는 / 2010년과 2020년 사이의 / 칠레보다 말레이시아가 더 적었다(→ 더 컸다)

⑤ Compared to Korea, / wheat consumption per capita / in Saudi Arabia / was more than 50 kilograms higher / in 2020.
한국과 비교하여 / 1인당 밀 소비량은 / 사우디아라비아의 / 50킬로그램 이상 더 많았다 / 2020년에

★ 독해가 쉬워지는 구문 풀이

In 2010, Russia had the second highest wheat consumption per capita, [**followed** by Saudi Arabia with the third highest].
　　　　　　　　　　　　과거분사

⇨ [ ]에는 수식 받는 명사 Russia가 follow가 나타내는 '따라가는' 행위의 대상이므로 과거분사 followed가 쓰였다.

어휘 wheat 밀　consumption 소비(량)　per capita 1인당
difference 차이　compared to ~와 비교하여

해석

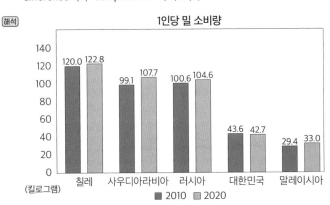

1인당 밀 소비량

위 도표는 2010년과 2020년에 서로 다른 5개국의 1인당 밀 소비량을 킬로그램 단위로 보여준다. ① 5개국 중에서, 칠레는 2010년과 2020년 모두 1인당 가장 많은 밀 소비량을 보였다. ② 2010년에, 러시아는 1인당 밀 소비량이 두 번째로 많았고, 세 번째로 많았던 사우디아라비아가 그 뒤를 이었다. ③ 한국을 제외한 모든 나라들에서는, 2010년보다 2020년에 1인당 소비된 밀이 더 많았다. ④ 2010년과 2020년 사이의 1인당 밀 소비량의 차이는 칠레보다 말레이시아가 더 적었다(→ 더 컸다). ⑤ 한국과 비교하여, 2020년에 사우디아라비아의 1인당 밀 소비량은 50킬로그램 이상 더 많았다.

해설 도표의 제목과 글의 도입부를 통해 이 도표가 서로 다른 5개국의 2010년과 2020년 1인당 밀 소비량에 관한 것임을 알 수 있다. 이 글에서는

①의 the highest, ②의 the second highest와 followed by ~ third highest, ③의 higher, ④의 smaller, ⑤의 more than 50 kilograms higher가 도표 내의 수치를 올바르게 설명하고 있는지 확인해야 한다. 칠레의 2010년 1인당 밀 소비량은 120.0이고, 2020년에는 122.8이었으므로 2010년과 2020년 사이의 밀 소비량 차이는 2.8이다. 말레이시아는 2010년에 29.4, 2020년에 33.0이었으므로 2010년과 2020년 사이의 밀 소비량 차이는 3.6으로 칠레보다 차이가 크므로, 도표의 내용과 일치하지 않는 것은 ④이다.

오답분석 ①은 2010년과 2020년 모두 칠레가 1인당 밀 소비량이 가장 많으므로 도표의 내용과 일치한다. ②은 2010년에 러시아의 1인당 밀 소비량이 두 번째로 많고, 세 번째로 많은 사우디아라비아가 그 뒤를 잇고 있으므로 도표의 내용과 일치한다. ③은 한국을 제외한 모든 나라들에서 2010년보다 2020년에 1인당 밀 소비량이 많았으므로 도표의 내용과 일치한다. ⑤은 2020년에 한국은 1인당 42.7킬로그램의 밀을 소비했고 사우디아라비아는 한국보다 50킬로그램 이상 더 많은 107.7킬로그램의 밀을 소비했으므로 도표의 내용과 일치한다.

07

지문분석

Moorhead Choir Auditions
Moorhead 합창단 오디션

★ The prestigious Moorhead School of Music / is looking for exceptional talents / who love to sing.
명망 있는 Moorhead 음악 학교는 / 특출한 인재들을 찾고 있습니다 / 노래 부르는 것을 사랑하는

We will be holding auditions / for the Concert Choir Group / from February 10 to March 28.
우리는 오디션을 개최할 예정입니다 / 연주회 합창단의 / 2월 10일부터 3월 28일까지

Requirements:
요건

-Must be a registered student
재학생이어야 함

-Must have sung / in at least one choir before
노래해본 적이 있어야 함 / 과거에 최소 한 곳의 합창단에서

-Must be able to attend rehearsals / (Every Tues. and Thurs., / 7-9 p.m.)
리허설에 참석할 수 있어야 함 / (매주 화요일과 목요일 / 오후 7시-9시)

The Audition Process
오디션 과정

-Sign up for an audition time
오디션 시간을 신청하세요

-Prepare to perform a singing exercise / in one of your vocal range / (bass, tenor, alto, or soprano)
노래 연습을 할 준비를 하세요 / 본인 음역대 중 하나에 맞는 / (베이스, 테너, 알토, 또는 소프라노)

-You will also be asked / to sight-read a song
당신은 또한 요청될 것입니다 / 즉석에서 노래를 한 곡을 하도록

For more information, / please contact Eric Kim. (ekimchoir@moorheaduni.com)
더 많은 정보를 얻으시려면 / Eric Kim (ekimchoir@moorheaduni.com)에게 연락 주세요

★ 독해가 쉬워지는 구문 풀이

The prestigious Moorhead School of Music is looking for exceptional **talents** [who love to sing].
　　　　　　　　　　　　주격 관계대명사

⇨ [ ]는 선행사 talents를 수식하는 주격 관계대명사절이다.

어휘 choir 합창단 prestigious 명망 있는 exceptional 특출한 talent 인재
requirement 요건 attend 참석하다 rehearsal 리허설, 예행연습
sign up for ~을 신청하다, 등록하다
sight-read (악보를 처음 보고) 즉석에서 노래하다

해석

Moorhead 합창단 오디션

명망 있는 Moorhead 음악 학교는 노래 부르는 것을 사랑하는 특출한 인재들을 찾고 있습니다. 우리는 2월 10일부터 3월 28일까지 연주회 합창단의 오디션을 개최할 예정입니다.

요건:
- 재학생이어야 함
- 과거에 최소 한 곳의 합창단에서 노래해본 적이 있어야 함
- 리허설에 참석할 수 있어야 함(매주 화요일과 목요일, 오후 7시-9시)

오디션 과정
- 오디션 시간을 신청하세요
- 본인 음역대(베이스, 테너, 알토, 또는 소프라노) 중 하나에 맞는 노래 연습을 할 준비를 하세요
- 당신은 또한 즉석에서 노래 한 곡을 하도록 요청될 것입니다

더 많은 정보를 얻으시려면, Eric Kim에게 연락 주세요.
(ekimchoir@moorheaduni.com)

해설 Must have sung in at least one choir before를 통해 지원 요건으로 과거에 최소 한 곳의 합창단에서 노래해본 적이 있어야 한다는 것을 알 수 있으므로, 글의 내용과 일치하는 것은 ② '지원자들은 과거에 합창단 경험이 있어야 한다.'이다.

오답분석 ①은 Must be a registered student라고 했으므로 글의 내용과 일치하지 않는다. ③은 attend rehearsals (Every Tues. and Thurs., 7-9 p.m.)라고 했으므로 글의 내용과 일치하지 않는다. ④은 Sign up for audition time이라고 했으므로 글의 내용과 일치하지 않는다. ⑤은 Prepare to perform a singing exercise in one of your vocal range라고 했으므로 글의 내용과 일치하지 않는다.

08   정답 ②

지문분석

Reality television, / entertaining though it may be, / ① does present problems / for society / as a whole.
리얼리티 TV / 이것은 재미있을 수는 있더라도 / 정말로 문제를 야기한다 / 사회에 / 전반적으로

To begin with, / the term "reality" is misleading.
우선 / "리얼리티"라는 용어는 오해의 소지가 있다

The cameras are supposedly on nonstop, / but the only footage / that ends up in shows / ② to be(→ is) shocking or dramatic / as that's what appeals to viewers.
아마도 카메라는 계속해서 켜져 있을 것이다 / 하지만 유일한 장면은 / 결국 쇼에 나오는 / 충격적이거나 극적인 것이다 / 그것이 시청자들의 관심을 끄는 것이기 때문이다

Furthermore, / the producers may introduce conflict / to encourage arguments / between cast members / or ③ focus only on the most sensational characters.
게다가 / 제작자들은 갈등을 끼워 넣을 수도 있다 / 말다툼을 조장하기 위해 / 출연자들 간의 / 또는 가장 화제인 인물에게만 초점을 맞춘다

The manipulation of reality / in this way / can suggest / to viewers / that certain extreme behaviors and questionable values / are normal.
현실 조작은 / 이러한 방식의 / 암시할 수 있다 / 시청자들에게 / 어떤 극단적인 행동이나 이상한 가치관이 / 일상적이라고

After all, / characters on reality shows / are ④ meant to be "regular people."
결국 / 리얼리티 쇼의 등장인물들은 / "평범한 사람"인 것처럼 의도된다

★ The notion / that cast members are just like everyone else / when most of them are attractive / and have / what society considers perfect bodies / ⑤ leads to low self-esteem / in viewers.
~한 생각은 / 출연자들이 그저 다른 사람들과 똑같다는 / 그들 중 대부분이 매력적임에도 / 그리고 지닐 때 / 사회가 완벽한 몸매라고 여기는 것을 / 낮은 자존감을 초래한다 / 시청자에게

★ 독해가 쉬워지는 구문 풀이

The notion [that cast members are just like everyone else when
　　주어　　　　　　　　　　동격의 that절
most of them **are** attractive and **have** what society considers
perfect bodies] leads to low self-esteem in viewers.
　　　　　　　　동사

⇨ [ ]는 The notion과 동격을 이룬다.
⇨ 동사 are와 have는 등위접속사 and로 연결되어 병렬구조를 이룬다.

어휘 entertaining 재미있는, 즐거운 as a whole 전반적으로, 전체적으로
misleading 오해의 소지가 있는 supposedly 아마도, 추정상
footage 장면, 화면 appeal 관심을 끌다, 호소하다
encourage 조장하다, 권장하다 argument 말다툼, 갈등 cast 출연자
sensational 화제의, 선정적인 manipulation 조작, 속임수
questionable 이상한, 의심스러운 self-esteem 자존감

해석 주제문 리얼리티 TV는 재미있을 수는 있더라도 정말로 사회에 전반적으로 문제를 야기한다. 우선, "리얼리티"라는 용어는 오해의 소지가 있다. 아마도 카메라는 계속해서 켜져 있을 것이지만, 결국 쇼에 나오는 유일한 장면은 충격적이거나 극적인 것인데, 이는 그것이 시청자들의 관심을 끄는 것이기 때문이다. 게다가, 제작자들은 출연자들 간의 말다툼을 조장하기 위해 갈등을 끼워 넣거나 가장 화제인 인물에게만 초점을 맞출 수도 있다. 이러한 방식의 현실 조작은 시청자들에게 어떤 극단적인 행동이나 이상한 가치관이 일상적임을 암시할 수 있다. 결국, 리얼리티 쇼의 등장인물들이 "평범한 사람"인 것처럼 의도된다. 그들 중 대부분이 매력적이면서 사회가 완벽한 몸매라고 여기는 것을 지님에도 출연자들이 그저 다른 사람들과 똑같다는 생각은 시청자들에게 낮은 자존감을 초래한다.

해설 절에는 반드시 주어와 동사가 있어야 하는데, 주어 the only footage의 동사가 없으므로 ②은 동사 자리이다. 동사 자리에는 '동사'나 '조동사 + 동사원형'이 와야 하므로, ②의 to be를 is로 고쳐야 한다.

오답분석 ①은 일반동사 present를 강조하고 있고 주어(Reality television)가 3인칭 단수이므로 강조를 위해 조동사 does를 사용한 것은 어법상 적절하다. ③은 같은 문장 성분을 대등하게 연결하는 등위접속사 or 앞에 동사원형 introduce가 있으므로 동사원형 focus를 사용한 것은 어법상 적절하다. ④은 '등장인물들이 의도된다'라는 의미의 수동 관계이므로 be동사와 함께 수동태를 만드는 과거분사 meant를 사용한 것은 어법상 적절하다. ⑤은 주어 자리에 단수명사 The notion이 왔으므로 단수동사 leads를 사용한 것은 어법상 적절하다. 동격절(that ~ perfect bodies)은 동사의 수 결정에 영향을 주지 않는다.

09   정답 ③

지문분석

Speaking confidently / paves the way / for success.
자신감 있게 말하는 것은 / 길을 열어준다 / 성공을 위한

★ If people appear nervous or uncertain / when they are talking, / the audience may not believe / what they are saying.
만약 사람들이 불안하거나 확실하지 않아 보인다면 / 말할 때 / 청중은 믿지 않을 수도 있다 / 그들이 말하는 것을

However, / if individuals speak with confidence, / they are more ① convincing / and get their messages across more clearly.
그러나 / 만약 사람들이 자신감을 가지고 말한다면 / 그들은 더 설득력 있게 된다 / 그리고 그들의 메시지가 더 명확히 전달된다

In a discussion, / people can gain confidence / by speaking up / at the beginning of a conversation.
토론 중에 / 사람들은 자신감을 얻을 수 있다 / 말함으로써 / 대화의 초반에

Anxiety increases over time, / so it is ② beneficial / to offer an opinion / early on.
불안감은 시간이 지나면서 커진다 / 그래서 도움이 된다 / 의견을 제안하는 것이 / 조기에

If you fail to do so, / discomfort grows, / and joining the conversation / will only become ③ easier(→ harder).
만약 당신이 이렇게 하지 못한다면 / 불편함이 커진다 / 그리고 대화에 참여하는 것은 / 쉬워질(→ 어려워질) 뿐이다

Practice also makes perfect.
또한 연습은 완벽을 만든다

Therefore, / prepare for an important discussion / by thinking / about what you want to express / ④ before you speak.
따라서 / 중요한 토론을 준비해라 / 생각함으로써 / 당신이 무엇을 표현하고 싶은지에 대해 / 당신이 말하기 전에

Lastly, / remind yourself / to slow down.
마지막으로 / 스스로에게 상기시켜라 / 속도를 늦출 것을

Speaking too ⑤ quickly / gives the impression / that you are unsure / of what you are saying.
너무 빠르게 말하는 것은 / ~한 인상을 준다 / 당신이 자신이 없다는 / 당신이 말하고 있는 것에 대해

> ★ 독해가 쉬워지는 구문 풀이
>
> If people appear nervous or uncertain when they are talking, the
> 　　　주어　 동사　　　　주격보어
> audience may not believe what they are saying.
>
> ⇨ appear는 주격보어를 취하는 동사이므로, 보어 자리에 형용사 nervous와 uncertain이 쓰였다.

[어휘] pave the way for ~을 위해 길을 열다　uncertain 확실하지 않은
get ~ across ~이 전달되다　anxiety 불안감　discomfort 불편함
prepare for ~을 준비하다　express 표현하다, 나타내다
remind 상기시키다　impression 인상

[해석] [주제문] 자신감 있게 말하는 것은 성공을 위한 길을 열어준다. 만약 사람들이 말할 때 불안하거나 확실하지 않아 보인다면, 청중은 그들이 말하는 것을 믿지 않을 수도 있다. 그러나, 만약 사람들이 자신감을 가지고 말한다면, 그들은 더 ① 설득력 있게 되고 그들의 메시지가 더 명확히 전달된다. 토론 중에, 사람들은 대화의 초반에 말함으로써 자신감을 얻을 수 있다. 불안감은 시간이 지나면서 커지기에, 조기에 의견을 제안하는 것이 ② 도움이 된다. 만약 당신이 이렇게 하지 못한다면, 불편함이 커지고, 대화에 참여하는 것은 ③ 쉬워질(→ 어려워질) 뿐이다. 또한 연습은 완벽을 만든다. 따라서, 당신이 말하기 ④ 전에 무엇을 표현하고 싶은지에 대해 생각함으로써 중요한 토론을 준비해라. 마지막으로, 스스로에게 속도를 늦출 것을 상기시켜라. 너무 ⑤ 빠르게 말하는 것은 당신이 말하고 있는 것에 대해 자신이 없다는 인상을 준다.

[해설] 불안감은 시간이 지나면서 커지기 때문에 조기에 의견을 제안하지 못한다면 불편함이 커지고 대화에 참여하는 것도 더 "어려워"질 뿐이라는 맥락이 되어야 하므로, ③의 easier를 harder와 같은 단어로 바꾸어야 문맥상 적절하다.

[오답분석] ①은 자신감을 가지고 말할 때 더 "설득력 있게" 되고, 메세지가 더 명확히 전달된다는 문맥이 되어야 하므로 convincing이 오는 것이 적절하다. ②은 불안감은 시간이 지날수록 커지기 때문에 조기에 의견을 제안하는 것이 "도움이 된다"는 문맥이 되어야 하므로 beneficial이 오는 것이 적절하다. ④은 연습이 완벽을 만들기 때문에 말하기 "전에" 무엇을 표현하

고 싶은지에 대해 생각하라는 문맥이 되어야 하므로 before가 오는 것이 적절하다. ⑤은 너무 "빠르게" 말하는 것은 당신이 말하고 있는 것에 대해 자신이 없다는 인상을 준다는 문맥이 되어야 하므로 quickly가 오는 것이 적절하다.

10　　　　　　　　　　　　　　　　정답 ⑤

> Some scientists believe / there is a link / between brain size and **climate change**.
> 몇몇 과학자들은 믿는다 / 연관이 있다고 / 뇌의 크기와 **기후 변화** 사이에
>
> The first members of the genus Homo / emerged about three million years ago / as *Australopithecus* went extinct.
> 인류의 첫 번째 구성원은 / 약 300만 년 전에 출현했다 / *오스트랄로피테쿠스*가 멸종하면서
>
> These early human ancestors / were responsible / for creating the first simple tools / associated with a higher level of thought.
> 이 인류의 초기 조상은 / ~한 역할을 했다 / 최초의 간단한 도구를 만들어 내는 / 보다 높은 수준의 사고와 관련된
>
> About a million and a half years later, / *Homo erectus*, / a species with a bigger brain, / appeared.
> 약 150만 년 이후, / *호모 에렉투스*가 / 더 큰 뇌를 가진 종인 / 등장했다
>
> ★ What's interesting is that / the appearance of both species occurred / at times when weather patterns had begun to vary drastically, / ushering in periods / of increasingly dry weather or colder temperatures.
> 흥미로운 점은 ~이다 / 두 종의 등장이 모두 일어났다는 것이다 / 기후 패턴이 급격하게 변화하기 시작했을 때 / 시기를 예고하며 / 점점 건조한 기후 또는 더 낮은 기온의
>
> This made life more unpredictable / as food and water were harder to find, / so our early ancestors / may have evolved bigger brains / to come up with solutions.
> 이것은 생활을 더 예측할 수 없게 만들었다 / 식량과 물을 찾는 것이 더 어려워지면서 / 그래서 우리의 초기 조상은 / 더 큰 뇌를 갖도록 진화했을 것이다 / 해결책을 찾아내기 위해
>
> It is speculated / that future shifts in environmental conditions / may lead to further adaptations / to the size of our brains.
> 짐작된다 / 미래의 환경 조건의 변화는 / 계속되는 적응을 이끌어 낼 것이라고 / 우리의 두뇌 크기의

> ★ 독해가 쉬워지는 구문 풀이
>
> **What**'s interesting is [that the appearance of both species occurred
> 　명사절 접속사
> at times {when weather patterns had begun to vary drastically},
> 　　　　　　　관계부사절
> ushering in periods of increasingly dry weather or colder temperatures].
>
> ⇨ 명사절 접속사 what은 선행사를 포함하며, the thing which(that)로 바꿔 쓸 수 있다.
> ⇨ 명사절 [ ]는 문장의 보어이며, { }는 선행사 times를 수식하는 관계부사절이다.

[어휘] emerge 출현하다　extinct 멸종된　responsible 역할을 하다
appear 등장하다　vary 변화하다　drastically 급격하게
usher in 예고하다, 안내하다　unpredictable 예측할 수 없는　evolve 진화하다
speculate 짐작하다　adaptation 적응　[선택지] lifespan 수명

[해석] [주제문] 몇몇 과학자들은 뇌의 크기와 **기후 변화** 사이에 연관이 있다고 믿는다. 인류의 첫 번째 구성원들은 약 300만 년 전에 오스트랄로피테쿠스가 멸종하면서 출현했다. 이 인류의 초기 조상은 보다 높은 수준의 사고와 관련된 최초의 간단한 도구를 만들어내는 역할을 했다. 약 150만 년 이후, 더 큰 뇌를 가진 종인 호모 에렉투스가 등장했다. 흥미로운 점은 두 종의 등장이 모두 점점 건조한 기후 또는 더 낮은 기온의 시기를 예고하며 기후 패턴이 급격하게 변화하기 시작했을 때 일어났다는 것이다. 식량과 물을 찾는 것이 더 어려워지면서 이것은 생활을 더 예측할 수 없게 만들었

고, 그래서 우리의 초기 조상은 해결책을 찾아내기 위해 더 큰 뇌를 갖도록 진화했을 것이다. 미래의 환경 조건의 변화는 두뇌 크기의 계속되는 적응을 이끌어 낼 것이라고 짐작된다.

① 비판적 사고
② 사회적 상호 작용
③ 신체적 발달
④ 더 길어진 수명
⑤ 기후 변화

[해설] 빈칸 문장은 이 글의 주제문이므로 이를 다시 언급한 문장이나 부연 설명하는 문장을 파악해야 한다. 빈칸 문장에서 몇몇 과학자들은 뇌의 크기와 '무엇' 사이에 연관이 있다고 믿는다고 하고, 글의 후반에서 미래의 환경 조건의 변화는 두뇌 크기의 계속되는 적응을 이끌어 낼 것으로 짐작된다고 했다. 따라서 빈칸에는 몇몇 과학자들은 뇌의 크기와 "기후 변화" 사이에 연관이 있다고 믿는다는 의미가 되어야 자연스러우므로 ⑤ climate change(기후 변화)가 정답이다.

[오답분석] ①의 '비판적 사고', ②의 '사회적 상호 작용', ④의 '더 길어진 수명'에 관한 내용은 글에서 언급되고 있지 않다. ③은 글에서 언급된 소재인 size of our brain과 연상되는 내용을 활용하여 혼동을 주는 오답이다.

11
정답 ③

지문분석

The English lexicon is constantly evolving, / with new terms coming / from various sources.
영어의 어휘는 끊임없이 변화하고 있다 / 새로운 용어들이 생겨남에 따라 / 다양한 원천으로부터

★ For instance, / technological innovations have often made it necessary / to combine existing words / in order to more accurately distinguish them.
예를 들어 / 기술 혁신은 종종 필요하도록 만들어왔다 / 기존의 단어들을 결합하는 것이 / 그것들(기술 혁신)을 더 정확하게 구별하기 위해

① Prior to the 1980s, / for example, / telephones were fixed / to one location / and could only be used there.
1980년대 이전에 / 예를 들면 / 전화기는 고정되어 있었다 / 한 장소에 / 그리고 그곳에서만 사용될 수 있었다

② But / when phones that could be used / while moving around / came along, / it became necessary to distinguish them / as "mobile phones."
하지만 / 사용될 수 있는 전화기가 ~했을 때 / 돌아다니면서 / 생겼다 / 그것들을 구별하는 것이 필요해졌다 / "휴대 전화"로

(③ Phone companies must license thousands of frequencies / to maximize / the number of simultaneous mobile phone calls.)
통신사는 수천 개의 주파수를 등록해야 한다 / 극대화하기 위해 / 휴대 전화 동시 통화량을

④ Similarly, / once computers became small / and affordable enough / for individual consumers to buy, / they became known / as "personal computers" or PCs.
마찬가지로 / 컴퓨터가 작아지자 / 그리고 가격이 충분히 적당한 / 개인 소비자들이 구매하기에 / 그것들은 알려지게 되었다 / "개인용 컴퓨터" 또는 PC로

⑤ More word combinations / like these / are sure to appear / in the future / as technology continues to advance / and new innovations are discovered.
더 많은 단어 결합은 / 이와 같은 / 분명히 나타날 것이다 / 미래에도 / 기술이 계속해서 발전할 것이기에 / 그리고 새로운 혁신적인 것들이 발견된다

★ 독해가 쉬워지는 구문 풀이

For instance, technological innovations have often made **it**
                                                      가목적어
necessary [to combine existing words] in order to more
목적격보어   진짜 목적어(to부정사)
accurately distinguish them.

⇨ 동사 make는 5형식 동사로 쓰일 때 'make + 목적어 + 목적격보어' 형태를 취하며, '~이 -하게 만들다'라는 의미를 나타낸다. 이때, to부정사구 목적어[ ]가 목적격보어(necessary)와 함께 오면 진짜 목적어를 목적격보어 뒤로 보내고, 목적어가 있던 자리에 가목적어 it을 쓰는 것이 일반적이다.

[어휘] evolve 변화하다, 진화하다 term 용어 innovation 혁신, 혁신적인 것
come along 생기다, 도착하다 license 등록하다, 인가하다
frequency 주파수, 빈도 maximize 극대화하다
affordable (가격이) 적당한, 감당할 수 있는 advance 발전

[해석] [주제문] 다양한 원천으로부터 새로운 용어들이 생겨남에 따라 영어의 어휘는 끊임없이 변화하고 있다. 예를 들어, 기술 혁신은 종종 그것들(기술 혁신)을 더 정확하게 구별하기 위해 기존의 단어들을 결합하는 것이 필요하도록 만들어왔다. ① 예를 들면, 1980년대 이전에, 전화기는 한 장소에 고정되어 있었고 그곳에서만 사용될 수 있었다. ② 하지만, 돌아다니면서 사용될 수 있는 전화기가 생겼을 때, 그것들을 "휴대 전화"로 구별하는 것이 필요해졌다. (③ 통신사는 휴대 전화 동시 통화량을 극대화하기 위해 수천 개의 주파수를 등록해야 한다.) ④ 마찬가지로, 컴퓨터가 작아지고 개인 소비자들이 구매하기에 가격이 충분히 적당해지자, 그것들은 "개인용 컴퓨터" 또는 PC로 알려지게 되었다. ⑤ 기술이 계속해서 발전하고 새로운 혁신적인 것들이 발견될 것이기에, 이와 같은 더 많은 단어 결합은 미래에도 분명히 나타날 것이다.

[해설] 이 글의 주제는 기술 혁신에 의해 새로운 용어들이 생겨남에 따라 영어의 어휘 또한 끊임없이 변화한다는 것이다. 대부분이 기술 혁신에 의해 생겨난 용어에 대한 내용으로 주제와 연관이 있는데, 통신사가 휴대 전화 동시 통화량을 극대화하기 위해 수천 개의 주파수를 등록해야 한다는 ③은 글의 흐름과 관계없는 문장이다.

[오답분석] ①과 ②은 휴대전화를, ④은 PC를 예로 들어 기술 혁신이 어떻게 새로운 용어를 만들어내는지를 설명하고 있으므로 글의 주제와 연관되어 있다. ⑤은 기술 혁신으로 인해 미래에도 더 많은 용어가 만들어질 것이라고 결론을 내리는 문장이므로 글의 흐름에 자연스럽다.

12
정답 ④

지문분석

★ Uncertainty avoidance describes / how well / people from different cultural backgrounds / tolerate unpredictable events.
불확실성 회피는 설명한다 / 얼마나 잘 / 서로 다른 문화적 배경을 가진 사람들이 / 예측할 수 없는 일을 견디는지를

It provides some insight / into how they might respond / to new and unfamiliar situations.
이는 약간의 이해를 제공한다 / 그들이 어떻게 반응할 지에 대해 / 새롭고 낯선 상황에

(A) To give an example / of how the measure works, / cultures with "high" uncertainty avoidance / usually try to avoid uncertainty.
한 가지 예를 들자면 / 그 기준이 작동하는 방식의 / 불확실성 회피가 "높은" 문화권은 / 일반적으로 불확실성을 피하려 한다

This means / that they have a low tolerance / for unpredictability / and are anxious / about the future and anything new.
이는 의미한다 / 그들이 더 낮은 내성을 가지고 있다는 것을 / 예측 불가능성에 대해 / 그리고 불안해한다 / 미래와 모든 새로운 것에 대해

They are / therefore / more likely to place an emphasis / on tradition, order, and stability.
그들은 / 따라서 / ~을 더 중요하게 생각할 가능성이 더 높다 / 전통, 질서, 그리고 안정성을

(B) The opposite is true of groups / with "low" uncertainty avoidance.
~한 집단에는 그 반대가 사실이다 / 불확실성 회피가 "낮은"

Such groups have a high tolerance / for unpredictability / and feel less fearful / about unexpected events.
이러한 집단은 높은 내성을 가진다 / 예측 불가능성에 대해 / 그리고 덜 두려워한다 / 예측할 수 없는 일에 대해

Thus, / they are generally / more adaptable, / innovative, / and open to innovative ideas.
따라서 / 그들은 보통 / 적응을 더 잘하고 / 혁신적이고 / 그리고 획기적인 발상에 개방적인

(C) The idea of uncertainty avoidance / was first proposed / by the Dutch sociologist Geert Hofstede / during his research / into cultural differences between countries.
불확실성 회피라는 개념은 / 처음 제시되었다 / 네덜란드의 사회학자 Geert Hofstede에 의해 / 연구를 하던 중에 / 국가 간 문화 차이에 대한

It is one of four measures / he used to compare one country / with another.
그것은 네 가지 기준 중 하나이다 / 그가 한 국가를 비교하기 위해 사용했던 / 다른 국가와

★ 독해가 쉬워지는 구문 풀이

Uncertainty avoidance describes [**how** well people from different
　　　　　　　　　　　　　　　의문사　　　　　주어
cultural backgrounds tolerate unpredictable events].
　　　　　　　　　　　　　　동사

▷ [ ]는 의문사 how가 사용된 간접 의문문으로, '의문사 + 주어 + 동사'의 어순을 갖는다.

어휘 uncertainty 불확실성　avoidance 회피　describe 설명하다
tolerate 견디다　unpredictable 예측할 수 없는　insight 이해, 통찰
measure 기준　tolerance 내성　unpredictability 예측 불가능성
place an emphasis on ~을 더 중요하게 생각하다　stability 안정성
opposite 반대　adaptable 적응을 잘 하는　innovative 혁신적인, 획기적인
open to ~에 개방적인　propose 제시하다　Dutch 네덜란드의
sociologist 사회학자

해석 **주제문** 불확실성 회피는 서로 다른 문화적 배경을 가진 사람들이 예측할 수 없는 일을 얼마나 잘 견디는지를 설명한다. 이는 새롭고 낯선 상황에 그들이 어떻게 반응할 지에 대해 약간의 이해를 제공한다. (C) 불확실성 회피라는 개념은 네덜란드의 사회학자 Geert Hofstede가 국가 간 문화 차이에 대한 연구를 하던 중에 그에 의해 처음 제시되었다. 그것은 그가 한 국가를 다른 국가와 비교하기 위해 사용했던 네 가지 기준 중 하나이다. (A) 그 기준이 작동하는 방식의 한 가지 예를 들자면, 불확실성 회피가 "높은" 문화권은 일반적으로 불확실성을 피하려 한다. 이는 그들이 예측 불가능성에 대해 더 낮은 내성을 가지고 있고 미래와 모든 새로운 것에 대해 불안해한다는 것을 의미한다. 따라서 그들은 전통, 질서, 그리고 안정성을 더 중요하게 생각할 가능성이 더 높다. (B) 불확실성 회피가 "낮은" 집단에서는 그 반대가 사실이다. 이러한 집단은 예측 불가능성에 대한 높은 내성을 가지고 예측할 수 없는 일에 대해 덜 두려워한다. 따라서, 그들은 보통 적응을 더 잘하고, 혁신적이며, 획기적인 발상에 개방적이다.

해설 주어진 글은 불확실성 회피가 서로 다른 문화적 배경을 가진 사람들이 예측할 수 없는 일을 얼마나 잘 견디는지를 설명한다는 내용이다. (C)의 The idea of uncertainty avoidance was first proposed(불확실성 회피라는 개념은 처음 제시되었다)는 주어진 글에서 묘사된 '불확실성 회피'의 창시자에 대해 설명하고 있으므로 주어진 글 바로 다음에 오는 것이 자연스럽다. (A)는 To give an example of how the measure works (그 기준이 작동하는 방식의 한 가지 예를 들자면)를 통해 (C)에서 언급된 네 가지 기준 중 하나인 불확실성 회피가 작동하는 방식의 예시를 설명하고 있으므로 (C) 다음에 오는 것이 자연스럽다. (B)는 The opposite을 통해 (A)의 내용과 대조되는 예시를 들고 있으므로 (A) 뒤에 오는 것이 자연스럽다. 따라서 글의 순서로 가장 적절한 것은 ④ (C)-(A)-(B)이다.

13
정답 ④

지문분석

Before the dawn of civilization, / people were predominantly nomads, / living in small groups / that acquired food / through hunting and gathering.
문명의 발단 이전에 / 사람들은 대부분 유목민이었다 / 작은 집단을 이루어 사는 / 식량을 얻는 / 수렵과 채집을 통해

(①) But / around 10,000 BC, / humans began to establish / agricultural hubs and more permanent settlements, / which resulted in numerous social changes.
하지만 / 기원전 10,000년 즈음 / 인간은 만들기 시작했다 / 농업 중심지와 더 영구적인 정착지를 / 이것은 다양한 사회적 변화를 낳았다

(②) Larger groups of people / came to live together, / and farming practices allowed for / excess food production.
더 큰 집단의 사람들이 / 함께 살게 되었다 / 그리고 농사법은 가능하게 했다 / 여분의 식량 생산을

(③) ★ Due to this abundance / of food, / not everyone had to / focus on providing nourishment, / and this enabled people to / pursue other "jobs."
이러한 풍부함 덕분에 / 식량의 / 모든 사람들이 ~할 필요가 없었다 / 음식물을 마련하는 것에 집중할 / 그리고 그것은 사람들이 ~할 수 있게 했다 / 다른 "일"에 종사하게

(④) (For example, / individuals started to invent tools, / establish a culture / and organize into societal groups / that began to live together.)
예를 들어 / 사람들은 도구를 발명하기 시작했다 / 문화를 확립하고 / 그리고 사회적 집단을 조직하다 / 함께 살기 시작한

Eventually, / villages and towns became massive cities / with dense populations.
결국 / 촌락과 마을은 거대한 도시가 되었다 / 인구가 밀집된

(⑤) Furthermore, / civilizations began to flourish / and advancements were made quickly, / enabling humans to prosper / rather than just survive.
더 나아가 / 문명은 번영하기 시작했다 / 그리고 발전이 빠르게 이루어졌다 / 인간이 번성할 수 있게 하며 / 단지 생존만 하기보다는

★ 독해가 쉬워지는 구문 풀이

[Due to this abundance of food, **not** everyone had to focus on
　　　　　　　　　　　　　　　부분 부정
providing nourishment,] and **this** enabled people to pursue other
　　　　　　　　　　　　　　　　지시대명사
"jobs."

▷ 부분 부정은 'not + every/all/always/both'의 형태로 쓰여 '모두/항상/둘 다 ~인 것은 아니다'라는 의미를 나타낸다.
▷ this는 지시대명사로 [ ]를 가리킨다.

어휘 dawn 발단, 새벽　civilization 문명　predominantly 대부분
nomad 유목민　gathering 채집　agricultural 농업의　settlement 정착지
excess 여분의　abundance 풍부함　nourishment 음식물, 영양
pursue 종사하다　dense 밀집된　flourish 번영하다, 번창하다
advancement 발전　prosper 번성하다

해석 문명의 발단 이전에, 사람들은 대부분 유목민이었고, 수렵과 채집을 통해 식량을 얻는 작은 집단을 이루어 살았다. 하지만 기원전 10,000년 즈음, 인간은 농업 중심지와 더 영구적인 정착지를 만들기 시작했고, 이것은 다양한 사회적 변화를 낳았다. 더 큰 집단의 사람들이 함께 살게 되었고, 농사법은 여분의 식량 생산을 가능하게 했다. 이러한 식량의 풍부함 덕분에, 모든 사람들이 음식물을 마련하는 것에 집중할 필요가 없었고, 이것은 사람들이 다른 "일"에 종사할 수 있게 했다. (예를 들어, 사람들은 도구를 발명하고, 문화를 확립하고, 그리고 함께 살기 시작한 사회적 집단을 조직하기 시작했다.) 결국, 촌락과 마을은 인구가 밀집된 거대한 도시가 되었다. 더 나아가, 문명은 번영하기 시작했고 발전이 빠르게 이루어졌으며, 인간이 단지 생존만 하기보다는 번성할 수 있게 했다.

해설 주어진 문장의 For example, individuals started ~(예를 들어, 사람들은 ~ 하기 시작했다)를 통해 주어진 문장 앞에는 사람들이 이러한 일들을 시작하게 된 설명이 나와야 한다는 것을 알 수 있다. 이 글에서는 ①~③ 뒤 문장까지 기원전 10,000년 즈음부터 사람들이 함께 살기 시작하고 여분의 식량 생산이 가능해지면서 생긴 변화에 대해 설명하고 있고, 주어진 문장의 For example은 앞에서 설명된 사람들이 다른 "일"에 종사할 수 있게 되었다는 것에 대한 예시를 제공하므로 주어진 문장이 들어가기에 가장 적절한 곳은 ④이다.

오답분석 ④ 앞 문장까지는 인간이 농업과 영구적인 정착지를 만들기 시작한 것이 어떻게 문명의 발전으로 이어졌는지를 설명하고 있으므로 흐름이 자연스럽다. ④ 뒤 문장들은 ④ 앞에서 나온 내용의 결과로 문명의 발전과 변화에 대해 언급하고 있으므로 흐름이 자연스럽다.

14 정답 ④

지문분석

In 1999, / two psychologists, / David Dunning and Justin Kruger, / conducted a number of tests / on a group of students, / evaluating their logic, humor, and grammar.
1999년에 / 두 명의 심리학자 / David Dunning과 Justin Kruger는 / 여러 시험을 실시했다 / 학생 집단에게 / 그들의 논리, 유머, 문법을 평가하기 위한

★ What they discovered was / that the students who performed the worst also believed / they had performed far better / than they actually did.
그들이 알아낸 것은 ~이었다 / 가장 못 한 학생들도 생각했다는 것 / 그들이 훨씬 더 잘 수행했다고 / 자신들이 실제로 한 것보다

They were not only incompetent / but also lacked the self-awareness / to judge their incompetence accurately.
그들은 유능하지 않았을 뿐만 아니라 / 자기 인식도 부족했다 / 그들의 무능력을 정확하게 평가하기 위한

This phenomenon has since become known / as the Dunning-Kruger effect.
이 현상은 그 이후로 알려져 왔다 / Dunning-Kruger 효과라고

According to Dunning and Kruger, / the effect may be caused / by something / they called the "dual burden."
Dunning과 Kruger에 따르면 / 그 효과는 야기될 수 있다 / 무언가에 의해 / 그들이 "이중 부담"이라고 부르는

The dual burden describes a condition / in which the knowledge that people need / to complete a task well / is the same knowledge / that they need / to evaluate themselves correctly.
이중 부담이란 ~한 상태를 설명한다 / 사람들이 필요로 하는 지식이 / 작업을 잘 마치게 하기 위해 / 동일한 지식이다 / 그들이 필요로 하는 / 스스로를 정확하게 평가하기 위해

It is as if / the incompetent students had two burdens or obstacles / to overcome.
그것은 마치 ~과 같다 / 유능하지 않은 학생들이 두 가지의 부담이나 상애물을 갖는 것 / 극복해야 할

First, / they did not know / enough to do well on the tests.
첫 번째로 / 그들은 알고 있지 않았다 / 시험에서 잘할 만큼 충분히

Second, / their lack of knowledge / caused them to be unaware / of how badly they did.
두 번째로 / 그들의 지식 부족은 / 그들이 알지 못하게 했다 / 그들이 얼마나 못했는지

⇩

According to the Dunning-Kruger effect, / people who perform (A) poorly / also lack the appropriate (B) awareness / to judge themselves accurately.
Dunning-Kruger 효과에 따르면 / 형편없이 수행하는 사람들은 / 또한 적절한 인식이 부족하다 / 스스로를 정확하게 평가하기 위한

★ 독해가 쉬워지는 구문 풀이

[What they discovered] was that the students who performed the worst also believed {they had performed far better than they 보어 actually did}.

⇨ 명사절 [ ]는 문장의 주어부이며, 단수 취급한다.
⇨ 명사절 { }는 동사 believed의 목적어이며 접속사 that은 생략되었다.

어휘 psychologist 심리학자, 정신 분석 의사 evaluate 평가하다
incompetent 유능하지 않은, 무능한 self-awareness 자기 인식
phenomenon 현상, 경이로운 것 burden 부담, 짐 knowledge 지식, 판단력

해석 1999년에, 두 명의 심리학자 David Dunning과 Justin Kruger는 학생 집단에게 그들의 논리, 유머, 문법을 평가하기 위한 여러가지 시험을 실시했다. 그들이 알아낸 것은 가장 못한 학생들도 자신들이 실제로 한 것보다 훨씬 더 잘 수행했다고 생각한다는 것이었다. **주제문** 그들은 유능하지 않았을 뿐만 아니라 그들의 무능력을 정확하게 평가하기 위한 자기 인식도 부족했다. 이 현상은 그 이후로 Dunning-Kruger 효과라고 알려져 왔다. Dunning과 Kruger에 따르면, 그 효과는 그들이 "이중 부담"이라고 부르는 무언가에 의해 야기될 수 있다. 이중 부담이란 사람들이 작업을 잘 마치게 하기 위해 필요로 하는 지식이 그들이 스스로를 정확하게 평가하기 위해 필요로 하는 지식과 동일한 상태를 설명한다. 그것은 마치 유능하지 않은 학생들이 극복해야 할 두 가지의 부담이나 장애물을 갖는 것과 같다. 첫 번째로, 그들은 시험에서 잘할 만큼 충분히 알고 있지 않았다. 두 번째로, 그들의 지식 부족은 그들이 얼마나 못했는지 알지 못하게 했다.

⇩

Dunning-Kruger 효과에 따르면 (A)형편없이 수행하는 사람들은 또한 스스로를 정확하게 평가하기 위한 적절한 (B)인식이 부족하다.

	(A)	(B)
①	잘 …	지식
②	잘 …	심리
③	형편없이 …	관심
④	형편없이 …	인식
⑤	평범하게 …	능력

해설 요약문은 Dunning-Kruger 효과에 따르면, '(A)하게' 수행하는 사람들은 또한 스스로를 정확하게 파악하기 위한 적절한 '(B)'가 부족하다는 내용이다. 글에서 Dunning과 Kruger는 가장 못한 학생들이 유능하지 않았을 뿐만 아니라 그들의 무능력을 정확하게 평가하기 위한 자기 인식도 부족했다고 했다. 따라서 요약문의 (A)에는 글에서 언급된 'performed the worst', 'did not know enough to do well'과 관련된 'poorly'가, (B)에는 글에서 언급된 'lacked the self-awareness', 'be unaware of'와 관련된 'awareness'가 적절하므로 ④ poorly(형편없이) - awareness(인식)가 정답이다.

오답분석 실력이 형편없는 사람들이 자신들이 실제로 한 것보다 훨씬 더 잘했다고 생각한다고 했으므로 ①과 ②의 well과 ⑤의 normally는 (A)에 들어갈 단어로 적절하지 않다. 또한 형편없는 실력을 보여준 상황에서 그들의 무능력을 정확하게 평가하기 위한 자기 인식도 부족했다고 했으므로 ②의 psychology, ③의 interest는 (B)에 들어갈 단어로 적절하지 않다.

지문분석

Although using a laptop / to take notes / is seemingly convenient, / taking notes the old-fashioned way / may boost your understanding / of the material.
비록 노트북을 사용하는 것이 ~하더라도 / 필기를 하기 위해 / 겉보기에 편리하다 / 옛날 방식으로 필기를 하는 것은 / 당신의 이해를 높일 수도 있다 / 자료에 대한

That's because / writing by hand is a slower process / than using a laptop.
그것은 ~하기 때문이다 / 손으로 쓰는 것이 더 느린 과정이다 / 노트북을 사용하는 것보다

Students who use laptops / are able to transcribe the material so quickly / that they often just type / what is said / word for word.
노트북을 사용하는 학생들은 / 자료를 매우 빠르게 기록할 수 있다 / 그래서 종종 타이핑하기만 한다 / 나온 내용을 / 글자 그대로

Students who put pen to paper, / on the other hand, / cannot write everything down, / so they learn to distinguish important details / from irrelevant ones.
글을 쓰는 학생들은 / 반면에 / 모든 것을 받아 적을 수 없다 / 그래서 중요한 세부 사항을 구분하는 것을 배운다 / 관련 없는 것과

They can also explain the concepts / discussed in a lecture / better afterwards / because they have to listen very carefully / and make sense of the material / before they summarize it / in their notes.
그들은 개념을 설명할 수도 있다 / 강의에서 논의된 / 이후에 더 잘 / 그들이 매우 주의 깊게 들어야 하기 때문에 / 그리고 자료를 이해한다 / 그것을 요약하기 전에 / 그들의 노트에

Furthermore, / students who take freehand notes / have more **freedom** / when it comes to note-taking / than students who use laptops.
게다가 / 손으로만 필기를 하는 학생들은 / 더 많은 **자유**가 있다 / 필기하는 것에 관한 한 / 노트북을 사용하는 학생들보다

For example, / when you take notes by hand, / you have the flexibility / to add sketches and diagrams / or to circle keywords.
예를 들어 / 당신이 손으로 필기를 할 때 / 당신은 융통성을 갖는다 / 스케치와 도표를 추가할 / 또는 키워드에 동그라미를 칠

Because / students may come to / associate concepts with them, / the end results / can be very useful.
~ 때문에 / 학생들이 ~할 수 있다 / 그것들을 개념과 연상시키다 / 최종 결과는 / 굉장히 유용할 수 있다

★ When you use a computer, / on the other hand, / all you can do / to improve your understanding of a concept / is describe it in writing.
당신이 컴퓨터를 사용한다면 / 반면 / 당신이 할 수 있는 것은 고작 ~이 전부이다 / 개념에 대한 이해를 증진시키기 위해 / 글로 표현하는 것이다

This is less effective / at helping them recall key details / when preparing for an exam later.
이것(컴퓨터를 사용하는 것)은 덜 효과적이다 / 그들이 주요한 사항들을 기억해내도록 돕는 데 / 추후 시험을 준비할 때

★ 독해가 쉬워지는 구문 풀이

When you use a computer, on the other hand, **all** [you can do to improve your understanding of a concept] is (to) **describe** it in writing.
(주어) / (수식어(관계절)) / (동사)

▷ 'all + ~ 대동사 do' 표현은 이어지는 보어 자리에 동사 원형을 쓰는 것이 원칙이나 to부정사도 사용할 수 있다.
▷ [ ]는 부정대명사 all을 수식하는 관계절이다.

어휘 take notes 필기를 하다, 메모하다 seemingly 겉보기에, 보아하니
old-fashioned 옛날식의, 구식의 transcribe 기록하다
word for word 글자 그대로 put pen to paper 글을 쓰다
irrelevant 관련 없는, 무관한 make sense of ~을 이해하다
flexibility 융통성, 적응성 diagram 도표, 도해 end result 최종 결과

---

recall 기억해내다, 상기하다

해석 **[주제문]** 필기를 하기 위해 노트북을 사용하는 것이 비록 겉보기에는 편리하더라도, 옛날 방식으로 필기를 하는 것은 자료에 대한 당신의 이해를 높일 수도 있다. 그것은 손으로 쓰는 것이 노트북을 사용하는 것보다 더 느린 과정이기 때문이다. 노트북을 사용하는 학생들은 자료를 매우 빠르게 기록할 수 있어서 나온 내용을 종종 글자 그대로 타이핑하기만 한다. 반면에, 글을 쓰는 학생들은 모든 것을 받아 적을 수 없어서 중요한 세부 사항을 관련 없는 것과 구분하는 것을 배운다. 그들은 노트에 자료를 요약하기 전에 매우 주의 깊게 듣고 그것을 이해해야 하기 때문에 강의에서 논의된 개념을 이후에 더 잘 설명할 수도 있다.

게다가, 손으로만 필기를 하는 학생들은 노트북을 사용하는 학생들보다 필기하는 것에 관한 한 더 많은 **자유**가 있다. 예를 들어, 당신이 손으로 필기를 할 때, 당신은 스케치와 도표를 추가하거나, 키워드에 동그라미를 칠 융통성을 갖는다. 학생들이 그것들을 개념과 연상시킬 수 있기 때문에, 최종 결과는 굉장히 유용할 수 있다. 반면, 당신이 컴퓨터를 사용한다면, 당신이 개념에 대한 이해를 증진시키기 위해 할 수 있는 것은 고작 글로 표현하는 것이 전부이다. 이것(컴퓨터를 사용하는 것)은 추후 시험을 준비할 때 그들이 주요한 사항들을 기억해내도록 돕는 데 덜 효과적이다.

15 정답 ②

해석 ① 온라인상에서 집중을 방해하는 것을 차단하고, 다시 집중 상태로 돌아가라!
② 노트북을 사용하는 것 대신 손으로 필기하는 것의 이점들
③ 강의 기반의 수업: 그것이 학습 과정에 도움이 되는가?
④ 가장 효율적인 필기 방식을 정하는 방법
⑤ 디지털 시대에서 손으로 글 쓰는 것을 가르치는 것의 중요성

어휘 distraction 집중을 방해하는 것, 주의 산만

해설 손으로 쓰는 옛날 방식으로 필기를 하는 것은 노트북으로 필기를 하는 것보다 자료에 대한 당신의 이해를 높일 수 있다는 내용의 글이므로, 글의 제목으로 가장 적절한 것은 ② The Benefits of Freehand Note-Taking over Using Laptops(노트북을 사용하는 것 대신 손으로 필기하는 것의 이점들)이다.

오답분석 ①, ③, ⑤는 글에서 언급되고 있지 않다. ④은 글의 핵심 소재 Note-Taking을 활용하여 혼동을 주는 오답이다.

16 정답 ①

해석 ① 자유 ② 에너지 ③ 스트레스
④ 능력 ⑤ 자신감

해설 이 글의 주제문인 '옛날 방식으로 필기를 하는 것은 자료에 대한 당신의 이해를 높일 수도 있다'를 다시 언급한 문장이나 부연 설명하는 문장을 파악해야 한다. 글의 후반부에서 손으로 필기를 할 때는 스케치와 도표를 추가하거나, 키워드에 동그라미를 칠 융통성을 갖게 되지만, 컴퓨터를 사용할 때는 고작 글로 표현하는 것이 전부라고 했다. 따라서 손으로만 필기를 하는 학생들은 노트북을 사용하는 학생들보다 필기하는 것에 관한 한 더 많은 "자유"가 있다는 의미가 되는 것이 자연스러우므로 ① freedom(자유)이 정답이다.

오답분석 ②, ③, ⑤은 글의 내용과 상관없는 오답이다. ④은 지문 후반부에 언급되는 "개념에 대한 이해", "주요한 사항들을 기억해내는 것"과 같은 소재를 활용하여 혼동을 주는 오답이다.

(A) Long ago, / a rich businessman decided to retire / and spend time / with his family.

오래전에 / 한 부유한 사업가는 퇴직하기로 결심했다 / 그리고 시간을 보내기로 / 그의 가족과

His wife had passed away, / but he had three sons.

그의 부인은 죽었다 / 하지만 그에게는 세 명의 아들이 있었다

His sons always said / they were very busy, / though, / so they only came twice a year.

그의 아들들은 항상 말했다 / 그들이 너무 바쁘다고 / 그러나 / 그래서 오로지 1년에 두 번만 왔다

As the man grew older, / his sons stopped by less and less / to see him.

그 남자가 나이가 들면서 / 그의 아들들은 점점 덜 들렀다 / 그를 보러

"They don't want to be with (a) me," / he thought sadly.

그들은 나와 함께 있고 싶어 하지 않아 / 라며 그가 슬프게 생각했다

"What can I do / about this?"

내가 무엇을 할 수 있을까 / 이것에 대해

(B) So, / the three sons took turns / living with their father, / taking care of him / and keeping him company.

그래서 / 세 아들은 교대로 했다 / 그들의 아버지와 살았다 / 그를 돌보았다 / 그리고 그의 곁에 있었다

(b) He eventually grew old / and died happily / after spending so much time / with his sons.

그는 결국 나이가 들었다 / 그리고 행복하게 죽었다 / 아주 많은 시간을 보낸 후에 / 그의 아들들과

After the funeral, / his sons finally opened the chest / and saw all the glass.

장례식 후에 / 그의 아들들은 마침내 그 상자를 열었다 / 그리고 모든 유리 조각을 보았다

"What a mean trick!" / the eldest complained.

정말 비열한 속임수잖아 / 라며 첫째가 불평했다

But / the middle son said / ★ "No, / we would have neglected him / if he hadn't done this."

그러나 / 둘째 아들이 말했다 / 아니야 / 우리는 아버지를 등한시했을 거야 / 그가 이렇게 하지 않았더라면

"You're right," / said the youngest.

형이 맞아 / 라고 막내가 말했다

"I'm so ashamed.

나는 너무 부끄러워

All he wanted / was our love."

그가 원한 건 오직 / 우리의 사랑이었어

(C) He finally came up with a clever plan.

그는 마침내 기발한 계획을 떠올렸다

The next day, / he went to the carpenter / and asked him for a large chest.

다음 날 / 그는 목수에게 갔다 / 그리고 그에게 큰 상자를 요청했다

Then, / (c) he visited the engineer / to make the strongest lock.

그 이후에 / 그는 기술자를 찾아갔다 / 가장 튼튼한 자물쇠를 만들기 위해

Finally, / he stopped by the glassmaker / and asked for broken pieces of glass.

마지막으로 / 그는 유리 제조업자에게 들렀다 / 그리고 깨진 유리 조각을 달라고 했다

The father went home, / filled the chest with glass, / locked it, / and set it / under the kitchen table.

그 아버지는 집에 갔다 / 유리로 그 상자를 채웠다 / 잠갔다 / 그리고 그것을 두었다 / 주방 식탁 아래에

(D) The next time / (d) his sons visited, / they saw it / and wondered / what was inside.

다음번에 ~했을 때 / 그의 아들들이 방문했다 / 그들은 그것을 보았다 / 그리고 궁금해했다 / 안에 무엇이 있을지

"It's just some things / I've been saving," / their father replied.

그건 그냥 몇몇 물건들이란다 / 내가 모아왔던 / 그들의 아버지가 답했다

Their feet hit the chest / as they sat down.

그들의 발이 상자를 쳤다 / 그들이 앉을 때

They could hear the glass clinking inside.

그들은 안에서 유리가 쨍그랑하는 소리를 내는 것을 들을 수 있었다

"Listen to those coins! / And it's so heavy!" / the eldest whispered / to (e) his brothers.

저 동전 소리 좀 들어봐 / 그리고 그건 아주 무거워 / 라고 첫째가 속삭였다 / 그의 남동생들에게

"It must be all the gold / he's saved / over the years."

그건 모두 금일 거야 / 아버지가 모아온 / 수년 동안

The sons decided / to take care of their father / to inherit the fortune.

그 아들들은 ~하기로 했다 / 그들의 아버지를 돌보기로 / 그 재산을 물려받기 위해

★ 독해가 쉬워지는 구문 풀이

"No, we would have neglected him if he hadn't done this."
                                        had p.p

⇨ 아버지가 속임수를 쓴 것은 과거에 이미 벌어진 사실이므로, 속임수를 쓰지 않았을 때와, 그에 따라 벌어졌을 세 아들의 행동을 가정하는 상황으로 가정법 과거완료 표현이 사용됐다. 가정법 과거완료 표현은 과거 사실에 대한 반대되는 일을 가정한다.

어휘 pass away 죽다, 사라지다 less and less 점점 덜 take turns 교대로 하다
keep somebody company ~의 곁에 있어 주다, ~의 친구가 되어 주다
mean 비열한, 심술궂은 neglect 등한시하다, 방치하다
come up with ~을 떠올리다, 제시하다 clever 기발한, 영리한
engineer 기술자, 공학자 clink 쨍그랑하는 소리를 내다
inherit 물려받다, 상속하다

해석 (A) 오래전에, 한 부유한 사업가는 퇴직하고 그의 가족과 시간을 보내기로 결심했다. 그의 부인은 죽었지만 그에게는 세 명의 아들이 있었다. 그러나, 그의 아들들은 항상 너무 바쁘다고 말했고 그래서 1년에 오로지 두 번만 왔다. 그 남자가 나이가 들면서, 그의 아들들은 점점 그를 보러 덜 들렀다. "그들은 (a) 나와 함께 있고 싶어 하지 않아"라며 그가 슬프게 생각했다. "이것에 대해 내가 무엇을 할 수 있을까?"
(C) 그는 마침내 기발한 계획을 떠올렸다. 다음 날, 그는 목수에게 가서 그에게 큰 상자를 요청했다. 그 이후에, (c) 그는 가장 튼튼한 자물쇠를 만들기 위해 기술자를 찾아갔다. 마지막으로, 그는 유리 제조업자에게 들러서 깨진 유리 조각들을 달라고 했다. 그 아버지는 집에 가서 유리로 그 상자를 채우고, 잠그고, 그것을 주방 식탁 아래에 두었다.
(D) (d) 그의 아들들이 다음번에 방문했을 때, 그들은 그것을 보았고 안에 무엇이 있을지 궁금해했다. "그건 그냥 내가 모아왔던 몇몇 물건들이란다"라고 그들의 아버지가 답했다. 그들이 앉을 때 그들의 빌이 싱자를 쳤다. 그들은 안에서 유리가 쨍그랑하는 소리를 내는 것을 들을 수 있었다. "저 동전 소리 좀 들어봐! 그리고 그건 아주 무거워!"라며 첫째가 (e) 그의 남동생들에게 속삭였다. "그건 모두 수년 동안 아버지가 모아온 금일 거야." 그 아들들은 그 재산을 물려받기 위해 그들의 아버지를 돌보기로 했다.
(B) 그래서, 세 아들은 교대로 그들의 아버지와 살면서 그를 돌보고 그의 곁에 있었다. (b) 그는 결국 나이가 들었고 그의 아들들과 아주 많은 시간을 보낸 후에 행복하게 죽었다. 장례식 후에, 그의 아들들은 마침내 그 상자를 열었고 모든 유리 조각을 보았다. "정말 비열한 속임수잖아!"라며 첫째가 불평했다. 그러나 둘째 아들이 "아니야, 그가 이렇게 하지 않았더라면 우리는 아버지를 등한시했을 거야"라고 말했다. "형이 맞아"라고 막내가 말했다. "나는 너무 부끄러워. 그가 원한 건 오직 우리의 사랑이었어."

17
정답 ③

[해설] (A)는 오래전에 한 부유한 사업가가 가족들과 더 많은 시간을 함께 보내고 싶어서 퇴직한 후에 세 아들이 자신을 더 자주 보러 오게 만들 방법을 고민하는 내용이다. (C)는 그가 기발한 계획을 떠올려 목수, 기술자, 유리 제조업자를 찾아갔다는 내용이므로 세 아들이 자신을 더 자주 보러 오게 할 수 있는 방법이 없을지 고민한 (A) 뒤에 오는 것이 자연스럽다. (D)의 they saw it에서 it은 (C)의 chest를 가리키므로 (C) 다음에 와야 한다. (B)는 세 아들이 교대로 그들의 아버지를 돌보며 곁에 있었고 나이가 들어 아버지가 죽은 후 아들들이 상자를 열어 진실을 알아냈다는 내용이므로 아들들이 상자 안의 내용물이 아버지의 재산인 줄 알고 그것을 물려받기 위해 아버지를 돌보기로 했다고 한 (D) 뒤에 오는 것이 자연스럽다. 따라서 글의 순서로 가장 적절한 것은 ③ (C)-(D)-(B)이다.

18
정답 ⑤

[해설] (a), (b), (c), (d)는 세 아들의 아버지인 부유한 사업가를 가리키지만 (e)는 첫째 아들을 가리키므로 ⑤가 정답이다.

19
정답 ⑤

[해설] The sons decided to take care of their father to inherit the fortune에서 아들들은 아버지의 재산을 물려받기 위해 그를 돌보기로 결심했다는 것을 알 수 있으므로, 글의 내용과 일치하지 않는 것은 ⑤ '아들들은 아버지의 외로운 모습을 보고 그를 돌보기로 했다.'이다.

[오답 분석] ①은 As the man grew older, his sons stopped by less and less to see him이라고 했으므로 글의 내용과 일치한다. ②은 the three sons took turns living with their father라고 했으므로 글의 내용과 일치한다. ③은 "You're right," said the youngest. "I'm so ashamed. All he wanted was our love."라고 했으므로 글의 내용과 일치한다. ④은 The father went home, filled the chest with glass라고 했으므로 글의 내용과 일치한다.

제3회 실전 모의고사
p.154

01
정답 ②

[지문분석]

To whom it may concern,
관계자분께

Hello, / my name is Kathy Owens.
안녕하세요 / 제 이름은 Kathy Owens입니다

I have been a longtime customer / of your airline.
저는 오랜 고객입니다 / 귀 항공사의

I was recently booked / on Flight 546 / from New York to Hong Kong.
저는 최근에 예약했습니다 / 546 항공편을 / 뉴욕에서 홍콩으로 가는

★ I had an important meeting / that I could not miss.
저는 중요한 회의가 있었습니다 / 놓칠 수 없는

Unfortunately, / when I arrived for my flight, / I found out / the plane had a serious mechanical problem.
안타깝게도 / 항공편에 탑승하기 위해 도착했을 때 / 저는 알게 되었습니다 / 그 비행기에 심각한 기계적인 결함이 있다는 것을

The flight was delayed / until the next day.
그 항공편은 지연되었습니다 / 다음 날까지

I had no choice but to / take a different flight, / and it still caused me / to miss my meeting.
저는 ~할 수밖에 없었습니다 / 다른 항공편을 타다 / 그럼에도 그것은 제가 ~하게 하였습니다 / 회의를 놓치게

As such, / I would like to / ask for a refund / for my original ticket.
이로써 / 저는 ~하고 싶습니다 / 환불을 요청하다 / 제 원래 티켓에 대해

Thank you for your time.
시간 내주셔서 감사합니다

Regards,
Kathy Owens
Kathy Owens 드림

★ 독해가 쉬워지는 구문 풀이

I had an important meeting [**that** I could not miss].

⇨ [ ]는 선행사 meeting을 수식하는 관계절이며, 목적격 관계대명사 that은 생략될 수 있다.

[어휘] customer 고객 book 예약하다 flight 항공편, 비행기 mechanical 기계적인 delay 지연시키다; 지연 have no choice but to ~할 수밖에 없다

[해석] 관계자분께,
안녕하세요, 제 이름은 Kathy Owens입니다. 저는 귀 항공사의 오랜 고객입니다. 저는 최근에 뉴욕에서 홍콩으로 가는 546 항공편을 예약했습니다. 저는 놓칠 수 없는 중요한 회의가 있었습니다. 안타깝게도, 항공편에 탑승하기 위해 도착했을 때, 저는 그 비행기에 심각한 기계적인 결함이 있다는 것을 알게 되었습니다. 그 항공편은 다음 날까지 지연되었습니다. 저는 다른 항공편을 탈 수밖에 없었고, 그럼에도 그것은 제가 회의를 놓치게 하였습니다. 이로써, 저는 제 원래 티켓에 대해 환불을 요청하고 싶습니다. 시간 내주셔서 감사합니다.
Kathy Owens 드림

[해설] 항공사에 구매했던 비행기 티켓의 환불을 요청하는 글이다. I would like to ask for a refund for my original ticket에서 '원래 구매했던 티켓에 대한 환불을 요청한다'고 했으므로, 정답은 ② '구매했던 비행기 티켓의 환불을 요청하려고'이다.

[오답 분석] ①, ④, ⑤은 글과 관련 없는 내용이다. ③은 '항공편 지연'을 다루고 있지만 승객들에게 사과하기 위한 글이 아니기 때문에 오답이다.

02
정답 ③

[지문분석]

Lauren looked at the map.
Lauren은 지도를 보았다

She couldn't understand it.
그녀는 그것을 이해할 수 없었다

Had she taken a wrong turn / somewhere along the hiking trail?
그녀는 길을 잘못 든 것일까 / 등산로 어딘가에서

She had been searching for the waterfall / for hours now / and, / according to the map, / she should be there.
그녀는 폭포를 찾고 있었다 / 지금 몇 시간째 / 그리고 / 지도에 따르면 / 그녀는 그곳(폭포)에 있어야 했다

She checked the map again / and walked in the other direction.
그녀는 지도를 다시 확인했다 / 그리고 다른 방향으로 걸어갔다

She had always been able to / get around the mountains, / so she didn't know / why she was having trouble now.
그녀는 항상 ~해왔다 / 산행을 완주하다 / 그래서 그녀는 몰랐다 / 왜 그녀가 지금 어려움을 겪고 있는지

★ She began to wonder / if the map was wrong, / when she heard / the loud snap of a tree branch.
그녀는 궁금해하기 시작했다 / 지도가 잘못된 것인지 / 그때 그녀는 들었다 / 나뭇가지가 탁 부러지는 큰 소리를

She looked around / but saw nothing.
그녀는 주위를 둘러보았다 / 하지만 아무것도 보이지 않았다

Suddenly, / she heard a low growl.
갑자기 / 그녀는 낮은 으르렁거리는 소리를 들었다

Her heart started pounding / and she could feel herself shaking.
그녀의 가슴이 쿵쿵 뛰기 시작했다 / 그리고 그녀는 자신이 떨고 있는 것을 느낄 수 있었다

★ 독해가 쉬워지는 구문 풀이

She began to wonder [if the map was wrong], when she heard the
　　　　　　　　　　　　간접 의문문
loud snap of a tree branch.

⇨ [ ]는 if나 whether로 시작되는 간접 의문문이며, 이때 어순은 <if/whether + 주어 + 동사>가 된다.

어휘 take a wrong turn 길을 잘못 들다 somewhere 어딘가에서
waterfall 폭포 direction 방향 wonder 궁금해하다 snap 탁 부러지는 소리
branch 가지 growl 으르렁거리는 소리 pound 쿵쿵 뛰다 shake 떨다
선택지 gloomy 우울한 irritated 짜증이 난 eager 열심인
confused 혼란스러워하는 satisfied 만족스러워하는 confident 자신 있는

해석 Lauren은 지도를 보았다. 그녀는 그것을 이해할 수 없었다. 그녀는 등산로 어딘가에서 길을 잘못 든 것일까? 그녀는 지금 몇 시간째 폭포를 찾고 있었고, 지도에 따르면, 그녀는 그곳(폭포)에 있어야 했다. 그녀는 지도를 다시 확인했고 다른 방향으로 걸어갔다. 그녀는 항상 산행을 완주해와서, 그녀는 왜 그녀가 지금 어려움을 겪고 있는지 몰랐다. 지도가 잘못된 것인지 궁금해하기 시작하던 그때, 그녀는 나뭇가지가 탁 부러지는 큰 소리를 들었다. 그녀는 주위를 둘러보았지만 아무것도 보이지 않았다. 갑자기, 그녀는 낮은 으르렁거리는 소리를 들었다. 그녀의 가슴이 쿵쿵 뛰기 시작했고 그녀는 자신이 떨고 있는 것을 느낄 수 있었다.

① 우울한　　　　　→ 짜증이 난
② 몹시 화가 난　　→ 열심인
③ 혼란스러워하는 → 겁먹은
④ 만족스러워하는 → 자신 있는
⑤ 신이 난　　　　→ 불안한

해설 Lauren이 등산 도중 길을 잘못 들어서 혼란스러워하다가, 나중에는 으르렁거리는 소리를 듣고 겁먹는 과정을 묘사하고 있는 글이다. 글의 중반부의 she didn't know why she was having trouble now를 통해 Lauren이 혼란스러워하는 것을 알 수 있고, 글의 후반부에서 Her heart started pounding and she could feel herself shaking을 통해 겁먹은 것을 알 수 있으므로, Lauren의 심경 변화로 가장 적절한 것은 ③ confused(혼란스러워하는) → frightened(겁먹은)이다.

오답분석 ①의 gloomy와 irritated, ②의 furious와 eager, ④의 satisfied와 confident, ⑤의 excited는 글 속의 상황에서 느낄 심경으로 적절하지 않다.

지문분석

Millions of people / all over the world / are becoming more and more concerned / about climate change.
수백만 명의 사람들이 / 전 세계 / 점점 더 관심을 갖고 있다 / 기후 변화에 대해

Unfortunately, / among developed countries, / only a few / are taking the necessary steps / against this issue.
안타깝게도 / 선진국들 중에서 / 몇몇만이 / 필요한 조치를 취하고 있다 / 이 문제에 대해

And / only one country has passed a policy / that aims to reduce / the country's carbon emissions / to 70 percent below its 1990 levels / by 2030.
그리고 / 오직 한 국가만이 정책을 통과시켰다 / 줄이는 것을 목표로 하는 / 그 나라의 탄소 배출량을 / 1990년 수치의 70퍼센트 이하로 / 2030년까지

★ Thus, / it is important / for countries and political leaders / to take more aggressive action.
따라서 / ~이 중요하다 / 국가와 정치 지도자들이 / 더 적극적인 조치를 취하는 것이

Experts say / that significant action needs to be adopted.
전문가들은 말한다 / 의미 있는 조치가 도입되어야 한다고

Rather than making promises / to try, / enacting a law is a powerful move / that can make a real difference.
약속을 하는 것보다는 / 노력하겠다는 / 법률을 제정하는 것이 강력한 움직임이다 / 실질적인 차이를 만들 수 있는

Hopefully, / making more powerful policies / will soon become the norm / rather than the exception.
바라건대 / 더 영향력 있는 정책을 만드는 것이 / 곧 표준이 될 것이다 / 예외가 아니라

★ 독해가 쉬워지는 구문 풀이

Thus, **it** is important for countries and political leaders [to take
　　　가주어
more aggressive action].
　　진짜 주어(to부정사구)

⇨ 주어가 '더 적극적인 조치를 취하는 것'이라는 의미로 길기 때문에, 긴 주어를 대신해서 가주어 역할을 할 수 있는 it으로 문장을 시작했다.

어휘 climate change 기후 변화 developed country 선진국
aim ~을 목표로 하다 carbon emission 탄소 배출(량)
aggressive 적극적인, 공격적인 action 조치, 행동 adopt 도입하다, 채택하다
enact 제정하다, 시행하다 norm 표준, 규범

해석 전 세계 수백만 명의 사람들이 기후 변화에 대해 점점 더 관심을 갖고 있다. 안타깝게도, 선진국들 중에서 몇몇만이 이 문제에 대해 필요한 조치를 취하고 있다. 그리고 오직 한 국가만이 2030년까지 그 나라의 탄소 배출량을 1990년 수치의 70퍼센트 이하로 줄이는 것을 목표로 하는 정책을 통과시켰다. [주제문] 따라서, 국가와 정치 지도자들이 더 적극적인 조치를 취하는 것이 중요하다 전문가들은 의미 있는 조치가 도입되어야 한다고 말한다. 노력하겠다는 약속을 하는 것보다는, 법률을 제정하는 것이 실질적인 차이를 만들 수 있는 강력한 움직임이다. 바라건대, 더 영향력 있는 정책을 만드는 것이 예외가 아니라 곧 표준이 될 것이다.

해설 국가와 정치 지도자들이 기후 변화에 대해 더 적극적이고 의미 있는 조치를 취해야 한다는 내용의 글이므로, 이 글의 요지로 가장 적절한 것은 ③ '기후 변화에 대응하기 위한 조치는 더욱 강력해져야 한다.'이다.

오답분석 ①, ②은 글의 핵심 소재 '기후 변화'를 활용하여 혼동을 주는 오답이다. ④은 글에서 언급된 '환경 정책'을 활용하여 혼동을 주는 오답이다. ⑤은 글의 핵심 소재 '탄소 배출'을 활용하여 혼동을 주는 오답이다.

04
정답 ③

It's natural / for individuals / to want to avoid conflict.
~은 자연스러운 것이다 / 사람들이 / 갈등을 회피하고 싶어 하는 것은

After all, / it can be / uncomfortable and awkward.
어쨌든 / 이것은 ~할 수 있다 / 불편하고 곤란한

But / clashing with other people / can benefit / rather than harm relationships.
그러나 / 다른 사람들과 부딪치는 것은 / 도움이 될 수도 있다 / 관계를 해치기보다 오히려

If you as an individual / disagree with someone / you know, / it might be better / to explain your perspective / on the situation.
만약 당신이 개인으로서 ~하다면 / 어떤 사람과 의견이 맞지 않다 / 당신이 아는 / 더 나을 수도 있다 / 당신의 관점을 설명하는 것이 / 그 상황에 대한

This is because / suppressing your thoughts, feelings, and opinions / in order to please someone else / can lead to / a buildup of angry feelings and an unhealthy relationship / over time.
이는 ~이기 때문이다 / 당신의 생각, 감정, 그리고 의견을 억누르는 것이 / 어떤 다른 사람을 만족시키기 위해 / ~으로 이어질 수 있다 / 화난 감정과 건강하지 못한 관계의 축적 / 시간이 흐르면서

★ Instead, / people should practice effective conflict resolution, / in which each person is open / and willing to hear their counterpart out.
대신에 / 사람들은 효과적인 갈등 해결 방법을 연습해야 한다 / 각자가 마음을 여는 / 그리고 그들의 상대의 말을 끝까지 들어주려는

This can result in / people understanding one another better / in the long run.
이것은 ~하는 결과로 이어질 수 있다 / 사람들이 서로를 더 잘 이해하다 / 장기적으로

Therefore, / accepting / that conflict occurs / doesn't mean / a relationship is doomed to fail; / in fact, / it is actually a necessary evil.
따라서 / 받아들이는 것은 / 갈등이 생긴다는 점을 / 의미하지 않는다 / 관계가 실패할 수밖에 없는 운명이라는 것을 / 사실 / 이것은 필요악이다

★ 독해가 쉬워지는 구문 풀이

Instead, people should practice effective conflict resolution, **in which** each person is open and willing to hear their counterpart out.
　　　　　　주어　　　　동사　　　　　　보어

⇨ 관계사 뒤에 완전한 절(each person ~ out)이 왔으므로 완전한 절을 이끄는 '전치사 + 관계대명사' 형태의 in which가 쓰였다.

어휘 awkward 곤란한 clash 부딪치다 perspective 관점 suppress 억누르다
buildup 축적 resolution 해결 방법
hear somebody out ~의 말을 끝까지 들어주다
counterpart 상대, 대응 관계에 있는 사람 doomed to ~할 수밖에 없는 운명인
선택지 temporary 일시적인 permanent 영원한 farewell 이별, 작별
settle 해결하다

해석 사람들이 갈등을 회피하고 싶어 하는 것은 자연스러운 것이다. 어쨌든, 이것은 불편하고 곤란할 수 있다. 주제문 그러나 다른 사람들과 부딪치는 것은 관계를 해치기보다 오히려 도움이 될 수도 있다. 만약 당신이 개인으로서 당신이 아는 어떤 사람과 의견이 맞지 않다면, 그 상황에 대한 당신의 관점을 설명하는 것이 더 나을 수도 있다. 이는 어떤 다른 사람을 만족시키기 위해 당신의 생각, 감정, 그리고 의견을 억누르는 것이 시간이 흐르면서 화난 감정과 건강하지 못한 관계의 축적으로 이어질 수 있기 때문이다. 대신에, 사람들은 각자가 마음을 열고 그들의 상대의 말을 끝까지 들어주려는 효과적인 갈등 해결 방법을 연습해야 한다. 이것은 장기적으로 사람들이 서로를 더 잘 이해하는 결과로 이어질 수 있다. 따라서, 갈등이 생긴다는 점을 받아들이는 것은 관계가 실패할 수밖에 없는 운명이라는 것을 의미하지 않으며, 사실, 이것은 필요악이다.

① 약점을 노출시키는 부정적인 사건
② 실패로 이어지는 일시적인 해결책
③ 영원한 이별을 피하기 위한 뼈아픈 방법
④ 낯선 사람들과 대화를 시작하기 위한 가이드
⑤ 사람들이 갈등을 해결하기 위한 즐거운 방법

해설 갈등은 불편하고 곤란할 수 있으나 관계에 도움이 될 수 있고, 장기적으로 서로를 이해하는 결과로 이어진다고 했으므로, 밑줄 친 a necessary evil(필요악)이 의미하는 바로 가장 적절한 것은 ③ a painful way to avoid permanent farewells(영원한 이별을 피하기 위한 뼈아픈 방법)이다.

오답 분석 ①과 ④은 글에서 언급된 내용이 아니다. ②은 갈등을 해결하려고 하는 것이 장기적으로 사람들이 서로를 더 잘 이해하는 결과가 될 수 있다고 한 글의 내용과 반대되는 내용을 다루고 있으므로 오답이다. ⑤은 글에서 언급된 conflict resolution과 연상되는 내용을 활용하여 혼동을 주는 오답이다.

05
정답 ④

Sports are beneficial / in so many ways, / from improving fitness / to offering individuals a sense of belonging.
스포츠는 유익하다 / 아주 많은 측면에서 / 건강을 증진시키는 것부터 / 사람들에게 소속감을 주는 것까지

★ For adolescents / in particular, / participating in sports / has proven / to be especially advantageous / for learning about peer cooperation.
청소년들에게 / 특히 / 스포츠에 참여하는 것은 / 증명되었다 / 더욱 이롭다고 / 또래와의 협동을 배우는 데

By working with their peers / to overcome challenges / and reducing stress / while doing so, / teenagers who engage in sports / see improvements in their mental health and self-confidence, / which can ultimately reduce their likelihood / of developing anti-social behavior.
또래와 협업함으로써 / 문제를 극복하기 위해 / 그리고 스트레스를 줄이고 / 그러는 동안 / 스포츠에 참여하는 십대들은 / 그들의 정신 건강과 자신감의 향상을 보게 된다 / 이는 궁극적으로 그들의 가능성을 줄일 수 있다 / 반사회적인 행동을 일으킬

In this way, / sports have even been shown / to assist in the fight / against crime / as they encourage adolescents / to spend their time / on the field or court / instead of engaging in illegal acts.
이러한 측면에서 / 스포츠는 심지어 증명되기도 했다 / 싸움에 도움이 된다고 / 범죄와의 / 그것들은 청소년을 ~하도록 장려하기 때문이다 / 그들의 시간을 보내도록 / 경기장이나 코트에서 / 불법 행위에 관여하는 대신에

Hence, / sports are / undoubtedly a useful asset / in youth-crime prevention.
따라서 / 스포츠는 의심할 여지없이 유용한 자산이다 / 청소년 범죄 예방에

★ 독해가 쉬워지는 구문 풀이

For adolescents in particular, participating in sports has **proven** to be especially advantageous for learning about peer cooperation.

⇨ 동사 prove는 '~이 되다, ~임이 드러나다'라는 의미의 2형식 동사이다.

어휘 beneficial 유익한, 이로운 sense of belonging 소속감
adolescent 청소년; 사춘기의 in particular 특히, 특별히 peer 또래, 동료
cooperation 협동, 협력 engage in ~에 참여하다, 종사하다
self-confidence 자신감, 자신 과잉 likelihood 가능성, 가망
anti-social 반사회적인 illegal 불법의, 비합법적인
undoubtedly 의심할 여지없이, 확실히 asset 자산, 유용한 것

해석 스포츠는 건강을 증진시키는 것부터 사람들에게 소속감을 주는 것까지, 아주 많은 측면에서 유익하다. 특히 청소년들에게, 스포츠에 참여하는 것

은 또래와의 협동을 배우는 데 더욱 이롭다고 증명되었다. 문제를 극복하기 위해 또래와 협업하고, 그러는 동안 스트레스를 줄임으로써 스포츠에 참여하는 십대들은 그들의 정신 건강과 자신감의 향상을 보게 되며, 이는 궁극적으로 그들의 반사회적인 행동을 일으킬 가능성을 줄일 수 있다. 이러한 측면에서, 스포츠는 청소년이 불법 행위에 관여하는 대신에 경기장이나 코트에서 그들의 시간을 보내도록 장려하기 때문에, 심지어 범죄와의 싸움에 도움이 된다고 증명되기도 했다. 〔주제문〕 따라서 스포츠는 의심할 여지없이 청소년 범죄 예방에 유용한 자산이다.

① 스포츠를 하는 것: 일부에겐 좋지만, 모두에게는 아니다
② 스포츠가 자신감에 주는 영향
③ 신체 회복 방법으로서의 스포츠
④ 스포츠: 청소년 범죄를 막는 해답
⑤ 팀 스포츠: 불법 행위의 숨겨진 원인

〔해설〕 청소년들이 스포츠에 참여하는 것은 또래와의 협업을 통해 스트레스를 줄이고 정신 건강과 자신감을 개선시키며, 심지어 청소년 범죄 예방에도 도움이 된다는 내용의 글이므로, 글의 제목으로 가장 적절한 것은 ④ Sports: The Key to Stopping Youth Crime(스포츠: 청소년 범죄를 막는 해답)이다.

〔오답분석〕 ①, ③은 글의 핵심 소재 중 하나인 '스포츠'만을 활용해 혼동을 주는 오답이다. ②은 글의 일부만을 다루는 지엽적 소재인 self-confidence를 활용하여 혼동을 주는 오답이다. ⑤은 스포츠가 불법 행위를 막는다는 글의 주제와 반대되는 내용이기 때문에 오답이다.

06
정답 ③

지문분석

The above charts show / the number of male and female deaths / caused by cancer, diabetes, asthma, or accidents.
위 도표는 보여준다 / 남성과 여성의 사망자 수를 / 암, 당뇨병, 천식, 또는 사고로 인한

① In both male and female deaths, / cancer was the largest cause of death / and accounted for / more than 75% of deaths each.
남성과 여성의 사망자 수 모두에서 / 암이 가장 큰 사망 원인이었다 / 그리고 차지했다 / 각 죽음의 75% 이상을

② ★ The percentage of deaths caused by accidents / exceeded / that of deaths caused by diabetes / for males.
사고로 인한 사망률은 / ~보다 컸다 / 당뇨병으로 인한 사망률 / 남성의

③ The percentage of death caused by asthma / was the lowest for females, / though it was still three times higher than(→ twice as high as) / asthma deaths in males.
천식으로 인한 사망률은 / 여성에게 있어 가장 낮았다 / 하지만 여전히 ~보다 3배가 높지만(→ 2배가 높지만) / 남성의 천식 사망률

④ Compared to that of females, / there were fewer deaths caused by diabetes / but more death caused by cancer / in males.
여성의 것에 비해 / 당뇨병으로 인한 사망은 더 적었다 / 하지만 암으로 인한 사망은 더 많았다 / 남성이

⑤ The number of deaths / caused by accidents and diabetes / combined / was still less than the deaths caused by cancer / for both males and females.
사망자 수 / 사고와 당뇨병으로 인한 / 합친 것은 / 여전히 암으로 인한 사망보다 적었다 / 남성과 여성 모두에서

★ 독해가 쉬워지는 구문 풀이

The percentage of deaths caused by accidents exceeded **that** of
        주어   동사
deaths caused by diabetes for males.
▷ 지시대명사 that은 앞의 The percentage를 가리키며, 동일한 명사의 반복을 피하기 위해 사용되었다.

〔어휘〕 cancer 암 diabetes 당뇨병 asthma 천식 accident 사고
account for 차지하다 exceed ~보다 크다, 초과하다 combine 합치다

〔해석〕

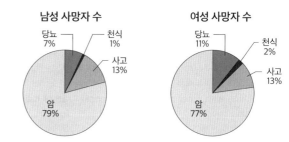

남성 사망자 수 / 여성 사망자 수

위 도표는 암, 당뇨병, 천식, 또는 사고로 인한 남성과 여성의 사망자 수를 보여준다. ① 남성과 여성의 사망자 수 모두에서, 암이 가장 큰 사망 원인이었고 각 죽음의 75% 이상을 차지했다. ② 사고로 인한 남성의 사망률은 당뇨병으로 인한 사망률보다 컸다. ③ 천식으로 인한 사망률은 여성에게 있어 가장 낮았지만, 여전히 남성의 천식 사망률보다 3배가 높았다(→ 2배가 높았다). ④ 여성의 것에 비해 당뇨병으로 인한 사망은 남성이 더 적었지만 암으로 인한 사망은 남성이 더 많았다. ⑤ 사고와 당뇨병으로 인한 사망자 수를 합친 것은 남성과 여성 모두에서 여전히 암으로 인한 사망보다 적었다.

〔해설〕 도표의 제목과 글의 도입부를 통해 이 도표가 암, 당뇨병, 천식, 또는 사고로 인한 남성과 여성 사망자 수에 관한 것임을 알 수 있다. 이 글에서는 ①의 the largest와 more than 75%, ②의 exceeded, ③의 the lowest와 three times higher, ④의 fewer와 more, ⑤의 still less than이 도표 내의 수치를 올바르게 설명하고 있는지 확인해야 한다. 천식으로 인한 여성의 사망률은 2%이고 남성의 사망률은 1%이므로, 천식으로 인한 여성의 사망률이 남성의 사망률보다 3배가 아닌 2배가 높기 때문에 도표의 내용과 일치하지 않는 것은 ③이다.

〔오답분석〕 ①은 남성과 여성 둘 다 각각 79%, 77%로 암이 가장 큰 사망 원인이었고 이는 75% 이상이므로 도표의 내용과 일치한다. ②은 사고로 인한 남성의 사망률은 13%로 당뇨병으로 인한 사망률 7%보다 크므로 도표의 내용과 일치한다. ④은 당뇨병으로 인한 사망은 여성과 남성 각각 11%, 7%로 여성이 남성보다 높고, 암으로 인한 사망은 여성과 남성 각각 77%, 79%로 남성이 여성보다 높으므로 도표의 내용과 일치한다. ⑤은 사고와 당뇨병으로 인한 사망자 수를 합친 것은 남성과 여성 각각 20%, 24%이며, 이는 암으로 인한 사망보다 적으므로 도표의 내용과 일치한다.

07
정답 ③

지문분석

Studio Rock's Beginner Pottery
Studio Rock의 초보자용 도예

If you're interested in / picking up a new hobby, / look no further than / our weekend pottery workshop / for beginners.
만약 당신이 ~하는 데 관심이 있다면 / 새로운 취미를 만드는 / 다른 곳 말고 바로 ~을 찾아주세요 / 저희의 주말 도예 공방을 / 초보자를 위한

It's the perfect way / to meet new people and unwind / after a long week / at work!
이것은 최고의 방법입니다 / 새로운 사람들을 만나고 긴장을 풀 / 길었던 한 주의 / 직장에서의

About classes:
수업과 관련해서

-Classes take place / on Saturdays and Sundays.
수업은 열립니다 / 토요일과 일요일마다

-Two classes each day: / Morning and Afternoon
하루에 2회 수업 / 오전과 오후

-$80 / per class / $290 / for 1 course (4 classes)
80달러 / 수업당 / 290달러 / 한 코스(4회 수업)에

*All materials and tools / will be provided.
모든 재료와 도구는 / 제공될 것입니다

Learn:
배우는 것

-Pottery wheel / (electric and manual)
도예 물레 / (전기 및 손)

-Painting
도색

-Decorating
장식

-Hand sculpting
손 빚음

★ You can register / online at our website / or call 555-0123 / between 8 a.m. and 5 p.m.
여러분은 등록하실 수 있습니다 / 온라인으로 저희 웹 사이트에서 / 또는 555-0123으로 전화를 주셔도 됩니다 / 오전 8시에서 오후 5시 사이에

*Class sizes are kept / to a maximum of five, / so sign up early / to participate.
수업 규모는 제한됩니다 / 최대 5명으로 / 그러므로 일찍 등록하세요 / 참여하려면

★ 독해가 쉬워지는 구문 풀이

You can [①register online at our website] or [②call 555-0123
　　　　　동사원형　　　　　　　　　　　　　　　동사원형
between 8 a.m. and 5 p.m].

⇨ [①]과 [②]는 등위접속사 and로 연결되어 병렬 구조를 이룬다. 따라서 조동사 can 뒤에는 동사원형(register, call)이 쓰였다.

[어휘] beginner 초보자　pottery 도예　workshop 공방, 작업장
unwind 긴장을 풀다　take place 열리다　wheel 물레
electric 자동의　manual 손으로 하는, 수동의　sculpt 빚다, 형태를 만들다
register 등록하다　sign up 등록하다

[해석]
Studio Rock의 초보자용 도예

만약 당신이 새로운 취미를 만드는 데 관심이 있다면, 다른 곳 말고 바로 초보자를 위한 저희의 주말 도예 공방을 찾아 주세요. 이것은 새로운 사람들을 만나고, 직장에서의 길었던 한 주의 긴장을 풀 최고의 방법입니다!

수업과 관련해서:
- 수업은 토요일과 일요일마다 열립니다.
- 하루에 2회 수업: 오전과 오후
- 수업당 80달러 / 한 코스(4회 수업)에 290달러
*모든 재료와 도구는 제공될 것입니다.

배우는 것:
- 도예 물레 (전기 및 손)
- 도색
- 장식
- 손 빚음

여러분은 저희 웹 사이트에서 온라인으로 등록하실 수 있고, 또는 오전 8시에서 오후 5시 사이에 555-0123으로 전화를 주셔도 됩니다. *수업 규모는 최대 5명으로 제한되므로, 참여하려면 일찍 등록하세요.

[해설] $290 for 1 course (4 classes)를 통해 한 코스는 4회 수업으로 이루어져 있다는 것을 알 수 있으므로, 글의 내용과 일치하는 것은 ③ '전체 한 코스는 4회 수업으로 이루어진다.'이다.

---

①은 pottery workshop for beginners라고 했으므로 글의 내용과 일치하지 않는다. ②은 Classes take place on Saturdays and Sundays라고 했으므로 글의 내용과 일치하지 않는다. ④은 Learn: Pottery wheel (electric and manual)이라고 했으므로 글의 내용과 일치하지 않는다. ⑤은 Class sizes are kept to a maximum of five라고 했으므로 글의 내용과 일치하지 않는다.

08　　정답 ③

[지문분석]

Although chimpanzees and bonobos are very ① closely related, / the fact / that they exhibit different behavioral traits / suggests / that their cognitive skills differ as well.
침팬지와 보노보가 매우 가까운 동족이더라도 / ~라는 사실은 / 그들이 다른 행동 특성을 보여준다는 / 나타낸다 / 그들의 인지 능력 또한 다르다는 것을

Because chimpanzees have the ability / to craft simple tools / to assist in ② their foraging, / for instance, / it stands to reason / that they understand cause and effect.
침팬지들은 능력이 있으므로 / 단순한 도구를 만들 / 그들의 수렵 채집을 도울 / 예를 들어 / ~은 누가 봐도 분명하다 / 그들이 원인과 결과를 이해한다는 것

In other words, / they comprehend / that using tools / such as sticks / ③ make(→ makes) a task easier.
다시 말해서 / 그들은 이해한다 / 도구를 이용하는 것이 ~라는 것을 / 막대기와 같은 / 일을 더 쉽게 만든다

Bonobos, / on the other hand, / ④ are believed to have a theory of mind, / which means / they can identify different feelings in others / and act accordingly.
보노보들은 / 반면에 / 마음 이론을 가진다고 여겨진다 / 그런데 이것은 의미한다 / 그들이 다른 개체의 여러 가지 감정을 분간할 수 있다는 것을 / 그리고 그에 따라 행동한다는 것을

★ Much of / what leads researchers to this conclusion / is ⑤ how bonobos interact / with one another.
~의 상당 부분은 / 연구원들을 이러한 결론으로 이끈 것 / 보노보들이 상호작용하는 방법에 있다 / 서로

They are well-known / for providing comfort / to others / and, unlike chimpanzees, / resolving conflicts / with affection rather than aggression.
그들은 잘 알려져 있다 / 위로를 해주는 것으로 / 다른 개체에게 / 그리고 침팬지들과 달리 / 갈등을 해결하는 것으로 / 공격보다는 애정으로

★ 독해가 쉬워지는 구문 풀이

Much of **what** leads researchers to this conclusion is how
　　　　　　주어　　　　　　　　　　　　　　　　　　　　동사
bonobos interact with one another

⇨ 관계대명사 what은 선행사를 포함하며, the thing which로 바꿔 쓸 수 있다.

[어휘] bonobo 보노보(난쟁이 침팬지)　related 동족인, 관련 있는
cognitive 인지의, 인식의　craft 만들다　foraging 수렵 채집
it stands to reason 누가 봐도 분명하다, 당연하다　identify 분간하다, 알아보다
accordingly 그에 따라, 따라서　interact 상호작용하다　one another 서로
affection 애정, 애착　aggression 공격, 침략

[해석] [주제문] 침팬지와 보노보가 매우 가까운 동족이더라도, 그들이 다른 행동 특성을 보여준다는 사실은 그들의 인지 능력 또한 다르다는 것을 나타낸다. 예를 들어, 침팬지들은 그들의 수렵 채집을 도울 단순한 도구를 만들 능력이 있으므로, 그들이 원인과 결과를 이해한다는 것은 누가 봐도 분명하다. 다시 말해서, 그들은 막대기와 같은 도구를 이용하는 것이 일을 더 쉽게 만든다는 것을 이해한다. 반면에, 보노보들은 마음 이론을 가진다고 여겨지는데, 이것은 그들이 다른 개체의 여러 가지 감정을 분간하고 그에 따라 행동할 수 있다는 것을 의미한다. 연구원들을 이러한 결론으로 이끈 것의 상당 부분은 보노보들이 서로 상호작용하는 방법에 있다. 그들은 다

른 개체에게 위로를 해주고, 침팬지들과 달리 공격보다는 애정으로 갈등을 해결하는 것으로 잘 알려져 있다.

[해설] 동명사 주어(using)는 단수 취급하고 동사 자리에 단수동사가 와야하므로 ③의 make를 makes로 고쳐야 한다. 참고로, 주어와 동사 사이의 수식어구(such as sticks)는 동사의 수 결정에 영향을 주지 않는다.

[오답분석] ①은 분사를 수식할 수 있는 것은 부사이므로 과거분사 related 앞에 부사 closely를 사용한 것은 어법상 적절하다. ②은 대명사가 지시하는 명사가 복수명사 chimpanzees이므로 복수대명사 their를 사용한 것은 어법상 적절하다. ④은 주어(Bonobos)와 동사가 '보노보들은 여겨진다'라는 의미의 수동 관계이므로 be동사(are)와 함께 수동태를 만드는 과거분사 believed를 사용한 것은 어법상 적절하다. ⑤은 완전한 절을 이끌며 be동사(is)의 보어 자리에 올 수 있는 의문사 how를 사용한 것은 어법상 적절하다.

09
정답 ④

[지문분석]

It's no coincidence / that a bad code in a computer / is called a virus.
~은 우연의 일치가 아니다 / 컴퓨터에 있는 나쁜 코드가 / 바이러스라고 불린다

Just like viruses infecting people, / the electronic variety infects computers.
사람들을 감염시키는 바이러스처럼 / 전자로 된 종류도 컴퓨터를 감염시킨다

A computer virus needs / a file or document / where it can "live."
컴퓨터 바이러스는 ~을 필요로 한다 / 파일이나 문서를 / 그것이 "살 수 있는"

It is ① similar to / how a human virus requires a host / or else it will die.
그것은 ~과 비슷하다 / 인간의 바이러스가 숙주를 필요로 하는 방식 / 그렇지 않으면 그것은 죽을 것이다

An external element, / such as double-clicking a file, / can easily ② awake a computer virus.
외부 요소는 / 파일을 더블 클릭하는 것과 같은 / 쉽게 컴퓨터 바이러스를 깨울 수 있다

However, / until then, / the virus remains ③ inactive.
하지만 / 그때까지 / 바이러스는 활동하지 않는 상태로 남아 있다

Sometimes, / a computer virus can be ④ found(→ hidden) for months / because it doesn't do anything.
때때로 / 컴퓨터 바이러스는 몇 달 동안 발견될(→ 숨어 있을) 수 있다 / 그것이 아무것도 하지 않기 때문에

★ You have no idea / it is in your computer, / concealed or buried / in a file somewhere.
당신은 알 수가 없다 / 그것이 당신의 컴퓨터에 있는지 / 숨겨져 있거나 묻혀 있는지 / 파일 어딘가에

Once it is initiated, / however, / ⑤ harmful issues start to show up / on your system.
일단 그것이 발동되면 / 그러나 / 유해한 문제들이 나타나기 시작한다 / 당신의 시스템에

For instance, / a really bad virus / can steal your personal information / or delete everything on the computer.
예를 들어 / 정말 심각한 바이러스는 / 당신의 개인 정보를 훔칠 수 있다 / 또는 컴퓨터에 있는 모든 것을 삭제한다

★ 독해가 쉬워지는 구문 풀이

You have no idea [(that) it is in your computer, concealed or buried
　　　　　　　　　　　동격의 that절
in a file somewhere].

⇨ [ ]는 명사 idea를 수식하는 동격절이며, 동격의 접속사 that이 생략되었다.

[어휘] coincidence 우연의 일치 infect 감염시키다 variety 종류, 다양성
document 문서, 서류 host 숙주 external 외부의 element 요소

awake 깨우다 inactive 활동하지 않는 conceal 숨기다, 감추다
bury 묻다, 숨기다 initiate 발동하다, 시작하다 show up 나타나다
personal information 개인 정보

[해석] **[주제문]** 컴퓨터에 있는 나쁜 코드가 바이러스라고 불리는 것은 우연의 일치가 아니다. 사람들을 감염시키는 바이러스처럼, 전자로 된 종류(바이러스)도 컴퓨터를 감염시킨다. 컴퓨터 바이러스는 그것이 "살 수 있는" 파일이나 문서를 필요로 한다. 그것은 인간의 바이러스가 숙주를 필요로 하는 방식과 ① 비슷한데 그렇지 않으면 그것은 죽을 것이다. 파일을 더블 클릭하는 것과 같은 외부 요소는 쉽게 컴퓨터 바이러스를 ② 깨울 수 있다. 하지만, 그때까지, 바이러스는 ③ 활동하지 않는 상태로 남아 있다. 때때로, 컴퓨터 바이러스는 아무것도 하지 않기 때문에 몇 달 동안 ④ 발견될 (→ 숨어 있을) 수 있다. 당신은 그것이 당신의 컴퓨터에 있는지, 파일 어딘가에 숨겨져 있거나 묻혀 있는지 알 수가 없다. 그러나, 일단 그것이 발동되면, 당신의 시스템에 ⑤ 유해한 문제들이 나타나기 시작한다. 예를 들어, 정말 심각한 바이러스는 당신의 개인 정보를 훔치거나 컴퓨터에 있는 모든 것을 삭제할 수 있다.

[해설] 컴퓨터 바이러스는 아무것도 하지 않기 때문에 때때로 몇 달 동안 "숨어 있을" 수 있다는 맥락이 되어야 하므로, ④의 found를 hidden과 같은 단어로 바꾸어야 문맥상 적절하다.

[오답분석] ①은 인간의 바이러스와 마찬가지로 숙주를 필요로 하고 (숙주가) 아니면 죽을 것이라는 점에서 컴퓨터 바이러스가 인간의 바이러스와 "비슷하다"는 문맥이 되어야 하므로 similar가 오는 것이 적절하다. ②은 파일을 더블 클릭하는 것과 같은 외부 요소가 쉽게 바이러스를 "깨울" 수 있다는 문맥이 되어야 하므로 awake가 오는 것이 적절하다. ③은 외부 요소가 바이러스를 깨울 때까지 바이러스는 "활동하지 않는" 상태로 남아있다는 문맥이 되어야 하므로 inactive가 오는 것이 적절하다. ⑤은 일단 바이러스가 발동되면 개인 정보를 훔치거나 컴퓨터에 있는 모든 것들을 삭제하는 등 당신의 시스템에 "유해한" 문제들이 나타나기 시작한다는 문맥이 되어야 하므로 harmful이 오는 것이 적절하다.

10
정답 ⑤

[지문분석]

We all have / a constant stream of thoughts / going through our head, / or a personal narrative we use / to give ourselves instructions / or make observations / about our surroundings.
우리는 모두 지닌다 / 끊임없는 생각의 흐름을 / 우리 머릿속을 지나가는 / 또는 우리가 사용하는 개인적인 서술 기법을 / 스스로에게 지시하기 위해 / 또는 관찰하기 위해 / 우리의 주변을

If what we tell ourselves is good, / this inner monologue, / known as self-talk, / can cheer us on / and have such a positive effect / that **our ability to function** / **improves**.
만약 우리가 스스로에게 말하는 것이 긍정적이라면 / 이 내적 독백은 / 자기대화라고 알려진 / 우리를 북돋아 줄 수 있다 / 그리고 매우 긍정적인 효과를 지녀서 / **제대로 기능하기 위한 우리의 능력이** / **향상된다**

For instance, / athletes / who engage in positive self-talk / can put themselves / in the right mental state / before a game.
예를 들어 / 운동선수들 / 긍정적인 자기대화를 하는 / 스스로를 만들 수 있다 / 적절한 정신 상태로 / 경기 전에

★ Any anxiety / they feel / about failing / to live up to the crowd's expectations / can lead to a very real inability / to perform properly.
어떠한 불안이라도 / 그들이 느끼는 / ~을 못할 것에 대해 / 군중의 기대에 부응하는 것 / 정말 실제적인 무능력으로 이어질 수 있다 / 제대로 경기하기에

But / engaging in self-talk / that calms, motivates, helps them focus, / and reminds them of techniques / they should use / can be incredibly reassuring.
하지만 / 자기대화를 하는 것은 / 그들을 진정시키고 동기 부여를 하고 그들이 집중하도록 돕는 / 그리고 기술을 상기시키는 / 그들이 이용해야 하는 / 용기를 엄청나게 북돋을 수 있다

This can translate to / overcoming any pre-game jitters / they might have / so they can play / to the best of their abilities.
이는 ~으로 바뀔 수 있다 / 경기 전의 어떠한 초조함도 극복하는 / 그들이 가지고 있을지 모르는 / 그래서 경기를 할 수 있는 / 그들의 힘이 닿는 데까지

★ 독해가 쉬워지는 구문 풀이

Any **anxiety** [they feel about failing to live up to the crowd's
<u>주어</u>
expectations] <u>can lead</u> to a very real inability to perform properly.
<u>동사</u>

⇨ [ ]는 선행사 anxiety를 수식하는 관계절로 뒤에 목적격 관계대명사 that 또는 which가 생략되어 있다.

어휘 narrative 서술(기법), 서사, 이야기 inner monologue 내적 독백
self-talk 자기대화 cheer somebody on ~를 북돋아 주다, ~를 응원하다
live up to ~에 부응하다 inability 무능력
incredibly 엄청나게, 믿을 수 없을 정도로 reassuring 용기를 북돋는, 안심시키는
translate (다른 형태로) 바뀌다, 바꾸다
to the best of one's ability ~의 힘이 닿는 데까지
선택지 harshly 엄격히, 엄하게 perception 인식, 자각
function (제대로) 기능하다

해석 우리는 모두 우리 머릿속을 지나가는 끊임없는 생각의 흐름, 또는 스스로에게 지시하거나 우리의 주변을 관찰하기 위해 사용하는 개인적인 서술 기법을 지닌다. 주제문 만약 우리가 스스로에게 말하는 것이 긍정적이라면, 자기대화라고 알려진 이 내적 독백은 우리를 북돋아 줄 수 있고 매우 긍정적인 효과를 지녀서 **제대로 기능하기 위한 우리의 능력이 향상된다**. 예를 들어, 긍정적인 자기대화를 하는 운동선수들은 경기 전에 스스로를 적절한 정신 상태로 만들 수 있다. 군중의 기대에 부응하지 못할 것에 대해 그들이 느끼는 어떠한 불안이라도 제대로 경기하기에 정말 실제적인 무능력으로 이어질 수 있다. 하지만 그들을 진정시키고 동기 부여를 하고 그들이 집중하도록 도우며, 그들이 이용해야 하는 기술을 상기시키는 자기대화를 하는 것은 용기를 엄청나게 북돋을 수 있다. 이는 그들이 가지고 있을지 모르는 경기 전의 어떠한 초조함도 극복해서 그들의 힘이 닿는 데까지 경기를 할 수 있는 것으로 바뀔 수 있다.

① 더 건강한 습관이 채택된다
② 우리는 우리의 실패를 덜 엄격하게 평가한다
③ 다른 사람들에 대한 우리의 인식이 바뀐다
④ 의사결정 기술이 향상된다
⑤ 제대로 기능하기 위한 우리의 능력이 향상된다

해설 빈칸 문장은 이 글의 주제문이므로 이를 다시 언급한 문장이나 부연 설명하는 문장을 파악해야 한다. 빈칸 문장에서 자기대화라고 알려진 내적 독백은 우리를 북돋아 줄 수 있고, 긍정적인 효과를 지녀서 '무엇'하다고 하고, 글의 후반에서 운동선수들의 예를 들어서 그들이 자기대화를 하는 것은 용기를 엄청나게 북돋우고 그들의 힘이 닿는 데까지 경기를 할 수 있게 한다고 했다. 따라서 빈칸에는 내적 독백이 우리를 북돋아 주고 긍정적인 효과를 지니므로 "제대로 기능하기 위한 우리의 능력이 향상된다"는 의미가 되는 것이 자연스러우므로 ⑤ our ability to function improves(제대로 기능하기 위한 우리의 능력이 향상된다)가 정답이다.

오답분석 ①의 "더 건강한 습관이 채택된다"와 ②의 "우리가 우리의 실패를 덜 엄격하게 평가한다" 것은 글의 내용과 관련이 없다. ③의 "다른 사람들에 대한 우리의 인식이 바뀐다"는 내용은 글에서 언급되고 있지 않다. ④의 "의사결정 기술이 향상된다"는 것은 글의 내용과 관련이 없다.

지문분석

Considering / how much social media influences / our perceptions, / it's not surprising / that it has a significant impact / on the tourism industry as well.
고려하면 / 소셜 미디어가 얼마나 많이 영향을 미치는지를 / 우리의 인식에 / ~은 놀랍지 않다 / 그것이 상당한 영향을 미친다는 것은 / 관광 산업에도

① Very few people / these days / rely solely on advertisements / or the advice of a travel agent / when planning a trip.
극히 소수의 사람들이 / 오늘날 / 광고에만 온전히 의존한다 / 또는 여행사의 조언에만 / 여행을 계획할 때

② ★ Instead, / most turn to sources / they trust on social media, / like family and friends, / who can provide firsthand advice / on where to go.
대신 / 대부분의 사람들은 출처에 의지한다 / 소셜 미디어상에서 그들이 신뢰하는 / 가족과 친구들 같은 / 직접 경험한 조언을 제공할 수 있는 / 어디로 가야 하는지에 대해

③ By doing so, / travelers can minimize / their risk of making a bad decision.
그렇게 함으로써 / 여행자들은 최소화할 수 있다 / 그들이 잘못된 결정을 내릴 위험을

④ (Some tourist destinations / are only popular at certain times of the year.)
몇몇 관광지들은 / 연중 특정 시기에만 인기가 있다

⑤ The tourism industry / has become increasingly aware of this / in recent years / and is posting / visually engaging content / and hiring influencers / to target potential customers directly.
관광 산업은 / 이 점을 점점 더 인지해 왔다 / 최근 몇 년 사이 / 그리고 게시하고 있다 / 시각적으로 매력적인 콘텐츠를 / 그리고 인플루언서들을 고용하고 있다 / 잠재적인 고객들을 직접적으로 공략하기 위해

★ 독해가 쉬워지는 구문 풀이

Instead, most turn to sources [①they trust on social media], [②like
          <u>주어</u> <u>동사</u>   <u>수식어(관계절)</u>
family and friends] ~

⇨ [①]은 선행사 sources를 수식하는 관계절이며, 목적격 관계대명사가 생략되었다.
⇨ [②]은 sources를 수식하는 전치사구이다.

어휘 significant 상당한 solely 온전히 travel agent 여행사
turn to ~에 의지하다 firsthand 직접 경험한 aware of ~을 인지하는
post 게시하다 engaging 매력적인 target 공략하다

해석 주제문 소셜 미디어가 우리의 인식에 얼마나 많이 영향을 미치는지를 고려하면, 그것이 관광 산업에도 상당한 영향을 미친다는 것은 놀랍지 않다. ① 오늘날 여행을 계획할 때 광고나 여행사의 조언에만 온전히 의존하는 사람들은 극히 소수이다. ② 대신, 대부분의 사람들은 어디로 가야 하는지에 대해 직접 경험한 조언을 제공할 수 있는 가족과 친구들 같은, 소셜 미디어상에서 그들이 신뢰하는 출처에 의지한다. ③ 그렇게 함으로써, 여행자들은 그들이 잘못된 결정을 내릴 위험을 최소화할 수 있다. (④ 몇몇 관광지들은 연중 특정 시기에만 인기가 있다.) ⑤ 관광 산업은 최근 몇 년 사이 이 점을 점점 더 인지해왔으며, 잠재적인 고객들을 직접적으로 공략하기 위해 시각적으로 매력적인 콘텐츠를 게시하고 있고 인플루언서들을 고용하고 있다.

해설 이 글의 주제는 소셜 미디어가 관광 산업에 상당한 영향을 미치고 있으며, 관광 산업은 이 점을 인지하여 잠재적인 고객들을 겨냥한 소셜 미디어상의 마케팅을 하고 있다는 것이다. 대부분의 문장들이 사람들이 여행 관련 정보를 얻기 위해 소셜 미디어에 의지한다는 것, 그리고 관광 산업이 이 점을 어떻게 이용해서 고객들을 공략하는지에 대한 내용으로 주제와 관련 있는데, 몇몇 관광지들은 연중 특정 시기에만 인기가 있다는 내용인 ④은 글의 흐름과 관계 없는 문장이다.

12 정답 ②

지문분석

★ One of the most important but underestimated inventions / is the nail, / which is a necessary component / in constructing furniture and houses.
가장 중요하지만 과소평가된 발명품 중 하나는 / 못이다 / 필수적인 구성 요소인 / 가구와 집을 만드는 데

(A) Our reliance on this method / lessened / once we were able to produce objects / made of metal.
이 방식에 대한 우리의 의존은 / 줄어들었다 / 우리가 물건을 생산할 수 있게 되자마자 / 금속으로 만들어진

Metal pieces could be hammered / on four sides / to form sharpened spikes, or nails.
금속 조각은 망치로 두드려질 수 있었다 / 네 가장자리가 / 날카로운 징, 또는 못의 형태가 되도록

(B) Prior to / the creation of the nail, / these types of structures were built / by interlocking wood / in different patterns / or joining them / with other wooden pieces.
~ 이전에 / 못의 발명 / 이러한 종류의 건축물들은 지어졌다 / 나무를 서로 맞물리게 함으로써 / 서로 다른 패턴으로 / 또는 그것들을 연결하면서 / 다른 나무 조각들과

They relied mainly on tension / to support weight and remain standing.
그것들은 주로 장력에 의존하였다 / 무게를 버티고 계속 서 있기 위해

(C) The nail's sharpened point / allowed it / to be driven through pieces of wood, / joining the pieces together quickly / and with far less difficulty / than before.
뾰족해진 못의 끝은 / ~ 할 수 있게 했다 / 그것이 나무 조각을 뚫고 들어가도록 / 빠르게 조각들을 연결하면서 / 그리고 훨씬 덜 어려운 방식으로 / 이전보다

So, / even though it may appear small and insignificant, / the nail has served societies / throughout the ages / by allowing permanent structures / to be built efficiently.
그래서 / 비록 그것이 작고 사소해 보일지라도 / 못은 사회에 기여해 왔다 / 여러 시대에 걸쳐 / 내구성 있는 건축물들이 ~하게 해줌으로써 / 효율적으로 지어지게

★ 독해가 쉬워지는 구문 풀이

One of the most important but **underestimated** inventions is the
　　　　　　　　　주어
nail, which is a necessary component in constructing furniture and
　　　　보어
houses.

⇨ 수식 받는 명사 inventions와 분사가 '과소평가된 발명품'이라는 의미의 수동 관계이므로 과거분사 underestimated가 쓰였다.

[어휘] underestimated 과소평가된　nail 못, 손톱　component 구성 요소, 부품　construct 만들다　reliance 의존　lessen 줄어들다, 감소하다　sharpen 날카롭게 하다　spike 징, 대못　interlock 서로 맞물리게 하다　insignificant 사소한　permanent 내구성 있는, 영구적인　efficiently 효율적으로

[해석] **[주제문]** 가장 중요하지만 과소평가된 발명품 중 하나는 가구와 집을 만드는 데 필수적인 구성 요소인 못이다.
(B) 못의 발명 이전에, 이러한 종류의 건축물들은 서로 다른 패턴으로 나무를 서로 맞물리게 하거나 그것들을 다른 나무 조각들과 연결하면서 지어졌다. 그것들은 무게를 버티고 계속 서 있기 위해 주로 장력에 의존하였다.
(A) 우리가 금속으로 만들어진 물건을 생산할 수 있게 되자마자 이 방식에 대한 우리의 의존은 줄어들었다. 금속 조각은 날카로운 징, 또는 못의 형태가 되도록 네 가장자리가 망치로 두드려질 수 있었다.
(C) 뾰족해진 못의 끝은 그것이 나무 조각을 뚫고 들어갈 수 있게 하면서, 이전보다 훨씬 덜 어려운 방식으로 빠르게 조각들을 연결했다. 그래서, 못은 비록 그것이 작고 사소해 보일지라도, 내구성 있는 건축물들이 효율적으로 지어지게 해줌으로써 여러 시대에 걸쳐 사회에 기여해왔다.

[해설] 주어진 글은 못이 가구와 집을 만드는 데 필수적인 구성 요소라는 내용이므로, 그 뒤에는 these types of structures(이러한 종류의 건축물들)를 통해 못이 발명되기 전의 가구와 집을 부연 설명하는 (B)가 오는 것이 자연스럽다. (A)의 this method(이 방식)는 (B)의 '나무를 서로 맞물리게 하거나 그것들을 다른 나무 조각들과 연결하는 것'을 가리키므로 (B) 바로 다음에 오는 것이 자연스럽다. (C)는 뾰족해진 못의 끝이 나무 조각들을 뚫고 들어갈 수 있게 한다는 내용이고, (A)의 마지막에서 금속 조각들의 네 가장자리를 망치로 두드려서 날카로운 못을 만들 수 있었다고 했으므로 (C)는 (A) 다음에 오는 것이 적절하다. 따라서 글의 순서로 가장 적절한 것은 ② (B) - (A) - (C)이다.

13 정답 ②

지문분석

Hand gestures play an important role / in communication / by allowing us to express ideas / for which we may not have the right words / at a given time.
손동작은 중요한 역할을 한다 / 의사소통에서 / 우리가 그 생각을 표현할 수 있게 해줌으로써 / ~에 해당하는 적당한 단어가 떠오르지 않을 경우 / 그 순간에

(①) Indeed, / people around the world / regularly depend on / a variety of hand gestures / in everyday interactions.
실제로 / 전 세계 사람들은 / ~에 자주 의존한다 / 다양한 손동작 / 일상적인 상호작용에서

(②) (To illustrate, / they may use three fingers / to quickly signal approval / without saying any words out loud.)
설명하자면 / 그들은 손가락 세 개를 이용할 수 있다 / 빠르게 승인 신호를 보내기 위해 / 어떤 말도 내뱉지 않고

But / care should be taken / to use appropriate gestures / for a particular cultural context.
그러나 / 주의가 기울여져야 한다 / 적절한 손동작을 사용하려면 / 특정 문화적 맥락에서

(③) ★ This is because / just as words carry different meanings / in different cultures, / so too can hand gestures / invite varied interpretations.
이것은 ~이기 때문이다 / 말이 서로 다른 의미를 전하는 만큼이나 / 서로 다른 문화에서 / 손동작도 ~할 수 있다 / 다양한 해석을 불러온다

(④) For instance, / crossing the index and middle fingers / has wildly divergent connotations / depending on / where you do it.
예를 들어 / 검지와 중지를 교차하는 것에는 / 매우 다양한 함의가 있다 / ~에 따라 / 당신이 어디서 그것을 하는지

(⑤) In America, / it is a positive expression / of good luck, / but in Vietnam, / a highly offensive insult!
미국에서 / 이것은 긍정적인 표현이다 / 행운을 비는 / 하지만 베트남에서는 / 매우 불쾌한 모욕이다

★ 독해가 쉬워지는 구문 풀이

This is because just as words carry different meanings in different cultures, [**so too** can hand gestures invite varied interpretations].
　　　　　　　　　　　　　　　　　조동사　　　주어　　　동사

⇨ [ ]는 so too가 '~도 그렇다'라는 의미로 쓰여 절 앞에 나온 도치 구문이다.

해석 손동작은 그 순간에 적당한 단어가 떠오르지 않을 경우 우리가 그 생각을 표현할 수 있게 해줌으로써 의사소통에서 중요한 역할을 한다. 실제로, 전 세계 사람들은 일상적인 상호작용에서 다양한 손동작에 자주 의존한다. (설명하자면, 어떤 말도 내뱉지 않고 빠르게 승인 신호를 보내기 위해 그들은 손가락 세 개를 이용할 수 있다.) 주제문 그러나 특정 문화적 맥락에서 적절한 손동작을 사용하려면 주의가 기울여져야 한다. 이것은 서로 다른 문화에서 말이 서로 다른 의미를 전하는 만큼이나, 손동작도 다양한 해석을 불러올 수 있기 때문이다. 예를 들어, 검지와 중지를 교차하는 것에는 당신이 어디서 그것을 하는지에 따라 매우 다양한 함의가 있다. 미국에서, 이것은 행운을 비는 긍정적인 표현이지만, 베트남에서는, 매우 불쾌한 모욕이다!

해설 주어진 문장의 To illustrate(설명하자면)를 통해 주어진 문장은 앞 문장의 예시를 드는 내용이라는 것을 알 수 있다. ② 앞 문장까지는 의사소통에서 손동작은 중요한 역할을 하며 많은 사람들이 의사소통할 때 다양한 손동작을 빈번하게 사용하고 있다는 내용이고, 주어진 문장은 ① 뒤 문장에서 언급한 다양한 손동작에 대한 예시이므로 ① 뒤 문장과 주어진 문장은 자연스럽게 연결된다. 따라서 주어진 문장이 들어가기에 가장 적절한 곳은 ②이다.

오답분석 ② 앞 문장까지는 손동작이 의사소통에 중요한 역할을 한다는 첫 문장에 대한 부연 설명을 하는 문장이므로 흐름이 자연스럽다. ② 뒤 문장에서는 But을 통해 문화적 맥락을 고려해서 손동작을 사용해야 한다는 내용으로 흐름을 전환하고 있고, ③ 뒤 문장부터는 ② 뒤 문장의 내용에 대한 부연 설명과 예시를 다루고 있으므로 자연스럽게 이어진다.

14 정답 ⑤

지문분석

Research into pitch perception, / or the ability / to detect slight variations / in musical sounds, / was recently conducted / on the Tsimane people, / an indigenous tribe / living in a remote area / of the Bolivian rainforest.
음높이 지각에 대한 연구 / 즉 능력 / 약간의 변화를 감지하는 / 음악적 소리에서 / 최근에 행해졌다 / Tsimane족 사람들을 상대로 / 토착 부족인 / 멀리 떨어진 지역에 사는 / 볼리비아 우림의

★ The researchers wanted to determine / if the Tsimane could recognize the link / between different versions of the same note, / like middle C and high C.
연구자들은 알아내고 싶었다 / Tsimane족이 관계를 인식할 수 있는지 / 같은 음의 서로 다른 버전들 사이의 / 가운데 C음과 높은 C음처럼

By playing Western music, / which is full of such variations, / the researchers determined / that they could not.
서양 음악을 연주하면서 / 그러한 변주가 가득한 / 연구자들은 알아냈다 / 그들이 할 수 없다는 것을

The Tsimane / had never listened to Western music before, / and their own music / does not contain such variations.
Tsimane족은 / 이전에 서양 음악을 들어본 적이 없었다 / 그리고 그들 고유의 음악은 / 그러한 변주를 담고 있지 않았다

This led the researchers to conclude / that pitch perception is not something / that we are born with / but acquire over time / if we are exposed to it.
이는 연구자들로 하여금 결론 내리게 했다 / 음높이 지각은 ~ 하는 것이 아니라 / 우리가 가지고 태어나는 / 시간이 흐르면서 습득하는 / 우리가 그것에 노출되면

⇩

The fact / that the Tsimane people could not (A) identify / different pitches of the same note / means / that this ability is (B) learned.
사실은 / Tsimane 족이 인식하지 못했다는 / 같은 음의 다른 음높이를 / 의미한다 / 이 능력이 학습되는 것임을

★ 독해가 쉬워지는 구문 풀이
The researchers wanted to determine [if the Tsimane could recognize the link between different versions of the same note, like middle C and high C].
           (명사절)
⇨ [ ]는 determine의 목적어 역할을 하는 명사절이다.

해석 음높이 지각, 즉 음악적 소리에서 약간의 변화를 감지하는 능력에 대한 연구가 최근에 볼리비아 우림의 멀리 떨어진 지역에 사는 토착 부족인 Tsimane족 사람들을 상대로 행해졌다. 연구자들은 Tsimane족이 가운데 C음과 높은 C음처럼 같은 음의 서로 다른 버전들 사이의 관계를 인식할 수 있는지 알아내고 싶었다. 그러한 변주가 가득한 서양 음악을 연주하면서, 연구자들은 그들이 (관계를 인식하는 것을) 할 수 없다는 것을 알아냈다. Tsimane족은 이전에 서양 음악을 들어본 적이 없었으며, 그들 고유의 음악은 그러한 변주를 담고 있지 않았다. 주제문 이는 연구자들로 하여금 음높이 지각은 우리가 가지고 태어나는 것이 아니라 우리가 그것에 노출되면 시간이 흐르면서 습득하는 것이라고 결론 내리게 했다.

⇩

Tsimane족이 같은 음의 다른 음높이를 (A) 인식하지 못했다는 사실은 이 능력이 (B) 학습되는 것임을 의미한다.

    (A)   (B)
① 알다   ⋯ 필수적인
② 즐기다   ⋯ 학습된
③ 기억하다 ⋯ 타고난
④ 두려워하다 ⋯ 타고난
⑤ 인식하다 ⋯ 학습된

해설 요약문은 Tsimane족이 같은 음의 다른 음높이를 '(A)하지' 못했다는 사실은 이 능력이 '(B)한' 것임을 의미한다는 내용이다. 글에서 연구자들이 Tsimane족 사람들을 대상으로 진행한 연구를 통해 음높이 지각은 우리가 가지고 태어나는 것이 아니라 우리가 다양한 음높이에 노출되면서 습득하는 것이라고 결론 내렸다고 했다. 따라서 요약문의 (A)에는 글에서 언급된 'recognize'와 관련된 'identify'가, (B)에는 글에서 언급된 'not something that we are born with', 'acquire over time'과 관련된 'learned'가 적절하므로 ⑤ identify(인식하다) - learned(학습된)가 정답이다.

오답분석 Tsimane족은 같은 음의 다른 음높이를 인식하지 못한다고 했으므로 ①의 know, ②의 enjoy, ③의 memorize, ④의 fear는 (A)에 들어갈 단어로 적절하지 않다. 연구자들이 음높이 지각은 우리가 다양한 음높이에 노출되면서 습득하는 것이라고 결론 내렸다고 했으므로 ①의 necessary와 ③, ④의 innate는 (B)에 들어갈 단어로 적절하지 않다.

지문분석

Across the industrialized world, / companies are testing / autonomous vehicles in large numbers, / suggesting that a driverless future / could soon be at hand.
산업화된 세계 전역에서 / 기업들은 시험하고 있다 / 수많은 자율 주행 차량들을 / 이는 운전자가 필요 없는 미래를 암시한다 / 곧 다다를 수 있음을

Apart from / helping business run more efficiently / and making long commutes bearable, / autonomous cars / could (a) reduce carbon emissions / and the alarming number of deaths / that occur each year in accidents.
~ 외에도 / 사업체들이 더 효율적으로 운영되도록 돕는 것 / 그리고 긴 통근을 견딜 수 있게 하는 것 / 자율 주행 자동차들 / 탄소 배출을 줄일 수 있다 / 그리고 어마어마한 수의 사망자들 / 매년 사고로 발생하는

Moreover, / most experts (b) doubt(→ expect) / development to spread more rapidly / in some areas than others.
더 나아가 / 대부분의 전문가들은 의심한다(→ 예측한다) / 발전이 더 빠르게 퍼질 것이라고 / 일부 분야에서는 다른 분야보다

For instance, / adoption will likely occur earlier / in highly controlled environments / such as factory floors, / and in places where physical dangers / (c) threaten human operators, / such as mines.
예를 들어 / (자율 주행 차량의) 채택이 우선적으로 일어날 것이다 / 극도로 통제된 환경에서 / 공장의 작업 현장처럼 / 그리고 물리적 위험이 있는 곳에서는 / 인간 노동자들을 위협하는 / 광산과 같이

They also predict / that driverless robotic vehicles / will become more common / than passenger cars, / since their speeds can easily be (d) limited / to run safely alongside pedestrians.
그들(전문가들)은 또한 전망한다 / 운전자가 필요 없는 로봇 자동차들이 ~라고 / 더 흔해질 것이다 / 승용차들보다 / 그들의 속도가 손쉽게 제한될 수 있기 때문이다 / 보행자들과 함께 안전하게 달릴 수 있도록

Still, / challenges remain.
그러나 / 여전히 난관들이 남아 있다

★ For one, / autonomous vehicles, / which are programmed to follow instructions, / have to contend with / the (e) unpredictable behavior of human drivers, / who do not always follow the rules / of the road.
첫째로 / 자율 주행 차량들 / 지시를 따르도록 설계된 / ~을 상대해야 한다 / 인간 운전자들의 예측 불가능한 행동 / 규범을 반드시 지키지는 않는 / 도로의

In addition, / bringing large numbers of driverless cars / to our streets safely / will require great changes / to policy and infrastructure.
게다가 / 많은 수의 운전자가 필요 없는 자동차들을 들여놓는 것 / 우리 주변의 도로에 안전하게 / 막대한 변화를 요구할 것이다 / 정책과 기반 시설에

The public, too, / will need to be convinced / of their safety.
대중들 역시 / 확신해야 할 것이다 / 그것들의 안전성을

Given these concerns, / it's not a good time for champagne yet.
이러한 우려들을 고려하면 / 아직 축배를 들기는 이르다

★ 독해가 쉬워지는 구문 풀이

For one, autonomous vehicles, [①which are programmed to follow
　　　　　　　주어
instructions], have to contend with the unpredictable behavior of
　　　　　　　　　동사
human drivers, [②who do not always follow the rules of the road].

⇨ [①]과, [②]은 각각 계속적 용법의 관계대명사가 사용된 관계절이다.
　 which는 앞의 autonomous vehicles를, who는 human drivers를 선
　 행사로 둔다.

어휘 autonomous vehicle 자율 주행 차량 driverless 운전자가 필요 없는
　　 be at hand 다다르다 commute 통근(거리); 통근하다 bearable 견딜 수 있는
　　 alarming 어마어마한, 놀라운 adoption 채택 pedestrian 보행자
　　 challenge 난관, 난제 contend with ~을 상대하다
　　 infrastructure 기반 시설 concern 우려 champagne 축배, 샴페인

해석 산업화된 세계 전역에서, 기업들은 수많은 자율 주행 차량들을 시험하고 있는데, 이는 운전자가 필요 없는 미래가 곧 다다를 수 있음을 암시한다. 사업체들이 더 효율적으로 운영되도록 돕고 긴 통근을 견딜 수 있게 하는 것 외에도, 자율 주행 자동차들은 탄소 배출 및 매년 사고로 발생하는 어마어마한 수의 사망자들도 (a) 줄일 수 있다. 더 나아가, 대부분의 전문가들은 일부 분야에서는 다른 분야보다 더 빠르게 발전이 퍼질 것이라고 (b) 의심한다(→ 예측한다). 예를 들어, 공장의 작업 현장처럼 극도로 통제된 환경이나, 광산과 같이 인간 노동자들을 (c) 위협하는 물리적 위험이 있는 곳에서는 (자율 주행 차량의) 채택이 우선적으로 일어날 것이다. 그들(전문가들)은 또한 승용차들보다 운전자가 필요 없는 로봇 자동차들이 더 흔해질 것이라 전망하는데, 이는 보행자들과 함께 안전하게 달릴 수 있도록 이 차량들의 속도가 손쉽게 (d) 제한될 수 있기 때문이다. 그러나 여전히 난관들이 남아 있다. 첫째로, 지시를 따르도록 설계된 자율 주행 차량들은 도로 규범을 반드시 지키지는 않는 인간 운전자들의 (e) 예측 불가능한 행동들을 상대해야 한다. 게다가, 많은 수의 운전자가 필요 없는 자동차들을 우리 주변의 도로에 안전하게 들여놓는 것은 정책과 기반 시설에 막대한 변화를 요구할 것이다. 대중들 역시 그것들의 안전성을 확신해야 할 것이다. 이러한 우려들을 고려하면, 아직 축배를 들기는 이르다.

15
정답 ①

해석 ① 운전자가 필요 없는 자동차: 아직 갈 길이 멀다
② 탄소 배출이 없는 자동차 생산의 어려움
③ 오늘날 자동차 산업의 가장 큰 걱정은 무엇인가?
④ 자동화: 기술의 미래
⑤ 왜 우리는 자율 주행 차량을 필요로 하는가

해설 자율 주행 차량은 탄소 배출을 줄이고 차 사고로 인한 사망자의 수를 줄일 수 있는 등의 여러 장점이 있지만, 인간 운전자의 예측할 수 없는 행동에 상대해야 하며, 정책 및 기반 시설에 막대한 변화가 요구되는 등, 다양한 난관들이 남아 있다는 내용의 글이므로, 글의 제목으로 가장 적절한 것은 ① Driverless Cars: Still A Long Way to Go(운전자가 필요 없는 자동차: 아직 갈 길이 멀다)이다.

오답분석 ②은 글에서 언급된 소재 Carbon을, ③은 글의 핵심 소재인 자동차와 연관된 Automotive Industry를, ④은 글의 핵심 소재인 Automation을 활용하여 혼동을 주는 오답이다. ⑤은 자율 주행 차량의 장점에 대해 언급한 글의 초반부까지의 내용만을 다루고 있는 오답이다.

어휘 carbon-free 탄소 배출이 없는 automotive 자동차의 automation 자동화

16
정답 ②

해설 ②앞에서 자율 주행 차량의 긍정적인 전망을 설명하고 있으며, Moreover를 통해 이러한 긍정적인 내용에 대한 부연 설명이 이어질 것임을 예상할 수 있다. 따라서 전문가들은 일부 분야에서 다른 분야보다 더 빠르게 발전이 퍼질 것으로 "예측한다"는 맥락이 되어야 하므로, ②의 doubt(의심하다)를 expect(예측하다)와 같은 어휘로 바꾸어야 문맥상 적절하다.

오답분석 ①은 자율 주행 차량들이 탄소 배출과 매년 사고로 발생하는 사망자 수를 "줄일" 수 있다는 문맥이 되어야 하므로 reduce가 오는 것이 적절하다. ③은 일부 분야에서는 다른 분야보다 더 빠르게 발전이 퍼질 것이며, 따라서 광산과 같이 인간 노동자들을 "위협하는" 물리적 위험이 있는 곳에서 자율 주행 차량의 채택이 우선적으로 일어날 것이라는 문맥이 되어야 하므로 threaten이 오는 것이 적절하다. ④은 승용차보다 무인 로봇 자동차들이 더 흔해질 것이라 전망되며, 이는 보행자들과 함께 안전하게 달릴 수 있도록 이 차량들의 속도가 손쉽게 "제한될" 수 있기 때문이라는 문맥이 되어야 하므로 limited가 오는 것이 적절하다. ⑤은 인간 운전자들이 도로 규범을 반드시 지키지는 않기 때문에 자율 주행 차량들은 이

들의 "예측 불가능한" 행동들을 상대해야 한다는 문맥이 되어야 하므로 unpredictable이 오는 것이 적절하다.

17 ~ 19

지문분석

(A) A man named Vincent / became seriously ill / one day / and had to stay in a hospital room / to recover.
Vincent라는 이름의 한 남자가 / 심각한 병에 걸렸다 / 어느 날 / 그래서 병실에 있어야만 했다 / 회복하기 위해

He was given / a shared room / with a bed by the door.
그는 제공받았다 / 다인실을 / 문 옆에 침대가 있는

Across from him, / on the opposite side of the room, / was another bed / by the window.
그의 바로 맞은 편이자 / 방 반대편에 / 또 다른 침대가 있었다 / 창가 쪽의

An old man occupied the bed / and greeted Vincent / as he came in.
한 노인이 그 침대를 사용했고 / Vincent에게 인사를 했다 / 그가 들어왔을 때

"It's nice to meet (a) you," / he said.
"당신과 만나서 반가워요" / 라고 그가 말했다

(B) Weeks went by / and Vincent awoke one day / to realize / that the old man had died.
몇 주가 흘렀다 / 어느 날 Vincent는 깨어나 / 알게 되었다 / 그 노인이 죽었다는 것을

Although this news / made Vincent sad, / he immediately thought / of the bed by the window.
비록 이 소식이 / Vincent를 슬프게 했지만 / 그는 즉시 생각했다 / 창가 쪽 침대를

Having had nothing / but an empty ceiling / to stare at for days, / (b) he liked / the idea of having the view from the window / for himself.
아무것도 없었기 때문에 / 텅 빈 천장 외에 / 며칠 동안 빤히 쳐다볼 수 있던 것은 / 그는 마음에 들었다 / 창가 쪽 풍경을 차지한다는 생각 / 자신을 위해

With the nurse's permission, / he moved to the empty bed / and looked outside.
간호사의 허락을 받아 / 그는 빈 침대로 이동했다 / 그리고 밖을 바라보았다

(C) Each day, / the old man by the window / sat up in bed / for an hour.
매일 / 창가 쪽의 그 노인은 / 침대에서 일어나 앉아 있었다 / 한 시간 동안

On those occasions, / he would look out the window / and describe / what he saw, / such as bright white clouds / against a perfectly blue sky / or colorfully dressed pedestrians / moving around like ants / in the street below.
그럴 때면 / 그는 창밖을 내다보며 / 묘사하곤 했다 / 자신이 본 것을 / 밝은 흰 구름과 같은 / 완벽하게 푸른 하늘을 배경으로 한 / 혹은 화려하게 차려입은 보행자들 / 개미처럼 돌아다니는 / 아래의 길거리에서

Vincent took pleasure / in hearing the old man speak.
Vincent는 즐거워했다 / 그 노인이 말하는 것을 듣는 것을

He imagined / the scenes / as if (c) he were looking at them / himself.
그는 상상했다 / 그 장면들을 / 마치 그가 그것들을 보고 있었던 것처럼 / 직접

(D) To (d) his amazement, / there was nothing outside / but a wall.
그에게 놀랍게도 / 밖에는 아무것도 없었다 / 벽 말고는

Vincent expressed some surprise / to his nurse, / who commented / that the man was completely blind / and was unable to see anything at all.
Vincent는 놀라움을 표현했다 / 그의 간호사에게 / ~을 말한 / 그 남자가 완전히 눈이 멀어서 / 아무것도 볼 수 없었다고

★ When Vincent wondered aloud / why (e) he would take the time / to describe / so many scenes / in detail, / the nurse said / that he was trying / to offer Vincent / words of encouragement.
Vincent가 소리 내어 궁금해하자 / 왜 그가 시간을 들였는지 / 묘사하는 데 / 그렇게 많은 장면들을 / 자세히 / 그 간호사는 말했다 / 그가 노력했다고 / Vincent에게 건네려 / 격려의 말을

★ **독해가 쉬워지는 구문 풀이**

[When Vincent wondered aloud {why he would take the time to
　　　　　　　　　　　　　　　　의문사 주어　　동사
describe so many scenes in detail}], the nurse said that he was trying to offer Vincent words of encouragement.

⇨ [ ]는 주절(the ~ encouragement)을 수식하는 부사절이다.
⇨ 명사절 { }는 동사 wondered의 목적어이며, 의문사가 포함된 간접의문문으로 <의문사 + 주어 + 동사>의 어순으로 쓰인다.

[어휘] immediately 즉시　stare 빤히 쳐다보다　permission 허락
take pleasure in ~을 즐거워하다　encouragement 격려

[해석] (A) Vincent라는 이름의 한 남자가 어느 날 심각한 병에 걸려서 회복하기 위해 병실에 있어야만 했다. 그는 문 옆에 침대가 있는 다인실을 제공받았다. 그의 바로 맞은 편이자 방 반대편에 또 다른 창가 쪽 침대가 있었다. 한 노인이 그 침대를 사용했고 Vincent가 들어왔을 때 인사를 했다. "(a) 당신과 만나서 반가워요."라고 그가 말했다.
(C) 매일, 창가 쪽의 그 노인은 한 시간 동안 침대에서 일어나 앉아 있었다. 그럴 때면, 그는 창밖을 내다보며 완벽하게 푸른 하늘을 배경으로 한 밝은 흰 구름이나 아래의 길거리에서 개미처럼 돌아다니는 화려하게 차려입은 보행자들과 같은 자신이 본 것을 묘사하곤 했다. Vincent는 그 노인이 말하는 것을 듣는 것을 즐거워했다. 그는 그것들을 마치 (c) 그가 직접 보고 있었던 것처럼 그 장면들을 상상했다.
(B) 몇 주가 흘렀고 어느 날 Vincent는 깨어나 그 노인이 죽었다는 것을 알게 되었다. 비록 이 소식이 Vincent를 슬프게 했지만, 그는 즉시 창가 쪽 침대를 생각했다. 며칠 동안 빤히 쳐다볼 수 있던 것은 텅 빈 천장 외에 아무것도 없었기 때문에, (b) 그는 자신을 위해 창가 쪽 풍경을 차지한다는 생각이 마음에 들었다. 간호사의 허락을 받아, 그는 빈 침대로 이동해 밖을 바라보았다.
(D) (d) 그에게 놀랍게도, 밖에는 벽 말고는 아무것도 없었다. Vincent는 그의 간호사에게 놀라움을 표현했는데, 간호사는 그 남자가 완전히 눈이 멀어서 아무것도 볼 수 없었다고 말했다. 왜 (e) 그가 그렇게 많은 장면들을 자세히 묘사하는 데 시간을 들였는지 Vincent가 소리 내어 궁금해하자 간호사는 그가 Vincent에게 격려의 말을 건네려 노력했다고 말했다.

17 정답 ②

[해설] (A)는 Vincent라는 남자가 심각한 병에 걸려 병원에 입원했고, 거기서 한 노인과 만났다는 내용이다. (C)의 the old man by the window는 (A)의 An old man을 가리키므로 (A) 다음에 와야 한다. (B)는 몇 주가 흐르고 Vincent가 그 노인이 죽었다는 사실을 알게 되었고 그 노인이 보던 창밖 풍경을 보러 창가 쪽 침대에 갔다는 내용이므로 창가 쪽 침대에 있던 노인이 Vincent에게 창밖 풍경을 묘사해줬다고 한 (C) 뒤에 오는 것이 자연스럽다. (D)에서 Vincent가 창밖에 벽 말고는 아무것도 없었다는 것을 안 것은 (B)의 마지막에서 Vincent가 빈 침대로 이동한 이후의 일이므로 (B) 뒤에 와야 한다. 따라서 글의 순서로 가장 적절한 것은 ② (C) - (B) - (D)이다.

18 정답 ⑤

[해설] (a), (b), (c), (d)는 Vincent를 가리키지만 (e)는 노인을 가리키므로 ⑤이 정답이다.

19 정답 ④

[해설] (C)의 Vincent took pleasure in hearing the old man speak를 통해 Vincent가 노인의 이야기를 듣는 것을 즐거워했다는 것을 알 수 있으므로, 글의 내용과 일치하지 않는 것은 ④ 'Vincent는 노인의 이야기에 싫증이 났다.'이다.

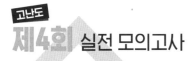

①은 He was given a shared room이라고 했으므로 글의 내용과 일치한다. ②는 ~this news made Vincent sad라고 했으므로 글의 내용과 일치한다. ③은 On those occasions, he would look out the window and describe what he saw라고 했으므로 글의 내용과 일치한다. ⑤은 the nurse said that he was trying to offer Vincent words of encouragement라고 했으므로 글의 내용과 일치한다.

고난도 제4회 실전 모의고사
p.162

01 ④　02 ④　03 ③　04 ④　05 ⑤　06 ⑤　07 ②　08 ③
09 ③　10 ③　11 ④　12 ②　13 ⑤　14 ④　15 ①　16 ⑤
17 ③　18 ①　19 ④

01
정답 ④

지문분석

Imagine / coming across two stories / in the news / —one about millions of children / suffering from severe poverty / and another about a single child / named Paul / who is also in the same situation.
상상해 보아라 / 두 가지 소식을 우연히 발견했다고 / 뉴스에서 / 하나는 수백만 명의 아이들에 대한 것이고 / 심각한 빈곤을 겪는 / 그리고 다른 하나는 한 아이에 대한 것이라고 / Paul이라는 이름의 / 역시나 같은 상황에 있는

If you are like most people, / you are more likely to / feel greater sympathy / for the suffering of Paul / than for the millions of other children.
만약 당신이 대부분의 사람들과 같다면 / 당신은 좀 더 ~할 것이다 / 더 큰 연민을 느낄 / Paul의 고통에 / 수백만 명의 다른 아이들보다

★ The reason for this is something / called the "identifiable victim effect," / which describes a common bias / people have / of feeling more empathy / for a victim / who is specific and identifiable / rather than another / who is largely faceless or nameless.
이것의 이유는 ~라는 것이다 / "인지 가능 희생자 효과"라고 불리는 / 일반적인 편견을 설명하는 / 사람들이 갖는 / 더 많은 공감을 느끼는 / 한 피해자에게 / 구체적이고 알아볼 수 있는 / 다른 사람보다 / 대체로 특징이 없거나 이름을 알 수 없는

The bias occurs / because our brains lack the capacity / to deal with tragedies / on a massive scale.
그 편견은 발생한다 / 우리의 뇌가 수용 능력이 부족하기 때문에 / 비극을 다룰 / 대규모의

And / because of the identifiable victim effect, / many people ignore problems / that affect a great number of victims.
그리고 / 인지 가능 희생자 효과로 인해 / 많은 사람들은 문제를 간과한다 / 엄청 많은 수의 피해자들에게 영향을 미치는

Instead, / they focus their attention / on the smaller number / who are identifiable / by name.
대신에 / 그들은 관심을 집중한다 / 더 적은 인원에 / 인식 가능한 / 이름으로

★ 독해가 쉬워지는 구문 풀이

The reason for this is **something** [called the "**identifiable victim effect**,"] {which describes a common bias people have of feeling more empathy for a victim who is specific and identifiable rather than another who is largely faceless or nameless}.
수식어(관계절)

▷ [ ]는 something을 수식하는 관계절이며, '주격 관계대명사 + be동사'가 생략되었다.
▷ { }에서 which는 관계대명사의 계속적 용법으로 쓰였고, 선행사 identifiable victim effect를 부연 설명한다.

어휘 come across ~을 우연히 발견하다 sympathy 연민, 동정, 공감 identifiable 인식 가능한, 알아볼 수 있는 victim 희생자, 피해자 bias 편견 empathy 공감, 감정 이입 faceless 특징이 없는, 정체불명의 nameless 이름을 알 수 없는, 익명의 capacity 수용 능력, 용량 deal with ~을 다루다, 처리하다 선택지 sympathetic 동정심이 있는, 공감하는 in time of crisis 위급 시에

해석 뉴스에서 두 가지 소식을 우연히 발견했는데, 하나는 심각한 빈곤을 겪는 수백만 명의 아이들에 대한 것이고, 다른 하나는 역시나 같은 상황에 있는 Paul이라는 이름의 한 아이에 대한 것이라고 상상해 보아라. 만약 당신이 대부분의 사람들과 같다면, 당신은 수백만 명의 다른 아이들보다 Paul의 고통에 더 큰 연민을 좀 더 느낄 것이다. 이것의 이유는 "인지 가능 희생자 효과"라고 불리는 것으로, 대체로 특징이 없거나 이름을 알 수 없는 다른 사람보다 구체적이고 알아볼 수 있는 한 피해자에게 더 많은 공감을 느끼는, 사람들이 갖는 일반적인 편견을 설명한다. 그 편견은 우리의 뇌가 대규모의 비극을 다룰 수용 능력이 부족하기 때문에 발생한다. 그리고 인지 가능 희생자 효과로 인해, 많은 사람들은 엄청 많은 수의 피해자들에게 영향을 미치는 문제를 간과한다. 대신에, 그들은 이름으로 인식 가능한 더 적은 인원에 관심을 집중한다.

① 신원을 알 수 없는 사람들이 더 동정심이 있는 이유
② 인지 가능 희생자 효과의 이점
③ 희생자들의 신원을 확인할 때 직면하는 문제들
④ 우리가 모르는 사람들에 대한 연민이 부족한 이유
⑤ 위급 시에 사람을 알아보는 방법

해설 사람들이 불특정한 다수보다 구체적이고 알아볼 수 있는 소수의 피해자에게 더 큰 연민을 느끼는 인지 가능 희생자 효과에 대해 설명하는 내용의 글이므로, 이 글의 주제로 가장 적절한 것은 ④ why we lack sympathy for unknown people(우리가 모르는 사람들에 대한 연민이 부족한 이유)이다.

오답분석 ①은 글의 핵심 소재 중 하나인 sympathy를, ③은 글에서 등장하는 identifiable과 글의 핵심 소재 중 하나인 victim을 활용하여 혼동을 주는 오답이다. ②은 인지 가능 희생자 효과의 문제점에 대해 다루는 글의 내용과 반대되므로 오답이다. ⑤은 글의 내용과 관련 없는 내용이므로 오답이다.

02
정답 ④

지문분석

Many animals use camouflage / to blend in with their surroundings.
많은 동물들은 위장을 이용한다 / 주변 환경과 조화를 이루기 위해

★ But / some, / like the tiger, / have such striking colors and markings / that one has to wonder / how they succeed.
하지만 / 일부 동물들은 / 호랑이 같은 / 매우 두드러진 색과 무늬를 가지고 있다 / 그래서 누군가는 의문을 품게 된다 / 이들이 어떻게 성공하는지

Part of the answer / has to do with / how animals see color.
그 답의 일부는 / ~과 관련이 있다 / 동물이 색을 보는 방법

For instance, / whereas human eyes can process / a full range of colors, / many of the animals / in the tiger's environment, / such as deer, / can only see green and blue.
예를 들어 / 인간의 눈은 처리할 수 있는 반면 / 모든 범주의 색을 / 많은 동물들은 / 호랑이의 영역에 사는 / 사슴과 같이 / 녹색과 파란색만 볼 수 있다

To the deer, / therefore, / the tiger appears nearly invisible / against the green background of the jungle.
사슴에게 / 따라서 / 호랑이는 거의 눈에 보이지 않는다 / 밀림의 녹색을 배경으로 하여

The tiger's bold stripes also play a part / by breaking up the tiger's outline.
호랑이의 선명한 줄무늬 역시 일조한다 / 호랑이의 외형을 분산시킴으로써

This helps it remain in camouflage / as it creeps / among tall grasses and plants / while it hunts.
이것은 그것(호랑이)이 위장한 상태를 유지하도록 도와준다 / 기어갈 때 / 키가 큰 수풀과 식물 사이로 / 사냥 중에

So, / though a tiger's coat may appear colorful and noticeable / to our eyes, / it is almost completely undetectable / to other animals.
따라서 / 비록 호랑이의 가죽이 화려하고 두드러져 보일지 몰라도 / 우리 눈에 / 거의 완전히 탐지 불가능하다 / 다른 동물들에게는

어휘　camouflage 위장, 분장　blend 조화를 이루다, 조화시키다
surrounding 주변 환경　striking 두드러진　have to do with ~와 관련이 있다
invisible 눈에 보이지 않는, 투명한　bold 선명한, 굵은　outline 외형
creep 기어가다　coat 가죽　noticeable 두드러진
undetectable 탐지 불가능한　선택지 prey 사냥감　perception 식별, 인지
distinguish 구분하다

해석　많은 동물들은 주변 환경과 조화를 이루기 위해 위장을 이용한다. 하지만, 호랑이 같은 일부 동물들은 매우 두드러진 색과 무늬를 가지고 있어서 누군가는 이들이 어떻게 성공하는지 의문을 품게 된다. 그 답의 일부는 동물이 색을 보는 방법과 관련이 있다. 예를 들어, 인간의 눈은 모든 범주의 색을 처리할 수 있는 반면, 사슴과 같이 호랑이의 영역에 사는 많은 동물들은 녹색과 파란색만 볼 수 있다. 따라서, 사슴에게 호랑이는 밀림의 녹색을 배경으로 하여 거의 눈에 보이지 않는다. 호랑이의 선명한 줄무늬 역시 호랑이의 외형을 분산시킴으로써 일조한다. 이것은 그것(호랑이)이 사냥 중에 키가 큰 수풀과 식물 사이로 기어갈 때 위장한 상태를 유지하도록 도와준다. 주제문 따라서, 비록 우리 눈에 호랑이의 가죽이 화려하고 두드러져 보일지 몰라도, 다른 동물들에게는 거의 완전히 탐지 불가능하다.

① 사슴: 호랑이가 제일 좋아하는 사냥감
② 왜 동물들은 위장이 필요할까
③ 동물 세계에서의 색채 식별
④ 호랑이의 위장에 담긴 비밀
⑤ 동물들은 어떻게 형체를 구분할까?

해설　비록 호랑이의 줄무늬가 우리에게는 두드러져 보여도 호랑이의 영역에 사는 많은 동물들이 녹색과 파란색만 볼 수 있으므로 호랑이는 밀림에서 위장한 상태를 유지할 수 있다는 내용의 글이므로, 글의 제목으로 가장 적절한 것은 ④ The Secrets Behind Tiger Camouflage(호랑이의 위장에 담긴 비밀)이다.

오답분석　①은 글에서 언급된 deer와 tiger를, ②은 글의 핵심 소재인 camouflage를 활용하여 혼동을 주는 오답이다. ③은 글의 일부 소재 color를 활용해 글의 내용을 지나치게 일반화한 오답이다. ⑤은 글에서 언급되고 있지 않다.

03　　　　　　　　　　　　　　　　　　정답 ③

지문분석

If you walk into a forest, / you may see / trees filled with fruits, / bushes with ripe berries, / or plenty of mushrooms and other vegetables / sprouting from the ground.
만약 당신이 숲속으로 걸어 들어간다면 / 당신은 보게 될지도 모른다 / 과일로 가득 찬 나무들 / 익은 산딸기가 달린 덤불 / 또는 많은 버섯과 다른 채소들 / 땅에서 자라나는

Such a harvest / has only one farmer: / Mother Nature.
그러한 수확물은 / 오직 하나의 농부만을 가진다 / 대자연이라는

This is the basis of natural farming, / also known as "do-nothing farming."
이것은 자연 농업의 기반이 된다 / "아무것도 하지 않는 농업"이라고도 알려진

★ It is an approach to agriculture / that encourages the laws of nature / and works alongside biodiversity, / so that plants can thrive / without humanity's touch.
그것은 농업에 대한 접근이다 / 자연의 법칙을 권장하는 / 그리고 생물의 다양성과 발맞춰 작업하는 / 식물이 잘 자랄 수 있도록 / 인간의 손길 없이

Natural farming does not use / any of the modern advancements / to farming, / like machines, pesticides, and fertilizer.
자연 농업은 사용하지 않는다 / 현대적인 발전 중 어느 것도 / 농작에 / 기계, 농약, 그리고 비료와 같은

Instead, / it tries to copy / what nature does / and allows crops to develop / on their own.
대신에 / 그것은 모방하려 노력한다 / 자연이 하는 것을 / 그리고 농작물이 성장할 수 있게 한다 / 혼자 힘으로

In this way, / it is a closed system, / which is more cost-efficient and environmentally-friendly.
이런 면에서 / 그것은 폐쇄적 시스템이다 / 그것은 더 비용 효율이 높고 환경친화적인

어휘　bush 덤불, 관목　ripe 익은　plenty of 많은　sprout 자라나다
harvest 수확(물)　Mother Nature 대자연　approach 접근
agriculture 농업　encourage 권장하다, 장려하다　alongside 발맞춰, 함께
biodiversity 생물의 다양성　thrive 잘 자라다　humanity 인간, 인류
advancement 발전, 진보　pesticide 농약, 살충제　fertilizer 비료
closed 폐쇄적인, 자급자족의　cost-efficient 비용 효율이 높은
environmentally-friendly 환경친화적인　선택지 abundant 풍부한, 많은
maintain 부양하다

해석　만약 당신이 숲속으로 걸어 들어간다면, 당신은 과일로 가득 찬 나무들, 익은 산딸기가 달린 덤불, 또는 땅에서 자라나는 많은 버섯과 다른 채소들을 보게 될지도 모른다. 그러한 수확물은 대자연이라는 오직 하나의 농부만을 가진다. 이것은 "아무것도 하지 않는 농업"이라고도 알려진 자연 농업의 기반이 된다. 그것은 인간의 손길 없이 식물이 잘 자랄 수 있도록 자연의 법칙을 권장하고 생물의 다양성과 발맞춰 작업하는 농업에 대한 접근이다. 자연 농업은 농작에 기계, 농약, 그리고 비료와 같은 현대적인 발전 중 어느 것도 사용하지 않는다. 대신에, 그것은 자연이 하는 것을 모방하려고 노력하고 농작물이 혼자 힘으로 성장할 수 있게 한다. 이런 면에서, 그것은 비용 효율이 더 높고 환경친화적인 폐쇄적 시스템이다.

① 농부의 지속적인 보살핌을 필요로 하는 과정
② 더 풍부한 채소를 위한 계획
③ 스스로를 부양할 수 있는 행위
④ 농업적으로 더 발전된 기술
⑤ 고대 농업 기술을 모방하는 방법

해설　자연 농업은 자연이 하는 것을 모방하려고 노력하고, 농작물이 인간의 손길 없이 혼자 힘으로 성장할 수 있게 한다고 했으므로 밑줄 친 a closed system(폐쇄적 시스템)이 의미하는 바로 가장 적절한 것은 ③ a practice that can maintain itself(스스로를 부양할 수 있는 행위)이다.

오답분석　①은 자연 농업이 인간의 손길 없이 식물이 잘 자랄 수 있도록 자연의 법칙을 권장한다고 언급한 글의 내용과 반대되므로 오답이다. ②은 글에서 언급된 plenty of ~ other vegetables를 활용하여 혼동을 주는 오답이

다. ④은 글에서 언급된 modern advancements to farming을 활용하여 혼동을 주는 오답이다. ⑤은 글에서 언급된 내용이 아니다.

04
정답 ④

지문분석

Participatory democracy is a political system / wherein the power to make political decisions / is given / to citizens completely.
참여 민주주의는 ~한 정치 체제이다 / 정치적인 결정을 하는 권력이 / 주어지는 / 시민들에게 완전히

A participatory democracy, / while similar to other forms of democracy / in that power rests in the hands of the people, / ① advocates for more participation and representation / than others.
참여 민주주의는 / 다른 민주주의의 형태와 비슷하지만 / 권력이 국민의 손에 있다는 점에서 / 더 많은 참여와 대표제를 지지한다 / 다른 것들보다

That is why / it is less likely to be ② corrupted / by politicians.
그것이 이유이다 / 부패될 가능성이 더 적은 / 정치인들에 의해

However, / critics say / that this type of democracy is not realistic.
하지만 / 비평가들은 말한다 / 이러한 유형의 민주주의는 현실적이지 않다고

In modern day, / managing a nation / is an ③ extremely complex and integrated endeavor.
현대에 / 국가를 운영하는 것은 / 극도로 복잡하고 통합적인 노력이다

It calls for time and effort / ④ what(→ that) the average citizen may not have.
그것은 시간과 노력을 필요로 한다 / 아마 보통의 시민이 가지고 있지 않을

★ As such, / representatives, / ⑤ whose job it is to understand the complexities and consequences of political policies, / need to represent the majority.
그러므로 / 대표들은 / 정치 정책의 복잡성과 결과를 이해하는 것이 그들의 일인 / 다수를 대리할 필요가 있다

> **★ 독해가 쉬워지는 구문 풀이**
>
> As such, **representatives**, [whose job it is to understand the
>   주어
> complexities and consequences of political policies], **need** to
>   동사
> represent the majority.
>
> ⇨ [ ]는 선행사 representatives를 수식하는 관계절이다.
> ⇨ [ ]은 본래 'It is their job to understand~'의 형태였으나, 선행사 representatives를 수식하는 관계절로 쓰이기 위해 their job이 '소유격 관계대명사 + 수식 받는 명사'(whose job)의 형태로 바뀌면서 문두로 나갔다.
> ⇨ 동사 need는 주절의 주어 representatives에 맞게 복수동사(need)가 쓰였다.

어휘 citizen 시민 completely 완전히 rest ~에 있다
    advocate 지지하다, 옹호하다 representation 대표(제) corrupt 부패하다
    politician 정치인 critic 비평가, 논평가 realistic 현실적인
    integrated 통합적인 endeavor 노력 call for ~을 필요로 하다
    complexity 복잡성 consequence 결과 majority 다수

해석 참여 민주주의는 정치적인 결정을 하는 권력이 시민들에게 완전히 주어지는 정치 체제이다. 참여 민주주의는 권력이 국민의 손에 있다는 점에서 다른 민주주의의 형태와 비슷하지만, 다른 것들보다 더 많은 참여와 대표제를 지지한다. 그것이 정치인들에 의해 부패될 가능성이 더 적은 이유이다. 하지만, 비평가들은 이러한 유형의 민주주의는 현실적이지 않다고 말한다. 현대에, 국가를 운영하는 것은 극도로 복잡하고 통합적인 노력이다. 그것은 아마 보통의 시민이 가지고 있지 않을 시간과 노력을 필요로 한다. 그러므로, 정치 정책의 복잡성과 결과를 이해하는 것이 그들의 일인 대표들은 다수를 대리할 필요가 있다.

해설 ④은 앞과 뒤에 각각 절이 하나씩 위치했으므로 접속사 혹은 관계대명사가 필요한 자리이다. 뒤에 나오는 절이 주어(the average citizen)와 타동사(may not have)만 있고 목적어가 없으므로 불완전한 절을 이끌 수 있는 관계대명사가 와야 하며, 선행사(time and effort)가 앞에 존재하므로 ④의 what을 that으로 고쳐야 한다.

오답분석 ①은 문장의 동사 자리이고 주어(A participatory democracy)가 단수이므로 단수동사 advocates를 사용한 것은 어법상 적절하다. ②은 문맥상 '정치인들에 의해 부패되다'라는 의미로 be동사와 함께 수동태를 이루는 과거분사 corrupted를 사용한 것은 어법상 적절하다. ③은 형용사를 수식할 수 있는 것은 부사이므로 형용사(complex) 앞에 부사 extremely를 사용한 것은 어법상 적절하다. ⑤은 선행사(representatives)가 사람이고, 관계절 내에서 job이 누구의 것인지 나타내므로 소유격 관계대명사 whose를 사용한 것은 어법상 적절하다.

05
정답 ⑤

지문분석

The principle of double effect / argues / that "intentional" harm is morally worse / than "unintentional" harm.
이중효과의 원리는 / 주장한다 / "의도적인" 피해가 도덕적으로 더 나쁘다고 / "의도적이지 않은" 피해보다

Take driving a car here, / for example.
차를 운전하는 것을 들어 보자 / 예로

Driving is a job requirement / for some people, / but for others, / it has ① become a way / for them to have fun.
운전하는 것이 일을 하기 위한 필수 요소이다 / 몇몇의 사람들에게는 / 하지만 다른 사람들에게 / 이것은 ~한 방법이 되었다 / 그들이 재미를 추구하는

However, / driving has been widely ② identified / as a leading contributor / to global warming.
그러나 / 운전은 널리 알려져 왔다 / 주요 원인 제공자로 / 지구 온난화의

Given / that both sets of drivers are polluters, / can we say / that both should have ③ equal blame?
~을 감안할 때 / 두 운전자 부류 모두가 오염 유발자임을 / 우리는 말할 수 있을까 / 양쪽 모두 동일한 책임을 가져야 한다고

At first, / their responsibility might seem similar, / since both groups knowingly ④ cause harm.
처음에는 / 그들의 책임이 비슷하게 보일지도 모른다 / 두 집단 모두 알고도 피해를 야기하기 때문에

★ However, / while the first group has no choice but to drive, / the second group has alternatives.
그러나 / 첫 번째 집단은 운전을 할 수밖에 없는 반면 / 두 번째 집단은 대안이 있다

By driving for fun, / they are intentionally choosing a ⑤ harmless (→ harmful) action / even though they can make a different choice.
재미로 운전함으로써 / 그들은 의도적으로 무해한(→ 유해한) 행동을 선택하고 있는 것이다 / 다른 선택을 할 수 있음에도 불구하고

Seen in this light, / we can argue / that the second group's actions are worse.
이러한 관점에서 봤을 때 / 우리는 주장할 수 있다 / 두 번째 집단의 행동이 더 나쁘다고

> **★ 독해가 쉬워지는 구문 풀이**
>
> However, while the first group **has no choice but to** drive, the second group has alternatives.
>
> ⇨ 'have no choice but + to부정사'는 '~할 수밖에 없다'를 의미하는 표현이다.

어휘 principle 원리 intentional 의도적인 morally 도덕적으로
    unintentional 의도적이지 않은
    job requirement (일을 하기 위한) 필수 요소, 자격요건
    identified ~으로 알려진 contributor 원인 제공자

global warming 지구 온난화 polluter 오염 유발자 blame 책임, 탓
responsibility 책임 knowingly 알고도, 고의로 alternative 대안
harmless 무해한

[해석] [주제문]이중효과의 원리는 "의도적인" 피해가 "의도적이지 않은" 피해보다 도덕적으로 더 나쁘다고 주장한다. 차를 운전하는 것을 예로 들어 보자. 몇몇의 사람들에게는 운전하는 것이 일을 하기 위한 필수 요소이지만, 다른 사람들에게 이것은 그들이 재미를 추구하는 방법이 ① 되었다. 그러나, 운전은 지구 온난화의 주요 원인 제공자로 널리 ② 알려져 왔다. 두 운전자 부류 모두가 오염 유발자임을 감안할 때, 우리는 양쪽 모두 ③ 동일한 책임을 가져야 한다고 말할 수 있을까? 처음에는, 두 집단 모두 알고도 피해를 ④ 야기하기 때문에, 그들의 책임이 비슷하게 보일지도 모른다. 그러나, 첫 번째 집단은 운전을 할 수밖에 없는 반면, 두 번째 집단은 대안이 있다. 재미로 운전함으로써, 그들은 다른 선택을 할 수 있음에도 불구하고 의도적으로 ⑤ 무해한(→ 유해한) 행동을 선택하고 있는 것이다. 이러한 관점에서 봤을 때, 우리는 두 번째 집단의 행동이 더 나쁘다고 주장할 수 있다.

[해설] 재미로 운전하는 사람들은 다른 선택을 할 수 있음에도 불구하고 의도적으로 "유해한" 선택을 하고 있다는 맥락이 되어야 하므로, ⑤의 harmless를 harmful과 같은 어휘로 바꾸어야 문맥상 적절하다.

[오답분석] ①은 몇몇의 사람들에게는 운전하는 것이 재미를 추구하는 방법이 "되었다"는 문맥이 되어야 하므로 become이 오는 것이 적절하다. ②은 운전은 지구 온난화의 주요 원인 제공자로 널리 "알려져 왔다"는 문맥이 되어야 하므로 identified가 오는 것이 적절하다. ③은 두 운전자 부류 모두가 오염 유발자이기 때문에 양쪽 모두 "동일한" 책임을 가져야 한다고 말할 수 있을까?라는 문맥이 되어야 하므로 equal이 오는 것이 적절하다. ④은 운전을 하는 두 집단 모두 알고도 피해를 "야기하는" 것이라는 문맥이 되어야 하므로 cause가 오는 것이 적절하다.

06

지문분석

An ever-expanding awareness of the nutrients / in various foods / is making some people reconsider / their previous views / on the vegetarian diet.
영양소에 대한 끊임없이 늘어나는 관심은 / 다양한 음식에 있는 / 몇몇 사람들을 다시 생각하게 만들고 있다 / 그들의 이전 견해를 / 채식에 대한

In the past, / their lack of knowledge / may have led them to believe / that being a vegetarian meant / eating only salad, / which may fail to satisfy / all of a person's nutritional requirements.
과거에 / 그들의 지식의 부족은 / 그들을 믿게 했을 수 있다 / 채식주의자가 된다는 것은 / ~을 의미한다고 / 오직 샐러드만 먹는 것을 / 충족시키지 못할 수 있다 / 한 사람의 모든 영양요구량을

However, / foods such as tofu, beans, and nuts / —common staples among most vegetarians— / are now commonly known to be excellent sources / of protein and other essential nutrients.
그러나 / 두부, 콩, 그리고 견과류와 같은 음식은 / 대부분의 채식주의자 사이에서 흔한 주식인 / 오늘날 훌륭한 공급원으로 흔히 알려져 있다 / 단백질과 다른 필수 영양소의

★ Meanwhile, / hardly can you go online / without coming across / an article on fruits and vegetables / that are considered super foods / and a list of all their vitamins, minerals, and benefits.
한편 / 당신은 온라인에 접속하기가 무척 어렵다 / 발견하지 않고 / 과일 및 채소에 관한 기사를 / 슈퍼푸드로 여겨지는 / 그리고 그들의 비타민, 미네랄, 그리고 효과에 대한 목록을

A meat-free diet does not suit / everyone's taste, / but more and more people / are beginning to realize / that a vegetarian diet doesn't have to be **insufficient**.
육류가 없는 식단이 맞는 것은 아니다 / 모든 사람의 취향에 / 하지만 점점 더 많은 사람들이 / 깨닫기 시작하고 있다 / 채식이 **불충분하지**만은 않다는 것을

★ 독해가 쉬워지는 구문 풀이

Meanwhile, [hardly can you go online] without coming across an
　　　　　 부정어 조동사 주어 동사
article on fruits and vegetables ~

⇨ [ ]는 부정의 의미를 가진 hardly가 강조를 위해 앞으로 나오면서 도치된 문장으로, <부정어 + 조동사/be동사 + 주어 + 동사>의 어순을 갖는다.

[어휘] ever-expanding 끊임없이 늘어나는 awareness 관심
vegetarian diet 채식 reconsider 다시 생각하다 satisfy 충족시키다
nutritional requirement 영양요구량 tofu 두부
hardly ~하기가 무척 어렵다, 거의 ~할 수가 없다 come across (우연히) 발견하다
meat-free 육류가 없는 suit ~에 맞다 [선택지] inconvenient 불편한
balanced 균형 잡힌 insufficient 불충분한

[해석] 다양한 음식에 있는 영양소에 대한 끊임없이 늘어나는 관심은 몇몇 사람들이 채식에 대한 그들의 이전 견해를 다시 생각하게 만들고 있다. 과거에, 그들의 지식의 부족은 채식주의자가 된다는 것은 오직 샐러드만 먹는 것을 의미하고, 이것이 한 사람의 모든 영양요구량을 충족시키지 못할 수 있다고 그들을 믿게 했을 수 있다. 그러나, 대부분의 채식주의자 사이에서 흔한 주식인 두부, 콩, 그리고 견과류와 같은 음식은, 오늘날 단백질과 다른 필수 영양소의 훌륭한 공급원으로 흔히 알려져 있다. 한편, 당신은 슈퍼푸드로 여겨지는 과일 및 채소에 관한 기사와 그들의 비타민, 미네랄, 그리고 효과에 대한 목록을 발견하지 않고 온라인에 접속하기가 무척 어렵다. [주제문]육류가 없는 식단이 모든 사람의 취향에 맞는 것은 아니지만, 점점 더 많은 사람들이 채식이 **불충분하지**만은 않다는 것을 깨닫기 시작하고 있다.

① 불편한
② 교육적인
③ 균형 잡힌
④ 비싼
⑤ 불충분한

[해설] 빈칸의 문장은 이 글의 주제문이므로 이를 다시 언급한 문장이나 부연 설명하는 문장을 파악해야 한다. 빈칸 문장에서 사람들은 채식이 '무엇'하지만은 않다는 것을 깨닫기 시작하고 있다고 하고, 글의 중반에서 대부분의 채식주의자들의 흔한 주식인 두부, 콩, 견과류는 단백질과 필수 영양소의 훌륭한 공급원으로 알려져 있다고 했다. 따라서 빈칸에는 사람들은 채식이 "불충분하지"만은 않다는 것을 깨닫기 시작하고 있다는 의미가 되는 것이 자연스러우므로 ⑤ insufficient(불충분한)가 정답이다.

[오답분석] ①의 "불편한"과 ②의 "교육적인", 그리고 ④의 "비싼"에 대한 내용은 글에서 언급되고 있지 않다. ③은 글에서 언급된 내용인 satisfy ~ nutritional requirements를 활용하여 혼동을 주는 오답이다.

07
정답 ②

지문분석

Although often taken for granted today, / the common mechanical clock represents / one of the most important steps forward / in humanity's economic success.
비록 오늘날에는 종종 당연시되지만 / 흔히 보이는 기계식 시계는 대표된다 / 가장 중요한 진보 중 하나로 / 인류의 경제 발전에서

(A) Unfortunately, / this method was extremely subjective, / and depended / not only on being able to see the sun, / but also on one's perception of its location.
안타깝게도 / 이 방식은 매우 주관적이었다 / 그리고 좌우되었다 / 태양을 볼 수 있는 것(상황)뿐 아니라 / 태양의 위치에 대한 개인의 지각에도

제4회 실전 모의고사 **179**

Businesspeople had no real way / to plan their activities.
사업가들은 실질적인 방법이 없었다 / 그들의 활동을 계획할

However, / once accurate mechanical clocks were invented, / time could be objectively measured and shared.
그러나 / 정확한 기계식 시계가 발명되자 / 시간은 객관적으로 측정되고 공유될 수 있었다

★ (B) Prior to the invention / of mechanical clocks, / time was measured / rather imprecisely, / which made business activity difficult / to coordinate.
발명 이전에 / 기계식 시계의 / 시간은 측정되었다 / 다소 부정확하게 / 이것은 경제활동을 힘들게 만들었다 / 조율하기

People determined / when to do things / by looking at the location / of the sun in the sky / and individually deciding / the general time of day, / such as sunup, midday, and sundown.
사람들은 정했다 / 언제 일을 할지 / 위치를 봄으로써 / 하늘에 뜬 태양의 / 그리고 각자 결정함 / 그날의 대략적인 시간을 / 동틀 녘, 한낮, 그리고 해 질 녘과 같이

(C) Having precise measurements of time / allowed businesspeople / to set their hours, schedule meetings, coordinate trade activities, / and monitor their production schedules.
시간의 정확한 측정값을 갖는 것은 / 사업가들이 ~ 할 수 있게 했다 / 그들의 시간을 정하거나 회의를 잡고, 무역 활동을 조율하여 / 그리고 그들의 생산 일정을 관리하게

All of these / made economic success possible.
이러한 모든 것들이 / 경제 발전을 가능케 했다

★ 독해가 쉬워지는 구문 풀이

Prior to the invention of mechanical clocks, [time was measured
　　　　　전치사구　　　　　　　주어　　　동사
rather imprecisely], **which** made business activity difficult to coordinate.

⇨ 계속적 용법으로 쓰인 관계대명사 which는, [ ]를 수식한다.

어휘 take for granted 당연시하다 humanity 인류 subjective 주관적인 perception 지각 businesspeople 사업가들 accurate 정확한 objectively 객관적으로 imprecisely 부정확하게 coordinate 조율하다, 조정하다 sunup 동틀 녘 midday 한낮 sundown 해 질 녘 precise 정확한 measurement 측정(값)

해석 〔주제문〕 비록 오늘날에는 종종 당연시되지만, 흔히 보이는 기계식 시계는 인류의 경제 발전에서 가장 중요한 진보 중 하나로 대표된다. (B) 기계식 시계의 발명 이전에, 시간은 다소 부정확하게 측정되었는데, 이것은 경제활동을 조율하기 힘들게 만들었다. 사람들은 하늘에 뜬 태양의 위치를 보고 동틀 녘, 한낮, 그리고 해 질 녘과 같이 그날의 대략적인 시간을 각자 결정함으로써 언제 일을 할지 정했다. (A) 안타깝게도, 이 방식은 매우 주관적이었고, 태양을 볼 수 있는 상황뿐만 아니라 태양의 위치에 대한 개인의 지각에도 좌우되었다. 사업가들은 그들의 활동을 계획할 실질적인 방법이 없었다. 그러나, 정확한 기계식 시계가 발명되자, 시간은 객관적으로 측정되고 공유될 수 있었다. (C) 시간의 정확한 측정값을 갖는 것은 사업가들이 그들의 시간을 정하거나 회의를 잡고, 무역 활동을 조율하여, 그들의 생산 일정을 관리할 수 있게 했다. 이러한 모든 것들이 경제 발전을 가능케 했다.

해설 주어진 글은 인류의 경제적 성공에서 가장 중요한 진보 중 하나인 기계식 시계에 대한 내용이고 (B)는 기계식 시계의 발명 이전에 시간을 측정했던 방법에 대한 내용이므로 주어진 글 뒤에 와야 한다. (A)의 this method(이 방식)는 (B)의 '태양의 위치를 바라보고 그날의 대략적인 시간을 정한 것'을 가리키므로 (B) 바로 다음에 오는 것이 적절하다. (C)는 시간의 정확한 측정값을 갖는 것이 사업가들에게 경제적 성공을 가능하게 했다는 내용이므로 정확한 기계식 시계가 발명되자 시간이 객관적으로 측정되고 공유될 수 있었다고 한 (A)의 뒤에 와야 자연스럽다. 따라서 글의 순서로 가장 적절한 것은 ② (B)-(A)-(C)이다.

지문분석

The distinction / between the words "empathy" and "sympathy" / is not very clear, / which often leads to confusion.
구분은 / "공감"과 "동정"이라는 단어 간의 / 그다지 명확하지 않다 / 이는 종종 혼동을 일으킨다

(①) However, / one key difference / is how we act / when we feel each one.
그러나 / 한 가지 핵심적인 차이점은 / 우리가 행동하는 방식이다 / 각각의 것을 느낄 때

(②) "Empathy" is generally used / to understand both positive and negative experiences, / resulting in pro-social (helping) behavior / towards the other.
"공감"은 일반적으로 사용된다 / 긍정적, 부정적인 경험 둘 다를 이해하기 위해 / 친사회적 (돕는) 행동을 야기한다 / 다른 사람들을 향한

(③) ("Sympathy," / in contrast, / is used / to mean a person's response / to the negative experiences (suffering) / of another individual.)
"동정"은 / 그에 반해서 / 사용된다 / 어떤 한 사람의 반응을 나타내기 위해 / 부정적인 경험 (고통)에 대한 / 다른 사람의

Unlike "empathy," / it doesn't necessarily involve / doing anything / about it (no pro-social behavior).
"공감"과는 달리 / 이것은 반드시 포함하지는 않는다 / 무언가 행동하는 것을 / 이것에 대해 (친 사회적인 태도가 아님)

(④) ★ Rather, / sympathizing allows a person / to acknowledge a situation / and just realize / the other person is going through / a difficult time.
오히려 / 동정하는 것은 어떤 한 사람이 ~하게 한다 / 상황을 인지하게 / 그리고 단순히 인식하게만 / 다른 사람이 겪고 있다는 것을 / 힘든 시간을

(⑤) So / while "empathy" may cause a person to directly react / to the other, / "sympathy" is more of a passive form / of simply feeling compassion.
그래서 / "공감"은 어떤 한 사람이 직접적으로 반응하게 하는 반면 / 다른 사람에게 / "동정"은 더 수동적인 형태이다 / 단순히 연민을 느끼는

★ 독해가 쉬워지는 구문 풀이

Rather, sympathizing allows a person to acknowledge a situation and just realize [the other person is going through a difficult time].
　　　　　　　　　　　　　　　　　　　　　　　　　　명사절

⇨ 명사절 [ ]는 동사 realize의 목적어이며, 앞에 명사절 접속사 that이 생략되었다.

어휘 distinction 구분 empathy 공감 sympathy 동정 confusion 혼동 pro-social 친사회적 response 반응 necessarily 반드시 suffering 고통 sympathize 동정하다 acknowledge 인지하다 passive 수동적인 compassion 연민

해석 "공감"과 "동정"이라는 단어 간의 구분은 그다지 명확하지 않아서 이는 종종 혼동을 일으킨다. 그러나, 한 가지 핵심적인 차이점은 우리가 각각의 것을 느낄 때 행동하는 방식이다. "공감"은 일반적으로 긍정적, 부정적인 경험 둘 다를 이해하기 위해 사용되고, 다른 사람들을 향한 친사회적 (돕는) 행동을 야기한다. (그에 반해서, "동정"은 다른 사람의 부정적인 경험 (고통)에 대한 어떤 한 사람의 반응을 나타내기 위해 사용된다.) "공감"과는 달리 이것은 반드시 이것에 대해 무언가 행동하는 것을 포함하지는 않는다(친 사회적인 태도가 아님). 오히려, 동정하는 것은 어떤 한 사람이 상황을 인지하고 다른 사람이 힘든 시간을 겪고 있다는 것을 단순히 인식하게만 한다. 그래서 "공감"은 어떤 한 사람이 다른 사람에게 직접적으로 반응하게 하는 반면, "동정"은 단순히 연민을 느끼는 더 수동적인 형태이다.

해설 주어진 문장의 "Sympathy," in contrast(그에 반해서 "동정"은)를 통해 주어진 문장 앞에는 동정과 대비되는 내용이 나와야 함을 알 수 있다. 이 글에서는 공감과 동정의 구분이 명확하지 않다는 첫 번째 문장에 이어

---

① 뒤에서 이들을 구분하는 한 가지 핵심적인 차이를 소개하고 있다. 이 어지는 ② 뒤에서는 공감을 먼저 언급하며, 공감이 긍정적인 경험과 부 정적인 경험 둘 다를 이해하기 위해 쓰인다고 했다. 그리고 ③과 ④ 뒤 에서는 공감과 대조되는 동정에 대한 내용이 이어지며, ⑤ 뒤에서는 앞 서 언급된 차이를 정리하고 있다. 따라서 ③ 앞에서 동정과 대비되는 공 감에 관한 내용이 언급되었으므로 주어진 문장이 들어가기에 가장 적절 한 곳은 ③이다.

<오답분석> ① 뒤 문장은 첫 번째 문장에 이어서 공감과 동정을 구분하는 한 가지 주 요한 차이를 소개하고 있으므로 주어진 문장이 들어가기에 적절하지 않 다. ② 뒤 문장은 공감에 관한 내용을 처음 언급하는 곳이므로 주어진 문 장이 들어가기에 적절하지 않다. ④ 뒤 문장은 공감과 달리 동정은 무언가 행동하는 것을 포함하지 않는다는 앞 내용을 부연 설명하고 있으므로 글 의 흐름이 자연스럽다. ⑤ 뒤 문장은 앞서 언급된 내용을 정리하고 있으므 로 주어진 문장이 들어가기에 적절하지 않다.

09
정답 ③

<지문분석>

If there was a drug / that could improve memory / and make it possible to concentrate / for hours on end, / one might ask, / "Would it be ethical to take it?"
만약 약이 있다면 / 기억력을 향상시킬 수 있는 / 그리고 집중하는 것을 가능하게 하는 / 몇 시간 동안 계속 / 누군가는 물어볼 수도 있다 / 그것을 먹는 것이 도덕적으로 옳을까

With regard to work, / it might help people / be more productive at the office / and finally get that promotion.
일에 관해서는 / 그것이 사람들을 도울 수도 있다 / 사무실에서 더 생산적이도록 / 그리고 마침내 승진하도록

But as the development of such a drug / becomes a reality, / it seems that / there may be an obstacle to overcome.
하지만 그런 약의 개발이 ~하면서 / 현실이 되다 / ~처럼 보인다 / 극복해야 할 장애물이 있을 수 있는 것

Some opponents say / that companies could start pressuring / their employees / to use it / against their will.
몇몇 반대자들은 말한다 / 회사가 압력을 가하기 시작할 수도 있다고 / 그들의 직원에게 / 그것을 사용하도록 / 그들의 의지에 반하여

In this day and age, / most people strive for / a healthy work-life balance.
요즘 같은 시대는 / 대부분의 사람들이 ~을 얻으려고 노력한다 / 건강한 일과 삶의 균형

★ However, / these drugs would likely only contribute to / the creation of a society / in which the main focus is work, / leaving people with little time / to relax / and do the things they want to do.
하지만 / 이러한 약들은 ~에만 기여할 것 같다 / 사회의 탄생 / 주된 초점이 일에 있는 / 사 람들에게 시간을 거의 남겨주지 않는다 / 휴식을 취할 / 그리고 그들이 하고 싶은 것을 할

> ★ 독해가 쉬워지는 구문 풀이
>
> However, these drugs would likely only contribute to the creation of a society in which the main focus is work, [leaving people with little time to relax and do the things they want to do].
>
> ⇨ [ ]는 주절(these ~ work)을 수식하는 분사구문의 부사절이며, 접속사 및 반복되는 주어(these drugs)가 생략되었다.

<어휘> drug 약, 마약 concentrate 집중하다 on end 계속
ethical 도덕적으로 옳은, 윤리적인 with regard to ~에 관해서는
productive 생산적인 development 개발 obstacle 장애(물)
overcome 극복하다 opponent 반대자, 적 pressure 압력을 가하다
employee 직원 against ~에 반하여 will 의지
in this day and age 요즘 같은 시대는, 지금은
strive for ~을 얻으려고 노력하다 work-life balance 일과 삶의 균형
contribute 기여하다 <선택지> likelihood 가능성 be willing to 기꺼이 ~하다

side effect 부작용 safely 아무 문제 없이, 틀림없이

<해석> 만약 기억력을 향상시킬 수 있고 몇 시간 동안 계속 집중하는 것을 가능하 게 하는 약이 있다면, 누군가는 "그것을 먹는 것이 도덕적으로 옳을까?"라 고 물어볼 수도 있다. 일에 관해서는, 그것이 사람들을 사무실에서 더 생 산적이도록, 그리고 마침내 승진하도록 도울 수도 있다. <주제문> 하지만 그 런 약의 개발이 현실이 되면서, 극복해야 할 장애물이 있을 수 있는 것처 럼 보인다. 몇몇 반대자들은 회사가 그들의 직원에게 그들의 의지에 반하 여 그것을 사용하도록 압력을 가하기 시작할 수도 있다고 말한다. 요즘 같 은 시대는, 대부분의 사람들이 건강한 일과 삶의 균형을 얻으려고 노력한 다. 하지만, 이러한 약들은 사람들이 휴식을 취하고 그들이 하고 싶은 것 을 할 시간을 거의 남겨주지 않으면서 주된 초점이 일에 있는 사회의 탄생 에만 기여할 것 같다.

① 그것이 절대 가능하지 않을 것이라는 상당한 가능성
② 사람들이 그것을 기꺼이 사용하지 않을 것이라는 희박한 가능성
③ 그것이 우리의 일과 삶의 균형을 파괴할 수도 있다는 가능성
④ 아무 문제 없이 무시될 수 있는 사소한 부작용
⑤ 생산 과정에서 발생할 수 있는 문제

<해설> 기억력을 향상시키고, 집중하게 해주는 약들은 사람들이 휴식을 취하거 나 하고 싶은 것을 할 시간을 거의 남겨주지 않으면서 결국 주된 초점이 일에 있는 사회의 탄생에만 기여할 것 같다고 했으므로, an obstacle to overcome(극복해야 할 장애물)이 의미하는 바로 가장 적절한 것은 ③ a possibility that it might destroy our work-life balance(그것이 우리의 일과 삶의 균형을 파괴할 수도 있다는 가능성)이다.

<오답분석> ①은 이러한 약의 개발이 점점 현실이 되고 있다고 한 글의 내용과 반대되 는 내용을 다루고 있으므로 오답이다. ②은 회사가 직원들의 의지와 상관 없이 그 약을 먹게 할 수도 있다는 내용을 활용하여 혼동을 주는 오답이 다. ④과 ⑤은 글에서 언급된 내용이 아니다.

10
정답 ③

<지문분석>

This is the story / of two frogs.
이것은 이야기이다 / 개구리 두 마리에 관한

One frog was fat / and the other skinny.
한 개구리는 뚱뚱했다 / 그리고 다른 개구리는 말랐다

One day, / while ① searching for food, / they inadvertently jumped into a vat of milk.
어느 날 / 먹이를 찾던 중에 / 그들은 실수로 우유 통에 뛰어들었다

★ The sides were so slippery / ② that it was hard for them / to hop out easily.
옆면이 너무 미끄러웠다 / 그래서 그들은 힘들었다 / 쉽게 뛰어넘기

They had nothing to do but swim.
그들은 수영할 수밖에 없었다

After paddling for hours, / the skinny frog grew tired, / ran out of breath, / and ③ crying(→ cried) for help.
몇 시간을 첨벙거리고 나서 / 마른 개구리는 지쳤다 / 숨이 가빠졌다 / 이윽고 도움을 요 청했다

But the fat frog said, / "Keep trying my friend.
하지만 뚱뚱한 개구리는 말했다 / 계속 노력해 친구야

Something good will happen."
무슨 좋은 수가 있을 거야

Another couple of hours passed.
또 몇 시간이 지나갔다

The skinny frog said, / "I can't go on any longer," / and he decided ④ to stop paddling.
마른 개구리는 말했다 / 난 더 이상 못하겠어 / 그리고 그는 첨벙거리는 것을 멈추기로 했다

Slowly, / he drowned in the milk / but the fat frog didn't give up.
천천히 / 그는 우유에 빠져 죽었다 / 그러나 뚱뚱한 개구리는 포기하지 않았다

Ten minutes later, / the fat frog felt / something ⑤ strange under his feet.
10분이 지난 후에 / 뚱뚱한 개구리는 느꼈다 / 그의 발밑에서 뭔가 이상한 것을

The milk turned into hard butter / at last, / and the fat frog / finally hopped out of the vat.
그 우유는 단단한 버터로 변했다 / 마침내 / 그리고 뚱뚱한 개구리는 / 마침내 그 통 밖으로 뛰어나왔다

★ 독해가 쉬워지는 구문 풀이

The sides were so slippery that it was hard for them to hop out easily.
　　　　　　　형용사　　가주어　　　　진짜 주어(to부정사구)

⇨ 'so + 형용사/부사 + that + 주어 + 동사'구문은 '매우 ~해서 -하다'라는 의미로 해석한다.
⇨ that절의 진짜 주어는 to hop out easily이고, 의미상의 주어는 for them 이다.

[어휘] inadvertently 실수로, 우연히 slippery 미끄러운 hop 뛰어넘다, 뛰다
run out of ~를 다 써버리다, 동나다 cry for help 도움을 청하다
drown 빠져 죽다, 익사하다 give up 포기하다 turn into ~으로 변하다
at last 마침내

[해석] 이것은 개구리 두 마리에 관한 이야기이다. 한 개구리는 뚱뚱했고 다른 개구리는 말랐다. 어느 날, 먹이를 찾던 중에, 그들은 실수로 우유 통에 뛰어들었다. 옆면이 너무 미끄러워서 그들은 쉽게 뛰어넘기 힘들었다. 그들은 수영할 수밖에 없었다. 몇 시간을 첨벙거리고 나서, 마른 개구리는 지쳤고, 숨이 가빠졌으며, 이윽고 도움을 요청했다. 하지만 뚱뚱한 개구리는 "계속 노력해 친구야. 무슨 좋은 수가 있을 거야."라고 말했다. 또 몇 시간이 지나갔다. 마른 개구리는 "난 더 이상 못하겠어"라고 말했고, 그는 첨벙거리는 것을 멈추기로 했다. 천천히, 그는 우유에 빠져 죽었으나 뚱뚱한 개구리는 포기하지 않았다. 10분이 지난 후에, 뚱뚱한 개구리는 그의 발밑에서 뭔가 이상한 것을 느꼈다. 그 우유는 마침내 단단한 버터로 변했고, 뚱뚱한 개구리는 드디어 그 통 밖으로 뛰어나왔다.

[해설] 동사 grew, ran, 그리고 crying은 등위접속사 and로 연결된 병렬 구조이며, 이들의 시제가 과거이므로 and 뒤에도 과거 동사가 와야 한다. 따라서 ③의 crying을 cried로 고쳐야 한다.

[오답 분석] ①은 주절의 주어 they와 분사구문의 searching이 나타내는 '먹이를 찾는' 행위의 주체이므로 현재분사 searching을 사용한 것은 어법상 적절하다. ②은 '너무 ~해서 -하다'를 의미하는 so ~ that 구문을 완성하는 that을 사용한 것으로 어법상 적절하다. ④은 동사 decide(decided)가 to부정사를 목적어로 취하는 동사이므로 to부정사 to stop을 사용한 것은 어법상 적절하다. ⑤은 -thing으로 끝나는 명사(something)는 형용사(strange)가 뒤에서 수식하므로 strange를 사용한 것은 어법상 적절하다.

11
정답 ④

지문분석

Philosophy of medicine / is a relatively recent field of study / that developed / in the 21st century.
의학 철학은 / 비교적 최신의 연구 분야이다 / 발달된 / 21세기에

Individuals / who study the philosophy of medicine / try to ① understand the intellectual aspects / of the medical industry / better.
사람들은 / 의학 철학을 공부하는 / 지적인 측면을 이해하려고 노력한다 / 의료 산업의 / 더 잘

For example, / philosophers of medicine might research / moral or ethical issues / about health, disease, or treatment.
예를 들어 / 의학 철학자들은 연구할 수 있다 / 도덕적이거나 윤리적인 문제들을 / 건강, 질병, 또는 치료에 관련된

They ask ② conceptual questions: / What is the meaning of health? / What is the nature of healing?
그들은 개념적인 질문을 던진다 / 건강의 의미는 무엇인가 / 치유의 본질은 무엇인가

★ Healthcare professionals ③ lack the time / to think about such abstract topics / since they have to focus on practical tasks / like writing prescriptions / and talking to patients.
의료 전문가들은 시간이 없다 / 그러한 추상적인 주제에 대해 생각할 / 그들은 실질적인 업무에 집중해야 하기 때문에 / 처방전을 쓰는 것과 같은 / 그리고 환자들과 이야기하는 것

So instead, / philosophers of medicine study theories / about ④ unimportant(→ important) decisions / that busy doctors and nurses cannot always consider.
그래서 그 대신 / 의학 철학자들이 이론을 연구한다 / 중요하지 않은(→ 중요한) 결정에 대한 / 바쁜 의사와 간호사들이 매번 고려하기는 힘든

Philosophers of medicine / thus / ⑤ have an essential purpose, / and contribute to advancements / in the medical field.
의학 철학자들은 / 따라서 / 필수적인 명분을 가진다 / 그리고 발전에 기여한다 / 의학 분야의

★ 독해가 쉬워지는 구문 풀이

Healthcare professionals lack the time to think about such abstract topics [since they have to focus on practical tasks like writing prescriptions and talking to patients].
　　　　　　　　　　　　　　　수식어(전치사구)

⇨ [ ]는 이유를 나타내는 부사절이다.

[어휘] medicine 의학 intellectual 지적인 aspect 측면 moral 도덕적인
ethical 윤리적인 treatment 치료 conceptual 개념적인
healthcare professional 의료 전문가 abstract 추상적인
practical 실질적인 prescription 처방전 purpose 명분, 목표
essential 필수적인, 근본적인 contribute 기여하다 advancement 발전

[해석] 의학 철학은 21세기에 발달된 비교적 최신의 연구 분야이다. [주제문] 의학 철학을 공부하는 사람들은 의료 산업의 지적인 측면을 더 잘 ① 이해하려고 노력한다. 예를 들어, 의학 철학자들은 건강, 질병, 또는 치료에 관련된 도덕적이거나 윤리적인 문제들을 연구할 수 있다. 그들은 '건강의 의미는 무엇인가?', '치유의 본질은 무엇인가?'와 같은 ② 개념적인 질문을 던진다. 의료 전문가들은 처방전을 쓰고 환자들과 이야기하는 것과 같은 실질적인 업무에 집중해야 하기 때문에 그러한 추상적인 주제에 대해 생각할 시간이 ③ 없다. 그래서 그 대신, 의학 철학자들이 바쁜 의사와 간호사들이 매번 고려하기는 힘든 ④ 중요하지 않은(→ 중요한) 결정에 대한 이론을 연구한다. 따라서 의학 철학자들은 필수적인 명분을 ⑤ 가지고, 의학 분야의 발전에 기여한다.

[해설] 의학 철학자들은 의사들과 간호사들이 실직적인 업무에 집중하느라 매번 고려하기는 힘든 중요한 결정에 대한 이론을 연구한다는 맥락이 되어야 하므로, ④의 unimportant를 important와 같은 어휘로 바꾸어야 문맥상 적절하다.

[오답 분석] ①은 의학 철학을 공부하는 사람들은 의학 산업의 지적인 측면을 "이해하려고" 노력한다는 문맥이 되어야 하므로 understand가 오는 것이 적절하다. ②은 의료 전문가들은 '건강의 의미는 무엇인가?' '치유의 본질은 무엇인가?'와 같은 "개념적인" 질문들을 던진다는 문맥이 되어야 하므로 conceptual이 오는 것이 적절하다. ③은 의료 전문가들은 실질적인 업무에 집중해야 하기 때문에 시간이 "부족하다"는 문맥이 되어야 하므로 lack이 오는 것이 적절하다. ⑤은 의학 철학자들은 필수적인 명분을 "가지고" 의학 분야에서의 발전에 기여한다는 문맥이 되어야 하므로 '가진다'를 의미하는 have가 오는 것이 적절하다.

지문분석

Algorithms on music streaming services / utilize users' playlists and listening history / to recommend new artists and albums.
음악 스트리밍 서비스의 알고리즘은 / 사용자의 재생목록과 청취 내역을 이용한다 / 새로운 음악가 및 앨범을 추천하기 위해

Recently, / research into the accuracy / of these recommendations / was conducted / using two groups of users / on a UK music website: / those who mostly listen to "mainstream" music / and those who mostly listen to non-mainstream music.
최근에 / 정확도에 대한 연구가 / 이러한 추천의 / 실행되었다 / 두 집단의 사용자를 활용하여 / 한 영국 음악 웹사이트에서 / 주로 "주류" 음악을 듣는 사람들 / 그리고 주로 비주류의 음악을 듣는 사람들

For the purpose of the study, / non-mainstream music was defined / as music featuring only acoustic instruments / or high-energy music like electronica or hard rock, / either with or without vocals.
연구의 목적을 위해 / 비주류 음악은 한정되었다 / 전자 장치를 쓰지 않는 악기만 포함하는 음악으로 / 또는 전자 악기 음악이나 하드 록과 같은 강렬한 음악으로 / 보컬이 있든지 없든지

★ The study found / that while the algorithms did well predicting / what mainstream music fans might like, / they were not as effective / at anticipating the same / for non-mainstream music listeners.
연구는 발견했다 / 알고리즘이 잘 예측한 반면에 / 주류 음악의 팬들이 좋아할 만한 것을 / 그들이 그다지 효과적이지 않음을 / 동일한 것(좋아할 만한 것)을 예측하는 것에는 / 비주류 음악 청취자들을 위해

It therefore appears / as though **recommendation systems are biased** / **toward popular music**.
그것은 따라서 ~으로 보인다 / 마치 **추천 시스템이 편향되어 있는 것처럼** / 대중음악에

This discovery could lead to the creation / of more effective algorithms / that could result in / better and more balanced music recommendations / for all users.
이러한 발견은 제작으로 이어질 수 있다 / 더 효과적인 알고리즘의 / ~이 될 수 있는 / 더 나은, 더 균형 잡힌 음악 추천 / 모든 사용자를 위해

★ 독해가 쉬워지는 구문 풀이

The study found [that {while the algorithms did well predicting
주어　　　　동사
what mainstream music fans might like}, they were not as effective
명사절 접속사
at anticipating the same for non-mainstream music listeners].

⇨ 명사절 [ ]는 동사 found의 목적어이다.
⇨ { }는 명사절을 수식하는 명사절 내부의 부사절이다.
⇨ 관계대명사 what은 선행사를 포함하며, the thing which(that)로 바꿔 쓸 수 있다.

어휘 algorithm 알고리즘 utilize 이용하다, 활용하다 accuracy 정확도, 정확 mainstream 주류의, 정통파의 high-energy 강렬한, 다이내믹한 electronica 전자 악기 음악 anticipate 예측하다, 예상하다
선택지 outnumber ~보다 수가 더 많다 biased 편향된, 선입견이 있는 alternative 대체의, 대안의 characterize 특징짓다, ~의 특성을 기술하다

해석 음악 스트리밍 서비스의 알고리즘은 새로운 음악가 및 앨범을 추천하기 위해 사용자의 재생목록과 청취 내역을 이용한다. 최근에, 이러한 추천의 정확도에 대한 연구가 한 영국 음악 웹사이트에서 주로 "주류" 음악을 듣는 사람들과 주로 비주류의 음악을 듣는 사람들, 두 집단의 사용자를 활용하여 실행되었다. 연구의 목적을 위해, 비주류 음악은 보컬이 있든지 없든지 전자 장치를 쓰지 않는 악기만 포함하는 음악, 또는 전자 악기 음악이나 하드 록과 같은 강렬한 음악으로 한정되었다. 연구는 알고리즘이 주류 음악의 팬들이 좋아할 만한 것을 잘 예측한 반면에 비주류 음악 청취자들을 위해 동일한 것(좋아할 만한 것)을 예측하는 것에는 그다지 효과

적이지 않았음을 발견했다. 주제문 따라서 그것은 마치 **추천 시스템이 대중음악에 편향되어 있는** 것처럼 보인다. 이러한 발견은 모든 사용자를 위해 더 나은, 더 균형 잡힌 음악 추천이 될 수 있는 더 효과적인 알고리즘의 제작으로 이어질 수 있다.

① 영국 음악 웹사이트의 사용자들은 알고리즘 도구에 영향을 많이 받는다
② 주류 음악가들이 비주류 음악가들보다 수가 더 많다
③ 추천 시스템이 대중음악에 편향되어 있다
④ 더 많은 대체 음악에 대한 수요는 대체로 무시되어왔다
⑤ 연구원들은 비주류 음악을 특징짓는 데 어려움이 있었다

해설 빈칸 문장은 이 글의 주제문이므로 이를 다시 언급한 문장이나 부연 설명하는 문장을 파악해야 한다. 빈칸 문장에서 알고리즘이 '무엇'인 것처럼 보인다고 하고, 빈칸 바로 앞 문장에서 알고리즘이 주류 음악의 팬들이 좋아할 만한 것은 잘 예측한 반면에 비주류 음악 청취자들이 좋아할 만한 것을 예측하는 데는 그다지 효과적이지 않음을 발견했다고 했다. 따라서 빈칸에는 알고리즘의 "추천 시스템이 대중음악에 편향되어 있는" 것처럼 보인다는 의미가 되는 것이 자연스러우므로 ③ recommendation systems are biased toward popular music(추천 시스템이 대중음악에 편향되어 있다)이 정답이다.

오답분석 ①은 글에서 언급된 music website를 활용하여 혼동을 주는 오답이다. ②, ⑤은 글의 빈출 단어 mainstream과 non-mainstream을 활용하여 혼동을 주는 오답이다. ④의 "더 많은 대체 음악에 대한 수요가 대체로 무시되어왔다"는 글의 내용과 관련이 없다.

지문분석

If the weather suddenly changes / and your knees start to ache, / are the two connected somehow?
만약 날씨가 갑자기 변한다면 / 그리고 당신의 무릎이 아프기 시작한다 / 그 둘은 어떻게든 연관이 있는 것일까

In fact, / they are, / and there may actually be / a scientific reason / behind it.
실제로 / 그들은 연관이 있다 / 그리고 정말로 있을 수도 있다 / 과학적인 이유가 / 그 이면에는

(A) We feel that tension / in places / like the hips, knees, hands, or shoulder joints.
우리는 그 긴장을 느끼게 된다 / ~한 부분에 / 허리, 무릎, 양손 및 어깨 관절과 같은

And that is / what produces the pain.
그리고 그것이 ~이다 / 고통을 만들어내는 것

★ So / when your grandfather says / he knows a storm is coming / because his knees hurt, / he is telling the truth!
따라서 / 만약 당신의 할아버지께서 ~라고 하신다면 / 폭풍이 올 것을 알고 있다고 / 그의 무릎이 아프기 때문에 / 그는 사실을 말하고 있는 것이다

(B) For instance, / when barometric pressure drops, / such as right before a thunderstorm, / there is less pressure / on our bodies, / allowing the tissue inside / to swell.
예를 들어 / 기압이 떨어지면 / 폭풍이 오기 직전처럼 / 압력이 줄어드는데 / 우리 몸에 가해지는 / 이는 내부 조직이 ~하게 한다 / 부풀어 오르게

This swollen tissue / puts pressure / on our joints.
이렇게 부풀어 오른 조직은 / 압력을 가한다 / 우리의 관절에

(C) Although we don't often think about it, / the air presses down / on everything below it, / including our bodies.
비록 우리가 흔히 신경 쓰지는 않지만 / 대기는 짓누른다 / 그 아래에 있는 모든 것을 / 우리의 몸을 포함하여

This is called barometric pressure.
이것은 기압이라고 불린다

Our bodies are so sensitive / to it / that any change has an effect / on us.
우리의 몸은 매우 예민해서 / 그것에 / 어떠한 변화든지 영향을 주게 된다 / 우리에게

★ 독해가 쉬워지는 구문 풀이

So [when your grandfather says {he knows a storm is coming <because his knees hurt>}], he is telling the truth!

⇨ [ ]은 주절(he is ~ truth!)을 수식하는 부사절이다.

⇨ 명사절 { }은 동사 says의 목적어이며, < >은 이 명사절을 수식하는 부사절이다.

어휘 somehow 어떻게든, 아무래도 tension 긴장 joint 관절
drop 줄어들다, 떨어지다 tissue (세포로 이뤄진) 조직 swell 부풀어 오르다
sensitive 예민한

해석 만약 날씨가 갑자기 변하고 당신의 무릎이 아프기 시작한다면, 그 둘은 어떻게든 연관이 있는 것일까? [주제문] 실제로, 그들은 연관이 있으며, 그 이면에는 정말로 과학적인 이유가 있을 수도 있다.
(C) 비록 우리가 흔히 신경 쓰지는 않지만, 대기는 우리의 몸을 포함하여 그 아래에 있는 모든 것을 짓누른다. 이것은 기압이라고 불린다. 우리의 몸은 그것에 매우 예민해서 어떠한 변화든지 우리에게 영향을 주게 된다.
(B) 예를 들어, 폭풍이 오기 직전처럼 기압이 떨어지면, 우리 몸에 가해지는 압력이 줄어드는데, 이는 내부 조직이 부풀어 오르게 한다. 이렇게 부풀어 오른 조직은 우리의 관절에 압력을 가한다.
(A) 우리는 허리, 무릎, 양손 및 어깨 관절과 같은 부분에 그 긴장을 느끼게 된다. 그리고 그것이 고통을 만들어내는 것이다. 따라서 만약 당신의 할아버지께서 그의 무릎이 아프기 때문에 폭풍이 올 것을 알고 있다고 하신다면, 그는 사실을 말하고 있는 것이다!

해설 주어진 글은 갑작스러운 날씨 변화에 무릎이 아프기 시작하는 것에는 과학적인 이유가 있을 수도 있다고 하는 내용이고, (C)에서 기압이 우리의 몸을 포함하여 모든 것을 짓누르는데 우리 몸은 이에 매우 예민하다는 내용을 통해 주어진 글의 마지막에서 언급한 과학적인 이유에 대해 부연 설명을 했으므로 (C)는 주어진 글 뒤에 와야 한다. (B)는 For instance를 통해 기압이 우리 몸에 영향을 미친다고 한 (C)의 내용에 대한 예시를 들고 있으므로 (C) 뒤에 오는 것이 적절하다. (A)의 that tension은 (B)의 기압에 의해 부풀어 오른 조직이 관절에 가하는 압력을 가리키므로 (B) 다음에 오는 것이 적절하다. 따라서 글의 순서로 가장 적절한 것은 ⑤ (C)-(B)-(A)이다.

14
정답 ④

지문분석

Over the past two decades, / online piracy has become increasingly widespread.
지난 20년에 걸쳐 / 온라인 저작권 침해는 점점 확산되어왔다

(①) Internet users can download or stream / all kinds of media, / including music, movies, and books / with just a few clicks.
인터넷 사용자들은 다운로드하거나 스트리밍할 수 있다 / 모든 종류의 미디어를 / 음악, 영화, 그리고 책을 포함하는 / 단지 몇 번의 클릭만으로

(②) Not surprisingly, / this trend has created friction / between entertainment companies and the online community.
놀랄 것도 없이 / 이러한 동향은 마찰을 빚어왔다 / 연예기획사와 온라인 커뮤니티 간에

(③) As a result, / a bill has been proposed / that would prevent all forms of copyright violations / on the Web / if passed.
그 결과 / 법안이 발의되었다 / 모든 종류의 저작권 침해를 막을 / 웹상에서 / 만약 통과된다면

(④) (★ The entertainment industry / supports this legislation / and argues / that users should pay for copyrighted materials / in whatever way that they are used.)
연예 산업은 / 이 법안을 지지한다 / 그리고 주장한다 / 사용자들은 저작권으로 보호되는 자료에 대가를 지불해야 한다고 / 그것들이 어떤 방식으로 이용되든지

Users, / on the other hand, / believe / that any new laws could ultimately block / the free flow of information / on the Internet.
사용자들은 / 반면에 / 생각한다 / 어떠한 새로운 법이든 결국 막을 것이라고 / 정보의 자유로운 흐름을 / 인터넷에서

(⑤) Clearly, / one side has something to gain / and the other has something to lose / depending on / which group the law favors.
분명히 / 한쪽은 얻는 것이 있다 / 그리고 다른 한쪽은 잃는 것이 있다 / ~에 따라 / 법이 어떤 집단의 편을 들어주는지

★ 독해가 쉬워지는 구문 풀이

The entertainment industry supports this legislation and argues
　주어　　　　　　　　　　 동사1　　　　　　　　　　 동사2
~ copyrighted materials **in whatever way that** they are used.

⇨ '어떤 방식으로 ~하든지'를 의미하는 in whatever way that은 복합관계부사 however로 바꿔 쓸 수 있다.

어휘 decade 10년 widespread 확산되다 stream 스트리밍하다 friction 마찰
bill 법안 propose 발의하다, 제안하다 violation 위반 legislation 법안
copyright 저작권으로 보호하는; 저작권 ultimately 결국
clearly 분명히, 뚜렷하게 favor ~의 편을 들어주다, ~에 유리하다

해석 지난 20년에 걸쳐, 온라인 저작권 침해는 점점 확산되어왔다. 인터넷 사용자들은 음악, 영화, 그리고 책을 포함하는 모든 종류의 미디어를 단지 몇 번의 클릭만으로 다운로드하거나 스트리밍할 수 있다. 놀랄 것도 없이, 이러한 동향은 연예기획사와 온라인 커뮤니티 간에 마찰을 빚어왔다. 그 결과, 만약 통과된다면 웹상에서 모든 종류의 저작권 침해를 막을 법안이 발의되었다. (연예 산업은 이 법안을 지지하며 저작권으로 보호되는 자료가 어떤 방식으로 이용되든지 사용자들이 그것들에 대가를 지불해야 한다고 주장한다.) 반면에, 사용자들은 어떠한 새로운 법이든 결국 인터넷에서 정보의 자유로운 흐름을 막을 것이라고 생각한다. 분명히, 법이 어떤 집단의 편을 들어주는지에 따라 한쪽은 얻는 것이 있고 다른 한쪽은 잃는 것이 있다.

해설 주어진 문장의 this legislation(이 법안)을 통해, 주어진 문장 앞에는 이 법안이 어떤 것인지에 대한 내용이 나와야 한다는 것을 알 수 있다. 이 글에서는 ② 뒤 문장까지 온라인 저작권 침해와 관련해 연예기획사와 온라인 커뮤니티 사이에 빚어온 마찰이 있었으며 ③ 뒤에서는 결과적으로 저작권 침해를 막기 위한 법안까지 발의되었다는 내용을 설명하고 있다. 따라서 주어진 문장의 this legislation은 ③ 뒤 문장의 a bill을 가리키므로 주어진 문장이 들어가기에 가장 적절한 곳은 ④이다.

오답분석 ③ 뒤 문장까지는 저작권 침해로 인해 연예기획사와 온라인 커뮤니티 간의 갈등으로 인해 결국 법안이 발의되었다는 내용이므로 문장의 흐름이 자연스럽다. ④ 뒤 문장은 저작권 침해를 방지하는 법안에 반대하는 사용자들의 입장에 대한 내용이므로 주어진 글 뒤에 자연스럽게 이어진다. ⑤ 뒤 문장은 앞에서 다룬 내용을 정리하는 결론에 해당하는 문장이므로 주어진 문장이 들어가기에 적절하지 않다.

15
정답 ①

지문분석

The subject of free will / has been debated / for centuries / by philosophers, / and none have taken a firmer stance / against it / than determinists.
자유 의지에 대한 문제는 / 논의되어 왔다 / 수 세기 동안 / 철학자들에 의해 / 그리고 그 누구도 더 확고한 입장을 취한 적이 없었다 / 그것에 반하는 / 결정론자들보다

Determinists do not believe / it is possible / to have free will / or to make independent choices / to alter your fate.
결정론자들은 생각하지 않는다 / ~이 가능하다고 / 자유 의지를 갖는 것 / 또는 독립적인 선택을 하는 것 / 당신의 운명을 바꾸기 위해

Rather, / they believe / that **everything is an outcome** / of prior events.
오히려 / 그들은 생각한다 / **모든 것은 결과라고** / 이전 사건들의

To use a metaphor / from science, / the earth, / year after year, / follows a predictable path / around the sun.
비유를 사용하자면 / 과학에서의 / 지구는 / 해마다 / 예측할 수 있는 경로를 따른다 / 태양 주변의

It has no choice but to / follow this path / because its orbit is influenced or determined / by the force of the sun's gravity.
그것은 ~할 수밖에 없다 / 이 경로를 따를 / 그것의 궤도는 영향을 받거나 결정되기 때문에 / 태양의 중력에 의해

Determinists believe / something similar occurs / with people.
결정론자들은 생각한다 / 이와 비슷한 일이 발생한다고 / 사람들에게도

People follow a path / in life / that has been influenced or determined / by the force of past actions.
사람들은 길을 따른다 / 인생의 / 영향을 받거나 결정된 / 앞선 행동의 영향력에 의해

★ Whenever they choose to do something, / they are not actually exercising their free will / but are behaving exactly / as they should, / given their particular circumstances.
그들이 무언가를 하기로 선택할 때마다 / 사실상 그들은 그들의 자유 의지를 행사하고 있는 것이 아니다 / 오히려 정확히 행동하고 있는 것이다 / 그들이 해야 하는 대로 / 그들의 특정 상황을 고려해봤을 때

★ 독해가 쉬워지는 구문 풀이

Whenever they choose to do something, they are not actually
복합관계부사
exercising their free will but are behaving exactly as they should, ~.

⇨ '~할 때마다'를 의미하는 복합관계부사 whenever는 시간부사절을 이끌며, at any time when으로 바꾸어 사용할 수 있다.

어휘 will 의지 firm 확고한 stance 입장, 자세 alter 바꾸다 fate 운명 metaphor 비유, 은유 year after year 해마다 predictable 예측할 수 있는 have no choice but to ~할 수밖에 없다 orbit 궤도; 궤도를 돌다 gravity 중력, 끌림 exercise 행사하다, 연습하다 given ~을 고려해볼 때 circumstance 상황, 환경

해석 자유 의지에 대한 문제는 수 세기 동안 철학자들에 의해 논의되어 왔고, 그 누구도 결정론자들보다 그것에 반하는 더 확고한 입장을 취한 적이 없었다. 결정론자들은 자유 의지를 갖는 것이나 당신의 운명을 바꾸기 위해 독립적인 선택을 하는 것이 가능하다고 생각하지 않는다. 〔주제문〕 오히려, 그들은 **모든 것이 이전 사건들의 결과**라고 생각한다. 과학에서의 비유를 사용하자면, 지구는 해마다 태양 주변의 예측할 수 있는 경로를 따른다. 그것의 궤도는 태양의 중력에 의해 영향을 받거나 결정되기 때문에 이 경로를 따를 수밖에 없다. 결정론자들은 사람들에게도 이와 비슷한 일이 발생한다고 생각한다. 사람들은 앞선 행동의 영향력에 의해 영향을 받거나 결정된 인생의 길을 따른다. 그들이 무언가를 하기로 선택할 때마다, 사실상 그들은 그들의 자유 의지를 행사하고 있는 것이 아니라 오히려 그들의 특정 상황을 고려할 때 그들이 해야 하는 대로 정확히 행동하고 있는 것이다.

① 모든 것이 이전 사건들의 결과이다
② 한 사람의 운명은 출생 시에는 불확실하다
③ 자유를 추구하는 것은 철학의 목표이다
④ 모든 결정들은 개인의 목표에 근거한다
⑤ 미래의 결과는 예측할 수 없다

해설 빈칸 문장은 이 글의 주제문이므로 이를 다시 언급한 문장이나 부연 설명하는 문장을 파악해야 한다. 빈칸 바로 앞 문장에서 결정론자들은 자유 의지를 갖는 것이나 운명을 바꾸기 위해 독립적인 선택을 하는 것이 가능하지 않다고 한 후 빈칸 문장에서 결정론자들은 오히려 '무엇이 어떠하다'

라고 생각한다고 했다. 이어서 사람도 이전 행동의 영향력에 의해 영향을 받거나 결정된 길을 따른다고 했으므로 빈칸에는 결정론자는 "모든 것이 이전 사건들의 결과"라고 생각한다는 의미가 되는 것이 자연스러우므로 ① everything is an outcome of prior events(모든 것은 이전 사건들의 결과이다)가 정답이다.

오답분석 ②의 '한 사람의 운명은 출생 시에는 불확실하다'와 ⑤의 '미래의 결과는 예측할 수 없다'는 모든 것은 이전 사건들의 결과라는 글의 주제와 반대되는 내용이므로 오답이다. ③은 글에서 언급된 '철학'과 '자유 의지'를 활용하여 혼동을 주는 오답이다. ④의 '모든 결정들은 개인의 목표에 근거한다'는 글의 내용과 관련이 없다.

16 정답 ⑤

지문분석

Free trade agreements, / or FTAs, / are essentially contracts drawn / to exchange goods and services.
자유무역협정 / 또는 FTA는 / 기본적으로 작성되는 계약서이다 / 상품 및 서비스를 교역하기 위해

(A) In the ideal scenario, / FTAs are mutually beneficial / for both.
이상적인 상황에서 / FTA는 상호적으로 이익이 된다 / 이 둘 모두에

Of course, / this isn't always the case / with imbalanced conditions, / but the major aim is / to foster prosperity / for all.
물론 / 항상 그렇지는 않다 / 불균형 상태에서는 / 하지만 주된 목표는 ~이다 / 번영을 도모하는 것 / 모두의

(B) Developing economies, / on the other hand, / benefit from FTAs / in other ways.
개발 도상국 / 반면 / FTA로부터 이익을 얻는다 / 다른 방식으로

★ FTAs give / access to foreign capital and technical support, / both of which can be put to use / growing local industries / and providing jobs to citizens.
FTA는 제공한다 / 해외 자본 및 기술적 지원으로의 접근을 / 모두 사용될 수 있다 / 지역 산업을 성장시키는 일에 / 그리고 주민들에게 일자리를 제공하는 일에

(C) In the case of developed economies, / FTAs allow them / to open up new markets / for their products / and outsource the production of goods / to countries / where costs are low.
선진국의 경우에 / FTA는 그들이 ~할 수 있게 한다 / 새로운 시장을 개척하도록 / 그들의 상품을 위한 / 그리고 상품 생산을 외부 위탁하도록 / ~한 국가들에 / 비용이 덜 드는

They are / thus able to use their capital / for other purposes, / such as investing / in new lines of business.
그들은 / 따라서 그들의 자본을 쓸 수 있다 / 다른 목적을 위해 / 투자와 같은 / 신사업 분야에 대한

★ 독해가 쉬워지는 구문 풀이

FTAs give access to **foreign capital and technical support**,
[both of which] can be put to use growing local industries and
수량 표현 관계대명사
providing jobs to citizens.

⇨ 선행사 foreign capital and technical support가 사물이고, both of 뒤에서 전치사 of의 목적어 역할을 하므로 목적격 관계대명사 which가 쓰였다.

어휘 free trade agreements 자유무역협정 essentially 기본적으로 contract 계약(서) draw (계약서 등을) 작성하다 ideal 이상적인 mutually 상호적으로 beneficial 이익이 되는 imbalanced 불균형의 foster 도모하다, 촉진하다 prosperity 번영 developing economies 개발 도상국 capital 자본 developed economies 선진국 outsource 외부 위탁하다 line (사업 등의) 분야

해석 자유무역협정, 또는 FTA는 기본적으로 상품 및 서비스를 교역하기 위해 작성되는 계약서이다.

(C) 선진국의 경우에, FTA는 선진국이 그들의 상품을 위한 새로운 시장을 개척하고 비용이 덜 드는 국가들에 상품 생산을 외부 위탁할 수 있게 한다. 따라서 그들은 신사업 분야에 대한 투자와 같은 다른 목적을 위해 그들의 자본을 쓸 수 있다.

(B) 반면, 개발 도상국은 다른 방식으로 FTA로부터 이익을 얻는다. FTA는 해외 자본 및 기술적 지원으로의 접근을 제공하는데, 이것은 모두 지역 산업을 성장시키고 주민들에게 일자리를 제공하는 일에 사용될 수 있다.

(A) 이상적인 상황에서, FTA는 이 둘 모두에 상호적으로 이익이 된다. 물론, 불균형 상태에서는 항상 그렇지는 않지만, 주된 목표는 모두의 번영을 도모하는 것이다.

해설 주어진 글은 FTA란 상품 및 서비스를 교역하기 위해 작성되는 계약서라고 설명하는 내용이다. (C)는 선진국의 경우에 FTA는 그들이 새로운 시장을 개척하고 상품 생산을 외부 위탁할 수 있게 한다는 내용이므로 FTA의 정의를 설명한 주어진 글의 뒤에 와야 한다. (B)는 on the other hand를 통해 개발 도상국에 대한 내용을 언급하며 (C)의 부연 설명을 하고 있으므로 (C) 뒤에 오는 것이 적절하다. (A)는 이상적인 상황에서 FTA는 둘 모두에 이익이 된다는 내용인데, (C)에서는 FTA가 선진국들에게 주는 이익을, 이어지는 (B)에서는 개발도상국에게 주는 이익을 언급했으므로 (A)는 마지막에 와야 한다. 따라서 글의 순서로 가장 적절한 것은 ⑤ (C)-(B)-(A) 이다.

17
정답 ③

지문분석

In 1959, / Leon Festinger and James Carlsmith had participants in an experiment / spend an hour performing tasks / that were designed to be boring and repetitive.
1959년 / Leon Festinger와 James Carlsmith는 실험 참가자들이 ~하도록 했다 / 과제를 수행하는 데에 한 시간을 보내다 / 지루하고 반복적이도록 설계된

★ When they were done, / the participants were paid either $1 or $20 / to tell the next participants / waiting for their turn / that the tasks had been interesting.
그들이 다 끝났을 때 / 참가자들은 1달러 또는 20달러를 지불 받았다 / 그다음 참가자들에게 말하도록 / 그들의 순서를 기다리는 / 그 과제들이 흥미로웠다고

Then, / the participants rated / how much they had enjoyed the tasks.
그다음에 / 그 참가자들은 평가했다 / 얼마나 그들이 과제를 즐겼는지

Those who were paid $1 / were more likely to claim / the tasks had been enjoyable / than those who were paid $20, / even if they did not believe this initially.
1달러를 지불 받은 사람들 / 주장하는 경우가 더 많았다 / 그 과제가 즐거웠다 / 20달러를 지불 받은 사람들보다 / 그들이 처음에 이렇게 믿지 않았더라도

They did this / because they were conflicted / about having wasted an hour of their time / for only $1.
그들은 이렇게 했다 / 그들은 마음의 갈등이 있었기 때문에 / 그들의 시간 중 한 시간을 낭비했다는 것에 대해 / 고작 1달러를 위해서

By saying / that the tasks had been fun, / participants were able to justify / having done them / and make themselves feel better / about the situation.
말함으로써 / 과제가 재미있었다고 / 참가자들은 정당화할 수 있었다 / 그것들을 한 것 / 그리고 자신이 더 만족스럽게 느낄 수 있도록 만들다 / 그 상황에 대해

This phenomenon / is known as cognitive dissonance, / and it tells us / that we try to manipulate our beliefs / to justify them.
이 현상은 / 인지 부조화로 알려져 있다 / 그리고 그것은 우리에게 말해준다 / 우리가 우리의 믿음을 조작하려 시도한다는 것 / 그것들(믿음)을 정당화하기 위해서

⇩

○

People (A) adjust the way they think / when they need a(n) (B) better reason / for a given situation.
사람들은 그들이 생각하는 방식을 조정한다 / 그들이 더 나은 이유가 필요할 때 / 주어진 상황에

★ 독해가 쉬워지는 구문 풀이

When they were done, the participants were paid either $1 or $20 to
　　　　　　　　　　　　주어　　　　　　　동사(수동태)
tell [①the next participants] waiting for their turn [②that the tasks
　　　간접 목적어　　　　　　　　　　　　　　　　　　직접 목적어
had been interesting].

⇨ 주어 participants가 동사 pay가 나타내는 '지불하는' 행위의 대상이므로 수동태 were paid가 쓰였다. 동사 pay는 목적어 2개가 올 수 있는 4형식 동사이므로, 수동태 표현 뒤에 동사 pay의 직접 목적어인 either $1 or $20가 남아 있음에 주의한다.

⇨ [①]은 tell의 간접 목적어, [②]는 직접 목적어로 쓰인 4형식 문장이다. tell은 3형식 문장으로도 사용할 수 있으며, 이때 어순은 tell [②] to [①]가 된다.

어휘 participant 참가자　experiment 실험　repetitive 반복적인　rate 평가하다
claim 주장하다　enjoyable 즐거운　initially 처음에
conflicted 마음에 갈등이 있는　waste 낭비하다　justify 정당화하다
phenomenon 현상　cognitive dissonance 인지 부조화
manipulate 조작하다　(선택지) uncertain 불확실한　adjust 조정하다

해석 1959년, Leon Festinger와 James Carlsmith는 실험 참가자들이 지루하고 반복적이도록 설계된 과제를 수행하는 데에 한 시간을 보내도록 했다. 그들이 다 끝냈을 때, 참가자들은 그들의 순서를 기다리는 그다음 참가자들에게 그 과제들이 흥미로웠다고 말하도록 1달러 또는 20달러를 지불 받았다. 그다음에, 그 참가자들은 얼마나 그들이 과제를 즐겼는지 평가했다. 그들이 처음에 이렇게 믿지 않았더라도, 1달러를 지불 받은 사람들이 20달러를 지불 받은 사람들보다 그 과제가 즐거웠다고 주장하는 경우가 더 많았다. 그들은 고작 1달러를 위해서 그들의 시간 중 한 시간을 낭비했다는 것에 대해 마음의 갈등이 있었기 때문에 이렇게 했다. 과제가 재미있었다고 말함으로써, 참가자들은 그것을 한 것을 정당화하고, 그 상황에 대해 자신이 더 만족스럽게 느낄 수 있도록 만들 수 있었다. (주제문) 이 현상은 인지 부조화로 알려져 있고, 그것은 우리에게 우리가 우리의 믿음을 정당화하기 위해서 그것들(믿음)을 조작하려고 시도한다는 것을 말해준다.

⇩

사람들은 주어진 상황에 (B) 더 나은 이유가 필요할 때 그들이 생각하는 방식을 (A) 조정한다.

　(A)　　　　　(B)
① 무시하다 … 불확실한
② 표현하다 … 더 나은
③ 조정하다 … 더 나은
④ 조정하다 … 더 나쁜
⑤ 표현하다 … 더 나쁜

해설 요약문은 사람들은 주어진 상황에 '(B)한' 이유가 필요할 때 그들이 생각하는 방식을 '(A)한다'는 내용이다. 글에서 우리가 우리의 믿음을 정당화하기 위해서 그것들(믿음)을 조작하려고 시도한다고 했다. 따라서 요약문의 (A)에는 글에서 언급된 'manipulate'와 관련된 'adjust'가, (B)에는 글에서 언급된 'to justify', 'feel better about the situation'과 관련된 'better'가 적절하므로 ③ adjust(조정하다) - better(더 나은)가 정답이다.

오답분석 우리의 믿음을 정당화하기 위해 그것을 조작하려고 시도한다고 했으므로 ①의 ignore, ②과 ⑤의 express는 (A)에 들어갈 단어로 적절하지 않다. 더

만족스럽게 느낄 수 있도록 정당화한다고 했으므로 ①의 uncertain, ④과 ⑤의 worse는 (B)에 들어갈 단어로 적절하지 않다.

18 ~ 19

지문분석

The movement of Romanticism began / in the late 18th century.
낭만주의 운동은 시작됐다 / 18세기 후반에

Departing from the traditional art of the time, / it focused heavily on emotions and imagination / as well as celebrating the common man.
당시의 전통 예술에서 벗어나서 / 그것은 감정과 상상력에 상당히 집중했다 / 일반인을 찬양하는 것뿐만 아니라 ~에도

This was in part a response to the Industrial Revolution / that (a) shifted society's focus / from the natural to innovation and science.
이것은 산업혁명에 대한 대응의 일부였다 / 사회의 초점을 바꿨던 / 자연 그대로의 것에서 혁신과 과학으로

Romanticists wanted to / instead / explore the (b) internal life.
낭만주의자들은 ~하고 싶어 했다 / 대신에 / 내적인 삶을 탐구하다

Thus, / to express this properly, / Romantic art had to come from / within the mind of the artist.
따라서 / 이것을 적절하게 표현하기 위해 / 낭만주의 예술은 ~에서 생겨나야 했다 / 예술가의 마음속에서

Therefore, / it should not be superficial or artificial.
그러므로 / 그것은 피상적이거나 인위적인 것이 되어서는 안 되었다

Much as its name implies, / Romanticism focused on love and joy.
그것의 이름이 암시하는 것만큼 / 낭만주의는 사랑과 기쁨에 초점을 맞췄다

However, / Romanticists also examined / the (c) opposite end of the spectrum / and delved deeply into / feelings of horror, isolation, and melancholy.
하지만 / 낭만주의자들은 또한 살펴보았다 / 스펙트럼의 반대편 끝을 / 그리고 깊이 탐구했다 / 공포, 고립, 그리고 우울의 감정을

A prime example of this / is the poem by Edgar Allen Poe / titled "The Raven," / in which a narrator mourning the loss of his love / is visited by a mysterious raven / in the middle of the night.
이것의 가장 적절한 예는 / Edgar Allen Poe가 쓴 시이다 / "The Raven"이라는 제목의 / 그것(이 시)에서 그의 사랑하는 사람을 잃은 것을 애도하는 서술자에게 / 신비한 까마귀가 찾아온다 / 한밤중에

The work centered on / heightened feelings / —in this case, / grief and mental instability— / that romanticists (d) denied (→ wanted) to convey / through literature and art.
그 작품은 초점을 맞췄다 / 고조된 감정에 / 이 경우에는 / 슬픔과 정서 불안 / 낭만주의자들이 전달하기를 부인했던(→ 원했던) / 문학과 예술을 통해

Romanticism eventually peaked in the 1800s / and gave way to Realism in the art world.
낭만주의는 마침내 1800년대에 절정에 달했다 / 그리고 예술계에서 현실주의에게 자리를 내 주었다

★ Still, / its characteristics (e) remained popular, / and its influence can be found everywhere / across film, television, literature, music, and art / to this today.
여전히 / 그것의 특징은 인기를 유지하고 있다 / 그리고 그것의 영향은 어디에서나 찾아볼 수 있다 / 영화, 텔레비전, 문학, 음악, 그리고 예술에 걸쳐 / 오늘날까지도

★ 독해가 쉬워지는 구문 풀이

Still, its characteristics remained popular, and its influence can be
　　　　주어1　　　　　동사1　주격보어　　　　　주어2　　　　동사2
found everywhere across film, television, literature, music, and art
to this today.

⇨ remain(remained)은 주격보어를 취할 수 있는 동사이므로, 뒤에 형용사 popular가 쓰였다. 주격보어 popular는 '인기가 있는'이라는 의미로 주어의 상태를 설명한다.

어휘 Romanticism 낭만주의 depart from ~에서 벗어나다
common man 일반인, 보통 사람 Industrial Revolution 산업혁명
internal 내적인, 내부의 superficial 피상적인, 외부의
artificial 인위적인, 인공의 imply 암시하다, 시사하다 joy 기쁨, 즐거움
delve 탐구하다 isolation 고립 melancholy 우울 prime 가장 적절한, 주요한
narrator 서술자, 이야기하는 사람 mysterious 신비한
center on ~에 초점을 맞추다 heighten 고조되다 grief 슬픔, 애도
mental instability 정서 불안 convey 전달하다, 전하다 literature 문학
give way to 자리를 내 주다, 바뀌다 Realism 현실주의
characteristic 특징, 특질

해석 **[주제문]** 낭만주의 운동은 18세기 후반에 시작됐다. 당시의 전통 예술에서 벗어나서, 그것은 일반인을 찬양하는 것뿐만 아니라 감정과 상상력에도 상당히 집중했다. 이것은 자연 그대로의 것에서 혁신과 과학으로 사회의 초점을 (a) 바꿨던 산업혁명에 대한 대응의 일부였다. 대신에 낭만주의자들은 (b) 내적인 삶을 탐구하고 싶어 했다. 따라서, 이것을 적절하게 표현하기 위해, 낭만주의 예술은 예술가의 마음속에서 생겨나야 했다. 그러므로, 그것은 피상적이거나 인위적인 것이 되어서는 안 되었다. 그것의 이름이 암시하는 것만큼, 낭만주의는 사랑과 기쁨에 초점을 맞췄다. 하지만, 낭만주의자들은 또한 스펙트럼의 (c) 반대편 끝을 살펴보며 공포, 고립, 그리고 우울의 감정을 깊이 탐구했다. 이것의 가장 적절한 예는 Edgar Allen Poe가 쓴 "The Raven"이라는 제목의 시인데, 이 시에서 그의 사랑하는 사람을 잃은 것을 애도하는 서술자에게 한밤중에 신비한 까마귀가 찾아온다. 그 작품은 낭만주의자들이 문학과 예술을 통해 전달하기를 (d) 부인했던 (→ 원했던), 고조된 감정에 초점을 맞췄는데, 이 경우에는 슬픔과 정서 불안이다. 낭만주의는 마침내 1800년대에 절정에 달했고 예술계에서 현실주의에게 자리를 내 주었다. 여전히, 그것의 특징은 인기를 (e) 유지하고 있고, 그것의 영향은 오늘날까지도 영화, 텔레비전, 문학, 음악, 그리고 예술에 걸쳐 어디에서나 찾아볼 수 있다.

18
정답 ①

해석 ① 낭만주의는 무엇이고, 그것이 우리에게 남긴 것은 무엇인가
② 낭만주의는 왜 대중매체에서 인기 있는가?
③ 낭만주의 예술가들의 흥망성쇠
④ 낭만주의: 놓친 기회
⑤ 오늘날 낭만주의 예술의 필요성

해설 18세기 후반에 시작된 낭만주의는 무엇이며, 낭만주의 예술가들은 무엇에 초점을 맞췄고, 오늘날에도 그 영향은 어디에서나 찾아볼 수 있다는 내용의 글이므로, 이 글의 제목으로 가장 적절한 것은 ① '낭만주의는 무엇이고, 그것이 우리에게 남긴 것은 무엇인가'이다.

오답분석 ②은 글의 마지막에서 낭만주의의 영향이 오늘날까지도 영화, 텔레비전, 문학, 음악, 예술 등에 남아있다고 한 내용을 활용하여 혼동을 주는 오답이다. ③과 ④은 글의 핵심 소재인 romanticism, romantic art, romanticists를 활용하여 혼동을 주는 오답이다. ⑤은 오늘날까지도 낭만주의의 영향이 여러 곳에 남아있다고 한 글의 내용과 반대되는 내용이므로 오답이다.

어휘 the rise and fall 흥망성쇠

19
정답 ④

해설 그 작품(Edgar Allen Poe의 시)이 낭만주의자들이 문학과 예술을 통해 전달하기를 "원했던" 슬픔과 정서 불안이라는 고조된 감정에 초점을 맞췄다는 맥락이 되어야 하므로, ④의 denied(부인했다)를 wanted(원했다)와 같은 어휘로 바꾸어야 문맥상 적절하다.

오답분석 ①은 이것(낭만주의 운동)이 자연 그대로의 것에서 혁신과 과학으로 사회의 초점을 "바꿨던" 산업혁명에 대한 대응의 일부였다는 맥락이 되어야

하므로 shifted가 오는 것이 적절하다. ②은 낭만주의 예술은 예술가의 마음속에서 생겨나야 했고 낭만주의자들은 "내적인" 삶을 탐구하고 싶어 했다는 맥락이 되어야 하므로 internal이 오는 것이 적절하다. ③은 낭만주의가 사랑과 기쁨에 초점을 맞추긴 했지만, 또한 스펙트럼의 "반대편" 끝을 살펴보며 공포, 고립, 그리고 우울의 감정을 깊이 탐구했다는 맥락이 되어야 하므로 opposite이 오는 것이 적절하다. ⑤은 오늘날 낭만주의의 영향을 어디에서나 찾아볼 수 있으며, 낭만주의의 특징은 여전히 인기를 "유지하고" 있다는 맥락이 되어야 하므로 remained가 오는 것이 적절하다.